D1237863

Your passport to proficiency

Sans frontières

Plan your itinerary for success

What's your **Destination?**

Communication!

Allez, viens! takes your classroom there.

It's even possible that **"What's next?"** becomes your students' favorite question!

Communication and culture in context

The clear structure of each chapter makes it easy for students to present, practice, and apply language skills—all in the context of the location where the chapter takes place!

Grammar support and practice in every lesson

Allez, viens! builds a proven communicative approach on a solid foundation of grammar and vocabulary so students become proficient readers, writers, and speakers of French. With the Travaux pratiques de grammaire, Grammar Tutor, and the CD-ROM and DVD Tutors, students can practice the way they learn best.

Technology that takes you there

Bring the world into your classroom with integrated audio, video, CD-ROM, DVD, and Internet resources that immerse students in authentic language and culture.

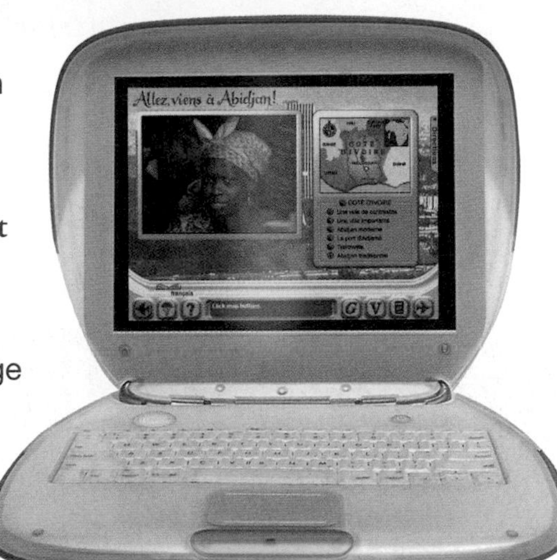

Assessment for state and national standards

To help you incorporate standardized test practice, the Standardized Assessment Tutor provides reading, writing, and math tests in French that target the skills students need. The Joie de lire Reader and Reading Strategies and Skills Handbook offer additional reading practice and reading skills development.

Easy lesson planning for all learning styles

Planning lessons has never been easier with a Lesson Planner with Substitute Teacher Lesson Plans, an editable One-Stop Planner® CD-ROM, and a Student Make-Up Assignments with Alternative Quizzes resource.

Travel a balanced program that's easy to navigate.

Le monde à votre portée!

Allez, viens!

Program components

Texts
- Pupil's Edition
- Annotated Teacher's Edition

Middle School Resources
- Middle School Teaching Resources
- Exploratory Guide

Planning and Presenting
- One-Stop Planner CD-ROM with Test Generator
- Lesson Planner with Substitute Teacher Lesson Plans
- Student Make-Up Assignments with Alternative Quizzes
- Teaching Transparencies

Grammar
- Travaux pratiques de grammaire
- Grammar Tutor for Students of French

Reading and Writing
- Reading Strategies and Skills Handbook
- Joie de lire Reader
- Cahier d'activités

Listening and Speaking
- Audio CD Program
- Listening Activities
- Activities for Communication
- TPR Storytelling Book (Levels 1 and 2)

Assessment
- Testing Program
- Alternative Assessment Guide
- Student Make-Up Assignments with Alternative Quizzes
- Standardized Assessment Tutor

Technology
- One-Stop Planner CD-ROM with Test Generator
- Audio CD Program
- Interactive CD-ROM Tutor
- Video Program
- Video Guide
- DVD Tutor (Levels 1 and 2)

Internet
- go.hrw.com
- www.hrw.com
- www.hrw.com/passport

ANNOTATED TEACHER'S EDITION

Allez, viens!®

HOLT FRENCH

LEVEL 2

HOLT, RINEHART AND WINSTON

A Harcourt Classroom Education Company

Austin • New York • Orlando • Atlanta • San Francisco • Boston • Dallas • Toronto • London

For permission to reprint copyrighted material in the Annotated Teacher's Edition, grateful acknowledgment is made to the following sources:

National Standards in Foreign Language Education Project: "National Standards Report" from *Standards for Foreign Language Learning: Preparing for the 21st Century.* Copyright © 1996 by National Standards in Foreign Language Education Project.

In the *Annotated Teacher's Edition,*

Cover and Title Page Photography Credits
Front Cover and Title Page: (background), © Robert Fried; (students), HRW Photo/John Langford

Back Cover: © Bob Yarbrough/Roving Eye/Painet; (frame)© 2003 Image Farm

Illustration Credits
All art, unless otherwise noted, by Holt Rinehart & Winston.
Chapter Four: Page 93C, Anne de Masson; 93H, Anne Stanley. **Chapter Five:** Page 127C, Françoise Amadieu; 127G, Gilles-Marie Baur. **Chapter Six:** Page 155C, Gilles-Marie Baur. **Chapter Seven:** Page 271H, Gilbert Gnangbel. **Chapter Nine:** Page 251H, Jocelyne Bouchard. **Chapter Ten:** Page 279G, Jocelyne Bouchard. **Chapter Twelve:** Page 341G, Anne Stanley.

Photography Credits
All photos HRW Photo/Marty Granger except:
Technology border: Digital imagery® © 2003 PhotoDisc, Inc.
Clock for pacing tips: Digital imagery® © 2003 PhotoDisc, Inc.
Chess piece for games feature: Digital imagery® © 2003 PhotoDisc, Inc.
House for Community Link feature: Courtesy Ellen Boelsche
Jeux interactifs computer: Digital imagery® © 2003 PhotoDisc, Inc.
All euros: © European Communities
All globes: Mountain High Maps® Copyright ©1997 Digital Wisdom, Inc.
Recipe card fabric: HRW Photo/Victoria Smith
Sage for recipe card: Corbis Images; Remaining herbs: Digital imagery® © 2003 PhotoDisc, Inc.

T1 (t), Corbis Images; T2 (b), HRW Photo/Sam Dudgeon; T3 (tl), Creatas; (tr), Courtesy Neel Heisel; (b), Corbis Images; T9, HRW Photo/Sam Dudgeon; T27 (b), Courtesy Neel Heisel; T41 (l), HRW Photo/Lance Schriner; T45, HRW Photo/Michelle Bridwell; T67 (r), Joe Viesti / Viesti Associates; 3D (r), Robert Fried; 3H (t), Ulrike Welsch/PhotoEdit; (b), Emmanuel Rongieras d'Usseau; 10, Courtesy Todd Loisé; 25, Courtesy Sandra Behensky; 31D, Robert Fried; 31H (tl), HRW Photo/John Langford; (cl), HBJ Photo/Oscar Buitrago; (cr), IPA/The Image Works; 37 and 54, Courtesy Deborah Zoernig; 59D (l), HRW Photo/Victoria Smith; (r), © Susan Van Etten/PhotoEdit; 59C, Mark Antman/The Image Works; 63, HRW Photo/Marty Granger/Edge Productions; 83, Courtesy Norah Jones; 93D, Robert Fried; 93G (t), Allan A. Philiba; (c), Robert Fried; 107, Courtesy Sue DiGiandomenico; 110, Courtesy Bill Heller; 127D (l), © Ric Ergenbright/CORBIS; (r), Robert Fried; 153, Courtesy Todd Bowen; 155D (l), © P. Somelet / DIAF; (r), Robert Fried; 165, Courtesy Jim Garland; 178, Courtesy Susan Hayden; 183D (l), © TempSport/CORBIS; (r), Robert Fried; 194, Courtesy Kim Peters; 196, Courtesy Alisa Glick; 217C (r), HRW Photo/Sam Dudgeon; 217D, Robert Fried; 217E (l), HRW Photo/Louis Boireau; 226, Courtesy Linda Hale; 251D, Robert Fried; 267, Courtesy Pam Seccombe; 273, Courtesy Nancy Rodman; 279D (l), © Owen Franken/CORBIS; 279D (r), Robert Fried; 279H, HRW Photo/Daniel Aubry; 281, Courtesy Maxine Stewart; 307C (l), *Paroles: Selected Poems by Jacques Prévert,* translated by Lawrence Ferlinghetti. Translation copyright © 1958 by Lawrence Ferlinghetti. Cover photo by Izis Bidermanas. Reprinted by permission of City Lights Books. HRW Photo by Sam Dudgeon; (c), *Les années métalliques* by Michel Demuth. Copyright © 1977 by Editions Robert Laffont, S.A. Reprinted by permission of Editions J'ai Lu. HRW Photo/Sam Dudgeon; (r), *La tragédie du Roi Christophe* by Aimé Césaire. Copyright © 1963 by Présence Africaine. Reprinted by permission of Présence Africaine. HRW Photo/Sam Dudgeon; 307D (both), © Robert Fried; 313, Courtesy Sharon Saam; 331, Courtesy Jeanne S. Jendrzejewski; 341D, Robert Fried; 354, Courtesy Todd Loisé.

ACKNOWLEDGMENTS continued on page R92, which is an extension of the copyright page.

Printed in the United States of America

ISBN 0-03-057329-7

1 2 3 4 5 6 7 048 05 04 03 02 01

Allez viens! Level 2 Annotated Teacher's Edition

CONTRIBUTING WRITERS

Gail Corder
Trinity Valley School
Fort Worth, TX

Ms. Corder was the principal writer of the Level 2 Annotated Teacher's Edition.

Judith Ryser
San Marcos High School
San Marcos, TX

Ms. Ryser wrote teaching suggestions and notes for the reading selections of the Level 2 Annotated Teacher's Edition.

Véronique Dupont
Westwood High School
Austin, TX

Ms. Dupont wrote answers to activities of the Level 2 Annotated Teacher's Edition.

Jayne Abrate
The University of Missouri
Rolla, MO

Ms. Abrate wrote teaching suggestions and notes for the Location Openers for the Level 2 Annotated Teacher's Edition.

TEACHER-TO-TEACHER CONTRIBUTORS

Sandra Behensky
Rock Island High School
Rock Island, IL

Todd Bowen
Adlai E. Stevenson High School
Lincolnshire, IL

Sue DiGiandomenico
Wellesley Middle School
Wellesley, MA

Jim Garland
Henry Clay High School
Lexington, KY

Alisa Glick
Greenwich Country Day School
Greenwich, CT

Linda Hale
Sonoma Valley High School
Sonoma, CA

Dr. Susan Hayden
Aloha High School
Beaverton, OR

Bill Heller
Perry High School
Perry, NY

Jeanne S. Jendrejewski
LSU Lab School
Baton Rouge, LA

Norah L. Jones
Rustberg High School
Rustberg, VA

Todd Losié
Renaissance High School
Detroit, MI

Kim Peters
Mooresville High School
Mooresville, IN

Nancy Rodman
The Blake School
Minneapolis, MN

Sharron Saam
Barrett Middle School Urban Academy
Columbus, OH

Pam Seccombe
Nathan Hale High School
West Allis, WI

Maxine Stewart
Genesis Preparatory School
New Port Richey, FL

Deborah Zoernig
Lutheran High School South
St. Louis, MO

REVIEWERS

John Billus
Weston High School
Weston, CT

Eugène Blé
Consultant
Austin, TX

Betty Clough
McCallum High School
Austin, TX

Robert H. Didsbury
Consultant
Raleigh, NC

Jennifer Jones
U.S. Peace Corps volunteer
Côte d'Ivoire 1991–1993
Austin, TX

Audrey O'Keefe
Jordan High School
Los Angeles, CA

Agathe Norman
Consultant
Austin, TX

Mayanne Wright
Consultant
Burnet, TX

Jo Anne S. Wilson
Consultant
Glen Arbor, MI

PROFESSIONAL ESSAYS

Standards for Foreign Language Learning
Paul Sandrock
Foreign Language Consultant
Department of Public Instruction
Madison, WI

Reading Strategies and Skills
Nancy A. Humbach
Miami University
Oxford, OH

Using Portfolios in the Language Classroom
Jo Anne S. Wilson
J. Wilson Associates
Glen Arbor, MI

Teaching Culture
Nancy A. Humbach
The Miami University
Oxford, OH

Dorothea Brushke, retired
Parkway School District
Chesterfield, MO

Learning Styles and Multi-Modality Teaching
Mary B. McGehee
Louisiana State University
Baton Rouge, LA

Multi-Level Classrooms
Dr. Joan H. Manley
The University of Texas
El Paso, TX

To the Teacher

Principles and Practices

> **We have seen significant advances in modern language curriculum practices:**
>
> **1.** a redefinition of the objectives of foreign language study involving a commitment to the development of proficiency in the four skills and in cultural awareness;
>
> **2.** a recognition of the need for longer sequences of study;
>
> **3.** a new student-centered approach that redefines the role of the teacher as facilitator and encourages students to take a more active role in their learning;
>
> **4.** the inclusion of students of all learning abilities.
>
> The new Holt, Rinehart and Winston World Languages programs take into account not only these advances in the field of foreign language education but also the input of teachers and students around the country.

As nations become increasingly interdependent, the need for effective communication and sensitivity to other cultures becomes more important. Today's youth must be culturally and linguistically prepared to participate in a global society. At Holt, Rinehart and Winston, we believe that proficiency in more than one language is essential to meeting this need.

The primary goal of the Holt, Rinehart and Winston World Languages programs is to help students develop linguistic proficiency and cultural sensitivity. By interweaving language and culture, our programs seek to broaden students' communication skills while at the same time deepening their appreciation of other cultures.

We believe that all students can benefit from foreign language instruction. We recognize that not everyone learns at the same rate or in the same way; nevertheless, we believe that all students should have the opportunity to acquire language proficiency to a degree commensurate with their individual abilities.

Holt, Rinehart and Winston's World Languages programs are designed to accommodate all students by appealing to a variety of learning styles.

We believe that effective language programs should motivate students. Students deserve an answer to the question they often ask: "Why are we doing this?" They need to have goals that are interesting, practical, clearly stated, and attainable.

Holt, Rinehart and Winston's World Languages programs promote success. They present relevant content in manageable increments that encourage students to attain achievable functional objectives.

We believe that proficiency in another language is best nurtured by programs that encourage students to think critically and to take risks when expressing themselves in the language. We also recognize that students should strive for accuracy in communication. While it is imperative that students have a knowledge of the basic structures of the language, it is also important that they go beyond the simple manipulation of forms.

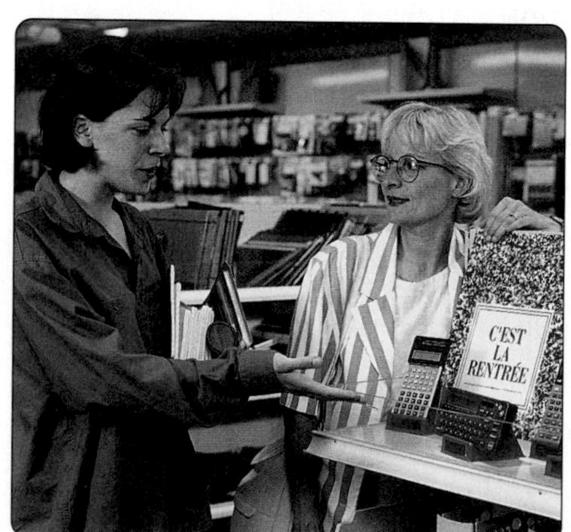

Holt, Rinehart and Winston's World Languages programs reflect a careful progression of activities that guide students from comprehensible input of authentic language through structured practice to creative, personalized expression. This progression, accompanied by consistent re-entry and spiraling of functions, vocabulary, and structures, provides students with the tools and the confidence to express themselves in their new language.

Finally, we believe that a complete program of language instruction should take into account the needs of teachers in today's increasingly demanding classrooms.

At Holt, Rinehart and Winston, we have designed programs that offer practical teacher support and provide resources to meet individual learning and teaching styles.

Contents

Pacing and Planning

Traditional Schedule

Days of instruction: 180

Location Opener	2 days per Location Opener x 6 Location Openers	12 days
Chapter	13 days per chapter x 12 chapters	156 days
		168 days

If you are teaching on a traditional schedule, we suggest following the plan above and spending 13 days per chapter. A complete set of lesson plans in the interleaf provides detailed suggestions for each chapter. For more suggestions, see the **Lesson Planner with Substitute Teacher Lesson Plans.**

Chapitre 9 : Tu connais la nouvelle?
Suggested Lesson Plans *50-Minute Schedule*

Day 1 | Day 2 | Day 3 | Day 4 | Day 5 | Day 6

251J SUGGESTED LESSON PLANS • 50-MINUTE SCHEDULE CHAPITRE 9

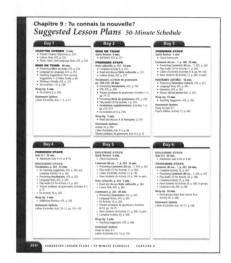

Block Schedule

Blocks of instruction: 90

Location Opener	1/2 block per Location Opener x 6 Location Openers	3 blocks
Chapter	7 blocks per chapter x 12 chapters	84 blocks
		87 blocks

If you are teaching on a block schedule, we suggest following the plan above and spending seven blocks per chapter. A complete set of lesson plans in the interleaf provides detailed suggestions for each chapter. For more suggestions, see the **Lesson Planner with Substitute Teacher Lesson Plans.**

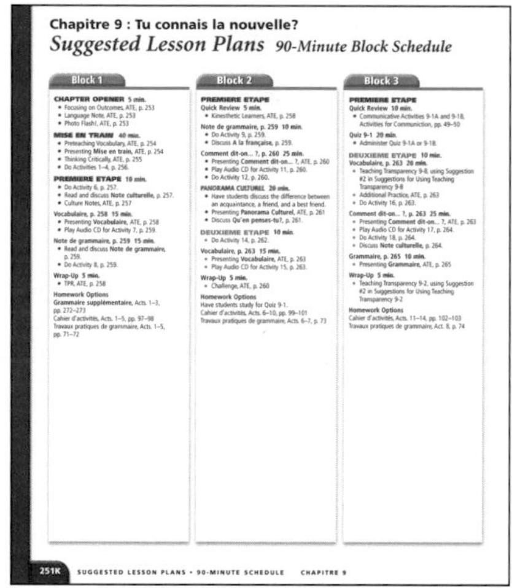
Chapitre 9 : Tu connais la nouvelle?
Suggested Lesson Plans *90-Minute Block Schedule*

Block 1 | Block 2 | Block 3

251K SUGGESTED LESSON PLANS • 90-MINUTE SCHEDULE CHAPITRE 9

One-Stop Planner CD-ROM

Use the **One-Stop Planner CD-ROM with Test Generator** to aid in lesson planning and pacing.

- Editable lesson plans with direct links to teaching resources
- Printable worksheets from resource books
- Direct launches to the HRW Internet activities
- Video and audio segments
- Test Generator
- Clip Art for vocabulary items

Pacing Tips

At the beginning of each chapter, you will find a Pacing Tip to help you plan your lessons.

Articulation Across Levels

The following chart shows how topics are repeated across levels in ***Allez, viens!*** from the end of Level 1 to the beginning of Level 3.

- In each level, the last chapter is a review chapter.
- In Levels 2 and 3, the first two chapters review the previous level.

LEVEL 1

CHAPTER 12
Review of Level 1

- Contractions with **de** and **à**
- The partitive
- The **passé composé**
- Possessive adjectives
- Asking for and giving directions
- Asking for advice
- Expressing need
- Family vocabulary
- Inviting
- Making requests
- Making suggestions
- Making excuses
- Pointing out places; things

LEVEL 2

CHAPTER 1 / CHAPTER 2
Review of Level 1

Chapter 1

- Adjective agreement
- **Avoir** and **être**
- **Choisir** and other **–ir** verbs
- The imperative
- The future with **aller**
- Asking for information
- Asking for and giving advice
- Asking for, making, and responding to suggestions
- Clothing and colors
- Describing yourself and others
- Expressing likes and dislikes
- Family vocabulary
- Relating a series of events
- Pronunciation: **liaison**

Chapter 2

- Using **tu** and **vous**
- Question formation
- Adjectives that precede the noun
- Contractions with **de** and **à**
- Prepositions of location
- Asking for and giving directions
- Asking how someone is feeling and telling how you are feeling
- Making suggestions
- Pointing out where things are
- Paying compliments
- Pronunciation: intonation

CHAPTER 12
Review of Level 2

- The **passé composé** and the **imparfait**
- Asking for and giving information
- Asking for and giving advice
- Clothing vocabulary
- Complaining
- Describing people and places
- Expressing discouragement and offering encouragement
- Giving directions
- Making and responding to suggestions
- Relating a series of events
- Sports and activities

LEVEL 3

CHAPTER 1 / CHAPTER 2
Review of Level 2

Chapter 1

- The **passé composé** and the **imparfait**
- Definite, indefinite, and partitive articles
- Question formation
- Describing what a place was like
- Exchanging information
- Expressing indecision
- Food vocabulary
- Inquiring; expressing enthusiasm and dissatisfaction
- Making recommendations
- Ordering and asking for details

Chapter 2

- The future with **aller**
- The imperative
- Pronouns and their placement
- Asking for and giving directions
- Asking about and telling where things are
- Expressing enthusiasm and boredom
- Expressing impatience
- Making, accepting, and refusing suggestions
- Reassuring someone

CHAPTER 12
Review of Level 3

- The future tense
- The subjunctive
- **Si** clauses
- Prepositions with countries
- Expressing anticipation
- Expressing certainty and doubt
- Expressing excitement and disappointment
- Greeting and introducing people
- Inquiring
- Making suppositions
- Offering encouragement

Allez, viens! French Level 1
Scope and Sequence

	FUNCTIONS	GRAMMAR	VOCABULARY	CULTURE	RE-ENTRY
	CHAPITRE PRELIMINAIRE Allez, viens!, *Pages xxvi–11*				
	• Introducing yourself • Spelling • Counting • Understanding classroom instructions	• French alphabet • French accent marks	• French names • French numbers 0–20 • French classroom expressions	• The French-speaking world • Famous French-speaking people • The importance of learning French • French gestures for counting	
Poitiers	**CHAPITRE 1 Faisons connaissance!, *Pages 16–45***				
	• Greeting people and saying goodbye • Asking how people are; telling how you are • Asking someone's name and age and giving yours • Expressing likes, dislikes, and preferences about things • Expressing likes, dislikes, and preferences about activities	• **Ne...pas** • The definite articles **le, la, l', and les** • The connectors **et** and **mais** • Subject pronouns • **-er** verbs	• Things you like or don't like • Activities you like or don't like to do	• Greetings and goodbyes • Hand gestures • Leisure time activities	• Introductions • Numbers 0–20 • Expressing likes, dislikes, and preferences about things
Poitiers	**CHAPITRE 2 Vive l'école!, *Pages 46–73***				
	• Agreeing and disagreeing • Asking for and giving information • Telling when you have class • Asking for and expressing opinions	• Using **si** instead of **oui** to contradict a negative statement • The verb **avoir**	• School subjects • School-related words • Class times • Parts of the school day • Numbers 21–59	• The French educational system/**le bac** • **L'heure officielle** • Curriculum in French schools • The French grading system	• Greetings • The verb **aimer** • Numbers for telling time

	FUNCTIONS	GRAMMAR	VOCABULARY	CULTURE	RE-ENTRY
Poitiers	**CHAPITRE 3 Tout pour la rentrée,** ***Pages 74–101***				
	• Making and responding to requests • Asking others what they need and telling what you need • Telling what you'd like and what you'd like to do • Getting someone's attention • Asking for information • Expressing thanks	• The indefinite articles **un, une,** and **des** • The demonstrative adjectives **ce, cet, cette,** and **ces** • Adjective agreement and placement	• School supplies • Things you might buy for school and fun • Colors • Numbers 60–201	• Bagging your own purchases • Buying school supplies in French-speaking countries • French currency (euros)	• The verb **avoir** • Expressing likes and dislikes • Numbers
Québec	**CHAPITRE 4 Sports et passe-temps,** ***Pages 106–135***				
	• Telling how much you like or dislike something • Exchanging information • Making, accepting, and turning down suggestions	• Expressions with **faire** and **jouer** • Question formation • **De** after a negative verb • The verb **faire** • The pronoun **on** • Adverbs of frequency	• Sports and hobbies • Weather expressions • Months of the year • Time expressions • Seasons	• Old and new in Quebec City • Celsius and Fahrenheit • Sports in francophone countries • **Maison des jeunes et de la culture**	• Expressing likes and dislikes • The verb **aimer;** regular **-er** verbs • Agreeing and disagreeing
Paris	**CHAPITRE 5 On va au café?,** ***Pages 140–167***				
	• Making suggestions and excuses • Making a recommendation • Getting someone's attention • Ordering food and beverages • Inquiring about and expressing likes and dislikes • Paying the check	• The verb **prendre** • The imperative	• Foods and beverages	• Food served in a café • Waitpersons as professionals • **La litote** • Tipping	• Accepting and turning down a suggestion • Expressing likes and dislikes • Numbers 20–100

	FUNCTIONS	GRAMMAR	VOCABULARY	CULTURE	RE-ENTRY
Paris	**CHAPITRE 6 Amusons-nous!, *Pages 168–197***				
	• Making plans • Extending and responding to invitations • Arranging to meet someone	• Using **le** with days of the week • The verb **aller** and **aller** + infinitive • Contractions with **à** • The verb **vouloir** • Information questions	• Places to go • Things to do	• Going out • Dating in France • Conversational time	• Expressing likes and dislikes • Days of the week • Making, accepting, and turning down suggestions • Sports and hobbies • **L'heure officielle**
Paris	**CHAPITRE 7 La famille, *Pages 198–225***				
	• Identifying people • Introducing people • Describing and characterizing people • Asking for, giving, and refusing permission	• Possession with **de** • Possessive adjectives • Adjective agreement • The verb **être**	• Family members • Adjectives to describe and characterize people	• Family life • Pets in France	• Asking for and giving people's names and ages • Adjective agreement
Abidjan	**CHAPITRE 8 Au marché, *Pages 230–259***				
	• Expressing need • Making, accepting, and declining requests • Telling someone what to do • Offering, accepting, or refusing food	• The partitive articles • **Avoir besoin de** • The verb **pouvoir** • **De** with expressions of quantity • The pronoun **en**	• Food items • Expressions of quantity • Meals	• The Ivorian market • Shopping for groceries in francophone countries • The metric system • Foods of Côte d'Ivoire • Mealtimes in francophone countries	• Food vocabulary • Activities • The imperative
Arles	**CHAPITRE 9 Au téléphone, *Pages 265–291***				
	• Asking for and expressing opinions • Inquiring about and relating past events • Making and answering a telephone call • Sharing confidences and consoling others • Asking for and giving advice	• The **passé composé** with **avoir** • Placement of adverbs with the **passé composé** • The **-re** verb: **répondre** • The object pronouns **le, la, les, lui,** and **leur**	• Daily activities	• History of Arles • The French telephone system • Telephone habits of French-speaking teenagers	• Chores • Asking for, giving, and refusing permission • **Aller** + infinitive

	FUNCTIONS	GRAMMAR	VOCABULARY	CULTURE	RE-ENTRY
Arles	**CHAPITRE 10 Dans un magasin de vêtements, *Pages 292–321***				
	• Asking for and giving advice • Expressing need; inquiring • Asking for an opinion; paying a compliment; criticizing • Hesitating; making a decision	• The verbs **mettre** and **porter** • Adjectives used as nouns • The **-ir** verbs: **choisir** • The direct object pronouns **le, la,** and **les** • **C'est** versus **il/elle est**	• Articles of clothing	• Clothing sizes • Fashion in francophone countries • Responding to compliments	• The future with **aller** • Colors • Likes and dislikes
Arles	**CHAPITRE 11 Vive les vacances!, *Pages 322–349***				
	• Inquiring about and sharing future plans • Expressing indecision; expressing wishes • Asking for advice; making, accepting, and refusing suggestions • Reminding; reassuring • Seeing someone off • Asking for and expressing opinions • Inquiring about and relating past events	• The prepositions **à** and **en** • The **-ir** verbs: **partir**	• Vacation places and activities • Travel items	• **Colonies de vacances** • Vacations	• **Aller** + infinitive • Asking for advice • Clothing vocabulary • The imperative • Weather expressions • The **passé composé** • The verb **vouloir**
Fort-de-France	**CHAPITRE 12 En ville, *Pages 354–383***				
REVIEW CHAPTER	• Pointing out places and things • Making and responding to requests • Asking for advice • Making suggestions • Asking for and giving directions	• The pronoun **y** • Contractions with **de**	• Buildings • Things to do or buy in town • Means of transportation • Locations	• Store hours in France and Martinique • Making "small talk" in francophone countries • Getting a driver's license in francophone countries • **DOMs** and **TOMs** • Public areas downtown	• Contractions with **à** • The partitive • Contractions with **de** • Family vocabulary • Possessive adjectives • The **passé composé** • Expressing need • Making excuses • Inviting

Allez, viens! French Level 2
Scope and Sequence

	FUNCTIONS	GRAMMAR	VOCABULARY	CULTURE	RE-ENTRY
Environs de Paris	**CHAPITRE 1 Bon séjour!, *Pages 4–31***				
REVIEW CHAPTER	• Describing and characterizing yourself and others • Expressing likes, dislikes, and preferences • Asking for information • Asking for and giving advice • Asking for, making, and responding to suggestions • Relating a series of events	• The verbs **avoir** and **être** • Adjective agreement • The interrogative adjective **quel** • **Choisir** and other **-ir** verbs • The imperative • The future with **aller**	• Travel items	• Travel documents for foreign countries • Studying abroad • Ethnic restaurants	• Adjectives to characterize people • Regular **-er** verbs • Pronunciation: **liaison** • Family vocabulary • Clothing and colors • Weather expressions and seasons
Environs de Paris	**CHAPITRE 2 Bienvenue à Chartres!, *Pages 32–59***				
REVIEW CHAPTER	• Welcoming someone and responding to someone's welcome • Asking about how someone is feeling and telling how you're feeling • Pointing out where things are • Paying and responding to compliments • Asking for and giving directions	• Using **tu** and **vous** • Question formation • Adjectives that precede the noun • Contractions with **à**	• Furniture and rooms • Places in town	• Polite behavior for a guest • Teenagers' bedrooms in France • Paying and receiving compliments • **Notre-Dame de Chartres** • Houses in francophone countries	• Pronunciation: intonation • Prepositions of location • Contractions with **de** • Making suggestions
Environs de Paris	**CHAPITRE 3 Un repas à la française, *Pages 60–89***				
	• Making purchases • Asking for, offering, accepting, and refusing food • Paying and responding to compliments • Asking for and giving advice • Extending good wishes	• The object pronoun **en** • The partitive articles • The indirect object pronouns **lui** and **leur**	• Places to shop • Food items to buy • Meals • Gift items	• Neighborhood stores • Typical meals in the francophone world • Courses of a meal • The euro • Special occasions	• Giving prices • Expressions of quantity • Food vocabulary • The verbs **vouloir** and **pouvoir**

	FUNCTIONS	GRAMMAR	VOCABULARY	CULTURE	RE-ENTRY
Martinique	**CHAPITRE 4 Sous les tropiques,** ***Pages 94–123***				
	• Asking for information and describing a place • Asking for and making suggestions • Emphasizing likes and dislikes • Relating a series of events	• Recognizing reflexive verbs • The reflexive pronouns **se** and **me** • The relative pronouns **ce qui** and **ce que** • The present tense of reflexive verbs • Adverbs of frequency	• Places, flora, and fauna • Vacation activities • Daily activities	• **La ville de Saint-Pierre** • Places to visit in different regions • **Yoles rondes** • The **créole** language • **Carnaval** • Music and dance in Martinique	• **De** with adjectives and plural nouns • Connectors for sequencing events • Adverbs of frequency • Pronunciation: **e muet** • Sports vocabulary • Weather expressions
Touraine	**CHAPITRE 5 Quelle journée!,** ***Pages 128–155***				
	• Expressing concern for someone • Inquiring; expressing satisfaction and frustration • Sympathizing with and consoling someone • Giving reasons and making excuses • Congratulating and reprimanding someone	• The **passé composé** with **avoir** • Introduction to the **passé composé** with **être**	• School day vocabulary	• **Carnet de correspondance** • Meals at school • French grades and report cards • School life in francophone countries	• Connector words • Sports and leisure activities • Pronunciation: the nasal sound [ɛ̃] • Question words • Reflexive verbs
Touraine	**CHAPITRE 6 A nous les châteaux!,** ***Pages 156–183***				
	• Asking for opinions; expressing enthusiasm, indifference, and dissatisfaction • Expressing disbelief and doubt • Asking for and giving information	• The phrase **c'était** • The **passé composé** with **être** • Formal and informal phrasing of questions • The verb **ouvrir**	• Weekend activities • Verbs that use **être** in the **passé composé**	• Types of châteaux in France • Studying historical figures in school • Buses and trains in France	• Pronunciation: [y] versus [u] • The **passé composé** with **avoir** • Expressing satisfaction and frustration • Telling time

	FUNCTIONS	GRAMMAR	VOCABULARY	CULTURE	RE-ENTRY
Touraine	**CHAPITRE 7 En pleine forme,** ***Pages 184–213***				
	• Expressing concern for someone and complaining • Giving advice; accepting and rejecting advice • Expressing discouragement and offering encouragement • Justifying your recommendations; advising against something	• Reflexive verbs in the **passé composé** • The pronoun **en** with activities • The verb **devoir** • The verb **se nourrir**	• Health expressions • Parts of the body • Injuries • Staying fit • Good and bad eating habits	• Pharmacies in France • Figures of speech • Teenagers' exercise habits • Staying healthy • Mineral water	• Expressing doubt • Telling how often you do something • Pronunciation: the [r] sound • Sports activities
Côte d'Ivoire	**CHAPITRE 8 C'était comme ça,** ***Pages 218–247***				
	• Telling what or whom you miss; reassuring someone • Asking and telling what things were like • Reminiscing • Making and responding to suggestions	• The **imparfait** of **avoir** and **être** • Formation of the **imparfait** • **Si on** + the **imparfait**	• Describing places • Childhood activities • Things to see and buy in Côte d'Ivoire	• Village life in Côte d'Ivoire • Ethnic groups in West Africa • High school in Côte d'Ivoire • Félix Houphouët-Boigny • City versus country living • Abidjan	• Pronunciation: the [ɛ] sound • Adjectives of physical traits and personality • Chores • Places in a city
Provence	**CHAPITRE 9 Tu connais la nouvelle?,** ***Pages 252–279***				
	• Wondering what happened; offering possible explanations • Accepting and rejecting explanations • Breaking some news; showing interest • Beginning, continuing, and ending a story	• **Avoir l'air** + adjective • The **passé composé** vs. the **imparfait** • The **passé composé** and the **imparfait** with interrupted actions • Using **être en train de** and the **imparfait**	• Feelings • Personal happenings	• The **cours Mirabeau,** Aix-en-Provence • Friendship • **Histoires marseillaises**	• School-related mishaps • The **passé composé** of reflexive verbs • Accidents and injuries • The relative pronouns **ce qui** and **ce que** • Explanations and apologies

Provence — **CHAPITRE 10 Je peux te parler?, *Pages 280–307***

FUNCTIONS	GRAMMAR	VOCABULARY	CULTURE	RE-ENTRY
• Sharing a confidence • Asking for and giving advice • Asking for and granting a favor; making excuses • Apologizing and accepting an apology; reproaching someone	• Object pronouns and their placement • Direct object pronouns with the **passé composé** • Object pronouns before an infinitive	• Apologetic actions • Party preparations	• Paul Cézanne • Roman ruins in Aix-en-Provence • **Provençale** cuisine • Talking about personal problems	• Accepting and refusing advice • Personal happenings • Pronunciation: the nasal sound [ã] • Making excuses

Provence — **CHAPITRE 11 Chacun ses goûts, *Pages 308–337***

FUNCTIONS	GRAMMAR	VOCABULARY	CULTURE	RE-ENTRY
• Identifying people and things • Asking for and giving information • Giving opinions • Summarizing	• The verb **connaître** • **C'est** versus **il/elle est** • The relative pronouns **qui** and **que**	• Songs and singers • Types of music • Types of movies • Types of books	• **La Fête de la musique** • Musical tastes • Movie theaters in France • The **Minitel**	• Emphasizing likes and dislikes • Making and responding to suggestions

Québec — **CHAPITRE 12 A la belle étoile, *Pages 342–371***

REVIEW CHAPTER

FUNCTIONS	GRAMMAR	VOCABULARY	CULTURE	RE-ENTRY
• Asking for and giving information; giving directions • Complaining; expressing discouragement and offering encouragement • Asking for and giving advice • Relating a series of events; describing people and places	• The verb **emporter** • The **passé composé** and the **imparfait**	• Animals • Outdoor activities • Camping equipment • Rules related to nature	• **Le parc de la Jacques-Cartier** • Ecology in Canada • Endangered animals • French-Canadian expressions	• Sports and activities • Clothing vocabulary • Making and responding to suggestions

Allez, viens! French Level 3
Scope and Sequence

la France — **CHAPITRE 1 France, les regions, *Pages 4–31***

REVIEW CHAPTER

FUNCTIONS	GRAMMAR	VOCABULARY	CULTURE	RE-ENTRY
• Renewing old acquaintances • Inquiring; expressing enthusiasm and dissatisfaction • Exchanging information • Asking and describing what a place was like • Expressing indecision • Making recommendations • Ordering and asking for details	• The **passé composé** • The **imparfait**	• French menu	• Traditional regional clothing • Regional specialties • Regional foods	• Sports and activities • Food vocabulary • Definite, indefinite, and partitive articles • Question formation

la Belgique — **CHAPITRE 2 Belgique, nous voilà!, *Pages 32–61***

REVIEW CHAPTER

FUNCTIONS	GRAMMAR	VOCABULARY	CULTURE	RE-ENTRY
• Asking for and giving directions • Expressing impatience • Reassuring someone • Expressing enthusiasm and boredom • Asking and telling where things are	• The verb **conduire** • The imperative • Pronouns and their placement	• At the gas station • Adjectives	• Languages in Belgium • Favorite comic book characters • Overview of Belgium	• The future with **aller** • Making, accepting, and refusing suggestions

la Suisse — **CHAPITRE 3 Soyons responsables!, *Pages 62–91***

FUNCTIONS	GRAMMAR	VOCABULARY	CULTURE	RE-ENTRY
• Asking for, granting, and refusing permission • Expressing obligation • Forbidding • Reproaching • Justifying your actions and rejecting others' excuses	• The subjunctive • **Ne...pas** + infinitive	• Household chores • Personal responsibilities • Social responsibilities	• Swiss work ethic • Switzerland's neutrality • Overview of Switzerland • Environmental issues • **La minuterie**	• The verb **devoir** • Complaining • Chores • Negative expressions

	FUNCTIONS	GRAMMAR	VOCABULARY	CULTURE	RE-ENTRY
la France	**CHAPITRE 4 Des goûts et des couleurs,** ***Pages 92–121***				
	• Asking for and giving opinions • Asking which one(s) • Pointing out and identifying people and things • Paying and responding to compliments • Reassuring someone	• The interrogative and demonstrative pronouns • The causative **faire**	• Clothing and styles • Describing clothing and hairstyles • Hair and hairstyles	• French clothing stores • Fashion and personal style • French sense of fashion	• Clothing vocabulary • Adjectives referring to clothing • Family vocabulary • Chores
le Sénégal	**CHAPITRE 5 C'est notre avenir,** ***Pages 126–155***				
	• Asking about and expressing intentions • Expressing conditions and possibilities • Asking about future plans • Expressing wishes • Expressing indecision • Giving advice • Requesting information • Writing a formal letter	• The future • The conditional • Question formation with inversion	• Future choices and plans • Careers	• Careers and education in Senegal • Overview of Senegal • Planning for a career • Types of job training	• The subjunctive • Giving advice • The **passé composé** • The imperfect • Making a telephone call • Expressing likes and preferences
le Maroc	**CHAPITRE 6 Ma famille, mes copains et moi,** ***Pages 156–185***				
	• Making, accepting, and refusing suggestions • Making arrangements • Making and accepting apologies • Showing and responding to hospitality • Expressing and responding to thanks • Quarreling	• Reciprocal verbs • The past infinitive	• Family relationships	• Bargaining in North Africa • Values of francophone teenagers • Overview of Morocco • Hospitality in Morocco	• Reflexive verbs • Expressing thanks

La République centrafricaine

CHAPITRE 7 Un safari-photo, *Pages 186–215*

FUNCTIONS	GRAMMAR	VOCABULARY	CULTURE	RE-ENTRY
• Making suppositions • Expressing doubt and certainty • Asking for and giving advice • Expressing astonishment • Cautioning someone • Expressing fear • Reassuring someone • Expressing relief	• Structures and their complements • Using the subjunctive • Irregular subjunctive forms	• Rainforest and savannah • Packing for a safari • African animals	• Overview of the Central African Republic • Animal conservation in the Central African Republic • Stereotypical impressions of francophone regions	• The subjunctive • Travel items • The conditional

la Tunisie

CHAPITRE 8 La Tunisie, pays de contrastes, *Pages 216–245*

FUNCTIONS	GRAMMAR	VOCABULARY	CULTURE	RE-ENTRY
• Asking someone to convey good wishes • Closing a letter • Expressing hopes or wishes • Giving advice • Complaining • Expressing annoyance • Making comparisons	• **Si** clauses • The comparative	• Traditional life • City life	• Overview of Tunisia • Traditional and modern life in Tunisia • Carthage • Modernization in francophone countries • Traditional and modern styles of dress in Tunisia	• The imperfect • Intonation • Adjective agreement • Describing a place

le Canada

CHAPITRE 9 C'est l'fun!, *Pages 250–279*

FUNCTIONS	GRAMMAR	VOCABULARY	CULTURE	RE-ENTRY
• Agreeing and disagreeing • Expressing indifference • Making requests • Asking for and making judgments • Asking for and making recommendations • Asking about and summarizing a story	• Negative expressions • The expression **ne...que** • The relative pronouns **qui, que,** and **dont**	• Television programming • The television • Types of movies	• Multilingual broadcasting in Canada • Overview of Montreal • Favorite types of movies • The Canadian film industry	• Expressing opinions • Quarreling • Agreeing and disagreeing • Types of films • Summarizing a story • Continuing and ending a story • Relating a series of events • Relative pronouns

	FUNCTIONS	GRAMMAR	VOCABULARY	CULTURE	RE-ENTRY
la Guadeloupe	**CHAPITRE 10 Rencontres au soleil,** ***Pages 280–309***				
	• Bragging; flattering • Teasing • Breaking some news; showing interest • Expressing disbelief; telling a joke	• The superlative • The past perfect	• Sea life • Everyday life	• Climate and natural assets of Guadeloupe • Overview of Guadeloupe • **La Fête des Cuisinières** • Daily routines of francophone teenagers • Greetings in Guadeloupe	• Forms of the comparative • Reciprocal verbs • Adjective agreement • Breaking some news
la Louisiane	**CHAPITRE 11 Laissez les bons temps rouler!,** ***Pages 310–339***				
	• Asking for confirmation • Asking for and giving opinions • Agreeing and disagreeing • Asking for explanations • Making observations • Giving impressions		• Musical instruments • Kinds of music • Cajun food	• **Mardi Gras** and festivals in Louisiana • Cajun French • Cajun music • History of Louisiana • Parties and celebrations in francophone countries	• Renewing old acquaintances • Food vocabulary • Types of music • Agreeing and disagreeing • Asking for and giving opinions • Emphasizing likes • Making suggestions • Expressing opinions • The relative pronouns **ce qui** and **ce que**
Autour du monde	**CHAPITRE 12 Echanges sportifs et culturels,** ***Pages 340–367***				
REVIEW CHAPTER	• Expressing anticipation • Making suppositions • Expressing certainty and doubt • Inquiring • Expressing excitement and disappointment	• The future after **quand** and **dès que**	• Sports and equipment • Places of origin	• International sporting events in francophone countries • Stereotypes of people in francophone countries	• Sports vocabulary • Making suppositions • **Si** clauses • Expressing certainty and doubt • The future • Prepositions with countries • Greeting people • Introducing people • Asking someone's name and age and giving yours • Offering encouragement

Pupil's Edition

***Allez, viens!** offers an integrated approach to language learning. Presentation and practice of functional expressions, vocabulary, and grammar structures are interwoven with cultural information, language learning tips, and realia to facilitate both learning and teaching. The technology, audiovisual materials, and additional print resources are integrated throughout each chapter.*

Allez, viens! Level 2

***Allez, viens!** Level 2* consists of twelve instructional chapters. To facilitate articulation from one level to the next, Chapters 1, 2, and 12 are review chapters and Chapter 11 introduces minimal new material.

Following is a description of the various features in ***Allez, viens!*** and suggestions on how to use them in the classroom.

Starting Out...

Location Opener In ***Allez, viens!***, chapters are arranged by location. Each new location is introduced by four pages of colorful photos and information about the region.

Chapter Opener These two-pages provide a visual introduction to the theme of the chapter and include a list of objectives students will be expected to achieve.

Setting The Scene...

Mise en train Language instruction begins with this comprehensible input that models language in a culturally authentic setting. Presented also on video and audio CD, the highly visual presentation allows students to practice their receptive skills and to begin to recognize some of the new functions and vocabulary they will encounter in the chapter. Following **Mise en train** is a series of activities to check comprehension.

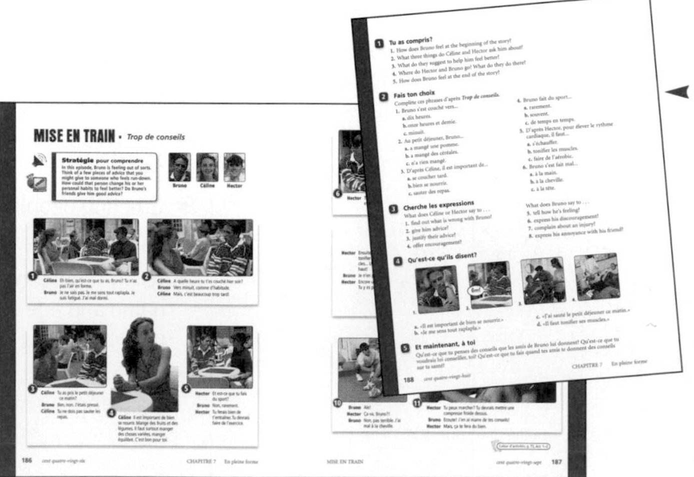

Building Proficiency Step By Step...

Première, Deuxième, and **Troisième étape** are the core instructional sections where most language acquisition will take place. The communicative goals in each chapter center on the functional expressions presented in **Comment dit-on...?** boxes. These expressions are supported by material in the **Vocabulaire, Grammaire,** and **Note de grammaire** sections. Activities following the above features are designed to practice recognition or to provide closed-ended practice. Activities then progress from controlled to open-ended practice where students are able to express themselves in meaningful communication.

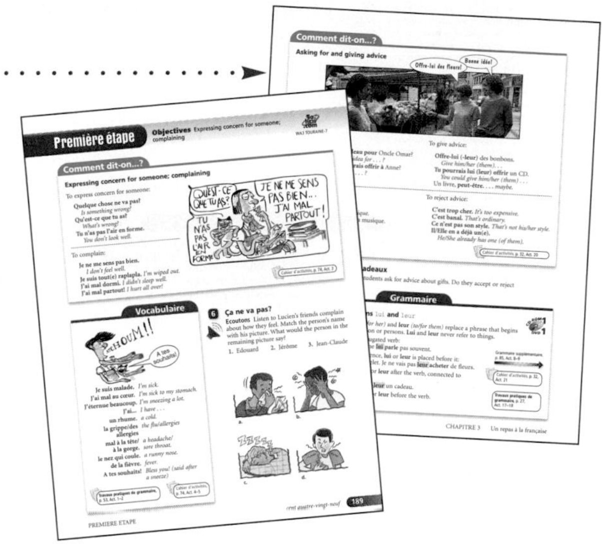

Discovering the People and the Culture...

There are also two major cultural features to help students develop an appreciation and understanding of the cultures of French-speaking countries.

Panorama Culturel presents interviews conducted throughout the French-speaking world on a topic related to the chapter theme. The interviews may be presented on video or done as a reading supplemented by the compact disc recording. Culminating activities on this page verify comprehension and encourage students to think critically about the target culture as well as their own.

Rencontre culturelle invites students to compare and contrast other cultures with their own.

Note culturelle helps students gain knowledge and understanding of other cultures.

Note culturelle

It is customary for guests to bring a gift when invited to a meal in a French home. Candy or flowers (other than chrysanthemums, which are associated with death) are always acceptable. When engaging in dinner conversation, there are several topics to avoid. These include asking about someone's age, profession, salary, or political affiliation.

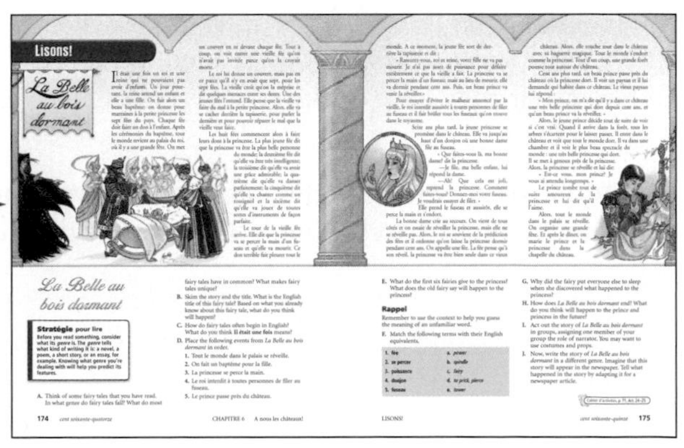

Understanding Authentic Documents...

Lisons! presents reading strategies that help students understand authentic French documents and literature presented in each chapter. The accompanying prereading, reading, and postreading activities develop students' overall reading skills and challenge their critical thinking abilities.

Targeting Students' Needs...

In each **étape** several special features may be used to enhance language learning and cultural appreciation.

De bons conseils suggests effective ways for students to learn a foreign language.

A la française provides students with tips for speaking more natural-sounding French.

Vocabulaire à la carte presents optional vocabulary related to the chapter theme.

Tu te rappelles? is a re-entry feature that lists and briefly explains previously learned vocabulary, functions, and grammar that students might need to review at the moment.

Si tu as oublié is a handy page reference to either an earlier chapter where material was presented or to a reference section in the back of the book.

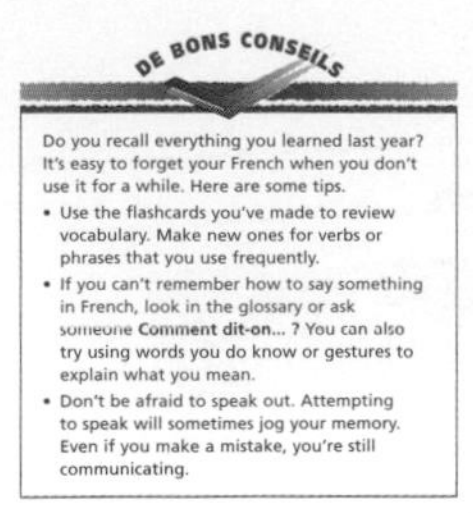

De bons conseils
Do you recall everything you learned last year? It's easy to forget your French when you don't use it for a while. Here are some tips.
• Use the flashcards you've made to review vocabulary. Make new ones for verbs or phrases that you use frequently.
• If you can't remember how to say something in French, look in the glossary or ask someone Comment dit-on... ? You can also try using words you do know or gestures to explain what you mean.
• Don't be afraid to speak out. Attempting to speak will sometimes jog your memory. Even if you make a mistake, you're still communicating.

A la française

There are many expressions you can use to show interest and get someone to continue a story in English. You can do the same in French. Say **Ah bon?** or **Ah oui?** *(Really?)*, **Et après?** *(And then what?)*, and **Et ensuite?** *(And what next?)*.

Vocabulaire à la carte

Zut!	*Darn!*
Oh là là!	*Oh my!*
Où je suis?	*Where am I?*
Qu'est-ce qui se passe?	*What's going on?*
Et alors?	*So what?*

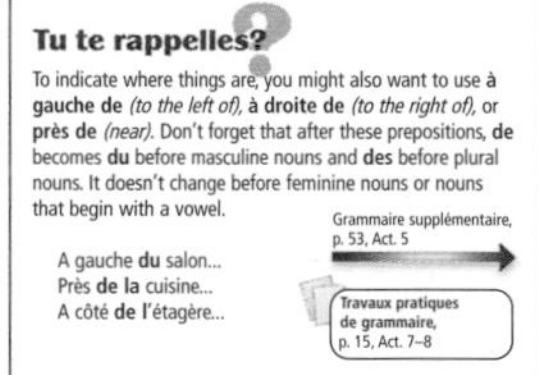

Tu te rappelles?
To indicate where things are, you might also want to use à gauche de (to the left of), à droite de (to the right of), or près de (near). Don't forget that after these prepositions, de becomes du before masculine nouns and des before plural nouns. It doesn't change before feminine nouns or nouns that begin with a vowel.
A gauche du salon...
Près de la cuisine...
A côté de l'étagère...
Grammaire supplémentaire, p. 53, Act. 5
Travaux pratiques de grammaire, p. 15, Act. 7–8

Wrapping It All Up...

Grammaire supplémentaire provides additional practice on the grammar concepts presented in the chapter.

Mise en pratique gives students the opportunity to review what they have learned and to apply their skills in new communicative contexts. Focusing on all four language skills as well as cultural awareness, the **Mise en pratique** can help you determine whether students are ready for the Chapter Test.

> **Ecrivons!** helps students develop their writing skills by focusing on the writing process. Each **Ecrivons!** gives students a topic related to the theme and functions of the chapter.

Que sais-je? is a checklist that students can use on their own to see if they have achieved the goals stated on the Chapter Opener.

Vocabulaire presents the chapter vocabulary grouped by **étape** and arranged according to function or theme.

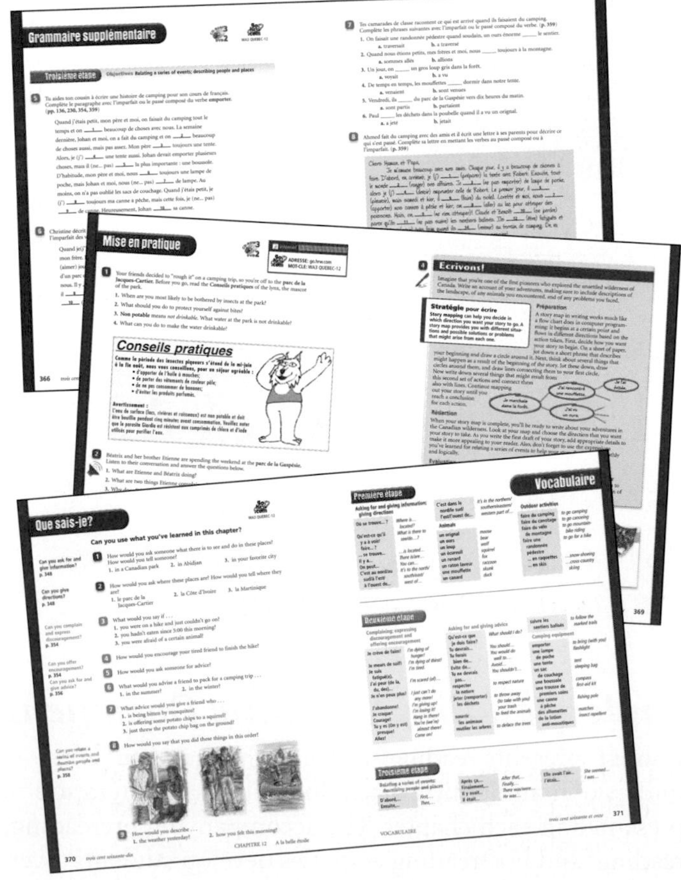

Technology Resources

Video Program-DVD Tutor

The *Video Program* and *DVD Tutor* provide the following video support:

- **Location Opener** documentaries
- **Mise en train** and **Suite** dramatic episodes
- **Panorama Culturel** interviews on a variety of cultural topics
- **Vidéoclips** which present authentic footage from target cultures

The *Video Guide* contains background information, suggestions for presentation, and activities for all portions of the *Video Program.*

Interactive CD-ROM Tutor

The *Interactive CD-ROM Tutor* offers:

- a variety of supporting activities correlated to the core curriculum of ***Allez, viens!*** and targeting all five skills
- a Teacher Management System (TMS) that allows teachers to view and assess students' work, manage passwords and records, track students' progress as they complete the activities, and activate English translations
- features such as a grammar reference section and a glossary to help students complete the activities

Internet Connection

Keywords in the *Pupil's Edition* provide access to two types of online activities:

- **Jeux interactifs** are directly correlated to the instructional material in the textbook. They can be used as homework, extra practice, or assessment.
- **Activités Internet** provide students with selected Web sites in French-speaking countries and activities related to the chapter theme. A printable worksheet in PDF format includes pre-surfing, surfing, and post-surfing activities that guide students through their research.

For easy access, see the keywords provided in the *Pupil's* and *Teacher's Editions.* For chapter-specific information, see the F page of the chapter interleaf.

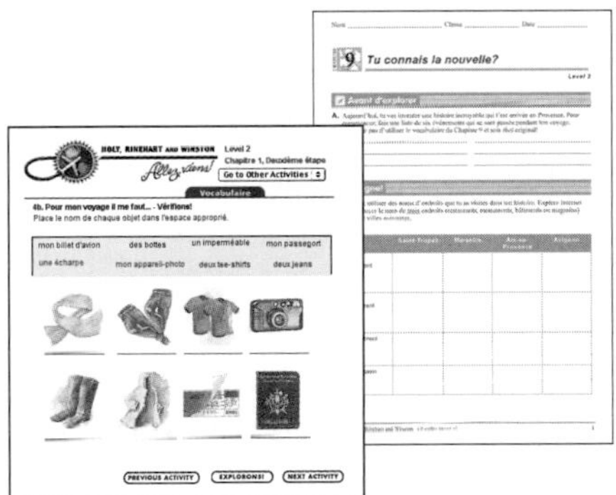

One-Stop Planner CD-ROM with Test Generator

The *One-Stop Planner CD-ROM* is a convenient tool to aid in lesson planning and pacing.

Easy navigation through menus or through lesson plans allows for a quick overview of available resources. For each chapter the *One-Stop Planner* includes:

- Editable lesson plans with direct links to teaching resources
- Printable worksheets from resource books
- Direct launches to the HRW Internet activities
- Video and audio segments
- Test Generator
- Clip Art for vocabulary items

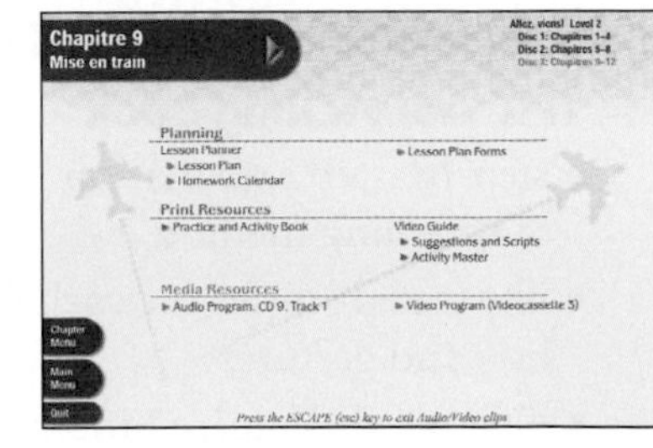

Ancillaries

The *Allez, viens!* French program offers a comprehensive ancillary package that addresses the concerns of today's teachers and is relevant to students' lives.

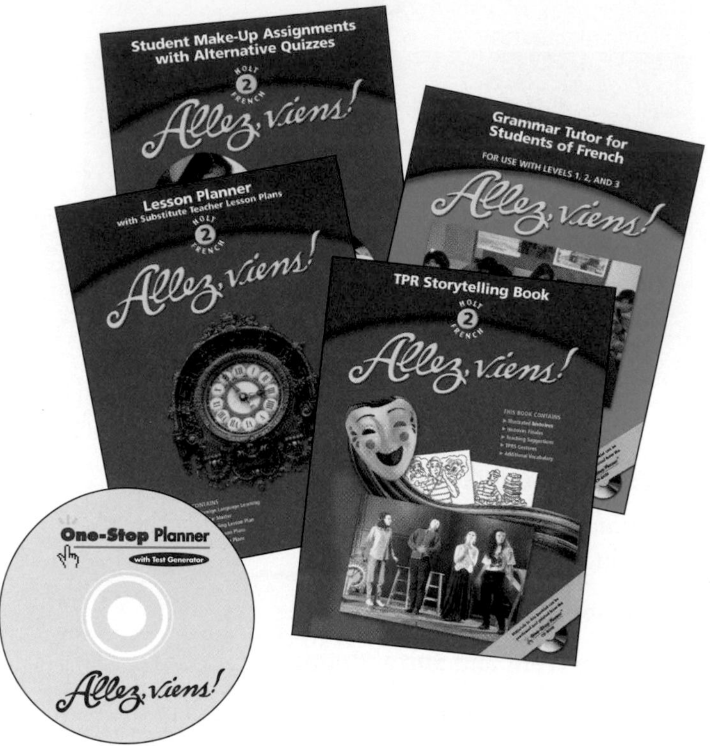

Lesson Planning

One-Stop Planner with Test Generator

- editable lesson plans
- printable worksheets from the resource books
- direct link to HRW Internet activities
- entire video and audio programs
- Test Generator
- Clip Art for vocabulary items

Lesson Planner with Substitute Teacher Lesson Plans
- complete lesson plans for every chapter
- block scheduling suggestions
- correlations to Standards for Foreign
- Language Learning
- a homework calendar
- chapter by chapter lesson plans for substitute teachers
- lesson plan forms for customizing lesson plans

Student Make-Up Assignments
- diagnostic information for students who are behind in their work
- copying masters for make-up assignments

Listening and Speaking

TPR Storytelling Book
- step-by-step explanation of the TPR Storytelling method
- illustrated stories for each **étape** with vocabulary lists and gestures
- illustrated **Histoire Finale** for each chapter
- teaching suggestions

Listening Activities
- print material associated with the *Audio Program*
- Student Response Forms for all Pupil's Edition listening activities
- Additional Listening Activities
- scripts, answers
- lyrics to each chapter's song

Audio Compact Discs
Listening activities for the *Pupil's Edition*, the Additional Listening Activities, and the *Testing Program*

Activities for Communication
- Communicative Activities for partner work based on an information gap
- Situation Cards to practice interviews and role-plays
- Realia: reproductions of authentic documents

Grammar

Travaux pratiques de grammaire
- re-presentations of major grammar points
- additional focused practice
- *Teacher's Edition* with overprinted answers

Grammar Tutor for Students of French
- presentations of grammar concepts in English
- re-presentations of French grammar concepts
- discovery and application activities

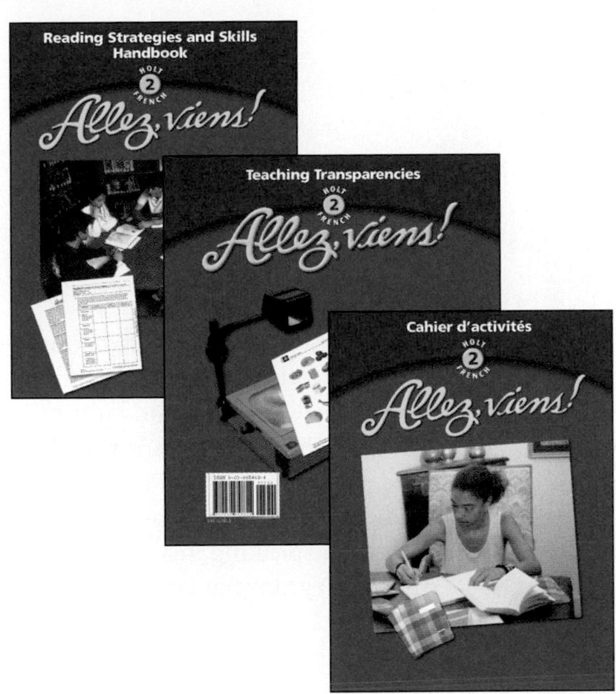

Reading and Writing

Reading Strategies and Skills Handbook

- explanations of reading strategies
- copying masters for application of strategies

Joie de lire 2

- readings on familiar topics
- cultural information
- additional vocabulary
- interesting and engaging activities

Cahier d'activités

- activities for practice
- *Teacher's Edition* with overprinted answers

Teaching Transparencies

- Colorful transparencies that help present and practice vocabulary, grammar, culture, and a variety of communicative functions
- **Mise en train**
- **Grammaire supplémentaire** Answers
- **Travaux pratiques de grammaire** Answers

Assessment

Testing Program

- Grammar and Vocabulary quizzes
- **Etape** quizzes that test the four skills
- Chapter Tests
- Speaking Tests
- Midterm and Final Exams
- Score sheets, scripts, answers

Alternative Assessment Guide

- Suggestions for oral and written Portfolio Assessment
- Performance Assessment
- CD-ROM Assessment
- rubrics, portfolio checklists, and evaluation forms

Student Make-Up Assignments

Alternative Grammar and Vocabulary quizzes for students who missed class and have to make up the quiz

Standardized Assessment Tutor

Reading, writing, and math tests in a standardized, multiple-choice format

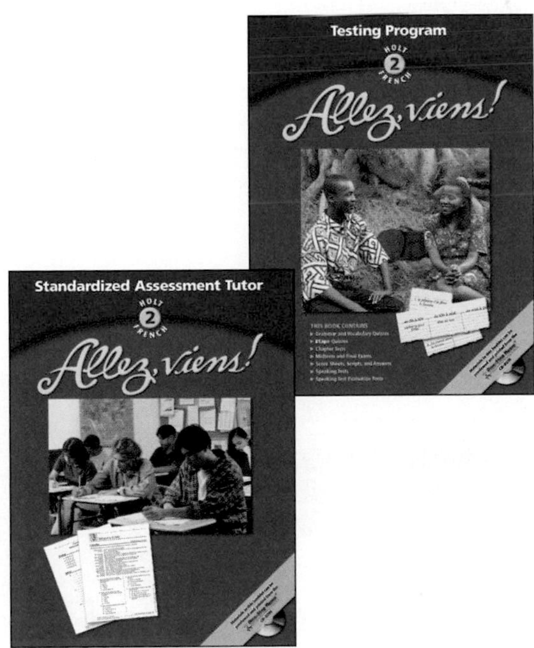

Annotated Teacher's Edition

Using the Chapter Interleaf

Each chapter of the ***Allez, viens!*** *Annotated Teacher's Edition* includes the following interleaf pages to help you plan, teach, and expand your lessons.

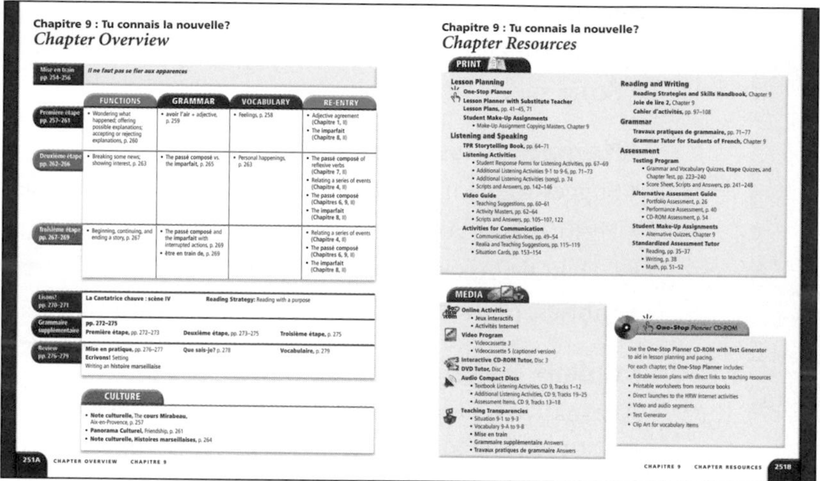

Chapter Overview

The Chapter Overview chart outlines at a glance the functions, grammar, vocabulary, re-entry, and culture featured in the chapter. You will also find a list of corresponding print and audiovisual resources organized by listening, speaking, reading, and writing skills, grammar, and assessment.

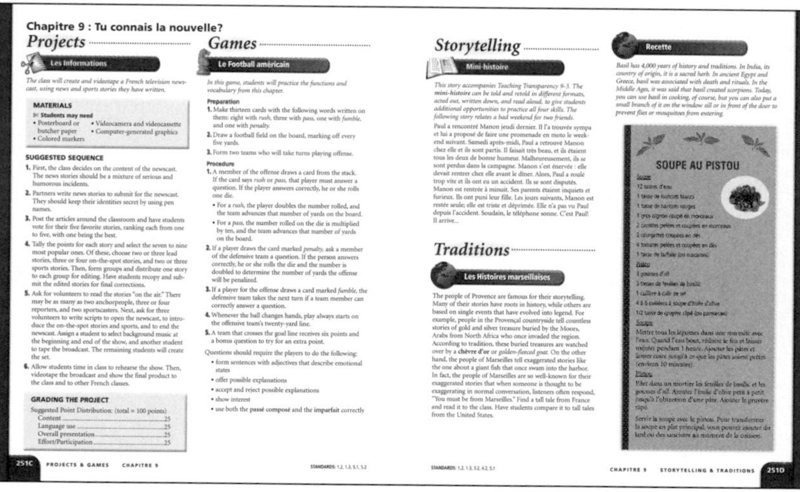

Projects/Games/ Storytelling/Traditions

Projects allow students to personalize and expand on the information from the chapter. Games reinforce the chapter content. In the Storytelling feature, you will find a story related to a *Teaching Transparency.* The Traditions feature concentrates on a unique aspect of the culture of the region. A recipe typical for the region accompanies this feature.

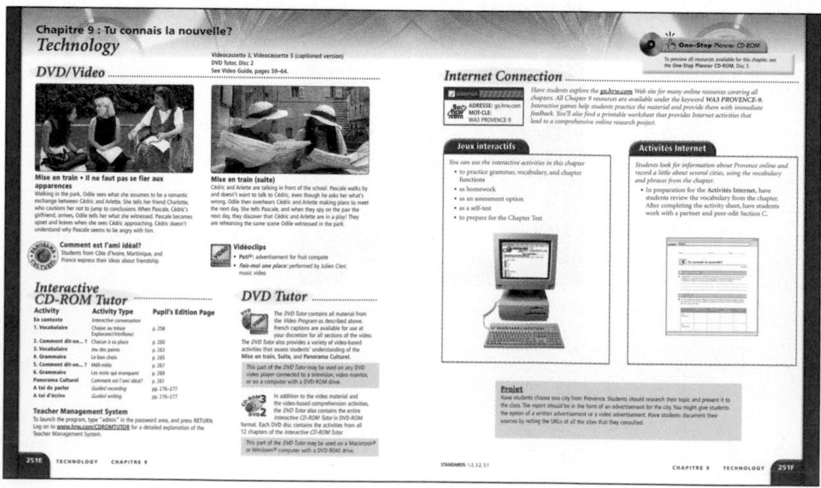

Technology

These pages assist you in integrating technology into your lesson plans. The Technology page provides a detailed list of video, DVD, CD-ROM, and Internet resources for your lesson. You will also find an Internet research project in each chapter.

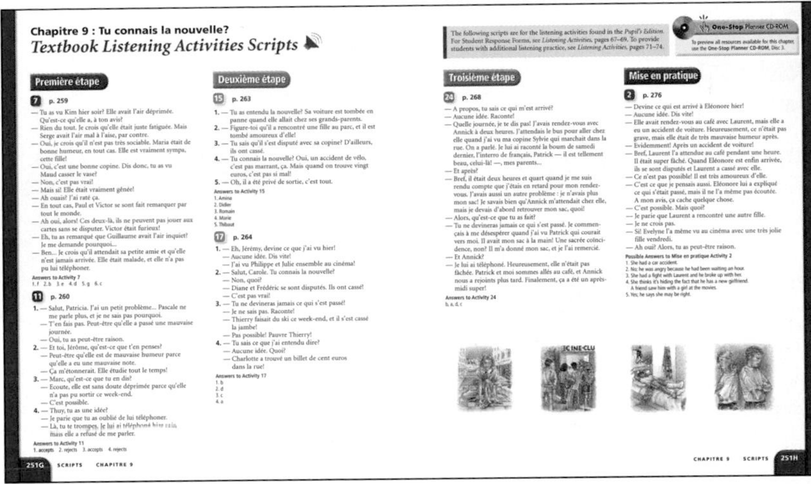

Textbook Listening Activities Scripts
Textbook Listening Activities Scripts provide the scripts of the chapter listening activities for reference or for use in class. The answers to each activity are provided below each script for easy reference.

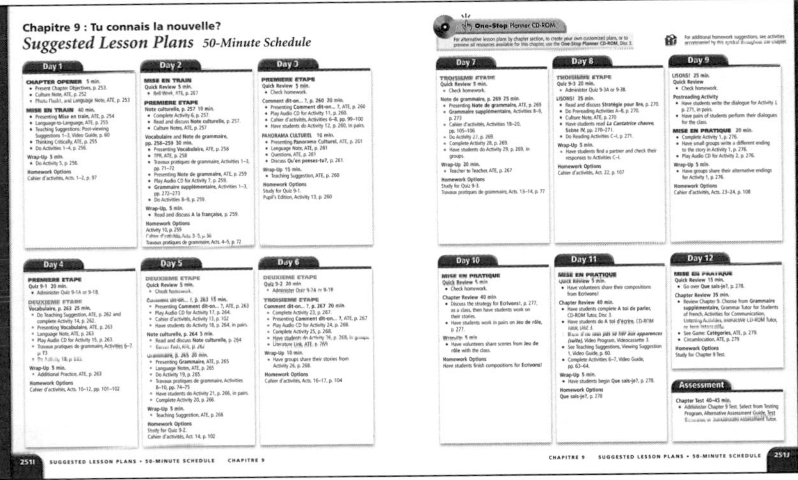

Suggested Lesson Plans—50-Minute Schedule
This lesson plan is used for classes with 50-minute schedules. Each lesson plan provides a logical sequence of instruction along with homework suggestions.

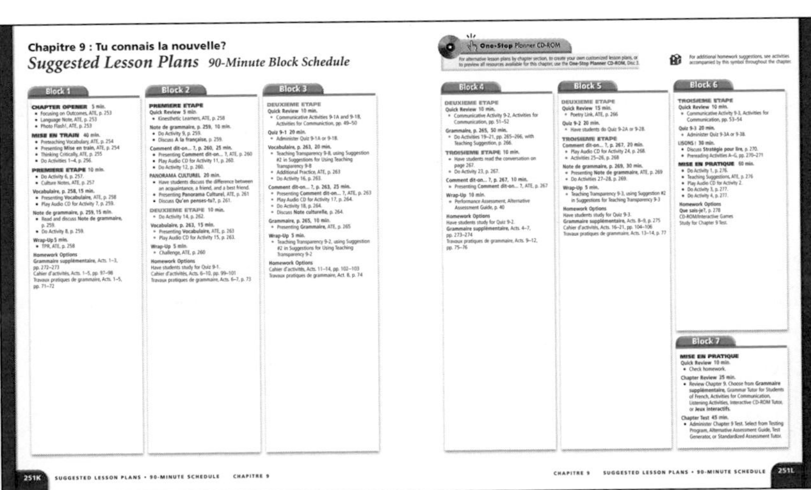

Suggested Lesson Plans—90-Minute Schedule
This lesson plan is used for classes with 90-minute schedules. Each lesson plan provides a logical sequence of instruction along with homework suggestions.

Using the Wrap-Around Teacher Text

Resource boxes provide a quick list of all the resources you can use for each chapter section.

Presenting boxes offer useful suggestions for presenting new material.

Première étape

CHAPITRE 5

Teaching Resources
pp. 133–137

PRINT 
- Lesson Planner, p. 22
- TPR Storytelling Book, pp. 32–33
- Listening Activities, pp. 35–36, 39
- Activities for Communication, pp. 25–26, 95, 98, 145–146
- Travaux pratiques de grammaire, pp. 37–40
- Grammar Tutor for Students of French, Chapter 5
- Cahier d'activités, pp. 50–52
- Testing Program, pp. 105–108
- Alternative Assessment Guide, p. 36
- Student Make-Up Assignments, Chapter 5

MEDIA
- One-Stop Planner
- Audio Compact Discs, CD 5, Trs. 3–5, 13, 19–20
- Teaching Transparencies: 5-1, 5-A; **Grammaire supplémentaire** Answers, Travaux pratiques de grammaire Answers
- Interactive CD-ROM Tutor, Disc 2

Presenting Grammaire

The passé composé Have students look at the sentences in the **Vocabulaire** on page 134. Explain that since the boy is talking about what *happened,* he's using the **passé composé.** Ask students how the **passé composé** is formed. List the past participles in the **Vocabulaire** and have students try to deduce the infinitives. Then, remind students how the negative is formed in the **passé composé** and call on individuals to make the sentences in the **Vocabulaire** on page 134 negative.

10 Qu'est-ce que tu dis?

Parlons/Ecrivons Imagine que tu rencontres Jean, Colette et Gérard à la fin de la journée. Demande-leur comment leur journée s'est passée. A ton avis, comment ils vont répondre?

Jean

Colette

Gérard

11 Encore en retard!

Parlons Tu es le proviseur du lycée! Ton/Ta camarade est un(e) élève qui arrive à l'école en retard. Demande-lui pourquoi il/elle est en retard et remplis un billet de retard. N'oublie pas de le signer! Ensuite, changez de rôle.

Ça n'a pas l'air d'aller. — en terminale
Vous vous appelez comment? — en seconde
Qu'est-ce qui vous est arrivé? — en première
Vous êtes en quelle classe?

Grammaire

The *passé composé* with *avoir*

CD-ROM 2 / DVD 1

You already know how to say that something happened in the past. For most verbs, you use a form of **avoir** and the past participle of the main verb.

j' **ai mangé**	nous **avons mangé**
tu **as mangé**	vous **avez mangé**
il/elle/on **a mangé**	ils/elles **ont mangé**

- To form past participles of **-er** verbs, drop **-er** from the infinitive and add **-é:**
  J'ai **raté** le bus.
- To form past participles of **-re** verbs, drop **-re** from the infinitive and add **-u:**
  Zut! On a **perdu** le match!
- To form past participles of **-ir** verbs, drop **-ir** from the infinitive and add **-i:**
  Enfin! On a **fini!**
- Many verbs have an irregular past participle, just as they do in English.
  Il a **été** collé aujourd'hui. (**être**)
  Vous avez **fait** vos devoirs? (**faire**)
  On a **eu** une interro. (**avoir**)
  J'ai **reçu** mon bulletin. (**recevoir**)
  Elle a **pris** un sandwich. (**prendre**)
  Il a **bu** de l'eau. (**boire**)
  Tu as **lu** ce roman? (**lire**)
  On a **vu** un film hier. (**voir**)
- To say that something didn't happen, put **ne... pas** around the form of **avoir:**
  Je **n'**ai **pas** entendu mon réveil.

Grammaire supplémentaire, pp. 148–149, Act. 1–4

Cahier d'activités, p. 52, Act. 8–9

Travaux pratiques de grammaire, pp. 39–40, Act. 5–8

Connections and Comparisons

Language-to-Language

In many languages, there are verbs that have irregular forms. If you have students who are native speakers of Spanish, have them identify some verbs that have irregular forms in the preterite in Spanish: **ser** *(to be),* **hacer** *(to make or to do),* **tener** *(to have),* **ver** *(to see).* Students may recognize that some of these corresponding verbs in French also have irregular forms in the **passé composé.** Ask students to identify some irregular verbs in English in the past tense. Ask them why they think certain verbs have historically become irregular.

136 CENT TRENTE-SIX PREMIERE ETAPE STANDARDS: 1.1, 4.1

Connections and Comparisons Under this head you will find helpful suggestions that connect what students are learning to other disciplines and provide critical thinking opportunities.

Correlations to the Standards for Foreign Language Learning are provided for your reference.

12 **Grammaire en contexte**

Ecoutons Listen to these students. Are they talking about something that is happening now or something that happened in the past?

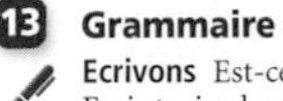

13 **Grammaire en contexte**

Ecrivons Est-ce que ces personnes ont passé une bonne ou une mauvaise journée? Ecris trois phrases pour décrire ce qui est arrivé à chaque personne.

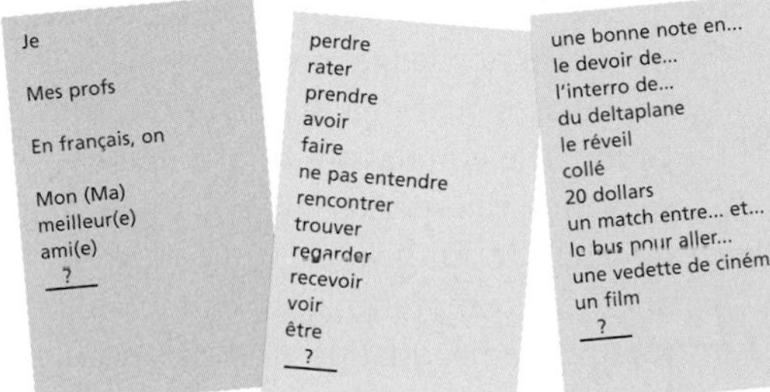

Je
Mes profs
En français, on
Mon (Ma) meilleur(e) ami(e)
?
perdre
rater
prendre
avoir
faire
ne pas entendre
rencontrer
trouver
regarder
recevoir
voir
être
?
une bonne note en...
le devoir de...
l'interro de...
du deltaplane
le réveil
collé
20 dollars
un match entre... et...
le bus pour aller...
une vedette de cinéma
un film
?

14 **L'heure de la sortie**

Ecrivons/Parlons Fais une liste de quatre activités que tes camarades font peut-être après l'école. Ensuite, demande à un(e) camarade s'il/si elle a fait ces activités hier.

EXEMPLE —**Tu as joué au foot hier?**
—**Non, j'ai joué au tennis.**

15 **Qu'est-ce qu'on a tous fait?**

Parlons In groups of four, try to find three things that everyone did last weekend and three things that no one did. Report your findings to the class, using **On a tous...** and **On n'a pas...** As the groups report, note the activities that most people did and didn't do.

16 **Jeu de rôle**

Parlons With a partner, choose two of these situations and take turns expressing concern for each other and asking and explaining what happened.

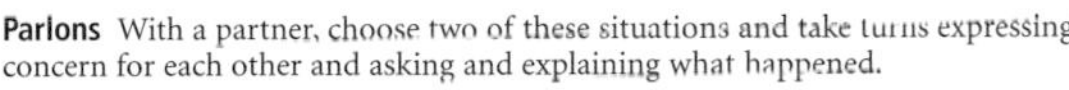

1. Tu arrives au cours de maths avec vingt minutes de retard. Le prof n'est pas content!
2. Tu n'étais pas à la boum de ton ami(e) samedi soir. Il/Elle veut savoir ce qui s'est passé.
3. Tu arrives chez toi à onze heures du soir. Ton père (ta mère) est furieux (furieuse).
4. Tu n'es pas allé(e) faire les magasins avec tes copains hier après l'école. Ton ami(e) te téléphone pour savoir pourquoi.

Communication for All Students

Challenge

12 Have students listen to the recording a second time and tell what happened or what is happening in each situation.

Group Work

Use Activity 16 to close this **étape.** Form small groups and assign one of the four situations to each one. Group members should work together to create the conversation and present it to the class.

Première étape

CHAPITRE 5

Additional Practice

12 On separate slips of paper, write an infinitive, the words **le présent** or **le passé composé,** and a subject in parentheses. Have pairs of students draw a slip of paper and work together to write a sentence, using the subject and the verb in the specified tense. Then, have one partner read the sentence aloud. The class will decide if the student is talking about something that is happening now or something that happened in the past.

Teaching Suggestion

14 For additional sports and weekend activities, refer students to the **Si tu as oublié...** section and the Additional Vocabulary in the back of the book.

Building on Previous Skills

15 To re-enter leisure activities and numbers, write several activities on the board. Have volunteers poll the class to see how many people did the activities last weekend. **(Qui a écouté de la musique?)** Have the poll takers count their classmates' raised hands aloud in French before they write the totals on the board.

Assess

- Testing Program, pp. 105–108
  Quiz 5-1A, Quiz 5-1B
  Audio CD 5, Tr. 13
- Student Make-Up Assignments, Chapter 5, Alternative Quiz
- Alternative Assessment Guide, p. 36

Possible Answers

10 Jean: —Qu'est-ce qui s'est passé?
—Je suis arrivé en retard au lycée.
Colette: —Qu'est-ce qui t'arrive?
—J'ai oublié mes devoirs.
Gérard: —Qu'est-ce qui s'est passé à l'école?
—J'ai eu huit à mon interro.

STANDARDS: 1.1, 1.3, 5.1, 5.2

The Annotated Teacher's Edition Wrap-Around Text offers helpful suggestions and information at point-of-use. You will also find annos, cultural information, correlations to the Standards for Foreign Language Learning, and references to other ancillaries.

Assessment
At the end of every **étape** and again at the end of the chapter, you will find references to all the assessment material available for that section of the chapter.

Communication for All Students
Under this head you will find helpful suggestions for students with different learning styles and abilities.

Bringing Standards into the Classroom

by Paul Sandrock, Foreign Language Consultant, Wisconsin Department of Public Education

The core question that guided the development of the National Standards and their accompanying goals was simply: what matters in instruction?

Each proposed standard was evaluated. Did the standard target material that will have application beyond the classroom? Was the standard too specific or not specific enough? Teachers should be able to teach the standard and assess it in multiple ways. A standard needs to provide a target for instruction and learning throughout a student's K–12 education.

In the development of standards, foreign languages faced other unique challenges. The writers could not assume a K–12 sequence available to all students. In fact, unlike other disciplines, they could not guarantee that all students would experience even any common sequence.

From this context, the National Standards in Foreign Language Education Project's task force generated the five C's, five goals for learning languages: communication, cultures, connections, comparisons, and communities. First presented in 1995, the standards quickly became familiar to foreign language educators across the US, representing our professional consensus and capturing a broad view of the purposes for learning another language.

To implement the standards, however, requires a shift from emphasizing the means to focusing on the ends. It isn't a matter of grammar versus communication, but rather how much grammar is needed to communicate. Instead of teaching to a grammatical sequence, teaching decisions become based on what students need to know to achieve the communicative goal.

The Focus on Communication

The first standard redefined communication, making its purpose **interpersonal, interpretive,** and **presentational** communication. Teaching to the purpose of interpersonal communication takes us away from memorized dialogues to spontaneous, interactive conversation, where the message is most important and where meaning needs to be negotiated between the speakers. Interpretive communication is not an exercise in translation, but asks beginners to tell the gist of an authentic selection that is heard, read, or viewed, while increasingly advanced learners tell deeper and deeper levels of detail and can interpret based on their knowledge of the target culture. In the presentational mode of communication, the emphasis is on the audience, requiring the speaker or writer to adapt language to fit the situation and to allow for comprehension without any interactive negotiation of the meaning.

Standards challenge us to refocus many of the things we've been doing all along. The requirements of speaking and our expectation of how well students need to speak change when speaking is for a different purpose. This focus on the purpose of the communication changes the way we teach and test the skills of listening, speaking, reading, and writing.

Standards help us think about how to help students put the pieces of language to work in meaningful ways. Our

Standards for Foreign Language Learning

Communication Communicate in Languages Other than English	**Standard 1.1** Students engage in conversations, provide and obtain information, express feelings and emotions, and exchange opinions. **Standard 1.2** Students understand and interpret written and spoken language on a variety of topics. **Standard 1.3** Students present information, concepts, and ideas to an audience of listeners or readers on a variety of topics.
Cultures Gain Knowledge and Understanding of Other Cultures	**Standard 2.1** Students demonstrate an understanding of the relationship between the practices and perspectives of the culture studied. **Standard 2.2** Students demonstrate an understanding of the relationship between the products and perspectives of the culture studied.
Connections Connect with Other Disciplines and Acquire Information	**Standard 3.1** Students reinforce and further their knowledge of other disciplines through the foreign language. **Standard 3.2** Students acquire information and recognize the distinctive viewpoints that are only available through the foreign language and its cultures.
Comparisons Develop Insight into the Nature of Language and Culture	**Standard 4.1** Students demonstrate understanding of the nature of language through comparisons of the language studied and their own. **Standard 4.2** Students demonstrate understanding of the concept of culture through comparisons of the cultures studied and their own.
Communities Participate in Multilingual Communities at Home and Around the World	**Standard 5.1** Students use the language both within and beyond the school setting. **Standard 5.2** Students show evidence of becoming life-long learners by using the language for personal enjoyment and enrichment.

standards answer *why* we are teaching various components of language, and we select *what* we teach in order to achieve those very standards.

The 5 C's

Originally the five C's were presented as five equal circles. During the years since the National Standards were printed, teachers implementing and using the standards to write curriculum, texts, and lesson plans have come to see that communication is at the core, surrounded by four C's that influence the context for teaching and assessing.

The four C's surrounding our core goal of **Communication** change our classrooms by bringing in real-life applications for the language learned:

- **Cultures:** Beyond art and literature, learning occurs in the context of the way of life, patterns of behavior, and contributions of the people speaking the language being taught.
- **Connections:** Beyond content limited to the culture of the people speaking the target language, teachers go out to other disciplines to find topics and ideas to form the context for language learning.
- **Comparisons:** Foreign language study is a great way for students to learn more about native language and universal principles of language and culture by comparing and contrasting their own to the target language and culture.
- **Communities:** This goal of the standards adds a broader motivation to the context for language learning. The teacher makes sure students use their new language beyond the class hour, seeking ways to experience the target culture.

Implementation at the Classroom Level: Assessment and Instruction

After the publication of the standards, states developed more specific performance standards that would provide evidence of the application of the national content standards. Standards provide the organizing principle for teaching and assessing. The standards-oriented teacher, when asked what she's teaching, cites the standard "students will sustain a conversation." With that clear goal in mind, she creates lessons to teach various strategies to ask for clarification and to practice asking follow-up questions that explore a topic in more depth.

Textbook writers and materials providers are responding to this shift. Standards provide our goals; the useful textbooks and materials give us an organization and a context. Standards provide the ends; textbooks and materials can help us practice the means. Textbooks can bring authentic materials into the classroom, real cultural examples that avoid stereotypes, and a broader exposure to the varicty of people who speak the language being studied. Textbooks can model the kind of instruction that will lead students to successful demonstration of the knowledge and skill described in the standards.

To really know that standards are the focus, look at the assessment. If standards are the target, assessment won't consist only of evaluation of the means (grammatical structures and vocabulary) in isolation. If standards are the focus, teachers will assess students' use of the second language in context. The summative assessment of our target needs to go beyond the specific and include open-ended, personalized tasks. Regardless of how the students show what they can do, the teacher will be able to gauge each student's progress toward the goal.

Assessment is like a jigsaw puzzle. If we test students only on the means, we just keep collecting random puzzle pieces. We have to test, and students have to practice, putting the pieces together in meaningful and purposeful ways. In order to learn vocabulary that will help students "describe themselves," for example, students may have a quiz on Friday with an expectation of close to 100% accuracy. But if that is all we ever do with those ten words, they will quickly be gone from students' memory, and we will only have collected a puzzle piece from each student. It is absolutely essential to have students use those puzzle pieces to complete the puzzle to provide evidence of what they "can do" with the language.

During this period of implementing our standards, we've learned that the standards provide a global picture, the essence of our goals. But they are not curriculum, nor are they lesson plans. The standards influence how we teach, but do not dictate one content nor one methodology. How can we implement the standards in our classrooms? Think about the targets; think about how students will show achievement of those targets through our evaluation measures; then think about what we need to teach and how that will occur in our classrooms. Make it happen in your classroom to get the results we've always wanted: students who can communicate in a language other than English.

Allez, viens!

supports the Standards for Foreign Language Learning in the following ways:

THE PUPIL'S EDITION

- Encourages students to take responsibility for their learning by providing clearly defined objectives at the beginning of each chapter.
- Provides a variety of pair- and group-work activities to give students an opportunity to use the target language in a wide range of settings and contexts.
- Offers culture-related activities and poses questions that develop students' insight and encourage them to develop observational and analytical skills.

THE ANNOTATED TEACHER'S EDITION

- Provides a broad framework for developing a foreign language program and offers specific classroom suggestions for reaching students with various learning styles.
- Offers ideas for multicultural and multidisciplinary projects as well as community and family links that encourage students to gain access to information both at school and in the community.

THE ANCILLARY PROGRAM

- Provides students with on-location video footage of native speakers interacting in their own cultural and geographic context.
- Includes multiple options for practicing new skills and assessing performance, including situation cards, portfolio suggestions, speaking tests, and other alternatives.
- Familiarizes students with the types of tasks they will be expected to perform on exit exams.

Reading Strategies and Skills

by Nancy Humbach, Miami University

Reading is the most enduring of the language skills. Long after a student ceases to study the language, the ability to read will continue to provide a springboard to the renewal of the other skills. We must consider all the ways in which our students will read and address the skills needed for those tasks.

How can we accomplish this goal? How can we, as teachers, present materials, encourage students to read, and at the same time foster understanding and build the student's confidence and interest in reading?

Selection of Materials

Reading material in the foreign language classroom should be relevant to students' backgrounds and at an accessible level of difficulty, i.e., at a level of difficulty only slightly above the reading ability of the student.

Authentic materials are generally a good choice. They provide cultural context and linguistic authenticity seldom found in materials created for students, and the authentic nature of the language provides a window on a new world. The problem inherent in the selection of authentic materials at early levels is obvious: the level of difficulty is frequently beyond the skill of the student. At the same time, however, readers are inspired by the fact that they can understand materials designed to be read by native speakers.

Presenting a Selection/ Reading Strategies

We assume that students of a second language already have a reading knowledge in their first language and that many of the skills they learned in their "reading readiness" days will serve them well. Too often, however, students have forgotten such skills as activating background knowledge, skimming, scanning, and guessing content based on context clues. Helping students to reactivate these skills is part of helping them become better readers.

Teachers should not assume their students' ability to transfer a knowledge set from one reading to another. Students use these skills on a regular basis, but often do not even realize they are doing so. To help students become aware of these processes, they need to be given strategies for reading. These strategies offer students a framework for the higher-level skills they need to apply when reading. Strategies also address learners of different learning styles and needs.

Advance Organizers

One way to activate the student's background knowledge is through advance organizers. They also serve to address the student's initial frustrations at encountering an unfamiliar text.

Advance organizers call up pertinent background knowledge, feelings, and experiences that can serve to focus the attention of the entire group on a given topic. In addition, they provide for a sharing of information among the students. Background information that includes cultural references and cultural information can reactivate in students skills that will help them with a text and provide for them clues to the meaning of the material.

A good advance organizer will provide some information and guide students to think about the scenarios being presented. An advance organizer might include photographs, drawings, quotations, maps, or information about the area where the story takes place. It might also be posed as a question, for example, "What would you do if you found yourself in....?" Having students brainstorm in advance, either as a whole class or in small groups, allows them to construct a scenario which they can verify as they read.

Prereading Activities

Prereading activities remind students of how much they really know and can prepare students in a number of ways to experience the language with less frustration. While we know that we must choose a reading selection that is not far beyond students' experience and skill level, we also know that no group of students reads at the same level. In the interest of assisting students to become better language learners, we can provide them with opportunities to work with unfamiliar structures and vocabulary ahead of time.

Preparing students for a reading selection can include a number of strategies that may anticipate but not dwell on potential problems to be encountered by students. Various aspects of grammar, such as differences in the past tenses and the meanings conveyed, can also cause problems. Alerting students to some of the aspects of the language allows them to struggle less, understand more quickly, and enjoy a reading selection to a greater degree.

Grouping vocabulary by category or simply choosing a short list of critical words for a section of reading is helpful. Providing an entire list of vocabulary items at one time can be overwhelming. With a bit of organization, the task becomes manageable to the point where students begin to master words they will find repeated throughout the selection.

Having students skim for a particular piece of information or scan for words, phrases, indicators of place or time, and names, and then asking them to write a sentence or two about the gist of a paragraph or story, gives them a sense of independence and success before they begin to read.

Getting into the Assignment

Teachers can recount the times they have assigned a piece of reading for homework, only to find that few students even attempted the work. Therefore, many teachers choose to complete the reading in class. Homework assignments should then be structured to have the student return to the selection and complete a assignment that requires critical thinking and imagination.

During class, several techniques assist students in maintaining interest and attention to the task. By varying these techniques, the teacher can provide for a lively class, during which students realize they *are* able to read. Partners can read passages to each other or students can take turns reading in small groups. The teacher might pose a question to be answered during that reading. Groups might also begin to act out short scenes, reading only the dialogue. Student might read a description of a setting and then draw what they imagine it to be. Of course, some selections might be silent reading with a specific amount of time announced for completion.

Reading aloud for comprehension and reading aloud for pronunciation practice are two entirely unrelated tasks. We can all recall classes where someone read aloud to us from weary lecture notes. Active engagement of the readers, on the other hand, forces them to work for comprehension, for the development of thought processes, and for improvement of language skills.

Postreading Activities

It is important to provide students with an opportunity to expand the knowledge they have gained from the reading selection. Students should apply what they have learned to their own personal experiences. How we structure activities can provide students more opportunities to reflect on their reading and learn how much they have understood. We often consider a written test the best way to ensure comprehension; however, many other strategies allow students to keep oral skills active. These might include acting out impromptu scenes from the story and creating dialogues that do not exist in a story, but might be imagined, based on other information. Consider the possibility of debates, interviews, TV talk show formats, telephone dialogues, or a monologue in which the audience hears only one side of the conversation.

Written assignments are also valid assessment tools, allowing students to incorporate the vocabulary and structures they have learned in the reading. Students might be encouraged to write journal entries for a character, create a new ending, or retell the story from another point of view. Newspaper articles, advertisements, and other creations can also be a means of following up. Comparisons with other readings require students to keep active vocabulary and structures they have studied previously. Encourage students to read their creations aloud to a partner, to a group, or to the class.

Conclusion

Reading can be exciting. The combination of a good selection that is relevant and rates high on the interest scale, along with good preparation, guidance, and postreading activities that demonstrate to the students the level of success attained, can encourage them to continue to read. These assignments also allow for the incorporation of other aspects of language learning, and incorporate the Five C's of the National Standards. Communication and culture are obvious links, but so are connections (advance organizers, settings, and so on), comparisons (with other works in the heritage or target language), and communities (learning why a type of writing is important in a culture).

Allez, viens!

offers reading practice and develops reading skills and strategies in the following ways:

THE PUPIL'S EDITION

- Provides an extensive reading section in each chapter called **Lisons!** Each **Lisons!** section offers a strategy students apply to an authentic text, as well as activities to guide understanding and exploration of the text.

THE ANNOTATED TEACHER'S EDITION

- Provides teachers with additional activities and information in every **Lisons!** section. Additional suggestions are provided for Pre-reading, Reading, and Postreading activities.

THE ANCILLARY PROGRAM

- ***Joie de lire*** This component offers reading selections of various formats and difficulty levels. Each chapter has a prereading feature, a reading selection with comprehension questions, and two pages of activities.
- The *Reading Strategies and Skills Handbook* offers useful strategies that can be applied to reading selections in the *Pupil's Edition,* ***Joie de lire,*** or a selection of your choosing.
- The ***Cahier d'activités*** contains a reading selection tied to the chapter theme, and reading activities for each chapter in ***Allez, viens!***

Using Portfolios in the Language Classroom

by Jo Anne S. Wilson, J. Wilson Associates

Portfolios offer a more realistic and accurate way to assess the process of language teaching and learning.

The communicative, whole-language approach of today's language instruction requires assessment methods that parallel the teaching and learning strategies in the proficiency-oriented classroom. We know that language acquisition is a process. Portfolios are designed to assess the steps in that process.

What Is a Portfolio?

A portfolio is a purposeful, systematic collection of a student's work. A useful tool in developing a student profile, the portfolio shows the student's efforts, progress, and achievements for a given period of time. It may be used for periodic evaluation, as the basis for overall evaluation, or for placement. It may also be used to enhance or provide alternatives to traditional assessment measures, such as formal tests, quizzes, class participation, and homework.

Why Use Portfolios?

Portfolios benefit both students and teachers because they:

- **Are ongoing and systematic.** A portfolio reflects the real-world process of production, assessment, revision, and reassessment. It parallels the natural rhythm of learning.
- **Offer an incentive to learn.** Students have a vested interest in creating the portfolios, through which they can showcase their ongoing efforts and tangible achievements. Students select the works to be included and have a chance to revise, improve, evaluate, and explain the contents.
- **Are sensitive to individual needs.** Language learners bring varied abilities to the classroom and do not acquire skills in a uniformly neat and orderly fashion. The personalized, individualized assessment offered by portfolios responds to this diversity.
- **Provide documentation of language development.** The material in a portfolio is evidence of student progress in the language learning process. The contents of the portfolio make it easier to discuss their progress with the students as well as with parents and others.
- **Offer multiple sources of information.** A portfolio presents a way to collect and analyze information from multiple sources that reflects a student's efforts, progress, and achievements in the language.

Portfolio Components

The language portfolio should include both oral and written work, student self-evaluation, and teacher observation, usually in the form of brief, nonevaluative comments about various aspects of the student's performance.

The Oral Component

The oral component of a portfolio might be an audio- or videocassette. It may contain both rehearsed and extemporaneous monologues and conversations. For a rehearsed speaking activity, give a specific communicative task that students can personalize according to their individual interests (for example, ordering a favorite meal in a restaurant). If the speaking activity is extemporaneous, first acquaint students with possible topics for discussion or even the specific task they will be expected to perform. (For example, tell them they will be asked to discuss a picture showing a sports activity or a restaurant scene.)

The Written Component

Portfolios are excellent tools for incorporating process writing strategies into the language classroom. Documentation of various stages of the writing process—brainstorming, multiple drafts, and peer comments—may be included with the finished product.

Involve students in selecting writing tasks for the portfolio. At the beginning levels, the tasks might include some structured writing, such as labeling or listing. As students become more proficient, journals, letters, and other more complicated writing tasks are valuable ways for them to monitor their progress in using the written language.

Student Self-Evaluation

Students should be actively involved in critiquing and evaluating their portfolios and monitoring their own progress.

The process and procedure for student self-evaluation should be considered in planning the contents of the portfolio. Students should work with you and their peers to design the exact format. Self-evaluation encourages them to think about what they are learning (content), how they learn (process), why they are learning (purpose), and where they are going in their learning (goals).

Teacher Observation

Systematic, regular, and ongoing observations should be placed in the portfolio after they have been discussed with the student. These observations provide feedback on the student's progress in the language learning process.

Teacher observations should be based on an established set of criteria that has been developed earlier with input from the student. Observation techniques may include the following:

- Jotting notes in a journal to be discussed with the student and then placed in the portfolio
- Using a checklist of observable behaviors, such as the willingness to take risks when using the target language or staying on task during the lesson
- Making observations on adhesive notes that can be placed in folders
- Recording anecdotal comments, during or after class, using a cassette recorder.

Knowledge of the criteria you use in your observations gives students a framework for their performance.

Electronic Portfolios

Technology can provide help with managing student portfolios. Digital or computer-based portfolios offer a means of saving portfolios in an electronic format. Students can save text, drawings, photographs, graphics, audio or video recordings, or any combination of multimedia information. Teachers can create their own portfolio templates or consult one of the many commercial software programs available to create digital portfolios. Portfolios saved on videotapes or compact discs provide a convenient way to access and store students' work. By employing technology, this means of alternative assessment addresses the learning styles and abilities of individual students. Additionally, electronic portfolios can be shared among teachers, and parents have the ability to easily see the students' progress.

Logistically, the hypermedia equipment and software available for students' use determine what types of entries will be included in the portfolios. The teacher or a team of teachers and students may provide the computer support.

How Are Portfolios Evaluated?

The portfolio should reflect the process of student learning over a specific period of time. At the beginning of that time period, determine the criteria by which you will assess the final product and convey them to the students. Make this evaluation a collaborative effort by seeking students' input as you formulate these criteria and your instructional goals.

Students need to understand that evaluation based on a predetermined standard is but one phase of the assessment process; demonstrated effort and growth are just as important. As you consider correctness and accuracy in both oral and written work, also consider the organization, creativity, and improvement revealed by the student's portfolio over the time period. The portfolio provides a way to monitor the growth of a student's knowledge, skills, and attitudes and shows the student's efforts, progress, and achievements.

How to Implement Portfolios

Teacher-teacher collaboration is as important to the implementation of portfolios as teacher-student collaboration. Confer with your colleagues to determine, for example, what kinds of information you want to see in the student portfolio, how the information will be presented, the purpose of the portfolio, the intended purposes (grading, placement, or a combination of the two), and criteria for evaluating the portfolio. Conferring among colleagues helps foster a departmental cohesiveness and consistency that will ultimately benefit the students.

The Promise of Portfolios

The high degree of student involvement in developing portfolios and deciding how they will be used generally results in renewed student enthusiasm for learning and improved achievement. As students compare portfolio pieces done early in the year with work produced later, they can take pride in their progress as well as reassess their motivation and work habits.

Allez, viens!

supports the use of portfolios in the following ways:

THE PUPIL'S EDITION

- Includes numerous oral and written activities that can be easily adapted for student portfolios, such as **Mon journal, Ecrivons!,** and **Jeu de rôle.**

THE ANNOTATED TEACHER'S EDITION

- Suggests activities in the Portfolio Assessment feature that may serve as portfolio items.

THE ANCILLARY PROGRAM

- Includes criteria in the *Alternative Assessment Guide* for evaluating portfolios.
- Provides Speaking Tests in the *Testing Program* for each chapter that can be adapted for use as portfolio assessment items.
- Offers several oral and written scenarios on the *Interactive CD-ROM Tutor* that students can develop and include in their portfolios.

Teaching Culture

by Nancy A. Humbach, Miami University, and Dorothea Bruschke, Parkway School District

We must integrate culture and language in a way that encourages curiosity, stimulates analysis, and teaches students to hypothesize.

The teaching of culture has undergone some important and welcome changes in recent years. Instead of teaching the standard notions of cultures, language and regions, we now stress the teaching of analysis and the critical thinking skills required to evaluate a culture, by comparing it to one's own, but within its own setting. The setting includes the geography, climate, history, and influences of peoples who have interacted within that cultural group.

The National Standards for the Teaching of Foreign Languages suggests organizing the teaching of culture into three categories: products, practices, and perspectives. Through the presentation of these aspects of culture, students should gain the skill to analyze the culture, evaluate it within its context, compare it to their culture and develop the ability to function comfortably in that culture.

Skill and practice in the analysis of cultural phenomena equip students to enter a cultural situation, assess it, create strategies for dealing with it, and accepting it as a natural part of the people. The ultimate goal of this philosophy is to reduce the "we vs. they" approach to culture. If students are encouraged to accept and appreciate the diversity of other cultures, they will be more willing and better able to develop the risk-taking strategies necessary to learn a language and to interact with people of different cultures.

There are many ways to help students become culturally knowledgeable and to assist them in developing an awareness of differences and similarities between the target culture and their own. Two of these approaches involve critical thinking, that is, trying to find reasons for a certain behavior through observation and analysis, and putting individual observations into larger cultural patterns. We must integrate culture and language in a way that encourages curiosity, stimutates analysis, and teaches students to hypothesize.

First Approach: Questioning

The first approach involves questioning as the key strategy. At the earliest stages of language learning, students begin to learn ways to greet peers, elders, and strangers, as well as the use of **tu** and **vous.** Students need to consider questions such as: "How do French-speaking people greet each other? Are there different levels of formality? Who initiates a handshake? When is a handshake or kisses on the cheeks **(la bise)** appropriate?" Each of these questions leads students to think about the values that are expressed through word and gesture. They start to "feel" the other culture, and at the same time, understand how much of their own behavior is rooted in their cultural background.

Magazines, newspapers, advertisements, and television commercials are all excellent sources of cultural material. For example, browsing through a French magazine, one finds a number of advertisements for food items and bottled water. Could this indicate a great interest in eating and preparing healthy food? Reading advertisements can be followed up with viewing videos and films, or with interviewing native speakers or people who have lived in French-speaking countries about customs involving food selection and preparation. Students might want to find answers to questions such as: "How much time do French people spend shopping for and preparing a meal? How long does a typical meal **en famille** last? What types of food and beverages does it involve?" This type of questioning might lead students to discover different attitudes toward food and mealtimes.

An advertisement for a refrigerator or a picture of a French kitchen can provide an insight into practices of shopping for food. Students first need to think about the refrigerator at home, take an inventory of what is kept in it, and consider when and where their family shops. Next, students should look closely at a French refrigerator. What is its size? What could that mean? (Shopping takes place more often, stores are within walking distance, and people eat more fresh foods.)

Food wrappers and containers also provide good clues to cultural insight. For example, since bread is often purchased fresh from a **boulangerie,** it is usually carried in one's hand or tote bag, with no packaging at all. Since most people shop daily and carry their own groceries home, heavier items like sodas often come in bottles no larger than one and one-half liters.

Second Approach: Associating Words with Images

The second approach for developing cultural understanding involves forming associations of words with the cultural images they suggest. Language and culture are so closely related that one might actually say that language *is* culture. Most words, especially nouns, carry a cultural connotation. Knowing the literal equivalent of a word in another language is of little use to students in understanding this connotation. For example, **ami** cannot be translated simply as *friend,* **pain** as *bread,* or **rue** as *street.* The French word **pain,** for instance, carries with it the image of a small local bakery stocked with twenty or thirty different varieties of freshly-baked bread, all warm from a brick oven. At breakfast, bread is sliced, covered with butter and jam, and eaten as a **tartine;** it is eaten throughout the afternoon and evening meals, in particular as an accompaniment to the cheese course. In French-speaking countries, "bread" is more than a grocery item; it is an essential part of every meal.

When students have acquired some sense of the cultural connotation of words—not only through teachers' explanations but, more importantly, through observation of visual images—they start to discover the larger underlying cultural themes, or what is often called deep culture.

These larger cultural themes serve as organizing categories into which individual cultural phenomena fit to form a pattern. Students might discover, for example, that French speakers, because they live in much more crowded conditions, have a great need for privacy (cultural theme), as reflected in such phenomena as closed doors, fences or walls around property, and sheers on windows. Students might also discover that love of nature and the outdoors is an important cultural theme, as indicated by such phenomena as flower boxes and planters in public places—even on small traffic islands—well-kept public parks in every town, and people going for a walk or going hiking.

As we teach culture, students learn not only to recognize elements of the target culture but also of their American cultural heritage. They see how elements of culture reflect larger themes or patterns. Learning what constitutes American culture and how that information relates to other people throughout the world can be an exciting journey for a young person.

As language teachers, we are able to facilitate that journey into another culture and into our own, to find our similarities as well as our differences from others. We do not encourage value judgments about others and their culture, nor do we recommend adopting other ways. We simply say to students, "Other ways exist. They exist for many reasons, just as our ways exist due to what our ancestors have bequeathed us through history, traditions, values, and geography."

Allez, viens!

develops cultural understanding and awareness in the following ways:

THE PUPIL'S EDITION

- Informs students about French-speaking countries through photo essays, maps, almanac boxes, and **Notes culturelles** that invite comparison with the students' own cultural experiences.
- Engages students in analysis and comparison of live, personal interviews with native speakers in the **Panorama Culturel** sections.
- Uses the **Rencontre culturelle** section to expose students to cross-cultural situations that require observation, analysis, and problem-solving.
- Helps students integrate the language with its cultural connotations through a wealth of authentic art, documents, and literature.

THE ANNOTATED TEACHER'S EDITION

- Provides the teacher with additional culture, history, and language notes, background information on photos and almanac boxes, and multicultural links.
- Suggests problem-solving activities and critical thinking questions that allow students to hypothesize, analyze, and discover larger underlying cultural themes.

THE ANCILLARY PROGRAM

- Includes additional realia to develop cultural insight by serving as a catalyst for questioning and direct discovery.
- Offers activities that require students to compare and contrast cultures.
- Provides songs, short readings, and poems as well as many opportunities for students to experience regional variation and idioms in the video, audio, and CD-ROM programs.

Learning Styles and Multi-Modality Teaching

by Mary B. McGehee, Louisiana State University

Incorporating a greater variety of activities to accommodate the learning styles of all students can make the difference between struggle and pleasure in the foreign language classroom.

The larger and broader population of students who are enrolling in foreign language classes brings a new challenge to foreign language educators, calling forth an evolution in teaching methods to enhance learning for all our students. Educational experts now recognize that every student has a preferred sense for learning and retrieving information: visual, auditory, or kinesthetic. Incorporating a greater variety of activities to accommodate the learning styles of all students can make the difference between struggle and pleasure in the foreign language classroom.

Accommodating Different Learning Styles

A modified arrangement of the classroom is one way to provide more effective and enjoyable learning for all students. Rows of chairs and desks must give way at times to circles, semicircles, or small clusters. Students may be grouped in fours or in pairs for cooperative work or peer teaching. It is important to find a balance of arrangements, thereby providing the most comfort in varied situations.

Since visual, auditory, and kinesthetic learners will be in the class, and because every student's learning will be enhanced by a multi-sensory approach, lessons must be directed toward all three learning styles. Any language lesson content may be presented visually, aurally, or kinesthetically.

Visual presentations and practice may include the chalkboard, charts, posters, television, overhead projectors, books, magazines, picture diagrams, flash cards, bulletin boards, films, slides, or videos. Visual learners need to see what they are to learn. Lest the teacher think he or she will never have the time to prepare all those visuals, Dickel and Slak (1983) found that visual aids generated by students are more effective than ready-made ones.

Auditory presentations and practice may include stating aloud the requirements of the lesson, oral questions and answers, paired or group work on a progression of oral exercises from repetition to communication, tapes, CDs, dialogues, and role-playing. Jingles, catchy stories, and memory devices using songs and rhymes are good learning aids. Having students record themselves and then listen as they play back the cassette allows them to practice in the auditory mode.

Kinesthetic presentations entail the students' use of manipulatives, chart materials, gestures, signals, typing, songs, games, and role-playing. These lead the students to associate sentence constructions with meaningful movements.

A Sample Lesson Using Multi-Modality Teaching

A multi-sensory presentation on greetings might proceed as follows:

For Visual Learners

As the teacher begins oral presentation of greetings and introductions, he or she simultaneously shows the written forms on transparencies, with the formal expressions marked with an adult's hat, and the informal expressions marked with a baseball cap.

The teacher then distributes cards with the hat and cap symbols representing the formal and informal expressions. As the students hear taped mini-dialogues, they hold up the appropriate card to indicate whether the dialogues are formal or informal. On the next listening, the students repeat the sentences they hear.

For Auditory Learners

A longer taped dialogue follows, allowing the students to hear the new expressions a number of times. They write from dictation several sentences containing the new expressions. They may work in pairs, correcting each other's work as they "test" their own understanding of the lesson at hand. Finally, students respond to simple questions using the appropriate formal and informal responses cued by the cards they hold.

For Kinesthetic Learners

For additional kinesthetic input, members of the class come to the front of the room, each holding a hat or cap symbol. As the teacher calls out situations, the students play the roles, using gestures and props appropriate to the age group they are portraying. Non-cued, communicative role-playing with props further enables the students to "feel" the differences between formal and informal expressions.

Helping Students Learn How to Use Their Preferred Mode

Since we require all students to perform in all language skills, part of the assistance we must render is to help them develop strategies within their preferred learning modes to carry out an assignment in another mode. For example, visual students hear the teacher assign an oral exercise and visualize what they must do. They must see themselves carrying out the assignment, in effect watching themselves as if there were a movie going on in their heads. Only then can they also hear themselves saying the right things. Thus, this assignment will be much easier for the visual learners who have been taught this process, if they have not already figured it out for themselves. Likewise, true auditory students, confronted with a reading/writing assignment, must talk themselves through it, converting the entire process into sound as they plan and prepare their work. Kinesthetic students presented with a visual or auditory task must first break the assignment into tasks and then work their way through them.

Students who experience difficulty because of a strong preference for one mode of learning are often unaware of the degree of preference. In working with these students, I prefer the simple and direct assessment of learning styles offered by Richard Bandler and John Grinder in their book *Frogs into Princes,* which allows the teacher and student to quickly determine how the student learns. In an interview with the student, I follow the assessment with certain specific recommendations of techniques to make the student's study time more effective.

The following is an example of an art-based activity from *Allez,viens!*

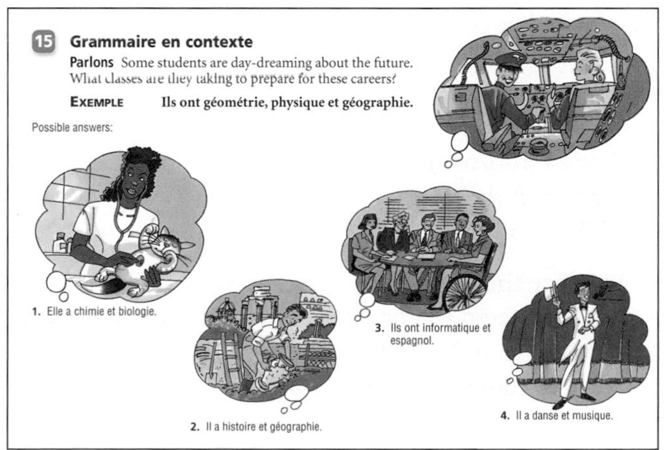

It is important to note here that teaching students to maximize their study does not require that the teacher give each student an individualized assignment. It does require that each student who needs it be taught how to prepare the assignment using his or her own talents and strengths. This communication between teacher and student, combined with teaching techniques that reinforce learning in all modes, can only maximize pleasure and success in learning a foreign language.

References

Dickel, M.J. and S. Slak. "Imaging Vividness and Memory for Verbal Material." *Journal of Mental Imagery* 7, i (1983):121–126.

Bandler, Richard, and John Grinder. *Frogs into Princes.* Real People Press, Moab, UT. 1978.

Allez, viens!

accommodates different learning styles in the following ways:

THE PUPIL'S EDITION

- Presents basic material in audio, video, print, and online formats.
- Includes role-playing activities and a variety of multi-modal activities, including an extensive listening strand and many art-based activities.

THE ANNOTATED TEACHER'S EDITION

- Provides suggested activities for visual, auditory, and kinesthetic learners as well as suggestions for slower-paced learning and challenge activities.
- Includes Total Physical Response activities.

THE ANCILLARY PROGRAM

- Provides additional reinforcement activities for a variety of learning styles.
- Presents a rich blend of audiovisual input through the video program, audio program, CD-ROM Tutor, transparencies, and blackline masters.

Multi-Level Classrooms

by Joan H. Manley

There are positive ways, both psychological and pedagogical, to make this situation work for you and your students.

So you have just heard that your third-period class is going to include both Levels 2 and 3! While this is never the best news for a foreign language teacher, there are positive ways, both psychological and pedagogical, to make this situation work for you and your students.

Relieving student anxieties

Initially, in a multi-level class environment, it is important to relieve students' anxiety by orienting them to their new situation. From the outset, let all students know that just because they "did" things the previous year, such as learn how to conjugate certain verbs, they may not yet be able to use them in a meaningful way. Students should not feel that it is demeaning or a waste of time to recycle activities or to share knowledge and skills with fellow students. Second-year students need to know they are not second-class citizens and that they can benefit from their classmates' greater experience with the language. Third-year students may achieve a great deal of satisfaction and become more confident in their own language skills when they have opportunities to help or teach their second-year classmates. It is important to reassure third-year students that you will devote time to them and challenge them with different assignments.

Easing your own apprehension

When you are faced with both Levels 2 and 3 in your classroom, remind yourself that you teach students of different levels in the same classroom every year, although not officially. After one year of classroom instruction, your Level 2 class will never be a truly homogeneous group. Despite being made up of students with the same amount of "seat time," the class comprises multiple layers of language skills, knowledge, motivation, and ability. Therefore, you are constantly called upon to make a positive experience out of a potentially negative one.

Your apprehension will gradually diminish to the extent that you are able to . . .

- make students less dependent on you for the successful completion of their activities.
- place more responsibility for learning on the students.
- implement creative group, pair, and individual activities.

How can you do this? Good organization will help. Lessons will need to be especially well-planned for the multi-level class. The following lesson plan is an example of how to treat the same topic with students of two different levels.

Teaching a lesson in a multi-level classroom

Lesson objectives

Relate an incident in the past that you regret.

Level 2: Express surprise and sympathy.

Level 3: Offer encouragement and make suggestions.

Lesson plan

1. **Review and/or teach the past tense.** Present the formation of the past tense. Model its use for the entire class or call upon Level 3 students to give examples.
2. **Practice the past tense.** Have Level 3 students who have mastered the past tense teach it to Level 2 students in pairs or small groups. Provide the Level 3 student instructors with several drill and practice activities they may use for this purpose.
3. **Relate your own regrettable past experience.** Recount a personal regrettable incident—real or imaginary—to the entire class as a model. For example, you may have left your automobile lights on, and when you came out of school, the battery was dead and you couldn't start your car. Or you

may have scolded a student for not doing the homework and later discovered the student had a legitimate reason for not completing the assignment.

4. **Prepare and practice written and oral narratives.** Have Level 2 students pair off with Level 3 students. Each individual writes about his or her experience, the Level 3 partner serving as a resource for the Level 2 student. Partners then edit each other's work and listen to each other's oral delivery. You might choose to have students record their oral narratives.

5. **Present communicative functions.**
   A. Ask for a volunteer to recount his or her own regrettable incident for the entire class.
   B. Model reactions to the volunteer's narrative.
      (1) Express surprise and sympathy (for Level 2): "Really! That's too bad!"
      (2) Offer encouragement and make suggestions (for Level 3): "Don't worry. You can still..."

6. **Read narratives and practice communicative functions.** Have Level 2 students work together in one group or in small groups, listening to classmates' stories and reacting with the prescribed communicative function. Have Level 3 students do the same among themselves. Circulate among the groups, listening, helping, and assessing.

7. **Assess progress.** Repeat your personal account for the entire class and elicit reactions from students according to their level. Challenge students to respond with communicative functions expected of the other level if they can.

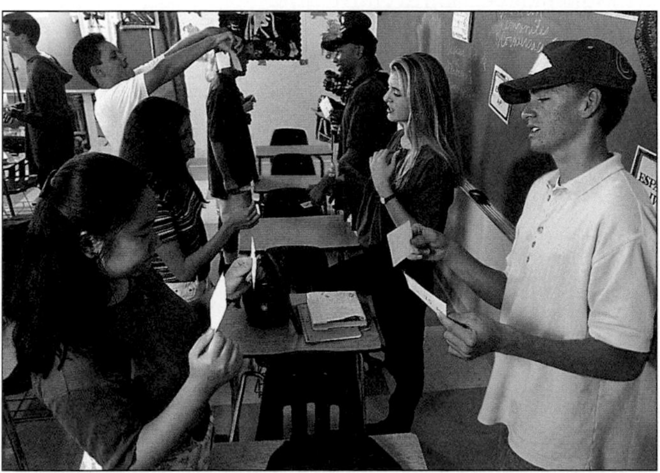

Every part of the above lesson plan is important. Both levels have been accommodated. The teacher has not dominated the lesson. Students have worked together in pairs and small groups, while Level 3 students have helped their Level 2 classmates. Individual groups still feel accountable, both within their level and across levels.

Any lesson can be adapted in this way. It takes time and effort, but the result is a student-centered classroom where students share and grow, and the teacher is the facilitator.

Allez, viens!

facilitates work in a multi-level classroom in the following ways:

THE PUPIL'S EDITION

- Provides creative activities for pair and group work that allow students at different levels to work together and learn from one another.

THE ANNOTATED TEACHER'S EDITION

- Offers practical suggestions for Projects and Cooperative Learning that engage students of different levels.
- Provides Communication for All Students teaching suggestions throughout the program. Second-year students will benefit from the Slower Pace activities, while third-year students will take advantage of the Challenge exercises.
- Provides a clear, comprehensive outline of the functions, vocabulary, and grammar that are recycled in each chapter. The Chapter Overview of each chapter is especially helpful to the teacher who is planning integrated or varied lessons in the multi-level classroom.

THE ANCILLARY PROGRAM

- Provides a variety of materials and activities to accommodate different levels in a multi-level classroom.
- Facilitates collective learning so that groups of students at different learning levels may work together, pacing an activity according to their specific abilities.

Professional References

This section provides information about several resources that can enrich your French class. Included are addresses of government offices of francophone countries, pen pal organizations, subscription agencies, and many others. Since addresses change frequently, you may want to verify them before you send your requests. You may also want to refer to the HRW web side at http://www.hrw.com for current information.

CULTURAL AGENCIES

For historic and tourist information about France and francophone countries, contact:

French Cultural Services
972 Fifth Ave.
New York, NY 10021
(212) 439-1400

French Cultural Services
540 Bush St.
San Francisco, CA 94108
(415) 397-4330

TOURIST OFFICES

French Government Tourist Office
444 Madison Ave.
New York, NY 10022
(212) 838-7800

Délégation du Québec
53 State Street
Exchange Place Bldg., 19th floor
Boston, MA 02109
(617) 723-3366

Caribbean Tourism Association
20 E. 46th St., 4th floor
New York, NY 10017
(212) 682-0435

INTERCULTURAL EXCHANGE

American Field Service
198 Madison Ave.
New York, NY 10016
(212) 299-9000

CIEE Student Travel Services
205 East 42nd St.
New York, NY 10017
(212) 661-1414

PEN PAL ORGANIZATIONS

For the names of pen pal groups other than those listed below, contact your local chapter of AATF. There are fees involved, so be sure to write for information.

Student Letter Exchange (League of Friendship)
211 Broadway, Suite 201
Lynbrook, NY 11563
(516) 887-8628

World Pen Pals
PO BOX 337
Saugerties, NY 12477
(914) 246-7828

PERIODICALS

Subscriptions to the following cultural materials are available directly from the publishers. See also the section on Subscription Services.

- ***Phosphore*** is a monthly magazine for high school students.
- ***Okapi*** is a bimonthly environmentally-oriented magazine for younger teenagers in France.
- ***Le Monde*** is the major daily newspaper in France.
- ***Le Figaro*** is an important newspaper in France. Daily or Saturday editions are available by subscription.
- ***Elle*** is a weekly fashion magazine for women.
- ***Paris Match*** is a general interest weekly magazine.
- ***Le Point*** is a current events weekly magazine.
- ***L'Express*** is a current events weekly magazine.

SUBSCRIPTION SERVICES

French-language magazines can be obtained through subscription agencies in the United States. The following companies are among the many that can provide your school with subscriptions.

EBSCO Subscription Services
5724 Hwy 280 E
Birmingham, AL 35242
(205) 991-6600

Continental Book Company
8000 Cooper Ave., Bldg. 29
Glendale, NY 11385
(718) 326-0560

PROFESSIONAL ORGANIZATIONS

The two major organizations for French teachers at the secondary-school level are:

The American Council on the Teaching of Foreign Languages (ACTFL)
6 Executive Blvd.
Upper Level
Yonkers, NY 10701
(914) 963-8830

The American Association of Teachers of French (AATF)
Mailcode 4510
Southern Illinois University
Carbondale, IL 61820

A Bibliography for the French Teacher

This bibliography is a compilation of several resources available for professional enrichment.

SELECTED AND ANNOTATED LIST OF READINGS

I. Methods and Approaches

Cohen, Andrew D. ***Assessing Language Ability in the Classroom,*** **(2nd ed.).** Boston, MA: Heinle, 1994.
- Assessment processes, oral interviews, role-playing situations, dictation, and portfolio assessment.

Hadley, Alice Omaggio. ***Teaching Language in Context,*** **(2nd ed.).** Boston, MA: Heinle, 1993.
- Overview of the proficiency movement and a survey of past language-teaching methods and approaches; application of the five skills in language education; includes sample activities, teaching summaries, and references.

Lafayette, R. (Ed.). ***National Standards: A Catalyst for Reform.*** Lincolnwood, IL: National Textbook Co., 1996.
- Outline and implications of the National Standards for the modern language classroom; addresses technology, teacher training, materials development, and the changing learning environment.

Lee, James F., and Bill VanPatten. ***Making Communicative Language Teaching Happen.*** New York: McGraw-Hill, 1995.
- Task-based approach to language education, includes activities and test sections to encourage communicative interaction in the classroom.

II. Second-Language Theory

Brown, H. Douglas. ***Principles of Language Learning and Teaching*** **(3rd. ed.).** Englewood Cliffs, NJ: Prentice Hall Regents, 1994.
- Addresses the cognitive, psychological, and sociocultural factors influencing the language-learning process; also includes theories of learning, styles and strategies, motivation, and culture; as well as assessment, error analysis, communicative competence, and theories of acquisition.

Ellis, Rod. ***The Study of Second Language Acquisition.*** Oxford: Oxford University Press, 1994.
- Provides an overview of second language acquisition: error analysis, acquisition orders, social factors, affective variables, individual differences, and the advantages and disadvantages of classroom instruction.

Krashen, Stephen. ***The Power of Reading.*** New York: McGraw, 1994.
- Updates Optimal Input Theory by incorporating the reading of authentic texts.

III. Technology-Enhanced instruction

Bush, Michael D., and Robert M. Terry, (Eds.), in conjunction with ACTFL. ***Technology Enhanced Language Learning.*** Lincolnwood, IL: National Textbook Co., 1997.
- Articles deal with the application of technology in the modern language classroom, including: computer-mediated communication, electronic discussions, hypermedia, the Internet, multimedia, videos, and the WWW.

Muyskens, Judith Ann. (Ed.). ***New Ways of Learning and Teaching: Focus on Technology and Foreign Language Education.*** Boston: Heinle and Heinle, 1997.
- Compilation of articles on the use of technology in the classroom; techniques for applying technology tools to the four skills and culture; also discusses implementation, teacher training, and language laboratories.

Steen, Douglas R., Mark R. Roddy, Derek Sheffield, and Michael Bryan Stout. ***Teaching With the Internet: Putting Teachers before Technology.*** Bellevue, WA: Resolution Business Press, Inc., 1995.
- Designed for K–12 teachers and based on educational theory, provides tips and strategies for using the Internet in and out of the classroom, cites specific case studies; topics include the Internet, e-mail, mailing lists, newsgroups, the WWW, creating a Web page, and other research services.

IV. Professional Journals

Calico
(Published by the Computer Assisted Language Instruction Consortium)
- Dedicated to the intersection of modern language learning and high technology. Research articles on videodiscs, using computer-assisted language learning, how-to articles, and courseware reviews.

The Foreign Language Annals
(Published by the American Council on the Teaching of Foreign Languages)
- Consists of research and how-to-teach articles.

The French Review
(Published by the American Association of Teachers of French)
- Articles on French-language literature.

The IALL Journal of Language Learning Technologies
(Published by the International Association for Learning Laboratories)
- Research articles as well as practical discussions pertaining to technology and language instruction.

The Modern Language Journal
- Primarily features research articles.

Allez, viens!®

HOLT FRENCH

HOLT, RINEHART AND WINSTON

A Harcourt Classroom Education Company

Austin • New York • Orlando • Atlanta • San Francisco • Boston • Dallas • Toronto • London

Cover and Title Page Photography Credits
Front Cover and Title Page: (background), © Robert Fried; (students), HRW Photo/John Langford

Back Cover: © Bob Yarbrough/Roving Eye/Painet; (frame)© 2003 Image Farm

Acknowledgments appear on page R92, which is an extension of the copyright page.

Printed in the United States of America

ISBN 0-03-056594-4

1 2 3 4 5 6 7 48 06 05 04 03 02 01

AUTHORS

John DeMado
Washington, CT

Mr. DeMado helped form the general philosophy of the French program and wrote activities to practice basic material, functions, grammar, and vocabulary.

Emmanuel Rongiéras d'Usseau
Le Kremlin-Bicêtre, France

Mr. Rongiéras d'Usseau contributed to the development of the scope and sequence for the chapters, created the basic material and listening scripts, selected realia, and wrote activities.

CONTRIBUTING WRITERS

Jayne Abrate
The University of Missouri
Rolla, MO

Jill Beede
Educational writer
Tahoma, CA

Judith Ryser
San Marcos High School
San Marcos, TX

REVIEWERS

Jeannette Caviness
Mount Tabor High School
Winston-Salem, NC

Jennie Chao
Consultant
Oak Park, IL

Gail Corder
Trinity Valley School
Ft. Worth, TX

Robert H. Didsbury
Consultant
Raleigh, NC

Jennifer Jones
U.S. Peace Corps volunteer
Côte d'Ivoire 1991–1993
Austin, TX

Joan H. Manley
The University of Texas at El Paso
El Paso, TX

Marie Line McGhee
Consultant
Austin, TX

Gail Montgomery
Foreign Language Program Administrator
Greenwich, CT Public Schools

Agathe Norman
Consultant
Austin, TX

Marc Prévost
Austin Community College
Austin, TX

Norbert Rouquet
Consultant
La Roche-sur-Yon, France

Robert Trottier
St. Johnsbury Academy
Saint Johnsbury, VT

Michèle Viard
The Dalton School
New York, NY

Jack Yerby
Farmington High School
Farmington, NM

FIELD TEST PARTICIPANTS

Marie Allison
New Hanover High School
Wilmington, NC

Gabrielle Applequist
Capital High School
Boise, ID

Jana Brinton
Bingham High School
Riverton, UT

Nancy J. Cook
Sam Houston High School
Lake Charles, LA

Rachael Gray
Williams High School
Plano, TX

Katherine Kohler
Nathan Hale Middle School
Norwalk, CT

Nancy Mirsky
Museum Junior High School
Yonkers, NY

Myrna S. Nie
Whetstone High School
Columbus, OH

Jacqueline Reid
Union High School
Tulsa, OK

Judith Ryser
San Marcos High School
San Marcos, TX

Erin Hahn Sass
Lincoln Southeast High School
Lincoln, NE

Linda Sherwin
Sandy Creek High School
Tyrone, GA

Norma Joplin Sivers
Arlington Heights High School
Fort Worth, TX

Lorabeth Stroup
Lovejoy High School
Lovejoy, GA

Robert Vizena
W.W. Lewis Middle School
Sulphur, LA

Gladys Wade
New Hanover High School
Wilmington, NC

Kathy White
Grimsley High School
Greensboro, NC

TO THE STUDENT

Some people have the opportunity to learn a new language by living in another country. Most of us, however, begin learning another language and getting acquainted with a foreign culture in a classroom with the help of a teacher, classmates, and a textbook. To use your book effectively, you need to know how it works.

Allez, viens! (*Come along!*) is organized to help you learn French and become familiar with the cultures of people who speak French. Each chapter presents concepts in French and strategies for learning a new language. This book also has six Location Openers set throughout the francophone world.

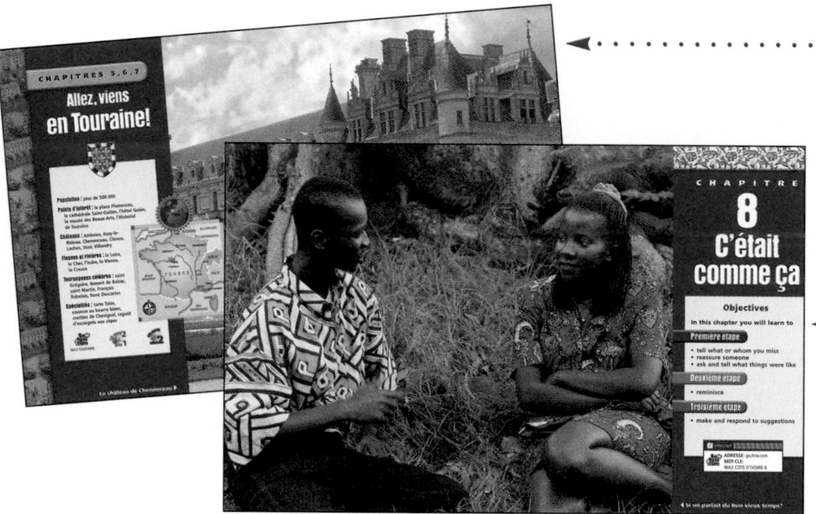

Location Opener You'll find six four-page photo essays called Location Openers that introduce different French-speaking places. You can also see these locations on video, the *CD-ROM Tutor,* and the *DVD Tutor.*

Chapter Opener The Chapter Opener pages tell you the chapter theme and goals.

Mise en train (*Getting started*) This illustrated story, which is also on video, shows you French-speaking people in real-life situations, using the language you'll learn in the chapter.

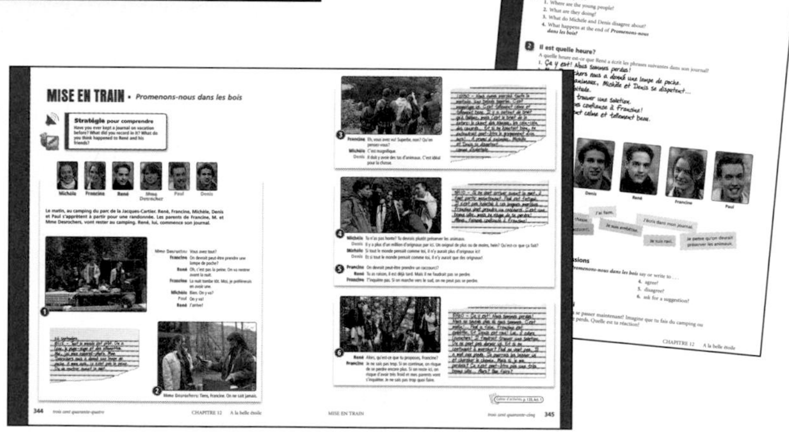

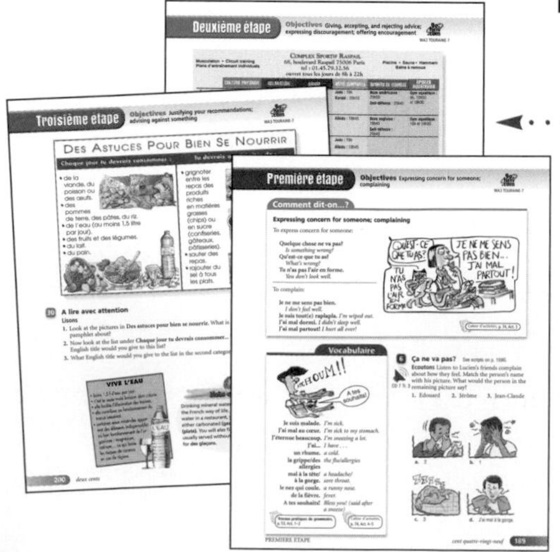

Première, Deuxième, and Troisième étape (*First, Second,* and *Third Part*) After the **Mise en train,** the chapter is divided into three sections called **étapes.** Within the **étape** are **Comment dit-on... ?** (*How do you say . . . ?*) boxes that contain the French expressions you'll need to communicate and **Vocabulaire** and **Grammaire/Note de grammaire** boxes that give you the French words and grammatical structures you'll need to know. Activities in each **étape** enable you to develop your skills in listening, reading, speaking, and writing.

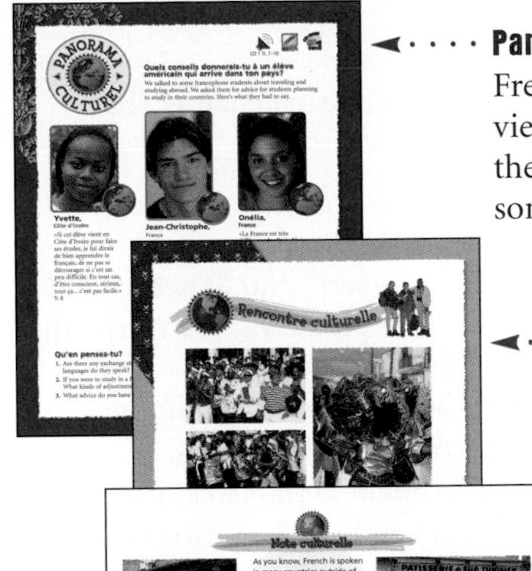

Panorama Culturel (*Cultural Panorama*) On this page are interviews with French-speaking people from around the world. You can watch these interviews on video or listen to them on audio CD. You can also watch them using the *CD-ROM tutor,* then check to see how well you understood by answering some questions about what the people say.

Rencontre culturelle (*Cultural Encounter*) This section, found in six of the chapters, gives you a firsthand encounter with some aspect of a French-speaking culture.

Note culturelle (*Culture Note*) In each chapter, there are notes with more information about the cultures of French-speaking people.

Lisons! (*Let's read!*) The reading section follows the three **étapes.** The selections are related to the chapter themes and help you develop your reading skills in French.

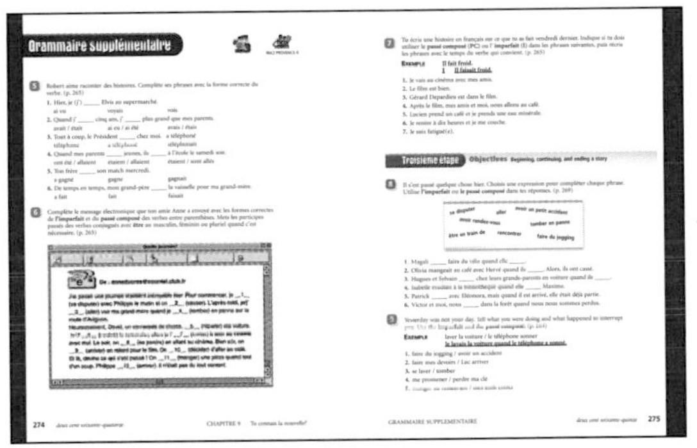

Grammaire supplémentaire (*Additional grammar practice*) This section begins the chapter review. You will find four pages of activities that provide additional practice on the grammar concepts you learned in the chapter.

Mise en pratique (*Review*) The activities on these pages practice what you've learned in the chapter and help you improve your listening, reading, and communicaton skills. You'll also review what you've learned about culture. A section called **Ecrivons!** *(Let's write!)* in each chapter will help develop your writing skills.

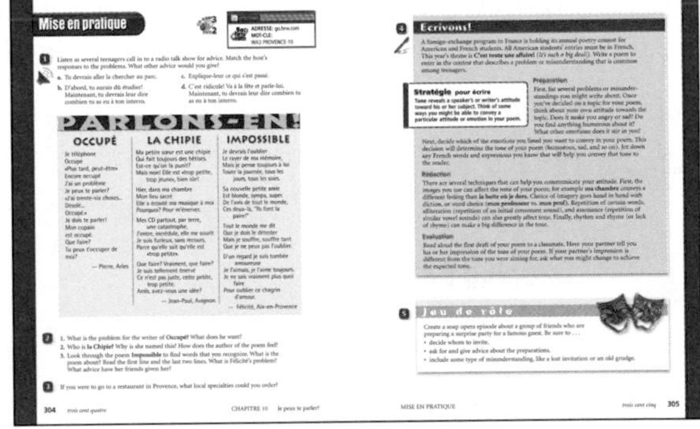

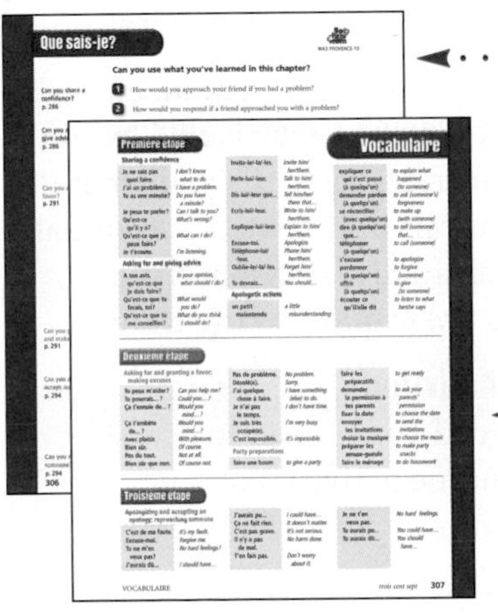

Que sais-je? (*Let's see if I can . . .*) This page at the end of each chapter contains a series of questions and short activities to help you see if you've achieved the chapter goals.

Vocabulaire (*Vocabulary*) On the French-English vocabulary list on the last page of the chapter, the words are grouped by **étape.** These words and expressions will be on the quizzes and tests.

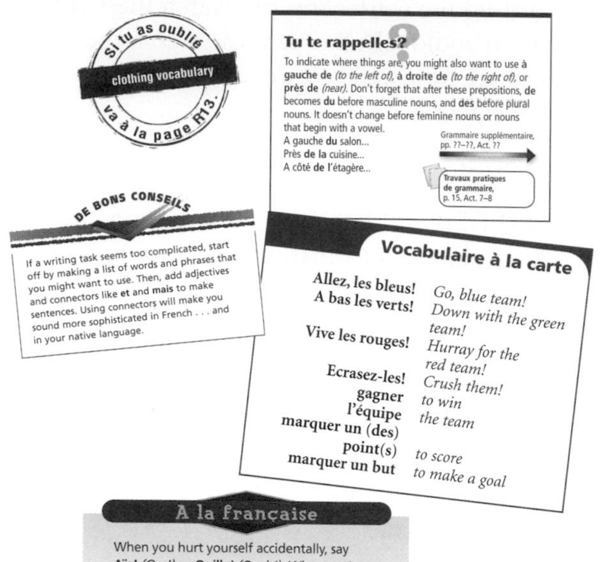

Si tu as oublié
clothing vocabulary
va à la page R13.
Tu te rappelles?
To indicate where things are, you might also want to use à gauche de (to the left of), à droite de (to the right of), or près de (near). Don't forget that after these prepositions, de becomes du before masculine nouns, and des before plural nouns. It doesn't change before feminine nouns or nouns that begin with a vowel.
A gauche du salon...
Près de la cuisine...
A côté de l'étagère...
Grammaire supplémentaire, pp. ??–??, Act. ??
Travaux pratiques de grammaire, p. 15, Act. 7–8
DE BONS CONSEILS
If a writing task seems too complicated, start off by making a list of words and phrases that you might want to use. Then, add adjectives and connectors like et and mais to make sentences. Using connectors will make you sound more sophisticated in French . . . and in your native language.
Vocabulaire à la carte
Allez, les bleus! Go, blue team!
A bas les verts! Down with the green team!
Vive les rouges! Hurray for the red team!
Ecrasez-les! Crush them!
gagner to win
l'équipe the team
marquer un (des) point(s) to score
marquer un but to make a goal
A la française
When you hurt yourself accidentally, say Aïe! (Ow!) or Ouille! (Ouch!). When you've finished doing something physically difficult, say Ouf! (Whew!).

You'll also find special features in each chapter that provide extra tips and reminders.

De bons conseils (*advice*) offers study hints to help you succeed in a language class.
Tu te rappelles? (*Do you remember?*) and **Si tu as oublié** (*If you forgot*) remind you of expressions, grammar, and vocabulary you may have forgotten.
A la française (*The French way*) gives you additional expressions to add more color to your speech.
Vocabulaire à la carte (*Additional Vocabulary*) lists extra words you might find helpful. These words will not appear on the quizzes and tests unless your teacher chooses to include them.

You'll also find French-English and English-French vocabulary lists at the end of the book. The words you'll need to know for the quizzes and tests are in boldface type.

At the end of your book, you'll find more helpful material, such as:

- a summary of the expressions you'll learn in the **Comment dit-on... ?** boxes
- a list of review vocabulary
- additional vocabulary words you might want to use
- a summary of the grammar you'll study
- a grammar index to help you find where structures are presented

Allez, viens! Come along on an exciting trip to new cultures and a new language!

Bon voyage!

Explanation of Icons in *Allez, viens!*

Throughout* Allez, viens!*, you'll see these symbols, or icons, next to activities and presentations. The following key will help you understand them.

Video/DVD Whenever this icon appears, you'll know there's a related segment in the *Allez, viens! Video* and *DVD Programs.*

Listening Activities

Pair Work/Group Work Activities

Writing Activities

Interactive Games and Activities Whenever this icon appears, you'll know there is a related activity on the Allez, viens! *Interactive CD-ROM Tutor.*

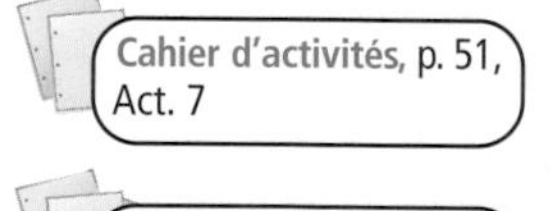

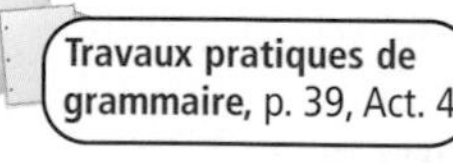

Practice Activities These icons tell you which activities from the *Cahier d'activités* and the *Travaux pratiques de grammaire* practice the material presented.

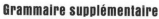

Grammaire supplémentaire, p. 240, Act. 1

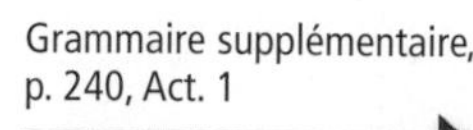

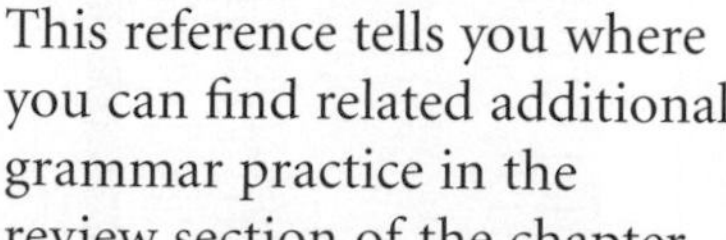

Grammaire supplémentaire This reference tells you where you can find related additional grammar practice in the review section of the chapter.

Internet Activities This icon provides the keyword you'll need to access related online activities at **go.hrw.com.**

ALLEZ, VIENS

aux environs de Paris!

Location for Chapitres 1, 2, 3 12

Chapitre 1

Bon séjour! 4

Chapitre 2

Bienvenue à Chartres! 32

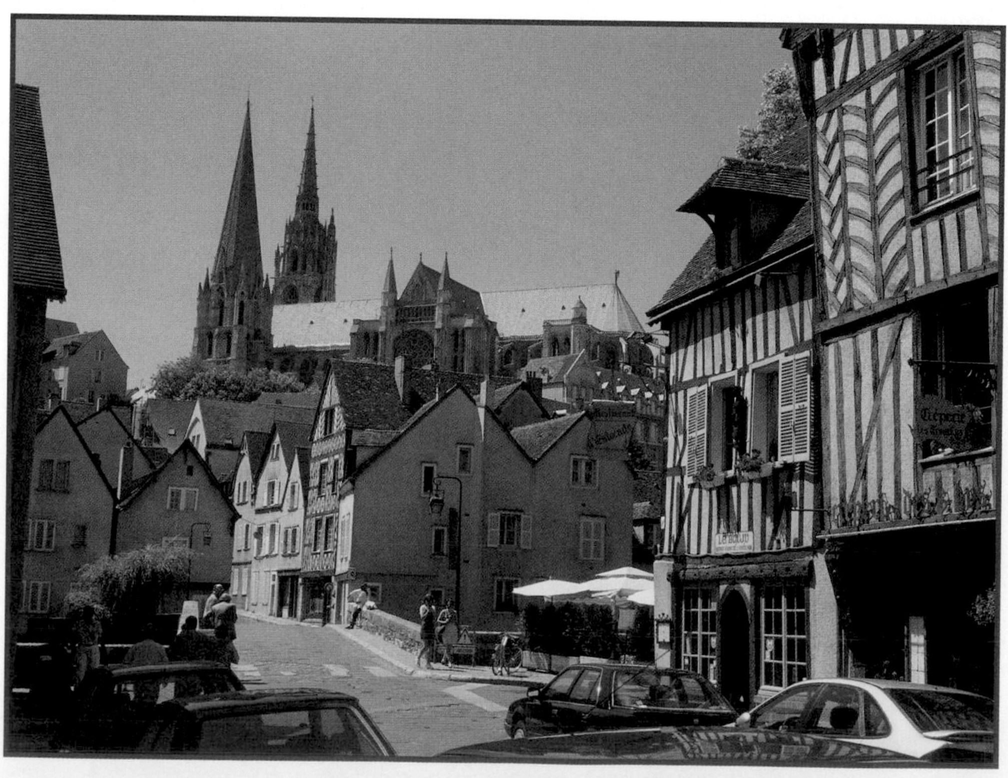

CHAPITRE 3

Un repas à la française 60

ALLEZ, VIENS
à la Martinique!

CHAPITRE 4

Sous les tropiques 94

ALLEZ, VIENS

en Touraine!

CHAPITRE 5

Quelle journée! 128

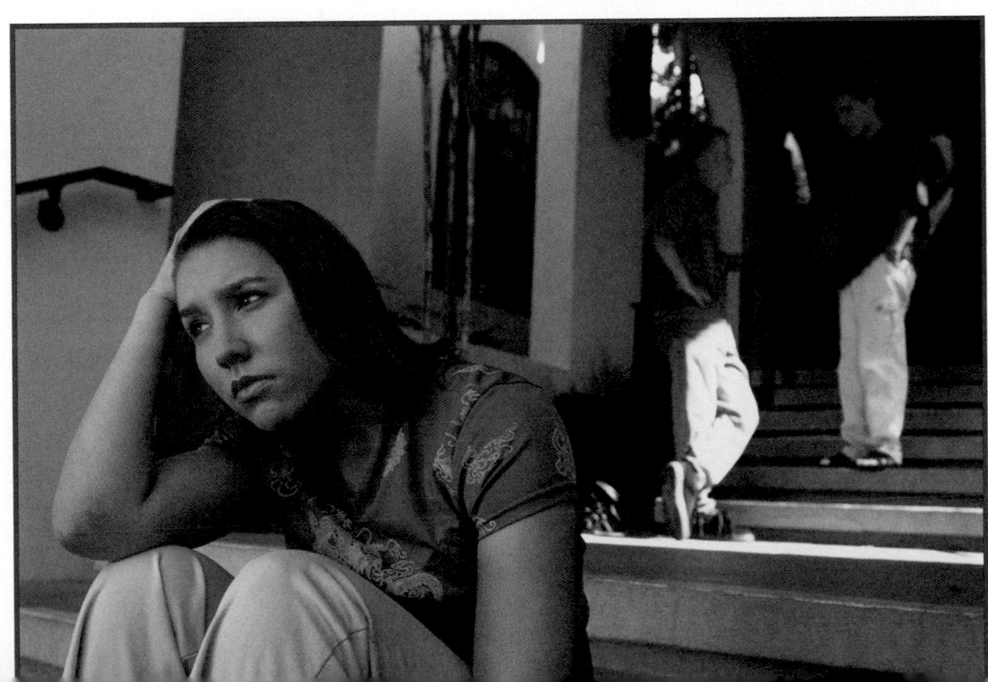

CHAPITRE 6

A nous les châteaux! 156

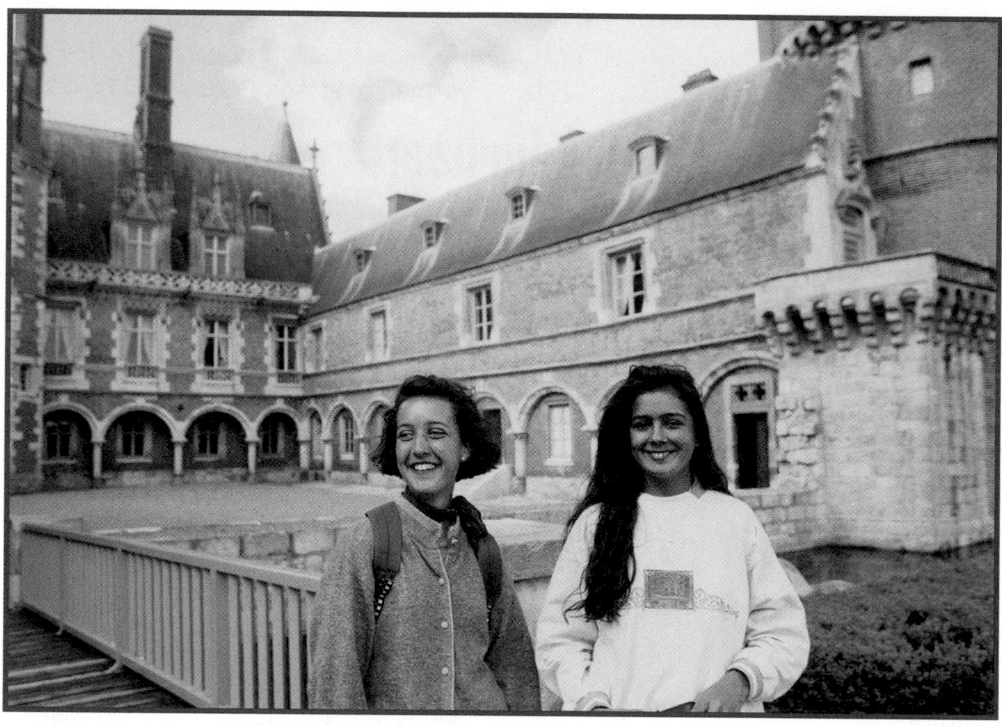

Chapitre 7

En pleine forme 184

ALLEZ, VIENS

en Côte d'Ivoire!

CHAPITRE 8

ALLEZ, VIENS

en Provence!

CHAPITRE 9

Tu connais la nouvelle? 252

CHAPITRE 10

Je peux te parler? 280

Chapitre 11

Chacun ses goûts 308

ALLEZ, VIENS

au Québec!

CHAPITRE 12

REFERENCE SECTION

Cultural References

Page numbers referring to material in the* Pupil's Edition *appear in regular type. When the material referenced is located in the* Annotated Teacher's Edition, *page numbers appear in boldface type.

HEALTH

LEISURE ACTIVITIES

MAPS

MUSIC

PARKS

PEOPLE

REGIONAL DIFFERENCES

SCHOOL LIFE

SHOPPING

SPORTS

TECHNOLOGY

TRANSPORTATION

TRAVEL

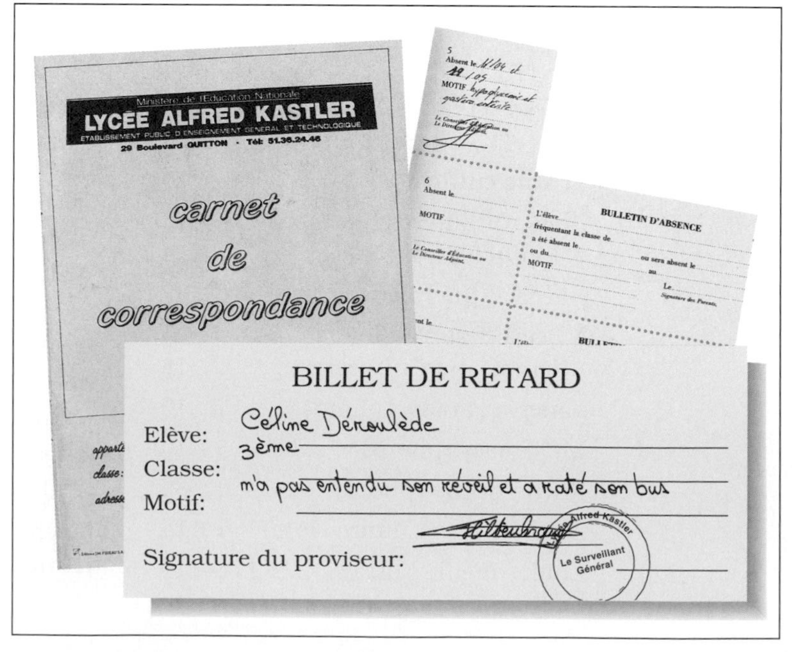

Maps

LA FRANCE

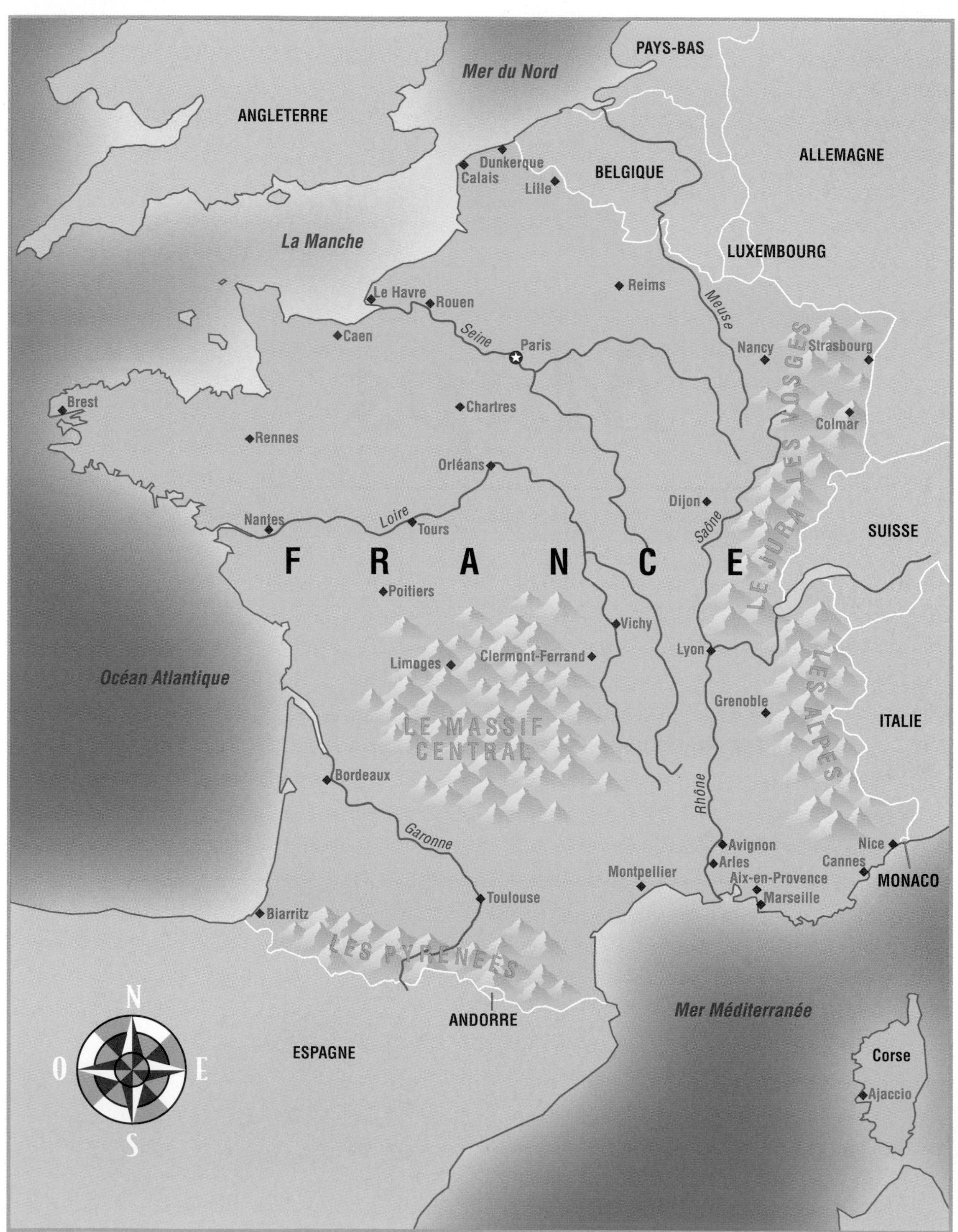

PAYS-BAS
Mer du Nord
ANGLETERRE
ALLEMAGNE
Dunkerque
Calais
Lille
BELGIQUE
LUXEMBOURG
La Manche
Reims
Meuse
Le Havre
Rouen
Caen
Seine
Paris
Nancy
Strasbourg
LES VOSGES
Brest
Chartres
Colmar
Rennes
Orléans
Dijon
Nantes
Loire
Tours
Saône
SUISSE
LE JURA
F R A N C E
Poitiers
Vichy
Lyon
Limoges
Clermont-Ferrand
Océan Atlantique
Grenoble
LES ALPES
ITALIE
LE MASSIF CENTRAL
Bordeaux
Rhône
Garonne
Avignon
Nice
Arles
Cannes
Montpellier
Aix-en-Provence
MONACO
Toulouse
Marseille
Biarritz
LES PYRÉNÉES
ANDORRE
Mer Méditerranée
N
O
E
S
ESPAGNE
Corse
Ajaccio

L'AFRIQUE FRANCOPHONE

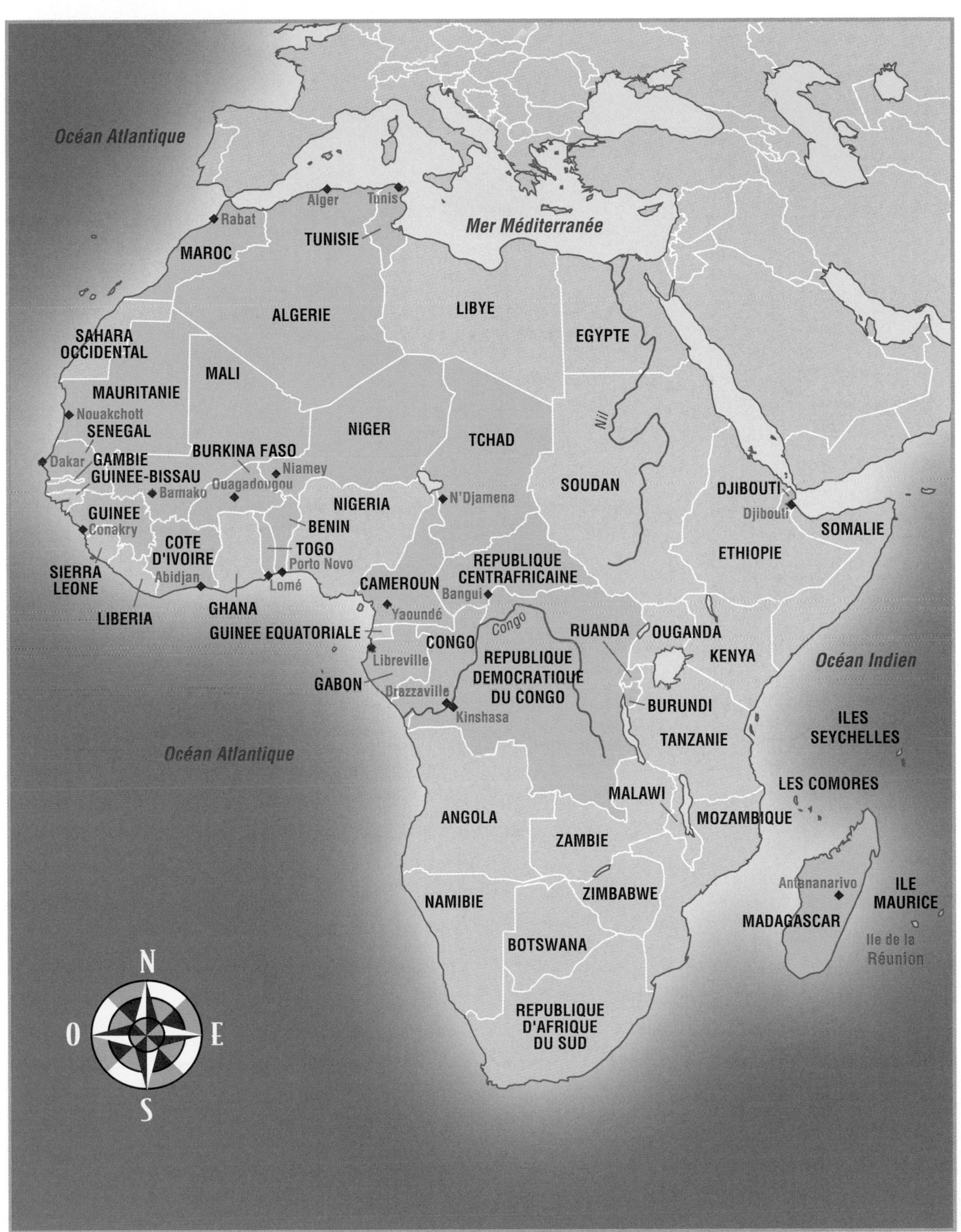
Océan Atlantique
Mer Méditerranée
Alger
Tunis
Rabat
TUNISIE
MAROC
ALGERIE
LIBYE
EGYPTE
SAHARA OCCIDENTAL
MALI
MAURITANIE
Nouakchott
SENEGAL
Dakar
GAMBIE
GUINEE-BISSAU
BURKINA FASO
Niamey
Ouagadougou
Bamako
NIGER
TCHAD
Nil
SOUDAN
DJIBOUTI
Djibouti
SOMALIE
ETHIOPIE
N'Djamena
NIGERIA
BENIN
TOGO
Porto Novo
Lomé
GUINEE
Conakry
COTE D'IVOIRE
Abidjan
SIERRA LEONE
LIBERIA
GHANA
CAMEROUN
Yaoundé
REPUBLIQUE CENTRAFRICAINE
Bangui
GUINEE EQUATORIALE
Congo
CONGO
Libreville
GABON
Brazzaville
Kinshasa
REPUBLIQUE DEMOCRATIQUE DU CONGO
RUANDA
OUGANDA
KENYA
BURUNDI
TANZANIE
Océan Indien
ILES SEYCHELLES
Océan Atlantique
LES COMORES
MALAWI
MOZAMBIQUE
ANGOLA
ZAMBIE
Antananarivo
ILE MAURICE
MADAGASCAR
Ile de la Réunion
NAMIBIE
ZIMBABWE
BOTSWANA
REPUBLIQUE D'AFRIQUE DU SUD
N
O
E
S

L'AMÉRIQUE FRANCOPHONE

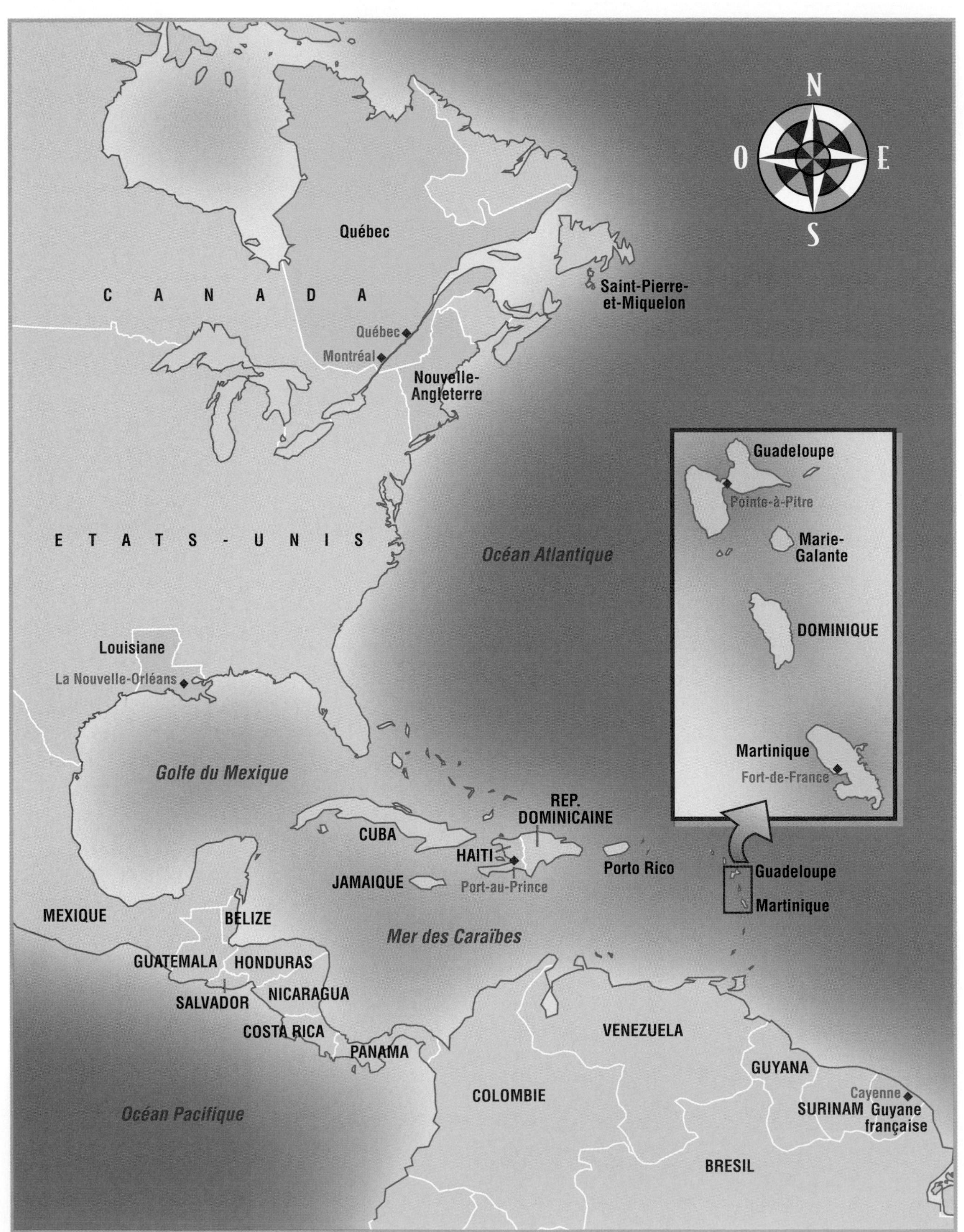
N
O
E
S
Québec
CANADA
Saint-Pierre-et-Miquelon
Québec
Montréal
Nouvelle-Angleterre
Guadeloupe
Pointe-à-Pitre
Marie-Galante
ETATS-UNIS
Océan Atlantique
DOMINIQUE
Louisiane
La Nouvelle-Orléans
Martinique
Fort-de-France
Golfe du Mexique
REP. DOMINICAINE
CUBA
HAITI
Porto Rico
Guadeloupe
JAMAIQUE
Port-au-Prince
Martinique
MEXIQUE
BELIZE
Mer des Caraïbes
GUATEMALA
HONDURAS
SALVADOR
NICARAGUA
COSTA RICA
VENEZUELA
PANAMA
GUYANA
COLOMBIE
Cayenne
SURINAM
Guyane française
Océan Pacifique
BRESIL

LE MONDE FRANCOPHONE

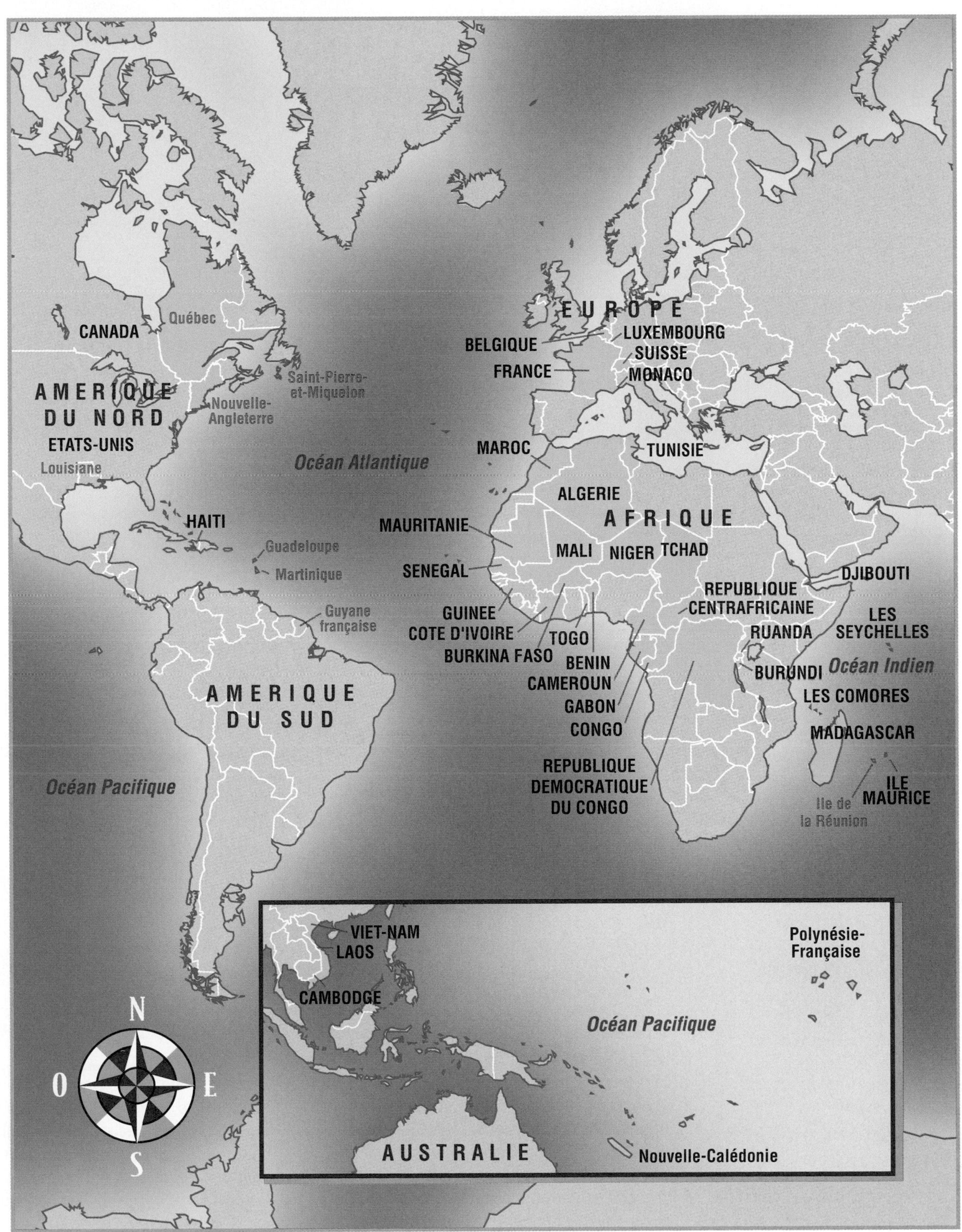

Teaching Resources
pp. T78–3

PRINT  
- Lesson Planner, p. 1
- Video Guide, pp. 1–2

MEDIA 
- One-Stop Planner
- Video Program
  Videocassette 1, 01:08–03:35
- DVD Tutor, Disc 1
- Interactive CD-ROM Tutor, Disc 1
- Map Transparency 1

 go.hrw.com
WA3 PARIS REGION

Using the Almanac and Map

Terms in the Almanac

- **Chantilly** is located just north of Paris. Products associated with Chantilly are lace, china, and whipped cream **(crème Chantilly).**
- **Versailles** was the showpiece of King Louis XIV. It satisfied his desire for grandeur and his wish to remove the court from Paris.
- Situated east of Paris, **le bois de Vincennes** was once a royal forest. It now houses the Paris zoo and the **parc floral de Paris.**
- **George Sand** (1804–1876), the pen name of Aurore Dupin, was a Romantic novelist. Her works include *Indiana* (1832) and *Lélia* (1833).
- **Simone de Beauvoir** (1908–1986) was a writer known for her existential themes (*L'Invitée,* 1943), her treatment of feminist issues (*Le Deuxième Sexe,* 1949), and her concern for the aged (*Une mort très douce,* 1964).
- **Marcel Proust** (1871–1922) is famous for his seven-volume work, *A la recherche du temps perdu.*

CHAPITRES 1, 2, 3

Allez, viens aux environs de Paris!

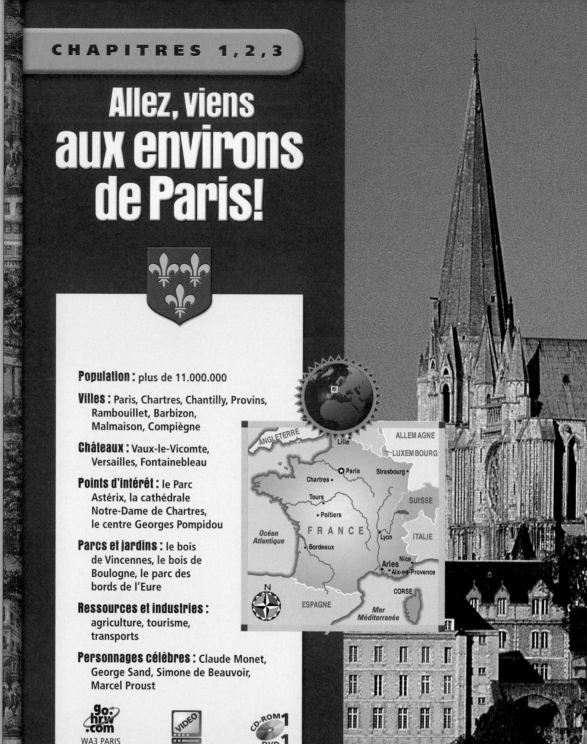

Population : plus de 11.000.000

Villes : Paris, Chartres, Chantilly, Provins, Rambouillet, Barbizon, Malmaison, Compiègne

Châteaux : Vaux-le-Vicomte, Versailles, Fontainebleau

Points d'intérêt : le Parc Astérix, la cathédrale Notre-Dame de Chartres, le centre Georges Pompidou

Parcs et jardins : le bois de Vincennes, le bois de Boulogne, le parc des bords de l'Eure

Ressources et industries : agriculture, tourisme, transports

Personnages célèbres : Claude Monet, George Sand, Simone de Beauvoir, Marcel Proust

ANGLETERRE
Lille
ALLEMAGNE
LUXEMBOURG
Paris
Strasbourg
Chartres
Tours
SUISSE
Poitiers
FRANCE
Océan Atlantique
Lyon
ITALIE
Bordeaux
Arles
Nice
Aix-en-Provence
CORSE
ESPAGNE
Mer Méditerranée
N

go.hrw.com
WA3 PARIS REGION
VIDEO
CD-ROM 1
DVD 1

La cathédrale Notre-Dame de Chartres

Cultures and Communities

Background Information

- The area surrounding Paris has been central to the political and economic life of France for centuries. The region, known as **Ile-de-France,** is composed of eight **départements.** Numerous churches and **châteaux** are located in the region. The wooded areas encircling the city are well-known, the most famous being the **bois de Vincennes** and the **bois de Boulogne.**
- **La cathédrale Notre-Dame de Chartres,** dedicated to the Virgin Mary, is famous for its differing towers, beautiful stained-glass windows with over 5,000 characters, and more than 4,000 impressive sculptures. The foundation and the Gothic facade of the church, built between 1140 and 1160, survived a series of fires, but the remainder of the church had to be rebuilt.

STANDARDS: 2.2, 3.1

Location Opener

CHAPTERS 1, 2, 3

Using the Map

Ask students where Paris is located in relation to the rest of France. Ask them to think of reasons why the city, which is located so far to the north and has long been the heart of French political and economic life, has gained such a position of prominence. (Possible reasons might include its position both on the Seine River and on the route from Italy, Spain, and Germany towards England.)

Map Activities

Ask students to recall what they already know about Paris: the monuments, cathedrals, museums, and so on. Then, ask them if they can name any cities or attractions in the area around Paris. You might refer students to the map of France on pupil page xxii or project *Map Transparency 1.*

Connections and Comparisons

Geography Link

Ask students to think of American and Canadian cities that have become prominent because of their location on rivers or other trade routes. (Students might mention cities such as Chicago or Duluth, MN on the Great Lakes, New Orleans on the Mississippi, steel and manufacturing towns in Ohio or Pennsylvania, and Quebec City and Montreal on the St. Lawrence River.)

STANDARDS: 2.2, 3.1, 5.1

Location Opener

CHAPTERS 1, 2, 3

Using the Photo Essay

❶ **L'Ile de la Cité** is the oldest part of Paris, and in fact, the city's ancient name, **Lutèce,** means *habitation surrounded by water.* In the Middle Ages, however, the population outgrew the confines of the island and spread to the river banks: **la rive droite** to the north and **la rive gauche** to the south. Together with **l'île Saint-Louis**, it is now an elegant residential area. The **bateaux-mouches,** pictured in the photo, are a popular way to view Paris as early river travelers must have seen it. *Notre-Dame, la Sainte-Chapelle,* and *La Conciergerie* are located on the island.

❷ **Le Dimanche d'été à la Grande Jatte** This painting by **Georges Seurat** shows a mixed crowd of people enjoying a Sunday afternoon on an island in the Seine River. The painting shows individuals engaged in a variety of activities: walking, sitting under trees, fishing, and boating. However, Seurat has given the painting an overall feeling of stillness and suspended motion. He concentrated mainly on the observation of light and color rather than on texture or facial detail.

❹ The two towers of the **cathédrale Notre-Dame de Chartres** were constructed at different times during the late twelfth and early thirteenth centuries. **Le clocher Vieux** on the left is the older of the two, while **le clocher Neuf** was constructed about 20 years later. The cathedral is a masterpiece of Gothic architecture, although it still shows evidence of Romanesque influence. It is the largest of all French cathedrals.

Les environs de Paris

Avec ses nombreux châteaux au milieu des forêts, ses cathédrales gothiques et sa merveilleuse campagne immortalisée par les peintres impressionnistes, la région parisienne est le cœur historique et culturel de la France.

internet

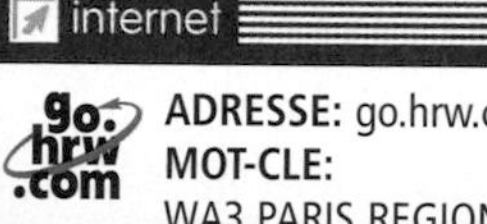

ADRESSE: go.hrw.com
MOT-CLE:
WA3 PARIS REGION

❶ **l'Ile de la Cité**
C'est à partir de cette île que la ville de Paris s'est développée petit à petit.

❷ **Le Dimanche d'été à la Grande Jatte**
En 1886, quand Georges Seurat a fini ce tableau, cet endroit n'était encore qu'une banlieue où les Parisiens aimaient aller se détendre.

❸ **Le Parc Astérix**
Astérix le Gaulois est devenu le sujet d'un parc d'attractions, qui se trouve à moins d'une heure de Paris.

Cultures and Communities

Culture Note

The French have a famous amusement park, **le Parc Astérix,** located near Roissy Airport. The theme park is inspired by the adventures of **Astérix,** the famous Gallic warrior of the **bandes dessinées** by Uderzo and Goscinny. **Astérix's** village includes the recreation of different periods of French history, as well as many of the places featured in the **Astérix** stories.

History Link

The sister island of **l'île de la Cité** is **l'île Saint-Louis,** which was formed in 1627 from two smaller islands. Among its former residents are Marie Curie, writers Charles Baudelaire and François Voltaire, and painter Honoré Daumier. On the island are aristocratic, seventeenth-century townhouses, mansions, and courtyards.

STANDARDS: 2.2, 3.1

4 **Chartres**
Une vue pittoresque de la ville et de sa belle cathédrale

5 **Le Château de Versailles**
Les grandes eaux, ou fontaines, consomment 3,8 millions de litres d'eau par heure.

Aux chapitres 1, 2 et 3,
tu vas faire la connaissance d'une élève américaine et de la famille chez qui elle va faire un séjour. Ils habitent à Chartres, à 77 kilomètres au sud-ouest de Paris. C'est dans la Beauce, une grande région agricole que l'on a surnommée «le grenier à grain» de la France.

7 **Giverny**
Le jardin de Claude Monet

6 **Le centre Georges Pompidou**
La modernité de cette grande structure mi-métal, mi-verre, attire de nombreux visiteurs à l'intérieur comme à l'extérieur.

Location Opener

CHAPTERS 1, 2, 3

5 The gardens at **Versailles,** covering 250 acres, were designed by André le Nôtre. The famous Hall of Mirrors **(la galerie des Glaces)** overlooking the grounds is lined with windows and mirrors that reflect both the light and the view. **Le Grand Canal** allowed Louis XV to take gondola rides with his courtiers and imagine he was in Venice. The thousands of fountains throughout the park are turned on for the public on summer weekends during **Les Grandes Eaux.** Also located on the grounds are **le Grand Trianon,** a small, pink, marble palace built by Louis XIV and **le Petit Trianon,** a favorite retreat of Marie-Antoinette.

6 **Le centre Georges Pompidou** was named after former French President Pompidou (1911–1974). It was completed in 1977. Because of its modernistic steel and glass construction, Parisians often refer to it as **"la raffinerie."** The escalators located outside the structure in glass tubes offer a panoramic view of Paris. It is often called the **centre Beaubourg** because of its location on the Beaubourg plateau.

7 The impressionist painter, **Claude Monet,** lived in the small village of **Giverny** from 1883 until his death in 1926 and is buried there. He was a brilliant innovator who excelled in presenting the effects of light at different times of the day. His paintings of the Rouen cathedral, water lilies, and haystacks at all times of the day are a few of his masterpieces.

Connections and Comparisons

Art Link

Georges Seurat painted in the nineteenth-century neo-impressionist style. His technique of portraying light by using tiny brushstrokes of contrasting colors was known as *pointillism.* The colors tend to blend when observed from a distance. In addition to *Le Dimanche d'été à la Grande Jatte* (seen on page 2), another of Seurat's masterpieces is *Baignade à Asnières.*

Chapitre 1 : Bon séjour!

Review Chapter

Chapter Overview

Mise en train pp. 6–8	***Une méprise***

	FUNCTIONS	GRAMMAR	VOCABULARY	RE-ENTRY
Première étape pp. 9–12	• Describing and characterizing yourself and others, p. 9 • Expressing likes, dislikes, and preferences, p. 11 • Asking for information, p. 12	• The verbs **avoir** and **être,** p. 10 • Adjective agreement, p. 11 • The interrogative adjective **quel,** p. 12		• Pronunciation: **liaison (Chapitre 2,** I) • Adjectives to characterize people **(Chapitre 7,** I) • Family vocabulary **(Chapitre 7,** I)
Deuxième étape pp. 13–17	• Asking for and giving advice, p. 15	• **-ir** verbs, p. 14 • The imperative, p. 15	• Clothing and travel items, p. 14	• Weather expressions and seasons **(Chapitre 4,** I) • Clothing and colors **(Chapitres 3, 10,** I)
Troisième étape pp. 18–21	• Asking for, making, and responding to suggestions, p. 18 • Relating a series of events, p. 20	• The future with **aller,** p. 21		• How to tell time **(Chapitres 2, 6,** I)

Lisons! pp. 22–23	**Une année scolaire aux USA**	**Reading Strategy:** Previewing and skimming	
Grammaire supplémentaire	**pp. 24–27** **Première étape,** pp. 24–25	**Deuxième étape,** pp. 26–27	**Troisième étape,** p. 27
Review pp. 28–31	**Mise en pratique,** pp. 28–29 **Ecrivons!** Making a writing plan Writing a letter	**Que sais-je?** p. 30	**Vocabulaire,** p. 31

CULTURE

- **Note culturelle,** Travel documents for foreign countries, p. 14
- **Panorama Culturel,** Studying abroad, p. 17
- Realia: **Les restaurateurs de la rue de la Porte-Morard,** p. 19
- **Note culturelle,** Ethnic restaurants, p. 19
- Realia: TV listings, p. 21

Chapitre 1 : Bon séjour!
Chapter Resources

PRINT

Lesson Planning

One-Stop Planner

Lesson Planner with Substitute Teacher

Lesson Plans, pp. 1–5, 63

Student Make-Up Assignments
- Make-Up Assignment Copying Masters, Chapter 1

Listening and Speaking

TPR Storytelling Book, pp. x–7

Listening Activities
- Student Response Forms for Listening Activities, pp. 3–5
- Additional Listening Activities 1-1 to 1-6, pp. 7–9
- Additional Listening Activities (song), p. 10
- Scripts and Answers, pp. 101–106

Video Guide
- Teaching Suggestions, pp. 4–5
- Activity Masters, pp. 6–8
- Scripts and Answers, pp. 85–87, 118

Activities for Communication
- Communicative Activities, pp. 1–6
- Realia and Teaching Suggestions, pp. 75–79
- Situation Cards, pp. 137–138

Reading and Writing

Reading Strategies and Skills Handbook, Chapter 1

Joie de lire 2, Chapter 1

Cahier d'activités, pp. 1–12

Grammar

Travaux pratiques de grammaire, pp. 1–11

Grammar Tutor for Students of French, Chapter 1

Assessment

Testing Program
- Grammar and Vocabulary Quizzes, **Etape** Quizzes, and Chapter Test, pp. 1–18
- Score Sheet, Scripts and Answers, pp. 19–26

Alternative Assessment Guide
- Portfolio Assessment, p. 18
- Performance Assessment, p. 32
- CD-ROM Assessment, p. 46

Student Make-Up Assignments
- Alternative Quizzes, Chapter 1

Standardized Assessment Tutor
- Reading, pp. 1–3
- Writing, p. 4
- Math, pp. 25–26

MEDIA

Online Activities
- **Jeux interactifs**
- **Activités Internet**

Video Program
- Videocassette 1
- Videocassette 5 (captioned version)

Interactive CD-ROM Tutor, Disc 1

DVD Tutor, Disc 1

Audio Compact Discs
- Textbook Listening Activities, CD 1, Tracks 1–13
- Additional Listening Activities, CD 1, Tracks 20–26
- Assessment Items, CD 1, Tracks 14–19

Teaching Transparencies
- Situation 1-1 to 1-3
- Vocabulary 1-A
- **Mise en train**
- **Grammaire supplémentaire** Answers
- **Travaux pratiques de grammaire** Answers

One-Stop Planner CD-ROM

Use the **One-Stop Planner CD-ROM with Test Generator** to aid in lesson planning and pacing.

For each chapter, the One-Stop Planner includes:
- Editable lesson plans with direct links to teaching resources
- Printable worksheets from resource books
- Direct launches to the HRW Internet activities
- Video and audio segments
- Test Generator
- Clip Art for vocabulary items

Projects

Mon/Ma correspondant(e)

Students will invent an exchange student from a francophone country who is coming to stay with them for a year.

MATERIALS

Students may need

- Magazines
- Old photographs
- Scissors
- Postcards
- Posterboard
- Colored markers

SUGGESTED SEQUENCE

1. Each student imagines a French-speaking exchange student and family. Have students use the map on page xxv (**Le Monde francophone**) to choose a French-speaking country and city. Students might research the country and city they choose in order to tell about the family members' lives there.
2. Students find pictures to use in their letters.
3. Students write a letter from the imaginary exchange student to themselves. The letter should include . . .
   - a description of the exchange student, including some of his or her likes and dislikes.
   - descriptions of his or her family members.
   - questions about the host student.
4. After students have proofread their letters, form groups for peer editing.
5. Students write postcards from the exchange student to someone back home. The postcards should tell how the student is enjoying his or her stay and describe four things that he or she and the host student are going to do this week, using **aller** + infinitive and the expressions **d'abord, puis, ensuite,** and **enfin.**
6. Repeat the peer-editing process with the postcards.
7. Students display the letter, the pictures, and the postcards on a sheet of posterboard.
8. Students introduce their exchange student to the class.

GRADING THE PROJECT

Suggested Point Distribution: (total = 100 points)

Content	20
Language use	20
Overall presentation	20
Comprehensibility	20
Presentation	20

Games

Le Mot juste

This game will help your students develop the skill of circumlocution, the linguistic art of communicating when a person doesn't know the precise word he or she needs. Explain to students that they will learn to paraphrase, use synonyms, describe essential elements, and apply key phrases to communicate when they find themselves at a loss for the exact word.

Materials To play this game, you will need index cards.

Preparation Create a list of words related to the vocabulary presented in the chapter or **étape.** On each card, write one word from the list. Arrange four desks at the front of the room so that the two partners from each team can face each other. Place the cards face down where they can easily be reached by the players from any of the desks. On the board or a transparency, write the following key phrases:

C'est un(e) truc, personne, animal que / qui...

Il/Elle est grand(e)/âgé(e). (C'est... rouge / grand.)

Ça ressemble à...

C'est le contraire de...

C'est un endroit où...

Il/Elle a...

... est fait(e) en plastique / bois / verre / coton.

On l'utilise pour...

Procedure Divide the class into two teams and select a scorekeeper and a timekeeper. Have two players from each team sit at the desks. A player from Team A selects a card and shows it to one of the players from Team B, but not to his own partner. Using circumlocution, the Team A player makes a statement to his or her partner about the vocabulary word without saying the word itself. (For *éléphant,* one could say **C'est un animal gris.**) If his or her partner guesses the word, Team A receives five points. (Allow 30 seconds per guess.) If not, the Team B player who has seen the card gives a clue to his or her partner. If the partner guesses correctly, Team B receives four points. Play alternates between the two teams, with point value dropping by one after each incorrect guess. If no team scores a point after five clues, any student on Team A may guess to earn one point. If Team A can't guess correctly, any student from Team B has the same opportunity. Announce the answer if no one guesses correctly. After four words, select four new players for the next round.

STANDARDS: 1.1, 1.3, 3.1, 3.2

Storytelling

Mini-histoire

This story accompanies Teaching Transparency 1-2. The ***mini-histoire*** *can be told and retold in different formats, acted out, written down, and read aloud, to give students additional opportunities to practice all four skills. The following story is about Alex's preparation for his trip to Paris.*

Alex va passer un an à Paris. Il demande à sa mère : «Qu'est-ce que je dois prendre?» Sa mère lui répond : «Tu arrives en automne : il pleut beaucoup. Prends ton imperméable, tes sweat-shirts et des jeans. En hiver, il fait froid : prends ton anorak, des pulls, tes gants et tes bottes noires. Au printemps, les journées sont plus chaudes : n'oublie pas de prendre tes nouveaux tee-shirts et tes baskets. En été, il fait très chaud : prends des shorts et bien sûr ton maillot de bain. Je vais chercher des chèques de voyage. Pense à prendre un dictionnaire et n'oublie pas ton appareil-photo.» «D'accord, Maman. Au fait, est-ce que tu peux m'aider à chercher mon passeport et mon billet d'avion? Je ne les trouve plus.»

Traditions

Chartres

Chartres, which derives its name from Carnutes, the Roman name for this area, has been attracting pilgrims for over 2,000 years. First, the Druids of Gaul gathered at a sanctuary built on the mound where today's cathedral stands. They were followed by the Romans, who came to a temple dedicated to Dea Mater (Mother Goddess). Soon afterwards, Christians began traveling to the site until eventually, the present-day cathedral, Notre-Dame de Chartres, was built. On the floor of the cathedral's central nave lies a labyrinth, or maze, in the shape of a spiral made of paving stones. For centuries, according to tradition, penitents who were unable to go on distant pilgrimages wound their way to the center of the labyrinth and out again in silent contemplation. This tradition remains strong as many of today's tourists come to the cathedral to do the same.

Recette

The **pâte à choux** is the basis for a large number of appetizers and desserts. Chocolate eclairs are made with the dough of the **choux.** The **choux** are used to make a wedding cake called a **pièce montée. Chou** is also a sweet name for your sweetheart.

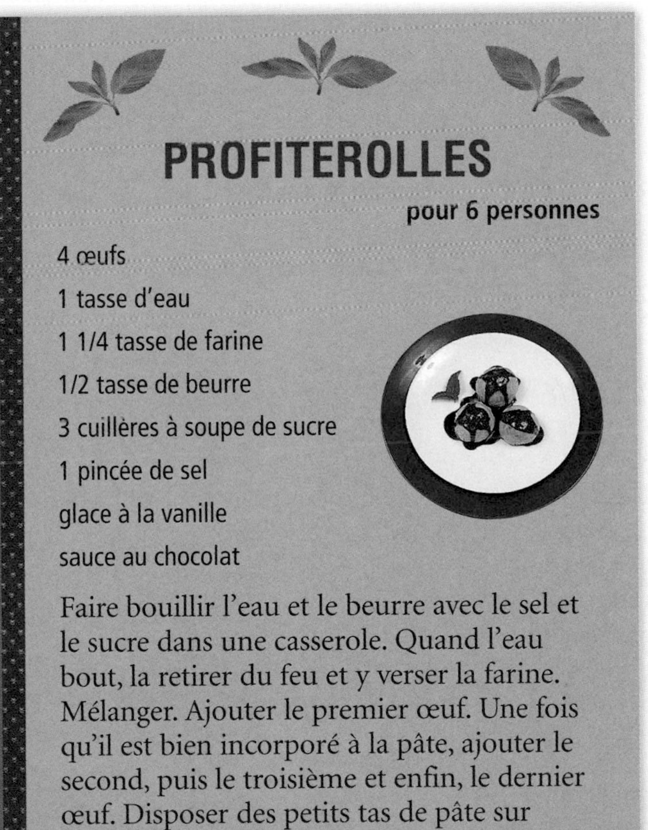

PROFITEROLLES

pour 6 personnes

4 œufs
1 tasse d'eau
1 1/4 tasse de farine
1/2 tasse de beurre
3 cuillères à soupe de sucre
1 pincée de sel
glace à la vanille
sauce au chocolat

Faire bouillir l'eau et le beurre avec le sel et le sucre dans une casserole. Quand l'eau bout, la retirer du feu et y verser la farine. Mélanger. Ajouter le premier œuf. Une fois qu'il est bien incorporé à la pâte, ajouter le second, puis le troisième et enfin, le dernier œuf. Disposer des petits tas de pâte sur la plaque du four. Faire cuire pendant 30 minutes au four à 375° F.

Ouvrir le chou et y ajouter une boule de glace à la vanille. Verser du chocolat liquide sur le tout. Servir.

Technology

DVD/Video

Videocassette 1, Videocassette 5 (captioned version)
DVD Tutor, Disc 1
See Video Guide, pages 3–8.

Mise en train • Une méprise
The Lepics go to the airport to pick up Pamela, their American guest. Sandra and her mother go inside to look for Pamela. Mr. Lepic, who stays in the van, greets a girl, Patricia, who fits Pamela's description, and puts her suitcase in the van. Sandra, her mother, and Pamela arrive. Mr. Lepic realizes his mistake and apologizes to Patricia. Patricia's French host arrives. Everyone says goodbye and the Lepics leave. Suddenly, Patricia notices that she has the wrong suitcase.

Quels conseils donnerais-tu à un élève américain qui arrive dans ton pays?
Students from Côte d'Ivoire and France give advice to an American student coming to their country.

Mise en train (suite)
Patricia and Bertrand manage to stop the Lepics, and they exchange suitcases. Mrs. Lepic suggests sightseeing in Paris before returning to Chartres. Sandra recommends taking a ride on a **bateau-mouche** on the Seine. The group sees some of the famous sights of Paris from the boat. After the boat ride, Mr. Lepic suggests having lunch.

Videoclips
- **EDF®**: advertisement for an electric company
- **Herta®**: advertisement for pie crust

Interactive CD-ROM Tutor

Activity	Activity Type	Pupil's Edition Page
En contexte	*Interactive conversation*	
1. Comment dit-on… ?	Chacun à sa place	p. 9
2. Grammaire	Les mots qui manquent	p. 11
3. Comment dit-on… ?	Le bon choix	p. 12
4. Vocabulaire	Jeu des paires	p. 14
5. Comment dit-on… ?	Chasse au trésor Explorons! Vérifions!	p. 18
6. Grammaire	Méli-mélo	pp. 10, 15, 21
Panorama Culturel	Qu'est-ce qu'il y a à visiter dans cette région?	p. 103
A toi de parler	*Guided recording*	pp. 28–29
A toi d'écrire	*Guided writing*	pp. 28–29

Teacher Management System
Launch the program, type "admin" in the password area, and press RETURN. Log on to www.hrw.com/CDROMTUTOR for a detailed explanation of the Teacher Management System.

DVD Tutor

The *DVD Tutor* contains all material from the *Video Program* as described above. French captions are available for use at your discretion for all sections of the video. The *DVD Tutor* also provides a variety of video-based activities that assess students' understanding of the **Mise en train, Suite,** and **Panorama Culturel.**

This part of the DVD Tutor may be used on any DVD video player connected to a television or video monitor.

In addition to the video material and the video-based comprehension activities, the *DVD Tutor* also contains the entire *Interactive CD-ROM Tutor* in DVD-ROM format. Each DVD disc contains the activities from all 12 chapters of the *Interactive CD-ROM Tutor.*

This part of the DVD Tutor may be used on a Macintosh® or Windows® computer with a DVD-ROM drive.

To preview all resources available for this chapter, use the **One-Stop Planner CD-ROM**, Disc 1.

Internet Connection

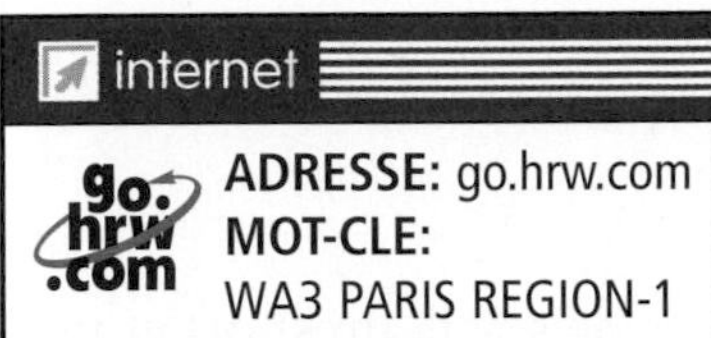

*Have students explore the **go.hrw.com** Web site for many online resources covering all chapters. All Chapter 1 resources are available under the keyword **WA3 PARIS REGION-1.** Interactive games help students practice the material and provide them with immediate feedback. You'll also find a printable worksheet that provides Internet activities that lead to a comprehensive online research project.*

Jeux interactifs

You can use the interactive activities in this chapter

- to practice grammar, vocabulary, and chapter functions
- as homework
- as an assessment option
- as a self-test
- to prepare for the Chapter Test

Activités Internet

Students look for information about the Paris region.

- In preparation for the **Activités Internet,** have students go over the names of cities, châteaux, and famous people of the Paris region listed on page xxvi of their textbook.

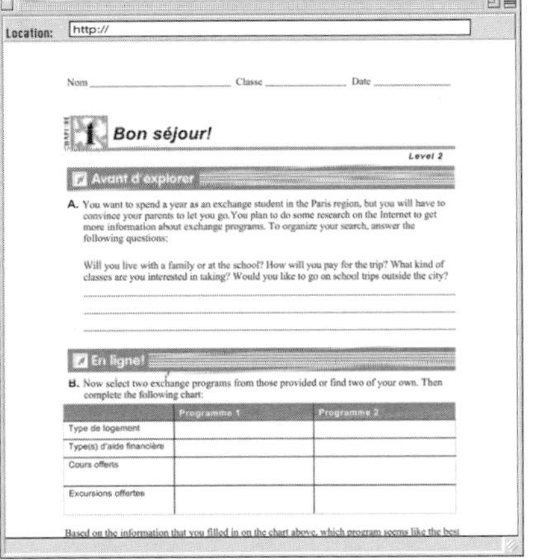

Location: http://

Nom ________ Classe ________ Date ________

1 Bon séjour!

Level 2

Avant d'explorer

A. You want to spend a year as an exchange student in the Paris region, but you will have to convince your parents to let you go. You plan to do some research on the Internet to get more information about exchange programs. To organize your search, answer the following questions:

Will you live with a family or at the school? How will you pay for the trip? What kind of classes are you interested in taking? Would you like to go on school trips outside the city?

En ligne!

B. Now select two exchange programs from those provided or find two of your own. Then complete the following chart:

	Programme 1	Programme 2
Type de logement		
Type(s) d'aide financière		
Cours offerts		
Excursions offertes		

Based on the information that you filled in on the chart above, which program seems like the best

Projet

Have the students choose one of the cities or châteaux from the Internet activity. They should do a Web search, gathering as much information as possible about the art, history, or tours of the city or château they have chosen. The students will then make a poster to present their information to the rest of the class. Have students document their sources by noting the URLs of all the sites that they consulted.

Chapitre 1 : Bon séjour!

Review Chapter

Textbook Listening Activities Scripts

Première étape

5 p. 9

1. —Pour lui, le sport est très important. Il a dix-sept ans, et il est très sympa.
2. —Il s'appelle Félix, et il est très gros.
3. —Elle a trente-neuf ans, mais elle est très jeune de caractère.
4. —Elle aime les magasins, le cinéma et la musique.
5. —Il a quarante-deux ans, et il travaille dans un bureau d'informatique.

Answers to Activity 5

1. c
2. a
3. d
4. e
5. b

6 p. 10

1. —Vanessa Paradis, une chanteuse célèbre, est grande et mince. Elle a les cheveux longs et châtains et les yeux marron. Elle est aussi actrice de cinéma.
2. —MC Solaar, alias Claude M'Barali, est rappeur. Il a les cheveux noirs et les yeux marron. Il est très populaire en France.
3. —Elsa, une Française d'origine italienne, aime chanter et faire du cinéma. Belle et mince, elle a les cheveux bruns et bouclés. Ses yeux sont bleus.
4. —Patrick Bruel est chanteur et acteur de cinéma. Il est grand. Il a les cheveux bruns, bouclés et assez longs.

Answers to Activity 6

1. a
2. d
3. b
4. c

9 p. 12

Bon, mon cousin Eric, il est très sympa. Il adore la musique, surtout la musique classique. Il va souvent aux concerts. Il aime aussi sortir avec des copains et jouer au basket-ball. Il adore aller se promener à la campagne avec son chien.

Ma cousine Caroline est très sociable; elle est toujours au téléphone. Elle adore sortir. Elle aime aller manger des hamburgers avec ses copains parce qu'elle est très gourmande. Caroline est aussi très sportive : elle joue souvent au tennis et au foot.

Answers to Activity 9

Caroline

Deuxième étape

16 p. 15

1. —Qu'est-ce que je dois prendre?
   —Pense à prendre des lunettes de soleil, un short et un tee-shirt. Prends aussi des sandales et un maillot de bain. Bon voyage!
2. —Voyons... qu'est-ce qu'il faut prendre?
   —Prends des pulls et des bottes. Oh, un anorak, bien sûr. Et prends ton bonnet, ton écharpe et tes gants. Et pense à prendre tes lunettes de soleil.
3. —Alors... je dois prendre des jeans, des pulls et mes baskets. Quoi d'autre?
   —Ben, n'oublie pas ton passeport! C'est essentiel pour aller aux Etats-Unis!

Answers to Activity 16

1. b
2. d
3. c

The following scripts are for the listening activities found in the *Pupil's Edition*. For Student Response Forms, see *Listening Activities*, pages 3–5. To provide students with additional listening practice, see *Listening Activities*, pages 7–10.

To preview all resources available for this chapter, use the **One-Stop Planner CD-ROM**, Disc 1.

Troisième étape

22 p. 19

Sandra	Où est-ce qu'on pourrait bien aller manger ce soir? Je n'ai pas très envie de faire la cuisine. Et toi?
Etienne	Moi non plus. Regardons dans le journal. Il y a une liste de bons restaurants. On pourrait aller dans un restaurant indien. Ça nous changerait.
Sandra	Ah, non, je n'aime pas la cuisine épicée. Il n'y a pas autre chose? Un restaurant traditionnel, peut-être?
Etienne	Si, mais nous n'allons pas au restaurant pour manger de la cuisine traditionnelle. Maman prépare ça tous les jours.
Sandra	Si tu veux, on peut aller à la Crêperie du Cygne. J'adore les crêpes!
Etienne	Non, je préfère le restaurant indochinois.
Sandra	Pas question!
Etienne	Alors? Qu'est-ce qu'on fait?
Sandra	Et une pizza, ça te dit?
Etienne	Oui, j'aime bien la cuisine italienne.
Sandra	Bien, allons à la Napolitaine. C'est pas loin d'ici.
Etienne	D'accord. Allons-y.

Answers to Activity 22

Etienne: an Indian or Indochinese restaurant
Sandra: a traditional restaurant, La Crêperie du Cygne
They decide to go to an Italian restaurant.

25 p. 20

Tiens, j'ai beaucoup de projets pour samedi! D'abord, le matin, je vais faire de la natation. Ensuite, je vais faire un pique-nique au parc avec des copains. On va prendre des sandwiches et des fruits. Puis, on va faire du vélo ensemble. Du vélo en plein air, c'est génial! Enfin, le soir, on va aller voir un film au cinéma. Ça va être une journée super!

Answers to Activity 25

b, c, a, d

Mise en pratique

3 p. 28

Ça y est. J'ai enfin mon billet. J'arrive jeudi à dix-huit heures. C'est le vol Air France cinquante-cinq. J'ai oublié de t'envoyer une photo de moi! Alors, j'ai les cheveux bruns, je suis de taille moyenne et je vais mettre un pull rouge. Mais vous allez me reconnaître facilement. Je suis le plus beau!

Answers to Mise en pratique Activity 3

He's arriving Thursday at 6:00 P.M. on Air France flight 55. He has dark hair, is of average height, and will be wearing a red sweater.

Chapitre 1 : Bon séjour!

Suggested Lesson Plans 50-Minute Schedule

Day 1

CHAPTER OPENER 5 min.
- Present Chapter Objectives, p. 5.
- Culture Notes, ATE, p. 4
- Thinking Critically, ATE, p. 5

MISE EN TRAIN 40 min.
- Presenting **Mise en train,** ATE p. 6
- Preteaching Vocabulary, ATE, p. 6
- Career Path, ATE, p. 7
- Language Note, ATE, p. 7
- Activities 1–4, p. 8
- Challenge, ATE, p. 8

Wrap-Up 5 min.
- Have students summarize the events from the **Mise en train,** using **Mise en train** Transparencies.

Homework Options
Cahier d'activités, Acts. 1–2, p. 1

Day 2

MISE EN TRAIN
Quick Review 5 min.
- Check homework.
- Play Audio CD for Activity 5, p. 9.

PREMIERE ETAPE
Comment dit-on... ?, p. 9 20 min.
- Presenting **Comment dit-on... ?,** ATE, p. 9
- Do Activity 6, p. 10.

Grammaire, p. 10 20 min.
- Presenting **Grammaire,** ATE, p. 10
- Do Activity 7, p. 10.
- **Grammaire supplémentaire,** p. 24, Activities 1–2

Wrap-Up, 5 min.
- Students describe a famous person to a partner who must guess the identity of the famous person

Homework Options
Cahier d'activités, Acts. 3–4, p. 2

Day 3

PREMIERE ETAPE
Quick Review 5 min.
- Check homework.

Grammaire, p. 11 25 min.
- Presenting **Grammaire,** ATE, p. 11
- Kinesthetic Learners, ATE, p. 11
- Do Activity 8, Part a., p. 11.
- **Grammaire supplémentaire,** pp. 24–25, Activities 3–4

Comment dit-on... ?, p. 11 10 min.
- Presenting **Comment dit-on... ?,** ATE, p. 11
- Play Audio CD for Activity 9, p. 12.

Wrap-Up 10 min.
- Activity 8, Part b., p. 11

Homework Options
Travaux pratiques de grammaire, Acts. 3–5, pp. 2–3
Pupil's Edition, Activity 10, p. 12

Day 4

PREMIERE ETAPE
Quick Review 10 min.
- Check homework.

Note de grammaire, p. 12 10 min
- Discuss **Note de grammaire,** p. 12.
- **Grammaire supplémentaire,** p. 25, Activity 6

Comment dit-on... ?, p. 12 25 min.
- Presenting **Comment dit-on... ?**; ATE, p. 12, using Teaching Transparency 1-1
- Language Note, ATE, p. 12
- Cahier d'activités, p. 4, Activity 8
- Review verbs ending in **-er**, using p. R33.
- Travaux pratiques de grammaire, p. 4, Activity 7
- Do Activity 11, p. 12.

Wrap-Up 5 min.
- Cahier d'activités, Act. 9, p. 4

Homework Options
Study for Quiz 1-1

Day 5

PREMIERE ETAPE
Quiz 20 min.
- Administer Quiz 1-1A, 1-1B, or a combination of the two.

DEUXIEME ETAPE
Vocabulaire, p. 14 15 min.
- Presenting **Vocabulaire,** ATE, p. 14
- Language-to-Language, ATE, p. 14
- Cahier d'activités, p. 5, Activities 10–11

Note de grammaire, p. 14 10 min.
- Present **Note de grammaire,** p. 14.
- Travaux pratiques de grammaire, p. 6, Activities 11–12

Wrap-Up 5 min.
- Read and discuss **Note culturelle,** p. 14.

Homework Options
Travaux pratiques de grammaire, Acts. 8–10, 13, pp. 5 and 7
Grammaire supplémentaire, Acts. 7–8, p. 26

Day 6

DEUXIEME ETAPE
Quick Review 10 min.
- Check homework.
- Read letter and complete Activity 13, p. 13.

Comment dit-on... ?, p. 15 15 min.
- Presenting **Comment dit-on... ?,** ATE, p. 15
- Play Audio CD for Activity 16, p. 15.
- Do Activity 17, p. 15.

Note de grammaire, p. 15 20 min.
- Discuss **Note de grammaire,** p. 15.
- Do TPR, ATE, p. 15.
- Review weather expressions and seasons.
- Travaux pratiques de grammaire, Activities 14–17, pp. 7–8.

Wrap-Up 5 min.
- Do Activity 18, p. 16, orally.

Homework Options
Study for Quiz 1-2.

For alternative lesson plans by chapter section, to create your own customized plans, or to preview all resources available for this chapter, use the **One-Stop Planner CD-ROM,** Disc 3.

For additional homework suggestions, see activities accompanied by this symbol throughout the chapter.

Day 7

DEUXIEME ETAPE

Quick Review 5 min.
- Game, ATE, p. 16

Quiz 1-2 20 min.
- Administer Quiz 1-2A, 1-2B, or a combination of the two.

PANORAMA CULTUREL 20 min.
- Present **Panorama Culturel,** p. 17, using Videocassette 1.
- **Panorama Culturel,** Interactive CD-ROM Tutor, Disc 1

Wrap-Up 5 min.
- Discuss **Qu'en penses-tu?** questions, p. 17.

Homework Options
Cahier d'activités, Acts. 15–16, p. 7

Day 8

TROISIEME ETAPE

Quick Review 5 min.
- Bell Work, ATE, p. 18

Comment dit-on... ?, p. 18 20 min.
- Presenting **Comment dit-on... ?,** ATE, p. 18
- Play Audio CD for Activity 22, p. 19.
- Discuss **Note culturelle,** p. 19, and Culture Note, ATE, p. 19.
- Do Activity 23, p. 19.

Comment dit-on... ?, p. 20 20 min.
- Presenting **Comment dit-on... ?,** ATE, p. 20
- Discuss Culture Notes, ATE, p. 21.
- Play Audio CD for Activity 25, p. 20.
- Complete Activity 26, p. 20.

Wrap-Up 5 min.
- Teaching Suggestion for Activity 26, ATE, p. 20

Homework Options
Cahier d'activités, Acts. 17–18, p. 8

Day 9

TROISIEME ETAPE

Quick Review 10 min.
- Check homework.

Note de grammaire, p. 21 30 min.
- Review how to tell time.
- Do Activity 27, p. 21.
- Presenting **Note de grammaire,** p. 21
- Do Activity 28, p. 21.
- Cahier d'activités, Activity 19, p. 9
- Travaux pratiques de grammaire, pp. 10–11, Activities 20–23.

Wrap-Up 10 min.
- Teaching Suggestion for Activity 27, ATE, p. 21

Homework Options
Study for Quiz 1-3.

Day 10

TROISIEME ETAPE

Quiz 1-3 20 min.
- Administer Quiz 1-3A, 1-3B, or a combination of the two.

LISONS! 25 min.
- Thinking Critically and Language Notes, ATE, p. 22
- Prereading Activity A, ATE, p. 22
- Reading Activities B–G, ATE, pp. 22–23

Wrap-Up 5 min.
- Discuss Culture Note, ATE, p. 23.

Homework Options
Cahier d'activités, Act. 24, p. 11

Day 11

LISONS!

Quick Review 5 min.
- Go over homework.

Postreading Activities 15 min.
- Complete Postreading Activities H–I, ATE, p. 23.

MISE EN PRATIQUE 20 min.
- Have students do Activities 1–2, p. 28, individually.
- Play Audio CD for Activity 3, p. 28.
- Discuss the strategy for **Ecrivons!,** p. 29, as a class and then have students work on their letters to Patrick.
- Have partners complete **Jeu de rôle,** p. 29.

Wrap-Up 10 min.
- Students complete letters for **Ecrivons!,** p. 29.

Homework Options
Que sais-je?, p. 30
Pupil's Edition Activity I, p. 23

Day 12

MISE EN PRATIQUE

Quick Review 15 min.
- See Game: **Sur la sellette,** ATE, p. 30.

Chapter Review 35 min.
- Review Chapter 1. Choose from **Grammaire supplémentaire,** Grammar Tutor for Students of French, Activities for Communication, Listening Activities, Interactive CD-ROM Tutor, or **Jeux interactifs.**

Homework Options
Study for Chapter 1 Test.

Assessment

Chapter Test 50 min.
- Administer Chapter 1 Test. Select from Testing Program, Alternative Assessment Guide, Test Generator, or Standardized Assessment Tutor.

Suggested Lesson Plans 90-Minute Block Schedule

Block 1

CHAPTER OPENER 5 min.
- Present Chapter Objectives, p. 5
- Culture Notes, ATE, p. 4
- Thinking Critically, ATE, p. 5

MISE EN TRAIN 35 min.
- Preteaching Vocabulary, ATE, p. 6
- Presenting **Mise en train,** ATE, p. 6, using Videocassette 1
- Do Activities 1–3, p. 8.

PREMIERE ETAPE 10 min.
- Read Sandra's letter on page 9 as students read along in their books. Then play Audio CD for Activity 5, p. 9.

Comment dit-on... ?, p. 9 15 min.
- Presenting **Comment dit-on... ?,** ATE, p. 9
- Play Audio CD for Activity 6, p. 10.

Grammaire, p. 10 20 min.
- Presenting **Grammaire,** ATE, p. 10
- Present **Tu te rappelles?,** p. 10, with Pronunciation, ATE, p. 11.
- Do Activity 7, p. 10.

Wrap-Up 5 min.
- Have students describe the characters from **Mise en train,** using **Mise en train** Transparencies.

Homework Options
Grammaire supplémentaire, Acts. 1–2, p. 24
Cahier d'activités, Acts. 1–4, pp. 1–2
Travaux pratiques de grammaire, Acts. 1–2, p. 1

Block 2

PREMIERE ETAPE
Quick Review 10 min.
- Teacher to Teacher, ATE, p. 10

Grammaire, p. 11 10 min.
- Presenting **Grammaire,** ATE, p. 11
- Activity 8, Part a., p. 11

Comment dit-on... ?, p. 11 20 min.
- Presenting **Comment dit-on... ?,** ATE, p. 11
- Play Audio CD for Activity 9, p. 12.
- Activity 10, p. 12

Comment dit-on... ?, p. 12 25 min.
- Presenting **Comment dit-on... ?,** ATE, p. 12
- Present **Note de grammaire,** p. 12. Discuss Language Note, ATE, p. 12.
- Do Activity 11, p. 12.

DEUXIEME ETAPE 10 min.
- Do Activity 13, using Slower Pace, ATE, p. 13.

Vocabulaire, p. 14 10 min.
- Presenting **Vocabulaire,** ATE, p. 14

Wrap-Up 5 min.
- Have students review material from the **Première étape** by describing the people represented in Teaching Transparency 1–1.

Homework Options
Have students study for Quiz 1-1.
Grammaire supplémentaire, Acts. 3–6, pp. 24–25
Cahier d'activités, Acts. 5–9, pp. 3–4
Travaux pratiques de grammaire, Acts. 3–7, pp. 2–4

Block 3

PREMIERE ETAPE
Quick Review 10 min.
- Bell Work, ATE, p. 13

Quiz 1-1 20 min.
- Administer Quiz 1-1A, 1-1B, or a combination of the two.

DEUXIEME ETAPE
Vocabulaire, p. 14 20 min.
- Have students read **De bons conseils,** p. 13.
- Language-to-Language, ATE, p. 14
- Review **Vocabulaire,** p. 14, by having students create illustrated flashcards for each of the vocabulary words.

Note de grammaire, p. 14 20 min.
- Present **Note de grammaire,** p. 14.
- Do Activity 14, p. 14.
- Discuss **Note culturelle,** p. 14.
- Do Activity 15, p. 15.

Comment dit-on... ?, p. 15 10 min.
- Presenting **Comment dit-on... ?,** ATE, p. 15
- Play Audio CD for Activity 16, p. 15.

Wrap-Up 10 min.
- Communicative Activity 1-1, Activities for Communication, pp. 1–2

Homework Options
Grammaire supplémentaire, Act. 7, p. 26
Cahier d'activités, Acts. 10–13, pp. 5–6
Travaux pratiques de grammaire, Acts. 8–13, pp. 5–7

One-Stop Planner CD-ROM

For alternative lesson plans by chapter section, to create your own customized plans, or to preview all resources available for this chapter, use the **One-Stop Planner CD-ROM,** Disc 1.

For additional homework suggestions, see activities accompanied by this symbol throughout the chapter.

Block 4

DEUXIEME ETAPE

Quick Review 10 min.
- Review clothing vocabulary with Game: Pictionnaire, ATE, p. 15.

Note de grammaire, p. 15 30 min.
- Present **Note de grammaire,** using the TPR suggestion, ATE, p. 15.
- Do Activities 17–19, pp. 15–16.

PANORAMA CULTUREL 15 min.
- Presenting **Panorama Culturel,** ATE, p. 17, using Videocassette 1
- Have students discuss the questions in **Qu'en penses-tu?,** p. 17.

TROISIEME ETAPE 5 min.
- Have students read Sandra's letter on p. 18, and then do Activity 21, p. 18.

Comment dit-on... ?, p. 18 20 min.
- Presenting **Comment dit-on... ?,** ATE, p. 18
- Have students read **Note culturelle,** p. 19.
- Play Audio CD for Activity 22, p. 19.
- Do Activity 23, p. 19.

Wrap-Up 10 min.
- Game, ATE, p. 16

Homework Options
Study for Quiz 1-2.
Grammaire supplémentaire, Act. 8, p. 26
Cahier d'activités, Acts. 14–16, pp. 6–7
Travaux pratiques de grammaire, Acts. 14–17, pp. 7–8

Block 5

DEUXIEME ETAPE

Quick Review 10 min.
- Review the **Deuxième étape,** using Teaching Transparency 1-2 and the fifth suggestion in Suggestions for Using Teaching Transparency 1-2.

Quiz 1-2 20 min.
- Administer Quiz 1-2A,1-2B, or a combination of the two.

TROISIEME ETAPE

Comment dit-on... ?, p. 18 15 min.
- Review by suggesting activities and places and having students respond according to your cue (thumbs-up or thumbs-down).
- Do Activity 24, p. 19.

Comment dit-on... ?, p. 20 20 min.
- Presenting **Comment dit-on... ?,** ATE, p. 20
- Play Audio CD for Activity 25, p. 20.
- Do Activity 26, p. 20.

Note de grammaire, p. 21 15 min.
- Presenting **Note de grammaire,** ATE, p. 21
- Do Activity 27, p. 21.

Wrap-Up 10 min.
- Create sentence strips, using the expressions for relating a series of events. Read the sentences aloud, and have students put the sentence strips in the correct order.

Homework Options
Study for Quiz 1-3.
Grammaire supplémentaire, Acts. 10–11, p. 27
Cahier d'activités, Acts. 17–23, pp. 8–10
Travaux pratiques de grammaire, Acts. 18–23, pp. 9–11

Block 6

TROISIEME ETAPE

Quick Review 10 min.
- Communicative Activity 1-3, Activities for Communication, pp. 5–6

Quiz 1-3 20 min.
- Administer Quiz 1-3A, 1-3B, or a combination of the two.

LISONS! 25 min.
- Culture Note, ATE, p. 23
- Prereading Activity A, p. 22. See Thinking Critically, ATE, 22
- Reading Activities B–G, pp. 22–23
- Postreading Activities H–I, p. 23

MISE EN PRATIQUE 35 min.
- Do Activities 1–2, p. 28
- Play Audio CD for Activity 3, p. 28.
- Have students do the first two steps of Activity 4, p. 29.
- Do Activity 5, p. 29.

Homework Options
Que sais-je?, p. 30
Finish **Ecrivons!,** Activity 4, p. 29.
Study for Chapter 1 Test.

Block 7

MISE EN PRATIQUE

Quick Review 10 min.
- Check homework.

Chapter Review 35 min.
- Review Chapter 1. Choose from **Grammaire supplémentaire,** Grammar Tutor for Students of French, Activities for Communication, Listening Activities, Interactive CD-ROM Tutor, or **Jeux interactifs.**

Chapter Test 45 min.
- Administer Chapter 1 Test. Select from Testing Program, Alternative Assessment Guide, Test Generator, or Standardized Assessment Tutor.

Chapter Opener

CHAPITRE 1

For resource information, see the **One-Stop Planner,** Disc 1.

Pacing Tips

This chapter is a review chapter, so students will recognize most of the functions, grammar, and vocabulary presented. The cultural information is primarily new, so you might plan your lessons accordingly. For Lesson Plans and timing suggestions, see pages 3I–3L.

Meeting the Standards

Communication

- Describing and characterizing yourself and others, p. 9
- Expressing likes, dislikes, and preferences, p. 11
- Asking for information, p. 12
- Asking for and giving advice, p. 15
- Asking for, making, and responding to suggestions, p. 18
- Relating a series of events, p. 20

Culture

- Culture Note, pp. 4, 16, 19, 21, 23
- Note culturelle, pp. 14, 19
- Panorama Culturel, p. 17

Connections

- Multicultural Link, pp. 17, 19, 28
- Math Link, p. 19

Comparisons

- Thinking Critically: Comparing and Contrasting, p. 22

Communities

- Family Link, p. 12
- Career Path, p. 7
- De l'école au travail, p. 21

Cultures and Communities

Culture Notes

- Point out that French and other European teenagers tend to spend more time visiting historical sites and monuments than American teenagers do. Since most of them grow up among buildings and streets that are many hundreds of years old, history has more of an immediate presence in their lives. Therefore, it is not unusual for French teenagers to ride their bicycles or mopeds to a neighboring town on the weekend for some sightseeing.
- During the school year at French high schools, one- and two-week exchanges are often arranged with schools in neighboring countries, especially in Germany and England. French high school students have the opportunity to participate in exchanges because of the French **lycée** vacation schedule.

CHAPITRE 1

Bon séjour!

Objectives

In this chapter you will review and practice how to

Première étape

- describe and characterize yourself and others
- express likes, dislikes, and preferences
- ask for information

Deuxième étape

- ask for and give advice

Troisième étape

- ask for, make, and respond to suggestions
- relate a series of events

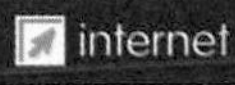

ADRESSE: go.hrw.com
MOT-CLE:
WA3 PARIS REGION-1

J'aime bien faire des photos... et j'adore Paris!

Connections and Comparisons

Thinking Critically

Analyzing Explain the difference between **Bon séjour!**, which refers to a stay, and **Bon voyage!**, which refers to a trip. Then, ask these questions:

- If you were going to spend a year with a family in a foreign country, what would you like them to know about you?
- Would it be difficult to pack for a year abroad? Why or why not? What would you need to know about the country and the family in order to pack well?
- What would you want to do once you arrived?

Chapter Opener

CHAPITRE 1

Focusing on Outcomes

Have students determine which chapter outcome is represented by the photo. Then, have them think of French expressions they may have learned that accomplish the functions listed. Have one student compile a list on the board of the various suggestions. NOTE: The self-check activities on page 30 help students assess their achievement of the objectives.

Teacher Note

Some activities suggested in the *Annotated Teacher's Edition* ask students to contact various people, businesses, and organizations in the community. Before assigning these activities, it is advisable to request parental permission. In some cases, you may also want to obtain permission from the parties the students will be asked to contact.

Chapter Sequence

Mise en train

CHAPITRE 1

Teaching Resources
pp. 6–8

PRINT

- Lesson Planner, p. 1
- Video Guide, pp. 4, 6
- Cahier d'activités, p. 1

MEDIA 

- One-Stop Planner
- Video Program
  Mise en train
  Videocassette 1, 03:37–07:22
  Videocassette 5 (captioned version), 00:45–04:31
  Suite
  Videocassette 1, 07:25–11:48
  Videocassette 5 (captioned version), 04:34–08:57
- DVD Tutor, Disc 1
- Audio Compact Discs, CD 1, Trs. 1–2
- **Mise en train** Transparencies

Presenting Mise en train

Have students view the video of the **Mise en train** with their book closed. Afterwards, ask them to name the characters in the story and their relationship to one another. Tell them to open their book and look at the title of the **Mise en train.** Have them try to deduce the meaning of the word **méprise** from what they saw in the video. Next, present the Preteaching Vocabulary suggestion below. Then, ask them to look at the photos on pages 6 and 7 and tell what mistakes are made. Finally, do the comprehension activities on page 8.

Mise en train Transparencies

The **roman-photo** is an abridged version of the video episode.

MISE EN TRAIN ▪ *Une méprise*

CD 1 Trs. 1–2

Stratégie pour comprendre

The Lepic family runs into some problems when they go to pick up their exchange student at the airport. After looking at the photos, guess what problems they encounter along the way. What does the title of this episode mean? What could have caused this **méprise** to happen?

Sandra

M. Lepic

Mme Lepic

Pamela

Bertrand

Patricia

1 **Chez la famille Lepic à Chartres : il est 9h du matin et on est en retard.**

Sandra Pamela arrive à l'aéroport à dix heures vingt. Dépêchez-vous!

M. Lepic N'oublie pas que d'abord elle va récupérer ses bagages et puis passer à la douane. Alors, comment est-elle? Brune? Blonde? Grande? Petite?

2 **Sandra** Elle a 16 ans. Elle est grande et elle a les cheveux bruns. D'après sa lettre, elle va porter une jupe rouge et elle aura une valise noire.

3 **A l'aéroport...**

M. Lepic Si tu veux, je peux vous retrouver ici.

Mme Lepic D'accord. Bonne idée.

M. Lepic Bien. Allez-y!

4 **Quelques minutes plus tard...**

M. Lepic Ah, c'est elle. Brune, une jupe rouge, une valise noire...

Preteaching Vocabulary

Activating prior knowledge

Ask students to think about experiences they have had in trying to arrange to meet someone they have never seen in person. Have them think about the information they would need (physical description, meeting time, and place...) in order to find this person. Before they read *Une méprise,* have them match each adjective with its English equivalent.

❶ **blonde**	a. short
❶ **petite**	b. tall
❷ **grande**	c. brunette
❹ **brune**	d. blond
❹ **rouge**	e. red

Can they see why there was a misunderstanding on the part of Monsieur Lepic?

STANDARDS: 1.2

5 **M. Lepic** Bonjour! Tu n'as pas vu ma femme et ma fille?

6 **Pendant ce temps...**

Sandra Alors, tu as fait bon voyage?
Pamela Oui. Excellent.
Mme Lepic Ça va? Pas trop fatiguée?
Pamela Non, ça va. Je suis très contente d'être en France! Je l'adore!

7 **Sandra** Je te présente Pamela. Mais, qui est-ce, Papa?
Patricia Eh bien,... je suis Patricia. Où est Bertrand?

8 **Sandra** Bertrand? Oh là là! Papa, mais qu'est-ce que tu as fait?
Bertrand Patricia?
Patricia Oui. Tu es bien Bertrand?
M. Lepic Oh, excusez-moi, mademoiselle. C'est une méprise.

9 **Mme Lepic** Alors, tout est bien qui finit bien!
M. Lepic Au revoir, Patricia. Et bon séjour à Paris!

10 **Patricia** Attends, ce n'est pas ma valise!
Bertrand Eh, monsieur! Arrêtez-vous!

Cahier d'activités, p. 1, Act. 1–2

Mise en train

CHAPITRE 1

Language Note

Passer à la douane means *to go through customs.* Passengers arriving in France on international flights must show their passports to customs officials **(les douaniers)** before claiming their luggage.

Teaching Suggestion

Ask students to guess the English equivalent of **Tout est bien qui finit bien.** *(All's well that ends well.)*

Visual Learners

Project quotations from ***Une méprise*** in random order on the overhead projector and have students give the number of the corresponding photo.

Career Path

For employees of an international airport or airline who deal daily with travelers from all over the world, knowledge of a foreign language is very important. Have students suggest specific jobs in these industries which involve speaking a foreign language.

Using the Captioned Video/DVD

If students have difficulty understanding French spoken at a normal speed, use Videocassette 5 to allow students to see the French captions for ***Une méprise*** and ***Une méprise (suite).*** Hearing the language and watching the story will reduce anxiety about the new language and facilitate comprehension. The reinforcement of seeing the written vocabulary words as they watch the gestures and actions will help prepare students to do the comprehension activities on page 8.

NOTE: The DVD Tutor contains captions for all sections of the *Video Program.*

Mise en train (suite)

When the story continues, Patricia and Bertrand manage to stop the Lepics, and they exchange suitcases. The Lepics then take Pamela on a tour of Paris by **bateau-mouche** before returning to Chartres.

STANDARDS: 1.2, 5.1

Mise en train

CHAPITRE 1

Challenge

4 Form small groups and have each group write an ending for *Une méprise.* A reporter from each group should read the ending the group imagined. You might have the class select the most probable and the most improbable endings. Show the continuation of *Une méprise* and compare the ending with those the students imagined.

Using the DVD Tutor

For extra practice, you might have pairs of students complete the **Mise en train Compréhension** activities on Disc 1 of the *DVD Tutor.*

These activities check for comprehension only. Students should not yet be expected to produce language modeled in **Mise en train.**

1 Tu as compris? See answers below.

1. Why does Sandra tell her family to hurry?
2. How does Sandra describe her friend?
3. When they arrive at the airport, what do Sandra and Mrs. Lepic do?
4. What is Mr. Lepic's first mistake? Why does he make it?
5. What happens at the end of *Une méprise?*

2 Arrange la scène

Choisis la photo qui correspond à chaque phrase. Ensuite, mets les phrases dans le bon ordre d'après *Une méprise.* 4, 3, 2, 1, 5

1. Pamela arrive à la voiture avec Mme Lepic et Sandra. e
2. Mme Lepic, Pamela et Sandra sortent de l'aéroport. d
3. M. Lepic voit Patricia. a
4. La famille Lepic arrive à l'aéroport. c
5. Patricia a la valise de Pamela. b

a.

b.

c.

d.

e.

3 Cherche les expressions

According to *Une méprise,* how do you . . .

1. tell what time it is? See answers below.
2. ask what someone looks like?
3. ask how someone's trip was?
4. express concern for someone?
5. introduce someone?
6. apologize for your mistake?

Je te présente...
Excusez-moi...
Il est neuf heures du matin.
Comment est-elle?
Ça va? Pas trop fatiguée?
Tu as fait bon voyage?

4 Et maintenant, à toi

With a partner, talk about what might happen next in *Une méprise.*

Answers

1
1. They're late picking up the exchange student.
2. sixteen, tall, brown hair, red skirt, black suitcase
3. go to look for Pamela
4. He thinks Patricia is Pamela. She fits Pamela's description.
5. Bertrand finds Patricia, and Mr. Lepic leaves with Patricia's suitcase.

3
1. Il est neuf heures du matin...
2. Comment est-elle?
3. Tu as fait bon voyage?
4. Ça va? Pas trop fatiguée?
5. Je te présente...
6. Excusez-moi...

Comprehension Check

Teaching Suggestion

2 Form small groups. Write the five sentences in random order on a piece of paper and make a copy for each group. Have the group cut the paper into strips, with one sentence per strip, and rearrange them in the correct sequence.

Kinesthetic/Auditory/Visual Learners

2 Read the sentences aloud one at a time and have students point to the photo that corresponds to each sentence they hear.

STANDARDS: 1.2

Première étape

Objectives Describing and characterizing yourself and others; expressing likes, dislikes, and preferences; asking for information

WA3 PARIS REGION-1

Moi, je m'appelle Sandra. J'ai 15 ans. Je suis brune et j'ai les yeux marron. Et toi, tu es comment? Dans ma famille, on est quatre. Mon père travaille dans l'informatique. Il a 42 ans. Ma mère travaille dans une boutique de souvenirs. Elle a 39 ans. Mon frère Etienne a 17 ans. Pour l'instant, il est au Texas. J'ai aussi un chat. Il s'appelle Félix. Moi, mon truc, c'est le cinéma. Et toi, qu'est-ce que tu aimes faire? J'ai plein de questions à te poser.

5 **Je te présente ma famille** See scripts and answers on p. 3G.

Ecoutons Ecoute Sandra qui parle de sa famille. De quelle photo est-ce qu'elle parle?

CD 1 Tr. 3

a.

b.

c.

d.

e.

Comment dit-on...?

Describing and characterizing yourself and others

CD-ROM 1 DVD 1

To describe yourself:

J'ai quinze **ans.**
J'ai les yeux bleus.
I have . . . eyes.
J'ai les cheveux courts/longs/noirs/roux.
I have short/long/black/red hair.
Je suis grand(e)/petit(e).

To describe others:

Elle a sept **ans.**
Elles ont les yeux marron/bleus/noirs.
Ils ont les cheveux blonds/bruns/châtains.
They have blond/dark brown/light brown hair.
Elle est forte.
Ils sont de taille moyenne.
They're of medium height.

To characterize yourself:

Je suis gourmand(e)!
I love to eat!

To characterize others:

Il est intelligent.
Elles sont sympas.

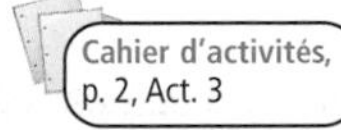

Cahier d'activités, p. 2, Act. 3

Communication for All Students

Slower Pace

5 Before you play the recording, have students look back at the **Mise en train** to identify Sandra and her parents in the photos.

Auditory Learners

Before presenting **Comment dit-on... ?**, review adjective agreement by reading a list of adjectives whose masculine and feminine forms are pronounced differently **(fort/forte).** Have students tell you which are masculine and which are feminine by listening to the forms you give them.

Première étape

CHAPITRE 1

Teaching Resources
pp. 9–12

PRINT

- Lesson Planner, p. 2
- TPR Storytelling Book, pp. x–1
- Listening Activities, pp. 3–4, 7
- Activities for Communication, pp. 1–2, 75, 78, 137–138
- Travaux pratiques de grammaire, pp. 1–4
- Grammar Tutor for Students of French, Chapter 1
- Cahier d'activités, pp. 2–4
- Testing Program, pp. 1–4
- Alternative Assessment Guide, p. 32
- Student Make-Up Assignments, Chapter 1

MEDIA

- One-Stop Planner
- Audio Compact Discs, CD 1, Trs. 3–5, 14, 20–21
- Teaching Transparencies: 1-1; **Grammaire supplémentaire** Answers; Travaux pratiques de grammaire Answers
- Interactive CD-ROM Tutor, Disc 1

Bell Work

Write some scrambled sentences from the **Mise en train** on the board. Students should unscramble and rewrite the sentences.

Presenting
Comment dit-on... ?

To present hair and eye color and age, use pictures of people whose hair and eye color are obvious. Tape a card with the person's age written on it to each picture. Then, describe the people. **(Elle a les cheveux bruns.)** Afterwards, ask either-or questions about each picture. **(Elle a les cheveux blonds ou bruns?)**

Première étape

CHAPITRE 1

Teaching Resources
pp. 9–12

PRINT 
- Lesson Planner, p. 2
- TPR Storytelling Book, pp. x–1
- Listening Activities, pp. 3–4, 7
- Activities for Communication, pp. 1–2, 75, 78, 137–138
- Travaux pratiques de grammaire, pp. 1–4
- Grammar Tutor for Students of French, Chapter 1
- Cahier d'activités, pp. 2–4
- Testing Program, pp. 1–4
- Alternative Assessment Guide, p. 32
- Student Make-Up Assignments, Chapter 1

MEDIA 
- One-Stop Planner
- Audio Compact Discs, CD 1, Trs. 3–5, 14, 20–21
- Teaching Transparencies: 1-1; **Grammaire supplémentaire** Answers; Travaux pratiques de Grammaire Answers
- Interactive CD-ROM Tutor, Disc 1

Presenting Grammaire

Avoir* and *Etre To review **être** and **avoir,** prepare two sets of cards. On the first set, write the subject pronouns. On the second set, write possible completions for sentences that would use **être** or **avoir (les yeux bleus, grand...).** Pick one card from each set and create a sentence that describes one or more of your students. **(Elles ont les yeux bleus.)** Ask for volunteers who match the description to stand up and rephrase the sentence you just said, using an appropriate pronoun and verb form. **(Nous avons les yeux bleus.)**

6 Le hit-parade des stars See scripts and answers on p. 3G.

CD 1 Tr. 4

Ecoutons Match the descriptions of these stars with their photos.

a.

b.

c.

d.

Tu te rappelles?

Do you remember how to make liaisons? You pronounce the final consonant of one word when the following word begins with a vowel sound, as in **les yeux** and **ils ont.**
(z) (z)

Grammaire

The verbs *avoir* and *être*

You may remember that **avoir** and **être** are irregular verbs. They follow different patterns than regular verbs.

avoir *(to have)*		**être** *(to be)*	
j'	**ai**	je	**suis**
tu	**as**	tu	**es**
il/elle/on	**a**	il/elle/on	**est**
nous	**avons**	nous	**sommes**
vous	**avez**	vous	**êtes**
ils/elles	**ont**	ils/elles	**sont**

Grammaire supplémentaire, p. 24, Act. 1–2

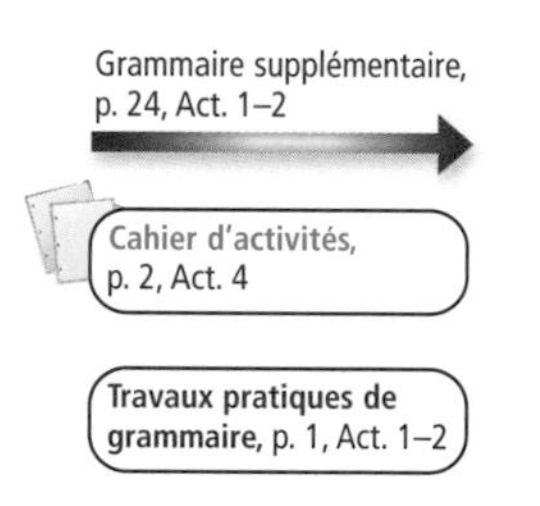
Cahier d'activités, p. 2, Act. 4

Travaux pratiques de grammaire, p. 1, Act. 1–2

7 Grammaire en contexte

a. **Ecrivons** Voici la première lettre de ton correspondant. Dans ce paragraphe, il fait sa description et la description de son meilleur ami. Complète sa lettre avec les formes appropriées d'**être** ou d'**avoir.**

1. ai 2. a 3. sommes 4. avons 5. est 6. suis 7. est 8. sommes 9. avons 10. es

Eh bien, moi, j' __1__ quinze ans et Claude __2__ seize ans. Nous ne __3__ ni grands ni petits. Nous __4__ les yeux marron, mais Claude __5__ brun et moi, je __6__ blond. Claude __7__ très intelligent, et moi aussi. Nous __8__ en seconde au lycée, et nous __9__ arts plastiques et espagnol ensemble. Et toi, comment tu __10__ ?

b. **Parlons** Décris ton/ta meilleur(e) ami(e) à ton groupe. Utilise **être** et **avoir** pour parler de la couleur de ses yeux, de la couleur de ses cheveux, de son âge et de sa taille.

Teacher to Teacher

Todd Losié
Renaissance High School
Detroit, MI

Todd suggests the following activity to practice describing people.

"To reinforce descriptions, I use pictures of celebrities from magazines that my students read. I have small groups describe the celebrities, or have one student describe a celebrity and the others guess who it is. I also select a short segment from one of the students' favorite television shows or movies and have the students view the segment without the sound. Students then describe the segment, including physical and personality attributes of the characters. I also have students perform voice-overs for the scene in French."

STANDARDS: 1.1, 1.2

Grammaire

Adjective agreement

As you remember, you often change the forms of adjectives in French according to the nouns they describe.

- You add an **e** to the masculine form of most adjectives to describe feminine nouns or pronouns. Adjectives that already end in a silent **e** don't change in the singular form.

  Il est **intelligent.** Elle est **intelligente.** Il est **jeune.** Elle est **jeune.**
- To describe plural nouns, you usually add an **s** to adjectives, unless they end in **s** or **x.**

  Ils sont **jeunes.** Elle a les cheveux **gris.** Ils sont **heureux.**
- Some adjectives have different feminine forms.

  Il est **beau.** Elle est **belle.** Il est **gentil.** Elle est **gentille.**

  Il est **sportif.** Elle est **sportive.**
- The singular forms of **sympa** are the same; an **-s** is added to make **sympa** plural. The adjective **châtain** is almost never used to describe anything but **les cheveux,** so you'll probably only see the plural form, **châtains.**

  Il/Elle est **sympa.** Ils/Elles sont **sympas.** Il a les cheveux **châtains.**
- Some adjectives don't change in the feminine or plural. Can you find one in **Comment dit-on... ?** on page 9?*

Grammaire supplémentaire, pp. 24–25, Act. 3–4

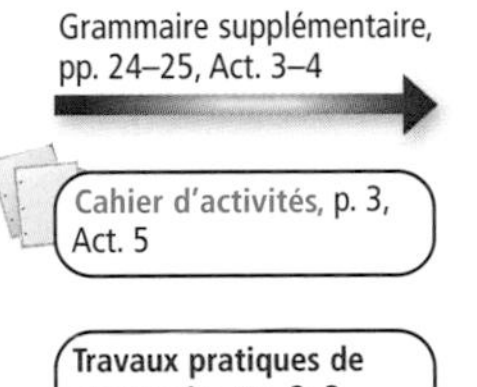

Cahier d'activités, p. 3, Act. 5

Travaux pratiques de grammaire, pp. 2–3, Act. 3–5

8 Grammaire en contexte

a. Ecrivons Tu as reçu une lettre de ta correspondante Karine. Complète la description de sa famille avec les formes appropriées des adjectifs entre parenthèses.

1. Ma sœur Anne est (pénible), mais elle est (mignon) aussi. pénible, mignonne
2. Mon frère Alain est très (grand) et (sportif). grand, sportif
3. Ma mère a les cheveux (blond) et mon père a les cheveux (châtain). blonds, châtains
4. Ma chatte s'appelle Fifi. Elle est (gentil) et très (intelligent). gentille, intelligente

b. Ecrivons Dans ton journal, écris un paragraphe où tu décris comment tu es. Ensuite, décris ta famille. Si tu préfères, tu peux décrire une famille imaginaire.

Comment dit-on...?

Expressing likes, dislikes, and preferences

To tell what you like:

J'adore le sport.
J'aime bien faire de la photo.

To tell what you prefer:

Je préfère jouer au foot.
J'aime mieux faire de la vidéo.

To tell what you dislike:

Je n'aime pas le tennis.

Cahier d'activités, pp. 3–4, Act. 6–7

Grammaire supplémentaire, p. 25, Act. 5

* marron

Communication for All Students

Kinesthetic Learners

Prepare sentences using third-person pronouns and various adjectives. **(Il est beau. Elles sont intelligentes.)** Seat four students in front of the room in groups of two: two boys and two girls. Read a sentence aloud and have the students in the chairs stand to represent its structure. Designate one boy and one girl to assume the responsibility of standing when singular subjects are read. For example, when he hears **Il est beau,** the designated boy stands. Both girls stand when they hear **Elles sont intelligentes.** Have students repeat each sentence while their classmates in front of the class are still standing in order to provide an audio-visual connection for auditory and visual learners or slower-paced learners.

Première étape

CHAPITRE 1

Language Note

Châtain is the French word for a hair color that is between brunette and blonde. Point out that you can say **Elle est blonde, Il est brun,** and **Elles sont rousses,** but you must say **Elle a les cheveux noirs, Il a les cheveux gris,** and **Ils ont les cheveux châtains.**

Pronunciation

Tu te rappelles? Have students reread the letter on page 9 and find examples of **liaison.**

Presenting Grammaire

Adjective agreement Prepare four sets of large cards. On the first set of four cards, write **il, elle, ils,** and **elles.** On the second set of two, write **est** and **sont.** On the third set of several cards, write adjectives in their masculine singular form. On the fourth set, write **-e, -s, -es, -le, -ve, -x,** and **no ending.** Have four students each take one set of cards. Student #1 chooses and shows a subject card. Student #2 then selects and shows the appropriate verb form. Student #3 holds up any adjective. Student #4 must choose the correct ending for the adjective.

Comment dit-on... ?

Show pictures of various activities and tell which activities you like or dislike. Then, ask students about their preferences as you show the pictures again. **(Tu aimes jouer au tennis, Jean?)**

Additional Practice

Have students make a collage on posterboard of magazine or catalogue pictures that represent their likes and dislikes. Then, have students explain their collage to the class. **(J'adore danser et écouter de la musique.)**

Première étape

CHAPITRE 1

Presenting Comment dit-on... ?

Ask students **Qu'est-ce que tu aimes faire?** If necessary, prompt with additional questions, such as **Tu aimes écouter de la musique? Tu aimes aller à la plage?** When students have heard several responses, ask them what other students like to do. **(Qu'est-ce que Paul aime faire?)** Repeat the process for each question in the function box, re-entering the preceding questions as you go.

Culture Note

10 Etienne was born in Dijon, the capital of Burgundy **(la Bourgogne),** in east central France. Dijon is known for its mustard, its vinegar, and its gingerbread. One of Etienne's favorite dishes is **bœuf bourguignon,** a specialty of the region, which is made by marinating beef cubes in flour, red wine, thyme, and bay leaves before cooking.

Teaching Suggestion

To close this **étape,** put the names of all the students in a box. Have them draw a name and give three sentences describing the person and telling what he or she likes.

Assess

- Testing Program, pp. 1–4 Quiz 1-1A, Quiz 1-1B, Audio CD 1, Tr. 14
- Student Make-Up Assignments Chapter 1, Alternative Quiz
- Alternative Assessment Guide, p. 32

See scripts and answers on p. 3G.

9 A qui est-ce que je ressemble?

CD 1 Tr. 5

Ecoutons Listen to Etienne describe his cousins Eric and Caroline. Look at his self-portrait and decide which cousin has more in common with him.

10 Un auto-portrait

Ecrivons Ecris une lettre à Etienne. Explique-lui comment tu es et dis ce que tu aimes et ce que tu n'aimes pas. Tu peux utiliser le portrait d'Etienne pour trouver des idées pour ta lettre. Tu peux aussi utiliser les expressions dans la boîte.

J'ai les cheveux...
Je n'aime pas...
Je suis...
Comme musique, j'aime...

Nom :	LEPIC
Prénom :	Etienne
Né(e) à :	Dijon
Résidence :	Chartres
Animaux domestiques :	un chat et deux poissons rouges
Sports pratiqués :	le tennis, le vélo, le foot
Plats préférés :	les hamburgers et le bœuf bourguignon
Passions :	le sport, la musique rock, les copains, la lecture
Ambition :	participer au Tour de France

Comment dit-on...?

Asking for information

CD-ROM 1 DVD 1

Qu'est-ce que tu aimes faire?
Qu'est-ce que tu fais comme sport?
Qu'est-ce que tu aimes comme musique?
Quel(le) est ton groupe/**ta** classe **préféré(e)?**
What is your favorite . . . ?
Qui est ton musicien/**ta** musicienne **préféré(e)?**
Who is your favorite . . . ?

Cahier d'activités, p. 4, Act. 8–9

Note de grammaire

The interrogative adjective **quel** has four forms: **quel, quelle, quels,** and **quelles.** It can mean *which* or *what*, and it agrees in number and gender with the noun it modifies.

Il a **quel** cours à dix heures?
Quelle jupe est-ce que tu préfères?

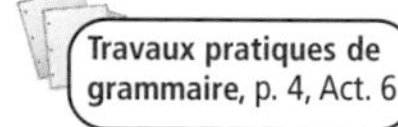

Travaux pratiques de grammaire, p. 4, Act. 6

Grammaire supplémentaire, p. 25, Act. 6

11 Sondage

Parlons Utilise les questions de **Comment dit-on... ?** pour interviewer trois camarades. Ensuite, dis quel(le) camarade est comme toi.

EXEMPLE —**Qui est ta musicienne préférée?**
—**Jennifer Lopez! J'adore la techno.**

Si tu as oublié
-er verbs
va à la page R33.

Travaux pratiques de grammaire, p. 4, Act. 7

12 Jeu de rôle

Parlons Avec un camarade, choisissez une personne célèbre qui vous intéresse et créez une interview. Ensuite, vous allez présenter votre interview à la classe. Utilisez des costumes, de la musique ou des objets appropriés pour amuser votre public.

Connections and Comparisons

Family Link

Have students teach a family member to describe himself or herself and to say what he or she likes in French. When assigning Family Link activities, keep in mind that some students and families may consider family matters private.

Language Note

Point out that **Qu'est-ce que** is followed by a subject and verb, **Quel est** by a thing, and **Qui est** by a person.

STANDARDS: 1.1, 1.2, 3.1, 5.1, 5.2

Objectives Asking for and giving advice

WA3 PARIS REGION-1

Ici, le climat est assez doux. Apporte quand même un manteau et deux ou trois gros pulls; il peut faire froid en hiver. Prends aussi un imperméable et des bottes parce qu'il pleut souvent. L'été, il fait chaud mais pas trop. Pense à prendre un maillot de bain. Quand il fait beau, on peut aller se baigner au lac. Pour l'école, on y va le plus souvent en jean et en tee-shirt.

13 **Pense à prendre...**

Lisons D'après la lettre de Sandra, quels vêtements est-ce que Pamela doit mettre...

1. en hiver? d **2.** quand il pleut? e, f **3.** pour aller à la piscine? a **4.** pour l'école? b, c

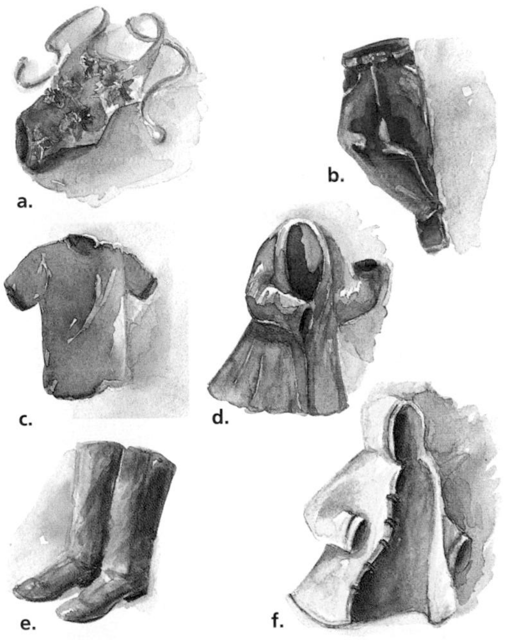

Do you recall everything you learned last year? It's easy to forget your French when you don't use it for a while. Here are some tips.

- Use the flashcards you've made to review vocabulary. Make new ones for verbs or phrases that you use frequently.
- If you can't remember how to say something in French, look in the glossary or ask someone **Comment dit-on... ?** You can also try using words you do know or gestures to explain what you mean.
- Don't be afraid to speak out. Attempting to speak will sometimes jog your memory. Even if you make a mistake, you're still communicating.

Communication for All Students

Slower Pace

13 Have students scan the letter and list the different weather conditions that are mentioned. Then, have them list the clothing Sandra asks Pamela to bring for each weather condition.

Auditory Learners

13 Read the letter aloud while students listen with their books closed. Each time students hear an expression about the weather, they should raise one hand. Each time they hear an article of clothing mentioned, they should raise both hands.

Deuxième étape

CHAPITRE 1

Teaching Resources

pp. 13–16

PRINT

- Lesson Planner, p. 3
- TPR Storytelling Book, pp. 2–3
- Listening Activities, pp. 4, 8
- Activities for Communication, pp. 3–4, 76, 78–79, 137–138
- Travaux pratiques de grammaire, pp. 5–8
- Grammar Tutor for Students of French, Chapter 1
- Cahier d'activités, pp. 5–7
- Testing Program, pp. 5–8
- Alternative Assessment Guide, p. 32
- Student Make-Up Assignments, Chapter 1

MEDIA 

- One-Stop Planner
- Audio Compact Discs, CD 1, Trs. 6, 15, 22–23
- Teaching Transparencies: 1-2, 1-A; **Grammaire supplémentaire** Answers; Travaux pratiques de grammaire Answers
- Interactive CD-ROM Tutor, Disc 1

Bell Work

Have students rewrite the following paragraph, changing the underlined items to describe their best friend or an imaginary friend.

Ma meilleure amie a quinze ans, et elle est très petite. Elle a les cheveux noirs et les yeux bleus. Elle adore jouer au tennis et faire du vélo.

STANDARDS: 1.2, 5.1

Deuxième étape

CHAPITRE 1

Teaching Resources
pp. 13–16

PRINT 
- Lesson Planner, p. 3
- TPR Storytelling Book, pp. 2–3
- Listening Activities, pp. 4, 8
- Activities for Communication, pp. 3–4, 76, 78–79, 137–138
- Travaux pratiques de grammaire, pp. 5–8
- Grammar Tutor for Students of French, Chapter 1
- Cahier d'activités, pp. 5–7
- Testing Program, pp. 5–8
- Alternative Assessment Guide, p. 32
- Student Make-Up Assignments, Chapter 1

MEDIA 
- One-Stop Planner
- Audio Compact Discs, CD 1, Trs. 6, 15, 21–23
- Teaching Transparencies: 1-2, 1-A; **Grammaire supplémentaire** Answers; Travaux pratiques de grammaire Answers
- Interactive CD-ROM Tutor, Disc 1

Presenting Vocabulaire

Bring to class a travel bag and as many of the items in the **Vocabulaire** as possible. Identify the items in French as you place them around the room where students can see them. Say that you are going to spend a year in France and you need to pack. On the board, write **A prendre.** Underneath, list all the items you have placed around the room. Then, pretend you can't find anything. Ask **Est-ce que quelqu'un a vu mon imperméable?** When a student hands you the correct item, ask other students **Qu'est-ce que Michel a trouvé?** Continue until your bag is packed.

Vocabulaire

Pour mon voyage, il me faut...

CD-ROM 1
DVD 1

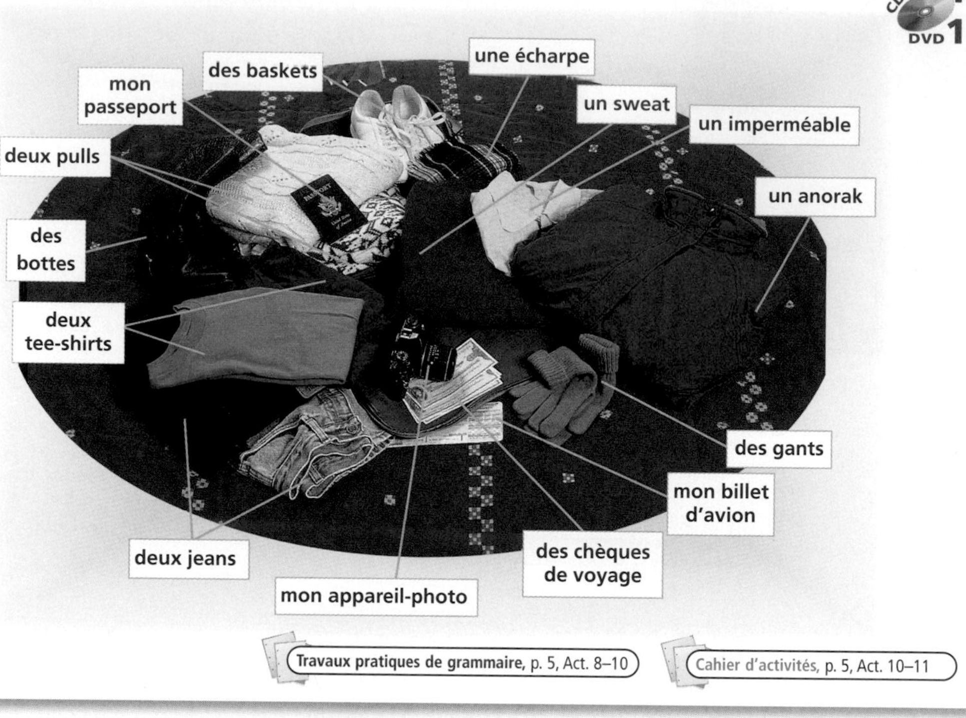

Travaux pratiques de grammaire, p. 5, Act. 8–10

Cahier d'activités, p. 5, Act. 10–11

Note de grammaire

To form the present tense of **-ir** verbs like **choisir,** drop the **-ir** and add these endings: **-is, -is, -it, -issons,-issez, -issent.** The past participle of **-ir** verbs ends in **-i:** il a chois**i.** Some **-ir** verbs you already know are **grandir, maigrir,** and **grossir.**

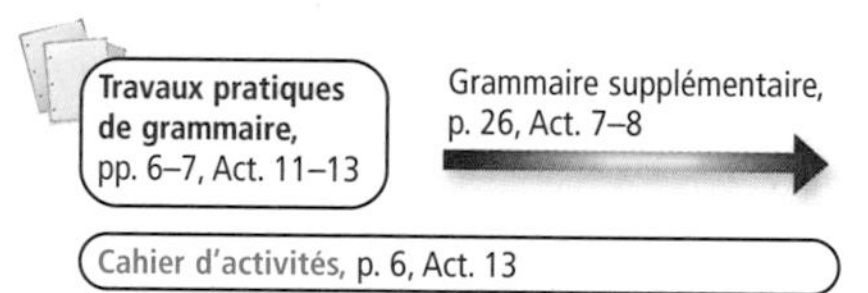

Note culturelle

Travel documents and visa requirements vary depending on the countries involved and the purpose of the stay. Students planning to stay more than three months in a country must have a visa, which can usually be obtained from the embassy or consulate of the country to be visited. Citizens of European Union countries now have the same passport, and they need only their national identity card to travel within Europe.

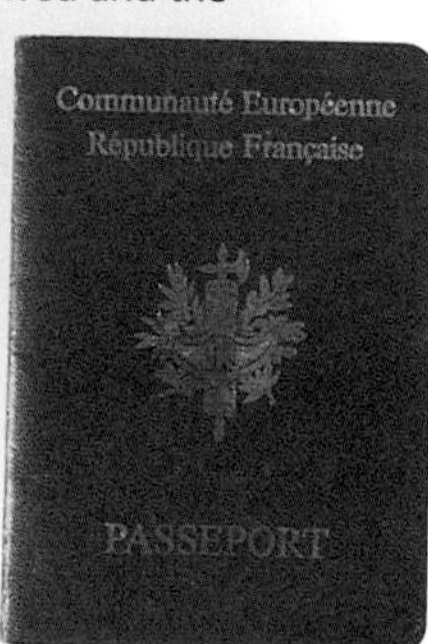

14 Que choisir?

Ecrivons Ton amie Pauline et toi, vous avez gagné à un jeu dans une boutique parisienne. Chaque personne peut choisir cinq articles dans le magasin. Pauline va aller faire du ski. Dis quels articles elle va prendre et en quelle(s) couleur(s). Ensuite, explique ce que toi, tu vas prendre. Utilise le verbe **choisir** dans ta réponse.

Connections and Comparisons

Language-to-Language

Have students find the cognates in the **Vocabulaire.** Have them think about the origin of each word. Which words do they think originated in English? **(baskets, sweat, tee-shirts, jeans)** Why? If you have native speakers of Spanish in your class, have them give the Spanish terms for clothing items that have cognates in the **Vocabulaire (un suéter, una blusa, unos pantalones).**

STANDARDS: 2.2, 4.1

15 Devinons!

Parlons Write down three activities that you'd like to do. Choose one of the activities. Then, tell your group what you're going to wear for the activity without naming it. The person who guesses what you're going to do takes the next turn.

EXEMPLE **—Je vais mettre un jean et un gros pull, un anorak, des gants et des bottes.**
—Tu vas faire du ski!
—Oui, c'est ça.

Comment dit-on...?

Asking for and giving advice

To ask for advice:

Qu'est-ce que je dois prendre?
What should I . . . ?

To give advice:

Pense à prendre ton passeport.
Remember to take . . .

Prends un dictionnaire bilingue.
N'oublie pas tes bottes.

Cahier d'activités, p. 7, Act. 15

Note de grammaire

One way to give advice is to use commands.

- When you're talking with a friend, use the **tu** form of the verb without **tu:** **Prends** ton maillot de bain.
- Don't forget to drop the final **s** when you're using the **tu** form of an **-er** verb as a command: **Pense** à moi!
- To make a command negative, put **ne... pas** around the verb: **N'**oublie **pas** ton billet!

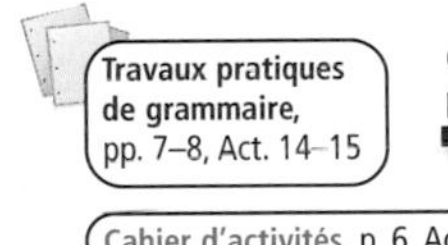
Travaux pratiques de grammaire, pp. 7–8, Act. 14–15
Grammaire supplémentaire, p. 26, Act. 9
Cahier d'activités, p. 6, Act. 14

16 Où vont-ils en vacances?

See scripts on p. 3G. 1. b 2. d 3. c

CD 1 Tr. 6

Ecoutons D'après ces conversations, où est-ce que ces gens vont pour les vacances?

a. à Paris
b. à la plage
c. à New York
d. à la montagne pour faire du ski

17 De bons conseils

Parlons Tes ami(e)s vont aller en vacances. Dis-leur quels articles ils doivent prendre.
See answers below.

Jérôme, tu vas avoir froid! ...

Dorothée, il pleut beaucoup dans cette région. ...

Sabine et Christian, vous voulez faire du sport, non? ..., alors.

Tu vas sûrement acheter des souvenirs, Julia. ...

Martin et Léa, ...! Il y a de belles photos à prendre là-bas.

Vous allez faire de l'équitation, non? Alors, ...

..., Alexandre. Tu en as besoin pour prendre l'avion!

Maxime et Tristan, ...pour les randonnées en skis!

Communication for All Students

Visual Learners

15 Assign each student a particular activity **(aller à l'école)** or type of weather **(Il neige.)**. Have them design and draw an outfit for that activity or weather condition, label it, and describe it to the class.

Note de grammaire

TPR To review the imperative, write on cards several commands using the **tu** and **vous** forms. They must be easily acted out, such as **Allez à la porte!** or **Fais du ski.** Select a leader to stand in front of the class. The other students stand by their desks. The leader reads the commands, addressing them either to one person, using the **tu** form, or to groups of students, using the **vous** form.

Deuxième étape

Game

Pictionnaire® Distribute sheets of butcher paper to small groups. Have each group write all the vocabulary words on slips of paper. Then, have a student draw a slip and sketch an illustration representing that word. The first student to guess the French word for that drawing scores a point. Students take turns drawing.

Presenting Comment dit-on... ?

First, ask students to recall the items they helped you "pack" (see Presenting **Vocabulaire** on page 14). They might add others. Then, write the expressions **Pense à prendre... , Prends... ,** and **N'oublie pas...** on the board. Tell students once again that you're going to France and ask **Qu'est-ce que je dois prendre?** Have students suggest items, using the expressions on the board. Mention specific activities you intend to do **(Je vais faire du ski.)** or types of weather you'll encounter **(Il pleut là-bas.)** to prompt students.

Possible Answers

17 Jérôme : Pense à prendre ton manteau!
Dorothée : N'oublie pas ton imperméable!
Sabine et Christian : Prenez vos baskets...
Julia : N'oublie pas des chèques de voyage.
Martin et Léa : ...prenez un appareil-photo!
Vous : ...prenez des bottes.
Alexandre : N'oublie pas ton billet d'avion.
Maxime et Tristan : Pensez à prendre vos gants...

STANDARDS: 1.3, 4.1, 5.2

Deuxième étape

CHAPITRE 1

Building on Previous Skills

Gather pictures of different weather conditions. Hold them up and ask either-or questions, such as **Il fait froid ou il fait chaud?** In addition, post several weather expressions on a bulletin board. Ask students to bring magazine pictures of outfits suitable for each kind of weather and display them under the appropriate expression.

Game

One student tells another what he or she is going to do. **(Je vais faire du ski.)** You might write suggestions on the board for students to refer to, such as **visiter Londres, faire de la natation,** and **aller au match de football américain.** The second student must give some appropriate advice. **(Prends des gants.)** The second student then tells a third student what he or she is going to do. The third student gives advice to the second, and so on. A student who cannot make an appropriate suggestion is out, but can get back in the game by helping another student who cannot respond.

Assess

- Testing Program, pp. 5–8 Quiz 1-2A, Quiz 1-2B, Audio CD 1, Tr. 15
- Student Make-Up Assignments Chapter 1, Alternative Quiz
- Alternative Assessment Guide, p. 32

18 A mon avis

Possible answers: Joseph: Prends des jeans, un tee-shirt et un maillot de bain. Marie-Claire: Prends des jeans, une écharpe et un manteau.

Parlons Tes amis Joseph et Marie-Claire font leurs valises pour partir en vacances, mais ils ont oublié plusieurs choses. Dis-leur ce qu'ils doivent prendre d'autre.

EXEMPLE **Marie-Claire, il va faire froid à Montréal. N'oublie pas tes gants...**

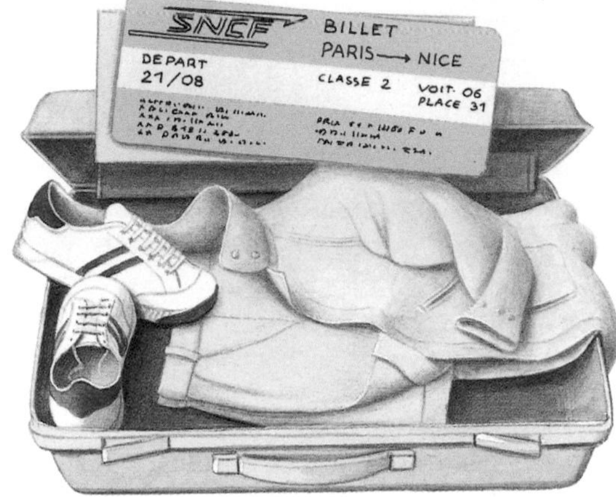

Joseph

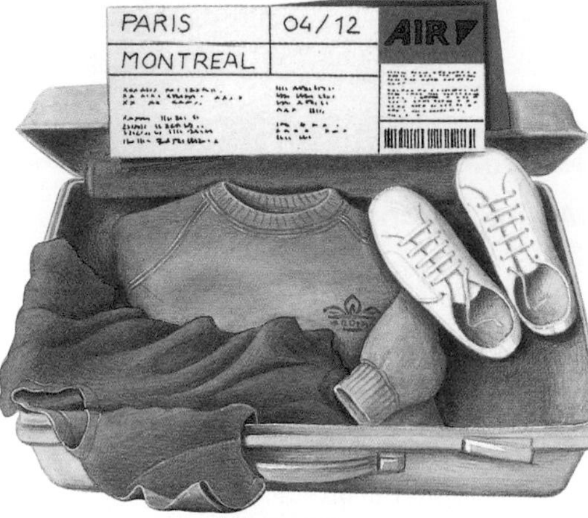

Marie-Claire

19 Qu'est-ce qu'on prend?

Parlons Ton ami(e) français(e) va passer une année chez toi. Il/Elle te téléphone pour savoir quoi prendre comme vêtements pour chaque saison. Joue la scène avec un(e) camarade.

EXEMPLE **—Qu'est-ce que je prends pour l'été?**
—Bon... Il fait très chaud ici. Pense à prendre des shorts et des tee-shirts.

Si tu as oublié
weather expressions and seasons
va à la page R15.

Travaux pratiques de grammaire, p. 8, Act. 16–17

20 Des cartes postales 

Ecrivons Imagine que tu es en vacances au Québec ou à la Martinique. Ton ami(e) va aussi y aller. Ecris-lui un petit mot pour lui donner des conseils. Dis-lui ce qu'il/elle doit prendre et parle du temps qu'il fait là-bas.

Cultures and Communities

Culture Note

18 Call attention to the dates on the train and airline tickets in the drawings. Explain that in France, the day is written before the month when writing dates. Therefore, it is important to understand that the date **04/12** on the plane ticket means *the fourth of December* and not *the twelfth of April.*

Family Link

Have students make a list of clothing their family members would pack for a trip. Be sure to have students write where the family members are going and why they would bring those articles of clothing. **(Mon frère Marc va au Canada. Il prend une écharpe et des gants parce qu'il adore faire du ski).**

STANDARDS: 1.1, 3.1, 4.1, 5.1

CHAPITRE 1

Teaching Resources
p. 17

PRINT
- Video Guide, pp. 5–7
- Cahier d'activités, p. 12

MEDIA
- One-Stop Planner
- Video Program
  Videocassette 1, 11:51–16:35
- DVD Tutor, Disc 1
- Audio Compact Discs, CD 1, Trs. 7–10
- Interactive CD-ROM Tutor, Disc 1

Presenting Panorama Culturel

On the board or on a transparency, write paraphrases of the advice given by the interviewees and number them. As students view the video, have them write the numbers in the order in which they hear the advice.

Questions

1. **D'après Yvette, qu'est-ce qu'il faut bien apprendre?** (le français)
2. **Selon Jean-Christophe, pourquoi est-il important de s'incorporer dans une famille?** (pour bien s'habituer à leurs manières, pour travailler avec eux, pour voir comment ils vivent)
3. **D'après Onélia, quelle est la différence entre la France et les Etats-Unis?** (La France est plus libérale.)

Quels conseils donnerais-tu à un élève américain qui arrive dans ton pays?

We talked to some francophone students about traveling and studying abroad. We asked them for advice for students planning to study in their countries. Here's what they had to say.

Yvette,
Côte d'Ivoire

«Si cet élève vient en Côte d'Ivoire pour faire ses études, je lui dirais de bien apprendre le français, de ne pas se décourager si c'est un peu difficile. En tout cas, d'être conscient, sérieux, tout ça... c'est pas facile.» Tr. 8

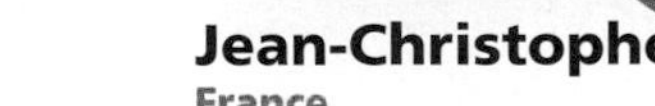

Jean-Christophe,
France

«Un conseil que je donnerais à un étudiant américain arrivant en France... ce serait de s'incorporer dans une famille pour bien s'habituer à leurs manières, pour travailler avec eux, pour voir comment nous vivons et de sortir parce que les jeunes Français savent s'amuser.» Tr. 9

Onélia,
France

«La France est très différente des Etats-Unis. Aux Etats-Unis, on n'a pas le droit de sortir [en boîte] avant 21 ans... [La France,] c'est un peu plus libéral que les Etats-Unis, donc, [il] faut faire attention. [Il ne] faut pas non plus abuser de l'alcool par exemple, et du tabac quand on arrive en France. Donc, voilà. C'est les conseils que je pourrais donner aux Américains.» Tr. 10

Qu'en penses-tu?

1. Are there any exchange students in your school? Where are they from? What languages do they speak?
2. If you were to study in a francophone country, how might your life be different? What kinds of adjustments might you have to make?
3. What advice do you have for foreign students who want to study in your area?

Connections and Comparisons

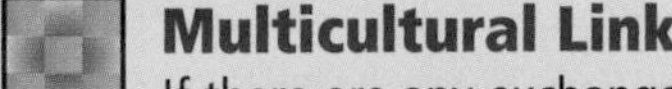

Multicultural Link

If there are any exchange students in your school, have your students interview them, asking the following questions:

- What surprised you most about American life?
- What do you like best about American life?
- What problems have you had because of language or cultural differences?
- What advice would you give to a student planning to spend time abroad?

STANDARDS: 2.1, 3.2, 4.2

CHAPITRE 1

Teaching Resources
pp. 18–21

PRINT

- Lesson Planner, p. 4
- TPR Storytelling Book, pp. 4–5
- Listening Activities, pp. 5, 9
- Activities for Communication, pp. 5–6, 77, 79, 137–138
- Travaux pratiques de grammaire, pp. 9–11
- Grammar Tutor for Students of French, Chapter 1
- Cahier d'activités, pp. 8–10
- Testing Program, pp. 9–12
- Alternative Assessment Guide, p. 32
- Student Make-Up Assignments, Chapter 1

MEDIA 

- One-Stop Planner
- Audio Compact Discs, CD 1, Trs. 11–12, 16, 24–25
- Teaching Transparencies: 1-3; **Grammaire supplémentaire** Answers; Travaux pratiques de grammaire Answers
- Interactive CD-ROM Tutor, Disc 1

Bell Work
Have students list as many clothes, travel accessories, and weather conditions as possible in three minutes.

Presenting
Comment dit-on... ?

On cards equal to the number of students, write the responses to suggestions and a plus or minus sign. Distribute the cards. Show pictures of activities and places, and suggest to individuals that they do the activity or go to the place. Students respond according to their card. Then students exchange cards until they get a different response, and repeat the process.

Troisième étape

Objectives Asking for, making, and responding to suggestions; relating a series of events

WA3 PARIS REGION-1

J'ai beaucoup de projets pour cette année avec toi. D'abord, je voudrais te présenter tous mes amis. Ils sont super sympas. Ensuite, tu vas voir Chartres, c'est une très jolie ville et il y a des tas de choses à faire. Si tu veux, on peut aller voir la cathédrale, aller au cinéma, écouter de la musique française... Tu n'as pas envie de manger du bon pain français?... Et pendant les vacances de Noël, on pourrait aller faire du ski avec mes cousins! Écris-nous vite. Pose toutes les questions que tu veux. Vivement ton arrivée! On va bien s'amuser!

Sandra

21 Que faire?

Lisons Qu'est-ce que Sandra veut faire avec Pamela? Qu'est-ce que toi, tu voudrais faire en France?

introduce her to friends, visit Chartres, go to the cathedral, go to the movies, listen to French music, eat French food, go skiing; Answers will vary.

Comment dit-on...?

Asking for, making, and responding to suggestions

CD-ROM 1 DVD 1

To ask for suggestions:

Qu'est-ce qu'on fait?
What should we do?

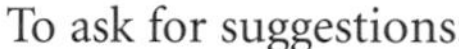

To make suggestions:

Si tu veux, on peut jouer au foot.
If you like, we can . . .
On pourrait aller au fast-food.
We could . . .
Tu as envie de faire les magasins?
Do you feel like . . . ?
Ça te dit de manger de la soupe?
Does . . . sound good to you?

To respond to suggestions:

D'accord.
C'est une bonne/excellente idée.
That's a good/excellent idea.
Je veux bien.
Je ne peux pas.
Ça ne me dit rien.
Non, je préfère...
No, I'd rather . . .
Pas question!

Cahier d'activités, p. 8, Act. 17–18

Communication for All Students

Challenge
Have students write questions in response to Sandra's statement: **Pose toutes les questions que tu veux.** Encourage students to write questions they would really want to ask if they were going to visit Sandra. You might also have them think of questions Sandra might have for an American student. Then have students exchange their lists of questions and try to come up with logical responses to each one.

22 On va au resto?

CD 1 Tr. 11

Ecoutons Sandra et Etienne vont manger au restaurant ce soir. D'abord, lis ces descriptions de restaurants. Ensuite, écoute Sandra et Etienne. Où est-ce qu'Etienne veut aller? Et Sandra? Qu'est-ce qu'ils décident de faire?

See scripts and answers on p. 3H.

Les restaurateurs de la rue de la Porte-Morard

Au cœur du Secteur Sauvegardé, en prolongement du pont St-Hilaire qui offre un beau panorama sur la rivière et la Cathédrale, les cinq restaurants de la rue de la Porte-Morard vous proposent cinq façons différentes d'apprécier une bonne table :

LE MAHARADJA- Spécialités indiennes et pakistanaises - Tél. 02 37 31 45 06.

LE CHENE FLEURI Hôtel-restaurant avec grande terrasse en saison - Cuisine traditionnelle - Tél. 02 37 35 25 70.

LA CREPERIE DU CYGNE Galettes de sarrasin - Crêpes - Salades - Grillades - Terrasse en été - Tél. 02 37 21 99 22.

LA NAPOLITAINE - Pizza et plats à emporter - Tél. 02 37 34 30 26.

LE TEMPLE- Restaurant indochinois, spécialités du Sud-Est Asiatique - Tél. 02 37 12 27 30.

Parking gratuit proche, place Morard.

Note culturelle

As you know, French is spoken In many countries outside of France. People from all over the world come to France to study or work, bringing with them the unique aspects of their cultures. In many French cities, it is common to find restaurants offering diverse ethnic specialties.

23 Qu'est-ce qu'on mange?

Parlons Tu es à Paris avec ton ami(e). Vous choisissez un restaurant, mais ce n'est pas facile!

EXEMPLE —**Tu as envie d'aller dans un restaurant chinois?**

—**Non, ça ne me dit rien. Je préfère un restaurant...**

marocain · indonésien · mexicain · russe · cambodgien · vietnamien · indien · français traditionnel · grec · thaïlandais · libanais · antillais

24 Qu'est-ce qu'on fait?

Parlons Tu as un(e) invité(e) français(e). Tes amis, ton invité(e) et toi, vous allez sortir samedi. Choisissez trois activités que vous avez envie de faire.

aller danser à... · faire les magasins · aller au cinéma pour voir... · aller au match de... · déjeuner au restaurant · faire du roller en ligne · faire un pique-nique au parc

Cultures and Communities

Culture Note

The restaurant **Le Dakar** serves African and Antillean specialties. Senegalese specialties include **poulet yassa** (chicken with onions and lemon juice), **mafé** (meat stew in peanut sauce), **tiebou dienne** (the Senegalese national dish consisting of rice, fish, and a variety of vegetables), and **bassi-saleté** (a Senegalese couscous made with millet).

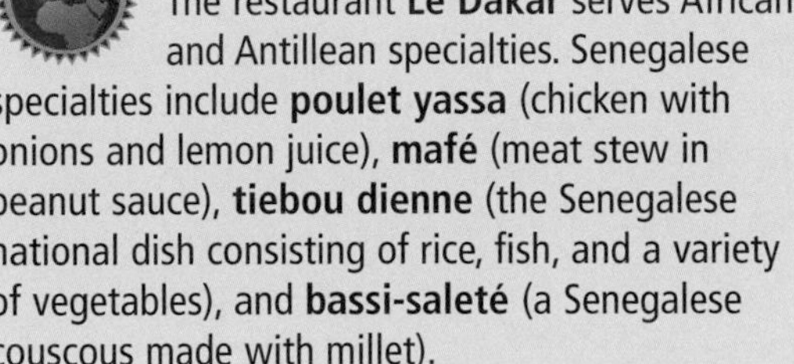

Multicultural Link

If there are any ethnic restaurants in your area, have students find out what their specialties are. Ask students who have been to one of these restaurants to tell the class what type of food they had and how they liked it. Encourage other students to consider trying one of these restaurants next time they go out to eat.

Troisième étape

CHAPITRE 1

Math Link

Divide the class into four groups. Have each group recall and list as many activities as possible. Then have them conduct a survey of their members to find out how many people like each activity a lot, a little, or not at all. **(Tu aimes beaucoup faire la cuisine, un peu, ou pas du tout?)** Have each group make graphs or charts to show the results of their survey.

Teaching Suggestion

24 Have each student write on a slip of paper an activity that he or she would like to do, such as **faire les magasins.** Then, have students circulate in the classroom to try to find another student who would like to do the same activity. Each student suggests doing the activity he or she has written. **(Si tu veux, on peut faire les magasins.)** If the other student has written the same activity, he or she should respond affirmatively **(C'est une bonne idée.)** or if not, negatively **(Ça ne me dit rien.).** When students find a match, they should report their activity to you. **(On va faire les magasins.)** For more activities, have students refer to the Additional Vocabulary on pages R16–R18 and the **Si tu as oublié...** list of sports on page R14.

Portfolio

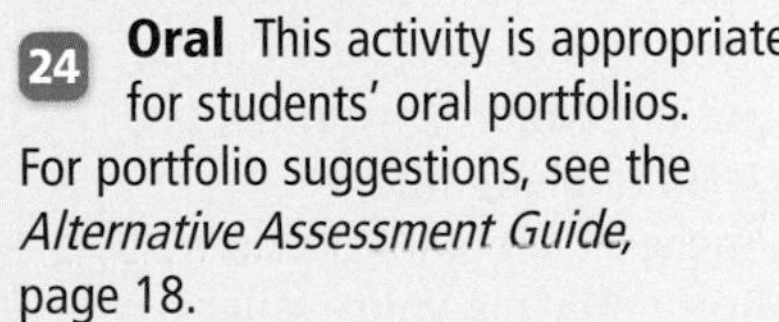

24 **Oral** This activity is appropriate for students' oral portfolios. For portfolio suggestions, see the *Alternative Assessment Guide,* page 18.

STANDARDS: 1.1, 1.2, 2.1, 2.2, 3.2, 4.2

Troisième étape

CHAPITRE 1

Teaching Resources
pp. 18–21

PRINT

- Lesson Planner, p. 4
- TPR Storytelling Book, pp. 4–5
- Listening Activities, pp. 5, 9
- Activities for Communication, pp. 5–6, 77, 79, 137–138
- Travaux pratiques de grammaire, pp. 9–11
- Grammar Tutor for Students of French, Chapter 1
- Cahier d'activités, pp. 8–10
- Testing Program, pp. 9–12
- Alternative Assessment Guide, p. 32
- Student Make-Up Assignments, Chapter 1

MEDIA 

- One-Stop Planner
- Audio Compact Discs, CD 1, Trs. 11–12, 16, 24–25
- Teaching Transparencies: 1-3; **Grammaire supplémentaire** Answers; Travaux pratiques de grammaire Answers
- Interactive CD-ROM Tutor, Disc 1

Presenting
Comment dit-on... ?

Write the following activities on the board and tell in what order you plan to do some of them, using **d'abord, ensuite, puis,** and **finalement.**
acheter un billet d'avion, préparer ma valise, aller à l'aéroport, prendre l'avion, visiter la ville, prendre le métro, aller au musée, aller voir la tour Eiffel, aller au café, faire des photos

Ask students what you are doing and what words you are using to do this. Then, have students select some activities from the list on the board and tell in what order they are going to do them.

Comment dit-on...?

Relating a series of events

D'abord, je vais visiter la tour Eiffel.	*First, . . .*
Ensuite, je vais manger des escargots dans un bon restaurant.	*Next, . . .*
Et puis, je vais voir la Joconde au Louvre.	*Then, . . .*
Finalement/Enfin, je vais acheter des cadeaux pour ma famille.	*Finally, . . .*

Cahier d'activités, p. 9, Act. 20–21

25 Projets de week-end
See scripts on p. 3H. b, c, a, d

Ecoutons Tarek raconte ses projets pour samedi. Mets les images en ordre.

CD 1 Tr. 12

a.

b.

c.

d.

26 Les vacances de mes rêves

Parlons Choisis un endroit où tu veux passer tes vacances. Explique à ton/ta camarade ce que tu vas faire là-bas, mais ne dis pas le nom de l'endroit où tu vas aller. Ton/Ta camarade doit deviner où tu veux aller.

EXEMPLE **—D'abord, je voudrais visiter la tour Eiffel.**
—Tu vas à Paris!

D'abord, Ensuite, Et puis, Finalement,	je vais je voudrais	manger... visiter... faire la connaissance de... voir... acheter... faire... aller à...

Communication for All Students

Challenge
25 Have students say as much as they can in French about each picture before they listen to the recording.

Teaching Suggestion
26 You might have partners volunteer to read their vacation plans to the class, who will guess where they are going.

STANDARDS: 1.1, 1.2

Note de grammaire

Use the appropriate form of **aller** followed by an infinitive to say that you're going to do something:

— Tu **vas sortir** ce soir?

— Oui, je **vais manger** au restaurant.

To say that you aren't going to do something, put **ne... pas** around the form of **aller.**

Je **ne vais pas** sortir ce soir.

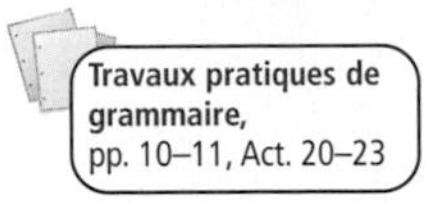

Travaux pratiques de grammaire, pp. 10–11, Act. 20–23

Grammaire supplémentaire, p. 27, Act. 10–11

Cahier d'activités, p. 9, Act. 19

27 Le petit écran

Tu es malade et tu dois rester chez toi. Fais une liste des émissions que tu vas regarder et à quelle heure. Ensuite, compare ta liste avec la liste de ton ami(e).

Exemple **D'abord, je vais regarder *Friends* à 18h20, puis *Journal* à 20h00. Ensuite,... Finalement,...**

Travaux pratiques de grammaire, pp. 9–10, Act. 18–19

19.05 Turbo
Au sommaire : La toute nouvelle Alfa Roméo 156. - Une MGF à 350 km/h. - Le MX OXBOW. - La Mercedes Classe A. - Gros plans sur les grands designers français. - Un handicapé engagé dans le championnat de France de super-tourisme.

19.40 Warning
Au sommaire : La pollution sonore. - Les fausses idées reçues sur l'ABS. - Les ouvertures d'autoroutes.

19.54 6 minutes/météo

20.00 Mode 6
Jean-Paul Gaultier.
Les collections de prêt-à-porter printemps-été.

20.05 Hot forme
Au sommaire : La digestion. - Comment bien se nourrir. - Les aliments.

20.35 Ciné 6

20.45 X-FILES : AUX FRONTIERES DU REEL
David Duchovny....... Fox Mulder
Gillian Anderson....... Dana Scully

18.20 Friends
Celui qui détestait le lait maternel. Pendant que Carol et Susan sont sorties, Ross et les amis gardent Ben. Phoebe prépare un biberon.

18.45 C'est l'heure
Un invité réagit à des reportages mettant en valeur une actualité divertissante.

19.25 C'est toujours l'heure
Des personnalités livrent leur regard sur l'actualité.

20.00 Journal

20.50 URGENCES
A. Edwards.................. Mark Greene
N. Wylie........................... John Carter

28 De l'école au travail

Ecrivons You're working in Paris as a coordinator for a student exchange program. Your job is to write a letter to an American student coming to Chartres giving him/her advice on what to pack. Tell how the student's host family will meet him/her and give a description of what the family looks like so that the student will recognize them.

Cultures and Communities

Culture Notes

Comment dit-on... ? The *Mona Lisa,* or *La Joconde* in French, is located in the Louvre museum in Paris. It is a masterpiece by Leonardo da Vinci, painted in the early sixteenth century, and is known for the mysterious smile of the woman in the portrait.

26 By law, French employees are entitled to five weeks of paid vacation per year. Generally, most French families take their vacation during the month of August when school is out. Tourists visiting France at this time might witness a mass exodus from Paris and the northern part of France to the south of France.

Troisième étape

CHAPITRE 1

Teaching Suggestion

27 Use the TV schedule for additional listening practice. Call out times and channels at random and have students write down the appropriate programs, or call out a program and have them write the channel and time.

Presenting Note de grammaire

The **futur proche** Conjugate the verb **aller** on the board. Then, form five or six groups. Give each group a card with an activity written on it in large letters **(aller au cinéma).** Move around the room, pointing to different groups and asking questions. Students will answer your questions according to their cards. For example, hold up the card of one group and ask the class **Qu'est-ce qu'ils vont faire ce week-end? Ils vont jouer au tennis ou ils vont faire du vélo? Et Alain,** (holding up another group's card and pointing to one student in the group) **qu'est-ce qu'il va faire? Il va au parc? Et nous?** (including yourself in the group and asking only your group). **Et vous?** (pointing to a group). **Et moi, je vais faire les magasins** (holding up your own card). **Et toi?** (pointing to an individual) and so on.

Assess

- Testing Program, pp. 9–12 Quiz 1-3A, Quiz 1-3B, Audio CD 1, Tr. 16
- Student Make-Up Assignments Chapter 1, Alternative Quiz
- Alternative Assessment Guide, p. 32

STANDARDS: 1.3, 2.1, 3.1, 4.1, 5.2

Lisons!

CHAPITRE 1

Teaching Resources
pp. 22–23

PRINT 

- Lesson Planner, p. 5
- Cahier d'activités, p. 11
- Reading Strategies and Skills Handbook, Chapter 1
- Joie de lire 2, Chapter 1
- Standardized Assessment Tutor, Chapter 1

MEDIA

- One-Stop Planner

Prereading

Activity A

Terms in Lisons!

Students may want to know the following terms from ***Une année scolaire aux USA:***

accueillants *(friendly)*
vous le faire mieux connaître *(to show (their country) to you)*
J'allais avoir 18 ans. *(I was almost 18.)*
J'aurais dû entrer en terminale. *(I would have been in my last year of high school.)*
une famille d'accueil *(a host family)*
que je m'y suis faits *(that I made)*
lors *(at the time of)*
souhaiter *(to wish)*

Reading

Activities B–G

Distinguishing Fact from Opinion

Challenge students to read carefully so that they will be able to judge how accurately these French students perceive the American high school. Which statements in the reading represent opinions and which ones represent facts?

Answers

B. *Where:* U.S.A.
Why: to show different aspects of an American high school

Lisons!

Une année scolaire aux USA

Stratégie pour lire
What are the first two things you should do when faced with a new text? A good reader *previews* the reading and then *skims* it. To *preview,* glance quickly at the layout of a reading to understand how it is organized. Next *skim* the sections of the text by reading the headings, captions, and the first sentences of paragraphs or blocks of text. Ask yourself: What is the reading about? Who was it written for? Where is it set? Why was it written?

A. Preview the article. What kind of text do you think it is?
  a. a pamphlet
  b. a pen pal letter
  c. an essay

B. Skim the reading to answer the *W* questions.
  1. Read the major headings. *What* is the article about?
    a. a scholar
    b. an academic year in a high school
    c. a year in France
  2. Look at the photos. *Where* and *why* do you think they were taken? See answers below.
  3. The major headings talk about **votre année** and the school year being **pour vous.** The headings of the first two paragraphs say "Live the American dream" and "Welcome to the United States." Look at the selections under Guillaume and Sonia's names. *Who* are the intended readers? students in France
  4. *Why* was this article written?
    a. to show American students how their schools differ from French schools

STUDENT TRAVEL SCHOOLS

Une année scolaire aux

Une année scolaire à l'étranger pour vous qui avez entre 15–18 ans

Vous serez rapidement la mascotte de l'école, tout le monde viendra vous poser des questions sur la France.

Vivez le "rêve américain"
"The American Dream" est un idéal de liberté, de bonheur et la possibilité de décider de son propre avenir. Une année dans une High School est pour vous l'occasion de découvrir "le pays où tout est possible". Celle-ci sera l'une des plus belles de votre vie! Profitez de cette occasion unique pour devenir américain pendant un an. Ce sera passionnant et vous en tirerez le plus grand profit.

Bienvenue aux Etats-Unis
L'Amérique est véritablement le pays de tous les contrastes. Plus de 250 millions d'Américains de toutes origines peuplent les Etats-Unis. S'il est bien difficile de décrire "l'Américain type", aucune confusion n'est possible quant à leur personnalité. Ils sont tous naturellement accueillants, ouverts et sont très positifs au sujet de la vie. Les Américains sont fiers de leur pays et vous le faire mieux connaître est une joie pour eux.

Participez au bal de la High School, le "Prom".

Connections and Comparisons

Language Notes

- Remind students of the definition of a cognate. Use **un idéal** as an example. Have students work in small groups to find as many cognates as they can in two minutes.
- Assure students they will not know every word or verb form, but encourage them to look for what they do know and to make guesses about unfamiliar words based on the context.

Thinking Critically

Comparing and Contrasting Ask students to list three ways in which they think French students might be different from American students. For example, unlike American teenagers, French teenagers usually do not have after-school jobs, they don't have cars, and they can't get their driver's license until they are 18 years old.

STANDARDS: 1.2, 3.1, 3.2, 4.2

STUDENT TRAVEL SCHOOLS

Votre année en High School aux USA

La fête de la "Graduation" restera un jour mémorable dans votre vie.

GUILLAUME

SONIA

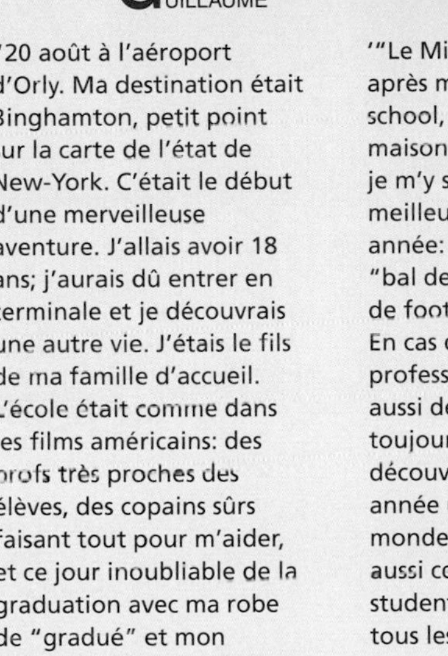

"20 août à l'aéroport d'Orly. Ma destination était Binghamton, petit point sur la carte de l'état de New-York. C'était le début d'une merveilleuse aventure. J'allais avoir 18 ans; j'aurais dû entrer en terminale et je découvrais une autre vie. J'étais le fils de ma famille d'accueil. L'école était comme dans les films américains: des profs très proches des élèves, des copains sûrs faisant tout pour m'aider, et ce jour inoubliable de la graduation avec ma robe de "gradué" et mon bonnet carré. Aujourd'hui je crois que j'ai rêvé mais les rêves sont peut-être ce qu'il y a de plus vrai."

'"Le Michigan est devenu, après mon année en high school, ma deuxième maison. Avec les amis que je m'y suis faits, j'ai vécu les meilleurs moments de mon année: la graduation, le "bal de prom", les matchs de foot-ball.
En cas de problème, les professeurs, devenus eux aussi des amis, étaient toujours là. J'ai également découvert lors de cette année un "nouveau monde", les U.S. mais aussi celui des exchange students. Ils venaient de tous les pays: de la Colombie à l'Australie en passant par les pays scandinaves... Je vous souhaite donc à tous de vivre la même expérience extraordinaire."

b. to describe the average American high school

c. to persuade a French student to consider a year abroad in an American high school

Vivez le «Rêve Américain»

C. What are some phrases used to describe "The American Dream"? Do you agree? See answers below.

Bienvenue aux Etats-Unis

D. If **accueillir** means *to welcome,* someone who is **accueillant** is __1__. welcoming

If **ouvrir** means *to open,* someone who is **ouvert** is __2__. open

If **la fierté** is *pride,* someone who is **fier** is __3__. proud

E. Are Americans described favorably? Are all Americans like this? Are you? Yes; Answers will vary.

Guillaume

F. Guillaume says his host school is like schools he's seen in American movies. In what way? Did Guillaume have a good time as an exchange student? How do you know? See answers below.

Sonia

G. See answers below.

G. How does Sonia describe her experience in the States?

H. If you were a French student, would you want to come to the United States after reading this article? Why or why not?

I. Make a pamphlet describing your school to attract French-speaking exchange students. Include events and distinctive features. Add photos or drawings with captions to your pamphlet.

Cahier d'activités, p. 11, Act. 24

Lisons!

CHAPITRE 1

Postreading
Activities H–I

Slower Pace
Have students work in pairs. For each of the three major photographs, have partners reduce the photo caption to one or two words that convey the gist of the whole caption.

Cooperative Learning
I. Have students work in groups of four to make the pamphlets. Assign the roles of leader, writer, proofreader, and artist. The leader heads a discussion of what to include in the pamphlet, group members dictate the text to the writer, the proofreader checks for errors, and the artist collects the art and arranges the layout of the pamphlet.

Teaching Suggestion
I. Have students add to their brochures mock interviews of what visiting students might say about their school. They might also include the interviews in their oral portfolios.

Answers
C. Freedom, happiness, and the opportunity to decide about your future

F. Teachers close to students, helpful friends, graduation ceremony and outfit; Yes; He speaks positively about his stay, calling it a marvelous adventure, and says he lived his dream.

G. Positively—she made new friends from around the world, she went to the prom, to football games. She discovered a new world, and Michigan became her second home.

Cultures and Communities

Making Generalizations
Discuss the notions of the "American Dream" and the American stereotype described in **Bienvenue aux Etats-Unis.** Remind students that many French and European teenagers know their American counterparts only through their exposure to American television shows that air in Europe.

Culture Note
Talk about some of the features of the French **lycée** and how it differs from the typical American high school. For example, **lycéens** do not have organized sports in school. There is no prom or yearbook. French high school students typically have Wednesday afternoon free, but they often go to school on Saturday morning.

STANDARDS: 1.2, 3.1, 3.2, 4.2

Grammaire supplémentaire

CHAPITRE 1

For **Grammaire supplémentaire** Answer Transparencies, see the *Teaching Transparencies* binder.

Answers

1
1. f
2. b
3. g
4. h
5. c
6. e
7. a

2
1. est
2. ont
3. avons
4. a
5. as
6. êtes
7. sont

3
1. Daniel
2. Danielle
3. Danielle
4. Daniel
5. Daniel
6. Danielle
7. Danielle
8. Daniel
9. Danielle

Grammaire supplémentaire

CD-ROM 1 DVD 1

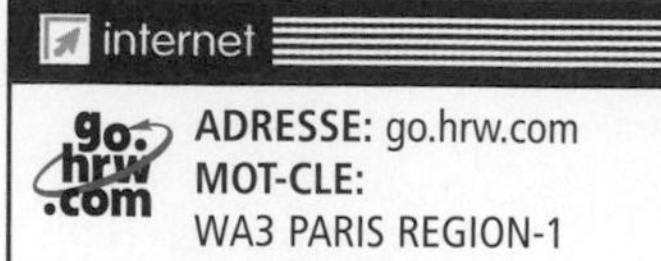

internet

ADRESSE: go.hrw.com
MOT-CLE:
WA3 PARIS REGION-1

Première étape

Objectives Describing and characterizing yourself and others; expressing likes, dislikes, and preferences; asking for information

1 Pour chaque début de phrase, choisis une fin logique. (**p. 10**)

1. Vous...	**a.** sont heureuses.
2. Tu...	**b.** as des amis.
3. Elle...	**c.** avons beaucoup de devoirs.
4. Didier...	**d.** sont canadiens.
5. Nous...	**e.** ai maths à dix heures.
6. Je/J'...	**f.** êtes sympa.
7. Christine et Stéphanie...	**g.** est mignonne.
	h. est amusant.

2 Complète les phrases suivantes avec le verbe approprié. (**p. 10**)

1. Martha _____ sportive.
   a sont est
2. Eric et Christian _____ des cours embêtants.
   sont a ont
3. Nous _____ classe le lundi.
   êtes sommes avons
4. Ta copine _____ beaucoup de devoirs.
   a ont est
5. Tu _____ français à onze heures.
   ai as es
6. Vous _____ méchant!
   avons êtes sont
7. Elles _____ mignonnes, tes amies.
   sont ont a

3 De qui est-ce qu'on parle dans les phrases suivantes? D'un garçon qui s'appelle Daniel ou d'une fille qui s'appelle Danielle? (**p. 11**)

EXEMPLE <u>Daniel</u> est intelligent.

1. _____ est beau.
2. _____ est gentille.
3. _____ est sportive.
4. _____ est roux.
5. _____ est grand.
6. _____ est blonde.
7. _____ est mignonne.
8. _____ est amusant.
9. _____ est heureuse.

Grammar Resources for Chapter 1

The **Grammaire supplémentaire** activities are designed as supplemental activities for the grammatical concepts presented in the chapter. You might use them as additional practice, for review, or for assessment.

For more grammar presentations, review, and practice, refer to the following:
- Travaux pratiques de grammaire
- Grammar Tutor for Students of French
- Grammar Summary on pp. R23–R42
- Cahier d'activités
- Grammar and Vocabulary quizzes (Testing Program)
- Test Generator
- Interactive CD-ROM Tutor
- DVD Tutor
- **Jeux interactifs** at go.hrw.com

Grammaire supplémentaire

CHAPITRE 1

4 Choisis un des adjectifs proposés pour compléter les phrases suivantes. Tu peux utiliser le même adjectif plus d'une fois. Fais attention à l'accord de l'adjectif avec le sujet de la phrase. (**p. 11**)

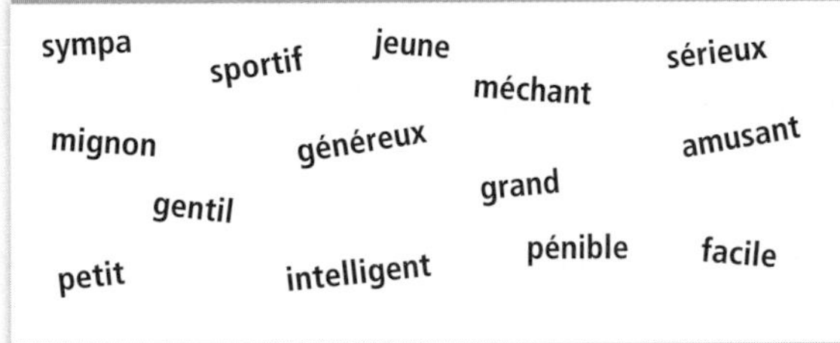

sympa
sportif
jeune
méchant
sérieux
mignon
généreux
amusant
gentil
grand
petit
intelligent
pénible
facile

1. Moi, je suis...
2. Le président des Etats-Unis est...
3. Mon/Ma meilleur(e) ami(e) est...
4. Mes cours sont...
5. Mon professeur est...
6. Mes chiens/chats sont...

5 Luc et Bruno parlent avec leurs amis de ce qu'ils font après l'école. Remets les phrases suivantes dans le bon ordre. N'oublie pas de mettre le verbe à la forme appropriée. (**p. 11**)

1. aimer / Serge / de la musique / écouter
2. la télé / regarder / souvent / tu
3. faire / nous / du sport / préférer
4. je / le français / à la bibliothèque / étudier
5. au volley / Florence / après l'école / jouer
6. mes amis / bien / danser / le tango
7. vous / téléphoner / à vos amis / souvent

6 Tu voudrais mieux connaître le nouvel élève. Pose-lui des questions. N'oublie pas d'utiliser la forme correcte de **quel.** (**p. 12**)

— __1__ est ton sport préféré?
— Je préfère le tennis.
— __2__ sont tes acteurs préférés?
— J'adore Gérard Depardieu et Juliette Binoche.
— Quand tu choisis des vêtements, __3__ sont tes couleurs préférées?
— En général, je préfère le bleu et le noir.
— __4__ est ta musique préférée?
— J'aime la musique techno.
— __5__ sont tes animaux préférés?
— Je préfère les lions et les girafes.

Answers

4 *Possible answers:*
1. grand(e) et sportif (sportive).
2. sérieux et généreux.
3. sérieux et intelligent/sérieuse et intelligente.
4. amusants et faciles.
5. amusant et intelligent.
6. mignons et amusants.

5
1. Serge aime écouter de la musique.
2. Tu regardes souvent la télé.
3. Nous préférons faire du sport.
4. J'étudie le français à la bibliothèque.
5. Florence joue au volley après l'école.
6. Mes amis dansent bien le tango.
7. Vous téléphonez souvent à vos amis.

6
1. Quel
2. Quels
3. quelles
4. Quelle
5. Quels

Teacher to Teacher

Sandra Behensky
Rock Island High School
Rock Island, IL

Sandra suggests the following activity to practice grammar.

"To review grammar, I play a Ladder Game. Divide the class into small teams. A member from each team goes to the board and draws a five-rung ladder for the team. The teacher asks a question. Each student at the board tries to be the first to answer correctly. The team who correctly answers first keeps their answer on the rung of the ladder. All other teams erase their answer. A new member of each team goes to the board, and the teacher asks a new question. Play continues until one team has all five rungs filled in."

Grammaire supplémentaire

CHAPITRE 1

For **Grammaire supplémentaire** Answer Transparencies, see the *Teaching Transparencies* binder.

Answers

7 **1.** grossit; picture of desserts
2. ai choisi; picture of bouquet
3. as grandi; picture of small pants
4. choisissez; picture of steak-frites
5. grandissent; picture of kitten

8 **1.** choisit
2. grossis
3. grandis
4. choisissent
5. maigrissez

Grammaire supplémentaire

WA3 PARIS REGION-1

Deuxième étape

Objectives Asking for and giving advice

7 Pour chaque phrase, choisis la forme correcte du verbe approprié. Ensuite, choisis la photo qui va avec chaque phrase. (**p. 14**)

as grandi	grandissent	ai choisi	grossit	choisissez

1. Quand on en mange trop, on _____ .
2. Je l'_____ pour ma mère. C'est son anniversaire aujourd'hui.
3. Mais tu _____ ! Il est trop court maintenant.
4. Quand vous allez au Restaurant Kléber quel plat _____ -vous?
5. Ils sont mignons mais ils _____ vite!

8 Complète les phrases suivantes avec le présent du verbe entre parenthèses. (**p. 14**)

1. Quelle chemise est-ce qu'elle _____ (choisir)?
2. Quand je mange trop de chocolat, je _____ (grossir).
3. Ton pantalon est trop court. Tu _____ (grandir) beaucoup!
4. Super! Mes amis _____ (choisir) un cadeau pour mon anniversaire.
5. Vous êtes au régime? Vous _____ (maigrir)?

Communication for All Students

Additional Practice

Give students a verb form **(grandit)** and have them write a sentence using this verb. This can also be done as an oral activity. As a challenge, have students use **et** or **mais** in every sentence they generate.

STANDARDS: 1.2

9 Complète les phrases suivantes avec l'impératif des verbes entre parenthèses. (**p. 15**)

EXEMPLE Catherine et Robert, **allez** (aller) dans vos chambres.

1. Nathalie et Robert, _____ (penser) à prendre vos imperméables.
2. Catherine, n'_____ (oublier) pas de faire tes devoirs.
3. Les filles, _____ (choisir) des vêtements chauds.
4. Robert, _____ (prendre) cet argent pour le week-end.
5. Les enfants, n'_____ (inviter) pas d'amis à la maison.
6. Nathalie, _____ (aller) au supermarché pour nous.

Troisième étape

Objectives **Asking for, making, and responding to suggestions; relating a series of events**

10 Pour chaque début de phrase, choisis la fin appropriée pour dire ce que ces gens vont faire. (**p. 21**)

1. Moi, je...	**a.** vas acheter un appareil-photo.
2. Elise et Sophie...	**b.** allons prendre des écharpes.
3. Et toi, tu...	**c.** allez voir un film au cinéma.
4. Nous, nous...	**d.** vais d'abord aller au restaurant.
5. Vous...	**e.** ne va pas aimer prendre l'avion.
6. Je crois que Paul...	**f.** vont aller en Italie cet été.

11 Dis ce que ces gens vont faire ce week-end. Utilise le verbe **aller.** (**p. 21**)

EXEMPLE Tu fais tes devoirs. **Tu vas faire tes devoirs.**

1. Marc achète des baskets. ____________
2. Je regarde un film. ____________
3. Nous allons au restaurant. ____________
4. Sylvie fait un pique-nique. ____________
5. Mes amis sortent après l'école. ____________
6. Tu visites le musée. ____________
7. Vous rencontrez des amis. ____________
8. Je danse à la discothèque. ____________
9. Les filles dorment. ____________

Review and Assess

You may wish to assign the **Grammaire supplémentaire** activities as additional practice or homework after presenting material throughout the chapter. Assign Activities 1–2 after **Grammaire** (p. 10), Activities 3–5 after **Grammaire** (p. 11), Activity 6 after **Note de grammaire** (p. 12), Activities 7–8 after **Note de grammaire** (p. 14), Activity 9 after **Note de grammaire** (p. 15), and Activities 10–11 after **Note de grammaire** (p. 21).

To prepare students for the **Etape** Quizzes and Chapter Test, we suggest doing the **Grammaire supplémentaire** activities in the following order. Have students complete Activities 1–6 before Quizzes 5-1A or 5-1B; Activities 7–9 before Quizzes 5-2A or 5-2B; and Activities 10–11 before Quizzes 5-3A or 5-3B.

Grammaire supplémentaire

CHAPITRE 1

Answers

9
1. pensez
2. oublie
3. choisissez
4. prends
5. invitez
6. va

10
1. d
2. f
3. a
4. b
5. c
6. e

11
1. Marc va acheter des baskets.
2. Je vais regarder un film.
3. Nous allons aller au restaurant.
4. Sylvie va faire un pique-nique.
5. Mes amis vont sortir après l'école.
6. Tu vas visiter le musée.
7. Vous allez rencontrer des amis.
8. Je vais danser à la discothèque.
9. Les filles vont dormir.

Mise en pratique

CHAPITRE 1

The **Mise en pratique** reviews and integrates all four skills and culture in preparation for the Chapter Test.

Teaching Resources
pp. 28–29

PRINT 

- Lesson Planner, p. 5
- TPR Storytelling Book, pp. 6–7
- Listening Activities, p. 5
- Video Guide, pp. 5, 8
- Grammar Tutor for Students of French, Chapter 1
- Standardized Assessment Tutor, Chapter 1

MEDIA

- One-Stop Planner
- Video Program, Videocassette 1, 16:37–18:22
- DVD Tutor, Disc 1
- Audio Compact Discs, CD 1, Tr. 13
- Interactive CD-ROM Tutor, Disc 1

Multicultural Link

2 Have groups create conversations in English, with one person playing the role of Patrick and the others playing his new American friends. The conversations should reflect the cultural differences between American and French lifestyles. For each topic, such as breakfast or what to wear, Patrick should express surprise and tell how things are done differently in France.

Answers

1
1. He will be spending a year in the United States.
2. He's 15 and athletic.
3. He lives in Poitiers.
4. He has a little brother.
5. He has a dog.
6. He enjoys tennis and soccer.
7. He wants to know what clothes to bring.
8. He wants to know if they're strict, because his English isn't very good.

Mise en pratique

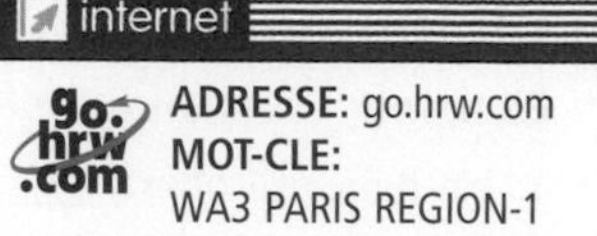

ADRESSE: go.hrw.com
MOT-CLE:
WA3 PARIS REGION-1

1 You're going to host Patrick, a French exchange student, in your home. He wrote to introduce himself and ask some questions. Read his letter and answer the following questions in English. See answers below.

Salut !

On m'a dit hier que je vais passer un an chez toi, en Amérique ! Je suis fou de joie et j'ai plein de questions.

Mais d'abord, je me présente. Je m'appelle Patrick. J'ai 15 ans et j'habite à Poitiers avec mes parents et mon petit frère Thomas. J'ai un chien aussi. Il s'appelle Léon.

Maintenant, mes questions ! Est-ce qu'il fait froid chez toi ? Quels types de vêtements est-ce que je dois prendre ? Est-ce qu'il y a un stade près de chez toi ? A ton avis, j'apporte ma raquette de tennis ou pas ? Est-ce qu'on peut jouer au foot dans ta ville ? Est-ce que les professeurs sont sévères ? Je m'inquiète un peu parce que mon anglais n'est pas très bon.

1. What did Patrick just find out?
2. How would you describe Patrick?
3. Where does he live?
4. How many brothers and sisters does he have?
5. What pets does he have?
6. What sports does he like?
7. Why does he ask about the weather?
8. What does he want to know about teachers? Why?

2 From what you know about life in France and what exchange students expect to find in the United States, what do you think Patrick might have trouble adjusting to? What might surprise him about your home and your school?

3 There's a message on your answering machine from Patrick to let you know when he's arriving, at what time, and on what flight. He also describes himself so you'll recognize him. Jot down the necessary information. See scripts and answers on p. 3H.

CD 1 Tr. 13

Apply and Assess

Teaching Suggestion

1 Have partners make up questions about Patrick's letter and take turns asking them to each other.

Slower Pace

3 Form small groups and make each group responsible for retrieving only one piece of information (when, what time, what flight, how Patrick is dressed) as they listen to the recording. Then, have students from each group report their findings. Write the information on the board and play the recording again.

STANDARDS: 1.2, 2.1

4 Ecrivons!

Answer Patrick's letter from Activity 1. Write about yourself, your home, and your school and tell him what you have planned for his visit. Don't forget to answer all of his questions.

Stratégie pour écrire
Making a writing plan will help make your writing task more manageable. For example, you might want to make a list of the topics you want to cover and jot down a few details related to each topic.

Préparation

After you've made your writing plan, organize your ideas in the order in which you'll talk about them in your letter. Use a cluster diagram to connect each topic with what you want to say about it, or group related topics together.

Rédaction

In Level 1, you learned words such as **et, mais,** and **surtout** to help you make longer, more sophisticated sentences. You also learned **d'abord** and **puis,** words that help you connect a series of events.

As you write to Patrick, use connecting words as effectively as possible to eliminate short, choppy sentences. In addition to the connecting words above, don't forget about the other words for relating a series of events presented on page 20.

Evaluation

After you've read your letter a couple of times, give it to a classmate to evaluate. It's a good idea to tell whoever is reading your letter some of your own concerns about your work. Many times a "fresh eye" can make suggestions you hadn't considered.

When your classmate returns your letter, proofread your work, make any necessary revisions, and complete your final draft.

5 Jeu de rôle

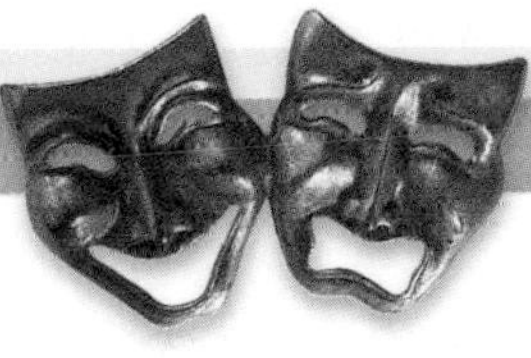

Patrick has arrived! It's the first day of school, and you're both getting ready. Create a conversation to include the following:

- Advise him on what to wear.
- Ask him what his favorite classes are.
- Describe your principal and your favorite teacher.
- Talk about what you're going to do after school.

Mise en pratique

CHAPITRE 1

Portfolio

4 **Written** This activity is appropriate for students' written portfolios. For portfolio information, see the *Alternative Assessment Guide,* pages iv–17.

Speaking Assessment

5 You might use the following rubric when grading your students on this activity.

Speaking Rubric	Points			
	4	3	2	1
Content (Complete–Incomplete)				
Comprehension (Total–Little)				
Comprehensibility (Comprehensible–Incomprehensible)				
Accuracy (Accurate–Seldom accurate)				
Fluency (Fluent–Not fluent)				

18–20: A	14–15: C	Under
16–17: B	12–13: D	12: F

Teacher Note

For additional practice and review, you might use the **Histoire Finale** for Chapter 1 on pages 6–7 of the *TPR Storytelling Book.*

Apply and Assess

Process Writing

4 You might have students work in groups of four or five to peer edit their letters. Assign each member of a group a different area to check, such as spelling and accents, verbs, nouns and adjectives, and correct use of vocabulary. Every member should read each letter and suggest corrections and/or improvements. You might use the Group Work Checklist from the *Alternative Assessment Guide,* page 13.

STANDARDS: 1.1, 1.3, 3.1, 5.1

CHAPITRE 1

Teaching Resources
p. 30

PRINT 

- Grammar Tutor for Students of French, Chapter 1

MEDIA 

- Interactive CD-ROM Tutor, Disc 1
- Online self-test

go.hrw.com
WA3 PARIS REGION-1

Teacher Note
This page is intended to help students prepare for the Chapter Test. It is a brief checklist of the major points covered in the chapter. The students should be reminded that this is only a checklist and does not necessarily include everything that will appear on the test.

Answers

2
1. *Like:* J'adore la salade. J'aime bien la salade. *Dislike:* Je n'aime pas la salade. *Prefer:* Je préfère... ; J'aime mieux...
2. *Like:* J'adore faire des photos. J'aime bien faire des photos. *Dislike:* Je n'aime pas faire des photos. *Prefer:* Je préfère... ; J'aime mieux...
3. *Like:* J'adore faire du roller en ligne. J'aime bien faire du roller en ligne. *Dislike:* Je n'aime pas faire du roller en ligne. *Prefer:* Je préfère... ; J'aime mieux...

3
1. Qu'est-ce que tu aimes faire?
2. Qu'est-ce que tu fais comme sport?
3. Qu'est-ce que tu aimes comme musique?
4. Quel est ton film préféré?

5 *Possible answers:*
Pense à prendre... ; Prends... ; N'oublie pas...
1. un maillot de bain, des sandales et des lunettes de soleil.
2. des bottes, des pantalons, des pulls, un manteau et des gants.
3. un imperméable, des jeans, des tee-shirts et des baskets.

Que sais-je?

WA3 PARIS REGION-1

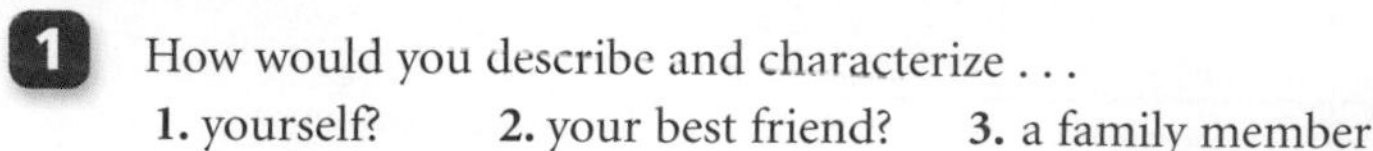

Can you use what you've learned in this chapter?

Can you describe and characterize yourself and others? p. 9

1 How would you describe and characterize . . .
1. yourself? 2. your best friend? 3. a family member?

Can you express likes, dislikes, and preferences? p. 11

2 How would you say that you like the following things? How would you say that you dislike them? That you prefer something else? See answers below.

1. 
2. 
3. 

Can you ask for information? p. 12

3 How would you ask someone . . . See answers below.
1. what he or she likes to do?
2. what sport he or she plays?
3. what type of music he or she likes?
4. what his or her favorite film is?

Can you ask for and give advice? p. 15

4 How would you ask someone what to take on a trip? Qu'est-ce que je dois prendre?

5 What would you advise a friend to bring to... See answers below.
1. the beach?
2. the mountains in the winter?
3. Chicago in the spring?

Can you ask for, make, and respond to suggestions? p. 18

6 How would you . . .
1. Qu'est-ce qu'on fait?
2. Si tu veux, on peut aller faire les magasins.

1. ask a friend what to do?
2. suggest that you can go shopping if your friend wants to?
3. suggest that you could play soccer? On pourrait jouer au football.
4. ask your friend if he or she would like to go to the movies?
Tu as envie d'aller au cinéma? Ça te dit d'aller au cinéma?

7 How would you respond to the following suggestions if you agreed? If you disagreed? If you preferred to do something else? Answers will vary.
1. On pourrait faire les magasins.
2. Tu as envie de regarder la télévision?

Can you relate a series of events? p. 20

8 How would your friend tell you that she is going to do these activities in this order? 1. D'abord, je vais faire de l'équitation. 2. Ensuite, je vais faire mes devoirs. 3. Enfin, je vais regarder la télévision.

1. 
2. 
3. 

Review and Assess

Game
Sur la sellette (The Hot Seat) Choose one student to sit in a chair in front of the class (the "hot seat"). The student answers questions asked by his or her classmates. After answering three questions correctly, the student chooses another classmate to sit in the "hot seat." Students might use the **Que sais-je?** section for their questions, or they might select questions from any part of the chapter.

STANDARDS: 1.2

Vocabulaire

Première étape

Describing and characterizing yourself and others

avoir... ans	*to be...years old*
J'ai...	*I have...*
Il/Elle a...	*He/She has...*
Ils/Elles ont...	*They have...*
les yeux marron	*brown eyes*
bleus	*blue*
verts	*green*
noirs	*black*
les cheveux blonds	*blond hair*
bruns	*dark brown*
châtains	*brown*
courts	*short*
longs	*long*
noirs	*black*
roux	*red*
Je suis...	*I am...*
Il/Elle est...	*He/She is...*
Ils/Elles sont...	*They are...*
beau (belle)	*handsome (beautiful)*
de taille moyenne	*of medium height*
fort(e)	*strong*
gourmand(e)	*someone who loves to eat*
grand(e)	*tall, big*
intelligent(e)	*smart*
jeune	*young*
petit(e)	*short, small*
sportif (sportive)	*athletic*
sympa	*nice*

Expressing likes, dislikes, and preferences

J'adore...	*I love...*
J'aime bien...	*I like...*
Je n'aime pas...	*I don't like...*
J'aime mieux...	*I prefer...*
Je préfère...	*I prefer...*

Asking for information

Qu'est-ce que tu aimes faire?	*What do you like to do?*
Qu'est-ce que tu fais comme sport?	*What sports do you play?*
Qu'est-ce que tu aimes comme musique?	*What music do you like?*
Quel(le) est ton/ta... préféré(e)?	*What is your favorite...?*
Qui est ton/ta... préféré(e)?	*Who is your favorite...?*

Deuxième étape

Asking for and giving advice

Qu'est-ce que je dois... ?	*What should I...?*
Pense à prendre...	*Remember to take...*
Prends...	*Take...*
N'oublie pas...	*Don't forget...*

Clothing and travel items

un imperméable	*a raincoat*
un jean	*a pair of jeans*
un tee-shirt	*a T-shirt*
des bottes (f.)	*a pair of boots*
des baskets (f.)	*a pair of sneakers*
un anorak	*a ski jacket*
un pull	*a sweater*
un sweat	*a sweatshirt*
une écharpe	*a scarf*
des gants (m.)	*a pair of gloves*
un appareil-photo	*a camera*
un passeport	*a passport*
un billet d'avion	*a plane ticket*
des chèques (m.) de voyage	*traveler's checks*

Troisième étape

Asking for, making, and responding to suggestions

Qu'est-ce qu'on fait?	*What should we do?*
Si tu veux, on peut...	*If you like, we can...*
On pourrait...	*We could...*
Tu as envie de... ?	*Do you feel like...?*
Ça te dit de... ?	*Does...sound good to you?*
D'accord.	*OK.*
C'est une bonne/excellente idée.	*That's a good/excellent idea.*
Je veux bien.	*I'd like to.*
Je ne peux pas.	*I can't.*
Ça ne me dit rien.	*That doesn't interest me.*
Non, je préfère...	*No, I'd rather...*
Pas question!	*No way!*

Relating a series of events

Qu'est-ce que tu vas faire... ?	*What are you going to do...?*
D'abord, je vais...	*First, I'm going to...*
Ensuite,...	*Next, ...*
Et puis,...	*Then, ...*
Finalement/Enfin,...	*Finally, ...*

Vocabulaire

CHAPITRE 1

Circumlocution

Have students play **Le Mot juste** on page 3C with the functions for describing people and the vocabulary for clothing items.

Teaching Suggestion

To review vocabulary, have students select two photos of people from this chapter and write a description of them and what they're wearing.

Chapter 1 Assessment

- **Testing Program**
  Chapter Test, pp. 13–18

  Audio Compact Discs, CD 1, Trs. 17–19
  Speaking Test, p. 343
- **Alternative Assessment Guide**
  Performance Assessment, p. 32
  Portfolio Assessment, p. 18
  CD-ROM Assessment, p. 46
- **Interactive CD-ROM Tutor, Disc 1**

  CD-ROM 1 A toi de parler
  DVD 1 A toi d'écrire
- **Standardized Assessment Tutor**
  Chapter 1
- **One-Stop Planner, Disc 1**
  Test Generator
  Chapter 1

Review and Assess

Game

J'en doute Form two teams. Students from one team call out a word from the vocabulary list, which a student from the opposing team must use in a sentence. The sentence must clearly illustrate the meaning of the word in order to receive a point. For example, **J'ai un imperméable** would not count. An acceptable answer might be **Je prends mon imperméable parce qu'il pleut.** If a student does not know the meaning of the word, he or she can try to bluff the other team by making up a sentence. The other team can call his or her bluff, however, by saying **J'en doute.** If they are right, and the player doesn't know the word, they receive two points. If they are wrong, and the player did know the word, they lose a point.

STANDARDS: 1.1

Chapitre 2 : Bienvenue à Chartres!

Review Chapter

Chapter Overview

Mise en train pp. 34–36	***Une nouvelle vie***

	FUNCTIONS	GRAMMAR	VOCABULARY	RE-ENTRY
Première étape pp. 37–39	• Welcoming someone; responding to someone's welcome, p. 37 • Asking how someone is feeling and telling how you are feeling, p. 38	• **Tu** versus **vous,** p. 38 • Intonation and **est-ce que,** p. 38		• Pronunciation: intonation **(Chapitre 1,** I) • Inquiring about and relating past events **(Chapitre 9,** I)
Deuxième étape pp. 40–45	• Pointing out where things are, p. 43 • Paying and responding to compliments, p. 44	• Adjectives that precede the noun, p. 43	• Rooms and furniture, p. 41	• Contractions with **de (Chapitre 12,** I) • Pointing out places and things **(Chapitre 12,** I) • Paying a compliment **(Chapitre 10,** I)
Troisième étape pp. 46–49	• Asking for and giving directions, p. 49	• Contractions with **à,** p. 48	• Places in town, p. 47	• Asking for and giving directions **(Chapitre 12,** I) • Making suggestions **(Chapitre 12,** I) • Places in town **(Chapitre 12,** I)

Lisons! pp. 50–51	**Passez une journée à Chartres**	**Reading Strategy:** Scanning	
Grammaire supplémentaire	**pp. 52–55** **Première étape,** pp. 52–53	**Deuxième étape,** pp. 53–54	**Troisième étape,** pp. 54–55
Review pp. 56–59	**Mise en pratique,** pp. 56–57 **Ecrivons!** Providing details Writing an ad	**Que sais-je?** p. 58	**Vocabulaire,** p. 59

CULTURE

- **Note culturelle,** Polite behavior for a guest, p. 39
- **Note culturelle,** Teens' bedrooms in France, p. 42
- **Note culturelle,** Paying and receiving compliments, p. 44
- **Panorama Culturel,** Houses in francophone countries, p. 45
- **Note culturelle,** Notre-Dame de Chartres, p. 48

Chapitre 2 : Bienvenue à Chartres!
Chapter Resources

PRINT

Lesson Planning

One-Stop Planner

Lesson Planner with Substitute Teacher

Lesson Plans, pp. 6–10, 64

Student Make-Up Assignments
- Make-Up Assignment Copying Masters, Chapter 2

Listening and Speaking

TPR Storytelling Book, pp. 8–15

Listening Activities
- Student Response Forms for Listening Activities, pp. 11–13
- Additional Listening Activities 2-1 to 2-6, pp. 15–17
- Additional Listening Activities (song), p. 18
- Scripts and Answers, pp. 107–111

Video Guide
- Teaching Suggestions, pp. 10–11
- Activity Masters, pp. 12–14
- Scripts and Answers, pp. 87–89, 118–119

Activities for Communication
- Communicative Activities, pp. 7–12
- Realia and Teaching Suggestions, pp. 80–84
- Situation Cards, pp. 139–140

Reading and Writing

Reading Strategies and Skills Handbook, Chapter 2

Joie de lire 2, Chapter 2

Cahier d'activités, pp. 13–24

Grammar

Travaux pratiques de grammaire, pp. 12–19

Grammar Tutor for Students of French, Chapter 2

Assessment

Testing Program
- Grammar and Vocabulary Quizzes, **Etape** Quizzes, and Chapter Test, pp. 27–44
- Score Sheet, Scripts and Answers, pp. 45–52

Alternative Assessment Guide
- Portfolio Assessment, p. 19
- Performance Assessment, p. 33
- CD-ROM Assessment, p. 47

Student Make-Up Assignments
- Alternative Quizzes, Chapter 2

Standardized Assessment Tutor
- Reading, pp. 5–7
- Writing, p. 8
- Math, pp. 25–26

MEDIA

Online Activities
- **Jeux interactifs**
- **Activités Internet**

Video Program
- Videocassette 1
- Videocassette 5 (captioned version)

Interactive CD-ROM Tutor, Disc 1

DVD Tutor, Disc 1

Audio Compact Discs
- Textbook Listening Activities, CD 2, Tracks 1–14
- Additional Listening Activities, CD 2, Tracks 21–27
- Assessment Items, CD 1, Tracks 15–20

Teaching Transparencies
- Situation 2-1 to 2-3
- Vocabulary 2-A to 2-C
- **Mise en train**
- **Grammaire supplémentaire** Answers
- **Travaux pratiques de grammaire** Answers

One-Stop Planner CD-ROM

Use the **One-Stop Planner CD-ROM with Test Generator** to aid in lesson planning and pacing.

For each chapter, the **One-Stop Planner** includes:
- Editable lesson plans with direct links to teaching resources
- Printable worksheets from resource books
- Direct launches to the HRW Internet activities
- Video and audio segments
- Test Generator
- Clip Art for vocabulary items

Projects

Ma ville

Students will create a map of a town on the classroom floor with masking tape. Afterwards, they will conduct a tour of their town, using the map to give and follow directions.

MATERIALS

Teacher and students may need

- Masking tape
- Transparency of town map
- Overhead projector
- Construction paper

SUGGESTED SEQUENCE

1. On the transparency of the map, overlay a nine-square grid. Then, make a similar grid on the floor, with masking tape, large enough so that students can walk on the streets.
2. Project the map on the overhead and assign two or three students to each section of the grid. They must then reproduce their section of the map on the corresponding section on the floor with masking tape, making sure that their section joins the others correctly. To label the streets, have students write the names of the streets on sheets of construction paper and tape them to the streets.
3. Now, add the buildings. Let students plan the town. Have students write the French names of the buildings on construction paper and tape them to the map.
4. The students responsible for each section will now conduct a tour of their section. They should point out the streets and buildings and tell where each building is in relation to another building.
5. Next, form two groups: residents and tourists. The resident gives the directions, and the tourist follows them. The resident should indicate a starting point for the tourist and choose a secret destination. Have the resident write the secret destination on a slip of paper. He or she then directs the tourist to the destination.

GRADING THE PROJECT

Suggested Point Distribution: (total = 100 points)

The resident:

Language use	25
Comprehensibility	25
Participation/effort	50

The tourist:

Comprehension	50
Participation/effort	50

Games

Mémoire

In this game, students will practice the vocabulary for rooms of a house or places in a town.

MATERIALS

Teacher may need

- 30 to 40 index cards
- Tape

Procedure Choose 12 vocabulary words for rooms of a house (**le salon**) or places in a town (**la gare**). For each room or place, write a short sentence telling what one does there. (**On regarde la télé. On prend le train.**) Write the words and their corresponding sentences on separate index cards. Tape the word cards to the board in random order, with the text facing the board. Number the cards 1–12. In a separate area of the board, do the same with the sentence cards. Divide the class into two teams. Teams take turns matching words and sentences from the two sides of the board. For example, a team member might call out **à gauche, treize et à droite, deux.** Turn over the two cards to see if they correspond to each other. If a match is made, the student must make a new sentence combining the two elements in order to receive credit for the match. (**Je vais à la gare pour prendre le train.**) If the sentence is correct, remove the two cards and mark a point for that team. Students on each team take turns guessing. If a team scores a point, they get another turn, but a team may not take more than three turns in a row. If no match is made, the next team takes a turn. When all the matches are found, the team with the most points wins.

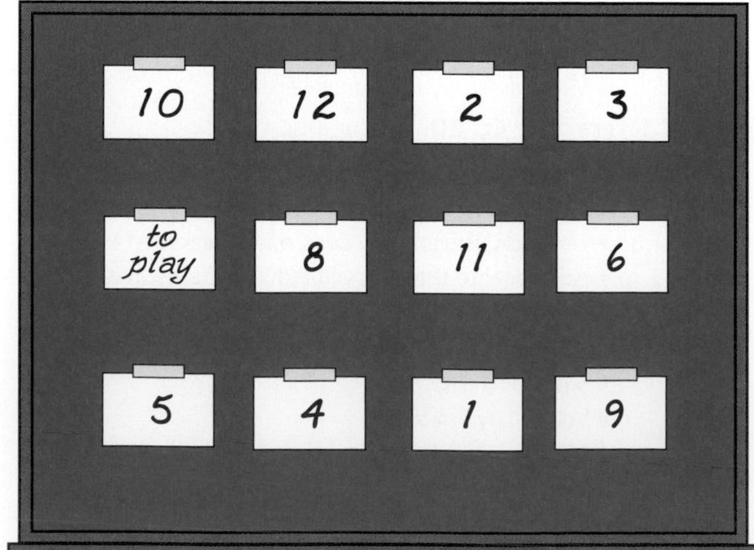

STANDARDS: 1.1, 1.2

Storytelling

Mini-histoire

This story accompanies Teaching Transparency 2-2. The ***mini-histoire*** *can be told and retold in different formats, acted out, written down, and read aloud, to give students additional opportunities to practice all four skills. The following story is about a boy named Antoine who is looking for his friend.*

Antoine veut parler à son amie Françoise. Il va dans la salle de séjour, mais elle n'est pas là. Antoine monte au premier étage et la cherche partout. Françoise n'est ni dans la salle de bains, ni dans les chambres, ni sur le balcon. Il regarde par la fenêtre, mais elle n'est pas non plus dans le jardin. Peut-être qu'elle se repose dans sa chambre. Antoine monte au deuxième étage et frappe à la porte. Pas de réponse. Il entre. Françoise a posé son sac sur le tapis et elle est partie. Antoine est déçu, car il voulait emmener son amie au cinéma. Il descend au rez-de-chaussée, va dans la cuisine, et surprise... Françoise est là. Elle boit tranquillement un café. Il lui demande : «Est-ce que tu veux venir au cinéma avec mes amis ce soir?» Elle répond : «Oui, bien sûr. J'adore aller au cinéma.»

Traditions

Les Marchés en plein air

Most towns and cities of France have **marchés en plein air** *(open-air markets)* once or twice a week, often in the town's main square. Products available in supermarkets or at smaller specialty stores can also be found in these markets; however, the produce, meats, and cheese usually come straight from the vendor's farm. Thus the quality is often higher than that found in supermarkets and the prices lower. Markets are important meeting places for local farmers and town residents. Like cafés, they give people the opportunity to catch up on the latest news. Bargaining is not customary, nor do customers handle the merchandise. Instead, customers state what they want and the vendor picks out the product for them. Ask students to compare and contrast the open-air markets of France with the farmer's markets of the United States.

Recette

Lentils come from the Mediterranean countries and have been cultivated for more than 2,000 years. There are three varieties of lentils: blond, brown, and green (most commonly found in France). Green lentils are dried in the sun while still in the fields. France produces 20,000 tons of green lentils per year.

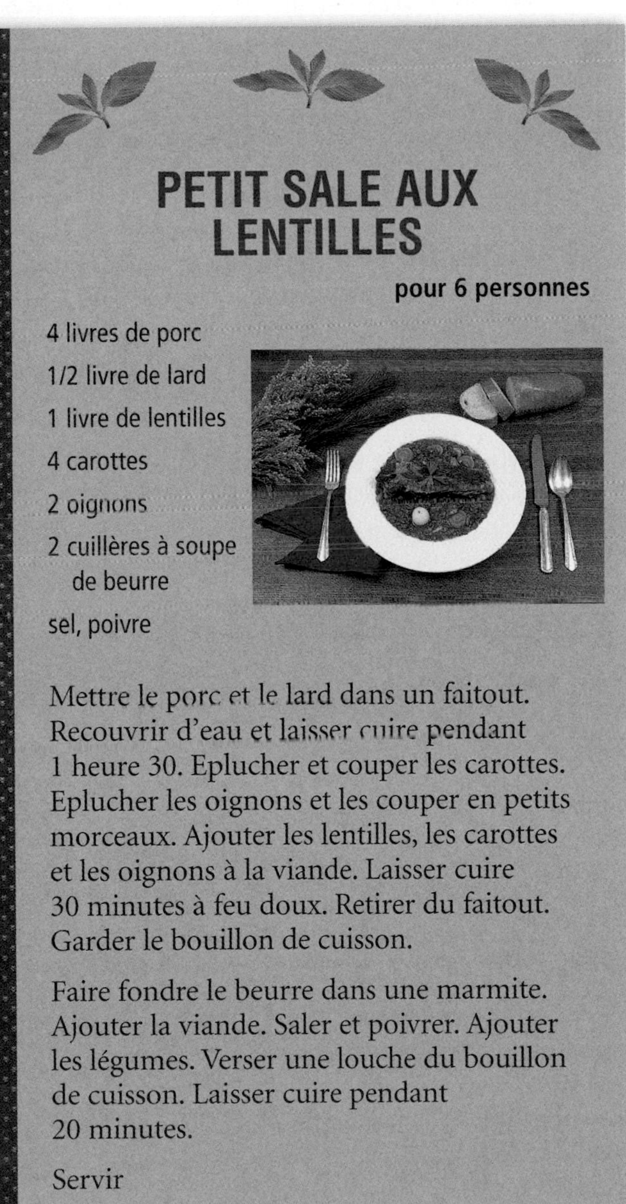

PETIT SALE AUX LENTILLES

pour 6 personnes

- 4 livres de porc
- 1/2 livre de lard
- 1 livre de lentilles
- 4 carottes
- 2 oignons
- 2 cuillères à soupe de beurre
- sel, poivre

Mettre le porc et le lard dans un faitout. Recouvrir d'eau et laisser cuire pendant 1 heure 30. Eplucher et couper les carottes. Eplucher les oignons et les couper en petits morceaux. Ajouter les lentilles, les carottes et les oignons à la viande. Laisser cuire 30 minutes à feu doux. Retirer du faitout. Garder le bouillon de cuisson.

Faire fondre le beurre dans une marmite. Ajouter la viande. Saler et poivrer. Ajouter les légumes. Verser une louche du bouillon de cuisson. Laisser cuire pendant 20 minutes.

Servir

STANDARDS: 1.3, 2.1, 3.2, 5.1

Technology

DVD/Video

Videocassette 1, Videocassette 5 (captioned version)
DVD Tutor, Disc 1
See Video Guide, pages 9–14.

Mise en train • Une nouvelle vie

The Lepic family arrives in Chartres with Pamela, and they welcome her to their home. Sandra gives Pamela a tour of her house. Sandra assumes that Pamela is exhausted and wants to rest, but Pamela says she wants to visit the cathedral. Sandra leaves Pamela to unpack. Later, when Sandra goes to get her, she discovers Pamela asleep on the bed.

Mise en train (suite)

Sandra takes Pamela out on her first day in Chartres. Pamela changes money at the **bureau de change,** then buys a guide book and some postcards at a local shop. They visit the cathedral and the old section of town, **le vieux Chartres.** Sandra keeps expecting Pamela to get tired, but she is full of energy and heads off to visit the tourist bureau!

Comment est ta maison?

Students from Quebec, Martinique, and Cameroun describe their homes.

Vidéoclips

- **Mérinos®:** advertisement for mattresses
- **Topps®:** advertisement for bathroom cleanser

Interactive CD-ROM Tutor

Activity	Activity Type	Pupil's Edition Page
En contexte	*Interactive conversation*	
1. Comment dit-on... ?	Chacun à sa place	pp. 37–38
2. Vocabulaire	Chasse au trésor Explorons! Vérifions!	pp. 41, 43
3. Comment dit-on... ?	Chasse au trésor Explorons! Vérifions!	pp. 41, 43
4. Grammaire	Les mots qui manquent	p. 43
5. Vocabulaire	Jeu des paires	p. 47
6. Comment dit-on... ?	Le bon choix	p. 49
Panorama Culturel	Comment est ta maison?	p. 45
A toi de parler	*Guided recording*	pp. 56–57
A toi d'écrire	*Guided writing*	pp. 56–57

Teacher Management System

Launch the program, type "admin" in the password area, and press RETURN. Log on to **www.hrw.com/CDROMTUTOR** for a detailed explanation of the Teacher Management System.

DVD Tutor

The *DVD Tutor* contains all material from the *Video Program* as described above. French captions are available for use at your discretion for all sections of the video. The *DVD Tutor* also provides a variety of video-based activities that assess students' understanding of the **Mise en train, Suite,** and **Panorama Culturel.**

This part of the *DVD Tutor* may be used on any DVD video player connected to a television or video monitor.

In addition to the video material and the video-based comprehension activities, the *DVD Tutor* also contains the entire *Interactive CD-ROM Tutor* in DVD-ROM format. Each DVD disc contains the activities from all 12 chapters of the *Interactive CD-ROM Tutor.*

This part of the *DVD Tutor* may be used on a Macintosh® or Windows® computer with a DVD-ROM drive.

To preview all resources available for this chapter, use the **One-Stop Planner CD-ROM**, Disc 1.

Internet Connection

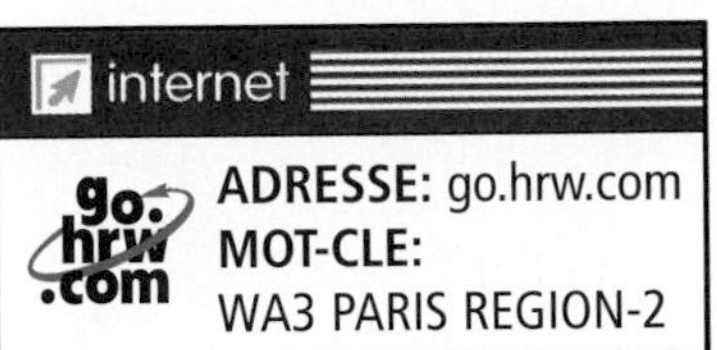

*Have students explore the **go.hrw.com** Web site for many online resources covering all chapters. All Chapter 2 resources are available under the keyword **WA3 PARIS REGION-2.** Interactive games help students practice the material and provide them with immediate feedback. You'll also find a printable worksheet that provides Internet activities that lead to a comprehensive online research project.*

Jeux interactifs

You can use the interactive activities in this chapter

- to practice grammar, vocabulary, and chapter functions
- as homework
- as an assessment option
- as a self-test
- to prepare for the Chapter Test

Activités Internet

Students look for information about famous French people from the Paris region.

- In preparation for the **Activités Internet,** have students pick a famous person from the list on page xxvi. They will then look for information on that person, using the links provided on the **go.hrw.com** Web site.

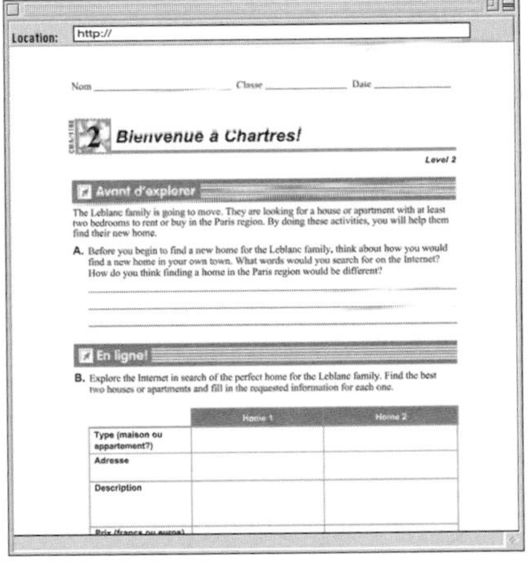

Location: http://

Nom ______ Classe ______ Date ______

2 Bienvenue à Chartres!

Level 2

Avant d'explorer

The Leblanc family is going to move. They are looking for a house or apartment with at least two bedrooms to rent or buy in the Paris region. By doing these activities, you will help them find their new home.

A. Before you begin to find a new home for the Leblanc family, think about how you would find a new home in your own town. What words would you search for on the Internet? How do you think finding a home in the Paris region would be different?

En ligne!

B. Explore the Internet in search of the perfect home for the Leblanc family. Find the best two houses or apartments and fill in the requested information for each one.

	Home 1	Home 2
Type (maison ou appartement?)		
Adresse		
Description		
Prix (francs ou euros)		

Projet

Students will do a Web search on Chartres. Then, have the students present their research in the form of an audio travelogue. They can record on an audiocassette what they saw on their cyber visit. Students should document their sources by noting the URLs of all the sites that they consulted.

STANDARDS: 1.2, 1.3, 3.2, 5.1

Chapitre 2 : Bienvenue à Chartres!

Review Chapter

Textbook Listening Activities Scripts 

Première étape

7 p. 37

1. —Bienvenue chez moi, Maryse!
—Merci.
—Fais comme chez toi.
—C'est gentil de ta part.
—Tu as fait bon voyage?
—C'était fatigant!
2. —Bienvenue à la maison, monsieur!
—Merci.
—Faites comme chez vous.
—C'est gentil.
—Oh, ça a été, mais je suis très fatigué!
3. —Bienvenue chez nous, Tante Monique!
—Merci.
—Tu as fait bon voyage?
—Excellent!

Answers to Activity 7
1. tiring
2. tiring
3. good

10 p. 39

1. —Bienvenue, Stéphanie. Tu as fait bon voyage?
—Oui, excellent.
—Alors, entre... Fais comme chez toi.
—C'est gentil de ta part.
—Dis, tu n'as pas faim?
—Si, un peu.
—Alors, on passe à table?
2. —Bonjour, madame. Bienvenue à Chartres!
—Oh, merci. Tu es gentil.
—Vous avez fait bon voyage?
—Oui, mais c'était fatigant.
—Alors, entrez. Vous n'avez pas soif?
—Si, un peu.
—Tenez, voilà un verre d'eau.
3. —Salut, Ginette. Tu as fait bon voyage?
—Oui, excellent.
—Alors, entre... fais comme chez toi. Il est déjà midi. Tu n'as pas faim?
—Non, ça va.

Answers to Activity 10
1. b
2. c
3. a

Deuxième étape

15 p. 42

1. Mettez-le dans le salon, s'il vous plaît.
2. Ça, ça va dans la salle à manger.
3. Mettez tout ça dans le jardin.
4. Mettez-le dans la cuisine, s'il vous plaît.
5. Oh, il va dans la chambre d'Antoine.

Answers to Activity 15

1. d 3. e 5. c
2. a 4. b

 18 p. 43

1. Le salon est au premier étage.
2. Les toilettes sont à côté de la salle de bains.
3. Les Morel ont un jardin et un balcon.
4. La salle à manger est au rez-de-chaussée, près de la cuisine.
5. La chambre des parents a un balcon.
6. Dans la chambre d'Antoine, il y a deux lits et un joli tapis rouge.

Answers to Activity 18

1. false 3. true 5. true
2. false 4. true 6. false

22 p. 44

1. SOLANGE Bon, ici, c'est le salon.
ARNAUD Oh, j'adore le tapis.
SOLANGE Vraiment?
2. SOLANGE Ensuite, il y a le bureau de Maman. Elle aime y travailler le soir.
ARNAUD Dis donc, elle a un super ordinateur, ta mère.
SOLANGE Tu trouves?
3. SOLANGE Et enfin, voilà ma chambre. Entre.
ARNAUD Merci. Tiens, j'aime beaucoup ce poster.
SOLANGE C'est vrai?
ARNAUD Oui, et tu sais, Céline Dion est ma chanteuse préférée.
4. ARNAUD Elle est chouette, ta chambre.
SOLANGE C'est gentil!

Answers to Activity 22

1. a rug 3. a poster
2. a computer 4. a bedroom

The following scripts are for the listening activities found in the *Pupil's Edition*. For Student Response Forms, see *Listening Activities*, pages 11–13. To provide students with additional listening practice, see *Listening Activities*, pages 15–17.

One-Stop Planner CD-ROM

To preview all resources available for this chapter, use the **One-Stop Planner CD-ROM**, Disc 1.

Troisième étape

26 p. 47

PATRICK Qu'est-ce qu'on va faire aujourd'hui?

CHANTAL On va visiter la cathédrale, bien sûr! Les vitraux sont magnifiques!

PATRICK D'accord... mais j'ai besoin d'aller à la poste. J'ai des cartes postales à envoyer.

CHANTAL D'accord, on va d'abord à la poste, puis à la cathédrale.

PATRICK Tu as envie d'aller au musée des Beaux-Arts?

CHANTAL Oui, pourquoi pas?

PATRICK D'accord, alors on va au musée après la cathédrale. Et ensuite?

CHANTAL Tu sais, c'est déjà beaucoup!

PATRICK Si on allait se reposer au parc? On pourrait faire un pique-nique.

CHANTAL Non, je n'ai pas très envie d'aller au parc. Si on allait à la piscine?

PATRICK A la piscine? C'est une bonne idée.

CHANTAL Alors c'est décidé. On y va!

Answers to Activity 26
la poste, la cathédrale, le musée des Beaux-Arts, la piscine;
e, b, a, f

29 p. 49

1. Bon, prenez le boulevard Chasles à droite. Traversez la place Pasteur. Continuez tout droit. C'est sur la droite, juste avant la rue des Bas-Bourgs.
2. Oh, ça, c'est facile. C'est tout près d'ici. Prenez la rue M. Violette. Vous ne pouvez pas la manquer, c'est le grand bâtiment sur la gauche.
3. Attendez... prenez le boulevard de la Résistance. Tournez à droite dans la rue de Gaulle. Ne la ratez pas, c'est une toute petite rue. Vous verrez, c'est sur la droite, après la rue Famin.

Answers to Activity 29
1. à la piscine
2. à la poste
3. à l'église Sainte-Foy

Mise en pratique

2 p. 56

Ah, le musée? C'est simple. Voyons... Vous êtes sur la place Saint-Michel. Prenez le boulevard Saint-Michel jusqu'au boulevard Saint-Germain. Tournez à droite. Allez tout droit. Tournez à droite dans la rue du Bac. Allez tout droit jusqu'au quai Voltaire. Le musée est là, à gauche.

Answers to Mise en pratique Activity 2
le musée d'Orsay

Chapitre 2 : Bienvenue à Chartres!

Review Chapter

Suggested Lesson Plans 50-Minute Schedule

Day 1

CHAPTER OPENER 5 min.
- Present Chapter Objectives, p. 33.
- Culture Notes, ATE, p. 32

MISE EN TRAIN 40 min.
- Presenting **Mise en train,** ATE, p. 34
- Complete Activities 1–5, p. 36.
- Challenge, ATE, p. 36
- Culture Note, ATE, p. 36

Wrap-Up 5 min.
- Teaching Suggestions: Post-viewing, Video Guide, p. 10

Homework Options
Cahier d'activités, Act. 1, p. 13

Day 2

MISE EN TRAIN
Quick Review 5 min.
- Bell Work, ATE, p. 37

PREMIERE ETAPE
Comment dit-on... ?, p. 37 20 min.
- Presenting **Comment dit-on... ?,** ATE, p. 37
- Play Audio CD for Activity 7, p. 37.
- Cahier d'activités, Activity 2, p. 14

Note de grammaire, p. 38 10 min.
- Read and discuss **Note de grammaire,** p. 38.
- **Grammaire supplémentaire,** Activity 1, p. 52

Comment dit-on... ?, p. 38 10 min.
- Presenting **Comment dit-on... ?,** ATE, p. 38
- TPR, ATE, p. 39

Wrap-Up, 5 min.
- Do Activity 9, p. 38.

Homework Options
Cahier d'activités, Acts. 3–5, pp. 14–15
Travaux pratiques de grammaire, Acts. 1–2, p. 12

Day 3

PREMIERE ETAPE
Quick Review 5 min.
- Check homework.

Comment dit-on... ?, and **Note de grammaire, p. 38** 25 min.
- Play Audio CD for Activity 10, p. 39.
- Review **Note de grammaire,** p. 38.
- See Language-to-Language, ATE, p. 38.
- **Grammaire supplémentaire,** Activity 3, p. 52
- Complete Activities 11–12, p. 39.
- Travaux pratiques de grammaire, Activities 3–4, p. 13

Note culturelle, p. 39 10 min.
- Read and discuss **Note culturelle,** p. 39.
- Culture Note, ATE, p. 39

Wrap-Up 10 min.
- Do Activity 13, p. 39.

Homework Options
Study for Quiz 2-1.

Day 4

PREMIERE ETAPE
Quiz 2-1 20 min.
- Administer Quiz 2-1A, 2-1B, or a combination of the two.

DEUXIEME ETAPE
Vocabulaire, p. 41 25 min.
- Presenting **Vocabulaire,** ATE, p. 41
- Culture Notes, ATE, p. 41
- Group Work and TPR, ATE, p. 42

Wrap-Up 5 min
- Cahier d'activités, Acts. 7–8, p. 16

Homework Options
Cahier d'activités, Act. 9, p. 17
Travaux pratiques de grammaire, Acts. 5–6, p. 14

Day 5

DEUXIEME ETAPE
Quick Review 5 min.
- Check homework.

Note culturelle, p. 42 10 min.
- Read and discuss **Note culturelle,** p. 42.
- Complete Activity 16, p. 42.

Comment dit-on... ?, p. 43 25 min.
- Presenting **Comment dit-on... ?,** ATE, p. 43
- Play Audio CD for Activity 18, p. 43.
- Cahier d'activités, Activity 10, p. 17
- Read and discuss **Tu te rappelles?,** p. 43.
- **Grammaire supplémentaire,** Activity 5, p. 53

Wrap-Up 10 min.
- Have students write Activity 19, p. 43. See Teaching Suggestion, ATE, p. 43.

Homework Options
Travaux pratiques de grammaire, Acts. 7–8, p. 15

Day 6

DEUXIEME ETAPE
Quick Review 5 min.
- Check homework.

Grammaire, p. 43 20 min.
- Presenting **Grammaire,** ATE, p. 43
- Language Note, ATE, p. 43
- Do Activity 20, p. 44.
- Cahier d'activités, Activities 11–12, pp. 17–18

Comment dit-on... ?, p. 44 20 min.
- Presenting **Comment dit-on... ?,** ATE, p. 44
- Play Audio CD for Activity 22, p. 44.
- Read and discuss **Note culturelle,** p. 44.
- Cahier d'activités, Activity 14, p. 19

Wrap-Up 5 min.
- Teaching Suggestion, ATE, p. 44

Homework Options
Travaux pratiques de grammaire, Acts. 9–10, p. 16
Grammaire supplémentaire, Act. 6, p. 53
Study for Quiz 2-2.

One-Stop Planner CD-ROM

For alternative lesson plans by chapter section, to create your own customized plans, or to preview all resources available for this chapter, use the **One-Stop Planner CD-ROM,** Disc 1.

For additional homework suggestions, see activities accompanied by this symbol throughout the chapter.

Day 7

DEUXIEME ETAPE

Quiz 2-2 20 min.
- Administer Quiz 2-2A, 2-2B, or a combination of the two.

PANORAMA CULTUREL 25 min.
- Present **Panorama Culturel,** p. 45, using Videocassette 1.
- Read and discuss **Qu'en penses-tu?** and **Savais-tu que… ?,** p. 45.
- **Panorama Culturel,** Interactive CD-ROM Tutor, (Disc 1)

Wrap-Up 5 min.
- Questions, ATE, p. 45

Homework Options
Video Guide, Post-viewing Activity 5, p. 13

Day 8

DEUXIEME ETAPE

Quick Review 10 min.
- Bell Work, ATE, p. 46

TROISIEME ETAPE

Vocabulaire, p. 47 25 min.
- Presenting **Vocabulaire,** ATE, p. 47
- Thinking Critically, ATE, p. 47
- Play Audio CD for Activity 26, p. 47.
- Cahier d'activités, Activity 17, p. 20
- Travaux pratiques de grammaire, Activities 11–13, pp. 17–18

Note de grammaire, p. 48 10 min.
- Presenting **Note de grammaire,** ATE, p. 48
- Complete Activity 27, p. 48.
- **Grammaire supplémentaire,** Activities 8–10, pp. 54–55

Wrap-Up 5 min.
- Teaching Suggestions, first suggestion, ATE, p. 47

Homework Options
Cahier d'activités, Acts. 18–19, p. 20
Travaux pratiques de grammaire, Acts. 14–16, pp. 18–19

Day 9

TROISIEME ETAPE

Quick Review 10 min.
- Check homework.

Note culturelle, p. 48 10 min.
- Read and discuss **Note culturelle,** p. 48.
- History Link, ATE, p. 48
- Architecture Link, ATE, p. 48

Comment dit-on... ?, p. 49 25 min.
- Presenting **Comment dit-on... ?,** ATE, p. 49
- Play Audio CD for Activity 29, p. 49.
- Complete Activity 30, p. 49, using the map on p. 46.
- Cahier d'activités, Activities 20–22, pp. 21–22

Wrap-Up 5 min.
- Do Activity 31, p. 49.

Homework Options
Cahier d'activités, Act. 23, p. 22
Study for Quiz 2-3.

Day 10

TROISIEME ETAPE

Quiz 2-3 20 min.
- Administer Quiz 2-3A, 2-3B or a combination of the two.

LISONS! 35 min.
- Prereading Activity A, p. 50, and Career Path, ATE, p. 50
- Reading Activities B–F, pp. 50–51

Wrap-Up 5 min.
- Discuss Science Link, ATE, p. 50 and Culture Notes, ATE, p. 51.

Homework Options
Cahier d'activités, Act. 24, p. 23

Day 11

LISONS!

Quick Review 5 min.
- Go over homework.

Postreading Activity 15 min.
- Do Postreading Activity G, ATE, p. 51.

MISE EN PRATIQUE 25 min.
- Do Activity 1, p. 56.
- Play Audio CD for Activity 2, p. 56.
- Discuss the strategy for **Ecrivons!**, p. 57, as a class, then have students work on their ads.
- Have partners do **Jeu de rôle,** p. 57.

Wrap-Up 5 min.
- Allow students to complete ads for **Ecrivons!**, p. 57.

Homework Options
Que sais-je?, p. 58

Day 12

MISE EN PRATIQUE

Quick Review 15 min.
- See Game: **C'est à toi!,** p. 58.

Chapter Review 35 min.
- Review Chapter 2. Choose from **Grammaire supplémentaire,** Grammar Tutor for Students of French, Activities for Communication, Listening Activities, Interactive CD-ROM Tutor, or **Jeux interactifs.**

Homework Options
Study for Chapter 2 Test.

Assessment

Chapter Test 40–45 min.
- Administer Chapter 2 Test. Select from Testing Program, Alternative Assessment Guide, Test Generator, Standardized Assessment Tutor.

Suggested Lesson Plans *90-Minute Block Schedule*

Block 1

CHAPTER OPENER 5 min.
- Present Chapter Objectives, p. 33.
- Thinking Critically, ATE p. 33

MISE EN TRAIN 30 min.
- Motivating Activity, ATE, p. 34
- Preteaching Vocabulary ATE, p. 34
- Presenting **Mise en train,** ATE, p. 34, using Videocassette 1
- Do Activities 1–4, p. 36.

PREMIERE ETAPE
Comment dit-on… ?, p. 37 30 min.
- Do Activity 6, p. 37.
- Presenting **Comment dit-on… ?,** ATE, p. 37
- Play Audio CD for Activity 7, p. 37.
- Present first **Note de grammaire,** p. 38.
- Do Activity 8, p. 38.

Comment dit-on… ?, p. 38 20 min.
- Presenting **Comment dit-on… ?,** ATE, p. 38
- Language-to-Language, ATE, p. 38
- Present second **Note de grammaire,** p. 38.

Wrap-Up 5 min.
- Have students work in pairs to improvise the arrival of an American student at the home of a francophone host family.

Homework Options
Grammaire supplémentaire, Acts. 1–3, p. 52
Cahier d'activités, Acts. 1–4, pp. 13–14
Travaux pratiques de grammaire, Acts. 1–4, pp. 12–13

Block 2

PREMIERE ETAPE
Quick Review 5 min.
- TPR, ATE, p. 39

Comment dit-on… ?, p. 38 30 min.
- Play Audio CD for Activity 10, p. 39.
- Do Activity 11, p. 39.
- Introduce **Note culturelle,** p. 39.
- Do Activity 12, p. 39.

DEUXIEME ETAPE
Vocabulaire, p. 41 30 min.
- Presenting **Vocabulaire,** ATE, p. 41
- Culture Notes, ATE, p. 41
- Discuss **Note culturelle,** p. 42.
- Play Audio CD for Activity 15, p. 42.
- Activity 16, p. 42

Comment dit-on… ?, p. 43 15 min.
- Presenting **Comment dit-on… ?,** ATE, p. 43
- Play Audio CD for Activity 18, p. 43.

Wrap-Up 10 min.
- Teaching Suggestion, ATE, p. 44

Homework Options
Have students study for Quiz 2-1.
Pupil's Edition, Activity 13, p. 39
Cahier d'activités, Acts. 5–9, pp. 15–17
Travaux pratiques de grammaire, Acts. 5–6, p. 14

Block 3

PREMIERE ETAPE
Quick Review 5 min.
- Communicative Activity 2-1, Activities for Communication, pp. 7–8

Quiz 2-1 20 min.
- Administer Quiz 2-1A, 2-1B, or a combination of the two.

DEUXIEME ETAPE
Vocabulaire, p. 41 15 min.
- Group Work, ATE, p. 42

Comment dit-on… ?, p. 43 25 min.
- Review **Comment dit-on… ?,** p. 43, by having students give a tour of the house in Teaching Transparency 2-2.
- Present **Tu te rappelles?,** p. 43.
- Do Activity 19, using Teaching Suggestion, ATE, p. 43.

Grammaire, p. 43 15 min.
- Presenting **Grammaire,** ATE, p. 43
- Do Activity 20, p. 44.

Wrap-Up 10 min.
- TPR, ATE, p. 42

Homework Options
Cahier d'activités, Acts. 10–12, pp. 17–18
Travaux pratiques de grammaire, Acts. 7–8, p. 15

One-Stop Planner CD-ROM

For alternative lesson plans by chapter section, to create your own customized plans, or to preview all resources available for this chapter, use the **One-Stop Planner CD-ROM,** Disc 1.

For additional homework suggestions, see activities accompanied by this symbol throughout the chapter.

Block 4

DEUXIEME ETAPE

Quick Review 10 min.

- Have students do Additional Listening Activities 2-3, Listening Activities, p. 16, and then check their work as a class.

PANORAMA CULTUREL 20 min.

- Presenting **Panorama Culturel,** ATE, p. 45, with Videocassette 1
- Read and discuss **Qu'en penses-tu?** and **Savais-tu que... ?**, p. 45

Grammaire, p. 43 10 min.

- **Grammaire supplémentaire,** Act. 6, p. 53

Comment dit-on... ?, p. 44 25 min.

- Presenting **Comment dit-on... ?**, ATE, p. 44
- Discuss **Note culturelle,** p. 44.
- Play Audio CD for Activity 22, p. 44.
- Do Activity 23, p. 44.

TROISIEME ETAPE

Vocabulaire, p. 47 **15 min.**

- Presenting **Vocabulaire,** ATE, p. 47
- Play Audio CD for Activity 26, p. 47.

Wrap-Up 10 min.

- Review, using Teaching Transparency 2-2. See suggestion #4 on Suggestions for Using Teaching Transparency 2-2.

Homework Options

Have students study for Quiz 2-2.
Pupil's Edition Activity 24, p. 44
Cahier d'activités, Acts. 13–17, pp. 18–20
Travaux pratiques de grammaire, Acts. 9–13, pp. 16–18

Block 5

DEUXIEME ETAPE

Quick Review 10 min.

- Project Transparency 2-A and have each student write four sentences describing the house. Have students share their sentences and work in pairs to correct any mistakes.

Quiz 2-2 20 min.

- Administer Quiz 2-2A, 2-2B, or a combination of the two.

TROISIEME ETAPE

Note de grammaire, p. 48 25 min.

- Presenting **Note de grammaire,** ATE, p. 48
- Do Activities 27–28, p. 48.
- Discuss **Note culturelle,** p. 48.

Comment dit-on... ?, p. 49 30 min.

- Presenting **Comment dit-on... ?,** ATE, p. 49
- Play Audio CD for Activity 29, p. 49.
- Activity 31, p. 49

Wrap-Up 5 min.

- Situation Cards 2-3: Role-plays, Activities for Communication, p. 140

Homework Options

Grammaire supplémentaire, Acts. 8–9, p. 54
Cahier d'activités, Acts. 18–23, pp. 20–22
Travaux pratiques de grammaire, Acts. 14–16, pp. 18–19
Have students study for Quiz 2-3.

Block 6

TROISIEME ETAPE

Quick Review 10 min.

- Communicative Activity 2-3, Activities for Communication, pp. 11–12

Quiz 2-3 20 min.

- Administer Quiz 2-3A, 2-3B, or a combination of the two.

LISONS! 30 min.

- **Stratégie pour lire,** p. 50
- Prereading Activity A, p. 50, and Career Path, ATE, p. 50
- Reading Activities B–F, pp. 50–51
- Postreading Activity G, p. 51

MISE EN PRATIQUE 30 min.

- Do Activity 1, p. 56.
- Play Audio CD for Activity 2, p. 56. See Slower Pace, ATE, p. 57.
- Do Activity 4, p. 57.
- Have students do the first two steps of **Ecrivons!,** Activity 3, p. 57.

Homework Options

Que sais-je?, p. 58
Interactive CD-ROM Tutor (Disc 1)
Study for Chapter 2 Test.
Finish Activity 3, p. 57.

Block 7

MISE EN PRATIQUE

Quick Review 10 min.

- Check homework.

Chapter Review 35 min.

- Review Chapter 2. Choose from **Grammaire supplémentaire,** Grammar Tutor for Students of French, Activities for Communication, Listening Activities, Interactive CD-ROM Tutor, or **Jeux interactifs.**

Chapter Test 45 min.

- Administer Chapter 2 Test. Select from Testing Program, Alternative Assessment Guide, Test Generator, or Standardized Assessment Tutor.

Chapter Opener

CHAPITRE 2

For resource information, see the **One-Stop Planner,** Disc 1.

Pacing Tips

This chapter is a review chapter, so students will recognize many of the functions presented. Students are presented with new vocabulary in the **Deuxième** and **Troisième étapes.** For Lesson Plans, and timing suggestions, see pages 31I–31L.

Meeting the Standards

Communication

- Welcoming someone; responding to someone's welcome, p. 37
- Asking how someone is feeling and telling how you are feeling, p. 38
- Pointing out where things are, p. 43
- Paying and responding to compliments, p. 44
- Asking for and giving directions, p. 49

Culture

- Culture Note, pp. 32, 33, 36, 39, 41, 47, 51, 57
- Note culturelle, pp. 39, 42, 44, 48
- Panorama Culturel, p. 45

Connections

- Multicultural Link, pp. 38, 45
- History Link, pp. 40, 47, 48
- Math Link, p. 43
- Architecture Link, p. 48
- Science Link, p. 50

Comparisons

- Thinking Critically: Comparing and Contrasting, p. 47
- Thinking Critically: Drawing Inferences, p. 50

Communities

- Career Path, p. 50
- De l'école au travail, p. 49

Cultures and Communities

Culture Notes

- France has had a serious shortage of housing since 1945. The problem is due in part to the antiquity of existing structures and also to the destruction of property during two world wars. From 1945 to 1974, France constructed more than 7 million new housing units, but gained more than 12 million new residents. As of 1990, there were estimated to be 26 million living accommodations in France.
- In 1962, only 41% of homes had indoor toilets **(des W.-C.)**, as compared to 94% in 1990. Only 29% had a shower or bathtub **(une douche, une baignoire)** in 1962, as compared to 94% in 1990, and only 11% had telephones. Even in 1990, only 76% of homes had a phone.

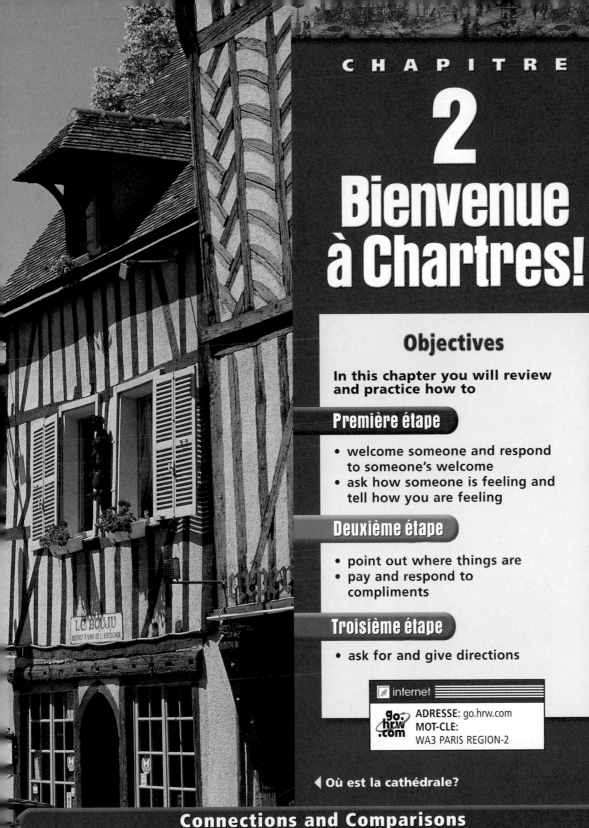

CHAPITRE 2

Bienvenue à Chartres!

Objectives

In this chapter you will review and practice how to

Première étape

- welcome someone and respond to someone's welcome
- ask how someone is feeling and tell how you are feeling

Deuxième étape

- point out where things are
- pay and respond to compliments

Troisième étape

- ask for and give directions

internet

go.hrw.com
ADRESSE: go.hrw.com
MOT-CLE:
WA3 PARIS REGION-2

◀ **Où est la cathédrale?**

CHAPITRE 2

Focusing on Outcomes

Have students match the photo caption with the correct outcome. Ask them to recall expressions they've already learned to accomplish these functions. NOTE: The self-check activities on page 58 help students assess their achievement of the objectives.

Culture Note

Many French homes are furnished with beautiful antiques, rich with history. Some common styles of furniture are Louis XIV **(Louis quatorze)** from the seventeenth century; Louis XVI **(Louis seize)** from the eighteenth century; **le style empire** and **le style second empire,** dating from the reigns of Napoleon I and III and Louis-Philippe from the nineteenth century. Many country homes have furniture in **le style rustique** (traditional, provincial style, which is simple, heavy, and unrefined).

Chapter Sequence

Connections and Comparisons

Thinking Critically

Analyzing If any of your students have participated in a foreign exchange program, have them describe some of the differences they found in family life or in the home where they stayed. If students have ever hosted an exchange student, have them tell what the visitor found different. If no one has had one of these experiences, share one of your own or ask students to imagine the adjustments they would have to make in these situations.

STANDARDS: 4.2

Mise en train

CHAPITRE 2

Teaching Resources
pp. 34–36

PRINT 
- Lesson Planner, p. 6
- Video Guide, pp. 10, 12
- Cahier d'activités, p. 13

MEDIA
- One-Stop Planner
- Video Program
  Mise en train
  Videocassette 1, 18:47–22:26
  Videocassette 5 (captioned version), 09:04–12:43
  Suite
  Videocassette 1, 22:31–27:10
  Videocassette 5 (captioned version), 12:49–17:29
- DVD Tutor, Disc 1
- Audio Compact Discs, CD 2, Trs. 1–2
- **Mise en train** Transparencies

Motivating Activity
Ask students to imagine themselves arriving at a host family's home in a foreign country. What are some of the things they would need to be able to say or ask in the first 30 minutes? On the first day? On later occasions?

Presenting
Mise en train
Before showing the video, ask students to identify the characters. Ask them what they remember about the characters from Chapter 1 and what they can tell you about this story based on the photos. You might also have students complete the Preteaching Vocabulary suggestion below. Then, have students view the video. Ask the questions in **Tu as compris?** on page 36 to check comprehension.

Mise en train Transparencies

The **roman-photo** is an abridged version of the video episode.

MISE EN TRAIN ▪ *Une nouvelle vie*

CD 2 Trs. 1–2

DVD VIDEO

Stratégie pour comprendre
Pamela is seeing the Lepic house for the first time. What are some of the phrases that Sandra uses to point things out? Pay attention to Sandra's gestures and to keywords to help you understand. What does Pamela want to do after seeing the house? What does she do instead?

Sandra

Pamela

Mme Lepic

1

Sandra Voici notre maison. Bienvenue chez nous.
Pamela C'est sympa ici.
Mme Lepic Tu trouves?
Sandra Viens, Pamela, on va visiter la maison.

2

Sandra Ça, c'est l'entrée… Et là, c'est le salon.
Pamela J'aime bien.

3

Sandra Ça, c'est la salle à manger…

4

Sandra Et voilà la cuisine…

Preteaching Vocabulary

Guessing words from context Ask students what words and expressions they would use to welcome someone to their home. Have them scan the pictures in the story and tell what Sandra is doing (she is welcoming Pamela and showing her guest around the house). Before students read *Une nouvelle vie,* have them guess the meaning of the following words based on the context.

2. le salon
3. la salle à manger
4. la cuisine
5. les toilettes
6. la salle de bains
7. la chambre

STANDARDS: 1.2

5 **Sandra** Alors, là, à droite, ce sont nos toilettes.

6 **Sandra** Notre salle de bains est à côté.

7 **Sandra** Et voilà ta chambre.
Pamela Elle est géniale.

8 **Sandra** Ça va? Pas trop fatiguée?
Pamela Non, ça va. J'ai envie de visiter la cathédrale. C'est loin d'ici?
Sandra Non, c'est tout près. Tu prends la rue du Soleil d'Or, à gauche. Puis tu tournes à droite. Et la cathédrale est sur ta droite.

9 **Pamela** On peut y aller aujourd'hui?
Sandra Euh… d'accord.

10 **Sandra** Bon, fais comme chez toi.
Pamela Merci. A tout de suite, alors.

11 **Une demi-heure plus tard…**
Sandra On y va, Pamela? … Pamela?

Cahier d'activités, p. 13, Act. 1

Mise en train

CHAPITRE 2

Teaching Suggestion

On the board or on a transparency, list in random order the rooms of the house that are introduced in the **Mise en train.** Number your random list. Then, have students view the video and write the numbers of the rooms in the order in which Sandra shows them to Pamela during the tour of the house.

Language Note

The top floor of many French homes is often directly under a pointed, steep roof. Therefore, rooms on the top floor with slanted interior walls (see Photo 7) are quite common. They are called **des chambres mansardées.**

Mise en train (suite)

When the story continues, Sandra and Pamela are in Chartres. Pamela changes money, buys a tourist guide, and she and Sandra visit the cathedral. Then they walk around the old section of town, **le Vieux Chartres.** Sandra keeps expecting Pamela to get tired, but she is full of energy!

Using the Captioned Video/DVD

If students have difficulty understanding French spoken at a normal speed, use Videocassette 5 to allow students to see the French captions for ***Une nouvelle vie*** and ***Une nouvelle vie (suite).*** Hearing the language and watching the story will reduce anxiety about the new language and facilitate comprehension. The reinforcement of seeing the written vocabulary words as they watch the gestures and actions will help prepare students to do the comprehension activities on page 36.

NOTE: The *DVD Tutor* contains captions for all sections of the *Video Program.*

Mise en train

CHAPITRE 2

Building on Previous Skills

3 Ask students to recall expressions for asking how someone is and for responding. **(Ça va? Comment ça va? Ça va bien. Très bien. Pas mal.)** Ask them if they remember how to express a desire for something **(Je voudrais...).**

Captioned Video

3 To complete this activity, you might play the captioned version of ***Une nouvelle vie*** on Videocassette 5 (or DVD Disc 1) and have students raise their hands when they identify one of the expressions from the activity.

Culture Note

Point out the difference between **les toilettes** and **la salle de bains. La salle de bains** is used only for washing and bathing. For this reason, one never refers to a public restroom as **la salle de bains.** It is called **les toilettes** or **les W.-C.**

Using the DVD Tutor

For additional practice with the **Mise en train,** have students complete the **Compréhension** activities on Disc 1 of the *DVD Tutor.*

These activities check for comprehension only. Students should not yet be expected to produce language modeled in **Mise en train.**

1 Tu as compris? See answers below.

1. Which rooms of the Lepic house does Pamela see?
2. What would Pamela like to do?
3. Why don't the girls visit the cathedral?

2 Qui...

1. trouve la maison sympa? Pamela
2. montre la maison à Pamela? Sandra
3. aimerait bien visiter la cathédrale? Pamela
4. explique comment aller à la cathédrale? Sandra

3 Cherche les expressions See answers below.

1. How does . . .
   - **a.** Sandra welcome Pamela?
   - **b.** Mrs. Lepic respond to a compliment?
   - **c.** Sandra ask how Pamela's feeling?
   - **d.** Sandra tell Pamela to make herself at home?
2. How does Pamela . . .
   - **a.** pay compliments?
   - **b.** say how she's feeling?
   - **c.** express a desire to do something?

4 C'est quelle pièce?

Qu'est-ce que Sandra dit pour montrer chaque pièce?

1. Ce sont nos toilettes.

2. Notre salle de bains est à côté.

3. Et voilà ta chambre.

4. Ça, c'est la salle à manger.

5. Et voilà la cuisine.

5 Et maintenant, à toi

Imagine que tu arrives dans une ville française. Qu'est-ce que tu aimerais faire?

Answers

1
1. entrance hallway, living room, dining room, kitchen, toilets, bathroom, Pamela's bedroom
2. visit the cathedral
3. Pamela falls asleep.

3
1. a. Bienvenue chez nous.
   b. Tu trouves?
   c. Ça va? Pas trop fatiguée?
   d. Fais comme chez toi.
2. a. C'est sympa ici.
   b. Non, ça va.
   c. J'ai envie de visiter la cathédrale.

Comprehension Check

Additional Practice

2 Have students work in pairs. One student reads aloud a sentence from the **Mise en train,** and the other, without looking in the book, tells who is speaking. They should take turns.

Challenge

2 Once students have correctly identified the person, ask them what the person said (or identify the frame number) that supports their response.

Auditory Learners

4 Randomly call out the rooms of the Lepic house represented in these illustrations and have students write down the numbers of the appropriate pictures.

Première étape

Objectives Welcoming someone; responding to someone's welcome; asking how someone is feeling and telling how you are feeling

WA3 PARIS REGION-2

BIENVENUE CHEZ NOUS, JEAN-CLAUDE!
...FAIS COMME CHEZ TOI...!

6 **Qu'en penses-tu?**

Parlons How does the guest act in the cartoon above? How should he act?

Possible answers: He acts as if he is at his own home. He should act with more respect and consideration.

Comment dit-on...?

Welcoming someone; responding to someone's welcome

To welcome someone:	To respond:
Bienvenue chez moi (chez nous). *Welcome to my home (our home).*	**Merci.** *Thank you.*
Faites comme chez vous.	**C'est gentil de votre part.**
Fais comme chez toi. *Make yourself at home.*	**C'est gentil de ta part.** *That's nice of you.*
Vous avez fait bon voyage?	**Oui, excellent.** *Yes, excellent.*
Tu as fait bon voyage? *Did you have a good trip?*	**C'était fatigant!** *It was tiring!*

Cahier d'activités, p. 14, Act. 2

7 **Bienvenue!** See scripts and answers on p. 31G.

Ecoutons Listen to the following dialogues in which people are being welcomed. Did they have a good trip or a tiring trip?

CD 2 Tr. 3

Teacher to Teacher

Deborah Zoernig
Lutheran High School South
St. Louis, MO

Deborah suggests this activity to practice the functions in this *étape*.

"Have groups of students make flashcards with clip art and photos from magazines. Cards should depict scenes from a student's arrival in a francophone home. The welcoming scene could be depicted by a graphic of a house; the house tour could be represented with pictures of different rooms; the "settling in" episode could be portrayed with graphics of food, drink, and a bed. Have groups of three students randomly choose a set of cards. One holds up the cards in random order as the other two say something appropriate for each scene. Students then redo the scenes in order."

Prem

CHAPIT

Teaching Resource

pp. 37–39

PRINT

- Lesson Planner, p. 7
- TPR Storytelling Book, pp. 8–9
- Listening Activities, pp. 11, 15
- Activities for Communication, pp. 7–8, 80, 83, 139–140
- Travaux pratiques de grammaire, pp. 12–13
- Grammar Tutor for Students of French, Chapter 2
- Cahier d'activités, pp. 14–15
- Testing Program, pp. 27–30
- Alternative Assessment Guide, p. 33
- Student Make-Up Assignments, Chapter 2

MEDIA

- One-Stop Planner
- Audio Compact Discs, CD 2, Trs. 3–4, 15, 21–22
- Teaching Transparencies: 2-1; **Grammaire supplémentaire** Answers; Travaux pratiques de grammaire Answers
- Interactive CD-ROM Tutor, Disc 1

Bell Work

Write sentences from the **Mise en train** in random order on the board. Ask students to rearrange them in the correct order to describe what happens in **Mise en train**.

Presenting Comment dit-on... ?

Write the new expressions on strips of transparency. Arrange some of the pieces on the projector to create a formal conversation and present each sentence. Then, shuffle the strips and have students place them in order. Finally, have students deduce the informal forms.

- TPR St[illegible] 8–9
- Listening Activit[illegible] 1, 15
- Activities for Communication, pp. 7–8, 80, 83, 139–140
- Travaux pratiques de grammaire, pp. 12–13
- Grammar Tutor for Students of French, Chapter 2
- Cahier d'activités, pp. 14–15
- Testing Program, pp. 27–30
- Alternative Assessment Guide, p. 33
- Student Make-Up Assignments, Chapter 2

MEDIA

- One-Stop Planner
- Audio Compact Discs, CD 2, Trs. 3–4, 15, 21–22
- Teaching Transparencies: 2-1; **Grammaire supplémentaire** Answers; Travaux pratiques de grammaire Answers
- Interactive CD-ROM Tutor, Disc 1

Teaching Suggestion

8 Students might work in pairs, taking turns being the host and the guest. You might also have individuals write out these conversations.

Presenting

Comment dit-on... ?

Write the words **fatigué, faim, soif, un peu, crevé,** and **meurs** on the board. Act out their meanings, saying **Je suis fatigué(e), J'ai faim,** and so on. Have students repeat the expressions, acting them out with you. Then, have individuals come to the front of the class to mime the various expressions. Have students tell you what is being mimed. **(Elle a soif. Il meurt de faim.)**

Note de grammaire

Remember to use **tu** when talking to a friend, a family member, or someone your age or younger. Use **vous** when talking to more than one person or to someone older than you.

As someone gets to know you better, he or she might suggest using the **tu** form: **Alors, on se tutoie?**

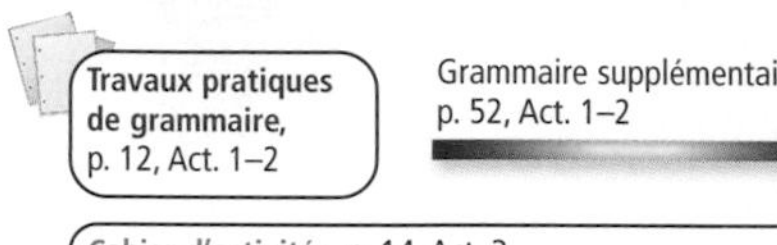

Cahier d'activités, p. 14, Act. 3

8 Grammaire en contexte

Parlons/Ecrivons Comment est-ce que tu accueilles ces gens quand ils arrivent chez toi? Qu'est-ce qu'ils te répondent?

Sandra

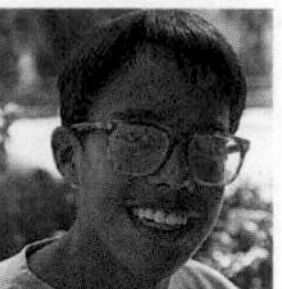
Thierry

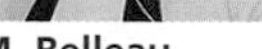
M. Belleau

Mme Ducharme

Comment dit-on...?

Asking how someone is feeling and telling how you are feeling

CD-ROM 1 DVD 1

To ask how someone is feeling:

Pas trop fatigué(e)? *(You're) not too tired?*
Vous n'avez pas faim?
Tu n'as pas faim? *Aren't you hungry?*
Vous n'avez pas soif?
Tu n'as pas soif? *Aren't you thirsty?*

To tell how you are feeling:

Non, ça va. *No, I'm fine.*
Si, je suis crevé(e). *Yes, I'm exhausted.*
Si, un peu. *Yes, a little.*
Si, j'ai très faim/soif! *Yes, I'm very hungry/thirsty!*
Si, je meurs de faim/soif! *Yes, I'm dying of hunger/thirst!*

Note de grammaire

When you make a statement in French, your voice usually falls at the end.

To ask a yes-or-no question, simply raise the pitch of your voice at the end of a statement.

Tu as fait bon voyage?

You can also add **est-ce que** to the beginning of the question.

Est-ce que tu as fait bon voyage?

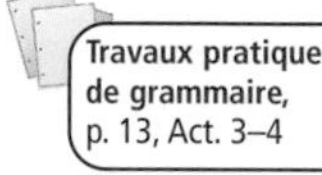

Grammaire supplémentaire, pp. 52–53, Act. 3–4

9 Les deux font la paire

Lisons/Parlons Avec ton/ta camarade, trouvez dans la colonne de droite la bonne réponse à chaque question ou commentaire de la colonne de gauche. Ensuite, crée une conversation logique avec ces phrases.

1. Tu as fait bon voyage? f	**a.** Non, ça va.
2. Tu n'as pas soif? b	**b.** Si, j'ai très soif.
3. Fais comme chez toi. d	**c.** Merci.
4. Bienvenue! c	**d.** C'est gentil de ta part.
5. Pas trop fatiguée? a	**e.** Si, je meurs de faim!
6. Tu n'as pas faim? e	**f.** Oui, excellent.

Connections and Comparisons

Language-to-Language

- Explain that the French often use the negative form of a verb to be more polite. For example, they might say **Tu n'as pas un stylo?** just as we might say in English *You wouldn't have a pen (I could borrow), would you?*
- Remind students that **si** is used to answer *yes* to a negative question.

Multicultural Link

Have students interview foreign exchange students, students of a different culture, relatives, or acquaintances to find out if there are both formal and familiar ways of saying *you* in their language. If so, have them find out when one may use the familiar form.

STANDARDS: 1.2, 4.1

Fais comme chez toi See scripts on p. 31G.

Ecoutons Il y a beaucoup de visiteurs chez Robert. Ecoute les conversations et choisis la scène qui représente chaque conversation. 1. b 2. c 3. a

CD 2 Tr. 4

a.

b.

c.

11 Ça ne va pas très bien!

Parlons/Ecrivons Comment est-ce que tu demandes à ces gens comment ça va? Qu'est-ce qu'ils répondent?

Caroline

Roberto

Mme Prévost

12 Jeu de rôle

Parlons Un(e) élève marocain(e) arrive chez toi. Accueille-le(la), demande-lui comment ça va et comment son voyage s'est passé. L'élève va te répondre. Continue la conversation. Joue cette scène avec un(e) camarade. Ensuite, changez de rôle.

Note culturelle

It is customary for guests to bring a gift when invited to a meal in a French home. Candy or flowers (other than chrysanthemums, which are associated with death) are always acceptable. When engaging in dinner conversation, there are several topics to avoid. These include asking about someone's age, profession, salary, or political affiliation.

13 Une bande dessinée

Ecrivons Crée une bande dessinée sur un(e) invité(e) qui n'est jamais content(e). Tu peux faire des dessins ou, si tu préfères, tu peux utiliser des images d'un magazine. Ecris la conversation entre cet(te) invité(e) et d'autres personnes dans des bulles ou sous les images.

Communication for All Students

Tactile/Visual Learners

9 Have students write the questions, comments, and responses on separate strips of paper. Then, have them arrange the strips to make a conversation.

TPR Tell students that they feel a certain way **(Vous avez faim!)** and have them act out their feelings to demonstrate their comprehension.

Première étape

CHAPITRE 2

Speaking Assessment

12 You might use the following rubric when grading your students on this activity.

Speaking Rubric	Points			
	4	3	2	1
Content (Complete–Incomplete)				
Comprehension (Total–Little)				
Comprehensibility (Comprehensible–Incomprehensible)				
Accuracy (Accurate–Seldom accurate)				
Fluency (Fluent–Not fluent)				

18–20: A 14–15: C Under
16–17: B 12–13: D 12: F

Teaching Suggestion

13 Students might assume the roles of the cartoon characters and present the cartoon to the class as a skit.

Culture Note

Because the French tend to be more guarded about their private lives than Americans, it is best to avoid personal questions altogether unless you know the person very well.

Assess

- Testing Program, pp. 27–30 Quiz 2-1A, Quiz 2-1B Audio CD 2, Tr. 15
- Student Make-Up Assignments, Chapter 2, Alternative Quiz
- Alternative Assessment Guide, p. 33

STANDARDS: 1.1, 1.3, 2.1, 3.1, 3.2, 4.2, 5.1, 5.2

Teaching Resources
pp. 40–44

PRINT
- Lesson Planner, p. 8
- TPR Storytelling Book, pp. 10–11
- Listening Activities, pp. 11–12, 16
- Activities for Communication, pp. 9–10, 81, 83–84, 139–140
- Travaux pratiques de grammaire, pp. 14–16
- Grammar Tutor for Students of French, Chapter 2
- Cahier d'activités, pp. 16–19
- Testing Program, pp. 31–34
- Alternative Assessment Guide, p. 33
- Student Make-Up Assignments, Chapter 2

MEDIA
- One-Stop Planner
- Audio Compact Discs, CD 2, Trs. 5–7, 16, 23–24
- Teaching Transparencies: 2-2, 2-A, 2-B; **Grammaire supplémentaire** Answers; Travaux pratiques de grammaire Answers
- Interactive CD-ROM Tutor, Disc 1

Bell Work
Write the following questions and responses on the board or on a transparency and have students rearrange them to make a conversation.
Si, un peu./C'était fatigant./ Vous avez fait bon voyage?/ Vous n'avez pas faim?/ Bienvenue chez nous./Faites comme chez vous./C'est gentil de votre part./Merci.

Additional Practice
14 Have students scan Pamela's journal entry and note what she says to give her impression of the Lepics and her new home.

Deuxième étape

Objectives Pointing out where things are; paying and responding to compliments

WA3 PARIS REGION-2

le 2 septembre

Cher journal,
Quelle journée! C'est aujourd'hui mon premier jour en France. La famille Lepic est super gentille.
Sandra m'a fait voir la maison. Elle est jolie, mais un peu bizarre. Ce n'est pas comme aux Etats-Unis. D'abord, quand on entre dans la maison, on n'est pas au premier étage, on est au rez-de-chaussée. Quand on monte l'escalier, on n'est pas au deuxième étage, on est au premier étage.

En plus, la salle de bains, c'est juste pour se laver. Les toilettes sont à part, de l'autre côté du couloir.
J'ai remarqué que les portes des chambres sont toujours fermées et qu'il faut frapper avant d'entrer. Dans ma chambre, mon lit est très confortable mais un des oreillers a une drôle de forme. Il est aussi large que mon lit. Ils appellent ça un traversin. Il n'y a pas de placard, mais une armoire pour les vêtements.
En tout cas, j'aime beaucoup la vie ici. C'est différent, mais c'est bien.

14 Ce n'est pas comme aux Etats-Unis!
Lisons Pamela a pris des photos pour illustrer son journal. Quelle photo correspond à ce qu'elle a écrit?
1. ...c'est juste pour se laver. b
2. Quand on monte l'escalier, on n'est pas au deuxième étage, on est au premier étage. c
3. Mon lit est très confortable... a
4. Il n'y a pas de placard, mais une armoire pour les vêtements. d

a.

b.

c.

d.

Connections and Comparisons

Language Note
Point out the expression **une drôle de forme** in Pamela's journal entry. Ask students to use this expression as they point out other things pictured in the chapter that look odd or different to them.

History Link
The word **armoire** was first used in the sixteenth century and sometimes denoted a cupboard set into the paneling of a room. These cupboards later evolved into free-standing cabinets, which were originally used to store arms. The cabinetmaker of Louis XIV, André-Charles Boulle, designed **armoires** that became examples of some of the most ornate, imposing pieces of Western furniture.

Vocabulaire

Pièces et meubles

CD-ROM 1 DVD 1

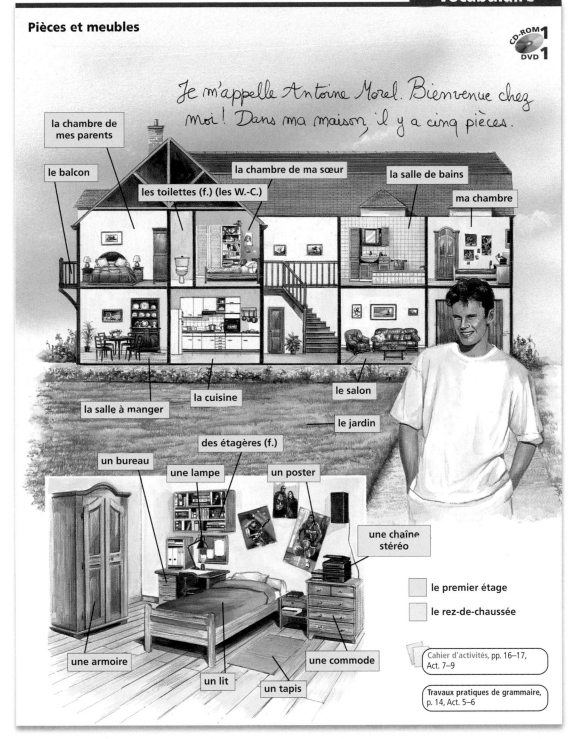

Je m'appelle Antoine Morel. Bienvenue chez moi! Dans ma maison, il y a cinq pièces.

la chambre de mes parents
le balcon
les toilettes (f.) (les W.-C.)
la chambre de ma sœur
la salle de bains
ma chambre
la salle à manger
la cuisine
le salon
le jardin
des étagères (f.)
un bureau
une lampe
un poster
une chaîne stéréo
le premier étage
le rez-de-chaussée
une armoire
un lit
un tapis
une commode

Cahier d'activités, pp. 16–17, Act. 7–9

Travaux pratiques de grammaire, p. 14, Act. 5–6

Presenting Vocabulaire

Show *Teaching Transparency 2-2* to teach the new words. Name each room as you point to it. Then, make statements about the different rooms and have students tell you whether the statements are true or false. **(Nous mangeons dans la salle à manger. Dans la cuisine, il y a une armoire.)** Then, point to the rooms and furnishings and ask either-or questions **(C'est la salle à manger ou la cuisine?)** to check comprehension.

Culture Notes

- Most French houses in the city are adjoining and have no front or side yard. The backyard is sometimes a courtyard shared by several houses.
- This house has five rooms **(cinq pièces)**. Point out that the French do not count the kitchen, bathroom, or W.-C. when counting rooms.

Communication for All Students

Additional Practice

Vocabulaire Give students a copy of the Transparency Master for *Teaching Transparency 2-2.* Have them cut out the various rooms and arrange them differently. Then, have students compare their version to the illustration in the book. **Dans le livre, il y a un lit dans la chambre, mais dans ma maison, il y a deux lits.**

Teacher Note

Have students name the floors of the house: **le rez-de-chaussée, le premier étage, le deuxième étage,** and so on. You might also refer students to the list of ordinal numbers on page R70.

Deuxième étape

CHAPITRE 2

Teaching Resources
pp. 40–44

PRINT

- Lesson Planner, p. 8
- TPR Storytelling Book, pp. 10–11
- Listening Activities, pp. 11–12, 16
- Activities for Communication, pp. 9–10, 81, 83–84, 139–140
- Travaux pratiques de grammaire, pp. 14–16
- Grammar Tutor for Students of French, Chapter 2
- Cahier d'activités, pp. 16–19
- Testing Program, pp. 31–34
- Alternative Assessment Guide, p. 33
- Student Make-Up Assignments, Chapter 2

MEDIA

- One-Stop Planner
- Audio Compact Discs, CD 2, Trs. 5–7, 16, 23–24
- Teaching Transparencies: 2-2, 2-A, 2-B; **Grammaire supplémentaire** Answers; Travaux pratiques de grammaire Answers
- Interactive CD-ROM Tutor, Disc 1

TPR Form groups of three to five. Each group should have a floor plan that another group has made and some pictures of furniture cut from magazines (see Group Work below). Have students take turns telling one another where to put the furniture. **(Mets la lampe dans le salon.)**

Possible Answers

16 Same things: bed, desk, stereo, chest of drawers, lamp
Different things: traversin/pillow, closet, blinds, bulletin board, doors, bookcase, poster, telephone, ceiling fan
Julie's bedroom; because of the blinds, homecoming corsage, telephone, and pillow

Note culturelle

You might be surprised at what you'll see—or won't see—in a typical French teenager's room. Some French homes don't have closets in the bedrooms, so clothes are hung in an armoire. Most families have just one television set, and it's in a room where everyone can watch it. In most French homes, the bathroom **(la salle de bains)** consists of a sink and a shower or bath. You will find the toilet **(les toilettes)** in a room separate from the bathroom. On many French beds, you will find a long pillow called a **traversin** that covers the width of the bed. Having a phone is expensive in France; there is a charge for each call made. For this reason, few young people have a phone in their room.

15 Dans quelle pièce? See scripts and answers on p. 31G.

Ecoutons The Morels are moving into their new home. Match the furniture with Mrs. Morel's instructions to the movers.

CD 2 Tr. 5

a.

b.

c.

d.

e.

16 Vive la différence!

Parlons/Ecrivons Julie et Nicole ont des choses semblables et des choses différentes dans leurs chambres. Qu'est-ce qu'elles ont qui est semblable? Qu'est-ce qui est différent? A ton avis, quelle chambre est sûrement la chambre d'une jeune Américaine? Pourquoi?
See answers below.

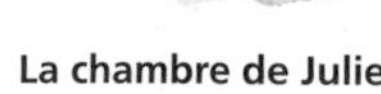
La chambre de Julie

La chambre de Nicole

Communication for All Students

Group Work

Form groups of three to five. Give each group a large sheet of butcher paper and have students draw an imaginary floor plan and label it. Then, have them cut out pictures of furniture from magazines to furnish the house and label them. Circulate around the room as they work and ask **Qu'est-ce que c'est?,** pointing to rooms or pieces of furniture in order to elicit the vocabulary. Do not have students glue or tape the furniture to the floor plan, however, as both can be used for other activities. Refer students to the Additional Vocabulary on page R14 for a list of house furnishings.

STANDARDS: 2.2, 3.2, 4.2

Dessiner, c'est gagner!

Parlons Dessine une section d'une maison, un meuble ou bien un objet de décoration. Utilise les nouveaux mots de vocabulaire à la page 41. Tes camarades vont deviner le mot en français. La personne qui répond en premier va faire un autre dessin.

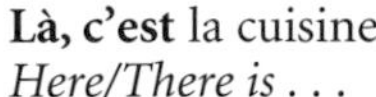

Comment dit-on...?

Pointing out where things are

CD-ROM 1 DVD 1

Là, c'est la cuisine.
Here/There is . . .

A côté de la cuisine, **il y a** la salle à manger.
Next to . . . there is . . .

Ça, c'est la chambre des parents, **en face des** toilettes.
This is . . . across from . . .

Cahier d'activités, p. 17, Act. 10

Chez les Morel

See scripts and answers on p.31G.

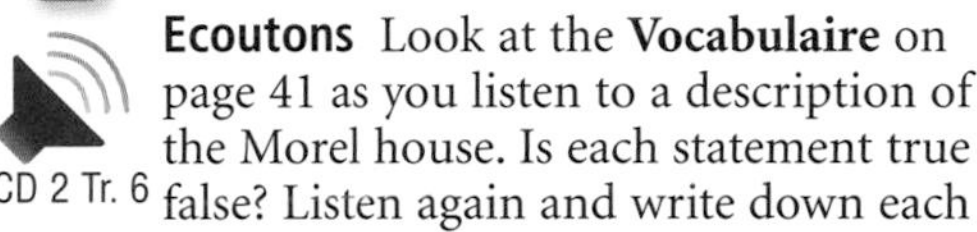

Ecoutons Look at the **Vocabulaire** on page 41 as you listen to a description of the Morel house. Is each statement true or false? Listen again and write down each statement, correcting those that are false.

CD 2 Tr. 6

Tu te rappelles?

To indicate where things are, you might also want to use **à gauche de** *(to the left of)*, **à droite de** *(to the right of)*, or **près de** *(near)*. Don't forget that after these prepositions, **de** becomes **du** before masculine nouns and **des** before plural nouns. It doesn't change before feminine nouns or nouns that begin with a vowel.

A gauche **du** salon...
Près **de la** cuisine...
A côté **de l'**étagère...

Grammaire supplémentaire, p. 53, Act. 5

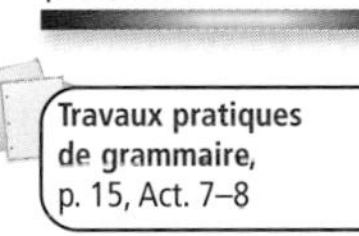

Travaux pratiques de grammaire, p. 15, Act. 7–8

C'est toi, le prof

Ecrivons Ecris cinq phrases (vraies ou fausses) sur la maison des Morel. Ensuite, lis tes phrases à un(e) camarade. Il/Elle va dire si chaque phrase est vraie ou fausse.

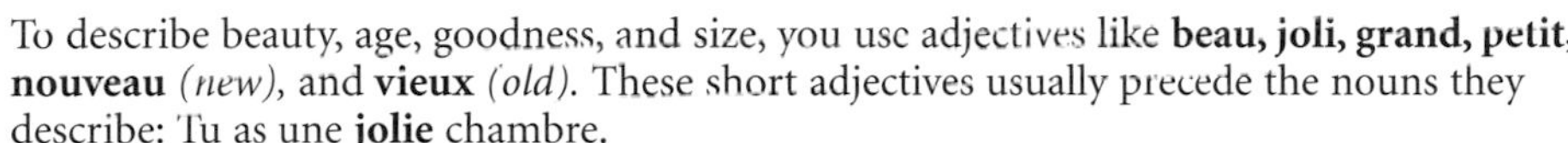

Grammaire

Adjectives that precede the noun

CD-ROM 1 DVD 1

To describe beauty, age, goodness, and size, you use adjectives like **beau, joli, grand, petit, nouveau** *(new)*, and **vieux** *(old)*. These short adjectives usually precede the nouns they describe: Tu as une **jolie** chambre.

- Some of these adjectives have irregular feminine forms: **beau/belle, nouveau/nouvelle, vieux/vieille**
- They also have irregular masculine forms that you place before nouns beginning with a vowel sound:

  (beau) un **bel** anorak **(vieux)** un **vieil** ami **(nouveau)** un **nouvel** hôtel
- To make **beau** and **nouveau** plural, add an **-x. Vieux,** however, doesn't change in the plural. To make **belle, nouvelle,** and **vieille** plural, simply add **–s.**

  Tu as vu ces **beaux** tapis? J'adore les **nouvelles** bottes de Sandrine!
- **Des** changes to **de** before an adjective that precedes a plural noun.

  Il y a **de** jolies fleurs dans ce jardin!

Grammaire supplémentaire, pp. 53–54, Act. 6–7

Cahier d'activités, pp. 17–18, Act. 11–12

Travaux pratiques de grammaire, p. 16, Act. 9–10

Connections and Comparisons

Math Link

Ask students to measure the length, width, and height of a room in their house (bedroom, living room) or a room at school (cafeteria, classroom) and convert feet and inches to meters and centimeters (1 m = 39.37 inches). Then, ask them to tell you the area of this room in square meters. They might also calculate the volume of the room in cubic meters.

Language Note

You might tell students that they can remember which adjectives precede the noun with the mnemonic device *BAGS* (Beauty, Age, Goodness, Size).

Deuxième étape

CHAPITRE 2

Presenting Comment dit-on... ?

Show a floor plan of a house on a transparency, such as *Teaching Transparency 2-2.* Point out the rooms and give their locations in reference to other rooms. Then, make some true-false statements about the house you've just described and have students reply **vrai** or **faux.** Next, ask questions, such as **Qu'est-ce qu'il y a en face de la chambre? Elle est où, la salle de bains?**

Teaching Suggestion

19 As an alternative activity, have students write sentences in a column labeled **Chez les Morel,** stating where the rooms are in the Morel house. Then, in a second column labeled **Chez moi,** have them give the locations of the same rooms in their own or an imaginary home.

Presenting Grammaire

Adjectives that precede the noun Write these sentences on the board:
J'ai un tapis rouge.
Carole est une fille sympa.
C'est un chien intelligent.
Have a volunteer circle the adjectives. Ask students where adjectives are usually placed in French. Next, distribute copies of the lyrics of ***Une perdriole*** *(Listening Activities,* page 90) and play the song. Have students circle the adjectives as they hear them. Ask students what they notice about the position of the adjectives. Read the **Grammaire** and have students name the adjectives in the song that are among those listed in the **Grammaire.**

STANDARDS: 1.2, 4.1, 5.2

Deuxième étape

CHAPITRE 2

Mon journal

21 Encourage students to use as many adjectives from the **Grammaire** as possible in their journal entries. Refer students to the Additional Vocabulary on page R16 for additional furnishings and adjectives. For an additional journal entry suggestion for Chapter 2, see *Cahier d'activités,* page 146.

Presenting
Comment dit-on... ?

Walk around the room, complimenting things that students have. Have students repeat the expressions after you. You might have students read the **Note culturelle** before they compliment one another.

Additional Practice

On a sheet of paper, have students use the adjectives in sentences. **(Elles sont belles. C'est une vieille armoire.)** Then, have them cut apart the words, shuffle them, and distribute them to a partner, who will rearrange the sentences.

Teaching Suggestion

To close this **étape,** have students imagine they are French students staying with an American family and write a journal entry similar to Pamela's on page 40. They should include a brief description of the house, a brief description of the room in which they are staying, and two compliments.

Assess

- Testing Program, pp. 31–34
  Quiz 2-2A, Quiz 2-2B
  Audio CD 2, Tr. 16
- Student Make-Up Assignments, Chapter 2, Alternative Quiz
- Alternative Assessment Guide, p. 33

20 Grammaire en contexte

Ecrivons Ta correspondante française Félicie t'a écrit une lettre. Elle décrit sa chambre. Complète sa description avec les formes appropriées des adjectifs entre parenthèses.

1. belle **2.** joli **3.** vieille **4.** nouveaux **5.** vieil **6.** petit **7.** nouvel **8.** beaux

J'ai une très __1__ (beau) chambre! D'abord, à côté de mon __2__ (joli) lit, il y a une __3__ (vieux) armoire que ma grand-mère m'a donnée. A droite de mon lit, j'ai de __4__ (nouveau) posters. Un __5__ (vieux) ami de mes parents m'a donné un __6__ (petit) bureau. A gauche de mon lit, il y a ma super chaîne stéréo, mes CD et mon __7__ (nouveau) appareil-photo que j'ai eu pour mon anniversaire. Voilà, je crois que je n'ai rien oublié... Ah si, j'ai aussi deux __8__ (beau) tapis de toutes les couleurs!

21 Mon journal

Ecrivons Imagine la chambre idéale. Fais-en une description dans ton journal. N'oublie pas les couleurs! Tu peux aussi faire un dessin.

Comment dit-on...?

Paying and responding to compliments

To pay a compliment:

Elle est vraiment bien, ta chambre.
Your . . . is really great.
Elle est cool, ta chaîne stéréo.
Il est beau, ton poster.
génial(e) *great*
chouette *very cool*

To respond:

Tu trouves?
Do you think so?
C'est vrai? (Vraiment?)
Really?
C'est gentil!
That's nice of you.

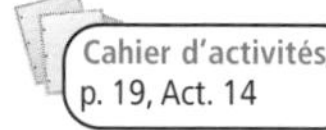

22 Quelle belle maison!

See scripts and answers on p. 31G.

CD 2 Tr. 7

Ecoutons Listen as Solange gives Arnaud a tour of her home. What does Arnaud compliment?

When you compliment a French person's home or possessions, the response will be the same as if you complimented the person's clothing or appearance. **Tu trouves? C'est vrai? Vraiment?** or **C'est gentil!** are standard responses to compliments. Remember that **merci** is not the only appropriate response.

23 Des compliments

Parlons Décris et «montre» ta chambre idéale à tes camarades. Utilise la description de l'activité 21. Chaque camarade va te faire un compliment. Chaque personne du groupe doit décrire sa chambre idéale et faire un compliment.

24 Elle est géniale, ta chambre!

Ecrivons Imagine que Nicole t'a envoyé un dessin de sa chambre (voir activité 16, p. 42). Ecris un petit mot à Nicole. Fais-lui des compliments sur sa chambre et sur les choses qu'elle a. Ensuite, décris ta chambre à Nicole. Dis-lui si tu as les mêmes choses ou si ta chambre est différente.

Communication for All Students

Auditory/Visual Learners

Have students describe their own home, or their ideal home, to a partner. First, have students draw unlabeled floorplans of the house they are going to describe. Then, one student should tell where several rooms are located in relation to others, while the other student fills in the names of the appropriate rooms on the drawing. Grades should be based on accuracy and comprehensibility.

STANDARDS: 1.1, 1.3, 2.1, 3.2, 5.1

Comment est ta maison?

We asked some young people to describe their homes. Here's what they said.

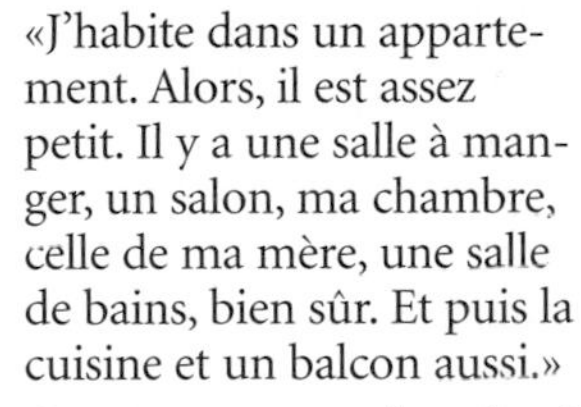

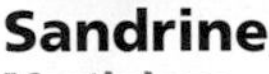

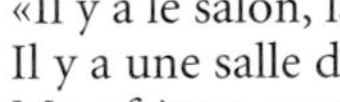

Geneviève,
Québec

«Il y a le salon, la cuisine. Il y a une salle de jeux. Mon frère a une chambre. J'en ai une. Euh... on a une salle pour nos bureaux. Après ça, il y a la salle de bains, il y a la salle de lavage.» Tr. 9

Sandrine,
Martinique

«J'habite dans un appartement. Alors, il est assez petit. Il y a une salle à manger, un salon, ma chambre, celle de ma mère, une salle de bains, bien sûr. Et puis la cuisine et un balcon aussi.»

Comment est ta chambre?

«Je pense qu'elle ressemble à la chambre d'à peu près toutes les filles de mon âge. Il y a des posters. J'ai une chaîne hi-fi aussi. Voilà.» Tr. 10

Adèle, **Cameroun**

«Ma chambre, je dirais d'abord qu'elle est assez belle. Ce sont mes goûts. Les murs sont blancs et on a fait des décorations en bleu parce que j'adore le bleu et le rose. Donc, j'ai assez de bleu et de rose dans ma chambre. J'ai d'abord comme meubles... j'ai une commode, mon bureau et c'est presque tout. Il n'y a pas grand-chose.» Tr. 11

Qu'en penses-tu?

1. How do homes in the United States differ from those described in the interviews? They are similar to those in the interviews.
2. What was not mentioned that is commonly found in American teenagers' rooms? Possible answers: telephone, television, computer

Savais-tu que...?

Homes in France are built of stone or cement blocks. In Quebec, houses are similar to American ones—often made of wood and painted in bright colors. Homes in Martinique and Guadeloupe can be large plantation-style houses or small cement-block houses. The porch is the central gathering place, and kitchens are sometimes separate to keep the rest of the house cool. In Côte d'Ivoire, villages are known for specific kinds of houses: some of clay, some of bamboo, and some built on stilts over lagoons. In cities, you'll see modern houses and apartments.

Connections and Comparisons

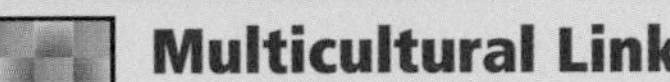

Multicultural Link

Ask students to find pictures of homes in different countries, provinces, or departments and to explain how the environment influenced the construction and design.

Thinking Critically

Ask students if they know of different ways in which houses are constructed in various regions of the United States. Ask how the different methods of construction are dependent upon the environment or other factors. (Coastal homes are built on stilts and basements are rare. On the east and west coasts, row houses are built to save space. In Alaska and California, homes are built to withstand earthquakes.)

CHAPITRE 2

Teaching Resources
p. 45

PRINT
- Video Guide, pp. 11–13
- Cahier d'activités, p. 24

MEDIA
- One-Stop Planner
- Video Program, Videocassette 1, 27:12–31:42
- DVD Tutor, Disc 1
- Audio Compact Discs, CD 2, Trs. 8–11
- Interactive CD-ROM Tutor, Disc 1

Presenting
Panorama Culturel

Have students list as many rooms and pieces of furniture in French as possible. Then, show the video and have students check off the items that they hear mentioned in the interviews.

Questions

1. **Qu'est-ce qu'il y a dans la chambre de Sandrine?** (des posters, une chaîne hi-fi)
2. **Qui a une salle de lavage dans sa maison?** (Geneviève)
3. **Les murs sont de quelle couleur dans la chambre d'Adèle?** (blancs)
4. **Adèle aime quelles couleurs?** (le bleu et le rose)

Using the DVD

For more practice with the **Panorama Culturel,** have students complete the **Panorama Culturel** section on the *DVD Tutor.*

STANDARDS: 1.2, 3.2, 4.2

Teaching Resources
pp. 46–49

PRINT

- Lesson Planner, p. 9
- TPR Storytelling Book, pp. 12–13
- Listening Activities, pp. 12–13, 17
- Activities for Communication, pp. 11–12, 82, 84, 139–140
- Travaux pratiques de grammaire, pp. 17–19
- Grammar Tutor for Students of French, Chapter 2
- Cahier d'activités, pp. 20–22
- Testing Program, pp. 35–38
- Alternative Assessment Guide, p. 33
- Student Make-Up Assignments, Chapter 2

MEDIA 

- One-Stop Planner
- Audio Compact Discs, CD 2, Trs. 12–13, 17, 25–26
- Teaching Transparencies: 2-3, 2-C; **Grammaire supplémentaire** Answers; Travaux pratiques de grammaire Answers
- Interactive CD-ROM Tutor, Disc 1

Bell Work

Write the following scrambled words on the board:

înache orésté/machber
arimero/rauube/strope

Have students unscramble the words. Then, ask them to imagine the items belong to a friend and write a compliment to their friend for each item. (Answers: **chaîne stéréo, chambre, armoire, bureau, poster)**

Troisième étape

Objectives Asking for and giving directions

go. hrw .com
WA3 PARIS REGION-2

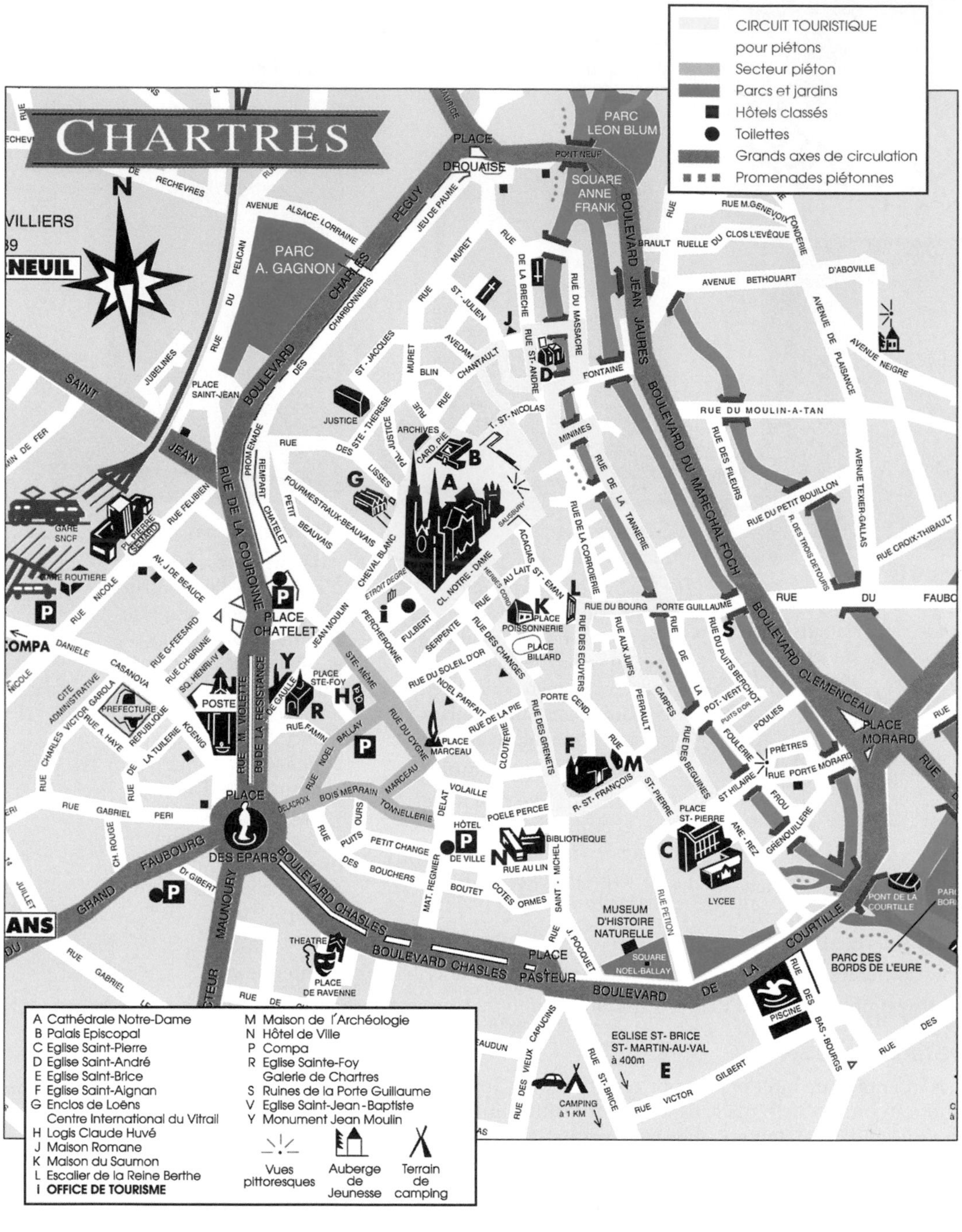

CHARTRES

CIRCUIT TOURISTIQUE pour piétons
Secteur piéton
Parcs et jardins
Hôtels classés
Toilettes
Grands axes de circulation
Promenades piétonnes

A Cathédrale Notre-Dame
B Palais Episcopal
C Eglise Saint-Pierre
D Eglise Saint-André
E Eglise Saint-Brice
F Eglise Saint-Aignan
G Enclos de Loëns
Centre International du Vitrail
H Logis Claude Huvé
J Maison Romane
K Maison du Saumon
L Escalier de la Reine Berthe
I **OFFICE DE TOURISME**
M Maison de l'Archéologie
N Hôtel de Ville
P Compa
R Eglise Sainte-Foy
Galerie de Chartres
S Ruines de la Porte Guillaume
V Eglise Saint-Jean-Baptiste
Y Monument Jean Moulin

Vues pittoresques
Auberge de Jeunesse
Terrain de camping

Communication for All Students

Auditory/Tactile Learners

Have pairs of students look at the map in their books as you describe the location of various buildings in relation to others, using **près de, à côté de, dans,** and **en face de.** Have partners point to the items on the map as you mention them. Then, ask students to complete sentences about the locations of the buildings. **(La bibliothèque est en face...)**

STANDARDS: 1.2, 3.1

25 Vrai ou faux?

Lisons Trouve les endroits suivants sur le plan de Chartres à la page 46. Ensuite, dis si les phrases suivantes sont vraies ou fausses.

1. La bibliothèque est à côté de la cathédrale. faux
2. La gare est près du parc des Bords de l'Eure. faux
3. La poste est dans la rue M. Violette. vrai
4. La piscine est près de la cathédrale. faux
5. Le lycée est à côté de l'église Saint-Pierre. vrai

Vocabulaire

En ville

un terrain de camping

une gare

une église

une piscine

une poste

un office de tourisme

une cathédrale	*a cathedral*	**un lycée**	*a high school*
un musée	*a museum*	**une auberge de jeunesse**	*a youth hostel*
un parc	*a park*	**une bibliothèque**	*a library*
une banque	*a bank*	**un théâtre**	*a theater*

Cahier d'activités, p. 20, Act. 17

Travaux pratiques de grammaire, pp. 17–18, Act. 11–13

26 Qu'est-ce qu'on fait? See scripts and answers on p. 31H.

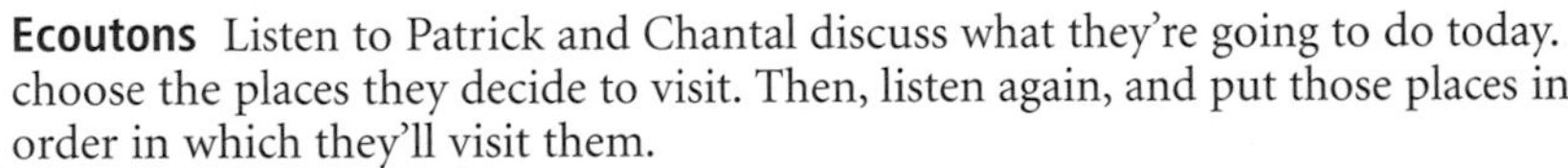

Ecoutons Listen to Patrick and Chantal discuss what they're going to do today. First, choose the places they decide to visit. Then, listen again, and put those places in the order in which they'll visit them.

CD 2 Tr. 12

a. le musée des Beaux-Arts
b. la cathédrale
c. le parc
d. l'office de tourisme
e. la poste
f. la piscine

Connections and Comparisons

Thinking Critically

Comparing and Contrasting Ask students to imagine why the street in the photo of the church is so narrow. (When the majority of French streets were constructed, they were built to accommodate pedestrians, horses, and carriages.) Ask them to think about the wide streets in the United States, particularly in the West, and how most of them were developed after the invention of the car.

History Link

Point out the contrast between the medieval church and the modern train station in the photos. Tell students that European towns exhibit both styles because of their ancient history. You might try to find pictures of some medieval towns, such as Carcassonne in the south of France, and Dinan in Bretagne, all of which clearly illustrate the contrast between medieval and modern architecture.

Presenting Vocabulaire

Using *Teaching Transparency 2-C,* say the new words and phrases aloud as you point to the corresponding picture. Then, make statements using the words **(On achète des livres dans un parc.)** and have students tell whether the statements are true or false.

Teaching Suggestions

- Have students write "clues" for each vocabulary word. For example, students might write **On y fait de la natation** for **la piscine.** Have students take turns reading their clues and having their classmates try to guess the places.
- Ask students if each of the places in the **Vocabulaire** exists in their town or neighborhood. If so, ask them what is next to it or across from it. **(Il y a une bibliothèque dans ta ville/ton quartier? Qu'est-ce qu'il y a en face de la bibliothèque?)**

Culture Notes

- Students may notice from the map of Chartres on page 46 that the town is not constructed on a north-south grid, thus forming city blocks as in the United States. Rather, French cities are generally built around a cathedral with the streets spiraling out from this central point.
- Students might like to know the meaning of the sign above the entrance to the post office. In France, you can have a savings account, purchase treasury bonds, and buy life insurance in the post office.

STANDARDS: 1.2, 3.1, 4.2

Teaching Resources
pp. 46–49

PRINT 

- Lesson Planner, p. 9
- TPR Storytelling Book, pp. 12–13
- Listening Activities, pp. 12–13, 17
- Activities for Communication, pp. 11–12, 82, 84, 139–140
- Travaux pratiques de grammaire, pp. 17–19
- Grammar Tutor for Students of French, Chapter 2
- Cahier d'activités, pp. 20–22
- Testing Program, pp. 35–38
- Alternative Assessment Guide, p. 33
- Student Make-Up Assignments, Chapter 2

MEDIA

- One-Stop Planner
- Audio Compact Discs, CD 2, Trs. 12–13, 17, 25–26
- Teaching Transparencies: 2-3, 2-C; **Grammaire supplémentaire** Answers; Travaux pratiques de grammaire Answers
- Interactive CD-ROM Tutor, Disc 1

Presenting
Note de grammaire

Contractions with *à* Clip pictures from magazines of the places pictured in the **Vocabulaire** on page 47. Mount them on colored construction paper, one color for pictures of feminine nouns, a second color for pictures of masculine nouns, and a third color for pictures of nouns that begin with a vowel sound. Tape the pictures around the room. Walk from picture to picture, telling students **Je vais à la gare** or **Je vais au parc.** Afterwards, ask students to deduce why you used **à la** or **au.**

Note de grammaire

When you're talking about going *to* a place, use **au** before masculine nouns, **à la** before feminine nouns, **à l'** before singular nouns that start with a vowel sound, and **aux** before all plural nouns.

Travaux pratiques de grammaire, pp. 18–19, Act. 14–16

Grammaire supplémentaire, pp. 54–55, Act. 8–10

Cahier d'activités, p. 20, Act. 18

27 Grammaire en contexte

Lisons/Parlons Où vas-tu pour…

1. envoyer une lettre?
2. faire du camping?
3. faire un pique-nique?
4. prendre le train?
5. nager?
6. admirer des œuvres d'art?
7. trouver un plan de la ville?
8. emprunter des livres?
9. voir des acteurs et des actrices?
10. admirer des sculptures?

28 Que faire?

Parlons Ton ami(e) et toi, vous arrivez à Chartres. Qu'est-ce que vous voulez faire le premier jour de votre visite? Choisissez trois choses.

EXEMPLE —**Tu as envie d'aller au parc des Bords de l'Eure?**
—**Non, ça ne me dit rien. Je préfère aller à la cathédrale.**
—**D'accord. Et après, on pourrait aller au théâtre sur la place de Ravenne.**

Si tu as oublié
making suggestions
va à la page 18.

Note culturelle

Notre-Dame de Chartres, one of the most famous Gothic cathedrals, was built in the thirteenth century on a site where a cathedral had stood since the sixth century. The cathedral can easily be recognized by its different towers—the plain Romanesque tower on the left and the more ornate Gothic tower on the right in the photo below. Spared in all major wars and conflicts, Chartres still has most of its original stained-glass windows, famous for their rich colors. The cathedral's flying buttresses, its great size, and its light-filled interior clearly illustrate the genius of Gothic construction.

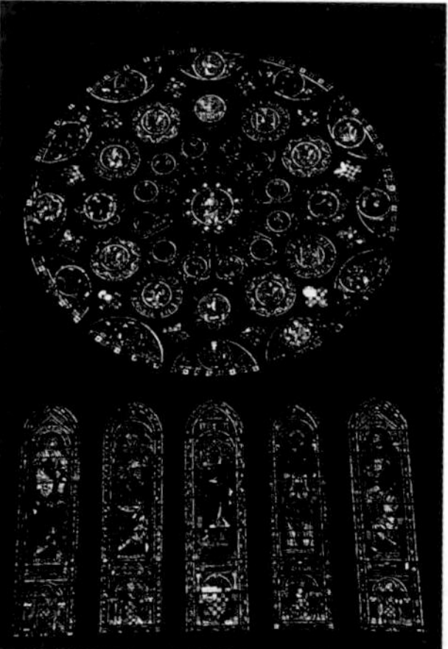

Connections and Comparisons

History Link

Note culturelle Ask students to imagine why the two towers are different. When the cathedral was destroyed by fire in 1194, only the crypts, western towers, and Royal Portal were left standing. The north tower was rebuilt in the later, High Gothic style. During World War II, the stained glass was dismantled and removed until the end of the war.

Architecture Link

The vaulted (pointed) arches of the Gothic cathedral support more weight than the rounded ones in earlier Romanesque architecture, allowing the walls to be thinner and the ceilings higher. Along with the wing-like exterior supports, called *flying buttresses,* the Gothic arch allowed for much larger openings in the walls for stained-glass windows, and a more open, airy atmosphere.

STANDARDS: 1.1, 2.2, 3.1

Comment dit-on...?

Asking for and giving directions

CD-ROM 1 DVD 1

To ask for directions:

Où est la gare, **s'il vous plaît?**

To give directions:

Traversez la place Châtelet et **prenez** la rue de la Couronne.
Cross . . . *take . . .*
Puis, tournez à gauche sur le boulevard de la Courtille.
Then, turn left on . . .
Allez/Continuez tout droit. La gare est **sur la droite** dans la rue Félibien.
Go/Keep going straight ahead. *on the right . . .*

Cahier d'activités, pp. 21–22, Act. 20–23

29 **C'est où?** See scripts and answers on p. 31H.

Ecoutons Look at the map of Chartres on page 46. Imagine you're at the **place des Epars.** Listen to the following directions and figure out where they lead.

CD 2 Tr. 13

à la cathédrale	à la poste	à la piscine
à l'église Sainte-Foy	au lycée	au parc Gagnon

30 **Comment y aller?**

Ecrivons Monsieur Dupont est en face de la cathédrale de Chartres, près des toilettes. Il veut aller au théâtre qui est sur la place de Ravenne, mais il ne sait pas comment on y va. Utilise le plan de Chartres à la page 46 pour compléter ce paragraphe pour aider Monsieur Dupont. **1.** à gauche **2.** à droite **3.** tout droit **4.** le boulevard Chasles **5.** à droite

Allez tout droit jusqu'à la rue Percheronne. Tournez __1__ dans la rue Percheronne. Ensuite, tournez __2__ dans la rue du Soleil d'Or. Continuez __3__ dans la rue Noël Ballay. A la place des Epars, tournez à gauche sur __4__. Le théâtre est __5__.

31 **Jeu de rôle**

You've just arrived at the train station in Chartres and can't wait to visit the town. Choose two places you'd like to go. Ask directions from people—who might not always send you the correct way! Act out a humorous scene. Use the map on page 46.

Vocabulaire à la carte

Zut!	*Darn!*
Oh là là!	*Oh my!*
Où je suis?	*Where am I?*
Qu'est-ce qui se passe?	*What's going on?*
Et alors?	*So what?*

32 **De l'école au travail**

Parlons Imagine que tu travailles à l'office de tourisme de Chartres cet été. Il y a beaucoup de touristes qui te demandent des renseignements pour trouver des sites touristiques. Ton/ta camarade va te demander comment trouver trois sites touristiques. Utilise le plan de Chartres sur la page 46 pour donner des renseignements pour aller de l'office de tourisme à quelques endroits. Ensuite, changez de rôle.

Communication for All Students

Game

Jeu d'obstacles To prepare for the game, create an obstacle course in the classroom by rearranging chairs, desks, and tables. Choose a finish line and two starting points equidistant from it. Form two teams. Choose one player from each team, blindfold them, and station them at their respective starting points. Have a member from the opposing team spin each blindfolded player around four or five times, then quickly call out **Allez!** The teammates of each blindfolded player must call out directions in French to get him or her safely to the finish line without hitting any of the obstacles. If the player hits an obstacle, he or she must stand in place for five seconds. The team whose player is first to reach the finish line wins. Repeat the process several times so that other team members may play.

Presenting
Comment dit-on... ?

Show *Teaching Transparency 2-3* to present the expressions. First, present the vocabulary as a conversation, asking where a place is and giving the directions. Trace the route with your finger on the transparency as you speak. Make statements about the places on the transparency and have students say whether your statements are true or false. Next, have students repeat each expression after you as you retrace the route on the map.

Language Notes

- Tell students that you say **sur le boulevard** and **sur l'avenue** but **dans la rue.**
- Other useful vocabulary items for Activity 32 are: **au coin** *(at the corner);* **au feu** *(at the stoplight);* **au carrefour** *(at the intersection).*
- Another acceptable way of expressing frustration is **Mince!** *(Darn!)*

Teaching Suggestion

Have students write and perform skits in which they give their classmates a tour of their town. They should re-enter expressions for asking how a student is feeling, such as **Pas trop fatigué(e)?** He or she might respond **Non, ça va.**

Assess

- Testing Program, pp. 35–38
  Quiz 2-3A, Quiz 2-3B
  Audio CD 2, Tr. 17
- Student Make-Up Assignments, Chapter 2, Alternative Quiz
- Alternative Assessment Guide, p. 33

CHAPITRE 2

Teaching Resources
pp. 50–51

PRINT 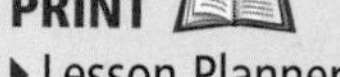
- Lesson Planner, p. 10
- Cahier d'activités, p. 23
- Reading Strategies and Skills Handbook, Chapter 2
- Joie de lire 2, Chapter 2
- Standardized Assessment Tutor, Chapter 2

MEDIA 
- One-Stop Planner

Prereading
Activity A

Career Path
Ask students if there are any international restaurants in their area. Have them imagine that they are employed by one of these restaurants. How would their knowledge of a foreign language help them in this career? Have them think about ordering supplies, creating menus, working with employees, and so on.

Reading
Activities B–F

Building on Previous Skills
Remind students of the French method of writing calendar dates using numerals. (The day is followed by the month. For example, the date **01/06** is read **le premier juin.**) Have students read aloud the dates in the brochures.

Answers
A. a tourist brochure; spend a day in Chartres; advertisements for tourist attractions in Chartres; use it to plan a day in Chartres

C. 1. Promotrain
2. Maison Picassiette
3. Centre International du Vitrail

Lisons!

PASSEZ UNE JOURNEE A CHARTRES

Stratégie pour lire
In Chapter 1 you reviewed the first two steps in reading a new selection: previewing and skimming. What should you do next? *Scan* to look for specific information. When you scan, you should look for key words to guide you to the specific information you want to find.

A. What kind of brochure do you see on these pages? What does the title mean? What kind of photos and art do you see? Who would use this information? See answers below.

B. Scan each section of the brochure briefly. Match the title of each section to the key word(s) that tell you what the section is about.

1. La Passacaille	a. les tours, découvrir
2. Le Musée des Beaux-Arts	b. cuisine traditionnelle
3. Au Plaisir d'offrir	c. cadeaux
4. La Sellerie	d. peintures, sculptures, art
5. Les Tours de la Cathédrale	e. pizzeria

C. Now that you have some key words in mind, scan the brochure again to figure out where you would go to . . . See answers below.
1. take a tour of Chartres.
2. see a house covered with pieces of pottery and glass.
3. learn about making stained-glass windows.

PASSEZ UNE JOURNEE A CHARTRES... VILLE D'ART

LE MUSEE DES BEAUX-ARTS
29, cloître Notre-Dame - 28000 CHARTRES
Tél. 02 37 36 41 39

Etabli dans l'ancien Palais Episcopal, le Musée des Beaux-Arts présente des collections conjuguant richesse et diversité : peintures (Holbein, Zurbaran, Chardin, une importante collection Vlaminck), sculptures, tapisseries, mobilier, émaux (XVIe s.), clavecins, arts décoratifs, art primitif océanien.

Accès : au chevet de la Cathédrale dans les jardins (secteur piétonnier).

Ouvert de 10 h à 12 h et de 14 h à 17 h toute l'année. Fermé mardi. Fermé dimanche matin du 1/11 au 31/03.

Plein tarif musée : 1,52€ Tarif réduit : 0,53€
Plein tarif exposition : 3,05€ Tarif réduit exposition : 1,52€

·R·E·S·T·A·U·R·A·N·T·
Au Chat qui Court
8 rue de la Couronne — Chartres — Tl. 02 37 28 55 10

UNE PROMENADE INSOLITE, SANS FATIGUE
Départ place de la Cathédrale. **Circuit commenté de 35 minutes** de **10 h à 19 h** dans le Vieux Chartres
de fin mars à la Toussaint (novembre)
Nocturnes en été
Prix :
4,57€ adultes
2,74€ enfants
Réservations groupes :
PROMOTRAIN
131, rue de Clignancourt
75018 PARIS - Tél. 01 42 62 24 00 - Fax 01 42 62 50 30

LA SELLERIE Restaurant
Cuisine traditionnelle dans un cadre rustique et incontournable
Salle de réception de 50 à 120 pers. - Aire de jeux enfants - Parking privé - Terrasse
48, RN 10 - 28630 THIVARS - Tél. 02 37 26 41 59
à 5 mn de Chartres
Menus à partir de 10€ tout compris
Menus enfants
Ouvert 7 j/7

Connections and Comparisons

Thinking Critically
Drawing Inferences Encourage students to skim each entry to determine what type of establishment is being discussed.

Science Link
Point out that the colors of the stained-glass windows **(les vitraux)** in the Gothic cathedrals were made by adding metal to the molten glass. Since different metals absorb light of different frequencies, the color of the glass varies according to the metal it contains. Copper was used for red, cobalt for blue, antimony for yellow, manganese for purple, and iron for green.

STANDARDS: 1.2, 2.2, 3.1

PIZZERIA
La Passacaille
Ouvert 7 jours sur 7
Salles climatisées
Spécialités italiennes
Pâtes fraîches maison
20 Pizzas au choix
30-32, rue Sainte-Même
entre la Place Châtelet et la Cathédrale
Tél. 02 37 21 52 10

LA MAISON PICASSIETTE

22, rue du Repos - 28000 CHARTRES - Tél. 02 37 34 10 76

Un univers surprenant : pas un centimètre de mur, pas un meuble qui ne soit tapissé d'éclats de vaisselle, faïence et verre divers. Un témoignage exceptionnel d'art populaire (classé Monument Historique).

Accès : entre la route de Paris et la route d'Orléans, proche du cimetière de Chartres.

Tous les jours sauf mardi 10 h - 12 h et 14 h - 18 h du 1/04 au 31/10.

Prix : 2,29€

LES TOURS DE LA CATHEDRALE

Découvrir Chartres et ses environs des tours de la cathédrale, base du "Clocher vieux" 800 ans d'âge, 103 m de haut et du "Clocher Neuf" élevé à 112 m au 16e s. par Jehan de Beauce.

Amateurs de photos, n'hésitez pas !

Accès : à l'intérieur de la Cathédrale près du portail nord (gauche).

Tous les jours excepté les matinées des dimanches et fêtes religieuses et durant certains offices et les 1/05, 1/11, 11/11, 25/12.

9 h 30 - 11 h 30, 14 h - 17 h 30 du 1/04 au 30/09

10 h 30 - 11 h 30, 14 h - 16 h du 1/10 au 31/03

Plein tarif : 3,81€
Tarif réduit : 1,52€

Au Plaisir d'offrir

Cadeaux - Souvenirs - Change - Toilettes

28, place Jean Moulin - Chartres

LE CENTRE INTERNATIONAL DU VITRAIL (C.I.V.)

5, rue du Cardinal Pie - 28000 CHARTRES - Tél. 02 37 21 65 72

Le Centre International du Vitrail a pour mission de promouvoir l'art du vitrail. Il offre au grand public les moyens de connaître et d'apprécier un art ancien que notre temps renouvelle. Il présente des expositions de vitraux de tous pays.

Accès : côté gauche rue parallèle à la Cathédrale.

Tous les jours de 9 h 30 à 12 h 30 et de 13 h 30 à 18 h

Fermeture du 1/04 au 12/04 et du 27/10 au 8/11 - Prix : 3,05€

D. Read more closely for the answers to these questions.

1. Where would you go if you wanted Italian food? La Passacaille
2. If you wanted to make a dinner reservation for a large group, which restaurant would you choose? La Sellerie
3. If you were an amateur photographer, would you be allowed to take pictures on the cathedral tours? Yes
4. If you plan to visit Chartres in July, will the train tour of Old Chartres run at night? Yes
5. Would you find the **Musée des Beaux-Arts** open on Tuesday? No

E. Choose activities that you can do on a Wednesday at 9:30 A.M., noon, 2 P.M., and 5 P.M. See answers below.

F. You and your friend Héloïse took photos of your day in Chartres. Complete these captions with information you scan from the brochure.

1. Me voilà à la Selleric. C'est la première fois que je mange...
2. Nous voilà au Musée des Beaux-Arts. Héloïse regarde...
3. C'est Héloïse et moi devant la cathédrale. On va...
4. C'est moi au Plaisir d'offrir. Si tu veux, on peut...

G. Create a travel brochure for French-speaking tourists about your town, city, or area. Draw and label pictures of places you think they would like to visit, or use photos from the newspaper. Be sure to include important information, such as times and days the places are open, the entrance fees, the type of food available, and so on. Before you make your final brochure, write a rough draft and have two classmates proofread it.

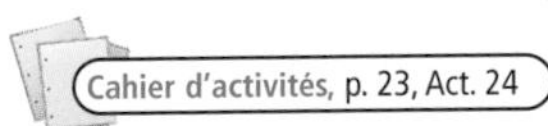
Cahier d'activités, p. 23, Act. 24

Lisons!

CHAPITRE 2

Postreading
Activity G

Cooperative Learning

Have students do this project in a group. Have the auditory learners survey the group and list the possible sights and activities from which the group will choose the contents of the brochure. Assign the visual/verbal learners the actual writing of the text. Kinesthetic learners will enjoy gathering and creating graphics for the brochure. Allow tactile learners to cut, paste, and arrange the brochure in its final form.

Language Note

Point out the word **change** in the ad for **Au Plaisir d'offrir** and have students try to guess what it means. (Tourists can exchange their foreign currency for local currency.)

Making Inferences

Ask students what kind of tourists would visit Chartres, according to the ads they see (i.e. photographers, art history majors, etc.). Have them point out specific ads and words in these ads to back up their inferences.

Answers

E. 9:30 a.m. — Le Centre International du Vitrail, visite des tours de la cathédrale
noon — Le Centre International du Vitrail, pizzeria, visite de Chartres en train
2 p.m. — le Musée des Beaux-Arts, visite de Chartres en train, La Maison Picassiette, visite des tours de la cathédrale, Le Centre International du Vitrail
5 p.m. — visite en train de Chartres, pizzeria, visite des tours de la cathédrale, La Maison Picassiette, Le Centre International du Vitrail

Cultures and Communities

Culture Notes

• Some of the most beautiful stained-glass windows in the world can be found in Paris in the **Sainte-Chapelle**, a tiny chapel built by Louis IX in the **Palais de Justice** on the **Ile de la Cité**. This chapel was built in the thirteenth century to house a relic believed to be Jesus' Crown of Thorns.

• **La Maison Picassiette** was the home of Raymond Isidore. In 1928, he was employed as the caretaker of the Chartres cemetery, near which he built his home. He began collecting glass and pottery shards and eventually decided to use them to mosaic the walls of his home. His work spread to the exterior walls of his home and to the surfaces of his yard. In 1952, his work was complete after more than 29,000 hours of work.

STANDARDS: 1.2, 1.3, 2.2, 3.1, 4.2, 5.2

Grammaire supplémentaire

CHAPITRE 2

For **Grammaire supplémentaire** Answer Transparencies, see the *Teaching Transparencies* binder.

Grammaire supplémentaire

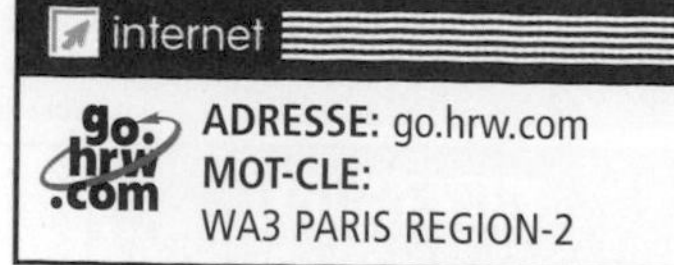

Première étape

Objectives Welcoming someone; responding to someone's welcome; asking how someone is feeling and telling how you are feeling

1 Décide si tu utilises **tu** ou **vous** pour parler aux personnes suivantes. Divise ta feuille en deux colonnes, l'une pour **tu,** l'autre pour **vous.** (**p. 38**)

EXEMPLE

tu	vous
	my teacher

your teacher — a classmate — your brother — your best friend — your friends Sabine and Robert — the family dog — your parents — your friend's mother — your 8-year-old sister — a police officer

2 Tu vas utiliser **tu** ou **vous** pour parler aux personnes mentionnées? Pose les questions suivantes et réponds aux questions en français. (**p. 38**)

1. Ask your best friend if he is not too tired.
2. Ask your parents if they are not hungry.
3. Tell your French teacher to make herself at home.
4. Ask your aunt if she had a good trip.
5. Respond to your older brother's welcome by saying, "That's nice of you."
6. Ask your family dog if he's thirsty.
7. Tell a classmate to make himself at home.
8. Ask your friends Marion and Diane if they had a nice trip.
9. Respond to your neighbors' welcome by saying, "That's nice of you."

3 Tu parles avec des amis à une fête. Tu poses une question à quelqu'un mais il/elle ne t'entend pas parce qu'il y a trop de bruit. Répète tes questions, avec **est-ce que.** (**p. 38**)

1. Paul aime la musique?
2. Tu as fait bon voyage?
3. Vous êtes français?
4. Tu es d'ici?
5. On va danser?
6. Tu as déjà mangé?

Answers

1 tu : the family dog, your best friend, a classmate, your 8-year-old sister, your brother
vous : my teacher, your friend's mother, a police officer, your parents, your friends Sabine and Robert

2
1. Pas trop fatigué?
2. Vous n'avez pas faim?
3. Faites comme chez vous.
4. Tu as fait bon voyage?
5. C'est gentil de ta part.
6. Tu n'as pas soif?
7. Fais comme chez toi.
8. Vous avez fait bon voyage?
9. C'est gentil de votre part.

3
1. Est-ce que Paul aime la musique?
2. Est-ce que tu as fait bon voyage?
3. Est-ce que vous êtes français?
4. Est-ce que tu es d'ici?
5. Est-ce qu'on va danser?
6. Est-ce que tu as déjà mangé?

Grammar Resources for Chapter 2

The **Grammaire supplémentaire** activities are designed as supplemental activities for the grammatical concepts presented in the chapter. You might use them as additional practice, for review, or for assessment.

For more grammar presentations, review, and practice, refer to the following:

- Travaux pratiques de grammaire
- Grammar Tutor for Students of French
- Grammar Summary on pp. R23–R42
- Cahier d'activités
- Grammar and Vocabulary quizzes (Testing Program)
- Test Generator
- Interactive CD-ROM Tutor
- DVD Tutor
- **Jeux interactifs** at go.hrw.com

STANDARDS: 1.2

4

Pose une question à chaque personne d'après leur réponse. Utilise est-ce que pour poser tes questions. Après, choisis la photo qui correspond à chaque phrase. (**p. 38**)

a. 
b. 
c. 
d. 

1. — ...?
— Si, je meurs de soif.

2. — ...?
— Oui, j'ai très faim.

3. — ...?
— Oui, elle a les cheveux bruns.

4. — ...?
— Si, elle est très fatiguée.

Deuxième étape

Objectives Pointing out where things are; paying and responding to compliments

5

Utilise les expressions entre parenthèses pour décrire où se trouvent les personnes ou les choses suivantes chez toi. (**p. 43**)

EXEMPLE Mon livre / le bureau (sur) **Mon livre est sur le bureau.**

1. Ma commode / mon lit (à côté de)
2. Les toilettes / la chambre de ma sœur (en face de)
3. Le salon / la cuisine (loin de)
4. La salle de bains / ma chambre (à gauche de)
5. La salle à manger / la cuisine (à droite de)
6. Mon lit / mon bureau et ma commode (entre)
7. Le poster / ma chaîne stéréo (près de)
8. Le jardin / la maison (devant)
9. Les étagères / mon bureau (derrière)
10. Le balcon / la chambre de mes parents (à côté de)

6

Lorette décrit où elle habite. Complète sa description avec la forme correcte des adjectifs entre parenthèses. (**p. 43**)

J'habite dans un ___1___ (vieux) appartement. Dans l'appartement, il y a trois ___2___ (grand) chambres. Dans ma chambre, j'ai un ___3___ (joli) lit confortable avec deux ___4___ (beau) tables de nuit. J'ai deux ___5___ (grand) posters sur le mur. Je les adore! J'aime lire et j'ai beaucoup de ___6___ (vieux) livres sur mon étagère. Par terre, il y a deux ___7___ (petit) tapis verts. Il y a une ___8___ (vieux) armoire où je mets mes vêtements près de la ___9___ (grand) fenêtre. J'ai aussi deux ___10___ (jeune) chats noirs qui aiment dormir sur mon lit.

Grammaire supplémentaire

CHAPITRE 2

Answers

4
1. Est-ce que tu n'as pas soif?; c
2. Est-ce que tu as faim?; a
3. Est-ce qu'elle a les cheveux bruns?; d
4. Est-ce qu'elle n'est pas fatiguée?; b

5
1. Ma commode est à côté de mon lit.
2. Les toilettes sont en face de la chambre de ma sœur.
3. Le salon est loin de la cuisine.
4. La salle de bains est à gauche de ma chambre.
5. La salle à manger est à droite de la cuisine.
6. Mon lit est entre mon bureau et ma commode.
7. Le poster est près de ma chaîne stéréo.
8. Le jardin est devant la maison.
9. Les étagères sont derrière mon bureau.
10. Le balcon est à côté de la chambre de mes parents.

6
1. vieil
2. grandes
3. joli
4. belles
5. grands
6. vieux
7. petits
8. vieille
9. grande
10. jeunes

Communication for All Students

Additional Practice

1 You might want to supplement Activity 1 by practicing **tu** and **vous** with pictures of people from a picture file or magazine. Hold up a picture and have students tell if they would use the **tu** or the **vous** form when addressing the subjects in your pictures.

Grammaire supplémentaire

CHAPITRE 2

For **Grammaire supplémentaire** Answer Transparencies, see the *Teaching Transparencies* binder.

Answers

7
1. J'ai un grand lit.
2. J'ai beaucoup de livres intéressants.
3. J'ai un tapis vert.
4. J'ai une belle lampe.
5. J'ai un vieil ordinateur.
6. J'ai deux tables de nuit super.
7. J'ai un joli bureau.
8. J'ai trois nouveaux disques.
9. J'ai de belles fleurs.
10. J'ai un petit téléphone.

8
1. à la
2. à la
3. au
4. au
5. à la
6. à l'
7. au
8. à la

9 *Possible answers:*
1. Je vais au terrain de camping.
2. Je vais au cinéma.
3. Je vais à la bibliothèque.
4. Je vais au lycée.
5. Je vais à la poste.
6. Je vais à la gare.
7. Je vais au parc.
8. Je vais au musée.

Grammaire supplémentaire

WA3 PARIS REGION-2

7 Utilise les mots proposés pour écrire une phrase qui décrit ce qu'il y a dans ta chambre. Utilise la forme correcte de l'adjectif et place-le correctement dans la phrase. (**p. 43**)

EXEMPLE une chaîne stéréo / nouveau
J'ai une nouvelle chaîne stéréo.

1. un lit / grand
2. beaucoup de livres / intéressant
3. un tapis / vert
4. une lampe / beau
5. un ordinateur / vieux
6. deux tables de nuit / super
7. un bureau / joli
8. trois disques / nouveau
9. des fleurs / beau
10. un téléphone / petit

Troisième étape

Objectives Asking for and giving directions

8 Manon essaie de décider où elle va aller demain. Utilise **au, à la** et **à l'** pour compléter les phrases suivantes. (**p. 48**)

EXEMPLE Elle veut voir une exposition. Elle va **au** musée.

1. Elle veut envoyer une lettre. Elle va _____ poste.
2. Elle veut emprunter des livres. Elle va _____ bibliothèque.
3. Elle veut faire du camping. Elle doit aller _____ terrain de camping.
4. Elle préfère étudier avec des amis. Elle va _____ lycée.
5. Elle va acheter des billets de train. Elle doit aller _____ gare.
6. Elle veut lire des brochures sur la ville. Elle va _____ office de tourisme.
7. Elle veut faire un pique-nique. Elle doit aller _____ parc.
8. Elle veut nager. Elle va _____ piscine.

9 Dis où tu vas pour faire les choses suivantes. (**p. 48**)

EXEMPLE nager? **Je vais à la piscine.**

1. faire du camping?
2. voir un film?
3. rendre des livres?
4. passer un examen?
5. acheter des timbres?
6. prendre le train?
7. jouer au foot?
8. admirer des tableaux?

Teacher to Teacher

Deborah Zoernig
Lutheran High School South
St. Louis, MO

Deborah suggests this activity to practice the grammar in the chapter.
"Use a digital camera to take pictures of objects in your classroom, including old, new, and beautiful things (for example, posters of France). Save the photos in a folder on the school's server and title the files with the names of the objects. Go to the computer lab and have the students access the files. Students should jot down each file name. For each file, they should write their own opinions, and, of course, use the correct forms of the adjectives that precede nouns! Save paper by requiring students to email their answers to you."

Grammaire supplémentaire

CHAPITRE 2

10 Tu visites la ville et tu as besoin de demander aux gens comment aller à certains endroits. Utilise **à la, au** et **à l'** pour compléter les phrases suivantes. Après, choisis les renseignements qui correspondent avec l'endroit où tu vas en ville. (**p. 48**)

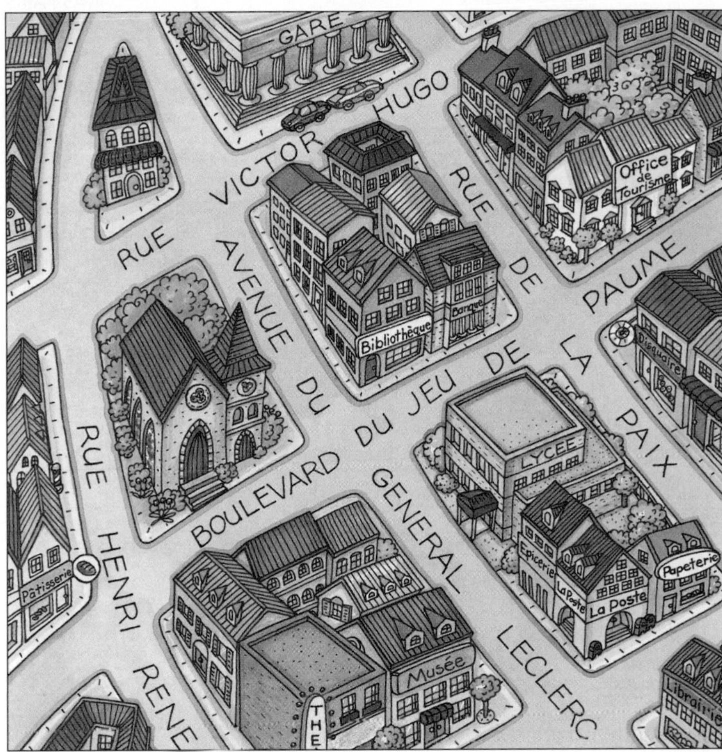

1. Tu es _____ office de tourisme et tu veux aller _____ église.
   _____

2. Tu es _____ banque et tu veux aller _____ lycée.
   _____

3. Tu es _____ gare et tu veux aller _____ poste.
   _____

4. Tu es _____ bibliothèque et tu veux aller _____ pâtisserie.
   _____

a. Prenez le boulevard du Jeu de Paume et tournez à gauche sur l'avenue du Général Leclerc. C'est à gauche.

b. Prenez le boulevard du Jeu de de Paume. Traversez l'avenue de Général Leclerc et la rue Henri René. C'est à droite.

c. Prenez le boulevard du Jeu de Paume. Traversez la rue de la Paix et l'avenue du Général Leclerc. C'est à droite.

d. Prenez la rue Victor Hugo, tournez à gauche sur l'avenue du Général Leclerc. Traversez le boulevard du Jeu de Paume et continuez tout droit. C'est à gauche.

Review and Assess

You may wish to assign the **Grammaire supplémentaire** activities as additional practice or homework after presenting material throughout the chapter. Assign Activities 1–2 after the first **Note de grammaire** (p. 38), Activities 3–4 after the second **Note de grammaire** (p. 38), Activities 5–7 after **Grammaire** (p. 43), and Activities 8–10 after **Note de grammaire** (p. 48).

To prepare students for the **Etape** Quizzes and Chapter Test, we suggest doing the **Grammaire supplémentaire** activities in the following order. Have students complete Activities 1–4 before Quizzes 2-1A or 2-1B; Activities 5–7 before Quizzes 2-2A or 2-2B; and Activities 8–10 before Quizzes 2-3A or 2-3B.

Answers

10
1. à l', à l'; c
2. à la, au; a
3. à la, à la; d
4. à la, à la; b

C H A P I T R E 2

The **Mise en pratique** reviews and integrates all four skills and culture in preparation for the Chapter Test.

Teaching Resources
pp. 56–57

PRINT

- Lesson Planner, p. 10
- TPR Storytelling Book, pp. 14–15
- Listening Activities, p. 13
- Video Guide, pp. 11, 14
- Grammar Tutor for Students of French, Chapter 2
- Standardized Assessment Tutor, Chapter 2

MEDIA 

- One-Stop Planner
- Video Program Videocassette 1, 31:44–32:40
- DVD Tutor, Disc 1
- Audio Compact Discs, CD 2, Tr. 14
- Interactive CD-ROM Tutor, Disc 1

Challenge/Auditory Learners

1 Have students imagine they are employees at the newspaper who take the ads over the phone. "Phone in" one or two of the ads and let them take dictation.

Language Note

1 Point out that **location** is a **faux ami.** It means *rental,* not *location.* The verb *to rent* is **louer.**

Mise en pratique

Echanges Location

Paris, Ile Saint-Louis : appartement 5 pièces, 3 chambres, 1 bain, 2 W.-C., vue Seine et Notre-Dame. Disponible fin juin-mi août contre logement en Californie. 01.45.15.92.38

Alpes, Brides-les-Bains : chalet en bois, 2 chambres, salon - coin cuisine, près des pistes de ski. Disponible hiver contre logement en Floride. 04.79.55.24.37

Côte d'Azur, Le Lavandou : villa, 7 pièces, cuisine équipée, piscine, jardin, 3 chambres, 2 bains, 2 W.- C., vue mer contre logement côte Est des Etats-Unis. 04.94.05.89.63

Franche-Comté, Marigny : ancienne ferme, 5 pièces, style rustique, cuisine moderne, grand jardin, recherche logement Mid-West. 03.84.25.74.47

Loire, Blois : Maison moderne centre-ville, cuisine, salon-salle à manger, 3 chambres, 1 bain-W.- C., jardin. Contre logement en Louisiane. 02.54.74.27.05

1 French people who would like to exchange homes with people in the United States placed the above ads. Which house would you like to stay in and why?

1. In what order is the following information given?

- **a.** type of home 1
- **b.** where the family would like to exchange 3
- **c.** phone number 4
- **d.** list of rooms 2

2. Which home(s) would be the best choice for you if . . . See answers below.

- **a.** you liked to swim?
- **b.** you lived in California?
- **c.** you preferred country living?
- **d.** you liked newer homes?
- **e.** you had a large family?
- **f.** you liked to ski?

2 Look at this map of Paris. You're at the **place St-Michel** in the **Quartier latin** and you're trying to find the museum at the **centre Georges Pompidou.** You ask a passer-by who, unfortunately, gives you the wrong directions. Listen to the directions and figure out where they would actually lead you. le musée d'Orsay See scripts on p. 31H.

CD 2 Tr. 14

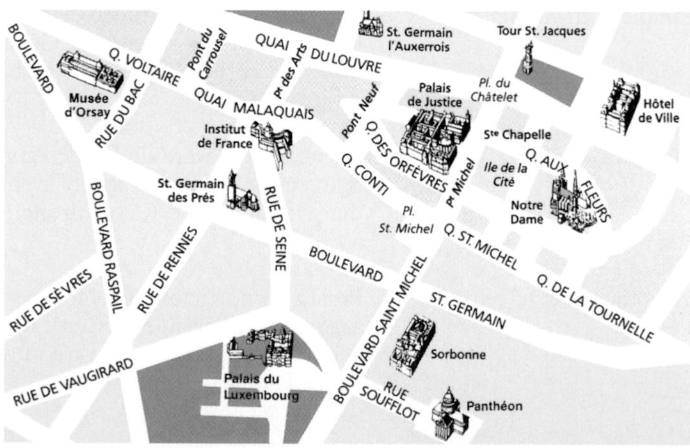

Apply and Assess

Teaching Suggestions

- To familiarize students with the newspaper ad, ask the following questions: **A Paris, l'appartement a combien de pièces? (cinq) Combien de chambres y a-t-il? (trois) Quel est le numéro de téléphone de l'immeuble à Paris? (01.45.15.92.83) Qu'est-ce qu'on peut faire à Brides-les-Bains? (du ski) Qu'est-ce qu'on peut voir de la villa sur la Côte d'Azur? (la mer)**
- You might write the following vocabulary words on the board for students to refer to as they do Activity 1: **une vue** *(a view);* **un chalet** *(a mountain cottage);* **en bois** *(made of wood);* **une piste de ski** *(ski slope);* **contre** *(a synonym for* **pour**); **équipée** *(equipped);* **une ferme** *(farm).*

Possible Answers

1 2. a. Côte d'Azur, Le Lavandou
b. Paris, Ile Saint-Louis
c. Franche-Comté, Marigny
d. Côte d'Azur, Le Lavandou; Loire, Blois
e. Paris, Ile Saint-Louis; Côte d'Azur, Le Lavandou; Franche-Comté, Marigny; Loire, Blois
f. Alpes, Brides-les-Bains

STANDARDS: 1.2, 3.1

3 Ecrivons!

Imagine you're an adult with your own home. For your vacation, you'd like to exchange houses with a French family, so you're going to place an ad in a French newspaper. Write an ad to encourage people to choose your home.

Stratégie pour écrire
Providing details will make your ad more appealing to prospective families. Sharp, specific details will grab your reader's eye immediately. Think about how you would describe your home to someone who has never seen it. You should include information about the climate where your house is located, the location itself, as well as the rooms in your home.

Préparation

Before you create your ad, you'll also want to think about your audience. Who will read your ad? What things might a French family visiting America look for in a house? Which of these features does your house possess? What other unique features does your house have? Jot down ideas for each of these questions.

Rédaction

Using your notes, write an ad persuading prospective families that your house is the one for them. When you give details, don't forget the adjectives you've learned. Remember also that organization is important in good persuasive writing. Point out what you feel is most appealing first and then progress toward points that are less important. You might refer to the ads on page 56 as a model.

Evaluation

After you've completed the first draft of your ad, read it over several times, but with a different purpose each time. Read through it once just to make sure you included all the important information. Next, make sure your ideas are arranged in a logical order. Finally, read for errors in punctuation, capitalization, and grammar.

4 Jeu de rôle

An American family has arranged to exchange homes with a French family. The Americans arrive at the French home before the French family leaves for the airport. Play the roles of the two families.

The French family should:

- welcome the American family.
- ask about their trip and how everyone is feeling.
- show the American family around their home.

The American family should:

- respond appropriately to the French family's welcome.
- tell how they are feeling.
- compliment the French family on their home and furnishings.

Mise en pratique

CHAPITRE 2

Culture Note

A **2 pièces** is the French equivalent of an American one-bedroom apartment or house. It includes a kitchen, bathroom, living room, and one separate bedroom. While the expression **une pièce** can be used to refer to an efficiency, people tend to use the word **studio** more often.

Slower Pace

2 Before you play the recording, have students locate on the map the square and the streets that they will hear mentioned **(la place Saint-Michel, le boulevard Saint-Michel, le boulevard Saint-Germain,** and **la rue du Bac).**

Teacher Note

For additional practice and review, you might use the **Histoire Finale** for Chapter 2 on pages 14–15 of the *TPR Storytelling Book.*

Portfolio

4 **Oral** This activity is appropriate for students' oral portfolios. For portfolio information, see the *Alternative Assessment Guide,* pages iv–17.

Apply and Assess

Process Writing

3 To extend this activity, ask groups of students to pretend they're real estate brokers who have just opened an agency specializing in vacation rentals. Have them create a "catalogue" of the homes they have available. They should group all their ads together in a folder and include photos or magazine cutouts. Then, have some students play the roles of the agents while others play the roles of tourists interested in renting one of the houses. Have students create a skit in which the tourists come to the agency and the agents show them the various homes that are available. The tourists should tell the agents what they're looking for, and the agents should describe and show the features of the various homes in their catalogues.

STANDARDS: 1.1, 1.3, 3.1, 5.1

CHAPITRE 2

Teaching Resources
p. 58

PRINT 

- Grammar Tutor for Students of French, Chapter 2

MEDIA  

- Interactive CD-ROM Tutor, Disc 1
- Online self-test

go.hrw.com
WA3 PARIS REGION-2

Teacher Note
This page is intended to help students prepare for the Chapter Test. It is a brief checklist of the major points covered in the chapter. The students should be reminded that this is only a checklist and does not necessarily include everything that will appear on the test.

Que sais-je?

WA3 PARIS REGION-2

Can you use what you've learned in this chapter?

Can you welcome someone and respond to someone's welcome? p. 37

1 What would you say to welcome . . . Possible answers:
1. your pen pal Jean-Louis? Bienvenue chez moi. Fais comme chez toi.
2. your mother's friend? Bienvenue chez nous. Faites comme chez vous.

2 How would you respond to your friend's father, who says . . . Possible answers:
1. Bienvenue chez nous. Merci.
2. Fais comme chez toi. C'est gentil de votre part.
3. Tu as fait bon voyage? Oui, excellent./C'était fatigant.

Can you ask how someone is feeling and tell how you are feeling? p. 38

3 How would you ask Etienne if he's . . .
1. not too tired? Pas trop fatigué?
2. hungry? Tu n'as pas faim?
3. thirsty Tu n'as pas soif?

4 How would you say that you're . . .
1. fine? Ça va.
2. very hungry? J'ai très faim.
3. a little thirsty? J'ai un peu soif.

Can you point out where things are? p. 43

5 When you're showing someone your home, how would you point out . . .
1. your room?
2. the bathroom?
3. the kitchen? See answers below.

Can you pay and respond to compliments? p. 44

6 How would you compliment someone on . . . ?
See answers below.

1.

2.

3.

7 How would you respond to a compliment?
Possible answers: Tu trouves? C'est vrai? Vraiment? C'est gentil!

Can you ask for and give directions? p. 49

8 How would you ask directions to . . .
1. the train station? Où est la gare, s'il vous plaît?
2. the post office? Où est la poste, s'il vous plaît?
3. the library? Où est la bibliothèque, s'il vous plaît?

9 How would you give someone directions from your school to . . .
1. your favorite fast-food restaurant?
2. the nearest movie theater?

Review and Assess

Game
C'est à toi! Form two teams and have the members of each team number themselves. Player one of Team A asks a question from **Que sais-je?** to player one of Team B. If the player answers correctly, Team B receives a point. If not, Team A may "steal" the point by answering the question correctly. Then, player two of Team B asks player two of Team A a question, and so on. Players may also make up additional questions based on the material in the chapter. Original questions are worth two points if answered correctly. Play for a predetermined length of time. The team with the most points at the end of play wins.

Possible Answers

5
1. Là, c'est ma chambre.
   Ça, c'est ma chambre.
2. Ça, c'est la salle de bains.
3. Là, c'est la cuisine.
   Ça, c'est la cuisine.

6
1. Elle est vraiment bien, ta chaîne stéréo.
2. Il est génial, ton poster.
3. Elle est cool, ta chambre.

 STANDARDS: 1.2

Première étape

Vocabulaire

Welcoming someone; responding to someone's welcome

Bienvenue chez moi (chez nous).	*Welcome to my home (our home).*
Faites/Fais comme chez vous (chez toi).	*Make yourself at home.*
Vous avez (Tu as) fait bon voyage?	*Did you have a good trip?*
Merci.	*Thank you.*
C'est gentil de votre/ta part.	*That's nice of you.*
Oui, excellent.	*Yes, excellent.*
C'était fatigant!	*It was tiring!*

Asking how someone is feeling and telling how you are feeling

Pas trop fatigué(e)?	*(You're) not too tired?*
Vous n'avez pas (Tu n'as pas) faim?	*Aren't you hungry?*
Vous n'avez pas (Tu n'as pas) soif?	*Aren't you thirsty?*
Non, ça va.	*No, I'm fine.*
Si, je suis crevé(e).	*Yes, I'm exhausted.*
Si, un peu.	*Yes, a little.*
Si, j'ai très faim/soif!	*Yes, I'm very hungry/thirsty.*
Si, je meurs de faim/soif!	*Yes, I'm dying of hunger/thirst!*

Deuxième étape

Pointing out where things are

Là, c'est...	*Here/There is . . .*
A côté de...	*Next to . . .*
Il y a...	*There is/are . . .*
Ça, c'est...	*This is/are . . .*
en face de	*across from*
à gauche de	*to the left of*
à droite de	*to the right of*
près de	*near*

Paying and responding to compliments

Il/Elle est vraiment bien, ton/ta...	*Your . . . is really great.*
cool	*cool*
beau (belle)	*beautiful*
génial(e)	*great*
chouette	*very cool*
Tu trouves?	*Do you think so?*
C'est vrai? (Vraiment?)	*Really?*
C'est gentil!	*That's nice of you.*

Furniture and rooms

l'armoire (f.)	*armoire, wardrobe*
le balcon	*balcony*
le bureau	*desk*
la chaîne stéréo	*stereo*
la chambre	*bedroom*
la commode	*chest of drawers*
la cuisine	*kitchen*
les étagères (f.)	*shelves*
le jardin	*yard*
la lampe	*lamp*
le lit	*bed*
la maison	*house*
la pièce	*room (of a house)*
le poster	*poster*
le premier étage	*second floor*
le rez-de-chaussée	*first (ground) floor*
la salle à manger	*dining room*
la salle de bains	*bathroom*
le salon	*living room*
le tapis	*rug*
les toilettes (f.) **(les W.-C.** (m.)**)**	*toilet, restroom*
beau (bel)(belle(s)) (beaux)	*beautiful*
nouveau (nouvel) (nouvelle(s)) (nouveaux)	*new*
vieux (vieil) (vieille(s))(vieux)	*old*

Troisième étape

Asking for and giving directions

Où est..., s'il vous plaît?	*Where is . . . , please?*
Traversez...	*Cross . . .*
Prenez...	*Take . . .*
Puis, tournez à gauche dans/sur...	*Then, turn left on . . .*
Allez/Continuez tout droit.	*Go/Keep going straight ahead.*
sur la droite/gauche	*on the right/left*

Places in town

l'auberge (f.) **de jeunesse**	*youth hostel*
la banque	*bank*
la bibliothèque	*library*
la cathédrale	*cathedral*
l'église (f.)	*church*
la gare	*train station*
le lycée	*high school*
le musée	*museum*
l'office (m.) **de tourisme**	*tourist information office*
le parc	*park*
la piscine	*pool*
la poste	*post office*
le terrain de camping	*campground*
le théâtre	*theater*

Review and Assess

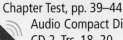

Circumlocution

Have students imagine they're visiting Chartres and need to ask for directions on how to get to a certain destination. Have students work with a partner, one playing the role of a tourist and the other playing the role of a passerby. The student playing the role of the tourist is having difficulty remembering how to say his or her destination in French and needs to circumlocute the word. Once the passerby guesses the destination, have students change roles.

Vocabulaire

CHAPITRE 2

Game

Pictionnaire® Form small groups and distribute a large sheet of butcher paper to each one. Have each group write all the vocabulary words under *Furniture and rooms* and *Places in town* on separate, small slips of paper and place them in a box. Then, have one student draw a slip of paper and draw an illustration representing the vocabulary word written on the slip of paper. The first student to guess the French word for the drawing scores a point. Have students take turns drawing. After a specified amount of time, the student with the most points wins.

Chapter 2 Assessment

- **Testing Program**
  Chapter Test, pp. 39–44
  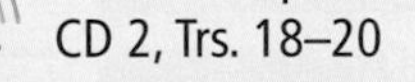
  Audio Compact Discs, CD 2, Trs. 18–20
  Speaking Test, p. 343
- **Alternative Assessment Guide**
  Performance Assessment, p. 33
  Portfolio Assessment, p. 19
  CD-ROM Assessment, p. 47
- **Interactive CD-ROM Tutor, Disc 1**

  A toi de parler
  A toi d'écrire
- **Standardized Assessment Tutor**
  Chapter 2
- **One-Stop Planner**

  Test Generator
  Chapter 2

STANDARDS: 1.1

Chapitre 3 : Un repas à la française
Chapter Overview

Mise en train pp. 62–64	***Une spécialité française***

	FUNCTIONS	GRAMMAR	VOCABULARY	RE-ENTRY
Première étape pp. 65–69	• Making purchases, p. 66	• The object pronoun **en,** p. 66	• Stores and products, 67	• Giving prices **(Chapitre 3,** I) • Expressions of quantity **(Chapitre 8,** I) • Food items **(Chapitre 8,** I) • Numbers **(Chapitre 3,** I)
Deuxième étape pp. 70–74	• Asking for, offering, accepting, and refusing food; paying and responding to compliments, p. 72	• The partitive articles, p. 73	• Meal vocabulary, p. 70	• Paying and responding to compliments **(Chapitre 10,** I) • Days of the week **(Chapitre 2,** I) • Meal vocabulary **(Chapitre 8,** I)
Troisième étape pp. 75–79	• Asking for and giving advice, p. 76 • Extending good wishes, p. 79	• The indirect object pronouns **lui** and **leur,** p. 76	• Gifts and shops, p. 77	• Asking for and giving advice **(Chapitre 1,** II) • Accepting and turning down suggestions **(Chapitre 4,** I)

Lisons! pp. 80–81	Recettes du monde francophone	**Reading Strategy:** Guessing meaning from visual clues and context	
Grammaire supplémentaire	**pp. 82–85** **Première étape,** p. 82	**Deuxième étape,** pp. 83–84	**Troisième étape,** p. 85
Review pp. 86–89	**Mise en pratique,** pp. 86–87 **Ecrivons!** Creating an outline Writing a restaurant critique	**Que sais-je?** p. 88	**Vocabulaire,** p. 89

CULTURE

- Realia: Grocery ad, p. 65
- **Note culturelle,** Neighborhood stores, p. 66
- **Panorama Culturel,** Typical meals in the francophone world, p. 69
- **Note culturelle,** French meals, p. 70
- Realia: Menu from **Le Lion d'Or,** p. 70
- Realia: School lunch menus from Martinique, p. 72
- **Rencontre culturelle,** The euro, p. 74
- **Note culturelle,** Meals for special occasions, p. 75
- Realia: Greeting cards, p. 79

Chapitre 3 : Un repas à la française
Chapter Resources

Lesson Planning

One-Stop Planner

Lesson Planner with Substitute Teacher

Lesson Plans, pp. 11–15, 65

Student Make-Up Assignments
- Make-Up Assignment Copying Masters, Chapter 3

Listening and Speaking

TPR Storytelling Book, pp. 16–23

Listening Activities
- Student Response Forms for Listening Activities, pp. 19–21
- Additional Listening Activities 3-1 to 3-6, pp. 23–25
- Additional Listening Activities (song), p. 26
- Scripts and Answers, pp. 112–116

Video Guide
- Teaching Suggestions, pp. 16–17
- Activity Masters, pp. 18–20
- Scripts and Answers, pp. 89–91, 119

Activities for Communication
- Communicative Activities, pp. 13–18
- Realia and Teaching Suggestions, pp. 85–89
- Situation Cards, pp. 141–142

Reading and Writing

Reading Strategies and Skills Handbook, Chapter 3

Joie de lire 2, Chapter 3

Cahier d'activités, pp. 25–36

Grammar

Travaux pratiques de grammaire, pp. 20–28

Grammar Tutor for Students of French, Chapter 3

Assessment

Testing Program
- Grammar and Vocabulary Quizzes, **Etape** Quizzes, and Chapter Test, pp. 53–70
- Score Sheet, Scripts and Answers, pp. 71–78

Alternative Assessment Guide
- Portfolio Assessment, p. 20
- Performance Assessment, p. 34
- CD-ROM Assessment, p. 48

Student Make-Up Assignments
- Alternative Quizzes, Chapter 3

Standardized Assessment Tutor
- Reading, pp. 9–11
- Writing, p. 12
- Math, pp. 25–26

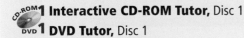

Online Activities
- **Jeux interactifs**
- **Activités Internet**

Video Program
- Videocassette 1
- Videocassette 5 (captioned version)

Interactive CD-ROM Tutor, Disc 1

DVD 1 **DVD Tutor,** Disc 1

Audio Compact Discs
- Textbook Listening Activities, CD 3, Tracks 1–14
- Additional Listening Activities, CD 3, Tracks 21–27
- Assessment Items, CD 3, Tracks 15–20

Teaching Transparencies
- Situation 3-1 to 3-3
- Vocabulary 3-A to 3-C
- **Mise en train**
- **Grammaire supplémentaire** Answers
- **Travaux pratiques de grammaire** Answers

One-Stop Planner CD-ROM

Use the **One-Stop Planner CD-ROM with Test Generator** to aid in lesson planning and pacing.

For each chapter, the **One-Stop Planner** includes:
- Editable lesson plans with direct links to teaching resources
- Printable worksheets from resource books
- Direct launches to the HRW Internet activities
- Video and audio segments
- Test Generator
- Clip Art for vocabulary items

Projects

Les Menus du monde

Groups of students will create a menu for a restaurant in a francophone country.

MATERIALS

✂ **Students may need**

- Posterboard or construction paper
- Markers
- Scissors
- Glue or tape
- Magazine pictures

SUGGESTED SEQUENCE

Form groups of four and assign the roles of organizer, writer, proofreader, and artist. Each group must choose a francophone country and create a restaurant menu that reflects the local cuisine. The menu should include:

- the French name, address, and logo of the restaurant
- at least four **à la carte** items under each of these categories: **entrées, plats principaux, salades, fruits, fromages, desserts,** and **boissons**
- a description of each dish, including the ingredients
- prices
- some artwork, either original or cut from magazines
- at least one house specialty
- **un menu à prix fixe**

When the menu has been completed, each group member must present a part of it to the class, describing some of the dishes and explaining how they represent the cuisine of the country.

GRADING THE PROJECT

Suggested Point Distribution: (total = 100 points)

Completion of requirements	20
Accuracy of written work	20
Overall appearance	20
Accuracy of oral presentation	20
Effort/Participation	20

Games

Loto!

In this game, students will practice the names of food and drink items and expressions for offering, accepting, or refusing food and drink.

Each student draws a grid with four squares across and four squares down. In each of the 16 squares, students draw a different food or drink. Then, students circulate around the room "offering" the foods and drinks on their cards to their classmates. (**Tu veux des fraises?**) If a classmate has drawn that item on his or her card, he or she must refuse. (**Merci, ça va.**) If the item is not on the classmate's card, then he or she must accept it. (**Oui, je veux bien.**) In this case, the student who offered the food crosses out that food on his or her card and writes in that square the name of the classmate who accepted it. The first person to write four names in a row, vertically, horizontally, or diagonally, calls out **Loto!** and then names the four foods he or she "offered" and the students who accepted them.

Que suis-je?

In this game, students will practice the vocabulary for food and drink items and descriptive adjectives.

Gather magazine pictures of food and drink items, one for each student in the class. Without letting students see the pictures, pin or tape them on their backs. Students then circulate around the classroom, asking one another questions to determine their identity. (**Je suis un légume? Je suis jaune?**) The other students can only answer **Oui** or **Non.** Continue until all have discovered their identity.

STANDARDS: 1.3, 3.2, 5.1, 5.2

Storytelling

Mini-histoire

This story accompanies Teaching Transparency 3-2. The ***mini-histoire*** *can be told and retold in different formats, acted out, written down, and read aloud, to give students additional opportunities to practice all four skills. The following story relates an American student's first day in France with her host family.*

Après ce long voyage, je suis fatiguée et j'ai faim, très faim. Chez moi, à Los Angeles on dîne toujours à six heures. Ici, à Paris, c'est bien différent, on ne dîne jamais avant sept heures. Madame Morel dit enfin : «Le dîner est prêt.» Je suis contente de passer à table. Florence me dit en souriant : «On a une surprise pour toi : en entrée, il y a des escargots». C'est mon premier repas en France et tout le monde me regarde. Je suis obligée de goûter. Je mets le premier escargot dans la bouche et, peut-être parce que j'ai très faim, je trouve ça délicieux! J'en mange une douzaine avec beaucoup de pain. Ensuite, le repas continue avec du poulet, des haricots verts, un gratin de pommes de terre et de la salade. Puis, on me propose des fromages. A la fin du repas, Florence me dit : «Pour ton arrivée, j'ai fait une mousse au chocolat. J'espère que tu vas l'aimer.» Je n'ai vraiment plus faim, mais le chocolat... c'est tellement bon!

Traditions

Poisson d'avril

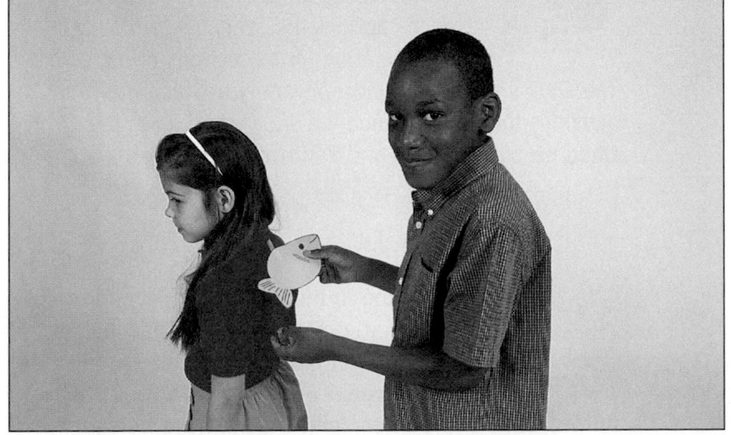

The French celebrate April 1 as **Poisson d'avril,** the equivalent of April Fool's Day in the United States. Instead of playing all kinds of practical jokes, people try to pin a paper fish on the back of someone without getting caught. If they succeed, they call out **Poisson d'avril** and the person who is fooled is supposed to give them a chocolate fish. According to legend, the holiday can be traced back to the day when Charles IX changed the beginning of the year from April 1 to January 1 in 1564. People protested the change by playing pranks and exchanging silly gifts. Candy and paper fish then became associated with the holiday because the zodiac sign for April 1 is Pisces. Declare a **Poisson d'avril** day, either on April 1 or on some other day. Students should try to pin a paper fish on the back of a classmate without their knowing.

Recette

For the past 20 years, in March, a **pot au feu** *or* **pot-bouille** *is prepared in a small village in the west of France. The tradition dates from over 200 years ago when a villager won a cow during a card game. He decided to give the cow to the poor of the village under one condition: make a gigantic* **pot au feu** *for everyone.*

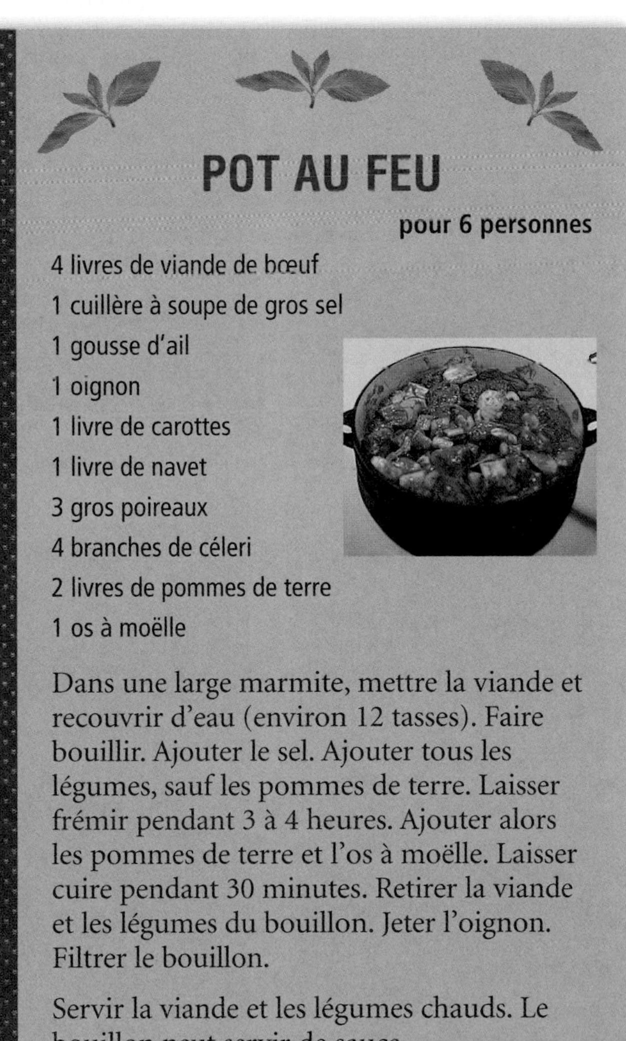

POT AU FEU

pour 6 personnes

4 livres de viande de bœuf
1 cuillère à soupe de gros sel
1 gousse d'ail
1 oignon
1 livre de carottes
1 livre de navet
3 gros poireaux
4 branches de céleri
2 livres de pommes de terre
1 os à moëlle

Dans une large marmite, mettre la viande et recouvrir d'eau (environ 12 tasses). Faire bouillir. Ajouter le sel. Ajouter tous les légumes, sauf les pommes de terre. Laisser frémir pendant 3 à 4 heures. Ajouter alors les pommes de terre et l'os à moëlle. Laisser cuire pendant 30 minutes. Retirer la viande et les légumes du bouillon. Jeter l'oignon. Filtrer le bouillon.

Servir la viande et les légumes chauds. Le bouillon peut servir de sauce.

STANDARDS: 1.3, 2.1, 3.2, 5.1

Technology

DVD/Video

Videocassette 1, Videocassette 5 (captioned version)
DVD Tutor, Disc 1
See Video Guide, pages 15–20.

Mise en train • Une spécialité française
Sandra, Pamela, and Mrs. Lepic are shopping for lunch. Mrs. Lepic decides to surprise Pamela with something typically French. Sandra and Pamela go to buy bread. They see some tempting pastries in one store window and snails in another, which Pamela doesn't find appetizing. Pamela buys carnations for Mrs. Lepic. At lunch, Mrs. Lepic brings out the surprise: **escargots!** Pamela tries to appear enthusiastic.

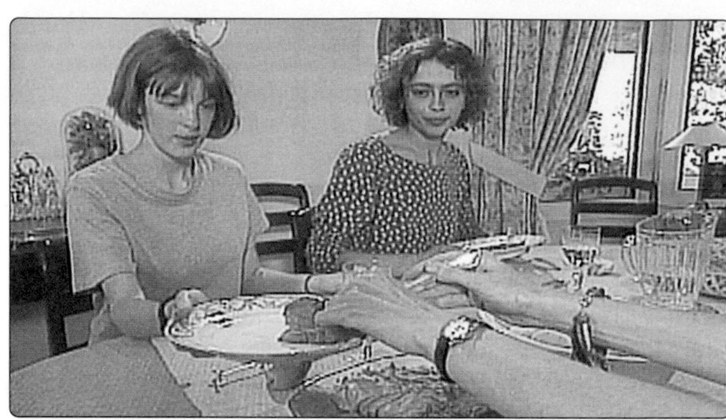

Mise en train (suite)
Pamela explains that she finds snails different from American food. The main course is served, followed by the salad course, the cheese course, and dessert. Pamela enjoys the meal and tells the Lepics that Americans eat their salad before or with the main course. She offers to make an American specialty, cheesecake, for the Lepics the next day.

Qu'est-ce qu'un petit déjeuner typique ici?
Students from Martinique and France talk about their meals.

Vidéoclips
- **Langouste de Cuba®**: advertisement for lobster
- **Carré frais®**: advertisement for cheese

Interactive CD-ROM Tutor

Activity	Activity Type	Pupil's Edition Page
En contexte	*Interactive conversation*	
1. Vocabulaire	Chacun à sa place	p. 67
2. Vocabulaire	Chasse au trésor Explorons! Vérifions!	p. 71
3. Comment dit-on... ?	Chacun à sa place	p. 72
4. Grammaire	Les mots qui manquent	p. 73
5. Grammaire	Méli-mélo	p. 76
6. Vocabulaire	Le bon choix	p. 77
Panorama Culturel	Qu'est-ce qu'un petit déjeuner typique ici?	p. 69
A toi de parler	*Guided recording*	pp. 86–87
A toi d'écrire	*Guided writing*	pp. 86–87

Teacher Management System
Launch the program, type "admin" in the password area, and press RETURN. Log on to www.hrw.com/CDROMTUTOR for a detailed explanation of the Teacher Management System.

DVD Tutor

The *DVD Tutor* contains all material from the *Video Program* as described above. French captions are available for use at your discretion for all sections of the video. The *DVD Tutor* also provides a variety of video-based activities that assess students' understanding of the **Mise en train, Suite,** and **Panorama Culturel.**

This part of the *DVD Tutor* may be used on any DVD video player connected to a television or video monitor.

In addition to the video material and the video-based comprehension activities, the *DVD Tutor* also contains the entire *Interactive CD-ROM Tutor* in DVD-ROM format. Each DVD disc contains the activities from all 12 chapters of the *Interactive CD-ROM Tutor.*

This part of the *DVD Tutor* may be used on a Macintosh® or Windows® computer with a DVD-ROM drive.

To preview all resources available for this chapter, use the **One-Stop Planner CD-ROM**, Disc 1.

Internet Connection

*Have students explore the **go.hrw.com** Web site for many online resources covering all chapters. All Chapter 3 resources are available under the keyword **WA3 PARIS REGION-3.** Interactive games help students practice the material and provide them with immediate feedback. You'll also find a printable worksheet that provides Internet activities that lead to a comprehensive online research project.*

Jeux interactifs

You can use the interactive activities in this chapter

- to practice grammar, vocabulary, and chapter functions
- as homework
- as an assessment option
- as a self-test
- to prepare for the Chapter Test

Activités Internet

Students look for information about a typical French meal.

- In preparation for the **Activités Internet,** have students review the different courses served in the **Mise en train** episode, ***Une spécialité française,*** on Videocassette 1 or DVD Disc 1.

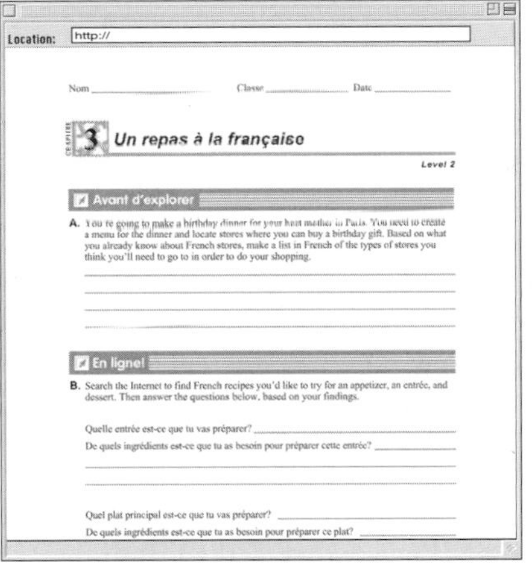

Location: http://

Nom ______ Classe ______ Date ______

CHAPITRE 3 *Un repas à la française*

Level 2

Avant d'explorer

A. You're going to make a birthday dinner for your host mother in Paris. You need to create a menu for the dinner and locate stores where you can buy a birthday gift. Based on what you already know about French stores, make a list in French of the types of stores you think you'll need to go to in order to do your shopping.

En ligne!

B. Search the Internet to find French recipes you'd like to try for an appetizer, an entrée, and dessert. Then answer the questions below, based on your findings.

Quelle entrée est-ce que tu vas préparer? ______

De quels ingrédients est-ce que tu as besoin pour préparer cette entrée? ______

Quel plat principal est-ce que tu vas préparer? ______

De quels ingrédients est-ce que tu as besoin pour préparer ce plat? ______

Projet

Have students do a scavenger hunt for French recipes, using the HRW Web site. The students should find one recipe with a picture of the dish for each course: **potage** *(soup),* **entrée** *(appetizer),* **plat principal** *(main dish),* **fromage** *(cheese),* **dessert** *(dessert).* The pictures and recipes could either be displayed on a poster board, or downloaded into a Powerpoint™ presentation. The project should then be presented to the rest of the class. Students should document their sources by noting the names of the URLs of all the sites they consulted.

STANDARDS: 1.3, 3.2, 5.1, 5.2

Chapitre 3 : Un repas à la française

Textbook Listening Activities Scripts 

Première étape

8 **p. 66**

1. —Pardon, vous avez des bananes?
—Oui, monsieur. Combien en voulez-vous?
—Un kilo, s'il vous plaît. Ça fait combien?

2. —Bonjour, monsieur. Je voudrais un kilo d'oranges, s'il vous plaît.
—Oui, bien sûr.
—Ça fait combien?

3. —Bonjour, madame. Il me faut des tomates et des pommes.
—Bon. Combien en voulez-vous?
—Je voudrais un kilo de tomates et un kilo de pommes Golden. Ça fait combien?

Answers to Activity 8

1. bananas; 0,90€
2. oranges; 0,75€
3. tomatoes, apples; 1 kilo of each; 1,47€

11 **p. 68**

1. —Maman, je vais en ville. Qu'est-ce que j'achète?
—J'ai besoin de lait et de beurre.
—D'accord.

2. —Marine, tu vas me chercher deux baguettes et un kilo de crevettes.
—Oui, Papa, j'y vais.

3. —Oh là là! J'ai oublié le pâté et la tarte! Vincent, tu peux aller les chercher pour moi?
—Bien sûr, Maman.

4. —Il faut m'acheter des œufs, un petit rôti et trois douzaines d'escargots, s'il te plaît.
—Bon. Allez, au revoir.

Answers to Activity 11

1. e
2. b, a
3. d, f
4. e, c, a

Deuxième étape

18 **p. 71**

1. —Oh, Papa! Tu as acheté des croissants!
—Oui, et j'ai aussi fait du chocolat pour toi.
—Youpi!

2. —Maman, il y a du lait dans le frigo?
—Bien sûr.
—Je ne trouve pas les œufs!
—Ah! Je crois que je sais ce que tu vas nous préparer!
—Et où est le fromage?
—Attends, je vais t'aider.

3. —C'était délicieux, Michel. J'adore le poulet préparé comme ça. Et ta quiche est toujours très bonne.
—C'est gentil. Tu veux encore de la mousse au chocolat?
—Merci, ça va.

4. —Oui, monsieur?
—Je voudrais un grand café, s'il vous plaît.
—Et avec ça?
—Des tartines à la confiture.

Answers to Activity 18

1. petit déjeuner
2. dîner
3. déjeuner ou dîner
4. petit déjeuner

20 **p. 72**

1. —Qu'est-ce qu'on sert à la cantine aujourd'hui?
—Du poisson avec des haricots verts et des carottes.
—Bof. Et comme dessert?
—Comme dessert, il y a du yaourt.
—Eh ben, ce n'est pas la cantine des gourmets ici!

2. —Qu'est-ce qu'il y a à la cantine?
—Euh... il y a du poisson.
—Toujours du poisson! Il y a un dessert intéressant au moins?
—Euh, non, c'est un fruit.
—Berk! Cette cantine est vraiment infecte.

3. —Tu aimes la salade de concombres?
—C'est pas mauvais. Il y en a aujourd'hui?
—Oui. Et du poisson, bien sûr...
—Encore?
—Oui, mais il y a de la glace au dessert!

Answers to Activity 20

1. Vauclin; jeudi
2. Rivière-Salée; mardi
3. Rivière-Salée; lundi

The following scripts are for the Listening Activities found in the *Pupil's Edition*. For Student Response Forms, see *Listening Activities,* pages 19–21. To provide students with additional listening practice, see *Listening Activities,* pages 23–25.

One-Stop Planner CD-ROM

To preview all resources available for this chapter, use the **One-Stop Planner CD-ROM**, Disc 1.

22 p. 73

1. —Encore de la salade?
—Merci, ça va.

2. —C'est vraiment bon! J'aime beaucoup votre tarte aux fraises!
—C'est gentil.

3. —Je pourrais avoir du pain, s'il te plaît?
—Voilà.

4. —Tu veux du pâté?
—Oui, je veux bien.

5. —C'était délicieux!
—Oh, ce n'est pas grand-chose.

6. —Tu pourrais me passer les haricots verts?
—Tiens.

Answers to Activity 22

1. offering food
2. paying a compliment
3. asking for food
4. offering food
5. paying a compliment
6. asking for food

Troisième étape

28 p. 76

1. —Eh bien, Maman, tu as une idée de cadeau pour Stéphane?
—Tu pourrais lui offrir des chaussettes. Il en a toujours besoin, j'en suis sûre!
—Des chaussettes? Oh Maman, c'est vraiment banal!

2. —Eh, Sabine! J'ai un petit problème. Je ne sais pas quoi offrir à Jean-Luc pour son anniversaire.
—Euh, ça, c'est dur. Un portefeuille, peut-être.
—Non, il en a déjà un.

3. —Salut, Karim. Dis, tu as une idée de cadeau pour ma sœur? C'est son anniversaire demain.
—Offre-lui un livre.
—Bonne idée. Elle aime beaucoup lire.

4. —Tu as une idée de cadeau pour Pierre? C'est son anniversaire demain.
—Ben, je ne sais pas. Il a peut-être besoin d'une cravate?
—Euh, non, ce n'est pas son style.

5. —Anne, qu'est-ce que je pourrais offrir à Rachida?
—Offre-lui un disque compact.
—Oui, tu as raison! Elle adore la musique!

Answers to Activity 28

1. reject
2. reject
3. accept
4. reject
5. accept

30 p. 78

1. —Oh, des fleurs! Merci, Pamela, c'est gentil.

2. —Oh, Etienne! Quel joli cadre!

3. —Tiens, un foulard! Qu'est-ce qu'il est chic! Bonne idée, Lionel!

4. —Oh, qu'il est beau, ce sac à main! Merci, Sandra.

Answers to Activity 30

1. e
2. d
3. a
4. b

Mise en pratique

2 p. 86

1. —Tu pourrais me passer le beurre? Je vais faire une tartine.
—Voilà. Tu veux encore du café?
—Oui, je veux bien. C'est vraiment bon!
—Alors Stéphanie, toi, tu vas aller à la boulangerie pour acheter des baguettes et à la crémerie pour acheter du fromage.
—Qu'est-ce que je prends comme fromage?
—Oh, je ne sais pas. Prends de gros morceaux de plusieurs fromages.
—Et toi? Qu'est-ce que tu vas faire?
—Je vais acheter du pâté et du jambon à la charcuterie.
—On ne prend pas de gâteau?
—Si, je vais acheter un gros gâteau à la pâtisserie. Dis, est-ce que Claude aime le chocolat?
—Elle adore le chocolat. Bon, je pars. Je dois aussi lui acheter un cadeau. Qu'est-ce que je pourrais lui offrir?
—Tu pourrais lui offrir un beau cadre ou va à la maroquinerie pour un portefeuille.
—C'est banal, non?
—Alors, offre-lui un foulard.
—Bonne idée.

Answers to Mise en pratique Activity 2

1. breakfast/afternoon snack
2. baguettes
3. at the pastry shop
4. He thinks it's ordinary.
5. a scarf

Chapitre 3 : Un repas à la française
Suggested Lesson Plans *50-Minute Schedule*

Day 1

CHAPTER OPENER 5 min.
- Present Chapter Objectives, p. 61.
- Culture Notes, ATE, p. 60
- Multicultural Link, ATE, p. 61

MISE EN TRAIN 40 min.
- Teaching Suggestions: Pre-viewing, Video Guide, p. 16
- Presenting **Mise en train,** ATE, p. 62
- Cahier d'activités, Activity 1, p. 25
- Do Activities 1–6, p. 64.
- Post-viewing Activity 2, Video Guide, p. 18

Wrap-Up 5 min.
- Teaching Suggestions: Post-viewing, Video Guide, p. 16

Homework Options
Challenge, ATE, p. 63

Day 2

MISE EN TRAIN
Quick Review 10 min.
- Bell Work, ATE, p. 65
- Discuss **Tu te rappelles?**, p. 65.
- Do Activity 7, p. 65.

PREMIERE ETAPE
Comment dit-on... ? and **Note de grammaire, p. 66** 30 min.
- Presenting **Comment dit-on... ?,** ATE, p. 66
- Present **Note de grammaire,** p. 66.
- Do Activity 8, p. 66.
- **Grammaire supplémentaire,** Activity 1, p. 82
- Have students do Activities 9–10, p. 66, in pairs.

Note culturelle, p. 66 5 min.
- Read and discuss **Note culturelle,** p. 66.

Wrap-Up, 5 min.
- Cahier d'activités, Activity 2, p. 26

Homework Options
Cahier d'activités, Acts. 3–5, pp. 26––27
Travaux pratiques de grammaire, Acts. 1–2, p. 20
Grammaire supplémentaire, Act. 2, p. 82

Day 3

PREMIERE ETAPE
Quick Review 5 min.
- Check homework.

Vocabulaire, p. 67 25 min.
- Presenting **Vocabulaire,** ATE, p. 67
- Play Audio CD for Activity 11, p. 68.
- Cahier d'activités, Activities 8–9, p. 28
- Do Activity 12, p. 68.
- Game: **C'est logique!,** ATE, p. 68

PANORAMA CULTUREL 15 min.
- Presenting **Panorama Culturel,** ATE, p. 69, with Videocassette
- **Questions,** ATE, p. 69

Wrap-Up 5 min.
- Discuss **Qu'en penses-tu?,** p. 69.

Homework Options
Study for Quiz 3-1.
Travaux pratiques de grammaire, Acts. 6–10, pp. 22–23
Cahier d'activités, Act. 10, p. 28

Day 4

PREMIERE ETAPE
Quiz 3-1 20 min.
- Administer Quiz 3-1A, 3-1B, or a combination of the two.

DEUXIEME ETAPE
Note culturelle, p. 70 5 min.
- Read and discuss **Note culturelle,** p. 70.

Vocabulaire, p. 71 20 min.
- Presenting **Vocabulaire,** ATE, p. 71
- Language Note, ATE, p. 71, and Culture Note, ATE, p. 70
- Play Audio CD for Activity 18, p. 71.
- Travaux pratiques de grammaire, Activities 11–12, p. 24
- Have students do Activity 19, p. 71, in pairs.

Wrap-Up 5 min.
- Review **Tu te rappelles?,** Pupil's Edition, p. 72.

Homework Options
Cahier d'activités, Acts. 11–12, p. 29
Grammaire supplémentaire, Acts. 3–4, p. 83

Day 5

DEUXIEME ETAPE
Quick Review 5 min.
- Check homework.

Comment dit-on... ?, p. 72 25 min.
- Presenting **Comment dit-on... ?,** ATE, p. 72
- Language Note, ATE, p. 73
- Play Audio CD for Activity 22, p. 73.
- Cahier d'activités, Activities 13–14, pp. 29–30

Note de grammaire, p. 73 15 min.
- Presenting **Note de grammaire,** ATE, p. 73
- **Grammaire supplémentaire,** Activity 6, p. 84
- Complete Activity 24, p. 73.
- Cahier d'activités, Activities 15–16, p. 30

Wrap-Up 5 min.
- Read and discuss **A la française,** p. 73.

Homework Options
Study for Quiz 3-2
Travaux pratiques de grammaire, Acts. 15–16, p. 26

Day 6

DEUXIEME ETAPE
Quiz 3-2 20 min.
- Administer Quiz 3-2A, 3-2B, or a combination of the two.

RENCONTRE CULTURELLE 20 min.
- Presenting **Rencontre culturelle,** ATE, p. 74
- Read and Discuss **Qu'en penses-tu?** and **Savais-tu que…?,** p. 74.
- Culture Notes, ATE, p. 74
- Economics Link, ATE, p. 74

Wrap-Up 10 min.
- Realia 3-2, Activities for Communication, pp. 86, 88–89

For alternative lesson plans by chapter section, to create your own customized plans, or to preview all resources available for this chapter, use the **One-Stop Planner CD-ROM,** Disc 1.

For additional homework suggestions, see activities accompanied by this symbol throughout the chapter.

Day 7

TROISIEME ETAPE

Quick Review 5 min.
- Bell Work, ATE, p. 75

Note culturelle, p. 75 5 min.
- Read and discuss **Note culturelle,** p. 75.

Comment dit-on... ?, p. 76 15 min.
- Presenting **Comment dit-on... ?,** ATE, p. 76
- Play Audio CD for Activity 28, p. 76.
- Cahier d'activités, Activity 20, p. 32

Grammaire, p. 76 20 min.
- Presenting **Grammaire,** p. 77
- Do Activities 8–9, **Grammaire supplémentaire,** p. 85.
- Complete Cahier d'activités, Activity 21, p. 32.
- Activity: **Méli-mélo,** CD-ROM Program, Disc 1

Wrap-Up 5 min.
- Teaching Suggestion, ATE, p. 75

Homework Options
Travaux pratiques de grammaire, Acts. 17–18, p. 27

Day 8

TROISIEME ETAPE

Quick Review 5 min.
- Check homework.

Vocabulaire, p. 77 25 min.
- Presenting **Vocabulaire,** ATE, p. 77
- Building on Previous Skills and Culture Note, ATE, p. 77
- Play Audio CD for Activity 30, p. 78.
- Travaux pratiques de grammaire, Activities 19–21, p. 28
- Have students do Activity 32, p. 78, in pairs.
- Culture Note, ATE, p. 79

Comment dit-on... ?, p. 79 15 min.
- Presenting **Comment dit-on... ?,** ATE, p. 79
- Cahier d'activités, Activities 26–27, p. 34

Wrap-Up 5 min.
- Language-to-Language, ATE, p. 79

Homework Options
Cahier d'activités, Acts. 23–25, pp. 33–34
Pupil's Edition, Act. 35, p. 79
Study for Quiz 3-3.

Day 9

TROISIEME ETAPE

Quiz 3-3 20 min.
- Administer Quiz 3-3A, 3-3B, or a combination of the two.

LISONS! 25 min.
- Do Prereading Activities A–B, p. 80.
- Have students read the recipes.
- Complete Reading Activities C–I, pp. 80–81.
- See TPR, ATE, p. 80.

Wrap-Up 5 min.
- Math Link, ATE, p. 81

Homework Options
Cahier d'activités, Act. 28, p. 35

Day 10

LISONS!

Quick Review 5 min.
- Discuss homework.

Postreading Activity 15 min.
- Do Postreading Activity J, p. 81.

MISE EN PRATIQUE 25 min.
- Do Activity 1, p. 86.
- Play Audio CD for Activity 2.
- Do Activity 3, p. 86.
- Discuss the strategy for **Ecrivons!,** p. 87, as a class, then have students work on their articles.
- Circumlocution, ATE, p. 89

Wrap-Up 5 min.
- Discuss Career Path, ATE, p. 87.

Homework Options
Have students finish articles for **Ecrivons!,** Pupil's Edition, p. 87.

Day 11

MISE EN PRATIQUE

Review 40 min.
- Have volunteers read their articles from **Ecrivons!,** p. 87.
- Have students prepare skits for **Jeu de rôle,** p. 87, in pairs or groups.
- Allow groups or pairs to act out their skits.

Wrap-Up 10 min.
- **A toi de parler,** Interactive CD-ROM Tutor, (Disc 1)

Homework Options
Que sais-je?, p. 88

Day 12

MISE EN PRATIQUE

Quick Review 15 min.
- Go over **Que sais-je?,** p. 88.

Chapter Review 35 min.
- Review Chapter 3. Choose from **Grammaire supplémentaire,** Grammar Tutor for Students of French, Activities for Communication, Listening Activities, Interactive CD-ROM Tutor, or **Jeux interactifs.**

Homework Options
Study for Chapter 3 Test.

Assessment

Chapter Test 50 min.
- Administer Chapter 3 Test. Select from Testing Program, Alternative Assessment Guide, Test Generator or Standardized Assessment Tutor.

Chapitre 3 : Un repas à la française

Suggested Lesson Plans 90-Minute Block Schedule

Block 1

CHAPTER OPENER 5 min.
- Present Chapter Objectives, p. 61.
- Building on Previous Skills, ATE, p. 60
- Culture Notes, ATE, p. 60
- Multicultural Link, ATE, p. 61

MISE EN TRAIN 35 min.
- Ask students what specialties from their region they would want to serve a guest from a foreign country.
- Preteaching Vocabulary, ATE, p. 62
- Presenting **Mise en train,** ATE, p. 62
- Do Activities 1–2, p. 64.
- Do Activity 4, using Slower Pace, ATE, p. 64.
- Do Activity 5, p. 64.

PREMIERE ETAPE 10 min.
- Do Activity 7, p. 65.
- Go over **Tu te rappelles?,** p. 65.

Comment dit-on... ?, p. 66 35 min.
- Presenting **Comment dit-on... ?,** ATE, p. 66
- Present **Note de grammaire,** p. 66.
- Ask students questions about things they have. **(Tu as combien de crayons?)** Possible student response: **J'en ai deux.**
- Play Audio CD for Activity 8, p. 66.
- Do Activity 9, p. 66.

Wrap-Up 5 min.
- Ask questions from **Comment dit-on... ?,** p. 66, and have students give a logical response.

Homework Options
Grammaire supplémentaire, Acts. 1–2, p. 82
Cahier d'activités, Acts. 1–5, pp. 25–27
Travaux pratiques de grammaire, Acts. 1–5, pp. 20–22

Block 2

PREMIERE ETAPE
Quick Review 5 min.
- Create a conversation between a salesperson and a customer, and put the sentences on a transparency in scrambled order. Have students write out the conversation in the correct order.

Vocabulaire, p. 67 30 min.
- Discuss **Note culturelle,** p. 66.
- Presenting **Vocabulaire,** ATE, p. 67
- Play Audio CD for Activity 11, p. 68.
- Activities 12–14, p. 68

DEUXIEME ETAPE
Vocabulaire, p. 71 30 min.
- **Note culturelle,** p. 70
- Presenting **Vocabulaire,** ATE, p. 71, using Slower Pace, ATE, p. 71
- Play Audio CD for Activity 18, p. 71.
- Activity 19, p. 71

PANORAMA CULTUREL 15 min.
- Ask students to describe a typical American breakfast. What do they consider the main meal of the day?
- Presenting **Panorama Culturel,** ATE, p. 69, using Videocassette 1
- Discuss **Qu'en penses-tu?** questions, p. 69.

Wrap-Up 10 min.
- Game: **C'est logique!,** ATE, p. 68

Homework Options
Have students study for Quiz 3-1.
Cahier d'activités, Acts. 6–12, pp. 27–29
Travaux pratiques de grammaire, Acts. 6–12, pp. 22–25

Block 3

PREMIERE ETAPE
Quick Review 10 min.
- Game: **Loto!,** ATE, p. 67

Quiz 3-1 20 min.
- Administer Quiz 3-1A, 3-1B, or a combination of the two.

DEUXIEME ETAPE
Comment dit-on... ? , p. 72 20 min.
- Presenting **Comment dit-on... ?,** ATE, p. 72
- Briefly review **Tu te rappelles?,** p. 72.
- Play Audio CD for Activity 22, p. 73.

Note de grammaire, p. 73 15 min.
- Presenting **Note de grammaire,** ATE, p. 73
- Activities 23 and 24, p. 73

TROISIEME ETAPE
Note culturelle, p. 75 5 min.
- Discuss **Note culturelle,** p. 75.

Comment dit-on... ?, p. 76 15 min.
- Presenting **Comment dit-on... ?,** ATE, p. 76
- Play Audio CD for Activity 28, p. 76.

Wrap-Up 5 min.
- Have students work in pairs to do Situation Card 3-2: Interview, Activities for Communication, p. 141.

Homework Options
Have students study for Quiz 3-2.
Grammaire supplémentaire, Acts. 3–7, pp. 83–84
Cahier d'activités, Acts. 13–20, pp. 29–32
Travaux pratiques de grammaire, Acts. 13–16, p. 26

One-Stop Planner CD-ROM

For alternative lesson plans by chapter section, to create your own customized plans, or to preview all resources available for this chapter, use the **One-Stop Planner CD-ROM,** Disc 1.

For additional homework suggestions, see activities accompanied by this symbol throughout the chapter.

Block 4

DEUXIEME ETAPE

Quick Review 10 min.
- Have students review the vocabulary and expressions from the **Deuxième étape,** using Teaching Transparency 3-2 and Suggestion #3 in Suggestions for Using Teaching Transparency 3-2.

Quiz 3-2 20 min.
- Administer Quiz 3-2A, 3-2B, or a combination of the two.

TROISIEME ETAPE

Grammaire, p. 76 25 min.
- Presenting **Grammaire,** ATE, p. 77
- **Grammaire supplémentaire,** Acts. 8–9, p. 85
- Do Activity 29, p. 77, using Building on Previous Skills, ATE, p. 77.

Vocabulaire, p. 77 30 min.
- Presenting **Vocabulaire,** ATE, p. 77
- Play Audio CD for Activity 30, p. 78.
- Culture Note, ATE, p. 77
- Do Activity 31, p. 78.

Wrap-Up 5 min.
- To review the indirect object pronouns and **Comment dit-on... ?,** p. 76, ask students to suggest gifts for various occasions.

Homework Options

Cahier d'activités, Acts. 21–25, pp. 32–34

Travaux pratiques de grammaire, Acts. 17–21, pp. 27–28

Block 5

TROISIEME ETAPE

Quick Review 10 min.
- Review the names of the stores from **Vocabulaire,** p. 77. Then, ask students what can be bought at each of the stores. On a blank transparency, make a list of the items they suggest.

RENCONTRE CULTURELLE 15 min.
- Presenting **Rencontre culturelle,** ATE, p. 74

Vocabulaire, p. 77 10 min.
- Do Activity 32, p. 78.
- Visual/Auditory Learners, ATE, p. 78

Comment dit-on... ?, p. 79 30 min.
- Presenting **Comment dit-on... ?,** ATE, p. 79
- Additional Listening Activity 3-6, Listening Activities, p. 25
- Do Activities 33 and 35, p. 79.

LISONS! 20 min.
- **Stratégie pour lire,** p. 80
- Prereading and Reading Activities A–E, p. 80
- TPR, ATE, p. 80

Wrap-Up 5 min.
- Hold up cards illustrating certain holidays and ask students to respond with the appropriate expression from **Comment dit-on... ?,** p. 79.

Homework Options

Activity 34, p. 79

Cahier d'activités, Acts. 26–27, p. 34

Block 6

TROISIEME ETAPE

Quick Review 10 min.
- Have students work in pairs to create and act out a scene based on Teaching Transparency 3-3.

Quiz 3-3 20 min.
- Administer Quiz 3-3A, 3-3B, or a combination of the two.

LISONS! 25 min.
- Reading and Postreading Activities F–J, p. 81

MISE EN PRATIQUE 35 min.
- Do Activity 1, p. 86.
- Play Audio CD for Activity 2.
- Activity 3, p. 86
- Do Activity 5, p. 87.
- Have students begin Activity 4, **Ecrivons!,** p. 87.

Homework Options

Que sais-je?, p. 88

Interactive CD-ROM Tutor (Disc 1)

Study for Chapter 3 Test.

Have students finish Activity 4, p. 87.

Block 7

MISE EN PRATIQUE

Quick Review 10 min.
- Go over homework.

Chapter Review 35 min.
- Review Chapter 3. Choose from **Grammaire supplémentaire,** Grammar Tutor for Students of French, Activities for Communication, Listening Activities, Interactive CD-ROM Tutor, or **Jeux interactifs.**

Chapter Test 45 min.
- Administer Chapter 3 Test. Select from Testing Program, Alternative Assessment Guide, Test Generator, or Standardized Assessment Tutor.

CHAPITRE 3

One-Stop Planner CD-ROM

For resource information, see the **One-Stop Planner,** Disc 1.

Pacing Tips

Chapter 3 has more new vocabulary than other chapters in Level 2. You might plan your lessons accordingly. For Lesson Plans and timing suggestions, see pages 59I–59L.

Meeting the Standards

Communication

- Making purchases, p. 66
- Asking for, offering, accepting, and refusing food; paying and responding to compliments, p. 72
- Asking for and giving advice, p. 76
- Extending good wishes, p. 79

Culture

- Culture Note, pp. 60, 70, 72, 74, 77, 79
- Note culturelle, pp. 66, 70, 75
- Panorama Culturel, p. 69

Connections

- Multicultural Link, pp. 61, 70
- Health Link, p. 71
- Math Link, pp. 66, 71, 81
- Economics Link, p. 74

Comparisons

- Thinking Critically: Analyzing, p. 69

Communities

- Career Path, p. 87
- De l'école au travail, p. 79

Building on Previous Skills

Distribute large sheets of paper to small groups and have them label four columns **Boissons, Fruits, Légumes,** and **Viandes.** Give each group thirty seconds to list in the first column as many drinks as they can recall. The group with the most entries wins. Repeat the procedure for the other categories.

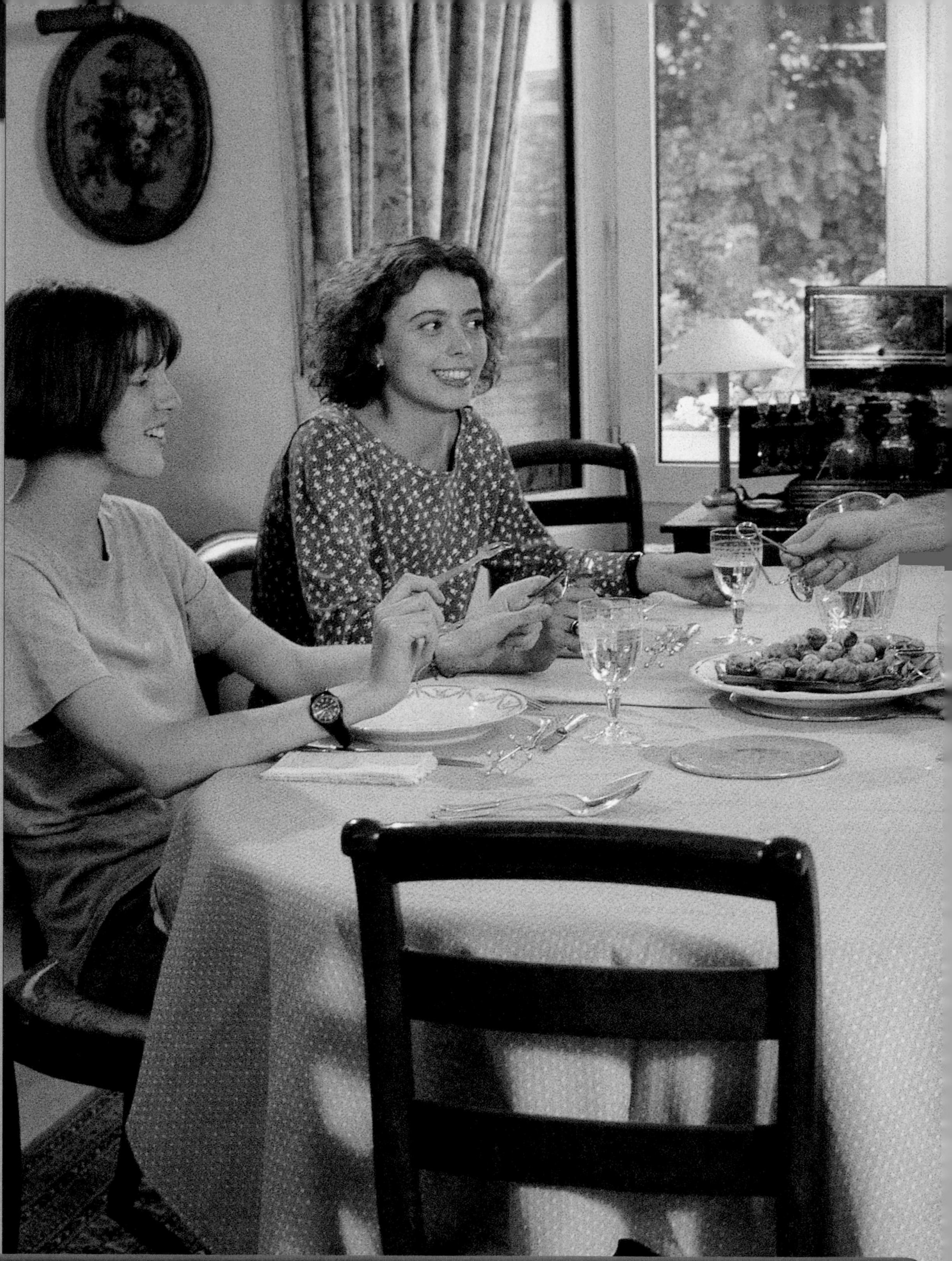

Cultures and Communities

Culture Notes

- You might point out that the French hold the fork in the left hand and the knife in the right at all times while eating. They don't switch the fork from the left to the right hand as right-handed Americans do. The French use the knife not only for cutting, but to scoop food onto the fork as well.
- In France, meals are usually served in separate courses and may last from one to three hours. If you're invited to dinner, it is customary to bring a small gift for the host. It is important to compliment the host on the meal.

CHAPITRE

3 Un repas à la française

Objectives

In this chapter you will learn to

Première étape

- make purchases

Deuxième étape

- ask for, offer, accept, and refuse food
- pay and respond to compliments

Troisième étape

- ask for and give advice
- extend good wishes

internet

ADRESSE: go.hrw.com
MOT-CLE:
WA3 PARIS REGION-3

◀ **C'est vraiment bon!**

Connections and Comparisons

Language Note

Ask students if they know why the nationality in **à la française** is in the feminine form. (The French words **la mode** and **la manière** in the expressions **à la mode** and **à la manière française** are feminine nouns.)

Multicultural Link

Ask if any students are familiar with table manners in other cultures. If so, ask them how they differ from American table manners. Students might recall from Level 1 that people in Côte d'Ivoire, especially those in the villages, and in much of Africa, often eat with their right hand out of a large bowl that is shared among those eating the meal.

Chapter Opener

CHAPITRE 3

Focusing on Outcomes

Give students the following sentences and have them match each one to an outcome.

C'est combien, les tomates!
La salade est délicieuse.
Encore du café?
Bon anniversaire!
Offre-lui des bonbons.

NOTE: The self-check activities on page 88 help students assess their achievement of the objectives.

Language Note

Have students look at the chapter title. Ask if they can guess the meaning of the word **repas** based on the photo. You might ask them if they have seen or heard the English word *repast,* meaning *meal.* Next, ask students if they know the expression **à la française.** Point out that **à la française** is short for **à la mode** or **à la manière française,** meaning *in the French style.*

Chapter Sequence

Teaching Resources
pp. 62–64

PRINT 
- Lesson Planner, p. 11
- Video Guide, pp. 16, 18
- Cahier d'activités, p. 25

MEDIA
- One-Stop Planner
- Video Program
  Mise en train
  Videocassette 1, 32:57–37:01
  Videocassette 5 (captioned version), 17:33–21:37
  Suite
  Videocassette 1, 37:05–41:01
  Videocassette 5 (captioned version), 21:42–25:38
- DVD Tutor, Disc 1
- Audio Compact Discs, CD 3, Trs. 1–2
- **Mise en train** Transparencies

Presenting Mise en train

Ask students to study the photos in the **Mise en train** for 30 seconds. Then, have them write a brief summary in English of what they think the story is about. Next, show the video. Finally, as individuals read their original ideas, have the class decide if they were correct. For more practice with the **Mise en train**, see the Preteaching Vocabulary suggestion below.

Mise en train Transparencies

The **roman-photo** is an abridged version of the video episode.

MISE EN TRAIN ▪ *Une spécialité française*

CD 3 Trs. 1–2

DVD

Stratégie pour comprendre
What French specialties do you see in these photos? Pay close attention to the French names for these foods. Do you already know what an escargot is? If you don't, try to guess what that word means by looking at the photos and considering Pamela's reaction to that dish.

Sandra

Pamela

Mme Lepic

M. Lepic

1
Mme Lepic Alors, qu'est-ce que vous voulez pour le déjeuner?
Pamela Je ne sais pas. J'aimerais manger quelque chose de bien français.

2
Mme Lepic Ah, je sais exactement ce que je vais faire.
Sandra Qu'est-ce que ça va être, Maman?
Mme Lepic C'est une surprise.

3
Mme Lepic Voyons, on n'a plus de pain.
Sandra Nous, on peut en acheter.
Mme Lepic D'accord. Moi, je vais chercher le reste des provisions.

4
Pamela Mmm... Regarde les pâtisseries!
Sandra Elles ont l'air bonnes, mais elles nous couperaient l'appétit.

Preteaching Vocabulary

Guessing words from context Ask students to look at the pictures to figure out what is happening in the **Mise en train.** What are Sandra and Pamela doing? Ask students to look for expressions related to food and shopping for food. Here are some examples they might find:

❶ **déjeuner**
❸ **pain, provisions**
❹ **pâtisseries, l'appétit**
❺ **escargots**
❿ **sers-toi**

Can students guess what the Lepics will be having for dinner from the pictures and the words they found?

STANDARDS: 1.2, 2.1, 2.2, 3.2

5

Sandra Voilà une spécialité française : les escargots!
Pamela On mange ça vraiment?
Sandra Mais oui, c'est délicieux.

6

Pamela Je voudrais faire un cadeau à ta mère. Qu'est-ce que je pourrais lui offrir?
Sandra Pourquoi est-ce que tu ne lui achètes pas des fleurs?
Pamela Bonne idée.

7

Pamela Je voudrais un bouquet d'œillets, s'il vous plaît.

8

Plus tard, chez les Lepic...

Pamela Tenez, c'est pour vous.
Mme Lepic Oh, c'est trop gentil! Je vais les mettre tout de suite dans un vase.

9

Sandra Pamela, tu veux du pain?
Pamela Oui, je veux bien.

10

Mme Lepic Et maintenant, la surprise. Les escargots!
Sandra Mmmm! J'adore les escargots!
M. Lepic Allez, sers-toi, Pamela.
Pamela ?!
Mme Lepic Bon appétit!

Cahier d'activités, p. 25, Act. 1

Using the Captioned Video/DVD

If students have difficulty understanding French spoken at a normal speed, use Videocassette 5 to allow students to see the French captions for ***Une spécialité française*** and ***Une spécialité française (suite).*** Hearing the language and watching the story will reduce anxiety about the new language and facilitate comprehension. The reinforcement of seeing the written vocabulary words as they watch the gestures and actions will help prepare students to do the comprehension activities on page 64.

NOTE: The *DVD Tutor* contains captions for all sections of the *Video Program.*

Mise en train

CHAPITRE 3

Slower Pace

On the board or on a transparency, write the following sentences. Have students rewrite them in the proper order to summarize the action of the story.

1. **Pamela offre des fleurs à Madame Lepic.**
2. **Pamela voudrait manger une spécialité française.**
3. **Sandra offre du pain à Pamela.**
4. **Madame Lepic sert des escargots.**
5. **Pamela achète des fleurs.**
6. **Sandra et Pamela regardent les pâtisseries.**

(*Answers:* 2, 6, 5, 1, 3, 4)

Challenge

Have students write a caption for each photo, summarizing the action.

Language Note

Ask students to find the expression Sandra uses to say that the pastries look good. **(Elles ont l'air bonnes.)** Point out that the expression **avoir l'air** can be used for people as well. **(Il a l'air fatigué.)**

Mise en train (suite)

When the story continues, Pamela tries the **escargots.** Mrs. Lepic offers her more, but she politely refuses. Mrs. Lepic serves the main course and after that, salad. With each course, Mrs. Lepic offers Pamela more food, but she refuses. After the salad, Mrs. Lepic brings out a plate of cheese, and then the dessert. At the end of the meal, Pamela offers to make an American dish for the Lepics.

Mise en train

CHAPITRE 3

Additional Practice

3 For additional listening practice, name the items pictured in random order and have students write the numbers of the corresponding pictures.

4 Write the sentences from Activity 4 (including missing words) out of order on an overhead transparency or on the board after students have done this activity. Have partners reconstruct the journal entry by putting the sentences in order.

Culture Note

The French pride themselves not only on the freshness and high quality of the ingredients they use in their cooking, but also on the presentation of their dishes, which they consider just as important. For a large majority of French people, cuisine is an art form as well as a ritual, with its own rules and methods that must be followed. The French culinary tradition dates back to the Renaissance, and the first restaurants to the French Revolution.

These activities check for comprehension only. Students should not yet be expected to produce language modeled in **Mise en train.**

1 Tu as compris?

1. Où sont Mme Lepic, Sandra et Pamela au début d'***Une spécialité française?*** on the street
2. Quelles courses est-ce que Pamela et Sandra font pour Mme Lepic? buy bread
3. Qu'est-ce que Pamela achète? Pourquoi? flowers; as a gift for Mme Lepic
4. Qu'est-ce que Mme Lepic a comme surprise pour Pamela? snails **(escargots)** for lunch

2 Vrai ou faux?

1. Pamela est allée chez le fleuriste pour acheter du pain. faux
2. Pamela et Sandra décident d'acheter des pâtisseries. faux
3. Mme Lepic achète du pain. faux
4. Pamela achète un bouquet de fleurs pour Mme Lepic. vrai
5. En France, on mange des escargots. vrai

3 C'est qui?

Qui a acheté les choses suivantes? Mme Lepic? Sandra? Pamela? Personne?

1. Pamela

2. Sandra et Pamela

3. Mme Lepic

4. Personne

4 Une journée intéressante

Dans son journal Pamela parle de sa journée. Mais elle a oublié quelques petites choses. Tu peux l'aider?

Aujourd'hui, je suis allée en ville avec Mme Lepic et __1__. On a acheté du __2__ à la boulangerie-pâtisserie, mais on n'a pas acheté de __3__ parce que ça coupe l'appétit. J'ai acheté des __4__ pour offrir à Mme Lepic. Elle était très contente. On a eu une surprise pour le déjeuner. Des __5__ !

5 Cherche les expressions

What do people in ***Une spécialité française*** say to . . . See answers below.

1. ask for advice?
2. make a suggestion?
3. accept a suggestion?
4. offer food?
5. accept food?

6 Et maintenant, à toi

Imagine que tu es invité(e) à dîner dans une famille française. On t'offre un plat que tu n'aimes pas. Qu'est-ce que tu fais?

Comprehension Check

Challenge

2 Scramble the statements and write them on the board or on a transparency. Have students unscramble them and then decide whether they are true or false.

Slower Pace

4 Write the missing words from Pamela's journal on the board or on a transparency in random order for students to choose from. You might also sketch illustrations of the nouns needed to complete the journal entry on the board in random order and label them **A** through **E.** Have students complete the journal entry with the letters that correspond to the pictures.

Answers

5
1. Qu'est-ce que je pourrais lui offrir?
2. Pourquoi est-ce que tu ne lui achètes pas des fleurs?
3. Bonne idée!
4. Tu veux du pain? Allez, sers-toi.
5. Oui, je veux bien.

STANDARDS: 1.2, 2.1, 2.2, 3.2

Objective Making purchases

go.hrw.com
WA3 PARIS REGION-3

E.LECLERC
2,30€
CAROTTES
le sachet de 2 kg
soit le kg 1,65€
2,87€
RAISINS
Italie, Sicile, le kg
0,90€
BANANES
le kg
1,05€
ENDIVES
le sachet de 1 kg
3,26€
CHOUX-FLEURS
les 2
0,75€
TOMATES
le kg
6,65€
ANANAS
cat. B, les 2
1,44€
POMMES GOLDEN
le sachet de 2 kg
soit le kg 0,72€
1,50€
ORANGES
le sachet de 2 kg
soit le kg 0,75€

7 **Les fruits et les légumes**

Lisons

1. Quels fruits et légumes est-ce que tu reconnais dans cette publicité? Est-ce qu'il y a des choses que tu n'as jamais vues?
2. Quelles quantités est-ce qu'on utilise pour vendre ces fruits et légumes? A ton avis, qu'est-ce que le mot **sachet** veut dire? 1 or 2 kilos; the bag
3. Imagine que tu as 5 euros. Tu veux faire une salade de fruits pour une fête. Quels fruits est-ce que tu vas acheter?

Tu te rappelles?

Do you remember how items are sold in French-speaking countries? Fruits and vegetables are priced by the pound **(une livre=500 grammes)** or the kilogram **(un kilo= 2 livres ou 1.000 grammes).** To give a price in French, say the amount of euros first, then the cents: **7€80=sept euros quatre-vingts.** To review numbers, practice counting by tens from 10 to 100: **dix, vingt, trente, quarante, cinquante, soixante, soixante-dix, quatre-vingts, quatre-vingt-dix, cent.**

Travaux pratiques de grammaire, pp. 20–21, Act. 1–3

Teaching Resources
pp. 65–68

PRINT

- Lesson Planner, p. 12
- TPR Storytelling Book, pp. 16–17
- Listening Activities, pp. 19, 23
- Activities for Communication, pp. 13–14, 85, 88, 141–142
- Travaux pratiques de grammaire, pp. 20–23
- Grammar Tutor for Students of French, Chapter 3
- Cahier d'activités, pp. 26–28
- Testing Program, pp. 53–56
- Alternative Assessment Guide, p. 34
- Student Make-Up Assignments, Chapter 3

MEDIA

- One-Stop Planner
- Audio Compact Discs, CD 3, Trs. 3–4, 15, 21–22
- Teaching Transparencies: 3-1, 3-A; **Grammaire supplémentaire** Answers; Travaux pratiques de grammaire Answers
- Interactive CD-ROM Tutor, Disc 1

Bell Work

Write the following sentences on the board. For each sentence, have students write the name of the character from the **Mise en train** who said it.

1. **J'adore les escargots!**
2. **J'aimerais manger quelque chose de bien français.**
3. **Pourquoi est-ce que tu ne lui achètes pas des fleurs?**
4. **Je vais les mettre tout de suite dans un vase.**
5. **Elles ont l'air bonnes, mais elles nous couperaient l'appétit.**
6. **Ah, je sais exactement ce que je vais faire.**

(*Answers:* 1. Sandra 2. Pamela 3. Sandra 4. Mme Lepic 5. Sandra 6. Mme Lepic)

Communication for All Students

TPR Display the pictures or the produce on a table. Ask individuals to give you the items. **(Luc, donne-moi la banane, s'il te plaît.)**

Challenge

7 Have students create their own food advertisement, substituting different food items and prices from the ad above. After presenting **Comment dit-on… ?** on page 66, have students use these ads to create conversations with the new expressions.

Teaching Resources
pp. 65–68

PRINT 

- Lesson Planner, p. 12
- TPR Storytelling Book, pp. 16–17
- Listening Activities, pp. 19, 23
- Activities for Communication, pp. 13–14, 85, 88, 141–142
- Travaux pratiques de grammaire, pp. 20–23
- Grammar Tutor for Students of French, Chapter 3
- Cahier d'activités, pp. 26–28
- Testing Program, pp. 53–56
- Alternative Assessment Guide, p. 34
- Student Make-Up Assignments, Chapter 3

MEDIA

- One-Stop Planner
- Audio Compact Discs, CD 3, Trs. 3–4, 15, 21–22
- Teaching Transparencies: 3-1, 3-A; **Grammaire supplémentaire** Answers; Travaux pratiques de grammaire Answers
- Interactive CD-ROM Tutor, Disc 1

Presenting
Comment dit-on... ?

Bring real or plastic fruits and vegetables to class and attach prices to them. Have a student play the role of the **vendeur (vendeuse)** while you play the role of the **client(e).** Write on the board under **vendeur (vendeuse): C'est un euro le kilo.** and **Combien en voulez-vous?** Then, ask for prices and quantities of various items, prompting students' responses by pointing at the board. Next, write on the board what a customer might say and have another student play that role.

Comment dit-on...?

Making purchases

To ask what quantity someone wants:

Combien en voulez-vous?
How many/much do you want?

To ask for a certain quantity of something:

Je voudrais une livre de tomates.
Je vais prendre un kilo de bananes.
Des pommes? **Je vais en prendre** deux kilos. *I'll take . . . (of them).*

To ask for a price:

C'est combien, s'il vous plaît?
Combien coûtent les pommes?
How much are . . . ?

To ask for the total cost:

Ça fait combien?

Cahier d'activités, p. 26, Act. 2–3

Note de grammaire

The object pronoun **en** means *of them.* You use it to replace the phrase **de(s)** + **a thing** or **things.**

—Vous voulez **des fraises?**
—Oui, je vais **en** prendre une livre.
—Et avec ça?
—**Des bananes,** s'il vous plaît.
—Combien **en** voulez-vous?
—Un kilo, s'il vous plaît.

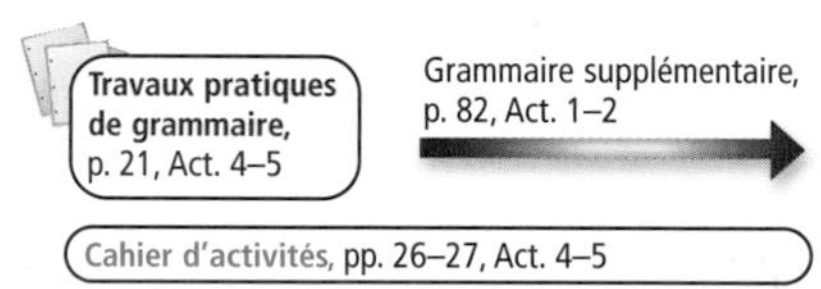

Travaux pratiques de grammaire, p. 21, Act. 4–5
Grammaire supplémentaire, p. 82, Act. 1–2
Cahier d'activités, pp. 26–27, Act. 4–5

Note culturelle

In France and in many French-speaking countries, people often do their grocery shopping in small neighborhood stores. Although convenience and lower prices are making supermarkets more popular, many people still prefer specialty shops for fresh food of high quality.

8 Grammaire en contexte

See scripts and answers on p. 59G.

CD 3 Tr. 3

Ecoutons Listen to the following conversations to find out what the people are buying at the supermarket. Then, listen a second time for how much they're buying. According to the ad on page 65, how much would each customer pay?

9 Méli-mélo!

Parlons Un marchand de fruits et légumes et un client ont une conversation. Mets leur conversation dans le bon ordre. Ensuite, joue la scène avec un(e) camarade, puis changez de rôle. Finalement, jouez cette scène encore une fois. Utilisez des fruits et des légumes différents chaque fois.

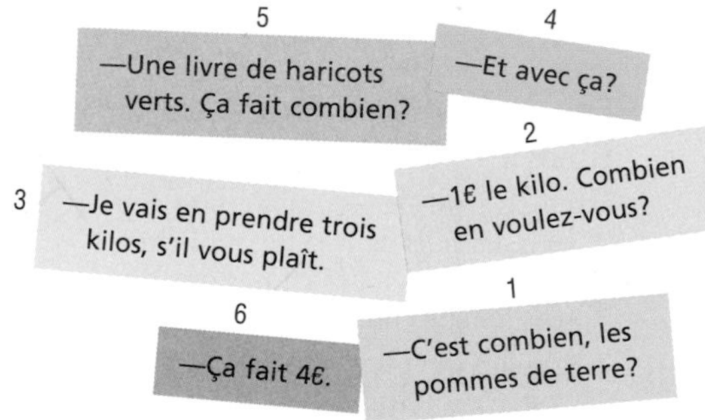

5
—Une livre de haricots verts. Ça fait combien?
4
—Et avec ça?
2
—1€ le kilo. Combien en voulez-vous?
3
—Je vais en prendre trois kilos, s'il vous plaît.
6
—Ça fait 4€.
1
—C'est combien, les pommes de terre?

10 A vos Caddies®

Ecrivons/Parlons Des amis végétariens vont venir manger chez toi. Fais une liste des fruits et des légumes nécessaires pour le repas. Ensuite, fais tes courses à **E. Leclerc.** Joue cette scène avec un(e) camarade, puis changez de rôle.

Connections and Comparisons

Math Link

To practice listening to and saying numbers, have students dictate simple addition and subtraction problems to one another. For example, have one student dictate a problem to another student at the board. **(Quinze et trente-deux font... ?)** The student at the board writes the problem, solves it, and reads it aloud. **(Quinze et trente-deux font quarante-sept.)** Then, he or she chooses another student to go to the board and dictates the next problem. **(Soixante moins deux font... ?)**

STANDARDS: 1.1, 1.2, 2.1, 3.1, 3.2, 4.1, 4.2

Où est-ce qu'on va pour acheter à manger?

A **la charcuterie,** on trouve...

A **la boulangerie,** on achète...

A **la crémerie,** on vend...

A **la pâtisserie,** on se régale avec...

A **la boucherie,** on peut acheter **de la viande** ou **de la volaille.**

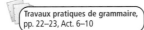

A **la poissonnerie,** on trouve du poisson et **des fruits de mer.**

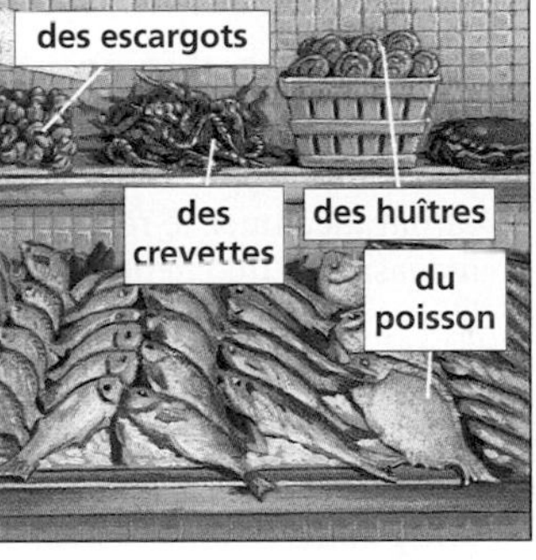

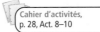

[1]pastries made of two iced cream puffs filled with chocolate or coffee cream
[2]rectangular pastries made of thin layers of puff pastry and cream filling

Travaux pratiques de grammaire, pp. 22–23, Act. 6–10

Cahier d'activités, p. 28, Act. 8–10

Communication for All Students

TPR Choose some of the students' drawings (see Presenting **Vocabulaire** above), reduce their size on a photocopier, and photocopy sets of the vocabulary items that students can cut apart into "cards." Or, you might use the Clip Art found on the *One-Stop Planner CD-ROM* to create the cards. Have students lay out the vocabulary cards on their desks and arrange them according to your instructions. **(Montrez-moi le pâté. Mettez le pain à côté du poulet.)**

Première étape

CHAPITRE 3

Presenting Vocabulaire

Before presenting this vocabulary, ask each student to draw one of the food items on construction paper and use their illustrations to present the vocabulary. Then, draw six storefronts on the board and write in the names of the stores. Show the pictures and ask where the items can be bought. **(Où est-ce qu'on achète du lait?)** As students point to the **crémerie,** have one student tape the picture to the board under the appropriate storefront. When you have used all the pictures in this manner, ask either-or questions about what is sold in each store. **(Qu'est-ce qu'on vend à la crémerie, du fromage ou du pâté?)**

Language Note

Remind students that the **-f** is pronounced in the French word **un œuf,** but that it is not pronounced in **des œufs.**

Teacher Note

You might point out that live **escargots** are found at the **poissonnerie,** while cooked and prepared **escargots** are found at the **charcuterie-traiteur,** where foods are already prepared for take-out.

Game

Loto! Have each student choose sixteen vocabulary cards (see TPR activity) and arrange four rows of four cards on his or her desk. Put one set of cards in a box for yourself and begin a bingo game. Draw cards from the box, call out the vocabulary items, and have students turn over the cards on their desks that correspond to the words you call. A student who turns over four cards in a row calls out **Loto!** and calls out the items in French.

Première étape

CHAPITRE 3

Game

C'est logique! Have each student make up six false statements about where one goes to buy something. **(On achète du lait à la boucherie.)** Then, form two teams. Have the first player from Team A read his or her sentence; the first player from Team B must correct it in order to score a point. **(Mais non, on achète du lait à la crémerie.)** If the sentence is not corrected appropriately, Team A scores a point.

Teaching Suggestion

To close this **étape,** have small groups write and perform the conversations in Activity 14 as skits.

Assess

- Testing Program, pp. 53–56
  Quiz 3-1A, Quiz 3-1B
  Audio CD 3, Tr. 15
- Student Make-Up Assignments, Chapter 3, Alternative Quiz
- Alternative Assessment Guide, p. 34

11 Les courses

CD 3 Tr. 4

Ecoutons Listen as some parents tell their children what to buy for dinner. Which store(s) will they have to visit?

a. la poissonnerie
b. la boulangerie
c. la boucherie
d. la charcuterie
e. la crémerie
f. la pâtisserie

12 L'intrus

Lisons Dans chaque groupe de mots, trouve le mot qui ne va pas avec les autres. Est-ce que tu peux expliquer pourquoi? See answers below.

1	2	3	4	5
du fromage	une religieuse	la volaille	des saucissons	des huîtres
du lait	un gâteau	la charcuterie	des crevettes	du poisson
du pâté	une tarte	la poissonnerie	du jambon	du poulet
du beurre	un rôti	la pâtisserie	du pâté	des escargots

13 Un cordon bleu attentionné

Lisons Toute la semaine, M. Lepic fait la cuisine! Qu'est-ce qu'il peut préparer pour les personnes suivantes? Qu'est-ce qu'il ne devrait pas préparer?

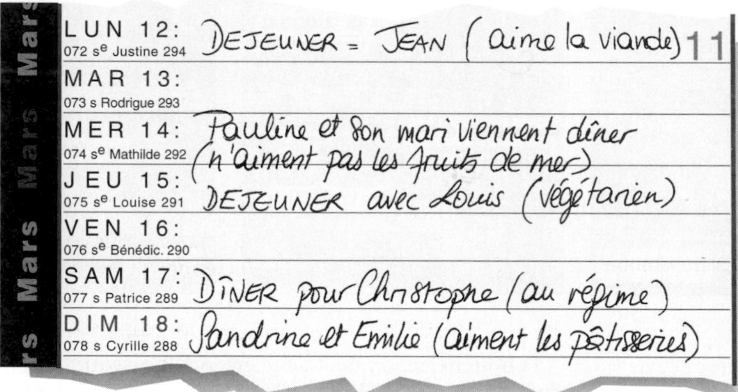

Mars Mars Mars
LUN 12: DEJEUNER = JEAN (aime la viande)
072 s[e] Justine 294
MAR 13:
073 s Rodrigue 293
MER 14: Pauline et son mari viennent dîner (n'aiment pas les fruits de mer)
074 s[e] Mathilde 292
JEU 15: DEJEUNER avec Louis (végétarien)
075 s[e] Louise 291
VEN 16:
076 s[e] Bénédic. 290
SAM 17: DîNER pour Christophe (au régime)
077 s Patrice 289
DIM 18: Sandrine et Emilie (aiment les pâtisseries)
078 s Cyrille 288

14 Vous en voulez combien?

Parlons Cet après-midi, tu vas faire les courses pour Mme Lepic avec un(e) ami(e). Avec un(e) camarade, jouez le rôle des marchands dans les magasins et du client. Achetez tous les produits sur la liste et choisissez des quantités appropriées.

une douzaine d'œufs
deux baguettes
un poulet
500 grammes de crevettes
2 litres de lait
1 kilo de pommes de terre
une tarte aux pommes
500 grammes de jambon

15 Une publicité

Ecrivons Choisis un magasin d'alimentation et crée une publicité pour ce magasin. Tu peux découper des images dans des magazines ou dans le journal, ou si tu préfères, tu peux faire des dessins. Fais la publicité de six produits au moins et n'oublie pas de donner les prix.

Communication for All Students

Slower Pace

11 Before playing the recording, have students name all the food items that can be bought at each store mentioned in the activity.

Challenge

13 Have students make up menus for each meal on the calendar. As an alternative activity, have students plan a menu for a friend or family member, taking into account that person's preferences, and list stores they would need to go to for each item.

Answers

12
1. **pâté;** not found at **crémerie**
2. **rôti;** not found at **pâtisserie**
3. **volaille;** not a store
4. **crevettes;** not found at **charcuterie**
5. **poulet;** not found at **poissonnerie**

STANDARDS: 1.1, 1.3, 5.1., 5.2

Qu'est-ce qu'un petit déjeuner typique ici?

What's a typical breakfast, lunch, or dinner where you live? We talked to francophone people around the world about their meals. Here's what they told us.

Chantal, Martinique

«Au petit déjeuner, je prends du chocolat, un jus de fruit. Je ne mange pas beaucoup, donc c'est tout ce que je prends.»

Quel est ton repas principal?

«Le déjeuner, soit à la cantine, ou bien chez moi, si je ne suis pas au lycée.»

Qu'est-ce que tu prends?

«D'habitude, enfin c'est varié, ça peut être des pâtes... Je ne sais pas... des pâtes, du riz, enfin c'est très varié. Il n'y a pas de trucs précis.» Tr. 6

Emmanuel, France

«Typiquement? Un déjeuner typiquement français, c'est en général [un] chocolat chaud avec des croissants. C'est tout différent des Américains. C'est... avec des croissants, des toasts, du pain, du beurre, de la confiture... Voilà.» Tr. 7

Sandrine, Martinique

«Au petit déjeuner, des tartines. Je prends des tartines au petit déjeuner, avec du chocolat.»

Quel est ton repas principal?

«Pour moi, c'est... le repas principal, c'est celui du midi.»

Qu'est-ce que tu prends?

«Le midi? C'est très varié, le midi. Je peux prendre du poisson, de la viande, du riz, des légumes du pays aussi.» Tr. 8

Qu'en penses-tu?

1. In what ways are these responses different or similar? *Different:* For breakfast, Chantal doesn't eat much. Emmanuel has **croissants**. Sandrine has **tartines**. *Same:* Each has hot chocolate for breakfast.
2. How do typical American meals compare with those mentioned in the interviews? Answers will vary.
3. How might the area in which people live influence their eating habits? The cuisine of a region is influenced by the products and ingredients available in that area and its local customs.

CHAPITRE 3

Teaching Resources p. 69

PRINT

- Video Guide, pp. 17–19
- Cahier d'activités, p. 36

MEDIA 

- One-Stop Planner
- Video Program Videocassette 1, 41:04–44:35
- DVD Tutor, Disc 1
- Audio Compact Discs, CD 3, Trs. 5–8
- Interactive CD-ROM Tutor, Disc 1

Presenting Panorama Culturel

On a sheet of paper, have students label two columns *Food* and *Beverages.* Have them view the video and list in the appropriate columns the food and drink items they hear mentioned. Show the video a second time and have students add more to their lists. Finally, ask the **Questions** below and have students choose the information listed that answers each question.

Questions

1. **Qu'est-ce que Chantal prend d'habitude au déjeuner?** (C'est très varié, des pâtes ou du riz.)
2. **D'après Emmanuel, qu'est-ce que c'est qu'un petit déjeuner typiquement français?** (un chocolat chaud, des croissants, des toasts, du pain, du beurre, de la confiture)
3. **Quel est le repas principal de Sandrine?** (celui de midi)

Connections and Comparisons

Thinking Critically

Analyzing Ask students what they would need to know if they were dinner guests of a French family. Then, ask them why table manners are important. Ask them what table manners are traditionally expected in the United States and if they think there are similar expectations in French homes.

Deuxième étape

CHAPITRE 3

Teaching Resources
pp. 70–73

PRINT
- Lesson Planner, p. 13
- TPR Storytelling Book, pp. 18–19
- Listening Activities, pp. 19–20, 24
- Activities for Communication, pp. 15–16, 86, 88–89, 141–142
- Travaux pratiques de grammaire, pp. 24–26
- Grammar Tutor for Students of French, Chapter 3
- Cahier d'activités, pp. 29–31
- Testing Program, pp. 57–60
- Alternative Assessment Guide, p. 34
- Student Make-Up Assignments, Chapter 3

MEDIA 
- One-Stop Planner
- Audio Compact Discs, CD 3, Trs. 9–11, 16, 23–24
- Teaching Transparencies: 3-2, 3-B; **Grammaire supplémentaire** Answers; Travaux pratiques de grammaire Answers
- Interactive CD-ROM Tutor, Disc 1

Bell Work
Write the names of the following stores on the board or on a transparency: **la boulangerie, la pâtisserie, la boucherie, la charcuterie, la crémerie,** and **la poissonnerie.** Have students list two food items that can be purchased at each store.

Deuxième étape

Objectives Asking for, offering, accepting, and refusing food; paying and responding to compliments

WA3 PARIS REGION-3

16 Au Lion d'Or
See answers below.

Lisons Regarde le menu du **Lion d'Or.** Combien de catégories est-ce qu'il y a sur le menu? Comment elles s'appellent? Quand tu vas au restaurant, combien de plats est-ce que tu prends? Comment tu appelles ces plats?

17 Et au petit déjeuner?
Parlons/Ecrivons D'habitude, qu'est-ce qu'on mange pour le petit déjeuner dans ta région? Est-ce que c'est la même chose qu'au **Lion d'Or** ou est-ce que c'est différent?

Note culturelle
Meals occupy a central place in French family and social life. Lunch and dinner usually consist of several courses: an appetizer, the main course, a simple green salad, cheese, and dessert. A special meal might have as many as nine courses! As an appetizer, the French might eat cold cuts, vegetables in a vinaigrette sauce, or soup. The main course consists of meat or seafood. The French eat a wide variety of meats, fowl, and game such as duck, goose, guinea hen, and rabbit. Potatoes are very common, and you may be served a variety of vegetables like turnips, endive, eggplant, or leeks. For dessert, fresh fruit is often served. Pastries or ice cream are usually reserved for special occasions. The evening meal is generally lighter and often meatless. Eggs are eaten at dinner, but rarely at breakfast.

LE LION D'OR

Entrées

Pâté de campagne	3,05 €
Saucisson sec pur porc	3,05 €
Sardines à l'huile	3,05 €
Carottes râpées	3,05 €
Œuf dur mayonnaise	3,05 €

Viandes-Volaille

Filet de bœuf	9,91 €
Carré d'agneau	9,91 €
Steak au poivre	9,15 €
Poulet garni	6,86 €
Daube de lapin	10,67 €
Filet de canard à l'orange	9,45 €
Tartare (préparé à la commande)	8,54 €

Tous nos plats sont accompagnés de frites ou de salade verte ou de haricots verts

Fromages

Camembert, Gruyère	2,90 €
Yaourt	1,52 €
Fromages Fermiers Sélectionnés	
St-Nectaire	3,35 €
Roquefort Papillon (Carte Noire)	3,81 €
Chèvre	4,12 €

Desserts

Crème de marrons	1,83 €
Mont-Blanc	2,44 €
Tarte aux fruits	3,96 €
Crème caramel	3,35 €
Mousse au chocolat	3,66 €

Boissons

Limonade	3,05 €
Eau minérale	3,35 €
Jus de fruit	3,66 €
Thé ou café glacé	3,96 €
Cidre	3,66 €
Milk shake	4,57 €

Au petit déjeuner

Croissant	1,83 €
Tartine	1,37 €
Gâteau Breton	1,37 €

Petit déjeuner complet à ..... 7,62 €
Double express ou crème ou chocolat ou thé, 1 croissant, 1 tartine, 1 orange pressée, confiture, beurre, miel

Cultures and Communities

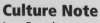

Culture Note
In a French restaurant, if you order **un café,** you will be served **un express,** very strong coffee in a small cup. For something less strong, people drink coffee with steamed milk **(un café-crème),** served in a large cup. French restaurants and cafés do not offer free refills of coffee. In the morning at home, people will drink coffee with hot milk **(un café au lait)** in a large bowl.

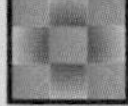

Multicultural Link
Have students interview people from several ethnic or cultural backgrounds different from their own. Have them ask the people to describe a typical breakfast, lunch, or dinner in their culture. Have students work in groups to share and compile their findings.

Answers

16 6 categories; appetizer, meat and poultry, cheese, dessert, drinks, breakfast; *Answers will vary; Possible answers:* appetizer, main course, dessert

STANDARDS: 1.2, 2.1, 3.2, 4.2

Vocabulaire

Les repas

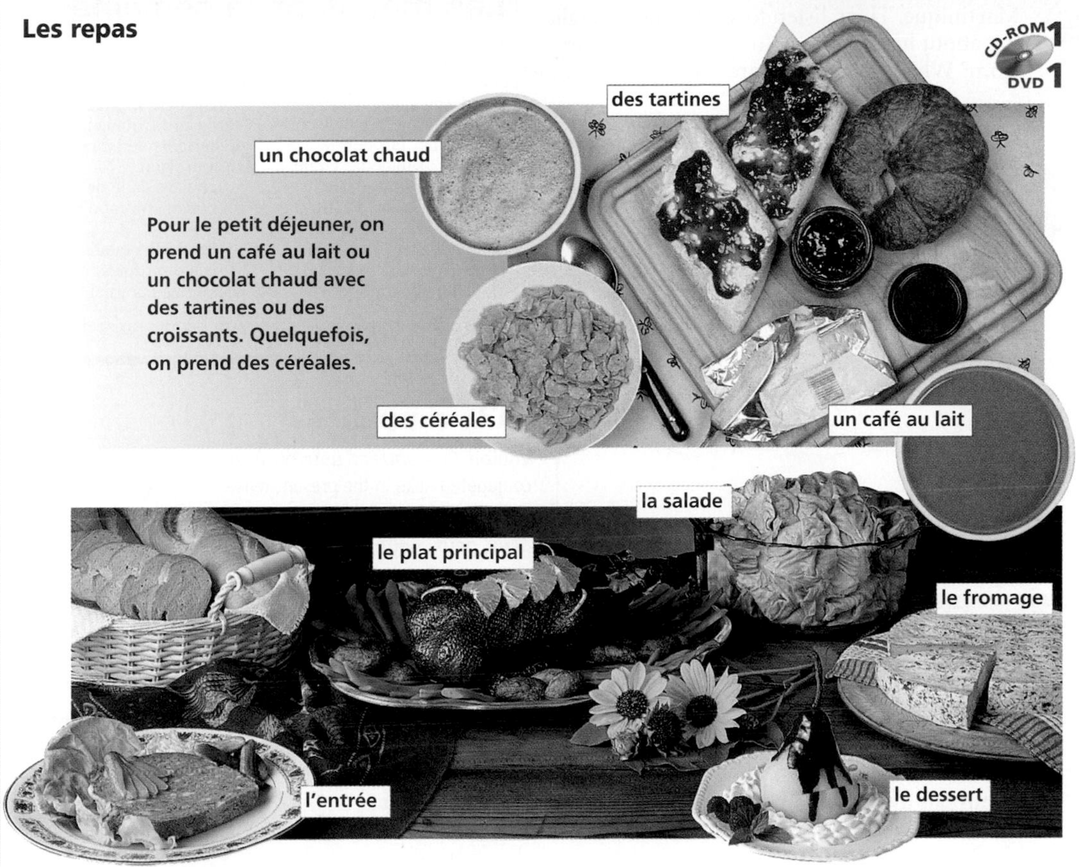

Pour le déjeuner et pour le dîner, on commence par une entrée. Ensuite, on sert le plat principal suivi d'une salade verte. A la fin du repas, on passe le plateau de fromages. Et pour terminer, on prend un dessert ou un fruit.

Cahier d'activités, p. 29, Act. 11–12

Travaux pratiques de grammaire, p. 24, Act. 11–12

18 Matin, midi ou soir? See scripts and answers on p. 59G.

Ecoutons Ecoute ces conversations. Est-ce qu'on parle du petit déjeuner, du déjeuner ou du dîner?

CD 3 Tr. 9

19 A la carte

Parlons Tu vas au **Lion d'Or** pour le déjeuner. Qu'est-ce que tu commandes? Joue la scène avec un(e) camarade.

Exemple —**Qu'est-ce que vous prenez comme entrée?**
—**Je voudrais…**

Qu'est-ce que vous prenez comme plat principal?

Pour le dessert?

Et comme fromage?

Et comme boisson?

Communication for All Students

Slower Pace

Referring to the display you used for **Presenting Vocabulaire** above, ask several either-or questions about what one eats for meals or various courses. Write the word next to each picture and ask **Quand est-ce qu'on mange de la salade? Au petit déjeuner ou au déjeuner? Qu'est-ce qu'on mange comme entrée? Une tarte aux pommes ou du pâté?**

Language Note

Point out that in French, **l'entrée** is the appetizer, while in English, *entrée* refers to the main dish. The main course in French is **le plat principal.**

Deuxième étape

CHAPITRE 3

Presenting Vocabulaire

Use the pictures students drew for the **Vocabulaire** on page 67 and create others to teach this vocabulary. Then, draw three columns on the board and label them **Petit déjeuner, Déjeuner,** and **Dîner.** Under **Déjeuner** and **Dîner,** write **entrée, plat principal, salade, fromage,** and **dessert.** Next, show a picture, ask **Quand est-ce qu'on mange une tartine?** and tape the picture to the board where students suggest. After all the pictures have been taped to the board, ask individuals **Qu'est-ce que tu voudrais manger comme entrée?** and so on.

Math Link

Have students convert the prices listed in the menu from euros to American dollars. The current rate of exchange can be found in the business section of the newspaper.

Health Links

- French meals are planned to facilitate digestion. The **entrée** wakes up the palate, and the **plat principal** is the main part of the meal. Next, the **salade,** made with an acidic dressing, helps digest the meat. The **fromages** and **fruits** that follow contain enzymes that also aid digestion.
- Obtain a chart from a health teacher that illustrates healthful meals. Use this to practice the vocabulary.

Deuxième étape

CHAPITRE 3

Teaching Resources
pp. 70–73

PRINT

- Lesson Planner, p. 13
- TPR Storytelling Book, pp. 18–19
- Listening Activities, pp. 19–20, 24
- Activities for Communication, pp. 15–16, 86, 88–89, 141–142
- Travaux pratiques de grammaire, pp. 24–26
- Grammar Tutor for Students of French, Chapter 3
- Cahier d'activités, pp. 29–31
- Testing Program, pp. 57–60
- Alternative Assessment Guide, p. 34
- Student Make-Up Assignments, Chapter 3

MEDIA 

- One-Stop Planner
- Audio Compact Discs, CD 3, Trs. 9–11, 16, 23–24
- Teaching Transparencies: 3-2, 3-B; **Grammaire supplémentaire** Answers; Travaux pratiques de grammaire Answers
- Interactive CD-ROM Tutor, Disc 1

Presenting
Comment dit-on... ?

Place pictures of food and beverages on a table. Ask a volunteer to pass you various items. **(Je pourrais avoir du sel, s'il te plaît?)** Prompt the student to respond **Tenez** or **Voilà** and pass you the picture of the item you requested. Take the picture and say **Merci.** Repeat with the other items. Then, distribute some pictures to students, asking **Tu pourrais me passer le beurre, s'il te plaît?** to elicit the appropriate response as they pass the items back to you.

20 Les menus de la cantine See scripts and answers on p. 59G.

CD 3 Tr. 10

Ecoutons Read this list of school menus from Martinique. Then, listen to some students talking about lunch. Which town are the speakers from? Which day's menu are they talking about?

CANTINES SCOLAIRES
Les menus de la semaine

VAUCLIN :
Lundi : fromage, lapin chasseur, haricots rosés, mandarines.
Mardi : melon, couscous au mouton, lait gélifié.
Jeudi : salade de laitue, poisson au four, haricots verts et carottes, yaourt.
Vendredi : salade de concombres, steak haché au four, chou vert sauce blanche, cocktail de fruits.

RIVIERE-SALEE :
Lundi : salade de concombres, haricots rosés, poisson grillé, glace.
Mardi : fromage, salade de haricots verts, poisson au four, fruit.
Jeudi : salade de carottes, riz blanc, colombo de cabri, glace.
Vendredi : salade de tomates, sardines, pâté en pot, île au caramel.

21 Une cantine quatre étoiles

Ecrivons Tu vas créer des menus pour une "semaine francophone" à ton école. Qu'est-ce qu'on va manger? Fais une liste des plats pour chaque jour de la semaine.

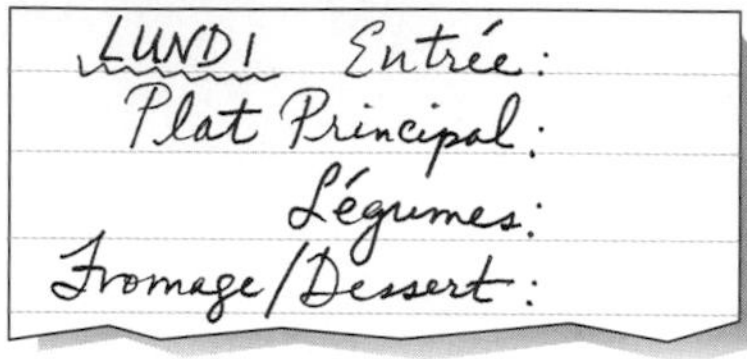

Tu te rappelles?

Vouloir *(to want)* and **pouvoir** *(can, to be able)* are conjugated alike in the present tense.

veux, veux, veut, voulons, voulez, veulent
peux, peux, peut, pouvons, pouvez, peuvent

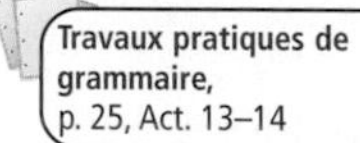
Travaux pratiques de grammaire, p. 25, Act. 13–14

Grammaire supplémentaire, p. 83, Act. 3–4

Comment dit-on...?

Asking for, offering, accepting, and refusing food; paying and responding to compliments

CD-ROM 1 DVD 1

To ask for food:	To respond:
Je pourrais avoir du pain, **s'il vous plaît (s'il te plaît)?** *May I have some . . . , please?*	**Voilà.** *Here it is.*
Vous pourriez (Tu pourrais) me passer le sel? *Would you pass me . . . ?*	**Tenez (Tiens).** *Here you are.*
To offer food or drink:	To accept:
Vous voulez (Tu veux) de la salade?	**Oui, je veux bien.**
	To refuse:
Encore du gâteau? *Some more . . . ?*	**Merci, ça va.** *Thank you, I've had enough.* **Je n'ai plus faim/soif.** *I'm not hungry/thirsty anymore.*
To pay a compliment about food:	To respond:
C'est vraiment bon! *This is really good!* **C'était délicieux!** *That was delicious!*	**Ce n'est pas grand-chose.** *It's nothing special.* **Merci, c'est gentil!**

Cahier d'activités, pp. 29–30, Act. 13–14

Cultures and Communities

Culture Note

20 Ask students why there is no menu listed for **mercredi.** Remind them that in many parts of France, Martinique, and Guadeloupe, **collège** and **lycée** students go to school only in the morning on Wednesday. Most students also go to school on Saturday morning. In some schools, however, the **cantine** still serves lunch on Wednesday and Saturday.

22 A table!

See scripts and answers on p. 59G.

Ecoutons Listen to the following conversations at the table. Is the first speaker asking for food, offering food, or paying a compliment?

CD 3 Tr. 11

Note de grammaire

CD-ROM 1 DVD 1

- When you're talking about a whole item, use the article **un, une,** or **des** *(a, an* or *some)* before the noun.
- When you're talking about a portion of an item, use the partitive articles **du, de la,** or **de l'** *(some)* before the noun.

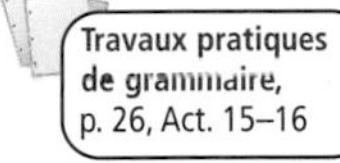

Travaux pratiques de grammaire, p. 26, Act. 15–16

Grammaire supplémentaire, pp. 83–84, Act. 5–7

Cahier d'activités, p. 30, Act. 15–16

23 Grammaire en contexte

Lisons Décide si on va entendre chaque commentaire **à table** ou **dans un magasin.**

1. Vous voulez encore du poulet? à table
2. Je vais prendre une tarte aux pommes. dans un magasin
3. Un rôti de bœuf, s'il vous plaît. dans un magasin
4. Encore de l'eau? à table
5. Je voudrais un kilo de pommes. dans un magasin
6. Je pourrais avoir du poisson? à table

24 Grammaire en contexte

Parlons Accepte ou refuse ces plats. Si tu reprends quelque chose, fais aussi un compliment!

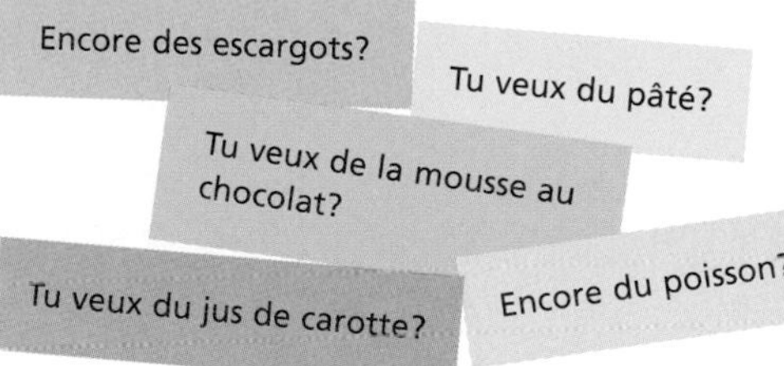

Encore des escargots?
Tu veux du pâté?
Tu veux de la mousse au chocolat?
Tu veux du jus de carotte?
Encore du poisson?

25 Un menu pour des amis

Ecrivons Tu as invité des amis à un déjeuner français. Qu'est-ce que tu vas faire comme entrée, comme plat principal et comme dessert? Crée le menu de ton repas.

26 Jeu de rôle

Parlons Tes invités de l'activité 25 sont arrivés. Accueille-les et sers le repas. Demande à tes invités s'ils veulent autre chose. Ils vont te répondre poliment. Ils vont aussi te faire des compliments sur le repas et dire s'il veulent reprendre de quelque chose.

A la française

If you'd like to try eating a meal the French way . . .

- wish everyone **Bon appétit!** before you start to eat.
- keep your hands on or above the table.
- place your bread next to your plate.
- don't change your fork to the other hand after cutting a piece of meat.
- eat French fries, pizza, and fruit with a knife and fork, not with your hands.
- ask for something politely and never point.
- eat slowly and enjoy the conversation.

Communication for All Students

Language Note

Point out that **Tiens!** is also used as an interjection meaning *Hey!* as in **Tiens, voilà Marie!** *(Hey, there's Marie!)*

Challenge

22 Have students offer appropriate responses for each request they hear in the activity.

Presenting Note de grammaire

The partitive Bring to class a cake, orange juice, and small serving cartons of apple juice. Demonstrate the difference between **un gâteau** (showing the cake) and **du gâteau** (cutting the cake). Do the same for the juice. Then, have students ask for some orange juice **(du jus d'orange),** an individual serving of apple juice **(un jus de pomme),** or some cake **(du gâteau).**

Writing Assessment

25 You might use the following rubric when grading your students on this activity.

Writing Rubric	Points			
	4	3	2	1
Content (Complete–Incomplete)				
Comprehensibility (Comprehensible–Incomprehensible)				
Accuracy (Accurate–Seldom accurate)				
Organization (Well organized–Poorly organized)				
Effort (Excellent–Minimal)				

18–20: A 14–15: C Under
16–17: B 12–13: D 12: F

Assess

- Testing Program, pp. 57–60 Quiz 3-2A, Quiz 3-2B Audio CD 3, Tr. 16
- Student Make-Up Assignments, Chapter 3, Alternative Quiz
- Alternative Assessment Guide, p. 34

STANDARDS: 1.1, 2.1, 3.2, 4.1, 4.2, 5.1, 5.2

CHAPITRE 3

Motivating Activity

Ask students if they've ever purchased items using a currency from a different country. Have them name the currencies of as many countries as they can think of. Students might refer to the list of countries in the Additional Vocabulary on pages R20–R21.

Presenting Rencontre culturelle

Display a map of Europe or project *Map Transparency 3: L'Europe francophone* (Level 3 *Teaching Transparencies).* Identify the countries currently using the euro. Read the introductory paragraph and **Savais-tu que... ?** with students. Then, have partners answer the questions in **Qu'en penses-tu... ?**

Economics Link

There are many reasons why a country might change its currency. Many countries have had to devalue or otherwise change their currencies in order to adapt to changing economic conditions. Ask students how they would react if a loaf of bread suddenly cost $10 and how their lives and values might change as a result of long-term inflation or recession.

In 2002, France adopted a new currency, replacing its own **francs** with the currency shared by most of the countries of Western Europe, the **euro.** What do you know about the euro?

Qu'en penses-tu? See answers below.

1. What items are illustrated on the bills and coins? What common element do you see on all the bills and coins?
2. How do these bills compare in design to U.S. dollars?
3. If several countries in the Western Hemisphere decided to use a common currency, how do you think it would affect travel, tourism, and banking?

Savais-tu que... ?

The adoption of a common currency is intended to strengthen Europe economically. One way the euro could do that is by making transactions easier between countries, thereby encouraging trade between them. Euro bills represent the major styles of European architecture with abstract designs of bridges and buildings. Why do you think the design of the bills favors abstract elements instead of real monuments? Euro coins have a common symbol on one face and unique symbols representing each country on the other. How do you think this new currency will affect the economy of Europe? How will it affect the economy of the United States?

Answers

1. architectural elements and maps; stars
2. *Possible answers:* Euro bills are more colorful than U.S. dollars; euro bills vary in size, but all U.S. bills are the same size.
3. Answers will vary.

Cultures and Communities

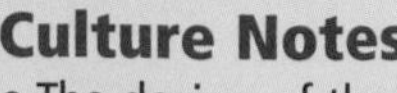

Culture Notes

• The design of the euro was a lengthy process that required the cooperation of all of the European Union countries in order to have a currency that would appeal to citizens of many cultures. Have students do a Web search, using the keywords **euro currency,** for the most recent information on the European Union and the exchange rate of the euro.

• Since France's overseas departments are covered by the Treaty on European Union, these departments use the euro as metropolitan France does. The euro is also in circulation in Monaco. Since France's overseas territories are not members of the European Union, they do not use the euro, nor do countries using the CFA **(franc de la Communauté financière africaine).**

Troisième étape

Objectives Asking for and giving advice; extending good wishes

WA3 PARIS REGION-3

Salut,

Juste un petit mot pour te demander de venir manger à la maison samedi soir. J'ai invité Jérôme et Béatrice aussi. On va faire une fondue. Ça te dit? Viens vers les sept heures. Tu n'es pas obligé d'apporter quelque chose, mais si tu y tiens, amène un dessert ou quelque chose à boire. A bientôt!

Sylvie

On fait une petite fête pour l'anniversaire de Gilles dimanche après-midi au parc de la Victoire. Ça va être une surprise, alors surtout ne lui dis rien! On s'occupe du gâteau et des bougies. J'espère que tu vas pouvoir venir. Plus on est de fous, plus on rit. A plus tard.

Jean-Pierre
Céline

1. un dessert ou une boisson **2.** un dîner **3.** samedi soir à sept heures **4.** une fondue **5.** chez Sylvie **6.** avec Jérôme, Béatrice et Sylvie

1. un cadeau **2.** une fête pour l'anniversaire de Gilles **3.** dimanche après-midi **4.** du gâteau **5.** au parc de la Victoire **6.** avec Céline et Jean-Pierre

27 Tu es invité(e)

Lisons Quelles sont les informations données dans chaque invitation?

1 Qu'est-ce qu'on apporte?
5 Où?
2 Qu'est-ce qu'on va faire?

3 Quand?

6 Avec qui?

4 Qu'est-ce qu'on va manger?

Note culturelle

In France, a meal is often a way to celebrate friendship or a special occasion. The New Year's dinner is usually spent with friends, while birthday and Christmas dinners are traditionally family celebrations when people exchange gifts and cards. Young people often receive a small gift on their saint's day as well.

Communication for All Students

Challenge

27 Have students imagine they are giving a dinner or birthday party, and then write an invitation, using those in the activity as models.

27 Have students work in pairs to answer the questions. Then, have one pair call out the answers and another pair call out the questions they answer. For example, one pair might call out **un dessert** and another pair would say **Qu'est-ce qu'on apporte?**

Troisième étape

CHAPITRE 3

Teaching Resources
pp. 75–79

PRINT
- Lesson Planner, p. 14
- TPR Storytelling Book, pp. 20–21
- Listening Activities, pp. 21, 25
- Activities for Communication, pp.17–18, 87, 89, 141–142
- Travaux pratiques de grammaire, pp. 27–28
- Grammar Tutor for Students of French, Chapter 3
- Cahier d'activités, pp. 32–34
- Testing Program, pp. 61–64
- Alternative Assessment Guide, p. 34
- Student Make-Up Assignments, Chapter 3

MEDIA
- One-Stop Planner
- Audio Compact Discs, CD 3, Trs. 12–13, 17, 25–26
- Teaching Transparencies: 3-3, 3-C; **Grammaire supplémentaire** Answers; Travaux pratiques de grammaire Answers
- Interactive CD-ROM Tutor, Disc 1

Bell Work

Write the following words on the board or on a transparency: **fromage, salade, entrée, fruits,** and **plat principal.** Have students write the courses in the proper order and add an appropriate food item for each one.

Teaching Suggestion

Before students read the letters, pretend you have just received an invitation. Open an envelope that contains an invitation similar to the ones on this page and read it aloud. Have students tell you who sent the invitation, to what event you are invited, and so on.

STANDARDS: 1.2, 2.1, 3.2, 4.2

Troisième étape

CHAPITRE 3

Teaching Resources pp. 75–79

PRINT

- Lesson Planner, p. 14
- TPR Storytelling Book, pp. 20–21
- Listening Activities, pp. 21, 25
- Activities for Communication, pp.17–18, 87, 89, 141–142
- Travaux pratiques de grammaire, pp. 27–28
- Grammar Tutor for Students of French, Chapter 3
- Cahier d'activités, pp. 32–34
- Testing Program, pp. 61–64
- Alternative Assessment Guide, p. 34
- Student Make-Up Assignments, Chapter 3

MEDIA 

- One-Stop Planner
- Audio Compact Discs, CD 3, Trs. 12–13, 17, 25–26
- Teaching Transparencies: 3-3, 3-C; **Grammaire supplémentaire** Answers; Travaux pratiques de grammaire Answers
- Interactive CD-ROM Tutor, Disc 1

Presenting Comment dit-on... ?

Write on a transparency several questions about what to give people as gifts. **(Tu as une idée de cadeau pour le président des Etats-Unis?)** Next to each question, give two possible answers: **a. Offre-lui un disque de rock. b. Offre-lui un livre sur l'histoire mondiale.** For each question, have students choose the letter of the most appropriate response. Finally, ask **Qu'est-ce que tu en penses? C'est une bonne idée ou c'est banal?**

Comment dit-on...?

Asking for and giving advice

To ask for advice:

Tu as une idée de cadeau pour Oncle Omar?
Have you got a gift idea for . . . ?
Qu'est-ce que je pourrais offrir à Anne?
What could I give to . . . ?

To give advice:

Offre-lui (-leur) des bonbons.
Give him/her (them). . .
Tu pourrais lui (leur) offrir un CD.
You could give him/her (them) . . .
Un livre, **peut-être.** . . . *maybe.*

To accept advice:

Bonne idée!
C'est original. *That's unique.*
Tu as raison, elle adore la musique.
You're right . . .
D'accord.
OK.

To reject advice:

C'est trop cher. *It's too expensive.*
C'est banal. *That's ordinary.*
Ce n'est pas son style. *That's not his/her style.*
Il/Elle en a déjà un(e).
He/She already has one (of them).

Cahier d'activités, p. 32, Act. 20

28 Quelques idées de cadeaux

See scripts and answers on p. 59H.

Ecoutons Listen as some students ask for advice about gifts. Do they accept or reject the suggestions?

CD 3 Tr. 12

Grammaire

The indirect object pronouns *lui* and *leur*

CD-ROM 1 DVD 1

The pronouns **lui** *(to/for him, to/for her)* and **leur** *(to/for them)* replace a phrase that begins with **à** or **pour** followed by a person or persons. **Lui** and **leur** never refer to things.

- Place **lui** or **leur** before the conjugated verb:
  Tu **leur offres** un cadeau? Je ne **lui parle** pas souvent.
- If there's an infinitive in the sentence, **lui** or **leur** is placed before it:
  Tu pourrais **lui offrir** un bracelet. Je ne vais pas **leur acheter** de fleurs.
- In a positive command, place **lui** or **leur** after the verb, connected to it with a hyphen:
  Offre-lui des bonbons! **Achète-leur** un cadeau.
- In a negative command, place **lui** or **leur** before the verb.
  Ne **lui** parle pas!

Grammaire supplémentaire, p. 85, Act. 8–9

Cahier d'activités, p. 32, Act. 21

Travaux pratiques de grammaire, p. 27, Act. 17–18

Communication for All Students

Kinesthetic Learners

Have students prepare index cards with these words: **Je/parle/à mon amie/à ma mère/à mes parents/à mes amis/à mon professeur/à mes cousins/lui/leur.** First, say a sentence with an indirect object and have students construct it with their cards **(Je parle à mon amie.).** Then have them take out the indirect object and replace it with the pronoun **lui** or **leur,** in the correct position.

STANDARDS: 1.2, 4.1

29 Grammaire en contexte 

Parlons Ton ami(e) ne sait pas quels cadeaux offrir à ces gens. Donne-lui des idées. See answers below.

1. Iman et Sylvie sont toujours à la dernière mode.
2. Catherine fait toujours des photos.
3. Vincent et Paul aiment bien manger.
4. Marc joue au foot tous les jours.
5. Il y a toujours des fleurs sur la table chez tante Marie.
6. Eric va étudier l'allemand à l'université.

Offre-lui...
Tu pourrais lui offrir...
Offre-leur...
Tu pourrais leur offrir...

un dictionnaire
un joli album de photos
des boucles d'oreilles
des chocolats
des baskets
un vase

Vocabulaire

Les magasins et les cadeaux

Oh là là, C'est l'anniversaire de maman. Il me faut des idées de cadeaux...

Des bonbons?
Une boîte de chocolats?

Des fleurs?

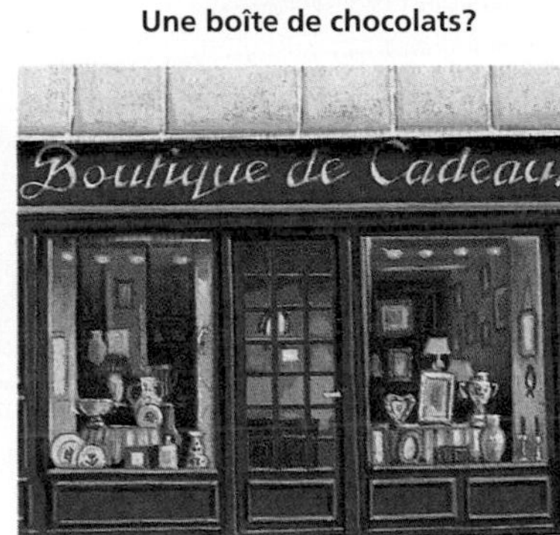

Un cadre?
Un vase?

Un foulard?
Un portefeuille?
Un sac à main?

Cahier d'activités, pp. 33–34, Act. 23–25

Travaux pratiques de grammaire, p. 28, Act. 19–21

Cultures and Communities

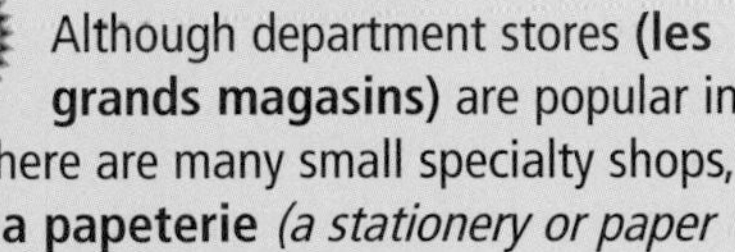

Culture Note

Although department stores **(les grands magasins)** are popular in France, there are many small specialty shops, such as **la papeterie** *(a stationery or paper goods store)*, **la carterie** *(a postcard shop)*, **la parfumerie** *(a perfume store)*, **la bijouterie** *(a jewelry store)*, and **le disquaire** *(a CD/music store)*. You might give students the words **(parfum, bijou, carte)** and have them guess the names of the shops.

Troisième étape

CHAPITRE 3

Presenting Grammaire

The indirect object pronouns *lui* and *leur* On large cards, write questions containing indirect objects underlined in different colored ink. **(Tu offres un cadeau <u>à tes parents</u>?)** Show each card and have students respond, using an indirect object pronoun. **(Oui, je leur offre un cadeau.)** Show the correct response you've written on the opposite side of the card, with the pronoun underlined.

Presenting Vocabulaire

Use pictures or objects to teach the words, having students repeat after you. Then, write the names of the stores on the board. Show an item **(des bonbons)** and ask **Qu'est-ce que c'est?** When students have answered, tell them where the item can be bought. **(On achète des bonbons à la confiserie.)** Then, tape the picture of that item to the board under the appropriate shop.

Building on Previous Skills

Re-enter the expressions used to ask someone to do something for you. **(Tu peux aller... ? Tu me rapportes... ?)** Tell students you are going to a certain store. **(Je vais à la maroquinerie.)** Have them ask you to buy something for them. **(Vous me rapportez un portefeuille?)**

Answers

29
1. Offre-leur des boucles d'oreilles.
2. Offre-lui un joli album de photos.
3. Offre-leur des chocolats.
4. Tu pourrais lui offrir des baskets.
5. Tu pourrais lui offrir un vase.
6. Offre-lui un dictionnaire.

Troisième étape

CHAPITRE 3

Teaching Resources
pp. 75–79

PRINT

- Lesson Planner, p. 14
- TPR Storytelling Book, pp. 20–21
- Listening Activities, pp. 21, 25
- Activities for Communication, pp. 17–18, 87, 89, 141–142
- Travaux pratiques de grammaire, pp. 27–28
- Grammar Tutor for Students of French, Chapter 3
- Cahier d'activités, pp. 32–34
- Testing Program, pp. 61–64
- Alternative Assessment Guide, p. 34
- Student Make-Up Assignments, Chapter 3

MEDIA 

- One-Stop Planner
- Audio Compact Discs, CD 3, Trs. 12–13, 17, 25–26
- Teaching Transparencies: 3-3, 3-C; **Grammaire supplémentaire** Answers; Travaux pratiques de grammaire Answers
- Interactive CD-ROM Tutor, Disc 1

Language Note
Remind students that with **fleuriste** and **disquaire,** they should use **chez** when referring to these words as stores. **(Je vais chez le fleuriste et à la confiserie.)**

Slower Pace
30 Before playing the recording, call out the names of these items and have students jot down the letters of the appropriate illustrations.

30 L'anniversaire de Mme Lepic See scripts and answers on p. 59H.

CD 3 Tr. 13

Ecoutons Qu'est-ce que chaque personne offre à Mme Lepic pour son anniversaire?

a.

b.

c.

d.

e.

31 Cadeau d'anniversaire

Parlons Mardi prochain, c'est l'anniversaire de ton meilleur ami (ta meilleure amie). Fais une description de ton ami(e), puis demande des conseils à tes camarades.

EXEMPLE — **Patrick aime la musique et le tennis. Qu'est-ce que je pourrais lui offrir?**
— **Offre-lui des baskets!**
— **Non, c'est trop cher.**
— **Tu pourrais lui offrir...**

32 Au grand magasin

Parlons Ton ami(e) et toi, vous faites des courses dans un grand magasin. Vous avez 75 euros chacun(e). Faites une liste de quatre personnes pour qui vous voulez acheter des cadeaux. Ensuite, fais tes suggestions à ton ami(e). Il/Elle va te donner des idées aussi.

Communication for All Students

Visual/Auditory Learners
32 For additional practice, have students write sentences telling what they are going to buy for six to eight people and for which occasions. **(Je vais acheter un portefeuille pour Papa pour la fête des Pères.)** You might make a list of holidays and special events on the board. Then, on a separate sheet of paper, have students label three columns: **cadeau, pour qui,** and **pourquoi.** Have them fill the columns with the gifts, people, and occasions they wrote about, but not in the same order. Then, have them pass the sheet of paper to a partner. The partner will draw lines from the gifts to the appropriate names and occasions as the student reads aloud his or her sentences.

Comment dit-on...?

Extending good wishes

Bonne fête! *Happy holiday! (Happy saint's day!)*
Joyeux (Bon) anniversaire! *Happy birthday!*
Bonne fête de Hanoukkah! *Happy Hanukkah!*
Joyeux Noël! *Merry Christmas!*
Bonne année! *Happy New Year!*
Meilleurs vœux! *Best wishes!*
Félicitations! *Congratulations!*
Bon voyage! *Have a good trip! (by plane, ship)*
Bonne route! *Have a good trip! (by car)*
Bon rétablissement! *Get well soon!*

Cahier d'activités, p. 34, Act. 26–27

33 Qu'est-ce que tu dis? See answers below.

Parlons/Ecrivons

1. C'est l'anniversaire de ton ami(e).
2. C'est le vingt-cinq décembre.
3. Ton professeur est malade.
4. On allume la menorah.
5. C'est la Fête des Pères.
6. C'est le premier janvier.
7. Ton ami(e) part pour la Côte d'Ivoire.
8. C'est le jour du mariage de ta cousine.
9. Tes parents vont faire du camping.
10. Ta mère a une promotion.

34 Les cartes de vœux

Ecrivons Fais une carte de vœux humoristique ou sérieuse pour quelqu'un.

35 De l'école au travail

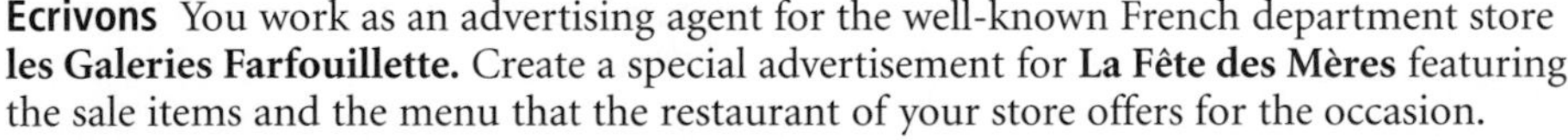

Ecrivons You work as an advertising agent for the well-known French department store **les Galeries Farfouillette.** Create a special advertisement for **La Fête des Mères** featuring the sale items and the menu that the restaurant of your store offers for the occasion.

Cultures and Communities

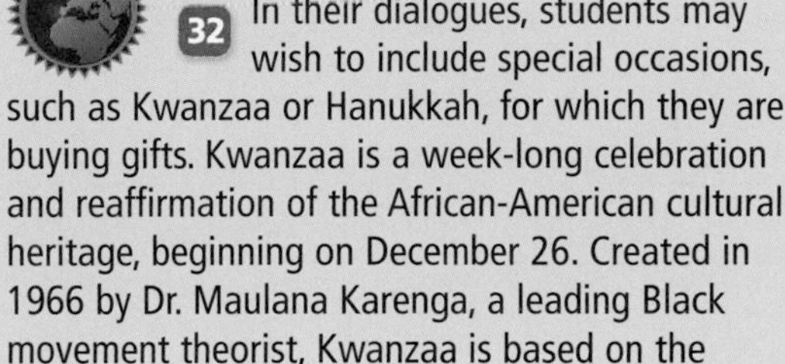

Culture Note

32 In their dialogues, students may wish to include special occasions, such as Kwanzaa or Hanukkah, for which they are buying gifts. Kwanzaa is a week-long celebration and reaffirmation of the African-American cultural heritage, beginning on December 26. Created in 1966 by Dr. Maulana Karenga, a leading Black movement theorist, Kwanzaa is based on the harvest festivals of African tribes, and in Swahili, the name means "first fruits of the harvest." Hanukkah, also celebrated in December, commemorates the second century B.C. victory of a small group of Jews against the armed forces of King Antioch. This group of Jews succeeded in the rededication of a Jewish temple in Jerusalem, which had been defiled by the King's army.

Troisième étape

CHAPITRE 3

Presenting Comment dit-on... ?

Say these expressions and have students repeat after you as they read along in their book. Then, have students illustrate each expression on a separate piece of paper. Display some of their illustrations on the bulletin board under headings you've prepared.

Teaching Suggestion

Students might hold up cards showing the dates of certain holidays **(le 25 décembre)** or illustrations representing them (a birthday cake), to which a partner would respond with the appropriate expression.

Language-to-Language

If you have Spanish-speaking students in your class, have them give the Spanish equivalents for the holiday expressions. **(¡Feliz cumpleaños!, ¡Feliz Navidad!)** Have students choose one or two of the expressions and try to find their equivalents in as many languages as they can.

Assess

- Testing Program, pp. 61–64
  Quiz 3-3A, Quiz 3-3B
  Audio CD 3, Tr. 17
- Student Make-Up Assignments, Chapter 3, Alternative Quiz
- Alternative Assessment Guide, p. 34

Answers

33
1. Joyeux anniversaire!
2. Joyeux Noël!
3. Bon rétablissement!
4. Bonne fête de Hanoukkah!
5. Bonne fête, Papa!
6. Bonne année!
7. Bon voyage!
8. Meilleurs vœux!
9. Bonne route!
10. Félicitations!

STANDARDS: 1.3, 2.1, 3.1

Lisons!

CHAPITRE 3

Teaching Resources
pp. 80–81

PRINT 
- Lesson Planner, p. 15
- Cahier d'activités, p. 35
- Reading Strategies and Skills Handbook, Chapter 3
- Joie de lire 2, Chapter 3
- Standardized Assessment Tutor, Chapter 3

MEDIA
- One-Stop Planner

Prereading
Activities A–B

Teaching Suggestion
B. Have students look at the photo of **pouding au pain et aux bleuets.** Have them guess what the title means and ask them to name some of the ingredients they might need to make this dish, without looking at the recipe. Write their responses on the board and compare them to the recipe in the book.

Reading
Activities C–I

Language Note
Students might want to know the following vocabulary from the recipes: **haché fin** *(finely chopped);* **des gousses d'ail écrasées** *(crushed cloves of garlic);* **râpé** *(grated);* **remuer** *(to stir);* **saupoudrer** *(to sprinkle);* **dorer** *(to brown);* **de la cannelle** *(cinnamon);* **des bleuets** *(the Canadian word for blueberries);* **des grains de poivre concassés** *(ground pepper);* **aplatir** *(to flatten).*

Possible Answers
A. Martinique, Canada, France, North Africa; *Answers will vary.*

B. *Ingredients:* soupe, grammes, cubes, granulé, crème, menthe, concentré; *Cooking:* couleur, bol, alterner, minutes

D. bananas, onions, butter, cheese

Lisons!

Gratin de bananes jaunes *Martinique*

INGREDIENTS
- 1 banane jaune [par personne] coupée en rondelles
- 1 oignon haché fin
- 2 gousses d'ail écrasées
- 50 grammes de beurre
- 3 cuillerées à soupe de farine
- 3/4 de litre de lait
- 110 grammes de fromage râpé
- sel et poivre

PREPARATION
1. Faire revenir l'oignon et l'ail dans le beurre, jusqu'à la couleur blonde. Ajouter un peu de sel et poivre.
2. En remuant constamment, rajouter la farine.
3. Hors du feu, ajouter le lait petit à petit.
4. Remettre sur le feu et amener à ébullition.
5. Retirer du feu et mettre la moitié du fromage.
6. Beurrer un plat qui va au four.
7. Alterner des couches de sauce et bananes, terminant avec la sauce.
8. Saupoudrer avec le reste du fromage.
9. Mettre au four à 425 degrés Fahrenheit et laisser dorer.

Servir chaud avec toutes viandes.

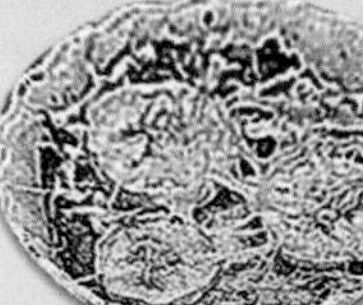

Steak au poivre — France

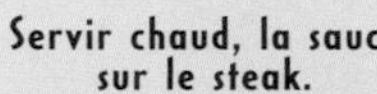

Ingrédients — par personne
- 1 steak
- 1/2 cuillerée à soupe de grains de poivre concassés
- 1/2 cuillerée à soupe de beurre
- 1/2 cuillerée à soupe d'huile
- 2 cuillerées à soupe de bouillon de bœuf
- 1/4 tasse de crème fraîche

Servir chaud, la sauce sur le steak.

Préparation
1. Répartir le poivre sur le steak.
2. Aplatir avec la main.
3. Saler le steak.
4. Faire cuire dans l'huile et le beurre.
5. Sortir le steak et réserver au chaud.
6. Dans la poêle ajouter le bouillon de bœuf et la crème fraîche.
7. Mélanger la sauce et ajouter un peu de sel.

Recettes du monde francophone

Stratégie pour lire
Even if you didn't speak any French at all, you could figure out the meaning of some of the words in the recipes. Become a great guesser! Learn to use visual clues and context to help you guess the meaning of unfamiliar vocabulary. You should try to anticipate the meaning of the words and think about how they fit into the context of what you're reading.

A. From what countries are these recipes? What do you think **soupe arabe** means? See answers below.

B. Scan the recipes and make a list of at least ten cognates. Which words are related to ingredients? Which words are related to cooking instructions? See answers below.

C. In what order is the information given?
- **a.** serving instructions 3
- **b.** ingredients 1
- **c.** cooking instructions 2

D. If you were going to make the **Gratin de bananes jaunes**, what are four ingredients that you would need? See answers below.

E. How long do you need to cook the **Pouding au pain et aux bleuets?** Is it served warm or cold? 30 minutes; warm

Communication for All Students

TPR Read the recipes, modeling each step with gestures. Have students mimic your gestures as they repeat the instructions. Choose several students to perform the gestures as you call out various instructions.

Pouding au pain et aux bleuets *Canada*

INGREDIENTS

- 4 tasses de cubes de pain
- 1 cuillerée à thé de cannelle
- 1/4 tasse de sucre granulé
- 3/4 tasse de beurre fondu
- 2 tasses de bleuets frais
- 1/2 tasse de sucre brun

PREPARATION

1. Chauffer le four à 350 degrés Fahrenheit.
2. Placer les cubes dans un grand bol.
3. Ajouter la cannelle et le sucre granulé.
4. Verser le beurre fondu et bien mêler.
5. Mélanger les bleuets et le sucre brun.
6. Dans un plat qui va au four, alterner des rangs de bleuets et pain.
7. Faire cuire au four pendant 30 minutes.

Servir chaud.

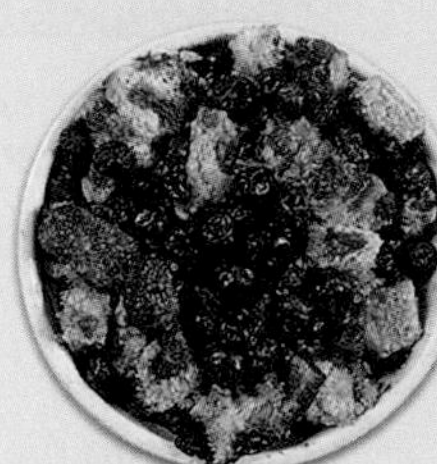

Chorba au poulet • *Soupe arabe*

INGREDIENTS (POUR 4 PERSONNES)

- 1 gousse d'ail hachée
- 2 oignons hachés
- 200 grammes de blancs de poulet en cubes
- 50 grammes de concentré de tomate
- 1 grosse boîte de tomates en morceaux
- 1 petite boîte de pois chiches
- 100 grammes de boulghour
- 1 botte de coriandre fraîche hachée
- 1 botte de menthe fraîche hachée
- 3 cuillerées à soupe d'huile d'olive
- 1,5 dl d'eau
- sel et poivre

PREPARATION

1. Faire fondre les oignons dans l'huile avec du sel et du poivre.
2. Ajouter le poulet et faire revenir.
3. Ajouter les tomates, le concentré de tomate et les pois chiches et cuire 10 minutes.
4. Ajouter l'eau, la coriandre, la menthe et le boulghour et laisser mijoter 30 minutes.

F. How many people will the recipe for **Steak au poivre** serve? 1

G. How much chicken do you need to purchase to make the **Chorba au poulet** for eight people? 400 grams

H. Match the following cooking instructions with the appropriate recipe.

c 1. Stir the sauce and add a little salt.
b 2. Heat the oven to 350°.
a 3. Remove from heat and add milk little by little.
b 4. Add the cinnamon and the granulated sugar.
d 5. Add the chicken and sauté.

a. *Gratin de bananes jaunes*
b. *Pouding au pain et aux bleuets*
c. *Steak au poivre*
d. *Chorba au poulet*

I. Which recipe(s) would you choose to make if you . . .

a. loved fruit? Gratin de bananes jaunes
b. were tired of the usual rice and potatoes? Gratin de bananes jaune
c. had a lot of leftover bread? Pouding au pain et aux bleuets
d. liked chicken? Chorba au poulet
e. liked spicy food? Steak au poivre
f. liked tomatoes? Chorba au poulet

J. Imagine that you're an exchange student in France. Select one of the recipes here to serve at a meal for your host family. Decide what you would like to have with the dish and create a menu. Then, write a shopping list for the items you need and tell where you will purchase the items.

Cahier d'activités, p. 35, Act. 28

Connections and Comparisons

Math Link

Have students convert the metric measurements in the recipe from Martinique to American equivalents, using the following approximations:

1 tablespoon = 15 milliliters
1 quart = 1 liter
1 ounce = 30 grams
1 pound = 450 grams

Have students convert the measurements in the recipes from Canada and France to their metric equivalents, using these approximations:

1 teaspoon = 5 milliliters
1 tablespoon = 15 milliliters
1 cup = 250 milliliters

Lisons!

CHAPITRE 3

Using Context Clues

Have students use the context to help them determine the meaning of words they do not know. Can they identify ingredients versus commands? Quantities? Have them justify their responses.

Teacher Notes

- **Chorba au poulet** is often made with lamb, which is commonly eaten in some North African countries. You might also tell students that **boulghour** is a grain found in many dishes in North Africa.
- Point out the use of the infinitive in written instructions, such as recipes, directions on product packages, and assembly instructions.

Postreading

Activity J

Teaching Suggestions

- Have groups of students create a skit in which they act out the dinner they're having with the exchange student. Remind them to use the expressions they've learned for asking for, offering, accepting, and refusing food and for paying and responding to compliments.
- Ask students to compile a list of their favorite foods, including fruit, vegetables, and meat or fish. Then, have them use the Internet to find a French recipe for a dish that contains these foods as ingredients. You might want to have students share their findings with the class and explain why they chose this particular recipe.

STANDARDS: 1.2, 2.2, 3.1, 4.1

Grammaire supplémentaire

CHAPITRE 3

For **Grammaire supplémentaire** Answer Transparencies, see the *Teaching Transparencies* binder.

Grammaire supplémentaire

CD-ROM 1
DVD 1

internet
ADRESSE: go.hrw.com
MOT-CLE:
WA3 PARIS REGION-3

Première étape

Objective Making purchases

1 Dans les phrases suivantes, remplace les mots soulignés par le pronom **en.** (**p. 66**)

EXEMPLE Combien <u>de bananes</u> voulez-vous?
<u>Combien en voulez-vous?</u>

1. Vous voulez <u>des œufs</u>?
2. Je vais prendre deux kilos <u>de tomates.</u>
3. Je veux six <u>oranges</u>, s'il vous plaît.
4. Il va acheter <u>du raisin</u>.
5. On ne trouve pas <u>de pain</u> là-bas.
6. Le pâtissier vend <u>des tartes aux fraises</u>.
7. Les végétariens ne mangent pas <u>de viande</u>.
8. Il achète une livre <u>de pommes de terre</u>.

2 Un étudiant canadien qui vit chez un de tes amis va faire les courses. Ton ami lui a écrit un mot pour lui dire ce qu'il doit acheter. Récris sa petite note. Pour éviter les répétitions, utilise le pronom **en** quand c'est possible. (**p. 66**)

> Passe à la pâtisserie pour acheter des baguettes. Prends trois baguettes. Ensuite, à la boucherie, achète des biftecks. Il nous faut six biftecks. Après ça, va à la poissonnerie. On a besoin de crevettes. Tu peux acheter 500 grammes de crevettes? Ah! N'oublie pas les escargots! Prends deux douzaines d'escargots. Pour finir, mon père voudrait du fromage. Est-ce que tu peux acheter du fromage à la crémerie? Merci beaucoup.

Answers

1
1. Vous en voulez?
2. Je vais en prendre deux kilos.
3. J'en veux six, s'il vous plaît.
4. Il va en acheter.
5. On n'en trouve pas là-bas.
6. Le pâtissier en vend.
7. Les végétariens n'en mangent pas.
8. Il en achète une livre.

2 Passe à la pâtisserie pour acheter des baguettes. <u>Prends-en trois.</u> Ensuite, à la boucherie, achète des biftecks. <u>Il nous en faut six.</u> Après ça, va à la poissonnerie. On a besoin de crevettes. <u>Tu peux en acheter 500 grammes?</u> Ah! N'oublie pas les escargots! <u>Prends-en deux douzaines.</u> Pour finir, mon père voudrait du fromage. <u>Est-ce que tu peux en acheter à la crémerie?</u> Merci beaucoup.

Grammar Resources for Chapter 3

The **Grammaire supplémentaire** activities are designed as supplemental activities for the grammatical concepts presented in the chapter. You might use them as additional practice, for review, or for assessment.

For more grammar presentations, review, and practice, refer to the following:

- Travaux pratiques de grammaire
- Grammar Tutor for Students of French
- Grammar Summary on pp. R23–R42
- Cahier d'activités
- Grammar and Vocabulary quizzes (Testing Program)
- Test Generator
- Interactive CD-ROM Tutor
- DVD Tutor
- **Jeux interactifs** at <u>**go.hrw.com**</u>

 STANDARDS: 1.2

Objectives Asking for, offering, accepting, and refusing food; paying and responding to compliments

Grammaire supplémentaire

CHAPITRE 3

3 Choisis le sujet approprié pour chacune des phrases suivantes. (**p. 72**)

1. voulons manger au restaurant.	**a.** Moi, je...
2. peuvent acheter du fromage.	**b.** Eric...
3. peut lui offrir un cadre.	**c.** Vous...
4. veux en prendre un kilo.	**d.** Suzanne et moi, nous...
5. pouvez me passer le sel?	**e.** Luc et Franck, ils...

4 Tes amis et toi, vous préparez une fête pour l'anniversaire de Claire. Dis ce que chaque personne fait en complétant les phrases suivantes avec la forme appropriée du verbe entre parenthèses. (**p. 72**)

Bonne et Heureuse Fête

1. François, tu _____ chercher des escargots? (vouloir)
2. Louise et moi, nous _____ acheter des baguettes après l'école. (pouvoir)
3. Stéphanie _____ acheter du pain. (vouloir)
4. Comme cadeau? Je _____ lui offrir un foulard pour son anniversaire. (pouvoir)
5. Vous _____ aller chercher un gâteau à la pâtisserie? (vouloir)
6. Ils _____ trouver des bonbons aux framboises. (vouloir)
7. Simon _____ acheter des fleurs. (vouloir)
8. Christa et Céline _____ emprunter un vase. (pouvoir)
9. _____ -vous apporter du parfum pour Claire? (pouvoir)
10. Julie, est-ce que tu _____ aller chercher des disques compacts? (vouloir)

5 You're having dinner with a friend. Is your friend offering you a) part of something or b) the whole item? (**p. 73**)

1. Encore une pomme?
2. Tu veux du gâteau au chocolat?
3. Tu veux encore de l'omelette?
4. Encore de l'eau minérale?
5. Tu veux une banane?
6. Encore de la salade?
7. Tu veux encore des petits pois?

Teacher to Teacher

Norah L. Jones
Rustburg High School
Rustburg, VA

Norah suggests the following activity to extend the *Grammaire supplémentaire* activities.

"As an alternative to doing the **Grammaire supplémentaire** activities individually, try a transparency race. Divide the class into teams, each with a transparency, pen, and tissues. Call out the number of one activity and one of the sentences in the activity (example: **Activité 4, phrase 3!**). Students should take turns writing the correct sentences as you call them out. The first team to project their *correct* transparency on the overhead is the winner."

Answers

3
1. d
2. e
3. b
4. a
5. c

4
1. veux
2. pouvons
3. veut
4. peux
5. voulez
6. veulent
7. veut
8. peuvent
9. Pouvez
10. veux

5
1. b
2. a
3. a
4. a
5. b
6. a
7. a

STANDARDS: 1.2

Grammaire supplémentaire

CHAPITRE 3

For **Grammaire supplémentaire** Answer Transparencies, see the *Teaching Transparencies* binder.

Grammaire supplémentaire

6 Voici une liste d'ingrédients pour faire une quiche. Fais une liste de ces ingrédients que tu vas acheter au supermarché cet après-midi. N'oublie pas d'employer les articles partitifs appropriés **(du, de la, des)**. (**p. 73**)

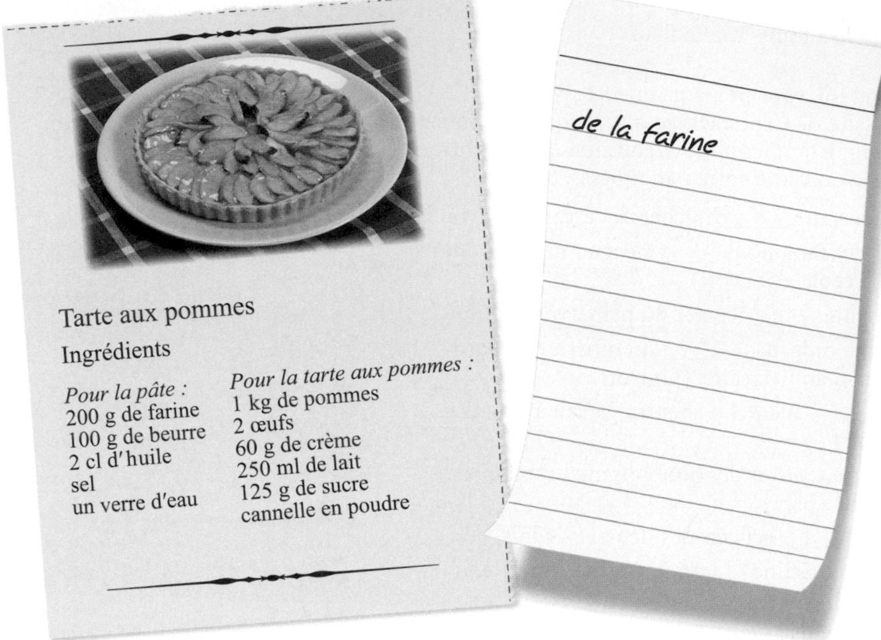

Tarte aux pommes

Ingrédients

Pour la pâte :	*Pour la tarte aux pommes :*
200 g de farine	1 kg de pommes
100 g de beurre	2 œufs
2 cl d'huile	60 g de crème
sel	250 ml de lait
un verre d'eau	125 g de sucre
	cannelle en poudre

7 Complète la conversation suivante avec les articles appropriés. (**p. 73**)

FRANCINE Qu'est-ce que tu vas prendre, _____ (du / de l' / de la) poulet ou _____ (un / une / des) bifteck?

THOMAS Je n'aime pas la viande. Je vais prendre _____ (un / une / des) omelette ou peut-être _____ (un / une / des) crevettes! C'est délicieux!

FRANCINE Moi, je vais prendre _____ (du / de l' / de la) poisson. Je veux aussi _____ (un / une / des) salade verte et _____ (du / de l' / de la) pain.

THOMAS Et comme dessert? _____ (Du / De l' / De la) tarte aux pommes, _____ (un / une / des) morceau de gâteau au chocolat ou _____ (un / une / des) religieuse?

FRANCINE _____ (Du / De l' / De la) mousse (f.) au chocolat, voilà.

THOMAS Bonne idée! Je vais en prendre aussi. Monsieur, je peux avoir _____ (du / de l' / de la) eau minérale, s'il vous plaît?

Communication for All Students

Additional Practice

For additional listening and speaking practice, ask questions containing indirect objects. **(Tu parles souvent à tes copains?)** Challenge volunteers to respond, using an indirect object pronoun. **(Oui, je leur parle souvent.)** You might also ask questions containing infinitives **(Tu vas offrir des fleurs à ton professeur de français?)** and questions to elicit the imperative. **(Qu'est-ce que je pourrais offrir à ma tante?)**

Answers

6 du beurre, de l'huile, du sel, des pommes, des œufs, de la crème, du lait, du sucre, de la cannelle,

7 du, un, une, des, du, une, du, De la, un, une, De la, de l'

STANDARDS: 1.2

Troisième étape

Objectives Asking for and giving advice, extending good wishes

Grammaire supplémentaire

CHAPITRE 3

8 Tes amis te demandent conseil. Complète les questions de tes amis et tes réponses en utilisant **lui** ou **leur.** (**p. 76**)

EXEMPLE —Marc aime le tennis. Qu'est-ce que je pourrais lui offrir?
—Offre-**lui** des baskets.

1. —Pamela et Luc aiment le chocolat. Qu'est-ce que je pourrais _____ offrir?
—Offre-_____ des bonbons au chocolat.
2. —Claude a toujours des fleurs dans la cuisine. Qu'est-ce que je pourrais _____ acheter?
—Achète-_____ un vase.
3. —Eric et Pierre viennent à la boum samedi. Je dois _____ parler?
—Oui, parle-_____ samedi!
4. —C'est l'anniversaire de Claire. Je fais un gâteau pour elle?
—Non, ne _____ fais pas de gâteau. Fais-_____ une tarte aux fraises.
5. —Tu as une idée de cadeau pour ma tante et mon oncle? Je _____ offre des fleurs?
—Non, ne _____ offre pas de fleurs.

9 Ton ami doit acheter des cadeaux pour les personnes suivantes. Dis ce qu'il devrait acheter ou ce qu'il ne devrait pas acheter pour ces personnes, d'après les phrases suivantes. Utilise **lui** ou **leur** dans tes réponses. (**p. 76**)

des disques — un foulard — un cadre — un livre — une cravate — une montre — des roses — des bonbons

EXEMPLE —Sa petite amie aime les photos.
Offre-lui un cadre. Ne lui offre pas de livre.

1. Sa mère aime les fleurs.
2. Ses grands-parents aiment lire.
3. Ses amis aiment danser.
4. Sa copine aime le chocolat.
5. Son voisin aime aller au théâtre.
6. Son frère est toujours en retard.
7. Ses grands-parents ont beaucoup de photos de lui.
8. Sa tante aime les vêtements féminins.

Answers

8
1. leur
leur
2. lui
lui
3. leur
leur
4. lui
lui
5. leur
leur

9
1. Offre-lui des roses. Ne lui offre pas de montre.
2. Offre-leur un livre. Ne leur offre pas de bonbons.
3. Offre-leur des disques. Ne leur offre pas de livre.
4. Offre-lui des bonbons. Ne lui offre pas de fleurs.
5. Offre-lui une cravate. Ne lui offre pas de disques.
6. Offre-lui une montre. Ne lui offre pas de livre.
7. Offre-leur un cadre. Ne leur offre pas de disques.
8. Offre-lui un foulard. Ne lui offre pas de cravate.

Review and Assess

You may wish to assign the **Grammaire supplémentaire** activities as additional practice or homework after presenting material throughout the chapter. Assign Activities 1–2 after **Note de grammaire** (p. 66), Activities 3–4 after **Tu te rappelles?** (p. 72), Activities 5–7 after **Note de grammaire** (p. 73), and Activities 8–9 after **Grammaire** (p. 76).

To prepare students for the **Etape** Quizzes and Chapter Test, we suggest doing the **Grammaire supplémentaire** activities in the following order. Have students complete Activities 1–2 before Quizzes 3-1A or 3-1B; Activities 3–7 before Quizzes 3-2A or 3-2B; and Activities 8–9 before Quizzes 3-3A or 3-3B.

STANDARDS: 1.2

Mise en pratique

CHAPITRE 3

The **Mise en pratique** reviews and integrates all four skills and culture in preparation for the Chapter Test.

Teaching Resources
pp. 86–87

PRINT 

- Lesson Planner, p. 15
- TPR Storytelling Book, pp. 22–23
- Listening Activities, p. 21
- Video Guide, pp. 17, 20
- Grammar Tutor for Students of French, Chapter 3
- Standardized Assessment Tutor, Chapter 3

MEDIA

- One-Stop Planner
- Video Program Videocassette 1, 44:36–45:46
- DVD Tutor, Disc 1
- Audio Compact Discs, CD 3, Tr. 14
- Interactive CD-ROM Tutor, Disc 1

Challenge

1 Have students write a restaurant review in French of a restaurant where they have recently eaten. Students might follow the example of the restaurant reviews in Activity 1.

Answers

1
1. name, address, prices, setting, type of cuisine
2. five
3. L'Air Marin
4. traditional French cuisine
5. chicken pâté, escargots, roast beef, apple tart
6. shrimp, oysters, pastries

3
1. inappropriate
2. appropriate
3. inappropriate
4. inappropriate

Mise en pratique

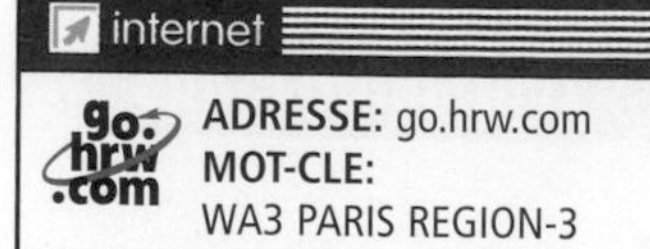

Le Fou du Roy

✪ ✪ ✪

Adresse : 12, rue de la Pie, Chartres

Les prix : menu à 21 euros (entrée, plat, fromage, dessert), carte
Le cadre : Un joli restaurant dans une ancienne cave. Musique classique et ambiance tamisée au rendez-vous.
La cuisine : Cuisine française traditionnelle. En entrée, le pâté au poulet et aux amandes est délicieux. Les escargots constituent aussi un choix excellent. Comme plats, ce restaurant offre une grande variété de viandes et de volaille. Nous recommandons le rôti de bœuf. Et pour finir, la tarte aux pommes est un vrai délice!

L'Air Marin

✪ ✪ ✪ ✪

Adresse : 38, place Saint-Pierre, Chartres

Les prix : menus à 20 euros et 25 euros
Le cadre : Le bleu est la couleur de la maison. Décor original avec toutes sortes d'objets insolites et grande terrasse ombragée en été.
La cuisine : De nombreuses spécialités de poissons et de fruits de mer. Pour 25 euros, vous pourrez déguster deux entrées, un plat principal, un assortiment de fromages et un dessert. Les crevettes au gingembre et les huîtres sont délicieuses. A essayer aussi, les religieuses et les millefeuilles faits maison.

1 Read the restaurant reviews and answer these questions. See answers below.

1. What information do the reviews give about the restaurants?
2. How many courses would you get if you ordered the **menu à 25 euros** at **L'Air Marin?**
3. Which restaurant would you go to if you liked seafood?
4. What type of food does **Le Fou du Roy** serve?
5. What are two specialties at **Le Fou du Roy?**
6. What does the critic recommend you try at **L'Air Marin?**

2 Martin-Alexandre and his sister, Stéphanie, are organizing a birthday party for Claude. Listen to their conversation and answer the following questions. See scripts on p. 59H.

CD 3 Tr. 14

1. What meal are they having together? breakfast/afternoon snack
2. What is Stéphanie going to buy at the **boulangerie?** baguettes
3. Where is Martin-Alexandre going to buy the dessert? at the pastry shop
4. What does Martin-Alexandre think about Stéphanie's first suggestion? He thinks that it's ordinary.
5. What does Martin-Alexandre decide to get for Claude? a scarf

3 If you were invited to dinner in a French home, which of the following would be appropriate? See answers below.

1. eating pizza with your hands
2. placing your bread next to your plate
3. pointing to something you'd like
4. eating with one hand resting in your lap

Apply and Assess

Teaching Suggestion

1 Read the **cuisine** section of each review to the class and take a poll of which restaurant the students prefer. Have students decide what they would order if they were to eat at the restaurant of their choice. Have them work in pairs to act out a scene that might take place at one of the restaurants reviewed. One partner should play the role of the customer and the other the role of the server. Students might refer to the school menus on page 72.

STANDARDS: 1.2, 2.1

Ecrivons!

Imagine that you have been hired as the food critic for a French newspaper. Write an article in which you review the food, service, and atmosphere of a new restaurant, **L'Escargot bleu.**

Stratégie pour écrire
Creating an outline is an effective way to arrange the information for your article in a logical order. A good outline will also help you avoid leaving out important information.

I. le déjeuner / le dîner
  A. l'entrée
    1.
    2.
  B. le plat principal
    1.
    2.

Préparation
First, put your ideas in related groups. In this case, the groups could be the meal (**le déjeuner** or **le dîner**), the service (**le service**), and the atmosphere (**l'ambiance**). Then, put these groups in the order in which you want to present them. Within each group, add subgroups to develop your ideas in more detail. For example, under **le déjeuner/le dîner,** you should tell what you had for each course and what you thought of the food.

Rédaction
Using the information from your outline, write the account of your experience at **L'Escargot bleu.** In your writing, try to avoid repetition and wordiness. A good way to do this is to use pronouns such as **en, y, lui,** and **leur** instead of repeating phrases over and over. Also, don't forget **le, la,** and **les,** the direct object pronouns you've learned.

Evaluation
A good way to evaluate your own writing is to read it aloud to yourself. This can often alert you to awkward wording or other problems with the flow of your writing. You might also read your work aloud to a classmate and have him or her point out anything that is unclear or difficult to follow.

5

Jeu de rôle

The French Club is planning a **soirée francophone.** Create a humorous skit as entertainment for the evening. Choose one of these scenarios or invent your own.
—A guest at a home in France does not act appropriately!
—Someone who knows little about French dining customs eats a meal in an elegant French restaurant.
—Two people meet for the first time, and one asks questions that shock the other.

Apply and Assess

Process Writing

4 You might have students write a review of a real restaurant in a francophone country. Have them research the Internet for restaurants. Many restaurant sites have photos and descriptions of their specialties.

Mise en pratique

CHAPITRE 3

Teacher Note

4 5 To help you assess performance on these activities, you might refer to the oral and written rubrics provided in the *Alternative Assessment Guide,* pages 1–8.

Family Link/Community Link

You might have students prepare a simple French meal for their family or friends with courses that follow the order of a French restaurant meal. For recipe ideas, see the interleaf pages in the *Annotated Teacher's Edition.* Their parents or friends could review the food, service, and atmosphere. Students could then share this review with the class. This could be done as an extra-credit project.

Career Path

A career in the restaurant business, as a critic or chef, for example, requires both an understanding of the culture and a knowledge of the language in order to truly understand the cuisine. Ask students how they think their knowledge of French would help them in a career as a chef. (In international restaurants, menu items are not always translated into English. Also, many of the finest culinary schools are in France and classes are conducted in French.)

Teacher Note

For additional practice and review, you might use the **Histoire Finale** for Chapter 3 on pages 22–23 of the *TPR Storytelling Book.*

Portfolio

5 **Written** This activity is appropriate for students' written portfolios. For portfolio information, see the *Alternative Assessment Guide,* pages iv–17.

Que sais-je?

CHAPITRE 3

Teaching Resources
p. 88

PRINT 
- Grammar Tutor for Students of French, Chapter 3

MEDIA
- Interactive CD-ROM Tutor, Disc 1
- Online self-test

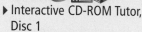

go.hrw.com
WA3 PARIS REGION-3

Answers

2
1. à la pâtisserie
2. à la crémerie
3. à la crémerie
4. à la charcuterie
5. à la boucherie
6. à la boulangerie

3 *Possible answers:*
Breakfast: croissants, tartines, café
Lunch: entrée, plat principal, fromage, dessert
Dinner: same as lunch

4 *Possible answers:*
1. Je pourrais avoir encore... ?
2. Tu pourrais me passer... ?
3. Tu veux de l'eau?

6 *Possible answers:*
C'était délicieux. C'est gentil.

8
1. Offre-lui un cadre.
2. Tu pourrais lui offrir un sac.
3. Tu peux lui offrir un foulard.

11
1. Bonne route!
2. Joyeux (Bon) anniversaire!
3. Bon rétablissement!

Que sais-je?

WA3 PARIS REGION-3

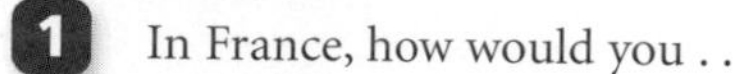

Can you use what you've learned in this chapter?

Can you make purchases? p. 66

1 In France, how would you . . .
1. ask how much the shrimp costs? Combien coûtent les crevettes?
2. ask for two kilograms (of them)? Je vais en prendre deux kilos.
3. ask how much all your purchases cost? Ça fait combien?

2 Where would you go to buy . . . See answers below.
1. a pastry?
2. eggs?
3. cheese?
4. ham?
5. chicken?
6. a croissant?

3 What would you expect to have for a typical French breakfast, lunch, and dinner? See answers below.

Can you ask for, offer, accept, and refuse food? p. 72

4 How would you . . . See answers below.
1. ask for more of your favorite dessert?
2. ask someone to pass your favorite main dish?
3. offer someone something to drink?

5 How would you respond if you were offered a second helping?
1. You'd like some more. Oui, je veux bien.
2. You just couldn't eat any more. Merci, je n'ai plus faim.

Can you pay and respond to compliments? p. 72

6 What would you say to compliment the meal you had just eaten? How would you respond to that compliment? See answers below.

Can you ask for and give advice? p. 76

7 How would you ask for advice about what to give someone for his or her birthday? Qu'est-ce que je pourrais offrir à... pour son anniversaire?

8 How would you advise your friend to give his or her grandmother these gifts? See answers below.

1.

2.

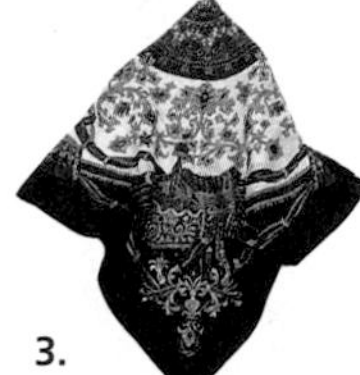
3.

9 At what stores would you buy the gifts in number 8?
1. à la boutique de cadeaux 2. à la maroquinerie 3. à la maroquinerie

10 How would you respond to a gift idea if . . . Possible answers:
1. you didn't like the idea? C'est banal. Ce n'est pas son style. Il/Elle en a déjà un(e).
2. you did like the idea? Bonne idée! C'est original. Tu as raison... ; D'accord.

Can you extend good wishes? p. 79

11 What would you say to someone who is . . . See answers below.
1. leaving by car on vacation?
2. having a birthday?
3. not feeling well?

Review and Assess

Teaching Suggestion

Type all of the answers to the questions in **Que sais-je?** in random order and number them according to their new order. Before distributing the copies, have students work in groups of three, reading the questions and deciding how to answer them. Next, distribute copies of the answers you've typed and have the groups match them to the questions. Finally, choose one student to come to the front of the class. Provide him or her with the answer key. Have the student call on individuals for answers and praise correct answers by saying **Oui, très bien! Excellent! C'est ça!**

STANDARDS: 1.2

Première étape

Making purchases

C'est combien, s'il vous plaît?	*How much is it, please?*
Combien coûte(nt)... ?	*How much is (are)...?*
Combien en voulez-vous?	*How many/much do you want?*
Je voudrais une livre (un kilo) de...	*I'd like a pound (kilo) of...*
Je vais (en) prendre...	*I'll take... (of them).*
Ça fait combien?	*How much does that make?*

Stores and products

la boucherie	*butcher shop*
la boulangerie	*bakery*
la charcuterie	*delicatessen*
la crémerie	*dairy*
la pâtisserie	*pastry shop*
la poissonnerie	*fish shop*
la baguette	*long loaf of bread*
le beurre	*butter*
le bifteck	*steak*
les crevettes (f.)	*shrimp*
les croissants (m.)	*croissants*
les escargots (m.)	*snails*
le fromage	*cheese*
les fruits de mer (m.)	*seafood*
les huîtres (f.)	*oysters*
le lait	*milk*
le jambon	*ham*
le mille-feuille	*layered pastry*
les œufs (m.)	*eggs*
le pain au chocolat	*croissant with a chocolate filling*
le pâté	*paté*
le poisson	*fish*
le poulet	*chicken*
la religieuse	*cream puff pastry*
le rôti de bœuf	*roast beef*
le saucisson	*salami*
la tarte aux pommes	*apple tart*
la viande	*meat*
la volaille	*poultry*

Vocabulaire

Deuxième étape

Asking for, offering, accepting, and refusing food

Je pourrais avoir..., s'il vous plaît?	*May I have some..., please?*
Vous pourriez (Tu pourrais) me passer... ?	*Would you pass...?*
Vous voulez (Tu veux)... ?	*Do you want...?*
Encore... ?	*Some more...?*
Voilà.	*Here it is.*
Tenez (Tiens).	*Here you are.*
Oui, je veux bien.	*Yes, I would.*
Merci, ça va.	*No thank you, I've had enough.*
Je n'ai plus faim/soif.	*I'm not hungry/ /thirsty any more.*

Paying and responding to compliments

C'est vraiment bon!	*This is really good!*
C'était délicieux!	*That was delicious!*
Ce n'est pas grand-chose.	*It's nothing special.*
Merci, c'est gentil!	*Thanks, that's nice of you!*

Meal vocabulary

la tartine	*bread, butter, jam*
le café au lait	*coffee with milk*
les céréales (f.)	*cereal*
le chocolat chaud	*hot chocolate*
l'entrée (f.)	*first course*
le plat principal	*main course*
le dessert	*dessert*

Troisième étape

Asking for and giving advice

Tu as une idée de cadeau pour... ?	*Have you got a gift idea for...?*
Qu'est-ce que je pourrais offrir à... ?	*What could I give to...?*
Offre-lui (-leur)...	*Give him/her (them)...*
Tu pourrais lui (leur) offrir...	*You could give him/her (them)...*
..., peut-être	*..., maybe*
Bonne idée!	*Good idea!*
C'est original.	*That's unique.*
Tu as raison...	*You're right...*
D'accord.	*OK.*
C'est trop cher.	*It's too expensive.*
C'est banal.	*That's ordinary.*
Ce n'est pas son style.	*That's not his/ her style.*
Il/Elle en a déjà un(e).	*He/She already has one (of them).*

Gifts and shops

les bonbons (m.)	*candies*
la boîte de chocolats	*box of chocolates*
le cadre	*photo frame*
les fleurs (f.)	*flowers*
le foulard	*scarf*
le portefeuille	*wallet*
le sac à main	*purse*
le vase	*vase*
la boutique de cadeaux	*gift shop*
la confiserie	*candy shop*
le fleuriste	*florist's shop*
la maroquinerie	*leather shop*

Extending good wishes

Bonne fête!	*Happy holiday! (Happy saint's day!)*
Joyeux (Bon) anniversaire!	*Happy birthday!*
Bonne fête de Hanoukkah!	*Happy Hanukkah!*
Joyeux Noël!	*Merry Christmas!*
Bonne année!	*Happy New Year!*
Meilleurs vœux!	*Best wishes!*
Félicitations!	*Congratulations!*
Bon voyage!	*Have a good trip! (by plane, ship)*
Bonne route!	*Have a good trip! (by car)*
Bon rétablissement!	*Get well soon!*

Review and Assess

Circumlocution

Have students imagine that they are exchange students helping to plan a dinner party for their host mother's birthday. They need to shop for a birthday gift and for some groceries to prepare the dinner. Have students work with a partner, one playing the role of the exchange student shopping for the items and the other playing the role of the salesperson. The exchange student should circumlocute the words for the items because he or she is having difficulty remembering the words in French. Have students switch roles once the salesperson has correctly guessed three of the items.

Vocabulaire

CHAPITRE 3

Game

Souviens-toi! Gather objects to represent as many of the vocabulary items as possible. Place twenty of them on a tray and cover the tray with a cloth. Form teams of five. Uncover the tray and show the objects to one team for one minute and then cover the tray again. Have the students in the team write down as many of the objects as they can remember. Repeat the process with each team. Finally, project on the overhead projector a list of the items on the tray. The team whose list most closely matches yours wins.

Chapter 3 Assessment

- **Testing Program**
  Chapter Test, pp. 65–70
   Audio Compact Discs, CD 3, Trs. 18–20
  Speaking Test, p. 344
- **Alternative Assessment Guide**
  Performance Assessment, p. 34
  Portfolio Assessment, p. 20
  CD-ROM Assessment, p. 48
- **Interactive CD-ROM Tutor, Disc 1**
  CD-ROM 1 A toi de parler
  DVD 1 A toi d'écrire
- **Standardized Assessment Tutor**
  Chapter 3
- **One-Stop Planner**
   Test Generator Chapter 3

Location Opener

CHAPTER 4

Teaching Resources
pp. 90–93

PRINT
- Lesson Planner, p. 16
- Video Guide, pp. 21–22

MEDIA 
- One-Stop Planner
- Video Program
  Videocassette 1, 00:54–03:29
- DVD Tutor, Disc 1
- Interactive CD-ROM Tutor, Disc 1
- Map Transparency 3

go.hrw.com
WA3 MARTINIQUE

Using the Almanac and Map

Terms in the Almanac
- **La Pagerie** was the estate of Napoléon Bonaparte's first wife Joséphine, who was born there in 1763.
- **La bibliothèque Schœlcher** is a library named after Victor Schœlcher, who worked in the nineteenth century to abolish slavery in Martinique.
- **La Savane,** a beautiful park in Fort-de-France, was once a battlefield where the French fought the English and the Dutch in the seventeenth century for possession of Martinique.
- **Aimé Césaire** is a poet and playwright who co-founded the literary movement called **Négritude,** which sought to restore the cultural identity of black Africans. His works include the poem *Cahier d'un Retour au pays natal* (1939) and the play *La Tragédie du roi Christophe* (1963).
- **Joséphine de Beauharnais** (1763–1814) was born in **la Pagerie.** She married Napoléon Bonaparte in 1796. When she was unable to provide him with the thé heir he so desperately wanted, Napoléon divorced her in 1809.

CHAPITRE 4

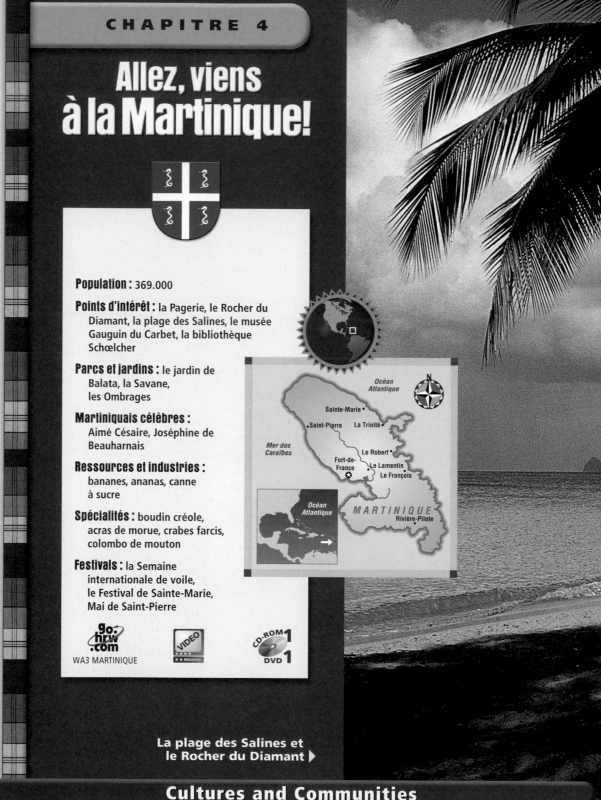

Allez, viens à la Martinique!

Population : 369.000

Points d'intérêt : la Pagerie, le Rocher du Diamant, la plage des Salines, le musée Gauguin du Carbet, la bibliothèque Schœlcher

Parcs et jardins : le jardin de Balata, la Savane, les Ombrages

Martiniquais célèbres : Aimé Césaire, Joséphine de Beauharnais

Ressources et industries : bananes, ananas, canne à sucre

Spécialités : boudin créole, acras de morue, crabes farcis, colombo de mouton

Festivals : la Semaine internationale de voile, le Festival de Sainte-Marie, Mai de Saint-Pierre

go.hrw.com
WA3 MARTINIQUE

VIDEO

CD-ROM 1
DVD 1

Océan Atlantique
Sainte-Marie
Saint-Pierre
La Trinité
Mer des Caraïbes
Le Robert
Fort-de-France
Le Lamentin
Le François
Océan Atlantique
MARTINIQUE
Rivière-Pilote

La plage des Salines et le Rocher du Diamant

Cultures and Communities

Culture Notes

- **La plage des Salines,** located at the southernmost tip of Martinique, is lined with coconut palms and is considered Martinique's best beach. It is located near a large salt pond and a petrified forest. The beach consists of approximately one and a half miles of white sand and calm waters.
- **Le Rocher du Diamant,** located off the southwest shore of the island opposite the fishing village of **Le Diamant,** was commandeered in 1804 by the British navy, who fortified it with cannons as they fought for possession of Martinique. After nearly 17 months of British occupation, the French commander Villeneuve finally recaptured the 575-foot rock in June of 1805.

STANDARDS: 2.2, 3.1

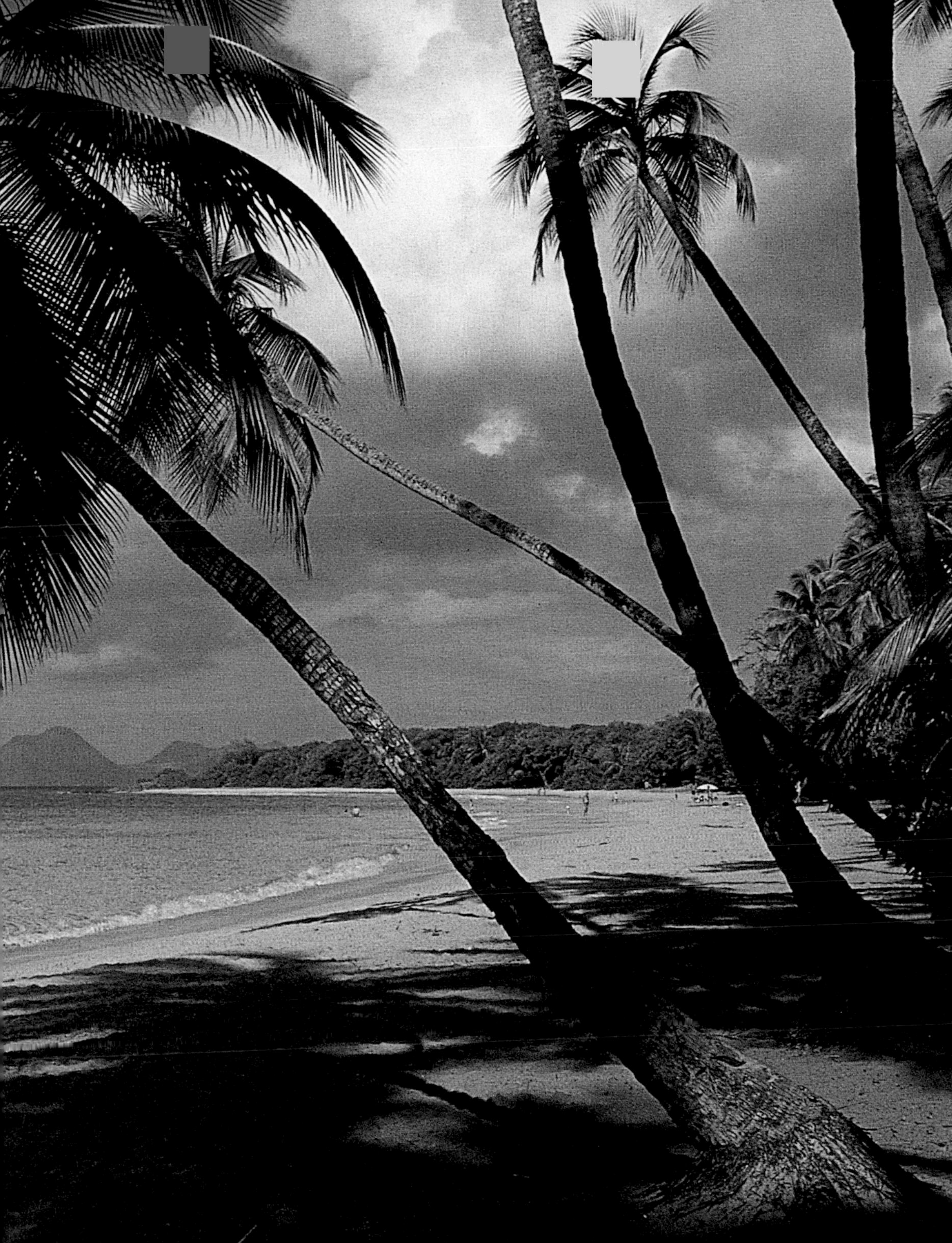

Location Opener

CHAPTER 4

Background Information

Madinina, the Carib Indian name of **la Martinique,** means *island of flowers.* The colorful flowers and plants contribute to the charm of the island. People of various racial and ethnic backgrounds live in Martinique: the **Créoles,** the largest ethnic group on the island, who are of mixed African and European descent; the **Békés,** or **Blancs-Pays,** who are white inhabitants born in Martinique; and the **Blancs-France,** or white residents from mainland France. There are also a number of Asian and Indian immigrants.

Some culinary specialties of Martinique include:

- **boudin créole:** a spicy sausage
- **acras de morue:** cod fritters
- **crabes farcis:** stuffed crab
- **colombo de mouton:** curried lamb stew with rice.

Map Activity

Have students locate Martinique on the map of the francophone world on pupil page xxv or on *Map Transparency 4.* Ask them what they think it would be like to live on a tropical island. Ask them what they remember about Martinique from Level 1. Remind them that Martinique and Guadeloupe are overseas departments **(départements d'outre-mer)** of France, and therefore are guaranteed the services of the French government and the educational system.

Connections and Comparisons

Art Link

Paul Gauguin (1848-1903) was a painter, sculptor, and printmaker who greatly influenced twentieth-century art. During his voyage to Martinique in 1887, he was influenced by the brilliant colors of the tropics. His paintings are generally simple, with many bright colors that he uses for expressive and symbolic purposes.

Geography Link

Ask students to name some agricultural products of Martinique. Then, ask them if they know where in the United States these same products are grown. (They might mention sugar cane in Louisiana and pineapples in Hawaii.) Ask students to name other foods native to the Americas (corn and popcorn, cranberries, blueberries, turkey, and various types of squash).

STANDARDS: 2.2, 3.1, 5.1

Location Opener

CHAPTER 4

Teaching Suggestion

2 Ask students to name common spices and tell where they think the following spices are grown. They might know that one of the reasons Columbus set out to discover a new route to the Orient was to search for spices. Have students research the origin and history of the spices listed below:

black pepper	**le poivre noir**
cinnamon	**la cannelle**
cloves	**les clous de girofle**
coriander	**la coriandre**
cumin	**le cumin**
curry	**le curry**
ginger	**le gingembre**
nutmeg	**la muscade**

Using the Photo Essay

3 Sugar cane **(canne à sucre)** was introduced to the West Indies during the 1600s. Slaves were later brought to Martinique from Africa to work on the sugar plantations. Pineapples were one of the first products from the New World presented at court by Spanish explorers in the sixteenth century. The word **ananas** is derived from the Carib word for fruit. Bananas **(bananes)** are plentiful on the islands. A larger variety of banana, the plantain, is starchy, not sweet. It must be cooked before it is eaten and is usually served as a side dish. The most common type of plantain is the "Martinique."

Thinking Critically

3 Observing Have students look at the photos on pages 92–93 and try to determine what products people might buy or sample when visiting a market in Martinique. (They might mention local fruits and vegetables, seafood, flowers, baskets, cloth, dolls, and art work.)

Martinique

La Martinique est une petite île de la mer des Caraïbes que l'on appelle aussi «la perle des Antilles françaises». On y vit au rythme créole : on danse la biguine et le zouk, on mange piquant, mais il ne faut pas oublier que la Martinique est un département de la France. Ses habitants sont français. Ils votent comme s'ils habitaient en France métropolitaine. Le français est la langue officielle et on paie ses achats en euros.

internet

go.hrw.com

ADRESSE: go.hrw.com
MOT-CLE: WA3 MARTINIQUE

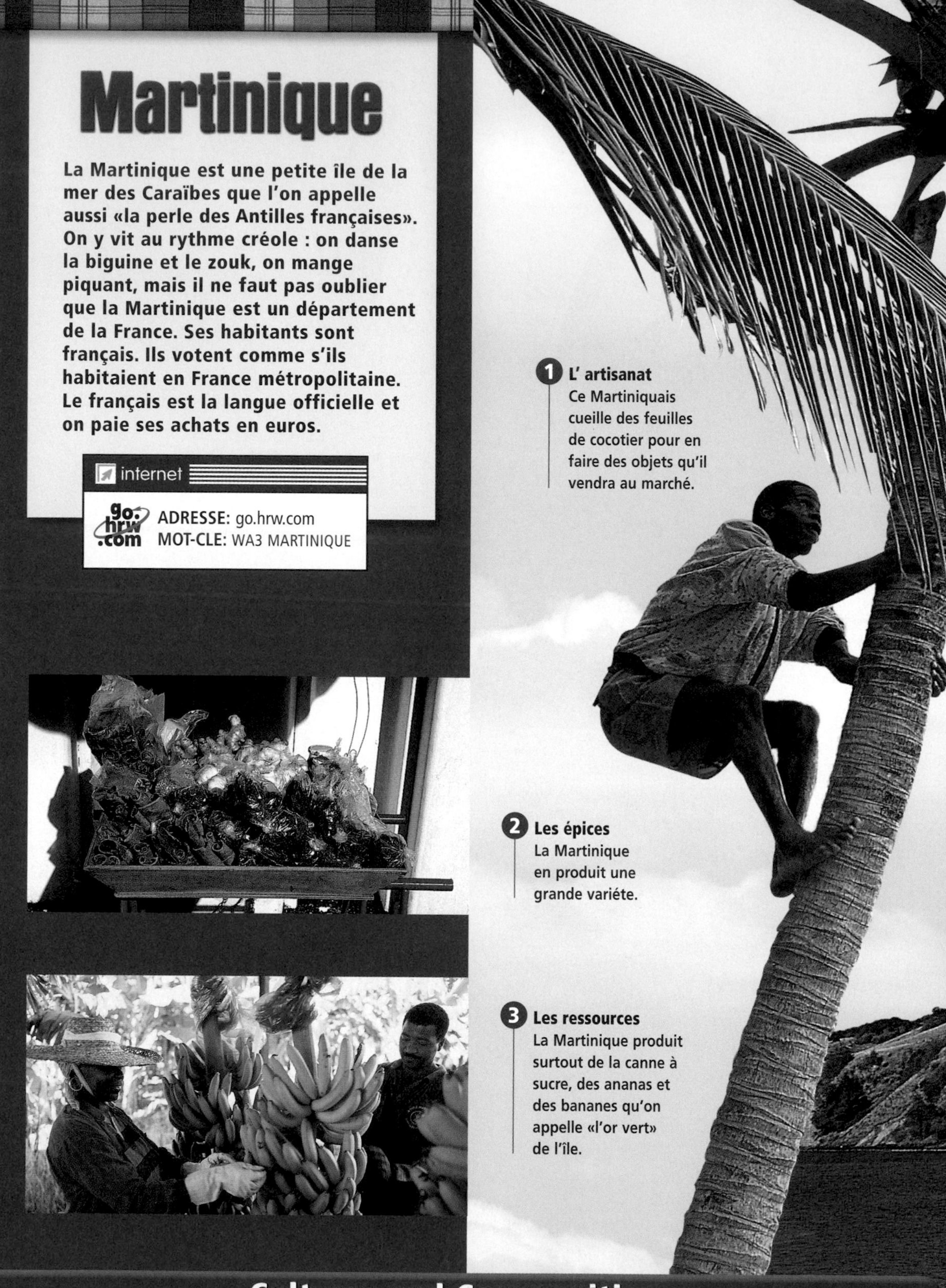

1 L' artisanat
Ce Martiniquais cueille des feuilles de cocotier pour en faire des objets qu'il vendra au marché.

2 Les épices
La Martinique en produit une grande variété.

3 Les ressources
La Martinique produit surtout de la canne à sucre, des ananas et des bananes qu'on appelle «l'or vert» de l'île.

Cultures and Communities

Teacher Note

1 The tree in the center photo is called a "traveler's palm." Originating in Madagascar, the tree has two vertical rows of leaves whose stalks contain large quantities of clear, watery sap from which comes a refreshing drink. Travelers who are short on water can always count on obtaining refreshment from this tree.

Culture Note

5 Gommier or **yole** races, which usually take place on Saints' days throughout the year, are a village tradition.

STANDARDS: 2.2, 3.1

Au chapitre 4, tu vas rencontrer Agnès, Stéphane, Jean-Philippe et Lisette, quatre jeunes Martiniquais qui vont te faire visiter leur merveilleuse île, appelée "l'île aux fleurs", avec ses magnifiques plages et sa forêt tropicale. Ils vont aussi te faire partager la vie quotidienne des Martiniquais, leur culture, leurs coutumes, etc... Bon voyage!

4 **Le jardin de Balata**
Des milliers d'espèces de fleurs poussent dans ce merveilleux jardin.

5 **Les gommiers**
Ces bateaux multicolores sont utilisés pour la pêche.

Location Opener

CHAPTER 4

4 Landscaper and horticulturist Jean-Philippe Thoze spent approximately 20 years developing **le jardin de Balata.** In the gardens are thousands of varieties of tropical flowers and plants. The term **balata** is the Carib name for a rare native tree. The town of Balata boasts a replica of the Sacré-Cœur basilica in Paris.

4 Martinique is known as **l'île aux fleurs,** and there is a rich array of flowers almost everywhere you turn. The orchids, frangipani, oleanders, hibiscus, jade vines, flamingo flowers, bougainvillea, and anthuriums paint the countryside with swatches of color. Trees such as the flame and tulip trees are magnificent when they are in bloom. Fruit trees abound, and tropical fruits such as mangoes, papayas, bright-red West Indian cherries, lemons, limes, and bananas are grown throughout the island.

5 Fishing is an important livelihood for many **Martiniquais.** Among the many varieties of sea life are the **oursins blancs** *(white sea urchins),* **étoiles de mer** *(starfish),* **dorades** *(sea bream),* and **poissons volants** *(flying fish).* The front part of the **gommiers** *(fishing boats)* is made of the trunk of the gum tree **(gommier),** with boards added to complete the structure of the boat.

Connections and Comparisons

Language Note

Bananas are referred to as **l'or vert** and sugar cane as **l'or blanc.** Ask students if they can imagine why. **(L'or** *(gold)* is a symbol of money or wealth and bananas are harvested when green. Since the island's economic prosperity is dependent upon bananas and sugar, their importance is implied by the expressions.) Ask students if they can imagine how the French sometimes refer to oil **(l'or noir).**

STANDARDS: 2.2, 3.1

Chapitre 4 : Sous les tropiques
Chapter Overview

Mise en train pp. 96–98	***Un concours photographique***

	FUNCTIONS	GRAMMAR	VOCABULARY	RE-ENTRY
Première étape pp. 99–103	• Asking for information and describing a place, p. 102		• Places, flora, and fauna, p. 100	• Using **de** before a plural noun **(Chapitre 2,** II) • Descriptive adjectives **(Chapitre 7,** I) • Weather expressions **(Chapitre 4,** I) • Asking for and giving directions **(Chapitre 2,** II)
Deuxième étape pp. 104–109	• Asking for and making suggestions, p. 106 • Emphasizing likes and dislikes, p. 107	• Recognizing reflexive verbs, p. 105 • The reflexive pronouns **se** and **me,** p. 107 • The relative pronouns **ce qui** and **ce que,** p. 108	• Vacation activities, p. 105	• Sports **(Chapitre 4,** I) • Making and responding to suggestions **(Chapitres 5, 6,** I)
Troisième étape pp. 110–113	• Relating a series of events, p. 111	• The present tense of reflexive verbs, p. 112 • Adverbs of frequency, p. 113	• Daily activities, p. 111	• Adverbs of frequency **(Chapitre 4,** I)

Lisons! pp. 114–115	**An sèl Zouk** (A **zouk** song by Kassav')	**Reading Strategy:** Looking for the main idea and decoding	
Grammaire supplémentaire	**pp. 116–119** **Première étape,** p. 116	**Deuxième étape,** pp. 117–118	**Troisième étape,** pp. 118–119
Review pp. 120–123	**Mise en pratique,** pp. 120–121 **Ecrivons!** Gathering information Creating a brochure	**Que sais-je?** p. 122	**Vocabulaire,** p. 123

CULTURE

- **Note culturelle, La ville de St-Pierre,** p. 99
- **Panorama Culturel,** Places to visit in different regions, p. 103
- **Note culturelle, Yoles rondes** *(fishing boats),* p. 104
- **Note culturelle,** The **créole** language, p. 106
- **Rencontre culturelle, Carnaval** in Martinique, p. 109
- **Note culturelle,** Music and dance in Martinique, p. 110

Chapitre 4 : Sous les tropiques
Chapter Resources

PRINT

Lesson Planning

One-Stop Planner

Lesson Planner with Substitute Teacher

Lesson Plans, pp. 16–20, 66

Student Make-Up Assignments
- Make-Up Assignment Copying Masters, Chapter 4

Listening and Speaking

TPR Storytelling Book, pp. 24–31

Listening Activities
- Student Response Forms for Listening Activities, pp. 27–29
- Additional Listening Activities 4-1 to 4-6, pp. 31–33
- Additional Listening Activities (song), p. 34
- Scripts and Answers, pp. 117–121

Video Guide
- Teaching Suggestions, pp. 24–25
- Activity Masters, pp. 26–28
- Scripts and Answers, pp. 91–94, 119

Activities for Communication
- Communicative Activities, pp. 19–24
- Realia and Teaching Suggestions, pp. 90–94
- Situation Cards, pp. 143–144

Reading and Writing

Reading Strategies and Skills Handbook, Chapter 4

Joie de lire 2, Chapter 4

Cahier d'activités, pp. 37–48

Grammar

Travaux pratiques de grammaire, pp. 29–36

Grammar Tutor for Students of French, Chapter 4

Assessment

Testing Program
- Grammar and Vocabulary Quizzes, **Etape** Quizzes, and Chapter Test, pp. 79–96
- Score Sheet, Scripts and Answers, pp. 97–104

Alternative Assessment Guide
- Portfolio Assessment, p. 21
- Performance Assessment, p. 35
- CD-ROM Assessment, p. 49

Student Make-Up Assignments
- Alternative Quizzes, Chapter 4

Standardized Assessment Tutor
- Reading, pp. 13–15
- Writing, p. 16
- Math, pp. 25–26

MEDIA

Online Activities
- **Jeux interactifs**
- **Activités Internet**

Video Program
- Videocassette 2
- Videocassette 5 (captioned version)

Interactive CD-ROM Tutor, Disc 1

DVD Tutor, Disc 1

Audio Compact Discs
- Textbook Listening Activities, CD 4, Tracks 1–11
- Additional Listening Activities, CD 4, Tracks 18–24
- Assessment Items, CD 4, Tracks 12–17

Teaching Transparencies
- Situation 4-1 to 4-3
- Vocabulary 4-A to 4-C
- **Mise en train**
- **Grammaire supplémentaire** Answers
- **Travaux pratiques de grammaire** Answers

One-Stop Planner CD-ROM

Use the **One-Stop Planner CD-ROM with Test Generator** to aid in lesson planning and pacing.

For each chapter, the One-Stop Planner includes:
- Editable lesson plans with direct links to teaching resources
- Printable worksheets from resource books
- Direct launches to the HRW Internet activities
- Video and audio segments
- Test Generator
- Clip Art for vocabulary items

Chapitre 4 : Sous les tropiques

Projects

Une publicité française

Students will create and perform a television commercial for the ***Office de tourisme de la Martinique*** *to encourage visitors to come to Martinique.*

MATERIALS

✂ **Students may need**

For making props:
- Posterboard
- Construction paper
- Glue or tape
- Markers
- Scissors

SUGGESTED SEQUENCE

1. To motivate students and give them ideas about the elements of a successful commercial, try to obtain videos from travel agencies that promote vacation packages.
2. Each group chooses a theme that determines which features of Martinique they will emphasize. The theme should be clearly stated in the commercial.
3. The script must include a physical description of the island and name at least five things to do there. Each group member should have a speaking part.
4. After the script is written, each group member should proofread it to check for variety of vocabulary and language accuracy.
5. When the script has been edited and recopied, students should gather and/or make props, and rehearse. Have students perform their commercials for the class. You might also videotape their commercials, if possible.

GRADING THE PROJECT

Suggested Point Distribution (total = 100 points)

Completion of requirements	20
Language use	20
Creativity/Presentation	20
Pronunciation	20
Effort/Participation	20

Games

Mot de passe

In this game, students will practice the vocabulary of the chapter.

Procedure Form two or three teams. Have one player from each team stand at the front of the classroom, facing his or her teammates. Choose a word from the chapter vocabulary to be the password and show it only to the players in front of the class. The first player may choose to pass or play. To play, he or she gives a one-word clue to try to get his or her teammates to say the password within ten seconds. If the player's teammates do not guess the word, the next player gives his or her teammates an additional clue and play continues. Give five points for guessing a word after the first clue, four points for guessing correctly after the second clue, and so on. On the next round, the other team gets the first turn.

Autour du monde

In this game, students will practice the vocabulary words and expressions from the chapter.

Preparation Prepare several one-word clues to elicit each vocabulary word or expression in the chapter. For example, **l'eau, le sel, les poissons,** or **le sable** could elicit **la mer.** Have the first student of the first row stand next to the student seated behind him or her. Call out a clue. The first of the two students who calls out the item you have in mind moves on to stand beside the desk of the next student. A student may continue moving "around the world," or he or she must take the seat of the one who guesses correctly before him or her. If neither student guesses correctly within five seconds, give the next clue. The first student to move "around the world" and return to his or her seat wins.

STANDARDS: 1.3, 3.1, 3.2

Storytelling

Mini-histoire

This story accompanies Teaching Transparency 4-3. The ***mini-histoire*** *can be told and retold in different formats, acted out, written down, and read aloud, to give students additional opportunities to practice all four skills. The following story is about Marcel's morning routine.*

Marcel a une vie très organisée. Il se lève tous les matins à six heures trente. D'abord, il prend une douche et se brosse les dents. Ensuite, il s'habille. Il n'a jamais trop de temps pour choisir ce qu'il va mettre : quelquefois, il choisit un short, mais souvent, il préfère mettre un pantalon avec un sweat-shirt. A sept heures et quart, il va dans la cuisine et prend son petit déjeuner. Il ne boit jamais de café : il n'aime pas ça. D'habitude, il se fait un chocolat. De temps en temps, pour changer, il se fait un café au lait ou un thé. Il mange aussi une tartine de beurre ou de confiture et quelquefois, un croissant. Il ne va jamais à l'école le ventre vide. A huit heures moins dix, il part au collège.

Traditions

The Biguine

Martinique is well known throughout the Caribbean for its traditional dances and music. Perhaps one of the most important folkdances of the country is the **biguine,** made internationally famous by the American composer Cole Porter in the 1930's when he wrote a song called "Begin the Biguine." The **biguine** is a lively partner dance which is believed to combine elements from the calenda, a dance with African roots, and the **menuet** and **branle,** ballroom dances introduced to the island by the French. The **biguine** has been popular for decades and is still danced everywhere on the island even though its popularity has been recently challenged by the more modern **zouk.** Find the music of the **biguine** and have students listen to it. Then have them imagine what the dance must be like, having heard the music.

Recette

Pineapples come from Central America and the Caribbean. They were introduced to Hawaii for the first time in the 18th century. Now, Hawaii is the largest producer of pineapples.

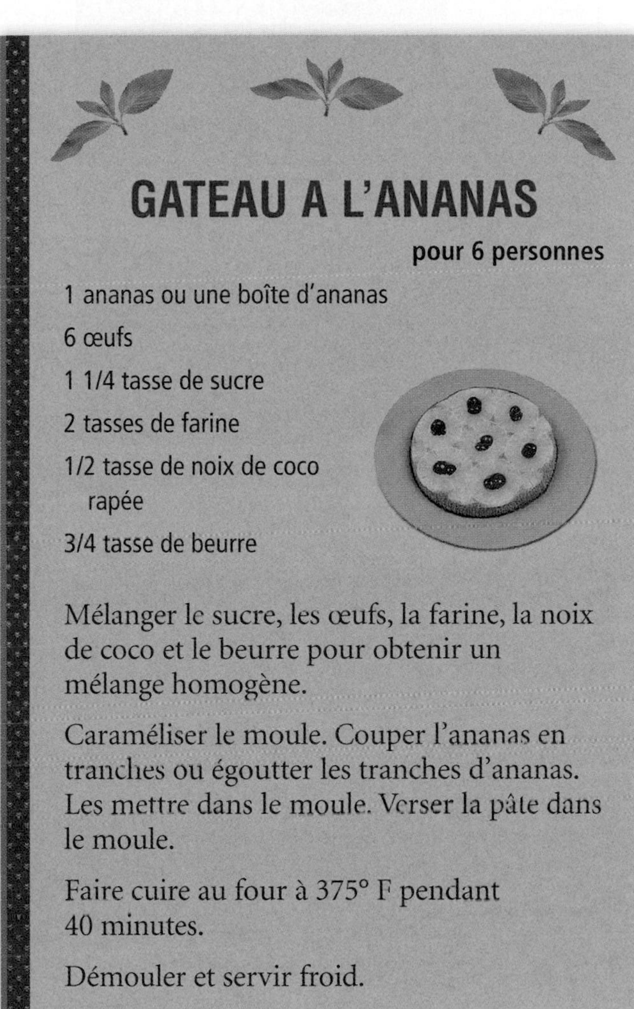

GATEAU A L'ANANAS

pour 6 personnes

1 ananas ou une boîte d'ananas
6 œufs
1 1/4 tasse de sucre
2 tasses de farine
1/2 tasse de noix de coco rapée
3/4 tasse de beurre

Mélanger le sucre, les œufs, la farine, la noix de coco et le beurre pour obtenir un mélange homogène.

Caraméliser le moule. Couper l'ananas en tranches ou égoutter les tranches d'ananas. Les mettre dans le moule. Verser la pâte dans le moule.

Faire cuire au four à 375° F pendant 40 minutes.

Démouler et servir froid.

STANDARDS: 1.3, 2.1, 3.2, 5.1

Technology

DVD/Video

Videocassette 2, Videocassette 5 (captioned version)
DVD Tutor, Disc 1
See Video Guide, pages 23–28.

Mise en train • Un concours photographique
Agnès and Jean-Philippe decide to enter a photo-essay contest at their school. They plan to photograph the beauty of Martinique. Lisette and Stéphane choose to focus on everyday life on the island. Agnès and Jean-Philippe photograph and describe the scenery. Stéphane and Lisette interview and photograph people at work. The four friends wonder who is going to win the contest!

Qu'est-ce qu'il y a à visiter dans cette région?
Students from the Côte d'Ivoire and France describe what there is to see in their area.

Mise en train (suite)
Lisette and Stéphane interview a bank employee. Agnès and Jean-Philippe take pictures of a rain forest and Mount Pelée in the north. Later, at school, the winning projects are displayed. The two pairs of friends both win prizes: Agnès and Jean-Philippe for their technical expertise, and Lisette and Stéphane for their originality.

Videoclips
- **La Liberté** performed by **Poglo:** music video

Interactive CD-ROM Tutor

Activity	Activity Type	Pupil's Edition Page
En contexte	*Interactive conversation*	
1. Vocabulaire	Chasse au trésor Explorons! Vérifions!	p. 100
2. Vocabulaire	Jeu des paires	p. 105
3. Comment dit-on… ?	Chacun à sa place	pp. 102, 106, 108
4. Comment dit-on… ?	Méli-mélo	p. 111
5. Grammaire	Les mots qui manquent	p. 112
6. Grammaire	Méli-mélo	pp. 111–112
Panorama Culturel	Qu'est-ce qu'il y a à visiter dans cette région?	p. 103
A toi de parler	*Guided recording*	pp. 120–121
A toi d'écrire	*Guided writing*	pp. 120–121

Teacher Management System
Launch the program, type "admin" in the password area, and press RETURN. Log in to www.hrw.com/CDROMTUTOR for a detailed explanation of the Teacher Management System.

DVD Tutor

The *DVD Tutor* contains all material from the *Video Program* as described above. French captions are available for use at your discretion for all sections of the video. The *DVD Tutor* also provides a variety of video-based activities that assess students' understanding of the **Mise en train, Suite,** and **Panorama Culturel.**

This part of the *DVD Tutor* may be used on any DVD video player connected to a television or video monitor.

In addition to the video material and the video-based comprehension activities, the *DVD Tutor* also contains the entire *Interactive CD-ROM Tutor* in DVD-ROM format. Each DVD disc contains the activities from all 12 chapters of the *Interactive CD-ROM Tutor.*

This part of the *DVD Tutor* may be used on a Macintosh® or Windows® computer with a DVD-ROM drive.

To preview all resources available for this chapter, use the **One-Stop Planner CD-ROM**, Disc 1.

Internet Connection

*Have students explore the **go.hrw.com** Web site for many online resources covering all chapters. All Chapter 4 resources are available under the keyword **WA3 MARTINIQUE-4.** Interactive games help students practice the material and provide them with immediate feedback. You'll also find a printable worksheet that provides Internet activities that lead to a comprehensive online research project.*

Jeux interactifs

You can use the interactive activities in this chapter

- to practice grammar, vocabulary, and chapter functions
- as homework
- as an assessment option
- as a self-test
- to prepare for the Chapter Test

Activités Internet

Students look for information about Martinique online and record interesting facts about the island, using the vocabulary from the chapter.

- In preparation for the **Activités Internet,** have students review the dramatic episode on Videocassette 2, or do the activities in the **Panorama Culturel** on page 103. After completing the activity sheet, have students work with a partner and share the information they gathered in Activity B on that sheet. Then ask each pair of students to share what they learned with the class.

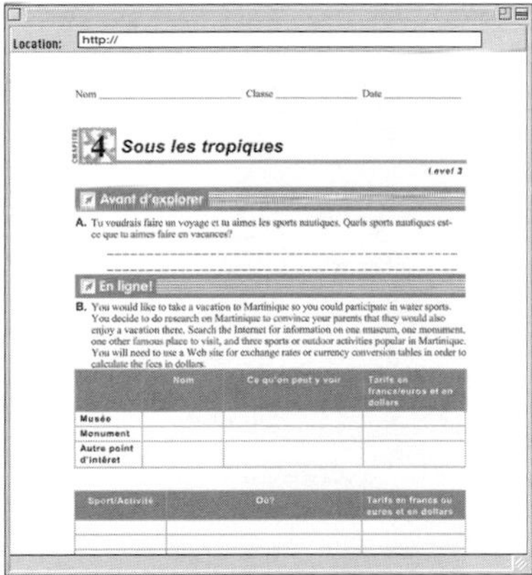

Location: http://

Nom ______ Classe ______ Date ______

CHAPITRE 4 **Sous les tropiques**

Level 3

Avant d'explorer

A. Tu voudrais faire un voyage et tu aimes les sports nautiques. Quels sports nautiques est-ce que tu aimes faire en vacances?

En ligne!

B. You would like to take a vacation to Martinique so you could participate in water sports. You decide to do research on Martinique to convince your parents that they would also enjoy a vacation there. Search the Internet for information on one museum, one monument, one other famous place to visit, and three sports or outdoor activities popular in Martinique. You will need to use a Web site for exchange rates or currency conversion tables in order to calculate the fees in dollars.

	Nom	Ce qu'on peut y voir	Tarifs en francs/euros et en dollars
Musée			
Monument			
Autre point d'intérêt			

Sport/Activité	Où?	Tarifs en francs ou euros et en dollars

Projet

Have students create a virtual guided tour of Martinique. They will search for maps, pictures, and historical information about Martinique. Have them also provide some outdoor activities. Students will then take their class on a virtual tour. They should document their sources by noting the names of the URLs of all the sites they consulted.

Chapitre 4 : Sous les tropiques
Textbook Listening Activities Scripts 

Première étape

8 **p. 101**

Venez à la Martinique! A vous la mer, le soleil, le ciel bleu, les plages et les cocotiers... A vous le poisson grillé, les fleurs, les épices! Visitez la forêt tropicale, escaladez les pentes de la montagne Pelée, regardez les magnifiques champs de canne à sucre. Venez à la Martinique, une histoire d'amour entre ciel et mer.

Answers to Activity 8
la mer, la forêt tropicale, les cocotiers, la montagne Pelée, les champs de canne à sucre

Deuxième étape

17 **p. 106**

MAGALI Alors, qu'est-ce que tu veux faire aujourd'hui?
CÉSAR Je ne sais pas... Ça te dit d'aller à la pêche?
MAGALI Non, c'est barbant. On attend pendant des heures, c'est tout!
CÉSAR Eh bien, tu as une autre idée?
MAGALI On pourrait faire du deltaplane. Ça, c'est original!
CÉSAR Pas question. Je n'ai pas envie de me casser une jambe! Pourquoi pas faire de la plongée?
MAGALI C'est une bonne idée... mais je n'ai pas de masque, moi.
CÉSAR On pourrait se promener sur la plage, alors.
MAGALI D'accord. On y va!

Answers to Activity 17
fishing, hang gliding, scuba diving, walking on the beach; walk on the beach

21 **p. 108**

1. — Qu'est-ce que tu aimes faire pendant les vacances?
— Ce que je préfère, c'est me lever tard parce que je dois me lever à six heures quand je vais à l'école. Et ça, je déteste!

2. — Et toi, qu'est-ce que tu aimes faire?
— Ce que j'aime bien, c'est faire de l'équitation le long de la plage.

3. — Qu'est-ce que tu aimes faire le week-end?
— Ben, ce qui me plaît, c'est de me baigner toute la journée.

4. — Et toi, qu'est-ce que tu aimes faire?
— J'aime rester à la maison. Tous mes copains aiment sortir, mais moi, ça ne me plaît pas.

Answers to Activity 21
1. getting up late; like
   getting up at 6:00 A.M.; dislike
2. horseback riding; like
3. swimming; like
4. staying at home; like
   going out; dislike

The following scripts are for the listening activities found in the *Pupil's Edition*. For Student Response Forms, see *Listening Activities*, pages 27–29. To provide students with additional listening practice, see *Listening Activities*, pages 31–33.

To preview all resources available for this chapter, use the **One-Stop Planner CD-ROM**, Disc 1.

Troisième étape

26 **p. 111**

Le matin? Ben, c'est assez banal. Je me lève à sept heures et demie. Puis, je me lave le visage pour me réveiller un peu. Ensuite, je vais à la cuisine pour prendre le petit déjeuner: des tartines et peut-être du chocolat, si j'ai le temps. Je m'habille, d'habitude en jean et en tee-shirt. Euh, enfin, je me brosse les dents super vite, et je cours au lycée.

Answers to Activity 26
e, b, c, d, a

Mise en pratique

2 **p. 120**

Il y a beaucoup de circuits pittoresques à faire. Je crois que celui-ci vous intéressera. On commence le matin par une visite de la Soufrière. Vous verrez un volcan actif de près. Ensuite, vous prendrez l'autocar pour aller déguster la cuisine locale dans un petit restaurant typique. Vers deux heures, visite de la forêt tropicale pour voir nos fameuses chutes d'eau, les chutes du Carbet. Enfin, vous pourrez visiter une plantation de café. Personnellement, c'est le circuit que je vous recommande.

Answers to Mise en pratique Activity 2
visit "La Soufrière" to see an active volcano, lunch at a typical restaurant, visit the tropical forest and the waterfalls of Le Carbet, visit a coffee plantation

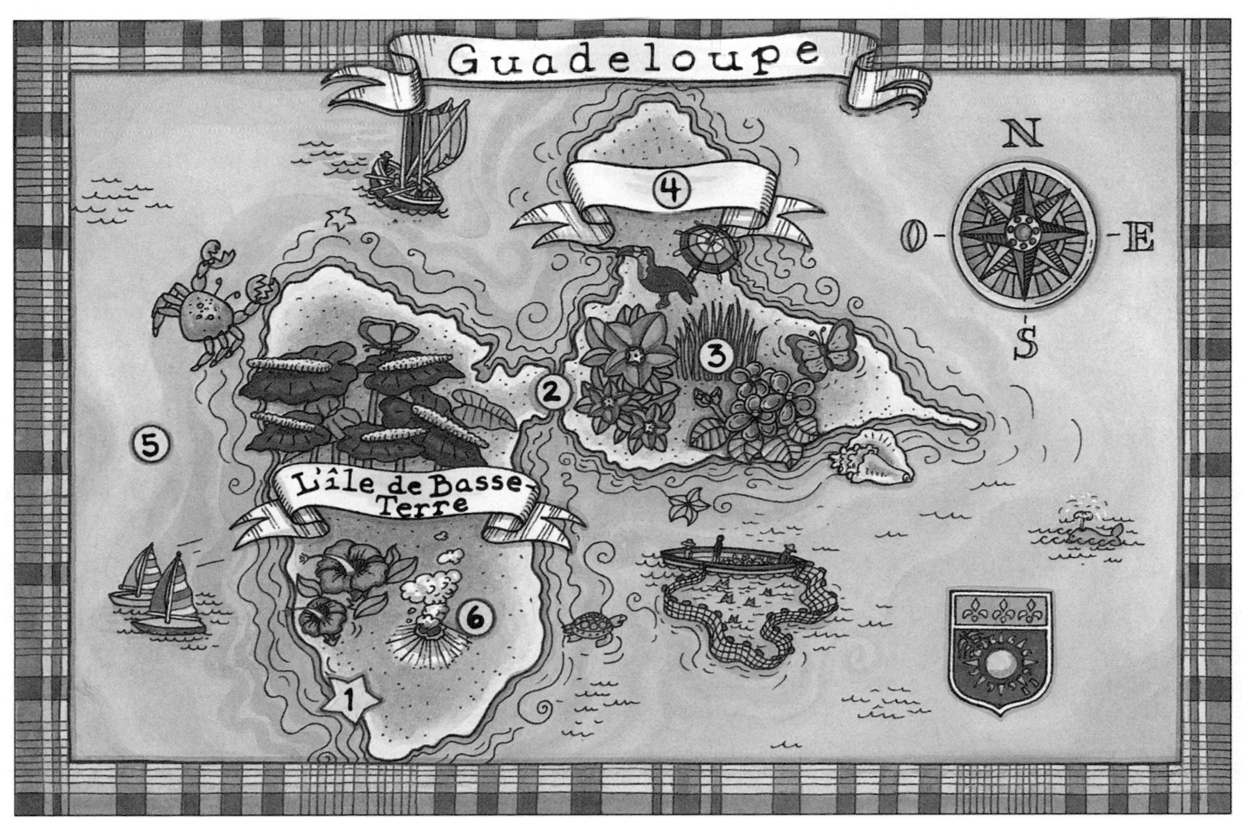

Chapitre 4 : Sous les tropiques

Suggested Lesson Plans 50-Minute Schedule

Day 1

CHAPTER OPENER 5 min.
- Present Chapter Objectives, p. 95.
- Culture Note, ATE, p. 94

MISE EN TRAIN 40 min.
- Presenting **Mise en train,** ATE, p. 97
- Thinking Critically, ATE, p. 96
- Do Activities 1–4, p. 98.
- Teaching Suggestions: **Mise en train** Post-viewing Suggestion 2, Video Guide, p. 24

Wrap-Up 5 min.
- Do Activity 5, p. 98.

Homework Options
Cahier d'activités, Acts. 1–2, p. 37

Day 2

PREMIERE ETAPE
Quick Review 10 min.
- Bell Work, ATE, p. 99
- Read and discuss **Note culturelle,** p. 99.

Vocabulaire, p. 100 35 min.
- Presenting **Vocabulaire,** ATE, p. 100
- Complete Activity 7, p. 100.
- Discuss **Tu te rappelles?,** p. 100.
- **Grammaire supplémentaire,** Activities 1–2, p. 116
- Play Audio CD for Activity 8, p. 101.
- Complete Activity 9, p. 101.
- Have students do Activity 11, p. 101, in pairs.

Wrap-Up 5 min.
- TPR, ATE, p. 101

Homework Options
Cahier d'activités, Acts. 3–4, p. 38
Travaux pratiques de grammaire, Acts. 1–4, pp. 29–30

Day 3

PREMIERE ETAPE
Quick Review 5 min.
- Check homework.

Comment dit-on... ?, p. 102 25 min.
- Presenting **Comment dit-on... ?,** ATE, p. 102
- Cahier d'activitiés, Activities 6–7, p. 39
- Music Link, ATE, p. 102
- Have students do Activity 13, p. 102, in small groups.

PANORAMA CULTUREL 15 min.
- Presenting **Panorama Culturel,** using Audio CD, ATE, p. 103
- **Questions,** ATE, p. 103

Wrap-Up 5 min.
- **Qu'en penses-tu?,** p. 103

Homework Options
Study for Quiz 4-1.
Pupil's Edition Act. 12, p. 102
Cahier d'activités, Act. 8, p. 40

Day 4

PREMIERE ETAPE
Quiz 4-1 20 min.
- Administer Quiz 4-1A, 4-1B, or a combination of the two.

DEUXIEME ETAPE
Note culturelle, p. 104 5 min.
- Read and discuss **Note culturelle,** p. 104.

Vocabulaire/Note de grammaire, p. 105 20 min.
- Presenting **Vocabulaire,** ATE, p. 105
- Language Notes, ATE, p. 105
- Presenting **Note de grammaire,** ATE, p. 105
- Play Audio CD for Activity 17, p. 106.
- Do Activity 18, p. 106.

Wrap-Up 5 min.
- Thinking Critically, ATE, p. 105

Homework Options
Cahier d'activités, Acts. 9–10, p. 41
Travaux pratiques de grammaire, Acts. 5–7, pp. 31–32
Grammaire supplémentaire, Act. 3, p. 117

Day 5

DEUXIEME ETAPE
Quick Review 5 min.
- Check homework.

Comment dit-on... ?, p. 106 15 min.
- Presenting **Comment dit-on... ?,** ATE, p. 106
- Cahier d'activités, Activity 11, p. 42
- Have students do Activity 19, p. 107, in pairs.
- Cahier d'activités, Activities 12–13, p. 42

Note culturelle, p. 106 5 min.
- Read and discuss **Note culturelle,** p. 106

Comment dit-on... ? and **Note de grammaire, p. 107** 20 min.
- Presenting **Comment dit-on... ?,** ATE, p. 107
- Language Note, ATE, p. 107
- Read and discuss **Note de grammaire,** p. 107.
- Play Audio CD for Activity 21, p. 108.

Wrap-Up 5 min.
- Cahier d'activités, Activity 14, p. 43

Homework Options
Pupil's Edition, Activity 20, p. 107

Day 6

DEUXIEME ETAPE
Quick Review 5 min.
- Have volunteers read the letters they wrote from Activity 20, p. 107.

Grammaire, p. 108 20 min.
- Read and discuss **Grammaire,** p. 108.
- Do Activity 22, p. 108.
- Travaux pratiques de grammaire, Activities 9–10, p. 33
- Have students do Activity 23, p. 108, in pairs.

De bons conseils, p. 108 5 min.
- Read and discuss **De bons conseils,** p. 108.
- Language-to-Language, ATE, p. 108

RENCONTRE CULTURELLE 15 min.
- Presenting **Rencontre culturelle,** p. 109
- History Link, Culture Note, and Teacher Note, ATE, p. 109
- Read and discuss **Qu'en penses-tu?** and **Savais-tu que… ?,** p. 109.

Wrap-Up 5 min.
- **Grammaire supplémentaire,** Activity 4, p. 117

Homework Options
Study for Quiz 4-2

One-Stop Planner CD-ROM

For alternative lesson plans by chapter section, to create your own customized plans, or to preview all resources available for this chapter, use the **One-Stop Planner CD-ROM,** Disc 1.

For additional homework suggestions, see activities accompanied by this symbol throughout the chapter.

Day 7

DEUXIEME ETAPE

Quiz 4-2 20 min.
- Administer Quiz 4-2A, 4-2B, or a combination of the two.

TROISIEME ETAPE

Note culturelle, p. 110 5 min.
- Read and discuss **Note culturelle,** p. 110.

Vocabulaire and **Comment dit-on... ?, p. 111 20 min.**
- Presenting **Vocabulaire** and **Comment dit-on... ?,** ATE, p. 111
- Read Agathe's schedule and do Activity 25, p. 110.
- Play Audio CD for Activity 26, p. 111.
- Do Activity 27, p. 112.

Wrap-Up 5 min.
- TPR, ATE, p. 111

Homework Options

Cahier d'activités, Acts. 16–17, p. 44

Day 8

TROISIEME ETAPE

Quick Review 5 min.
- Check homework.

Grammaire, p. 112 25 min.
- Presenting **Grammaire,** ATE, p. 112
- Do Activity 28, p. 112.
- **Grammaire supplémentaire,** Act. 7–8, p. 118
- Travaux pratiques de grammaire, Acts. 13–15, pp. 35–36
- Read and discuss **Tu te rappelles?,** p. 112.
- Do Activity 29, p. 113, in small groups.

Note de grammaire, p. 113 10 min.
- Read and discuss **Note de grammaire,** p. 113.
- **Grammaire supplémentaire,** Act. 10, p. 119

Wrap-Up 10 min.
- Game: **A toi!,** ATE, p. 118

Homework Options

Pupil's Edition, Acts. 30 and 31, p. 113
Cahier d'activités, Acts. 18–21, pp. 45–46
Study for Quiz 4-3.

Day 9

TROISIEME ETAPE

Quiz 4-3 20 min.
- Administer Quiz 4-3A, 4-3B, or a combination of the two.

LISONS! 25 min.
- Complete Prereading Activities A–C, p. 114.
- Culture Notes, ATE, p. 114.
- Have students read lyrics, focusing on main idea.
- Do Reading Activities D–G, ATE, pp. 114–115.
- Language Note, ATE, p. 115.

Wrap-Up 5 min.
- Career Path, ATE, p. 114

Homework Options

Cahier d'activités, Acts. 23–24, p. 47

Day 10

LISONS!

Quick Review 5 min.
- Discuss homework.

Postreading Activity 15 min.
- Do Postreading Activities H–I, ATE, p. 115.

MISE EN PRATIQUE 25 min.
- Do Activity 1, p. 120.
- Play Audio CD for Activity 2, p. 120.
- Discuss the strategy for **Ecrivons!,** p. 121, as a class, then have students work on their brochures.

Wrap-Up 5 min.
- Discuss Geography Link and Government Link, ATE, p. 120.

Homework Options

Have students finish brochures for **Ecrivons!,** Pupil's Edition, p. 121.

Day 11

MISE EN PRATIQUE

Review 40 min.
- Have volunteers present their brochures from **Ecrivons!,** p. 121.
- Have students prepare interview questions for **Jeu de rôle,** p. 121.
- Have students conduct their interviews with a partner.

Wrap-Up 10 min.
- **A toi d'écrire,** Interactive CD-ROM Tutor (Disc 1)

Homework Options

Que sais-je?, p. 122

Day 12

MISE EN PRATIQUE

Quick Review 15 min.
- Go over **Que sais-je?,** p. 122.

Chapter Review 35 min.
- Review Chapter 4. Choose from **Grammaire supplémentaire,** Grammar Tutor for Students of French, Activities for Communication, Listening Activities, Interactive CD-ROM Tutor, or **Jeux interactifs.**

Homework Options

Study for Chapter 4 Test.

Assessment

Chapter Test 50 min.
- Administer Chapter 4 Test. Select from Testing Program, Alternative Assessment Guide, Test Generator, or Standardized Assessment Tutor.

Chapitre 4 : Sous les tropiques

Suggested Lesson Plans *90-Minute Block Schedule*

Block 1

CHAPTER OPENER **5 min.**
- Present Chapter Objectives, p. 95.
- Culture Note, ATE, p. 94

MISE EN TRAIN **40 min.**
- Preteaching Vocabulary, ATE, p. 96
- Presenting **Mise en train,** ATE, p. 97
- Activities 1–5, p. 98, using Thinking Critically, ATE, p. 98

PREMIERE ETAPE

Vocabulaire, p. 100 35 min.
- Read and discuss **Note culturelle,** p. 99.
- Presenting **Vocabulaire,** ATE, p. 100
- Present **Tu te rappelles?,** p. 100.
- Activity 7, p. 100
- Play Audio CD for Activity 8 and do Activity 9, p. 101.

Wrap-Up 10 min.
- Thinking Critically, ATE, p. 96

Homework Options
Grammaire supplémentaire, Acts. 1–2, p. 116
Cahier d'activités, Acts. 1–5, pp. 37–39
Travaux pratiques de grammaire, Acts. 1–4, pp. 29–30

Block 2

PREMIERE ETAPE

Quick Review 5 min.
- TPR, ATE, p. 101

Vocabulaire, p. 100 20 min.
- Activities 10–11, p. 101

Comment dit-on... ?, p. 102 25 min.
- Presenting **Comment dit-on... ?,** ATE, p. 102
- Do Activities 12–13, p. 102.

PANORAMA CULTUREL 20 min.
- Presenting **Panorama Culturel,** using Videocassette 2, ATE, p. 103
- Discuss **Qu'en penses-tu?** questions, p. 103, and Community Link, ATE, p. 103.

DEUXIEME ETAPE

Vocabulaire, p. 105 15 min.
- Presenting **Vocabulaire,** ATE, p. 105
- Language Notes, ATE, p. 105
- Play Audio CD for Activity 17, p. 106.

Wrap-Up 5 min.
- Ask students questions about various places around the world. Students should respond using expressions from **Comment dit-on... ?,** p. 102.

Homework Options
Have students study for Quiz 4-1.
Pupil's Edition, Activity 14, p. 102
Cahier d'activités, Acts. 6–9, pp. 39–41
Travaux pratiques de grammaire, Acts. 5–6, pp. 31–32

Block 3

PREMIERE ETAPE

Quick Review 10 min.
- Communicative Activity 4-1, Activities for Communication, pp. 19–20

Quiz 4-1 20 min.
- Administer Quiz 4-1A, 4-1B, or a combination of the two.

DEUXIEME ETAPE

Vocabulaire, p. 105 10 min.
- Show pictures of the vocabulary items to students and have them identify the activities in French.
- TPR, ATE, p. 105

Note de grammaire, p. 105 15 min.
- Presenting **Note de grammaire,** ATE, p. 105
- **Grammaire supplémentaire,** Activity 3, p. 117
- Do Activity 18, p. 106.

Comment dit-on... ?, p. 106 30 min.
- Presenting **Comment dit-on... ?,** p. 106
- Discuss **Note culturelle,** using Teaching Suggestion, ATE, p. 106.
- Do Activities 19–20, p. 107, using the first Teaching Suggestion for Activity 19, ATE, p. 107

Wrap-Up 5 min.
- Ask students to suggest various activities, using the expressions from **Comment dit-on... ?,** p. 106.

Homework Options
Cahier d'activités, Acts. 10–13, pp. 41–42
Travaux pratiques de grammaire, Acts. 7–8, p. 32

One-Stop Planner CD-ROM

For alternative lesson plans by chapter section, to create your own customized plans, or to preview all resources available for this chapter, use the **One-Stop Planner CD-ROM**, Disc 1.

For additional homework suggestions, see activities accompanied by this symbol throughout the chapter.

Block 4

DEUXIEME ETAPE

Quick Review 10 min.

- Teaching Transparency 4-2, using the fourth suggestion in Suggestions for Using Teaching Transparency 4-2

Comment dit-on… ?/Grammaire, p. 107 40 min.

- Presenting **Comment dit-on… ?**, ATE, p. 107
- Read and discuss **Grammaire,** p. 107.
- Play Audio CD for Activity 21, p. 108.
- Read and discuss **Grammaire,** p. 108.
- Do Activities 22–23, p. 108.

TROISIEME ETAPE 10 min.

- Have students read Agathe's schedule, p. 110.
- Do Activity 25, p. 110.

Vocabulaire/Comment dit-on… ?, p. 111 25 min.

- Presenting **Vocabulaire/Comment dit-on… ?**, ATE, p. 111
- TPR, ATE, p. 111
- Play Audio CD for Activity 26, p. 111.
- Do Activity 27, p. 112.

Wrap-Up 5 min.

- Have students make a list of what they really like and dislike, using **ce qui** and **ce que.** Then, have them share their sentences with the class.

Homework Options

Have students study for Quiz 4-2.
Grammaire supplémentaire, Act. 4, p. 117
Cahier d'activités, Acts. 14–16, pp. 43–44
Travaux pratiques de grammaire, Acts. 9–12, pp. 33–34

Block 5

DEUXIEME ETAPE

Quick Review 5 min.

- Have students do Situation 4-2: Interview Activities in Communication, p. 143, in pairs.

Quiz 4-2 20 min.

- Administer Quiz 4-2A, 4-2B, or a combination of the two.

TROISIEME ETAPE

Vocabulaire/Comment dit-on… ?, p. 111 10 min.

- Teaching Transparency 4-3 and the third suggestion in Suggestions for Using Transparency 4-3

Grammaire, p. 112 45 min.

- Presenting **Grammaire,** ATE, p. 112
- Discuss **Tu te rappelles?**, p. 112.
- Do Activities 28–29, pp. 112–113.
- Present **Note de grammaire,** p. 113.
- Do Activities 30 and 31, using Teaching Suggestion and Cooperative Learning, ATE, p. 113.

Wrap-Up 10 min.

- Game: **A toi!**, ATE, p. 118

Homework Options

Have students study for Quiz 4-3.
Grammaire supplémentaire, Acts. 7–8, p. 118
Cahier d'activités, Acts. 17–22, pp. 44–46
Travaux pratiques de grammaire, Acts. 13–16, pp. 35–36

Block 6

TROISIEME ETAPE

Quick Review 10 min.

- Communicative Activity 4-3, Activities for Communication, pp. 23–24,

Quiz 4-3 20 min.

- Administer Quiz 4-3A, 4-3B, or a combination of the two.

RENCONTRE CULTURELLE 10 min.

- Presenting **Rencontre culturelle,** ATE, p. 109
- Game: **Mot de passe,** ATE, p. 93C

LISONS! 30 min.

- Activity A, p. 114
- Activities B–E, pp. 114–115
- Activity F, p. 115
- Activity H, p. 115

MISE EN PRATIQUE 20 min.

- Do Activity 1, p. 120, using Visual/Tactile Learners, ATE, p. 120.
- Play Audio CD for Activity 2, p. 120.
- Begin **Ecrivons!**, p. 121.

Homework Options

Que sais-je?, p. 123
Finish **Ecrivons!**, p. 121.
Study for Chapter 4 Test.

Block 7

MISE EN PRATIQUE

Quick Review 10 min.

- Go over homework.

Chapter Review 35 min.

- Review Chapter 4. Choose from **Grammaire supplémentaire,** Grammar Tutor for Students of French, Activities for Communication, Listening Activities, Interactive CD-ROM Tutor, or **Jeux interactifs.**

Chapter Test 45 min.

- Administer Chapter 4 Test. Select from Testing Program, Alternative Assessment Guide, Test Generator, or Standardized Assessment Tutor.

Chapter Opener

CHAPITRE 4

For resource information, see the **One-Stop Planner,** Disc 1.

Pacing Tips

The amount of new content is equal in all three **étapes,** so you might plan your lessons accordingly. For Lesson Plans and timing suggestions, see pages 93I–93L.

Meeting the Standards

Communication

- Asking for information and describing a place, p. 102
- Asking for and making suggestions, p. 106
- Emphasizing likes and dislikes, p. 107
- Relating a series of events, p. 111

Culture

- Culture Note, pp. 98, 104, 109, 111, 114
- Note culturelle, pp. 99, 104, 110
- Panorama Culturel, p. 103
- Rencontre culturelle, p. 109

Connections

- Multicultural Link, pp. 96, 109, 114
- Science Link, p. 101
- Music Link, p. 102
- History Link, p. 109
- Geography Link, p. 120
- Math Link, p. 120
- Government Link, p. 120

Comparisons

- Thinking Critically: Comparing and Contrasting, p. 96
- Thinking Critically: Synthesizing, p. 98
- Thinking Critically: Comparing and Contrasting, p. 105

Communities

- Community Link, p. 121
- De l'école au travail, p. 113

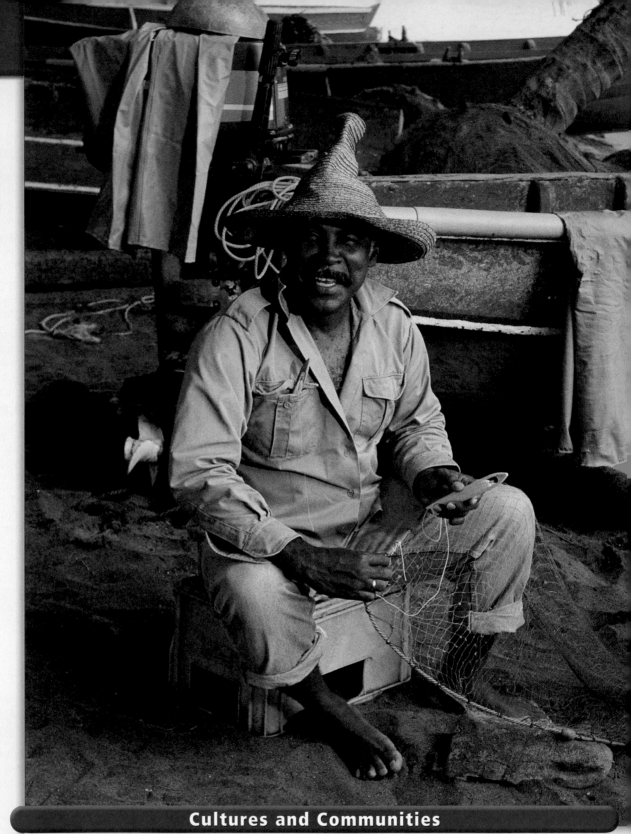

Cultures and Communities

Culture Note

All of Martinique's beaches are open to the public, but hotels charge a fee for non-guests to use their changing rooms or facilities. The soft, white-sand beaches begin south of Fort-de-France. To the north, the beaches are made up of hard-packed gray, or even black, volcanic sand. **Pointe-du-Bout** is a man-made, soft white beach lined with luxury resorts. South of **Pointe-du-Bout** is **Anse-Mitan,** a natural white-sand beach surrounded by perfect snorkeling waters. Some beaches offer the convenience of picnic tables and nearby **bistros** and **cafés,** while others are more secluded and offer nothing but sea and sand.

C H A P I T R E

4

Sous les tropiques

Objectives

In this chapter you will learn to

Première étape

- ask for information and describe a place

Deuxième étape

- ask for and make suggestions
- emphasize likes and dislikes

Troisième étape

- relate a series of events

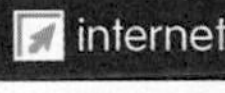

ADRESSE: go.hrw.com
MOT-CLE:
WA3 MARTINIQUE-4

◀ **Qu'est-ce qu'on peut faire à la Martinique?**

Chapter Opener

C H A P I T R E 4

Focusing on Outcomes

Have students match the photo caption to the correct outcome. NOTE: The self-check activities on page 122 help students assess their achievement of the objectives.

Chapter Sequence

Connections and Comparisons

Teacher Note

Call attention to the colorful fabric border on the top of this page. This material is called **madras,** a brightly-colored, woven, cotton plaid of various designs. This fabric is used to make the traditional costume of Martinique, as well as everyday clothing. You might challenge students to find another appearance of this unique cloth in the chapter (page 110, Agathe's skirt).

Mise en train

CHAPITRE 4

Teaching Resources
pp. 96–98

PRINT 

- Lesson Planner, p. 16
- Video Guide, pp. 24, 26
- Cahier d'activités, p. 37

MEDIA

- One-Stop Planner
- Video Program
  Mise en train
  Videocassette 2, 03:32–08:49
  Videocassette 5 (captioned version), 25:47–31:04
  Suite
  Videocassette 2, 08:52–16:35
  Videocassette 5 (captioned version), 31:07–38:50
- DVD Tutor, Disc 1
- Audio Compact Discs, CD 4, Trs. 1–2
- **Mise en train** Transparencies

Teaching Suggestion
Have students scan the flyer and ask them these questions: Who is sponsoring the contest? What is its theme? Whom do you contact for information?

Multicultural Link
Ask students what opinions they have of other countries and why they hold these opinions. Ask how the media (TV programs, commercials, advertisements, newspapers, magazines) influence what they think about other people and places.

Thinking Critically
Comparing and Contrasting
Have students compare the two sets of photos in the **Mise en train.** Ask them what has been emphasized in each set and which one they prefer.

This is an abridged version of the video episode.

MISE EN TRAIN ▪ *Un concours photographique*

CD 4 Trs. 1–2

Stratégie pour comprendre
Can you guess the theme of each one of the two photo projects?

Agnès **Jean-Philippe** **Stéphane** **Lisette**

1

Agnès C'est une bonne idée, ce concours photographique. Ça te tente de le faire avec moi? J'ai mon nouvel appareil-photo!
Jean-Philippe Pourquoi pas? Il y a beaucoup de choses à voir.

CONCOURS
Reportage Photographique
Le Club Photo vous invite à participer à son concours annuel
Thème:
Découvrir la Martinique
Nombreux prix!
Alors, à vos appareils-photos et vive l'imagination!
Pour tous renseignements, contactez M. Lucas, salle 310

LA MARTINIQUE...
autrefois appelée Madinina, l'île aux fleurs. Une île parmi tant d'autres, mais si belle, colorée, chaleureuse...

On se promène, on se baigne, on se bronze. La mer, le sable, le soleil, les cocotiers, l'eau couleur turquoise, les sports nautiques... La Martinique — c'est magnifique!

Chez nous, il fait beau, chaud même parfois, mais il y a toujours un peu de pluie. C'est pour ça que notre île est si verte toute l'année. Il y a des fleurs de toutes les couleurs : rouges, jaunes, mauves, bleues, et blanches!

Plus vers le nord, c'est la jungle tropicale, les arbres immenses, le paradis des plantes et des moustiques.

C'est l'éternel printemps. Quand on a vu le soleil se coucher sur la mer ou bien se lever au petit matin, déjà on est amoureux.

Preteaching Vocabulary

Identifying Keywords
Have students look at the different photo essays and try to come up with general differences based on the photos. Then have them look at the text more closely and identify keywords within each essay that shows distinct differences between the two versions **(Essay 1: île aux fleurs; Essay 2: île des Martiniquais).**

 STANDARDS: 1.2, 2.1, 3.1

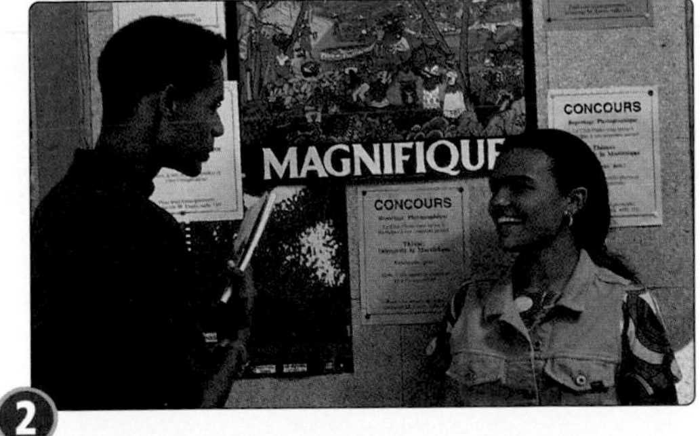

Stéphane Tu sais, la Martinique, c'est plus qu'une île touristique. Pour vraiment l'apprécier, on doit voir comment on vit ici.

Lisette Tu as raison. Il vaut mieux montrer la vie de tous les jours à la Martinique.

LES VISAGES DE LA MARTINIQUE

La Martinique, c'est plus qu'un paradis pour les touristes. C'est aussi l'île des Martiniquais...

La vie des jeunes

Pour nous, les jeunes, c'est l'école. Le soir, on apprend les leçons. Parfois, on aide les parents au travail. Mais on préfère, bien sûr, faire du vélo ou aller à la plage.

La vie en famille

Le samedi après-midi ou le dimanche, c'est quand la famille peut être réunie. On aime bien jouer aux jeux de société ou se balader ensemble.

La vie en ville

Beaucoup de gens se lèvent à 4h parce que leur travail commence très tôt. Le soir, on prépare le repas en famille. D'habitude, on se couche de bonne heure, mais on a toujours le temps de s'amuser. Cette employée de banque aime danser, surtout le zouk.

La vie près de la mer

Avec la mer toujours bleue et le climat doux, la Martinique est un paradis pour les pêcheurs. On pêche toute l'année: des daurades, des thons, des poissons rouges... Ça change selon la saison. Puis on va les vendre au marché.

Cahier d'activités, p. 37, Act. 1–2

Using the Captioned Video/DVD

If students have difficulty understanding French spoken at a normal speed, use Videocassette 5 to allow students to see the French captions for ***Un concours photographique*** and ***Un concours photographique (suite).*** Hearing the language and watching the story will reduce anxiety about the new language and facilitate comprehension. The reinforcement of seeing the written vocabulary words as they watch the gestures and actions will help prepare students to do the comprehension activities on page 98.

NOTE: The *DVD Tutor* contains captions for all sections of the *Video Program.*

Mise en train

CHAPITRE 4

Presenting Mise en train

Before they view the video, tell students that the teenagers they're going to see are entering a contest. Ask students to try to answer these questions as they watch the episode: 1. Are all the students going to do the same thing? 2. What are they going to do differently? Then, have students look at the photos and read the text in the **Mise en train.** Ask them to determine which participants in the photo contest took which group of photos and for what reason. See Preteaching Vocabulary on page 96 for more practice with the **Mise en train.**

Challenge

Have groups of three write one-sentence captions for the photos, using their own words. Write their captions on the board or on a transparency and have the class choose the best ones.

Mise en train (suite)

When the story continues, Lisette and Stéphane interview a bank employee. Agnès and Jean-Philippe take pictures of a rainforest and Mount Pelée in the north. Later, at school, the winning projects are displayed. The two pairs of friends both win prizes: Agnès and Jean-Philippe for their technical expertise, and Lisette and Stéphane for their originality.

Mise en train

CHAPITRE 4

Challenge

2 Have students work in pairs to make up additional sentence starters based on the **Mise en train.** Have them write their work on a transparency and ask their classmates to complete the sentences.

Thinking Critically

3 **Synthesizing** Have students explain why they believe certain photos belong to one or the other photo essay theme. Then, ask them which photos they prefer and why.

Culture Note

3 Refer students to Photo 3. Head wraps in Martinique are more than a fashion. They also convey information about the women who wear them. Traditionally, a wrap with one peak indicates a woman is single. Two peaks indicate she is engaged, and three show that she is married.

These activities check for comprehension only. Students should not yet be expected to produce language modeled in **Mise en train.**

1 Tu as compris?

1. Why are the students taking pictures? for a photo essay contest
2. What do Agnès and Jean-Philippe take pictures of? nature
3. What do they emphasize in their presentation of Martinique? the beauty of the island
4. What do Stéphane and Lisette take pictures of? people
5. What are they trying to show in their photo-essay? everyday life

2 Pourquoi?

Complète les phrases suivantes.

1. L'île est verte toute l'année... d
2. C'est un paradis pour les pêcheurs... c
3. Beaucoup de gens se lèvent à 4h... e
4. C'est une île très colorée... a
5. On aime se balader ensemble le samedi après-midi ou le dimanche... b

a. parce qu'il y a des fleurs de toutes les couleurs.
b. parce que c'est quand la famille peut être réunie.
c. parce que le climat est doux et la mer est toujours bleue.
d. parce qu'il y a toujours un peu de pluie.
e. parce que le travail commence très tôt.

3 A qui, les photos?

Voici des photos prises par Agnès, Jean-Philippe, Stéphane et Lisette. D'après ce que tu sais sur les thèmes de leurs reportages photographiques, dis qui a pris chaque photo.

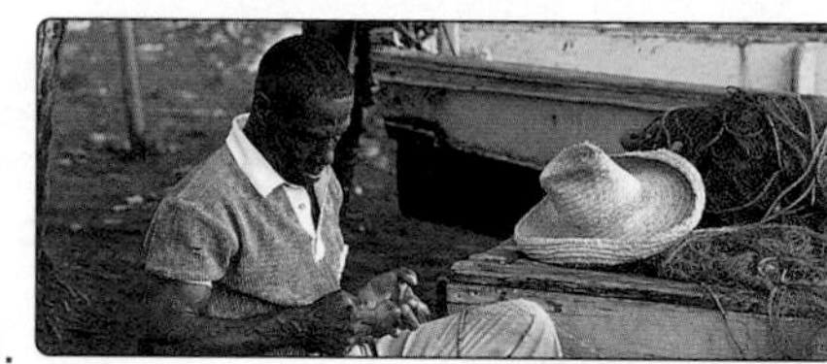
1.

2.

3.

4.

5.

Stéphane, Lisette: 1, 3, 5; Agnès, Jean-Philippe: 2, 4

4 Cherche les expressions

In *Un concours photographique* what do the students say to . . . See answers below.

1. suggest that they participate in the photo contest?
2. accept a suggestion?
3. describe what's on the island?
4. describe the weather?
5. tell when and how often they do something?

5 Et maintenant, à toi

Imagine que tu vas faire un reportage photographique sur ta ville ou sur ton état. Qu'est-ce que tu vas prendre comme photos?

Answers

4
1. Ça te tente de le faire avec moi?
2. Pourquoi pas?
3. *Possible answers:* Il y a beaucoup de choses à voir! La mer, le sable, le soleil, les cocotiers, l'eau couleur turquoise, les sports nautiques...
4. Il fait beau, chaud même parfois, mais il y a toujours un peu de pluie.
5. *Possible answers:* le soir, le samedi après-midi, le dimanche, à quatre heures, très tôt, d'habitude, toute l'année

Comprehension Check

Tactile/Visual Learners

2 Have students write the sentence starters on strips of paper of one color, and the sentence completions on strips of paper of a second color. Encourage students to add their own sentence starters and completions on the appropriate colored strips. Then, have students shuffle the strips and pass them to a partner who will match the strips.

Teaching Suggestion

3 Describe the photos one at a time in random order and have students write the number of the photo that matches your description.

STANDARDS: 1.2, 2.1, 3.1, 4.2

Première étape

Objectives Asking for information and describing a place

WA3 MARTINIQUE-4

Salut Norbert!
On visite Saint-Pierre aujourd'hui. La ville a été détruite par une éruption volcanique en 1902. Sur la plage, le sable est noir. Ça fait bizarre. Il fait beau, on passe de bonnes vacances et on t'embrasse très fort,
Paul

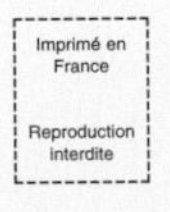

Norbert ROUQUET
6 Rue PASCAL
85000 LA ROCHE-SUR-YON

Un petit mot de la Martinique où il fait un temps magnifique. Je t'écris de la plage à l'ombre des cocotiers. C'est un vrai paradis ici. On rentre dans l'eau comme dans son bain, et il y a des fleurs incroyables, immenses. Le seul problème, c'est les moustiques. Vous verrez mes jambes! Bisous.
Florence

Imprimé en France
Reproduction interdite

M et Mme LEPOULAIN
12 Boulevard du Fort
59650 VILLENEUVE D'ASCQ

6 Les cartes postales See answers below.

Lisons

1. Qu'est-ce que Florence pense de la Martinique? Quel est son problème?
2. Paul visite quelle ville? Qu'est-ce qui est arrivé en 1902 dans cette ville?
3. Qu'est-ce que Paul trouve bizarre? Pourquoi?

You know the present-day capital of Martinique is Fort-de-France, but did you know that until 1902 the capital was the city of Saint-Pierre? Saint-Pierre was a very rich and glamorous city, known as **le Petit Paris** of the West Indies. But on the morning of May 8, 1902, Mount Pelée exploded, and in three minutes the entire city of 30,000 people was destroyed. Only one person, a prisoner protected by his cell walls, survived the eruption.

Communication for All Students

Challenge

Type the postcard messages, but leave out some keywords and list them as choices at the bottom of the paper. Distribute copies to students and have them fill in the blanks without looking at their books. Then, have them open their books and correct their papers.

Auditory Learners

Distribute copies of the postcard messages (see Challenge), but this time read each message aloud. Have students listen and fill in the blanks with their choices.

Première étape

CHAPITRE 4

Teaching Resources
pp. 99–102

PRINT

- Lesson Planner, p. 17
- TPR Storytelling Book, pp. 24–25
- Listening Activities, pp. 27, 31
- Activities for Communication, pp. 19–20, 90, 93, 143–144
- Travaux pratiques de grammaire, pp. 29–30
- Grammar Tutor for Students of French, Chapter 4
- Cahier d'activités, pp. 38–40
- Testing Program, pp. 79–82
- Alternative Assessment Guide, p. 35
- Student Make-Up Assignments, Chapter 4

MEDIA 

- One-Stop Planner
- Audio Compact Discs, CD 4, Trs. 3, 12, 18–19
- Teaching Transparencies: 4-1, 4-A; **Grammaire supplémentaire** Answers; Travaux pratiques de grammaire Answers
- Interactive CD-ROM Tutor, Disc 1

Bell Work

Write the following in two columns on the board or on a transparency. Have students match the expressions on the left with those on the right.

Left: **Madinina/la jungle tropicale/l'appareil-photo/les poissons/danser**

Right: **le zouk/le concours photographique/l'île aux fleurs/le paradis des plantes et des moustiques/des daurades, des thons, des poissons rouges**

Answers

6
1. C'est un paradis.; Il y a des moustiques.
2. Saint-Pierre; une éruption volcanique
3. le sable; parce qu'il est noir

STANDARDS: 1.2, 3.1

Teaching Resources
pp. 99–102

PRINT 

- Lesson Planner, p. 17
- TPR Storytelling Book, pp. 24–25
- Listening Activities, pp. 27, 31
- Activities for Communication, pp. 19–20, 90, 93, 143–144
- Travaux pratiques de grammaire, pp. 29–30
- Grammar Tutor for Students of French, Chapter 4
- Cahier d'activités, pp. 38–40
- Testing Program, pp. 79–82
- Alternative Assessment Guide, p. 35
- Student Make-Up Assignments, Chapter 4

MEDIA

- One-Stop Planner
- Audio Compact Discs, CD 4, Trs. 3, 12, 18–19
- Teaching Transparencies: 4-1, 4-A; **Grammaire supplémentaire** Answers; Travaux pratiques de grammaire Answers
- Interactive CD-ROM Tutor, Disc 1

Presenting Vocabulaire

Sketch a map of the United States on the board. Add several major cities and a compass labeled **nord, sud, ouest,** and **est.** Have students repeat the compass directions after you. Then, ask either-or questions **(Los Angeles est dans l'est ou dans l'ouest des Etats-Unis?)** and questions to elicit information **(C'est où, New York?).** Have students open their books and repeat the vocabulary after you. Then, ask questions about the map of Martinique similar to those you asked about the United States.

Vocabulaire

CD-ROM 1 DVD 1

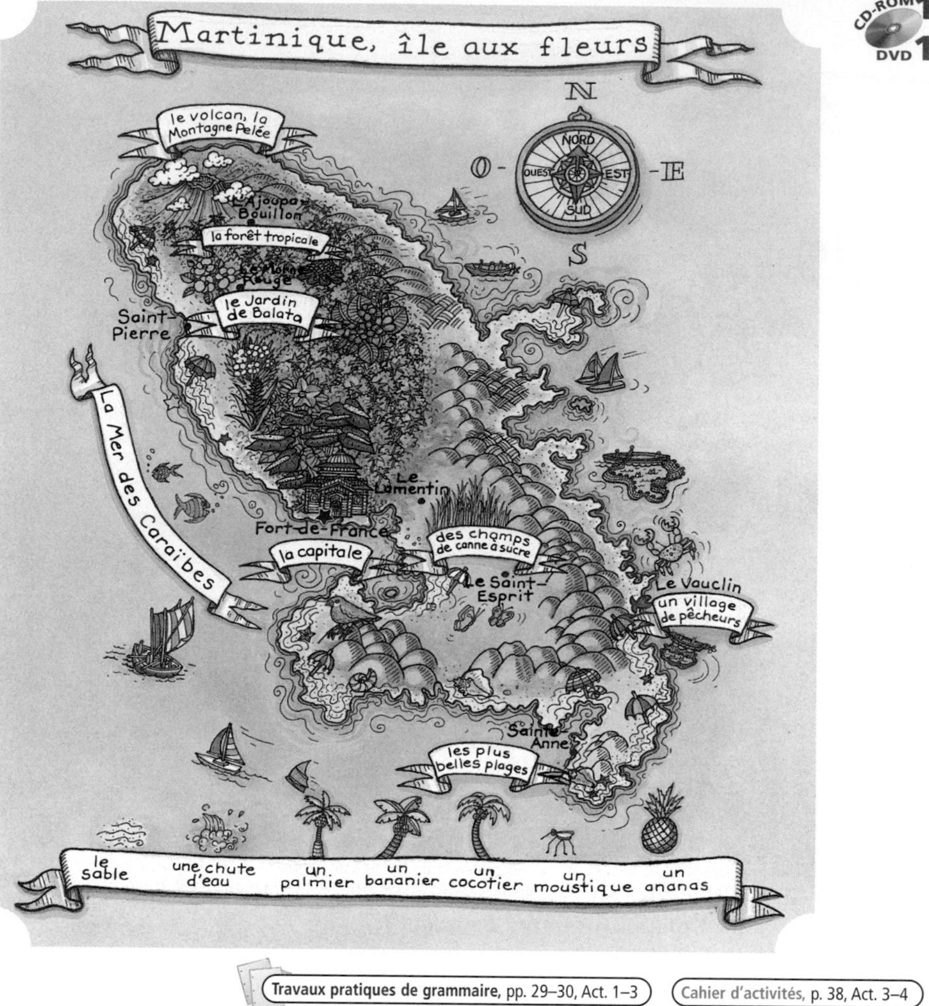

Travaux pratiques de grammaire, pp. 29–30, Act. 1–3

Cahier d'activités, p. 38, Act. 3–4

7 Vrai ou faux?

Lisons

1. La Martinique est dans la mer des Caraïbes. vrai
2. La capitale de la Martinique est la montagne Pelée. faux
3. Dans le sud, il y a de belles plages. vrai
4. Dans le nord de la Martinique, il y a une forêt tropicale. vrai
5. Il y a des villages de pêcheurs dans l'ouest de la Martinique. faux

Tu te rappelles?

When you want to say *some,* simply use **de** if there's an adjective before a plural noun:

des conseils → **de bons** conseils
des plages → **de belles** plages

Travaux pratiques de grammaire, p. 30, Act. 4

Grammaire supplémentaire, p. 116, Act. 1–2

Cahier d'activités, p. 39, Act. 5

Communication for All Students

Tactile/Visual/Auditory Learners

Trace an outline of Martinique on a transparency and label several cities. Draw several features on small, separate pieces of transparency (tropical forest, mosquitos, sugar cane field). Have students draw the same map on a sheet of paper and the features on small, separate pieces of paper. Describe Martinique, using the vocabulary, and ask students to place the features on the map as you describe them in French. **(Au Morne Rouge, il y a le jardin de Balata. Au nord du jardin, il y a une forêt tropicale. Dans la forêt tropicale, il y a beaucoup de moustiques!)** Turn on the overhead projector after every two or three sentences and place the features on your map so that students can check theirs.

STANDARDS: 1.2, 3.1, 4.1

8 Une île tropicale

See scripts and answers on p. 93G.

CD 4 Tr. 3

Ecoutons While in France, you hear the following ad for Martinique on the radio. Which features of the island are mentioned?

les bananiers | la montagne Pelée | Fort-de-France | le sable | la forêt tropicale | les cocotiers | une chute d'eau | les villages de pêcheurs | les champs de canne à sucre

9 A la Martinique

Lisons/Ecrivons Complète les phrases suivantes avec les mots et les expressions présentés dans l'activité 8. Ensuite, invente d'autres phrases avec les mots et expressions que tu n'as pas utilisés.

1. Le volcan qui a détruit l'ancienne capitale s'appelle ______. la montagne Pelée
2. Si vous adorez le poisson, visitez ______. les villages de pêcheurs
3. Il pleut beaucoup dans ______. la forêt tropicale
4. Attention à ta tête quand tu marches sous ______. les cocotiers
5. A la Martinique il y a des plages où ______ est noir. le sable
6. La capitale de la Martinique s'appelle ______. Fort-de-France

10 Vingt questions

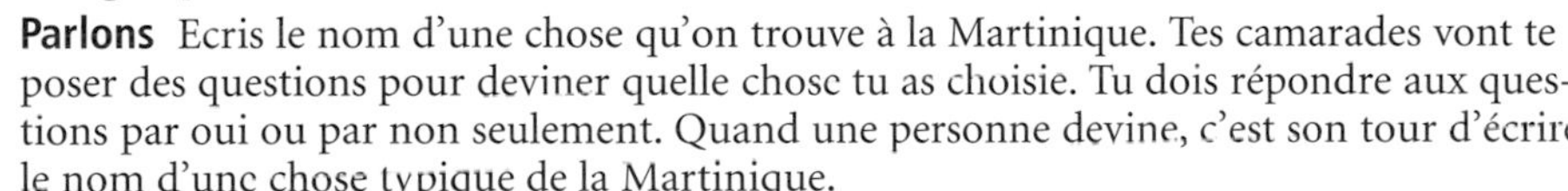

Parlons Ecris le nom d'une chose qu'on trouve à la Martinique. Tes camarades vont te poser des questions pour deviner quelle chose tu as choisie. Tu dois répondre aux questions par oui ou par non seulement. Quand une personne devine, c'est son tour d'écrire le nom d'une chose typique de la Martinique.

EXEMPLE **—C'est un fruit? —Non. —C'est une ville? —Oui.**
—C'est un arbre? —Non. —C'est Fort-de-France? —Oui.
—C'est un lieu? —Oui.

11 Une visite guidée

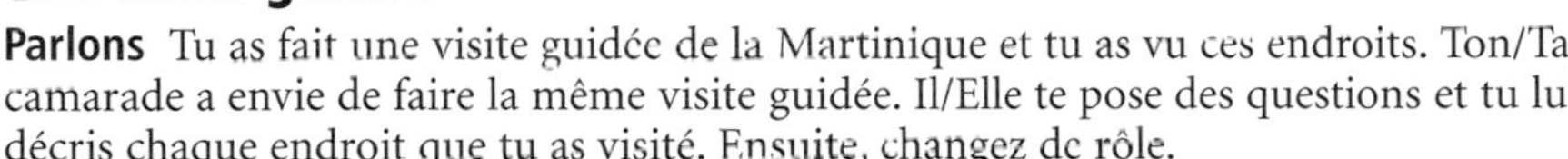

Parlons Tu as fait une visite guidée de la Martinique et tu as vu ces endroits. Ton/Ta camarade a envie de faire la même visite guidée. Il/Elle te pose des questions et tu lui décris chaque endroit que tu as visité. Ensuite, changez de rôle.

EXEMPLE **—C'est comment, la plage des Salines?**
—C'est magnifique! Le sable est blanc et il y a des palmiers.

la ville de Saint-Pierre

le jardin de Balata

le marché

la forêt tropicale

Première étape

CHAPITRE 4

TPR On a large sheet of butcher paper, sketch an outline of Martinique, label the towns, and tape it to the board. On small, separate pieces of butcher paper, have students draw the vocabulary items (a waterfall, a pineapple, a fishing village). Tell students where to tape the pictures on the map. **(Max, mets le sable à Sainte-Anne.)**

Teaching Suggestion

8 On the board or on a transparency, list all of the features in random order and number each one. Then, play the recording and have students number the features in the order they are mentioned.

Challenge

9 Have students design a crossword puzzle that uses these sentence starters as clues. Have them create additional clues and supply the answers.

Building on Previous Skills

11 To re-enter the pronoun **en,** have partners secretly choose one of the four places in the photos. One student asks questions to try to guess the place his or her partner has chosen. **(Il y a du sable?)** The other must answer, using the pronoun **en. (Oui, il y en a. Non, il n'y en a pas.)**

Connections and Comparisons

Science Link

The climate of the mountainous northern region of Martinique is typical of the subtropical rain forest. Between 160 and 200 inches of annual rainfall and high humidity produce lush vegetation, consisting of palm, rosewood, logwood, breadfruit, and mahogany trees, oleander, ferns, and orchids. Volcanoes tend to produce rich soil. However, the permanently moist rain forest soil is not very fertile, since the hot and humid weather causes organic matter to decompose rapidly and to be quickly absorbed. Plants in rain forests exhibit stratification, developing a high canopy of foliage sometimes extending beyond 100 feet, with little vegetation underneath. Most trees have a very shallow root system because rain falls in the forest, drips down the leaves, and trickles down the tree trunk to the ground, moistening but not drenching it.

STANDARDS: 1.1, 1.2, 3.1, 3.2, 5.2

Première étape

CHAPITRE 4

Presenting
Comment dit-on... ?

Sketch a map of the United States on the board and add several cities and attractions, such as Disney World® and the Grand Canyon. Point to one of the features you drew and describe its location on the map, its size, or its climate. **(La ville de San Diego se trouve dans l'ouest des Etats-Unis. Le Texas est plus grand que la Louisiane. Il fait beau en Floride.)** Then, have students answer simple questions about various places pictured on the map. **(Est-ce que la Virginie est dans l'ouest? Est-ce qu'il fait chaud en Alaska?)**

Portfolio

15 **Oral** This activity is appropriate for students' oral portfolios. For portfolio suggestions, see the *Alternative Assessment Guide,* page 21.

Assess

- Testing Program, pp. 79–82 Quiz 4-1A, Quiz 4-1B Audio CD 4, Tr. 12
- Student Make-Up Assignments, Chapter 4, Alternative Quiz
- Alternative Assessment Guide, p. 35

Comment dit-on...?

Asking for information and describing a place

To ask about a place:	To describe a place:
Où se trouve la Martinique? *Where is . . . located?* **Qu'est-ce qu'il y a** à voir? *What is there . . . ?*	La Martinique **se trouve** dans la mer des Caraïbes. **Dans le nord,** il y a la forêt tropicale et **dans le sud,** il y a de belles plages. La capitale se trouve **dans l'ouest** et il y a des villages de pêcheurs **dans l'est.**
Il fait chaud?	**Il fait** toujours très chaud et il pleut souvent.
C'est comment? *What's it like?*	C'est **plus grand que** New York. *. . . bigger than . . .* C'est **moins grand qu'**Oahu. *. . . smaller than . . .* La Martinique est une île **charmante, colorée** et **vivante!** *. . . charming, colorful, lively*

Cahier d'activités, p. 39, Act. 6–7

12 Ma ville

Ecrivons Complète les phrases pour faire une description de ta ville.

_____ se trouve dans l'état de/d' _____. Dans le nord, il y a _____ et dans le sud, il y a _____. Il fait _____ chez nous. Ma ville est plus grande que _____ et moins grande que _____. C'est une ville _____ et _____.

13 Jeu d'identification

Parlons Pense à une ville importante aux Etats-Unis ou ailleurs. Tes camarades de classe vont te poser des questions pour deviner le nom de cette ville.

Où se trouve cette ville? | C'est petit? | Qu'est-ce qu'il y a à voir? | C'est comment? | C'est plus grand que... ? | Il fait froid en hiver?

14 Mon journal

Ecrivons Est-ce que tu as envie de voyager? Où est-ce que tu voudrais aller? Décris l'endroit que tu aimerais visiter. Dis ce qu'il y a à faire et à voir là-bas. Ajoute des images à ta description si tu veux.

15 Et toi, tu voudrais aller où?

Parlons Maintenant, pose cinq questions à un(e) camarade sur l'endroit où il/elle voudrait aller. Tu peux poser des questions sur la géographie, le climat et les activités locales. Ensuite, changez de rôle.

Connections and Comparisons

Music Link

After presenting the expressions in **Comment dit-on... ?**, you might play the song *Vive la rose* on Audio CD 10 and have students listen for sentences that use **plus... que** with an adjective. Then, give students copies of the lyrics, and have them circle these sentences. Finally, have small groups of students write a short paragraph in which they describe two places of their choice, using the expressions from **Comment dit-on... ?** and the comparative forms **plus... que** and **moins... que**.

CD-ROM 1 DVD 1

Qu'est-ce qu'il y a à visiter dans cette région?

We asked some francophone people what there is to see in their area. Here's what they had to say.

Célestine, Côte d'Ivoire

«En Côte d'Ivoire, ce qu'il y a à voir en touriste je dirais... Je pense souvent au niveau de Man, c'est-à-dire, le pays, la ville de Man. Il y a les montagnes et puis, il y a des cascades et ensuite, il y a la ville de Korhogo qui recouvre beaucoup de culture, c'est-à-dire les danses. Et il y a beaucoup de choses à apprendre, surtout pour les étrangers. Il y a les masques à découvrir. Il y en a plein. Il y a trop de choses. On ne peut pas les citer.» Tr. 5

Thomas, France

«[Paris,] c'est une ville de touristes quand même. C'est une grande ville parce que c'est la capitale de la France quand même. C'est une des plus belles villes du monde et il y a beaucoup de lieux touristiques. Il y a beaucoup de musées. Il y a des sculptures. Il y a des cinémas, beaucoup de cinémas pour les sorties entre copains. Et il y a la tour Eiffel, la tour Montparnasse, les grands sites.» Tr. 6

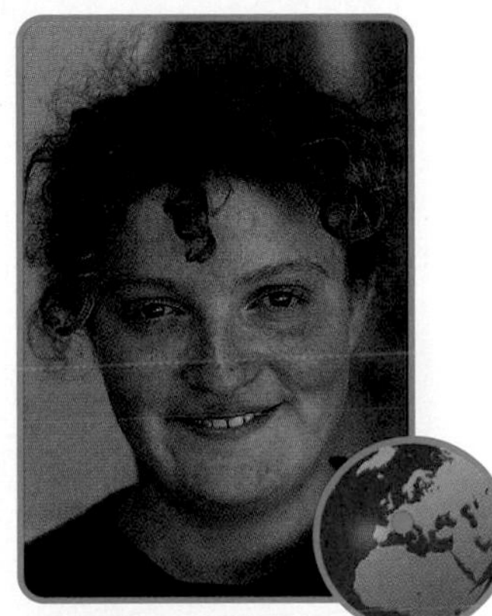

Marie, France

«En Provence, il y a surtout la mer. Moi, j'aime bien. C'est pas très loin. C'est à une demi-heure d'ici. Il y a la mer. On peut se baigner. Aussi, il y a toutes les villes de Côte d'Azur qui sont très jolies, où on peut aller se promener. Voilà.» Tr. 7

Qu'en penses-tu?

1. Which of the places mentioned would you most like to visit? What makes it attractive to you?
2. What is there to see and do where you live? Are the sights and activities similar to those the interviewees mentioned?
3. Imagine that you're a teenager living in Martinique and you were just asked the question **Qu'est-ce qu'il y a à visiter dans cette région?** Using these interviews as models, write an answer to the question.

Cultures and Communities

Community Link

Ask students what there is to see and do in their area. Is their town or city considered a popular place for tourists? What would they want to show people who were visiting them?

CHAPITRE 4

Teaching Resources
p. 103

PRINT
- Video Guide, pp. 25–27
- Cahier d'activités, p. 48

MEDIA
- One-Stop Planner
- Video Program, Videocassette 2, 16:37–21:30
- DVD Tutor, Disc 1
- Audio Compact Discs, CD 4, Trs. 4–7
- Interactive CD-ROM Tutor, Disc 1

Presenting Panorama Culturel

After students have seen the video, write several of the interviewee's comments on the board in random order and number each one. Show the video again and have students match the numbers of the comments with the names of the interviewees.

Questions

1. **D'après Célestine, qu'est-ce qu'il y a à voir à Man?** (les montagnes et les cascades) **Et à Korhogo?** (la culture et la danse)
2. **Qu'est-ce que Thomas pense de Paris?** (C'est une ville de touristes et c'est une des plus belles villes du monde.)
3. **Qu'est-ce qu'il y a à Paris pour les touristes?** (des musées, des sculptures, des cinémas, la tour Eiffel, la tour Montparnasse, les grands sites)
4. **D'après Marie, quelle est l'attraction touristique principale de la Provence?** (la mer)

STANDARDS: 1.2, 2.2, 3.2, 4.2, 5.1

Teaching Resources
pp. 104–108

PRINT

- Lesson Planner, p. 18
- TPR Storytelling Book, pp. 26–27
- Listening Activities, pp. 27–28, 32
- Activities for Communication, pp. 21–22, 91, 93–94, 143–144
- Travaux pratiques de grammaire, pp. 31–33
- Grammar Tutor for Students of French, Chapter 4
- Cahier d'activités, pp. 41–43
- Testing Program, pp. 83–86
- Alternative Assessment Guide, p. 35
- Student Make-Up Assignments, Chapter 4

MEDIA 

- One-Stop Planner
- Audio Compact Discs, CD 4, Trs. 8–9, 13, 20–21
- Teaching Transparencies: 4-2, 4-B; **Grammaire supplémentaire** Answers; Travaux pratiques de grammaire Answers
- Interactive CD-ROM Tutor, Disc 1

Bell Work

Have students identify the following: **un arbre tropical/un fruit tropical/un volcan/l'ancien nom de la Martinique/le contraire de nord/on fait du sucre avec** (*Answers:* **un cocotier, un palmier, un bananier/un ananas, une banane/la montagne Pelée/Madinina/sud/la canne à sucre)**

Teaching Suggestion

16 Read the brochure with students and ask the following questions: **Qui aime faire de la plongée? Qui aime faire de la voile? Tu as un bateau? Qui aime faire les boutiques?** Then, have students make substitutions in the captions of the brochure to adapt them to their own city or state.

Deuxième étape

Objectives Asking for and making suggestions; emphasizing likes and dislikes

WA3 MARTINIQUE-4

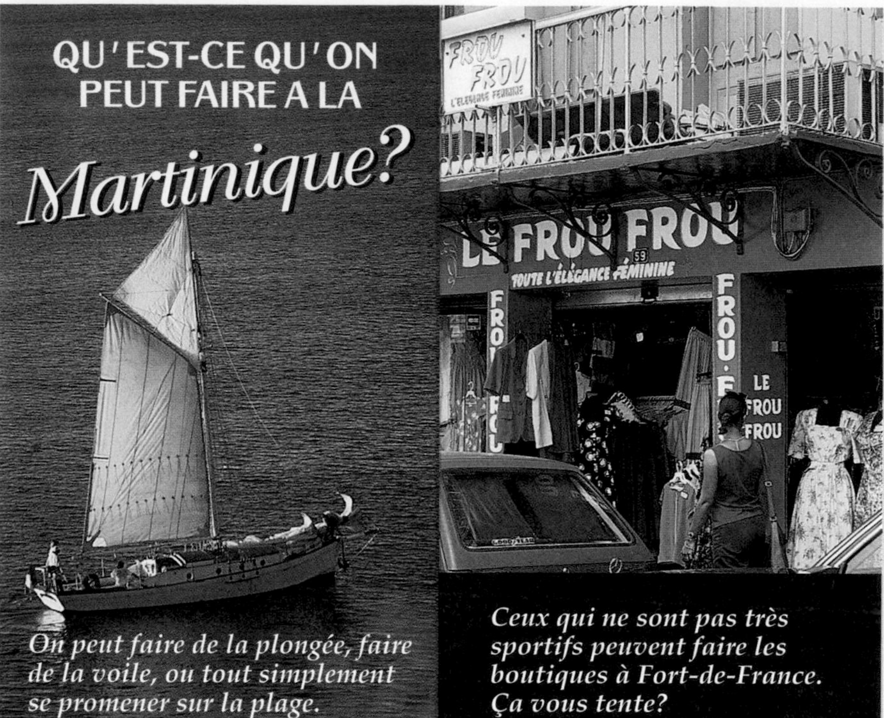

QU'EST-CE QU'ON PEUT FAIRE A LA
Martinique?
LE FROU FROU
TOUTE L'ÉLÉGANCE FÉMININE
FROU FROU
On peut faire de la plongée, faire de la voile, ou tout simplement se promener sur la plage.
Ceux qui ne sont pas très sportifs peuvent faire les boutiques à Fort-de-France. Ça vous tente?

16 Tu veux visiter la Martinique?

Lisons Est-ce que cette brochure te donne envie d'aller à la Martinique? Pourquoi ou pourquoi pas?

Among the most beautiful sights in Martinique are the **yoles rondes,** or **gommiers,** the traditional fishing boats that are also used for racing. People come from all over the world to watch the "nautical ballet" of these brightly painted boats that are unique to Martinique.

Cultures and Communities

Culture Note

Shoppers can find good buys in Fort-de-France on designer scarves, French fragrances, fine china, crystal, and leather goods. The area around the cathedral has many small boutiques that carry luxury items. The **Centre des métiers d'art** and the **marché artisanal sur la Savane** in Fort-de-France carry local crafts, including dolls, straw goods, tapestries, pottery, jewelry, and beads. A **collier chou** is a traditional style necklace, and a **chaîne forçat** is a traditional bracelet.

STANDARDS: 2.2, 3.2

Vocabulaire

A la Martinique, on aime bien...

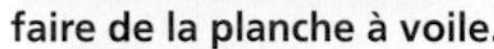

faire de la planche à voile.

faire du deltaplane.

faire de la plongée sous-marine.

aller à la pêche.

faire de la plongée avec un tuba.

danser le zouk.

déguster des fruits tropicaux.

se promener.

se baigner.

s'amuser.

Travaux pratiques de grammaire, pp. 31–32, Act. 5–7

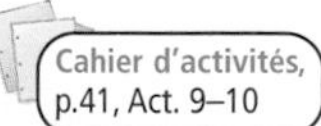

Cahier d'activités, p.41, Act. 9–10

Note de grammaire

Did you notice the word **se** before some of the verbs in the **Vocabulaire?** The pronoun **se** tells you that the subject of the sentence receives the action of the verb. Verbs with this pronoun before them are called *reflexive verbs.* You'll learn how to make the forms of the reflexive verbs later in this chapter.

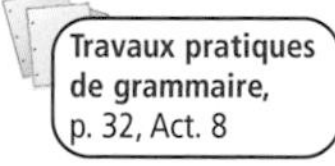

Travaux pratiques de grammaire, p. 32, Act. 8

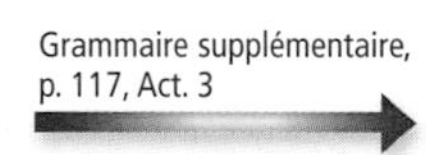

Grammaire supplémentaire, p. 117, Act. 3

Presenting Vocabulaire

Show pictures of the vocabulary items and have students repeat after you. Then, ask questions about the activities, such as **Qui a déjà fait du deltaplane? Qui voudrait essayer? Qui aime aller à la pêche?** Next, draw a grid on the board, listing several activities vertically and several questions horizontally, such as **Qui a déjà fait... ? Qui aime beaucoup... ? Qui n'aime pas du tout... ?** Ask a student to poll the class and tally the results on the board.

TPR Tell students to do these activities **(Jean, danse le zouk!)** and have them respond physically to demonstrate their comprehension.

Thinking Critically

Comparing and Contrasting
Ask students which of these activities they can do in or near their own town and which ones are limited to a particular environment. Ask them what they do in their area that they couldn't do on a tropical island.

Presenting Note de grammaire

The pronoun *se* Demonstrate the difference between **promener** and **se promener** by drawing stick figures on the board or on a transparency. Point to an appropriate drawing, saying **Le garçon se promène. Ici, il promène son chien.** Do the same with the verbs **amuser** and **s'amuser. (La fille s'amuse. Ici, elle amuse le bébé.)**

Connections and Comparisons

Language Notes

- Call attention to the word **tropicaux** and ask students to try to guess the singular form **(tropical).** Discuss the formation of this adjective and its plural form. Have students suggest other nouns that might be used with **tropical. (une île/des îles, un arbre/des arbres, une forêt/des forêts, un menu/des menus)**
- **Déguster** means much more than **manger.** It means to *savor* whatever you eat or drink and to truly appreciate it. **Une dégustation** implies a *sampling* of something. Sometimes, a grocery store will offer **une dégustation gratuite** of samples of a new product. **Un dégustateur/une dégustatrice** is a person who tests the quality of wine.

Teaching Resources
pp. 104–108

PRINT 

- Lesson Planner, p. 18
- TPR Storytelling Book, pp. 26–27
- Listening Activities, pp. 27–28, 32
- Activities for Communication, pp. 21–22, 91, 93–94, 143–144
- Travaux pratiques de grammaire, pp. 31–33
- Grammar Tutor for Students of French, Chapter 4
- Cahier d'activités, pp. 41–43
- Testing Program, pp. 83–86
- Alternative Assessment Guide, p. 35
- Student Make-Up Assignments, Chapter 4

MEDIA

- One-Stop Planner
- Audio Compact Discs, CD 4, Trs. 8–9, 13, 20–21
- Teaching Transparencies: 4-2, 4-B; **Grammaire supplémentaire** Answers; Travaux pratiques de grammaire Answers
- Interactive CD-ROM Tutor, Disc 1

Presenting
Comment dit-on... ?

Type and distribute copies of the script for listening Activity 17. Draw three columns on the board or on a transparency and label them as follows: *Asking for suggestions, Making suggestions,* and *Accepting and Refusing suggestions.* Have students pick out the sentences from the listening script that accomplish these functions and write them in the appropriate columns. Finally, introduce the expressions in **Comment dit-on... ?** and ask students which ones they recall from Chapter 1.

17 Qu'est-ce qu'on fait aujourd' hui? See scripts and answers on p. 93G.

Ecoutons Listen as Magali and César decide what to do today. List two things they suggest. What do they finally decide to do?
CD 4 Tr. 8

18 Qu'est-ce qu'ils aiment?

Parlons/Ecrivons Regarde les bureaux de José et de Jocelyne. A ton avis, qu'est-ce qu'ils aiment faire?

Le bureau de José
écouter de la musique, faire de la natation, faire du deltaplane, aller à la pêche, faire de la plongée

Le bureau de Jocelyne
déguster des fruits, faire de la plongée, faire de la voile

Comment dit-on...?

Asking for and making suggestions

To ask for suggestions about what to do:

Qu'est-ce qu'on peut faire?

To make suggestions:

On peut se promener sur la plage.
We can . . .
Ça te dit d'aller manger une glace?
What do you think of going . . . ?
Si on allait se baigner?
How about going . . . ?

Cahier d'activités, p. 42, Act. 11–13

Note culturelle

In Martinique, people speak French and **créole,** a mixture of French and African languages with some Spanish, English, and Portuguese words. Here's how to respond in Creole to someone's suggestions:

Oui / Non ***Ouai / Han-Han***
Chouette! ***I bon!***
D'accord. ***D'accó.***
C'est une bonne idée. ***Ce'an bon bagaï.***
Je ne peux pas. ***Mwen pé pa.***
Ça ne me dit rien. ***Sa pa ka di mwen ayen.***
Pas question! ***Awa!***

Cultures and Communities

Teaching Suggestion

Note culturelle Before reading the **Note culturelle** with students, write the expressions on the board or on a transparency. Put the French expressions in one column and the Creole expressions in random order in a second column. Have students try to match the French expressions to their Creole equivalents.

Teacher Note

For more information on the Creole language, see **Lisons!** on page 114.

STANDARDS: 1.2, 2.1, 3.2

Une journée touristique

Parlons Fais des projets pour une journée touristique à la Martinique avec un(e) camarade. Choisissez ce que vous allez faire le matin, l'après-midi et le soir.

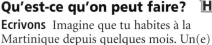

- déguster des spécialités antillaises
- visiter Saint-Pierre
- faire des photos des chutes d'eau
- écouter de la musique antillaise et danser
- aller voir la forêt tropicale
- visiter un village de pêcheurs
- — ? —
- s'amuser sur la plage
- se promener à Fort-de-France

Qu'est-ce qu'on peut faire?

Ecrivons Imagine que tu habites à la Martinique depuis quelques mois. Un(e) ami(e) américain(e) va venir te voir. Ecris une lettre à ton ami(e) pour lui dire ce qu'il y a à faire et à voir à la Martinique. Suggère six activités que vous pouvez faire pendant son séjour.

If a writing task seems too complicated, start off by making a list of words and phrases that you might want to use. Then, add adjectives and connectors like **et** and **mais** to make sentences. Using connectors will make you sound more sophisticated in French . . . and in your native language.

Comment dit-on...?

Emphasizing likes and dislikes

To emphasize what you like:

Ce que j'aime bien le week-end, **c'est** me coucher très tard.
What I like is . . .

Ce que je préfère, c'est me promener sur la plage.
What I prefer is . . .

Ce qui me plaît à la Martinique, **c'est** la mer!
What I like is . . .

To emphasize what you don't like:

Ce que je n'aime pas, c'est les maths!
What I don't like is . . .

Ce qui ne me plaît pas, c'est de me lever à 6h du matin.
What I don't care for is . . .

Ce qui m'ennuie, c'est de rester à la maison le week-end.
What bores me is . . .

Cahier d'activités, p. 43, Act. 14

Ce qui me plaît, c'est de jouer au frisbee®!

CD-ROM 1 DVD 1

Note de grammaire

When you're using a reflexive verb to talk about yourself, use **me** before the verb instead of **se.** Can you figure out what **me lever** and **me coucher** mean in **Comment dit-on... ?** if **se lever** means *to get up* and **se coucher** means *to go to bed?*

Teacher to Teacher

Sue DiGiandomenico
Wellesley Middle School
Wellesley, MA

Sue suggests the following activity to practice the vocabulary in this étape.

"Using PowerPoint®, students work in pairs to create a wonderful weekend full of activities. Have students imagine that they have a chance to visit Martinique for a weekend. Have them plan and illustrate (using PowerPoint® layout and graphics from the Internet) 5–7 slides. Ask them to include the activities they want to do, what they want to see, and what they plan to eat. Students present the project to the class."

Deuxième étape

CHAPITRE 4

Teaching Suggestions

19 Encourage students to respond to their partner's suggestions in Creole (see **Note culturelle** on page 106). Students might present their conversations to the class.

19 After students have finished their pair work, have them ask their classmates questions to find out whose plans are similar to theirs. **(Qui va visiter Saint-Pierre le matin? Qui va danser le soir?)**

Presenting
Comment dit-on... ?

Write the following question and answers on the board or on a transparency: *What do you like to do on the weekend?*
1. I like to go shopping.
2. What I really like to do is go shopping.
Ask students to explain the difference between the two responses. Model each statement in **Comment dit-on... ?,** telling what you really like or dislike. Have students repeat each expression after you, substituting their own likes or dislikes. Then, write times on the board, such as **le week-end** or **le samedi soir.** Have students tell what they really like or dislike doing at these times. **(Ce que j'aime le week-end, c'est me lever très tard.)** Finally, have partners ask each other questions, using the expressions and the times on the board.

Language Note

Remind students to use **de** before the infinitive in the expressions in **Comment dit-on... ?** that use the verbs **plaire** and **ennuyer (Ce qui me plaît, c'est de dormir tard. Ce qui m'ennuie, c'est de rester à la maison.)**

Deuxième étape

CHAPITRE 4

Language-to-Language

De bons conseils Ask students if they have ever used a French or Spanish dictionary, or any other language dictionary. You might point out that most verbs in French dictionaries are listed in the infinitive form. French dictionaries also usually give the gender of the noun following the entry. Ask students to examine dictionaries in the library, such as the *Petit Robert®* or *Larousse®*, and tell what other helpful information they could find.

Additional Practice

Have students make a list of what they really like and dislike, using **ce qui** and **ce que.** Then, have them ask classmates about their likes and dislikes until they find someone with similar interests.

Assess

- Testing Program, pp. 83–86 Quiz 4-2A, Quiz 4-2B Audio CD 4, Tr. 13
- Student Make-Up Assignments, Chapter 4, Alternative Quiz
- Alternative Assessment Guide, p. 35

21 Ce que j'aime bien... See scripts and answers on p. 93G.

CD 4 Tr. 9

Ecoutons What activities are these people talking about? Do they like or dislike the activities?

Grammaire

The relative pronouns *ce qui* and *ce que*

The relative pronouns **ce qui** and **ce que** both mean *what.*

- **Ce qui** is the subject of the clause it introduces. Notice that expressions with **plaire** and **ennuyer** require **de** before an infinitive.
  - **Ce qui** me plaît, c'est **de** faire de la plongée sous-marine.
  - **Ce qui** m'ennuie, c'est **de** me lever tôt.
- **Ce que** is the direct object of the clause it introduces. It is usually followed by a subject.
  - **Ce que** j'aime bien, c'est danser le zouk avec mes amis.

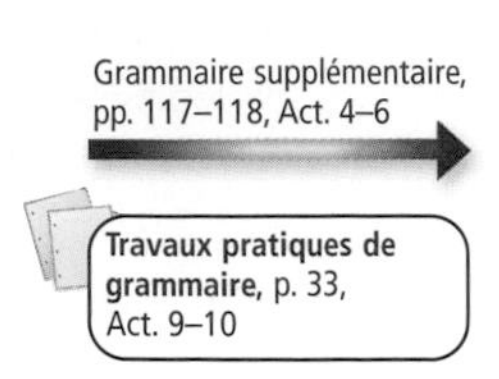

Grammaire supplémentaire, pp. 117–118, Act. 4–6

Travaux pratiques de grammaire, p. 33, Act. 9–10

22 Grammaire en contexte

Ecrivons Mélanie, ta nouvelle correspondante martiniquaise, te dit ce qu'elle aime et ce qu'elle n'aime pas. Complète sa lettre avec **ce qui** et **ce que.** **1.** ce que **2.** Ce qui **3.** Ce que **4.** Ce que **5.** ce que **6.** Ce qui **7.** Ce qui

Je m'appelle Mélanie et j'habite à Fort-de-France. La Martinique, c'est super! Moi, ___1___ j'aime, c'est faire du sport. ___2___ me plaît surtout ici, c'est tous les sports nautiques qu'on peut faire. ___3___ je préfère, c'est la planche à voile. ___4___ je n'aime pas par contre, c'est faire du deltaplane. Avec mes amis, ___5___ nous aimons bien, c'est nous promener sur la plage. ___6___ ne me plaît pas trop à la Martinique, c'est la pluie; il pleut toujours un peu ici. ___7___ m'ennuie aussi, c'est la pêche. Et toi, tu aimes le sport? C'est comment, les Etats-Unis? Ecris-moi vite!

23 Qu'est-ce que tu aimes faire?

Parlons Qu'est-ce que tu aimes faire dans les situations suivantes? Pose des questions à un(e) camarade et puis, changez de rôles.

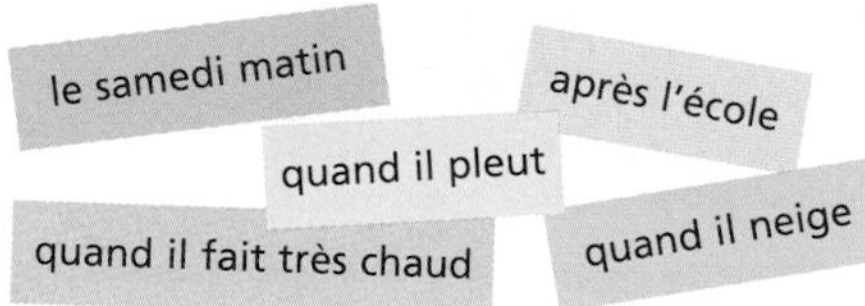

le samedi matin
après l'école
quand il pleut
quand il fait très chaud
quand il neige

24 Une publicité

Ecrivons Crée une publicité pour attirer les touristes dans un des endroits que tu préfères. Décris cet endroit et dis ce qu'il y a à faire et ce que tu préfères là-bas. Utilise des photos, des dessins, de la musique ou des objets pour encourager les gens à visiter cet endroit.

DE BONS CONSEILS

If you look up specific words or phrases in an English-French dictionary, here are a few hints:

- Some words can have several different meanings in English or in French. If you look up the word *pool* for example, do you mean a *swimming pool* or a *billiard game*? Be sure to choose the correct French equivalent.
- Pay attention to the part of speech of the word you're looking for. Are you looking for the noun *snack,* as in a *quick snack,* or the verb *snack,* as in *I snack between meals*?
- To be sure you have the appropriate definition, look up the French word you want to use in the French-English part of the dictionary. Is the English equivalent what you had in mind?

Communication for All Students

Teaching Suggestion

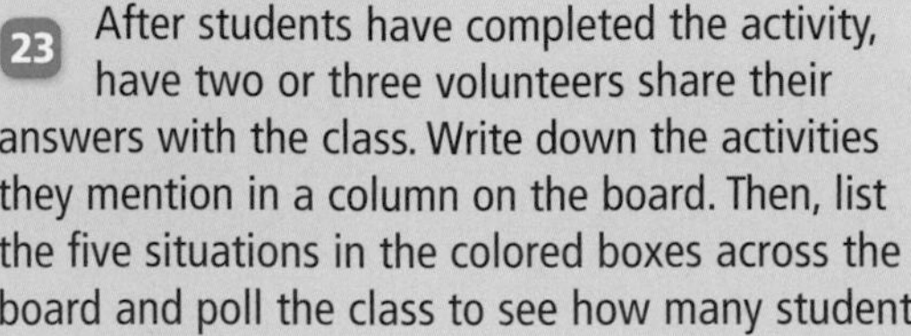

23 After students have completed the activity, have two or three volunteers share their answers with the class. Write down the activities they mention in a column on the board. Then, list the five situations in the colored boxes across the board and poll the class to see how many students also do the activities the volunteers suggested for each situation. Tally the results to see which activities are the most popular. For an extra challenge, have students write a short paragraph summarizing the results of the poll.

STANDARDS: 1.2, 1.3, 3.1, 4.1, 5.1, 5.2

Qu'en penses-tu?

1. What celebration is pictured above? Carnival
2. What festivals and celebrations do you have in your area?

Savais-tu que... ?

Carnival (**Carnaval**) is a well-known tradition in French-speaking countries. It takes place the week before Lent (**le Carême**), ending on Shrove Tuesday (**Mardi gras**), at the stroke of midnight. In Martinique, however, Carnival lasts until midnight of Ash Wednesday (**Mercredi des cendres**), and is celebrated with parades, music, dancing, feasting, and colorful costumes. Queens are elected to reign over the festivals, and on the Sunday before Ash Wednesday, they parade through the streets of the city to the beat of Creole songs. On Monday, mock weddings are held in which the participants dress in burlesque costumes. On Tuesday, Carnival performers dance wildly in red costumes decorated with mirrors. Finally, on Ash Wednesday, people dress in black and white costumes to mourn the death of the cardboard king, **Roi Vaval,** who symbolizes the spirit of Carnival. At the stroke of midnight, the dancing and music stop, and Lent begins. Other cities famous for their Carnival celebrations are Nice in France, Quebec City in Canada, and New Orleans in Louisiana.

Presenting Rencontre culturelle

Ask students to look at the photos and to guess what celebration is pictured. Read **Savais-tu que... ?** with them. Then, ask students why they think **Carnaval** is also celebrated in Quebec City and New Orleans (because of the strong French influence in these two cities).

History Link

French colonists introduced **Mardi gras** to North America in the early 1700s. It became especially popular in the south and is a legal holiday in Alabama, Florida, and parts of Louisiana. It dates back to the ancient Roman custom of celebrating before a period of fasting. In French, **Mardi gras** means *Fat Tuesday,* referring to the custom of parading a fat ox through the streets of Paris on Shrove Tuesday.

Culture Note

In New Orleans, during the two weeks before **Mardi gras,** elaborate parades and masked balls are held every night. They are sponsored by civic clubs called Krewes. Each club chooses a king, usually a senior member, and a queen, usually the daughter of a member, to reign over the festivities. This is considered such an honor that some of the members put their daughters' names on a list the day they are born, so that they might be queen 18 years later.

Cultures and Communities

Teacher Note

Lent **(le Carême)** is a Christian, religious season of spiritual discipline and renewal; it lasts approximately 40 days. Ash Wednesday marks the first day of penitence that begins the season of Lent. On this day in many churches, the priest or pastor blesses ashes from burned palm fronds and uses them to mark a cross on the worshiper's forehead, symbolizing purification and penitence. Shrove Tuesday, the day before Ash Wednesday, originated with the custom of seeking forgiveness for sin (being *shriven*) on that day.

Multicultural Link

Have students do research to find out about **Carnaval** or **Mardi gras** in other parts of the world, such as Rio de Janeiro, Nice, and Quebec, where the largest celebrations occur.

STANDARDS: 2.1, 3.2, 4.2

CHAPITRE 4

Teaching Resources
pp. 110–113

PRINT
- Lesson Planner, p. 19
- TPR Storytelling Book, pp. 28–29
- Listening Activities, pp. 28, 33
- Activities for Communication, pp. 23–24, 92, 94, 143–144
- Travaux pratiques de grammaire, pp. 34–36
- Grammar Tutor for Students of French, Chapter 4
- Cahier d'activités, pp. 44–46
- Testing Program, pp. 87–90
- Alternative Assessment Guide, p. 35
- Student Make-Up Assignments, Chapter 4

MEDIA 
- One-Stop Planner
- Audio Compact Discs, CD 4, Trs. 10, 14, 22–23
- Teaching Transparencies: 4-3, 4-C; **Grammaire supplémentaire** Answers; Travaux pratiques de grammaire Answers
- Interactive CD-ROM Tutor, Disc 1

Bell Work
Write the following scrambled conversation on the board and have students rewrite it in the correct order.

— **Bonne idée. L'aventure, j'adore!**
— **Non, il fait trop chaud. Si on allait faire du deltaplane?**
— **On pourrait regarder une vidéo.**
— **Qu'est-ce qu'on peut faire cet aprèm?**
— **Non, c'est barbant. Ça te dit d'aller à la plage?**

Teacher Note
For more information on Antillean music and dance, see **Lisons!** on page 114.

Troisième étape

Objective Relating a series of events

WA3 MARTINIQUE-4

SALUT, JE M'APPELLE AGATHE ET JE T'INVITE A PASSER UNE JOURNÉE TYPIQUE AVEC MOI, ALLEZ, VIENS!

D'abord, je me lève à 7h du matin.

Puis, je me lave.

Je me brosse les dents.

Vers 7h30, je m'habille.

Ensuite, je prends mon petit déjeuner et je vais au lycée.

Après l'école, je rentre chez moi. Le mercredi et le vendredi, je vais à un cours de percussions. Après, on mange en famille.

Enfin, en semaine, je me couche assez tôt, vers 9h. Mais le weekend, je me couche beaucoup plus tard.

25 Et toi?

Parlons Est-ce que ta routine quotidienne est comme celle d'Agathe? Qu'est-ce qui est différent?

Note culturelle

Music and dance are an integral part of life in Martinique. A popular saying is that in Martinique **tout finit par une chanson.** Much of the music arises from the time the first Africans were brought as slaves to work in the sugar cane fields. The rhythms of the songs and the steps of the dances they created are still in existence today in the **biguine, mazurka,** and the internationally popular **zouk.**

Teacher to Teacher

Bill Heller
Perry High School
Perry, NY

Bill suggests the following activity to practice reflexive verbs.

"Give students several days to collect magazine pictures of as many reflexive verbs as possible from Chapter 4. Divide the class into teams who pool their pictures together. Call out a sentence with a reflexive verb, using *il, elle, ils,* or *elles.* The first team to produce an appropriate picture earns two points. Other teams with an appropriate picture earn one point. The team with the most points at the end of the game wins. As an additional assignment, have each team select five of the pictures from their pool and create a story."

STANDARDS: 2.1, 2.2, 3.2

Vocabulaire

se lever	*to get up*	**Je me lève.**	*I get up.*
se laver	*to wash (oneself)*	**Je me lave.**	*I wash (myself).*
se brosser les dents	*to brush one's teeth*	**Je me brosse les dents.**	*I brush my teeth.*
s'habiller	*to get dressed*	**Je m'habille.**	*I get dressed.*
se coucher	*to go to bed*	**Je me couche.**	*I go to bed.*
		tôt	*early*
		tard	*late*

Travaux pratiques de grammaire, p. 34, Act. 11–12

Comment dit-on...?

Relating a series of events

CD-ROM 1 DVD 1

To start:

D'abord, je me lève.

To continue:

Ensuite, je me lave.
Et puis, je m'habille.
Vers 8h, je mange.
At about . . .
Après ça, j'attends le bus.
After that, . . .

To end:

Enfin/Finalement,
je vais au lycée.
Finally, . . .

Cahier d'activités, p. 44, Act. 16–17

26 Les matins d'André See scripts on p. 93H.

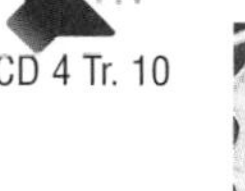

CD 4 Tr. 10

Ecoutons André décrit ses préparatifs du matin. Mets les images en ordre. e, b, c, d, a

a.

b.

c.

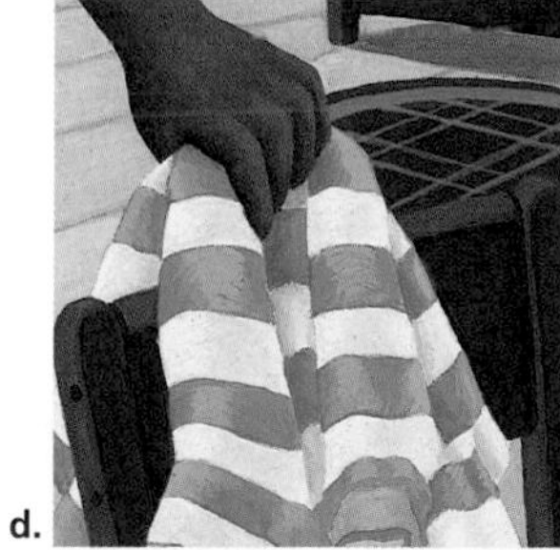
d.

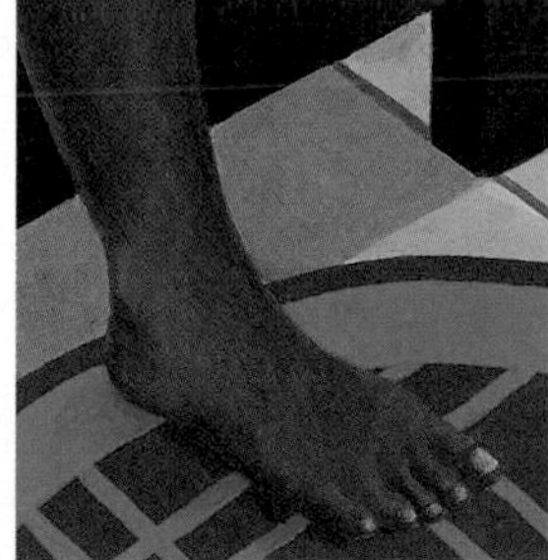
e.

Communication for All Students

Additional Practice

Comment dit-on... ?/Vocabulaire Tell the class they are all going to describe a day's activities. Point to one student and say **D'abord,...** The student should repeat the word and add a daily activity. **D'abord, je me lève.** Point to another student and say **Ensuite,...** The student might say **Ensuite, je me lave.** Continue the procedure, cueing responses with the other sequencing words. You might repeat the activity, focusing on household chores or a visit to Martinique.

Presenting Vocabulaire, Comment dit-on... ?

Name and act out the activities in the **Vocabulaire.** You might use props to illustrate your actions (an alarm clock, a washcloth). Have students repeat after you and imitate your actions. Repeat the process, this time including sequencing words and times of day in your sentences. Then, have a student come to the front of the classroom to act out your sentences. **(D'abord, je me lève à sept heures. Ensuite, je me lave. A sept heures et demie, je prends mon petit déjeuner...)** He or she may look at the book for support.

TPR Give commands using the **Vocabulaire (Brossez-vous les dents! Levez-vous!)** and have students act out the commands at their desks.

Slower Pace

26 Before you play the recording, have students suggest a sentence from the **Vocabulaire** to describe each illustration.

Culture Note

Call attention to the **gant de toilette** in illustration **b.** The French use a washcloth that is sewn together to fit over the hand and worn like a glove. Students might also notice the bowl pictured in the third illustration. Usually, the French drink their hot chocolate **(chocolat chaud),** or coffee **(café au lait)** in a large bowl.

STANDARDS: 1.2, 3.2

Troisième étape

CHAPITRE 4

Teaching Resources
pp. 110–113

PRINT 

- Lesson Planner, p. 19
- TPR Storytelling Book, pp. 28–29
- Listening Activities, pp. 28, 33
- Activities for Communication, pp. 23–24, 92, 94, 143–144
- Travaux pratiques de grammaire, pp. 34–36
- Grammar Tutor for Students of French, Chapter 4
- Cahier d'activités, pp. 44–46
- Testing Program, pp. 87–90
- Alternative Assessment Guide, p. 35
- Student Make-Up Assignments, Chapter 4

MEDIA

- One-Stop Planner
- Audio Compact Discs, CD 4, Trs. 10, 14, 22–23
- Teaching Transparencies: 4-3, 4-C; **Grammaire supplémentaire** Answers; Travaux pratiques de grammaire Answers
- Interactive CD-ROM Tutor, Disc 1

Presenting Grammaire

Reflexive verbs After reading the **Grammaire** with students, act out your daily routine, asking **Qu'est-ce que je fais?** as you do each activity. Prompt students to reply **Vous vous levez.** Confirm each reply: **Oui, je me lève.** Then, ask a volunteer to act out his or her daily routine. Ask students **Qu'est-ce qu'il/elle fait?** to elicit **Il/Elle se lève.** Finally, have students work in pairs to act out their daily routine and tell each other what they are doing. **(Tu te lèves.)**

27 Un matin typique

Lisons Mets les activités suivantes dans l'ordre où tu les fais le matin. Ajoute d'autres activités que tu fais d'habitude.

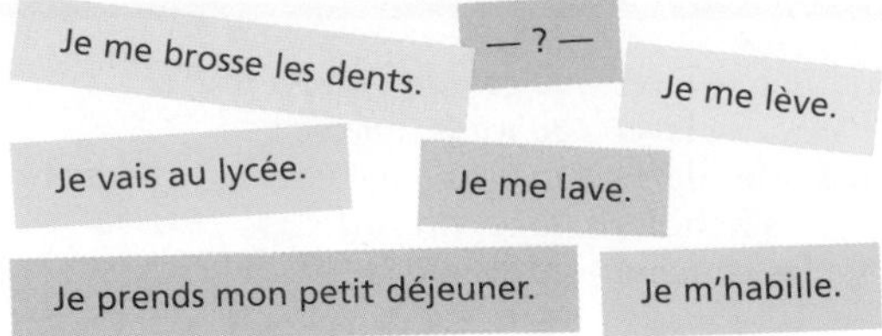

Je me brosse les dents.
— ? —
Je me lève.
Je vais au lycée.
Je me lave.
Je prends mon petit déjeuner.
Je m'habille.

Grammaire

The present tense of reflexive verbs

CD-ROM 1 DVD 1

- To make the forms of a reflexive verb, use the reflexive pronoun that refers to the subject of the verb. The verb forms follow the patterns already familiar to you.

je **me** lave	nous **nous** lavons
tu **te** laves	vous **vous** lavez
il/elle/on **se** lave	ils/elles **se** lavent

- The reflexive pronoun changes with the subject, even when you use the infinitive form of a reflexive verb: Je vais **me** promener.
- The reflexive pronouns sometimes have an English equivalent, such as *myself, yourself, herself,* and so on.

  Je **m'**habille. *I dress (myself).*
  Tu **te** laves. *You wash (yourself).*

  But often, there is no English equivalent.

  Ils **s'**amusent. *They're having fun.*

- To make a reflexive verb negative, put **ne... pas** around the reflexive pronoun and the verb: Le samedi, je **ne** me lève **pas** à 6h!
- The verbs **se promener** and **se lever** add an **accent grave** in some forms:

je me prom**è**ne/l**è**ve	nous nous promenons/levons
tu te prom**è**nes/l**è**ves	vous vous promenez/levez
il/elle/on se prom**è**ne/l**è**ve	ils/elles se prom**è**nent/l**è**vent

Grammaire supplémentaire, pp. 118–119, Act. 7–9

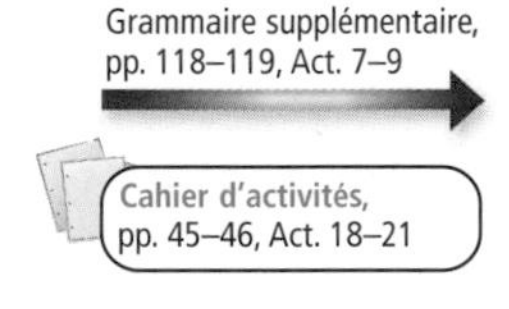
Cahier d'activités, pp. 45–46, Act. 18–21

Travaux pratiques de grammaire, pp. 35–36, Act. 13–15

28 Grammaire en contexte

Lisons Yvan, un jeune Martiniquais, décrit ce qu'il fait avec sa famille et ses amis pendant le week-end. Complète chaque phrase d'Yvan.

1. Le matin, je... f
2. Sophie ne... b
3. Mes parents... d
4. Pour aller au parc, mon frère... e
5. Le dimanche, nous... c
6. Et vous,... a

a. vous vous couchez vers dix heures.
b. se lève pas tôt le samedi matin.
c. nous amusons sur la plage.
d. se promènent souvent au jardin de Balata.
e. s'habille en jean.
f. me lave vers sept heures.

Tu te rappelles?

When you're listening to people or reading books and magazines, keep in mind that the unaccented **e** is often dropped:

Je me lave.	*Je m'lave.*
On se promène.	*On s'promène.*
Tu te couches?	*Tu t'couches?*

Communication for All Students

Tactile/Visual Learners

27 Have students write the activities on separate, small strips of paper. On other small pieces of paper, have students sketch representations of each activity. Finally, have them match the sketches to the strips and arrange them in the order in which they do the activities.

29 Grammaire en contexte

Ecrivons Martine et Maxine sont jumelles, mais leurs routines sont différentes. Complète le paragraphe de Martine avec les formes appropriées des verbes entre parenthèses. **1.** me lève **2.** se lève **3.** me lave **4.** se lave **5.** s'habille **6.** m'habille **7.** nous couchons **8.** se couchent

En semaine, je __1__ (se lever) vers sept heures, mais Maxine __2__ (se lever) vers huit heures. Moi, je __3__ (se laver) le matin, mais Maxine __4__ (se laver) le soir. En général, Maxine __5__ (s'habiller) très chic pour aller à l'école, mais moi, je __6__ (s'habiller) relax. Ma mère et moi, nous __7__ (se coucher) très tôt, mais Maxine et mon père __8__ (se coucher) plus tard.

Note de grammaire

Use adverbs of frequency to tell how often you do something:

Grammaire supplémentaire, p. 119, Act. 10

d'habitude	*usually*	**ne... jamais**	*never*
souvent	*often*	**de temps en temps**	*from time to time*
quelquefois	*sometimes*	**... fois par semaine**	*. . . times a week*

Travaux pratiques de grammaire, p. 36, Act. 16

Although adverbs are generally placed after the verb, longer adverbs may be placed at the beginning or end of a sentence. Treat **ne... jamais** just as you would **ne... pas.**

30 Chère Marie-Line, ...

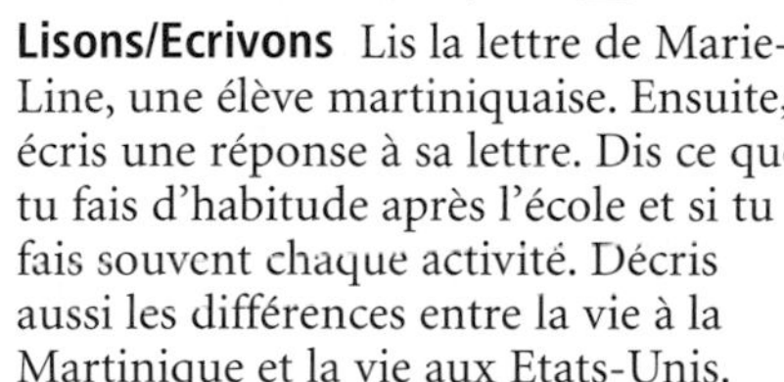

Lisons/Ecrivons Lis la lettre de Marie-Line, une élève martiniquaise. Ensuite, écris une réponse à sa lettre. Dis ce que tu fais d'habitude après l'école et si tu fais souvent chaque activité. Décris aussi les différences entre la vie à la Martinique et la vie aux Etats-Unis.

Après l'école, je rentre chez moi. D'abord, je prends mon goûter : souvent des tartines ou un fruit et quelquefois, de la canne à sucre. Puis, je fais mes devoirs. Comme je ne suis pas très forte en maths, je dois passer beaucoup de temps à faire mes devoirs de maths et je n'aime pas beaucoup ça. Vers 8h, mon père rentre à la maison et toute la famille dîne ensemble. Après, si j'ai le temps, je regarde la télé. J'aime surtout les films américains et les clips vidéo de Zouk Machine, mon groupe préféré. Enfin, vers 10h, je vais me coucher car je dois me lever à 6h les jours de classe. C'est dur!

Et toi, qu'est-ce que tu fais après l'école? Tu as beaucoup de devoirs? C'est comment, ta vie aux Etats-Unis? Raconte-moi. J'attends ta lettre.

Je t'embrasse,
Marie-Line

31 Mon emploi du temps

Parlons/Ecrivons

Qu'est-ce que tu fais en général...

1. à 10h le samedi matin?
2. à 8h le vendredi soir?
3. à midi le dimanche?
4. à 7h le mercredi matin?
5. à 11h le jeudi soir?
6. à 9h le lundi matin?

32

De l'école au travail

Ecrivons Tu travailles pour l'Office de Tourisme de la Martinique. Tu dois faire une brochure pour les touristes qui visitent l'île. Fais une liste des points d'intérêt et des activités qu'un touriste peut y faire.

Troisième étape

CHAPITRE 4

Building On Previous Skills

Re-enter the names of rooms in the house and places in town by asking **Où est-ce qu'on se lave? Où est-ce qu'on s'habille? Où est-ce qu'on déjeune?** and so on.

Teaching Suggestion

30 You might first use the letter for a reading activity. Have students read the letter and then respond to your questions, true-false statements, or other means of assessing their comprehension.

Cooperative Learning

30 Form groups of four and have students peer-edit their letters. Have one student check for accents and spelling, one for subject-verb agreement, one for correct use of possessive adjectives, and one for correct use of connectors and adverbs of frequency. All students should check for comprehensibility and make suggestions for improvement.

Teaching Suggestion

Have students write a paragraph describing their daily routine. Have them peer-edit their paragraphs as they did in Activity 30 and then rewrite each sentence of their own letter on a strip of paper. Have them shuffle the strips of paper and pass them to a partner. The partner rearranges the strips in the original or a logical order. The writer of the paragraph then checks for accuracy and offers corrections, if necessary. **(Non, d'abord, ma mère rentre du travail et après, mon père prépare le dîner.)**

Connections and Comparisons

Critical Thinking

Comparing and Contrasting Have students make a Venn Diagram after they complete Activity 30. In the left circle, they should list activities that only they do, in the right circle, activities that only Marie-Line does, and in the intersecting circle, activities that both they and Marie-Line do. Have students reports their comparisons to another student or the class.

Assess

- Testing Program, pp. 87–90 Quiz 4-3A, Quiz 4-3B Audio CD 4, Tr. 14
- Student Make-Up Assignments, Chapter 4, Alternative Quiz
- Alternative Assessment Guide, p. 35

STANDARDS: 1.1, 1.2, 1.3, 3.1, 4.2, 5.1, 5.2

Lisons!

CHAPITRE 4

Teaching Resources
pp. 114–115

PRINT

- Lesson Planner, p. 20
- Cahier d'activités, p. 47
- Reading Strategies and Skills Handbook, Chapter 4
- Joie de lire 2, Chapter 4
- Standardized Assessment Tutor, Chapter 4

MEDIA 

- One-Stop Planner

Prereading
Activities A–C

Making Predictions
Have students recall what they have learned about Martinique. Have them predict what **zouk** music is like by trying to answer these questions: Is it fast or slow? What could the lyrics be about? In what language(s) will the lyrics be?

Multicultural Link
B. Ask students if they are familiar with music from a different culture. Ask them if any of their favorite songs are British, Canadian, or Australian, and if they can detect different accents or word usage.

Career Path
A career in the music industry provides opportunities to meet people from different countries and cultures. Musicians travel all over the world to perform concerts and to film music videos. Have students ever heard any songs sung in French? What languages would be helpful for a music career and why?

Answers

B. a song; French and Creole; Creole; Tékitizi; take it easy

D. Guadeloupe; *Possible answers:* love, warmth, beauty, sweetness; "Elles ont de l'allure, elles nous donnent de la douceur, de la chaleur, de l'amour."

Lisons!

An sèl zouk

Stratégie pour lire
Reading in a foreign language can be intimidating. After previewing, skimming, and scanning, look for the main idea of what you're reading. Then, it's easier to figure out the details.

Music allows people to express the feelings and ideas closest to their hearts and minds. That's the basis of **zouk,** a music unique to the French West Indies.

A. What would you write a song about? Your feelings? Global politics? Injustice? Your home? The things you love, or things that bother you? List three things you might write about in a song.

B. What are you going to read here? Can you tell what two languages are represented? Do you think Kassav' sings *An sèl zouk* in French or in Creole? What's the title of the CD? Do you know what it means? (hint: it's from English) See answers below.

C. Skim the French lyrics. Which of the following do you think is the focus of the song?

a. the songwriter's feelings about France

b. Martinique, Guadeloupe, the Caribbean

c. life as a sailor

D. Where is the songwriter from? How does he feel about his homeland? What words and phrases tell you this? See answers below.

AN SÈL ZOUK
UN SEUL ZOUK

Fout' sa jéyan / lè mwen Gwadloup' / Mwen a kaze an mwen / Mwen byen kontan / Ké ni bon tan / Tchè mwen souri pou Matinik / Sé kon si sé la mwen wè jou / Bondyé / Sa ou pé di di sa zanmi / Yo tou piti /Sé la nou grandi / Epi mizik an tout' kwen kaÿ la / **An sèl Gwadloup ki ni / Sé an sèl Matinik / Pou an zèl Zouk nou ni / Madikéra** / Pa lé kwè dé bèl péyi kon sa / Fo nou pa viv' kon nou yé a / Rété tou sa / Sa ou ka di ya / Mwen ja réfléchi asou tou sa / Mé pa ka konpwann / éti nou kaÿ épi sa / Yo pa byen gran / Mé yo ni balan / E yo ka ba dousè chalè lov' / **Ki nou la Gwadloup / Ki nou Matinik / Ki nou Guyann / Nou sé karayib / An nou mété nou / O dyapazon** / Lésé tchè nou palé / Pou nou pé sanblé / **An sèl Gwadloup ki ni / Sé an sèl Matinik / Pou an zèl Zouk nou ni / Madikéra** / An gran makè té di / Yo kon pousyè lò épi lajan / Ki tonbé dépi zétwal / E pozé an lan mè / Lè an ka sonjé sé la nou vwè jou / Bondyé mèsi / An mété an jounou /I ka fè révé / I ka fè chanté / Bondyé mèsi sé la nou vwè jou /**Woyoyoÿ / An nou alé / woyoyoÿ / Bagaÿ la fè zip zip / Biten la fè zip zip zip** /

Paroles & Musique César DURCIN

Cultures and Communities

Culture Notes

- **Zouk** is an integral part and a unique expression of French Antillean culture. Immigrants from Martinique and Guadeloupe brought their island music with them to Paris, where they encountered the rhythms of French-speaking Africa. Catalyzed by the high-energy tunes of Parisian discos, the hybrid sound was christened *zouk,* the Creole term for *party.* Dynamic groups like Kassav' and Zouk Machine have brought this music world-wide attention.
- The basic sound of **zouk** comes from the traditional **gwo ka** drums, which are made from barrels that once held salted meat, once the food of slaves. The rhythm of **zouk** comes from the French West Indies, and the guitar and vocal arrangements have their roots in West Africa.

STANDARDS: 1.2, 2.2, 3.1, 3.2, 4.1, 4.2, 5.2

C'est super / Lorsque je suis à la Guadeloupe / Je suis chez moi / Content / Je prends du bon temps / J'ai le cœur qui sourit pour la Martinique / C'est comme si j'y étais né / Qu'en dis-tu / Elles sont petites / C'est là que nous avons grandi / Avec de la musique dans toute la maison / **Il n'y a qu'une seule Guadeloupe / Une seule Martinique / Pour un seul zouk / Madikera** / Mais je ne peux admettre / Que nous vivons comme nous le faisons / Il faut que ça change / J'ai déjà pensé à tout ce dont tu parles / Et je ne vois pas / Où celà nous mène / Elles ne sont pas très grandes / Mais elles ont de l'allure / Et elles nous donnent de la douceur, de la chaleur, et de l'amour /**Que nous soyons à la Guadeloupe / à la Martinique / En Guyane / Dans la Caraïbe / Accordons nos violons** / Laissons parler nos cœurs / Pour nous rassembler / **Il n'y a qu'une seule Guadeloupe / Une seule Martinique / Pour un seul zouk / Madikera** / Un grand écrivain a dit / Qu'elles sont comme des pièces d'or et d'argent / Tombées de la bourse aux étoiles / Et posées sur la mer / Lorsque je pense que c'est là que nous avons vu le jour / Je me mets à genoux / Pour remercier Dieu /

For Activities E and H, see answers below.

E. Which lines of the song are the chorus? How do you know? **Madikera** is a word made from **Madinina,** a name for Martinique, and **Karukéra,** a name for Guadeloupe. What is the message of the chorus?

F. Try to pronounce each Creole word below and find its French equivalent. If you can't figure out the word's meaning by its sound, compare the Creole text with the French text. Which Creole word comes from English?

1. Gwadloup d	**a.** les étoiles
2. Matinik f	**b.** content
3. kontan b	**c.** la mer
4. piti g	**d.** Guadeloupe
5. mizik e	**e.** musique
6. zétwal a	**f.** Martinique
7. lan mè c	**g.** petites
8. lov' h	**h.** l'amour

Try to match these phrases. 1. a 2. c 3. b

1. Mwen byen kontan.	**a. Je suis bien content.**
2. Pou an zèl Zouk.	**b. C'est là que nous avons grandi.**
3. Sé la nou grandi.	**c. Pour un seul zouk.**

G. Write a list of other Creole words you can figure out and pass it to a classmate, who will try to write the French words next to the Creole ones.

H. Looking at all the words and phrases you have decoded, what are the songwriter's feelings about **zouk?** How does the title of the song relate to his ideas?

I. Write a brief song in French about one of the topics you listed in Activity A and set it to a favorite piece of music. Use some of the expressions you've learned in this chapter to express what you like and dislike about your topic.

Cahier d'activités, p. 47, Act. 23–24

Lisons!

CHAPITRE 4

Reading

Activities D–G

Determining the Main Idea

E. Have students use the context to determine the main idea of the song. Ask how the chorus relates to the main idea and title of the song.

Postreading

Activities H–I

Challenge

Type the lyrics of the Creole song and number the lines. Type the lines of the French song in a different order and precede each one with a letter of the alphabet. Have students match the Creole lyrics with their French equivalents.

Language-to-Language

The Creole that is spoken in Martinique, Guadeloupe, and Haiti is of French and African origin. Words written in Creole are usually spelled phonetically. These words often resemble (in spelling and pronunciation) words in one of the languages of origin. Examples in Creole/French include **jou/jour, mèsi/merci, lajan/l'argent,** and **konpwann/comprendre.** Creole languages often originate when the speakers of two different languages attempt to communicate, resulting in a simplified form of one of the languages.

Connections and Comparisons

Language Note

Write the following Kassav' song titles on the board or on a transparency. Have students pronounce them the way they are written, and then ask students if they recognize any French words in the Creole: **Palé mwen dous'** *(Tell Me Sweet Things);* **Zôt Vini Pou** *(Others Come For . . .);* **Lévé Tèt' Ou** *(Lift Your Head Up);* **Mwen Alé** *(I'm Going/Leaving);* **Ou Chanjé** *(You've Changed).*

Answers

E. "Il n'y a qu'une seule Guadeloupe... Madikera."; it repeats itself, and it's in bold type; to present a strong, unified Guadeloupe and Martinique.

H. *Possible answers:* He wants to unify all of the French-speaking areas of the Carribean.; He uses the word "un seul," *only one (all together).*

Grammaire supplémentaire

CHAPITRE 4

For **Grammaire supplémentaire** Answer Transparencies, see the *Teaching Transparencies* binder.

Grammaire supplémentaire

internet

go.hrw.com

ADRESSE: go.hrw.com
MOT-CLE:
WA3 MARTINIQUE-4

Première étape

Objectives Asking for information and describing a place

1 Tu regardes les photos que ton ami a prises pendant ses vacances. Utilise un des adjectifs proposés pour décrire ce que tu vois sur chaque photo. (**p. 100**)

EXEMPLE des fleurs **Il y a de jolies fleurs.**

1. des chutes d'eau
2. des Martiniquais
3. des arbres tropicaux
4. des fruits
5. des cocotiers

joli bon jeune grand
nouveau beau petit

2 Ecris six phrases pour décrire la Martinique. N'utilise les mots et les adjectifs proposés qu'une seule fois. (**p. 100**)

EXEMPLE **A la Martinique, il y a de magnifiques plages.**

délicieux bon joli
grand immense beau

cocotiers ananas fleurs de toutes les couleurs
arbres tropicaux
poissons champs de canne à sucre

Grammar Resources for Chapter 4

The **Grammaire supplémentaire** activities are designed as supplemental activities for the grammatical concepts presented in the chapter. You might use them as additional practice, for review, or for assessment.

For more grammar presentations, review, and practice, refer to the following:

- Travaux pratiques de grammaire
- Grammar Tutor for Students of French
- Grammar Summary on pp. R23–R42
- Cahier d'activités
- Grammar and Vocabulary quizzes (Testing Program)
- Test Generator
- Interactive CD-ROM Tutor
- DVD Tutor
- **Jeux interactifs** at go.hrw.com

Possible Answers

1
1. Il y a de belles chutes d'eau.
2. Il y a de jeunes Martiniquais.
3. Il y a de grands arbres tropicaux.
4. Il y a de bons fruits.
5. Il y a de grands cocotiers.

2 Answers will vary.

STANDARDS: 1.2

Deuxième étape

Objectives Asking for and making suggestions; emphasizing likes and dislikes

3 Decide whether a) **the subject** of the following sentences receives the action of the verb or b) **something other than the subject** receives the action of the verb. (**p. 105**)

Exemple Ils s'amusent. a

1. Ils dansent le zouk.
2. Elle fait du deltaplane.
3. Il se promène.
4. Elles se baignent.
5. Il déguste des fruits tropicaux.
6. Je me promène.
7. Ils vont au parc.

4 Irène demande à son cousin Pascal ce qu'il aime et ce qu'il n'aime pas. Utilise **ce qui** ou **ce que** et le verbe qu'Irène utilise dans sa question pour compléter les réponses de Pascal. (**p. 108**)

1. Qu'est-ce qui ne te plaît pas dans ta routine de la semaine?
   ______ , c'est de me lever à 6h du matin.
2. Qu'est-ce que tu n'aimes pas à l'école?
   ______ , c'est la géographie!
3. Qu'est-ce que tu préfères faire le matin en vacances?
   ______ , c'est me promener sur la plage.
4. Qu'est-ce qui te plaît à la Martinique?
   ______ à la Martinique, c'est la mer!
5. Qu'est-ce qui t'ennuie le week-end?
   ______ , c'est de rester à la maison le week-end.
6. Qu'est-ce que tu aimes faire le week-end?
   ______ bien le week-end, c'est me coucher tard.

5 Complète ces phrases où chaque personne dit ce qu'il/elle aime ou n'aime pas faire pendant les vacances. Utilise **ce que** ou **ce qui** et les activités proposées. (**p. 108**)

aller à la pêche — faire du deltaplane — faire de la planche à voile — danser le zouk — faire de la plongée avec un tuba — s'amuser — faire de la plongée sous-marine — se baigner — se promener

1. PAUL ______ m'ennuie, c'est de ______.
2. JOËL ______ je préfère, c'est ______.
3. MIREILLE ______ ne me plaît pas, c'est de ______.
4. DANIEL ______ j'aime bien, c'est ______.
5. LAURENT ______ me plaît, c'est de ______.
6. SANDRINE ______ je n'aime pas, c'est ______.

Communication for All Students

Auditory Learners

5 Have students complete each expression, using **ce qui** and **ce que** in **Comment dit-on… ?** according to their own likes and dislikes. Have them read their sentences to the class and have others respond **Moi aussi!** or **Moi non plus!**

Answers

3
1. b
2. b
3. a
4. a
5. b
6. a
7. b

4
1. Ce qui ne me plaît pas
2. Ce que je n'aime pas
3. Ce que je préfère
4. Ce qui me plaît
5. Ce qui m'ennuie
6. Ce que j'aime

5 *Possible Answers:*
1. Ce qui, faire du deltaplane
2. Ce que, me baigner
3. Ce qui, d'aller à la pêche
4. Ce que, me promener
5. Ce qui, danser le zouk
6. Ce que, faire de la planche à voile

STANDARDS: 1.2

Grammaire supplémentaire

CHAPITRE 4

For **Grammaire supplémentaire** Answer Transparencies, see the *Teaching Transparencies* binder.

Answers

6
1. Ce que
2. Ce qui
3. Ce qui
4. Ce que
5. Ce que
6. Ce que
7. Ce qui
8. Ce que

7
1. m'
2. Vous
3. te
4. il
5. elles
6. nous
7. se
8. vous
9. me
10. se

8
1. André se lève tôt.
2. Je me brosse les dents.
3. Tu te couches tard.
4. Ils s'habillent rapidement.
5. Mon ami se promène le matin.
6. Vous vous lavez tous les soirs vers 8 heures.

Grammaire supplémentaire

WA3 MARTINIQUE-4

6 Complète les phrases suivantes avec **ce que** ou **ce qui.** (**p. 108**)

1. _____ j'aime manger, c'est de la pizza.
2. _____ me plaît quand je suis fatigué, c'est de dormir tard le samedi.
3. _____ m'ennuie à la maison, c'est de faire le ménage.
4. _____ je préfère faire quand il fait beau, c'est aller à la plage.
5. _____ je déteste le week-end, c'est faire mes devoirs.
6. _____ je n'aime pas, c'est jouer au foot.
7. _____ ne me plaît pas, c'est de me coucher tard.
8. _____ j'aime bien en vacances, c'est sortir tous les soirs.

Troisième étape

Objective **Relating a series of events**

7 Tes amis et toi, vous parlez de votre routine quotidienne. Complète les phrases suivantes avec le sujet ou le pronom réfléchi approprié. (**p. 112**)

EXEMPLE Sophie, **elle** se lève à 7 heures.

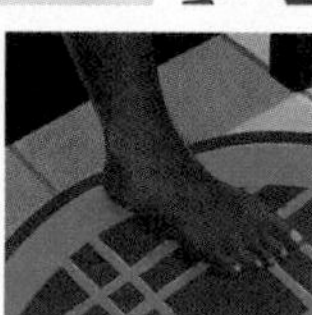

1. Je _____ habille rapidement.
2. _____ vous brossez les dents après le petit déjeuner?
3. Tu vas _____ coucher tôt?
4. Luc, _____ se lave avant de prendre son petit déjeuner.
5. Claire et Christiane, _____ s'amusent beaucoup.
6. Nous _____ promenons sur la plage.
7. Mon ami aime _____ promener tous les jours!
8. A quelle heure est-ce que vous aimez _____ lever?
9. Je ne veux pas _____ brosser les cheveux.
10. Mes parents _____ baignent souvent en mer.

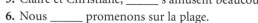

8 Récris les phrases suivantes où ces personnes décrivent leur routine quotidienne. Choisis le pronom réfléchi qui correspond au sujet. (**p. 112**)

1. tôt / se / André / lever
2. les dents / je / brosser / se
3. se / tu / tard / coucher
4. ils / se / rapidement / habiller
5. promener / mon ami / le matin / se
6. tous les soirs vers 8 heures / se / vous / laver

Communication for All Students

Game

A toi! To practice reflexive verbs, have students form a circle (or two). Call out a sentence containing a reflexive verb. **(Nous nous levons à six heures.)** Then, toss a beach ball to a student as you call out a different subject **(mon père)**. The student catches the ball, replaces the subject of the original sentence with the new one, and says the new sentence. **(Mon père se lève à six heures.)** Then, he or she tosses the ball to another student, calling out a new subject. A student who does not respond within five seconds is out of the game, but may get back in by correcting another's error. After several tosses, start a new sentence. You might also substitute different verbs in addition to subjects, saying **Je me lave** and calling out **s'habiller** as you throw the ball.

STANDARDS: 1.2

9 Stéphanie a envoyé une lettre à son copain Emmanuel. Elle parle d'un jour typique pendant ses vacances à la Martinique. Complète les phrases de sa lettre avec les verbes entre parenthèses au présent. (**p. 112**)

Cher Emmanuel,

Salut! Comment ça va? Ici, à la Martinique, ça va très bien. C'est "I bon"! (Ça veut dire "chouette" en créole). Il __1__ (faire) très beau ici. C'est un vrai paradis. D'habitude, je __2__ (se lever) tôt le matin et je __3__ (se promener) sur la plage. Quelquefois, je me baigne dans la mer l'après-midi. Après ma promenade, je __4__ (prendre) mon petit déjeuner avec ma grand-mère. Ensuite, je __5__ (s'habiller) pour sortir en ville. Trois fois par semaine, je __6__ (faire) des courses avec ma grand-mère. De temps en temps, je __7__ (sortir) avec des amis et on __8__ (s'amuser) bien sur la plage ou en ville. J'ai un copain qui __9__ (s'appeler) Jean-François. Il est très gentil et il me __10__ (montrer) tout Fort-de-France. D'habitude, je __11__ (rentrer) le soir pour dîner avec ma grand-mère. Je __12__ (se coucher) tôt parce que je suis toujours fatiguée après une journée magnifique. Demain, je __13__ (aller) faire de la plongée. C'est super, non? Et toi, qu'est-ce que tu fais pendant tes vacances? Raconte-moi!

Je t'embrasse
Stéphanie

10 Choose an adverb from the word box to tell how often you do the following activities. (**p. 113**)

souvent	le lundi, le mardi,...	toujours	beaucoup
d'habitude	ne... jamais	quelquefois	

EXEMPLE s'amuser? **Je m'amuse souvent.**

1. se promener?
2. se laver?
3. se coucher tard?
4. sortir avec des amis?
5. se lever tôt?
6. danser le zouk?

Review and Assess

You may wish to assign the **Grammaire supplémentaire** activities as additional practice or homework after presenting material throughout the chapter. Assign Activities 1–2 after **Tu te rappelles?** (p. 100), Activity 3 after **Note de grammaire** (p. 105), Activities 4–6 after **Grammaire** (p. 108), Activities 7–9 after **Grammaire** (p. 112), and Activity 10 after **Note de grammaire** (p. 113).

To prepare students for the **Etape** Quizzes and Chapter Test, we suggest doing the **Grammaire supplémentaire** activities in the following order. Have students complete Activities 1–2 before Quizzes 4-1A or 4-1B; Activities 3–6 before Quizzes 4-2A or 4-2B; and Activities 7–10 before Quizzes 4-3A or 4-3B.

Grammaire supplémentaire

CHAPITRE 4

Answers

9
1. fait
2. me lève
3. me promène
4. prends
5. m'habille
6. fais
7. sors
8. s'amuse
9. s'appelle
10. montre
11. rentre
12. me couche
13. vais

10 Answers will vary.

Mise en pratique

CHAPITRE 4

The **Mise en pratique** reviews and integrates all four skills and culture in preparation for the Chapter Test.

Teaching Resources
pp. 120–121

PRINT 

- Lesson Planner, p. 20
- TPR Storytelling Book, pp. 30–31
- Listening Activities, p. 29
- Video Guide, pp. 25, 28
- Grammar Tutor for Students of French, Chapter 4
- Standardized Assessment Tutor, Chapter 4

MEDIA

- One-Stop Planner
- Video Program Videocassette 2, 21:32–25:21
- DVD Tutor, Disc 1
- Audio Compact Discs, CD 4, Tr. 11
- Interactive CD-ROM Tutor, Disc 1

Government Link
Guadeloupe, like Martinique, is a French overseas **département**, or *administrative district*, which is represented in the French National Assembly by four deputies, and in the French senate by two senators. The citizens of Guadeloupe are entitled to the same social welfare programs as in France, including old-age and disability pensions, family allowances, unemployment relief, and health insurance.

Geography Link
Guadeloupe consists of two main islands, Grande-Terre and Basse-Terre. Basse-Terre, twenty-seven miles long and fifteen miles wide, is thickly forested and mountainous. The dormant volcanic summit, La Soufrière, which is 4,813 feet above sea level, is located on this island.

Mise en pratique

Qu'est-ce qu'il y a à voir à la Guadeloupe? Il y a deux îles, Basse-Terre et Grande-Terre. Les deux îles sont liées par la Rivière Salée. A l'ouest, en Basse-Terre, il y a le volcan de la Soufrière, près de la ville de Basse-Terre, qui est la capitale de la Guadeloupe. A l'est, en Grande-Terre, il y a des champs de canne à sucre. Comme à la Martinique, il fait toujours chaud, entre 16 et 27 degrés Celsius. La Guadeloupe est plus grande que la Martinique, mais moins grande que Porto Rico. C'est une île accueillante, vivante et tout à fait charmante!

1 Comme la Martinique, la Guadeloupe est une île des Antilles. Comment est l'île de la Guadeloupe? Lis cette brochure, puis fais correspondre les numéros du plan avec chaque élément de la liste. welcoming, lively, charming

a. les champs de canne à sucre 3
b. la mer des Caraïbes 5
c. la Soufrière 6
d. la Rivière Salée 2
e. l'île de Grande-Terre 4
f. la ville de Basse-Terre 1

2 A travel agent in Guadeloupe is describing a tour you're interested in taking. As she speaks, write down, in order, what you will do on the tour. See scripts and answers on p. 93H.

CD 4 Tr. 11

Apply and Assess

Math Link
Have students convert the Celsius temperatures in the brochure to Fahrenheit to find out how warm it is in Guadeloupe and Martinique. To convert Celsius into degrees Fahrenheit, multiply Celsius by 1.8 and add 32. Then, have students convert the average seasonal temperatures where they live into Celsius. To convert degrees Fahrenheit into Celsius, subtract 32 from Fahrenheit and divide by 1.8.

Visual/Tactile Learners
1 Read the brochure with students and ask them to find and touch the areas on the map that the brochure refers to. Students might work with partners to verify that they've found the correct area.

STANDARDS: 1.2, 3.1

3 Ecrivons!

Choose a city in either Martinique or Guadeloupe and create a brochure about it. Describe the city and its inhabitants and make suggestions about things to do and sights to visit. You could also illustrate your brochure with drawings or magazine clippings.

Stratégie pour écrire
Gathering information is an important first step when writing about places and people. Which sources would best provide you with accurate information and authentic illustrations?

Préparation

List the various types of information you need for your brochure and try to think of sources for each specific type of information. Your textbook is a good place to start, but if you're looking for information on sights to visit, you might also look in travel guides or try to find Internet web pages that deal with the area you're writing about.

On a chart like the one below, keep track of where you find each piece of information. If you find something in a book, write down the title and the page number where you found the information. Write down the web address for information you find on the Internet.

Source Name	Type of Information	Page Number/ Web Address	Information
Allez, viens!, Level 2	sights and monuments	p. 93	Des milliers d'espèces de fleurs poussent dans le jardin de Balata.

Rédaction

Once you've gathered all the information you need from your various sources, you're ready to create your brochure. You should include information that you think would be most appealing to your reader as well as eye-catching illustrations or pictures. But remember: while you want to entice your reader, you also want to provide accurate information. When writing your brochure, don't forget the expressions you know for making suggestions.

Evaluation

When you present information as fact, it's a good idea to go back and double check your work for accuracy. Check the source of every piece of information you've presented in your brochure to make sure it's correct. Then, proofread your work. You might also have a classmate evaluate what you've created.

4 Jeu de rôle

If you were rich and famous, would you change your daily routine? Imagine that you and your partner have suddenly become rich and famous. Take turns interviewing each other about your new lifestyles. Be sure to ask your partner when he or she gets up and goes to bed, what he or she eats for breakfast, lunch, and dinner, and how he or she spends the rest of the day.

Apply and Assess

Process Writing

3 If your students are using the Internet to gather information, you might have them brainstorm a list of keywords to help in their searches. Or, if you have access to the Internet and your students do not, consider printing information from your findings for them.

Mise en pratique

CHAPITRE 4

Community Link

Arrange to have your students visit an elementary school classroom and share what they have learned about Martinique with younger students.

Challenge

3 Have students use their brochures to perform a skit in which they discuss plans for a day of sightseeing. Have them first choose one of the places to visit, and then three things to do, according to the brochure they've created. They should ask for and make suggestions, emphasize likes and dislikes, and relate a series of events.

Writing Assessment

3 You might use the following rubric when grading your students on this activity.

Writing Rubric	Points			
	4	3	2	1
Content (Complete–Incomplete)				
Comprehensibility (Comprehensible–Incomprehensible)				
Accuracy (Accurate–Seldom accurate)				
Organization (Well organized–Poorly organized)				
Effort (Excellent–Minimal)				

18–20: A 14–15: C Under
16–17: B 12–13: D 12: F

Teacher Note

For additional practice and review, you might use the **Histoire finale** for Chapter 4 on pages 30–31 of the *TPR Storytelling Book.*

Que sais-je?

CHAPITRE 4

Teaching Resources
p. 122

PRINT 
- Grammar Tutor for Students of French, Chapter 4

MEDIA  
- Interactive CD-ROM Tutor, Disc 1
- Online self-test

go.hrw.com WA3 MARTINIQUE-4

Que sais-je?

WA3 MARTINIQUE-4

Can you use what you've learned in this chapter?

Can you ask for information? p. 102

1 How would you ask . . . See answers below.
1. the location of a place?
2. what it's like?
3. what attractions there are?
4. what the weather is like?

Can you describe a place? p. 102

2 How would you describe your state? Tell . . .
1. where it's located.
2. what's in the north, south, east, and west.
3. how big it is in relation to others.
4. what there is to do there.
5. what there is to see there.

Can you ask for and make suggestions? p. 106

3 How would you ask what there is to do in Martinique?
Qu'est-ce qu'on peut faire à la Martinique?

4 How would you suggest these activities to your friend? See answers below.

1.

2.

3.

4.

Can you emphasize likes and dislikes? p. 107

5 How would you tell someone what you really like to do . . . See answers below.
1. on Saturday mornings?
2. on weekends?

6 How would you tell someone what you really don't like to do . . . See answers below.
1. on Sundays?
2. when it's cold?
3. at school?

Can you relate a series of events? p. 111

7 How would you tell someone . . .
1. what you do first thing in the morning? D'abord,...
2. what you do after that? Ensuite,... ; Et puis,... ; Après ça,...
3. what you finally do before leaving for school? Enfin/Finalement,...

8 Explain what you usually do after school.

Possible Answers

1
1. Où se trouve... ?
2. C'est comment?
3. Qu'est-ce-qu'il y a à voir?
4. Il fait... ?

4
1. Ça te dit d'aller se baigner à la plage?
2. Si on allait faire du deltaplane?
3. On peut aller se promener?
4. Si on allait faire de la plongée?

5
1. Ce que j'aime bien le samedi matin, c'est...
2. Ce qui me plaît le week-end, c'est...

6
1. Ce que je n'aime pas le dimanche, c'est...
2. Ce qui ne me plaît pas quand il fait froid, c'est...
3. Ce qui m'ennuie à l'école, c'est...

Review and Assess

Game

Serpent! Prepare a game on a sheet of paper on which squares "snake" across the page. Number each square and label the first one **Départ**, and the last one, **Arrivée.** In each square, write an answer to one of the questions in **Que sais-je?** On a separate sheet of paper, type the numbers of the questions in **Que sais-je?** that correspond to the squares on the sheet. Give each group one board for two players and an answer sheet for the judge. The players will need one die and two game pieces. Have them take turns rolling the die. They must read what's on the square, look at the **Que sais-je?,** and determine which question is answered by that square. The judge must verify the players' responses. The first person to reach **Arrivée** wins!

STANDARDS: 1.2

Vocabulaire

Première étape

Asking for information and describing a place

Où se trouve... ?	*Where is...?*
Qu'est-ce qu'il y a... ?	*What is there...?*
Il fait...?	*Is it...? (weather)*
C'est comment?	*What's it like?*
...se trouve...	*...is located...*
dans le nord	*in the north*
dans le sud	*in the south*
dans l'est	*in the east*
dans l'ouest	*in the west*
plus grand(e) que...	*bigger than...*
moins grand(e) que...	*smaller than...*
charmant(e)	*charming*
coloré(e)	*colorful*
vivant(e)	*lively*

Places, flora, and fauna

un ananas	*pineapple*
un bananier	*banana tree*
la capitale	*capital*
des champs (m.) **de canne à sucre**	*sugar cane fields*
une chute d'eau	*waterfall*
un cocotier	*coconut tree*
la forêt tropicale	*tropical rain forest*
l'île	*island*
la mer	*sea*
un moustique	*mosquito*
un palmier	*palm tree*
les plages (f.)	*beaches*
le sable	*sand*
un village de pêcheurs	*fishing village*
le volcan	*volcano*

Deuxième étape

Asking for and making suggestions

Qu'est-ce qu'on peut faire?	*What can we do?*
On peut...	*We can...*
Ça te dit d'aller... ?	*What do you think of going...?*
Si on allait... ?	*How about going...?*

Emphasizing likes and dislikes

Ce que j'aime bien, c'est...	*What I like is...*
Ce que je préfère, c'est...	*What I prefer is...*
Ce qui me plaît, c'est (de)...	*What I like is...*
Ce que je n'aime pas, c'est...	*What I don't like is...*
Ce qui ne me plaît pas, c'est (de)...	*What I don't care for is...*
Ce qui m'ennuie, c'est (de)...	*What bores me is...*

Activities

aller à la pêche	*to go fishing*
danser le zouk	*to dance the zouk*
faire du deltaplane	*to hang glide*
faire de la planche à voile	*to windsurf*
faire de la plongée sous-marine	*to scuba dive*
faire de la plongée avec un tuba	*to snorkel*
déguster	*to taste, enjoy*
s'amuser	*to have fun*
se baigner	*to go swimming*
se promener	*to go for a walk*

Troisième étape

Relating a series of events

D'abord,...	*First,...*
Ensuite,...	*Next,...*
Et puis,...	*And then,...*
Vers...	*About (a certain time)...*
Après ça,...	*After that,...*
Enfin/ Finalement,...	*Finally, ...*

Daily activities

se brosser les dents	*to brush one's teeth*
se coucher	*to go to bed*
s'habiller	*to get dressed*
se lever	*to get up*
se laver	*to wash (oneself)*
tôt	*early*
tard	*late*

Review and Assess

Circumlocution

Have students work in pairs. One student should play the role of the travel agent, while the other plays the role of a customer. The customer is trying to decide where to go on vacation but can't remember the names of the cities. The customer should describe a city and its location without naming it. **(Cette ville se trouve dans le sud de la France. Il fait chaud.)** The travel agent should help the customer remember the name of the city.

STANDARDS: 1.1

Vocabulaire

CHAPITRE 4

Challenge

To review vocabulary, have students group words and expressions from the vocabulary list that are related. For example, **la mer** and **se baigner,** or **les plages** and **le sable.** Then, have them write sentences showing the relationship between the two words they have chosen to group together. **(On se baigne dans la mer. C'est une plage de sable blanc.)**

Chapter 4 Assessment

- **Testing Program**
  Chapter Test, pp. 91–96

  Audio Compact Discs, CD 4, Trs. 15–17
  Speaking Test, p. 344
- **Alternative Assessment Guide**
  Performance Assessment, p. 35
  Portfolio Assessment, p. 21
  CD-ROM Assessment, p. 49
- **Interactive CD-ROM Tutor, Disc 1**
  CD-ROM 1 A toi de parler
  DVD 1 A toi d'écrire
- **Standardized Assessment Tutor**
  Chapter 4
- **One-Stop Planner**

  Test Generator
  Chapter 4

Teaching Resources
pp. 124–127

PRINT

- Lesson Planner, p. 21
- Video Guide, pp. 29–30

MEDIA 

- One-Stop Planner
- Video Program
  Videocassette 2, 25:49–28:38
- DVD Tutor, Disc 1
- Interactive CD-ROM Tutor, Disc 2
- Map Transparency 1

go.hrw.com
WA3 TOURAINE

Using the Almanac and Map

Terms in the Almanac

- **La cathédrale Saint-Gatien,** built between the thirteenth and sixteenth centuries, displays the evolution of Gothic architecture.
- **Le musée des Beaux-Arts,** built during the seventeenth and eighteenth centuries, displays paintings by artists such as Rubens, Rembrandt, Delacroix, Monet, and Degas.
- **La Loire,** the longest river in France, is more than 1,020 kilometers long.
- **Le Cher,** a tributary of the Loire River, joins it at Tours. The château of Chenonceau is built over the Cher River.
- **François Rabelais** (c. 1494–1553), priest, doctor, and author, wrote *Gargantua* and *Pantagruel,* which satirized the society of his time and presented his views on education, religion, and philosophy.
- **René Descartes** (1596–1650) was a philosopher and mathematician known for his famous phrase "Cogito ergo sum" (**«Je pense, donc je suis»**).

CHAPITRES 5,6,7

Allez, viens en Touraine!

Population : plus de 500.000

Points d'intérêt : la place Plumereau, la cathédrale Saint-Gatien, l'hôtel Goüin, le musée des Beaux-Arts, l'Historial de Touraine

Châteaux : Amboise, Azay-le-Rideau, Chenonceau, Chinon, Loches, Ussé, Villandry

Fleuves et rivières : la Loire, le Cher, l'Indre, la Vienne, la Creuse

Tourangeaux célèbres : saint Grégoire, Honoré de Balzac, saint Martin, François Rabelais, René Descartes

Spécialités : tarte Tatin, saumon au beurre blanc, crottins de Chavignol, ragoût d'escargots aux cèpes

go.hrw.com WA3 TOURAINE

VIDEO

CD-ROM 2 DVD 1

Le château de Chenonceau

Cultures and Communities

Background Information

Touraine was recaptured from the English by Joan of Arc in 1429 during the Hundred Years' War (1337–1453). The region was long a favorite getaway of French kings because of its mild climate, beautiful countryside, numerous rivers, and fine forests for hunting. From the fifteenth to the seventeenth centuries, medieval and Renaissance rulers from Charles VII to Henri III built their châteaux in this region. In fact, within a 60-kilometer radius of the city of Tours, there are over 200 châteaux. Also known for its flowers, fruits, vegetables, and vineyards, Touraine is called **le jardin de la France.**

STANDARDS: 2.2

Culture Notes

- Tours is located within 60 kilometers (37 miles) of some of the loveliest châteaux in France. Because of its location, Tours is an excellent central point from which to visit the châteaux of the Loire Valley.
- The Chenonceau château is built across the Cher River, which is a tributary of the Loire. During World War II, the Cher formed part of the boundary between northern, occupied France and the southern, unoccupied zone. The château was sometimes used by members of the French resistance to smuggle Jews, prisoners, and downed Allied aviators out of the occupied zone. They would cross the river through the gallery that Catherine de Médicis had built, and exit safely through the door on the other side of the river.

Teacher Note

The following are some of the regional food specialties of Touraine:

- **tarte Tatin:** a caramelized, upside-down apple tart, originally made at the hôtel Tatin in the Loire Valley by two sisters **(les demoiselles Tatin),** who accidentally cooked an apple tart upside down and created a culinary sensation. For recipe, see page 183D.
- **saumon au beurre blanc:** salmon cooked in a sauce of butter, wine, and shallots. For recipe, see page 127D.
- **crottins de Chavignol:** a popular goat cheese **(chèvre).**
- **ragoût d'escargots aux cèpes:** a stew made with snails **(escargots)** known as **petits gris,** and wild mushrooms **(cèpes)** peculiar to Touraine.

Connections and Comparisons

History Link

The Chenonceau château was constructed in the sixteenth century. It is referred to as the **château des six femmes** because of six influential women who lived there at one time or another until the nineteenth century. Its two gardens are named after two of the women: Catherine de Médicis and Diane de Poitiers. Catherine de Médicis's contribution to the château was a gallery she had built on the bridge that crosses the Cher River. Its floor is made of black and white diamond-shaped stones. (See Photo 7 on page 159.)

STANDARDS: 2.2, 3.1

Location Opener

CHAPTER 5

Using the Photo Essay

1 **La place Plumereau,** located in the center of Tours, is known for its fifteenth-century houses. The wooden beams supporting the structures are covered with slate tiles to protect them from the weather. Numerous cafés, boutiques, galleries, concerts, and other types of entertainment make the square a popular gathering place.

2 **Honoré de Balzac** (1799–1850) was a French novelist known for the detailed, accurate descriptions of his more than 2,000 characters, who were portrayed as the product of their heredity and environment. His most famous work is the 90-volume *La Comédie humaine.* Other works by Balzac include *Le Curé de Tours* (1829), *Le Père Goriot* (1834), and *Les Illusions perdues* (1837–1843).

3 The **château d'Ussé** has beautiful terraces facing the Indre River. The château was used as a model for the castle in *Sleeping Beauty (La Belle au bois dormant).* Several rooms in the château display various scenes of the story. The château, built at the beginning of the Renaissance, has a variety of steeples, turrets, towers, chimneys, and dormer windows set upright in a sloping roof.

4 **Chenonceau,** constructed around 1520, is built over the Cher River. The approach to Chenonceau is a magnificent shaded **allée,** and its **son et lumière** show is highlighted by the reflection of the bridge's illuminated arches in the water. The town of Chenonceaux is spelled with an **-x,** whereas the château of Chenonceau does not have a final **-x.**

Touraine

La Touraine, célèbre pour ses abondantes cultures de fruits et de légumes et pour ses vignes, est souvent appelée «le jardin de la France». C'est aussi une importante région historique. Les rois aimaient y séjourner en raison de son climat doux et de ses forêts abondantes en gibier. Ils y ont construit de merveilleux châteaux que l'on connaît aujourd'hui sous le nom de «châteaux de la Loire».

internet

go.hrw.com

ADRESSE: go.hrw.com
MOT-CLE: WA3 TOURAINE

1 La place Plumereau
Cette place située au cœur de la ville de Tours est un des endroits préférés des étudiants.

2 Honoré de Balzac
Ce grand écrivain a écrit certains de ses romans au château de Saché, prés de la ville de Tours.

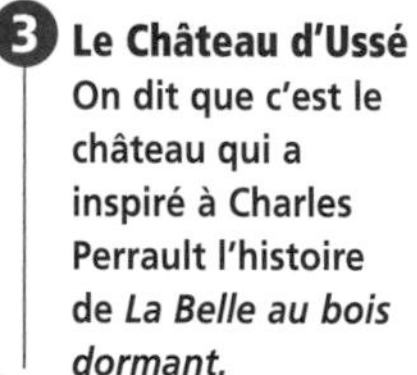

3 Le Château d'Ussé
On dit que c'est le château qui a inspiré à Charles Perrault l'histoire de *La Belle au bois dormant.*

Cultures and Communities

Culture Note

There were both royal châteaux and private châteaux built in Touraine. In general, the king had only one set of furnishings, which was transported from château to château as he traveled. That is why many of the royal châteaux are today quite sparsely furnished. In most private châteaux, a guest room was always set aside for the king.

Teaching Suggestion

You might have students work in groups to look up additional information on the châteaux shown on these pages, or any of the other châteaux located in Touraine and the Loire Valley. These include Langeais, Blois, Chambord, Chaumont, and others. Encourage students to find interesting stories connected with the châteaux. To expand this activity, see the project on page 155C.

STANDARDS: 2.2, 3.2

4 Chenonceau

5 Villandry

6 Montrésor

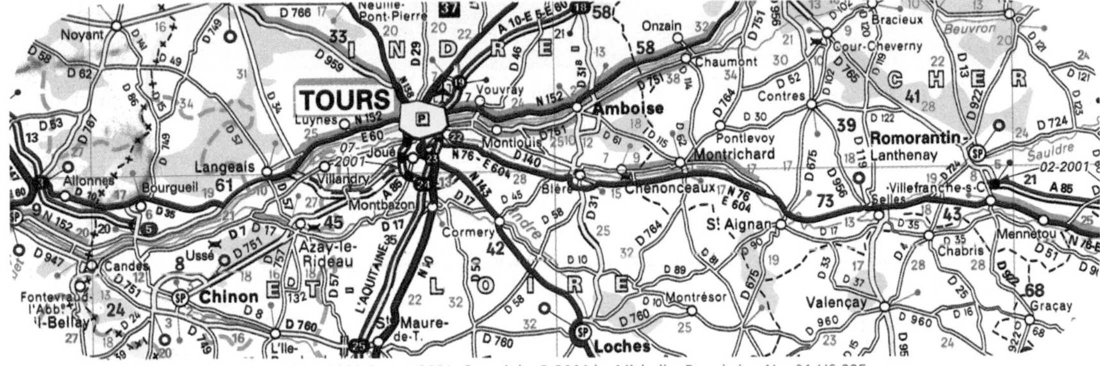

From *Map #989 France 2001*. Copyright © 2001 by Michelin. Permission No. 01-US-005

7 Azay-le-Rideau

8 Amboise

Aux chapitres 5, 6 et 7,

tu vas faire la connaissance de quatre lycéens qui habitent Tours. Cette ville est située dans la région qu'on appelle la Touraine. Pour commencer, tu vas visiter la Touraine avec tes nouveaux copains. Après, tu vas voir un peu Tours, une ville historique et très vivante.

9 **Le Clos-Lucé**
Léonard de Vinci a habité ce beau manoir près du château d'Amboise.

Connections and Comparisons

Thinking Critically

Observing Point out to students that most of the châteaux were built along rivers. Have them suggest reasons why this was done (transportation, water supply, fishing, defense, scenery).

Drawing Inferences Have students imagine what it would be like to live in an ancient building. How would it be different from a modern home? (Even when ancient structures are modernized with electricity and conveniences, there are certain characteristics of these old buildings that cannot be changed. The thick stone walls are very humid and cold, especially if the building is built in water or has a moat. There is a musty smell that is hard to eradicate. Floors and walls are often uneven or cracked. Stone staircases become worn and uneven.)

Location Opener

CHAPTER 5

5 **Villandry** is famous for its sixteenth-century Renaissance gardens, built in three terraces with a large lake at the top that provides water pressure for irrigation and the fountains. Ask students if they can tell which part of the château dates from a period earlier than the Renaissance (the heavily fortified tower that was built for defense).

6 Located on the Indrois River, **Montrésor** is a medieval fortress that once belonged to the counts of Anjou. The village at the foot of the château is known today for its collection of medieval furniture.

7 **Azay-le-Rideau** was built partly in the Indre River during the Renaissance. In fact, the **donjon** *(castle tower)* is in the middle of the river. The château is known for its main staircase, which is straight rather than spiral. There is an excellent **son et lumière** show during which spectators stroll around the château, following the performers who re-enact its history.

8 **Amboise,** a royal château, was the preferred residence of Louis XI, Charles VIII, and François I. After the **Conjuration d'Amboise,** a massacre of French Protestants in 1560, it was abandoned by the monarchy. The tower on the left side has a huge spiral ramp that allowed men on horseback to ride up to meet with the king.

9 **Le manoir du Clos-Lucé** is a fifteenth-century house made of brick and stone. François I convinced Leonardo da Vinci, whom he named "the great master in all forms of art and science," to live and work there. The lower level contains scale models made by IBM® from some of da Vinci's drawings: the first airplane, the first self-propelled vehicle, the helicopter, the parachute, the tank, the machine gun, and the swing bridge.

Chapitre 5 : Quelle journée!

Chapter Overview

Mise en train pp. 130–132	***C'est pas mon jour!***

	FUNCTIONS	GRAMMAR	VOCABULARY	RE-ENTRY
Première étape pp. 133–137	• Expressing concern for someone, p. 135	• The **passé composé** with **avoir,** p. 136	• School-day vocabulary, p. 134	• Relating a series of events **(Chapitre 9,** I) • Sports and leisure activities **(Chapitre 4,** I, II)
Deuxième étape pp. 138–141	• Inquiring; expressing satisfaction and frustration, p. 139 • Sympathizing with and consoling someone, p. 141	• Introduction to the **passé composé** with **être,** p. 140		• Pronunciation: the nasal sound [ɛ̃] **(Chapitre 7,** I) • Reflexive verbs **(Chapitre 4,** II) • Inquiring about and relating past events **(Chapitre 9,** I)
Troisième étape pp. 142–145	• Giving reasons and making excuses, p. 143 • Congratulating and reprimanding someone, p. 143			• Question words **(Chapitre 6,** I) • School subjects **(Chapitre 2,** I)

Lisons! pp. 146–147	**Le Cancre** and **Page d'écriture** Two poems by Jacques Prévert	**Reading Strategy:** Deducing the main idea	
Grammaire supplémentaire	**pp. 148–151** **Première étape,** pp. 148–149	**Deuxième étape,** pp. 149–151	**Troisième étape,** p. 151
Review pp. 152–155	**Mise en pratique,** pp. 152–153 **Ecrivons!** Effective introductions Writing about the best and worst day of the year	**Que sais-je?** p. 154	**Vocabulaire,** p. 155

CULTURE

- **Note culturelle, Carnet de correspondance,** p. 133
- Realia: French tardy slip, p. 133
- **Note culturelle,** Meals at school, p. 138
- Realia: **Bulletin trimestriel,** p. 142
- **Note culturelle,** French grades and report cards, p. 142
- **Panorama Culturel,** School life in francophone countries, p. 145

Chapitre 5 : Quelle journée!
Chapter Resources

Lesson Planning

One-Stop Planner

Lesson Planner with Substitute Teacher

Lesson Plans, pp. 21–25, 67

Student Make-Up Assignments
- Make-Up Assignment Copying Masters, Chapter 5

Listening and Speaking

TPR Storytelling Book, pp. 32–39

Listening Activities
- Student Response Forms for Listening Activities, pp. 35–37
- Additional Listening Activities 5-1 to 5-6, pp. 39–41
- Additional Listening Activities (song), p. 42
- Scripts and Answers, pp. 122–126

Video Guide
- Teaching Suggestions, pp. 32–33
- Activity Masters, pp. 34–36
- Scripts and Answers, pp. 95–97, 120

Activities for Communication
- Communicative Activities, pp. 25–30
- Realia and Teaching Suggestions, pp. 95–99
- Situation Cards, pp. 145–146

Reading and Writing

Reading Strategies and Skills Handbook, Chapter 5

Joie de lire 2, Chapter 5

Cahier d'activités, pp. 49–60

Grammar

Travaux pratiques de grammaire, pp. 37–44

Grammar Tutor for Students of French, Chapter 5

Assessment

Testing Program
- Grammar and Vocabulary Quizzes, **Etape** Quizzes, and Chapter Test, pp. 105–122
- Score Sheet, Scripts and Answers, pp. 123–130

Alternative Assessment Guide
- Portfolio Assessment, p. 22
- Performance Assessment, p. 36
- CD-ROM Assessment, p. 50

Student Make-Up Assignments
- Alternative Quizzes, Chapter 5

Standardized Assessment Tutor
- Reading, pp. 17–19
- Writing, p. 20
- Math, pp. 25–26

Online Activities
- **Jeux interactifs**
- **Activités Internet**

Video Program
- Videocassette 2
- Videocassette 5 (captioned version)

Interactive CD-ROM Tutor, Disc 2

DVD Tutor, Disc 1

Audio Compact Discs
- Textbook Listening Activities, CD 5, Tracks 1–12
- Additional Listening Activities, CD 5, Tracks 19–25
- Assessment Items, CD 5, Tracks 13–18

Teaching Transparencies
- Situation 5-1 to 5-3
- Vocabulary 5-A
- **Mise en train**
- **Grammaire supplémentaire** Answers
- **Travaux pratiques de grammaire** Answers

One-Stop Planner CD-ROM

Use the **One-Stop Planner CD-ROM with Test Generator** to aid in lesson planning and pacing.

For each chapter, the **One-Stop Planner** includes:
- Editable lesson plans with direct links to teaching resources
- Printable worksheets from resource books
- Direct launches to the HRW Internet activities
- Video and audio segments
- Test Generator
- Clip Art for vocabulary items

Chapitre 5 : Quelle journée!

Projects

Une bande dessinée

In groups of four, students will create, write, and illustrate a comic strip of ten frames, entitled ***Une journée horrible.*** *Students should use at least six of the nine functions in this chapter and the* ***passé composé*** *of verbs conjugated with both* ***être*** *and* ***avoir.*** *Assign the roles of leader/creator, writer, proofreader, and artist. All group members will participate in all aspects of the project, but these roles will define the principal tasks of the group members.*

MATERIALS

✄ Students may need

- Posterboard or butcher paper
- Scissors
- Glue or tape
- Markers or colored pencils

SUGGESTED SEQUENCE

1. Each group creates the characters for its comic strip.
2. Students create the story and outline what will happen in each frame of the comic strip.
3. Two members begin to write the script while the others sketch possible illustrations or find pictures from magazines or catalogues. Each member proofreads the finished script for accuracy and makes suggestions for improvement. Students then submit the rewritten copy and drawings of each character.
4. Correct the rough draft, using correction symbols so that the group is held accountable for correcting its grammatical errors. For example, use **sp** to indicate a spelling error, or **ag** to signal incorrect subject-verb or noun-adjective agreement.
5. Group members then rewrite the rough draft and complete the comic strip. The frames can be drawn on separate sheets of paper and glued to a posterboard. Each frame should be large enough to accommodate the speech bubbles and/or captions. The title and the names of the creators, writers, and illustrators of the comic strip should be clearly written on the posterboard.

GRADING THE PROJECT

Suggested Point Distribution (total = 100 points)

Inclusion of requirements	20
Language use	20
Vocabulary	20
Creativity/Overall appearance	20
Effort/Participation	20

Games

Course de relais

In this game, students will practice the vocabulary from the chapter.

Procedure Label two sides of the board **Equipe 1** and **Equipe 2.** On each side, list expressions from the **Vocabulaire** (page 155), deleting some letters from each word. If you delete accented letters, put the accent above or below the blank space where it belongs. Then, form two teams. The first team to complete all of the words correctly wins. One player at a time from each team goes to the board to fill in the space in one expression. The next player may not go to the board until the preceding player is seated. A player may fill in an expression or correct another's mistake, but not both. Students may not call out answers, but may encourage their teammates. (**Allez! Vite! Cours!**)

Tic Tac Toe

This game will help students practice the ***passé composé.***

Preparation Make three or four tic tac toe grids and one answer sheet. You may also want to draw the grid on a transparency to play as a class. In each square write an infinitive in parentheses followed by a sentence without the verb. (**voir—J'_____ Marc.**) Distribute copies to groups of two players and one judge. Players take turns reading aloud a sentence and supplying the verb in the **passé composé.** The judge verifies the answers. When the answer is correct, a student puts a marker in that square. (A coin works well.) A student wins when three squares in a row are marked horizontally, vertically, or diagonally.

STANDARDS: 1.3, 5.2

Storytelling

Mini-histoire

This story accompanies Teaching Transparency 5-2. The ***mini-histoire*** *can be told and retold in different formats, acted out, written down, and read aloud, to give students additional opportunities to practice all four skills. The following story relates Olivier's good day and Louise's frustrating day.*

Olivier a passé une journée formidable! Son professeur de maths a rendu les interrogations écrites : il a eu une note excellente. Après le cours d'histoire, il a rencontré Sophie, une fille très cool. Il lui a téléphoné et lui a demandé : «Qu'est-ce que tu fais ce soir? Est-ce-que tu veux aller au cinéma?». «D'accord.» a répondu Sophie. Ils se sont retrouvés à sept heures et quart devant le cinéma.

Louise a passé une journée épouvantable! D'abord, son réveil n'a pas sonné et elle s'est levée à huit heures. Ensuite, elle n'a pas eu le temps de déjeuner : elle est partie très vite, elle a raté le bus et elle est arrivée en retard à l'école. En classe, son professeur a donné les carnets de notes. Louise est intelligente mais n'étudie pas, alors, elle a de très mauvaises notes. Elle appelle son ami Christophe et ils se donnent rendez-vous au café. Au café, elle l'attend pendant une heure. Christophe n'est jamais arrivé.

Traditions

River Travel

Throughout history, people and freight have traveled along France's vast system of rivers, smaller tributaries, and canals. Today France has approximately 7,957 km of navigable rivers and canals. One of the eight major rivers in this system is the Loire. Measuring over 1,000 km, it is the longest river in France. Although only about one-half of the Loire is still navigable, it was one of France's greatest highways for over 2,000 years. Phoenicians, Greeks, Romans, and even Vikings have all used the Loire's waters to transport their goods. River traffic on the Loire reached its zenith in the 17th–19th centuries, the construction of railroads finally bringing on its demise. However, with the support of the French government, traditional river travel for commerce and pleasure remains active today. Find a map of France's river and canal system, then have students plot a week-long barge trip, traveling in part on the Loire.

Recette

France is surrounded on three sides by water and it has numerous rivers and streams. Therefore, fish is an important part of French gastronomy.

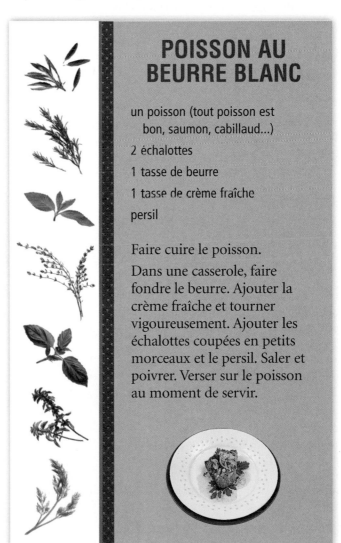

POISSON AU BEURRE BLANC

un poisson (tout poisson est bon, saumon, cabillaud...)

2 échalottes

1 tasse de beurre

1 tasse de crème fraîche

persil

Faire cuire le poisson.

Dans une casserole, faire fondre le beurre. Ajouter la crème fraîche et tourner vigoureusement. Ajouter les échalottes coupées en petits morceaux et le persil. Saler et poivrer. Verser sur le poisson au moment de servir.

Chapitre 5 : Quelle journée!
Technology

DVD/Video

Videocassette 2, Videocassette 5 (captioned version)
DVD Tutor, Disc 1
See Video Guide, pages 31–36.

Mise en train • C'est pas mon jour!
At a café after school, Céline tells Hector that nothing has gone right for her today. First, she woke up late. She missed her bus and arrived late to school. Then she realized she didn't have her homework. Finally, she got a low grade on a math quiz. Hector consoles her. Céline says she's going home to go to bed so nothing else can happen to her.

Mise en train (suite)
Now everything goes wrong for Hector. A bookstore doesn't have the books he needs. While at a café, he notices his sack is missing and follows a man leaving with an identical sack. The waiter thinks Hector is leaving without paying, and Hector can't find his money! Luckily, Céline arrives and pays Hector's bill. The waiter finds Hector's sack with his money inside.

Qu'est-ce que tu aimes à l'école?
Students from Martinique and France give their opinion of school, what they like and what they dislike.

Vidéoclips
- **Hansaplast®**: advertisement for first-aid supplies
- **Crédit Lyonnais®**: advertisement for a bank

Interactive CD-ROM Tutor

Activity	Activity Type	Pupil's Edition Page
En contexte	*Interactive conversation*	
1. Vocabulaire	Chasse au trésor Explorons!/Vérifions!	p. 134
2. Grammaire	Les mots qui manquent	p. 136
3. Comment dit-on… ?	Méli-mélo	pp. 135, 139
4. Grammaire	Le bon choix	p. 140
5. Comment dit-on… ?	Chacun à sa place	pp. 139, 141
6. Comment dit-on… ?	Méli-mélo	p. 143
Panorama Culturel	Qu'est-ce que tu aimes à l'école?	p. 145
A toi de parler	*Guided recording*	pp. 152–153
A toi d'écrire	*Guided writing*	pp. 152–153

Teacher Management System

Launch the program, type "admin" in the password area, and press RETURN. Log on to www.hrw.com/CDROMTUTOR for a detailed explanation of the Teacher Management System.

DVD Tutor

The *DVD Tutor* contains all material from the *Video Program* as described above. French captions are available for use at your discretion for all sections of the video. The *DVD Tutor* also provides a variety of video-based activities that assess students' understanding of the **Mise en train, Suite,** and **Panorama Culturel.**

This part of the *DVD Tutor* may be used on any DVD video player connected to a television or video monitor.

In addition to the video material and the video-based comprehension activities, the *DVD Tutor* also contains the entire *Interactive CD-ROM Tutor* in DVD-ROM format. Each DVD disc contains the activities from all 12 chapters of the *Interactive CD-ROM Tutor.*

This part of the *DVD Tutor* may be used on a Macintosh® or Windows® computer with a DVD-ROM drive.

To preview all resources available for this chapter, use the **One-Stop Planner CD-ROM,** Disc 2.

Internet Connection

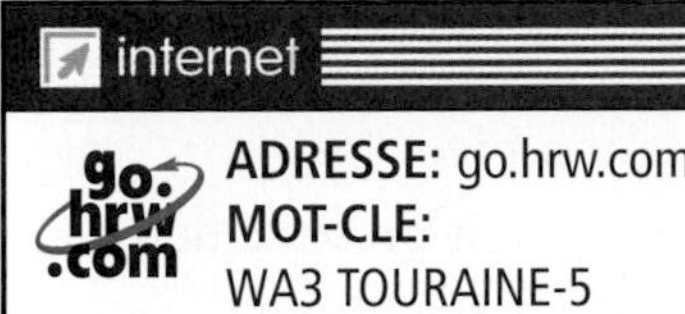

Have students explore the ***go.hrw.com*** *Web site for many online resources covering all chapters. All Chapter 5 resources are available under the keyword* ***WA3 TOURAINE-5.*** *Interactive games help students practice the material and provide them with immediate feedback. You'll also find a printable worksheet that provides Internet activities that lead to a comprehensive online research project.*

Jeux interactifs

You can use the interactive activities in this chapter

- to practice grammar, vocabulary, and chapter functions
- as homework
- as an assessment option
- as a self-test
- to prepare for the Chapter Test

Activités Internet

Students look online for information about French schools.

- In preparation for the **Activités Internet,** have students review school vocabulary, or complete the activities in the **Panorama Culturel** on page 145. After they complete the activity sheet, have students work with a partner and share the information they gathered in Activity B on that sheet. Then, ask each pair of students to share what they learned with the class.

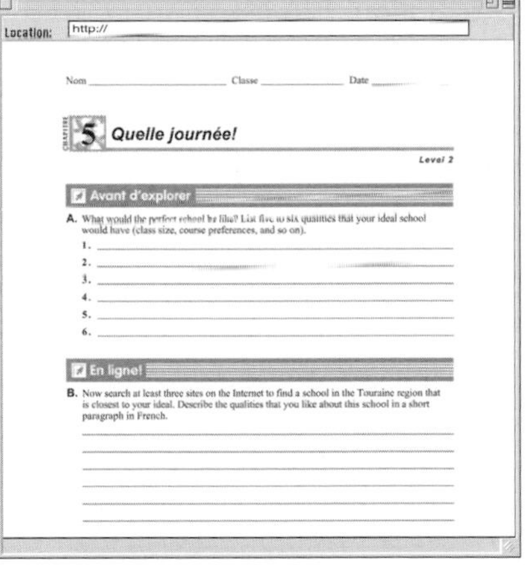

Location: http://

Nom ______ Classe ______ Date ______

5 Quelle journée!

Level 2

Avant d'explorer

A. What would the perfect school be like? List five to six qualities that your ideal school would have (class size, course preferences, and so on).

1. ______
2. ______
3. ______
4. ______
5. ______
6. ______

En ligne!

B. Now search at least three sites on the Internet to find a school in the Touraine region that is closest to your ideal. Describe the qualities that you like about this school in a short paragraph in French.

Projet

Have students choose one of the **Points d'intérêt** or one of the **Tourangeaux célèbres** from page 124 in their book. Students should research their topic online. Have the class make a timeline. Each student can then place their research result with a picture on the timeline and present their findings to the class. Have students document their sources by noting the URLs of all the sites that they consulted.

STANDARDS: 1.2, 1.3, 2.1, 3.2, 5.1

Chapitre 5 : Quelle journée!
Textbook Listening Activities Scripts 

Première étape

7 p. 135

1. —Tu n'as pas tes devoirs aujourd'hui, Sara?
   —Excusez-moi, monsieur, mais j'ai perdu mon livre d'anglais.
2. —Pourquoi tu n'es pas venue avec nous hier après-midi? On a fait les magasins!
   —Désolée, mais c'était impossible. J'ai été collée.
3. —Tu en fais une tête. Qu'est-ce qui se passe?
   —Ben, j'ai eu une mauvaise note en maths après tout le temps que j'ai passé à étudier!
4. —Pourquoi tu es arrivé en classe avec quinze minutes de retard?
   —J'ai raté le bus.

Answers to Activity 7

1. c
2. d
3. a
4. b

9 p. 135

FRANCINE Salut, Luc. Te voilà enfin. Dis donc, ça n'a pas l'air d'aller. Qu'est-ce qui t'arrive?

LUC Désolé d'être en retard. Tout a été de travers ce matin!

FRANCINE Qu'est-ce qui s'est passé?

LUC J'avais oublié mon livre d'histoire, donc à midi, je suis rentré chez moi pour aller le chercher.

FRANCINE Et après?

LUC Ben, je ne l'ai pas trouvé et en plus, en descendant l'escalier, j'ai raté une marche, je suis tombé et j'ai déchiré mon pantalon.

FRANCINE Pauvre vieux!

LUC Attends! J'ai vite mis un autre pantalon, et j'ai couru pour attraper le bus. Mais je l'ai raté, donc, j'ai décidé de venir à pied.

FRANCINE Tu es venu à pied? Mais ça fait presque deux kilomètres! Tu aurais dû me téléphoner.

Answers to Activity 9

1,3

12 p. 137

1. —Tiens, Marie, qu'est-ce qui t'arrive?
   —J'ai eu une interro de français et j'ai eu sept!
2. —J'ai attendu le bus pendant vingt minutes aujourd'hui. Et toi?
   —Moi, je l'ai attendu un quart d'heure!
3. —Salut, Marc! Tu attends le bus?
   —Non, j'attends ma mère. Elle vient me chercher.
4. —Eh ben, qu'est-ce qui s'est passé?
   —D'abord, je n'ai pas entendu mon réveil. Ensuite, j'ai eu une interro de français, et après l'école, on a perdu le match de basket.
5. —Tu as été collé aujourd'hui?
   —Oui, malheureusement.

Answers to Activity 12

1. past
2. past
3. now
4. past
5. past

The following scripts are for the listening activities found in the *Pupil's Edition.* For Student Response Forms, see *Listening Activities,* pages 35–37. To provide students with additional listening practice, see *Listening Activities,* pages 39–42.

One-Stop Planner CD-ROM

To preview all resources available for this chapter, use the **One-Stop Planner CD-ROM,** Disc 2.

Deuxième étape

18 **p. 139**

1. —Salut, Georges. Comment ça s'est passé, ton week-end au lac?
—Oh, tout a été de travers!

2. —Salut, Eliane. Comment s'est passé ton week-end?
—Ça s'est très bien passé, merci.

3. —Et toi, comment s'est passé ton week-end?
—Moi? J'ai travaillé tout le week-end. C'était horrible!

4. —Martine, comment s'est passé ton week-end?
—J'ai fait de la natation et je suis allée à la boum de Denise. C'était super!

5. —Et toi, Bruno?
—J'ai vu un bon film comique au cinéma et j'ai regardé un match de foot à la télé. Mon équipe a gagné! Quel week-end formidable!

Answers to Activity 18

1. bad
2. good
3. bad
4. good
5. good

Troisième étape

30 **p. 144**

1. —Combien tu as eu à ta rédaction de français?
—A ma rédaction? Ben, j'ai eu seize.
—Seize? Bravo!

2. —Eh, salut! Combien tu as eu à ton interro d'histoire?
—J'ai eu quinze.
—Félicitations! Moi, j'ai eu onze.

3. —Et à l'interro de sciences-éco? Combien tu as eu?
—Euh, ce n'est pas mon fort. J'ai eu dix.
—C'est pas terrible, ça. Tu dois mieux travailler.

4. —Combien tu as eu en biologie?
—J'ai eu huit. Je ne suis pas doué pour les sciences.
—Mais, c'est inadmissible! Tu ne dois pas faire le clown en classe!

Answers to Activity 30

1. congratulating
2. congratulating
3. reprimanding
4. reprimanding

Mise en pratique

2 **p. 135**

LE PERE Je vous ai demandé un rendez-vous parce que je ne suis pas content des notes de Ginette. Elle a eu huit à la dernière interro. Qu'est-ce qui se passe?

LE PROF Le huit, c'est qu'elle n'a pas assez étudié. Et la semaine passée, elle est arrivée en retard tous les jours!

LE PERE Eh bien, elle dit que l'histoire, ce n'est pas son fort. Elle dit aussi que vous ne l'aimez pas!

LE PROF N'importe quoi! Ce n'est pas du tout vrai! Elle est très intelligente, mais elle doit mieux travailler. Elle doit être plus sérieuse, et surtout, elle ne doit pas faire le clown en classe!

LE PERE Bon, je vais lui parler. C'est inadmissible, un huit en histoire-géo!

Answers to Mise en pratique Activity 2

1. faux
2. faux
3. faux
4. vrai
5. faux
6. vrai

Chapitre 5 : Quelle journée!

Suggested Lesson Plans 50-Minute Schedule

Day 1

CHAPTER OPENER 5 min.
- Present Chapter Objectives, p. 129.
- Language-to-Language and Culture Notes, ATE, pp. 128–129

MISE EN TRAIN 40 min.
- Presenting **Mise en train,** ATE, p. 130
- Teacher Note and Culture Note, ATE, p. 131
- Teaching Suggestions: Viewing Suggestion 2, Video Guide, p. 32
- Do Activities 1–4, p. 132.
- Teaching Suggestions: Post-viewing Suggestions 1–2, Video Guide, p. 32

Wrap-Up 5 min.
- Do Activity 5, p. 132.

Homework Options
Cahier d'activités, Act. 1, p. 49

Day 2

MISE EN TRAIN
Quick Review 10 min.
- Bell Work, ATE, p. 133
- Motivate: Ask students to name some excuses they might give for arriving late to school or for not having their homework completed when it is due. Which of those excuses would their teacher find acceptable?
- Read and discuss **Note culturelle**, p. 133.

PREMIERE ETAPE
Vocabulaire, p. 134 35 min.
- Presenting **Vocabulaire,** ATE, p. 134
- Play Audio CD for Activity 7, p. 135.
- Complete Activity 8, p. 135.
- Travaux pratiques de grammaire, Activities 1–2, p. 37
- See Game: **Qu'est-ce qui se passe?,** ATE, p. 135.

Wrap-Up, 5 min.
- Discuss Culture Note, ATE, p. 135.

Homework Options
Cahier d'activités, Acts. 2–5, pp. 50–51
Travaux pratiques de grammaire, Acts. 3–4, p. 38

Day 3

PREMIERE ETAPE
Quick Review 5 min.
- Check homework.

Comment dit-on... ?, p. 135 15 min.
- Presenting **Comment dit-on... ?,** ATE, p. 135
- Play Audio CD for Activity 9, p. 135.
- Complete Activity 10, p. 136.
- Cahier d'activités, Activity 7, p. 51

Grammaire, p. 136 25 min.
- Presenting **Grammaire,** ATE, p. 136
- Discuss Language-to-Language, ATE, p. 136.
- Play Audio CD for Activity 12, p. 137.
- **Grammaire supplémentaire,** Activities 1–2, p. 148
- Have students do Activity 14, p. 137, in pairs.

Wrap-Up 5 min.
- Building on Previous Skills, ATE, p. 137

Homework Options
Study for Quiz 5-1.
Pupil's Edition, Activity 13, p. 137
Cahier d'activités, Acts. 8–9, p. 52
Travaux pratiques de grammaire, Acts. 5–8, pp. 39–40

Day 4

PREMIERE ETAPE
Quiz 5-1 20 min.
- Administer Quiz 5-1A, 5-1B, or a combination of the two.

DEUXIEME ETAPE
Note culturelle, p. 138 5 min.
- Read and discuss **Note culturelle,** p. 138.

Comment dit-on... ?, p. 139 20 min.
- Presenting **Comment dit-on... ?,** ATE, p. 139
- Teacher Note, ATE, p. 139
- Play Audio CD for Activity 18, p. 139.
- Cahier d'activités, Activities 11–12, p. 53
- Have students do Activity 19, p. 139, in groups.

Wrap-Up 5 min.
- Read and discuss **Tu te rappelles?** and **A la française,** p. 139.

Homework Options
Travaux pratiques de grammaire, Acts. 9–10, p. 41

Day 5

DEUXIEME ETAPE
Quick Review 5 min.
- Check homework.

Grammaire, p. 140 25 min.
- Presenting **Grammaire,** ATE, p. 140
- **Grammaire supplémentaire,** Activities 5–8, pp. 149–150
- Have students do Activity 23, p. 141, in groups.

Comment dit-on... ?, p. 141 15 min.
- Presenting **Comment dit-on... ?,** ATE, p. 141
- Cahier d'activités, Activities 16–17, p. 55
- Complete Activities 24–25, p. 141.

Wrap-Up 5 min.
- Have pairs do Activity 26, p. 141, using lists from Activity 25.

Homework Options
Study for Quiz 5-2.
Pupil's Edition, Activities 21–22, p. 140
Travaux pratiques de grammaire, Acts. 11–14, pp. 42–43
Cahier d'activités, Acts. 13–14, pp. 53–54

Day 6

DEUXIEME ETAPE
Quiz 5-2 20 min.
- Administer Quiz 5-2A or 5-2B, or a combination of the two.

TROISIEME ETAPE
Note culturelle, p. 142 10 min.
- Read and discuss **Note culturelle,** p. 142.
- Thinking Critically, ATE, p. 142
- Culture Notes, ATE, p. 142
- Do Activity 27, p. 142.

Comment dit-on... ?, p. 143 15 min.
- Presenting **Comment dit-on... ?,** ATE, p. 143 (top)
- Cahier d'activités, Activities 19–21, p. 56
- Have students do Activity 28, p. 143, in pairs.

Wrap-Up 5 min.
- Have students begin the writing segment of Activity 29, ATE, p. 143.

Homework Options
Complete Activity 29, p. 143.

For alternative lesson plans by chapter section, to create your own customized plans, or to preview all resources available for this chapter, use the **One-Stop Planner CD-ROM,** Disc 2.

For additional homework suggestions, see activities accompanied by this symbol throughout the chapter.

Day 7

TROISIEME ETAPE

Quick Review 10 min.
- Have partners do the oral segment of Activity 29, p. 143.

Comment dit-on... ?, p. 143 20 min.
- Presenting **Comment dit-on... ?,** ATE, p. 143 (bottom)
- Play Audio CD for Activity 30, p. 144.
- Do Activity 31, p. 144.
- **Grammaire supplémentaire,** Activity 10, p. 151
- Have students do Activities 32–33, p. 144, in pairs.

PANORAMA CULTUREL, p. 145 15 min.
- Presenting **Panorama Culturel,** ATE, p. 145
- Culture Note, ATE, p. 145
- Questions, ATE, p. 145

Wrap-Up 5 min.
- Discuss **Qu'en penses-tu?,** p. 145

Homework Options
Study for Quiz 5-3.
Cahier d'activités, Acts. 22–23, pp. 57–58
Travaux pratiques de grammaire, Acts. 15–17, p. 44

Day 8

TROISIEME ETAPE

Quiz 5-3 20 min.
- Administer Quiz 5-3A, 5-3B, or a combination of the two.

LISONS!, 25 min.
- Read and discuss **Stratégie pour lire,** p. 146.
- Do Prereading Activities A–C, p. 146.
- Literature Link, ATE, p. 146
- Read **Le Cancre** and complete Reading Activities D–K, pp. 146–147.
- Thinking Critically, ATE, p. 146

Wrap-Up 5 min.
- Teacher Notes, ATE, p. 146

Homework Options
Cahier d'activités, Act. 25, p. 59

Day 9

LISONS!

Quick Review 10 min.
- Check homework.

Postreading Activity 35 min.
- Read **Page d'écriture** and complete Postreading Activity L, p. 147.
- Discuss Culture Note and Language Note, ATE, p. 147.
- Group Work suggestion, ATE, p. 147

Wrap-Up 5 min.
- Have groups share their illustrations with the class.

Homework Options
Have students write their own school-related poems.

Day 10

LISONS!

Quick Review 5 min.
- Have volunteers share their poems with the class.

MISE EN PRATIQUE 40 min.
- Do Activity 1, p. 152.
- Play Audio CD for Activity 2, p. 152.
- Discuss Teacher Note and Language Note, ATE, p. 152, and Culture Note, ATE, p. 153.
- Discuss **Stratégie pour écrire** for **Ecrivons!,** p. 153. Then have students work on journal entries.

Wrap-Up 5 min.
- Discuss Career Path, ATE, p. 153.

Homework Options
Complete journal entries for **Ecrivons!,** p. 153.

Day 11

MISE EN PRATIQUE

Quick Review 10 min.
- Have volunteers share their journal entries from **Ecrivons!**

Chapter Review 35 min.
- Have students complete **A toi de parler,** Interactive CD-ROM Tutor, Disc 2.
- Have students do **A toi d'écrire,** Interactive CD-ROM Tutor, Disc 2.
- See Teaching Suggestions, Pre-viewing Suggestions 1–2, Video Guide, p. 32.
- Show ***C'est pas mon jour! (suite),*** Video Program, Videocassette 2.
- Video Guide, Activities 6–8, pp. 35–36

Wrap-Up 5 min.
- Have students begin **Que sais-je?,** p. 154.

Homework Options
Que sais-je?, p. 154

Day 12

MISE EN PRATIQUE

Quick Review 15 min.
- Check homework and do **Jeu de rôle,** p. 153.

Chapter Review 35 min.
- Review Chapter 5. Choose from **Grammaire supplémentaire,** Grammar Tutor for Students of French, Activities for Communication, Listening Activities, Interactive CD-ROM Tutor, or **Jeux interactifs.**

Homework Options
Study for Chapter 5 Test.

Assessment

Chapter Test 50 min.
- Administer Chapter 5 Test. Select from Testing Program, Alternative Assessment Guide, Test Generator, or Standardized Assessment Tutor.

Chapitre 5 : Quelle journée!

Suggested Lesson Plans *90-Minute Block Schedule*

Block 1

CHAPTER OPENER 5 min.
- Present Chapter Objectives, p. 129
- Read and discuss Culture Notes and Language-to-Language, ATE, pp. 128–129.

MISE EN TRAIN 40 min.
- Preteaching Vocabulary, ATE, p. 130
- Presenting **Mise en train,** ATE, p. 130
- Do Activities 1–5, p. 132, using Tactile/Visual Learners Suggestion for Activity 2, ATE, p. 132.

PREMIERE ETAPE 10 min.
- Do Activity 6, p. 133.
- Discuss **Note culturelle,** p. 133.

Vocabulaire, p. 134 25 min.
- Presenting **Vocabulaire,** ATE, p. 134
- Play Audio CD for Activity 7, p. 135, using Slower Pace, ATE, p. 134.
- Do Activity 8, p. 135.

Wrap-Up 10 min.
- Teaching Transparency 5-A and Suggestion #2 in Suggestions for Using Teaching Transparency 5-A

Homework Options
Cahier d'activités, Acts. 1–5, pp. 49–51
Travaux pratiques de grammaire, Acts. 1–4, pp. 37–38

Block 2

PREMIERE ETAPE
Quick Review 10 min.
- Game: **Qu'est-ce qui se passe?,** ATE, p. 135

Comment dit-on… ?, p. 135 30 min.
- Presenting **Comment dit-on… ?,** ATE, p. 135
- Play Audio CD for Activity 9, p. 135.
- Teaching Suggestion, Activity 9, ATE, p. 135
- Do Activities 10–11, p. 136.

Grammaire, p. 136 45 min.
- Presenting **Grammaire,** ATE, p. 136
- Play Audio CD for Activity 12, p. 137.
- Additional Practice, ATE, p. 137
- Do Activities 13–14, p. 137.

Wrap-Up 5 min.
- Building on Previous Skills, ATE, p. 137

Homework Options
Have students study for Quiz 5-1.
Grammaire supplémentaire, Acts. 1–4, pp. 148–149
Cahier d'activités, Acts. 6–10, pp. 51–52
Travaux pratiques de grammaire, Acts. 5–8, pp. 39–40

Block 3

PREMIERE ETAPE
Quick Review 5 min.
- Teaching Transparency 5-1 and Suggestion #2 in Suggestions for Using Teaching Transparency 5-1

Quiz 5-1 20 min.
- Administer Quiz 5-1A, 5-1B, or a combination of the two.

DEUXIEME ETAPE 10 min.
- Have students read the conversation on page 138.
- Do Activity 17, p. 138.
- Discuss **Note culturelle,** p. 138.

Comment dit-on… ?, p. 139 30 min.
- Presenting **Comment dit-on… ?,** ATE, p. 139
- Play Audio CD for Activity 18, p. 139.
- **A la française,** p. 139
- Do Activity 20, p. 139.

Grammaire, p. 140 20 min.
- Presenting **Grammaire,** ATE, p. 140
- Do Activity 21, p. 140.

Wrap-Up 5 min.
- In random order, read expressions for expressing satisfaction and expressing frustration from **Comment dit-on… ?,** p. 139. Have students give a thumbs-up sign for expressions of satisfaction and a thumbs-down sign for expressions of frustration.

Homework Options
Cahier d'activités, Acts. 11–13, p. 53
Travaux pratiques de grammaire, Acts. 9–12, pp. 41–42

For alternative lesson plans by chapter section, to create your own customized plans, or to preview all resources available for this chapter, use the **One-Stop Planner CD-ROM,** Disc 2.

For additional homework suggestions, see activities accompanied by this symbol throughout the chapter.

Block 4

DEUXIEME ETAPE

Quick Review 10 min.
- Visual Learners/Slower Pace, ATE, p. 139

Grammaire, p. 140 25 min.
- Additional Practice, ATE, p. 150
- Do Activity 22, p. 140.

Comment dit-on… ?, p. 141 25 min.
- Presenting **Comment dit-on… ?,** ATE, p. 141
- Activities 24–26, p. 141

TROISIEME ETAPE

Comment dit-on… ?, p. 143 20 min.
- Presenting **Comment dit-on… ?,** ATE, p. 143 (top)
- Do Activity 28, p. 143.
- Discuss **Note culturelle,** p. 142.
- Culture Notes and Teacher Note, ATE, p. 142

Wrap-Up 10 min.
- Have students read the **bulletins trimestriels,** p. 142. Have students imagine what Jean and Caroline might say to give reasons or excuses for their grades.

Homework Options
Have students study for Quiz 5-2.
Grammaire supplémentaire, Acts. 5–8, pp. 149–150
Cahier d'activités, Acts. 14–21, pp. 54–56
Travaux pratiques de grammaire, Acts. 13–14, p. 43

Block 5

DEUXIEME ETAPE

Quick Review 10 min.
- Teaching Transparency 5-2 and Suggestion #1 in Suggestions for Using Teaching Transparency 5-2

Quiz 5-2 20 min.
- Administer Quiz 5-2A, 5-2B, or a combination of the two.

TROISIEME ETAPE

Comment dit-on… ?, p. 143 15 min.
- Review expressions from **Comment dit-on… ?,** p. 143 (top).
- Do Activity 29, p. 143.

Comment dit-on… ?, p. 143 20 min.
- Presenting **Comment dit-on… ?,** ATE, p. 143 (bottom)
- Play Audio CD for Activity 30, p. 144.
- Do Activity 32, p. 144.

PANORAMA CULTUREL 15 min.
- Presenting **Panorama Culturel,** ATE, p. 145, using Videocassette 2
- Discuss Questions, ATE, p. 145, and **Qu'en penses-tu?,** p. 145.

Wrap-Up 10 min.
- Teaching Transparency 5-3, using the third suggestion in Suggestions for Using Teaching Transparency 5-3

Homework Options
Have students study for Quiz 5-3.
Grammaire supplémentaire, Act. 10, p. 151
Cahier d'activités, Acts. 22–24, pp. 57–58
Travaux pratiques de grammaire, Acts. 15–17, p. 44

Block 6

TROISIEME ETAPE

Quick Review 10 min.
- Communicative Activity 5-3A and 5-3B, Activities for Communication, pp. 29–30

Quiz 5-3 20 min.
- Administer Quiz 5-3A, 5-3B, or a combination of the two.

LISONS! 35 min.
- **Stratégie pour lire,** p. 146
- Prereading Activities A–C, p. 146
- Making Predictions, ATE, p. 146
- Do Reading Activities D–F, pp. 146–147.

MISE EN PRATIQUE 25 min.
- Do Activity 1, p. 152.
- Play Audio CD for Activity 2, p. 152.

Homework Options
Que sais-je?, p. 154
Pupil's Edition, Acts. 4–5, p. 153
Study for Chapter 5 Test.

Block 7

MISE EN PRATIQUE

Quick Review 10 min.
- Collect homework and have students share their responses to Activity 3, p. 152.

Chapter Review 35 min.
- Review Chapter 5. Choose from **Grammaire supplémentaire,** Grammar Tutor for Students of French, Activities for Communication, Listening Activities, Interactive CD-ROM Tutor, or **Jeux interactifs.**

Chapter Test 45 min.
- Administer Chapter 5 Test. Select from Testing Program, Alternative Assessment Guide, Test Generator, or Standardized Assessment Tutor.

Chapter Opener

CHAPITRE 5

One-Stop Planner CD-ROM

For resource information, see the **One-Stop Planner,** Disc 2.

Pacing Tips

In this chapter, students will revisit the **passé composé.** In the **Deuxième étape,** students will be introduced to the **passé composé** with **être,** so you might plan your lessons accordingly. For Lesson Plans and timing suggestions, see pages 127I–127L.

Meeting the Standards

Communication

- Expressing concern for someone, p. 135
- Inquiring; expressing satisfaction and frustration, p. 139
- Sympathizing with and consoling someone, p. 141
- Giving reasons and making excuses, p. 143
- Congratulating and reprimanding someone, p. 143

Culture

- Culture Note, pp. 128, 129, 131, 133, 135, 142, 145, 147, 153
- Note culturelle, pp. 133, 138, 142
- Panorama Culturel, p. 145

Connections

- Music Link, p. 140
- Multicultural Link, p. 145
- Literature Link, p. 146

Comparisons

- Thinking Critically: Comparing and Contrasting, p. 142
- Thinking Critically: Analyzing, p. 146

Communities

- Career Path, p. 153
- De l'école au travail, p. 144

Cultures and Communities

Culture Note

Les écoles maternelles accept children from ages two to six. Children then attend **l'enseignement élémentaire** for five years. **L'enseignement secondaire** in the **collège** lasts for four years and is for students from ages eleven to fifteen. In the first two years, **sixième** and **cinquième**, students have a common curriculum. In grades **quatrième** and **troisième,** students begin to choose **options** to orient themselves towards a particular course of study. After **collège**, students may choose a vocational **lycée** that prepares them for a professional certificate. Students may also opt for a three-year, academic cycle that prepares them for the **baccalauréat,** a rigorous exam that guarantees successful students the right to enter a French university.

CHAPITRE

5 Quelle journée!

Objectives

In this chapter you will learn to

Première étape

- express concern for someone

Deuxième étape

- inquire
- express satisfaction and frustration
- sympathize with and console someone

Troisième étape

- give reasons and make excuses
- congratulate and reprimand someone

internet

ADRESSE: go.hrw.com
MOT-CLE: WA3 TOURAINE-5

◀ **J'ai passé une journée horrible!**

Chapter Opener

CHAPITRE 5

Focusing on Outcomes

As you read each of the outcomes for the chapter, ask students in what situations they would use these functions. Then have students look at the photo and describe what they see. Which outcome best matches the photo? NOTE: The self-check activities on page 154 help students assess their achievement of the objectives.

Culture Note

From elementary through junior high, French schools provide students with books, which must be covered and returned at the end of the school year. High school students, however, must buy their own books. They commonly buy used books from classmates, who post notices in the hallways announcing the books they have for sale.

Chapter Sequence

Connections and Comparisons

Language-to-Language

Point out that the word **journée** is a **faux ami;** it is not the equivalent of the English word *journey.* Have students guess the root word **(jour). Journée** is used to talk about the duration of a day **(J'ai lu toute la journée.),** whereas **jour** refers to the day as a period of time. **(Quel jour on est?)**

Mise en train

CHAPITRE 5

Teaching Resources
pp. 130–132

PRINT 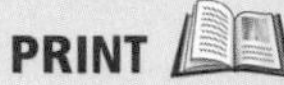
- Lesson Planner, p. 21
- Video Guide, pp. 32, 34
- Cahier d'activités, p. 49

MEDIA  
- One-Stop Planner
- Video Program
  Mise en train
  Videocassette 2, 28:42–32:17
  Videocassette 5 (captioned version), 38:56–42:31
  Suite
  Videocassette 2, 32:20–36:57
  Videocassette 5 (captioned version), 42:34–47:11
- DVD Tutor, Disc 1
- Audio Compact Discs, CD 5, Trs. 1–2
- **Mise en train** Transparencies

Presenting Mise en train

Write the sentences that explain what happened to Céline on the board in random order. Convey the meaning through gestures or mime with props. You might also complete the Preteaching Vocabulary suggestion below. Then, show the video and have students reorder the actions as they occur in the video. Finally, have students answer the questions in Activity 1 on page 132.

Mise en train Transparencies

The **roman-photo** is an abridged version of the video episode.

MISE EN TRAIN ▪ *C'est pas mon jour!*

CD 5 Trs. 1–2
DVD

Stratégie pour comprendre
What are some bad things that can happen to you on a school day? See if you can relate to what happened to Céline. If Hector says that 10/20 is a decent score on a test, how do you think French teachers grade?

Céline

Hector

C'est mercredi et il est midi et demi. Céline et Hector n'ont pas cours.

1
Céline Salut, Hector.
Hector Salut, Céline. Désolé d'être en retard.
Céline T'en fais pas.

2
Céline Oh, c'est pas vrai!
Hector Oh, excuse-moi!
Céline T'inquiète pas. C'est pas grave.

3
Céline Tu sais, depuis ce matin, ça ne s'arrête pas. C'est pas mon jour!
Hector Ah, oui? Qu'est-ce qui s'est passé? Raconte!
Céline Oh, tout a été de travers!

4
7h45 du matin :
Céline Mon réveil n'a pas sonné. Alors, je me suis réveillée en retard...
Je n'ai pas eu le temps de prendre mon petit déjeuner. J'ai juste pris une pomme.
J'ai couru pour attraper le bus, mais je l'ai raté. Alors, bien sûr, je suis arrivée à l'école en retard.

Preteaching Vocabulary

Guessing words from context

Have students guess what the title ***C'est pas mon jour!*** means. Then have students discuss what could happen on a bad day for a typical teenager. Using this as a context, have students look at the photos and read the text to come up with four events that contributed to Céline's bad day. Here are some examples of what students might find:

- ❹ **Mon réveil n'a pas sonné.**
- ❹ **...je suis arrivée à l'école en retard.**
- ❺ **J'avais oublié mes devoirs!**
- ❻ **...j'ai eu à mon interro de maths... 10!**

 STANDARDS: 1.2

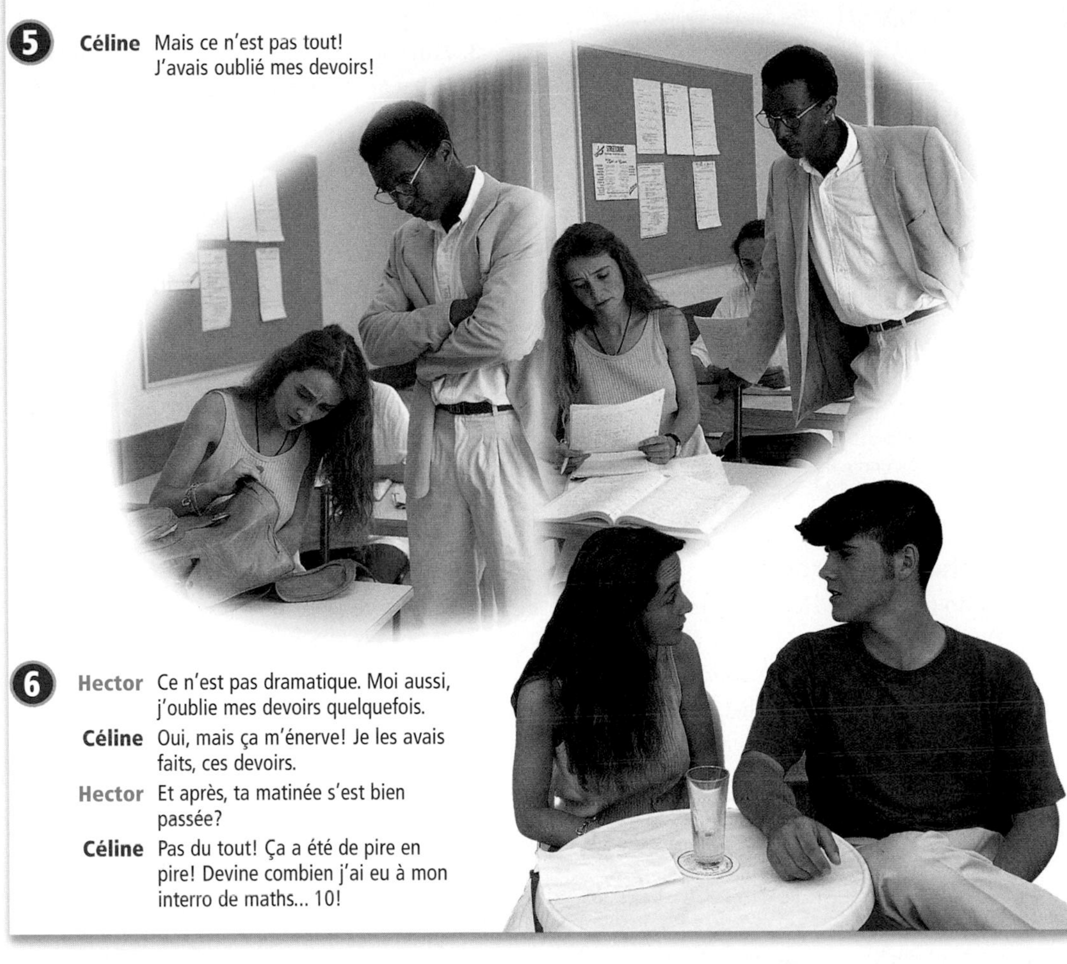

5 **Céline** Mais ce n'est pas tout! J'avais oublié mes devoirs!

6 **Hector** Ce n'est pas dramatique. Moi aussi, j'oublie mes devoirs quelquefois.
Céline Oui, mais ça m'énerve! Je les avais faits, ces devoirs.
Hector Et après, ta matinée s'est bien passée?
Céline Pas du tout! Ça a été de pire en pire! Devine combien j'ai eu à mon interro de maths... 10!

7 **Hector** C'est pas mal!
Céline Pas mal? D'habitude, j'ai 15.
Hector Pas moi. Les maths, ce n'est pas mon fort.

8 **Hector** Tu sais, il y a des jours comme ça. Ça va aller mieux!
Céline Je ne sais pas. Cet après-midi, je vais me coucher. Comme ça, je ne risque rien.

Cahier d'activités, p. 49, Act. 1

Using the Captioned Video/DVD

If students have difficulty understanding French spoken at a normal speed, use Videocassette 5 to allow students to see the French captions for ***C'est pas mon jour!*** and ***C'est pas mon jour! (suite).*** Hearing the language and watching the story will reduce anxiety about the new language and facilitate comprehension. The reinforcement of seeing the written vocabulary words as they watch the gestures and actions will help prepare students to do the comprehension activities on page 132.

NOTE: The *DVD Tutor* contains captions for all sections of the *Video Program.*

Mise en train

CHAPITRE 5

Teacher Note

Remind students that the French grading system is based on 20, so Céline's grade of 10 is considered average. A score of 18 or 19 is very rare and considered exceptional.

Culture Note

Students might notice that Céline's classroom seems bare and undecorated. French junior high/middle school **(collège)** or high school **(lycée)** classrooms are not reserved for a particular teacher or class. Instead, students and teachers move about from room to room. Classes are usually one or two hours long, and students have about five minutes between classes, which is called **l'interclasse.** Usually, the same students change classes together, since they are grouped according to the course of study they have chosen.

Mise en train (suite)

When the story continues, everything starts to go wrong for Hector. First, the bookstore doesn't have the books he needs, so he buys a different book. While at a café, Hector notices his sack is missing and sees a man leaving with what he thinks is his sack. He follows and stops the man. The waiter thinks Hector, who can't find his money, is leaving without paying! At that moment, Céline arrives. She pays Hector's bill, and the waiter finds Hector's sack with his money inside.

STANDARDS: 1.2, 2.1

Mise en train

CHAPITRE 5

Auditory Learners

4 Create other unfortunate situations to read to the class in addition to the ones written in Activity 4. (**J'ai perdu mon livre d'histoire. Je n'ai pas fait mes devoirs. Je n'ai pas entendu mon réveil. Je n'ai pas eu le temps de prendre mon petit déjeuner. Je n'ai pas fini mes devoirs. J'ai raté le bus.**) Have individuals respond to each sentence with one of the responses presented in the activity. (**Ça m'arrive aussi. Ça ne risque pas de m'arriver.**)

These activities check for comprehension only. Students should not yet be expected to produce language modeled in **Mise en train.**

1 Tu as compris?
See answers below.

1. What kind of mood is Céline in? Why?
2. Name three unfortunate things that happened to Céline.
3. How does Hector react to Céline's story?
4. What are Céline's plans for the afternoon?

2 Mets en ordre

Mets les phrases dans le bon ordre d'après la journée de Céline dans ***C'est pas mon jour!*** See answers below.

1. D'abord,...
2. Ensuite,...
3. Et puis,...
4. Après ça,...
5. Et puis,...
6. Finalement,...

elle n'avait pas ses devoirs.

son réveil n'a pas sonné.

Hector a renversé son verre sur sa jupe.

elle est arrivée à l'école en retard.

elle a raté son bus.

elle a eu dix à son interro de maths.

3 Cherche les expressions

What do Céline and Hector say in each of these situations?

1. Hector apologizes.
2. Céline makes light of an accident.
3. Hector wants to know what happened to Céline.
4. Céline complains about her bad day.
5. Céline is annoyed.
6. Hector consoles Céline.

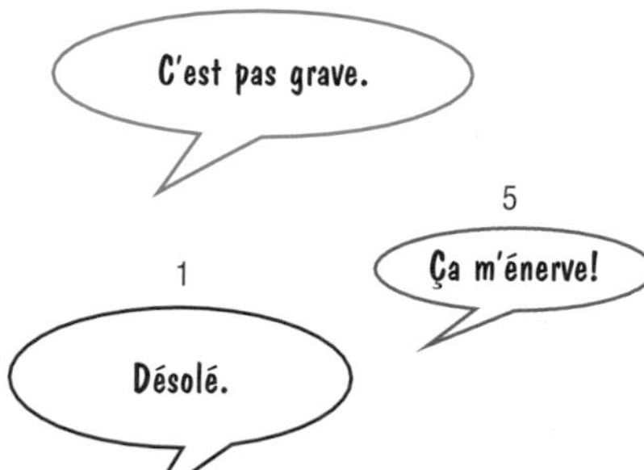

4 Ça t'arrive aussi?

Si Céline et Hector te disent les choses suivantes, comment est-ce que tu réponds? Est-ce que tu dis **Ça m'arrive aussi** *(That happens to me, too)* ou **Ça ne risque pas de m'arriver** *(That will never happen to me)?*

Je me suis réveillé(e) en retard.

Je suis arrivé(e) à l'école en retard.

J'ai couru pour attraper le bus.

J'oublie mes devoirs quelquefois.

5 Et maintenant, à toi

Est-ce que, comme Céline, tu as déjà passé une très mauvaise journée? Qu'est-ce qui est arrivé? Qu'est-ce que tu as fait?

Answers

1
1. bad mood; Everything went wrong.
2. *Possible answers:* Her alarm didn't go off, she woke up late, she didn't have time for breakfast, she missed her bus, she got to school late, she forgot her homework, she got a 10 on her math quiz, Hector spilled his drink on her.
3. He sympathizes with her and consoles her.
4. to go to bed so nothing else can happen to her

2
1. D'abord, son réveil n'a pas sonné.
2. Ensuite, elle a raté son bus.
3. Et puis, elle est arrivée à l'école en retard.
4. Après ça, elle n'avait pas ses devoirs.
5. Et puis, elle a eu dix à son interro de maths.
6. Finalement, Hector a renversé son verre sur sa jupe.

Comprehension Check

Tactile/Visual Learners

2 Have students write the sequencing expressions, as well as the sentence fragments, on separate, small strips of paper. Then, have them put the sentences in order, according to Céline's day, and attach the appropriate sequencing expressions.

Teaching Suggestion

3 Have students pair off to do this activity. Assign each pair numbers 1 and 2, 3 and 4, or 5 and 6.

STANDARDS: 1.2

Objective Expressing concern for someone

WA3 TOURAINE-5

Ministère de l'Education Nationale
LYCÉE ALFRED KASTLER
ETABLISSEMENT PUBLIC D'ENSEIGNEMENT GENERAL ET TECHNOLOGIQUE
29 Boulevard GUITTON · Tél: 02.51.36.24.46

carnet de correspondance

5
Absent le 11/04 et 12/05
MOTIF hypoglycémie et gastro-entérite
Le Conseiller d'Education ou Le Directeur Adjoint,

6
Absent le ....
MOTIF ....
Le Conseiller d'Education ou Le Directeur Adjoint,

BULLETIN D'ABSENCE
L'élève ....
fréquentant la classe de ....
a été absent le .... ou sera absent le ....
ou du .... au ....
MOTIF ....
Le ....
Signature des Parents,

BILLET DE RETARD

Elève: Céline Déroulède
Classe: 3ème
Motif: n'a pas entendu son réveil et a raté son bus
Signature du proviseur:

Alfred Kastler
Le Surveillant Général

6 **Qu'est-ce que c'est?**

Lisons/Parlons A ton avis, qu'est-ce que c'est, **un billet de retard?** Quelles informations il y a sur un billet de retard? Qu'est-ce qui est arrivé à Céline ce matin?

a tardy slip; name of student, grade level, reason for being late, signature of principal; Céline did not hear her alarm clock, and she missed her bus.

Note culturelle

If you're late to school in France, you're required to go to the principal's office to explain your tardiness. The person in charge fills out a form in your **carnet de correspondance,** a special notebook in which your behavior is recorded. The **carnet** is used less with older students. Parents must sign any notes written in the **carnet** to show that they are aware of their child's conduct.

Cultures and Communities

Culture Note

Le proviseur (Madame le proviseur) is the director of the **lycée.** Most students might never see the **proviseur.** In **école primaire,** the head of the school is called **le directeur (la directrice).**

Teaching Suggestion

After students have done Activity 6 and read the **Note culturelle,** ask the following questions: **Céline est en quelle classe? Quel est son nom de famille? Elle va à quel lycée? Qu'est-ce qu'on lui a donné? Qui a signé le billet? Pourquoi est-ce que Céline est arrivée en retard?**

Teaching Resources
pp. 133–137

PRINT

- Lesson Planner, p. 22
- TPR Storytelling Book, pp. 32–33
- Listening Activities, pp. 35–36, 39
- Activities for Communication, pp. 25–26, 95, 98, 145–146
- Travaux pratiques de grammaire, pp. 37–40
- Grammar Tutor for Students of French, Chapter 5
- Cahier d'activités, pp. 50–52
- Testing Program, pp. 105–108
- Alternative Assessment Guide, p. 36
- Student Make-Up Assignments, Chapter 5

MEDIA 

- One-Stop Planner
- Audio Compact Discs, CD 5, Trs. 3–5, 13, 19–20
- Teaching Transparencies: 5-1, 5-A; **Grammaire supplémentaire** Answers; Travaux pratiques de grammaire Answers
- Interactive CD-ROM Tutor, Disc 2

Bell Work

Write the following scrambled monologue on the board or on a transparency. Have students rearrange the sentences to form a logical sequence of events.

1. **Donc, je suis arrivée au lycée en retard.**
2. **Je n'ai pas pris mon petit déjeuner.**
3. **Mon réveil n'a pas sonné.**
4. **J'ai couru pour attraper le bus.**
5. **Je me suis réveillée en retard.**
6. **Mais bien sûr, je l'ai raté.**

(*Answers:* 3, 5, 2, 4, 6, 1)

STANDARDS: 1.2, 2.1, 3.2, 4.2

Teaching Resources
pp. 133–137

PRINT

- Lesson Planner, p. 22
- TPR Storytelling Book, pp. 32–33
- Listening Activities, pp. 35–36, 39
- Activities for Communication, pp. 25–26, 95, 98, 145–146
- Travaux pratiques de grammaire, pp. 37–40
- Grammar Tutor for Students of French, Chapter 5
- Cahier d'activités, pp. 50–52
- Testing Program, pp. 105–108
- Alternative Assessment Guide, p. 36
- Student Make-Up Assignments, Chapter 5

MEDIA 

- One-Stop Planner
- Audio Compact Discs, CD 5, Trs. 3–5, 13, 19–20
- Teaching Transparencies: 5-1, 5-A; **Grammaire supplémentaire** Answers; Travaux pratiques de grammaire Answers
- Interactive CD-ROM Tutor, Disc 2

Presenting Vocabulaire

Gather props to present the sentences. Act out each sentence and have students repeat after you, mimicking your gestures. Then, call out sentences in random order and have students mime the appropriate gestures for each sentence. Next, ask nine volunteers to come to the front of the class. Have each one repeat a sentence after you and mime the gestures. The other students should continue to participate by repeating and miming as well.

Vocabulaire

Quelle journée!

CD-ROM 2 DVD 1

J'ai passé une journée épouvantable!

D'abord, **je n'ai pas entendu mon réveil.**

Ensuite, **j'ai raté une marche. Je suis tombé.**

J'ai déchiré ma chemise...

... et **j'ai perdu** mon livre de maths.

Après ça, **j'ai raté le bus** et **je suis arrivé** à l'école **en retard.**

Ensuite, **le prof a rendu les interros** et **j'ai eu une mauvaise note...**

... donc, **j'ai été collé.**

Finalement, **j'ai reçu mon bulletin trimestriel.** Quelle journée!

Cahier d'activités, pp. 50–51, Act. 2–5

Travaux pratiques de grammaire, pp. 37–38, Act. 1–4

Communication for All Students

Slower Pace

7 Before you play the recording, ask students to imagine what excuse each illustration might suggest. Then, ask questions about the illustrations. **(Sept sur vingt, c'est une bonne ou une mauvaise note? Le bus arrive ou il part? Le bureau est bien rangé ou il est en désordre? La fille est heureuse ou triste?)**

Challenge

8 Have partners create additional sentence starters and completions and present them to the class on a transparency for other students to match.

7 **Quelle est ton excuse?** See scripts on p. 127G. **1.** c **2.** d **3.** a **4.** b

CD 5 Tr. 3

Ecoutons Listen to these dialogues and decide which of the excuses illustrated below is given in each one.

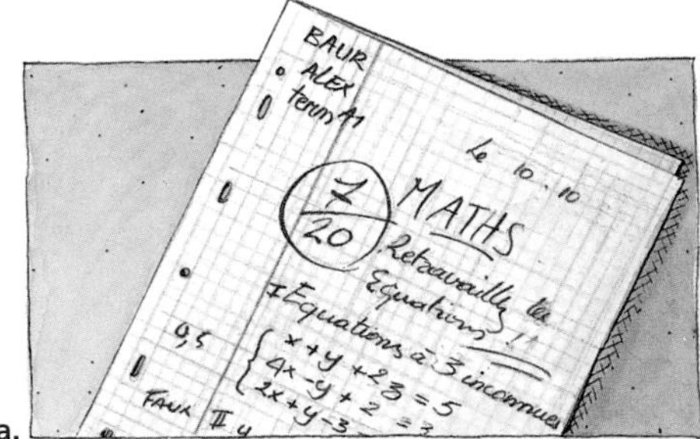

a.

b.

c.

d.

8 **La suite**

Lisons Complète chaque phrase de façon logique.

1. J'ai déchiré mon jean... c
2. J'ai reçu mon bulletin trimestriel... d
3. J'ai perdu mes devoirs d'histoire... a
4. Je n'ai pas entendu mon réveil... e
5. Mon prof n'était pas content... b

a. donc, mon prof était furieux, et j'ai eu zéro.
b. parce que j'ai perdu mon livre de français.
c. quand je suis tombé(e).
d. et j'ai eu de très bonnes notes!
e. donc, j'ai raté le bus.

Comment dit-on...?

Expressing concern for someone

Ça n'a pas l'air d'aller. *You look like something's wrong.*
Qu'est-ce qui t'arrive? *What's wrong?*
Qu'est-ce qui se passe? *What's going on?*
Raconte! *Tell me!*

Cahier d'activités, p. 51, Act. 7

9 **Les excuses de Luc** See scripts on p. 127G.

CD 5 Tr. 4

Ecoutons Luc is late for his lunch meeting with Francine at a café. Listen to his excuses and decide which of the following happened to make him late.

(1.) Luc est rentré chez lui à midi.
2. Il a trouvé son livre d'histoire.
(3.) Il a raté une marche et il est tombé.
4. Il a pris le bus pour aller au café.

Cultures and Communities

Culture Note

Call attention to illustration **a** in Activity 7. In labeling their school papers, French students usually write their last names first in capital letters, followed by their first names in lowercase letters. They usually don't write their class periods since the school day isn't divided into class periods. The **term A1** below this student's name refers to **terminale A1,** which means that the student is in **terminale** and has chosen section **A1** of the **baccalauréat.** However, in 1993, the French government simplified the nomenclature of **bac** choices, which had ranged from **A** to **E,** and from **1** to **3** for each letter. Currently, there are only three sections for the general **bac: ES (économique et social), L (littéraire),** and **S (scientifique).** There are also four technological sections.

Première étape

CHAPITRE 5

Game

Qu'est-ce qui se passe? On a photocopy of *Teaching Transparency Master 5-A,* number the illustrations 1–9. Then, distribute photocopies of the numbered transparency master to each student. Select one student to be the "judge" and have the other students form groups of four or five. Give each group of students a container of slips of paper on which are written the numbers 1–12. To play the game, students take turns drawing a slip of paper and telling what happened in the illustration that corresponds to the number they drew. For example, if a student draws the number two, he or she would say **Je n'ai pas entendu mon réveil,** and two points would be awarded for the correct answer. The judge makes final decisions about the acceptability of the answers. A student who draws the numbers 10, 11, or 12 loses a turn.

Presenting
Comment dit-on... ?

Ask students to imagine that something unfortunate just happened to them and to be prepared to talk about it. Then, go around the room asking students what's wrong. **(Ça n'a pas l'air d'aller, Paul. Qu'est-ce qui t'arrive? Qu'est-ce qui se passe, Anne?)**

Teaching Suggestion

9 Have students listen to the recording a second time and identify the expressions of concern that Francine uses. Then, have them correct the false statements.

Teaching Resources
pp. 133–137

PRINT 

- Lesson Planner, p. 22
- TPR Storytelling Book, pp. 32–33
- Listening Activities, pp. 35–36, 39
- Activities for Communication, pp. 25–26, 95, 98, 145–146
- Travaux pratiques de grammaire, pp. 37–40
- Grammar Tutor for Students of French, Chapter 5
- Cahier d'activités, pp. 50–52
- Testing Program, pp. 105–108
- Alternative Assessment Guide, p. 36
- Student Make-Up Assignments, Chapter 5

MEDIA 

- One-Stop Planner
- Audio Compact Discs, CD 5, Trs. 3–5, 13, 19–20
- Teaching Transparencies: 5-1, 5-A; **Grammaire supplémentaire** Answers, Travaux pratiques de grammaire Answers
- Interactive CD-ROM Tutor, Disc 2

Presenting Grammaire

The passé composé Have students look at the sentences in the **Vocabulaire** on page 134. Explain that since the boy is talking about what *happened,* he's using the **passé composé**. Ask students how the **passé composé** is formed. List the past participles in the **Vocabulaire** and have students try to deduce the infinitives. Then, remind students how the negative is formed in the **passé composé** and call on individuals to make the sentences in the **Vocabulaire** on page 134 negative.

10 Qu'est-ce que tu dis?

Parlons/Ecrivons Imagine que tu rencontres Jean, Colette et Gérard à la fin de la journée. Demande-leur comment leur journée s'est passée. A ton avis, comment ils vont répondre?
See answers below.

Jean

Colette

Gérard

11 Encore en retard!

Parlons Tu es le proviseur du lycée! Ton/Ta camarade est un(e) élève qui arrive à l'école en retard. Demande-lui pourquoi il/elle est en retard et remplis un billet de retard. N'oublie pas de le signer! Ensuite, changez de rôle.

Ça n'a pas l'air d'aller.
Vous vous appelez comment?
Qu'est-ce qui vous est arrivé?
Vous êtes en quelle classe?
en terminale
en seconde
en première

Grammaire

The *passé composé* with *avoir*

CD-ROM 2 DVD 1

You already know how to say that something happened in the past. For most verbs, you use a form of **avoir** and the past participle of the main verb.

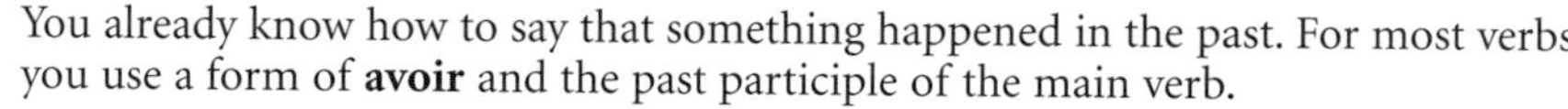
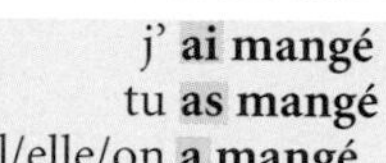
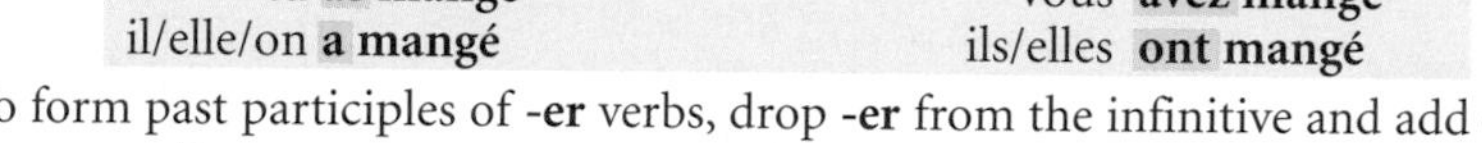

j' **ai mangé**	nous **avons mangé**
tu **as mangé**	vous **avez mangé**
il/elle/on **a mangé**	ils/elles **ont mangé**

- To form past participles of **-er** verbs, drop **-er** from the infinitive and add **-é:**
  J'ai **raté** le bus.
- To form past participles of **-re** verbs, drop **-re** from the infinitive and add **-u:**
  Zut! On a **perdu** le match!
- To form past participles of **-ir** verbs, drop **-ir** from the infinitive and add **-i:**
  Enfin! On a **fini!**
- Many verbs have an irregular past participle, just as they do in English.
  Il a **été** collé aujourd'hui. (**être**)
  Vous avez **fait** vos devoirs? (**faire**)
  On a **eu** une interro. (**avoir**)
  J'ai **reçu** mon bulletin. (**recevoir**)
  Elle a **pris** un sandwich. (**prendre**)
  Il a **bu** de l'eau. (**boire**)
  Tu as **lu** ce roman? (**lire**)
  On a **vu** un film hier. (**voir**)
- To say that something didn't happen, put **ne... pas** around the form of **avoir:**
  Je **n'ai pas** entendu mon réveil.

Grammaire supplémentaire, pp. 148–149, Act. 1–4

Cahier d'activités, p. 52, Act. 8–9

Travaux pratiques de grammaire, pp. 39–40, Act. 5–8

Connections and Comparisons

Language-to-Language

In many languages, there are verbs that have irregular forms. If you have students who are native speakers of Spanish, have them identify some verbs that have irregular forms in the preterite in Spanish: **ser** *(to be),* **hacer** *(to make* or *to do),* **tener** *(to have),* **ver** *(to see).* Students may recognize that some of these corresponding verbs in French also have irregular forms in the **passé composé.** Ask students to identify some irregular verbs in English in the past tense. Ask them why they think certain verbs have historically become irregular.

STANDARDS: 1.1, 4.1

12 **Grammaire en contexte** See scripts and answers on p. 127G.

Ecoutons Listen to these students. Are they talking about something that is happening now or something that happened in the past?

CD 5 Tr. 5

13 **Grammaire en contexte** 

Ecrivons Est-ce que ces personnes ont passé une bonne ou une mauvaise journée? Ecris trois phrases pour décrire ce qui est arrivé à chaque personne.

Je	perdre	une bonne note en...
Mes profs	rater	le devoir de...
En français, on	prendre	l'interro de...
Mon (Ma) meilleur(e) ami(e)	avoir	du deltaplane
?	faire	le réveil
	ne pas entendre	collé
	rencontrer	20 dollars
	trouver	un match entre... et...
	regarder	le bus pour aller...
	recevoir	une vedette de cinéma
	voir	un film
	être	?
	?	

14 **L'heure de la sortie**

Ecrivons/Parlons Fais une liste de quatre activités que tes camarades font peut-être après l'école. Ensuite, demande à un(e) camarade s'il/si elle a fait ces activités hier.

Exemple **—Tu as joué au foot hier?**
—Non, j'ai joué au tennis.

15 **Qu'est-ce qu'on a tous fait?**

Parlons In groups of four, try to find three things that everyone did last weekend and three things that no one did. Report your findings to the class, using **On a tous...** and **On n'a pas...** As the groups report, note the activities that most people did and didn't do.

16 **Jeu de rôle**

Parlons With a partner, choose two of these situations and take turns expressing concern for each other and asking and explaining what happened.

1. Tu arrives au cours de maths avec vingt minutes de retard. Le prof n'est pas content!
2. Tu n'étais pas à la boum de ton ami(e) samedi soir. Il/Elle veut savoir ce qui s'est passé.
3. Tu arrives chez toi à onze heures du soir. Ton père (ta mère) est furieux (furieuse).
4. Tu n'es pas allé(e) faire les magasins avec tes copains hier après l'école. Ton ami(e) te téléphone pour savoir pourquoi.

Additional Practice

12 On separate slips of paper, write an infinitive, the words **le présent** or **le passé composé,** and a subject in parentheses. Have pairs of students draw a slip of paper and work together to write a sentence, using the subject and the verb in the specified tense. Then, have one partner read the sentence aloud. The class will decide if the student is talking about something that is happening now or something that happened in the past.

Teaching Suggestion

14 For additional sports and weekend activities, refer students to the **Si tu as oublié...** section and the Additional Vocabulary in the back of the book.

Building on Previous Skills

15 To re-enter leisure activities and numbers, write several activities on the board. Have volunteers poll the class to see how many people did the activities last weekend. **(Qui a écouté de la musique?)** Have the poll takers count their classmates' raised hands aloud in French before they write the totals on the board.

Assess

- Testing Program, pp. 105–108
  Quiz 5-1A, Quiz 5-1B
  Audio CD 5, Tr. 13
- Student Make-Up Assignments, Chapter 5, Alternative Quiz
- Alternative Assessment Guide, p. 36

Communication for All Students

Challenge

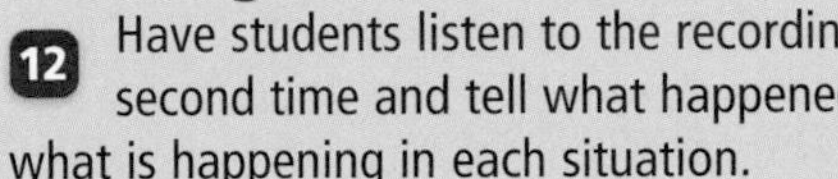

12 Have students listen to the recording a second time and tell what happened or what is happening in each situation.

Group Work

Use Activity 16 to close this **étape.** Form small groups and assign one of the four situations to each one. Group members should work together to create the conversation and present it to the class.

Possible Answers

10 Jean: —Qu'est-ce qui s'est passé?
—Je suis arrivé en retard au lycée.
Colette: —Qu'est-ce qui t'arrive?
—J'ai oublié mes devoirs.
Gérard: —Qu'est-ce qui s'est passé à l'école?
—J'ai eu huit à mon interro.

Teaching Resources
pp. 138–141

PRINT 

- Lesson Planner, p. 23
- TPR Storytelling Book, pp. 34–35
- Listening Activities, pp. 36, 40
- Activities for Communication, pp. 27–28, 96, 98–99, 145–146
- Travaux pratiques de grammaire, pp. 41–43
- Grammar Tutor for Students of French, Chapter 5
- Cahier d'activités, pp. 53–55
- Testing Program, pp. 109–112
- Alternative Assessment Guide, p. 36
- Student Make-Up Assignments, Chapter 5

MEDIA

- One-Stop Planner
- Audio Compact Discs, CD 5, Trs. 6, 14, 21–22
- Teaching Transparencies: 5-2; **Grammaire supplémentaire** Answers; Travaux pratiques de grammaire Answers
- Interactive CD-ROM Tutor, Disc 2

Bell Work
Have students write down three things that happened to them during the week or on the weekend.

Teaching Suggestion
Play the role of Benoît and tell the class about your bad day, using gestures and props. Then, smile and play the role of Yves, telling the class about your good day. Distribute typed copies of randomly ordered sentences from Yves and Benoît's conversation. Have students label two columns on a sheet of paper: **une bonne journée** and **une mauvaise journée.** Have them rewrite the sentences from the conversation in the appropriate column.

Deuxième étape

Objectives Inquiring; expressing satisfaction and frustration; sympathizing with and consoling someone

WA3 TOURAINE-5

YVES — Oh là là, ça a pas l'air d'aller, toi! Qu'est-ce qui s'est passé?

BENOIT — Ben, j'ai reçu un ballon dans la figure en gym et j'ai dû aller à l'infirmerie! Décidément, c'est pas mon jour, aujourd'hui!

YVES — Ah, bon? Qu'est-ce qui t'est arrivé d'autre?

BENOIT — Tout a été de travers! D'abord, je suis arrivé en retard à l'école. Ensuite, je suis tombé dans l'escalier. Et puis, à la cantine, quelqu'un a renversé une assiette de spaghettis sur mon pantalon.

YVES — Pauvre vieux!

BENOIT — Enfin... Et toi, au fait? J'espère que ta journée s'est mieux passée que la mienne.

YVES — Oui, elle s'est même très bien passée. En géo, j'ai eu 18. Ensuite, en français, j'ai eu 16. Le prof a même lu ma rédaction à la classe! Après, à la récré, Julien m'a invité à son anniversaire. Et finalement, en anglais, on a vu un bon film.

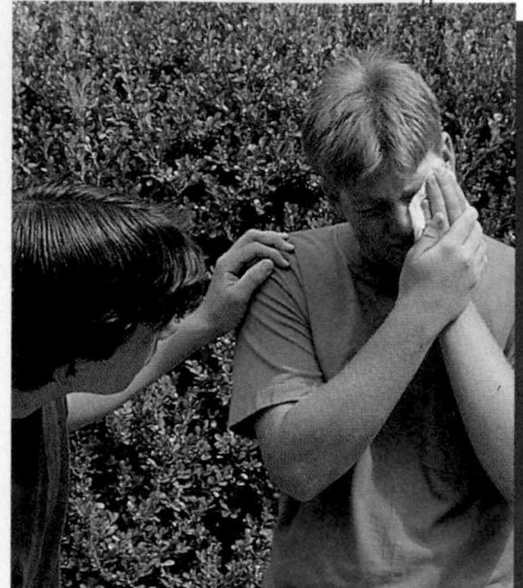

17 C'est Yves ou Benoît?
Lisons

1. Il a eu une bonne note en géo. Yves
2. Il est allé à l'infirmerie. Benoît
3. Il a vu un bon film. Yves
4. Quelqu'un a renversé une assiette de spaghettis sur son pantalon. Benoît
5. Il est arrivé en retard à l'école. Benoît
6. Il a eu 16 en français. Yves
7. Il va aller à une fête. Yves
8. Il est tombé dans l'escalier. Benoît

Many students who do not live close enough to go home for lunch eat in the school cafeteria **(la cantine).** The meals served follow the French sequence: a first course, a main dish with vegetables, then cheese, fruit, or yogurt. Students might stand in line for their meals, or they might be served at their table. Since the lunch period lasts for about two hours, students usually have time to study, play a game, or go to a café after they eat.

Communication for All Students

Slower Pace
17 Have students divide a piece of paper in half vertically. The first column should be labeled "+" and the second column "–". Then have students look at the sentences in Activity 17. They should determine which sentences recount happy occurrences and which relate unhappy incidents. They should then write the former in the plus column and the latter in the minus column. Finally, have them read the dialogue and decide whether something good or bad happened to Yves or Benoît.

Challenge
17 After students have completed the activity, have them imagine they had a particularly good or bad day at school yesterday. Ask them to write a short paragraph about four things that happened to them.

STANDARDS: 2.1, 3.2, 4.2

Comment dit-on...?

Inquiring; expressing satisfaction and frustration

CD-ROM 2 DVD 1

To inquire:

Comment ça s'est passé? *How did it go?*
Comment s'est passée ta journée? *How was your day?*
Comment s'est passé ton week-end? *How was your weekend?*
Comment se sont passées tes vacances? *How was your vacation?*

To express satisfaction:

C'était... *It was . . .*
incroyable! *amazing!*
super!
génial!
Ça s'est très bien passé!
It went really well!
Quelle journée (formidable)!
What a (great) day!
Quel week-end (formidable)!
What a (great) weekend!

To express frustration:

C'était incroyable!
It was unbelievably bad!
J'ai passé une journée horrible!
I had a terrible day!
C'est pas mon jour!
It's just not my day!
Tout a été de travers!
Everything went wrong!
Quelle journée!/Quel week-end!
What a (bad) day!/ . . . weekend!

Cahier d'activités, p. 53, Act. 11–12

Travaux pratiques de grammaire, p. 41, Act. 9–10

18 Comment s'est passé leur week-end? See scripts and answers on p. 127H.

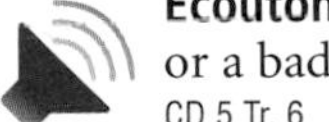

Ecoutons Listen as some friends disuss their weekends. Did they have a good weekend or a bad one?
CD 5 Tr. 6

19 Sondage

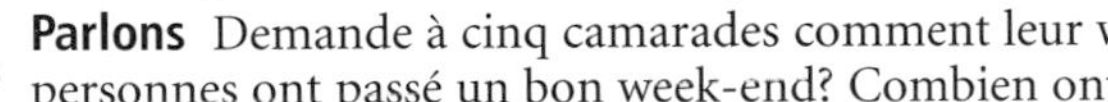

Parlons Demande à cinq camarades comment leur week-end s'est passé. Combien de personnes ont passé un bon week-end? Combien ont passé un mauvais week-end?

20 Et toi, qu'est-ce que tu as fait?

Parlons Demande à un(e) camarade comment sa journée s'est passée hier. Ton/Ta camarade va décrire sa journée et parler de trois choses positives ou négatives.

Tu te rappelles?

Do you remember how to pronounce the nasal sound [ɛ̃] in **incroyable?** When you see the letters **in, im, ain, aim,** or **(i)en,** don't pronounce the *n* sound as in the English word *fine,* but make a pure nasal sound where part of the air goes through the back of your mouth and nose, as in the French word **fin.** Try pronouncing these words with the nasal [ɛ̃]: **bulletin, bien, faim, soudain.** Remember that if another vowel follows the **n** or **m, (inadmissible),** there is no nasal sound.

A la française

There are many expressions you can use to show interest and get someone to continue a story in English. You can do the same in French. Say **Ah bon?** or **Ah oui?** *(Really?),* **Et après?** *(And then what?),* and **Et ensuite?** *(And what next?).*

Communication for All Students

Visual Learners/Slower Pace

Write the expressions from **Comment dit-on... ?** on separate strips of transparency and label three columns on a transparency: *To inquire, To express satisfaction,* and *To express frustration.* Place the transparency on the overhead projector and the strips one at a time in random order. Have students tell you under which heading to place each strip. You might read each expression aloud with the appropriate intonation to help auditory learners.

Challenge

18 Play the recording again and have students tell what the speakers did over the weekend.

Deuxième étape

CHAPITRE 5

Presenting Comment dit-on... ?

Have students ask you how your day was, using the informal questions in the dialogue on page 138 as a model. Smile or look sad as you respond with one of the expressions in **Comment dit-on... ?** Then, say several expressions and have students tell whether you are inquiring, expressing satisfaction, or expressing frustration.

Teacher Note

Explain that **Quel week-end!/Quelle journée!** and **C'était incroyable!** can be used to express both satisfaction and frustration. Tell students that they will need to rely on context, gestures, facial expressions, and intonation to determine whether each expression is used to convey satisfaction or frustration.

Teaching Suggestions

20 After the pairs have finished their conversation, ask volunteers to come to the front of the class and tell about their partner's day. **(Hier, Claire a passé une bonne journée. Elle...)** Have the class take notes during the presentations. Then, question students about what happened to their classmates, according to their presentations. **(Qui a été collé? Qui a eu cent à son interro d'algèbre?)**

Tu te rappelles? Have students look at the Additional Vocabulary at the back of the book to find as many words as possible that contain the nasal [ɛ̃] sound. Then, have them write and act out short skits, using as many of the words as possible.

STANDARDS: 1.1, 1.2, 4.1, 5.1, 5.2

Teaching Resources
pp. 138–141

PRINT

- Lesson Planner, p. 23
- TPR Storytelling Book, pp. 34–35
- Listening Activities, pp. 36, 40
- Activities for Communication, pp. 27–28, 96, 98–99, 145–146
- Travaux pratiques de grammaire, pp. 41–43
- Grammar Tutor for Students of French, Chapter 5
- Cahier d'activités, pp. 53–55
- Testing Program, pp. 109–112
- Alternative Assessment Guide, p. 36
- Student Make-Up Assignments, Chapter 5

MEDIA 

- One-Stop Planner
- Audio Compact Discs, CD 5, Trs. 6, 14, 21–22
- Teaching Transparencies: 5-2; **Grammaire supplémentaire** Answers; Travaux pratiques de grammaire Answers
- Interactive CD-ROM Tutor, Disc 2

Presenting Grammaire

The *passé composé* with *être* Prepare two sets of large cards of two different colors. On one set, write verbs that use **avoir** as their helping verb in the **passé composé.** On the other set, write verbs that use **être.** Draw two columns on the board (one for **avoir** and the other for **être).** Choose a card and create a sentence in the **passé composé** using the verb you selected. Write the sentence in the appropriate column and tape the card next to it. When you have at least six sentences in each column, ask students what difference they notice between the verbs.

Grammaire

Introduction to the *passé composé* with *être*

You already know how to form the **passé composé** with **avoir** by using the present-tense form of **avoir** and the past participle of the verb you want to use.

However, some verbs use **être** instead of **avoir** as the helping verb in the **passé composé.** Many of the verbs that use **être** in the **passé composé** are verbs of motion, such as **tomber, aller, arriver, sortir,** and **partir.** Notice that when you write these forms, the past participle agrees with the subject of the verb. You'll learn more about this in Chapter 6.

je	**suis tombé(e)**	nous	**sommes tombé(e)s**
tu	**es tombé(e)**	vous	**êtes tombé(e)(s)**
il/elle/on	**est tombé(e)(s)**	ils/elles	**sont tombé(e)s**

You also use **être** to form the **passé composé** of all reflexive verbs. You'll learn more about reflexive verbs in the **passé composé** in Chapter 7.

je me	**suis levé(e)**	nous nous	**sommes levé(e)s**
tu t'	**es levé(e)**	vous vous	**êtes levé(e)(s)**
il/elle/on s'	**est levé(e)(s)**	ils/elles se	**sont levé(e)s**

Grammaire supplémentaire, pp. 149–151, Act. 5–9

Cahier d'activités, pp. 53–54, Act. 13–14

Travaux pratiques de grammaire, pp. 42–43, Act. 11–14

21 Grammaire en contexte

Ecrivons Tu n'es pas allé(e) à l'école hier parce que tu étais malade. Alors ton ami Patrick t'a écrit un petit mot. Il te raconte ce qui s'est passé à l'école. Complète le petit mot de Patrick avec le passé composé des verbes entre parenthèses. Utilise le passé composé avec l'auxiliaire qui convient. N'oublie pas de faire l'accord du participe passé quand c'est nécessaire.

1. ai passé **2.** ai eu **3.** suis allé **4.** ai rencontré **5.** a raté **6.** est tombée **7.** est arrivée **8.** a été **9.** est sortis **10.** a vu **11.** est partie **12.** sommes allés

Moi, hier, je (j') __1__ (passer) une journée formidable! A l'école, je (j') __2__ (avoir) une très bonne note en histoire-géo. L'après-midi, je (j') __3__ (aller) à la bibliothèque et je (j') __4__ (rencontrer) une fille super! Par contre, pour Sophie, tout a été de travers! D'abord, elle __5__ (rater) une marche et elle __6__ (tomber). Et puis, elle __7__ (arriver) à l'école en retard, alors elle __8__ (être) collée. Pauvre Sophie! Le soir, Sophie et moi, on __9__ (sortir) avec Yves, Laura et Aline. On __10__ (voir) un film super au cinéma. Sophie __11__ (partir) tout de suite après le film pour étudier pour son interro de maths, mais nous, nous __12__ (aller) au café. C'était sympa!

22 Comment se sont passées tes vacances?

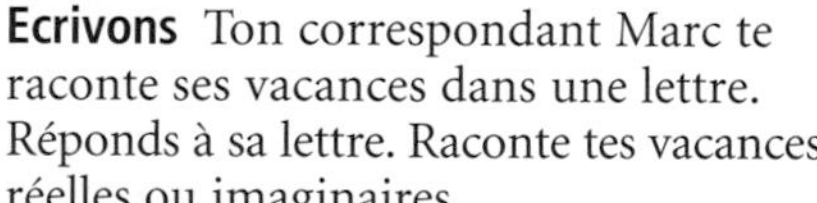

Ecrivons Ton correspondant Marc te raconte ses vacances dans une lettre. Réponds à sa lettre. Raconte tes vacances, réelles ou imaginaires.

Salut!
Comment ça s'est passé, tes vacances? Nous, on est partis faire du ski dans les Alpes. C'était super! J'ai fait du ski pour la première fois. Je suis souvent tombé. Les montagnes sont magnifiques. Attends de voir mes photos. Et toi? Tu as passé de bonnes vacances? Qu'est-ce que tu as fait? Raconte-moi!
Marc

Connections and Comparisons

Music Link

After presenting the **Grammaire,** distribute copies of the song *A la claire fontaine (Listening Activities,* Level 1, page 34). Play the song on Audio CD 5 (Level 1) as students read the lyrics. Then, ask students to underline the verbs that are in the **passé composé.** For each verb, have a volunteer tell you which helping verb is used and why.

STANDARDS: 1.3, 3.1, 4.1

23 Devine!

Lisons/Parlons Put the letters you wrote for Activity 22 together face down. Each person selects a letter and reads it silently. The rest of the group asks yes-no questions to determine where the writer went and what he or she did on vacation.

Exemple **—Cette personne est allée en France?** **—Oui.**
—Elle est allée à la plage? **—Non.**
—Elle a fait du ski? **—Non.**
— ___?___

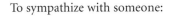

Comment dit-on...?

Sympathizing with and consoling someone

CD-ROM 2 DVD 1

To sympathize with someone:

Oh là là! *Oh no!*
C'est pas de chance, ça! *Tough luck!*
Pauvre vieux/vieille! *You poor thing!*

To console someone:

Courage! *Hang in there!*
Ça va aller mieux. *It'll get better.*
T'en fais pas. *Don't worry.*
C'est pas grave. *It's not serious.*

Cahier d'activités, p. 55, Act. 16–17

24 Les pauvres!

Parlons/Ecrivons What would you say to sympathize with these people and console them? See answers below.

1.

2.

3.

25 Une mauvaise journée

Ecrivons Fais une liste de cinq choses qui peuvent arriver quand on passe une mauvaise journée.

Exemple **Ma journée se passe mal si je ne prends pas mon petit déjeuner.**

26 La plus mauvaise journée de ma vie

Parlons Tout ce que tu as écrit dans ta liste de l'activité 25 est arrivé hier! Raconte ta journée à un(e) ami(e). Ton ami(e) veut savoir tout ce qui est arrivé. Il/Elle te répond et essaie de te consoler. Ensuite, changez de rôle.

Communication for All Students

Visual Learners

Have students bring to class a magazine picture of someone who is sad, hurt, or upset. Tell them to mount it on construction paper and attach to it a caption telling what happened. Form groups of five and have group members show their picture and read the caption to the group. They then pass the pictures to the other group members, who each write an expression of sympathy or consolation under the caption. Students should vary the expressions they use.

Deuxième étape

CHAPITRE 5

Presenting Comment dit-on... ?

Have students find the expressions in the **Mise en train** on pages 130 and 131 that Hector uses to sympathize with and console Céline. **(T'inquiète pas. C'est pas grave. Ce n'est pas dramatique. Ça va aller mieux.)** Write them on the board and add others from **Comment dit-on... ?** Have students say the expressions.

Group Work

Form groups of six. In each group, distribute six different paragraph-starters. **(Hier, quand je suis arrivé(e) chez moi,...)** To start, each member completes the sentence and continues writing for one minute. When you call time, students pass their papers to the next student in the group, who adds to the paragraph. With each pass, extend the time. When everyone has written on every paper, have students choose the best paragraph within their group and read it to the class.

Assess

- Testing Program, pp. 109–112 Quiz 5-2A, Quiz 5-2B Audio CD 5, Tr. 14
- Student Make-Up Assignments, Chapter 5, Alternative Quiz
- Alternative Assessment Guide, p. 36

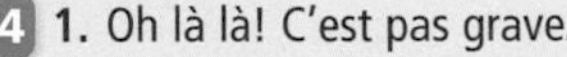

Possible Answers

24
1. Oh là là! C'est pas grave.
2. C'est pas de chance ça!
3. Courage, t'en fais pas!

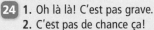

Teaching Resources
pp. 142–144

PRINT
- Lesson Planner, p. 24
- TPR Storytelling Book, pp. 36–37
- Listening Activities, pp. 37, 41
- Activities for Communication, pp. 29–30, 97, 99, 145–146
- Travaux pratiques de grammaire, p. 44
- Grammar Tutor for Students of French, Chapter 5
- Cahier d'activités, pp. 56–58
- Testing Program, pp. 113–116
- Alternative Assessment Guide, p. 36
- Student Make-Up Assignments, Chapter 5

MEDIA 
- One-Stop Planner
- Audio Compact Discs, CD 5, Trs. 7, 15, 23–24
- Teaching Transparencies: 5-3; **Grammaire supplémentaire** Answers; Travaux pratiques de grammaire Answers
- Interactive CD-ROM Tutor, Disc 2

Bell Work
Have students list in French four good and two unfortunate things that happened to them during the past week.

Teaching Suggestion
For listening and speaking practice, ask the following questions about the **bulletins: Comment s'appelle leur lycée? Caroline est en quelle classe? Elle a combien de cours? Combien Jean a eu en latin? Que dit son prof de latin?**

Thinking Critically
Comparing and Contrasting
Ask students how the **bulletins** are similar to or different from their own report cards.

Troisième étape

Objectives Giving reasons and making excuses; congratulating and reprimanding someone

WA3 TOURAINE-5

Lycée Balzac
Académie de Tours

BULLETIN TRIMESTRIEL

NOM et prénom : PUECH Jean Classe de 2de 7

MATIERES D'ENSEIGNEMENT	MOYENNE DE L'ELEVE	APPRECIATIONS
Français	15	Travail sérieux
Mathématiques	12	A fait beaucoup de progrès
Physique-Chimie	15	Bon élève
SVT*	9	Travail moyen.
Histoire-Géographie	16	Bon travail
Anglais	13	Résultats encourageants
Latin	11	A fait beaucoup de progrès
Arts plastiques	10	Peut mieux faire
Education physique	10	Doit s'appliquer davantage

Lycée Balzac
Académie de Tours

BULLETIN TRIMESTRIEL

NOM et prénom : GUY Caroline Classe de 2de 7

MATIERES D'ENSEIGNEMENT	MOYENNE DE L'ELEVE	APPRECIATIONS
Français	12	Satisfaisant
Mathématiques	14	A fait beaucoup de progrès
Physique-Chimie	15	Bon travail
SVT	9	Peut mieux faire.
Histoire-Géographie	18	Très bonne élève!
Allemand	15	Travail sérieux
Anglais	11	Assez bien
Musique	17	Elève très sérieuse
Education physique	12	A fait beaucoup de progrès

*SVT is an abbreviation for **sciences de la vie et de la terre,** another name for **sciences naturelles.** The course SVT includes topics in biology, geology, and ecology.

27 Tu comprends?
Lisons

1. Qui a eu la meilleure note en français? En maths?
2. En quelle matière est-ce que Jean est le plus fort? Et Caroline?
3. En quelle matière est-ce qu'il est le moins bon? Et Caroline?
4. Tu es comme Jean ou comme Caroline?

1. Jean; Caroline
2. histoire-géographie; histoire-géographie
3. SVT; SVT

Note culturelle
Report cards come out three times a year: in December, before the Easter break, and at the end of the school year in June or July. Written or oral tests **(les interros écrites ou orales),** (pop) quizzes **(les interros(surprises)),** compositions **(les rédactions),** oral presentations **(les exposés),** and homework **(les devoirs)** are all graded assignments.

Cultures and Communities

Culture Notes
- French high school students usually have at least two hours of homework every day.
- French high school teachers generally teach fewer hours per week and are provided with more preparation time at school than their American counterparts.

Teacher Note
On the report cards pictured on this page, **2de 7** refers to a grade level **(seconde)** and class number **(7).** Students in **2de 7** take almost all of their courses together as a group.

Comment dit-on...?

Giving reasons and making excuses

To give reasons:

Je suis assez bon (bonne) en français.
I'm pretty good at . . .
C'est en maths **que je suis le/la meilleur(e).**
I'm best in . . .
L'anglais, **c'est mon fort!**
. . . is my strong point.

To make excuses:

L'histoire, **c'est pas mon fort.**
. . . isn't my best subject.
J'ai du mal à comprendre.
I have a hard time understanding.
Je suis pas doué(e) pour les sciences.
I don't have a talent for . . .

Cahier d'activités, p. 56, Act. 19–21

28 Comment tu trouves tes cours?

Ecrivons/Parlons Fais une liste de tous les cours que tu as cette année et écris tes commentaires sur chaque cours. Montre ta liste à un(e) camarade. Est-ce que vous avez les mêmes opinions de vos cours?

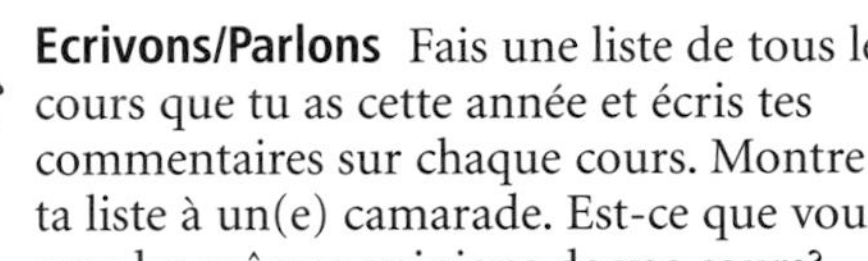

Je suis fort(e) en...
chouette
J'adore...
C'est intéressant!
difficile
amusant
Le prof est super.
facile

29 Le jour des bulletins trimestriels

a. **Ecrivons** C'est toi, le professeur! Fais une liste de six cours et donne des notes à un(e) camarade. Ecris aussi tes appréciations pour chaque cours.

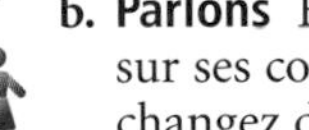

b. **Parlons** Echange ton bulletin trimestriel avec un(e) camarade. Pose-lui des questions sur ses cours et ses notes. Il/Elle va te dire pourquoi il/elle a eu ces notes. Ensuite, changez de rôle.

EXEMPLE —**Combien tu as eu en maths?**
—**J'ai eu 15. Je suis assez bon (bonne) en maths. Et toi?**
—**Moi, j'ai eu 8. C'est pas mon fort!**

Comment dit-on...?

Congratulating and reprimanding someone

CD-ROM 2 DVD 1

To congratulate someone:

Félicitations! *Congratulations!*
Bravo! *Terrific!*
Chapeau! *Well done!*

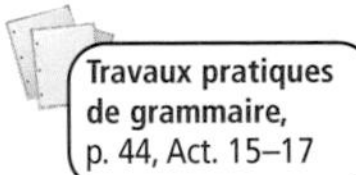

Travaux pratiques de grammaire, p. 44, Act. 15–17

Grammaire supplémentaire, p. 151, Act. 10

Cahier d'activités, pp. 57–58, Act. 22–23

To reprimand someone:

C'est inadmissible. *That's unacceptable.*
Tu dois mieux travailler en classe.
You have to work harder in class.
Tu ne dois pas faire le clown en classe!
You can't be goofing off in class!
Ne recommence pas. *Don't do it again.*

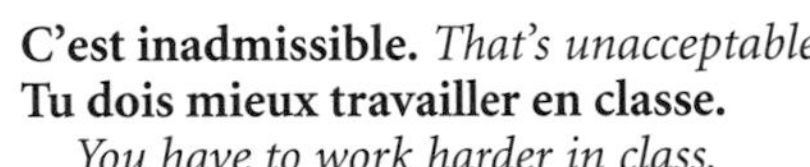

Presenting

Comment dit-on... ?

Write the expressions on the board in two columns: *To give reasons* and *To make excuses.* Then, ask who has a particular class **(Qui a algèbre?)** and how they do in it. **(Tu es assez bon (bonne) en algèbre ou tu as du mal à comprendre?)** Students might answer with a thumbs-up or thumbs-down gesture.

Comment dit-on... ?

Circulate among the students, handing them papers with French grades written on them, some good, some bad. As you hand a paper to a student, show the grade to the class and congratulate or reprimand the student, based on the grade. Then write the expressions from **Comment dit-on... ?** on the board. Have each student write a school subject in French on a slip of paper and next to it, a grade based on 20 points. Have students exchange their slips and then circulate around the room, talking about their grades and congratulating or reprimanding one another.

Language Note

In the expression **faire le clown,** the word **clown** is pronounced *cloon.*

Communication for All Students

Challenge

Have students write a short sentence describing a situation that would elicit congratulations or a reprimand. **(J'ai eu 16 en maths!)** Have them read their sentence to the class and have students suggest various congratulations or reprimands.

Role-Play

Have students take turns acting out the following scenario. One is a student who comes home and tells a parent about various events that took place during the day. The other is the parent who congratulates or reprimands the student.

STANDARDS: 1.1, 1.3, 5.1

Troisième étape

CHAPITRE 5

Teaching Suggestion

To close this **étape,** have students write letters to a French pen pal in which they tell about a fictitious report card. They should give excuses for any bad grades and give reasons for good ones.

Portfolio

33 **Oral** This activity is appropriate for students' oral portfolios. For portfolio suggestions, see the *Alternative Assessment Guide,* page 22.

Speaking Assessment

34 You might use the following rubric when grading your students on this activity.

Speaking Rubric	Points			
	4	3	2	1
Content (Complete–Incomplete)				
Comprehension (Total–Little)				
Comprehensibility (Comprehensible–Incomprehensible)				
Accuracy (Accurate–Seldom accurate)				
Fluency (Fluent–Not fluent)				

18–20: A 14–15: C Under
16–17: B 12–13: D 12: F

Assess

- Testing Program, pp. 113–116 Quiz 5-3A, Quiz 5-3B Audio CD 5, Tr. 15
- Student Make-Up Assignments, Chapter 5, Alternative Quiz
- Alternative Assessment Guide, p. 36

30 Les notes de Gilbert See scripts and answers on p. 127H.

Ecoutons Listen as Gilbert's father and friends ask him about his schoolwork. Are they reprimanding or congratulating him?

CD 5 Tr. 7

31 Vraiment, Gilbert...

Lisons/Parlons Regarde les notes de Gilbert. Qu'est-ce que tu peux lui dire à propos de ses notes?

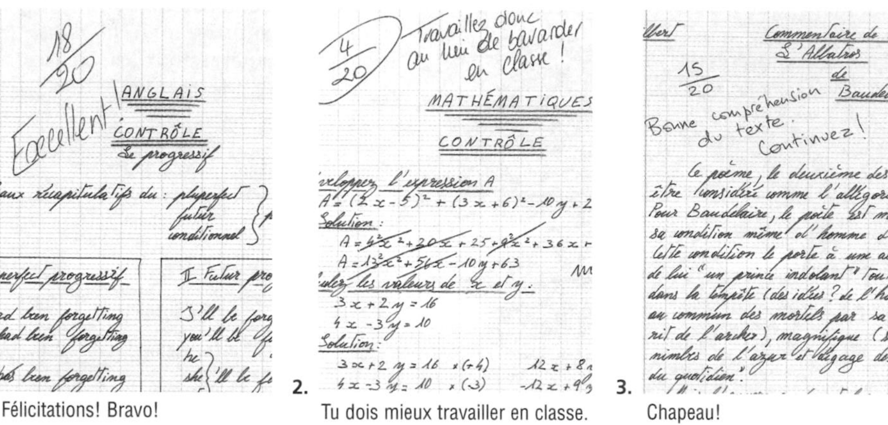

Possible answers: 1. Félicitations! Bravo! 2. Tu dois mieux travailler en classe. 3. Chapeau!

32 Le meilleur et le pire

Parlons Ecris le nom de deux cours et invente une note (une bonne note et une mauvaise note) pour chaque cours. Ton/Ta camarade va jouer le rôle d'un de tes parents. Il/Elle va te demander quelles notes tu as eues. Explique-lui pourquoi tu as eu ces notes. Dis-lui les vraies raisons ou invente des excuses.

33 Ta semaine à l'école

Parlons Demande à un(e) camarade comment sa semaine à l'école s'est passée. Il/Elle va te raconter ce qui est arrivé. Console ton/ta camarade ou gronde-le/la. Ensuite, changez de rôle.

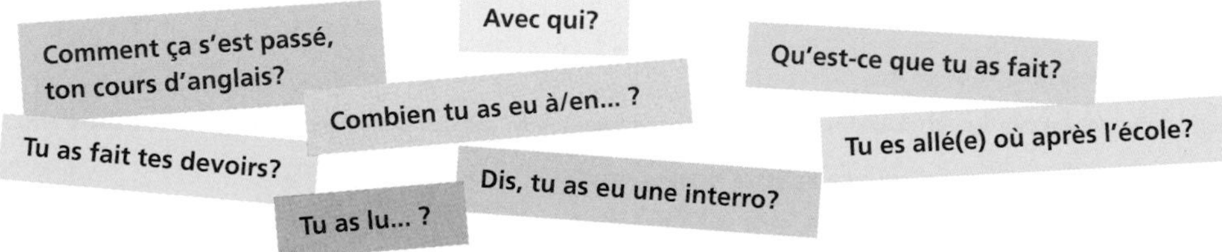

Comment ça s'est passé, ton cours d'anglais?
Avec qui?
Qu'est-ce que tu as fait?
Combien tu as eu à/en... ?
Tu es allé(e) où après l'école?
Tu as fait tes devoirs?
Dis, tu as eu une interro?
Tu as lu... ?

34 De l'école au travail

Parlons You're a French teaching assistant and you have to evaluate some of your students. Discuss their grades with them and congratulate them or encourage them to study more.

EXEMPLE —Eh bien, Marc, 7/20 en sciences! Qu'est-ce qui se passe?
—C'est que... les sciences, c'est pas mon fort....

Communication for All Students

Visual Learners

30 Before you play the recording, write the congratulations and reprimands on an overhead transparency, in a different order than students will hear them. Add two more congratulations and reprimands that are not part of the dialogues **(Chapeau!/Ne recommence pas!)**. Show students the transparency and have partners decide whether they are congratulations or reprimands. Finally, play the CD without the aid of the transparency.

Challenge

30 Play the recording a second time and have students write each school subject and grade they hear mentioned.

STANDARDS: 1.1, 1.2, 1.3, 3.1, 5.2

Qu'est-ce que tu aimes à l'école?

What do you like and dislike about school? We asked several francophone students for their opinions. Here's what they had to say.

Franck,
Martinique

«Les mathématiques. J'aime bien. On travaille. Ça permet de réfléchir. J'aime bien.»

Et tes professeurs, ils sont comment?

«En général, assez sympathiques; ils sont très proches de nous. Ils nous comprennent le plus souvent. Ils nous aident si on a des petits problèmes. S'ils voient que ça ne va pas trop, ils nous conseillent. Ils sont très sympathiques.» Tr. 9

Virginie, France

«Ce que j'aime à l'école? Les récréations... parce qu'on peut se voir entre copains. Ça fait une pause entre chaque heure de cours. Et puis, on peut discuter, se désaltérer, tout ça... Mon cours préféré, c'est l'anglais, parce que j'aime la langue anglaise.»

Qu'est-ce que tu n'aimes pas à l'école?

«Ce que je n'aime pas à l'école? Les sciences physiques. J'aime pas du tout.» Tr. 10

Emmanuel, France

«Ben, à l'école, ce que j'aime en particulier, c'est les copains. C'est tout, hein. Parce que, bon, il y a certains profs qui sont sympas... Autrement le lycée... [ce que j'aime,] c'est les copains, et se retrouver entre nous, j'aime bien.»

Qu'est-ce que tu n'aimes pas à l'école?

«Les surveillants. Je n'aime pas les surveillants à l'école, parce que... bon il y en a qui sont sympas, mais il y en a d'autres qui sont trop stricts, et puis ils sont même pénibles, quoi.» Tr. 11

Qu'en penses-tu?

1. What do these students say they like most about school? nice teachers, breaks, friends
2. What complaints do they have? The supervisors are too strict.
3. Are your likes and dislikes similar to or different from those mentioned by these students? How?

Cultures and Communities

Culture Note

Student/teacher relationships in French schools tend to be more formal than in American schools. French students are expected to use **vous** when addressing their teachers, raise their hands before talking, and not eat or drink in class. Teachers, especially at the high school level, usually use **vous** and they often use students' last names. Some even use **Monsieur** or **Mademoiselle** plus the student's last name.

Multicultural Link

Have students interview people from other countries or do research about their educational systems. Have them report their findings to the class.

CHAPITRE 5

Teaching Resources
p. 145

PRINT
- Video Guide, pp. 33–35
- Cahier d'activités, p. 60

MEDIA 
- One-Stop Planner
- Video Program, Videocassette 2, 37:00–41:22
- DVD Tutor, Disc 1
- Audio Compact Discs, CD 5, Trs. 8–11
- Interactive CD-ROM Tutor, Disc 2

Presenting Panorama Culturel

Have students view the video and listen for one or two things that each interviewee likes or dislikes. Ask the **Questions** below to check for comprehension. Then have students discuss **Qu'en penses-tu?** in small groups. Finally, ask them which of the three students they identify with the most and why.

Questions

1. **Pourquoi est-ce que Franck aime les maths?** (Ça permet de réfléchir.)
2. **Pourquoi est-ce que Franck trouve que les profs sont sympas?** (Ils aident les élèves.)
3. **Quel est le cours préféré de Virginie?** (l'anglais)
4. **Qu'est-ce qu'Emmanuel préfère à l'école?** (les copains) **Qu'est-ce qu'il n'aime pas?** (les surveillants)

Lisons!

CHAPITRE 5

Teaching Resources
pp. 146–147

PRINT 
- Lesson Planner, p. 25
- Cahier d'activités, p. 59
- Reading Strategies and Skills Handbook, Chapter 5
- Joie de lire 2, Chapter 5
- Standardized Assessment Tutor, Chapter 5

MEDIA
- One-Stop Planner

Prereading
Activities A–C

Making Predictions
After students do Activities A–C, read *Le Cancre* aloud to the class. Pass out typed copies of the poem and have students underline every word they do know (including the words translated in Activity C). Then, have them read the poem to themselves, trying to determine meaning from the underlined words and make predictions about what the poems will be about before looking up new words in the dictionary.

Reading
Activities D–K

Teacher Notes
- You and your students may be interested in a book called *La Foire aux cancres* (by Jean-Charles, published in Paris by Calmann-Lévy). It is a compilation of the humorous mistakes made by **cancres** in French classrooms.
- Call students' attention to the donkey ears that the boy is wearing in the illustration. French children wore them as punishment, just as American children once wore the dunce cap.

Lisons!

Poèmes de Jacques Prévert

Stratégie pour lire
Sometimes, in order to understand what you've read, you have to understand the separate parts of it first. In a poem, it's helpful to examine the words, images, and symbols before you decide what the main idea or message is.

Do you have days when you would rather be anywhere else than in school? If you have, you can relate to these poems by Jacques Prévert.

A. What do you think these poems will be about?

B. What drives you crazy about school? Make a list. What words can you find in the two poems that relate to what you don't like about school?

C. Here's some vocabulary you might need to understand these poems. Write a sentence with each of these words.

le rire	*laugh*
le visage	*face*
les chiffres	*numbers*
le pupitre	*desk*
la craie	*chalk*
effacer	*to erase*
le maître	*grade school teacher*
faire le pitre	*to goof off*
ils s'en vont	*they leave*

Le Cancre
See answers below.

D. **Un cancre** is *a dunce.* What is a dunce? French schoolchildren who got into trouble used to have to wear donkey ears. What donkey-like quality is the boy in

Le Cancre

Il dit non avec la tête
mais il dit oui avec le cœur
il dit oui à ce qu'il aime
il dit non au professeur
il est debout
on le questionne
et tous les problèmes sont posés
soudain le fou rire le prend
et il efface tout
les chiffres et les mots
les dates et les noms
les phrases et les pièges
et malgré les menaces du maître
sous les huées des enfants prodiges
avec des craies de toutes les couleurs
sur le tableau noir du malheur
il dessine le visage du bonheur

Page d'écriture

Deux et deux quatre
quatre et quatre huit
huit et huit font seize...
Répétez ! dit le maître
Deux et deux quatre
quatre et quatre huit
huit et huit font seize.
Mais voilà l'oiseau-lyre
qui passe dans le ciel
l'enfant le voit
l'enfant l'entend
l'enfant l'appelle :
Sauve-moi
joue avec moi
oiseau !
Alors l'oiseau descend
et joue avec l'enfant
Deux et deux quatre...
Répétez ! dit le maître
et l'enfant joue
l'oiseau joue avec lui...
Quatre et quatre huit
huit et huit font seize
    et seize et seize
    qu'est-ce qu'ils font?
Ils ne font rien seize et seize

Connections and Comparisons

Literature Link
Jacques Prévert (1900–1977) was a popular French poet who published a highly successful volume of poetry: *Les Paroles (Words).* Some of these poems were put to music. Young people related to Prévert because he wrote about happiness and love, lashed out at hypocrisy and stupidity, and playfully mocked respected human institutions. He wrote in free verse, irregular verse, occasional rhymes, and puns.

Thinking Critically
Analyzing Ask students if they think it's a good idea to single out young students as a dunce **(un cancre)** and why or why not?

STANDARDS: 1.2, 2.2, 3.1, 3.2

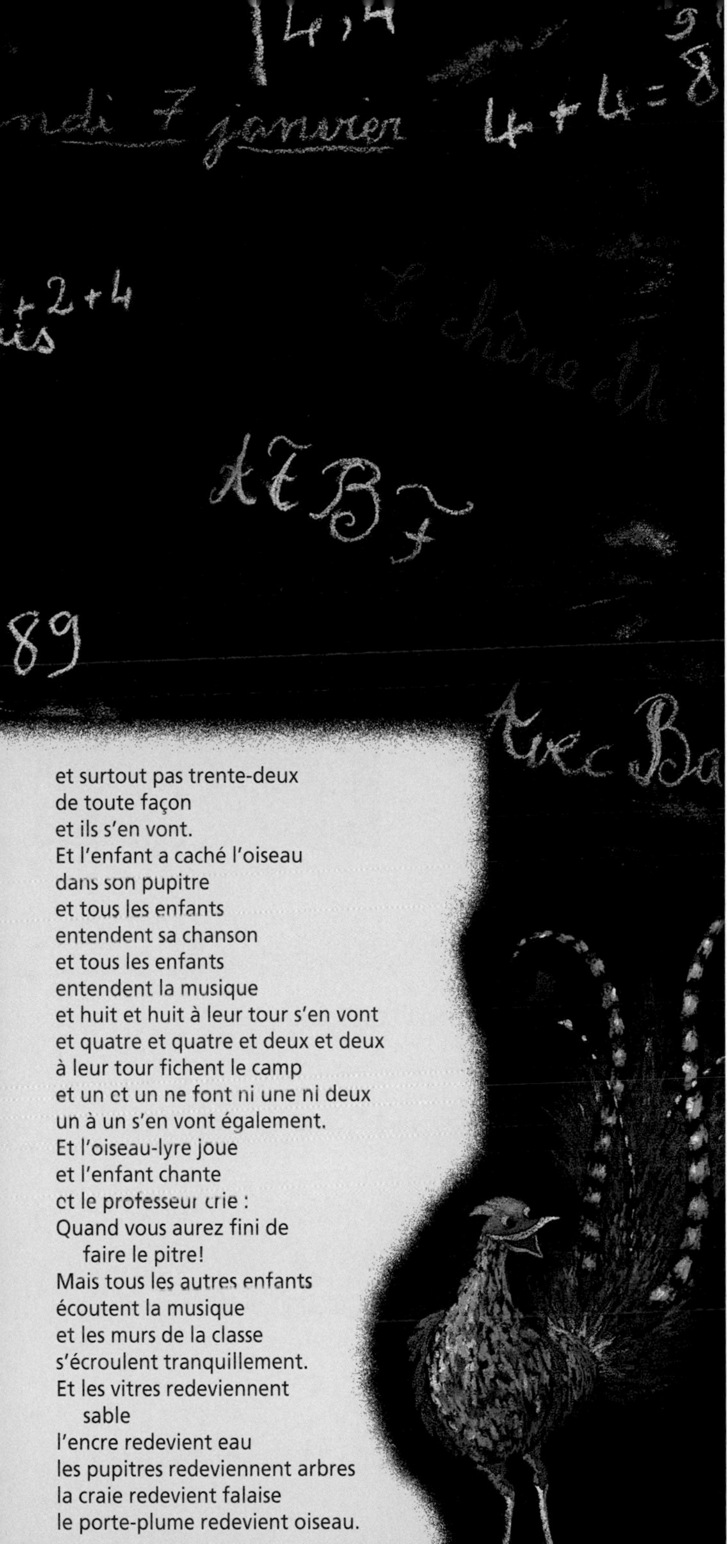

et surtout pas trente-deux
de toute façon
et ils s'en vont.
Et l'enfant a caché l'oiseau
dans son pupitre
et tous les enfants
entendent sa chanson
et tous les enfants
entendent la musique
et huit et huit à leur tour s'en vont
et quatre et quatre et deux et deux
à leur tour fichent le camp
et un et un ne font ni une ni deux
un à un s'en vont également.
Et l'oiseau-lyre joue
et l'enfant chante
et le professeur crie :
Quand vous aurez fini de
faire le pitre!
Mais tous les autres enfants
écoutent la musique
et les murs de la classe
s'écroulent tranquillement.
Et les vitres redeviennent
sable
l'encre redevient eau
les pupitres redeviennent arbres
la craie redevient falaise
le porte-plume redevient oiseau.

the poem displaying? What lines in the poem tell you this?

E. What else does the boy do to express his negative attitude toward school? See answers below.

F. These are some expressions that show the poet has the same attitude. Can you match them to their English equivalents?

1. **les phrases et les pièges** c
2. **les menaces du professeur** a
3. **les huées des enfants prodiges** d
4. **le tableau noir du malheur** b

a. *the teacher's threats*
b. *the blackboard of unhappiness*
c. *the sentences and the traps*
d. *the boos of the gifted students*

G. Despite his negative attitude about school, the boy has an essentially positive attitude about life. How do you know? Is he really **un cancre?** See answers below.

H. Draw **le visage du bonheur** as you imagine it.

Page d'écriture

I–L: See answers below.

I. How does the poem begin? Do you do these kinds of drills in class? What happens to these numbers as the poem goes on?

J. Other classroom objects are transformed at the end of the poem. What quietly falls down? What turns into sand? What does the ink turn into? The desks? The chalk? The pen?

K. What does the student invite into the classroom that causes these transformations? In your opinion, what does this guest in the classroom symbolize?

L. What is the common theme that links these two poems? How does the student in each poem escape from the routine of the classroom?

Cahier d'activités, p. 59, Act. 25

Lisons!

CHAPITRE 5

Postreading
Activity L

Group Work
Have groups of five divide the text of *Page d'écriture* evenly among themselves and illustrate each sentence of the poem. Give students the option of using magazine cut-outs. You might need to help them decide what constitutes a sentence. Have students use one piece of paper for each illustration, drawing anything they think represents the meaning of the sentence. Have them write the sentence on the back of and below the illustration. Then, have groups sit in front of the class and show their illustrations as they read their lines of the poem. Students might choose the best illustrations from different groups to represent the entire poem and display them in the classroom.

Language Note
Un vers is a line of poetry **(au troisième vers:** *in the third line;* **vers blancs/libres:** *blank/free verse).* **Une strophe** is a *stanza.*

Cultures and Communities

Culture Note
Long ago, French schoolchildren used to write with a quill **(une plume)**, a feather made into a pen that was dipped in ink. The quill was attached to a wooden holder called a **porte-plume.** Good handwriting was emphasized. Even today, French children learn cursive writing before they learn to print. This was also the case with American children until about 1940.

Connecting Literature to Cinema
You might show *Les Quatre Cents Coups (400 Blows),* a 1959 film by director François Truffaut, which depicts a 1950s classroom setting.

Answers
D. a bad student; stubbornness; "Il dit non avec la tête... ," "Il dit non au professeur... "

E. He's rebellious. He erases "knowledge" off the board.

G. He draws "the face of happiness" on the chalkboard. Answers will vary.

I. with addition problems; Answers will vary.; They leave the classroom.

J. the classroom walls; the windows; water; trees; stone; bird

K. bird; *Possible answers:* freedom, the power of the pen to transport you to another place through the imagination.

L. children seeking liberation from the classroom; by using the imagination

STANDARDS: 1.2, 2.2, 3.1, 3.2

Grammaire supplémentaire

CHAPITRE 5

For **Grammaire supplémentaire** Answer Transparencies, see the *Teaching Transparencies* binder.

Grammaire supplémentaire

internet

ADRESSE: go.hrw.com
MOT-CLE: WA3 TOURAINE-5

Première étape

Objective Expressing concern for someone

1 Tous les élèves sont arrivés en retard en classe aujourd'hui, mais ils ont tous une bonne excuse. Choisis le participe passé du verbe approprié pour compléter leurs phrases. (**p. 136**)

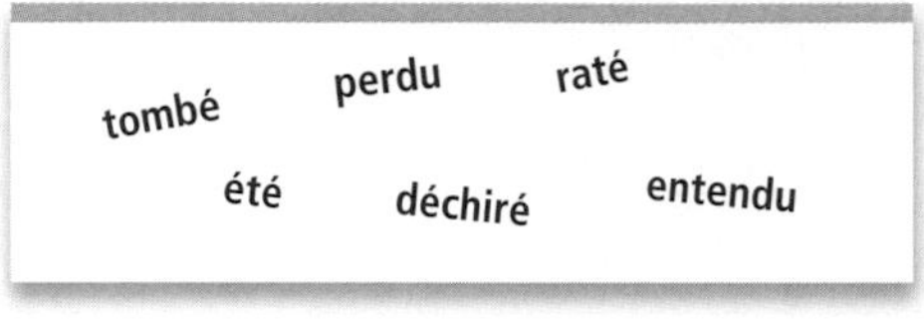

1. J'ai _____ le bus.
2. Je n'ai pas _____ mon réveil.
3. J'ai _____ mon livre d'histoire.
4. J'ai _____ mon pantalon.
5. Je suis _____ quand j'ai raté une marche.
6. J'ai _____ collé.

2 Sébastien a passé une très mauvaise journée à l'école aujourd'hui. Qu'est-ce qu'il écrit dans son journal pour décrire sa journée? (**p. 136**)

EXEMPLE perdre mon livre de français **<u>J'ai perdu mon livre de français.</u>**

1. rater le bus
2. oublier mes devoirs
3. avoir une mauvaise note
4. déchirer mon pantalon
5. recevoir mon bulletin trimestriel

3 La journée de Paul a été tout à fait le contraire de celle de Sébastien. Qu'est-ce qu'il dit pour décrire sa journée? Utilise **ne... pas** dans tes réponses. (**p. 136**)

1. rater le bus
2. oublier mes devoirs
3. avoir une mauvaise note
4. déchirer mon pantalon
5. recevoir mon bulletin trimestriel

Answers

1
1. raté
2. entendu
3. perdu
4. déchiré
5. tombé
6. été

2
1. J'ai raté le bus.
2. J'ai oublié mes devoirs.
3. J'ai eu une mauvaise note.
4. J'ai déchiré mon pantalon.
5. J'ai reçu mon bulletin trimestriel.

3
1. Je n'ai pas raté le bus.
2. Je n'ai pas oublié mes devoirs.
3. Je n'ai pas eu de mauvaise note.
4. Je n'ai pas déchiré mon pantalon.
5. Je n'ai pas reçu mon bulletin trimestriel.

Grammar Resources for Chapter 5

The **Grammaire supplémentaire** activities were designed as supplemental activities for the grammatical concepts presented in the chapter. You might use them as additional practice, for review, or for assessment.

For more grammar presentations, review, and practice, refer to the following:

- Travaux pratiques de grammaire
- Grammar Tutor for Students of French
- Grammar Summary on pp. R23–R42
- Cahier d'activités
- Grammar and Vocabulary quizzes (Testing Program)
- Test Generator
- Interactive CD-ROM Tutor
- DVD Tutor
- **Jeux interactifs** at <u>go.hrw.com</u>

Grammaire supplémentaire

CHAPITRE 5

4 Karima et Ahmed parlent de leur journée. Complète leur dialogue avec le **passé composé** des verbes entre parenthèses. (**p. 136**)

KARIMA C'était super. En classe, on __1__ (voir) un bon film et mon prof __2__ (rendre) les interros. Moi, j' __3__ (avoir) une bonne note.

AHMED Ah oui? Moi, j'__4__ (passer) une journée épouvantable.

KARIMA Ah bon? Qu'est-ce qui s'est passé? Raconte!

AHMED Mon frère et moi, nous __5__ (ne pas entendre) notre réveil. Ensuite, mon frère __6__ (rater) une marche à l'école et il __7__ (déchirer) sa chemise!

KARIMA Quelle journée! Vous __8__ (ne pas avoir) de chance. Et après l'école, tu __9__ (jouer) au foot?

AHMED Non, mes profs nous __10__ (donner) trop de devoirs et puis en rentrant de l'école, j' __11__ (recevoir) mon bulletin trimestriel. Il est pas terrible!

Deuxième étape

Objectives Inquiring; expressing satisfaction and frustration; sympathizing with and consoling someone

5 Colette te raconte son week-end à Paris. Complète ses phrases avec l'auxiliaire **être** ou l'auxiliaire **avoir.** (**p. 140**)

1. Ma mère, ma sœur et moi, nous _____ allées à Paris le week-end dernier.
2. Mon père _____ resté seul à la maison.
3. On _____ pris un taxi de l'aéroport.
4. Je me _____ couchée tôt parce que j'étais fatiguée.
5. Samedi, ma mère et moi, nous _____ visité la tour Eiffel.
6. Ma mère et ma sœur _____ pris beaucoup de photos.
7. On s' _____ beaucoup amusées.

Communication for All Students

Additional Practice

To give students practice forming the **passé composé,** prepare several flashcards. On one side, write sentences in the present tense. **(Sophie prend une tartine.)** Have students read the card and restate the sentence in the **passé composé. (Sophie a pris une tartine.)** To help visual learners, show the sentence in the **passé composé** that you've written on the other side of the card.

Challenge

Have students arrange photographs or magazine cut-outs of an actual or imaginary vacation on posterboard. Have them write a caption for each picture, using the **passé composé**.

Answers

4
1. a vu
2. a rendu
3. ai eu
4. ai passé
5. n'avons pas entendu
6. a raté
7. a déchiré
8. n'avez pas eu
9. as joué
10. ont donné
11. ai reçu

5
1. sommes
2. est
3. a
4. suis
5. avons
6. ont
7. est

STANDARDS: 1.2

Grammaire supplémentaire

CHAPITRE 5

For **Grammaire supplémentaire** Answer Transparencies, see the *Teaching Transparencies* binder.

Grammaire supplémentaire

WA3 TOURAINE-5

6 Paul a passé une très mauvaise journée hier. Imagine que tu es Paul et dis ce qui t'est arrivé et pourquoi en utilisant le vocabulaire proposé. (**p. 140**)

EXEMPLE tomber / rater une marche
Je suis tombé parce que j'ai raté une marche.

1. avoir un zéro / perdre mon livre de français
2. arriver en retard / entendre mon réveil
3. aller au café / perdre mon argent
4. avoir de bonnes notes / oublier mes devoirs
5. voir mes amis / être collé(e)

7 Tes parents veulent savoir ce que tes amis et toi, vous avez fait hier soir. Dans les phrases suivantes, remplace les verbes par les verbes réfléchis proposés. N'oublie pas d'utiliser le **passé composé.** (**p. 140**)

se coucher | se lever | se baigner | s'habiller | se laver | s'amuser

EXEMPLE Marie est allée au parc. **Elle s'est promenée au parc.**

1. Luc et David sont allés au lit de bonne heure.
2. J'ai nagé à la piscine.
3. Monique a pris un bain.
4. Nous ne sommes pas sortis du lit après minuit.
5. Karine et Simone sont allées à la boum.

8 You're at the beach and you write to a friend about what you did during your first day of vacation, but some of the words got washed out. Fill them in using the **passé composé.** (**p. 140**)

Salut,

Mon premier jour de vacances __1__ (se passer) super bien. Je __2__ (se lever) à midi et je __3__ (se promener) sur la plage avec des amis. Ensuite, nous __4__ (se baigner). L'eau était très chaude. C'était formidable. Puis nous avons fait du deltaplane. Moi, j'avais peur mais mes copains m'ont aidé(e) et finalement on __5__ (s'amuser). Le soir, on a mangé dans un restaurant près de la plage. On a mangé un poisson délicieux et beaucoup de fruits. Enfin, on est allés danser dans la discothèque de la plage et on __6__ (se coucher) à deux heures du matin. Le jour suivant on __7__ (se lever) très tard. Et toi, comment __8__ (se passer) tes vacances? Qu'est-ce que tu as fait? Raconte-moi!

Answers

6
1. J'ai eu un zéro parce que j'ai perdu mon livre de français.
2. Je suis arrivé en retard parce que je n'ai pas entendu mon réveil.
3. Je ne suis pas allé au café parce que j'ai perdu mon argent.
4. Je n'ai pas eu de bonnes notes parce que j'ai oublié mes devoirs.
5. Je n'ai pas vu mes amis parce que j'ai été collé.

7
1. Ils se sont couchés de bonne heure.
2. Je me suis baigné(e).
3. Monique s'est lavée.
4. Nous ne nous sommes pas levés après minuit.
5. Elles se sont amusées.

8
1. s'est passé
2. me suis levé(e)
3. me suis promené(e)
4. nous sommes baignés
5. s'est amusés
6. s'est couchés
7. s'est levés
8. se sont passées

Review and Assess

Additional Practice

Type and distribute copies of the following paragraph and have students supply the **passé composé** of the verbs in parentheses.

Ce matin, le réveil de Sylvie ____ (ne pas sonner). Donc, elle ____ (se réveiller) tard. Puis, elle ____ (se laver) et ____ (s'habiller) très vite. Elle ____ (ne pas avoir) le temps de prendre son petit déjeuner, alors elle ____ (manger) juste une pomme et elle ____ (boire) du jus d'orange. Elle ____ (aller) à l'arrêt de bus, mais elle ____ (rater) le bus. Pauvre Sylvie! A cause de tout ça, elle ____ (arriver) en retard à l'école, et en plus, en entrant dans la salle de classe, elle ____ (ne pas voir) la marche, et elle ____ (tomber). Quel désastre!

STANDARDS: 1.2

Grammaire supplémentaire

CHAPITRE 5

9 Regarde les illustrations et complète les phrases suivantes en utilisant le **passé composé.** (**pp. 136, 140**)

1. Elle __________ le match de tennis.
2. Il __________ et il a cassé toutes les assiettes.
3. Elle __________ ses devoirs d'espagnol.
4. Il __________ de l'argent dans la rue.

Troisième étape

Objectives Giving reasons and making excuses; congratulating and reprimanding someone

10 Luc parle avec ses parents de ses notes et des notes de ses camarades. D'après les raisons qu'il donne pour expliquer leurs mauvaises notes, dis ce que chaque personne doit faire pour avoir de meilleures notes. Utilise le verbe **aller** + **infinitif** dans tes réponses. (**pp. 21, 143**)

1. —Combien tu as eu en histoire?
   —J'ai eu 11. Je n'ai pas fait mes devoirs.
   —Tu dois mieux travailler en classe!
   —C'est vrai, je...
2. —Combien Paul a eu en anglais?
   —Il a eu 8. Il a fait le clown en classe.
   —C'est inadmissible!
   —C'est vrai, il...
3. —Combien Julien et François ont eu en français?
   —Ils ont eu 11.
   —Ils doivent mieux travailler!
   —C'est vrai, ils...
4. —Toi et Pamela, combien vous avez eu en maths?
   —Nous avons eu 10, tous les deux.
   —C'est inadmissible!
   —C'est vrai, nous...

Review and Assess

You may wish to assign the **Grammaire supplémentaire** activities as additional practice or homework after presenting material throughout the chapter. Assign Activities 1–4 after **Grammaire** (p. 136), and Activities 5–9 after **Grammaire** (p. 140).

To prepare students for the **Etape** Quizzes and Chapter Test, we suggest doing the **Grammaire supplémentaire** activities in the following order. Have students complete Activities 1–4 before Quizzes 5-1A or 5-1B; Activities 5–9 before Quizzes 5-2A or 5-2B; and Activity 10 before Quizzes 5-3A or 5-3B.

Answers

9
1. a gagné
2. est tombé
3. a perdu
4. a trouvé

10 *Possible answers:*
1. vais faire mes devoirs tous les jours.
2. ne va pas faire le clown en classe.
3. vont écouter le professeur.
4. allons mieux travailler.

Mise en pratique

C H A P I T R E 5

The **Mise en pratique** reviews and integrates all four skills and culture in preparation for the Chapter Test.

Teaching Resources
pp. 152–153

PRINT

- Lesson Planner, p. 25
- TPR Storytelling Book, pp. 38–39
- Listening Activities, p. 37
- Video Guide, pp. 33, 36
- Grammar Tutor for Students of French, Chapter 5
- Standardized Assessment Tutor, Chapter 5

MEDIA 

- One-Stop Planner
- Video Program Videocassette 2, 41:24–42:57
- DVD Tutor, Disc 1
- Audio Compact Discs, CD 5, Tr. 12
- Interactive CD-ROM Tutor, Disc 2

Teacher Note

You might remind students that **seconde** is the first year of the **lycée, première** is the second year, and **terminale** is the last.

Language Note

Tell students that the **c** in **seconde** is pronounced as a hard **[g]** sound.

Answers

1
1. to excuse a student from PE class; gives student's name, class, class date, reason for excuse, if a doctor's note is attached, date excuse was signed, and parental signature; excuses her from gym class
2. gives student's name, date, class grade, time she arrived, how many minutes late, the excuse, and whether or not she will be admitted to class; she did not hear her alarm clock and missed the bus; arrived at 8:30; missed the bus
3. Ginette's day was bad.

Mise en pratique

1. What is the purpose of the first document? What information does it give? What does this note excuse Ginette from?
2. What information does the second document give? What happened to Ginette? At what time did Ginette arrive at school? Why?
3. How was Ginette's day?

DEMANDE DE DISPENSE EXCEPTIONNELLE D'EDUCATION PHYSIQUE
(à remplir par les parents et à remettre au Conseiller d'Education avant le cours)

Nom de l'élève GARIN Prénom Ginette Classe 2nde
Date du cours 12/11
Motif de la demande s'est fait mal à la main – dispense d'EPS
Ci-joint certificat médical: (1) Oui - ~~Non~~
Date 12/11 *Signature,* Mme Garin

Lycée Balzac Tours — INFIRMERIE

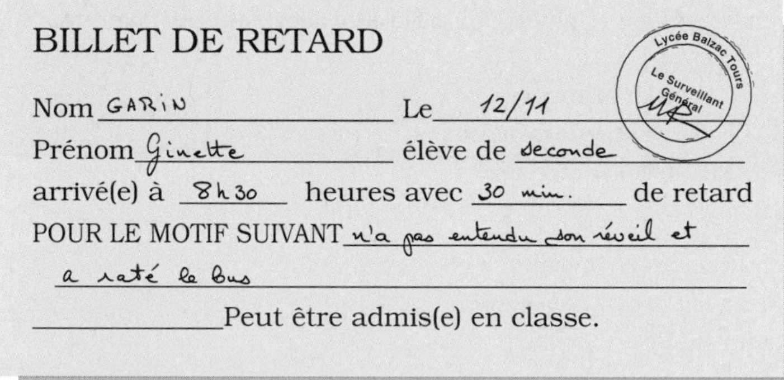

BILLET DE RETARD

Nom GARIN Le 12/11
Prénom Ginette élève de seconde
arrivé(e) à 8h30 heures avec 30 min. de retard
POUR LE MOTIF SUIVANT n'a pas entendu son réveil et a raté le bus
________ Peut être admis(e) en classe.

Lycée Balzac Tours — Le Surveillant Général

2 Ecoute la conversation entre le père de Ginette et son professeur d'histoire-géo. Décide si les phrases suivantes sont vraies ou fausses. See scripts and answers on p. 127H.

CD 5 Tr. 12

1. Ginette a eu 9 à l'interro d'histoire-géo.
2. La semaine passée, elle est arrivée en classe à l'heure.
3. D'après Ginette, l'histoire est son fort.
4. D'après Ginette, le prof ne l'aime pas.
5. Le prof de Ginette ne l'aime pas.
6. D'après le prof, Ginette ne doit pas faire le clown en classe.

3 Qu'est-ce que tu sais sur les écoles françaises? Est-ce que tu aimerais être élève dans un lycée français? Explique pourquoi ou pourquoi pas.

Apply and Assess

Slower Pace

For listening and reading practice, assign a number to each document. Make random statements about the documents and have students write the number(s) of the document(s) to which each of your statements refers. **(L'élève est en seconde. Elle n'a pas sport aujourd'hui. L'élève s'appelle Ginette. L'infirmier ou l'infirmière a signé. L'élève est arrivée avec trente minutes de retard. L'élève s'est fait mal à la main. L'élève n'a pas entendu son réveil.)**

STANDARDS: 1.2

4
Ecrivons!

Imagine that your school is preparing a time capsule to be opened by students in the year 2099. Your French class has been asked to keep a journal describing the lives of teenagers in your time period. Write a journal entry describing the best or worst day of your school year.

Stratégie pour écrire
Effective introductions are important when writing a narrative piece, such as a journal entry. A good introduction will "hook" your reader so that he or she will want to read more.

Préparation

Before you begin to write, recall as many details about the day as you can. List details to include and group them together in categories. Think about the individual events that made up the experience; sensory details like sights, sounds, and feelings; and significant people and places.

Rédaction

An effective introduction in narrative writing generally has three main components: a snappy opening, some background information, and just a hint of the event's importance. You might begin with a thought-provoking question or an exclamation. Then, briefly describe what led to the day's being good or bad. Try to hint at the outcome of the day without giving it away completely.

The body of your writing will contain most of the details of the event. Think of the French words and phrases you know that would best allow your reader to see, feel, and hear your experience. If you don't know the word for a certain thing, think about how you could use what you do know to express it differently.

Finally, conclude your journal entry by explaining the outcome of your day. You might tell whether or not this day changed your life in some way and if you would do anything differently now.

Evaluation

When you evaluate your work, put yourself in your reader's shoes. Consider how a student in the year 2099 might react to your writing and ask yourself: Does the introduction grab my attention? Is there enough background information? Does the order of events make sense?

5
Jeu de rôle

You've been having problems in one of your classes, so you decide to meet with your teacher after school today. Act out the situation with a partner.

- Be sure to bring up your latest grades, good and bad.
- Give reasons for tardiness, bad grades, or lost homework.
- The teacher may be sympathetic, reprimanding, or both.

Teacher to Teacher

Todd Bowen
Adlai E. Stevenson High School
Lincolnshire, IL

Todd suggests the following activity to review material from this chapter.

"I use Learning Centers to wrap up a chapter. Each center has an activity that practices a skill that will be on the test and can be completed in about five minutes. The students rotate to each center until they work their way through all activities (usually 5 or 6). I use half-sheet worksheets for structure skills, an additional listening activity, a speaking activity, a vocabulary review, and a culture quiz. Students check the answer key before moving on to the next center."

Mise en pratique

CHAPITRE 5

Culture Note

The **surveillant général** stamp on the **billet de retard** probably contains the signature or initials of the **surveillant** rather than the **surveillant général. Surveillants,** familiarly called **les pions** by students, are usually university students who take on part-time jobs to help the **lycée** administration with various tasks, such as monitoring halls and signing various student forms. Above the **surveillants** is the **surveillant général** or the **conseiller d'éducation,** who is on campus at all times and is responsible for scheduling classes.

Process Writing

4 You might show students some examples of good introductions from various English and French short stories to help them with their own introductions.

Career Path

There are many options for people who choose to teach foreign language(s) as a career. You can teach in public, private, or independent language schools in the U.S. or abroad. Some international companies employ language teachers to teach their employees. Knowledge of a foreign language is also helpful for people who teach English as a Second Language. Considering today's market in international business, what three languages do students think it would be most important to learn?

Teacher Note

For additional practice and review, you might use the **Histoire Finale** for Chapter 5 on pages 38–39 of the *TPR Storytelling Book.*

Que sais-je?

CHAPITRE 5

Teaching Resources
p. 154

PRINT 

- Grammar Tutor for Students of French, Chapter 5

MEDIA  

- Interactive CD-ROM Tutor, Disc 2
- Online self-test

go.hrw.com
WA3 TOURAINE-5

Teaching Suggestion
Have students work in pairs to find as many responses as possible to each of the questions in **Que sais-je?**

Possible Answers

3
1. Comment ça s'est passé hier?
2. Comment s'est passé ton week-end?
3. Comment se sont passées tes vacances?

6
1. Oh là là!
2. C'est pas de chance, ça! Ça va aller mieux.
3. Pauvre vieux! T'en fais pas. C'est pas grave.

7
1. L'informatique, c'est pas mon fort!
2. L'anglais, c'est mon fort!
3. Je suis pas doué(e) pour le français.

Que sais-je?

WA3 TOURAINE-5

Can you use what you've learned in this chapter?

Can you express concern for someone? p. 135

1 How would you show concern for someone by asking what happened? Possible answers: Ça n'a pas l'air d'aller. Qu'est-ce qui se passe? Qu'est-ce qui t'arrive?

2 How would your friend answer you if the following happened to him?

1. J'ai déchiré ma chemise.

2. J'ai raté le bus.

3. J'ai reçu mon bulletin trimestriel.

Can you inquire? p. 139

3 How would you inquire about your friend's . . . See answers below.
1. day yesterday?
2. weekend?
3. vacation?

Can you express satisfaction and frustration? p. 139

4 How would you respond to someone's question about your weekend if it went really well? Possible answers: C'était incroyable/super/génial! Ça s'est très bien passé! Quel week-end formidable!

5 How would you respond to someone's question about your vacation if everything went wrong? Tout a été de travers!

Can you sympathize with and console someone? p. 141

6 What would you say to sympathize with and console these people? See answers below.
1. Céline a raté le bus.
2. Véronique a été collée.
3. Henri est arrivé en retard au cours de français.

Can you give reasons and make excuses? p. 143

7 How would you explain the following grades on your report card? See answers below.

MATIERES	MOYENNE	APPRECIATIONS
Informatique	9	Peu d'effort!
Anglais	16	Bon travail
Français	8	Travail moyen

Can you congratulate and reprimand someone? p. 143

8 What would you say to a friend who . . . Possible answers:
1. got a good grade in French? Bravo!
2. won an athletic competition? Félicitations!
3. received a scholarship to college? Chapeau!

9 How would you reprimand a friend who . . .
1. got a low grade in English? Tu dois mieux travailler en classe.
2. is always joking in class? Tu ne dois pas faire le clown en classe!

Review and Assess

Game

Tic Tac Toe Create three to five transparencies of tic tac toe grids. Number the squares and write one of the questions from **Que sais-je?** in each square. You might write the same question in two squares and require different responses for each one. You might also turn the questions into instructions: *Show concern for someone and ask what happened.* Then, project a grid on the overhead. Form two teams and have them take turns choosing a square trying to respond correctly in order to place their team's X or O in that square. Individuals should choose a square **(J'aimerais le numéro sept, s'il vous plaît),** and you mark an X or an O in the square if they respond appropriately. The first team to mark three squares in a row wins!

STANDARDS: 1.1, 1.2

Vocabulaire

Première étape

Expressing concern for someone

Ça n'a pas l'air d'aller.	*You look like something's wrong.*
Qu'est-ce qui se passe?	*What's going on?*
Qu'est-ce qui t'arrive?	*What's wrong?*
Raconte!	*Tell me!*

School day vocabulary

passer une journée épouvantable	*to have a horrible day*
entendre le réveil	*to hear the alarm clock*
rater le bus	*to miss the bus*
rater une marche	*to miss a step*
tomber	*to fall*
déchirer	*to rip, to tear*
arriver en retard à l'école	*to arrive late to school*
rendre les interros	*to return tests*
avoir une mauvaise note	*to get a bad grade*
être collé(e)	*to have detention*
perdre	*to lose*
recevoir le bulletin trimestriel	*to receive one's report card*

Deuxième étape

Inquiring; expressing satisfaction and frustration

Comment ça s'est passé?	*How did it go?*
Comment s'est passée ta journée?	*How was your day?*
Comment s'est passé ton week-end?	*How was your weekend?*
Comment se sont passées tes vacances?	*How was your vacation?*
C'était incroyable!	*It was amazing!/unbelievably bad!*
Ça s'est très bien passé!	*It went really well!*
Quelle journée (formidable)!	*What a (great) day!*
Quel week-end (formidable)!	*What a (great) weekend!*
J'ai passé une journée horrible!	*I had a terrible day!*
C'est pas mon jour!	*It's just not my day!*
Tout a été de travers!	*Everything went wrong!*
Quelle journée!	*What a (bad) day!*
Quel week-end!	*What a (bad) weekend!*

Sympathizing with and consoling someone

Oh là là!	*Oh no!*
C'est pas de chance, ça!	*Tough luck!*
Pauvre vieux/vieille!	*You poor thing!*
Courage!	*Hang in there!*
Ça va aller mieux.	*It'll get better.*
T'en fais pas.	*Don't worry.*
C'est pas grave.	*It's not serious.*

Other expressions

arriver	*to arrive, to happen*

Troisième étape

Giving reasons and making excuses

Je suis assez bon (bonne) en...	*I'm pretty good at...*
C'est en... que je suis le/la meilleur(e).	*I'm best in...*
..., c'est mon fort.	*...is my strong point.*
..., c'est pas mon fort.	*...isn't my best subject.*
J'ai du mal à comprendre.	*I have a hard time understanding.*
Je suis pas doué(e) pour...	*I don't have a talent for...*

Congratulating someone

Félicitations!	*Congratulations!*
Bravo!	*Terrific!*
Chapeau!	*Well done!*

Reprimanding someone

C'est inadmissible.	*That's unacceptable.*
Tu dois mieux travailler en classe.	*You have to work harder in class.*
Tu ne dois pas faire le clown en classe!	*You can't be goofing off in class!*
Ne recommence pas.	*Don't do it again.*

Review and Assess

Circumlocution/ Building on Previous Skills

To review vocabulary from previous chapters, have students use circumlocution to describe terms to a partner who will try to guess them. See **Le Mot juste** and a list of circumlocution expressions on page 3C.

Vocabulaire

CHAPITRE 5

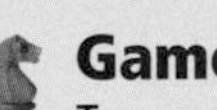

Game

To practice the vocabulary from the chapter, play **Course de relais,** described on page 127C.

Teaching Suggestion

Have students write scrambled sentences **(passé/j'ai/horrible/journée/une)** with several of the expressions on this vocabulary page. Have them exchange sentences with a partner who must then write the words in the correct order. Students could prepare the scrambled sentences as part of a homework assignment.

Chapter 5 Assessment

- **Testing Program**
  Chapter Test, pp. 117–122

  Audio Compact Discs, CD 5, Trs. 16–18
  Speaking Test, p. 345
- **Alternative Assessment Guide**
  Performance Assessment, p. 36
  Portfolio Assessment, p. 22
  CD-ROM Assessment, p. 50
- **Interactive CD-ROM Tutor, Disc 2**

  A toi de parler
  A toi d'écrire
- **Standardized Assessment Tutor**
  Chapter 5
- **One-Stop Planner, Disc 2**

  Test Generator, Chapter 5

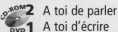

STANDARDS: 1.1

Chapitre 6 : A nous les châteaux!
Chapter Overview

Mise en train pp. 158–160	***Le disparu***

	FUNCTIONS	GRAMMAR	VOCABULARY	RE-ENTRY
Première étape pp. 161–165	• Asking for opinions; expressing enthusiasm, indifference, and dissatisfaction, p. 164	• The phrase **c'était,** p. 164	• Weekend activities, p. 162	• Pronunciation: **[y]** versus **[u] (Chapitre 4,** I) • Inquiring about and relating past events **(Chapitre 5,** II)
Deuxième étape pp. 166–170	• Expressing disbelief and doubt, p. 168	• The **passé composé** with **être,** p. 167	• Verbs that use **être** in the **passé composé,** p. 167	• The **passé composé** with **avoir** **(Chapitre 5,** II)
Troisième étape pp. 171–173	• Asking for and giving information, p. 172	• Formal and informal phrasing of questions, p. 172 • The verb **ouvrir,** p. 173		• Question words **(Chapitre 6,** I, **Chapitre 5,** II) • Telling time **(Chapitres 2, 6,** I) • Making purchases **(Chapitre 3,** II)

Lisons! pp. 174–175	**La Belle au bois dormant**	**Reading Strategy:** Understanding **genre**	
Grammaire supplémentaire	**pp. 176–179** **Première étape,** pp. 176–177	**Deuxième étape,** pp. 177–178	**Troisième étape,** p. 179
Review pp. 180–183	**Mise en pratique,** pp. 180–181 **Ecrivons!** Summarizing Writing about a famous person	**Que sais-je?** p. 182	**Vocabulaire,** p. 183

CULTURE

- **Note culturelle,** Types of **châteaux** in France, p. 161
- **Panorama Culturel,** Studying historical figures in school, p. 170
- Realia: Brochure of bus tours in Touraine, p. 171
- **Note culturelle,** Buses and trains in France, p. 171
- Realia: **Renseignements pratiques** for Fontainebleau, p. 173
- Realia: Train schedule, p. 173

Chapitre 6 : A nous les châteaux!
Chapter Resources

PRINT

Lesson Planning

One-Stop Planner

Lesson Planner with Substitute Teacher

Lesson Plans, pp. 26–30, 68

Student Make-Up Assignments
- Make-Up Assignment Copying Masters, Chapter 6

Listening and Speaking

TPR Storytelling Book, pp. 40–47

Listening Activities
- Student Response Forms for Listening Activities, pp. 43–45
- Additional Listening Activities 6-1 to 6-6, pp. 47–49
- Additional Listening Activities (song), p. 50
- Scripts and Answers, pp. 127–131

Video Guide
- Teaching Suggestions, pp. 38–39
- Activity Masters, pp. 40–42
- Scripts and Answers, pp. 97–99, 120

Activities for Communication
- Communicative Activities, pp. 31–36
- Realia and Teaching Suggestions, pp. 100–104
- Situation Cards, pp. 147–148

Reading and Writing

Reading Strategies and Skills Handbook, Chapter 6

Joie de lire 2, Chapter 6

Cahier d'activités, pp. 61–72

Grammar

Travaux pratiques de grammaire, pp. 45–52

Grammar Tutor for Students of French, Chapter 6

Assessment

Testing Program
- Grammar and Vocabulary Quizzes, **Etape** Quizzes, and Chapter Test, pp. 131–148
- Score Sheet, Scripts and Answers, pp. 149–156
- Midterm Exam, pp. 157–164
- Score Sheet, Scripts and Answers, pp. 165–170

Alternative Assessment Guide
- Portfolio Assessment, p. 23
- Performance Assessment, p. 37
- CD-ROM Assessment, p. 51

Student Make-Up Assignments
- Alternative Quizzes, Chapter 6

Standardized Assessment Tutor
- Reading, pp. 21–23
- Writing, p. 24
- Math, pp. 25–26

MEDIA

Online Activities
- **Jeux interactifs**
- **Activités Internet**

Video Program
- Videocassette 2
- Videocassette 5 (captioned version)

Interactive CD-ROM Tutor, Disc 2

DVD Tutor, Disc 1

Audio Compact Discs
- Textbook Listening Activities, CD 6, Tracks 1–12
- Additional Listening Activities, CD 6, Tracks 24–30
- Assessment Items, CD 6, Tracks 13–18
- Midterm Exam, CD 6, Tracks 19–23

Teaching Transparencies
- Situation 6-1 to 6-3
- Vocabulary 6-A and 6-B
- **Mise en train**
- **Grammaire supplémentaire** Answers
- **Travaux pratiques de grammaire** Answers

One-Stop Planner CD-ROM

Use the **One-Stop Planner CD-ROM with Test Generator** to aid in lesson planning and pacing.

For each chapter, the **One-Stop Planner** includes:
- Editable lesson plans with direct links to teaching resources
- Printable worksheets from resource books
- Direct launches to the HRW Internet activities
- Video and audio segments
- Test Generator
- Clip Art for vocabulary items

Projects

Des châteaux vivants

Students will give an oral presentation in English on the château of their choice. Groups of four will present a colorful history of the château. Their presentations might include original songs, raps, skits, puppet shows, computer-generated material, or any other imaginative ideas.

MATERIALS

✂ **Students may need**
(depending upon the chosen format)

- Posters
- Slides
- Videocassettes
- Computer-generated graphics
- Costumes/Props
- Puppets and stage

SUGGESTED SEQUENCE

1. Each group chooses and researches a château. You might give students the following guidelines.
   - Tell when the château was built and by whom.
   - Name three features of the architecture of this château.
   - Talk about two important people who lived there.
   - Tell why you like the château and if you would like to have lived there. Give reasons.
2. Groups decide on the format for their presentation.
3. Students write and edit the script for their presentation.
4. Members prepare the visual aids and rehearse their presentation. The group hands in a final copy of the script before performing.

GRADING THE PROJECT

Suggested Point Distribution (total = 100 points)

Content	40
Creativity/Overall presentation	20
Effort/Participation	20
Written test grades	20

TEACHER NOTE

There are many travel guides that provide information about châteaux, such as *Let's Go France* (Saint Martin's Press) and *Frommer's Comprehensive Travel Guide* (Prentice Hall Travel). You might write or call the tourist office in Tours at: Office de Tourisme, Hôtel de Ville, rue Bernard Palissy, 37000 Tours (Tel. 02.47.70.37.37). You might also refer students to the Location Opener on pages 124–127 for the names and photos of several châteaux.

Games

Dessiner, c'est gagner!

In this game, students will practice the vocabulary from this chapter and the ***passé composé*** *with* ***avoir*** *and* ***être****.*

Procedure Copy on a transparency the vocabulary for activities from the **Première étape** (page 162) and the verbs from the **Deuxième étape** (page 167) of the *Pupil's Edition.* Form two teams. Have students on each team agree on a character for a story. Each team will imagine what their character did last weekend, using at least eight of the verbs and expressions from the transparency. The first person in each team begins by writing one or two sentences introducing the team's character and telling about one thing that happened to the character over the weekend. The first player then passes the paper to the next player on the team. The second player writes another sentence and passes it to the next player. Continue until all players on each team have had a chance to add an event to the story. When both teams have finished, collect their papers. Have a volunteer from the first team come to the board, read the other team's paper silently, and then draw a representation of the first event of the story. Only players on the drawer's team may try to guess what the event is. When a player guesses correctly, the volunteer draws the next event on the board. When students have guessed all the events, another volunteer from the same team must summarize the story, based on the illustrations and guesses. Keep track of how long it takes students to guess the entire story. Repeat this process with the second team. The team that finishes in the shortest time wins the game.

STANDARDS: 1.1, 2.2, 3.2

Storytelling

Mini-histoire

*This story accompanies Teaching Transparency 6-1. The **mini-histoire** can be told and retold in different formats, acted out, written down, and read aloud, to give students additional opportunities to practice all four skills. The following story relates Audrey's vacation in France.*

Audrey est à Paris depuis une semaine chez sa correspondante. Elle envoie un email à son frère pour lui raconter comment se passe son séjour.

Je vais bien. Ma copine Clothilde habite tout près du Louvre. Elle est très sympa. Le jour de mon arrivée, elle m'a dit : « Si tu n'es pas trop fatiguée, je t'emmène sur la grande roue. Ça va te plaire!». La grande roue se trouve place de la Concorde. Quel spectacle!

Le week-end dernier, la sœur de Clothilde nous a emmenées avec ses amies voir les châteaux de la Loire. Nous avons visité Blois, Chenonceau et Chambord. Le midi, nous avons pique-niqué dans la forêt.

Demain, on doit emmener Romain, le petit frère de Clothilde, au zoo de Vincennes. Je passe des vacances super! Donne-moi de tes nouvelles.

Traditions

Troglodytes

The Loire Valley lies on a bed of chalky white limestone called *tufa* or **tuffeau.** Since Neolithic times, people have been using tufa to build their homes. At first, the tufa was hollowed out to make caves in which the valley's first residents lived. Then during the Renaissance, tufa was mined from the bluffs to build the region's many **châteaux.** The mining during this time and subsequent centuries left a network of caves resembling large blocks of Swiss cheese. Today the residents of the Loire have found multiple uses for these caves. Some have been converted into modern homes, restaurants, and hotels. Ask students to imagine what it would be like to live in a troglodyte (cave) home. Then have them find out where else in the world people have built homes in caves.

Recette

The most famous crêpe is the "Crêpe Suzette". It was actually created by mistake. The future King Edward VII, Prince of Wales, was enjoying dinner when the cook accidentally spilled orange liqueur on the crêpe and set it on fire. Instead of admitting his mistake when the future king asked what was happening, the cook decided to say that it was a new recipe in honor of the king, and he named it "Crêpe Prince de Galles". The future king loved it, but preferred to rename it "Crêpe Suzette" in honor of the charming woman with whom he was sharing his dinner.

CREPES

1 œuf

2 tasses de lait

2 tasses de farine

1/2 tasse de sucre

une pincée de sel

beurre

Pour la garniture, utiliser de la confiture, de la sauce au chocolat ou du sucre

Mettre la farine dans une saladier. Faire un puit. Y mettre l'œuf, le sel et le sucre. Ajouter un petit peu de lait. Mélanger, et continuer à ajouter le lait petit à petit jusqu'à l'obtention d'une pâte relativement liquide (doit ressembler à de la pâte à pancake).

Faire chauffer une poêle. Ajouter une petite noix de beurre dans la poêle. Verser une louche de pâte à crêpe. Etaler la pâte. Faire cuire d'un côté pendant une ou deux minutes. La retourner. Faire cuire de l'autre côté.

Servir avec de la confiture, du sucre ou de la sauce chocolat.

STANDARDS: 1.3, 2.2, 3.2, 5.1

Chapitre 6 : A nous les châteaux!

Technology

DVD/Video

Videocassette 2, Videocassette 5 (captioned version)
DVD Tutor, Disc 1
See Video Guide, pages 37–42.

Mise en train • Le disparu

Céline tells Bruno about her weekend excursion to the château de Chenonceau with Hector and Virginie. The three friends took a bus to the town of Chenonceaux, rented bicycles, and rode the rest of the way. Céline read aloud from her guidebook, and they toured the château. At the end of the segment, Céline and Virginie noticed that Hector was missing!

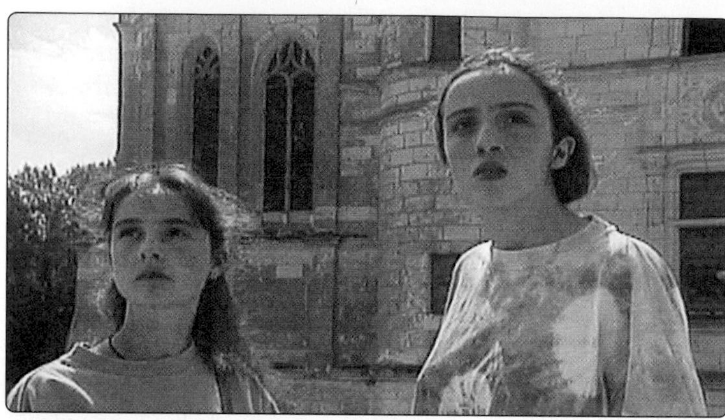

Mise en train (suite)

Searching for Hector, Céline and Virginie find a note with a riddle directing them to the garden of Diane de Poitiers. A second note sends them to the garden of Catherine de Médicis, and a third, around the château. They can't find Hector, but they hear a voice calling for help from the bank below. It's Hector, who can't get back up to the bridge. The trick Hector played backfired on him!

Qui sont les personnages historiques que tu as étudiés?

Students from Martinique and France talk about famous people they have studied in school.

Vidéoclips

- **Banania®**: advertisement for chocolate-flavored powder
- **Persil®**: advertisement for laundry soap

Interactive CD-ROM Tutor

Activity	Activity Type	Pupil's Edition Page
En contexte	*Interactive conversation*	
1. Vocabulaire	Chasse au trésor Explorons!/Vérifions!	p. 162
2. Comment dit-on... ?	Chacun à sa place	p. 164
3. Vocabulaire	Jeu des paires	p. 167
4. Grammaire	Les mots qui manquent	p. 167
5. Comment dit-on... ?	Le bon choix	p. 172
6. Grammaire	Méli-mélo	p. 172
Panorama Culturel	Qui sont les personnages historiques que tu as étudiés?	p. 170
A toi de parler	*Guided recording*	pp. 180–181
A toi d'écrire	*Guided writing*	pp. 180–181

Teacher Management System

Launch the program, type "admin" in the password area, and press RETURN. Log on to www.hrw.com/CDROMTUTOR for a detailed explanation of the Teacher Management System.

DVD Tutor

The *DVD Tutor* contains all material from the *Video Program* as described above. French captions are available for use at your discretion for all sections of the video. The *DVD Tutor* also provides a variety of video-based activities that assess students' understanding of the **Mise en train, Suite,** and **Panorama Culturel.**

This part of the *DVD Tutor* may be used on any DVD video player connected to a television or video monitor.

In addition to the video material and the video-based comprehension activities, the *DVD Tutor* also contains the entire *Interactive CD-ROM Tutor* in DVD-ROM format. Each DVD disc contains the activities from all 12 chapters of the *Interactive CD-ROM Tutor.*

This part of the *DVD Tutor* may be used on a Macintosh® or Windows® computer with a DVD-ROM drive.

To preview all resources available for this chapter, use the **One-Stop Planner CD-ROM,** Disc 2.

Internet Connection

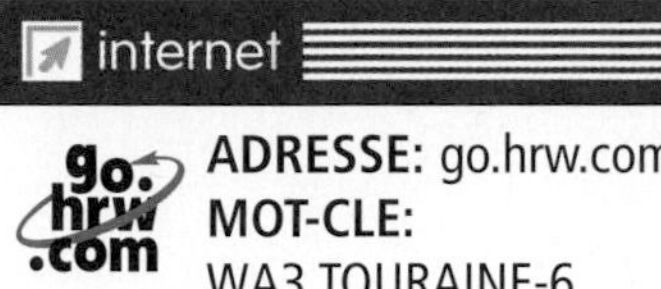

Have students explore the ***go.hrw.com*** *Web site for many online resources covering all chapters. All Chapter 6 resources are available under the keyword* ***WA3 TOURAINE-6.*** *Interactive games help students practice the material and provide them with immediate feedback. You'll also find a printable worksheet that provides Internet activities that lead to a comprehensive online research project.*

Jeux interactifs

You can use the interactive activities in this chapter

- to practice grammar, vocabulary, and chapter functions
- as homework
- as an assessment option
- as a self-test
- to prepare for the Chapter Test

Activités Internet

Students look for information about the Loire Valley châteaux online and record a little about each castle, using the vocabulary from the chapter.

- In preparation for the **Activités Internet**, have students review **Allez, viens en Touraine!** on Videocassette 2. After they complete the activity sheet, have students work with a partner and share the information they gathered in Activity B on that sheet. Then ask each pair of students to share what they learned with the class.

Location: http://

Nom ______ Classe ______ Date ______

6 *A nous les châteaux!*

Level 2

Avant d'explorer

En ligne!

	1	2	3	4
Nom ou activité				
Adresse				
Heures d'opération/ prix				
Ce qu'on peut voir et faire				

Projet

Have students work in groups of three or four. Students will make a small tourist brochure for their favorite château from page 127 in the textbook. They will reconstruct the history of their château, record their findings on audiocassette, and make a small brochure. The brochure should include at least one picture of the château, who the château was built for, one unique feature of the architecture, and one important event that occurred there. Have students document their sources by noting the URLs of all the sites that they consulted.

Chapitre 6 : A nous les châteaux!

Textbook Listening Activities Scripts 

Première étape

7 p. 163

1. Elle a donné à manger aux animaux.
2. Elle a fait un tour sur la grande roue.
3. Elle a assisté à un spectacle son et lumière.
4. Elle est montée dans des tours.
5. Elle est allée dans un parc d'attractions.
6. Elle a fait une visite guidée.

Answers to Activity 7

1. Han
2. Perrine
3. Mariyam
4. Mariyam
5. Perrine
6. Han

10 p. 164

1. — Eh, Dien, tu as passé un bon week-end?
   — Ben, oui.
   — Qu'est-ce que tu as fait?
   — Ben, je suis allé au château de Fontainebleau.
   — Vraiment? Ça t'a plu?
   — Oui, beaucoup. C'était magnifique.
2. — Salut, Bertrand. C'était comment, ton week-end?
   — Oh, pas mal. Je suis allé au zoo.
   — Tu t'es bien amusé?
   — Oh, plus ou moins.
3. — C'était comment, la boum hier soir?
   — La fête de Béatrice? C'était sensass! Je me suis beaucoup amusée.
4. — Salut, Amina. Qu'est-ce que tu as fait hier?
   — Je suis allée dans un parc d'attractions.
   — Tu t'es bien amusée?
   — Pas vraiment. Je me suis plutôt ennuyée. C'était nul.

Answers to Activity 10

1. enthusiastic
2. indifferent
3. enthusiastic
4. dissatisfied

Deuxième étape

16 p. 167

1. — Dis, tu as vu Paul?
   — Paul? Je crois qu'il est retourné dans l'autocar.
2. — Bon. Et Laurence? Où est-elle?
   — Je crois qu'elle est restée au café.
   — Va la chercher, s'il te plaît.
3. — Où est Ali?
   — Il est descendu au bord de la rivière.
   — Oh là là! Va le chercher tout de suite!
4. — Et Guillaume?
   — Euh, je ne sais pas. Peut-être qu'il est monté au premier étage?
   — Bon... va le chercher.
5. — Et Mireille? Tu l'as vue?
   — Oui... elle est allée dans le jardin de Diane de Poitiers. Je vais la chercher.
6. — Enfin, il n'y a plus que Marcel qui manque.
   — Je crois qu'il est parti avec les Américains!

Answers to Activity 16

1. in the bus
2. at a café
3. at the riverbank
4. on the second floor
5. in the castle garden
6. with some Americans

20 p. 169

1. Mai — Salut, Daniel. Comment s'est passé ton week-end?
Daniel — Très bien, merci.
Mai — Qu'est-ce que tu as fait?
Daniel — D'abord, je suis allé au supermarché. Et tu ne vas pas croire qui j'ai vu! J'ai fait la connaissance de Vanessa Paradis!
Mai — Ça m'étonnerait!

2. Mai — Eh bien, Agnès, qu'est-ce qui s'est passé?
Agnès — Oh, je suis tombée, et j'ai déchiré ma robe.
Mai — Oh là là! Pauvre vieille!

The following scripts are for the listening activities found in the *Pupil's Edition.* For Student Response Forms, see *Listening Activities,* pages 43–45. To provide students with additional listening practice, see *Listening Activities,* pages 47–50.

To preview all resources available for this chapter, use the **One-Stop Planner CD-ROM,** Disc 2.

3. MAI Salut, Richard. Tu as passé un bon week-end?

RICHARD Oui, c'était super! Je suis allé visiter le château de Versailles, et j'ai vu le fantôme de Louis Quatorze.

MAI Mon œil!

4. MAI Et toi, Valérie, comment ça s'est passé, ton week-end?

VALÉRIE Bof. J'ai lu un roman, et j'ai fait du vélo, c'est tout.

MAI Oh, c'est pas si mal.

5. MAI Mohammed, qu'est ce que tu as fait ce week-end?

MOHAMMED J'ai fait un vidéoclip avec Kassav'.

MAI N'importe quoi!

MOHAMMED Mais si, c'est vrai! Tu vas voir!

Answers to Activity 20

1. no
2. yes
3. no
4. yes
5. no

Troisième étape

26 p. 172

L'EMPLOYE Bonjour, mademoiselle.

NATHALIE Bonjour, monsieur. A quelle heure est-ce que le train pour Paris part?

L'EMPLOYE Dans une demi-heure. A quatorze heures vingt-cinq.

NATHALIE Combien coûte un aller simple?

L'EMPLOYE Onze euros.

NATHALIE Bon, alors un aller simple, s'il vous plaît. Le train part de quel quai?

L'EMPLOYE Du quai dix, par là.

NATHALIE Bien. Merci beaucoup.

Answers to Activity 26

1. Paris
2. quatorze heures vingt-cinq
3. aller simple
4. onze euros
5. dix

Mise en pratique

2 p. 180

Horaires pour samedi et dimanche. Ligne douze, destination Blois avec arrêts à Amboise et Monteaux. Départ de la gare routière de Tours à neuf heures. Arrivée Amboise à neuf heures trente, Monteaux à neuf heures cinquante-cinq, Blois à dix heures quarante-cinq. Pour le retour, départ Blois à quinze heures trente, Monteaux à seize heures vingt, Amboise à seize heures quarante-cinq, arrivée Tours à dix-sept heures quinze. Prix aller simple : huit euros, six euros pour les enfants de moins de huit ans. Prix aller-retour : quatorze euros, dix euros pour les enfants de moins de huit ans.

Answers to Mise en pratique Activity 2

To Amboise: 9:00
From Amboise: 4:45
Price of ticket: 14 euros

Chapitre 6 : A nous les châteaux!

Suggested Lesson Plans 50-Minute Schedule

Day 1

CHAPTER OPENER 5 min.
- Present Chapter Objectives, p. 157.
- Thinking Critically and Teacher Note, ATE, p. 157

MISE EN TRAIN 40 min.
- Presenting **Mise en train,** ATE, p. 159
- Culture Note, ATE, p. 158
- Thinking Critically, ATE, p. 159
- Teaching Suggestions: Viewing Suggestion 2, Video Guide, p. 38
- Do Activities 1–4, p. 160.

Wrap-Up 5 min.
- Do Activity 5, p. 160.

Homework Options
Cahier d'activités, Acts. 1–2, p. 61

Day 2

MISE EN TRAIN
Quick Review 10 min.
- Bell Work, ATE, p. 161
- Read and discuss **Note culturelle,** p. 161.
- Do Activity 6, p. 161.

PREMIERE ETAPE
Vocabulaire, p. 162 35 min.
- Presenting **Vocabulaire,** ATE, p. 162
- Play Audio CD for Activity 7, p. 163.
- Language Notes, ATE, p. 163
- Complete Activity 8, p. 163.
- Culture Notes, ATE, pp. 162–163
- Travaux pratiques de grammaire, pp. 45–46, Activities 1–3
- Have students do Activity 9, p. 163, in pairs.

Wrap-Up, 5 min.
- Career Path, ATE, p. 163

Homework Options
Cahier d'activités, Acts. 3–4, pp. 62–63
Travaux pratiques de grammaire, Act. 4, p. 46

Day 3

PREMIERE ETAPE
Quick Review 5 min.
- Check homework.

Comment dit-on... ?, and **Note de grammaire, p. 164** 40 min.
- Presenting **Comment dit-on... ?,** ATE, p. 164
- Language Note, ATE, p. 165
- Cahier d'activités, p. 64, Activities 7–8
- Read and discuss **Note de grammaire,** p. 164.
- Play Audio CD for Activity 10, p. 164.
- Do Activity 11, p. 164.
- Do Activity 13, p. 165.
- Have students do Activity 14, p. 165.

Wrap-Up 5 min.
- Write the name of several places to visit on index cards. Distribute one to each student. Have each student tell what he or she did at the place on the card, and what he or she thought of it.

Homework Options
Study for Quiz 6-1.
Pupil's Edition, Activity 12, p. 165
Travaux pratiques de grammaire, Act. 5, p. 144

Day 4

PREMIERE ETAPE
Quiz 6-1 20 min.
- Administer Quiz 6-1A, 6-1B, or a combination of both.

DEUXIEME ETAPE
Vocabulaire, p. 167 20 min.
- Bell Work, ATE, p. 166
- Presenting **Vocabulaire,** ATE, p. 167
- Travaux pratiques de grammaire, Activities 6–8, pp. 47–48
- Cahier d'activités, Activities 10–11, p. 65

Wrap-Up 10 min.
- Do Activity 17, p. 167.

Homework Options
Travaux pratiques de grammaire, Acts. 9–10, pp. 48–49

Day 5

DEUXIEME ETAPE
Quick Review 5 min.
- Check homework.

Grammaire, p. 167 25 min.
- Presenting **Grammaire,** ATE, p. 167
- Teaching Suggestion, ATE, p. 167
- **Grammaire supplémentaire,** Activities 4–5, p. 177
- Do Activity 18, p. 168.
- Have students do Activity 19, part a, p. 168, in groups.

Comment dit-on... ?, p. 168 15 min.
- Presenting **Comment dit-on... ?,** ATE, p. 168
- Play Audio CD for Activity 20, p. 169.
- Do Activity 21, p. 169.
- Have students do Activity 23, p. 169, in groups.

Wrap-Up 5 min.
- Culture Note, ATE, p. 169, and Language-to-Language, ATE, p. 168

Homework Options
Study for Quiz 6-2.
Pupil's Edition, Activity 19, part b, p. 168
Travaux pratiques de grammaire, Acts. 11–13, pp. 49–50
Cahier d'activités, Acts. 12–13, p. 66

Day 6

DEUXIEME ETAPE
Quiz 6-2 20 min.
- Administer Quiz 6-2A, 6-2B, or a combination of both.

PANORAMA CULTUREL, 15 min.
- Presenting **Panorama Culturel,** ATE, p. 170
- Thinking Critically, ATE, p. 170
- Questions, ATE, p. 170
- Discuss **Qu'en penses–tu?** questions, p. 170.

TROISIEME ETAPE
Note culturelle, p. 171 10 min.
- Read and discuss **Note culturelle,** p. 171.
- Do Activity 25, p. 171.
- Culture Note, ATE, p. 171

Wrap-Up 5 min.
- Describe a tour you took from the brochure, on page 171, without naming the place. Have students tell you where you went.

For alternative lesson plans by chapter section, to create your own customized plans, or to preview all resources available for this chapter, use the **One-Stop Planner CD-ROM,** Disc 2.

For additional homework suggestions, see activities accompanied by this symbol throughout the chapter.

Day 7

TROISIEME ETAPE

Quick Review 5 min.
- Bell Work, ATE, p. 171

Comment dit-on... ? and Note de grammaire, p. 172 30 min.
- Presenting **Comment dit-on... ?**, ATE, p. 172
- Play Audio CD for Activity 26, p. 172.
- Cahier d'activités, Activities 17–19, pp. 68–69
- Present **Note de grammaire,** p. 172.
- Do Activity 27, p. 172.
- **Grammaire supplémentaire,** Acts. 9–10, p. 179
- Have students do Activity 28, p. 172, in pairs.

Note de grammaire, p. 173 10 min.
- Read and discuss **Note de grammaire,** p. 173.
- Do Activity 29, p. 173.
- Language Notes, ATE, p. 173
- Have students do Activity 31, p. 173, in pairs.

Wrap-Up 5 min.
- Teaching Suggestion, ATE, p. 173

Homework Options
Study for Quiz 6-3
Cahier d'activités, Acts. 20–21, p. 69
Travaux pratiques de grammaire, Acts. 14–17, pp. 51–52

Day 8

TROISIEME ETAPE

Quiz 6-3 20 min.
- Administer Quiz 6-3A, 6-3B, or a combination of the two.

LISONS! 25 min.
- Read and discuss **Stratégie pour lire,** p. 174.
- Do Prereading Activities A–C, p. 174.
- Have students read ***La Belle au bois dormant,*** pp. 174–175.

Wrap-Up 5 min.
- Culture Note, ATE, p. 174

Homework Options
Cahier d'activités, Acts. 24–25, p. 71

Day 9

LISONS!

Quick Review 5 min.
- Check homework.

Reading and Postreading Activities 40 min.
- Review ***La Belle au bois dormant,*** pp. 174–175.
- Complete Reading Activities D–H, pp. 174–175.
- Have students do Postreading Activity I, p. 175, using Cooperative Learning, ATE, p. 175.

Wrap-Up 5 min.
- Have students begin Activity J, p. 175.

Homework Options
Complete Activity J, p. 175.

Day 10

LISONS!

Quick Review 5 min.
- Have volunteers share the newspaper articles they wrote with the class.

MISE EN PRATIQUE 40 min.
- Do Activity 1, p. 180.
- Play Audio CD for Activity 2, p. 180.
- Do Activity 3, p. 180.
- Discuss Culture Note, ATE, p. 181.
- Discuss the strategy for **Ecrivons!,** p. 181, as a class, then have students work on their summaries.
- Game, ATE, p. 181

Wrap-Up 5 min.
- Show **Vidéoclips,** Video Program, Videocassette 2.
- Complete Activities 9–10, Video Guide, p. 42.

Homework Options
Have students finish summaries for **Ecrivons!,** p. 181.

Day 11

MISE EN PRATIQUE

Quick Review 10 min.
- Have volunteers share their summaries from **Ecrivons!**

Chapter Review 35 min.
- Have students complete **A toi de parler,** CD-ROM Tutor, Disc 2.
- Have students do **A toi d'écrire,** CD-ROM Tutor, Disc 2.
- See Teaching Suggestions, Pre–viewing Suggestions 1–2, Video Guide, p. 38.
- Show ***Le disparu (suite),*** Video Program, Videocassette 2.
- Complete Activities 6–8, Video Guide, pp. 41–42.

Wrap-Up 5 min.
- Have students begin **Que sais-je?,** p. 182.

Homework Options
Que sais-je?, p. 182

Day 12

MISE EN PRATIQUE

Quick Review 20 min.
- Go over **Que sais-je?,** p. 182.
- Do **Jeu de rôle,** p. 181, in groups.

Chapter Review 30 min.
- Review Chapter 6. Choose from **Grammaire supplémentaire,** Grammar Tutor for Students of French, Activities for Communication, Listening Activities, Interactive CD-ROM Tutor, or **Jeux interactifs.**

Homework Options
Study for Chapter 6 Test

Assessment

Chapter Test 40–45 min.
- Administer Chapter 6 Test. Select from Testing Program, Alternative Assessment Guide, Test Generator, Standardized Assessment Tutor.

Chapitre 6 : A nous les châteaux!

Suggested Lesson Plans *90-Minute Block Schedule*

Block 1

CHAPTER OPENER 5 min.
- Present Chapter Objectives, p. 157.
- Thinking Critically, ATE, p. 157
- Teacher Note, ATE, p. 157

MISE EN TRAIN 40 min.
- Preteaching Vocabulary, ATE, p. 158
- Presenting **Mise en train,** ATE, p. 159
- Thinking Critically, ATE, p. 159
- Culture Note, ATE, p. 158
- Math Link, ATE, p. 158
- Do Activities 1–4, p. 160.

PREMIERE ETAPE
Vocabulaire, p. 162 30 min.
- Presenting **Vocabulaire,** ATE, p. 162
- Culture Notes, ATE, pp. 162–163
- Discuss **Note culturelle,** p. 161.
- Do Activity 8, p. 163.
- Play Audio CD for Activity 7, p. 163.

Comment dit-on... ?, p. 164 10 min.
- Presenting **Comment dit-on... ?,** ATE, p. 164

Wrap-Up 5 min.
- Bell Work, ATE, p. 161

Homework Options
Grammaire supplémentaire, p. 176, Acts. 1–2
Cahier d'activités, Acts. 1–4, pp. 61–63
Travaux pratiques de grammaire, Acts. 1–4, pp. 45–46

Block 2

PREMIERE ETAPE
Quick Review 10 min.
- Teaching Transparency 6-1, using the first suggestion in Suggestions for Using Teaching Transparency 6-1

Vocabulaire, p. 162 10 min.
- Do Activity 9, p. 163.

Comment dit-on... ?, p. 164 45 min.
- Read and discuss **Note de grammaire,** p. 164.
- Play Audio CD for Activity 10, p. 164.
- Do Activity 11, p. 164.
- Read and discuss **Tu te rappelles?,** p. 164.
- Do Activities 12–14, p. 165.

DEUXIEME ETAPE
Vocabulaire, p. 167 15 min.
- Presenting **Vocabulaire,** ATE, p. 167
- Teaching Suggestion, ATE, p. 167

Wrap-Up 10 min.
- Write the names of several places to visit on index cards. Distribute one to each student. Have each student tell what he or she did at the place on the card, and what he or she thought of it. The others will try to guess where the student went.

Homework Options
Have students study for Quiz 6-1.
Cahier d'activités, Acts. 5–9, pp. 63–64
Travaux pratiques de grammaire, Act. 5, p. 46

Block 3

PREMIERE ETAPE
Quick Review 10 min.
- Communicative Activity 6-1 and 6-1B, Activities for Communication, pp. 31–32

Quiz 6-1 20 min.
- Administer Quiz 6-1A, 6-1B, or a combination of both.

DEUXIEME ETAPE
Vocabulaire, p. 167 20 min.
- Have students read the photo album entries on page 166.
- Play Audio CD for Activity 16, p. 167.
- Do Activity 17, p. 167.

Grammaire, p. 167 30 min.
- Presenting **Grammaire,** ATE, p. 167
- Teaching Suggestion, ATE, p. 167
- Do Activity 18, p. 168.
- Read and discuss **De bons conseils,** p. 168.

Wrap-Up 10 min.
- Game: **Faites voir!,** p. 177

Homework Options
Grammaire supplémentaire, Acts. 4–6, pp. 177–178
Cahier d'activités, Acts. 10–11, p. 65
Travaux pratiques de grammaire, Acts. 6–11, pp. 47–49

One-Stop Planner CD-ROM

For alternative lesson plans by chapter section, to create your own customized plans, or to preview all resources available for this chapter, use the **One-Stop Planner CD-ROM,** Disc 2.

For additional homework suggestions, see activities accompanied by this symbol throughout the chapter.

Block 4

DEUXIEME ETAPE

Quick Review 10 min.
- Communicative Activity 6-2A and 6-2B, Activities for Communication, pp. 33–34

Grammaire, p. 167 10 min.
- Do Activity 19, part a, p. 168.

Comment dit-on... ?, p. 168 25 min.
- Presenting **Comment dit-on... ?,** ATE, p. 168
- Play Audio CD for Activity 20, p. 169.
- Do Activities 21–22, p. 169.

TROISIEME ETAPE 10 min.
- Do Activity 25, p. 171.
- Read and discuss **Note culturelle,** p. 171.

Comment dit-on... ?, p. 172 25 min.
- Presenting **Comment dit-on... ?,** ATE, p. 172
- Play Audio CD for Activity 26, p. 172.
- Present **Note de grammaire,** p. 172.

Wrap-Up 10 min.
- Teaching Transparency 6-2, using Suggestion #3 in Suggestions for Using Teaching Transparency 6-2

Homework Options
Have students study for Quiz 6-2.
Grammaire supplémentaire, Acts. 7–8, p. 178
Cahier d'activités, Acts. 12–19, pp. 66–69
Travaux pratiques de grammaire, Acts. 12–15, pp. 50–51

Block 5

DEUXIEME ETAPE

Quick Review 10 min.
- Situation Card 6-2: Role–play, Activities for Communication, p.148

Quiz 6-2 20 min.
- Administer Quiz 6-2A, 6-2B, or a combination of the two.

TROISIEME ETAPE

Comment dit-on... ?, p. 172 15 min.
- Do Activities 27–28, p. 172.

Note de grammaire, p. 173 20 min.
- Go over **Note de grammaire,** p. 173, with students.
- Do Activities 29–30, p. 173.

PANORAMA CULTUREL 20 min.
- Presenting **Panorama Culturel,** ATE, p. 170
- Read and discuss the questions in **Qu'en penses-tu?,** p. 170.

Wrap-Up 5 min.
- Additional Listening Activity 6-6, Listening Activities, p. 49

Homework Options
Have students study for Quiz 6-3.
Grammaire supplémentaire, Act. 11, p. 179
Cahier d'activités, Acts. 20–23, pp. 69–70
Travaux pratiques de grammaire, Acts. 6–7, p. 52

Block 6

TROISIEME ETAPE

Quick Review 10 min.
- Communicative Activity 6-3A and 6-3B, Activities for Communication, pp. 35–36

Quiz 6-3 20 min.
- Administer Quiz 6-3A, 6-3B, or a combinaton of the two.

LISONS! 30 min.
- Read and discuss **Stratégie pour lire,** p. 174.
- Prereading Activities A–C, p. 174
- Reading Activities D–H, pp. 174–175

MISE EN PRATIQUE 30 min.
- Do Activity 1, using Slower Pace, ATE, p. 180.
- Do Activities 3 and 5, pp. 180–181.
- Play Audio CD for Activity 2, p. 180.

Homework Options
Que sais-je?, p. 182
Pupil's Edition, Activity 4, p. 181
Study for Chapter 6 Test.

Block 7

MISE EN PRATIQUE

Quick Review 10 min.
- Go over homework and do Game, ATE, p. 181.

Chapter Review 35 min.
- Review Chapter 6. Choose from **Grammaire supplémentaire,** Grammar Tutor for Students of French, Activities for Communication, Listening Activities, Interactive CD-ROM Tutor, or **Jeux interactifs.**

Chapter Test 45 min.
- Administer Chapter 6 Test. Select from Testing Program, Alternative Assessment Guide, Test Generator, or Standardized Assessment Tutor.

Chapter Opener

CHAPITRE 6

For resource information, see the **One-Stop Planner,** Disc 2.

Pacing Tips

In this chapter, the **Deuxième étape** presents verbs that require **être** with the **passé composé.** The **Troisième étape** is lighter in the amount of new content, so you might plan your lessons accordingly. For Lesson Plans and timing suggestions, see pages 155I–155L. After Chapter 6, you might give students the Midterm Exam on pages 157–164 of the *Testing Program.*

Meeting the Standards

Communication

- Asking for opinions; expressing enthusiasm, indifference, and dissatisfaction, p.164
- Expressing disbelief and doubt, p. 168
- Asking for and giving information, p. 172

Culture

- Culture Note, pp. 156, 158, 162, 163, 169, 171, 172, 174, 181
- Note culturelle, pp. 161, 171
- Panorama Culturel, p. 170

Connections

- Math Link, p. 158
- Multicultural Link, p. 170
- History Link, p. 170
- Radio-Television-Film Link, p. 175

Comparisons

- Thinking Critically: Comparing and Contrasting, p. 157
- Thinking Critically: Drawing Inferences, p. 159
- Thinking Critically: Comparing and Contrasting, p. 170

Communities

- Career Path, p. 163
- De l'école au travail, p. 173

Cultures and Communities

Culture Note

While there are many châteaux in the Touraine region, there are also many châteaux located in other regions of France, such as the Château de Maintenon pictured on these pages. Located between Chartres and Versailles, the Château de Maintenon was built in the early 16th century on the banks of the Eure. It became the property of Françoise d'Aubigné, better known as Madame de Maintenon in 1674. In 1686, Madame de Maintenon created Saint-Cyr-l'Ecole, which became a famous military school in 1808.

CHAPITRE

6

A nous les châteaux!

Objectives

In this chapter you will learn to

Première étape

- ask for opinions
- express enthusiasm, indifference, and dissatisfaction

Deuxième étape

- express disbelief and doubt

Troisième étape

- ask for and give information

C'est magnifique, le château de Maintenon!

Chapter Opener

CHAPITRE 6

Focusing on Outcomes

Ask students to say as much as they can in French about the photo. Read the list of outcomes with students and have them try to match the photo with the correct outcome. NOTE: The self-check activities on page 182 help students assess their achievement of the objectives.

Teacher Note

You might remind students that the town of Chenonceaux is spelled with an **–x**, whereas the château of Chenonceau does not have a final **–x**.

Chapter Sequence

Connections and Comparisons

Thinking Critically

Comparing and Contrasting Have students look at the photo. Ask them what they think the students in the photographs did over the weekend and whether it is something they would do. Explain that while French teenagers also go out with friends, go shopping, go to the movies and to parties as American teenagers do, it is not unusual for them to visit a historical site or a museum.

Mise en train

CHAPITRE 6

Teaching Resources
pp. 158–160

PRINT 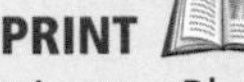

- Lesson Planner, p. 26
- Video Guide, pp. 38, 40
- Cahier d'activités, p. 61

MEDIA 

- One-Stop Planner
- Video Program
  Mise en train
  Videocassette 2, 43:24–48:10
  Videocassette 5 (captioned version), 47:28–52:14
  Suite
  Videocassette 2, 48:13–52:58
  Videocassette 5 (captioned version), 52:17–57:02
- DVD Tutor, Disc 1
- Audio Compact Discs, CD 6, Trs. 1–2
- **Mise en train** Transparencies

Math Link
Call attention to the road signs in Photo 4. The numbers on the signs indicate the distance in kilometers to the destination. Have students calculate the distance in miles by multiplying the number of kilometers by 0.62 (Loches, 16.74 miles; Chisseaux, 1.24 miles; Montrichard, 6.2 miles).

Culture Note
Students may notice the tourists at the château in Photo 8. The Chenonceau château is one of the most frequently visited châteaux in France. It receives visitors, not only from France, but frequently from the United States, Japan, and all the western European countries.

The **roman-photo** is an abridged version of the video episode.

MISE EN TRAIN • *Le disparu*

CD 6 Trs. 1–2

DVD

Stratégie pour comprendre
Listen for keywords in ***Le disparu*** that will help you understand what Céline and Hector are talking about. What words signal that she is talking about something in the past? What did Céline and her friends do over the weekend? What happened to Hector?

Bruno

Céline

Hector

Virginie

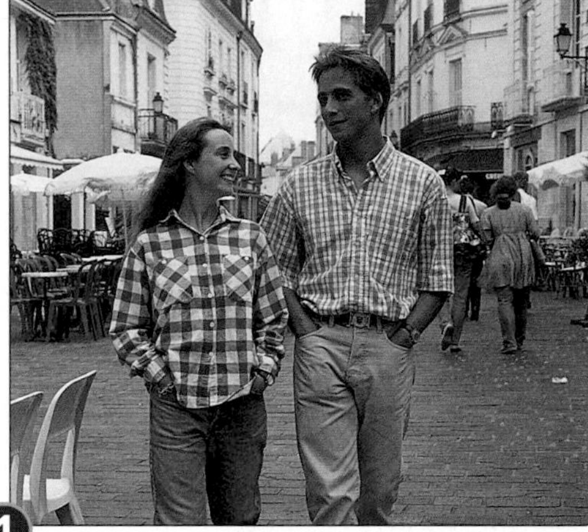

1

Bruno Alors, Céline, qu'est-ce que tu as fait pendant le week-end?
Céline Je suis allée visiter le château de Chenonceau avec Hector et Virginie.
Bruno C'était comment? Ça t'a plu?
Céline Oui! C'était magnifique! Quelle aventure, je te dis!

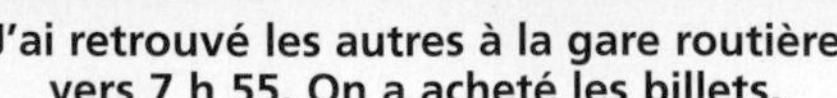
2 J'ai retrouvé les autres à la gare routière vers 7 h 55. On a acheté les billets.

3 Le car est parti à 8 h 10.

Preteaching Vocabulary

Identifying Keywords
First ask students to guess the context of the **Mise en train** (a visit to Chenonceau). Then, have them use the photos on pages 158–159 and identify words or phrases to tell them what is happening. Once they have understood the basic storyline, have them tell what happens to Hector at the end of the story. Have them identify words and phrases related to disappearing in the story. Students might identify the following:

6 **disparaissent**
8 **n'était plus là**
9 **On l'a perdu?**
9 **Il a disparu!**

4 **On est arrivés à Chenonceaux à 8 h 55. Ensuite, on a loué des vélos.**

Hector C'est par là!

5 **Céline** «Le château a été construit entre 1513 et 1521 par Thomas Bohier». On l'appelle «le château des six femmes». Eh, Hector, tu m'écoutes?

6 **Hector** Oui, oui... Vous savez, on dit qu'il y a des gens qui disparaissent dans ces châteaux.

Virginie Sans blague? Tu plaisantes!

Céline Je ne te crois pas.

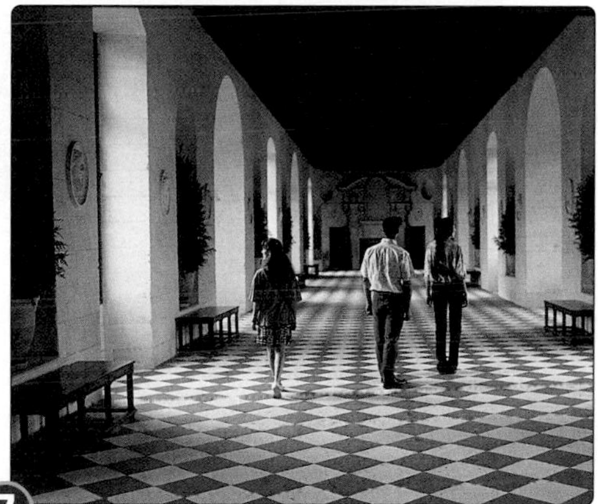

7 **On a visité le château...**

8 **Et puis, on a remarqué qu'Hector n'était plus là!**

Virginie Tiens. Où est Hector?

Céline Je ne sais pas.

9 **On a cherché partout, mais on ne l'a pas trouvé.**

Céline On l'a perdu?

Virginie Il a disparu!

Cahier d'activités, p. 61, Act. 1–2

Using the Captioned Video/DVD

If students have difficulty understanding French spoken at a normal speed, use Videocassette 5 to allow students to see the French captions for ***Le disparu*** and ***Le disparu (suite).*** Hearing the language and watching the story will reduce anxiety about the new language and facilitate comprehension. The reinforcement of seeing the written vocabulary words as they watch the gestures and actions will help prepare students to do the comprehension activities on page 160.

NOTE: The *DVD Tutor* contains captions for all sections of the *Video Program.*

Mise en train

CHAPITRE 6

Presenting Mise en train

Before showing the video, you might present the Preteaching Vocabulary suggestion on page 158. Show the video and ask the questions in Activity 1 on page 160. Then, play the recording and have students read along.

Mise en train Transparencies

Thinking Critically

Drawing Inferences Ask students how often they use buses and trains to get around town. Point out that most Americans tend to depend more on cars than on public transportation and that French teenagers rely more on public transportation than on cars. Ask students to imagine why. (French teenagers can't get a driver's license until they're eighteen. Cars and gasoline are expensive. The public transportation system is more convenient and much more developed.

Mise en train (suite)

When the story continues, Céline and Virginie find a note from Hector near the bicycles. It's a riddle telling them to go to the garden of Diane de Poitiers. There, they find another riddle directing them to go to the garden of Catherine de Médicis. They can't find Hector, but they hear a voice calling for help. On the bank below, they see Hector, who needs help getting back up to the bridge. The trick Hector played on them didn't work out exactly as he had planned!

STANDARDS: 1.2, 2.1, 4.2

Mise en train

CHAPITRE 6

Challenge

3 Have students cover the word box before they complete Céline's journal. Afterwards, list on the board or on a transparency the words students used to complete the journal so that they can compare them with those in the box.

Teaching Suggestion

5 Form small groups and ask each one to imagine how this episode might end. Have them write down the endings. Then, either now or later, read them the synopsis of ***Le disparu (suite)*** on page 159 and have them compare their endings to what really happens. Have the class select the ending they prefer.

Language Note

Point out the use of the word **le car** for the intercity bus that Céline and her friends took to Chenonceaux. **Le bus** refers only to city buses.

Teacher Note

For more practice with the **Mise en train,** have students complete the **Compréhension** questions on Disc 1 of the *DVD Tutor.*

These activities check for comprehension only. Students should not yet be expected to produce language modeled in **Mise en train.**

1 Tu as compris?

1. Where did Céline and her friends go for the day? to visit Chenonceau
2. How did they get there? by bus and by bicycle
3. How did they find out about the history of the château? from a guide book
4. What did they do at the château? They explored it.
5. What happens at the end of the story? Hector disappears.

2 Qui...

1. n'est pas allé au château? Bruno
2. a visité le château? Céline, Hector, Virginie
3. a trouvé Chenonceau magnifique? Céline
4. a lu le guide du château? Céline
5. a dit qu'il y a des gens qui disparaissent? Hector
6. a disparu? Hector
7. a cherché Hector partout? Céline, Virginie

Virginie

Bruno

Céline

Hector

3 Le journal de Céline

Complète le journal de Céline.

est parti, visiter, est arrivés, des vélos, a remarqué, magnifique, a cherché, a acheté

See answers below.

Ce week-end, je suis allée ______ le château de Chenonceau. C'était ______ ! On ______ les billets à la gare et le car ______ à 8h10. On ______ à Chenonceaux à 8h55. On est allés directement louer ______. J'ai lu mon guide du château à haute voix, mais Hector n'écoutait pas. Il nous a dit que des gens disparaissent dans les châteaux, mais je ne l'ai pas cru.
Après la visite guidée du château, on ______ qu'Hector n'était plus là ! On l'______ partout, mais il avait disparu sans laisser de traces !
La suite au prochain numéro...

4 Cherche les expressions

What do the teenagers in ***Le disparu*** say to . . . See answers below.

1. ask for an opinion?
2. express enthusiasm?
3. express disbelief?

5 Et maintenant, à toi

A ton avis, qu'est-ce qui est arrivé à Hector? Qu'est-ce que tu ferais à la place de Céline et de Virginie?

Comprehension Check

Slower Pace

3 Read the letter aloud and have students listen with their books closed. As you read the letter, fill in the blanks, so students hear the letter as it should be. Convey the meaning with gestures, actions, and intonation as you read. Then, have students open their books and do the activity. You might have them work with a partner.

Answers

3 visiter, magnifique, a acheté, est parti, est arrivés, des vélos, a remarqué, a cherché

4
1. C'était comment?
2. C'était magnifique!
3. Sans blague? Tu plaisantes! Je ne te crois pas.

Première étape

Objectives Asking for opinions; expressing enthusiasm, indifference, and dissatisfaction

WA3 TOURAINE-6

Es-tu déjà allé à Loches? On a vu des cachots et je suis montée dans la vieille tour en ruine. C'est très intéressant... on se sent vraiment transporté au Moyen Age. Au fait, je t'ai acheté un souvenir... mais c'est une surprise! Je t'embrasse.

Adèle

LOCHES

Jean Brami
Bâtiment Le Fanal n°8
Esplanade de l'Europe
34000 MONTPELLIER

Le château d'Azay-le-Rideau

Si tu voyais Azay-le-Rideau! C'est incroyable comme château. On s'est promenés dans le parc, puis on a fait un pique-nique. Le spectacle son et lumière sur la vie dans un château de la Renaissance était superbe. C'est vraiment à voir!

Frédéric

Véronique Fabre
8, rue de Liège
75009 PARIS

Note culturelle

Most castles in France fall into two categories. **Châteaux forts,** such as Loches, were built for protection in the Middle Ages. They are massive buildings with thick walls, often surrounded by a moat and built in a strategic location. **Châteaux de la Renaissance,** such as Chenonceau or Azay-le-Rideau, date from the sixteenth century when more thought was given to comfort than to defense. **Châteaux de la Renaissance** feature large windows, ornate sculptures or stonework, and often highly decorated interiors.

6 C'est Loches ou Azay-le-Rideau?

Lisons/Parlons

1. **a.** On peut monter dans une vieille tour. *a. Loches*
   b. C'est un château du Moyen Age. *Loches*
   c. On peut se promener dans le parc ou pique-niquer. *Azay-le-Rideau*
   d. On peut descendre voir les cachots. *Loches*
   e. On l'a construit à l'époque de la Renaissance. *Azay-le-Rideau*
2. Quel château est-ce que tu préfères? Pourquoi?

Communication for All Students

Auditory Learners

If possible, display large photos of Azay-le-Rideau and Loches, either from travel posters or books. Read the two postcards aloud, omitting the names of the châteaux. Have students listen with their books closed and try to identify the château each postcard describes.

Première étape

CHAPITRE 6

Teaching Resources
pp. 161–165

PRINT
- Lesson Planner, p. 27
- TPR Storytelling Book, pp. 40–41
- Listening Activities, pp. 43, 47
- Activities for Communication, pp. 31–32, 100, 103, 147–148
- Travaux pratiques de grammaire, pp. 45–46
- Grammar Tutor for Students of French, Chapter 6
- Cahier d'activités, pp. 62–64
- Testing Program, pp. 131–134
- Alternative Assessment Guide, p. 37
- Student Make-Up Assignments, Chapter 6

MEDIA
- One-Stop Planner
- Audio Compact Discs, CD 6, Trs. 3–4, 13, 24–25
- Teaching Transparencies: 6-1, 6-A; **Grammaire supplémentaire** Answers; Travaux pratiques de grammaire Answers
- Interactive CD-ROM Tutor, Disc 2

Bell Work

Draw two columns on the board or on a transparency. Have students match the questions and statements with the appropriate responses.
In the left column, write: **C'est combien un aller-retour pour Chenonceaux? Ça t'a plu? Qu'est-ce que tu as fait pendant le week-end? Où est Hector?**
In the right column, write: **Je suis allée visiter le château de Chenonceau. Il a disparu! Quatre euros. Oui, je me suis beaucoup amusée!**

STANDARDS: 1.2, 2.2, 3.1, 3.2

Teaching Resources
pp. 161–165

PRINT 

- Lesson Planner, p. 27
- TPR Storytelling Book, pp. 40–41
- Listening Activities, pp. 43, 47
- Activities for Communication, pp. 31–32, 100, 103, 147–148
- Travaux pratiques de grammaire, pp. 45–46
- Grammar Tutor for Students of French, Chapter 6
- Cahier d'activités, pp. 62–64
- Testing Program, pp. 131–134
- Alternative Assessment Guide, p. 37
- Student Make-Up Assignments, Chapter 6

MEDIA

- One-Stop Planner
- Audio Compact Discs, CD 6, Trs. 3–4, 13, 24–25
- Teaching Transparencies: 6-1, 6-A; **Grammaire supplémentaire** Answers; Travaux pratiques de grammaire Answers
- Interactive CD-ROM Tutor, Disc 2

Presenting Vocabulaire

First, relate each of these experiences in the **Vocabulaire** as if it were yours. Sketch on the board as you speak or use pictures you've gathered. Then, write **au parc d'attractions, au zoo,** and **aux châteaux** on the board. Tell students again what you did **(J'ai donné à manger aux animaux.)** and have them tell you where you went by identifying the correct place written on the board.

Vocabulaire

Qu'est-ce que tu as fait pendant le week-end?

Perrine :
Je suis allée dans un parc d'attractions.

J'ai fait un tour sur les montagnes russes...

et sur la grande roue.

Han :
Ce week-end, moi, je suis allée au zoo!

J'ai fait une visite guidée,...

on a fait un pique-nique...

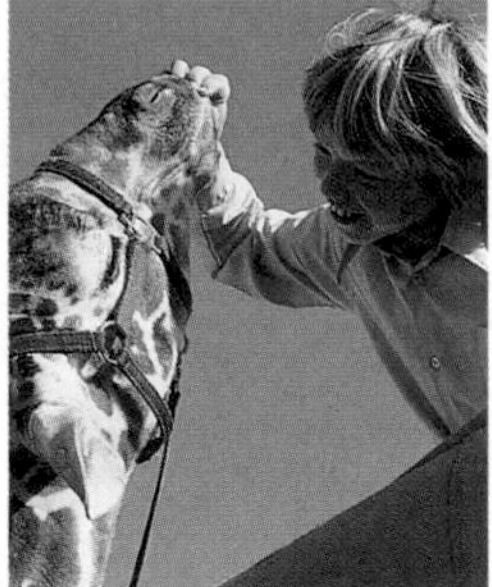

et on a donné à manger aux animaux. Ça m'a beaucoup plu!

Mariyam :
Moi, je suis allée faire un circuit des châteaux!

Je suis montée dans des tours...

et après, on a assisté à un spectacle son et lumière. C'était magnifique!

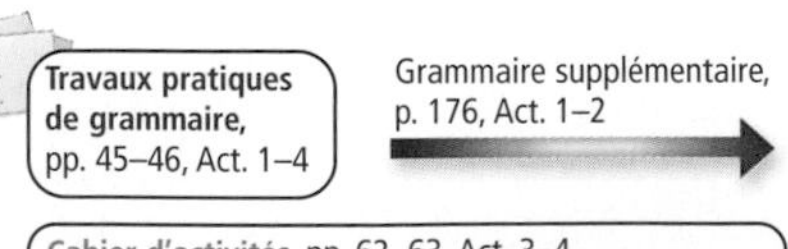

Travaux pratiques de grammaire, pp. 45–46, Act. 1–4

Grammaire supplémentaire, p. 176, Act. 1–2

Cahier d'activités, pp. 62–63, Act. 3–4

Cultures and Communities

Culture Note

There are three major theme parks in France. **Euro Disney,** located in Marne-la-Vallée, is 32 kilometers (20 miles) east of Paris. The park covers 99 acres of the 1,500 acre resort. It has five themes: Frontierland, Adventureland, Main Street USA, Fantasyland, and Discoveryland. The resort has numerous restaurants, hotels, and sports and camping facilities. **Parc Astérix,** located a short distance north of the Charles-de-Gaulle Airport in Paris, was inspired by the popular heroes from the comic strip. Fairground attractions range from high-speed water rides to merry-go-rounds. The **Rue de Paris** leads visitors through a historical reconstruction of Paris over the centuries. **Futuroscope,** near Poitiers, is an extraordinary theme park that features modern, visual technology in a futuristic setting.

7 Qu'est-ce qu'elles ont fait? See scripts and answers on p. 155G.

Ecoutons Regarde le Vocabulaire à la page 162 et écoute Alain et Monique qui parlent des activités de leurs amies. Est-ce qu'ils parlent de Perrine, d'Han ou de Mariyam?
CD 6 Tr. 3

8 L'album de photos de Fatima

Lisons Fatima est allée en vacances et elle veut te montrer ses photos. Mais quand elle ouvre son album, toutes les photos tombent. Aide Fatima à trouver la description qui va avec chaque photo.

a.

b.

c.

d.

1. On a fait une visite guidée du château et on a vu un spectacle son et lumière le soir. C'était génial! a
2. Samedi midi au parc. Comme il faisait beau, on a décidé de faire un pique-nique. Mélanie et Franck ont apporté des fruits et nous, on a fait des sandwiches. c
3. Ça, c'est le zoo qu'on a visité. Il y a plein d'animaux super là-bas! Et si on veut, on peut même donner à manger aux singes. b
4. Karim et Gina n'ont pas voulu monter sur les montagnes russes. Mais Franck et moi, on s'est beaucoup amusés au parc d'attractions. d

9 Alors, tu as fait le circuit...

Lisons/Parlons Imagine que tu as fait un de ces circuits. Ton/Ta camarade va te poser des questions pour essayer de deviner quel circuit tu as fait. Ensuite, changez de rôle.

EXEMPLE —Tu es allé(e) dans un parc d'attractions? — Oui.
—Tu as fait une visite guidée des châteaux? — Non.
—Alors, tu as fait le circuit vert! — ?

Faites le circuit jaune! On va... faire une visite guidée des châteaux, monter dans une tour, aller au zoo et donner à manger aux animaux!

ESSAYEZ LE CIRCUIT BLEU! VOUS POUVEZ... aller au zoo, donner à manger aux animaux, faire un pique-nique et aller dans un parc d'attractions!

Choisissez le circuit rose où vous pouvez... faire un pique-nique, aller au zoo, donner à manger aux animaux et assister à un spectacle son et lumière!

Amusez-vous en faisant le circuit vert! Vous pouvez... aller dans un parc d'attractions, faire un tour sur les montagnes russes, faire un pique-nique et assister à un spectacle son et lumière!

ON VA FAIRE LA FÊTE SUR LE CIRCUIT ORANGE! ALLONS... FAIRE UN PIQUE-NIQUE, ASSISTER À UN SPECTACLE SON ET LUMIÈRE, FAIRE UNE VISITE GUIDÉE DES CHÂTEAUX ET MONTER DANS UNE TOUR!

Première étape

CHAPITRE 6

Teaching Suggestion

8 Before students begin the activity, ask them to describe the four photos in French, giving as much detail as they can.

Language Notes

- **Un cachot** is the French word for *dungeon.* **Un donjon** is a **faux ami. Le donjon** is *the castle keep,* a high, fortified tower.
- The word **zoo** in French is pronounced **[zo]** as in **zoologique [zo o lo jik].**
- Call students' attention to the false cognate **assister.** It means *to attend,* not *to help*, which is **aider.**

Career Path

Working as an employee at a theme park is a great way to meet and work with people from all over the world. Ask students to name some jobs in a theme park that might require knowledge of a foreign language. What languages would be important to know?

Culture Note

Sound and light shows **(des spectacles son et lumière)** are a popular form of summer entertainment in France. They often use actors and props in addition to film, audio recordings, and light displays. The lights and film are projected onto historic cathedrals, monuments, and châteaux. The shows usually have historic themes, so they are educational, as well as entertaining.

Communication for All Students

Auditory Learners

8 After students have described the photos in the activity, read aloud the four monologues and have students match each one with the appropriate photo.

Visual Learners

9 Have students sketch an illustration of all the things they could do on one of the excursions. Then, have them show the sketch to a partner, who will try to guess which trip they have chosen. **(Tu as choisi le circuit rose.)**

Première étape

CHAPITRE 6

Teaching Resources
pp. 161–165

PRINT

- Lesson Planner, p. 27
- TPR Storytelling Book, pp. 40–41
- Listening Activities, pp. 43, 47
- Activities for Communication, pp. 31–32, 100, 103, 147–148
- Travaux pratiques de grammaire, pp. 45–46
- Grammar Tutor for Students of French, Chapter 6
- Cahier d'activités, pp. 62–64
- Testing Program, pp. 131–134
- Alternative Assessment Guide, p. 37
- Student Make-Up Assignments, Chapter 6

MEDIA 

- One-Stop Planner
- Audio Compact Discs, CD 6, Trs. 3–4, 13, 24–25
- Teaching Transparencies: 6-1, 6-A; **Grammaire supplémentaire** Answers; Travaux pratiques de grammaire Answers
- Interactive CD-ROM Tutor, Disc 2

Presenting
Comment dit-on... ?

On a transparency, write the new expressions in three columns. Above the appropriate columns, draw a smiling face, an indifferent face, and a frowning face. Then, list places that are commonly visited in your area. Ask students **Tu es allé(e) au musée ce week-end? C'était comment?** Point to the sentences that express enthusiasm, gesture thumbs-up, and ask **C'était superbe? C'était sensass?** Have students answer, **(Oui, c'était sensass!)**, making the appropriate gesture. Continue with the other expressions.

Comment dit-on...?

Asking for opinions; expressing enthusiasm, indifference, and dissatisfaction

CD-ROM 2 DVD 1

To ask for an opinion:

C'était comment? *How was it?*
Ça t'a plu? *Did you like it?*
Tu t'es bien amusé(e)? *Did you have fun?*

To express indifference:

C'était... *It was . . .*
assez bien. *OK.*
comme ci comme ça. *so-so.*
pas mal. *all right.*
Mouais. *Yeah.*
Plus ou moins. *More or less.*

To express enthusiasm:

C'était... *It was . . .*
magnifique! *beautiful!*
incroyable! *incredible!*
superbe! *gorgeous!*
sensass! *sensational!*
Ça m'a beaucoup plu. *I really liked it.*
Je me suis beaucoup amusé(e). *I had a lot of fun.*

To express dissatisfaction:

C'était... *It was . . .*
ennuyeux. *boring.*
mortel. *deadly dull.*
nul. *lame.*
sinistre. *awful.*
Sûrement pas! *Definitely not!*
Je me suis ennuyé(e). *I was bored.*

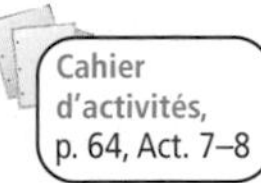
Cahier d'activités, p. 64, Act. 7–8

10 Ils se sont amusés?

See scripts and answers on p. 155G.

CD 6 Tr. 4

Ecoutons Listen to several friends discuss what they did over the weekend. Are they enthusiastic, indifferent, or dissatisfied? Listen again and write down each response.

Note de grammaire

You've probably noticed that **c'était** *(it was)* uses a form of the verb **être** you haven't studied yet. To describe what things were like in the past, you use a verb tense called the **imparfait** *(imperfect)*. You'll learn more about it in Chapter 8.

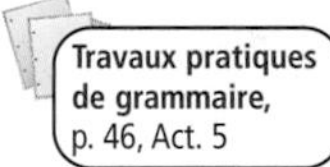
Travaux pratiques de grammaire, p. 46, Act. 5

Grammaire supplémentaire, p. 177, Act. 3

Tu te rappelles?

- Two of the most difficult sounds for English speakers to produce in French are the sound [y] in **tu** and the sound [u] in **tout.**
- To produce the [y] sound, start by saying *me* in English, then round your lips, keeping your tongue pressed behind your lower teeth. Practice by saying **Ça t'a plu?** and **Sûrement pas!** There's no equivalent to this sound in English, so it takes some practice to get it right.
- The [u] sound is like the vowel sound in the English word *fool.* Practice this sound by saying **beaucoup** and **un tour.**
- Learning to distinguish between these sounds is important. There's a big difference between a **pull** and a **poule** *(a hen)* in French!

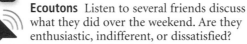

11 Grammaire en contexte

Lisons Complète chaque phrase.

1. Je me suis beaucoup ennuyé pendant mes vacances. __c__
2. La plage? Bof... __d__
3. —Tu t'es bien amusé à Paris?
   —__a__
4. —Chambord? __b__

a. Oui, ça m'a beaucoup plu.
b. C'était magnifique!
c. C'était mortel!
d. C'était comme ci comme ça.

Communication for All Students

Visual Learners

Write the four functions on the board and have students copy them. Scatter transparency strips with the expressions from **Comment dit-on... ?** written on them on the overhead projector. Have students copy the expressions under the appropriate function.

STANDARDS: 1.2, 4.1

12 En famille

Parlons/Ecrivons Ces familles sont parties en week-end. Où est-ce qu'elles sont allées? Qu'est-ce qu'elles ont fait? C'était comment pour chaque personne dans la famille?

See answers below.

1.

3.

2.

4.

13 C'était comment?

Parlons/Ecrivons Ton ami(e) te pose la question **C'était comment?** Comment est-ce que tu réponds si...

1. tu es allé(e) à une boum chez ton/ta meilleur(e) ami(e) hier soir?
2. tu as fait une visite guidée d'une maison historique?
3. tu as vu un film français avec Gérard Depardieu?
4. tu es allé(e) à un concert de jazz?
5. tu es allé(e) dans un musée d'art moderne?
6. tu as fait un pique-nique à la plage avec ta famille?
7. tu as passé un examen de français?

14 Nos distractions

Ecrivons/Parlons Fais une liste de six attractions touristiques dans ta région. Demande à tes camarades s'ils sont allés dans ces endroits. Demande-leur aussi s'ils ont aimé chaque attraction. D'après ton sondage, quel endroit est le plus populaire? Quelle attraction est la moins populaire?

EXEMPLE —**Tu es déjà allé(e) à Mount Rushmore?**
—**Oui.**
—**Ça t'a plu?**
—**Beaucoup. C'était superbe!**

15 Le week-end

Parlons Prépare un dialogue avec un(e) camarade de classe. Qu'est-ce que tu as fait ce week-end? Où es-tu allé(e)? Qu'est-ce que tu as fait là-bas? C'était comment? Et ton/ta camarade?

Teacher to Teacher

Jim Garland
Henry Clay High School
Lexington, KY

Jim suggests the following activity to review material from this chapter.

"Create a computerized Jeopardy™ board, using PowerPoint®, with five categories and five questions per category. You might save this to use as a template in other chapters. Type in an answer or question on each slide and include the point value. The game can be customized for each lesson of the textbook, and it is a great way to review and have fun at the same time. Divide the class into three teams and appoint a captain to give the official response. Prizes may be given to the winning team at the end of the game."

Language Note

Point out that the word **mouais** is slang and should only be used in informal situations, not in written language. It is a combination of the hesitative sound **Hmmm** and the word **ouais,** which is slang for **oui.**

Speaking Assessment

15 You might use the following rubric when grading your students on this activity.

Speaking Rubric	Points			
	4	3	2	1
Content (Complete–Incomplete)				
Comprehension (Total–Little)				
Comprehensibility (Comprehensible–Incomprehensible)				
Accuracy (Accurate–Seldom accurate)				
Fluency (Fluent–Not fluent)				

18–20: A 14–15: C Under
16–17: B 12–13: D 12: F

Assess

- Testing Program, pp. 131–134
  Quiz 6-1A, Quiz 6-1B
  Audio CD 6, Tr. 13
- Student Make-Up Assignments, Chapter 6, Alternative Quiz
- Alternative Assessment Guide, p. 37

Possible Answers

12
1. au zoo; Pour le garçon, c'était nul! Pour sa sœur, c'était magnifique!
2. faire un pique-nique; C'était comme ci comme ça/superbe!
3. sur les montagnes russes; C'était incroyable/sinistre!
4. visiter les châteaux; C'était mortel/pas mal.

STANDARDS: 1.1, 1.3, 5.1

Teaching Resources
pp. 166–169

PRINT

- Lesson Planner, p. 28
- TPR Storytelling Book, pp. 42–43
- Listening Activities, pp. 44, 48
- Activities for Communication, pp. 33–34, 101, 103–104, 147–148
- Travaux pratiques de grammaire, pp. 47–50
- Grammar Tutor for Students of French, Chapter 6
- Cahier d'activités, pp. 65–67
- Testing Program, pp. 135–138
- Alternative Assessment Guide, p. 37
- Student Make-Up Assignments, Chapter 6

MEDIA 

- One-Stop Planner
- Audio Compact Discs, CD 6, Trs. 5–6, 14, 26–27
- Teaching Transparencies; 6-2, 6-B; **Grammaire supplémentaire** Answers; Travaux pratiques de grammaire Answers
- Interactive CD-ROM Tutor, Disc 2

Bell Work

Write the following sentences on the board or on a transparency. Have students try to guess where each person went.

1. **Han a donné à manger aux animaux.**
2. **Anne a fait un tour sur les montagnes russes.**
3. **Marc a visité des cachots.**
4. **Marie a vu un film français.**
5. **Jean a fait un pique-nique.**

Teaching Suggestion

Ask students what they notice about the verbs in the **passé composé (être** is the helping verb). Then, call their attention to the past participles and ask them why there are letters added to some of them.

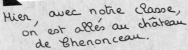

Deuxième étape

Objective Expressing disbelief and doubt

go.hrw.com
WA3 TOURAINE-6

Le 21 avril à Chenonceau...

Hier, avec notre classe, on est allés au château de Chenonceau.

On est arrivés au château de bonne heure. Jean-Claude n'est pas venu avec nous.

Than et Mathieu sont entrés pour la visite guidée. Ali est directement monté au premier étage.

Anaïs est descendue au bord du Cher.

Charlotte est tombée dans le jardin de Diane de Poitiers.

Catherine et Surya sont restées longtemps au café.

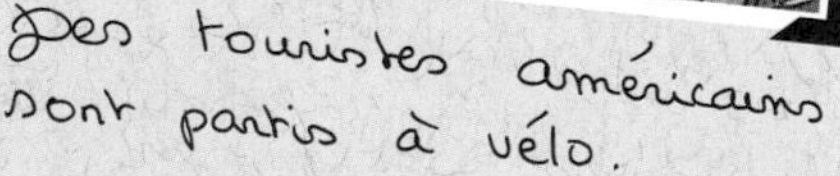

Des touristes américains sont partis à vélo.

On est rentrés très contents!

Communication for All Students

Tactile/Auditory Learners

Have students copy the captions of the illustrations on separate slips of paper and cover the captions in their book with paper. Students should then shuffle the slips, select one, and read aloud the caption to a partner, who will point to the illustration that fits the caption.

Kinesthetic Learners

Ask for volunteers to come to the front of the room and act out one of the captions. Classmates try to guess the caption that corresponds to the gestures.

16 Où sont-ils? See scripts and answers on p. 155G.

CD 6 Tr. 5

Ecoutons Listen as the teacher tries to locate all the students to head back to the bus. Where are these students?

1. Paul **2.** Laurence **3.** Ali **4.** Guillaume **5.** Mireille **6.** Marcel

Vocabulaire

CD-ROM 2 DVD 1

entrer (entré)	*to enter*	**mourir (mort)**	*to die*
venir (venu)	*to come*	**sortir (sorti)**	*to go out*
rester (resté)	*to stay*	**partir (parti)**	*to leave*
monter (monté)	*to go up*	**rentrer (rentré)**	*to go back (home)*
descendre (descendu)	*to go down*	**revenir (revenu)**	*to come back*
naître (né)	*to be born*	**retourner (retourné)**	*to return*
devenir (devenu)	*to become*		

Travaux pratiques de grammaire, pp. 47–49, Act. 6–10 | Cahier d'activités, p. 65, Act. 10–11

17 Un message de Paris

H 1. partis 2. montés 3. resté 4. venu 5. descendus 6. entrés 7. rentrés

Lisons/Ecrivons Ton correspondant Loïc et ses amis sont allés à Paris hier. Lis le message électronique de Loïc et choisis le verbe approprié pour compléter chaque phrase.

Hier, mes copains et moi, on est allés à Paris. On est __1__ (partis/retournés) de Rouen vers huit heures. A Paris, on est tout de suite allés à la tour Eiffel. On est __2__ (nés/montés) tout en haut par les escaliers. Yann, lui, il est __3__ (resté/devenu) au deuxième étage parce qu'il était fatigué. Après, on a décidé d'aller au musée, mais Paul n'est pas __4__ (venu/mort). On a pris le bus et on est __5__ (revenus/descendus) à l'arrêt du Louvre. On est __6__ (entrés/sortis) dans le musée et on a fait une visite guidée. Vers quatre heures, on a repris le train et on est __7__ (rentrés/devenus) à la maison.

Grammaire

The *passé composé* with *être*

- To form the **passé composé** of some verbs, you use **être** instead of **avoir** as the helping verb. The verbs you've just learned follow this pattern, as do the verbs **aller, tomber,** and **arriver** from Chapter 5.

je **suis rentré(e)**	nous **sommes rentré(e)s**
tu **es rentré(e)**	vous **êtes rentré(e)(s)**
il/elle/on **est rentré(e)(s)**	ils/elles **sont rentré(e)s**

Grammaire supplémentaire, pp. 177–178, Act. 4–8

- When you form the **passé composé** with **être,** the past participle agrees in gender and number with the subject, just as an adjective agrees with the noun it describes. If the subject of the verb is feminine, add an **-e** to the past participle. If the subject is feminine plural, add **-es.** If it's masculine plural, add an **-s.** Don't forget that a compound subject with one masculine element is considered masculine plural.

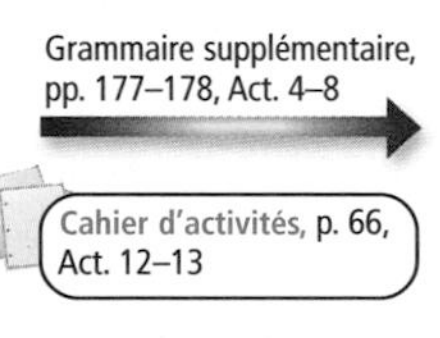

Cahier d'activités, p. 66, Act. 12–13

Travaux pratiques de grammaire, pp. 49–50, Act. 12–13

Connections and Comparisons

Teaching Suggestion

You might give students a mnemonic device to help them remember which verbs are conjugated with **être** in the **passé composé.** A common one is *DR. & MRS. VANDERTRAMP.* Each letter in the name is the first letter of a verb: **D-devenir, R-rester, M-monter,** and so on.

Presenting Vocabulaire

Make a house out of a cardboard box or poster with an opening for a door. Use a stuffed animal to enact the story below in the **passé composé.** On the board, draw the Eiffel Tower and whatever else you may need to tell the story. Write the sentences in scrambled order and ask for volunteers to reconstruct the story. **(M. Ours est né à Chartres. Un jour, il est sorti de sa maison. Il est descendu en ville et il est allé à la gare. Son train est parti pour Paris à six heures. Il est revenu à Chartres vers midi et il est retourné chez lui. A deux heures, il est reparti pour Paris. Il est monté au troisième étage de la tour Eiffel. Il est tombé! Aïe! Il est mort. Il n'est jamais rentré chez lui.)**

Grammaire

The *passé composé* with *être* On strips of transparency, write several sentences in large letters, using verbs in the **passé composé** conjugated with both **être** and **avoir.** Cut the strips into subject pronouns, helping verbs, past participles, and past participle endings, and shuffle the pieces. After reading **Grammaire,** have two students come up to the overhead projector and try to rearrange the pieces into sentences. You might prepare index cards instead of strips of transparency for small groups to use.

Group Work

Have groups create a story, using verbs that are conjugated with **être** in the **passé composé.** They might present the stories to the class, using props and illustrations.

Teaching Resources
pp. 166–169

PRINT

- Lesson Planner, p. 28
- TPR Storytelling Book, pp. 42–43
- Listening Activities, pp. 44, 48
- Activities for Communication, pp. 33–34, 101, 103–104, 147–148
- Travaux pratiques de grammaire, pp. 47–50
- Grammar Tutor for Students of French, Chapter 6
- Cahier d'activités, pp. 65–67
- Testing Program, pp. 135–138
- Alternative Assessment Guide, p. 37
- Student Make-Up Assignments, Chapter 6

MEDIA 

- One-Stop Planner
- Audio Compact Discs, CD 6, Trs. 5–6, 14, 26–27
- Teaching Transparencies: 6-2, 6-B; **Grammaire supplémentaire** Answers; Travaux pratiques de grammaire Answers
- Interactive CD-ROM Tutor, Disc 2

Additional Practice
After presenting **De bons conseils,** have students do Activity 7 on page 48 of the *Travaux pratiques de grammaire.* This activity uses the house diagram to review the verbs that require **être** in the **passé composé.**

Presenting
Comment dit-on... ?
Have partners think of two unbelievable things that have happened to them. Then, as students tell you about them, react with the expressions of disbelief and doubt in **Comment dit-on... ?**

18 Grammaire en contexte
Parlons/Ecrivons Tes copains et toi, vous êtes allés au château samedi dernier. Décris ce que chacun de vous a fait.

Je On Les filles Les garçons ? ? et ?	arriver aller monter descendre rester tomber retourner ?	au château de ? à pied/à vélo/en train dans une tour dans le jardin dans la chambre du roi dans la boutique de souvenirs dans l'escalier ?

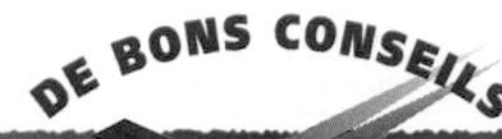

How can you remember when to use **avoir** to form the past tense and when to use **être?** A general rule of thumb is that you often associate **être** with verbs of motion. Think of a house. You use **être** with any verb that will get you *into* the house, *upstairs* and *downstairs* (even by falling!), and *out* of the house. Also, if you *stay* in the house, and are *born* or *die* in the house, you will use **être** with these verbs. Draw a picture to illustrate this and keep it as a study guide.

19 Qu'est-ce qu'il/elle a fait?

a. **Ecrivons/Parlons** Choisis une personne célèbre et fais une liste de trois choses que cette personne a faites. Lis la liste à ton groupe, mais ne dis pas le nom de la personne. Tes camarades doivent deviner qui tu as choisi. Ensuite, c'est le tour de la personne qui a deviné.

Elle a trouvé... — Il a chanté... — Elle a joué... — Elle a découvert... — Il a inventé... — Elle est allée... pour... — Il est devenu célèbre grâce à ...

b. **Ecrivons** Trouve trois autres informations intéressantes au sujet de ta personne célèbre. Ensuite, écris un paragraphe sur cette personne.

Comment dit-on...?
Expressing disbelief and doubt
To express disbelief and doubt:

Tu plaisantes! *You're joking!*
C'est pas vrai. *You're kidding.*
N'importe quoi! *That's ridiculous!*

Pas possible! *No way!*
Ça m'étonnerait. *I doubt it.*
Mon œil! *Yeah, right!*

Cahier d'activités, p. 67, Act. 15

Connections and Comparisons
Language-to-Language
Tell students that **Mon œil!** literally means *My eye!* Have them think of expressions in English that use body parts. *(I'm up to my ears in work. He's a pain in the neck.)* You might share the following French expressions with your students: **avoir le bras long** *(to have pull);* **au pied levé** *(at the drop of a hat).* You might share these Spanish expressions with your students, too: **Ojos que no ven, corazón que no siente** *(out of sight, out of mind);* **En boca cerrada no entran moscas.** *(Keep your mouth shut so you don't stick your foot in it.)*

20 C'est pas vrai! See scripts and answers on p. 155G.

Ecoutons Listen to Mai as she asks her friends about their weekends. Does she believe what they tell her or not?
CD 6 Tr. 6

21 C'est vrai?

Parlons/Ecrivons Qu'est-ce que tu réponds à un(e) ami(e) qui te dit les choses suivantes? Possible answers:

1.
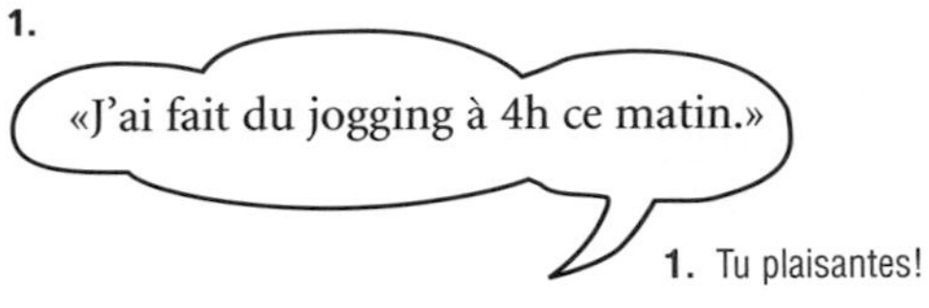

«J'ai fait du jogging à 4h ce matin.»

1. Tu plaisantes!

2.
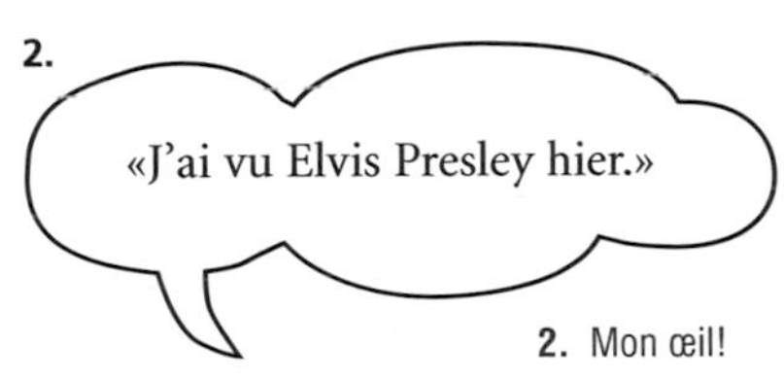

«J'ai vu Elvis Presley hier.»

2. Mon œil!

3.

«La France est en Afrique.»

3. C'est pas vrai!

4.
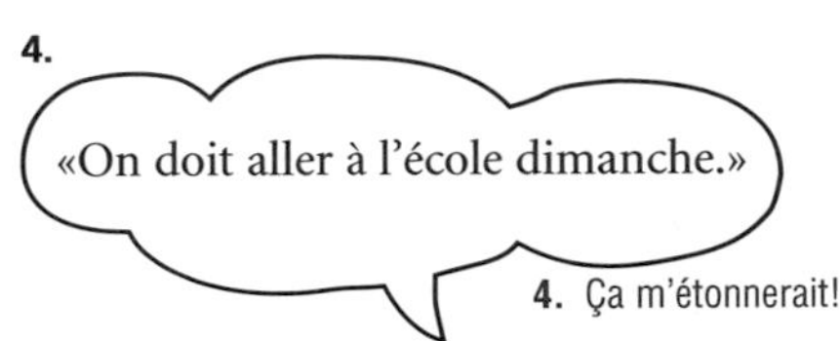

«On doit aller à l'école dimanche.»

4. Ça m'étonnerait!

5.
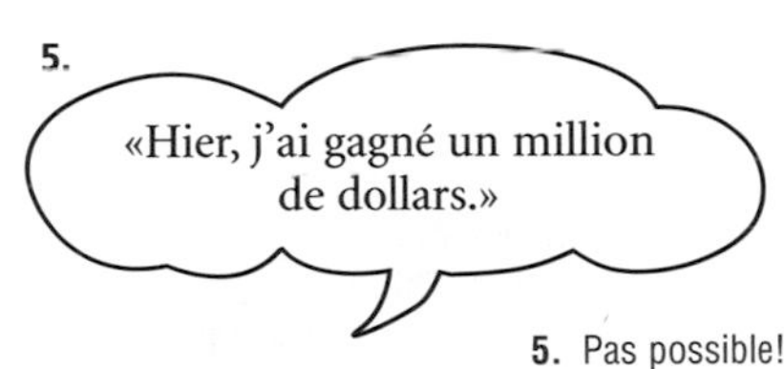

«Hier, j'ai gagné un million
de dollars.»

5. Pas possible!

6.
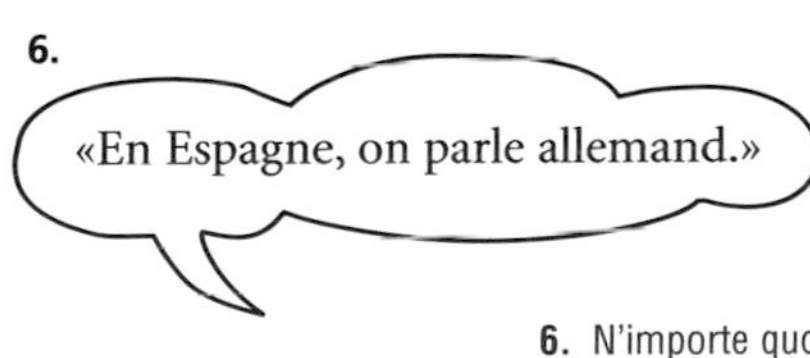

«En Espagne, on parle allemand.»

6. N'importe quoi!

22 Un jour...

Parlons Invente trois choses incroyables qui sont arrivées. Raconte à un(e) camarade ce qui s'est passé. Ton/Ta camarade ne te croit pas et il/elle va te demander plus de détails. Ensuite, changez de rôle.

EXEMPLE —**Un jour, je suis arrivé(e) à l'école avec le président de la République française.**
—**Tu plaisantes! Pourquoi est-ce qu'il est venu avec toi?**
—...

23 Mon œil!

Parlons In your group, take turns telling tall tales about yourselves. The entire group will respond with expressions of doubt and disbelief. When you have told your stories, choose the best one from your group.

24 Un journal bizarre!

Ecrivons Créez un journal avec des histoires incroyables. Chaque groupe raconte sa meilleure histoire. Ajoutez d'autres détails pour rendre l'histoire encore plus intéressante et incroyable.

Communication for All Students

Teaching Suggestion

On index cards, write several unusual activities that your students did on an imaginary field trip **(revenir tout(e) seul(e), rester dans le car).** Write each activity on two cards, so that two students will have a card with the same activity. Distribute one card to each student. Have students circulate around the room, trying to find the person who did the same thing they did. If a student's card reads **arriver en retard,** he or she asks **Tu es arrivé(e) en retard?** Students should answer according to their own card. **(Oui, moi aussi, je suis arrivé(e) en retard. Non, je suis venu(e) à pied.)** If the cards don't match, students should react with disbelief. **(Mon œil!)** When students find their match, they should report to you.

Additional Practice

20 Have students listen to the recording a second time and tell what each person did or where he or she went.

Teacher Note

22 23 A source of true, extraordinary accomplishments that students might use is the *Guinness Book of World Records.*

Portfolio

24 **Written** This activity is appropriate for students' written portfolios. For portfolio suggestions, see the *Alternative Assessment Guide,* page 23.

Culture Note

To express disbelief, French people will often place their index finger just below their eye, pull down the bottom lid slightly, and say **Mon œil!** Sometimes they will make this gesture and frown, without speaking, to convey their meaning. The French will protrude their jaw and lips and say **Peuh!** to express disbelief. This gesture is often accompanied by the expression **N'importe quoi!** *(That's ridiculous!).*

Assess

- Testing Program, pp. 135–138
  Quiz 6-2A, Quiz 6-2B
  Audio CD 6, Tr. 14
- Student Make-Up Assignments, Chapter 6, Alternative Quiz
- Alternative Assessment Guide, p. 37

CHAPITRE 6

Teaching Resources
p. 170

PRINT 

- Video Guide, pp. 39–41
- Cahier d'activités, p. 72

MEDIA 

- One-Stop Planner
- Video Program, Videocassette 2, 53:02–57:50
- DVD Tutor, Disc 1
- Audio Compact Discs, CD 6, Trs. 7–10
- Interactive CD-ROM Tutor, Disc 2

Presenting
Panorama Culturel

Before you show the video, have students list all the French historical figures they know. Then, show the video. Have students list all the names they hear mentioned and compare the two lists.

Questions

1. **Avec qui est-ce que l'impératrice Joséphine s'est mariée?** (avec Napoléon)
2. **Quel auteur est-ce que Pauline admire le plus?** (Victor Hugo)
3. **Qui a étudié Jules César?** (Evelyne)
4. **Qui est Maupassant?** (C'est un auteur.)
5. **Pourquoi est-ce qu'Hervé, qui est Martiniquais, connaît les personnages français?** (La Martinique est un département français.)

Qui sont les personnages historiques que tu as étudiés?

We asked students what famous people they have studied in school. Here are their responses.

Hervé, Martinique

«Je connais tous les personnages historiques français et je vais en citer quelques-uns. Bien, on peut parler des rois de France, par exemple de Louis XIV, de Louis XV, d'Henri IV en Angleterre et en Martinique, notre impératrice Joséphine qui s'est mariée avec l'empereur Napoléon.»

Il y a quelqu'un que tu admires en particulier?

«J'apprécie beaucoup Joséphine, l'impératrice, tout d'abord parce que c'est une compatriote et voilà.» Tr. 8

Pauline, France

«On a étudié surtout des auteurs, comme Victor Hugo ou Maupassant, mais aussi des personnages historiques de l'histoire de France, comme Napoléon.»

Il y a quelqu'un que tu admires en particulier?

«Que j'admire... Je vois pas spécialement. J'aime bien Victor Hugo. J'aime bien les poètes.» Tr. 9

Evelyne, France

«Les personnages qu'on a étudiés en histoire sont Hitler, Mussolini, Vercingétorix et Jules César... Louis XVI et tous les rois de France et les rois d'Angleterre aussi.» Tr. 10

Qu'en penses-tu?

1. Which of the famous people mentioned have you studied? What did they do?
2. Which of these famous people do you find most interesting? Why?
3. What other French-speaking historical figures do you know about? What did they do?
4. Choose a well-known francophone person you have not studied and find out why he or she is famous.

Connections and Comparisons

Thinking Critically

Comparing and Contrasting Ask students how the history they learn differs from the history the interviewees learn.

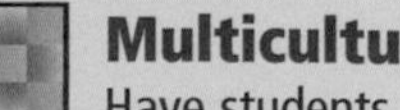

Multicultural Link

Have students research historical figures from other cultures and present their findings to the class.

History Link

Point out that America and France have been linked many times throughout history. Ask students if they can think of any examples. (Benjamin Franklin was ambassador to France. He and others gleaned many of our democratic principles from the writings of Diderot, Rousseau, and Montesquieu. The French helped us fight our revolution, and then staged their own thirteen years later.)

STANDARDS: 1.2, 2.1, 3.1, 3.2, 4.2

Objectives Asking for and giving information

go.hrw.com WA3 TOURAINE-6

CIRCUITS D'UNE JOURNEE	CIRCUITS D'UNE DEMI-JOURNEE
Départ à 9 h 00, place de la Gare, quai n° 6	**Départ à 13 h 15, place de la Gare, quai n° 6**
10 - TOURS, Cormery, vallée de l'Indre, **LOCHES** (visite, déjeuner libre), **CHENONCEAU** (visite), **AMBOISE** (visite), Montlouis, TOURS (vers 18 h 45). *Les samedis, du 10 avril au 25 septembre. Les mardis, du 6 juillet au 28 septembre.* Car : **22 €** Droits d'entrée : **10 €**	12 - TOURS, Vouvray, **CHAUMONT** (visite), **LE CLOS-LUCE** à Amboise, demeure de Léonard de Vinci (visite), TOURS (vers 18 h 45). *Les samedis, du 3 juillet au 11 septembre.* Car : **14 €** Droits d'entrée : **6, 50 €**
11 - TOURS, Amboise (vue sur le château), Chaumont, **BLOIS** (visite, déjeuner libre), Ménars, **CHAMBORD** (visite), **CHEVERNY** (visite), vallée du Cher, TOURS (vers 18 h 45). *Les lundis et vendredis, du 12 avril au 27 septembre.* Car : **22 €** Droits d'entrée : **10 €**	13 - TOURS, Savonnières, Villandry, **USSE** (visite), **LANGEAIS** (visite), TOURS (vers 18 heures). *Les mardis, du 6 juillet au 31 août.* Car : **14 €** Droits d'entrée : **5, 50 €**

SPECTACLES *SON ET LUMIERE*

Départ place de la Gare, quai n° 6

14 - **LE LUDE :** "Les glorieuses et fastueuses soirées au bord du Loir". Départ à 21 heures jusqu'au 31 juillet, à 20 h 30 au mois d'août. *Les samedis, du 26 juin au 21 août. Les vendredis, du 25 juin au 20 août.* Car et droits d'entrée : **21 € 50**

15 - **AMBOISE :** "A la Cour du Roy François". Départ à 21 h 30 jusqu'au 31 juillet, à 21 heures à partir du 1er août. *Les mercredis, du 7 juillet au 25 août.* Car et droits d'entrée : **18 €**

Les circuits de jour sont accompagnés et commentés par des guides-interprètes de Touraine (français-anglais).

25 A lire avec attention

Lisons Ces gens choisissent quel(s) tour(s)?

1. Julien voudrait visiter Chaumont et Clos-Lucé. 12
2. Francine veut voir un spectacle son et lumière mercredi. 15
3. Hélène a 19, 50 € pour le car et l'entrée. 13, 15
4. Cam voudrait assister à un spectacle son et lumière vendredi. 14
5. Luc veut voir Amboise et visiter Chambord. 11
6. En avril, Marion voudrait visiter des châteaux. 10, 11
7. Robert veut faire une visite guidée en anglais. 10, 11

Note culturelle

The intercity bus **(le car)** and the train **(le train)** are two excellent ways to see France. Trains run frequently between larger towns and cities. They are known for running on time. Nearly all train lines are electrified and computerized. The **train à grande vitesse (TGV),** a high-speed train that covers long distances with only a few stops, is the most popular. At the **gare routière,** usually located at the train station, you can take the bus to the smaller towns in the region you are visiting. Some of the bus stations also offer tours, like the ones you see here in the brochure.

Cultures and Communities

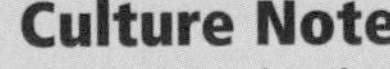

Culture Note

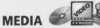

The national railroad in France is operated by a government agency called the **Société Nationale des Chemins de Fer Français,** or **SNCF.** The TGV travels at speeds up to 185 miles per hour. **TGV Nord-Europe** from Paris's **Gare du Nord** travels due north through Normandy. **TGV Atlantique** from Paris's **Gare Montparnasse** branches west to Brittany **(Bretagne)** and southwest from Bordeaux to the Spanish border. **TGV Sud-Est** from Paris's **Gare de Lyon** travels southeast through Lyon to the Côte d'Azur.

Teaching Resources
pp. 171–173

PRINT

- Lesson Planner, p. 29
- TPR Storytelling Book, pp. 44–45
- Listening Activities, pp. 45, 49
- Activities for Communication, pp. 35–36, 102, 104, 147–148
- Travaux pratiques de grammaire, pp. 51–52
- Grammar Tutor for Students of French, Chapter 6
- Cahier d'activités, pp. 68–70
- Testing Program, pp. 139–142
- Alternative Assessment Guide, p. 37
- Student Make-Up Assignments, Chapter 6

MEDIA

- One-Stop Planner
- Audio Compact Discs, CD 6, Trs. 11, 15, 28–29
- Teaching Transparencies: 6-3; **Grammaire supplémentaire** Answers; Travaux pratiques de grammaire Answers
- Interactive CD-ROM Tutor, Disc 2

Bell Work

Write the mnemonic device *Dr. & Mrs. Vandertramp* on the board or on a transparency. Have students use this device as an aid to list the infinitives and the past participles of the verbs that are conjugated with **être** in the **passé composé.**

Teaching Suggestion

Ask questions about the tour schedules, such as: **Il y a combien de spectacles son et lumière? Le car pour Cormery part à quelle heure? C'est combien, le car pour Vouvray? Qu'est-ce qu'on peut faire au mois de juin? C'est combien, les circuits d'une journée?**

Teaching Resources
pp. 171–173

PRINT

- Lesson Planner, p. 29
- TPR Storytelling Book, pp. 44–45
- Listening Activities, pp. 45, 49
- Activities for Communication, pp. 35–36, 102, 104, 147–148
- Travaux pratiques de grammaire, pp. 51–52
- Grammar Tutor for Students of French, Chapter 6
- Cahier d'activités, pp. 68–70
- Testing Program, pp. 139–142
- Alternative Assessment Guide, p. 37
- Student Make-Up Assignments, Chapter 6

MEDIA 

- One-Stop Planner
- Audio Compact Discs, CD 6, Trs. 11, 15, 28–29
- Teaching Transparencies: 6-3; **Grammaire supplémentaire** Answers; Travaux pratiques de grammaire Answers
- Interactive CD-ROM Tutor, Disc 2

Presenting
Comment dit-on... ?

Draw a train schedule on the board and label the towns the trains go to, the departure and arrival times, the **quais** the trains leave from, and the prices of one-way and round-trip tickets. On another section of the board, draw a ticket window for the entrance to a château and post the visiting hours and the entrance fee. Then, have two students play the roles of the ticket agents at the station and at the château. Play the role of a tourist, pointing to the information on the board to prompt responses.

Comment dit-on...?

Asking for and giving information

Cahier d'activités, pp. 68–69, Act. 17–19

To ask for information:	To respond:
A quelle heure est-ce que le train (le car) pour Blois part? *What time does the train (the bus) for . . . leave?*	**A** 14**h**40.
De quel quai? *From which platform?*	**Du quai** 5.
A quelle heure est-ce que vous ouvrez (fermez)? *What time do you open (close)?*	**A** 10**h** (**à** 18**h**).

To ask for prices:	To ask for what you want:
Combien coûte un aller-retour? *How much is a round-trip ticket?*	**Je voudrais un aller-retour.** *I'd like a round-trip ticket.*
Combien coûte un aller simple? *How much is a one-way ticket?*	**Un aller simple, s'il vous plaît.** *A one-way ticket, please.*
C'est combien, l'entrée? *How much is the entrance fee?*	**Trois tickets, s'il vous plaît.** *Three (entrance) tickets, please.*

26 A la gare See scripts and answers on p. 155H.

CD 6 Tr. 11

Ecoutons Nathalie achète un billet à la gare. Ecoute sa conversation avec l'employé de la gare. Ensuite, complète les phrases suivantes.

1. Nathalie veut aller à...
2. Le train part à...
3. Elle voudrait un...
4. Ça coûte...
5. Le train part du quai...

Note de grammaire

- To ask a question formally, use the question word(s) followed by **est-ce que: A quelle heure est-ce que le train arrive?**
- To ask a question informally, put the question word(s) at the end of the question: **Le train arrive à quelle heure?**

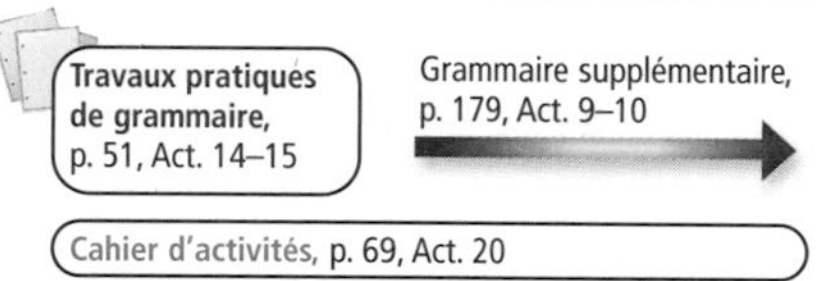

27 Grammaire en contexte

Lisons Mets en ordre cette conversation entre l'employée de la gare routière et un touriste. Answers will vary.

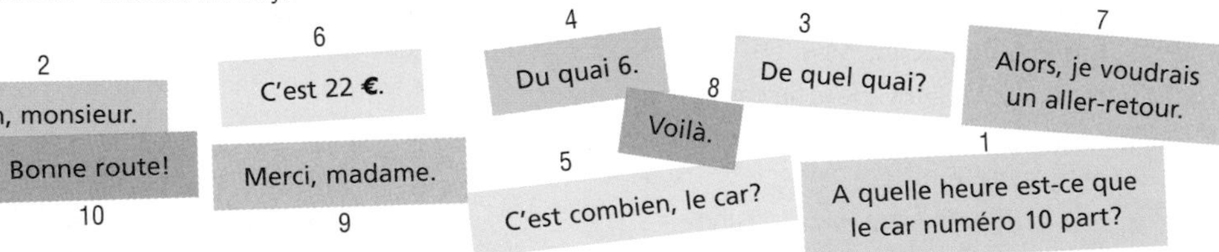

28 Une excursion

Lisons/Parlons Regarde la brochure à la page 171. Choisis un circuit que tu voudrais faire et achète ton ticket à la gare routière. Demande à l'employé(e) toutes les informations importantes. Joue cette scène avec un(e) camarade, puis changez de rôle.

Cultures and Communities

Culture Note

Although trains and buses are commonly used by tourists, some take advantage of the extensive road system in France and rent cars. On the national highways **(les autoroutes)**, the speed limit **(la limite de vitesse)** is 130 kilometers per hour; on divided highways, it's 110 kilometers per hour; on rural roads, it's 90 kilometers per hour; in all towns, the speed limit is 50 kilometers per hour.

STANDARDS: 1.1, 1.2, 4.1

Note de grammaire

Ouvrir *(to open)* ends in **-ir,** but it's conjugated like a regular **-er** verb. Drop the **-ir** and add the endings **-e, -es, -e, -ons, -ez,** or **-ent.**

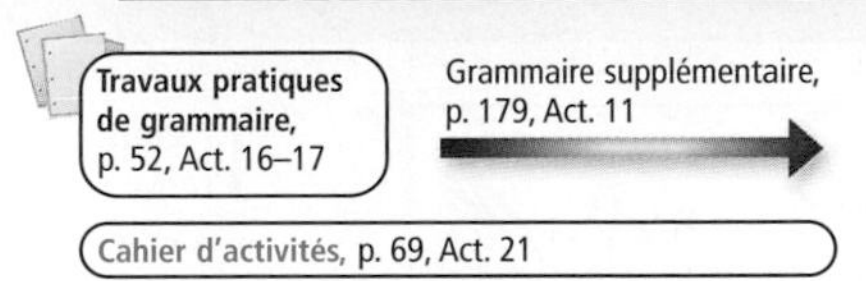

Cahier d'activités, p. 69, Act. 21

29 Grammaire en contexte

Lisons Lis les renseignements pratiques pour Fontainebleau et réponds aux questions. See answers below.

1. Les jardins ouvrent à quelle heure?
2. A quelle heure est-ce qu'ils ferment? Pourquoi est-ce que l'heure de fermeture change?
3. Le château ouvre à quelle heure? Il ferme à quelle heure pour le déjeuner?
4. A quelle heure est-ce que le château rouvre? Il ferme à quelle heure le soir?

RENSEIGNEMENTS PRATIQUES:

Les cours et jardins sont ouverts tous les jours dès 8 h du matin et ferment entre 17 et 20 h 30 suivant la saison.

Le château est ouvert tous les jours (sauf mardi) de 9 h 30 à 12 h 30 et de 14 h à 17 h. Fermeture des caisses à 11 h 30 et 16 h.

L'entrée générale pour les grands et petits appartements, le Musée Napoléon et le Musée Chinois se fait au milieu du bâtiment de droite de la cour du cheval blanc.

Renseignements : tél. 01 64 22 27 40.

30 A la boutique de cadeaux

Parlons Tu vas ouvrir une boutique de cadeaux. Décide à quelle heure tu vas ouvrir et fermer. N'oublie pas l'heure du déjeuner! Ton/Ta camarade va jouer le rôle d'un(e) touriste qui te téléphone pour savoir quand ton magasin est ouvert. Ensuite, changez de rôle.

31 Jeu de rôle

Lisons/Parlons Tu habites à Tours. Samedi, tu vas aller visiter le château d'Azay-le-Rideau. D'abord, choisis le train que tu vas prendre. Ensuite, ton père ou ta mère va te demander ce que tu vas faire et à quelle heure tu vas partir. Réponds à ses questions. Joue cette scène avec un(e) camarade, puis changez de rôle.

SEMAINE

	•	⦿ CAR	• CAR	AQLS 1	• AQLS 2	• CAR	○ AQLS 3	○ AQLS 4	○	⦿ AQLS	• INTERLOIRE	⦿	⦿	○	•	⦿	AQLS 5	AQLS 6	⦿
Tours (SNCF)	5:45								9:08			12:17	12:21			14:07			16:37
Tours (Halte Routière)	│	6:40	7:15			9:17			│			│	│			│			│
St-Pierre-des Corps (S	│	│	│			9:27			│			│	│			│			│
Joué-lès-Tours (SNCF)	5:52	│	│			│			9:15			12:24	12:28			14:14			16:45
Joué-lès-Tours (Mairie	│	6:57	7:33			│			│				│			│			│
Ballan	5:58	7:05	7:41			9:49			9:21				12:34			14:20			16:52
Druye	│	│	│			│			│				12:41			│			│
Azay-le-Rideau (SNCF)	6:10	│	│			│			9:33				12:49			14:32			17:05
Azay-le-Rideau (Mairie	│	7:22	7:57			10:05			│				│			│			│
Rivarennes	│	│	│			│			│				12:56			│			│
St-Benoît-la-Forét (Hô	│	7:35	│			10:18			│				│			│			│
Chinon (SNCF)	6:28	7:50	8:25			10:27			9:51				13:09			14:50			17:22

• du lundi au vendredi ○ le samedi ⦿ du lundi au samedi INTERLOIRE : TER circulant à 200 km/h. AQUALYS : Paris/Orléans/Tours

Source SNCF 2000

32 De l'école au travail

You work for a tour company. You recently took one of the tours offered by the company, and your boss has asked you to write a short summary of your trip. Tell when you left, how you got there, what you did, and whether or not you had a good time.

Communication for All Students

Teaching Suggestion

To close this **étape,** hand out copies of the following sentences and have students rearrange them to create a dialogue. Afterwards, project the dialogue on the overhead and have students check their papers. **Du quai six./Voilà, mademoiselle./C'est 5 euros./De quel quai est-ce que le train part?/Alors, une place pour le train de 8h20, s'il vous plaît./Pardon, monsieur. Combien coûte un aller-retour pour Blois?**

Troisième étape

CHAPITRE 6

Teacher Note

Note de grammaire, p. 172 You might tell students that a third, more formal way to form questions in French is by using *inversion,* reversing the order of the subject pronoun and the verb. Tell them that a **-t-** is inserted after a third person singular verb that ends with a vowel. **(Je prends le train pour Paris. A quelle heure arrive-t-il?)** Inversion will be covered in more detail in Level 3.

Language Notes

29 Point out that **rouvre** is a form of the verb **ouvrir** with the prefix **re-,** meaning *again,* attached to it; the **-e** is dropped because **ouvre** begins with a vowel sound. Other words formed in this manner are **récrire, rhabiller, rasseoir,** and **rassurer.** If the prefix is **ré-,** the **-é** is not always dropped before a vowel, as in **réinventer** and **réarmer.**

- The English word *overture,* meaning the music played at the beginning or *opening* of a performance, comes from the French word **l'ouverture.**

Assess

- Testing Program, pp. 139–142
  Quiz 6-3A, Quiz 6-3B
  Audio CD 6, Tr. 15
- Student Make-Up Assignments, Chapter 6, Alternative Quiz
- Alternative Assessment Guide, p. 37

Answers

29
1. à 8h
2. entre 17h et 20h30 suivant la saison
3. 9h30; 12h30
4. 14h; 17h

CHAPITRE 6

Teaching Resources
pp. 174–175

PRINT 

- Lesson Planner, p. 30
- Cahier d'activités, p. 71
- Reading Strategies and Skills Handbook, Chapter 6
- Joie de lire 2, Chapter 6
- Standardized Assessment Tutor, Chapter 6

MEDIA

- One-Stop Planner

Prereading
Activities A–C

Teaching Suggestion
Have students list other types of literature that might fall in the same genre as fairy tales (fables, short stories, fantasy stories).

Monitoring Comprehension
A. Have students break down the title by words that they know or recognize. For example, while they may not know the word **dormant,** they should be able to recognize the stem **dorm- (dormir),** and thus deduce that **dormant** has something to do with sleeping.

B. Challenge You might name some other fairy tales in French and have students try to determine the English equivalents. Some possibilities are: ***Boucles d'Or*** *(Goldilocks)* and ***Le Petit Chaperon rouge*** *(Little Red Riding Hood).*

Possible Answers

A. Fairy tales are short stories. Most fairy tales are set in the past, and they usually begin with "Once upon a time..." and end with "They lived happily ever after." Fairy tales are popular with children.

Lisons!

Il était une fois un roi et une reine qui ne pouvaient pas avoir d'enfants. Un jour pourtant, la reine attend un enfant et elle a une fille. On fait alors un beau baptême; on donne pour marraines à la petite princesse les sept fées du pays. Chaque fée doit faire un don à l'enfant. Après les cérémonies du baptême, tout le monde revient au palais du roi, où il y a une grande fête. On met un couvert en or devant chaque fée. Tout à coup, on voit entrer une vieille fée qu'on n'avait pas invitée parce qu'on la croyait morte.

Le roi lui donne un couvert, mais pas en or parce qu'il n'y en avait que sept, pour les sept fées. La vieille croit qu'on la méprise et dit quelques menaces entre ses dents. Une des jeunes fées l'entend. Elle pense que la vieille va faire du mal à la petite princesse. Alors, elle va se cacher derrière la tapisserie, pour parler la dernière et pour pouvoir réparer le mal que la vieille veut faire.

Les huit fées commencent alors à faire leurs dons à la princesse. La plus jeune fée dit que la princesse va être la plus belle personne du monde; la deuxième fée dit qu'elle va être très intelligente; la troisième dit qu'elle va avoir une grâce admirable; la quatrième dit qu'elle va danser parfaitement; la cinquième dit qu'elle va chanter comme un rossignol et la sixième dit qu'elle va jouer de toutes sortes d'instruments de façon parfaite.

Le tour de la vieille fée arrive. Elle dit que la princesse va se percer la main d'un fuseau et qu'elle va mourir. Ce don terrible fait pleurer tout le

La Belle au bois dormant

> **Stratégie pour lire**
> Before you read something, consider what its *genre* is. The *genre* tells what kind of writing it is: a novel, a poem, a short story, or an essay, for example. Knowing what genre you're dealing with will help you predict its features.

A. Think of some fairy tales that you have read. In what genre do fairy tales fall? What do most fairy tales have in common? What makes fairy tales unique? See answers below.

B. Skim the story and the title. What is the English title of this fairy tale? Based on what you already know about this fairy tale, what do you think will happen? *Sleeping Beauty,* Answers will vary.

C. How do fairy tales often begin in English? What do you think **Il était une fois** means? Once upon a time . . .

D. Place the following events from *La Belle au bois dormant* in order.

1. Tout le monde dans le palais se réveille. 5
2. On fait un baptême pour la fille. 1
3. La princesse se perce la main. 3
4. Le roi interdit à toutes personnes de filer au fuseau. 2
5. Le prince passe près du château. 4

Cultures and Communities

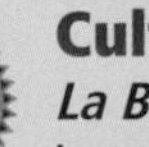

Culture Note
La Belle au bois dormant appeared in a collection of fairy tales compiled and translated into French by Charles Perrault in 1697. The collection also includes ***Cendrillon*** *(Cinderella),* ***Le Petit Chaperon rouge*** *(Little Red Riding Hood),* and ***La Belle et la Bête*** *(Beauty and the Beast).* Part of the title of the collection, ***Contes de ma mère l'oye,*** was translated over one hundred years later by British publisher John Newbery for a collection of nursery rhymes entitled *Mother Goose's Melody.*

STANDARDS: 1.2, 2.2, 3.1, 3.2, 4.1, 4.2

monde. A ce moment, la jeune fée sort de derrière la tapisserie et dit :

« Rassurez-vous, roi et reine, votre fille ne va pas mourir. Je n'ai pas assez de puissance pour défaire entièrement ce que la vieille a fait. La princesse va se percer la main d'un fuseau; mais au lieu de mourir, elle va dormir pendant cent ans. Puis, un beau prince va venir la réveiller.»

Pour essayer d'éviter le malheur annoncé par la vieille, le roi interdit aussitôt à toutes personnes de filer au fuseau et il fait brûler tous les fuseaux qu'on trouve dans le royaume.

Seize ans plus tard, la jeune princesse se promène dans le château. Elle va jusqu'au haut d'un donjon où une bonne dame file au fuseau.

« Que faites-vous là, ma bonne dame? dit la princesse.

—Je file, ma belle enfant, lui répond la dame.

—Ah! Que cela est joli, reprend la princesse. Comment faites-vous? Donnez-moi votre fuseau. Je voudrais essayer de filer. »

Elle prend le fuseau et aussitôt, elle se perce la main et s'endort.

La bonne dame crie au secours. On vient de tous côtés et on essaie de réveiller la princesse, mais elle ne se réveille pas. Alors, le roi se souvient de la prédiction des fées et il ordonne qu'on laisse la princesse dormir pendant cent ans. On appelle une fée. La fée pense qu'à son réveil, la princesse va être bien seule dans ce vieux château. Alors, elle touche tout dans le château avec sa baguette magique. Tout le monde s'endort comme la princesse. Tout d'un coup, une grande forêt pousse tout autour du château.

Cent ans plus tard, un beau prince passe près du château où la princesse dort. Il voit un paysan et il lui demande qui habite dans ce château. Le vieux paysan lui répond :

« Mon prince, on m'a dit qu'il y a dans ce château une très belle princesse qui dort depuis cent ans, et qu'un beau prince va la réveiller. »

Alors, le jeune prince décide tout de suite de voir si c'est vrai. Quand il arrive dans la forêt, tous les arbres s'écartent pour le laisser passer. Il entre dans le château et voit que tout le monde dort. Il va dans une chambre et il voit le plus beau spectacle du monde : une très belle princesse qui dort. Il se met à genoux près de la princesse. Alors, la princesse se réveille et lui dit:

« Est-ce vous, mon prince? Je vous ai attendu longtemps. »

Le prince tombe tout de suite amoureux de la princesse et lui dit qu'il l'aime.

Alors, tout le monde dans le palais se réveille. On organise une grande fête. Et après le dîner, on marie le prince et la princesse dans la chapelle du château.

E. What do the first six fairies give to the princess? What does the old fairy say will happen to the princess? See answers below.

Rappel

Remember to use the context to help you guess the meaning of an unfamiliar word.

F. Match the following terms with their English equivalents.

1. fée c	**a.** *power*
2. se percer d	**b.** *spindle*
3. puissance a	**c.** *fairy*
4. donjon e	**d.** *to prick, pierce*
5. fuseau b	**e.** *tower*

G. Why did the fairy put everyone else to sleep when she discovered what happened to the princess? See answers below.

H. How does *La Belle au bois dormant* end? What do you think will happen to the prince and princess in the future? See answers below.

I. Act out the story of *La Belle au bois dormant* in groups, assigning one member of your group the role of narrator. You may want to use costumes and props.

J. Now, write the story of *La Belle au bois dormant* in a different genre. Imagine that this story will appear in the newspaper. Tell what happened in the story by adapting it for a newspaper article.

Cahier d'activités, p. 71, Act. 24–25

Connections and Comparisons

Radio-Television-Film Link

If possible, you might show an animated version of *Sleeping Beauty.* French versions are available through several foreign language educational video distributors. After they have viewed the video, have students compare the story line and ending to the written version above. Have students discuss what might account for some of the differences.

Lisons!

CHAPITRE 6

Reading

Activities D–H

Using Context Clues

Rappel Have students use the context to determine the meanings of these words: **la marraine** *(godmother);* **les dons** *(gifts);* **un rossignol** *(nightingale);* **le paysan** *(peasant).*

H. Have students tell how the ending of this fairy tale is different from the endings of most fairy tales with which they're familiar. (Most English fairy tales end with the phrase, *"And they all lived happily ever after.")* Tell students that this fairy tale does not reflect the endings of most French fairy tales: **Ils eurent beaucoup d'enfants et ils vécurent très heureux.**

Postreading

Activities I–J

Cooperative Learning

I. You might have groups of students write a complete script for ***La Belle au bois dormant.*** As an alternative, divide the story into manageable parts or "acts" and assign one to each group. When all the scripts are done, have students rehearse and perform ***La Belle au bois dormant*** for other classes. Or, have students perform the skits for an elementary school class.

Answers

E. The first six fairies give the princess beauty, intelligence, and grace, as well as the ability to dance, to sing, and to play many instruments perfectly. The old fairy says she will prick her finger and die.

G. The fairy put everyone else to sleep because she didn't want the princess to wake up alone in 100 years.

H. The prince arrives and kneels down beside the sleeping princess, waking her. Everyone in the palace awakens, and the young couple are married. *Answers may vary.*

Grammaire supplémentaire

CHAPITRE 6

For **Grammaire supplémentaire** Answer Transparencies, see the *Teaching Transparencies* binder.

Grammaire supplémentaire

Première étape

Objectives Asking for opinions; expressing enthusiasm, indifference, and dissatisfaction

1 Au début de l'été dernier, tes amis et toi avez fait une liste de choses à faire. Regarde la liste et dis qui as fait chaque activité pendant l'été. Mets les verbes au passé composé. (**pp. 136, 140, 162**)

1. aller dans un parc d'attractions / Monique
2. faire un tour sur les montagnes russes / elle
3. faire un pique-nique / Luc et sa famille
4. assister à un concert / ils
5. aller au zoo / tu
6. donner à manger aux animaux / les enfants
7. aller en France / Béatrice
8. visiter un château / elle
9. faire des tas de choses / on

2 Yves, ton correspondant canadien, passe l'été en France. Complète sa carte postale avec les verbes appropriés. Utilise le passé composé. (**pp. 136, 140, 162**)

Un petit bonjour de France où nous passons des vacances super. Jeudi, ma famille et moi, nous ___1___ dans un parc d'attractions. On ___2___ un tour sur les montagnes russes. J'ai eu très peur! Vendredi, mon père et mon frère ___3___ au zoo. Ils ___4___ une visite guidée. Ma mère n'aime pas beaucoup les zoos, alors nous, nous ___5___ un circuit des châteaux. C'était chouette. Demain, nous allons à Paris. On va sûrement visiter le Louvre. Bon, je dois te laisser. A bientôt.

Yves

Chelsea Monroe
2513 Franklin St.
San Diego, CA
92107

Answers

1
1. Monique est allée dans un parc d'attractions.
2. Elle a fait un tour sur les montagnes russes.
3. Luc et sa famille ont fait un pique-nique.
4. Ils ont assisté à un concert.
5. Tu es allé(e) au zoo.
6. Les enfants ont donné à manger aux animaux.
7. Béatrice est allée en France.
8. Elle a visité un château.
9. On a fait des tas de choses.

2
1. sommes allés
2. a fait
3. sont allés
4. ont fait
5. avons fait

Grammar Resources for Chapter 6

The **Grammaire supplémentaire** activities were designed as supplemental activities for the grammatical concepts presented in the chapter. You might use them as additional practice, for review, or for assessment.

For more grammar presentations, review, and practice, refer to the following:
- Travaux pratiques de grammaire
- Grammar Tutor for Students of French
- Grammar Summary on pp. R23–R42
- Cahier d'activités
- Grammar and Vocabulary quizzes (Testing Program)
- Test Generator
- Interactive CD-ROM Tutor
- DVD Tutor
- **Jeux interactifs** at go.hrw.com

STANDARDS: 1.2

3 Tes amis te racontent leurs vacances. Comment est-ce qu'ils ont trouvé leurs vacances? Utilise **C'était** et un des adjectifs suggérés. (**p. 164**)

incroyable — sensass — ennuyeux — comme ci comme ça

1. Nous sommes allés dans un parc d'attractions. Nous avons fait un tour sur les montagnes russes. Nous nous sommes beaucoup amusés. ...
2. Nous avons rendu visite à mes grands-parents. Nous avons fait les magasins et nous avons mangé au restaurant. Nous avons aussi vu une pièce. ...
3. Nous sommes allés en Afrique. Nous avons fait une visite guidée. Nous avons vu des éléphants, des zèbres et même des lions! ...
4. Nous sommes allés à la campagne. Je n'ai rien fait de spécial. J'ai lu un peu, et j'ai beaucoup dormi. ...

Deuxième étape

Objective Expressing disbelief and doubt

4 Tu as été très occupé(e) ce week-end. Tes amis et toi, vous vous racontez les dernières nouvelles de l'école. Choisis le verbe auxiliaire approprié pour compléter les phrases suivantes au passé composé. (**p. 167**)

1. Je (J') _____ perdu mon portefeuille.
   as — ai — suis
2. François et Emile, ils _____ allés au zoo.
   ont — a — sont
3. Nous nous _____ amusés.
   sommes — avons — avez
4. Monique et Suzanne, vous _____ vu un bon film?
   êtes — avez — avons
5. Julie, elle _____ tombée dans l'escalier.
   ont — est — sont
6. Tu _____ rentré trop tard.
   est — as — es

5 Ton camarade de classe, Martin, te dis ce qu'il a fait avec sa famille aujourd'hui. Complète chaque phrase avec le sujet logique. (**p. 167**)

On	Vous
Martine et Claire	Nous
Luc et Pierre	Mme Baril
Je	Tu

Exemple <u>Luc et Pierre</u> sont descendus dans le jardin.

1. _____ sommes allés dans une boutique de vêtements.
2. _____ suis allé au parc promener le chien.
3. _____ sont allées au café.
4. _____ est tombée dans l'escalier.
5. _____ êtes rentrés tard.
6. _____ es resté chez toi.
7. _____ est restés longtemps au café.

Communication for All Students

Game

Faites voir! Give several sheets of construction paper to groups of four. Write sentences in the **passé composé** on a transparency, but do not project it. Read aloud each sentence in the present tense. Each group writes the sentence on the construction paper in the **passé composé**. Say **Faites voir!** and have each group hold up its paper. Give a point to groups that show a correct sentence. Finally, project the correct sentence.

Grammaire supplémentaire

CHAPITRE 6

Answers

3
1. C'était sensass.
2. C'était comme ci comme ça.
3. C'était incroyable.
4. C'était ennuyeux.

4
1. ai
2. sont
3. sommes
4. avez
5. est
6. es

5
1. Nous
2. Je
3. Martine et Claire
4. Mme Baril
5. Vous
6. Tu
7. On

STANDARDS: 1.2

CHAPITRE 6

For **Grammaire supplémentaire** Answer Transparencies, see the *Teaching Transparencies* binder.

Grammaire supplémentaire

WA3 TOURAINE-6

6 Marion te raconte son week-end. Complète ses phrases avec les participes passés proposés. Utilise chaque participe seulement une fois. (**p. 167**)

sortie	fait	allés	amusés
assisté	montée	joué	

EXEMPLE J'ai **joué** au volley-ball après l'école.

1. Mon frère et moi, nous sommes _____ au parc d'attractions!
2. Ma sœur est _____ dans une tour d'un vieux château.
3. Mes amies ont _____ un pique-nique au parc.
4. Je suis _____ avec des amis.
5. Mon frère et ma sœur se sont bien _____ à la boum.
6. On a _____ à un spectacle son et lumière.

7 Daniel et ses amis sont allés en France. Avant les vacances, Daniel avait fait une liste de ce que chaque personne voulait faire. Ils ont fait tout ce qu'ils voulaient faire. Récris les phrases suivantes et mets les verbes au passé composé. (**pp. 136, 167**)

EXEMPLE Betty et Suzie veulent faire les magasins.
Betty et Suzie ont fait les magasins.

1. Kristen, Luke et moi, nous voulons faire un circuit des châteaux.
2. Michael veut monter dans une vieille tour d'un château.
3. Moi, je veux prendre beaucoup de photos.
4. Nous voulons sortir le soir.
5. Marc et Adrienne veulent assister à un concert.
6. Gabrielle et moi, nous voulons visiter des musées.

8 Magali fait un album de photo. Elle t'a demandé de l'aider à écrire des descriptions de ses photos. Ecris deux phrases pour décrire chaque photo. (**pp. 136, 167**)

EXEMPLE **Magali est allée à Chenonceaux.**
Magali est montée dans une vieille tour.

Answers

6
1. allés
2. montée
3. fait
4. sortie
5. amusés
6. assisté

7
1. Kristen, Luke et moi, nous avons fait un circuit des châteaux.
2. Michael est monté dans une vieille tour d'un château.
3. Moi, j'ai pris beaucoup de photos.
4. Nous sommes sorti(e)s le soir.
5. Marc et Adrienne ont assisté à un concert.
6. Gabrielle et moi, nous avons visité des musées.

8 *Possible answers:*
1. Magali a visité Paris. Magali est montée dans la tour Eiffel.
2. Magali est allée à la plage. Magali a nagé dans la mer.
3. Magali a fait les magasins. Magali a acheté des vêtements.

Teacher to Teacher

Dr. Susan Hayden
Aloha High School
Beaverton, OR

Susan suggests this activity to review grammar from this chapter.

"After students have seen the "house of **être**" organizer from the *Cahier d'activités,* have them design and draw their own organizer to help them remember which verbs use **être.** Our students created the "airplane of **être**", the "farm of **être**", the "tree of **être**", and many more. I let them draw their creation on a later test for a few extra points."

Troisième étape

Objectives Asking for and giving information

Grammaire supplémentaire

CHAPITRE 6

9 Indicate whether the question being asked is **a) formal** or **b) informal.** (**p. 172**)

1. Le train arrive à quelle heure?
2. Le magasin ouvre quand?
3. De quel quai est-ce que le train part?
4. C'est combien, le billet?
5. A quelle heure est-ce que vous fermez?
6. On y va comment?
7. Le car qui retourne à six heures est où?
8. Avec qui est-ce qu'on monte dans cette tour?
9. Pendant combien de temps est-ce que le bus reste à la gare routière?
10. Le TGV revient d'où?

10 Julie et ses camarades sont à la gare. Il y a trop de bruit et Julie n'entend pas toute la conversation. Quelle était la question? Utilise l'intonation pour les questions des camarades de Julie et **est-ce que** pour les questions posées à l'employé. (**p. 172**)

1. JEAN-LUC _____
   LISETTE On y va en train.
2. LISETTE _____
   L'EMPLOYE Le train part à quinze heures.
3. LISETTE _____
   L'EMPLOYE Le train part du quai numéro 5.
4. JEAN-LUC _____
   L'EMPLOYE Nous ouvrons à six heures du matin.
5. JEAN-LUC _____
   LISETTE Le train arrive à Paris à 21 heures.

11 Monique et toi, vous voulez ouvrir un magasin de souvenirs à Chenonceaux. Complète la conversation sur les horaires d'ouverture avec la forme appropriée du verbe **ouvrir.** (**p. 173**)

TOI A quelle heure est-ce qu'on _____ le matin?

MONIQUE Je ne veux pas _____ trop tôt, peut-être vers onze heures?

TOI Non, onze heures, c'est trop tard. Les autres magasins _____ à neuf heures.

MONIQUE J'ai une idée! Toi, tu _____ le matin à neuf heures et moi, je viens travailler l'après-midi. On ferme à midi pour le déjeuner et je peux _____ le magasin l'après-midi.

TOI D'accord, mais le week-end, nous _____ tous (toutes) les deux à neuf heures, d'accord?

MONIQUE Ça va.

Review and Assess

You may wish to assign the **Grammaire supplémentaire** activities as additional practice or homework after presenting material throughout the chapter. Assign Activity 3 after **Note de grammaire** (p. 164), Activities 4–8 after **Grammaire** (p. 167), Activities 9–10 after **Note de grammaire** (p. 172), and Activity 11 after **Note de grammaire** (p. 173.).

To prepare students for the **Etape** Quizzes and Chapter Test, we suggest doing the **Grammaire supplémentaire** activities in the following order. Have students complete Activities 1–3 before Quizzes 6-1A or 6-1B; Activities 4–8 before Quizzes 6-2A or 6-2B; and Activities 9–11 before Quizzes 6-3A or 6-3B.

Answers

9
1. b
2. b
3. a
4. b
5. a
6. b
7. b
8. a
9. a
10. b

10
1. On y va comment?
2. A quelle heure est-ce que le train part?
3. De quel quai est-ce que le train part?
4. A quelle heure est-ce que vous ouvrez?
5. Le train arrive à Paris à quelle heure?

11
1. ouvre
2. ouvrir
3. ouvrent
4. ouvres
5. ouvrir
6. ouvrons

Mise en pratique

CHAPITRE 6

The **Mise en pratique** reviews and integrates all four skills and culture in preparation for the Chapter Test.

Teaching Resources
pp. 180–181

PRINT

- Lesson Planner, p. 30
- TPR Storytelling Book, pp. 46–47
- Listening Activities, p. 45
- Video Guide, pp. 39, 42
- Grammar Tutor for Students of French, Chapter 6
- Standardized Assessment Tutor, Chapter 6

MEDIA 

- One-Stop Planner
- Video Program, Videocassette 2, 57:53–59:10
- DVD Tutor, Disc 1
- Audio Compact Discs, CD 6, Tr. 12
- Interactive CD-ROM Tutor, Disc 2

Slower Pace

1 You might have students work in pairs to do this activity. In addition, you might translate the following expressions if students find they prevent their comprehension of the text: **Depuis toujours, les châtelaines recevaient...** *(The ladies of the château had always received . . .);* **ainsi que la façon dont elles étaient traitées...** *(as well as the way they were treated . . .);* **et attendait de tous les hommes... qu'ils en fassent autant...** *(and expected all the men . . . to do the same . . .).*

Mise en pratique

ADRESSE: go.hrw.com
MOT-CLE: WA3 TOURAINE-6

1 Quand tu es arrivé(e) au château d'Amboise, tu as acheté cette brochure. Lis-la et réponds aux questions suivantes.

Un homme de goût

Depuis toujours, les châtelaines recevaient peu de respect et d'attention de la part des hommes de la cour. Mais, sous François Ier, leur rôle dans la société ainsi que la façon dont elles étaient traitées ont commencé à changer. Le roi François aimait les femmes, les respectait et attendait de tous les hommes de sa cour qu'ils en fassent autant. Si un homme disait du mal d'une femme, il était pendu. François Ier dépensait beaucoup pour les vêtements de ses courtisanes. Il voulait qu'elles montrent leur beauté. Sous son règne, la Cour de France est devenue une école d'élégance, de goût et de culture où les arts, les sciences et la poésie étaient célébrés lors des nombreux festivals organisés par le roi lui-même.

1. How were women treated before the reign of Francis I? without much respect
2. How did he treat the women in his court? with respect
3. How did their role change when Francis I became king? They became a more visible part of court life.
4. What did he spend a lot of money on? Why? clothes; to show the beauty of the women in his court
5. How did the French court change under his reign? It became a place where the arts and sciences flourished.
6. What did he organize? festivals

2 You call the bus station in Tours, but you get a recorded message. Listen carefully and note the times you'll need to catch the bus to and from Amboise and how much your ticket will be. See scripts and answers on p. 155H.

CD 6 Tr. 12

3 How much cultural information do you remember from this chapter? Match the people, places, and things on the left with the terms on the right.

1. Azay-le-Rideau c	**a.** poète
2. Joséphine e	**b.** gare routière
3. le TGV f	**c.** château de la Renaissance
4. Victor Hugo a	**d.** château fort
5. Moyen Age d	**e.** Martinique
6. le car b	**f.** train à grande vitesse

Review and Assess

Additional Practice

2 For additional listening practice, list in random order on the board the times, destinations, prices, and ages mentioned in the recording. Have students listen to the recording again and match the times with the destinations and the prices with the ages.

STANDARDS: 1.2, 3.1

4 ## Ecrivons!

You've been hired by a local tourism office to write materials for French tourists who visit your area. Your first assignment is to write a summary of the life and accomplishments of a famous person from your region.

Stratégie pour écrire

A summary is a brief version of the details of an event or of a person's life, told in your own words. A good summary will give your readers the important facts about the famous person you've chosen without including too many unnecessary details.

Préparation

To write your summary, you'll first need to find information on the famous person you've chosen to write about. Narrow down your sources to avoid wasting time. For example, if the person you've chosen was well known only in your region, an American history book probably wouldn't be a good source to consult. Instead, you might try sources that deal strictly with your state or region's history.

Believe it or not, your summary actually begins *before* you start to write. How? It begins with your research, because it's here that you decide which points about this person's life are important enough to include in your summary. As you learn about the person, take notes about events or accomplishments in his or her life that are truly significant.

Rédaction

Using the notes you've compiled, write your summary about the individual you selected. The key to writing a good summary is to be concise; say as much as possible in a few words. Remember, you're not trying to document every fact about your famous person's life; you only want to feature the high points.

Evaluation

When you are writing about historical figures, accuracy is very important. Go back to the sources you consulted and make sure the dates you've cited are correct and that the facts you've presented are accurate.

After you've completed the first draft of your summary, give it to a classmate to read. Have him or her point out any sentences or phrases that are unclear. You might also ask your classmate to point out any details in your summary that he or she feels are unnecessary.

5 ## Jeu de rôle

While you're at Amboise, one of your friends disappears! Act out the scene with two classmates.

- Make suggestions about what might have happened to your friend.
- React with doubt to the suggestions.
- Resolve the problem.

Review and Assess

Game

After students have completed **Ecrivons!,** you might have them play **Vingt Questions!** Form four teams. Each team secretly chooses a famous historical figure and the other teams try to guess the identity of the person by asking only yes-no questions in French. Before beginning, students might create a list of questions and question starters they can use to play the game. **(C'est un homme/une femme? Il/Elle est mort(e)? Il/Elle a inventé/découvert... ? Il/Elle était chanteur/chanteuse/acteur/actrice?)** The teams take turns asking questions, but all the teams combined may ask only twenty questions. The first team to guess the identity of the historical figure wins.

Culture Note

Amboise was the first French castle to reflect the style of the Italian Renaissance. The structure of the château is a mixture of both the Gothic and Renaissance styles. Two squat towers were built with ramps to accommodate horses and carriages. The château was built in the fifteenth century by Charles VIII, who died in 1498 after banging his head on a very low door in the château. The château enjoyed its hey-day under King Francis I, who was known as the Chevalier King. He sponsored many outlandish festivals, the most memorable of which was in honor of the arrival of the Holy Roman Emperor Charles V in 1539. Torchbearers led the way as the emperor made a grand entrance up one of the tower's ramps. A torch ignited one of the fabric-draped towers and nearly burned Charles V alive.

Process Writing

4 The Internet is a good place to find information on a variety of subjects. Many Internet search engines, such as Yahoo® and Alta Vista®, have specific regional and city sites that may be of benefit, especially if students choose persons of regional fame for their summaries.

Teacher Note

For additional practice and review, you might use the **Histoire Finale** for Chapter 6 on pages 46–47 of the *TPR Storytelling Book.*

STANDARDS: 1.1, 1.3, 3.1, 5.1, 5.2

Que sais-je?

CHAPITRE 6

Teaching Resources
p. 182

PRINT 

- Grammar Tutor for Students of French, Chapter 6

MEDIA

- Interactive CD-ROM Tutor, Disc 2
- Online self-test

go.hrw.com
WA3 TOURAINE-6

Slower Pace

6 Have students organize the information in a chart to help them as they do this activity.

Answers

2 *Possible answers:*
1. C'était sensass!
2. Je me suis beaucoup amusé(e)!
3. C'était pas mal.

4
1. Pas possible!
2. Mon œil!
3. C'est pas vrai!
4. Tu plaisantes!

5
1. Combien coûte un aller-retour pour Paris?
2. De quel quai est-ce que le train part?
3. A quelle heure est-ce que le train part?
4. A quelle heure est-ce que vous ouvrez et fermez?
5. Combien coûte l'entrée?

6
1. A quelle heure est-ce que le musée ouvre?
2. A quelle heure est-ce que le musée ferme au printemps?
3. Combien coûte l'entrée?
4. Combien coûte l'entrée pour les enfants de treize à dix-huit ans?

7
1. Le musée ouvre à dix heures.
2. Le musée ferme à douze heures trente et à dix-huit heures trente.
3. 3 €
4. 2 €

Que sais-je?

WA3 TOURAINE-6

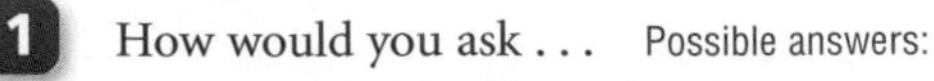

Can you use what you've learned in this chapter?

Can you ask for opinions? **p. 164**

1 How would you ask . . . Possible answers:
1. how your friend's weekend was? C'était comment, ton week-end?
2. if your friend liked what he or she did? Ça t'a plu?
3. if your friend had fun? Tu t'es bien amusé(e)?

Can you express enthusiasm, indifference, and dissatisfaction? **p. 164**

2 You're just back from a trip, and your friend asks you how it was. How would you respond if you had visited these places? See answers below.

1.

2.

3.

3 How would you tell what you did on your last vacation and how you liked it?

Can you express disbelief and doubt? **p. 168**

4 How would you respond if your friend told you . . . See answers below.
1. she got lost in the dungeon while visiting a castle?
2. he saw the ghost of Francis I arguing with Leonardo da Vinci?
3. she found 100 gold coins in the gardens at Chenonceau?
4. he just inherited the château of Azay-le-Rideau?

Can you ask for and give information? **p. 172**

5 How would you find out . . . See answers below.
1. the cost of a round-trip ticket to your destination?
2. which platform the train leaves from?
3. at what time the train leaves?
4. when a place opens and closes?
5. how much it costs to get into a place?

6 Can you ask someone . . . See answers below.
1. at what times this museum opens?
2. at what time it closes in the spring?
3. what the regular entrance fee is?
4. what the fee for teenagers is?

7 Can you give the information above? See answers below.

(Musée Archéologique de l'Hôtel Goüin) 25 rue de Commerce - Tél. 02.47.66.22.32
Du 1er février au 14 mars et du 1er octobre au 30 novembre de 10h à 12h30 et de 14h à 17h30, fermé le vendredi. Tous les jours du 15 mars au 14 mai de 10h à 12h30 et de 14h à 18h30. Du 15 mai au 30 septembre de 10h à 19h. Entrée : Plein tarif : 3 € - Groupes + 15 pers. et 3e âge : 2 € 50 - Enfants de 7 à 18 ans : 2 € - Scolaires : 0, 75 €.

Apply and Assess

Teaching Suggestion

Have partners answer all the questions in **Que sais-je?** Then, have them write humorous skits which include all of the functions in **Que sais-je?** For example, John asks Mary about her weekend (#1), and Mary asks John about a recent trip he took (#2). Then, Mary talks about her last trip (#3). She talks about the unusual things that happened during her vacation, and John responds with disbelief (#4). Finally, John and Mary discuss the next trip they're going to take and ask each other questions about tourist information (#5 and #6). Have the pairs present the skits to the class.

Vocabulaire

Première étape

Asking for opinions; expressing enthusiasm, indifference, and dissatisfaction

C'était comment?	*How was it?*
C'était...	*It was...*
magnifique	*beautiful*
incroyable	*incredible*
superbe	*gorgeous*
sensass	*sensational*
assez bien	*OK*
comme ci comme ça	*so-so*
pas mal	*all right*
ennuyeux	*boring*
mortel	*deadly dull*
nul	*lame*
sinistre	*awful*
Ça t'a plu?	*Did you like it?*
Ça m'a beaucoup plu.	*I really liked it.*
Mouais.	*Yeah.*
Sûrement pas!	*Definitely not!*
Tu t'es amusé(e)?	*Did you have fun?*
Je me suis beaucoup amusé(e).	*I had a lot of fun.*
Plus ou moins.	*More or less.*
Je me suis ennuyé(e).	*I was bored.*

Activities

assister à un spectacle son et lumière	*to attend a sound and light show*
donner à manger aux animaux	*to feed the animals*
faire un circuit des châteaux	*to tour some châteaux*
faire un pique-nique	*to have a picnic*
faire un tour sur la grande roue	*to ride on the ferris wheel*
faire un tour sur les montagnes russes	*to ride on the roller coaster*
faire une visite guidée	*to take a guided tour*
monter dans une tour	*to go up in a tower*
visiter un parc d'attractions	*to visit an amusement park*
visiter un zoo	*to visit a zoo*

Deuxième étape

Expressing disbelief and doubt

Tu plaisantes!	*You're joking!*
Pas possible!	*No way!*
Ça m'étonnerait.	*I doubt it.*
C'est pas vrai!	*You're kidding!*
N'importe quoi!	*That's ridiculous!*
Mon œil!	*Yeah, right!*

Verbs

entrer	*to enter*
venir	*to come*
rester	*to stay*
monter	*to go up*
descendre	*to go down*
partir	*to leave*
sortir	*to go out*
rentrer	*to go back (home)*
revenir	*to come back*
retourner	*to return*
naître	*to be born*
devenir	*to become*
mourir	*to die*

Troisième étape

Asking for and giving information

A quelle heure est-ce que le train (le car) pour... part?	*What time does the train (the bus) for... leave?*
De quel quai?	*From which platform?*
Du quai...	*From platform...*
A quelle heure est-ce que vous ouvrez (fermez)?	*What time do you open (close)?*
Combien coûte... ?	*How much is...?*
un aller-retour	*a round-trip ticket*
un aller simple	*a one-way ticket*
C'est combien, l'entrée?	*How much is the entrance fee?*
Je voudrais...	*I'd like...*
Un..., s'il vous plaît.	*A..., please.*
...tickets, s'il vous plaît.	*...(entrance) tickets, please.*

Apply and Assess

Circumlocution

Tell students to imagine they spent the weekend at a great amusement park. They want to tell the French exchange student about the weekend, but they don't know the French names for all the rides and events at the park. Have students use circumlocution to describe the weekend to a partner. Their partner (the exchange student) will try to guess the rides or events they are trying to describe.

Vocabulaire

CHAPITRE 6

Challenge

Have students create a crossword puzzle that uses the verbs in the **Vocabulaire.** Students might give clues to the meaning of a verb found in the puzzle. **(C'est le contraire de «monter».)** They might also create incomplete sentences as clues to indicate that the missing helping verb, past participle, or subject pronoun is found in the puzzle. **(Les filles sont _____ (aller). Christian ____ venu avec moi. _____suis sorti avec mes amis.)**

Chapter 6 Assessment

- **Testing Program**
  Chapter Test, pp. 143–148

  Audio Compact Discs, CD 6, Trs. 16–18
  Speaking Test, p. 345
  Midterm Exam, pp. 157–164

  Audio Compact Discs, CD 6, Trs. 19–23
- **Alternative Assessment Guide**
  Performance Assessment, p. 37
  Portfolio Assessment, p. 23
  CD-ROM Assessment, p. 51
- **Interactive CD-ROM Tutor, Disc 2**
  CD-ROM 2 A toi de parler
  DVD 1 A toi d'écrire
- **Standardized Assessment Tutor**
  Chapter 6
- **One-Stop Planner, Disc 2**

  Test Generator
  Chapter 6

Chapitre 7 : En pleine forme
Chapter Overview

Mise en train pp. 186–188	***Trop de conseils***			
	FUNCTIONS	**GRAMMAR**	**VOCABULARY**	**RE-ENTRY**
Première étape pp. 189–193	• Expressing concern for someone; complaining, p. 189	• Reflexive verbs in the **passé composé,** p. 192	• Illnesses, p. 189 • Aches, pains, and injuries, pp. 190–191	• Expressing doubt **(Chapitre 6,** II) • Sympathizing with and consoling someone **(Chapitre 5,** II) • Reflexive verbs **(Chapitre 4,** II)
Deuxième étape pp. 194–199	• Giving advice; accepting and rejecting advice, p. 197 • Expressing discouragement; offering encouragement, p. 198	• The pronoun **en** with activities, p. 196 • The verb **devoir,** p. 197	• At the gym, p. 195	• Telling how often you do something **(Chapitre 4,** II) • Sports activities **(Chapitre 4,** I) • Pronunciation: the **[r]** sound **(Chapitre 3,** I) • The pronoun **en, (Chapitre 3,** II)
Troisième étape pp. 200–203	• Justifying your recommendations; advising against something, p. 202	• The verb **se nourrir,** p. 201	• Eating right, p. 201	• Food vocabulary **(Chapitre 3,** II)

Lisons! pp. 204–205	**Pourquoi manger?**		**Reading Strategy:** Using background knowledge
Grammaire supplémentaire	**pp. 206–209** **Première étape,** pp. 206–207	**Deuxième étape,** pp. 207–208	**Troisième étape,** pp. 208–209
Review pp. 210–213	**Mise en pratique,** pp. 210–211 **Ecrivons!** Identifying your audience Creating a health brochure	**Que sais-je?** p. 212	**Vocabulaire,** p. 213

CULTURE

- **Note culturelle,** Pharmacies in France, p. 191
- **Rencontre culturelle,** Figures of speech, p. 193
- **Note culturelle,** Teens' exercise habits, p. 195
- **Panorama Culturel,** Staying healthy, p. 196
- **Note culturelle,** Mineral water, p. 200
- Realia: **Test Super-Forme!** (health quiz), p. 201
- Realia: Government health poster, p. 203

Chapitre 7 : En pleine forme
Chapter Resources

Lesson Planning

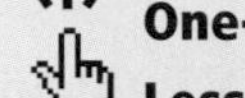

One-Stop Planner

Lesson Planner with Substitute Teacher

Lesson Plans, pp. 31–35, 69

Student Make-Up Assignments
- Make-Up Assignment Copying Masters, Chapter 7

Listening and Speaking

TPR Storytelling Book, pp. 48–55

Listening Activities
- Student Response Forms for Listening Activities, pp. 51–53
- Additional Listening Activities 7-1 to 7-6, pp. 55–57
- Additional Listening Activities (song), p. 58
- Scripts and Answers, pp. 132–136

Video Guide
- Teaching Suggestions, pp. 44–45
- Activity Masters, pp. 46–48
- Scripts and Answers, pp. 99–101, 120–121

Activities for Communication
- Communicative Activities, pp. 37–42
- Realia and Teaching Suggestions, pp. 105–109
- Situation Cards, pp. 149–150

Reading and Writing

Reading Strategies and Skills Handbook, Chapter 7

Joie de lire 2, Chapter 7

Cahier d'activités, pp. 73–84

Grammar

Travaux pratiques de grammaire, pp. 53–61

Grammar Tutor for Students of French, Chapter 7

Assessment

Testing Program
- Grammar and Vocabulary Quizzes, **Etape** Quizzes, and Chapter Test, pp. 171–188
- Score Sheet, Scripts and Answers, pp. 189–196

Alternative Assessment Guide
- Portfolio Assessment, p. 24
- Performance Assessment, p. 38
- CD-ROM Assessment, p. 52

Student Make-Up Assignments
- Alternative Quizzes, Chapter 7

Standardized Assessment Tutor
- Reading, pp. 27–29
- Writing, p. 30
- Math, pp. 51–52

Online Activities
- **Jeux interactifs**
- **Activités Internet**

Video Program
- Videocassette 3
- Videocassette 5 (captioned version)

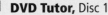

Interactive CD-ROM Tutor, Disc 2

DVD Tutor, Disc 1

Audio Compact Discs
- Textbook Listening Activities, CD 7, Tracks 1–15
- Additional Listening Activities, CD 7, Tracks 22–28
- Assessment Items, CD 7, Tracks 16–21

Teaching Transparencies
- Situation 7-1 to 7-3
- Vocabulary 7-A to 7-E
- **Mise en train**
- **Grammaire supplémentaire** Answers
- **Travaux pratiques de grammaire** Answers

One-Stop Planner CD-ROM

Use the **One-Stop Planner CD-ROM with Test Generator** to aid in lesson planning and pacing.

For each chapter, the **One-Stop Planner** includes:
- Editable lesson plans with direct links to teaching resources
- Printable worksheets from resource books
- Direct launches to the HRW Internet activities
- Video and audio segments
- Test Generator
- Clip Art for vocabulary items

Projects

A votre santé!

In groups of four, students will create a "slide" presentation to promote a fictitious health resort. They are to send slides and an audiocassette to health resorts in France in order to attract potential visitors to the United States. The slides will actually be transparencies that students draw and project on the overhead projector.

MATERIALS

Students may need
- Transparencies
- Colored transparency pens
- An audiocassette
- An audiocassette recorder

SUGGESTED SEQUENCE

1. The groups name their resort, choose its location, and invent an address and phone number.
2. The group members decide what features to highlight in their presentation. They should describe the meals served and the activities offered, telling how each is beneficial to the participants.
3. Students write the script for the presentation. All group members proofread the script. Students write a final draft and hand it in.
4. While you correct their papers, students should prepare the transparencies and the audiocassette. Students might use background music or sound effects in their recording as long as it doesn't render their speech inaudible. Students might complete the recording outside of class. If students don't have access to an audiocassette recorder, they should arrange a time to use one before or after school.
5. Students hand in a final copy before the presentation.
6. One or more of the members will change the slides during the presentation. Students might include an auditory signal in the recording to indicate slide changes.

GRADING THE PROJECT

Suggested Point Distribution: (total = 100 points)

Content	20
Accuracy of written work	20
Creativity/Presentation	20
Comprehensibility	20
Effort/Participation	20

Games

Mémoire

In the two games on this page, students will practice the vocabulary and expressions from this chapter.

Procedure Choose several expressions from the **Vocabulaire** of the **Première étape** on page 213. Write each expression on two separate index cards. Distribute one card to every student, except two to six students whom you ask to serve as the players in front of the class. These players take turns asking the others **Quelque chose ne va pas?** or **Qu'est-ce que tu as?** The object of the game is for players to find two students who respond in the same way **(J'ai un rhume.)**, according to the expression written on their card. When a player finds two students in the class who answer in the same way, he or she collects their cards. When all of the cards have been collected, the player who holds the most cards wins.

Charades

Procedure Have students write on separate slips of paper the expressions that can be mimed from the **Vocabulaire** on page 213. Form teams of five. A player from one team goes to the front of the room and draws a slip of paper. The player mimes the word or expression written on the paper for his or her team members, who call out their guesses. (**Qu'est-ce que tu as?** or **J'ai mal au dos.**) The object of the game is to get your team members to say the word or expression in the least amount of time. Time students, using a watch or a stopwatch. Keep score by recording the number of seconds it takes a team to guess the correct word or expression. If a team cannot guess the word or expression in one minute, record a score of sixty seconds. In this case, you might give other teams a chance to erase five seconds from their total by trying to guess the word or expression. As the ultimate bonus, you might give the team that guesses correctly the opportunity to subtract ten seconds from their score by writing the word or expression correctly on the board. The team with the least amount of recorded time after a set number of rounds is the winner.

STANDARDS: 1.3, 5.1, 5.2

Storytelling

Mini-histoire

This story accompanies Teaching Transparency 7-1. The ***mini-histoire*** *can be told and retold in different formats, acted out, written down, and read aloud, to give students additional opportunities to practice all four skills. The following story is about several animals waiting to see their veterinarian.*

Le vétérinaire a beaucoup de travail aujourd'hui.
Le gorille lui dit : Je me suis coupé le doigt. L'éléphant a le nez qui coule et il éternue souvent. Il a sûrement un rhume! Le grand kangourou a mal au cou et le petit kangourou s'est cassé le bras. Le serpent est tout raplapla car il a mal à la tête et le crocodile a mal aux dents. Le lion a mal au ventre, mal au cœur, mal à la gorge... il a mal partout! Il a la grippe. Le zèbre est fatigué : il ne mange plus et ne dort pas bien. Il a besoin de vitamines.

Traditions

Sports to Stay in Shape

Increasing numbers of French people spend their free time in the pursuit of physical fitness. Soccer, or **football,** is the most popular recreational team sport played in France, followed by rugby. People of all ages play soccer in one of the thousands of soccer clubs around the country. Although team sports are popular, most people prefer individual sports for fitness. Some of the most popular sports are cycling, tennis, skiing, hiking, and horseback riding. Have students research one of last year's important sporting events in France, such as the **Tour de France** or the French Open, and report how French athletes performed.

Recette

The Tatin family had a hotel in Lamotte-Beuvron at the turn of the century. Caroline was in charge of welcoming guests, while her sister Isabelle was in the kitchen preparing meals. One day, Isabelle forgot to put the dough in the pie dish before putting the apples in. When she realized her mistake, she decided to throw the dough on top of the apples. She created the "Tarte Tatin" (upside-down tart).

TARTE TATIN

Pâte à tarte	Garniture
2 tasses de farine	3/4 tasse de beurre
1/2 tasse de sucre	2/3 tasse de sucre
1/2 tasse de beurre	4 pommes épluchées et coupées en lamelles
1 œuf	

Pâte à tarte
Faire fondre le beurre. Placer la farine dans un saladier. Faire un puits. Y mettre le sucre et l'œuf. Commencer à mélanger doucement. Ajouter le beurre petit à petit. Faire une boule du mélange. Si la boule est trop beurrée, ajouter une ou deux cuillères à soupe de farine. Laisser reposer pendant que vous préparez les pommes et le reste de la garniture.

Garniture
Allumer le four à 350° F. Placer le beurre dans un moule. Mettre le moule au four pendant 5 minutes. Ajouter le sucre. Mettre de nouveau le moule dans le four pendant 5 minutes. Mélanger de temps en temps. Sortir le moule du four et ajouter les pommes coupées. Etaler la pâte et la placer sur les pommes. Mettre au four pendant 20 à 30 minutes. Retirer du four. Démouler la tarte sur le plat de service.

Servir tiède.

Chapitre 7 : En pleine forme
Technology

DVD/Video

Videocassette 3, Videocassette 5 (captioned version)
DVD Tutor, Disc 1
See Video Guide, pages 43–48.

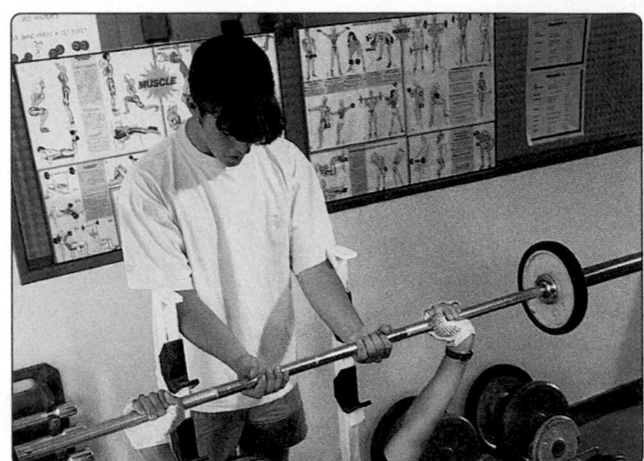

Mise en train • Trop de conseils

At a café, Bruno complains that he is not feeling well. Céline and Hector question him about his diet, his exercise regimen, and his sleeping habits. Bruno reveals that he doesn't do much to stay in good health. Hector suggests that Bruno join him at the gym to work out. At the gym, after several exercises, Bruno twists his ankle. Hector tries to help, but Bruno is fed up with his friend's suggestions.

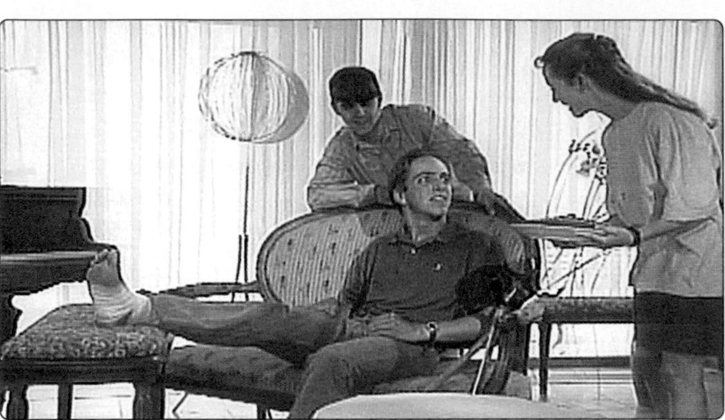

Mise en train (suite)

Céline and Hector visit Bruno, whose ankle is bandaged, at his home. They bring him a healthful cake and carrot juice, which Bruno accepts without much enthusiasm. While trying to help, Hector bumps Bruno's injured foot and Céline drops cake on his new pants. Bruno tries to be gracious, but he is glad when his friends finally leave!

Qu'est-ce qu'il faut faire pour être en forme?

Students from Quebec and France talk about what they do to stay in shape.

Vidéoclips

- **Fumer, c'est pas ma nature!**: anti-smoking advertisement
- **Taillefine®**: advertisement for yogurt

Interactive CD-ROM Tutor

Activity	Activity Type	Pupil's Edition Page
En contexte	*Interactive conversation*	
1. Vocabulaire	Chasse au trésor Explorons!/Vérifions!	pp. 189–191
2. Grammaire	Les mots qui manquent	p. 192
3. Vocabulaire	Jeu des paires	p. 195
4. Comment dit-on... ?	Chacun à sa place	pp. 189, 198
5. Vocabulaire	Le bon choix	p. 201
6. Comment dit-on... ?	Chacun à sa place	pp. 197, 202
Panorama Culturel	Qu'est-ce qu'il faut faire pour être en forme?	p. 199
A toi de parler	*Guided recording*	pp. 210–211
A toi d'écrire	*Guided writing*	pp. 210–211

Teacher Management System

Launch the program, type "admin" in the password area, and press RETURN. Log on to www.hrw.com/CDROMTUTOR for a detailed explanation of the Teacher Management System.

DVD Tutor

The *DVD Tutor* contains all material from the *Video Program* as described above. French captions are available for use at your discretion for all sections of the video. The *DVD Tutor* also provides a variety of video-based activities that assess students' understanding of the **Mise en train, Suite,** and **Panorama Culturel.**

This part of the *DVD Tutor* may be used on any DVD video player connected to a television or video monitor.

In addition to the video material and the video-based comprehension activities, the *DVD Tutor* also contains the entire *Interactive CD-ROM Tutor* in DVD-ROM format. Each DVD disc contains the activities from all 12 chapters of the *Interactive CD-ROM Tutor.*

This part of the *DVD Tutor* may be used on a Macintosh® or Windows® computer with a DVD-ROM drive.

One-Stop Planner CD-ROM

To preview all resources available for this chapter, use the **One-Stop Planner CD-ROM,** Disc 2.

Internet Connection

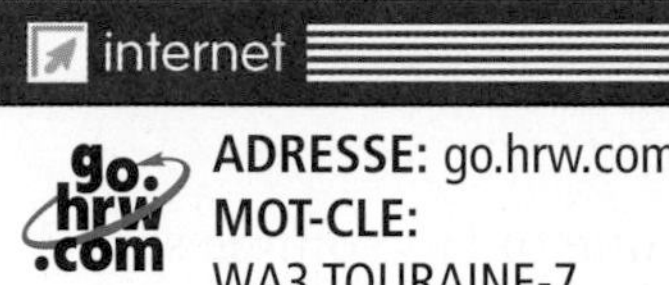

internet
go.hrw.com
ADRESSE: go.hrw.com
MOT-CLE:
WA3 TOURAINE-7

Have students explore the ***go.hrw.com*** *Web site for many online resources covering all chapters. All Chapter 7 resources are available under the keyword* ***WA3 TOURAINE-7.*** *Interactive games help students practice the material and provide them with immediate feedback. You'll also find a printable worksheet that provides Internet activities that lead to a comprehensive online research project.*

Jeux interactifs

You can use the interactive activities in this chapter

- to practice grammar, vocabulary, and chapter functions
- as homework
- as an assessment option
- as a self-test
- to prepare for the Chapter Test

Activités Internet

Students look for and record information about health issues, using the vocabulary from the chapter.

- In preparation for the **Activités Internet,** have students review the chapter vocabulary, or redo the activities in the **Panorama Culturel.** After they complete the activity sheet, have students work with a partner and share the information they gathered in Activity B on that sheet. Then ask each pair of students to share what they learned with the class.

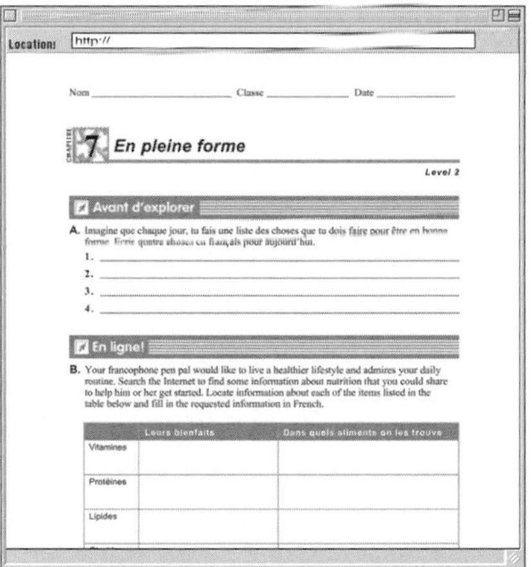

Location: http://

Nom ______ Classe ______ Date ______

CHAPITRE 7 *En pleine forme*

Level 2

Avant d'explorer

A. Imagine que chaque jour, tu fais une liste des choses que tu dois faire pour être en bonne forme. Écris quatre choses en français pour aujourd'hui.

1. ______
2. ______
3. ______
4. ______

En ligne!

B. Your francophone pen pal would like to live a healthier lifestyle and admires your daily routine. Search the Internet to find some information about nutrition that you could share to help him or her get started. Locate information about each of the items listed in the table below and fill in the requested information in French.

	Leurs bienfaits	Dans quels aliments on les trouve
Vitamines		
Protéines		
Lipides		

Projet

Have students create a food pyramid, using the Internet to find the names of different categories of food in French and examples of each category. Students should use a variety of items. Once the project is completed, each student should point out at least one item per category to the class. Have students document their sources by noting the URLs of all the sites that they consulted.

STANDARDS: 1.2, 1.3, 5.1

Chapitre 7 : En pleine forme
Textbook Listening Activities Scripts 

Première étape

6 p. 189

1. — Salut, Edouard. Ça ne va pas?
— Oh, j'ai mal à la tête.
— Tu devrais boire de l'eau et prendre de l'aspirine.

2. — Eh bien, Jérôme, qu'est-ce que tu as?
— J'ai un rhume. Je n'arrête pas d'éternuer et j'ai le nez qui coule.
— Pauvre vieux!

3. — Jean-Claude. Jean-Claude! Psst! Tu n'as pas l'air en forme, toi. Quelque chose ne va pas?
— Oh, j'ai mal dormi hier soir. J'ai passé une nuit blanche.
— Tu devrais te reposer!

Answers to Activity 6
1. b 3. c
2. a d. J'ai mal à la gorge.

9 p. 190

1. — Et vous, qu'est-ce que vous avez?
— Aïe, j'ai mal aux dents!

2. — Qu'est-ce que vous avez?
— J'ai mal au bras et à la main. Je jouais au foot pendant le cours de sport et je suis tombé.

3. — Qu'est-ce qu'il y a?
— J'ai fait de la natation hier et maintenant, j'ai vraiment mal à l'oreille.

4. — Qu'est-ce que vous avez?
— J'ai joué au volley pendant le cours de sport et maintenant, j'ai mal à la main.

Answers to Activity 9
1. d 3. a
2. c, b 4. b

13 p. 192

1. On a pas mal de clients ce matin! D'abord, quelqu'un s'est foulé la cheville en faisant une randonnée.

2. Et il y a quelqu'un qui s'est fait mal au coude, mais ça va maintenant.

3. Il y a aussi quelqu'un qui s'est coupé le doigt, mais ce n'est pas grave.

Answers to Activity 13
1. Véronique
2. Fatima
3. Tranh

Deuxième étape

19 p. 196

1. — Salut, Josée. Dis, qu'est-ce que tu fais comme sport?
— Ben, moi, j'aime surtout faire du jogging. J'en fais deux ou trois fois par semaine. Quelquefois, je fais aussi de l'aérobic.

2. — Et toi, Christelle?
— Le mardi et le jeudi, je fais de la gymnastique et je fais de la musculation trois fois par semaine.

3. — Khalid, qu'est-ce que tu fais comme sport?
— J'aime faire de la natation de temps en temps. En ce moment, je m'entraîne tous les jours au football américain.

Answers to Activity 19
Josée: jogging two or three times a week, aerobics sometimes
Christelle: gymnastics twice a week, weightlifting three times a week
Khalid: swimming from time to time, football every day

23 p. 197

1. — Ben, Bertrand, tu dois vraiment te mettre en condition. Pourquoi tu ne joues pas au tennis avec moi?
— Oh, je n'ai pas le temps! En plus, je déteste le sport.

2. — Hélène? Ça n'a pas l'air d'aller.
— Je suis toute raplapla.
— Mais tu n'es pas en forme! Tu pourrais faire de l'exercice, faire de la gymnastique. C'est génial!
— C'est une bonne idée. Peut-être que j'irai à la MJC demain.

3. — Ça va, Michel?
— Non, je n'ai pas bien dormi hier soir.
— Tu devrais peut-être te coucher plus tôt.
— Tu as raison. Ce soir, je me couche à neuf heures!

4. — Tu sais, Cécile, tu devrais faire du sport. Pourquoi tu ne fais pas de la musculation ou au moins de l'exercice? On peut en faire ensemble!
— C'est gentil, mais ce n'est pas mon truc, la musculation.

Answers to Activity 23
1. refuse 3. accepte
2. accepte 4. refuse

The following scripts are for the listening activities found in the *Pupil's Edition*. For Student Response Forms, see *Listening Activities,* pages 51–53. To provide students with additional listening practice, see *Listening Activities,* pages 55–58.

One-Stop Planner CD-ROM

To preview all resources available for this chapter, use the **One-Stop Planner CD-ROM,** Disc 2.

26 p. 198

SABRINA Salut, Emile.

EMILE Salut, Sabrina. On commence?

SABRINA Oui, alors, tu vois, je commence par des pompes. Voilà, je te montre comment on fait. J'en fais... cinq. Alors... une, deux, trois, quatre... Et cinq! Ouf!

EMILE Bon. A mon tour. J'en fais cinq aussi! Une, deux, trois,... Oh, je n'en peux plus!

SABRINA Tu y es presque!

EMILE Quatre...

SABRINA Encore un effort!

EMILE Cinq!

Answers to Activity 26
Sabrina encourage Emile.

Troisième étape

32 p. 201

1. — Et toi, Marie-Ange, tu te nourris bien?
— Bof. Je ne sais pas. Je suis toujours pressée, donc, je saute souvent le petit déjeuner.
— Est-ce que tu grignotes entre les repas?
— Oui, des frites ou des chips. Mais au moins, je ne mange jamais de confiseries; je n'aime pas ça.

2. — Tu crois que tu te nourris bien, Ali?
— Oui, je mange toujours des crudités et je bois deux litres d'eau par jour. Je fais aussi beaucoup de sport.
— Tu grignotes entre les repas?
— Oui, mais c'est toujours des fruits.

3. — Et toi, Philippe, tu te nourris bien?
— Ben, je ne sais pas. Je mange souvent du riz et des pâtes pour avoir de l'énergie. J'évite de manger des produits riches en matières grasses.
— Tu grignotes entre les repas?
— Oui, malheureusement, j'adore les pâtisseries!

Answers to Activity 32
Good habits: Ali, Philippe
Bad habits: Marie-Ange, Philippe
Ali is the healthiest.

35 p. 202

JULIE Mais qu'est-ce que tu as, David? Tu n'as pas l'air en forme!

DAVID Je me sens tout raplapla.

JULIE Alors, ça te fera du bien de m'accompagner au gymnase.

DAVID Quoi, faire de l'exercice? Non, c'est pas mon truc, ça.

JULIE On peut jouer au tennis, alors. Le tennis, c'est une bonne façon de se mettre en condition.

DAVID D'accord, d'accord. Un match, c'est tout.

JULIE Et après, tu devrais venir manger végétarien chez moi. Manger beaucoup de légumes, c'est bon pour la santé!

DAVID Bonne idée. J'aime bien les légumes... mais pas de petits pois, d'accord?

JULIE D'accord. Et tu devrais boire beaucoup d'eau... tiens, bois de l'eau minérale. C'est meilleur que le coca! Tu devrais éviter les boissons sucrées!

DAVID Merci. Alors, on va le faire, ce match?

Answers to Activity 35
de l'accompagner au gymnase, de faire du tennis, de manger beaucoup de légumes, de boire beaucoup d'eau, d'éviter les boissons sucrées

Mise en pratique

2 p. 210

Venez au Centre Equilibre Santé! Vous voulez vous mettre en forme et vous reposer en même temps? Chez nous, on offre des activités pour tous. On vous proposera un programme individuel en fonction de vos possibilités physiques : musculation, gymnastique, natation et des exercices de relaxation. Après, le sauna et les massages sont à votre disposition. Si vous téléphonez maintenant, on vous propose des excursions spéciales : choisissez l'excursion rafting, l'équitation ou le vélo tout terrain. Téléphonez maintenant pour profiter de ces excursions à prix spécial! Combattez le stress! Vous deviendrez une nouvelle personne!

Answers to Mise en pratique Activity 2
1. weightlifting, gymnastics, swimming, relaxation exercises
2. sauna and massage
3. rafting, horseback riding, mountain biking
4. call now

Chapitre 7 : En pleine forme

Suggested Lesson Plans 50-Minute Schedule

Day 1

CHAPTER OPENER 5 min.
- Present Chapter Objectives, p. 185.
- Culture Notes, ATE, pp. 184–185

MISE EN TRAIN 40 min.
- Presenting **Mise en train,** ATE, p. 187
- Culture Note, ATE, p. 187
- Teaching Suggestions: Post-viewing Suggestion 2, Video Guide, p. 44
- Activities 1–4, p. 188

Wrap-Up 5 min.
- Activity 5, p. 188

Homework Options
Cahier d'activités, Acts. 1–2, p. 73

Day 2

MISE EN TRAIN
Quick Review 5 min.
- Bell Work, ATE, p. 189

PREMIERE ETAPE
Comment dit-on... ? and **Vocabulaire, p. 189 25 min.**
- Presenting **Comment dit-on... ?** and **Vocabulaire,** ATE, p. 189
- Play Audio CD for Activity 6, p. 189.
- Do Activities 1–2, Travaux pratiques de grammaire, p. 53.
- Complete Activity 7, p. 190.
- Have students do Activity 8, p. 190, in pairs.

Vocabulaire, p. 190 15 min.
- Presenting **Vocabulaire,** ATE, p. 190
- Play Audio CD for Activity 9, p. 190.
- Complete Activity 10, p. 191.
- Read and discuss **A la française,** p. 191.
- Have students do Activity 12, p. 191, in pairs.

Wrap-Up, 5 min.
- Read and discuss **Note culturelle,** p. 191.

Homework Options
Cahier d'activités, Acts. 3–7, pp. 74–75
Travaux pratiques de grammaire, Acts. 3–5, pp. 54–55

Day 3

PREMIERE ETAPE
Quick Review 5 min.
- Check homework.

Vocabulaire, p. 191 15 min.
- Presenting **Vocabulaire,** ATE, p. 191
- Play Audio CD for Activity 13, p. 192.
- Complete Activity 6, Travaux pratiques de grammaire, p. 55.
- Do Activity 14, p. 192.

Note de grammaire, p. 192 15 min.
- Presenting **Note de grammaire,** ATE, p. 192
- Complete Activities 7–8, Travaux pratiques de grammaire, p. 56.
- Have students do Activity 16, p. 192, in pairs.

RENCONTRE CULTURELLE, p. 193 10 min.
- Presenting **Rencontre culturelle,** ATE, p. 193
- Language-to-Language and Language Arts Link, ATE, p. 193

Wrap-Up 5 min.
- Share other idiomatic expressions with the class.

Homework Options
Study for Quiz 7-1.
Grammaire supplémentaire, Acts. 1–2, p. 206

Day 4

PREMIERE ETAPE
Quiz 20 min.
- Administer Quiz 7-1A, 7-1B, or a combination of the two.

DEUXIEME ETAPE
Vocabulaire, p. 195 25 min.
- Complete Activities 17–18, p. 194.
- Read and discuss **Note culturelle,** p. 195.
- Presenting **Vocabulaire,** ATE, p. 195
- Play Audio CD for Activity 19, p. 196.
- Read and discuss **Tu te rappelles?,** p. 196.
- Complete Activity 20, p. 196.

Wrap-Up 5 min.
- Activity 21, p. 196

Homework Options
Cahier d'activités, Act. 11, p. 77
Travaux pratiques de grammaire, Acts. 9–12, pp. 57–58

Day 5

DEUXIEME ETAPE
Quick Review 5 min.
- Check homework.

Note de grammaire, p. 196 10 min.
- Presenting **Note de grammaire,** ATE, p. 196
- **Grammaire supplémentaire,** Activities 4–5, pp. 207–208
- Have students do Activity 22, p. 196, in groups.

Comment dit-on... ? and **Note de grammaire, p. 197 30 min.**
- Presenting **Comment dit-on... ?,** ATE, p. 197
- Play Audio CD for Activity 23, p. 197.
- Read and discuss **Tu te rappelles?,** p. 197.
- Complete Activities 13–14, Cahier d'activités, p. 78.
- Read and discuss **Note de grammaire,** p. 197.
- Do Activity 15, Travaux pratiques de grammaire, p. 59.
- Complete Activity 24, p. 197.

Wrap-Up 5 min.
- Do Activity 25, p. 197, using Additional Practice.

Homework Options
Travaux pratiques de grammaire, Acts. 13–14, pp. 58–59
Grammaire supplémentaire, Act. 6, p. 208

Day 6

DEUXIEME ETAPE
Quick Review 5 min.
- Check homework.

Comment dit-on... ?, p. 198 25 min.
- Presenting **Comment dit-on... ?,** ATE, p. 198
- Play Audio CD for Activity 26, p. 198.
- Complete Activities 16–17, Cahier d'activités, p. 79.
- Have students do Activity 29, p. 198, in groups.

PANORAMA CULTUREL, p. 199 15 min.
- Presenting **Panorama Culturel,** ATE, p. 199
- Thinking Critically, ATE, p. 199
- Questions, ATE, p. 199
- **Qu'en penses-tu?,** p. 199

Wrap-Up 5 min.
- Teaching Suggestion, ATE, p. 198

Homework Options
Study for Quiz 7-2.
Act. 27, p. 198

One-Stop Planner CD-ROM

For alternative lesson plans by chapter section, to create your own customized plans, or to preview all resources available for this chapter, use the **One-Stop Planner CD-ROM,** Disc 2.

For additional homework suggestions, see activities accompanied by this symbol throughout the chapter.

Day 7

DEUXIEME ETAPE

Quiz 20 min.
- Administer Quiz 7-2A, 7-2B, or a combination of the two.

TROISIEME ETAPE

Vocabulaire, p. 201 15 min.
- Complete Activity 30, p. 200.
- Read and discuss **Note culturelle,** p. 200.
- Presenting **Vocabulaire,** ATE, p. 201
- Complete Activity 31, p. 201.
- Play Audio CD for Activity 32, p. 201.

Note de grammaire, p. 201 10 min.
- Read and discuss **Note de grammaire,** p. 201.
- Complete Activities 7–9, **Grammaire supplémentaire,** pp. 208–209.
- Do Activity 21, Cahier d'activités, p. 81.

Wrap-Up 5 min.
- Activity 34, p. 202

Homework Options
Act. 33, p. 202
Cahier d'activités, Act. 18, p. 80
Travaux pratiques de grammaire, Acts. 18–19, p. 61

Day 8

TROISIEME ETAPE

Quick Review 10 min.
- Check homework.

Comment dit-on... ?, p. 202 30 min.
- Presenting **Comment dit-on... ?,** ATE, p. 202
- Language Note, ATE, p. 202
- Play Audio CD for Activity 35, p. 202.
- Complete Activities 22–23, Cahier d'activités, pp. 81–82.
- Do Activity 36, p. 203, using Group Work, ATE, p. 203.
- Present **Vocabulaire à la carte,** p. 203.
- Have students do Activity 38, p. 203, in pairs.

Wrap-Up 10 min.
- Begin Activity 37, p. 203.

Homework Options
Study for Quiz 7-3
Complete brochures for Act. 37, p. 203.

Day 9

TROISIEME ETAPE

Quiz 20 min.
- Administer Quiz 7-3A, 7-3B, or a combination of the two.

LISONS!, pp. 204–205 25 min.
- Read and discuss **Stratégie pour lire,** p. 204.
- Complete Activities A–B, p. 204.
- Have students read **Pourquoi manger?,** pp. 204–205.
- Do Activities C–I, pp. 204–205.
- Have students begin Activity J, p. 205.

Wrap-Up 5 min.
- Teacher Note, ATE, p. 205

Homework Options
Complete article for Act. J, p. 205.

Day 10

LISONS!

Quick Review 5 min.
- Have volunteers share their articles with the class.

MISE EN PRATIQUE 40 min.
- Do Activities 1–3, p. 210.
- Discuss the strategy for **Ecrivons!,** p. 211, as a class, then have students work on their brochures.
- Have students work in pairs on **Jeu de rôle,** p. 211.

Wrap-Up 5 min.
- Show **Vidéoclips,** Video Program, Videocassette 3.
- Complete Activities 9–11, Video Guide, p. 48.

Homework Options
Have students finish brochures for **Ecrivons!**.

Day 11

MISE EN PRATIQUE

Quick Review 10 min.
- Have volunteers share their brochures from **Ecrivons!**.

Chapter Review 35 min.
- Have students complete **A toi de parler,** CD-ROM Tutor, Disc 2.
- Have students do **A toi d'écrire,** CD-ROM Tutor, Disc 2.
- Show ***Trop de conseils (suite),*** Video Program, Videocassette 3.
- See Teaching Suggestions, Viewing Suggestion 1, Video Guide, p. 44.
- Complete Activities 6–8, Video Guide, pp. 47– 48.

Wrap-Up 5 min.
- Have students begin **Que sais-je?,** p. 212.

Homework Options
Que sais-je?, p. 212

Day 12

MISE EN PRATIQUE

Quick Review 15 min.
- Go over **Que sais-je?,** p. 212.

Chapter Review 35 min.
- Review Chapter 7. Choose from **Grammaire supplémentaire,** Grammar Tutor for Students of French, Activities for Communication, Listening Activities, Interactive CD-ROM Tutor, or **Jeux interactifs.**
- See Game: **Loto!,** ATE, p. 213
- Circumlocution, ATE, p. 213

Homework Options
Study for Chapter 7 Test.

Assessment

Chapter Test 40–45 min.
- Administer Chapter 7 Test. Select from Testing Program, Alternative Assessment Guide, Test Generator, or Standardized Assessment Tutor.

Chapitre 7 : En pleine forme

Suggested Lesson Plans 90-Minute Block Schedule

Block 1

CHAPTER OPENER 5 min.

- Present Chapter Objectives, p. 185.
- Career Path, ATE, p. 184

MISE EN TRAIN 40 min.

- Draw two columns on the board and label them **De bonnes habitudes** and **De mauvaises habitudes.** Ask students to name all the good and bad health habits they can think of. Write their suggestions in the appropriate column. You might provide the French equivalents for the expressions they give.
- Preteaching Vocabulary, ATE, p. 186
- Presenting **Mise en train,** ATE, p. 187
- Activities 1–4, p. 188

PREMIERE ETAPE

Comment dit-on... ?, p. 189 10 min.

- Presenting **Comment dit-on... ?,** p. 189

Vocabulaire, p. 189 30 min.

- Presenting **Vocabulaire,** ATE, p. 189
- Play Audio CD for Activity 6, p. 189.
- Activity 7, p. 190
- Discuss **Note culturelle,** p. 191.

Wrap-Up 5 min.

- Kinesthetic Learners, ATE, p. 189

Homework Options

Cahier d'activités, Acts. 1–5, pp. 73–74

Travaux pratiques de grammaire, Acts. 1–2, p. 53

Block 2

PREMIERE ETAPE

Quick Review 5 min.

- Teaching Transparency 7-1 and Suggestion #2 in Suggestions for Using Teaching Transparency 7-1

Vocabulaire, p. 189 10 min.

- Activity 8, p. 190

Vocabulaire, p. 190 25 min.

- Presenting **Vocabulaire,** ATE, p. 190
- Play Audio CD for Activity 9, p. 190.
- Activity 10, p. 191

Vocabulaire, p. 191 45 min.

- Presenting **Vocabulaire,** ATE, p. 191
- Language Note, ATE, p. 191
- Play Audio CD for Activity 13, p. 192.
- Activity 14, p. 192
- Presenting **Note de grammaire,** ATE, p. 192
- Activity 15, p. 192

Wrap-Up 5 min.

- TPR, ATE, p. 191

Homework Options

Have students study for Quiz 7-1.

Grammaire supplémentaire, Acts. 1–2, p. 206

Cahier d'activités, Acts. 6–9, pp. 75–76

Travaux pratiques de grammaire, Acts. 3–8, pp. 54–56

Block 3

PREMIERE ETAPE

Quick Review 5 min.

- Teaching Transparency 7-C and Suggestion #4 in Suggestions for Using Teaching Transparency 7-C

Quiz 7-1 20 min.

- Administer Quiz 7-1A, 7-1B, or a combination of the two.

RENCONTRE CULTURELLE 10 min.

- Presenting **Rencontre culturelle,** ATE, p. 193
- **Savais-tu que...?,** p. 193

DEUXIEME ETAPE

Vocabulaire, p. 195 35 min.

- Presenting **Vocabulaire,** ATE, p. 195
- Play Audio CD for Activity 19, p. 196.
- **Note culturelle,** p. 195
- **Tu te rappelles?,** p. 196
- Activities 20–21, p. 196

Note de grammaire, p. 196 10 min.

- Presenting **Note de grammaire,** ATE, p. 196

Wrap-Up 10 min.

- Additional Practice, ATE, p. 197

Homework Options

Grammaire supplémentaire, Acts. 4–5, pp. 207–208

Cahier d'activités, Acts. 10–11, p. 77

Travaux pratiques de grammaire, Acts. 9–13, pp. 57–58

One-Stop Planner CD-ROM

For alternative lesson plans by chapter section, to create your own customized plans, or to preview all resources available for this chapter, use the **One-Stop Planner CD-ROM,** Disc 2.

For additional homework suggestions, see activities accompanied by this symbol throughout the chapter.

Block 4

DEUXIEME ETAPE

Quick Review 10 min.
- Teaching Transparency 7-2 and Suggestion #1 in Suggestions for Using Teaching Transparency 7-2

Note de grammaire, p. 196 10 min.
- Activity 22, p. 196

Comment dit-on... ?, p. 197 35 min.
- Presenting **Comment dit-on... ?,** ATE, p. 197
- Play Audio CD for Activity 23, p. 197.
- Present **Note de grammaire,** p. 197.
- Activities 24–25, p. 197

Comment dit-on... ?, p. 198 20 min.
- Presenting **Comment dit-on... ?,** ATE, p. 198
- Play Audio CD for Activity 26, p. 198.
- Activity 27, p. 198

PANORAMA CULTUREL 10 min.
- Ask students "Qu'est-ce qu'il faut faire pour être en forme?" and "Qu'est-ce qu'il faut éviter de manger?"
- Presenting **Panorama Culturel,** ATE, p. 199

Wrap-Up 5 min.
- Teaching Suggestion, ATE, p. 197

Homework Options

Have students study for Quiz 7-2.
Act. 28, p. 198
Grammaire supplémentaire, Act. 6, p. 208
Cahier d'activités, Acts. 12–17, pp. 77–79
Travaux pratiques de grammaire, Acts. 14–15, p. 59

Block 5

DEUXIEME ETAPE

Quick Review 5 min.
- Additional Listening Activity 7-4, Listening Activities, p. 56

Quiz 7-2 20 min.
- Administer Quiz 7-2A, 7-2B, or a combination of the two. Options: Test Generator, Alternative Assessment Program.

TROISIEME ETAPE

Vocabulaire, p. 201 40 min.
- Presenting **Vocabulaire,** ATE, p. 201
- Discuss **Note culturelle,** p. 200.
- Present **Note de grammaire,** p. 201.
- Activities 31 and 33, pp. 201–202
- Play Audio CD for Activity 32, p. 201.

Comment dit-on... ?, p. 202 15 min.
- Presenting **Comment dit-on... ?,** ATE, p. 202
- Play Audio CD for Activity 35, p. 202.
- Activity 36, p. 203

Wrap-Up 10 min.
- Teaching Transparency 7-E, using Suggestion #1 in Suggestions for Using Teaching Transparency 7-E

Homework Options

Have students study for Quiz 7-3.
Acts. 34 and 37, pp. 202–203
Grammaire supplémentaire, Acts. 7–9, pp. 208–209
Cahier d'activités, Acts. 18–24, pp. 80–82
Travaux pratiques de grammaire, Acts. 16–19, pp. 60–61

Block 6

TROISIEME ETAPE

Quick Review 10 min.
- Communicative Activity 7-3, Activities for Communication, pp. 41–42

Quiz 7-3 20 min.
- Administer Quiz 7-3A, 7-3B, or a combination of the two. Options: Test Generator, Alternative Assessment Program.

LISONS! 30 min.
- Discuss **Stratégie pour lire,** p. 204.
- Activity A, p. 204, using Teaching Suggestion, ATE, p. 204
- Activities B–G, pp. 204–205

MISE EN PRATIQUE 30 min.
- Activity 1, p. 210
- Play Audio CD for Activity 2, p. 210.
- Activity 5, p. 211

Homework Options

Que sais-je?, p. 212
CD-ROM/Interactive Games
Study for Chapter 7 Test.

Block 7

MISE EN PRATIQUE

Quick Review 10 min.
- Check homework.

Chapter Review 35 min.
- Review Chapter 7. Choose from **Grammaire supplémentaire,** Grammar Tutor for Students of French, Activities for Communication, Listening Activities, Interactive CD-ROM Tutor, or **Jeux interactifs.**

Chapter Test 40–45 min.
- Administer Chapter 7 Test. Select from Testing Program, Alternative Assessment Guide, Test Generator, or Standardized Assessment Tutor.

Chapter Opener

CHAPITRE 7

One-Stop Planner CD-ROM

For resource information, see the **One-Stop Planner,** Disc 2.

Pacing Tips

Chapter 7 has several vocabulary presentations, particularly in the **Première étape,** so you might plan your lessons accordingly. For Lesson Plans and timing suggestions, see pages 183I–183L.

Meeting the Standards

Communication

- Expressing concern for someone; complaining, p. 189
- Giving, accepting, and rejecting advice, p. 197
- Expressing discouragement; offering encouragement, p. 198
- Justifying your recommandations; advising against something, p. 202

Culture

- Culture Note, pp. 184, 185, 187
- Note culturelle, pp. 191, 195, 200
- Rencontre culturelle, p. 193
- Panorama Culturel, p. 199

Connections

- Music Link, p. 190
- Language Arts Link, p. 193
- Health Link, pp. 195, 204
- Math Link, p. 195

Comparisons

- Thinking Critically: Drawing Inferences, p. 188
- Thinking Critically: Analyzing, p. 199

Communities

- Career Path, p. 184
- Community Link, pp. 199, 203
- De l'école au travail, p. 203

Cultures and Communities

Culture Note

Soccer was introduced to France in 1890 and has since become the most popular sport there. Each year, the French Federation of Soccer organizes championships and the **Coupe de France.** Its final match is attended by the president of France. There are more than two million soccer players in France, of whom 650 are professionals. French soccer enthusiasts can choose from among 20,000 soccer clubs.

Career Path

Athletic trainers have the opportunity to work with professional athletes from all over the world. Ask students if they can name any sports that might provide the opportunity to work with French-speaking athletes **(hockey, soccer, tennis).**

STANDARDS: 2.2, 5.1

CHAPITRE

7 En pleine forme

Objectives

In this chapter you will learn to

Première étape

- express concern for someone
- complain

Deuxième étape

- give, accept, and reject advice
- express discouragement
- offer encouragement

Troisième étape

- justify your recommendations
- advise against something

internet

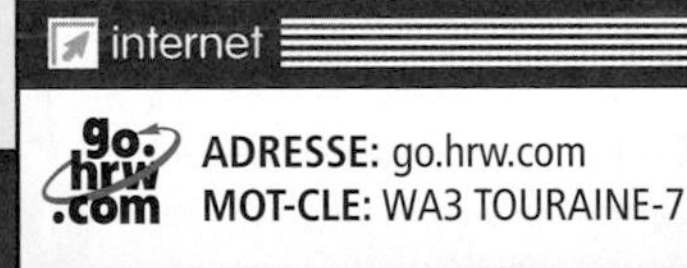

ADRESSE: go.hrw.com
MOT-CLE: WA3 TOURAINE-7

◀ Tu devrais faire du sport!

Chapter Opener

CHAPITRE 7

Focusing on Outcomes

Ask students to say as much as they can in French about the photo. Read the list of outcomes with students and have them try to match the photo with the correct outcome. NOTE: The self-check activities on page 212 help students assess their achievement of the objectives.

Teacher Note

For more information on soccer in France, see page 183D.

Chapter Sequence

Cultures and Communities

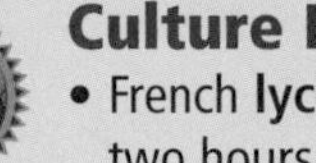

Culture Notes

- French **lycéens** are required to take two hours of physical education a week. There is usually a choice among track and field **(athlétisme)**, gymnastics, soccer, volleyball, and basketball. However, schools do not have teams that compete against teams from other schools. Therefore, there are no cheerleaders, marching bands, or student athletes, even at the university level. Students who wish to compete in team sports must join city leagues or clubs outside of school.
- The French generally eat fruits and vegetables at both lunch and dinner. Even busy working families tend to buy and prepare fresh produce rather than frozen or canned goods.

CHAPITRE 7

Teaching Resources
pp. 186–188

PRINT 

- Lesson Planner, p. 31
- Video Guide, pp. 44, 46
- Cahier d'activités, p. 73

MEDIA  

- One-Stop Planner
- Video Program
  Mise en train
  Videocassette 3, 00:49–04:29
  Videocassette 5 (captioned version), 57:20–1:01:00
  Suite
  Videocassette 3, 04:32–08:39
  Videocassette 5 (captioned version), 1:01:03–1:05:10
- DVD Tutor, Disc 1
- Audio Compact Discs, CD 7, Trs. 1–2
- **Mise en train** Transparencies

Language Note
The word **raplapla** comes from the word **raplati,** meaning *flattened.* Other related French words are **plat** *(flat);* **l'eau minérale plate** *(flat, non-carbonated mineral water);* **à plat ventre** *(lying flat);* and **un plateau** *(a flat tray, raised flat surface, plateau).*

Challenge/Auditory Learners
Type the text of the **Mise en train,** changing some of the words and numbering the lines. For example, for the first line, instead of **Eh bien, qu'est-ce que tu as, Bruno?,** type **Alors, qu'est-ce que tu vois, Annick?** As a listening exercise, play the recording and have students cross out the words on the typed copy of the text that are different from those they hear.

The **roman-photo** is an abridged version of the video episode.

MISE EN TRAIN • *Trop de conseils*

CD 7 Trs. 1–2
DVD

Stratégie pour comprendre
In this episode, Bruno is feeling out of sorts. Think of a few pieces of advice that you might give to someone who feels run-down. How could that person change his or her personal habits to feel better? Do Bruno's friends give him good advice?

Bruno

Céline

Hector

1
Céline Eh bien, qu'est-ce que tu as, Bruno? Tu n'as pas l'air en forme.
Bruno Je ne sais pas. Je me sens tout raplapla. Je suis fatigué. J'ai mal dormi.

2
Céline A quelle heure tu t'es couché hier soir?
Bruno Vers minuit, comme d'habitude.
Céline Mais, c'est beaucoup trop tard!

3
Céline Tu as pris le petit déjeuner ce matin?
Bruno Ben, non. J'étais pressé.
Céline Tu ne dois pas sauter les repas.

4
Céline Il est important de bien se nourrir. Mange des fruits et des légumes. Il faut surtout manger des choses variées, manger équilibré. C'est bon pour toi.

5
Hector Et est-ce que tu fais du sport?
Bruno Non, rarement.
Hector Tu ferais bien de t'entraîner. Tu devrais faire de l'exercice.

Preteaching Vocabulary

Recognizing Cognates
The new vocabulary presented in this story contains many cognates that students will recognize. Before students read the **Mise en train,** have them scan the story to find cognates related to diet and exercise. Here are some examples of what they might find:

- 4 des fruits
- 5 le sport
- 5 t'entraîner
- 5 l'exercice
- 6 le gymnase
- 8 tonifier les muscles
- 9 l'aérobic
- 9 le rythme cardiaque

STANDARDS: 1.2

6 **Hector** Tiens, pourquoi tu ne viens pas avec moi au gymnase?

7 **Au gymnase...**
Hector Au début, il faut s'échauffer. Doucement, il ne faut pas forcer. Va à ton propre rythme.

Hector Ensuite, il faut tonifier les muscles... Un peu plus haut!
Bruno Je n'en peux plus!
Hector Encore un effort. Tu y es presque.

8

9 **Hector** On fait de l'aérobic pour élever le rythme cardiaque.
Bruno Ouf! Je suis déjà crevé.
Hector Courage!

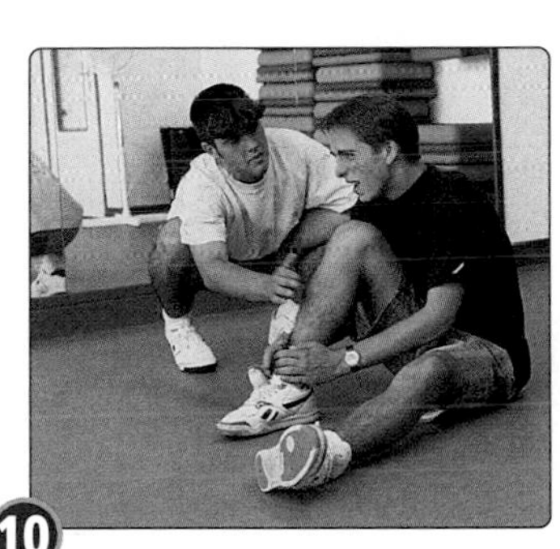

10 **Bruno** Aïe!
Hector Ça va, Bruno?!
Bruno Non, pas terrible. J'ai mal à la cheville.

11 **Hector** Tu peux marcher? Tu devrais mettre une compresse froide dessus.
Bruno Ecoute! J'en ai marre de tes conseils!
Hector Mais, ça te fera du bien.

Cahier d'activités, p. 73, Act. 1–2

Using the Captioned Video/DVD

If students have difficulty understanding French spoken at a normal speed, use Videocassette 5 to allow students to see the French captions for ***Trop de conseils*** and ***Trop de conseils (suite).*** Hearing the language and watching the story will reduce anxiety about the new language and facilitate comprehension. The reinforcement of seeing the written vocabulary words as they watch the gestures and actions will help prepare students to do the comprehension activities on page 188.

NOTE: The *DVD Tutor* contains captions for all sections of the *Video Program.*

Mise en train

CHAPITRE 7

Presenting Mise en train

To begin, have students view the video with their books closed. Then, play the audio recording as students read along. Ask the questions in Activity 1 on page 188. Finally, ask questions such as **Qui n'est pas en pleine forme? Est-ce qu'il mange bien? Est-ce qu'il fait de l'exercice? Qui lui donne des conseils? Est-ce qu'ils lui donnent trop de conseils?** You might also present the Preteaching Vocabulary suggestion on page 186.

Mise en train Transparencies

Culture Note

Most of the gymnasiums and sports complexes in France **(les salles et les centres de sport)** that offer aerobics, body-building, water aerobics, and weightlifting have appeared only in recent years.

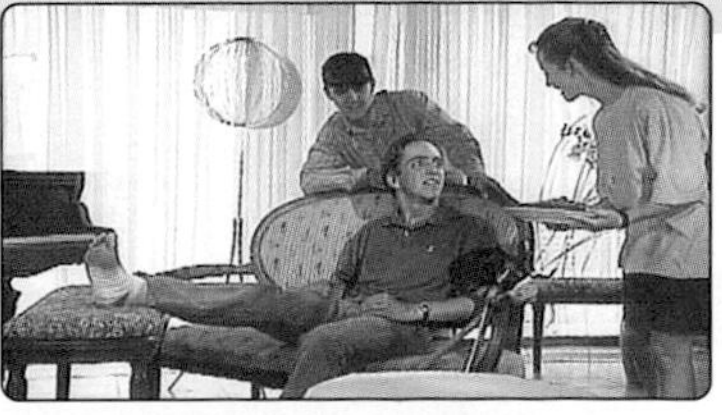

Mise en train (suite)

When the story continues, Bruno is at home with his ankle bandaged. Céline and Hector bring him a cake and fruit juice. They are trying to help, but Hector bumps Bruno's foot, and Céline spills cake on Bruno's new pants. Bruno tries to be gracious, but he's glad when Céline and Hector finally leave!

Mise en train

CHAPITRE 7

Thinking Critically

Drawing Inferences Ask students if they think Americans are concerned with their diet because of health or for other reasons. Ask them to imagine why these French teenagers are so concerned about their friend's health.

Language-to-Language

To help students understand and remember the verb **sauter** *(to skip, to jump),* point out that we use this word in English *(to sauté vegetables).* (When vegetables are sautéed, the hot butter or oil makes them jump around in the pan.) Call students' attention to the difference in pronunciation between the French **sauté** and the English *sauté.*

These activities check for comprehension only. Students should not yet be expected to produce language modeled in **Mise en train.**

1 Tu as compris? See answers below.

1. How does Bruno feel at the beginning of the story?
2. What three things do Céline and Hector ask him about?
3. What do they suggest to help him feel better?
4. Where do Hector and Bruno go? What do they do there?
5. How does Bruno feel at the end of the story?

2 Fais ton choix

Complète ces phrases d'après ***Trop de conseils.***

1. Bruno s'est couché vers...
   a. dix heures.
   b. onze heures et demie.
   c. minuit.
2. Au petit déjeuner, Bruno...
   a. a mangé une pomme.
   b. a mangé des céréales.
   c. n'a rien mangé.
3. D'après Céline, il est important de...
   a. se coucher tard.
   b. bien se nourrir.
   c. sauter des repas.
4. Bruno fait du sport...
   a. rarement.
   b. souvent.
   c. de temps en temps.
5. D'après Hector, pour élever le rythme cardiaque, il faut...
   a. s'échauffer.
   b. tonifier les muscles.
   c. faire de l'aérobic.
6. Bruno s'est fait mal...
   a. à la main.
   b. à la cheville.
   c. à la tête.

3 Cherche les expressions See answers below.

What does Céline or Hector say to . . .

1. find out what is wrong with Bruno?
2. give him advice?
3. justify their advice?
4. offer encouragement?

What does Bruno say to . . .

5. tell how he's feeling?
6. express his discouragement?
7. complain about an injury?
8. express his annoyance with his friend?

4 Qu'est-ce qu'ils disent? 1. b 2. c 3. a 4. d

1. 

2. 

3. 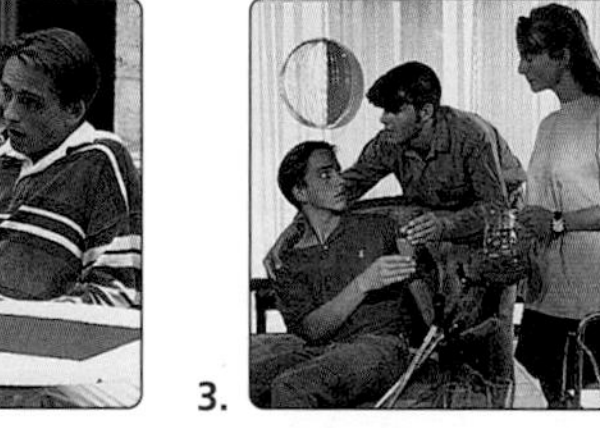

4. 

a. «Il est important de bien se nourrir.»
b. «Je me sens tout raplapla.»
c. «J'ai sauté le petit déjeuner ce matin.»
d. «Il faut tonifier ses muscles.»

5 Et maintenant, à toi

Qu'est-ce que tu penses des conseils que les amis de Bruno lui donnent? Qu'est-ce que tu voudrais lui conseiller, toi? Qu'est-ce que tu fais quand tes amis te donnent des conseils sur ta santé?

Answers

1
1. tired
2. what time he went to bed, whether he ate breakfast that morning, if he plays sports
3. Don't skip meals. Eat a balanced diet with lots of fruits and vegetables. Exercise.
4. to a gym; ride stationary bicycles, lift weights, do aerobics
5. He is fed up with his friends' advice.

3
1. Qu'est-ce que tu as?
2. Tu ne dois pas sauter les repas. Mange des fruits et des légumes. Tu ferais bien de t'entraîner. Tu devrais faire de l'exercice. Pourquoi tu ne viens pas avec moi au gymnase?
3. C'est bon pour toi. Ça te fera du bien.
4. Encore un effort. Tu y es presque! Courage!
5. Je me sens tout raplapla. Je suis fatigué. J'ai mal dormi.
6. Je n'en peux plus. Ouf! Je suis déjà crevé!
7. J'ai mal à la cheville.
8. J'en ai marre de tes conseils.

Comprehension Check

Auditory Learners

2 Read this activity aloud and have volunteers answer. For non-auditory learners, you might give students the option of looking at their books as you read aloud.

Teaching Suggestion

4 Have students select additional quotations from ***Trop de conseils*** and take turns with a partner reading them aloud and trying to guess who the speaker is.

Première étape

Objectives Expressing concern for someone; complaining

WA3 TOURAINE-7

Comment dit-on...?

Expressing concern for someone; complaining

To express concern for someone:

Quelque chose ne va pas?
Is something wrong?
Qu'est-ce que tu as?
What's wrong?
Tu n'as pas l'air en forme.
You don't look well.

To complain:

Je ne me sens pas bien.
I don't feel well.
Je suis tout(e) raplapla. *I'm wiped out.*
J'ai mal dormi. *I didn't sleep well.*
J'ai mal partout! *I hurt all over!*

Cahier d'activités, p. 74, Act. 3

Vocabulaire

Je suis malade. *I'm sick.*
J'ai mal au cœur. *I'm sick to my stomach.*
J'éternue beaucoup. *I'm sneezing a lot.*
J'ai... *I have . . .*
un rhume. *a cold.*
la grippe/des allergies *the flu/allergies*
mal à la tête/ à la gorge. *a headache/ sore throat.*
le nez qui coule. *a runny nose.*
de la fièvre. *fever.*
A tes souhaits! *Bless you! (said after a sneeze)*

Travaux pratiques de grammaire, p. 53, Act. 1–2
Cahier d'activités, p. 74, Act. 4–5

6 Ça ne va pas? See scripts on p. 183G.

CD 7 Tr. 3

Ecoutons Listen to Lucien's friends complain about how they feel. Match the person's name with his picture. What would the person in the remaining picture say?

1. Edouard 2. Jérôme 3. Jean-Claude

a. 2

b. 1

c. 3

d. J'ai mal à la gorge.

Communication for All Students

Kinesthetic Learners

Tell students they have a complaint or illness. **(Tu as un rhume.)** Have them respond by making an appropriate gesture or facial expression.

Challenge

One student says: **Je suis malade.** A second student says **Je suis malade** and adds an illness: **J'ai la grippe.** A third student says **Je suis malade; j'ai la grippe** and adds another illness **J'ai le nez qui coule.** The challenge continues in this way until a student cannot repeat the sentences in the order in which they were presented.

Première étape

CHAPITRE 7

Teaching Resources
pp. 189–193

PRINT

- Lesson Planner, p. 32
- TPR Storytelling Book, pp. 48–49
- Listening Activities, pp. 51, 55
- Activities for Communication, pp. 37–38, 105, 108, 149–150
- Travaux pratiques de grammaire, pp. 53–56
- Grammar Tutor for Students of French, Chapter 7
- Cahier d'activités, pp. 74–76
- Testing Program, pp. 171–174
- Alternative Assessment Guide, p. 38
- Student Make-Up Assignments, Chapter 7

MEDIA 

- One-Stop Planner
- Audio Compact Discs, CD 7, Trs. 3–5, 16, 22–23
- Teaching Transparencies: 7-1, 7-A, 7-B, 7-C; **Grammaire supplémentaire** Answers; Travaux pratiques de grammaire Answers
- Interactive CD-ROM Tutor, Disc 2

Bell Work

Have students find expressions in the **Mise en train** to tell how Bruno is feeling.

Presenting
Comment dit-on... ?

Tell students how you're feeling, using facial expressions and gestures. Write each new expression on the board as you use it. Express concern for a student and prompt him or her to tell you what's wrong.

Vocabulaire

Act out these illnesses to convey their meaning. Have students repeat after you and mimic your gestures.

Teaching Resources
pp. 189–193

PRINT

- Lesson Planner, p. 32
- TPR Storytelling Book, pp. 48–49
- Listening Activities, pp. 51, 55
- Activities for Communication, pp. 37–38, 105, 108, 149–150
- Travaux pratiques de grammaire, pp. 53–56
- Grammar Tutor for Students of French, Chapter 7
- Cahier d'activités, pp. 74–76
- Testing Program, pp. 171–174
- Alternative Assessment Guide, p. 38
- Student Make-Up Assignments, Chapter 7

MEDIA

- One-Stop Planner
- Audio Compact Discs, CD 7, Trs. 3–5, 16, 22–23
- Teaching Transparencies: 7-1, 7-A, 7-B, 7-C; **Grammaire supplémentaire** Answers; Travaux pratiques de grammaire Answers
- Interactive CD-ROM Tutor, Disc 2

Presenting Vocabulaire

Teach **le bras** by pointing to your arm and having students repeat as they touch their arm. Continue in this manner for other parts of the body. Then, use a doll to teach ailments by making cause-and-effect statements. **(Elle a fait du jogging, et maintenant, elle a mal aux pieds.)** Point to where the doll hurts.

7 Tu n'as pas l'air en forme!

Parlons/Ecrivons Tu n'as pas l'air en forme aujourd'hui et ton ami(e) te demande ce que tu as. Qu'est-ce que tu réponds si...

1. tu t'es couché(e) à deux heures du matin? Je suis tout(e) raplapla.
2. tu es allergique aux chats? J'ai des allergies.
3. tu es fatigué(e)? J'ai mal dormi.
4. tu as besoin d'aspirine? J'ai mal à la tête.
5. tu éternues et tu as le nez qui coule?
6. tu es allé(e) au championnat de foot hier soir et tu as beaucoup crié?
7. tu as la grippe? J'ai mal partout.

5. J'ai un rhume. **6.** J'ai mal à la gorge.

8 C'est pas de chance, ça!

Parlons Tu es venu(e) à l'école malade aujourd'hui. Ton ami(e) te console et te donne des conseils. Joue cette scène avec un(e) camarade, puis changez de rôle.

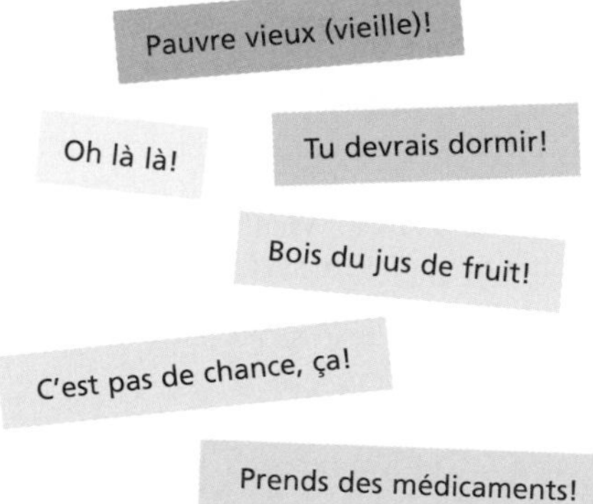

Pauvre vieux (vieille)!
Oh là là!
Tu devrais dormir!
Bois du jus de fruit!
C'est pas de chance, ça!
Prends des médicaments!

Vocabulaire

J'ai mal partout!
J'ai mal...

Travaux pratiques de grammaire, pp. 54–55, Act. 3–5

Grammaire supplémentaire, p. 206, Act. 1

Cahier d'activités, p. 75, Act. 6–7

9 Qu'est-ce que vous avez? See scripts and answers on p. 183G.

Ecoutons Listen as several students talk to the pharmacist. Where are their aches and pains?

CD 7 Tr. 4

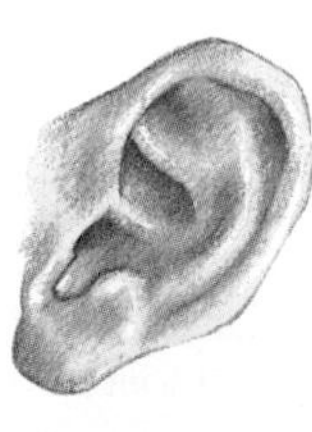
a.

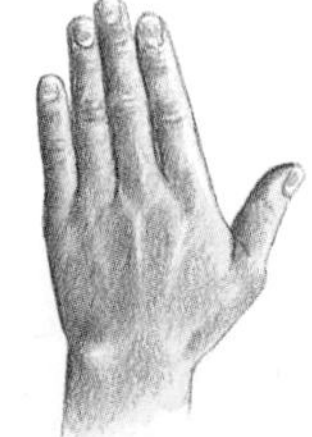
b.

c.

d.

Connections and Comparisons

Music Link

Distribute copies of the lyrics of the song *Alouette (Listening Activities,* Level 1, page 50). Play the song and have students underline the French words for body parts they already know. Then, tell students that **une alouette** is a bird and briefly explain the meaning of the song. Ask students what other words they think they will find in the song, knowing it's about a bird (wings, beak, tail, legs). Have them go over the lyrics again and try to guess what these words are in French. You might tell students that in French, the word **patte** is used instead of **pied** when talking about animals. Finally, have pairs of students create humorous skits in which the **alouette** complains about its aches and pains to another bird.

STANDARDS: 1.1, 1.2, 3.1, 5.1

Note culturelle

In France, you go to the pharmacy **(la pharmacie)** for both over-the-counter medicines, such as cough syrup and aspirin, and for prescription medication. You can't get a prescription filled at the grocery store as you can in the United States. Only the pharmacy, easily spotted on the street by its green sign in the shape of a cross, will honor a doctor's prescription.

10 J'ai mal à...

Parlons/Ecrivons Qu'est-ce qui te fait mal si... See answers below.

1. tu as mangé trop de pizza?
2. tu as joué au volley-ball toute la journée?
3. tu as fait cent abdominaux?
4. tu as passé deux heures à faire du jogging?
5. tu as dansé jusqu'à minuit?
6. tu as passé la nuit à étudier?
7. tu es allé(e) chez le dentiste?
8. tu es assis(e) tout près des enceintes à un concert de rock?

11 Jacques a dit

Parlons Your group leader tells you where you ache: **Vous avez mal au dos.** The group acts it out, but only if the leader begins by saying **Jacques a dit.** You're out if you act out a pain when the leader doesn't begin by saying **Jacques a dit.** The winner becomes the next leader.

12 Aïe! J'ai mal partout!

Parlons Hier soir, tu as fait du sport. Maintenant, tu as mal partout. Ton ami(e) te demande comment tu vas. Explique où tu as mal. Ton ami(e) va te consoler. Ensuite, changez de rôle.

Exemple —**Qu'est-ce que tu as?**
—**J'ai mal dormi et maintenant, j'ai mal à la tête.**

A la française

When you hurt yourself accidentally, say **Aïe!** *(Ow!)* or **Ouille!** *(Ouch!).* When you've finished doing something physically difficult, say **Ouf!** *(Whew!).*

Vocabulaire

Qu'est-ce qui t'est arrivé?

CD-ROM 2
DVD 1

Travaux pratiques de grammaire, p. 55, Act. 6

Communication for All Students

Visual Learners/Slower Pace

10 Write the questions on a transparency and project them on the overhead. Have a student come up to the projector and call on volunteers to answer the questions. The student-teacher should write the answers beside or underneath each question.

Challenge

10 Have students work in groups to write causes and their effects on separate index cards. **(J'ai mangé trop de pizza. J'ai mal au ventre.)** Challenge them to invent additional causes for pains or aches and their effects. Then, have them pass the shuffled cards to another group, who will match the causes to the effects.

Première étape

CHAPITRE 7

TPR Give students commands to follow, such as **Touchez votre pied droit avec la main gauche.** Then, have students give their classmates commands to follow.

Presenting Vocabulaire

Using bandages or small strips of an old bedsheet, bandage your elbow, leg, ankle, and finger. Pointing to the bandages, act out the expressions and have students repeat them after you. You might use a crutch and bandage to help illustrate the different verbs or add context, such as **Ce week-end, j'ai fait du ski et je me suis cassé la jambe.** Then, ask students to substitute other parts of the body in each expression. **(Je me suis cassé le bras.)** Finally, hand out the bandages, ask students to create their own injuries, and circulate around the room, asking individuals **Qu'est-ce qui t'est arrivé?** Allow them to look at their books as they respond.

Language Note

Point out that you use the definite article, not the possessive adjective, with parts of the body after the verbs **se couper, se casser,** and **se fouler. (Je me suis cassé <u>la</u> jambe.)**

Possible Answers

10
1. le ventre
2. les mains, les bras
3. le ventre
4. les jambes, les pieds
5. les jambes, les pieds
6. la tête, les yeux, le dos
7. les dents
8. les oreilles

STANDARDS: 1.1, 2.1, 3.2, 4.1, 4.2, 5.2

Première étape

CHAPITRE 7

Presenting Note de grammaire

Reflexive verbs in the *passé composé* On strips of transparency, write the sentences in the **Note de grammaire** in large letters and cut them apart into words. Guide volunteers through the process of putting the sentences together. Explain the difference between **Elle s'est coupée** and **Elle s'est coupé le doigt**. Afterwards, you might have small groups complete a similar exercise, using photocopied sentence strips cut apart into words.

Group Work

Form groups of five and have each group write on separate index cards 25 expressions from the **Comment dit-on... ?** and **Vocabulaire** sections of this **étape** that relate to an injury or illness. Have each student in the group draw five line drawings of a human figure on a sheet of paper. Each group member chooses five cards and reads them to the group. **(Il a mal au dos. Il a un rhume.)** The other group members draw the injuries or illnesses described on their human figures. Afterwards, students should take turns explaining the injuries and illnesses of each person in their drawings. The students who read the cards should compare what the members say with what is written on the cards.

Assess

- Testing Program, pp. 171–174 Quiz 7-1A, Quiz 7-1B Audio CD 7, Tr. 16
- Student Make-Up Assignments, Chapter 7, Alternative Quiz
- Alternative Assessment Guide, p. 38

Note de grammaire

CD-ROM 2
DVD 1

- Many of the verbs you use to tell about injuries are reflexive. They follow the same pattern in the past tense as other reflexive verbs you've learned:

  Je **me suis cassé** la jambe.
  Tu **t'es cassé** le doigt.
  Elle **s'est cassé** la cheville.
  Nous **nous sommes cassé** la jambe.
  Vous **vous êtes cassé** le bras.
  Ils **se sont cassé** les doigts.

- When a direct object follows a reflexive verb, as in the sentences above, the past participle does not change to agree with the subject.

  Elle s'est **coupée.** *but*
  Elle s'est **coupé** le doigt.

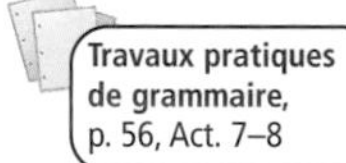

Travaux pratiques de grammaire, p. 56, Act. 7–8

Grammaire supplémentaire, pp. 206–207, Act. 2–3

Cahier d'activités, p. 76, Act. 8

13 Grammaire en contexte

See scripts and answers on p. 183G.

CD 7 Tr. 5

Ecoutons You're helping out the nurse at a **colonie de vacances** this summer. Listen as she tells you about the patients who have come in this morning. Which of the people in the **Vocabulaire** on page 191 is she talking about? Fatima? Guy? Véronique? Tranh?

14 Grammaire en contexte

Lisons Un accident, ça arrive! Complète ces phrases avec tous les mots appropriés.

1. Quand mes amis et moi sommes allés faire du ski, je n'ai pas eu de chance! Je me suis cassé ___?___. la jambe, le bras...
2. Mon amie faisait la cuisine et elle s'est coupé ___?___. le doigt
3. A la fin de la soirée, mon meilleur ami s'est foulé ___?___. la cheville
4. En rentrant chez moi, je me suis fait mal ___?___. au dos, au pied...

15 Grammaire en contexte

Ecrivons Ton ami Pascal a passé un mauvais week-end. Qu'est-ce qui lui est arrivé? Complète ce paragraphe.

J'ai passé un week-end épouvantable! D'abord, vendredi, je [... me suis foulé la cheville], donc je n'ai pas pu aller faire du ski avec mes copains. Ensuite, samedi après-midi, je faisais un sandwich quand je [... me suis coupé le doigt]. Et c'est pas tout! Samedi soir, en entrant dans ma chambre, je [... me suis fait mal à la jambe]. Dimanche, j'allais répondre au téléphone quand je suis tombé dans l'escalier et je [... me suis cassé le bras]. Je craque, moi!

16 Qu'est-ce qui s'est passé?

Parlons You phone a friend to find out why he or she didn't meet you after school. Your friend says he or she is hurt and tells you what's wrong. React with sympathy, or express disbelief if you think your friend is making excuses. Then, reverse roles.

EXEMPLE —**Salut, Emmanuelle. Pourquoi tu n'es pas venue aujourd'hui?**
—**C'est que je suis tombée dans l'escalier...**

Si tu as oublié
how to express doubt
va à la page 168.

Communication for All Students

Slower Pace

14 Write possible answers to this activity in random order on an overhead transparency. Allow students to refer to it while they complete the exercise.

Challenge

15 Have one student at the board write the answers to this activity as they are given in class. Check for correct spelling. Then have partners give each other a dictation. One partner sits with his or her back to the board and writes all or part of the original exercise as the other partner reads the text of Activity 15, referring to the board for the missing vocabulary. Then have students look at the board and their textbook to correct their work.

STANDARDS: 1.1, 1.2, 5.1

Rencontre culturelle

1. Elle a un chat dans la gorge.

2. Il a pris ses jambes à son cou!

3. Ça coûte les yeux de la tête!

4. Tu me casses les pieds!

Qu'en penses-tu?

1. How would you translate these expressions literally? Can you figure out what the expressions mean figuratively? What would the English equivalents be?
2. Think of expressions like these in English. Then, find out what they are in French.

Savais-tu que... ?

Different cultures sometimes use very different images to convey the same idea. Did you figure out the English equivalents of the French expressions above?

1. Literal meaning:
   She's got a cat in her throat.
   English equivalent:
   She's got a frog in her throat.
2. Literal meaning:
   He took his legs to his neck.
   English equivalent:
   He ran like the wind.
3. Literal meaning:
   It costs the eyes from the head.
   English equivalent:
   It costs an arm and a leg.
4. Literal meaning:
   You're breaking my feet!
   English equivalent:
   You're a pain in the neck!

Connections and Comparisons

Language-to-Language

Have students recall expressions in English that refer to parts of the body. *(My eye! My foot! You're pulling my leg! My eyes are bigger than my stomach. I put my foot in my mouth. I made it by the skin of my teeth. Could you give me a hand? He'd cut off his nose to spite his face. You're shooting yourself in the foot.)* Ask students how such expressions add to a language. (They make it more expressive and colorful.) Ask why students should learn these kinds of expressions in a foreign language. (It makes their informal speech more authentic.)

Teaching Suggestion

Have students try to match the following figures of speech and their equivalents: **Il n'a pas mis le nez dehors de la journée. (Il n'est pas sorti pendant toute la journée.) Ils se sont bouffé le nez. (Ils se sont fâchés.) Il a la langue bien pendue. (Il parle beaucoup.) Je donne ma langue au chat. (Dis-moi la réponse. Je ne peux pas deviner.) Il conduit comme un pied. (Il conduit très mal.) Il a fait ça les doigts dans le nez. (Il a fait ça facilement.) Il a le cœur sur la main. (Il est très généreux.) Il a réussi haut la main. (Il a réussi facilement.) La moutarde me monte au nez. (Je suis très fâché(e).)**

Presenting Rencontre culturelle

For each illustration, ask **Qu'est-ce que ça veut dire?** and prompt students to give an explanation of each expression in French. **(Elle ne peut pas parler. Il va très vite. C'est très cher. Elle l'embête.)** Then, ask the questions in **Qu'en penses-tu?**

Visual Learners

Have students draw or find descriptive or humorous pictures to illustrate the idioms on the pupil's page as well as those listed in the Teaching Suggestion on this page. Have them write the idiom below their illustration. You might display the pictures in the classroom.

Language Arts Link

Point out that the figures of speech on this page are called *idiomatic expressions* and cannot be translated literally.

Deuxième étape

CHAPITRE 7

Teaching Resources
pp. 194–198

PRINT

- Lesson Planner, p. 33
- TPR Storytelling Book, pp. 50–51
- Listening Activities, pp. 52, 56
- Activities for Communication, pp. 39–40, 106, 108–109, 149–150
- Travaux pratiques de grammaire, pp. 57–59
- Grammar Tutor for Students of French, Chapter 7
- Cahier d'activités, pp. 77–79
- Testing Program, pp. 175–178
- Alternative Assessment Guide, p. 38
- Student Make-Up Assignments, Chapter 7

MEDIA 

- One-Stop Planner
- Audio Compact Discs, CD 7, Trs. 6–8, 17, 24–25
- Teaching Transparencies: 7-2, 7-D; **Grammaire supplémentaire** Answers; Travaux pratiques de grammaire Answers
- Interactive CD-ROM Tutor, Disc 2

Bell Work

Project a transparency of a person with an injury or ailment. Have students write a six-line conversation they might have with this person.

Answers

17
1. to give the schedule of activities at a health club
2. six categories; fitness classes, relaxation exercises, dance classes, martial arts classes, combat sports, water sports
3. stretching, aerobics, yoga, self-defense
4. individual training plans

18
1. a. abdominaux, boxe américaine, aérobic
   b. gym aquatique
   c. yoga, gym douce, stretching

Deuxième étape

Objectives Giving, accepting, and rejecting advice; expressing discouragement; offering encouragement

WA3 TOURAINE-7

COMPLEX SPORTIF RASPAIL
68, boulevard Raspail 75006 Paris
tel : 01.45.79.32.56
ouvert tous les jours de 8h à 22h

Musculation • Circuit training
Plans d'entraînement individuels

Piscine • Sauna • Hammam
Bains à remous

	CULTURE PHYSIQUE	RELAXATION	DANSE	ARTS MARTIAUX	SPORTS DE COMBAT	SPORTS AQUATIQUES
Lundi	**Abdominaux :** 11h15, 13h et 19h30 **Aérobic :** 8h30, 15h 18h30 et 20h	**Yoga :** 9h, 12h30 et 18h45 **Gym douce :** 10h15, 15h45 et 19h45	**Modern'jazz :** 19h30 **Danse africaine :** 18h45	**Judo :** 19h **Karaté :** 20h15	**Boxe américaine :** 20h30 **Self-défense :** 20h45	**Gym aquatique :** 9h, 12h30 et 18h30
Mardi	**Stretching :** 12h30 et 18h15 **Abdominaux :** 11h, 15h et 20h30	**Yoga :** 9h, 12h30, 16h45 et 18h45	**Modern'jazz :** 18h30 **Danse de salon :** 20h45	**Aïkido :** 18h45	**Boxe anglaise :** 18h45 **Self-défense :** 20h45	**Gym aquatique :** 15h et 19h30
Mercredi	**Abdominaux :** 11h15 et 19h30 **Aérobic :** 8h30, 15h, 18h30 et 20h	**Yoga :** 8h, 12h30 et 19h30 **Gym douce :** 12h, 15h45 et 20h	**Modern'jazz :** 19h45 **Danse africaine :** 20h45	**Judo :** 19h **Aïkido :** 18h45		
Jeudi	**Abdominaux :** 11h15, 15h et 20h30 **Aérobic :** 9h30, 16h, 18h30 et 21h		**Rock :** 18h45 **Danse africaine :** 19h45 et 21h	**Judo :** 19h	**Boxe américaine :** 18h30 **Self-défense :** 19h45	**Gym aquatique :** 10h45 et 20h30
Vendredi	**Aérobic :** 8h30, 15h, 18h30 et 20h **Step :** 9h, 16h et 19h45	**Yoga :** 11h45, 13h30 et 19h45 **Gym douce :** 10h15, 15h45 et 20h45	**Danse de salon :** 20h30 **Danse africaine :** 18h45	**Karaté :** 20h15 **Aïkido :** 18h45	**Boxe américaine :** 19h30 **Self-défense :** 19h45	
Samedi	**Abdominaux :** 11h45, 14h et 19h30 **Aérobic :** 10h30, 15h, 18h30 et 19h30	**Yoga :** 9h, 12h30, 15h45, 17h et 18h45 **Gym douce :** 10h15, 13h, 17h15 et 19h45	**Modern'jazz :** 14 h et 19h30 **Danse africaine :** 14h et 18h45	**Judo :** 10h45, 14h, 16h et 19h **Aïkido :** 12h, 15h45, 16h30 et 18h45	**Boxe américaine :** 11h45 et 20h30 **Boxe anglaise :** 10h, 18h45 et 21h	**Gym aquatique :** 8h45, 10h45, 13h, 15h45 et 18h30
Dimanche	**Aérobic :** 9h30, 15h, 18h45 et 20h **Step :** 9h, 16h et 19h45	**Yoga :** 8h, 14h30 et 18h45 **Gym douce :** 10h15, 15h45	**Rock :** 19h30 **Danse africaine :** 18h45	**Judo :** 19h30 **Karaté :** 20h45	**Boxe américaine :** 18h30 **Self-défense :** 19h45	**Gym aquatique :** 9h, 10h45, 12h et 18h30

17 **A lire avec attention** See answers below.

Lisons

1. What's the purpose of this brochure?
2. How many major categories are there? What are they?
3. Can you guess what the courses are?
4. What do you think **Plans d'entraînement individuels** means?

18 **Qu'est-ce qu'on choisit?** See answers below.

Lisons

1. Au Complex Sportif Raspail, quels cours est-ce qu'on choisit...
   a. pour se tonifier les muscles?
   b. si on aime la piscine?
   c. si on est stressé(e)?
2. Tu choisis quelles activités? Quels jours? Pourquoi?

Teacher to Teacher

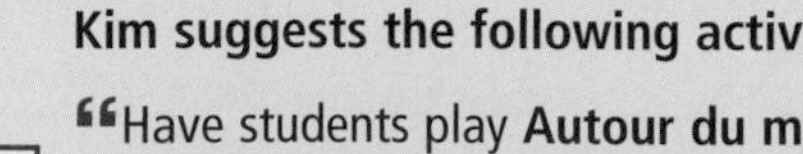

Kim Peters
Mooresville High School
Mooresville, IN

Kim suggests the following activity to practice vocabulary.

"Have students play **Autour du monde** to practice vocabulary. One student stands next to a seated student. A flash card with a picture illustrating a vocabulary word is shown. The first student to say the French equivalent moves to stand next to the desk of the student behind him or her. A student that goes through one row is the winner. The last student in the row who lost against the winner then stands up to try to win against the next student/row."

STANDARDS: 1.2, 3.1, 4.1

Deuxième étape

CHAPITRE 7

Group Work

Note culturelle Have students work in groups to conduct a school-wide poll to determine the exercise habits of students in their school. Have them write a list of questions to ask a predetermined percentage of the student body. Have them compile their results and submit them to the school newspaper.

Presenting Vocabulaire

Draw or gather pictures of people doing the activities in the **Vocabulaire.** Attach an index card to each picture with the name of a boy or girl written on it. Attach another card on which you've written an expression of frequency, such as **souvent** or **deux fois par semaine.** Show each picture and tell what the person is doing and how frequently. **(Eric fait des pompes tous les jours.)** Then, tape the pictures and cards to the board and ask questions, such as **Qui aime faire des pompes?** and **Combien de fois par semaine est-ce que Surya fait de la gymnastique?** Finally, personalize the questions and ask students **Qui fait des abdominaux? Tu en fais souvent?** and so on.

There has been a growing interest among French teenagers in both individual and team sports. Although there are no athletic teams that represent the **lycées,** students can join informal teams in their town or city. Many students have some sort of regular athletic activity, and some belong to private sports clubs like **Gymnase Club.** People can also take a variety of dance, martial arts, and weight-training classes at the **Maison des jeunes et de la culture (MJC).**

Vocabulaire

Qu'est-ce que tu fais pour te mettre en condition?

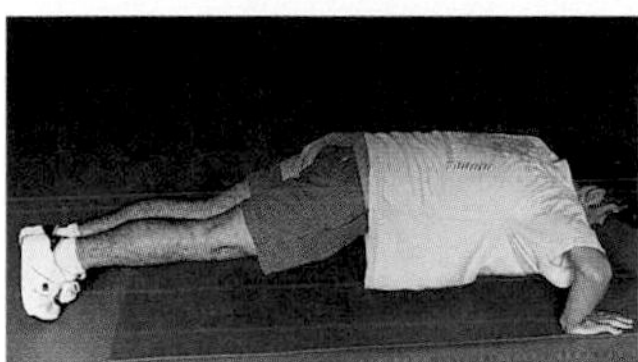

Quelquefois, **je fais de l'exercice.** J'aime **faire des pompes.**

Moi, je fais de la musculation.

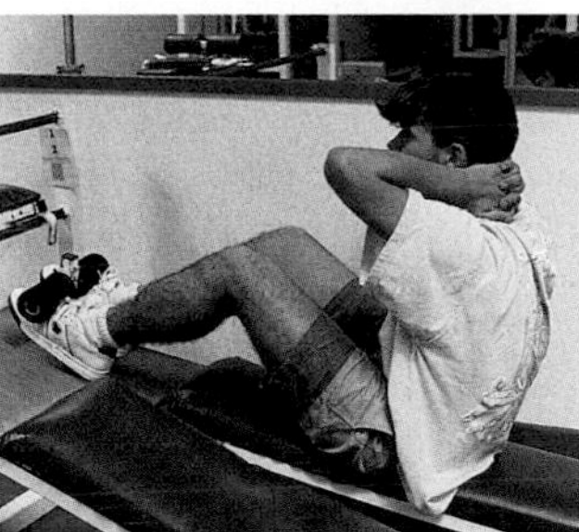

Moi, je fais des abdominaux tous les jours!

Moi, je fais souvent **de la gymnastique.**

Moi, je m'entraîne au basket.

Je fais de l'aérobic deux fois par semaine.

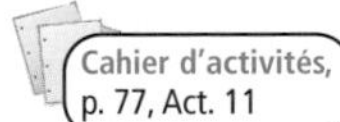

Travaux pratiques de grammaire, p. 57, Act. 9–11

Cahier d'activités, p. 77, Act. 11

Connections and Comparisons

Health Link

Obtain from the health or physical education teacher a chart that gives the number of calories burned per hour during various physical activities. Have students calculate how many calories the people in the photos would burn in an hour doing the activities pictured. Some students might calculate how many calories they burn in a week according to their own physical activity.

Math Link

Once students have finished their calculations (see Health Link), have them draw a graph demonstrating the relationship between physical activity and calories burned and have them write an explanation.

STANDARDS: 1.2, 2.1, 3.1, 4.2

Deuxième étape

CHAPITRE 7

Teaching Resources
pp. 194–198

PRINT

- Lesson Planner, p. 33
- TPR Storytelling Book, pp. 50–51
- Listening Activities, pp. 52, 56
- Activities for Communication, pp. 39–40, 106, 108–109, 149–150
- Travaux pratiques de grammaire, pp. 57–59
- Grammar Tutor for Students of French, Chapter 7
- Cahier d'activités, pp. 77–79
- Testing Program, pp. 175–178
- Alternative Assessment Guide, p. 38
- Student Make-Up Assignments, Chapter 7

MEDIA 

- One-Stop Planner
- Audio Compact Discs, CD 7, Trs. 6–8, 17, 24–25
- Teaching Transparencies: 7-2, 7-D; **Grammaire supplémentaire** Answers; Travaux pratiques de grammaire Answers
- Interactive CD-ROM Tutor, Disc 2

Presenting
Note de grammaire

Write the questions and answers from the **Note de grammaire** in large letters on strips of posterboard and cut them into words. Have students come to the front of the class and form a question with the words. Have students rearrange themselves to form the response with **en.**

Possible Answers

21
1. Il doit faire de la musculation et des pompes.
2. Elle doit faire de la musculation, de la danse et de l'aérobic.
3. Ils doivent faire de la danse et de la musculation.

19 Qu'est-ce que tu fais comme sport?

CD 7 Tr. 6

Ecoutons See scripts and answers on p. 183G.

a. Simone asked her friends Josée, Christelle, and Khalid what they do to keep in shape. What does each person do?

b. Listen again to Josée, Christelle, and Khalid and write down how often they do each activity.

Tu te rappelles?

Here are some expressions you've already learned to tell how often you do something:

Je m'entraîne à la natation **tous les jours.**
Je fais de l'exercice **trois fois par semaine.**
Je joue au tennis **deux fois par mois.**
Je **ne** fais **jamais** d'aérobic.
Je fais de la gymnastique **le lundi** et **le jeudi.**

Travaux pratiques de grammaire, p. 58, Act. 12

20 Sportif ou pas?

Parlons/Ecrivons Décris ce que ta famille, tes amis et toi, vous faites comme sports. Choisis un mot ou une expression dans chaque boîte et fais des phrases.

Je	faire de la musculation	tous les jours
Ma mère/Mon père	faire de l'aérobic	deux fois par semaine
Ma meilleure amie	faire des abdominaux	ne... jamais
Mon meilleur ami	faire de la gymnastique	le matin
Ma sœur/Mon frère	faire de l'exercice	l'après-midi
Avec l'équipe de..., on...	s'entraîner au/à la...	le soir
?	?	?

21 Les sportifs
See answers below.

Parlons/Ecrivons Qu'est-ce qu'ils doivent faire pour se mettre en condition?

1. 

2. 

3. 

Note de grammaire

You can use **en** to replace a phrase beginning with **de la, du, de l',** or **des** that refers to an activity:

—Tu fais **de la natation?**
—Non, je n'**en** fais pas. Et toi?
—Moi, j'**en** fais souvent.

Travaux pratiques de grammaire, pp. 58–59, Act. 13–14

Grammaire supplémentaire, pp. 207–208, Act. 4–5

22 Grammaire en contexte

Parlons Est-ce que tes camarades de classe sont sportifs? Fais une liste de cinq sports et activités. Ensuite, demande à trois de tes camarades s'ils en font et s'ils en font souvent. Qui est le plus sportif?

EXEMPLE
— **Tu fais de la gymnastique?**
— **Oui.**
— **Tu en fais souvent?**
— **Ben... deux fois par semaine.**

Teacher to Teacher

Alisa Glick
Greenwich Country Day School
Greenwich, CT

Alisa suggests the following activity to practice material from this chapter.

"Exit pass" As the students are leaving the classroom, ask them a question related to the objective of the day. If the objective was asking for and giving advice, you might ask: **Pourquoi tu ne fais pas de sport?** Each student answers the question in order to exit the class. For a large class, you could have students ask one another the Exit Pass question.

STANDARDS: 1.2, 5.1

Comment dit-on...?

Giving, accepting, and rejecting advice

To give advice:

Tu dois te mettre en condition.
You've got to . . .
Tu devrais faire du sport.
You should . . .
Tu ferais bien de t'entraîner au basket.
You would do well to . . .
Tu n'as qu'à te coucher plus tôt.
All you have to do is . . .
Pourquoi tu ne fais **pas** de la gymnastique?
Why don't you . . . ?

To accept advice:

Tu as raison.
Bonne idée!
D'accord.

To reject advice:

Je ne peux pas.
Non, je n'ai pas très envie.
Non, je préfère faire de la musculation!
Pas question!
Je n'ai pas le temps.
I don't have time.
Ce n'est pas mon truc.
It's not my thing.

Cahier d'activités, p. 78, Act. 13–14

23 Les conseils d'Olivier

CD 7 Tr. 7

Ecoutons Olivier donne des conseils à ses amis. Est-ce qu'ils acceptent ou refusent ses conseils? See scripts and answers on p. 183G.

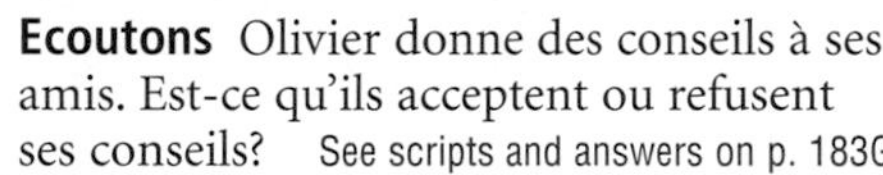

Note de grammaire

Devoir is an irregular verb that means *must, to have to.*

je	**dois**	nous	**devons**
tu	**dois**	vous	**devez**
il/elle/on	**doit**	ils/elles	**doivent**

- The past participle of **devoir** is **dû.**
- **Tu devrais** *(You should)* is a polite form of **devoir.**

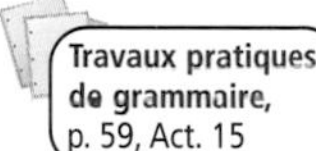
Travaux pratiques de grammaire, p. 59, Act. 15

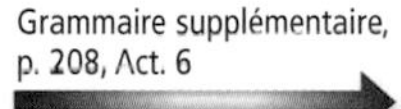
Grammaire supplémentaire, p. 208, Act. 6

24 Grammaire en contexte

Ecrivons Utilise les mots et les expressions proposés et crée six phrases pour expliquer ce que toi et tes amis, vous devez faire pour vous mettre en forme. Utilise le verbe **devoir** dans tes phrases.

nous	faire de la musculation
tu	faire des abdominaux
Luc et Stéphanie	faire des pompes
vous	s'entraîner au football
Martine	faire de l'aérobic
je	faire de la gymnastique

25 Tu ferais bien de...

See answers below.

Donne des conseils à tes amis.

1. Jean-Paul s'est endormi en maths.
2. Cam ne peut pas porter ses gros livres.
3. Arnaud a grossi pendant l'hiver.
4. Mireille est crevée à la fin de la journée.
5. Raoul a des difficultés à monter l'escalier.
6. André ne peut pas toucher ses pieds.

Tu te rappelles?

When you're pronouncing the French **r**, keep the tip of your tongue pressed against your lower front teeth. Arch the back of your tongue upward, almost totally blocking the passage of air in the back of your throat. Practice by saying **tu ferais** and **tu devrais.** Then try **tu as raison, très envie,** and **mon truc.**

Communication for All Students

Additional Practice

25 For additional listening practice to help auditory learners, you might first read the sentences aloud as students listen with their books closed.

Presenting Comment dit-on... ?

On separate strips of transparency, write sentences that state a health problem, give advice, and either accept or reject advice. Color-code the sentences according to the function they serve. For example, write **Je suis tout raplapla** (stating a health problem) in black, **Tu n'as qu'à te coucher plus tôt** (giving advice) in green, **Tu as raison** (accepting advice) in blue, and **Je ne peux pas** (rejecting advice) in red. Arrange the strips to form conversations, read them, and have students repeat after you. Then, ask students which sentences state a health problem (black), which ones give advice, and so on. Finally, place the strips randomly on the overhead projector and have students rearrange them to form other conversations.

Teaching Suggestion

Have each student write a complaint from the **Première étape** on a sheet of paper and pass it to a classmate. The classmate writes a reply, giving some advice from **Comment dit-on... ?** and passes it back. The first student then writes back, accepting or rejecting the advice. Allow students to continue their correspondence as long as they can. Circulate around the classroom, checking the notes. You might read humorous ones to the class.

Possible Answers

25
1. Tu devrais te coucher plus tôt.
2. Tu ferais bien de faire de la musculation.
3. Pourquoi tu ne fais pas de l'exercice?
4. Tu n'as qu'à te coucher plus tôt.
5. Tu dois te mettre en condition.
6. Pourquoi tu ne fais pas de la gymnastique?

Presenting
Comment dit-on... ?

Prepare a short skit in which two people are exercising. One person is out of shape and gets discouraged. The other one offers encouragement. Act out both sides of the conversation for the class, alternatively miming aerobic activities while expressing discouragement and giving encouragement. Use gestures and facial expressions to convey the meaning of the new expressions. Then, show magazine pictures of people who are exhausted or discouraged. For each picture, ask **Qu'est-ce qu'il/elle dit?,** give an appropriate answer **(J'abandonne.),** and ask students to repeat it after you. Finally, show the pictures again and have volunteers supply the appropriate responses.

Teaching Suggestion

To close this **étape,** gather several pictures of people engaged in physical activity, some who are out of shape or tired, and some who are discouraged. Show the pictures and ask a variety of questions about them in order to elicit the functional expressions from this **étape.** For example, for a picture of someone doing push-ups, ask **Qu'est-ce qu'il fait? Combien de fois par semaine est-ce qu'il en fait?** For a picture of a tired person, say **Quels conseils est-ce que tu lui donnes?** and so on.

Assess

- Testing Program, pp. 175–178 Quiz 7-2A, Quiz 7-2B Audio CD 7, Tr. 17
- Student Make-Up Assignments, Chapter 7, Alternative Quiz
- Alternative Assessment Guide, p. 38

Comment dit-on...?

Expressing discouragement; offering encouragement

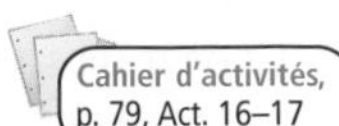

To express discouragement:

Je n'en peux plus! *I just can't do any more!*
J'abandonne. *I give up.*
Je craque! *I'm losing it!*

To offer encouragement:

Allez! *Come on!*
Courage! *Hang in there!*
Encore un effort! *One more try!*
Tu y es presque! *You're almost there!*

Cahier d'activités, p. 79, Act. 16–17

26 Courage! See scripts and answers on p. 183H.

Ecoutons Sabrina et Emile sont au gymnase. Qui encourage qui?
CD 7 Tr. 8

27 Qu'est-ce qu'ils disent?  *Possible answers:*
Parlons/Ecrivons

1\. Encore un effort!/Je n'en peux plus!

2\. J'abandonne./Courage!

3\. Allez! Tu y es presque!

28 Allez-y, allez-y!

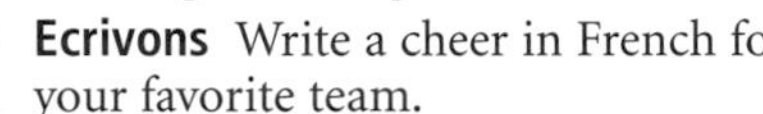

Ecrivons Write a cheer in French for your favorite team.

Vocabulaire à la carte

Allez, les bleus!	*Go, blue team!*
A bas les verts!	*Down with the green team!*
Vive les rouges!	*Hurray for the red team!*
Ecrasez-les!	*Crush them!*
gagner	*to win*
l'équipe	*the team*
marquer un (des) point(s)	*to score*
marquer un but	*to make a goal*

29 Les copains d'abord

Parlons Chaque personne dans ton groupe est découragée pour une des raisons suivantes. Les autres l'encouragent et lui donnent des conseils. Joue la scène avec trois de tes camarades.

Je me sens tout(e) raplapla et je n'arrive pas à dormir.

Je voudrais être en forme mais je n'aime pas le sport.

Mon équipe de football ne gagne jamais.

Je suis toujours en retard pour l'école le matin et mes notes ne sont pas très bonnes.

Communication for All Students

Visual Learners

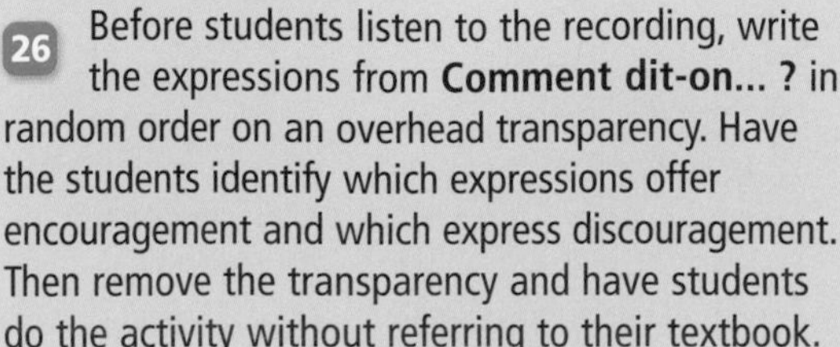

26 Before students listen to the recording, write the expressions from **Comment dit-on... ?** in random order on an overhead transparency. Have the students identify which expressions offer encouragement and which express discouragement. Then remove the transparency and have students do the activity without referring to their textbook.

STANDARDS: 1.2, 1.3, 5.2

Qu'est-ce qu'il faut faire pour être en forme?

We asked some francophone people what to do to stay in shape. Here's what they had to say.

Mélanie, Québec

«Pour être en forme, il faut faire beaucoup d'exercice. Il faut bien manger. C'est important. Et après ça, il faut... Moi, je fais un régime alimentaire... Il faut faire très attention à ce qu'on mange et puis il faut se coucher de bonne heure. Il faut dormir.» Tr. 10

Patricia, Québec

«Alors, il faut pratiquer au moins un sport ou une activité physique trois fois par semaine, à raison d'une heure à la fois et de façon assez intensive.»

Qu'est-ce qu'il faut éviter de manger?

«Eh bien, des chips, du chocolat, des liqueurs, des choses comme ça. Il faut surtout s'alimenter avec des fruits, des légumes, manger de la viande en portion réduite, etc.»
Tr. 11

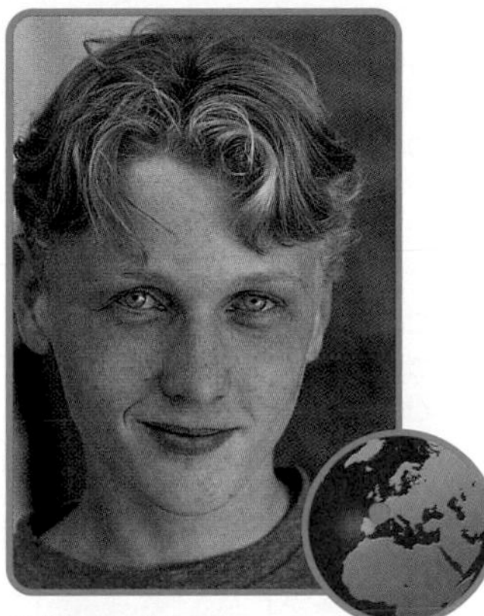

Sébastien, France

«Pour être en forme, je fais beaucoup de sport. Surtout du basket, du foot et du tennis. Sinon, je mange bien, le petit déjeuner surtout, et voilà.» Tr. 12

Qu'en penses-tu?

1. What do these people do to stay healthy?
2. What else might someone do to stay in shape?
3. In your opinion, what is a healthy lifestyle?

1. exercise, participate in sports, play basketball, soccer, and tennis, eat fruits and vegetables, eat breakfast and eat less meat, avoid unhealthy food, go to bed early

CHAPITRE 7

Teaching Resources
p. 199

PRINT

- Video Guide, pp. 45–47
- Cahier d'activités, p. 84

MEDIA 

- One-Stop Planner
- Video Program
  Videocassette 3, 08:42–12:53
- DVD Tutor, Disc 1
- Audio Compact Discs, CD 7, Trs. 9–12
- Interactive CD-ROM Tutor, Disc 2

Presenting Panorama Culturel

Show the video and ask students what they can tell about each interviewee. Then have students answer the **Questions** below.

Questions

1. **Qui dit qu'il faut beaucoup dormir pour être en forme?** (Mélanie)
2. **D'après Patricia, qu'est-ce qu'il faut éviter de manger ou de boire?** (des chips, du chocolat, des liqueurs)
3. **Selon Patricia, qu'est-ce qu'il faut manger?** (des fruits, des légumes, de la viande en portion réduite)
4. **Quels sports est-ce que Sébastien fait pour être en forme?** (du basket, du foot et du tennis)

Connections and Comparisons

Community Link

If there is a gym, fitness club, or community center in your town that offers sports activities, have a group of students visit it and interview people who attend. Have them find out why people exercise and what else they do to stay healthy. Other groups could interview student athletes. Have the groups report the information to the class and compare their answers with those of Mélanie, Patricia, and Sébastien.

Thinking Critically

Analyzing Ask students which they think is more important, looking good or feeling good, and why. Ask how the media can influence our attitudes about feeling or looking good.

CHAPITRE 7

Teaching Resources
pp. 200–203

PRINT

- Lesson Planner, p. 34
- TPR Storytelling Book, pp. 52–53
- Listening Activities, pp. 53, 57
- Activities for Communication, pp. 41–42, 107, 109, 149–150
- Travaux pratiques de grammaire, pp. 60–61
- Grammar Tutor for Students of French, Chapter 7
- Cahier d'activités, pp. 80–82
- Testing Program, pp. 179–182
- Alternative Assessment Guide, p. 38
- Student Make-Up Assignments, Chapter 7

MEDIA 

- One-Stop Planner
- Audio Compact Discs, CD 7, Trs. 13–14, 18, 26–27
- Teaching Transparencies: 7-3, 7-E; **Grammaire supplémentaire** Answers; Travaux pratiques de grammaire Answers
- Interactive CD-ROM Tutor, Disc 2

Bell Work
Ask students to imagine they have a friend who has very unhealthy habits. Have them write five sentences, offering the person advice on what to do to get in shape.

Kinesthetic/Auditory Learners
30 After students have read the realia and answered the questions, call out the foods mentioned in the realia and have students gesture thumbs-up, if they should consume the food, or thumbs-down, if they should avoid the food.

Troisième étape

Objectives Justifying your recommendations; advising against something

WA3 TOURAINE-7

DES ASTUCES POUR BIEN SE NOURRIR

Chaque jour tu devrais consommer :

- de la viande, du poisson ou des œufs.
- des pommes de terre, des pâtes, du riz.
- de l'eau (au moins 1,5 litre par jour).
- des fruits et des légumes.
- du lait.
- du pain.

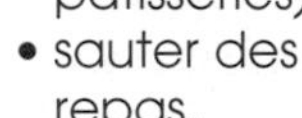

Tu devrais aussi éviter de :

- grignoter entre les repas des produits riches en matières grasses (chips) ou en sucre (confiseries, gâteaux, pâtisseries).
- sauter des repas.
- rajouter du sel à tous les plats.

30 **A lire avec attention**
Lisons

1. Look at the pictures in **Des astuces pour bien se nourrir.** What is the pamphlet about? how to eat well
2. Now look at the list under **Chaque jour tu devrais consommer...** What English title would you give to this list? Foods You Should Eat Every Day
3. What English title would you give to the list in the second category? Foods You Should Avoid

VIVE L'EAU

- boire 1,5 l d'eau par jour.
- c'est la seule vraie boisson zéro calorie.
- elle facilite l'élimination des toxines.
- elle contribue au fonctionnement du transit intestinal.
- certaines eaux minérales apportent des éléments indispensables au bon fonctionnement de l'organisme : magnésium, calcium,... ce qui limite les risques de carence en cas de régime.

L'EAU

Note culturelle

Drinking mineral water has long been part of the French way of life. If you ask for mineral water in a restaurant, you have a choice of either carbonated **(gazeuse)** or non-carbonated **(plate).** You will also find that beverages are usually served without ice. If you want ice, ask for **des glaçons.**

Connections and Comparisons

Language Notes

- Have students deduce the meaning of the word **astuces** *(ways, tricks, tips).* Point out that the word **trucs** *(things)* may be used to mean the same thing in informal conversation.
- Tell students that if they want tap water in restaurants, they should ask for **une carafe d'eau** *(a pitcher of water)* or **de l'eau du robinet** *(tap water).* In either case, the server will bring tap water served in a pitcher. If they just ask for **de l'eau,** the server may bring bottled water, which they will have to pay for.

STANDARDS: 1.2, 2.1, 3.1, 3.2, 4.1, 4.2

Vocabulaire

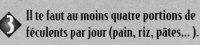

On doit...	*Everyone should . . .*	Evitez de...	*Avoid . . .*
bien se nourrir.	*eat well.*	grignoter entre les repas.	*snacking between meals.*
manger des légumes.	*eat vegetables.*	sauter des repas.	*skipping meals.*
manger des pâtes.	*eat pasta.*	consommer trop de sucre,	*eating too much sugar,*
manger du riz.	*eat rice.*	de sel,	*salt,*
boire de l'eau.	*drink water.*	de matières grasses.	*fat.*
		suivre un régime trop strict.	*following a diet that's too strict.*

CD-ROM 2 DVD 1

Travaux pratiques de grammaire, p. 60, Act. 16–17

Cahier d'activités, p. 80, Act. 18

31 Le test super-forme

Lisons Est-ce que tu te nourris bien? Essaie ce petit test.

Test Super-Forme!

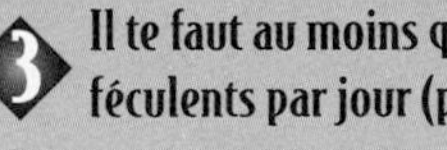

Est-ce que tu connais les habitudes alimentaires et le style de vie qui sont bons pour la santé? Réponds par «vrai» ou par «faux», puis compare avec les réponses données à la fin du test.

1 Il te faut au moins cinq portions de légumes et de fruits par jour.

2 Le lait, le fromage et les yaourts sont de bonnes sources de calcium.

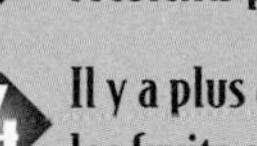
3 Il te faut au moins quatre portions de féculents par jour (pain, riz, pâtes...).

4 Il y a plus de matières grasses dans les fruits secs que dans les noix (amandes, noix de pacane, cacahuètes...).

5 Il faut boire un litre d'eau par jour.

6 C'est mieux de grignoter des bretzels que des chips.

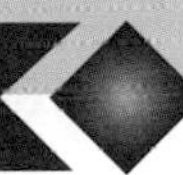

RÉPONSES: 1. vrai 2. vrai 3. faux (Il te faut 6-11 portions) 4. faux 5. faux (Il te faut au moins 1,5 litre) 6. vrai

Note de grammaire

The verb **se nourrir** is a regular -**ir** verb. It follows the same pattern as **choisir** and **finir.** It's also a reflexive verb.

Je **me nourris** bien, mais mes amis **se nourrissent** mal.

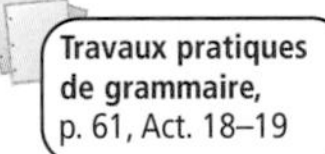

Travaux pratiques de grammaire, p. 61, Act. 18–19

Grammaire supplémentaire, pp. 208–209, Act. 7–9

Cahier d'activités, p. 81, Act. 21

See scripts and answers on p. 183H.

32 Grammaire en contexte

CD 7 Tr. 13

Ecoutons André is asking his friends Marie-Ange, Ali, and Philippe about their eating habits for a class project. Who has good habits? Who has bad ones? Who is the most healthy?

Presenting Vocabulaire

Bring as many of the vocabulary items as possible to class. You might show and talk about sugar and butter, incorporating the new expressions. **(C'est du sucre. Où est-ce qu'on trouve du sucre? Dans les pâtisseries? Qu'est-ce qu'il y a d'autre dans les pâtisseries? Beaucoup de matières grasses? Pour bien se nourrir, il faut consommer beaucoup de sucre? Il faut consommer beaucoup de matières grasses?** and so on.) Then, have students draw two columns on a sheet of paper and label them **On doit...** and **Evitez de...** Read aloud a numbered list of recommendations you have prepared. **(1. Manger beaucoup de sucre.)** Have students write the number of your statement in the appropriate column.

Building on Previous Skills

- Tell students that **éviter, sauter,** and **consommer** are regular **-er** verbs. You might have students conjugate them and use them in sentences for practice.
- Have students guess from the context what **la santé** *(health)* and **les féculents** *(starchy food)* mean. Then, tell students the meaning of **les noix** *(nuts)* and have them try to guess what **les amandes** *(almonds)* and **les noix de pécan** *(pecans)* are.

Communication for All Students

Auditory Learners/Challenge

32 Have students draw a chart with three columns. In the first column, they write the names of the three friends, and they label the other two columns **De bonnes habitudes** and **De mauvaises habitudes.** Play the recording and have students write in the appropriate columns the good and bad habits mentioned. Then, project the same chart on a transparency and ask students how to fill it in.

— **Quelles sont les bonnes habitudes de Marie-Ange?**

— **Elle ne mange pas de confiseries.**

STANDARDS: 1.2, 3.1

Troisième étape

CHAPITRE 7

Teaching Resources pp. 200–203

PRINT

- Lesson Planner, p. 34
- TPR Storytelling Book, pp. 52–53
- Listening Activities, pp. 53, 57
- Activities for Communication, pp. 41–42, 107, 109, 149–150
- Travaux pratiques de grammaire, pp. 60–61
- Grammar Tutor for Students of French, Chapter 7
- Cahier d'activités, pp. 80–82
- Testing Program, pp. 179–182
- Alternative Assessment Guide, p. 38
- Student Make-Up Assignments, Chapter 7

MEDIA 

- One-Stop Planner
- Audio Compact Discs, CD 7, Trs. 13–14, 18, 26–27
- Teaching Transparencies: 7-3, 7-E; **Grammaire supplémentaire** Answers; Travaux pratiques de grammaire Answers
- Interactive CD-ROM Tutor, Disc 2

Presenting Comment dit-on... ?

With one hand, hold up a vegetable, or a picture of one, and say **C'est bon pour toi!** with appropriate inflection and gesture. With the other hand, hold up a picture of a cigarette and say **Ce n'est pas bon pour toi! Evite de fumer!** Present the remaining expressions in this manner, using pictures or objects.

Language Note

Point out the difference between **C'est mieux que de** + infinitive and **C'est meilleur que** + noun.

33 Mes habitudes 

Lisons Le professeur de danse de Charlotte lui a demandé d'écrire un paragraphe sur ses habitudes alimentaires et sur les sports et les activités qu'elle pratique. Lis ce que Charlotte a écrit, puis complète son paragraphe avec les mots proposés.

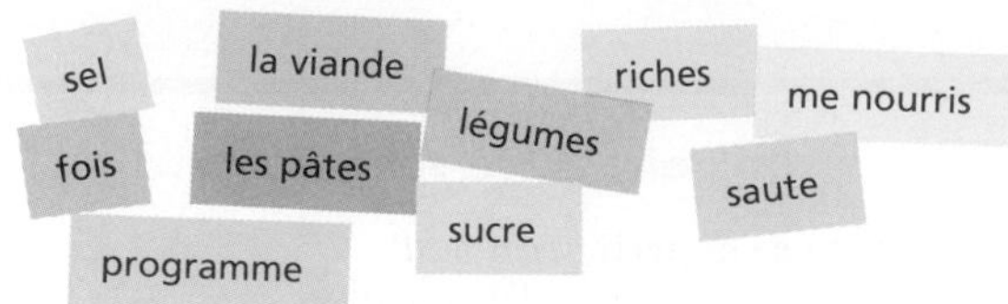

Je ne _1_ pas toujours très bien. Je n'aime pas _2_, donc, je ne mange pas trop souvent de bifteck; je préfère _3_ : les spaghettis, par exemple. Je mange rarement des fruits et des _4_ ; je préfère les chips. Je suis souvent pressée, donc, je _5_ parfois le petit-déjeuner ou le dîner. Mais au déjeuner, je prends toujours du poulet ou du poisson et je ne rajoute jamais de _6_ aux plats. Je n'aime pas trop les produits _7_ en _8_ : les confiseries, les gâteaux. Mon faible, c'est les chips et les frites. Je suis assez sportive. Je fais de la natation deux _9_ par semaine et je joue quelquefois au foot avec des copains. Je n'ai jamais fait de danse, mais j'ai très envie de commencer un nouveau _10_ sportif!

34 Mon journal

Ecrivons Décris tes habitudes alimentaires et dis quelles activités tu pratiques. Ensuite, explique ce que tu voudrais changer dans tes habitudes.

EXEMPLE **Je fais de la natation deux ou trois fois par mois. Je voudrais en faire plus souvent.**

Comment dit-on...?

Justifying your recommendations; advising against something

To justify your recommendations:

C'est bon pour toi. *It's good for you.*
C'est bon pour la santé. *It's healthy.*
Ça te fera du bien. *It'll do you good.*
C'est mieux que de manger dans un fast-food. *It's better than . . .*

To advise against something:

Evite de fumer. *Avoid...*
Ne saute pas de repas. *Don't skip . . .*
Tu ne devrais pas te faire bronzer. *You shouldn't . . .*

Cahier d'activités, pp. 81–82, Act. 22–23

35 David n'est pas en forme

See scripts and answers on p. 183H.

Ecoutons Julie et David sont au café. Ecoute leur conversation. Qu'est-ce que Julie conseille à David?

CD 7 Tr. 14

Communication for All Students

Slower Pace

33 Before students look at this activity, read the letter aloud, filling in the blanks with the correct words. Use pictures, gestures, and intonation to get the meaning across. Then, have students open their books and complete the paragraph.

34 Before students begin the activity, have them list their habits in one column and the changes they would like to make in another. Circulate to check their notes and offer help. Then, have them use their notes to write the journal entry.

STANDARDS: 1.2, 1.3

36 A toi de donner des conseils

Parlons/Ecrivons Donne des conseils à ces gens. Qu'est-ce qu'ils devraient éviter de faire? Qu'est-ce qu'ils devraient faire? See answers below.

1. 

2. 

3. 

37 En pleine forme!

Ecrivons Crée une brochure sur la santé. Tu peux faire des dessins ou si tu préfères, tu peux utiliser des images de magazines. Explique ce qu'on doit faire et ce qu'on ne doit pas faire pour être en forme.

Vocabulaire à la carte

se ronger les ongles	*to bite one's nails*
mâcher du chewing-gum	*to chew gum*
boire de l'alcool	*to drink alcohol*
fumer	*to smoke*
se faire bronzer	*to get a tan*

Sans tabac ça va!
Alcool, ras-le-bol.
Céréales, on se régale
Légumes et fruits, c'est oui!
Il n'y a pas de tabac sans dégâts!
Jeu de vin, jeu de vilains
Je mange, donc je suis!

38  De l'école au travail 

Parlons You're working at a gym as a fitness trainer, and you've developed a group of clients who are French speakers. Act out a training session where you evaluate the fitness habits of one of your French-speaking clients (played by your partner). Ask your client questions in French about what he/she eats, how often he/she exercises, etc. and give advice. Then, change roles.

EXEMPLE **—Qu'est-ce que vous mangez à midi?**
—Pas grand-chose. Mais je grignote l'après-midi avant de venir au gym.
—Eh bien, vous devriez manger à midi.

Troisième étape

CHAPITRE 7

Group Work

36 Form small groups and assign one photo to each group. Have the groups create a conversation between the person(s) shown in their photo and a friend. Have groups present their conversations to the class. The class should select the best conversation for each photo.

Portfolio

37 **Written** This activity is appropriate for students' written portfolios.

38 **Oral** This activity is appropriate for students' oral portfolios. For portfolio suggestions, see the *Alternative Assessment Guide,* page 24.

Teaching Suggestion

To close this **étape,** ask an artistic student to draw pictures of a person doing all the things listed in the **Vocabulaire à la carte.** Ask another to draw a picture of a person eating a variety of unhealthy foods. Make transparencies of the pictures and project them. Have the class give these people advice about what they should and should not do and then justify their advice.

Assess

- Testing Program, pp. 179–182
  Quiz 7-3A, Quiz 7-3B
  Audio CD 7, Tr. 18
- Student Make-Up Assignments, Chapter 7, Alternative Quiz
- Alternative Assessment Guide, p. 38

Connections and Comparisons

Community Link

37 Have students display their posters in elementary or other schools. They might make their posters bilingual if French isn't offered at these schools.

Possible Answers

36
1. Evite de manger trop de sel. Ce n'est pas bon pour toi.
2. Evite de te faire bronzer. Tu devrais mettre un tee-shirt.
3. Tu ne devrais pas manger de matières grasses. Mange de la salade. Ça te fera du bien.

STANDARDS: 1.1, 1.3, 5.1, 5.2

Teaching Resources
pp. 204–205

PRINT

- Lesson Planner, p. 35
- Cahier d'activités, p. 83
- Reading Strategies and Skills Handbook, Chapter 7
- Joie de lire 2, Chapter 7
- Standardized Assessment Tutor, Chapter 7

MEDIA 

- One-Stop Planner

Prereading
Activities A–B

Motivating Activity
Ask students to name the four food groups that make up a well-balanced daily diet and the recommended quantities.

Teaching Suggestion
A. Write students' answers to **Pourquoi manger?** on the board. Read the first sentence of the article to the students and check off the students' answers that match the sentence.

Reading
Activities C–I

Terms in Lisons!
Students might want to know the following words: **la croissance** *(growth);* **le foie** *(liver);* **la sueur** *(sweat);* **les larmes** *(tears);* **des os** *(bones).*

Answers

B. *Possible answers:* Vegetables: green vegetables, spinach, parsley, and salad; Fruit and dairy products: yogurt, cheese, milk, oranges, and kiwis

D. fish, meat, cheese, yogurt, milk, eggs, liver, green vegetables, potatoes, water, nuts, bread, rice, cereal, nuts, parsley, salad, kiwis, and oranges

F. Ham contains more protein.; You should not eat Camembert, Brie, or Emmenthal if you are trying to lose weight.

Lisons!

Pourquoi manger?

Pour grandir, pour réfléchir, pour avoir du tonus, pour vivre, nous avons besoin de manger. Les aliments contiennent des substances qui nous sont nécessaires : ce sont les nutriments, les vitamines, les minéraux... Découvrez où se cachent ces éléments indispensables à notre santé...

Le sucre, le chocolat et la confiture contiennent des glucides rapides qui donnent de l'énergie et du tonus.

La viande, mais aussi le poisson, les œufs, le lait et le fromage contiennent des protéines, indispensables à la croissance et à l'entretien des muscles et d'organes comme le cœur ou le cerveau.

Les pommes de terre et les légumes verts contiennent de la vitamine K dont notre sang a besoin pour coaguler.

Le poisson, comme les œufs et le foie, contient de la vitamine A, recommandée pour avoir une bonne vue et une peau en bon état. La vitamine A est très utile pour la croissance.

La salade et les céréales contiennent des fibres qui facilitent le transit intestinal.

Le pain, le riz et les pâtes contiennent des glucides lents. Nous en avons besoin pendant l'effort sportif.

Pourquoi manger?

Stratégie pour lire

Background knowledge is the information you already know about a subject. Before you read something, take a minute to recall what you already know about the topic. Doing this will make it easier to guess the meanings of unfamiliar words or phrases.

A. What would be your answer to **Pourquoi manger?** What do you expect the article to be about?

B. Make a short list of the foods you think are healthful. Now, scan the article. How many of the food items from the article appear on your list? See answers below.

C. What vegetables are mentioned in the article? What fruit and dairy products are mentioned?

D. Which food items contain vitamins and/or minerals that help muscles? See answers below.

E. What should you avoid eating at night? Why? Vitamin C; it's a stimulant.

F. Look at the section titled **Le saviez-vous?** Which contains more protein in 100 grams: ham or tuna? Which cheeses would you probably not eat if you were trying to lose weight? See answers below.

Connections and Comparisons

Health Link
Bring to class a chart showing the recommended daily amounts of the various food groups. Have pairs or small groups create a "healthy menu" for one day, including food items to be eaten at breakfast, lunch, and dinner. They might refer to the article for food items to feature in their menus. You might assign a country to each pair or group and tell them to choose food items that reflect their country's eating habits. For listening practice, ask students to read their menus aloud and have the class guess which country they were assigned, based on the items in their menus.

STANDARDS: 1.2, 3.1, 3.2, 4.2

Les noix, les légumes secs et le foie contiennent de la vitamine B 1 : elle favorise l'attention et le calme et elle permet un bon fonctionnement musculaire.

L'eau constitue les trois quarts de notre corps. Elle s'élimine par la sueur, l'urine et les larmes. L'eau est indispensable pour la circulation du sang et pour l'hydratation des cellules. Ce sont les reins qui régulent l'eau dans le corps; ils filtrent aussi les minéraux dont nous avons besoin.

Les oranges, les kiwis, le persil et la salade contiennent de la vitamine C, qui lutte contre des infections, notamment les rhumes. La vitamine C est un excitant : il faut éviter de la consommer le soir!

Les céréales complètes, comme les légumes secs et la viande rouge, contiennent de la vitamine B 6, qui aide au bon fonctionnement des muscles et du système nerveux.

Les légumes verts, comme les épinards, contiennent du fer. Le fer est un des constituants des globules rouges dont le rôle est de transporter l'oxygène dans le sang. La vitamine B 12 contenue dans le foie et les coquillages intervient dans la fabrication des globules rouges.

Le lait ainsi que le fromage et les yaourts contiennent du calcium, indispensable à la construction de notre corps. Le calcium est particulièrement important pour la constitution des os et la solidité des dents. Pour bien fixer ce calcium, nous avons besoin de vitamine D, contenue dans le poisson, la viande.

Le saviez-vous?

- Dans 100 grammes de cacahuètes ou d'amandes grillées, il y a environ 50 grammes de lipides (graisses).
- Dans une meringue de 100 grammes, il y a 90 grammes de glucides (sucres).
- Dans une tranche de jambon cuit de 100 grammes, on trouve 30 grammes de protéines, autant que dans 100 grammes de thon en conserve.
- Le camembert, le brie, l'emmental sont des fromages plus gras que les pâtes fondues (La Vache qui rit®) ou le fromage de chèvre.
- Dans 100 grammes de chips, il y a 49 grammes de glucides et 35 grammes de lipides.

Source : "Le guide du bien maigrir en gardant la santé", par le docteur Jacques Fricker, aux Éditions Odile Jacob-guide.

G. Match each of the following foods with its health benefit, according to the article.

1. le poisson c	**a.** ***gives energy***
2. le chocolat a	**b.** ***hydrates cells***
3. l'eau b	**c.** ***contains vitamin A***
4. le lait d	**d.** ***builds strong teeth***
5. la salade e	**e.** ***contains fiber***

H. Look back at the article and use the context to define the following words.

1. «... pour avoir du *tonus*...» vigor
2. «... indispensable à la construction de notre *corps*.» body
3. «... dont notre *sang* a besoin pour *coaguler*.» blood; coagulate
4. «... les kiwis, le *persil* et la salade contiennent...» parsley

I. Look at the illustrations of the food items. Are the items similar to what you would see in the United States? Which ones are different? If this article were to be printed in the United States, would the same food items be included? Why or why not? See answers below.

J. Now, create your own response to the question **Pourquoi manger?** Choose three or four items that you feel are important and write your own article. You may want to illustrate your selection.

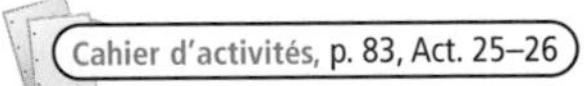
Cahier d'activités, p. 83, Act. 25–26

Communication for All Students

Cooperative Learning

J. Some students may prefer to work in groups so that the task of writing the article is broken down into smaller steps. Create a cooperative learning assignment in which one student is the writer, one gathers the artwork, and another arranges the layout of the article.

Lisons!

CHAPITRE 7

Thinking Critically

I. Comparing and Contrasting

Before they do this activity, have students create lists of food items that are typically French, uniquely American, and common to both countries. For example, students should be able to remember that the French eat a wide variety of vegetables and meats that aren't as commonly served in the United States. After students have created their lists, have them use the information in the article and their background knowledge of the topic to come up with at least two vitamins or minerals each food item on their lists provides.

Postreading

Activity J

Teacher Note

You might tell students that **Emmenthal** is a type of cheese made from cow's milk. It originated in the Emme River valley in Switzerland. Similar to Swiss cheese, it is made in the shape of a large wheel and kept at a temperature of 72° to 80° F. Complete ripening takes three to six months. This sweetcurd cheese is slightly salty when fresh and pleasingly sharp when fully ripened.

Possible Answers

I. The items that are different are the sugar cubes, the bread, and the milk bottle. Sugar cubes are not used as often in the United States, bread usually is sold sliced, and milk comes in a differently shaped container. If this article were to be printed in the United States, the food items would be similar because the same healthful food items are sold in the United States.

STANDARDS: 1.2, 1.3, 3.1, 3.2, 4.2

Grammaire supplémentaire

CHAPITRE 7

For **Grammaire supplémentaire** Answer Transparencies, see the *Teaching Transparencies* binder.

Grammaire supplémentaire

CD-ROM 2 DVD 1

internet
ADRESSE: go.hrw.com
MOT-CLE: WA3 TOURAINE-7

Première étape

Objectives Expressing concern for someone; complaining

1 Regarde les illustrations suivantes et dis si quelque chose ne va pas chez ces personnes. (**p. 190**)

Juliette

Hervé

Patricia

Martine

1.
2.
3.
4.

2 Daniel et sa sœur jumelle font toujours la même chose. D'après ce que Daniel a fait, dis ce qui est arrivé à Dominique. N'oublie pas de faire l'accord du participe passé quand c'est nécessaire. (**p. 192**)

EXEMPLE Daniel s'est promené au parc.
Dominique s'est promenée au parc aussi.

1. Daniel s'est coupé le doigt.
2. Daniel s'est couché tard.
3. Daniel s'est cassé la jambe.
4. Daniel s'est lavé.
5. Daniel s'est amusé.
6. Daniel s'est foulé la cheville.

Answers

1
1. Juliette a de la fièvre.
2. Hervé s'est cassé la jambe.
3. Patricia a mal au cœur.
4. Martine a mal à la gorge.

2
1. Dominique s'est coupé le doigt aussi.
2. Dominique s'est couchée tard aussi.
3. Dominique s'est cassé la jambe aussi.
4. Dominique s'est lavée aussi.
5. Dominique s'est amusée aussi.
6. Dominique s'est foulé la cheville aussi.

Grammar Resources for Chapter 7

The **Grammaire supplémentaire** activities were designed as supplemental activities for the grammatical concepts presented in the chapter. You might use them as additional practice, for review, or for assessment.

For more grammar presentations, review, and practice, refer to the following:

- Travaux pratiques de grammaire
- Grammar Tutor for Students of French
- Grammar Summary on pp. R23–R42
- Cahier d'activités
- Grammar and Vocabulary quizzes (Testing Program)
- Test Generator
- Interactive CD-ROM Tutor
- DVD Tutor
- **Jeux interactifs** at go.hrw.com

STANDARDS: 1.2

3 Véronique est aux sports d'hiver avec sa copine Marie. Elle écrit un petit mot à ses parents. Complète sa lettre avec le **passé composé** des verbes entre parenthèses. **(p. 192)**

Maman et Papa,

Quel week-end! Hier soir, ma camarade de chambre et moi, nous ___1___ (se coucher) très tard. On est allées à une fête organisée par l'hôtel. Je ___2___ (s'amuser)! A la fête, j'ai rencontré un garçon très sympa qui s'appelle Lucien. Il n'a pas pu danser parce qu'il ___3___ (se casser) la jambe quand il est tombé en faisant du ski. Marie a beaucoup dansé à la fête et elle ___4___ (se faire) mal au pied en dansant. Dimanche matin, on a décidé de faire du ski. Ce n'était pas une bonne idée parce que j'étais fatiguée et Marie avait mal partout. Nos amis Pierre et Jean-Marc n'ont pas eu de chance! Ils ont eu un accident sur la piste. Heureusement, Pierre ___5___ (ne pas se casser) le bras, mais Jean-Marc ___6___ (se fouler) la cheville! Quel week-end!

Marie

Deuxième étape

Objectives Giving, accepting, and rejecting advice; expressing discouragement; offering encouragement

4 Robert is very athletic. Look at his exercise schedule, and then tell which activity he is talking about based on how often he says he does it. **(p. 196)**

lundi	mardi	mercredi	jeudi	vendredi
pompes abdominaux natation	jogging pompes natation	abdominaux pompes	pompes jogging	musculation abdominaux pompes

1. J'en fais trois fois par semaine.
2. J'en fais tous les jours.
3. J'en fais le mardi et le jeudi.
4. J'en fais une fois par semaine.
5. J'en fais deux fois par semaine.

Communication for All Students

Additional Practice

Have students conduct a chain activity in which they ask one another if they participate in certain sports activities, using the pronoun **en** or an expression of frequency in their responses. One student begins by asking **Tu fais de la musculation, Sophie?** Sophie answers **Non, je n'en fais pas** or **Oui, j'en fais souvent**. Sophie then asks a student another question, and so on. You might list sports or activities on the board as prompts.

Answers

3
1. nous sommes couchées
2. me suis amusée
3. s'est cassé
4. s'est fait
5. ne s'est pas cassé
6. s'est foulé

4 *Possible answers:*
1. des abdominaux
2. des pompes
3. du jogging ou des pompes
4. de la musculation
5. de la natation, du jogging

Grammaire supplémentaire

CHAPITRE 7

For **Grammaire supplémentaire** Answer Transparencies, see the *Teaching Transparencies* binder.

Answers

5
1. Oui, j'en fais tous les jours.
2. Non, je n'en fais jamais.
3. Oui, j'en fais trois fois par semaine.
4. Oui, j'en fais souvent.
5. Non, j'en fais rarement.

6
1. dois
2. dois
3. doivent
4. devez
5. doit

7
1. vous nourrissez
2. me nourris
3. choisis
4. finis
5. se nourrit

Grammaire supplémentaire

WA3 TOURAINE-7

5 Ton ami(e) te demande ce qu'il/elle doit faire pour être en forme. Réponds-lui en utilisant le pronom **en** et les expressions entre parenthèses. (**p. 196**)

EXEMPLE Tu fais du jogging? (souvent) **<u>Oui, j'en fais souvent.</u>**

1. Tu fais de la musculation? (tous les jours)
2. Tu fais de l'équitation? (ne... jamais)
3. Tu fais des abdominaux? (trois fois par semaine)
4. Tu fais des pompes? (souvent)
5. Tu fais de la gymnastique? (rarement)

6 Simon dit à tous ses amis ce qu'ils doivent faire pour être en forme. Complète ses phrases avec la forme correcte du verbe **devoir.** (**p. 197**)

1. Toi, tu _____ faire de l'aérobic trois fois par semaine.
2. Moi, je _____ faire de l'exercice tous les jours.
3. François et son frère, ils _____ faire beaucoup d'abdominaux.
4. Julie et Christine, vous _____ faire de la danse.
5. Lucien veut être en forme. Il _____ faire de la musculation.

Troisième étape

Objectives Justifying your recommendations; advising against something

7 You and your classmates are completing a survey about eating habits. Unscramble the letters in the questions and comments to reveal the correct forms of the verbs **se nourrir, choisir,** and **finir.** (**p. 201**)

1. Comment est-ce que vous [S N O O U U R R S S Z I E V]?
2. J'aime manger des fruits et des légumes. Je [I S R N O E M U R] bien.
3. Tu [S C O H S I I] un fruit ou un gâteau?
4. A quelle heure est-ce que tu [S F I I N] le petit déjeuner?
5. Elle boit un litre d'eau par jour? Elle [U O N R I E R S T] très bien.

Review and Assess

Teaching Suggestion

Write the conjugations of **choisir** and **finir** on the board, and then write the infinitive **se nourrir** and the subject pronouns. Have one student write the reflexive pronouns next to the subject pronouns. Have another write the stem of the verb next to each reflexive pronoun. Have a third student add the ending of each verb form to the stem of the verb. All students should follow the same procedure on a sheet of paper.

STANDARDS: 1.2

Grammaire supplémentaire

CHAPITRE 7

8 D'après ce que ces gens mangent, dis s'ils se nourrissent bien ou mal. (**p. 201**)

1. Je mange toujours beaucoup de sucre.
2. Alice mange des fruits et des légumes à tous les repas.
3. Marc et Pierre grignotent entre les repas.
4. Nous suivons un régime trop strict.
5. Tu manges souvent du riz et des pâtes.

9 Complete each sentence with the appropriate verb from the word box below. Then match the sentences to the photos. (**p. 201**)

grossis	finissons	se nourrir	ai grossi	maigrissent

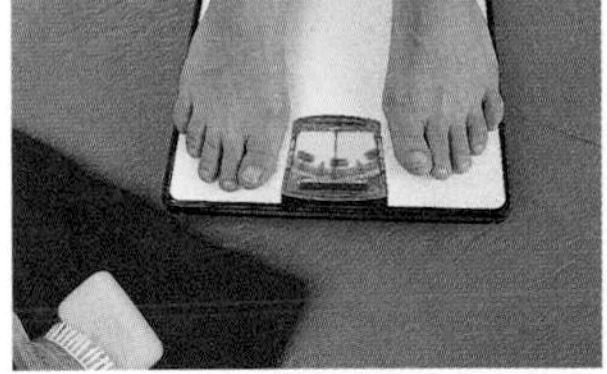
a.

b.

c.

d.

e.

1. On doit bien __________ pour être en bonne santé : il faut manger des fruits et des légumes frais tous les jours.
2. Zut! Je/J'_______ encore ________!
3. Quand j'en mange trop, je __________.
4. Nous __________ la salade avant de commander un dessert.
5. Elles __________ quand elles font beaucoup d'exercice.

Review and Assess

You may wish to assign the **Grammaire supplémentaire** activities as additional practice or homework after presenting material throughout the chapter. Assign Activities 2–3 after **Note de grammaire** (p. 192), Activities 4–5 after **Note de grammaire** (p. 196), Activity 6 after **Note de grammaire** (p. 197), and Activities 7–9 after **Note de grammaire** (p. 201).

To prepare students for the **Etape** Quizzes and Chapter Test, we suggest doing the **Grammaire supplémentaire** activities in the following order. Have students complete Activities 1–3 before Quizzes 7-1A or 7-1B; Activities 4–6 before Quizzes 7-2A or 7-2B; and Activities 7–9 before Quizzes 7-3A or 7-3B.

Answers

8
1. Tu te nourris mal.
2. Elle se nourrit bien.
3. Ils se nourrissent mal.
4. Vous vous nourrissez mal.
5. Je me nourris bien.

9
1. se nourrir; c
2. ai… grossi; a
3. grossis; e
4. finissons; d
5. maigrissent; b

STANDARDS: 1.2

Mise en pratique

C H A P I T R E 7

The **Mise en pratique** reviews and integrates all four skills and culture in preparation for the Chapter Test.

Teaching Resources
pp. 210–211

PRINT 

- Lesson Planner, p. 35
- TPR Storytelling Book, pp. 54–55
- Listening Activities, p. 53
- Video Guide, pp. 45, 48
- Grammar Tutor for Students of French, Chapter 7
- Standardized Assessment Tutor, Chapter 7

MEDIA

- One-Stop Planner
- Video Program, Videocassette 3, 12:56–14:29
- DVD Tutor, Disc 1
- Audio Compact Discs, CD 7, Tr. 15
- Interactive CD-ROM Tutor, Disc 2

Challenge

3 Have students incorporate all of the answers to these questions in a letter to a friend or relative back home describing their home-stay in France.

Answers

1 1. how to stop dieting/how to choose a healthy lifestyle instead of dieting
2. grease/fat
3. chips, sauces made from butter, and bread with chocolate
4. snacking between meals; having too many sugary drinks

Mise en pratique

ADRESSE: go.hrw.com
MOT-CLE: WA3 TOURAINE-7

1 Lis cet article et réponds aux questions suivantes. See answers below.

Gare au régime!

Si vous vous sentez "mal dans votre peau" à cause de quelques kilos en trop, ne commencez jamais un régime sans prendre l'avis d'un médecin.
À votre âge, le poids n'est pas stable. Patientez. Tout se mettra bientôt en place.
En attendant, faites la chasse aux graisses : éliminez les chips ou les sauces au beurre, évitez les pains au chocolat au goûter (ils contiennent des sucres et des graisses et la combinaison des deux fait particulièrement grossir!).
Perdez aussi l'habitude de grignoter entre les repas, et n'abusez pas des boissons sucrées.
Facile, non?

1. D'après le titre et les illustrations, de quoi parle cet article, à ton avis?
2. Qu'est-ce que ça veut dire **graisses,** d'après toi?
3. Quels aliments est-ce que l'article conseille d'éviter?
4. Quelles sont les mauvaises habitudes qu'il faut aussi éviter, d'après l'article?

2 Listen to a radio commercial for the health spa **Centre Equilibre Santé** and answer the following questions. See scripts and answers on p. 183H.

CD 7 Tr. 15

1. What exercise activities are offered?
2. What is available after you work out?
3. What special excursions are offered?
4. What do you have to do to get the excursions in the package?

3 If you were in France, . . .

1. where would you go to have a prescription filled? to a pharmacy
2. what symbol would you look for to find that place? a green cross
3. where could you go to take an aerobics class? gym club
4. what two kinds of mineral water could you order in a restaurant? carbonated or non-carbonated
5. when would you tell someone **J'ai un chat dans la gorge!**? when you cannot talk
6. when would you say **Aïe!** and **Ouf!**? **Aïe!** when you are hurt; **Ouf!** after doing something physical to express relief

Review and Assess

Challenge

2 Type the listening script, substituting blanks for ten to twelve words, and distribute copies to students. Play the recording two or three times and have students fill in the blanks with words they hear or can guess from the context.

Slower Pace

2 Distribute the listening script as suggested for the Challenge activity, but supply the missing words at the end of the script for students to use in completing the sentences.

STANDARDS: 1.2, 3.1

Ecrivons!

You've been hired as a fitness advisor by a French health clinic. Your first duty is to create a brochure that provides general fitness guidelines for new clients. Your brochure should mention exercise, diet, and healthful habits.

Stratégie pour écrire
Identifying your audience is a primary consideration when you do any type of writing. Having a good idea of who will read what you've written will help you to determine its length, content, and tone.

Préparation

Begin by brainstorming a list of suggestions that you might make to someone who wants to pursue a healthful lifestyle. Group your ideas by categories, such as **exercice, alimentation,** and **habitudes.**

Now, consider who will be reading your guidelines. Will your audience be people who are already fit or individuals who may be in poor physical condition? Will they be more likely to respond positively to a few good suggestions or to a lot of information? The answers to these questions should help you tailor your brochure to your reader's needs.

Rédaction

After you've decided what to include in your brochure, you're ready to design it. You may want to group your guidelines in separate categories like the ones you created earlier. Also, to make it more attractive, illustrate your brochure with your own drawings or pictures cut from magazines.

Before creating your final draft, make a mock-up of your brochure. Pencil in your guidelines where you want them to go. Then, attach any illustrations you plan to use with paper clips or tape. This will allow you to evaluate your work without being committed to a set format.

Evaluation

Set your mock-up aside for awhile before you evaluate your brochure. It's much easier to be objective about your work after a little time away from it. After evaluating your work, have a classmate look at it. Ask your classmate to imagine that he or she is a new client at the health clinic and to give you feedback on the strengths and weaknesses of your brochure.

When you're satisfied with the layout and content of your brochure, proofread it, make any necessary corrections, and then create the final product.

5

Jeu de rôle

Play the role of a whining (or accident-prone!) patient who comes to a doctor with several ailments or injuries, thinking that everything is extremely serious. The doctor asks what happened and what is wrong, and then gives advice on what the patient should and shouldn't do.

Review and Assess

Process Writing

4 To help students focus on their target audience, have them break down the three main categories into subcategories. For example, the category **alimentation** might be broken down into subcategories such as **à manger** and **à éviter.**

Mise en pratique

CHAPITRE 7

Teaching Suggestion

5 Have the patient be someone famous, but do not mention the celebrity's name in the role-play. The ailments or injuries should be associated with something that would seriously hamper the celebrity's career (Tiger Woods: **Je pense que je me suis cassé la main!**). After the conversation is performed, have the class guess who the celebrity is.

Speaking Assessment

5 You might use the following rubric when grading your students on this activity.

Speaking Rubric	Points			
	4	3	2	1
Content (Complete–Incomplete)				
Comprehension (Total–Little)				
Comprehensibility (Comprehensible–Incomprehensible)				
Accuracy (Accurate–Seldom accurate)				
Fluency (Fluent–Not fluent)				

18–20: A 16–17: B 14–15: C 12–13: D Under 12: F

Teacher Note

For additional practice and review, you might use the **Histoire Finale** for Chapter 7 on pages 54–55 of the *TPR Storytelling Book.*

STANDARDS: 1.1, 1.3, 3.1, 5.1, 5.2

C H A P I T R E 7

Teaching Resources
p. 212

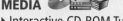

PRINT
- Grammar Tutor for Students of French, Chapter 7

MEDIA
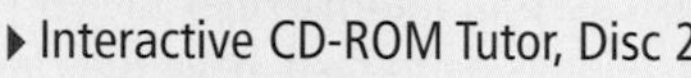
- Interactive CD-ROM Tutor, Disc 2
- Online self-test

go.hrw.com
WA3 TOURAINE-7

Teaching Suggestion
Have students work in pairs to answer the questions in **Que sais-je?**

Possible Answers

3 1. Tu dois faire des pompes.
2. Tu ferais bien de faire de la musculation.
3. Pourquoi tu ne manges pas des fruits?

4 *Accept:* Tu as raison. Bonne idée! D'accord.
Reject: Je ne peux pas. Non, je n'ai pas très envie. Non, je préfère... ; Pas question! Je n'ai pas le temps. Ce n'est pas mon truc.

7 Tu devrais faire du sport parce que c'est bon pour toi. Tu ferais bien de te coucher plus tôt. Ça te fera du bien. Pourquoi tu ne manges pas des fruits et des légumes? C'est mieux que de manger des hamburgers et des frites.

Que sais-je?

WA3 TOURAINE-7

Can you use what you've learned in this chapter?

Can you express concern for someone and complain? p. 189

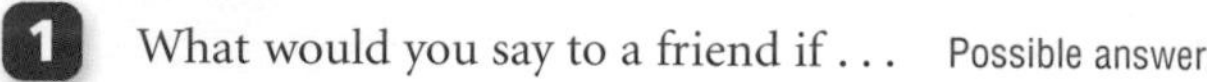

1 What would you say to a friend if . . . Possible answers:
1. he didn't look well? Tu n'as pas l'air en forme.
2. something seemed to be wrong? Quelque chose ne va pas?
3. she were on crutches? Qu'est-ce que tu as?

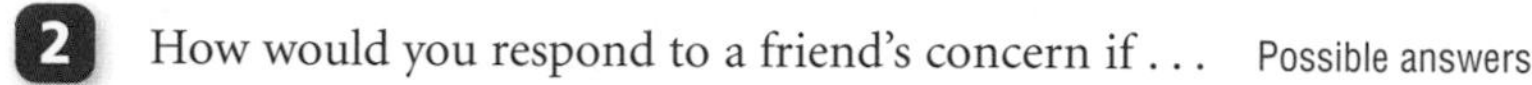

2 How would you respond to a friend's concern if . . . Possible answers:
1. you were very tired? J'ai mal dormi. Je suis tout(e) raplapla.
2. you weren't feeling well? Je ne me sens pas bien.
3. your arm were in a sling? Je me suis cassé le bras.
4. you had a cold? J'ai un rhume.
5. you'd cut your finger? Je me suis coupé le doigt.
6. you'd lifted weights for the first time? J'ai mal partout!

Can you give advice? p. 197

3 How would you suggest that your friend do the following? See answers below.

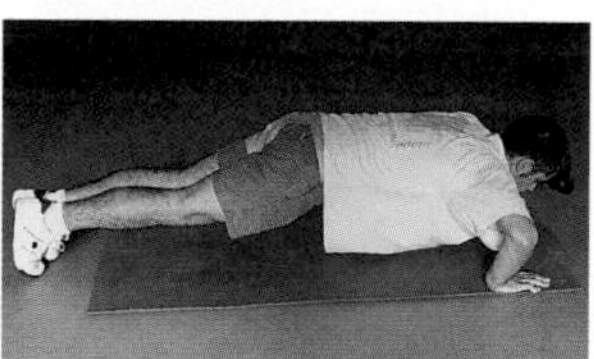
1.

2.

3.

Can you accept and reject advice? p. 197

4 How would you respond to the suggestions you made in number 3? See answers below.

Can you express discouragement and offer encouragement? p. 198

5 How would you express discouragement if you were . . . Possible answers:
1. on the last mile of a marathon? Je n'en peux plus!
2. studying for final exams? Je craque!
3. in the final minutes of your aerobics class? J'abandonne!

6 How would you encourage someone who . . . Possible answers:
1. can't go on? Encore un effort!
2. is almost finished? Tu y es presque!
3. is discouraged about grades? Courage!

Can you justify your recommendations and advise against something? p. 202

7 How would you tell someone what he or she should do on a regular basis and explain why? See answers below.

8 If a friend were trying to lead a healthy lifestyle, what are three things you would advise him or her to avoid? Possible answers: Evite de fumer! Ne saute pas de repas! Tu ne devrais pas te faire bronzer!

Apply and Assess

Game
Que sais-je? Form two teams and have the members of each team count off. Have the first student from each team go to the board. Call out a question at random from **Que sais-je?** The first student to write a complete, correct answer wins a point for his or her team. Continue with the second player from each team, and so on. The team with the most points at the end of the game wins.

STANDARDS: 1.2

Vocabulaire

Première étape

Expressing concern for someone; complaining

Quelque chose ne va pas?	*Is something wrong?*
Qu'est-ce que tu as?	*What's wrong?*
Tu n'as pas l'air en forme.	*You don't look well.*
Je ne me sens pas bien.	*I don't feel well.*
Je suis tout(e) raplapla.	*I'm wiped out.*
J'ai mal dormi.	*I didn't sleep well.*
J'ai mal partout!	*I hurt all over!*

Illnesses, aches, pains, and injuries

J'éternue beaucoup.	*I'm sneezing a lot.*
A tes souhaits!	*Bless you!*
Je suis malade.	*I'm sick.*
J'ai mal au cœur.	*I'm sick to my stomach.*
J'ai le nez qui coule.	*I've got a runny nose.*
J'ai un rhume.	*I've got a cold.*
J'ai la grippe.	*I've got the flu.*
J'ai des allergies.	*I have allergies.*
J'ai de la fièvre.	*I have fever.*
J'ai mal...	*My...hurts.*
à la gorge	*throat*
à la tête	*head*
au dos	*back*
au genou	*knee*
au pied	*foot*
au bras	*arm*
à la main	*hand*
au ventre	*stomach*
à l'oreille (f.)	*ear*
aux dents (f.)	*teeth*
au cou	*neck*
à la jambe	*leg*
se faire mal à...	*to hurt one's...*
se casser...	*to break one's...*
se fouler la cheville	*to sprain one's ankle*
se couper le doigt	*to cut one's finger*

Deuxième étape

Giving, accepting, and rejecting advice

Tu dois...	*You've got to...*
Tu devrais...	*You should...*
Tu ferais bien de...	*You would do well to...*
Tu n'as qu'à...	*All you have to do is...*
Pourquoi tu ne... pas... ?	*Why don't you...?*
Tu as raison.	*You're right.*
Bonne idée!	*Good idea!*
D'accord.	*OK.*
Je ne peux pas.	*I can't.*
Non, je n'ai pas très envie.	*No, I don't feel like it.*
Non, je préfère...	*No, I prefer...*
Pas question!	*No way!*
Je n'ai pas le temps.	*I don't have time.*
Ce n'est pas mon truc.	*It's not my thing.*

Expressing discouragement; offering encouragement

Je n'en peux plus!	*I just can't do any more!*
J'abandonne.	*I give up.*
Je craque!	*I'm losing it!*
Allez!	*Come on!*
Courage!	*Hang in there!*
Encore un effort!	*One more try!*
Tu y es presque!	*You're almost there!*

At the gym

se mettre en condition	*to get into shape*
faire des abdominaux	*to do sit-ups*
faire de l'aérobic	*to do aerobics*
faire de l'exercice	*to exercise*
faire de la gymnastique	*to do gymnastics*
faire de la musculation	*to lift weights*
faire des pompes	*to do push-ups*
s'entraîner à...	*to train for*

Troisième étape

Justifying your recommendations; advising against something

C'est bon pour toi.	*It's good for you.*
C'est bon pour la santé.	*It's healthy.*
Ça te fera du bien.	*It'll do you good.*
C'est mieux que de...	*It's better than...*
Evite de...	*Avoid...*
Ne saute pas...	*Don't skip...*
Tu ne devrais pas...	*You shouldn't...*

Eating right

On doit...	*Everyone should...*
bien se nourrir	*eat well*
manger des légumes/des pâtes/du riz	*eat vegetables/pasta/rice*
devoir	*to have to, must*
Evitez de...	*Avoid...*
suivre un régime trop strict	*following a diet that's too strict*
consommer trop	*eating too much*
de sucre	*sugar*
de sel	*salt*
de matières grasses	*fat*
grignoter entre les repas	*snacking between meals*
sauter des repas	*skipping meals*

Vocabulaire

CHAPITRE 7

Game

Loto! So that students can practice writing, reading, and hearing the expressions and vocabulary from this chapter, have them draw a large 5 × 5 grid on a sheet of paper and write in each square one of the expressions from the **Vocabulaire.** While students are making their grids, write the expressions on separate slips of paper and place them in a box. When students have completed their grids, begin the game of Bingo. The first student to mark five squares in a row (with small bits of paper), calls out **Loto!** and should then read aloud the French expressions he or she marked.

Chapter 7 Assessment

- **Testing Program**
  Chapter Test, pp. 183–188

  Audio Compact Discs, CD 7, Trs. 19–21
  Speaking Test, p. 346
- **Alternative Assessment Guide**
  Performance Assessment, p. 38
  Portfolio Assessment, p. 24
  CD-ROM Assessment, p. 52
- **Interactive CD-ROM Tutor, Disc 2**
  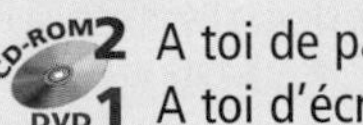
  A toi de parler
  A toi d'écrire
- **Standardized Assessment Tutor**
  Chapter 7
- **One-Stop Planner, Disc 2**
  Test Generator
  Chapter 7

Apply and Assess

Circumlocution

Have students imagine that they are traveling in France and they accidentally hurt themselves. Have students work with a partner, one playing the role of the traveler and the other playing the role of the doctor the traveler visits. The traveler doesn't know the exact word for his or her illness or injury and must circumlocute the word by describing his or her symptoms without naming the ailment. The student playing the role of the doctor should try to guess the illness or injury.

STANDARDS: 1.1

Location Opener

CHAPTER 8

Teaching Resources
pp. 214–217

PRINT 

- Lesson Planner, p. 36
- Video Guide, pp. 49–50

MEDIA 

- One-Stop Planner, Disc 2
- Video Program
  Videocassette 3, 15:00–17:39
- DVD Tutor, Disc 2
- Interactive CD-ROM Tutor, Disc 2
- Map Transparency 2

go.hrw.com
WA3 COTE D'IVOIRE

Using the Almanac and Map

Terms in the Almanac

- **Yamoussoukro,** the administrative capital of Côte d'Ivoire since 1983, is the hometown of former President **Félix Houphouët-Boigny.**
- The **Baoulé,** the largest ethnic group in Côte d'Ivoire, migrated from Ghana over two hundred years ago. They are known as excellent goldsmiths and weavers.
- The **Agni** also originated in Ghana and settled primarily in eastern Côte d'Ivoire.
- The **Bété,** who settled in the south-western forest region of Côte d'Ivoire more than 1,000 years ago, are known for their masks.
- The **Sénoufo** settled in the northern part of the country in the sixteenth century. They are known for their elaborate statues and masks.
- The **Malinké,** originally from what is now Guinea and Mali, live in northern Côte d'Ivoire and are famous for their rich musical heritage and pottery.
- **Le parc national de la Comoë** is the largest game park in West Africa.

CHAPITRE 8

Allez, viens en Côte d'Ivoire

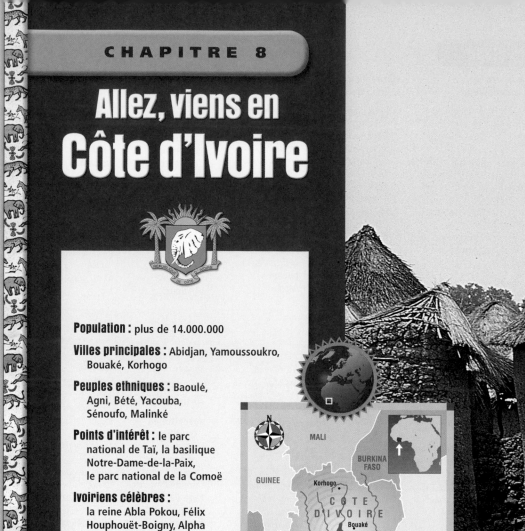

Population : plus de 14.000.000

Villes principales : Abidjan, Yamoussoukro, Bouaké, Korhogo

Peuples ethniques : Baoulé, Agni, Bété, Yacouba, Sénoufo, Malinké

Points d'intérêt : le parc national de Taï, la basilique Notre-Dame-de-la-Paix, le parc national de la Comoë

Ivoiriens célèbres : la reine Abla Pokou, Félix Houphouët-Boigny, Alpha Blondy, Désiré Ecaré

Ressources et industries : café, cacao, bois, bananes

Festivals : la Fête des ignames, la Fête de génération, la Fête des masques

WA3 COTE D'IVOIRE

Un village Sénoufo ▸

Cultures and Communities

Culture Note

Have students look at the Sénoufo village on pages 214–215. The structure of the buildings is economical, practical, and comfortable at the same time. Villagers use straw from the surrounding fields for the roofs and beaten or stabilized earth bricks for the walls. With this kind of structure, air-conditioning is not needed, despite the hot temperatures, since the straw roof ensures that the temperature is spread out evenly, and the gap between the top of the walls and the roof provides for a cooling flow of air. The narrower structures in the photo are granaries used to store sorghum, millet, and other grains. They are elevated on clay supports **(pieds de terre)** in order to protect the grains from the humidity and rodents **(rongeurs).**

STANDARDS: 2.2, 3.2, 5.1

Using the Map

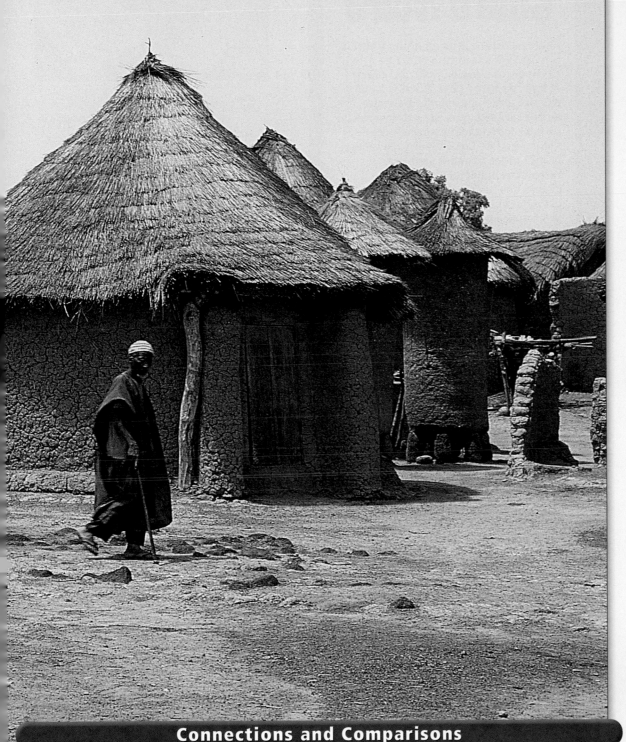

Have students look at the map of Côte d'Ivoire on this page. Ask them why they think it is hotter and drier the farther north you go, and wetter and more humid as you travel south. (As you travel north, you move towards the desert, so you encounter fewer trees and less rain. As you travel south, you see more and more tropical rain forest. Also, Côte d'Ivoire is located approximately seven degrees north of the equator.) Ask students if they know the capitals of the countries surrounding Côte d'Ivoire (Monrovia, Liberia; Conakry, Guinea; Bamako, Mali; Ouagadougou, Burkina Faso; Accra, Ghana).

Culture Note

La reine Abla Pokou, the famous queen of the **Baoulé** people, led the migration of the Baoulé from Ghana to Côte d'Ivoire in the eighteenth century.

Connections and Comparisons

Background Information

Côte d'Ivoire got its name from the ivory trade, which once flourished, but has since been banned in many countries around the world. Consisting mostly of rain forest, the southern half of the country has a tropical climate with oppressive humidity and abundant rainfall. The northern half, which is savannah, tends to be hotter and drier. In addition to French, which is the national language, more than 60 ethnic languages are spoken in Côte d'Ivoire. **Djoula,** the market language, is spoken at least minimally by most Ivorians.

STANDARDS: 2.2

Using the Photo Essay

❶ **L'artisanat** Korhogo, located in northern Côte d'Ivoire, is the main city of the Sénoufo. The Korhogo region is surrounded by artisan villages, known for their weavers, blacksmiths, potters, woodcarvers, and painters of tapestry and cloth. **Batiks** *(tapestry or painted cloth pictures),* or **toiles** *(painted canvas or cloth),* similar to the one shown in this photo, are made in the villages of Fakaha and Katia. These tapestries, or cloth pictures, are generally pieces of canvas, burlap, or gunnysack with images of black and brown animals and other patterns painted on them.

❷ In western Côte d'Ivoire, travelers encounter various **ponts de liane,** which enable them to cross the streams and rivers. These swinging bridges are made of tough, slender vines called **liane,** rope, and several thin branches. Since they are considered sacred and must not be touched by the soles of shoes, the bridges must be crossed barefoot. Although they are destroyed every year by torrential rains, they are patiently rebuilt by the local villagers, sometimes overnight!

❸ **La pêche** One of Côte d'Ivoire's most interesting fishing villages is Sassandra, located on the Atlantic coast five to six hours west of Abidjan. Sassandra is assumed to be a contraction of San Andrea, a name given by the Portuguese, who were visitors to the area in the fifteenth and sixteenth centuries. The town is inhabited by the Néyo people, who are well-known as fishermen **(pêcheurs).**

Art Link

❶ The paint used for the **batiks** is made with various dyes taken from millet. The different colors are made by mixing the dyes together to produce blacks, browns, and whites.

Côte d'Ivoire

Au XVe siècle, des navigateurs français sont arrivés sur la côte ouest de l'Afrique, une région riche en ivoire, et l'ont baptisée Côte d'Ivoire. La Côte d'Ivoire a été une colonie française de 1893 à 1960, puis elle est devenue un pays indépendant sous le nom de République de Côte d'Ivoire. Le cacao, le café et les bananes sont des ressources importantes pour l'économie ivoirienne. La Côte d'Ivoire est aussi un grand exportateur de bois précieux comme l'ébène et l'acajou.

internet
go.hrw.com
ADRESSE: go.hrw.com
MOT-CLE: WA3 COTE D'IVOIRE

❶ **L'artisanat**
Les artisans de Côte d'Ivoire font beaucoup de produits originaux comme les batiks.

❷ **Les ponts suspendus**
Ce pont de liane se trouve près de la ville de Man.

❸ **La pêche**
La pêche est une activité traditionnelle et les pêcheurs tiennent à leur indépendance.

Cultures and Communities

Culture Notes

Various tribal dance performances and numerous festivals are held throughout Côte d'Ivoire during the year.

- **La Fête des ignames** is a harvest ritual observed by the Agni and the Abron, who belong to the Akan ethnic group.
- **La Fête des générations** is a celebration of various generations throughout the country. The Adioukrou hold this festival just before the children return to school.
- During **la Fête des masques,** held in Man every November, one can see more than 100 masks from nearby villages. Throughout West Africa, it is believed that masks appease the ancestors and minor deities who are intermediaries between people and God. They are also thought to ward off evil.

STANDARDS: 2.1, 2.2, 3.1

4 Abidjan
Cette ville est un des grands centres commerciaux de l'Afrique occidentale.

5 La plage d'Assinie
Voici un des endroits préférés non seulement des touristes étrangers mais aussi des Ivoiriens.

6 La basilique Notre-Dame-de-la-Paix
Située à Yamoussoukro, cette basilique est la plus grande église du monde.

7 La cascade du mont Tonkoui
C'est une des merveilles de la Côte d'Ivoire.

Au chapitre 8, tu vas faire la connaissance de Sandrine et de Koffi qui vont te parler de leur vie en Côte d'Ivoire. Promène-toi avec eux dans les rues d'Abidjan, goûte la cuisine locale et visite les marchés d'artisans où tu vas pouvoir admirer des pagnes colorés et de magnifiques masques. Amuse-toi bien!

8 Les danseurs yacoubas
Ces danseurs traditionnels sont réputés pour leurs talents d'acrobates.

Connections and Comparisons

Thinking Critically

4 Observing Ask students if the skyline of Abidjan resembles that of an American or a European city. Have them look for clues in the photo to justify their answers. Ask if they notice anything in the photo that suggests Abidjan is an African city.

Culture Note

Another attraction in the Man region, especially for hikers, is the **Dent de Man,** a steep, jagged, tooth-shaped mountain located 14 kilometers northeast of town. To climb this 75-foot summit, known as the "guardian angel of Man," visitors will need a guide to avoid losing the jungle path.

Location Opener

CHAPTER 8

4 Abidjan, former capital of Côte d'Ivoire, remains the diplomatic and economic center of the country. The city grew rapidly after the Vridi Canal was built in 1950. The canal connected the city to the lagoon and created a protected, deep-water port.

5 La plage d'Assinie, located two hours east of Abidjan, is reputed to be one of the best beaches in Côte d'Ivoire.

7 La cascade du mont Tonkoui, the most famous attraction in the Man region, is a waterfall located in a bamboo forest five kilometers outside of the city. Approximately 20 kilometers from Man is **mont Tonkoui,** which, at 1,218 meters, is the highest point in Côte d'Ivoire. From this vantage point, one can see neighboring Guinea and its dense forests and rolling hills.

8 The **Yacouba** people who live primarily in western Côte d'Ivoire in and around the city of Man, are admired for their acrobatic dancing. You might point out to students the numerous, decorative cowry shells that adorn the costumes of the dancers in this photo. Their ceremonial masks, often featuring plumes, shells, and even tin cans, can be seen in museums all over the world.

Architecture Link

6 La basilique Notre-Dame-de-la-Paix, a replica of St. Peter's Basilica in Rome, is larger than St. Peter's and is the world's largest church. It was built in only three years, compared to 100 years for St. Peter's. Designed to hold 7,000 people, the basilica contains 30 acres of marble and four times the amount of stained glass found in the Notre-Dame Cathedral in Chartres, France. It is also the world's largest air-conditioned space.

STANDARDS: 2.2, 3.1, 4.2

Chapitre 8 : C'était comme ça
Chapter Overview

Mise en train pp. 218–222	***La Nostalgie***

	FUNCTIONS	GRAMMAR	VOCABULARY	RE-ENTRY
Première étape pp. 223–227	• Telling what or whom you miss; reassuring someone, p. 225 • Asking and telling what things were like, p. 226	• The **imparfait** of **être** and **avoir**, p. 227	• Describing places, p. 226	• Sympathizing with and consoling someone **(Chapitres 5, 7,** II) • The phrase **c'était (Chapitre 6,** II) • Asking and telling what things were like **(Chapitre 6,** II)
Deuxième étape pp. 228–233	• Reminiscing, p. 229	• The **imparfait,** p. 230	• Childhood activities, p. 228	• Pronunciation: The [ɛ] sound **(Chapitre 9,** I) • Adjectives of physical traits and personality **(Chapitre 1,** II)
Troisième étape pp. 234–237	• Making and responding to suggestions, p. 237	• **Si on** + the **imparfait,** p. 237	• Things to see and buy in Abidjan, p. 236	• Responding to suggestions **(Chapitre 1,** II) • Locations **(Chapitre 2,** II)

Lisons! pp. 238–239	An excerpt from **La belle histoire de Leuk-le-Lièvre**	**Reading Strategy:** Linking words and pronouns	
Grammaire supplémentaire	**pp. 240–243** **Première étape,** p. 240	**Deuxième étape,** pp. 241–242	**Troisième étape,** p. 243
Review pp. 244–247	**Mise en pratique,** pp. 244–245 **Ecrivons!** Point of view Writing an account of a trip back in time	**Que sais-je?** p. 246	**Vocabulaire,** p. 247

CULTURE

- **Rencontre culturelle,** Village life in Côte d'Ivoire, p. 223
- **Note culturelle,** Ethnic groups in West Africa, p. 224
- **Note culturelle,** High school in Côte d'Ivoire, p. 229
- **Note culturelle,** Félix Houphouët-Boigny and his birthplace, Yamoussoukro, p. 231
- **Panorama Culturel,** City living versus country living, p. 233
- Markets in Abidjan, pp. 234–235
- **Note culturelle,** Abidjan, p. 235

Chapitre 8 : C'était comme ça
Chapter Resources

Lesson Planning

One-Stop Planner

Lesson Planner with Substitute Teacher

Lesson Plans, pp. 36–40, 70

Student Make-Up Assignments

- Make-Up Assignment Copying Masters, Chapter 8

Listening and Speaking

TPR Storytelling Book, pp. 56–63

Listening Activities

- Student Response Forms for Listening Activities, pp. 59–61
- Additional Listening Activities 8-1 to 8-6, pp. 63–65
- Additional Listening Activities (song), p. 66
- Scripts and Answers, pp. 137–141

Video Guide

- Teaching Suggestions, pp. 52–53
- Activity Masters, pp. 54–56
- Script and Answers, pp. 102–104, 121

Activities for Communication

- Communicative Activities, pp. 43–48
- Realia and Teaching Suggestions, pp. 110–114
- Situation Cards, pp. 151–152

Reading and Writing

Reading Strategies and Skills Handbook, Chapter 8

Joie de lire 2, Chapter 8

Cahier d'activités, pp. 85–96

Grammar

Travaux pratiques de grammaire, pp. 62–70

Grammar Tutor for Students of French, Chapter 8

Assessment

Testing Program

- Grammar and Vocabulary Quizzes, **Etape** Quizzes, and Chapter Test, pp. 197–214
- Score Sheet, Scripts and Answers, pp. 215–222

Alternative Assessment Guide

- Portfolio Assessment, p. 25
- Performance Assessment, p. 39
- CD-ROM Assessment, p. 53

Student Make-Up Assignments

- Alternative Quizzes, Chapter 8

Standardized Assessment Tutor

- Reading, pp. 31–33
- Writing, p. 34
- Math, pp. 51–52

MEDIA

Online Activities

- **Jeux interactifs**
- **Activités Internet**

Video Program

- Videocassette 3
- Videocassette 5 (captioned version)

Interactive CD-ROM Tutor, Disc 2

DVD Tutor, Disc 2

Audio Compact Discs

- Textbook Listening Activities, CD 8, Tracks 1–12
- Additional Listening Activities, CD 8, Tracks 19–26
- Assessment Items, CD 7, Tracks 13–18

Teaching Transparencies

- Situation 8-1 to 8-3
- Vocabulary 8-A to 8-C
- **Mise en train**
- **Grammaire supplémentaire** Answers
- **Travaux pratiques de grammaire** Answers

One-Stop Planner CD-ROM

Use the **One-Stop Planner CD-ROM with Test Generator** to aid in lesson planning and pacing.

For each chapter, the **One-Stop Planner** includes:

- Editable lesson plans with direct links to teaching resources
- Printable worksheets from resource books
- Direct launches to the HRW Internet activities
- Video and audio segments
- Test Generator
- Clip Art for vocabulary items

Chapitre 8 : C'était comme ça

Projects

Livres pour enfants

*Students will write and illustrate a children's book in French, using the **imparfait** and the present tense. The story should be about a character whose situation has recently changed.*

MATERIALS

Students may need

- Construction paper
- Markers or colored pencils
- Magazine or catalogue pictures
- Scissors, glue or tape
- Hole punch
- Yarn or ribbon

SUGGESTED SEQUENCE

1. Each student creates characters (people, animals, or animated objects) and a story line that meets the specifications given above. The students should turn in a plan in French or English, in which they briefly describe the story line and the characters.
2. Students might hand in a rough draft of each page of the story as it is completed.
3. When students have corrected and rewritten the entire text, they should complete the illustrations, create a title page, and assemble the book.
4. When the books are completed, students might circulate them in class for others to read.

GRADING THE PROJECT

Suggested Point Distribution: (total = 100 points)

Content	20
Language use	20
Variety of vocabulary	20
Creativity/Effort	20
Overall appearance	20

COMMUNITY LINK

As a community-service project, you might send the book to an elementary school with a cassette tape of students reading the story, complete with music and sound effects.

Games

Awalé

Awalé** is a traditional game, similar to backgammon, that was originally played in Egypt thousands of years ago. **Awalé** is representative of African culture and is also an intellectually challenging source of entertainment. Played by Africans of all ages, it is known by different names, depending on the country. In Côte d'Ivoire, the game is called **awalé.

MATERIALS

Students may need

- An egg carton (with two rows of six cups each)
- Two paper cups, one for each end of the carton
- 48 beans, pebbles, or seeds

Procedure

1. To begin, players place four beans in each cup of the egg carton. Players will sit on opposite sides of the game board. They can start from any cup on their side that contains beans.
2. Either player may start the game. Moves are made counterclockwise around the board. Player A starts by picking up all the beans from one of the cups on his or her side of the board and dropping them one at a time in each consecutive cup to the right.
3. The two cups at either end of the board are for captured beans. Beans are captured when the last bean (or beans) falls into a cup (or cups) containing one or two beans. Potentially, a player may capture the beans of several cups at a time, if <u>each</u> of those cups contains one or two beans prior to the move. For example, if the player's last three beans fall into three consecutive cups, each containing one or two beans, he or she would capture the beans in those three cups, including the bean that completed the move.

   However, if the player's last three beans fall into three cups containing two, four, and two beans respectively, he or she would only capture the two beans in the last cup, since the <u>four</u> beans in the next-to-last cup break the

STANDARDS: 1.3, 3.2, 5.1

sequence. To prevent the capture of beans, players should either try to fill as many cups as possible with more than two beans or try to leave several cups empty.

4. Players take turns until one player has no beans on his or her side, and the other player cannot reach the other side of the board with two consecutive moves.
5. At the end of the game, players count their captured beans, plus any beans left on their opponent's side of the board. One point is given for each captured bean.
6. A match can consist of a particular number of games (4), or points (50, 100, 200, . . .), or a certain amount of time (30 minutes).

Storytelling

Mini-histoire

*This story accompanies Teaching Transparency 8-3. The **mini-histoire** can be told and retold in different formats, acted out, written down, and read aloud, to give students additional opportunities to practice all four skills. The following story tells about a Saturday morning spent in the market of Cocody.*

Maman et moi, nous sommes allés au marché de Cocody samedi matin. Tout de suite, Maman a acheté un pagne adorable. Nous nous sommes promenés dans le marché très longtemps. Soudain, je n'ai plus vu Maman. Je regarde de tous les côtés et ne la vois pas. Une femme habillée d'un pagne me fait signe d'approcher. Elle est près de la marchande de masques. J'ai peur de m'approcher et je vais regarder les paniers à côté des masques. La femme m'appelle. Je regarde et je reconnais Maman. Elle porte son nouveau pagne! Il est presque midi. J'ai faim et nous décidons de quitter le marché pour rentrer à la maison.

Traditions

Les griots

The **Malinké** of Côte d'Ivoire have a long tradition of transmitting their people's history by word of mouth from one generation to the next. The professional historians and praise singers that perform this task are called **jeli** in the Malinké language, or **griots** in French. Their histories are poetic and often accompanied by the **kora,** a harp-like instrument and a **tam-tam,** or "talking drum." Considered "word-smiths," **griots** form part of the artisan class in Malinké society. Like many traditional professions, their role in the community is passed down from generation to generation. Without the stories of the **griots,** we would know very little about the Malinké, since their history has only just recently been written down. Have students imagine they are **griots** and tell the class a family story or community legend that has been passed down to their generation.

Recette

Eggplant comes from Asia, and it was already used 2,500 years ago. It was first introduced in North Africa before spreading thoughout the whole continent. It came to Europe at the beginning of the Middle Ages. However, eggplant was not mentioned in cookbooks until the 19th century.

SAUCE A L'AUBERGINE

Ingrédients

1 tasse d'oignons

1 livre de poisson frais

1 livre d'aubergines

1/2 livre de tomates

8 ou 9 grosses crevettes

1 cuillère à café de piment

Faire cuire les oignons. Ajouter le poisson et les crevettes et laisser cuire pendant 15 minutes. Eplucher et couper les aubergines et les tomates. Les ajouter au poisson. Recouvrir d'eau. Faire cuire. Egouter les légumes et les écraser. Servir avec du riz ou du foutou.

Technology

Videocassette 3, Videocassette 5 (captioned version)
DVD Tutor, Disc 2
See Video Guide, pages 51–56.

DVD/Video

Mise en train • La Nostalgie
Sandrine and her friend Koffi meet at a park in Abidjan. Sandrine has just moved to the city from a village, and she's homesick. She describes her village and its people to Koffi. She compares village and city life. Koffi reassures her that she will grow to like Abidjan and offers to show her around.

Mise en train (suite)
Several weeks later, Sandrine's sister Albertine arrives for a visit. Albertine is amazed and overwhelmed by the city, but Sandrine is now a confident city-dweller. Sandrine takes Albertine to Treichville and then to have lunch in a **maquis.** Koffi joins them, and they make plans to go to the movies that evening.

Est-ce que tu préfères la vie en ville ou à la campagne? Pourquoi?
Students from Quebec, France, and Vietnam tell whether they prefer the city or the country and why.

Vidéoclip
- *Le Chant du riz pilé* performed by Pierre Perret: music video

Interactive CD-ROM Tutor

Activity	Activity Type	Pupil's Edition Page
En contexte	*Interactive conversation*	
1. Vocabulaire	Chasse au trésor Explorons!/Vérifions!	pp. 222–226
2. Grammaire	Chacun à sa place	p. 227
3. Comment dit-on… ?	Chacun à sa place	pp. 226, 228–229
4. Grammaire	Les mots qui manquent	p. 230
5. Vocabulaire	Jeu des paires	p. 236
6. Vocabulaire	Le bon choix	p. 236
Panorama Culturel	Est-ce que tu préfères la vie en ville ou à la campagne? Pourquoi?	p. 233
A toi de parler	*Guided recording*	pp. 244–245
A toi d'écrire	*Guided writing*	pp. 244–245

Teacher Management System
Launch the program, type "admin" in the password area, and press RETURN. Log on to www.hrw.com/CDROMTUTOR for a detailed explanation of the Teacher Management System.

DVD Tutor

The *DVD Tutor* contains all material from the *Video Program* as described above. French captions are available for use at your discretion for all sections of the video. The *DVD Tutor* also provides a variety of video-based activities that assess students' understanding of the **Mise en train, Suite,** and **Panorama Culturel.**

This part of the *DVD Tutor* may be used on any DVD video player connected to a television or video monitor.

In addition to the video material and the video-based comprehension activities, the *DVD Tutor* also contains the entire *Interactive CD-ROM Tutor* in DVD-ROM format. Each DVD disc contains the activities from all 12 chapters of the *Interactive CD-ROM Tutor.*

This part of the *DVD Tutor* may be used on a Macintosh® or Windows® computer with a DVD-ROM drive.

To preview all resources available for this chapter, use the **One-Stop Planner CD-ROM,** Disc 2.

Internet Connection

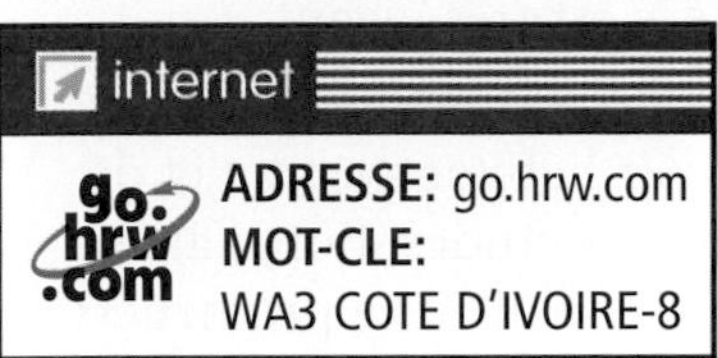

*Have students explore the **go.hrw.com** Web site for many online resources covering all chapters. All Chapter 8 resources are available under the keyword **WA3 COTE D'IVOIRE-8.** Interactive games help students practice the material and provide them with immediate feedback. You'll also find a printable worksheet that provides Internet activities that lead to a comprehensive online research project.*

Jeux interactifs

You can use the interactive activities in this chapter

- to practice grammar, vocabulary, and chapter functions
- as homework
- as an assessment option
- as a self-test
- to prepare for the Chapter Test

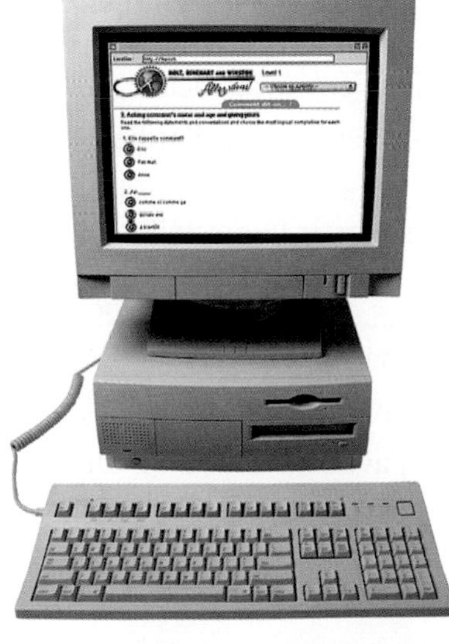

Activités Internet

Students look for information about Côte d'Ivoire. Using the vocabulary from the chapter, students write an account of their imaginary trip to Côte d'Ivoire.

- In preparation for the **Activités Internet,** have students review the dramatic episode on Videocassette 3, complete the activities in the **Panorama Culturel,** or go over the information presented in the Location Opener. After they complete the activity sheet, have students work with a partner and peer-edit Section D.

Location: http://

Nom ______ Classe ______ Date ______

CHAPITRE 8 *C'était comme ça*

Level 2

Avant d'explorer

A. Imagine that you are spending a year in Côte d'Ivoire as an exchange student. What activities do you do in Côte d'Ivoire? How is your life different?

En ligne!

B. Maintenant, cherche trois choses que tu peux faire ou trois endroits que tu peux visiter pendant ton séjour dans ta famille ivoirienne. Décris chaque activité en détail et dis ce qu'il y a à faire ou à voir dans les endroits que tu mentionnes.

Endroit ou activité	Ce qu'on peut y faire

Projet

Have students select three places they would like to visit in Côte d'Ivoire and research these places on the Internet. Tell the students to imagine they have just returned from a long trip in Africa and are telling their friends what they did, what they liked, and what they now miss about Côte d'Ivoire. Have students document their sources by noting the URLs of all the sites that they consulted.

Chapitre 8 : C'était comme ça
Textbook Listening Activities Scripts 

Première étape

7 p. 225

1. —Qu'est-ce qu'il y a, Sylvie?
   —Oh, mon village me manque. C'était tellement calme là-bas.
   —T'en fais pas! Tu vas t'y faire. Tu vas voir, il y a beaucoup de choses à voir et à faire ici.
2. —Ça va, Emile?
   —Tu vois, mes copains me manquent. On jouait toujours ensemble dans le village.
   —Mais tu vas te plaire ici aussi! Tout le monde est très sympa.
3. —Pourquoi tu fais la tête, Francine?
   —Ce qui me manque, c'est de faire du ski. Mais c'est impossible ici! Il ne neige jamais!
   —Allez! Fais-toi une raison. Pourquoi pas faire du ski nautique? Tu vas voir, c'est super cool!
4. —Ça va, Bertrand?
   —Oh, je regrette les repas en famille. Toute la famille se réunissait pour le dîner. Ici, je mange seul.
   —Tu vas voir, tu vas te faire des amis.

Answers to Activity 7

1. a
2. c
3. b
4. d

11 p. 227

JUSTIN Alors Mamadou, comment tu trouves notre grande ville? Géniale, hein?

MAMADOU Euh... C'est très différent de mon village, ça c'est sûr! C'est beaucoup plus animé.

JUSTIN Tu vois, je t'avais dit qu'Abidjan te plairait.

MAMADOU Oui, c'est vrai, mais qu'est-ce que je suis fatigué! Avec toutes ces voitures, c'est impossible de bien dormir. C'est beaucoup trop bruyant!

JUSTIN Ben moi, je préfère ça à un petit village isolé et mortel. Tu verras, d'ici peu, tu t'habitueras au bruit.

MAMADOU Et puis, mon village était quand même plus propre et moins dangereux, et ça, ça me manque vraiment.

JUSTIN Ecoute, on ne peut pas tout avoir! En tout cas, moi, j'adore Abidjan. C'est peut-être un peu moins tranquille et un peu plus sale que chez toi, mais au moins, c'est très vivant.

MAMADOU Oui, tu as raison. Après tout, j'ai beaucoup de chance de pouvoir habiter avec toi et de pouvoir continuer mes études. Bon, j'arrête de me plaindre! Et si on allait se promener?

JUSTIN Oui, bonne idée! Je vais te montrer des endroits que tu n'as encore jamais vus. Ça va être super!

MAMADOU D'accord, allons-y!

Answers to Activity 11

His village was quieter, cleaner, and safer; go for a walk in the city

Deuxième étape

17 p. 229

YAPO Alors, Mme Koré, vous étiez comment quand vous étiez enfant?

MME KORE Oh, j'étais parfois pénible. Je posais constamment des questions à ma mère. Oui, je l'ennuyais beaucoup.

YAPO Et est-ce que vous l'aidiez aussi?

MME KORE Oui, j'avais des responsabilités à la maison. Je devais sortir la poubelle, balayer la terrasse et aider ma mère à faire la cuisine. J'aimais faire tout ça. C'était amusant de faire la cuisine avec ma mère.

YAPO Vous aviez des frères et sœurs?

MME KORE Oui, j'avais deux frères. On s'entendait très bien. Je ne les taquinais jamais. Ils étaient gentils.

YAPO Vous faisiez des bêtises?

MME KORE Bien sûr, comme tous les enfants! J'étais parfois embêtante, mais pas trop. Mais je n'avais pas de soucis! Ah, que c'était bien, quand j'étais petite.

Answers to Activity 17

Elle ne taquinait pas ses frères. Elle faisait des bêtises.

The following scripts are for the listening activities found in the *Pupil's Edition*. For Student Response Forms, see *Listening Activities*, pages 59–61. To provide students with additional listening practice, see *Listening Activities*, pages 63–66.

To preview all resources available for this chapter, use the **One-Stop Planner CD-ROM,** Disc 2.

19 **p. 230**

Oh, pour vous, les jeunes d'aujourd'hui, la vie est plus facile qu'avant. Quand j'étais enfant, la vie était dure. Les filles n'avaient pas le droit d'aller à l'école; ça, c'était pour les garçons. Nous, les filles, on restait à la maison, on faisait le ménage et on s'occupait de nos frères et sœurs. C'était beaucoup plus difficile que maintenant. Je devais travailler tous les jours! Oh, la vie était dure! Je ne la regrette pas.

Answers to Activity 19
1. faux 2. faux 3. vrai 4. faux

Troisième étape

27 **p. 236**

1. JUSTIN Tu sais, l'architecture à Abidjan n'est pas toujours moderne. Là, par exemple, ce style est très différent de celui de la cathédrale que tu as vue tout à l'heure.
   MAMADOU Oui, c'est beaucoup plus traditionnel. Je préfère ça.
2. MAMADOU Où est-ce qu'on va maintenant?
   JUSTIN C'est une surprise, mais je suis sûr que tu vas aimer.
   MAMADOU Allez, dis-moi.
   JUSTIN Sois patient. Tu verras, c'est un endroit super où on peut trouver des tas de choses géniales, surtout des tissus. Voilà. On y est.
3. MAMADOU Dis donc, qu'est-ce qu'il fait chaud!
   JUSTIN Oui, tu as raison. Et puis, on a aussi beaucoup marché. Je suis un peu fatigué, moi. Pas toi?
   MAMADOU Si. On s'arrête quelques minutes pour se reposer? Et si on allait boire un verre?
   JUSTIN D'accord.
4. MAMADOU Oh là là! Avec tout ça, j'ai complètement oublié d'acheter des cadeaux pour mes frères.
   JUSTIN Ce n'est pas trop tard. On peut s'arrêter ici, si tu veux.
   MAMADOU Bonne idée. Comme ça, je pourrai acheter un masque pour Henri et un tam-tam pour Félix. Ça lui fera plaisir, il adore la musique.

Answers to Activity 27
1. b 2. e 3. a 4. c

Mise en pratique

2 **p. 244**

Quand j'étais jeune, j'habitais à Abidjan. Maintenant, j'habite dans un petit village au nord de Bouaké. La vie au village, c'est pas mal. C'est propre et très tranquille. Et puis, tout le monde se connaît. Bien sûr, en ville, il y avait plus de choses à faire. J'avais beaucoup d'amis et je sortais souvent. On allait voir des concerts ou bien on allait au théâtre. Je conduisais une voiture super. Le week-end, mes amis et moi, nous allions à la plage. C'était bien, mais on avait plus de soucis. Ici, j'ai des responsabilités aussi, mais c'est moins stressant.

Possible Answers to Mise en pratique Activity 2
Three things he used to do in Abidjan: see concerts, go to the theater, drive a great car, go with friends to the beach
Two things he mentions about the village: it's clean and calm, everyone knows each other

Chapitre 8 : C'était comme ça

Suggested Lesson Plans 50-Minute Schedule

Day 1

CHAPTER OPENER 5 min.
- Present Chapter Objectives, p. 219.
- Culture Note, ATE, p. 218

MISE EN TRAIN 40 min.
- Presenting **Mise en train,** ATE, p. 220
- Culture Note, ATE, p. 221
- Teaching Suggestions: Post-viewing Suggestions 3–4, Video Guide, p. 52
- Activities 1–4, p. 222

Wrap-Up 5 min.
- Activity 5, p. 222

Homework Options
Cahier d'activités, Activities 1–2, p. 85

Day 2

MISE EN TRAIN
Quick Review 5 min.
- Check homework.

RENCONTRE CULTURELLE 10 min.
- Presenting **Rencontre culturelle,** ATE, p. 223
- Culture Note, ATE, p. 223
- Thinking Critically: Synthesizing, ATE, p. 223

PREMIERE ETAPE
Note culturelle, p. 224 10 min.
- Complete Activity 6, p. 224.
- Read and discuss **Note culturelle,** p. 224.
- Language-to-Language, ATE, p. 224
- Thinking Critically, ATE, p. 224

Comment dit-on... ?, p. 225 20 min.
- Presenting **Comment dit-on... ?,** ATE, p. 225
- Language Note, ATE, p. 225
- Play Audio CD for Activity 7, p. 225.
- Complete Activity 3, Cahier d'activités, p. 86
- Do Activities 8–9, p. 225.
- Have students do Activity 10, p. 226, in pairs.

Wrap-Up, 5 min.
- Do Activity 4, Cahier d'activités, p. 86.

Homework Options
Cahier d'activités, Act. 5, p. 86

Day 3

PREMIERE ETAPE
Quick Review 5 min.
- Check homework.

Comment dit-on... ? and **Vocabulaire, p. 226** 15 min.
- Presenting **Comment dit-on... ?** and **Vocabulaire,** ATE, p. 226
- Language Note, ATE, p. 227
- Play Audio CD for Activity 11, p. 227.

Grammaire, p. 227 20 min.
- Presenting **Grammaire,** ATE, p. 227
- Do Activity 13, p. 227.
- Complete Activities 1–3, **Grammaire supplémentaire,** p. 240.
- Do Activity 14, p. 227.
- Complete Activities 8–9, Cahier d'activités, p. 88.

Wrap-Up 10 min.
- Play **Catégories,** ATE, p. 227.

Homework Options
Study for Quiz 8-1.
Travaux pratiques de grammaire, Acts. 1–6, pp. 62–64

Day 4

PREMIERE ETAPE
Quiz 20 min.
- Administer Quiz 8-1A, 8-1B, or a combination of the two.

DEUXIEME ETAPE
Vocabulaire, p. 228 20 min.
- Presenting **Vocabulaire,** ATE, p. 228
- Culture Notes, ATE, p. 228
- Complete Activities 7–8, Travaux pratiques de grammaire, p. 65.
- Have students do Activity 16, p. 229, in pairs.
- Play Audio CD for Activity 17, p. 229.
- Complete Activities 10–11, Cahier d'activités, p. 89.

Note culturelle, p. 229 5 min
- Read and discuss **Note culturelle,** p. 229.
- Culture Notes, ATE, p. 228

Wrap-Up 5 min.
- Travaux pratiques de grammaire, Activity 9, p. 66

Homework Options
Travaux pratiques de grammaire, Act. 10, p. 66

Day 5

DEUXIEME ETAPE
Quick Review 5 min.
- Check homework.

Comment dit-on... ? and **Vocabulaire à la carte, p. 229** 10 min.
- Presenting **Comment dit-on... ?** and **Vocabulaire à la carte,** ATE, p. 229
- Do Activity 18, p. 229.

Grammaire, p. 230 25 min.
- Presenting **Grammaire,** ATE, p. 230
- Play Audio CD for Activity 19, p. 230.
- Read and discuss **De bons conseils,** p. 230.
- Complete Activities 11–15, Travaux pratiques de grammaire, pp. 67–68.
- Do Activity 21, p. 231.
- Have students do Activity 22, p. 231, in pairs.

Wrap-Up 10 min.
Game: **Course de relais,** ATE, p. 241

Homework Options
Cahier d'activités, Acts. 13–15, pp. 90–91

Day 6

DEUXIEME ETAPE
Quick Review 10 min.
- Check homework.
- Music Link, ATE, p. 231

Note culturelle, p. 231 10 min.
- Read and discuss **Note culturelle,** p. 231.
- Culture Notes and Career Path, ATE, p. 231

Vocabulaire à la carte, p. 232 10 min.
- Presenting **Vocabulaire à la carte,** ATE, p. 232
- Do Activity 25, p. 232.
- Building on Previous Skills, ATE, p. 232

PANORAMA CULTUREL 10 min.
- Presenting **Panorama Culturel,** ATE, p. 233
- Questions, ATE, p. 233
- **Qu'en penses-tu?,** p. 233

Wrap-Up 10 min.
- Play Charades, ATE, p. 232.

Homework Options
Study for Quiz 8-2

For alternative lesson plans by chapter section, to create your own customized plans, or to preview all resources available for this chapter, use the **One-Stop Planner CD-ROM,** Disc 2.

For additional homework suggestions, see activities accompanied by this symbol throughout the chapter.

Day 7

DEUXIEME ETAPE

Quiz 20 min.
- Administer Quiz 8-2A, 8-2B, or a combination of the two.

TROISIEME ETAPE

Note culturelle, p. 235 10 min.
- Read and discuss **Note culturelle,** p. 235.
- Culture Notes, ATE, p. 235
- Do Activity 26, p. 235.

Vocabulaire, p. 236 15 min.
- Presenting **Vocabulaire,** ATE, p. 236
- Play Audio CD for Activity 27, p. 236.
- Complete Activities 16–17, Travaux pratiques de grammaire, p. 69.
- Do Activity 29, p. 237.

Wrap-Up 5 min.
- Activity 28, p. 236

Homework Options
Cahier d'activités, Acts. 16–18, pp. 92–93

Day 8

TROISIEME ETAPE

Quick Review 10 min.
- Check homework.

Comment dit-on... ? and **Note de grammaire, p. 237 20 min.**
- Presenting **Comment dit-on... ?,** ATE, p. 237
- Read and discuss **Note de grammaire,** p. 237.
- Complete Activities 19–21, Cahier d'activités, pp. 93–94.
- Do Activities 8–10, **Grammaire supplémentaire,** p. 243.
- Have students do Activities 30–31, p. 237, in pairs.

Wrap-Up 20 min.
- Teaching Suggestion, ATE, p. 237

Homework Options
Study for Quiz 8-3
Travaux pratiques de grammaire, Acts. 18–19, p. 70

Day 9

TROISIEME ETAPE

Quiz 20 min.
- Administer Quiz 8-3A, 8-3B, or a combination of the two.

LISONS! 25 min.
- Read and discuss **Stratégie pour lire,** p. 238.
- Complete Activities A–B, pp. 238–239.
- Culture Note, Teacher Note, and Language Note, ATE, p. 238
- Have students read **Les questions difficiles (suite),** pp. 238–239.
- Do Activities C–E, p. 239.
- Have students complete Activity F, p. 239.

Wrap-Up 5 min.
- Thinking Critically: Synthesizing, ATE, p. 239

Homework Options
Cahier d'activités, Acts. 23–24, p. 95

Day 10

LISONS!

Quick Review 5 min.
- Check homework.

MISE EN PRATIQUE 40 min.
- Do Activity 1, p. 244.
- Play Audio CD for Activity 2, p. 244.
- Do Activity 3, p. 245.
- Discuss the strategy for **Ecrivons!,** p. 245, as a class, then have students work on their compositions.
- Have students work in pairs on **Jeu de rôle,** p. 245.

Wrap-Up 5 min.
- Have volunteers share scenes from **Jeu de rôle** with the class.

Homework Options
Have students finish compositions for **Ecrivons!**.

Day 11

MISE EN PRATIQUE

Review 40 min.
- Have volunteers share their compositions from **Ecrivons!**
- Have students complete **A toi de parler,** CD-ROM Tutor, Disc 2.
- Have students do **A toi d'écrire,** CD-ROM Tutor, Disc 2.
- Show ***La Nostalgie (suite),*** Video Program, Videocassette 3.
- See Teaching Suggestions, Viewing Suggestions 1–2, Video Guide, p. 52.
- Complete Activities 6–7, Video Guide, pp. 55– 56.

Wrap-Up 10 min.
- Have students begin **Que sais-je?,** p. 246.

Homework Options
Que sais-je?, p. 246

Day 12

MISE EN PRATIQUE

Quick Review 15 min.
- Go over **Que sais-je?,** p. 246.

Chapter Review 35 min.
- Review Chapter 8. Choose from **Grammaire supplémentaire,** Grammar Tutor for Students of French, Activities for Communication, Listening Activities, Interactive CD-ROM Tutor, or **Jeux interactifs.**

Homework Options
Study for Chapter 8 Test.

Assessment

Chapter Test 40–45 min.
- Administer Chapter 8 Test. Select from Testing Program, Alternative Assessment Guide, Test Generator, or Standardized Assessment Tutor.

Chapitre 8 : C'était comme ça

Suggested Lesson Plans 90-Minute Block Schedule

Block 1

CHAPTER OPENER 10 min.
- Present Objectives, p. 219.
- Thinking Critically, ATE, p. 219

MISE EN TRAIN 45 min.
- Preteaching Vocabulary, ATE, p. 220
- Presenting **Mise en train,** ATE, p. 220
- Activities 1–2, p. 222 using the Teaching Suggestion for Activity 2, ATE, p. 222
- Activities 3–4, p. 222
- Read and discuss **Note culturelle,** p. 224.

PREMIERE ETAPE
Comment dit-on... ?, p. 225 30 min.
- Presenting **Comment dit-on... ?,** ATE, p. 225
- Play Audio CD for Activity 7, p. 225.
- Language Note, ATE, p. 225
- Activity 8, p. 225

Wrap-Up 5 min.
- Read expressions from **Comment dit-on... ?,** p. 225, at random, and have students indicate whether each expression falls under "Telling what or whom you missed" or "Reassuring someone."

Homework Options
Cahier d'activités, Acts. 1–5, pp. 85–86

Block 2

PREMIERE ETAPE
Quick Review 5 min.
- Tell students something you miss and ask them to reassure you, using as many expressions as they can from **Comment dit-on... ?,** p. 225.

Comment dit-on... ?, p. 225 10 min.
- Activity 10, p. 226

Comment dit-on... ?, p. 226 10 min.
- Presenting **Comment dit-on... ?,** ATE, p. 226

Vocabulaire, p. 226 20 min.
- Presenting **Vocabulaire,** ATE, p. 226
- Play Audio CD for Activity 11, p. 227.
- Language Note, ATE, p. 227
- Activity 12, p. 227

PANORAMA CULTUREL 20 min.
- Presenting **Panorama Culturel,** ATE, p. 233

Grammaire, p. 227 20 min.
- Presenting **Grammaire,** ATE, p. 227
- Activities 13–14, p. 227

Wrap-Up 5 min.
- Teaching Transparency 8-1, using Suggestion #2 in Suggestions for Using Teaching Transparency 8-1

Homework Options
Have students study for Quiz 8-1.
Activity 15, p. 227
Grammaire supplémentaire, Acts. 1–3, p. 240
Cahier d'activités, Acts. 6–9, pp. 87–88
Travaux pratiques de grammaire, Acts. 1–6, pp. 62–64

Block 3

PREMIERE ETAPE
Quick Review 10 min.
- Communicative Activity 8-1, Activities for Communication, pp. 43–44

Quiz 8-1 20 min.
- Administer Quiz 8-1A, 8-1B, or a combination of the two. Options: Test Generator, Alternative Assessment Program

DEUXIEME ETAPE
Vocabulaire, p. 228 25 min.
- Presenting **Vocabulaire,** ATE, p. 228
- Activity 16, p. 229
- Play Audio CD for Activity 17, p. 229.
- Discuss **Note culturelle,** p. 229.

Comment dit-on... ?, p. 229 15 min.
- Presenting **Comment dit-on... ?/Vocabulaire à la carte,** ATE, p. 229
- Activity 18, p. 229

Grammaire, p. 230 15 min.
- Presenting **Grammaire,** ATE, p. 230
- **De bons conseils,** p. 230
- Play Audio CD for Activity 19, p. 230.

Wrap-Up 5 min.
- Teaching Transparency 8-2, using Suggestion #2 in Suggestions for Using Teaching Transparency 8-2

Homework Options
Cahier d'activités, Acts. 10–11, p. 89
Travaux pratiques de grammaire, Acts. 7–10, pp. 65–66

For alternative lesson plans by chapter section, to create your own customized plans, or to preview all resources available for this chapter, use the **One-Stop Planner CD-ROM,** Disc 2.

For additional homework suggestions, see activities accompanied by this symbol throughout the chapter.

Block 4

DEUXIEME ETAPE

Quick Review 10 min.

- Teaching Transparency 8-B, using Suggestion #4 in Suggestions for Using Teaching Transparency 8-B

Grammaire, p. 230 55 min.

- Review the forms of the **imparfait.**
- Activity 20, p. 230
- Discuss **Tu te rappelles?,** p. 231.
- Activities 21–23, pp. 231–232
- Discuss **Note culturelle,** p. 231.

TROISIEME ETAPE

Note culturelle 15 min.

- Discuss **Note culturelle,** p. 235.
- Have students read the letter and photo captions, pp. 234–235.
- Activity 26, p. 235

Wrap-Up 10 min.

- Music Link, ATE, p. 231

Homework Options

Have students study for Quiz 8-2.
Activity 25, p. 232
Grammaire supplémentaire, Acts. 4–6, pp. 241–242
Cahier d'activités, Acts. 12–15, pp. 90–91
Travaux pratiques de grammaire, Acts. 11–15, pp. 67–68

Block 5

DEUXIEME ETAPE

Quick Review 10 min.

- Game: **Course de relais,** ATE, p. 241

Quiz 8-2 20 min.

- Administer Quiz 8-2A, 8-2B, or a combination of the two. Options: Test Generator, Alternative Assessment Program

TROISIEME ETAPE

Vocabulaire, p. 236 20 min.

- Presenting **Vocabulaire,** ATE p. 236
- Play Audio CD for Activity 27, p. 236.
- Activity 28, p. 236

Comment dit-on... ?, p. 237 30 min.

- Presenting **Comment dit-on... ?,** ATE, p. 237
- Read and discuss **Note de grammaire,** p. 237.
- Activities 30–31, p. 237

Wrap-Up 10 min.

- Teaching Transparency 8-3, using Suggestion #1 in Suggestions for Using Teaching Transparency 8-3

Homework Options

Have students study for Quiz 8-3.
Grammaire supplémentaire, Acts. 8–10, p. 243
Cahier d'activités, Acts. 16–22, pp. 92–94
Travaux pratiques de grammaire, Acts. 16–19, pp. 69–70

Block 6

TROISIEME ETAPE

Quick Review 10 min.

- Communicative Activity 8-3, Activities for Communication, pp. 47–48

Quiz 8-3 20 min.

- Administer Quiz 8-3A, 8-3B, or a combination of the two. Options: Test Generator, Alternative Assessment Guide

RENCONTRE CULTURELLE 10 min.

- Presenting **Rencontre culturelle,** ATE, p. 223

LISONS! 30 min.

- Discuss **Stratégie pour lire,** p. 238.
- Activities A–E, pp. 238–239

MISE EN PRATIQUE 20 min.

- Activity 1, p. 244
- Play Audio CD for Activity 2, p. 244.
- Activity 5, p. 245

Homework Options

- **Que sais-je?,** p. 246
- CD-ROM/Interactive Games
- Study for Chapter 8 Test.

Block 7

MISE EN PRATIQUE

Quick Review 10 min.

- Check homework.

Chapter Review 35 min.

- Review Chapter 8. Choose from **Grammaire supplémentaire,** Grammar Tutor for Students of French, Activities for Communication, Listening Activities, Interactive CD-ROM Tutor, or **Jeux interactifs.**

Chapter Test 45 min.

- Administer Chapter 8 Test. Select from Testing Program, Alternative Assessment Guide, Test Generator, or Standardized Assessment Tutor.

Chapter Opener

CHAPITRE 8

One-Stop Planner CD-ROM

For resource information, see the **One-Stop Planner,** Disc 2.

Pacing Tips

Students will be introduced to the **imparfait** in this chapter. In the **Première étape,** they learn the imperfect forms of **être** and **avoir.** In the **Deuxième étape,** they learn how to form the imperfect tense of all verbs. For Lesson Plan suggestions, see pages 217I–217L.

Meeting the Standards

Communication

- Telling what or whom you miss; reassuring someone, p. 225
- Asking and telling what things were like, p. 226
- Reminiscing, p. 229
- Making and responding to suggestions, p. 237

Culture

- Culture Note, pp. 218, 221, 223, 228, 231, 235, 236, 238
- Note culturelle, pp. 224, 229, 231, 235
- Rencontre culturelle, p. 223
- Panorama Culturel, p. 233

Connections

- Multicultural Link, pp. 223, 244
- Music Link, p. 231
- Language Arts Links, p. 238

Comparisons

- Thinking Critically: Synthesizing, pp. 223, 224, 235, 239
- Thinking Critically: Comparing and Contrasting, p. 230
- Thinking Critically: Analyzing, p. 244

Communities

- Career Path, p. 231
- De l'école au travail, p. 237

Cultures and Communities

Culture Note

You might tell students how people from Côte d'Ivoire use cowry shells to decorate their jewelry. During the eighteenth century, Djoula traders brought the cowry shell, originally from the Indian Ocean, to Côte d'Ivoire. These shells were used as currency in parts of the country until World War II. Because of their history, today they are a symbol of success. They are used not only to make jewelry, but also to decorate elaborate costumes worn in tribal rituals.

STANDARDS: 2.2

CHAPITRE 8
C'était comme ça

Objectives

In this chapter you will learn to

Première étape

- tell what or whom you miss
- reassure someone
- ask and tell what things were like

Deuxième étape

- reminisce

Troisième étape

- make and respond to suggestions

internet

ADRESSE: go.hrw.com
MOT-CLE:
WA3 COTE D'IVOIRE-8

◀ **Si on parlait du bon vieux temps?**

CHAPITRE 8

Focusing on Outcomes

Ask students to read the chapter outcomes and, taking into account the meaning of **du bon vieux temps,** tell what they think the two people in the photo are talking about.
NOTE: The self-check activities on page 246 help students assess their achievement of the objectives.

Photo Flash!

Koffi and Sandrine, two students in Abidjan, are talking about Sandrine's recent move to Abidjan. She is telling Koffi about the village she is from. Although more than three million people live in Côte d'Ivoire's largest city, Abidjan, more than half of the country's population lives in rural areas **(en brousse,** *in the bush).*

Chapter Sequence

Connections and Comparisons

Thinking Critically

Analyzing Have students work in groups to list all the problems or difficulties they imagine a young Ivorian from a small town or village might encounter when coming to live in the city for the first time.

Teaching Resources
pp. 220–222

PRINT 
- Lesson Planner, p. 36
- Video Guide, pp. 52, 54
- Cahier d'activités, p. 85

MEDIA
- One-Stop Planner
- Video Program
- **Mise en train**
  Videocassette 3, 17:40–21:23
  Videocassette 5 (captioned version), 1:05:16–1:08:59
- **Suite**
  Videocassette 3, 21:26–29:13
  Videocassette 5 (captioned version), 1:09:02–1:16:49
- DVD Tutor, Disc 2
- Audio Compact Discs, CD 8, Trs. 1–2
- **Mise en train** Transparencies

Presenting Mise en train

Have students view the first segment of the video. Ask students what Sandrine misses about her village. Then, play the rest of the video and have students give Sandrine's impression of the city of Abidjan. Next, play the audio recording and have students read along as they listen. Finally, have students answer the questions in Activity 1 on page 222. You might also present the Preteaching Vocabulary suggestion below.

Mise en train Transparencies

Culture Note

All students in Côte d'Ivoire wear uniforms. In high school, boys wear khaki shirts and pants, and girls generally wear blue skirts and white blouses. In elementary school, girls wear blue or brown gingham dresses.

This is an abridged version of the video episode.

MISE EN TRAIN • *La Nostalgie*

CD 8 Trs. 1–2

Stratégie pour comprendre

In this episode, what do you think Sandrine is talking to Koffi about? Does she seem happy or sad?

Sandrine

Koffi

1

Koffi et Sandrine sont camarades de classe. Sandrine est née dans un village en Côte d'Ivoire. Ça fait trois semaines qu'elle habite à Abidjan.

Koffi C'était comment, là-bas dans ton village?

Sandrine Oh, c'était tellement mieux. J'avais beaucoup d'amis. Ils me manquent beaucoup.

2 **J'allais au collège de Sakassou. C'était un petit collège. Nous étions une cinquantaine d'élèves.**

3 **Après l'école, j'avais des responsabilités. On travaillait...**

4 **mais on s'amusait aussi. On ne faisait pas grand-chose, mais c'était bien. On se promenait ensemble. On écoutait de la musique...**

Preteaching Vocabulary

Using Prior Knowledge

In the **Mise en train,** Sandrine reminisces about where she used to live. While students have not yet learned the **imparfait,** they should be able to understand Sandrine based on their prior knowledge of the vocabulary. Have them give the infinitive or English equivalent of the following list:

- 2 allais
- 3 travaillait
- 4 faisait
- 4 se promenait
- 4 écoutait
- 5 chantait
- 5 discutait

STANDARDS: 1.2, 2.1, 3.2

5 De temps en temps, on organisait des fêtes. Ça me plaisait beaucoup. On chantait et on dansait. On discutait. C'était super.

6 Il y avait des animaux : des vaches, des chèvres, des poules...

7 On se réunissait souvent : les cousins, les oncles et les tantes, les grands-parents. C'était merveilleux.

8 Ici à Abidjan, j'ai l'impression que les gens sont plus seuls qu'en brousse. On vit dans des appartements. On ne se connaît pas autant.

9 Ici, c'est tellement plus grand! Si on veut aller voir quelqu'un, il faut prendre le bus. Là-bas, tout le monde se connaît dans le village.

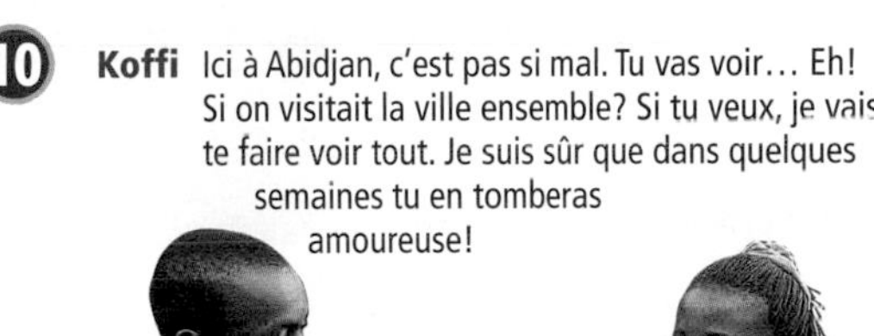

10 **Koffi** Ici à Abidjan, c'est pas si mal. Tu vas voir… Eh! Si on visitait la ville ensemble? Si tu veux, je vais te faire voir tout. Je suis sûr que dans quelques semaines tu en tomberas amoureuse!

Cahier d'activités, p. 85, Act. 1–2

Using the Captioned Video/DVD

If students have difficulty understanding French spoken at a normal speed, use Videocassette 5 to allow students to see the French captions for ***La Nostalgie*** and ***La Nostalgie (suite).*** Hearing the language and watching the story will reduce anxiety about the new language and facilitate comprehension. The reinforcement of seeing the written vocabulary words as they watch the gestures and actions will help prepare students to do the comprehension activities on page 222.

NOTE: The *DVD Tutor* contains captions for all sections of the *Video Program.*

Mise en train

CHAPITRE 8

Slower Pace

Draw two columns on the board or on a transparency and label them **En brousse** and **En ville.** For visual learners, put a symbol next to each label, such as a palm tree next to **En brousse** and a skyscraper next to **En ville.** Have students do the same on a sheet of paper. Then, have partners find the sentences in the **Mise en train** that refer to Sandrine's village and those that refer to Abidjan and write them in the appropriate column. Afterwards, have them tell you what to write in the columns on the board or on the transparency.

Culture Note

Ebony is the heartwood of many tropical trees common in western Africa. The bark of these trees is jet-black, yet the wood just under the bark is white. It is the interior heartwood of the tree, the dark brown ebony streaked with black, that is commonly used for many Ivorian crafts. This hard, close-grained wood typically polishes to a high gloss and is ideal for cabinet-making, piano keys, and knife handles, as well as statues and masks.

Mise en train (suite)

When the story continues, it is several weeks later and Sandrine's sister, Albertine, has just arrived from the village to visit. Albertine is excited but completely unaccustomed to being in a big city. Sandrine, however, has changed. She is confident and very much at home in Abidjan. Sandrine gives her sister a tour, and Albertine is amazed at how she has become a city-dweller.

Mise en train

CHAPITRE 8

Auditory Learners

4 Assign each question to a different group of students. Then, read aloud one of the answers and have students stand up or raise their hands when they hear an expression that serves the function they were assigned.

Teaching Suggestion

5 If students have ever moved, tell them to copy all of the sentences from ***La Nostalgie*** that they themselves might have said about their experience. If students have never moved, have them tell what they would miss and/or what they would look forward to.

These activities check for comprehension only. Students should not yet be expected to produce language modeled in **Mise en train.**

1 **Tu as compris?** See answers below.

1. Where did Sandrine move from? Where does she live now?
2. Where does Koffi live? Does he like it there?
3. What was it like where Sandrine used to live? What did she do there?
4. According to Sandrine, what is Abidjan like?
5. What does Koffi offer to do?

2 **Ville ou village?**

Est-ce que Sandrine parle de son village ou d'Abidjan?

1. «Il y avait des chèvres.» de son village
2. «On organisait des fêtes.» de son village
3. «C'est tellement grand!» d'Abidjan
4. «Nous étions une cinquantaine d'élèves.» de son village
5. «On vit dans des appartements.» d'Abidjan
6. «Les gens sont plus seuls.» d'Abidjan

3 **C'était le bon vieux temps**

Sandrine parle de quelle image?

1. «On se promenait ensemble.» a
2. «On chantait et on dansait.» c
3. «On se réunissait souvent.» b

a.

b.

c.

4 **Cherche les expressions** See answers below.

1. What does Sandrine say to . . .
   a. tell what she thinks of her life in the village?
   b. recall what she used to do?
   c. give her impressions of Abidjan?
2. What does Koffi say to . . .
   a. ask how life was in Sandrine's village?
   b. reassure Sandrine?

5 **Et maintenant, à toi**

Et toi, est-ce que tu as déjà déménagé? Qu'est-ce que tu regrettes? Est-ce que tu aimerais déménager maintenant? Pourquoi ou pourquoi pas?

Answers

1
1. a small village; in Abidjan
2. Abidjan; yes
3. a small, close-knit community; go to school, work, get together with her friends and family, take walks, listen to music, dance, sing songs, organize parties
4. lonely, too big, people don't know one another
5. take her on a tour of Abidjan

4
1. a. ... c'était tellement mieux.
   b. J'allais... ; J'avais... ; On travaillait... ; ... on s'amusait... ; ... on faisait... ; On se promenait... ; On écoutait... ; ... on organisait... ; On chantait... ; ... on dansait; On discutait; On se réunissait...
   c. ... j'ai l'impression que... ; Ici, c'est tellement plus grand!
2. a. C'était comment... ?
   b. ... c'est pas si mal; Tu vas voir... ; Je suis sûr que dans quelques semaines tu en tomberas amoureuse!

Comprehension Check

Teaching Suggestions

2 Ask students if they can tell from the verbs in the sentences if Sandrine is talking about her life in the village or her life in Abidjan. Point out the imperfect endings that indicate she is talking about what used to happen.

3 Before they complete this activity, ask students to write three short paragraphs in French describing the three pictures, using as much detail as they can. Then, have volunteers read their paragraphs aloud and have other students try to identify the pictures that are being described.

3 Have students find additional statements in the **Mise en train** relevant to each picture.

STANDARDS: 1.2, 2.1, 3.2

What can you tell about everyday life in an African village from these photos?

Qu'en penses-tu?

1. What are these people from different villages in Côte d'Ivoire doing?
2. How does this differ from the way things are done in the United States?

1. spinning yarn, carving wood, preparing food, carrying fruit
2. In the United States, people buy what they need from stores, whereas in a small village in Côte d'Ivoire, people make many of the things they need from raw materials.

Savais-tu que... ?

Small villages in Côte d'Ivoire are plentiful and rich in local culture. Certain regions of Côte d'Ivoire, as well as individual towns, villages, and ethnic groups, are known for their particular customs, crafts, and costumes. The town of Korhogo is famous for its painted woven fabrics; the Sénoufo are known for their weaving; the people in Katiola are noted for their pottery. In areas where electricity and machinery are not available, everyday life requires many physical tasks. Life is simpler; people cook over open fires, carry water, use large communal bowls in place of table settings and silverware, and walk instead of riding in cars.

Cultures and Communities

Culture Note

In Côte d'Ivoire, living in the city has its advantages, especially in Abidjan. There are better health-care facilities, a greater selection of food, more social activities, and better educational opportunities. Unfortunately, as in the United States, city life is also more stressful and expensive. Village life, on the other hand, can be quite simple. Villages can range in size from less than 100 inhabitants to more than 25,000. Larger villages are likely to have water and electricity, whereas people living in smaller villages may have to depend on a well or stream for water, and campfires and lanterns for cooking and lighting.

CHAPITRE 8

Thinking Critically

Comparing and Contrasting Ask students to imagine living in a small, rural village like those pictured. Ask them what they think they would like or dislike about the lifestyle. Ask them to compare city life and country life in the United States. Ask them which they prefer in the United States, city or country life, and why.

Presenting Rencontre culturelle

Have students look at the pictures and tell what the people are doing. Ask them to recall the expression that tells where these people live **(en brousse).** (Refer to the Photo Flash! on page 219.) Discuss the questions in **Qu'en penses-tu?** and the information in **Savais-tu que... ?** with students. Afterwards, ask them to imagine what a typical day might be like for a teenager living **en brousse.** You might have them discuss this in groups.

Thinking Critically

Synthesizing Ask students to name some of the ways in which life would be less complicated in a small village. Ask them if they think it would be easier for them to adjust to the village or for the villagers to adjust to the city and why. Then, ask students if they think it's possible to live a less complicated life in this country. How? Is it desirable? Why or why not?

Multicultural Link

Have students research villages or peoples in other parts of Africa, or the world, to find out what particular craft(s), if any, they are known for. Students might then report their findings to the class.

CHAPITRE 8

Teaching Resources
pp. 224–227

PRINT 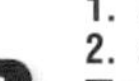

- Lesson Planner, p. 37
- TPR Storytelling Book, pp. 56–57
- Listening Activities, pp. 59, 63
- Activities for Communication, pp. 43–44, 110, 113, 151–152
- Travaux pratiques de grammaire, pp. 62–64
- Grammar Tutor for Students of French, Chapter 8
- Cahier d'activités, pp. 86–88
- Testing Program, pp. 197–200
- Alternative Assessment Guide, p. 39
- Student Make-Up Assignments, Chapter 8

MEDIA 

- One-Stop Planner
- Audio Compact Discs, CD 8, Trs. 3–4, 13, 19–20
- Teaching Transparencies: 8-1, 8-A; **Grammaire supplémentaire** Answers; Travaux pratiques de grammaire Answers
- Interactive CD-ROM Tutor, Disc 2

Bell Work

Write the following sentences on the board or on a transparency. Students decide whether each sentence describes life **en brousse, en ville,** or **les deux.**

1. **Il n'y a pas de voitures.**
2. **On y écoute de la musique.**
3. **Tout le monde se connaît.**
4. **Il faut prendre le bus pour aller voir quelqu'un.**
5. **On organise des fêtes.**
6. **Il y a une cinquantaine d'élèves dans le collège.**
7. **On discute avec des amis.**

Première étape

Objectives Telling what or whom you miss; reassuring someone; asking and telling what things were like

WA3 COTE D'IVOIRE-8

ADJOUA Alors, ça va, Adama? Tu te débrouilles dans notre grande ville?

ADAMA Oui, mais je regrette mon village. Il me manque beaucoup.

ADJOUA Je comprends. Dis-moi, il se trouve où, ton village?

ADAMA Koni est dans le nord, près de Korhogo.

ADJOUA C'était tellement différent là-bas?

ADAMA Oui, la vie était plus tranquille, on était moins pressés. Il y avait des coutumes, des cérémonies avec des danses traditionnelles.

ADJOUA Mais il y a des danses ici aussi! Et il y a tant d'autres choses à voir... et beaucoup de monde!

ADAMA Là-bas, j'avais un tas d'amis. On jouait au foot... on jouait aux cartes... et à l'awalé, j'étais le champion!

ADJOUA T'en fais pas! Tu vas avoir des amis ici aussi. Et c'est bien de vivre en ville. Tu vas voir, c'est plus animé ici.

1. Koni
2. son village
3. différente, plus tranquille, on était moins pressés
4. On dansait, on jouait au foot, aux cartes et à l'awalé.
5. plus animée

6 Tu as compris?
Lisons

1. Adama est d'où?
2. Qu'est-ce qu'Adama regrette?
3. Comment était la vie là-bas?
4. Qu'est-ce qu'on faisait là-bas?
5. D'après Adjoua, comment est la vie à Abidjan?

Note culturelle

Most high schools in West Africa are in large cities or towns, so students have to leave their home village if they want to continue their studies beyond the junior high level. Students who go to a big city to study usually live with a relative or friend from the same village who will take them in as a family member. People from the same ethnic group often live in the same neighborhood. You can usually tell a person's ethnic group from his or her name: **Adjoua** and **Koffi** are Baoulé names, and **Adama** is a Sénoufo name. French West Africans often have both an African and French first name. They give their family name first, followed by their African first name and then their French first name: **TRAORE Adama Eric** or **KOUASSI Adjoua Désirée.**

Connections and Comparisons

Thinking Critically

Synthesizing Have students discuss the advantages and the disadvantages of living at home and living on campus while attending college.

Language-to-Language

Have students discuss how names are given in various countries. If you have native speakers of Spanish in your class, you might discuss how Spaniards and Latin Americans tend to have two last names, the first being the father's name, and the second being the mother's maiden name. Ask students to think about names in the United States that have French origins.

STANDARDS: 1.2, 2.1, 3.1, 3.2, 4.1, 4.2

Comment dit-on...?

Telling what or whom you miss; reassuring someone

To tell what or whom you miss:

Je regrette la campagne. *I miss . . .*
Mon école **me manque.** *I miss . . .*
Mes copains **me manquent.**
Ce qui me manque, c'est mon ancienne maison. *What I really miss is . . .*

To reassure someone:

Tu vas t'y faire. *You'll get used to it.*
Fais-toi une raison. *Make the best of it.*
Tu vas te plaire ici. *You're going to like it here.*
Tu vas voir que tout le monde est sympa ici. *You'll see . . .*

Cahier d'activités, p. 86, Act. 3–5

7 **Ce qui me manque** See scripts on p. 217G.

Ecoutons Ecoute ces élèves. Qu'est-ce qui leur manque?

CD 8 Tr. 3

1. Sylvie a
2. Emile c
3. Francine b
4. Bertrand d

c

b

a

d

8 **Qu'est-ce que tu as?** Possible answers:

Parlons/Ecrivons

a. Tes amis veulent savoir ce qui ne va pas. Utilise les verbes **manquer** et **regretter** pour exprimer tes sentiments si...
   1. ton/ta meilleur(e) ami(e) vient de déménager? Mon meilleur ami (Ma meilleure amie) me manque.
   2. ton chien a disparu? Mon chien me manque.
   3. il n'y a plus de neige et tu adores faire du ski? Je regrette le ski et la neige.
   4. ta mère est partie en voyage pour son travail? Ma mère me manque.
   5. ton professeur préféré a quitté ton école? Mon prof me manque.

b. Qu'est-ce que tes amis te disent pour te réconforter? Tu vas t'y faire. Fais-toi une raison.

9 **Ils ont le mal du pays**

Ecrivons Il y a de nouveaux élèves à ton école. Fais des phrases pour dire ce qui manque à chaque élève, d'après toi. Inclus au moins trois choses par personne.

Lisa est de Tours.
Philippe vient de Québec.
Karine est de Paris.
José vient de la Martinique.

Communication for All Students

Additional Practice

7 Ask students what each person in the recording misses. **(Qu'est-ce que Sylvie regrette? Qu'est-ce qu'Emile regrette?)** Then, tell students to imagine they are the individuals in the recording and ask them what they miss.

Première étape

CHAPITRE 8

Presenting Comment dit-on... ?

Ask students to bring in pictures of people or things (or magazine cutouts) they would miss about their hometown if they had to move somewhere else. Write the new expressions in two columns on the board and tell students you have just moved away. Then, have a student give you the pictures he or she brought. Holding up the various pictures, tell what or whom you miss, using the new expressions. Repeat this process several times and have students say each expression after you. Next, have volunteers show and tell you what or whom they miss, using one of their pictures. Reassure them, using the new expressions.

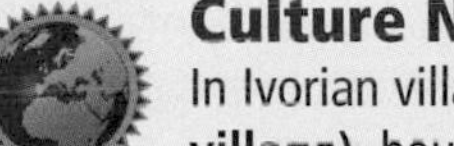

Culture Note

In Ivorian villages **(au village)**, houses might be made of cement, cinder blocks, mud bricks, and even bamboo. Animals, such as goats, dogs, and chickens, can be seen everywhere and may even travel with their owners in cars and in taxis!

Language Note

Call students' attention to the verb forms in **Mon école me manque** and **Mes copains me manquent.** Ask them how **manquer** is used in French as opposed to the way *to miss* is used in English. (Literally, **me manque(nt)** means *is (are) lacking to me.)* Finally, ask students how they would say *I miss you* in French. **(Tu me manques. Vous me manquez.)**

Possible Answers

9 *José:* la plage, la mer, la planche à voile
Lisa: ses copains, sa maison, ses profs, les châteaux
Karine: la tour Eiffel, le métro, les musées
Philippe: le ski, la neige, le hockey

STANDARDS: 2.2, 4.1

Première étape

CHAPITRE 8

Teaching Resources
pp. 224–227

PRINT 

- Lesson Planner, p. 37
- TPR Storytelling Book, pp. 56–57
- Listening Activities, pp. 59, 63
- Activities for Communication, pp. 43–44, 110, 113, 151–152
- Travaux pratiques de grammaire, pp. 62–64
- Grammar Tutor for Students of French, Chapter 8
- Cahier d'activités, pp. 86–88
- Testing Program, pp. 197–200
- Alternative Assessment Guide, p. 39
- Student Make-Up Assignments, Chapter 8

MEDIA 

- One-Stop Planner
- Audio Compact Discs, CD 8, Trs. 3–4, 13, 19–20
- Teaching Transparencies: 8-1, 8-A; **Grammaire supplémentaire** Answers; Travaux pratiques de grammaire Answers
- Interactive CD-ROM Tutor, Disc 2

Presenting
Comment dit-on... ?

Describe an imaginary town where you once lived, using magazine pictures or drawings. Then, ask if anyone has ever lived in another home or city. Ask students several either-or questions to elicit the expressions in **Comment dit-on... ?**

Vocabulaire

To illustrate the adjectives, gather magazine pictures and describe them. Then, ask either-or questions about them. Next, have students repeat the vocabulary after you.

10 Fais-toi une raison

Parlons Tu viens de déménager pour aller habiter à Abidjan. Décris à ton/ta nouveau/nouvelle ami(e) ivoirien(ne) trois choses qui te manquent. Ton ami(e) va te rassurer. Joue cette scène avec un(e) camarade, puis changez de rôle.

EXEMPLE —**Qu'est-ce que tu as?**
—**Ma ville me manque.**
—**Ah, bon? Pourquoi?**
—...

la cuisine américaine — ma meilleure amie — __?__ — mon chat — mon lycée — la neige — les fêtes — mon chien — mon meilleur ami

Comment dit-on...?

Asking and telling what things were like

To ask what things were like:

C'était comment? *What was it like?*
C'était tellement/si différent?
Was it really so different?

To tell what things were like:

C'était beau. *It was . . .*
Il y avait de jolies maisons. *There were . . .*
La vie était plus simple, **moins** compliquée!
Life was more . . . , less . . .

Vocabulaire

CD-ROM 2
DVD 2

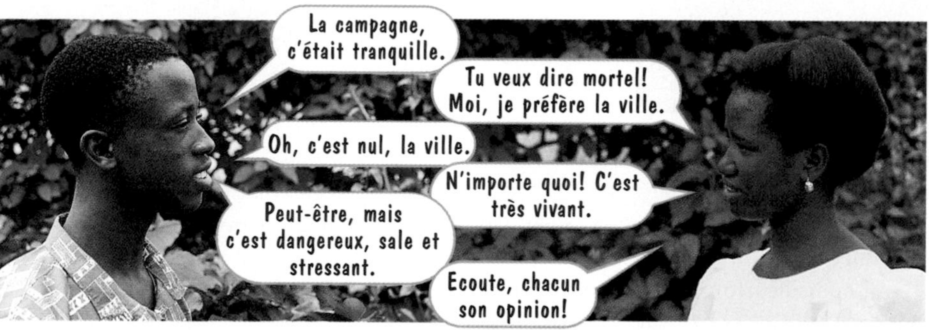
La campagne, c'était tranquille.
Tu veux dire mortel! Moi, je préfère la ville.
Oh, c'est nul, la ville.
N'importe quoi! C'est très vivant.
Peut-être, mais c'est dangereux, sale et stressant.
Ecoute, chacun son opinion!

génial(e)	*great*	**très vivant(e)**	*very lively*
calme	*calm*	**bruyant(e)**	*noisy*
tranquille	*peaceful*	**sale**	*dirty*
propre	*clean*	**stressant(e)**	*stressful*
relaxant(e)	*relaxing*	**animé(e)**	*lively*
mortel (mortelle)	*deadly dull*	**dangereux (dangereuse)**	*dangerous*
nul (nulle)	*worthless*		

Travaux pratiques de grammaire, pp. 62–63, Act. 1–4
Cahier d'activités, p. 87, Act. 6–7

Teacher to Teacher

Linda Hale
Sonoma Valley High School
Sonoma, CA

Linda suggests the following activity to practice the vocabulary in this étape.

"My students make large flash cards with 8"x11" construction paper to illustrate opposites like those in the **Vocabulaire** box on this page. Have students illustrate one pair of opposites on each side of a sheet of construction paper. Students can quiz one another using the flashcards. Keep the best drawings for a class set to practice and review for final exams."

STANDARDS: 1.1, 5.1

11 Ville ou village? See scripts and answers on p. 217G.

CD 8 Tr. 4

Ecoutons Listen to the conversation between Justin and his cousin Mamadou, who has just moved to Abidjan to go to school. List three things Mamadou misses about his village. What do he and Justin decide to do?

12 La vie en ville

Parlons/Ecrivons Adjoua compare sa vie en ville à sa vie au village. Dis si tu es d'accord ou pas d'accord avec elle et donne ton opinion personnelle.

EXEMPLE **—La vie en ville, c'est super.**
—Oui, c'est génial. ou Mais non, c'est nul.

1. La ville, c'est super.
2. La vie à la campagne, c'est tranquille.
3. La ville, c'est toujours bruyant.
4. La campagne, c'est relaxant.

Grammaire

The *imparfait* of être and *avoir*

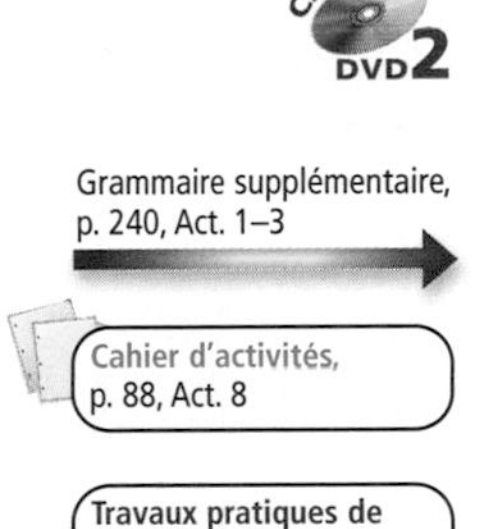

CD-ROM 2
DVD 2

To describe what things were like in the past or how they used to be, you'll use the imperfect tense (**l'imparfait**) of **être** and **avoir.** You've already seen two forms, **c'était** and **il y avait.** Here are the imperfect forms of **être** and **avoir:**

être		avoir	
j'**étais**	nous **étions**	j'**avais**	nous **avions**
tu **étais**	vous **étiez**	tu **avais**	vous **aviez**
il/elle/on **était**	ils/elles **étaient**	il/elle/on **avait**	ils/elles **avaient**

To make an imperfect form negative, place **ne... pas** around the verb: La vie en ville **n'**était **pas** tranquille. You'll learn how to form other verbs in the **imparfait** later in this chapter.

Grammaire supplémentaire, p. 240, Act. 1–3

Cahier d'activités, p. 88, Act. 8

Travaux pratiques de grammaire, p. 64, Act. 5–6

13 Grammaire en contexte

Lisons Relis la conversation entre Adjoua et Adama à la page 224 et fais la liste des formes d'**avoir** et d'**être** qui sont à l'imparfait. C'était, était, était, avait, avais, étais

14 Grammaire en contexte

Ecrivons Monique est allée faire du camping. Complète son journal avec l'imparfait du verbe **être** ou du verbe **avoir.** **1.** avait **2.** avions **3.** avaient **4.** étions **5.** étaient **6.** étais

Ce week-end, je suis allée faire du camping. Quand on est arrivés au terrain de camping, on __1__ très faim, alors on a fait un pique-nique. Ensuite, comme nous __2__ nos vélos de montagne, on s'est promenés dans la forêt. Mes parents __3__ leur appareil-photo, alors ils ont fait des photos. Le soir, nous __4__ très fatigués, alors on s'est couchés tôt. Ma sœur et moi, on a rencontré deux autres filles. Elles __5__ très sympas. Moi, j' __6__ très contente de mon week-end!

15 Tu vas t'y faire 

Ecrivons Ton/Ta correspondant(e) d'Abidjan va venir habiter dans ta ville et il/elle va aller à ton école. Il/Elle est un peu inquiet (inquiète). Ecris-lui une lettre pour le/la rassurer. Décris les avantages de ton école et de ta ville.

Communication for All Students

Game

Catégories Write on the board the four functions from this **étape** plus *describing places.* Form two teams. Name a category *(reassuring someone)* and have the two teams take turns reassuring someone about something. **(Tu vas voir, c'est sympa ici.)** Continue until a team cannot add another appropriate expression. The last team to say something appropriate to the category scores a point. When students have exhausted a category, choose another one and start a new round.

Language Note

Remind students that an adjective is invariable when it directly follows **c'est** and **c'était. (La ville, c'est amusant.)** However, the adjective must reflect the gender and number when a noun or **il(s)/elle(s)** are used: **Les villes sont bruyantes. Elles sont animées.**

Presenting Grammaire

The *imparfait* of *être* and *avoir* Write on a transparency a short description of your childhood or an imaginary past event, using the **imparfait** forms of **être** and **avoir.** Read it aloud as students read along with you. Ask them whether your story describes something in the present or the past. Go over the **Grammaire** with students. Then, ask them to reread ***La Nostalgie*** on pages 220–221 to find all the forms of **être** and **avoir** in the **imparfait.** Finally, read the poem *Le Petit Chameau (Listening Activities,* Level 3, page 66) aloud and have students raise their hands when they hear an **imparfait** form of **être** or **avoir.**

Portfolio

15 Written This activity is suitable for students' written portfolios. For portfolio information, see the *Alternative Assessment Guide,* pages iv–17.

Assess

- Testing Program, pp. 197–200
  Quiz 8-1A, Quiz 8-1B
  Audio CD 8, Tr. 13
- Student Make-Up Assignments, Chapter 8, Alternative Quiz
- Alternative Assessment Guide, p. 39

STANDARDS: 1.2, 1.3, 4.1, 5.2

Teaching Resources
pp. 228–232

PRINT

- Lesson Planner, p. 38
- TPR Storytelling Book, pp. 58–59
- Listening Activities, pp. 60, 64
- Activities for Communication, pp. 45–46, 111, 113–114, 151–152
- Travaux pratiques de grammaire, pp. 65–68
- Grammar Tutor for Students of French, Chapter 8
- Cahier d'activités, pp. 89–91
- Testing Program, pp. 201–204
- Alternative Assessment Guide, p. 39
- Student Make-Up Assignments, Chapter 8

MEDIA 

- One-Stop Planner
- Audio Compact Discs, CD 8, Trs. 5–6, 14, 21–22
- Teaching Transparencies: 8-2, 8-B; **Grammaire supplémentaire** Answers; Travaux pratiques de grammaire Answers
- Interactive CD-ROM Tutor, Disc 2

Bell Work

Ask students to imagine they have just moved and write five sentences describing the town they left and telling what and whom they miss.

Presenting Vocabulaire

Use puppets to tell Yapo's story. Tell students that Yapo is reminiscing about his childhood. Introduce his mother and brother and proceed to tell the story, using the puppets and other props to get the meaning across. Then, have students open their books and read silently as you read the sentences aloud.

Deuxième étape

Objective Reminiscing

WA3 COTE D'IVOIRE-8

Vocabulaire

Quand j'étais petit(e)...

Yapo

je faisais la sieste tous les jours.

Je faisais toujours **des bêtises.**

Je taquinais mon frère...

et **je conduisais une voiture** super.

J'ennuyais ma mère.

Je n'avais pas de responsabilités, pas de soucis.

Travaux pratiques de grammaire, pp. 65–66, Act. 7–10

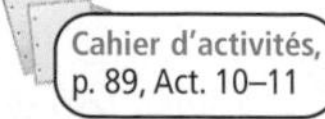

Cahier d'activités, p. 89, Act. 10–11

Cultures and Communities

Culture Notes

- Other pastimes of Ivorian teenagers include dancing, singing, discussing current events, playing a variety of sports, and card or board games. Girls enjoy braiding one another's hair, which can be a very elaborate, time-consuming procedure.
- In West African countries, it is very common for children to share a bed or a mat, since there are often not enough for each child to have his or her own.
- In Côte d'Ivoire, students often write their school work on small chalkboards. They are issued books and study a variety of subjects, including three languages in high school. Course work is usually rigorous, and lessons are given in French. This can be difficult for children who grow up speaking their ethnic language and little or no French.

STANDARDS: 1.2, 2.1

Moi aussi!

Lisons/Parlons Est-ce que tu étais comme Yapo quand tu étais enfant? Avec un(e) camarade, lis ce qu'il a dit dans le Vocabulaire à la page 228 et réponds **Moi aussi! Moi, non! Moi non plus!** ou **Moi, si!** à chaque phrase. Est-ce que toi et ton/ta camarade, vous aviez le même caractère quand vous étiez jeunes?

Vous étiez comment?

CD 8 Tr. 5

Ecoutons Yapo interviewe son professeur sur son enfance. Ecoute l'interview. Ensuite, lis ses notes. Sont-elles correctes? Corrige les erreurs s'il y en a. See scripts and answers on p. 217G.

Elle était pénible; elle ennuyait sa mère.
Elle aidait sa mère; elle faisait la cuisine avec elle.
Elle taquinait ses deux frères.
Elle ne faisait jamais de bêtises.

Note culturelle

Some families in Côte d'Ivoire may only be able to send one child to high school, so being a student like Yapo is a respected privilege. High school is very competitive, and students devote most of their time to their studies. When they do have free time, they often visit relatives and friends, play soccer, or get together to listen to music and discuss the latest family events, such as marriages, initiations, and baptisms.

Comment dit-on...?

Reminiscing

Quand j'étais petit(e), j'étais très pénible! *When I was little, . . .*
Quand ma meilleure amie **était petite,** elle était gentille. *When . . . was little, . . .*
Quand j'avais deux **ans,** je n'étais pas facile! *When I was . . . years old, . . .*

18 La vie à cinq ans

Parlons/Ecrivons Un(e) reporter du journal de ton école te pose des questions sur ton enfance. Réponds à ses questions.

1. Quand tu avais cinq ans, tu étais comment?
2. Tu avais un ou une meilleur(e) ami(e)?
3. Il ou elle était comment?
4. Comment était ta vie quand tu avais cinq ans?

Vocabulaire à la carte

rigolo/rigolote	*funny*
polisson (polissonne)	*naughty*
toujours mal luné(e)	*always in a bad mood*
capricieux (capricieuse)	*temperamental*
coquin(e)	*mischievous*
sage	*well-behaved*
timide	*shy*
calme	*calm*
un petit diable	*a little devil*
un petit ange	*a little angel*

Communication for All Students

Slower Pace

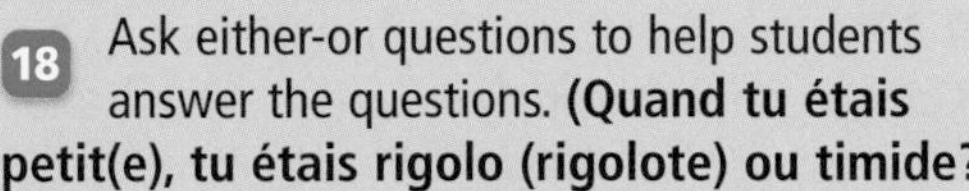

18 Ask either-or questions to help students answer the questions. **(Quand tu étais petit(e), tu étais rigolo (rigolote) ou timide?)**

Challenge

18 Ask students to imagine and describe what their favorite celebrities were like when they were little **(Quand Tom Cruise était petit, il était...).**

Teaching Suggestion

17 As a variation, have students listen to the recording before they open their books. Tell them to take notes (not complete sentences) as the teacher describes her childhood. Then, have students open their books and compare their notes with Yapo's.

Presenting

Comment dit-on... ?, Vocabulaire à la carte

Label two columns on the board **Un petit diable** and **Un petit ange** and draw a picture to illustrate each label. Write the other vocabulary words on separate flashcards. Then, describe how you were and how your imaginary brother or sister was when you were little. **(Moi, quand j'étais petit(e), j'étais un petit ange, bien sûr! Mon frère/ma sœur, par contre, était un petit diable!)** Tape the vocabulary words under the appropriate columns as you use them. **(Moi, j'étais sage. Mais mon frère/ma sœur était polisson(ne)!)** Use facial expressions, gestures, and intonation to help convey the meaning of the words.

Deuxième étape

CHAPITRE 8

Teaching Resources
pp. 228–232

PRINT

- Lesson Planner, p. 38
- TPR Storytelling Book, pp. 58–59
- Listening Activities, pp. 60, 64
- Activities for Communication, pp. 45–46, 111, 113–114, 151–152
- Travaux pratiques de grammaire, pp. 65–68
- Grammar Tutor for Students of French, Chapter 8
- Cahier d'activités, pp. 89–91
- Testing Program, pp. 201–204
- Alternative Assessment Guide, p. 39
- Student Make-Up Assignments, Chapter 8

MEDIA

- One-Stop Planner
- Audio Compact Discs, CD 8, Trs. 5–6, 14, 21–22
- Teaching Transparencies: 8-2, 8-B; **Grammaire supplémentaire** Answers; Travaux pratiques de grammaire Answers
- Interactive CD-ROM Tutor, Disc 2

Presenting Grammaire

The imperfect On the board or on a transparency, write several irregular verbs in the **imparfait**, using all the subject pronouns. Ask students if they can figure out what stem is used to form the **imparfait**. Next, write several infinitives on the board and ask students to give the **nous** form of the verb in the present tense. Draw a line through the **-ons** to show how to form the stem. Show flashcards with infinitives and subject pronouns written on them and have students give the **imparfait**. Turn the flashcard to reveal the correct form.

Grammaire

The imperfect

CD-ROM 2 DVD 2

You've already learned to use the imperfect of **être** and **avoir** to tell what things were like in the past or how they used to be. You also use the imperfect when you're talking about *what used to happen* in the past.

- To form the imperfect, you add the appropriate ending to a verb stem.
- The stem of most verbs is the **nous** form of the verb in the present tense without **-ons.** All verbs use the same imperfect endings: **-ais, -ais, -ait, -ions, -iez,** and **-aient.**

faire → nous faisons → **fais-**
aller → nous allons → **all-**

je fais**ais**	nous fais**ions**
tu fais**ais**	vous fais**iez**
il/elle/on fais**ait**	ils/elles fais**aient**

- To make an imperfect form negative, place **ne... pas** around the verb:
  Quand j'étais petit, je **ne** faisais **pas** la sieste.

Grammaire supplémentaire, pp. 241–242, Act. 4–7

Cahier d'activités, pp. 90–91, Act. 13–15

Travaux pratiques de grammaire, pp. 67–68, Act. 11–15

19 Grammaire en contexte

See scripts and answers on p. 217G.

CD 8 Tr. 6

Ecoutons Ecoute la grand-mère de Sandrine qui parle de son enfance. Est-ce que ces phrases sont vraies ou fausses?

1. According to Sandrine's grandmother, life was easier when she was young.
2. Girls went to school.
3. Girls worked harder.
4. She misses her childhood.

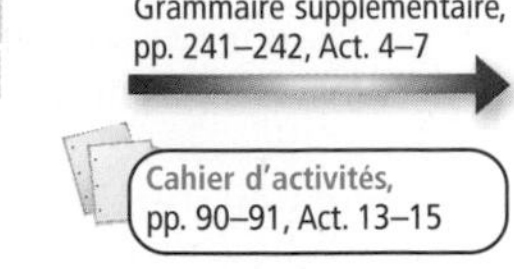

When you're learning the forms of a new verb or verb tense, it often helps to look for patterns to help you remember how to spell the verbs. For example, to remember the endings of the imperfect tense, notice that the **nous** and **vous** stems have the familiar present tense endings with just one difference: an added **i** for imperfect. How could you remember the other endings? Taking a minute to analyze verb forms makes it easy to recall them when you want to communicate in French.

20 Grammaire en contexte

Ecrivons Aimé est un jeune Ivoirien qui a grandi dans un village de Côte d'Ivoire. Dans une lettre à ta classe, il décrit sa vie dans son village. Complète sa lettre avec l'imparfait des verbes proposés. 1. avais 2. était 3. allais 4. rentrait 5. préparait 6. faisions 7. aimais 8. préférait 9. jouaient 10. allions 11. lisait 12. aimiez

lire, avoir, préférer, aimer, rentrer, devoir, être, jouer, aller, préparer, faire, aimer

Quand je (j') __1__ cinq ans, la vie __2__ beaucoup plus facile! Je (J') __3__ à l'école le matin seulement. A midi, mon frère et moi, on __4__ à la maison pour manger. Ma mère __5__ le déjeuner. Après, nous __6__ la sieste. Moi, je (j') __7__ beaucoup dormir, mais mon frère, il __8__ s'amuser. L'après-midi, mon frère et ses amis __9__ au foot. Le soir, nous __10__ souvent chez nos grands-parents. Ma grand-mère nous __11__ toujours des histoires passionnantes. Et vous, est-ce que vous __12__ votre vie quand vous étiez petits?

Connections and Comparisons

Thinking Critically

19 Comparing and Contrasting Ask students to compare the childhood of Sandrine's grandmother with that of Yapo's teacher (Activity 17, page 229). Ask students what they think contributed to the differences. (Sandrine's grandmother grew up in a village, and she is older. Yapo's teacher may have grown up in more modern times.)

STANDARDS: 1.2, 4.1

21 Grammaire en contexte

Parlons/Ecrivons Qu'est-ce que Yapo faisait quand il était plus jeune?

1. Il étudiait avec un copain.

2. Il jouait à l'awalé.

3. Il se baignait.

4. Il allait à l'école.

22 Tu avais une vie facile?

Parlons L'année dernière, qu'est-ce que tu faisais chez toi? Pose des questions à un(e) camarade pour savoir quelles responsabilités il/elle avait. Il/Elle va répondre avec **jamais, quelquefois, d'habitude,** ou **toujours.** Qui avait la vie la plus facile?

1. Tu faisais la vaisselle?
2. Tu gardais ton frère ou ta sœur?
3. Tu lavais la voiture?
4. Tu promenais le chien?
5. Tu sortais la poubelle?
6. Tu faisais la lessive?
7. Tu rangeais ta chambre?
8. Tu passais l'aspirateur?
9. Tu faisais la cuisine?
10. Tu tondais le gazon?

Tu te rappelles?

Do you remember how to pronounce the [ɛ] sound represented by the letters **ais, ait, ê** and **è?** It sounds like the *e* in *pet.* Don't let the sound glide; keep it tense and short. Practice saying this sentence: **Il faisait des bêtises et ennuyait sa mère.**

Note culturelle

Félix Houphouët-Boigny, affectionately called **Papa Houphouët** or **Le Vieux,** was elected as Côte d'Ivoire's first president in 1960 when the country gained independence from France. His presidency was marked by economic prosperity, owing to his support of agriculture and his willingness to foster a close relationship with France. Houphouët-Boigny served as president of Côte d'Ivoire until his death in December 1993. His funeral was held in Yamoussoukro. Because of its distinction as the native village of the president, Yamoussoukro has been built up more than any other town in Côte d'Ivoire, with the exception of Abidjan. Some impressive sights in Yamoussoukro are the Presidential Palace, **la basilique Notre-Dame-de-la-Paix** (the largest basilica in the world), and large four-lane highways lined with towering street lights and trees for miles in both directions.

Deuxième étape

CHAPITRE 8

Teaching Suggestion

21 Ask students to bring in a photo of themselves at a younger age that shows what they used to do. Have them tell their classmates about it. Give students the option of bringing in magazine or catalogue pictures instead of a photo so they can "invent" their childhood, if they prefer.

Music Link

For additional practice with the **imparfait,** play the song *Le bon roi Dagobert* (Audio CD 9, Track 25) for students, asking them to pay attention to the verbs. Then, distribute copies of the lyrics *(Listening Activities,* page 74) to pairs of students. Have them read the song, underline the verbs that are in the **imparfait,** and write the infinitives of the verbs next to them.

Career Path

Working for the Peace Corps is an exciting way to meet people in other countries and to learn about their culture. The Peace Corps is present in countries all over the world, but if you speak French, there is a chance you could work in Africa. Depending on their skills, Peace Corps volunteers might help repair or build homes, provide medical assistance, or teach French and/or English. Ask students what other types of humanitarian organizations they know of and why it's so important that people of those organizations speak more than one language.

Cultures and Communities

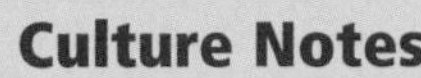

Culture Notes

- Before Côte d'Ivoire's independence in 1960, Félix Houphouët-Boigny became the first African to hold a cabinet post in the French government. While his West African counterparts were stressing nationalism in the early post-independence years (1960s), the Ivorian president continued to use France's resources to aid in the growth and modernization of his country and the betterment of his people.
- When foreign dignitaries would visit Côte d'Ivoire, the president would take them to Yamoussoukro. These days were declared holidays, and school children would line the streets waving and greeting the president and his guests.

STANDARDS: 1.1, 2.2, 5.1, 5.2

Deuxième étape

CHAPITRE 8

Presenting Vocabulaire à la carte

Draw or gather pictures or objects to represent the vocabulary. Show the pictures or objects, say the French name, and have students repeat after you. Then, while holding up the picture or object, ask questions, such as **Tu jouais aux billes quand tu étais petit(e)? Qui avait une poupée? Comment est-ce qu'elle s'appelait? Tu avais un nounours? Il était comment?**

Building on Previous Skills

25 Help students transfer the expressions for emphasizing they learned in the present tense to the **imparfait. (Ce que j'aimais surtout, c'était... , Ce qui me plaisait, c'était...)**

Game

Charades Form groups of five. Have students take turns acting out what they did when they were little. The others should try to guess, using the **imparfait. (Tu faisais la sieste.)** The student who guesses correctly scores a point.

Assess

- Testing Program, pp. 201–204 Quiz 8-2A, Quiz 8-2B Audio CD 8, Tr. 14
- Student Make-Up Assignments, Chapter 8, Alternative Quiz
- Alternative Assessment Guide, p. 39

23 Devine!

Lisons D'abord, trouve les mots suivants dans le questionnaire. A ton avis, qu'est-ce qu'ils veulent dire en anglais? Ensuite, réponds aux questions du sondage.

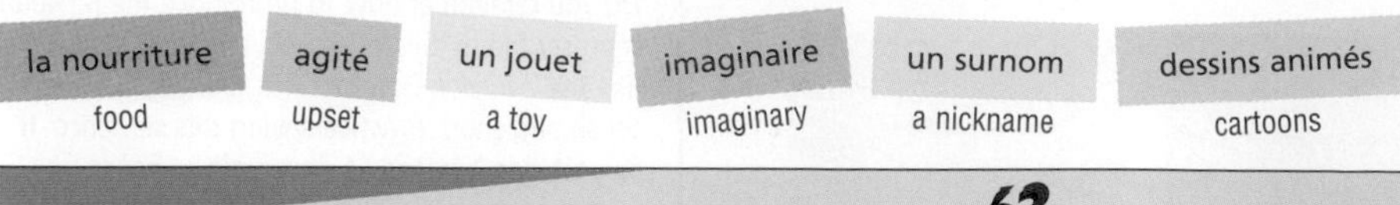

la nourriture
food
agité
upset
un jouet
a toy
imaginaire
imaginary
un surnom
a nickname
dessins animés
cartoons

Connais-tu bien ton passé?
Tu étais comment quand tu étais enfant... mignon(ne)? pénible? Fais ce jeu-test pour te rappeler ton enfance. Est-ce que tu t'en souviens bien?
1. Quelle était ta nourriture préférée quand tu étais bébé?
2. Tu étais calme ou agité(e) comme bébé?
3. A deux ans, est-ce que tu avais un jouet préféré? Lequel?
MON P'TIT BICHON, MON POULET... MON BIQUET...
MA PUCE... MON POUSSIN.. MON FITOU..
4. Est-ce que tu avais un surnom quand tu étais petit(e)? Lequel?
5. Est-ce que tu avais un(e) ami(e) imaginaire? Comment s'appelait-il ou elle? Qu'est-ce qu'il ou elle faisait?
SCHTROUMPFS®
MICKEY MOUSE®
ASTERIX®
SNOOPY®
BABAR®
BANDES DESSINÉES
6. Tu lisais des bandes dessinées ou tu regardais des dessins animés? Lesquels? Quels étaient tes personnages préférés?

24 Une enquête

Parlons Utilise le sondage de l'activité 23 pour interviewer quatre camarades. Pour chaque question, fais une liste des réponses populaires.

25 Mon journal

Ecrivons Comment étais-tu quand tu étais enfant? Qu'est-ce que tu faisais? Comment était ta vie? Qu'est-ce que tu regrettes de ton enfance?

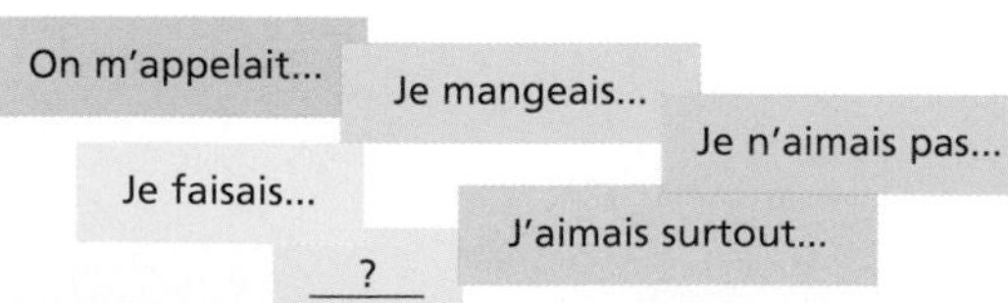

On m'appelait...
Je mangeais...
Je n'aimais pas...
Je faisais...
J'aimais surtout...
?

Vocabulaire à la carte

un tricycle	*a tricycle*
un nounours	*a teddy bear*
une couverture	*a blanket*
un bac à sable	*a sandbox*
une poupée	*a doll*
un train électrique	*a train*
un ballon	*a ball*
des cubes (m.)	*blocks*
des billes (f.)	*marbles*

Cultures and Communities

Family Link

Have students bring in a baby picture of themselves. If they prefer, they could draw a picture of themselves when they were a baby. Have them ask a parent or other family members what they used to do when they were younger, using the questions from Activity 23 as a guide. Then have students write a story about themselves when they were young. When finished, they should exchange papers with a partner for proofreading. Students then write a final copy and attach their baby picture/drawing to the page. Finally, have students display their story on their desk and ask one another questions about when they were young.

STANDARDS: 1.1, 1.3, 3.1, 5.1, 5.2

Est-ce que tu préfères la vie en ville ou à la campagne? Pourquoi?

We asked some French-speaking people whether they would prefer to live in the city or the country and why. Here's what they had to say.

Jacques, Québec

«J'aime les deux. J'aime bien vivre à la ville à cause de toutes les commodités qu'on y retrouve, mais j'aime bien partir les fins de semaines, ou durant les vacances, pour me rendre à la campagne.»
Tr. 8

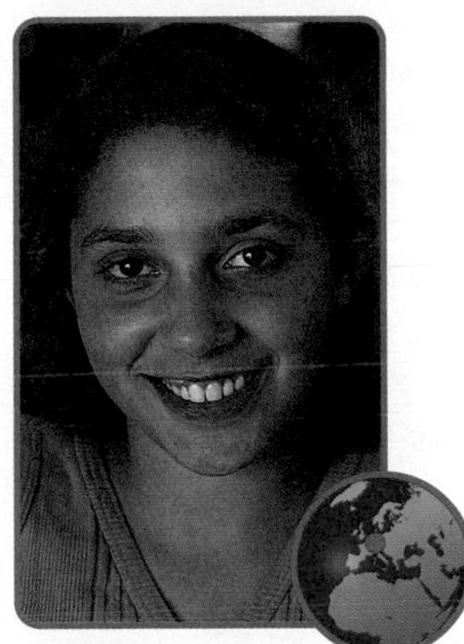

Onélia, France

«[En ville,] on peut sortir quand on veut. On n'a pas besoin des parents qui nous emmènent et nous ramènent en voiture. C'est plus pratique. On peut inviter des amis et sortir ensemble. Je trouve que c'est un avantage.»
Tr. 9

Céline, Viêt-nam

«[A la campagne,] il n'y a pas de pollution. C'est plus... C'est mieux pour respirer. C'est plus agréable et, par exemple, il n'y a pas de bruit comme tout à l'heure là. Et on est plus au calme et il y a moins de voleurs, aussi.» Tr. 10

Qu'en penses-tu?

1. According to these people, what are the advantages and disadvantages of living in the city? In the country? *In the city:* more convenient; teenagers don't need rides from their parents; it's easy to go out with friends *In the country:* no pollution; not as noisy; people are calmer; less crime
2. Do you agree or disagree with the interviewees? Why?
3. Which of these advantages or disadvantages apply to where you live? Which don't?
4. Can you think of other reasons why you might prefer living in the country or in the city?
5. How might your life be different if you lived in a small town, a big city, or an African village?

Communication for All Students

Challenge

Ask a few students who feel strongly about either city or country life to try to convince their classmates that their preference is the better lifestyle. You might form two teams and debate the topic. **(Vivre en ville ou à la campagne. Que choisir?)**

CHAPITRE 8

Teaching Resources
p. 233

PRINT

- Video Guide, pp. 53–55
- Cahier d'activités, p. 96

MEDIA

- One-Stop Planner
- Video Program, Videocassette 3, 29:15–34:12
- DVD Tutor, Disc 2
- Audio Compact Discs, CD 8, Trs. 7–10
- Interactive CD-ROM Tutor, Disc 2

Presenting
Panorama Culturel

Have students view the video and say as much as they can about the interviews. Ask them the **Questions** below to check comprehension. Finally, have students work in small groups to discuss the questions in **Qu'en penses-tu?**

Questions

1. **Qui préfère la campagne? La ville? Qui aime les deux?** (Céline; Onélia; Jacques)
2. **Quand est-ce que Jacques aime aller à la campagne?** (les fins de semaine ou pendant les vacances)
3. **Pourquoi est-ce qu'Onélia préfère la ville?** (On peut sortir quand on veut.)
4. **Pourquoi est-ce que Céline préfère la campagne?** (Il n'y a pas de pollution, c'est moins bruyant et c'est plus calme.)

STANDARDS: 1.2, 2.1, 3.2, 4.2

Teaching Resources
pp. 234–237

PRINT

- Lesson Planner, p. 39
- TPR Storytelling Book, pp. 60–61
- Listening Activities, pp. 61, 65
- Activities for Communication, pp. 47–48, 112, 114, 151–152
- Travaux pratiques de grammaire, pp. 69–70
- Grammar Tutor for Students of French, Chapter 8
- Cahier d'activités, pp. 92–94
- Testing Program, pp. 205–208
- Alternative Assessment Guide, p. 39
- Student Make-Up Assignments, Chapter 8

MEDIA 

- One-Stop Planner
- Audio Compact Discs, CD 8, Trs. 11, 15, 23–24
- Teaching Transparencies: 8-3, 8-C; **Grammaire supplémentaire** Answers; Travaux pratiques de grammaire Answers
- Interactive CD-ROM Tutor, Disc 2

Bell Work
Have students copy and complete the following sentence starters, using different verbs in the **imparfait.**

1. **Quand j'avais six ans...**
2. **Quand ma grand-mère était jeune...**
3. **Quand nous étions jeunes, mon meilleur ami (ma meilleure amie) et moi...**

Teaching Suggestion
Read the letter and the photo captions aloud as students listen with their books closed. Then, ask them if Sandrine still feels the way she did in the **Mise en train.** Have them describe her mood and tell what she is doing in Abidjan.

Troisième étape

Objectives Making and responding to suggestions

WA3 COTE D'IVOIRE-8

Chers Papa et Maman,

J'espère que vous allez bien. Ici, tout va bien. Abidjan, c'est pas mal comme ville et je commence à m'y faire. J'ai pensé que ça vous ferait plaisir si je vous envoyais quelques photos pour vous donner une idée de ce que je fais. Ici, c'est très animé comme vous pouvez le remarquer et il y a des tas de choses à voir. Je n'ai vraiment pas le temps de m'ennuyer, mais je pense quand même beaucoup à vous, et je dois dire que notre petit village me manque un peu. Bon, je dois vous quitter. Tante Adela m'appelle pour le dîner. Donnez mon bonjour à tout le monde.

A bientôt. Grosses bises.
Sandrine

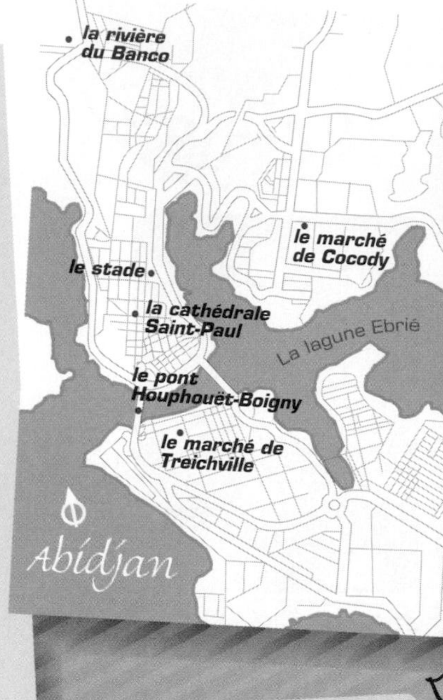

A Abidjan, il y a des mosquées dont l'architecture est très traditionnelle.

On voit aussi des bâtiments super modernes comme cette cathédrale, par exemple.

Ça, c'est le marché de Treichville. On peut y acheter toutes sortes de choses.

Communication for All Students

Teaching Suggestion
Read aloud the captions of the photos as students read along in their books. Then, ask questions about the photos. **(Où est-ce qu'on peut boire quelque chose? Où est-ce qu'il y a des poteries? Où est-ce qu'on vend des tissus? Où voyez-vous un pagne?)** Have students point to the photo in their book that answers each question. Next, have students work in pairs. Have one partner cover the captions of the photos in his or her book with pieces of paper and the other read the captions aloud in random order one at a time. The first partner will point to the photo that matches the caption being read.

STANDARDS: 1.2, 2.2, 3.1

A Cocody, on vend surtout des tissus. Il y en a de toutes les couleurs.

D'ailleurs, j'y ai acheté un pagne. Comment vous le trouvez?

Ça, c'est un maquis. Quand il fait chaud, c'est agréable d'y boire une boisson rafraîchissante.

C'est un marché d'artisans. J'adore la poterie, les paniers et les masques.

Note culturelle

Abidjan is Côte d'Ivoire's main city, although in 1983 the political capital was officially transferred to Yamoussoukro, the birthplace of former president Félix Houphouët-Boigny. As Abidjan's population has grown from just a few hundred thousand to over 2 million today, so has its diversity. Now you can see modern skyscrapers and European-style office buildings in the Plateau and Cocody regions as well as traditional African-style marketplaces in Treichville. Known as the "melting pot" of Africa, Abidjan is home to many people from Côte d'Ivoire's 60 different ethnic groups.

26 Qu'est-ce qu'il y a? See answers below.

Parlons/Ecrivons Qu'est-ce qu'il y a sur les photos de Sandrine? Qu'est-ce que tu voudrais voir à Abidjan? Réponds en anglais.

Culture Notes

- Abidjan, located on the inland Ebrié Lagoon, was a small town until 1950, when a canal was completed to link the lagoon with the ocean, making Abidjan a major port.
- Towns, villages, and ethnic groups are known for their particular crafts. The town of Man, in western Côte d'Ivoire, is known for its masks and panther-dance dolls. In and around Yamoussoukro and Bouaké, north of Yamoussoukro, the Baoulé are known for their gold jewelry and beautiful woven blankets.

Thinking Critically

Synthesizing Have students suggest American cities that would be considered a "melting pot."

Cultures and Communities

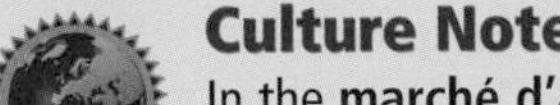

Culture Note

In the **marché d'artisans,** prices are rarely marked, since merchants expect customers to bargain for what they buy. **Pagnes** and **tissu** *(fabric/cloth)* can be made of cotton, rayon, blends, or wax, which is the most expensive. Authentic masks can be quite expensive, especially if made of ebony **(ébène)** (see Culture Note on page 221). Bracelets, necklaces, and earrings can be made of wood, silver, gold, bronze, bone, plastic, or glass beads.

Answers

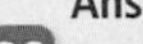

26 a mosque, a cathedral, the Treichville market, cloth from the Cocody market, an outdoor restaurant; *Answers will vary.*

Teaching Resources
pp. 234–237

PRINT

- Lesson Planner, p. 39
- TPR Storytelling Book, pp. 60–61
- Listening Activities, pp. 61, 65
- Activities for Communication, pp. 47–48, 112, 114, 151–152
- Travaux pratiques de grammaire, pp. 69–70
- Grammar Tutor for Students of French, Chapter 8
- Cahier d'activités, pp. 92–94
- Testing Program, pp. 205–208
- Alternative Assessment Guide, p. 39
- Student Make-Up Assignments, Chapter 8

MEDIA 

- One-Stop Planner
- Audio Compact Discs, CD 8, Trs. 11, 15, 23–24
- Teaching Transparencies: 8-3, 8-C; **Grammaire supplémentaire** Answers; Travaux pratiques de grammaire Answers
- Interactive CD-ROM Tutor, Disc 2

Presenting Vocabulaire

Talk about each picture, using synonyms, gestures, and drawings, and then ask questions about them. **(Avez-vous déjà visité une mosquée? Quel tissu préférez-vous? Que porte la femme dans son pagne? Combien de masques voyez-vous? Que font les gens au maquis? Avez-vous déjà fait de la poterie?**

Language Note

Tell students that **une poterie/des poteries** is used to refer to objects, whereas **de la poterie** refers to the craft.

Vocabulaire

Au marché à Abidjan

CD-ROM 2 DVD 2

une mosquée

des tissus (m.)

un pagne*

un masque

un maquis

des poteries (f.)

des tam-tam (m.)

des paniers (m.)

* a 2½-meter piece of Ivorian cloth used to make skirts, shirts, head wraps, or baby slings

Travaux pratiques de grammaire, p. 69, Act. 16–17

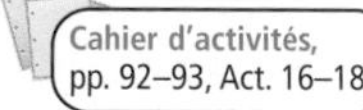
Cahier d'activités, pp. 92–93, Act. 16–18

27 En visite à Abidjan See scripts and answers on p. 217H.

CD 8 Tr. 11

Ecoutons Justin is giving Mamadou a tour of Abidjan. Listen to the following conversations. Where is each one taking place?

a. devant un maquis
b. devant une mosquée
c. près d'un marché d'artisans
d. à la cathédrale
e. près du marché de Cocody

28 Bienvenue à Abidjan!

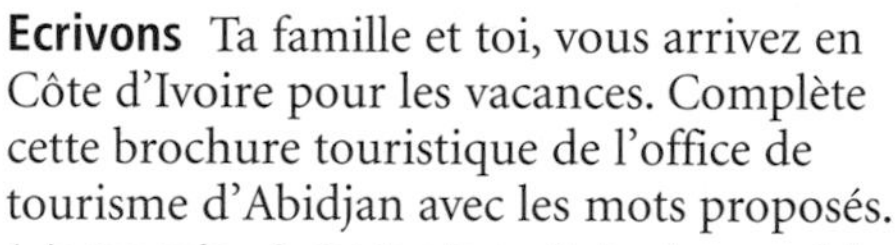

Ecrivons Ta famille et toi, vous arrivez en Côte d'Ivoire pour les vacances. Complète cette brochure touristique de l'office de tourisme d'Abidjan avec les mots proposés.

les masques | la mosquée | des pagnes | un panier | un maquis | la poterie | des tissus | des tam-tam

1. la mosquée 2. des tam-tam 3. des tissues 4. la poterie

Voici quelques attractions à ne pas manquer : si vous aimez les monuments, allez visiter __1__ . Au marché de Treichville, on peut trouver toutes sortes d'objets : __2__ pour faire de la musique; __3__ de toutes les couleurs pour faire des vêtements; des vases, si vous aimez __4__ . N'oubliez pas d'aller admirer __5__ en bois qu'on porte pendant les fêtes. A Treichville, les dames qui veulent s'habiller à l'ivoirienne peuvent aussi acheter __6__ . Et pour porter tous les magnifiques cadeaux que vous avez trouvés au marché, achetez __7__ . Finalement, allez déguster des spécialités ivoiriennes dans __8__ .

5. les masques 6. des pagnes 7. un panier 8. un maquis

Cultures and Communities

Culture Note

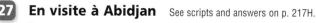

A **maquis** is an outdoor restaurant where people socialize. At a typical **maquis,** there are usually several wooden tables covered with plastic tablecloths and surrounded by wooden chairs. A menu lists what is served, but what is actually available depends on the season of the year, the time of day, the day of the week, and when the owner last went to the market. There is loud music and good food: chicken and rice with various sauces; fried plantains **(aloco);** spaghetti with a sauce of palm oil and tomato paste; rice made with tomato paste, palm oil, and hot pepper **(riz gras);** and omelettes served with bread.

STANDARDS: 1.2, 2.1, 3.2

29 Des souvenirs

Ecrivons Imagine que tu es Thomas, un élève parisien en vacances à Abidjan. Ecris une lettre à ta mère. Décris où tu es allé, ce que tu as fait et dis quels souvenirs tu as achetés.

Comment dit-on...?

Making and responding to suggestions

To make suggestions:

Si on allait au stade pour voir un match de foot?
Si on achetait un pagne au marché?
Si on visitait la mosquée?
Si on jouait du tam-tam?

To respond to suggestions:

D'accord.
C'est une bonne idée.
Bof.
Comme tu veux. *It's up to you.*
Non, je préfère...
Non, je ne veux pas.

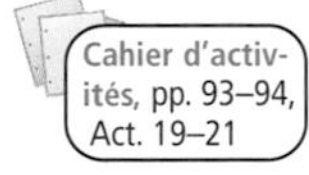

Cahier d'activités, pp. 93–94, Act. 19–21

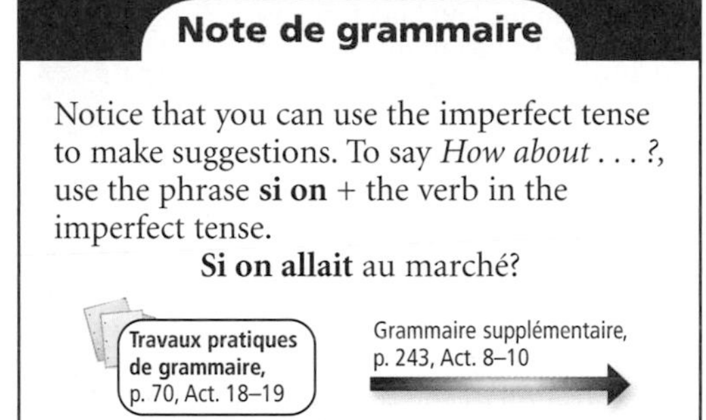

Note de grammaire

Notice that you can use the imperfect tense to make suggestions. To say *How about . . . ?*, use the phrase **si on** + the verb in the imperfect tense.

Si on allait au marché?

Travaux pratiques de grammaire, p. 70, Act. 18–19

Grammaire supplémentaire, p. 243, Act. 8–10

30 Grammaire en contexte

Parlons Propose ces activités à ton ami(e). Il/Elle va accepter ou refuser. Ensuite, changez de rôle. Possible answers:

1. Si on jouait du tam-tam?

2. Si on jouait au foot?

3. Si on achetait des poteries?

4. Si on mangeait dans un maquis?

31 Que faire en ville?

Parlons Aujourd'hui, tu vas visiter Abidjan avec ton correspondant ivoirien (ta correspondante ivoirienne). Choisissez ce que vous allez faire le matin, l'après-midi et le soir.

32 De l'école au travail

Parlons Imagine que tu travailles pour une agence de voyages ivoirienne. Tu dois organiser une visite d'Abidjan pour un groupe d'étudiants français. Qu'est-ce que tu vas leur suggérer?

Communication for All Students

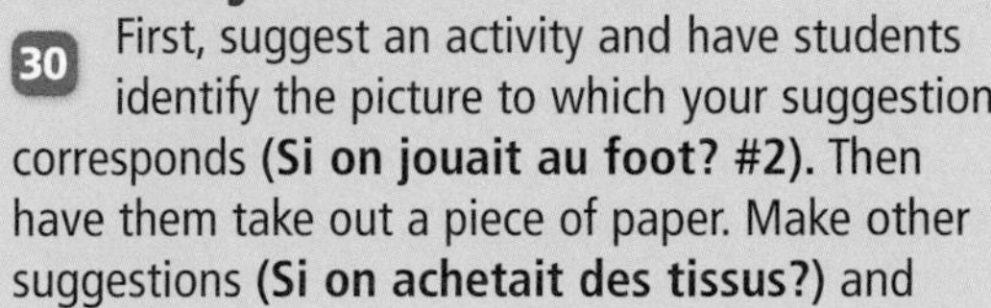

Auditory/Visual Learners

30 First, suggest an activity and have students identify the picture to which your suggestion corresponds **(Si on jouait au foot? #2).** Then have them take out a piece of paper. Make other suggestions **(Si on achetait des tissus?)** and have students illustrate the suggestions you are making. After you have finished, students refer to their illustrations to make suggestions to a partner. The partner should point to the picture that prompted the suggestion.

Teaching Suggestion

29 Ask students to suggest what an Ivorian student visiting their town might buy as a souvenir to take back home.

Presenting
Comment dit-on... ?

On a transparency, draw several places to visit in Abidjan. On another transparency, draw and cut out some smiling faces, frowning faces, and indifferent faces. Then, propose things to do **(Si on allait au musée?)** and respond in a different voice. **(Bof.)** Put a face that represents your answer in the appropriate place on the transparency. Then, repeat the suggestions and have students answer, using the faces as cues. Next, read **Comment dit-on... ?** with students. Suggest going somewhere and have individuals respond.

Teaching Suggestion

Have students draw a map of Abidjan like the one on page 234. Then, have them draw and cut out small pictures of things to buy at the places labeled on the map. Next, have them suggest doing something with a partner **(Si on allait au marché pour acheter un panier?),** placing the object they mention **(le panier)** on the map in the appropriate place **(le marché).** The partner accepts and the cutout is left in place, or he or she refuses and the cutout is changed or removed. Students take turns.

Assess

- Testing Program, pp. 205–208
  Quiz 8-3A, Quiz 8-3B
  Audio CD 8, Tr. 15
- Student Make-Up Assignments, Chapter 8, Alternative Quiz
- Alternative Assessment Guide, p. 39

Lisons!

CHAPITRE 8

Teaching Resources
pp. 238–239

PRINT 
- Lesson Planner, p. 40
- Cahier d'activités, p. 95
- Reading Strategies and Skills Handbook, Chapter 8
- Joie de lire 2, Chapter 8
- Standardized Assessment Tutor, Chapter 8

MEDIA
- One-Stop Planner

Prereading
Activity A

Teaching Suggestion
You might give students a short passage in English and ask them to identify linking words and pronouns before beginning the fable.

Reading
Activities B–E

Language Arts Links/ Paraphrasing
B. • Review the definition of *paraphrasing* before beginning this activity. Make sure students know what a *synonym* is.

• Point out the narrative structure of the tale. The quotation marks indicate that it is a story told within a story. At the end of the tale, students discover the name of the narrator (Leuk-le-Lièvre).

Language Note
Point out the use of the **passé simple** in the fifth paragraph **(partirent, déclara).** Tell students that this is a written, not a spoken, verb form used instead of the **passé composé** in literary and historical texts. Students will learn more about the **passé simple** in Level 3.

Answers
A. 3. to explain new vocabulary, to check for understanding, to discuss the story, to practice grammar functions

Lisons!

Une fable africaine

Stratégie pour lire
If you drive a car, you know that signs are important. Signs tell you when and where to go, what streets you're looking for, and how fast you may drive. When you're reading, look for *linking words* and *pronouns.* These signs help you understand a story. Linking words indicate when events occur, and pronouns help you keep track of who's doing what.

A. Preview the pictures, titles, and organization of the reading.
1. What kind of book is this?
   a. a textbook about rabbits
   b. a reading book for young students
   c. an African history book
2. What is the hare's name?
   a. Senghor **c.** Leuk
   b. Sadji
3. What is the purpose of the activities at the end of the story? See answers below.

B. Paraphrase the definitions in the **Que signifie?** activity by choosing synonyms for the words or phrases in italics in the following sentences. Based on these words, can you guess what the story will be about?
1. **Un philtre** est ***un breuvage*** qui possède un pouvoir extraordinaire.
   a. une boisson **b.** un homme
2. **Un prétendant** est celui qui veut ***épouser*** une jeune fille.
   a. rencontrer
   b. se marier avec

L. SENGHOR & A. SADJI
LA BELLE HISTOIRE DE
LEUK-LE-LIÈVRE
Cours Elémentaire
des écoles d'Afrique Noire
HACHETTE · EDICEF

78. – Les questions difficiles (suite)

« Trois jeunes hommes aimaient une même jeune fille et chacun d'eux voulait l'épouser. Tous trois possédaient un savoir très étendu.

« Le premier pouvait voir ce qui se passait à des milliers de kilomètres. Son regard traversait les forêts les plus épaisses, passait par-dessus la montagne la plus haute et rien ne pouvait l'arrêter.

« Le deuxième possédait une peau de mouton qui, rapide comme l'éclair, vous transportait d'un lieu à un autre, instantanément. Sur cette peau, pouvait prendre place un nombre considérable de personnes.

« Le troisième avait un philtre• qui redonnait la vie aux morts. Il suffisait d'en verser quelques gouttes dans leurs narines.

« Les trois jeunes hommes partirent ensemble pour rendre visite à la belle jeune fille. Chacun d'eux cachait aux autres le pouvoir qu'il détenait. Chacun croyait qu'à leur arrivée il triompherait de ses camarades. En chemin, ils causaient comme de bons amis, lorsque, tout à coup, le prétendant• qui avait la vue longue et perçante déclara :

« — Tiens, tiens, la jeune fille vers qui nous allons est décédée. Je vois qu'on l'a emmenée au cimetière. La fosse est déjà creusée, le cortège• est debout et les fossoyeurs• s'apprêtent à l'enterrer. Quel malheur, les amis! Je vois cela, mais nous n'avons aucun moyen, ni vous ni moi, d'arracher cette jeune et belle personne à la mort.

« — J'ai, dit le second, le moyen de vous

Cultures and Communities

Culture Note
The stories in this book are based on African folktales, retold in French for elementary school children who are learning French. The main character in this tale is Leuk, a clever hare who sets out on a journey during which he meets all kinds of animals and people who teach him lessons about life.

Teacher Note
Léopold Sédar Senghor, born in Senegal in 1906 to a wealthy merchant family, was educated by Europeans, first in Dakar, and finally, in France. He taught in a French **lycée.** Although he was influenced by European philosophy, he became the leader of a group of Africans who wanted to return to the source of their culture. Senghor was the first president of Senegal from 1960 until 1981.

STANDARDS: 1.2, 2.2, 3.1, 3.2

transporter immédiatement à ce cimetière. Mais à quoi bon puisque nous ne pourrons que regarder enterrer la jeune fille? Aucun de nous, en effet, n'est capable de la ressusciter.

« — Emmène-nous toujours, si tu le peux, jusqu'au cimetière, dit le troisième. Nous verrons bien.»

« L'homme tire, de son vêtement, la peau de mouton sur laquelle les trois compagnons prennent place. En un clin d'œil, les voilà arrivés au cimetière, près de la fosse ouverte où la jeune fille doit être ensevelie.

« Alors le troisième prétendant prend le philtre magique, le philtre qui ressuscite les morts. Il en verse quelques gouttes dans les narines de la morte. Aussitôt celle-ci se redresse, éternue trois fois, et regarde tout le monde, l'air étonné. Elle est sauvée.

« On demande, dit encore Leuk, quel est, de ces trois prétendants, celui qui méritait d'épouser la jeune fille. »

Que signifie? philtre : breuvage qui possède un pouvoir extraordinaire — **prétendant :** celui qui veut épouser une jeune fille — **cortège :** ensemble des personnes qui accompagnent un vivant ou un mort — **fossoyeur :** homme chargé de creuser la tombe d'un mort.

Pourquoi et comment?
1. Dites quel pouvoir possédait chacun des trois prétendants.
2. Pourquoi chacun cachait-il son secret?
3. Quel est celui des trois que la jeune fille va épouser et pourquoi?

Ecrivez. — Grammaire : Accord du sujet avec le verbe. Les pronoms personnels du singulier sont : je, tu, il ou elle, moi, toi, lui ou elle.

Exercice : Accorder, à l'indicatif présent, les verbes avec les pronoms sujets. — Je (partir) pour un long voyage — Tu (vouloir) épouser la belle fille — Elle (habiter) très loin — Il (posséder) un philtre magique — Tu (avoir) une vue perçante — C'est moi qui (voir) la jeune fille morte — C'est toi qui (offrir) la peau.

3. **Un cortège** est ***l'ensemble*** des personnes qui accompagnent un vivant ou un mort.
   a. plusieurs   b. le groupe
4. **Un fossoyeur** est un homme chargé de ***creuser*** la tombe d'un mort.
   a. faire   b. acheter

C. In **Les questions difficiles,** three suitors vie for the hand of a beautiful girl. Read the story and make a chart of the powers and actions of each suitor. See answers below.

D. Look for the following linking words in the story and figure out what's happening at the point where they appear. See answers below.

en chemin	*on the way*
lorsque	*when*
en effet	*in fact, indeed*
en un clin d'œil	*in the wink of an eye*
aussitôt	*right away*

E. Find the following sentences in the story. Then, identify what the italicized pronouns refer to.
   1. Trois jeunes hommes aimaient une même jeune fille et chacun d'eux voulait ***l'***épouser.
      a. chacun des hommes
      b. la jeune fille
   2. Emmène-***nous*** toujours...
      a. le troisième jeune homme et la jeune fille
      b. les trois jeunes hommes
   3. Aussitôt ***celle-ci*** se redresse...
      a. la peau   b. la morte
   4. ... quel est, de ces trois prétendants, ***celui*** qui méritait d'épouser la jeune fille.
      a. le prétendant   b. la fille

F. Answer the questions in the **Pourquoi et comment?** activity. Take a poll to find out who the class thinks will marry the girl. See answers below.

Cahier d'activités, p. 95, Act. 23–24

Lisons!

CHAPITRE 8

Language Note

E. Stress the importance of pronouns in order to avoid repetition. Ask students to imagine how it would sound if a story always referred to its characters by name.

Postreading
Activity F

Terms in Lisons!

Students might want to know the following vocabulary: **épaisse** *(thick);* **une peau de mouton** *(lambskin);* **l'éclair** *(lightning);* **cacher** *(to hide);* **détenir** *(to hold);* **décédée** *(deceased);* **emmener** *(to take away);* **enterrer, ensevelir** *(to bury);* **arracher** *(to rescue from).*

Answers

C. **Le premier:** He had extraordinary vision; He saw the girl being buried in the cemetery.
Le deuxième: He had a magic sheepskin that could transport people anywhere; He transported the other two men and himself to the cemetery.
Le troisième: He had a drink that brought the dead back to life. He brought the girl back to life.

D. **en chemin** — They're going to visit the girl.
lorsque — The man with extraordinary vision notices that the girl is dead.
en effet — The second man is saying that the men are not able to bring the girl back to life.
en un clin d'œil — They arrive at the cemetery.
aussitôt — The girl is saved.

F. 1. **Le premier:** He had extraordinary vision.
Le deuxième: He had a magic sheepskin that could transport people anywhere.
Le troisième: He had a drink that brought the dead back to life.
2. They wanted to impress the girl.
3. Answers will vary.

Connections and Comparisons

Thinking Critically

Drawing Inferences Before they begin Activity B, have students read ***Que signifie?*** at the end of the story. Ask them what they think the four words mean. Ask if they can make any predictions about the plot of the story based on their understanding of these words.

Synthesizing Point out that the story is about three young men and that the number three is also a common element in our fairytales and folklore. Ask students to name other folktales where there is a group of three characters or elements. (Examples include *Goldilocks and the Three Bears, The Three Little Pigs,* and *Three wishes from a genie.)*

Grammaire supplémentaire

CHAPITRE 8

For **Grammaire supplémentaire** Answer Transparencies, see the *Teaching Transparencies* binder.

Answers

1
1. b
2. a
3. a
4. a
5. b
6. b
7. a
8. b
9. a
10. a

2
1. ais, ais
2. ait
3. ait
4. aient
5. aient
6. iez, iez
7. ait, ions
8. ais, ait

3
1. étais
2. avais
3. était
4. étions
5. avait
6. étaient
7. n'avais pas
8. aviez
9. étiez

Grammaire supplémentaire

CD-ROM 2 DVD 2

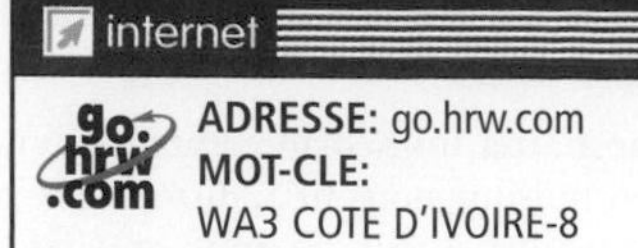

internet
ADRESSE: go.hrw.com
MOT-CLE:
WA3 COTE D'IVOIRE-8

Première étape

Objectives Telling what or whom you miss; reassuring someone; asking and telling what things were like

1 Ton grand-père te parle de sa vie. Lis chaque phrase et dis s'il parle a) de maintenant ou b) de sa jeunesse. (**p. 227**)

1. C'était calme, la campagne.
2. La ville, c'est bruyant.
3. Il y a beaucoup de pollution.
4. Ce n'est pas relaxant.
5. Il y avait de jolies maisons.
6. La vie était plus simple.
7. J'ai beaucoup de temps libre.
8. On avait deux chiens.
9. J'ai beaucoup de choses à faire.
10. C'est plus stressant.

2 Your mother is helping you remember your childhood. Write the endings of the **imparfait** for the verbs **être** and **avoir.** (**p. 227**)

1. Quand tu ét _____ petit tu av _____ un jeune chien.
2. Il ét _____ mignon mais polisson.
3. C'ét _____ vraiment un petit diable.
4. Quelquefois tes grands-parents n'ét _____ pas contents parce que vous faisiez souvent des bêtises dans le jardin.
5. Ils n'av _____ plus de belles fleurs parce que le chien les mangeait.
6. Vous n'av _____ pas de responsabilités et vous ét _____ heureux.
7. Mais notre vie n'ét _____ pas tranquille et nous av _____ beaucoup de soucis.
8. Quand tu ét _____ à l'école, le chien ét _____ triste et toi aussi.

3 Annie décrit sa jeunesse dans son journal. Complète son paragraphe avec l'imparfait des verbes entre parenthèses. (**p. 227**)

Quand j' __1__ (être) jeune, j' __2__ (avoir) beaucoup d'amis. Ma meilleure amie, c' __3__ (être) ma voisine Sandrine. Nous __4__ (être) très bonnes amies. Elle __5__ (avoir) trois frères. Ils __6__ (être) assez pénibles, mais moi, je __7__ (ne pas avoir) de frère, alors j'aimais jouer avec eux. Et vous, vous __8__ (avoir) une amie comme Sandrine quand vous __9__ (être) jeune?

Review and Assess

The **Grammaire supplémentaire** activities were designed as supplemental activities for the grammatical concepts presented in the chapter. You might use them as additional practice, for review, or for assessment.

For more grammar presentations, review, and practice, refer to the following:

- Travaux pratiques de grammaire
- Grammar Tutor for Students of French
- Grammar Summary on pp. R23–R42
- Cahier d'activités
- Grammar and Vocabulary quizzes (Testing Program)
- Test Generator
- Interactive CD-ROM Tutor
- DVD Tutor
- **Jeux interactifs** at go.hrw.com

Deuxième étape

Objective Reminiscing

4 You and your friends are discussing what things were like when you were younger. Complete each sentence below with the appropriate imperfect ending. (**p. 230**)

1. Nous sort _____ souvent le week-end.
2. Colette et Francine fais _____ leurs devoirs dans leur chambre.
3. J'ét _____ très timide.
4. Vous habit _____ à la campagne.
5. Tu all _____ au café avec tes amis.
6. Elles se lav _____ tous les jours à sept heures.
7. Elle av _____ beaucoup d'amis.
8. Nous taquin _____ nos frères et nos sœurs.
9. Je jou _____ au volley-ball.
10. Ton frère ét _____ pénible.

5 Chantal pose des questions à André sur sa vie quand il était petit. Complète leur conversation avec l'imparfait des verbes entre parenthèses. (**p. 230**)

CHANTAL Quand tu __1__ (avoir) cinq ans, où est-ce que tu habitais?

ANDRE Mes parents, mon frère et moi, nous __2__ (habiter) à Paris.

CHANTAL Paris? C' __3__ (être) comment?

ANDRE Il y __4__ (avoir) de jolies maisons dans notre quartier, mais les rues __5__ (être) très bruyantes.

CHANTAL Est-ce que tu __6__ (être) polisson?

ANDRE Non, j'__7__ (être) timide et calme, mais quelquefois je __8__ (taquiner) mon petit frère!

CHANTAL Ton frère et toi, est-ce que vous __9__ (ennuyer) vos parents?

ANDRE De temps en temps, nous __10__ (faire) des bêtises, mais nos parents n' __11__ (avoir) pas vraiment de soucis!

CHANTAL Est-ce que vous regrettez ce temps-là?

ANDRE Oui, c'__12__ (être) le bon temps! Nous n'__13__ (avoir) pas de responsabilités!

MON P'TIT BICHON, MON POULET... MON BIQUET...
MA PUCE... MON POUSSIN.. MON FITOU..

Answers

4
1. ions
2. aient
3. ais
4. iez
5. ais
6. aient
7. ait
8. ions
9. ais
10. ait

5
1. avais
2. habitions
3. était
4. avait
5. étaient
6. étais
7. étais
8. taquinais
9. ennuyiez
10. faisions
11. avaient
12. était
13. avions

Communication for All Students

Game

Course de relais On two sides of the board, write several different sentences with blanks where the verbs should be. Precede each sentence with the infinitive of the verb in parentheses: **(faire) Tu ___ du vélo.** One student at a time from each team goes to the board to write the correct **imparfait** form of the verb in one of the team's sentences. The next team member goes to the board when the preceding player is seated. A student may correct a teammate's mistake or fill in a new blank. Teammates may not call out answers. They may only encourage their teammates. **(Allez! Vite!)** When all sentences are completed on one side, the last student on that team says **Fini!** Stop the race and compare answers. The team with the fewest mistakes wins. You might give different weight to mistakes and blanks left unfilled.

CHAPITRE 8

For **Grammaire supplémentaire** Answer Transparencies, see the *Teaching Transparencies* binder.

Grammaire supplémentaire

WA3 COTE D'IVOIRE-8

6 Certaines choses ne changent jamais. Tes camarades de classe ont les mêmes tâches domestiques que quand ils étaient plus jeunes. Lis ce qu'ils doivent faire maintenant et dis ce qu'ils devaient faire quand ils étaient jeunes. (**p. 230**)

1. Sandrine fait la vaisselle.
2. Paul et Luc tondent le gazon.
3. Vous rangez votre chambre.
4. Je lave la voiture.
5. Tu gardes ton petit frère.
6. Colette et Gérard font la lessive.
7. Christine va au supermarché.
8. Nous avons des responsabilités.
9. Arnaud sort la poubelle.
10. Elles promènent le chien.

7 Antoine était un enfant mal élevé quand il était petit. Lis les phrases suivantes et dis s'il faisait ces choses ou non quand il était petit. (**p. 230**)

EXEMPLE ennuyer sa mère **Antoine ennuyait sa mère.**

1. faire la sieste tous les jours
2. être très méchant
3. jouer avec ses amis
4. faire des bêtises
5. taquiner sa sœur
6. ennuyer son chien
7. conduire la voiture avant d'avoir 18 ans
8. manger des légumes
9. casser tous ses jouets
10. étudier pour l'école

Answers

6
1. Sandrine faisait la vaisselle.
2. Paul et Luc tondaient le gazon.
3. Vous rangiez votre chambre.
4. Je lavais la voiture.
5. Tu gardais ton petit frère.
6. Colette et Gérard faisaient la lessive.
7. Christine allait au supermarché.
8. Nous avions des responsabilités.
9. Arnaud sortait la poubelle.
10. Elles promenaient le chien.

7
1. Antoine ne faisait pas la sieste tous les jours.
2. Antoine était très méchant.
3. Antoine ne jouait pas avec ses amis.
4. Antoine faisait des bêtises.
5. Antoine taquinait sa sœur.
6. Antoine ennuyait son chien.
7. Antoine conduisait la voiture avant d'avoir 18 ans.
8. Antoine ne mangeait pas de légumes.
9. Antoine cassait tous ses jouets.
10. Antoine n'étudiait pas pour l'école.

Review and Assess

Teaching Suggestion

Display magazine pictures of various activities on the chalk tray. Briefly review the imperfect with **Si on... ?** Give students sentences like **Si on faisait les magasins?** and have a volunteer go to the chalk tray and pick up the corresponding picture. The student then gives the picture to another volunteer. When all the pictures have been given to students, review the formation of the imperfect with third-person singular. Then have students at their seats hold up their pictures. Ask questions such as **Qui faisait les magasins?** and have students name the person who is holding the picture of the activity.

STANDARDS: 1.2

Troisième étape

Objectives Making and responding to suggestions

Grammaire supplémentaire

CHAPITRE 8

8 Qu'est-ce que Koffi suggère à Sandrine? Complète ses phrases avec les expressions proposées. (**p. 237**)

un pique-nique sur la plage d'Assinie	dans le quartier du Plateau	à l'awalé
des cadeaux pour tes parents	des chansons traditionnelles de ton village	
la cathédrale Saint Paul	à tes cousins à Korhogo	un jus de fruit au maquis
faire des courses au marché de Treichville	les danseurs yacoubas à la télévision	

1. Si on allait _____ ?
2. Si on achetait _____ ?
3. Si on visitait _____ ?
4. Si on jouait _____ ?
5. Si on buvait _____ ?
6. Si on téléphonait _____ ?
7. Si on regardait _____ ?
8. Si on se promenait _____ ?
9. Si on écoutait _____ ?
10. Si on organisait _____ ?

9 Tu dois suggérer des activités à des étudiants américains qui arrivent en Côte d'Ivoire. D'après ce que chaque personne aime, suggère-leur quelque chose à faire. (**p. 237**)

1. Karen aime beaucoup les jolis vases.
2. Martin aime la musique africaine.
3. Joan aime faire des vêtements.
4. Ethan aime les objets en bois.
5. Myrna aime dîner au restaurant.
6. Patrick aime visiter des monuments.

a. Si on visitait la mosquée?
b. Si on allait voir des masques?
c. Si on allait au maquis?
d. Si on achetait du tissu?
e. Si on allait écouter les joueurs de tam-tam?
f. Si on achetait des poteries?

10 Ton ami et toi, vous essayez de trouver quelque chose à faire aujourd'hui. Lis ce que ton ami dit et fais-lui une suggestion en utilisant **Si on... ?** (**p. 237**)

EXEMPLE J'ai soif. **Si on allait boire un jus d'orange?**

1. J'ai envie de voir un peu la ville.
2. Je suis très fatigué(e).
3. J'ai un examen de français demain.
4. J'ai besoin de faire de l'exercice.
5. C'est l'anniversaire de ma mère.
6. Il y a un bon film au ciné à cinq heures.

Answers

8
1. faire des courses au marché de Treichville
2. des cadeaux pour tes parents
3. la cathédrale Saint-Paul
4. à l'awalé
5. un jus de fruit au maquis
6. à tes cousins à Korhogo
7. les danseurs yacoubas à la télévision
8. dans le quartier du Plateau
9. des chansons traditionnelles de ton village
10. un pique-nique sur la plage d'Assinie

9
1. f
2. e
3. d
4. b
5. c
6. a

10
1. Si on se promenait en ville?
2. Si on faisait une sieste?
3. Si on étudiait à la bibliothèque?
4. Si on faisait du jogging?
5. Si on lui achetait un cadeau?
6. Si on allait voir un film?

Review and Assess

You may wish to assign the **Grammaire supplémentaire** activities as additional practice or homework after presenting material throughout the chapter. Assign Activities 1–3 after **Grammaire** (p. 227), Activities 4–7 after **Grammaire** (p. 230), and Activities 8–10 after **Note de grammaire** (p. 237).

To prepare students for the **Etape** Quizzes and Chapter Test, we suggest doing the **Grammaire supplémentaire** activities in the following order. Have students complete Activities 1–3 before Quizzes 8-1A or 8-1B; Activities 4–7 before Quizzes 8-2A or 8-2B; and Activities 8–10 before Quizzes 8-3A or 8-3B.

CHAPITRE 8

The **Mise en pratique** reviews and integrates all four skills and culture in preparation for the Chapter Test.

Teaching Resources
pp. 244–245

PRINT 

- Lesson Planner, p. 40
- TPR Storytelling Book, pp. 62–63
- Listening Activities, p. 61
- Video Guide, pp. 53, 56
- Grammar Tutor for Students of French, Chapter 8
- Standardized Assessment Tutor, Chapter 8

MEDIA 

- One-Stop Planner
- Video Program Videocassette 3, 34:14–37:19
- DVD Tutor, Disc 2
- Audio Compact Discs, CD 8, Tr. 12
- Interactive CD-ROM Tutor, Disc 2

Thinking Critically

1 Analyzing If students were to write their own African folk tale, in which country would it take place and why? Ask students where the story of Mamy Wata takes place and if they usually think of water when they think of Africa. Ask them why this might be a popular folktale in Africa. (Since water is scarce in many parts of Africa, folktales dealing with an abundance of water are prevalent. In this tale, the queen of water provided the animals with plenty of water and allowed the men to fish where they pleased.)

Answers

1
1. the queen of the waters, very generous; She let animals drink from all the bodies of water and let men fish wherever they wanted.
2. He was unhappy; He was crying and groaning.
3. She played with him, taught him how to play the drums, sing, and dance. He was a young man who had been turned into a monster by an evil sorceress.

Mise en pratique

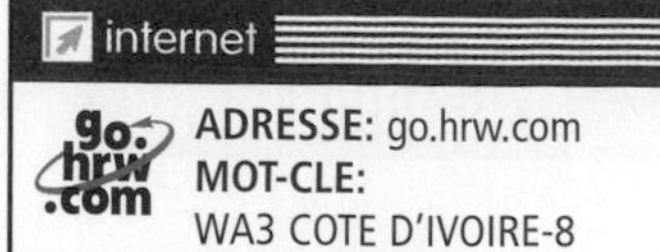

L'HISTOIRE DE MAMY WATA

Mamy Wata, reine des eaux, était très généreuse. Elle laissait les animaux boire dans tous les points d'eau et les hommes avaient en plus le droit de pêcher partout où ils le désiraient.

Un jour, quand Mamy Wata nageait paisiblement dans une rivière avec quelques gros poissons, on est venu l'avertir qu'à plusieurs kilomètres de là, un horrible monstre terrorisait les habitants des villages riverains.

Mamy Wata a décidé d'aller voir ce qui se passait. On lui a indiqué la grotte dans laquelle le monstre se retirait la nuit pour dormir. Elle s'est cachée dans un coin. Lorsque le monstre est rentré se coucher, elle s'est mise à l'observer. Le monstre ne pouvait pas dormir. Il pleurait et grondait beaucoup, et faisait beaucoup de bruit en respirant.

Mamy Wata a compris que le monstre était malheureux. Elle a inventé des jeux. Elle lui a appris à jouer du tam-tam. Elle lui a appris à chanter et à danser. Le monstre était tellement content d'avoir une amie qu'il s'est mis à rire.

Soudain, alors qu'il riait encore, il s'est aperçu qu'il avait complètement changé. Il était redevenu le jeune homme d'avant! C'était en réalité un jeune homme qu'une méchante sorcière avait un jour changé en monstre!

1 Read *L'histoire de Mamy Wata* and answer the questions. See answers below.

1. Who was Mamy Wata? What was she like? What did she do for animals? And for people?
2. When Mamy Wata first sees the monster, what is he like? What is he doing in his cave?
3. What does Mamy Wata do for the monster? What had happened to the monster?

2 Adamou just moved from Abidjan to a small village. Listen as he talks about what life was like in the city and what it's like now that he lives in a village. Then, list three things in English that Adamou used to do in Abidjan and two things he mentions about the village. See scripts and answers on p. 217H.

CD 8 Tr. 12

Review and Assess

Language Note
Students may want to know the following vocabulary words from *L'histoire de Mamy Wata:* **une reine** *(a queen);* **le droit** *(the right/privilege);* **paisiblement** *(peacefully);* **avertir** *(to warn);* **une grotte** *(a cave);* **se mettre à** *(to begin);* **gronder** *(to groan);* **s'apercevoir** *(to notice).*

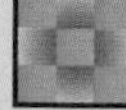

Multicultural Link
Have students find out about folktales from different cultures. Students might do research to find folktales or ask people they know from other cultures. Students might then tell these tales to the class.

STANDARDS: 1.2, 4.2

3 From what you know about the culture of Côte d'Ivoire, answer the following questions. See answers below.

1. How can you tell to which ethnic group someone belongs?
2. If you were a high school student, how would you spend your free time?
3. What are Ivorian villages like?

Ecrivons!

You've just returned from a trip back in time to a culture very different from your own. Write a brief account of what your visit to a different time and place was like.

Stratégie pour écrire
Point of view is a major consideration in describing your experiences. The narrator who tells your story can make a difference in how it's received.

Préparation

You'll first want to choose a time and place for your story and jot down what your visit was like. What was there? What were the people like? Consider which would make more sense, grouping similar ideas together or telling the story in chronological order.

Rédaction

Whom will you choose to tell your story? In the first person point of view, your narrator would most likely be you. You'd use the first person **je** and speak directly to your reader. In the third person point of view, your narrator would be an "outsider looking in" on your story. Characters would be referred to with third person pronouns like **il, elle, ils,** and **elles.** Whichever point of view you choose, make sure you're consistent throughout your story.

Evaluation

To help you decide on an appropriate point of view, you might write two first drafts: one in the first person and one in the third person. Ask a classmate to read both versions or read both versions aloud to a group of classmates and ask them which version is more believable. Based on their comments, you can decide which is better for your story.

Jeu de rôle

With a partner, act out a scene in which a travel agent tries to convince a customer who knows nothing about Africa to visit Abidjan.

- The travel agent suggests Abidjan and describes its advantages.
- The customer asks what there is to see, do, and buy there.
- The customer has false, preconceived notions about the city and Côte d'Ivoire. The agent corrects the customer's false impressions.

Review and Assess

Process Writing

4 To help practice the writing strategy, have students look back at *Leuk-le-Lièvre* and *Mamy Wata* to determine the point of view of each story. You might show them other examples of stories told from different points of view.

Teacher Note

For additional practice and review, you might use the **Histoire Finale** for Chapter 8 on pages 62–63 of the *TPR Storytelling Book.*

Mise en pratique

CHAPITRE 8

Captioned Video/DVD

As a chapter review, write out the conversation from a section of ***La Nostalgie*** and leave out targeted expressions that students have learned in the chapter. Play the video and have students fill in the expressions. Then, play the captioned version on Videocassette 5 or DVD Disc 2 and have students check their answers.

Writing Assessment

4 You might use the following rubric when grading your students on this activity.

Writing Rubric	Points			
	4	3	2	1
Content (Complete–Incomplete)				
Comprehension (Total–Little)				
Comprehensibility (Comprehensible–Incomprehensible)				
Accuracy (Accurate–Seldom accurate)				
Fluency (Fluent–Not fluent)				

18–20: A 14–15: C Under
16–17: B 12–13: D 12: F

Possible Answers

3
1. from their names
2. studying, visiting relatives and friends, playing soccer, listening to music and discussing the latest family events with friends
3. quiet, clean, everyone knows one another; usually the same ethnic group; people make many of the things they need; chickens and goats are common; people cook over open fires; they walk rather than drive; bowls are used without silverware; there are usually no high schools.

CHAPITRE 8

Teaching Resources
p. 246

PRINT 
- Grammar Tutor for Students of French, Chapter 8

MEDIA
- Interactive CD-ROM Tutor, Disc 2
- Online self-test

go.hrw.com
WA3 COTE D'IVOIRE-8

Cooperative Learning
Have students work in groups to answer the questions in **Que sais-je?** Assign one student to read aloud each question to the group. Have another student turn to the page where the answer is found and suggest two answers for each question. Designate a third student to decide on and choose the best answer. Finally, a fourth student should write down the answer chosen as the best response to each question. Have students rotate roles with each question.

Answers
5 1. Yapo taquinait son frère.
2. Nous jouions du tam-tam.
3. Yapo faisait des bêtises.

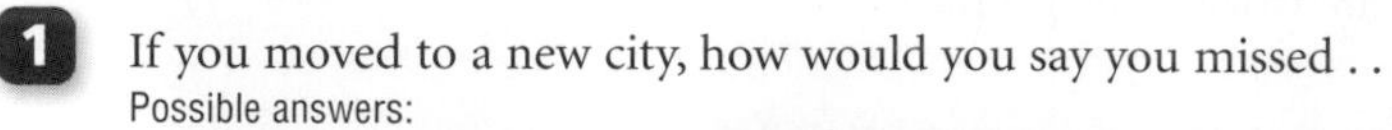

Que sais-je?

WA3 COTE D'IVOIRE-8

Can you use what you've learned in this chapter?

Can you tell what or whom you miss? p. 225

1 If you moved to a new city, how would you say you missed . . .
Possible answers:

1. Ce qui me manque, c'est ma maison.

2. Mon chat me manque.

3. Mes copains me manquent.

Can you reassure someone? p. 225

2 How would you reassure someone who had just moved to your town and was homesick? Possible answers: Tu vas t'y faire. Fais-toi une raison. Tu vas te plaire ici. Tu vas voir, tout le monde est sympa ici.

Can you ask and tell what things were like? p. 226

3 How would you ask your homesick friend what his or her former town was like? Ta ville, c'était comment?

4 How would you describe how things were . . .
1. in medieval times?
2. when you were five?

Can you reminisce? p. 229

5 How would you tell what these people used to do when they were young?
See answers below.

1. Yapo et son frère

2. Tes amis et toi

3. Yapo

6 How would you tell what you usually did after school when you were ten years old? Quand j'avais dix ans, après l'école, je (j')...

Can you make and respond to suggestions? p. 237

7 How would you suggest . . .
1. visiting a place in Abidjan? Si on visitait... ?
2. buying something from the market? Si on achetait... ?
3. playing your favorite game or sport? Si on jouait... ?

8 How would you respond if a friend invited you to . . . Possible answers:
1. play tennis?
2. eat barbecue?
3. visit a museum?
D'accord. C'est une bonne idée. Non, je préfère... Bof. Non, je ne veux pas.

Apply and Assess

Game
Que sais-je? Write the questions from **Que sais-je?** on separate index cards and shuffle them. Form six teams and number them one through six. Have a member of the first team choose a card and read the question aloud. If he or she answers the question correctly, his or her team receives two points and play passes to the next team. If he or she cannot answer the question correctly, the first player on the next team may try to answer for one point. If he or she does not succeed, the question is placed back in the stack of questions. The game is over when all of the questions have been answered.

Vocabulaire

Première étape

Telling what or whom you miss

Je regrette...	*I miss...*
... me manque.	*I miss... (singular)*
... me manquent.	*I miss... (plural)*
Ce qui me manque, c'est...	*What I really miss is...*

Reassuring someone

Tu vas t'y faire.	*You'll get used to it.*
Fais-toi une raison.	*Make the best of it.*
Tu vas te plaire ici.	*You're going to like it here.*
Tu vas voir...	*You'll see...*

Asking and telling what things were like

C'était comment?	*What was it like?*
C'était tellement/si différent?	*Was it really so different?*
C'était...	*It was...*
Il y avait...	*There were...*
La vie était plus..., moins...	*Life was more... , less...*

Describing places

animé(e)	*exciting*
bruyant(e)	*noisy*
calme	*calm*
dangereux (dangereuse)	*dangerous*
génial(e)	*great*
mortel (mortelle)	*deadly dull*
nul (nulle)	*worthless*
propre	*clean*
relaxant(e)	*relaxing*
sale	*dirty*
stressant(e)	*stressful*
tranquille	*peaceful*
très vivant(e)	*very lively*

Deuxième étape

Reminiscing

Quand j'étais petit(e),...	*When I was little, . . .*
Quand il/elle était petit(e),...	*When he/she was little,...*
Quand j'avais... ans,...	*When I was... years old,...*

Activities

avoir des responsabilités	*to have responsibilities*
avoir des soucis	*to have worries*
conduire une voiture	*to drive a car*
faire des bêtises	*to do silly things*
faire la sieste	*to take a nap*
ennuyer	*to bother*
taquiner	*to tease*

Troisième étape

Making and responding to suggestions

Si on allait... ?	*How about going...?*
Si on achetait... ?	*How about buying...?*
Si on visitait... ?	*How about visiting...?*
Si on jouait... ?	*How about playing...?*
D'accord.	*OK.*
C'est une bonne idée.	*That's a good idea.*
Bof.	*(expression of indifference)*
Comme tu veux.	*It's up to you.*
Non, je préfère...	*No, I prefer...*
Non, je ne veux pas.	*No, I don't want to.*

Things to see and buy in Abidjan

un maquis	*popular Ivorian outdoor restaurant*
un masque	*mask*
une mosquée	*mosque*
un pagne	*piece of Ivorian cloth*
des paniers (m.)	*baskets*
des poteries (f.)	*pottery*
un tam-tam	*African drum*
du tissu	*fabric, cloth*

Apply and Assess

Game

Pick phrases to complete and questions to answer from the **Vocabulaire.** Divide the class into two teams. Have a student from each team come to the front of the class. Give the students a phrase to complete or a question to answer, for example: **Quand j'étais petit(e)...** The student who raises his or her hand first gets to answer. If an appropriate response **(Je faisais des bêtises. Je taquinais les autres.)** is given, a point is earned for the team. If not, the other student has a chance to answer and win a point for his or her team. Continue the game until a set number of points is reached.

Vocabulaire

CHAPITRE 8

Circumlocution

Have students work with a partner, one playing the role of a tourist and the other the role of a market vendor. The tourist has lost a bag containing some items purchased at the **marché d'artisans** and is retracing his or her steps to recover the lost bag. The tourist is trying to describe the items that were in the bag, but can't remember the exact words in French. The tourist must use circumlocution to communicate the words that he or she wants the market vendor to understand. Have students switch roles once the vendor has correctly guessed at least two of the words.

Chapter 8 Assessment

- **Testing Program**
  Chapter Test, pp. 209–214

  Audio Compact Discs, CD 8, Trs. 16–18
  Speaking Test, p. 346
- **Alternative Assessment Guide**
  Performance Assessment, p. 39
  Portfolio Assessment, p. 25
  CD-ROM Assessment, p. 53
- **Interactive CD-ROM Tutor, Disc 2**

  A toi de parler
  A toi d'écrire
- **Standardized Assessment Tutor**
  Chapter 8
- **One-Stop Planner, Disc 2**
  Test Generator
  Chapter 8

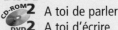

STANDARDS: 1.2

Location Opener

CHAPTER 9

Teaching Resources
pp. 248–251

PRINT 

- Lesson Planner, p. 41
- Video Guide, pp. 57–58

MEDIA

- One-Stop Planner
- Video Program
  Videocassette 3, 37:47–40:31
- DVD Tutor, Disc 2
- Interactive CD-ROM Tutor, Disc 3
- Map Transparency 1

 go.hrw.com
WA3 PROVENCE

Using the Almanac and Map

Terms in the Almanac

- **Marseille,** one of the oldest French cities, is the second largest city in France and the primary seaport.
- **Avignon** gained prominence in 1309 when the French Pope Clement V moved the papal court there, where it remained until 1377.
- **St-Tropez** is known for its beautiful coast and beaches.
- **Cannes** has hosted the world-renowned International Film Festival for more than 40 years.
- **Paul Cézanne** (1839–1906), born in Aix-en-Provence, was an impressionist painter.
- **Marcel Pagnol** (1895–1974), a significant novelist, playwright, and film director, wrote *Jean de Florette* and *Manon des Sources.*
- **bouillabaisse:** a traditional fish soup made with fish and shellfish
- **soupe au pistou:** a vegetable and bean soup flavored with **pistou,** a sauce of basil, garlic, and olive oil
- **daube provençale:** a stew traditionally made with **herbes provençales,** tomatoes, and lamb
- **aïoli:** a strong garlic mayonnaise made with olive oil

CHAPITRES 9,10,11

Allez, viens en Provence!

Population : plus de 4.000.000

Villes principales : Marseille, Aix-en-Provence, Arles, Avignon, Toulon, Saint-Tropez, Nice, Cannes, Nîmes

Ressources et industries : parfum, lavande, olives, herbes provençales

Provençaux célèbres : Paul Cézanne, Marcel Pagnol, Le Corbusier

Spécialités : bouillabaisse, soupe au pistou, daube provençale, aïoli, pissaladière, saucissons, fruits confits, calissons

WA3 PROVENCE

Un paysage provençal typique ▶

Cultures and Communities

Culture Note

The photo spread on pages 248–249 shows a lavender field, a common sight in the Provence region. Because of an abundance of flowers, such as lavender, jasmine, tuberoses, violets, and orange blossom, Provence, and particularly the town of Grasse, has become known for its perfume. Distillation of the essences of the flowers in Grasse began in the sixteenth century. Then, in the nineteenth century, Paris became the center for perfume production, while Grasse continued to provide the raw materials. Three perfumeries in Provence that still offer tours are **Galimard, Molinard,** and **Fragonard.**

STANDARDS: 2.2, 3.1, 5.1

Connections and Comparisons

Thinking Critically

Comparing and Contrasting Have students share what they know about southern France, and then have them look at the photos on pages 248–251. Ask them how **la Provence** is different from the French regions they have previously studied **(Paris et ses environs,** pages xxvi–3; **la Touraine,** pages 124–127).

Language Notes

- **Aix** is a derivation of the Latin word for water **(aquae),** which is **eaux** in modern French. Many towns that include the name **Aix** or **Ax** are famous for their mineral springs: Aix-la-Chapelle (Aachen in German), Aix-les-Bains, and Aix-les-Thermes.
- The city of **Marseille** is written with a final **-s** in English (Marseilles).

Background Information

- Equally influenced by the Greeks and the Romans, **Provence** is known for the beauty and variety of its countryside, the Mediterranean nature of the weather and crops, and the vestiges of past civilizations found at every turn. The rugged areas of the region are dotted with tiny villages, many of which are built on cliffs, and most of the houses are built of limestone and have roofs made of terra-cotta tiles.
- *La Marseillaise,* the French national anthem, was adopted and sung by a regiment from **Marseille,** which is how the song got its name. It was composed in Strasbourg by Rouget de Lisle.
- Most French cities have tourist offices **(Syndicats d'Initiative)** that sell posters **(affiches)** of the region. One poster for Aix-en-Provence bears a reproduction of Cézanne's painting, *la Montagne Sainte-Victoire.*

Teacher Note

For more practice with the Location Opener, have students complete the **Compréhension** questions on Disc 2 of the *DVD Tutor.*

STANDARDS: 2.2, 3.1, 4.1

Location Opener

CHAPTER 9

Using the Photo Essay

1 **Gordes,** a Provençal village built high on a cliff, boasts the Renaissance **château de Gordes,** which is really a fortress. The château was built in the eleventh century and rebuilt in the sixteenth century. Inside the château is the **musée Vasarely,** named after the artist Victor Vasarely, one of the founders of kinetic art. The museum houses many tapestries and works of art.

2 **Les gorges du Verdon** A tributary of the Durance River, the Verdon River has carved out a canyon, the Grand Canyon of the Verdon, which varies in depth from 250 to 700 meters. It is the deepest canyon in Europe, and the view from Point Sublime is breathtaking. A walking path was built in 1928, and a corniche road was built in 1947 to accommodate automobile traffic.

3 **Le pont du Gard,** a remnant of the aqueduct that once brought fresh water from a spring at Uzès to the city of Nîmes, was built in 19 B.C. by the Romans, a testimony to their desire for large quantities of fresh water and to their engineering skills. The entire aqueduct was over 17 kilometers (10.5 miles) long, and therefore vulnerable during times of war. By the fourth century, the bridge was no longer maintained, and local people carried off stones for building. Napoléon III had the bridge restored in the nineteenth century. The aqueduct is made of enormous dry blocks set together with no mortar, and the arches vary in size.

Geography Link

3 A **corniche** is a roadway that winds along a cliff or steep slope.

Provence

La Provence offre une grande variété de paysages : la Côte d'Azur a de belles plages, la Haute-Provence a les Alpes et la Camargue a des chevaux sauvages et des flamants roses. En Provence, on peut aussi voir des forêts de pins et des champs de lavande. Depuis les années 1900, les touristes viennent en grand nombre y passer leurs vacances. Chaque été, des centaines de festivals de toutes sortes attirent aussi un grand nombre de personnes.

internet

go.hrw.com
ADRESSE: go.hrw.com
MOT-CLE: WA3 PROVENCE

1 Les villages perchés
La plupart de ces villages, comme Gordes, ont été construits il y a 500 ans à cause de fréquentes attaques de maraudeurs.

2 Les gorges du Verdon
C'est le Grand Canyon français. A 700 mètres plus bas se trouve la rivière où l'on fait du canoë.

Cultures and Communities

Culture Notes

- The **Camargue** consists of over 300,000 acres of wetlands, pastures, dunes, and salt flats. It is home to an incredible collection of flora, such as tamarisk and narcissi, and fauna, including the egret (similar to a heron) and the ibis (a large wading bird).
- During the Dark Ages (the fifth through the tenth century A.D.), one of the Romance languages that evolved was the **langue d'oc,** or **Occitan.** The numerous variations of **Provençal,** which are spoken today throughout Provence, are dialects of this language.

STANDARDS: 2.2, 3.1

3 Le pont du Gard
C'est un aqueduc de 49 mètres de haut construit par les Romains il y a 2.000 ans.

4 Les calanques de Cassis
A trente minutes de Marseille, les calanques de Cassis offrent un total dépaysement : falaises blanches plongeant dans l'eau turquoise.

5 La Côte d'Azur
Elle est célèbre pour ses plages, ses hôtels et ses boutiques de grand luxe. La Promenade des Anglais à Nice est un lieu touristique très connu.

Aux chapitres 9, 10 et 11, quelques élèves d'Aix-en-Provence vont te montrer leur belle ville. Depuis l'époque des Romains, Aix-en-Provence est la capitale de la Provence. Aujourd'hui, c'est surtout une ville d'art, peuplée d'étudiants en raison de sa célèbre université.

6 Aix-en-Provence
Les jeunes aiment bien se retrouver dans les cafés du **cours Mirabeau,** l'avenue principale de cette belle ville. La célèbre **montagne Sainte-Victoire,** ici peinte par Paul Cézanne, est située à l'est de la ville. Elle attire beaucoup de monde le week-end.

Location Opener

CHAPTER 9

4 Cassis is a fishing port east of Marseilles. The **calanques,** which are deep, narrow arms of the sea enclosed by rugged white limestone cliffs, are sometimes used as natural yacht harbors. They also provide a real challenge for rock climbers. The **calanques** are celebrated in the poem *Calendal,* by Frédéric Mistral, the famous Provençal poet.

5 La Promenade des Anglais, a famous boulevard that extends from one end of Nice's waterfront to the other, is lined with luxury hotels. This eight-lane, five-kilometer highway was built in 1830, and its name reflects the influx of the English, who established Nice as a major resort. It is also the central parade route of Nice and the site of the Carnaval celebration for Mardi Gras and the **bataille de fleurs** in the summer.

5 Nice, located on the **baie des Anges,** is the capital of the Côte d'Azur. The city was founded in 350 B.C. by the Greeks and later colonized by the Romans. In 1814, France lost possession of Nice to the Italians until 1861, when it was reclaimed by the French after the people voted in favor of its return. As a result, there is a distinctive Italian influence in the city.

6 Aix-en-Provence was founded by the Romans in 122 B.C. and became the capital of Provence in the twelfth century. The town's university was built in 1409, and the area became a part of France in 1486.

Language Note

4 The final **-s** in the name of the town **Cassis** is not pronounced, while the final **-s** is pronounced in the name of the fruit, **cassis** *(black currants).*

Connections and Comparisons

Thinking Critically

Observing Ask students to determine from the photos the kinds of activities that are available to residents and tourists in Provence.

Comparing and Contrasting Ask students to think of popular tourist resorts in the United States and compare them to Provence. Have them compare the kinds of activities available in both places and the people who go there.

STANDARDS: 2.2, 3.1, 4.2

Chapitre 9 : Tu connais la nouvelle?

Chapter Overview

Mise en train pp. 254–256	***Il ne faut pas se fier aux apparences***			
	FUNCTIONS	**GRAMMAR**	**VOCABULARY**	**RE-ENTRY**
Première étape pp. 257–261	• Wondering what happened; offering possible explanations; accepting or rejecting explanations, p. 260	• **avoir l'air** + adjective, p. 259	• Feelings, p. 258	• Adjective agreement **(Chapitre 1,** II) • The **imparfait (Chapitre 8,** II)
Deuxième étape pp. 262–266	• Breaking some news; showing interest, p. 263	• The **passé composé** vs. the **imparfait,** p. 265	• Personal happenings, p. 263	• The **passé composé** of reflexive verbs **(Chapitre 7,** II) • Relating a series of events **(Chapitre 4,** II) • The **passé composé (Chapitres 6, 9,** II) • The **imparfait (Chapitre 8,** II)
Troisième étape pp. 267–269	• Beginning, continuing, and ending a story, p. 267	• The **passé composé** and the **imparfait** with interrupted actions, p. 269 • **être en train de,** p. 269		• Relating a series of events **(Chapitre 4,** II) • The **passé composé (Chapitres 6, 9,** II) • The **imparfait (Chapitre 8,** II)

Lisons! pp. 270–271	**La Cantatrice chauve : scène IV**	**Reading Strategy:** Reading with a purpose	
Grammaire supplémentaire	**pp. 272–275** **Première étape,** pp. 272–273	**Deuxième étape,** pp. 273–275	**Troisième étape,** p. 275
Review pp. 276–279	**Mise en pratique,** pp. 276–277 **Ecrivons!** Setting Writing an **histoire marseillaise**	**Que sais-je?** p. 278	**Vocabulaire,** p. 279

CULTURE

- **Note culturelle,** The **cours Mirabeau,** Aix-en-Provence, p. 257
- **Panorama Culturel,** Friendship, p. 261
- **Note culturelle, Histoires marseillaises,** p. 264

Chapitre 9 : Tu connais la nouvelle?

Chapter Resources

Lesson Planning

One-Stop Planner

Lesson Planner with Substitute Teacher

Lesson Plans, pp. 41–45, 71

Student Make-Up Assignments

- Make-Up Assignment Copying Masters, Chapter 9

Listening and Speaking

TPR Storytelling Book, pp. 64–71

Listening Activities

- Student Response Forms for Listening Activities, pp. 67–69
- Additional Listening Activities 9-1 to 9-6, pp. 71–73
- Additional Listening Activities (song), p. 74
- Scripts and Answers, pp. 142–146

Video Guide

- Teaching Suggestions, pp. 60–61
- Activity Masters, pp. 62–64
- Scripts and Answers, pp. 105–107, 122

Activities for Communication

- Communicative Activities, pp. 49–54
- Realia and Teaching Suggestions, pp. 115–119
- Situation Cards, pp. 153–154

Reading and Writing

Reading Strategies and Skills Handbook, Chapter 9

Joie de lire 2, Chapter 9

Cahier d'activités, pp. 97–108

Grammar

Travaux pratiques de grammaire, pp. 71–77

Grammar Tutor for Students of French, Chapter 9

Assessment

Testing Program

- Grammar and Vocabulary Quizzes, **Etape** Quizzes, and Chapter Test, pp. 223–240
- Score Sheet, Scripts and Answers, pp. 241–248

Alternative Assessment Guide

- Portfolio Assessment, p. 26
- Performance Assessment, p. 40
- CD-ROM Assessment, p. 54

Student Make-Up Assignments

- Alternative Quizzes, Chapter 9

Standardized Assessment Tutor

- Reading, pp. 35–37
- Writing, p. 38
- Math, pp. 51–52

Online Activities

- **Jeux interactifs**
- **Activités Internet**

Video Program

- Videocassette 3
- Videocassette 5 (captioned version)

Interactive CD-ROM Tutor, Disc 3

DVD Tutor, Disc 2

Audio Compact Discs

- Textbook Listening Activities, CD 9, Tracks 1–12
- Additional Listening Activities, CD 9, Tracks 19–25
- Assessment Items, CD 9, Tracks 13–18

Teaching Transparencies

- Situation 9-1 to 9-3
- Vocabulary 9-A to 9-B
- **Mise en train**
- **Grammaire supplémentaire** Answers
- **Travaux pratiques de grammaire** Answers

One-Stop Planner CD-ROM

Use the **One-Stop Planner CD-ROM with Test Generator** to aid in lesson planning and pacing.

For each chapter, the **One-Stop Planner** includes:

- Editable lesson plans with direct links to teaching resources
- Printable worksheets from resource books
- Direct launches to the HRW Internet activities
- Video and audio segments
- Test Generator
- Clip Art for vocabulary items

Chapitre 9 : Tu connais la nouvelle?

Projects

Les Informations

The class will create and videotape a French television newscast, using news and sports stories they have written.

MATERIALS

✄ **Students may need**

- Posterboard or butcher paper
- Colored markers
- Videocamera and videocassette
- Computer-generated graphics

SUGGESTED SEQUENCE

1. First, the class decides on the content of the newscast. The news stories should be a mixture of serious and humorous incidents.
2. Partners write news stories to submit for the newscast. They should keep their identities secret by using pen names.
3. Post the articles around the classroom and have students vote for their five favorite stories, ranking each from one to five, with one being the best.
4. Tally the points for each story and select the seven to nine most popular ones. Of these, choose two or three lead stories, three or four on-the-spot stories, and two or three sports stories. Then, form groups and distribute one story to each group for editing. Have students recopy and submit the edited stories for final corrections.
5. Ask for volunteers to read the stories "on the air." There may be as many as two anchorpeople, three or four reporters, and two sportscasters. Next, ask for three volunteers to write scripts to open the newscast, to introduce the on-the-spot stories and sports, and to end the newscast. Assign a student to select background music at the beginning and end of the show, and another student to tape the broadcast. The remaining students will create the set.
6. Allow students time in class to rehearse the show. Then, videotape the broadcast and show the final product to the class and to other French classes.

GRADING THE PROJECT

Suggested Point Distribution: (total = 100 points)

Content	25
Language use	25
Overall presentation	25
Effort/Participation	25

Games

Le Football américain

In this game, students will practice the functions and vocabulary from this chapter.

Preparation

1. Make thirteen cards with the following words written on them: eight with *rush,* three with *pass,* one with *fumble,* and one with *penalty.*
2. Draw a football field on the board, marking off every five yards.
3. Form two teams who will take turns playing offense.

Procedure

1. A member of the offense draws a card from the stack. If the card says *rush* or *pass,* that player must answer a question. If the player answers correctly, he or she rolls one die.
   - For a *rush,* the player doubles the number rolled, and the team advances that number of yards on the board.
   - For a *pass,* the number rolled on the die is multiplied by ten, and the team advances that number of yards on the board.
2. If a player draws the card marked *penalty,* ask a member of the defensive team a question. If the person answers correctly, he or she rolls the die and the number is doubled to determine the number of yards the offense will be penalized.
3. If a player for the offense draws a card marked *fumble,* the defensive team takes the next turn if a team member can correctly answer a question.
4. Whenever the ball changes hands, play always starts on the offensive team's twenty-yard line.
5. A team that crosses the goal line receives six points and a bonus question to try for an extra point.

Questions should require the players to do the following:

- form sentences with adjectives that describe emotional states
- offer possible explanations
- accept and reject possible explanations
- show interest
- use both the **passé composé** and the **imparfait** correctly

STANDARDS: 1.2, 1.3, 5.1, 5.2

Storytelling

Mini-histoire

*This story accompanies Teaching Transparency 9-3. The **mini-histoire** can be told and retold in different formats, acted out, written down, and read aloud, to give students additional opportunities to practice all four skills. The following story relates a bad weekend for two friends.*

Paul a rencontré Manon jeudi dernier. Il l'a trouvée sympa et lui a proposé de faire une promenade en moto le week-end suivant. Samedi après-midi, Paul a retrouvé Manon chez elle et ils sont partis. Il faisait très beau, et ils étaient tous les deux de bonne humeur. Malheureusement, ils se sont perdus dans la campagne. Manon s'est énervée : elle devait rentrer chez elle avant le dîner. Alors, Paul a roulé trop vite et ils ont eu un accident. Ils se sont disputés. Manon est rentrée à minuit. Ses parents étaient inquiets et furieux. Ils ont puni leur fille. Les jours suivants, Manon est restée seule; elle est triste et déprimée. Elle n'a pas vu Paul depuis l'accident. Soudain, le téléphone sonne. C'est Paul! Il arrive...

Traditions

Les Histoires marseillaises

The people of Provence are famous for their storytelling. Many of their stories have roots in history, while others are based on single events that have evolved into legend. For example, people in the Provençal countryside tell countless stories of gold and silver treasure buried by the Moors, Arabs from North Africa who once invaded the region. According to tradition, these buried treasures are watched over by a **chèvre d'or** or *golden-fleeced goat.* On the other hand, the people of Marseilles tell exaggerated stories like the one about a giant fish that once swam into the harbor. In fact, the people of Marseilles are so well-known for their exaggerated stories that when someone is thought to be exaggerating in normal conversation, listeners often respond, "You must be from Marseilles." Find a tall tale from France and read it to the class. Have students compare it to tall tales from the United States.

Recette

Basil has 4,000 years of history and traditions. In India, its country of origin, it is a sacred herb. In ancient Egypt and Greece, basil was associated with death and rituals. In the Middle Ages, it was said that basil created scorpions. Today, you can use basil in cooking, of course, but you can also put a small branch of it on the window sill or in front of the door to prevent flies or mosquitoes from entering.

SOUPE AU PISTOU

Soupe

12 tasses d'eau
1 tasse de haricots blancs
1 tasse de haricots rouges
1 gros oignon coupé en morceaux
2 carottes pelées et coupées en morceaux
2 courgettes coupées en dés
4 tomates pelées et coupées en dés
1 tasse de farfalle (ou macaroni)

Pistou

3 gousses d'ail
3 tasses de feuilles de basilic
1 cuillère à café de sel
4 à 6 cuillères à soupe d'huile d'olive
1/2 tasse de gruyère râpé (ou parmesan)

Soupe

Mettre tous les légumes dans une marmite avec l'eau. Quand l'eau bout, réduire le feu et laisser mijoter pendant 1 heure. Ajouter les pâtes et laisser cuire jusqu'à ce que les pâtes soient prêtes (environ 10 minutes).

Pistou

Piler dans un mortier les feuilles de basilic et les gousses d'ail. Ajouter l'huile d'olive petit à petit jusqu'à l'obtention d'une pâte. Ajouter le gruyère râpé.

Servir la soupe avec le pistou. Pour transformer la soupe en plat principal, vous pouvez ajouter du lard ou des saucisses au moment de la cuisson.

STANDARDS: 1.2, 1.3, 3.2, 4.2, 5.1

Technology

DVD/Video

Videocassette 3, Videocassette 5 (captioned version)
DVD Tutor, Disc 2
See Video Guide, pages 59–64.

Mise en train • Il ne faut pas se fier aux apparences

Walking in the park, Odile sees what she assumes to be a romantic exchange between Cédric and Arlette. She tells her friend Charlotte, who cautions her not to jump to conclusions. When Pascale, Cédric's girlfriend, arrives, Odile tells her what she witnessed. Pascale becomes upset and leaves when she sees Cédric approaching. Cédric doesn't understand why Pascale seems to be angry with him.

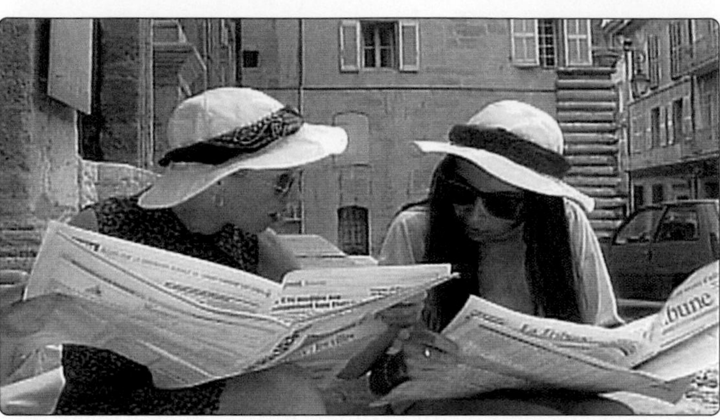

Mise en train (suite)

Cédric and Arlette are talking in front of the school. Pascale walks by and doesn't want to talk to Cédric, even though he asks her what's wrong. Odile then overhears Cédric and Arlette making plans to meet the next day. She tells Pascale, and when they spy on the pair the next day, they discover that Cédric and Arlette are in a play! They are rehearsing the same scene Odile witnessed in the park.

Comment est l'ami idéal?

Students from Côte d'Ivoire, Martinique, and France express their ideas about friendship.

Vidéoclips

- **Poti®**: advertisement for fruit compote
- ***Fais-moi une place:*** performed by Julien Clerc music video

Interactive CD-ROM Tutor

Activity	Activity Type	Pupil's Edition Page
En contexte	*Interactive conversation*	
1. Vocabulaire	Chasse au trésor Explorons!/Vérifions!	p. 258
2. Comment dit-on... ?	Chacun à sa place	p. 260
3. Vocabulaire	Jeu des paires	p. 263
4. Grammaire	Le bon choix	p. 265
5. Comment dit-on... ?	Méli-mélo	p. 267
6. Grammaire	Les mots qui manquent	p. 269
Panorama Culturel	Comment est l'ami idéal?	p. 261
A toi de parler	*Guided recording*	pp. 276–277
A toi d'écrire	*Guided writing*	pp. 276–277

Teacher Management System

Launch the program, type "admin" in the password area, and press RETURN. Log on to www.hrw.com/CDROMTUTOR for a detailed explanation of the Teacher Management System.

DVD Tutor

The *DVD Tutor* contains all material from the *Video Program* as described above. French captions are available for use at your discretion for all sections of the video. The *DVD Tutor* also provides a variety of video-based activities that assess students' understanding of the **Mise en train, Suite,** and **Panorama Culturel.**

This part of the *DVD Tutor* may be used on any DVD video player connected to a television, video monitor, or on a computer with a DVD-ROM drive.

In addition to the video material and the video-based comprehension activities, the *DVD Tutor* also contains the entire *Interactive CD-ROM Tutor* in DVD-ROM format. Each DVD disc contains the activities from all 12 chapters of the *Interactive CD-ROM Tutor.*

This part of the *DVD Tutor* may be used on a Macintosh® or Windows® computer with a DVD-ROM drive.

To preview all resources available for this chapter, use the **One-Stop Planner CD-ROM**, Disc 3.

Internet Connection

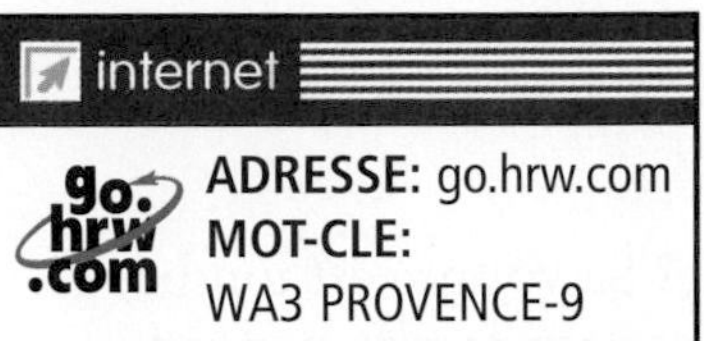

*Have students explore the **go.hrw.com** Web site for many online resources covering all chapters. All Chapter 9 resources are available under the keyword **WA3 PROVENCE-9.** Interactive games help students practice the material and provide them with immediate feedback. You'll also find a printable worksheet that provides Internet activities that lead to a comprehensive online research project.*

Jeux interactifs

You can use the interactive activities in this chapter

- to practice grammar, vocabulary, and chapter functions
- as homework
- as an assessment option
- as a self-test
- to prepare for the Chapter Test

Activités Internet

Students look for information about Provence online and record a little about several cities, using the vocabulary and phrases from the chapter.

- In preparation for the **Activités Internet,** have students review the vocabulary from the chapter. After completing the activity sheet, have students work with a partner and peer-edit Section C.

Location: http://

Nom ________ Classe ________ Date ________

CHAPITRE 9 *Tu connais la nouvelle?*

Level 2

Avant d'explorer

A. Aujourd'hui, tu vas inventer une histoire incroyable qui t'est arrivée en Provence. Pour commencer, fais une liste de six événements qui se sont passés pendant ton voyage. N'oublie pas d'utiliser le vocabulaire du Chapitre 9 et sois *(be)* original!

En ligne!

B. Tu veux utiliser des noms d'endroits que tu as visités dans ton histoire. Explore Internet pour trouver le nom de trois endroits (restaurants, monuments, bâtiments ou magasins) pour les villes suivantes.

	Saint-Tropez	Marseille	Aix-en-Provence	Avignon
Un restaurant				
Un monument				

Projet

Have students choose one city from Provence. Students should research their topic and present it to the class. The report should be in the form of an advertisement for the city. You might give students the option of a written advertisement or a video advertisement. Have students document their sources by noting the URLs of all the sites that they consulted.

STANDARDS: 1.3, 3.2, 5.1

Chapitre 9 : Tu connais la nouvelle?

Textbook Listening Activities Scripts 

Première étape

7 p. 259

— Tu as vu Kim hier soir? Elle avait l'air déprimée. Qu'est-ce qu'elle a, à ton avis?
— Rien du tout. Je crois qu'elle était juste fatiguée. Mais Serge avait l'air mal à l'aise, par contre.
— Oui, je crois qu'il n'est pas très sociable. Maria était de bonne humeur, en tout cas. Elle est vraiment sympa, cette fille!
— Oui, c'est une bonne copine. Dis donc, tu as vu Maud casser le vase?
— Non, c'est pas vrai!
— Mais si! Elle était vraiment gênée!
— Ah ouais? J'ai raté ça.
— En tout cas, Paul et Victor se sont fait remarquer par tout le monde.
— Ah oui, alors! Ces deux-là, ils ne peuvent pas jouer aux cartes sans se disputer. Victor était furieux!
— Eh, tu as remarqué que Guillaume avait l'air inquiet? Je me demande pourquoi...
— Ben... Je crois qu'il attendait sa petite amie et qu'elle n'est jamais arrivée. Elle était malade, et elle n'a pas pu lui téléphoner.

Answers to Activity 7
1. f 2. b 3. e 4. d 5. g 6. c

11 p. 260

1. — Salut, Patricia. J'ai un petit problème... Pascale ne me parle plus, et je ne sais pas pourquoi.
— T'en fais pas. Peut-être qu'elle a passé une mauvaise journée.
— Oui, tu as peut-être raison.
2. — Et toi, Jérôme, qu'est-ce que t'en penses?
— Peut-être qu'elle est de mauvaise humeur parce qu'elle a eu une mauvaise note.
— Ça m'étonnerait. Elle étudie tout le temps!
3. — Marc, qu'est-ce que tu en dis?
— Ecoute, elle est sans doute déprimée parce qu'elle n'a pas pu sortir ce week-end.
— C'est possible.
4. — Thuy, tu as une idée?
— Je parie que tu as oublié de lui téléphoner.
— Là, tu te trompes. Je lui ai téléphoné hier soir, mais elle a refusé de me parler.

Answers to Activity 11
1. accepts 2. rejects 3. accepts 4. rejects

Deuxième étape

15 p. 263

1. — Tu as entendu la nouvelle? Sa voiture est tombée en panne quand elle allait chez ses grands-parents.
2. — Figure-toi qu'il a rencontré une fille au parc, et il est tombé amoureux d'elle!
3. — Tu sais qu'il s'est disputé avec sa copine? D'ailleurs, ils ont cassé.
4. — Tu connais la nouvelle? Oui, un accident de vélo, c'est pas marrant, ça. Mais quand on trouve vingt euros, c'est pas si mal!
5. — Oh, il a été privé de sortie, c'est tout.

Answers to Activity 15
1. Amina
2. Didier
3. Romain
4. Marie
5. Thibaut

17 p. 264

1. — Eh, Jérémy, devine ce que j'ai vu hier!
— Aucune idée. Dis vite!
— J'ai vu Philippe et Julie ensemble au cinéma!
2. — Salut, Carole. Tu connais la nouvelle?
— Non, quoi?
— Diane et Frédéric se sont disputés. Ils ont cassé!
— C'est pas vrai!
3. — Tu ne devineras jamais ce qui s'est passé!
— Je ne sais pas. Raconte!
— Thierry faisait du ski ce week-end, et il s'est cassé la jambe!
— Pas possible! Pauvre Thierry!
4. — Tu sais ce que j'ai entendu dire?
— Aucune idée. Quoi?
— Charlotte a trouvé un billet de cent euros dans la rue!

Answers to Activity 17
1. b
2. d
3. c
4. a

The following scripts are for the listening activities found in the *Pupil's Edition*. For Student Response Forms, see *Listening Activities,* pages 67–69. To provide students with additional listening practice, see *Listening Activities,* pages 71–74.

One-Stop Planner CD-ROM

To preview all resources available for this chapter, use the **One-Stop Planner CD-ROM**, Disc 3.

Troisième étape

24 **p. 268**

— A propos, tu sais ce qui m'est arrivé?
— Aucune idée. Raconte!
— Quelle journée, je te dis pas! J'avais rendez-vous avec Annick à deux heures. J'attendais le bus pour aller chez elle quand j'ai vu ma copine Sylvie qui marchait dans la rue. On a parlé. Je lui ai raconté la boum de samedi dernier, l'interro de français, Patrick — il est tellement beau, celui-là! —, mes parents...
— Et après?
— Bref, il était deux heures et quart quand je me suis rendu compte que j'étais en retard pour mon rendez-vous. J'avais aussi un autre problème : je n'avais plus mon sac! Je savais bien qu'Annick m'attendait chez elle, mais je devais d'abord retrouver mon sac, quoi!
— Alors, qu'est-ce que tu as fait?
— Tu ne devineras jamais ce qui s'est passé. Je commençais à me désespérer quand j'ai vu Patrick qui courait vers moi. Il avait mon sac à la main! Une sacrée coïncidence, non? Il m'a donné mon sac, et je l'ai remercié.
— Et Annick?
— Je lui ai téléphoné. Heureusement, elle n'était pas fâchée. Patrick et moi sommes allés au café, et Annick nous a rejoints plus tard. Finalement, ça a été un après-midi super!

Answers to Activity 24
b, a, d, c

Mise en pratique

2 **p. 276**

— Devine ce qui est arrivé à Eléonore hier!
— Aucune idée. Dis vite!
— Elle avait rendez-vous au café avec Laurent, mais elle a eu un accident de voiture. Heureusement, ce n'était pas grave, mais elle était de très mauvaise humeur après.
— Evidemment! Après un accident de voiture!
— Bref, Laurent l'a attendue au café pendant une heure. Il était super fâché. Quand Eléonore est enfin arrivée, ils se sont disputés et Laurent a cassé avec elle.
— Ce n'est pas possible! Il est très amoureux d'elle.
— C'est ce que je pensais aussi. Eléonore lui a expliqué ce qui s'était passé, mais il ne l'a même pas écoutée. A mon avis, ça cache quelque chose.
— C'est possible. Mais quoi?
— Je parie que Laurent a rencontré une autre fille.
— Je ne crois pas.
— Si! Evelyne l'a même vu au cinéma avec une très jolie fille vendredi.
— Ah oui? Alors, tu as peut-être raison.

Possible Answers to Mise en pratique Activity 2
1. She had a car accident.
2. No; he was angry because he had been waiting an hour.
3. She had a fight with Laurent and he broke up with her.
4. She thinks it's hiding the fact that he has a new girlfriend. A friend saw him with a girl at the movies.
5. Yes; he says she may be right.

Chapitre 9 : Tu connais la nouvelle?

Suggested Lesson Plans 50-Minute Schedule

Day 1

CHAPTER OPENER 5 min.
- Present Chapter Objectives, p. 253.
- Culture Note, ATE, p. 252
- Photo Flash!, and Language Note, ATE, p. 253

MISE EN TRAIN 40 min.
- Presenting **Mise en train,** ATE, p. 254
- Language-to-Language, ATE, p. 255
- Teaching Suggestions: Post-viewing Suggestions 1–3, Video Guide, p. 60
- Thinking Critically, ATE, p. 255
- Do Activities 1–4, p. 256.

Wrap-Up 5 min.
- Do Activity 5, p. 256.

Homework Options
Cahier d'activités, Acts. 1–2, p. 97

Day 2

MISE EN TRAIN
Quick Review 5 min.
- Bell Work, ATE, p. 257

PREMIERE ETAPE
Note culturelle, p. 257 10 min.
- Complete Activity 6, p. 257.
- Read and discuss **Note culturelle,** p. 257.
- Culture Notes, ATE, p. 257

Vocabulaire and **Note de grammaire, pp. 258–259** 30 min.
- Presenting **Vocabulaire,** ATE, p. 258
- TPR, ATE, p. 258
- Travaux pratiques de grammaire, Activities 1–3, pp. 71–72
- Presenting **Note de grammaire,** ATE, p. 259
- Play Audio CD for Activity 7, p. 259.
- **Grammaire supplémentaire,** Activities 1–3, pp. 272–273
- Do Activities 8–9, p. 259.

Wrap-Up 5 min.
- Read and discuss **A la française,** p. 259.

Homework Options
Activity 10, p. 259
Cahier d'activités, Acts. 3–5, p. 98
Travaux pratiques de grammaire, Acts. 4–5, p. 72

Day 3

PREMIERE ETAPE
Quick Review 5 min.
- Check homework.

Comment dit-on... ?, p. 260 20 min.
- Presenting **Comment dit-on... ?,** ATE, p. 260
- Play Audio CD for Activity 11, p. 260.
- Cahier d'activités, Activities 6–8, pp. 99–100
- Have students do Activity 12, p. 260, in pairs.

PANORAMA CULTUREL 10 min.
- Presenting **Panorama Culturel,** ATE, p. 261
- Language Note, ATE, p. 261
- Questions, ATE, p. 261
- Discuss **Qu'en penses-tu?,** p. 261.

Wrap-Up 15 min.
- Teaching Suggestion, ATE, p. 260

Homework Options
Study for Quiz 9-1.
Pupil's Edition, Activity 13, p. 260

Day 4

PREMIERE ETAPE
Quiz 9-1 20 min.
- Administer Quiz 9-1A or 9-1B.

DEUXIEME ETAPE
Vocabulaire, p. 263 25 min.
- Do Teaching Suggestion, ATE, p. 262 and complete Activity 14, p. 262.
- Presenting **Vocabulaire,** ATE, p. 263
- Language Note, ATE, p. 263
- Play Audio CD for Activity 15, p. 263.
- Travaux pratiques de grammaire, Activities 6–7, p. 73
- Do Activity 16, p. 263.

Wrap-Up 5 min.
- Additional Practice, ATE, p. 263

Homework Options
Cahier d'activités, Acts. 10–12, pp. 101–102

Day 5

DEUXIEME ETAPE
Quick Review 5 min.
- Check homework.

Comment dit-on... ?, p. 263 15 min.
- Presenting **Comment dit-on... ?,** ATE, p. 263
- Play Audio CD for Activity 17, p. 264.
- Cahier d'activités, Activity 13, p. 102
- Have students do Activity 18, p. 264, in pairs.

Note culturelle, p. 264 5 min.
- Read and discuss **Note culturelle,** p. 264.
- Career Path, ATE, p. 262

Grammaire, p. 265 20 min.
- Presenting **Grammaire,** ATE, p. 265
- Language Notes, ATE, p. 265
- Do Activity 19, p. 265.
- Travaux pratiques de grammaire, Activities 8–10, pp. 74–75
- Have students do Activity 21, p. 266, in pairs.
- Complete Activity 20, p. 266.

Wrap-Up 5 min.
- Teaching Suggestion, ATE, p. 266

Homework Options
Study for Quiz 9-2.
Cahier d'activités, Act. 14, p. 102

Day 6

DEUXIEME ETAPE
Quiz 9-2 20 min.
- Administer Quiz 9-2A or 9-2B.

TROISIEME ETAPE
Comment dit-on... ?, p. 267 20 min.
- Complete Activity 23, p. 267.
- Presenting **Comment dit-on... ?,** ATE, p. 267
- Play Audio CD for Activity 24, p. 268.
- Complete Activity 25, p. 268.
- Have students do Activity 26, p. 268, in groups.
- Literature Link, ATE, p. 269

Wrap-Up 10 min.
- Have groups share their stories from Activity 26, p. 268.

Homework Options
Cahier d'activités, Acts. 16–17, p. 104

For alternative lesson plans by chapter section, to create your own customized plans, or to preview all resources available for this chapter, use the **One-Stop Planner CD-ROM**, Disc 3.

For additional homework suggestions, see activities accompanied by this symbol throughout the chapter.

Day 7

TROISIEME ETAPE

Quick Review 5 min.
- Check homework.

Note de grammaire, p. 269 25 min.
- Presenting **Note de grammaire,** ATE, p. 269
- **Grammaire supplémentaire,** Activities 8–9, p. 275
- Cahier d'activités, Activities 18–20, pp. 105–106
- Do Activity 27, p. 269.
- Complete Activity 28, p. 269.
- Have students do Activity 29, p. 269, in groups.

Wrap-Up 20 min.
- Teacher to Teacher, ATE, p. 267

Homework Options
Study for Quiz 9-3.
Travaux pratiques de grammaire, Acts. 13–14, p. 77

Day 8

TROISIEME ETAPE

Quiz 9-3 20 min.
- Administer Quiz 9-3A or 9-3B.

LISONS! 25 min.
- Read and discuss **Stratégie pour lire,** p. 270.
- Do Prereading Activities A–B, p. 270.
- Culture Note, ATE, p. 270
- Have students read ***La Cantatrice chauve,* Scène IV,** pp. 270–271.
- Do Reading Activities C–I, p. 271.

Wrap-Up 5 min.
- Have students find a partner and check their responses to Activities C–I.

Homework Options
Cahier d'activités, Act. 22, p. 107

Day 9

LISONS! 25 min.

Quick Review
- Check homework.

Postreading Activity
- Have students write the dialogue for Activity J, p. 271, in pairs.
- Have pairs of students perform their dialogues for the class.

MISE EN PRATIQUE 20 min.
- Complete Activity 1, p. 276.
- Have small groups write a different ending to the story in Activity 1, p. 276.
- Play Audio CD for Activity 2, p. 276.

Wrap-Up 5 min.
- Have groups share their alternative endings for Activity 1, p. 276.

Homework Options
Cahier d'activités, Acts. 23–24, p. 108

Day 10

MISE EN PRATIQUE

Quick Review 5 min.
- Check homework.

Chapter Review 40 min.
- Discuss the strategy for **Ecrivons!,** p. 277, as a class, then have students work on their stories.
- Have students work in pairs on **Jeu de rôle,** p. 277.

Wrap-Up 5 min.
- Have volunteers share scenes from **Jeu de rôle** with the class.

Homework Options
Have students finish compositions for **Ecrivons!**

Day 11

MISE EN PRATIQUE

Quick Review 5 min.
- Have volunteers share their compositions from **Ecrivons!**

Chapter Review 40 min.
- Have students complete **A toi de parler,** CD-ROM Tutor, Disc 3.
- Have students do **A toi d'écrire,** CD-ROM Tutor, Disc 3.
- Show ***Il ne faut pas se fier aux apparences (suite),*** Video Program, Videocassette 3.
- See Teaching Suggestions, Viewing Suggestion 1, Video Guide, p. 60.
- Complete Activities 6–7, Video Guide, pp. 63–64.

Wrap-Up 5 min.
- Have students begin **Que sais-je?,** p. 278.

Homework Options
Que sais-je?, p. 278

Day 12

MISE EN PRATIQUE

Quick Review 15 min.
- Go over **Que sais-je?,** p. 278.

Chapter Review 35 min.
- Review Chapter 9. Choose from **Grammaire supplémentaire,** Grammar Tutor for Students of French, Activities for Communication, Listening Activities, Interactive CD-ROM Tutor, or **Jeux interactifs.**
- See Game: **Catégories,** ATE, p. 279.
- Circumlocution, ATE, p. 279

Homework Options
Study for Chapter 9 Test.

Assessment

Chapter Test 40–45 min.
- Administer Chapter 9 Test. Select from Testing Program, Alternative Assessment Guide, Test Generator, or Standardized Assessment Tutor.

Chapitre 9 : Tu connais la nouvelle?

Suggested Lesson Plans *90-Minute Block Schedule*

Block 1

CHAPTER OPENER 5 min.
- Focusing on Outcomes, ATE, p. 253
- Language Note, ATE, p. 253
- Photo Flash!, ATE, p. 253

MISE EN TRAIN 40 min.
- Preteaching Vocabulary, ATE, p. 254
- Presenting **Mise en train,** ATE, p. 254
- Thinking Critically, ATE, p. 255
- Do Activities 1–4, p. 256.

PREMIERE ETAPE 10 min.
- Do Activity 6, p. 257.
- Read and discuss **Note culturelle,** p. 257.
- Culture Notes, ATE, p. 257

Vocabulaire, p. 258 15 min.
- Presenting **Vocabulaire,** ATE, p. 258
- Play Audio CD for Activity 7, p. 259.

Note de grammaire, p. 259 15 min.
- Read and discuss **Note de grammaire,** p. 259.
- Do Activity 8, p. 259.

Wrap-Up 5 min.
- TPR, ATE, p. 258

Homework Options
Grammaire supplémentaire, Acts. 1–3, pp. 272–273
Cahier d'activités, Acts. 1–5, pp. 97–98
Travaux pratiques de grammaire, Acts. 1–5, pp. 71–72

Block 2

PREMIERE ETAPE
Quick Review 5 min.
- Kinesthetic Learners, ATE, p. 258

Note de grammaire, p. 259 10 min.
- Do Activity 9, p. 259.
- Discuss **A la française,** p. 259.

Comment dit-on... ?, p. 260 25 min.
- Presenting **Comment dit-on... ?,** ATE, p. 260
- Play Audio CD for Activity 11, p. 260.
- Do Activity 12, p. 260.

PANORAMA CULTUREL 20 min.
- Have students discuss the difference between an acquaintance, a friend, and a best friend.
- Presenting **Panorama Culturel,** ATE, p. 261
- Discuss **Qu'en penses-tu?,** p. 261.

DEUXIEME ETAPE 10 min.
- Do Activity 14, p. 262.

Vocabulaire, p. 263 15 min.
- Presenting **Vocabulaire,** ATE, p. 263
- Play Audio CD for Activity 15, p. 263.

Wrap-Up 5 min.
- Challenge, ATE, p. 260

Homework Options
Have students study for Quiz 9-1.
Cahier d'activités, Acts. 6–10, pp. 99–101
Travaux pratiques de grammaire, Acts. 6–7, p. 73

Block 3

PREMIERE ETAPE
Quick Review 10 min.
- Communicative Activities 9-1A and 9-1B, Activities for Communiction, pp. 49–50

Quiz 9-1 20 min.
- Administer Quiz 9-1A or 9-1B.

DEUXIEME ETAPE 10 min.
Vocabulaire, p. 263 20 min.
- Teaching Transparency 9-B, using Suggestion #2 in Suggestions for Using Teaching Transparency 9-B
- Additional Practice, ATE, p. 263
- Do Activity 16, p. 263.

Comment dit-on... ?, p. 263 25 min.
- Presenting **Comment dit-on... ?,** ATE, p. 263
- Play Audio CD for Activity 17, p. 264.
- Do Activity 18, p. 264.
- Discuss **Note culturelle,** p. 264.

Grammaire, p. 265 10 min.
- Presenting **Grammaire,** ATE, p. 265

Wrap-Up 5 min.
- Teaching Transparency 9-2, using Suggestion #2 in Suggestions for Using Teaching Transparency 9-2

Homework Options
Cahier d'activités, Acts. 11–14, pp. 102–103
Travaux pratiques de grammaire, Act. 8, p. 74

For alternative lesson plans by chapter section, to create your own customized lesson plans, or to preview all resources available for this chapter, use the **One-Stop Planner CD-ROM**, Disc 3.

For additional homework suggestions, see activities accompanied by this symbol throughout the chapter.

Block 4

DEUXIEME ETAPE

Quick Review 10 min.
- Communicative Activity 9-2, Activities for Communication, pp. 51–52

Grammaire, p. 265 50 min.
- Do Activities 19–21, pp. 265–266, with Teaching Suggestion, ATE, p. 266.

TROISIEME ETAPE 10 min.
- Have students read the conversation on page 267.
- Do Activity 23, p. 267.

Comment dit-on... ?, p. 267 10 min.
- Presenting **Comment dit-on... ?**, ATE, p. 267

Wrap-Up 10 min.
- Performance Assessment, Alternative Assessment Guide, p. 40

Homework Options
Have students study for Quiz 9-2.
Grammaire supplémentaire, Acts. 4–7, pp. 273–275
Travaux pratiques de grammaire, Acts. 9–12, pp. 75–76

Block 5

DEUXIEME ETAPE

Quick Review 15 min.
- Poetry Link, ATE, p. 266

Quiz 9-2 20 min.
- Have students do Quiz 9-2A or 9-2B.

TROISIEME ETAPE

Comment dit-on... ?, p. 267 20 min.
- Play Audio CD for Activity 24, p. 268.
- Activities 25–26, p. 268

Note de grammaire, p. 269 30 min.
- Presenting **Note de grammaire,** ATE, p. 269
- Do Activities 27–28, p. 269.

Wrap-Up 5 min.
- Teaching Transparency 9-3, using Suggestion #2 in Suggestions for Using Teaching Transparency 9-3

Homework Options
Have students study for Quiz 9-3.
Grammaire supplémentaire, Acts. 8–9, p. 275
Cahier d'activités, Acts. 16–21, pp. 104–106
Travaux pratiques de grammaire, Acts. 13–14, p. 77

Block 6

TROISIEME ETAPE

Quick Review 10 min.
- Communicative Activity 9-3, Activities for Communication, pp. 53–54

Quiz 9-3 20 min.
- Administer Quiz 9-3A or 9-3B.

LISONS! 30 min.
- Discuss **Stratégie pour lire,** p. 270.
- Prereading Activities A–B, p. 270
- Activities C–G, pp. 270–271

MISE EN PRATIQUE 30 min.
- Do Activity 1, p. 276.
- Teaching Suggestion, ATE, p. 276
- Play Audio CD for Activity 2, p. 276.

Homework Options
Que sais-je?, p. 278
CD-ROM/Interactive Games
Study for Chapter 9 Test.

Block 7

MISE EN PRATIQUE

Quick Review 10 min.
- Check homework.

Chapter Review 35 min.
- Review Chapter 9. Choose from **Grammaire supplémentaire,** Grammar Tutor for Students of French, Activities for Communication, Listening Activities, Interactive CD-ROM Tutor, or **Jeux interactifs.**

Chapter Test 45 min.
- Administer Chapter 9 Test. Select from Testing Program, Alternative Assessment Guide, Test Generator, or Standardized Assessment Tutor.

CHAPITRE 9

One-Stop Planner CD-ROM

For resource information, see the **One-Stop Planner,** Disc 3.

Pacing Tips

In this chapter, students will learn when to use the **passé composé** and when to use the **imparfait.** Since this topic can be fairly difficult for students to understand, you might allot more time for the **Deuxième** and **Troisième étapes** in this chapter. Students will also review this topic in future chapters. For suggested Lesson Plans and timing suggestions, see pages 251I–251L.

Meeting the Standards

Communication

- Wondering what happened; offering possible explanations; accepting or rejecting explanations, p. 260
- Breaking some news; showing interest, p. 263
- Beginning, continuing, and ending a story, p. 267

Culture

- Culture Note, pp. 252, 257, 270
- Note culturelle, pp. 257, 264
- Panorama Culturel, p. 261

Connections

- Literature Link, p. 269
- Multicultural Link, p. 270
- Drama Link, p. 271

Comparisons

- Thinking Critically: Analyzing, p. 255

Communities

- Career Path, p. 262
- De l'école au travail, p. 269

Cultures and Communities

Culture Note

Aix-en-Provence is known as the historical and cultural capital of Provence. Its history dates to 122 B.C., when a Roman consul named Caius Sextius Calvinus founded the thermal baths of **Aquae Sextiae** in Aix.

STANDARDS: 3.1

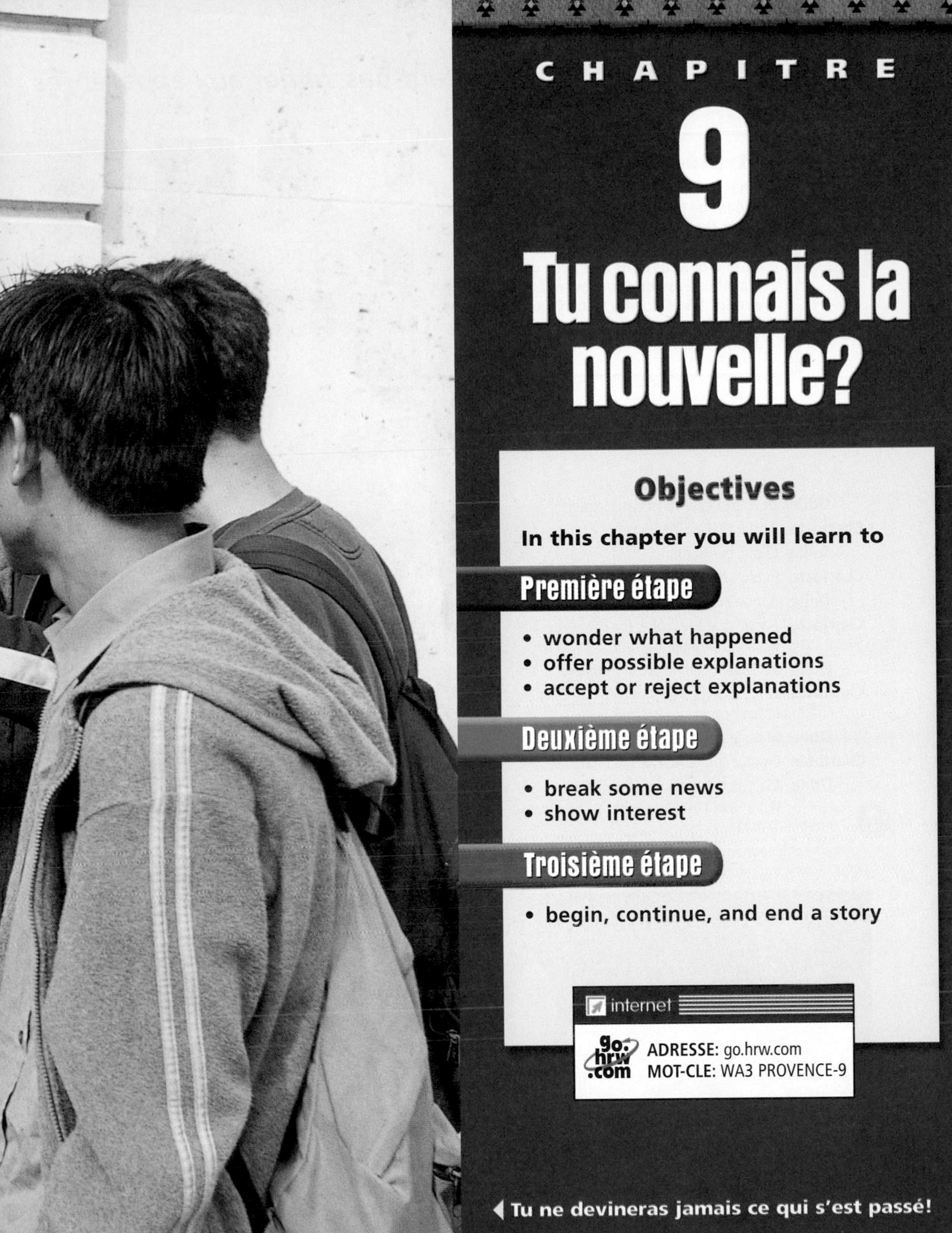

CHAPITRE 9

Tu connais la nouvelle?

Objectives

In this chapter you will learn to

Première étape

- wonder what happened
- offer possible explanations
- accept or reject explanations

Deuxième étape

- break some news
- show interest

Troisième étape

- begin, continue, and end a story

internet

go.hrw.com ADRESSE: go.hrw.com
MOT-CLE: WA3 PROVENCE-9

◀ Tu ne devineras jamais ce qui s'est passé!

Chapter Opener

CHAPITRE 9

Focusing on Outcomes

As you read each of the outcomes for the chapter, ask students in what situations they would use these functions. Then have students look at the photo and describe what they see. Which outcome best matches the caption? NOTE: The self-check activities on page 278 help students assess their achievement of the objectives.

Photo Flash!

Some **lycées,** such as this one, open onto the street and are difficult to distinguish from the other buildings on the city block. Other **lycées** might have large campuses surrounded by walls, with a gated entrance.

Chapter Sequence

Connections and Comparisons

Language Note

Explain that **nouvelle** also means *news.* Then, ask students to guess the meaning of **Tu connais la nouvelle?** *(Did you hear the latest?)*

STANDARDS: 4.1

CHAPITRE 9

Teaching Resources
pp. 254–256

PRINT 

- Lesson Planner, p. 41
- Video Guide, pp. 60, 62
- Cahier d'activités, p. 97

MEDIA 

- One-Stop Planner
- Video Program
  Mise en train
  Videocassette 3, 40:34–44:04
  Videocassette 5 (captioned version), 1:16:53–1:20:23
  Suite
  Videocassette 3, 44:07–48:35
  Videocassette 5 (captioned version), 1:20:25–1:24:53
- DVD Tutor, Disc 2
- Audio Compact Discs, CD 9, Trs. 1–2
- **Mise en train** Transparencies

Presenting Mise en train

Before students read the **Mise en train,** have them complete the Preteaching Vocabulary suggestion below. Ask if they can guess who is making assumptions about whom and what those assumptions might be. Ask students to suggest some possible explanations for Cédric's and Arlette's behavior. Then, show the video and ask the questions in Activity 1 on page 256. Have students compare the story with the assumptions they made before reading.

Mise en train Transparencies

The **roman-photo** is an abridged version of the video episode.

MISE EN TRAIN • *Il ne faut pas se fier aux apparences*

CD 9 Trs. 1–2

Stratégie pour comprendre

What does it mean for Cédric to be the *petit copain de Pascale*? Why is Odile so intrigued when she sees him with Arlette in the park? Have you ever made assumptions about people or situations and then discovered that those assumptions were completely wrong? What do you think Charlotte means when she says *Il ne faut pas se fier aux apparences?*

Odile

Charlotte

Pascale

Cédric

Arlette

1

Odile Devine qui j'ai vu ici dans le parc.
Charlotte Aucune idée... Dis un peu!
Odile Cédric et Arlette.
Charlotte Et alors?
Odile A mon avis, ça cache quelque chose.
Charlotte J'ai du mal à le croire. Toi, tu vois des histoires d'amour partout.
Odile Ils avaient l'air de bien s'entendre.
Charlotte Je n'y crois pas. Tu sais bien que Cédric est le petit copain de Pascale.
Odile Mais, je t'assure que c'est vrai.
Charlotte En tout cas, ça ne nous regarde pas...
Odile Mais, je les ai vus. Ils se parlaient tendrement et puis, Cédric lui a embrassé la main.

2

Charlotte Ecoute, il ne faut pas se fier aux apparences.
Odile Bon, comme tu veux... Pauvre Pascale!
Charlotte Chut! La voilà!

3

Odile Bonjour! Comment vas-tu?
Pascale Super. Qu'est-ce que vous avez à me regarder comme ça? Qu'est-ce que j'ai?
Charlotte Rien du tout.

Preteaching Vocabulary

Guessing Words from Context

Have students guess what the title ***Il ne faut pas se fier aux apparences*** means. Have them look at the photos to try and guess what is happening. Have students tell if they ever had problems with a friend over a misunderstanding. When students have a general idea of the story in the **Mise en train,** have them use the context to guess the meaning of the following expressions.

- ❶ Devine qui j'ai vu...
- ❶ J'ai du mal à le croire.
- ❺ Qu'est-ce que vous racontez?
- ❼ Elle est fâchée?

STANDARDS: 1.2

4

Pascale Allez, quoi! Dites-le-moi!
Odile On a vu Cédric et Arlette dans le parc...
Charlotte ...en train de se parler.
Pascale Et alors?
Charlotte Alors, rien.

5

Pascale Mais quoi? Je ne comprends rien. Qu'est-ce que vous racontez? Ah, je commence à comprendre. Vous voulez dire que Cédric et Arlette...
Charlotte Mais non, pas du tout!

6

Odile Tiens, le voilà, Cédric!
Pascale Eh bien, au revoir! J'ai du travail à faire. A lundi. Salut.

7

Cédric Salut. Où est-ce que Pascale est partie? Elle va revenir?
Odile Non, elle est rentrée chez elle.
Cédric Pourquoi? Elle est fâchée? Elle ne m'a même pas dit bonjour.
Odile Elle avait du travail à faire.

8

Cédric Pascale!!
Odile Moi, j'adore quand ça se complique!

Cahier d'activités, p. 97, Act. 1–2

Using the Captioned Video/DVD

If students have difficulty understanding French spoken at a normal speed, use Videocassette 5 to allow students to see the French captions for ***Il ne faut pas se fier aux apparences*** and ***Il ne faut pas se fier aux apparences (suite).*** Hearing the language and watching the story will reduce anxiety about the new language and facilitate comprehension. The reinforcement of seeing the written vocabulary words as they watch the gestures and actions will help prepare students to do the comprehension activities on page 256.

NOTE: The *DVD Tutor* contains captions for all sections of the *Video Program.*

Mise en train

CHAPITRE 9

Thinking Critically

Analyzing Ask students to analyze the factors that contributed to the misunderstanding in the **Mise en train.** Have them suggest what certain characters might have done to prevent a misunderstanding. (Odile might have asked Cédric and Arlette what they were doing. Pascale might have asked Odile to explain her implication. Charlotte and Odile might have told Cédric why Pascale left.)

Language-to-Language

Call attention to the way Charlotte warns Odile to be quiet in Photo 2. Point out that where we say *Shhh!* in English, the French say **Chut!,** pronouncing the **–t.** In German, people say **Pft!** or **Still!** while in Spanish, you might hear **Tsss!, Ch-Ch-Ch-Ch!,** or **Shhh!**

Mise en train (suite)

When the story continues, Cédric and Arlette are talking in front of school. Pascale walks by, and Cédric asks her what's wrong. She doesn't want to talk to him and continues walking. Cédric can't understand what's wrong. Then, Odile overhears Cédric and Arlette making plans to meet the next day. She tells Pascale, and the next day, they discover that Cédric and Arlette are in a play! They are rehearsing the same scene Odile witnessed in the park.

Mise en train

These activities check for comprehension only. Students should not yet be expected to produce language modeled in **Mise en train.**

1 Tu as compris? See answers below.

1. What did Odile see in the park?
2. What does Odile think is going on?
3. What does Charlotte think is going on?
4. Why does Pascale leave so quickly?
5. How does Odile feel about what happened?

2 Mets en ordre

Mets l'histoire dans le bon ordre.

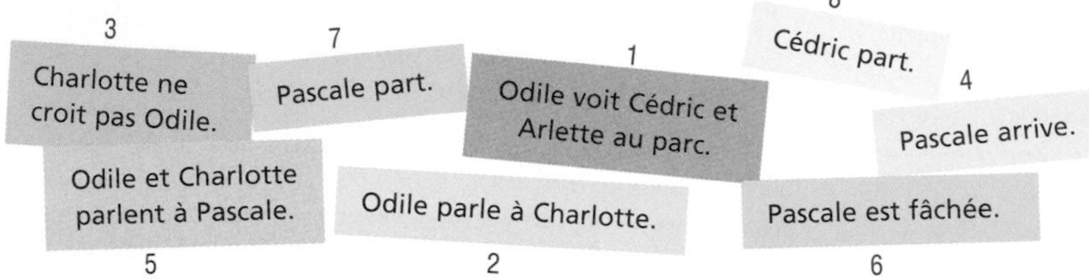
3 Charlotte ne croit pas Odile.
7 Pascale part.
1 Odile voit Cédric et Arlette au parc.
8 Cédric part.
4 Pascale arrive.
5 Odile et Charlotte parlent à Pascale.
2 Odile parle à Charlotte.
6 Pascale est fâchée.

3 Qui suis-je?

Cédric

Arlette

Odile

Charlotte

Pascale

1. «Moi, j'adore quand ça se complique!» Odile
2. «Je vois des histoires d'amour partout.» Odile
3. «Nous avions l'air de bien nous entendre.» Cédric et Arlette
4. «J'ai embrassé la main d'Arlette.» Cédric
5. «Je suis fâchée.» Pascale
6. «Je suis le petit copain de Pascale.» Cédric
7. «Je ne crois pas que Cédric et Arlette flirtaient.» Charlotte
8. «J'ai dit que j'avais du travail à faire.» Pascale

4 Cherche les expressions

What do the people in ***Il ne faut pas se fier aux apparences*** say to . . .

1. break some news? Devine qui j'ai vu...
2. show interest in hearing some news? Aucune idée... Dis un peu!
3. reject explanations for what might have happened? J'ai du mal à le croire. Je n'y crois pas.
4. ask what's going on? Allez, quoi! Dites-le-moi!

5 Et maintenant, à toi

Imagine que tu es Pascale. Comment tu réagis à cette situation?

CHAPITRE 9

Visual/Tactile Learners

2 Have pairs of students write the sentences on separate index cards and then arrange them in the correct order. You might write the sentences on strips of transparency and have individuals arrange them in the correct order on the overhead.

Kinesthetic/Auditory Learners

2 Form groups of eight. Give each group member a card on which you've written one of the sentences in the activity. Then, have the group members stand up and arrange themselves in a line to represent the order of the sentences in the story. Tell students that they may only say what is written on their cards to accomplish the task, but not show their cards to one another.

Group Work

3 Form groups of five. Have each group write the names of the five characters on slips of paper. Each group member draws a slip and assumes the identity of that character. Students prepare several statements their characters might say, including those listed in this activity. Then, students take turns saying the statements, giving clues to their identity. The other students in the group try to guess which role each student has assumed.

Comprehension Check

Captioned Video/DVD

3 To complete this activity, you might play the captioned version of ***Il ne faut pas se fier aux apparences*** on Videocassette 5 or DVD Disc 2 and have students raise their hand when they recognize one of the expressions from the activity. Then, have them identify the person who said the expression.

Teaching Suggestion

3 Write the names of the characters on a transparency. Then, write the sentences on separate strips of transparency and scatter them on the projector. Have one student at a time place one strip next to the appropriate character's name.

Answers

1
1. She saw Cédric kissing Arlette's hand.
2. Cédric has found a new girlfriend.
3. nothing
4. She is angry at Cédric.
5. She is enjoying the situation.

STANDARDS: 1.2, 1.3

Objectives Wondering what happened; offering possible explanations; accepting or rejecting explanations

go.
hrw
.com

WA3 PROVENCE-9

A mon avis, il est amoureux d'elle.
Je crois que ça cache quelque chose. Pascale va être furieuse!
Mais non! Je parie que Cédric s'amuse!
Peut-être que Pascale et Cédric se sont disputés... alors, Cédric s'est trouvé une nouvelle copine!

6 **A ton avis...**

Lisons/Parlons Qu'est-ce que leurs amies disent pour expliquer l'attitude de Cédric et d'Arlette? Comment est-ce que toi, tu expliques leur attitude? Cédric is in love with Arlette. Cédric is having fun. Pascale and Cédric had an argument, and Cédric has found a new girlfriend. Answers will vary.

Note culturelle

Where do you go to see and talk about what's happening in your town? In Aix-en-Provence, the **cours Mirabeau** provides entertainment and refreshment to tourists and inhabitants alike. Often called one of the most beautiful streets in Europe, the **cours Mirabeau** is the main street in Aix. Plane trees and fountains run the length of the broad boulevard, making it a cool place even in the summer when the **provençal** sun is strong. One side of the street has banks and mansions **(hôtels particuliers)** from the seventeenth and eighteenth centuries, while the other side of the street is famous for its shops and sidewalk cafés. One of these, the **Deux Garçons,** is the place in Aix to see and be seen.

Cultures and Communities

Culture Notes

- **Les Deux Garçons,** a café on the **cours Mirabeau,** is a favorite spot among local inhabitants and university students, who refer to it as **Les Deux G.** The University of Aix enjoys a reputation for academic excellence, especially in the fields of law, economics, and literary studies. Many foreign students study at this university and visit **Les Deux G,** making the café an even livelier location for socializing.
- Wide, shady avenues **(cours)** were built with the advent of the horse-drawn carriage in the seventeenth century. The **cours Mirabeau** was named for Honoré Riquetti, Comte de Mirabeau, one of the leaders of the French Revolution.

Première étape

CHAPITRE 9

Teaching Resources
pp. 257–260

PRINT

- Lesson Planner, p. 42
- TPR Storytelling Book, pp. 64–65
- Listening Activities, pp. 67, 71
- Activities for Communication, pp. 49–50, 115, 118, 153–154
- Travaux pratiques de grammaire, pp. 71–72
- Grammar Tutor for Students of French, Chapter 9
- Cahier d'activités, pp. 98–100
- Testing Program, pp. 223–226
- Alternative Assessment Guide, p. 40
- Student Make-Up Assignments, Chapter 9

MEDIA 

- One-Stop Planner
- Audio Compact Discs, CD 9, Trs. 3–4, 13, 19–20
- Teaching Transparencies: 9-1, 9-A; **Grammaire supplémentaire** Answers; Travaux pratiques de grammaire Answers
- Interactive CD-ROM Tutor, Disc 3

Bell Work

Write these sentences on the board or on a transparency. Students decide which character from the **Mise en train** would most likely say each sentence.

1. **Je crois qu'Odile voit des histoires d'amour partout.**
2. **Pascale est furieuse contre moi, mais je ne sais pas pourquoi.**
3. **Je suis la petite amie de Cédric.**
4. **Cédric m'a embrassé la main.**
5. **J'ai vu Arlette et Cédric ensemble dans le parc.**

(*Answers:* 1. Charlotte 2. Cédric 3. Pascale 4. Arlette 5. Odile)

Language Note

You might point out that **copain** and **copine** are also used for *boyfriend* and *girlfriend.*

Première étape

CHAPITRE 9

Teaching Resources
pp. 257–260

PRINT

- Lesson Planner, p. 42
- TPR Storytelling Book, pp. 64–65
- Listening Activities, pp. 67, 71
- Activities for Communication, pp. 49–50, 115, 118, 153–154
- Travaux pratiques de grammaire, pp. 71–72
- Grammar Tutor for Students of French, Chapter 9
- Cahier d'activités, pp. 98–100
- Testing Program, pp. 223–226
- Alternative Assessment Guide, p. 40
- Student Make-Up Assignments, Chapter 9

MEDIA 

- One-Stop Planner
- Audio Compact Discs, CD 9, Trs. 3–4, 13, 19–20
- Teaching Transparencies: 9-1, 9-A; **Grammaire supplémentaire** Answers; Travaux pratiques de grammaire Answers
- Interactive CD-ROM Tutor, Disc 3

Presenting Vocabulaire

Demonstrate these emotions yourself, telling the class in French how you feel, using appropriate intonation and facial expressions. **(Je suis fâché(e)!)** Then, ask students how they feel, using these expressions. **(Tu es gêné(e)?)** Have them answer in French, exhibiting the appropriate emotion with facial expressions and body language to show they understand.

TPR Suggest an emotion **(Vous êtes fâchés!)** and have students act it out to show their comprehension.

Vocabulaire

Les émotions

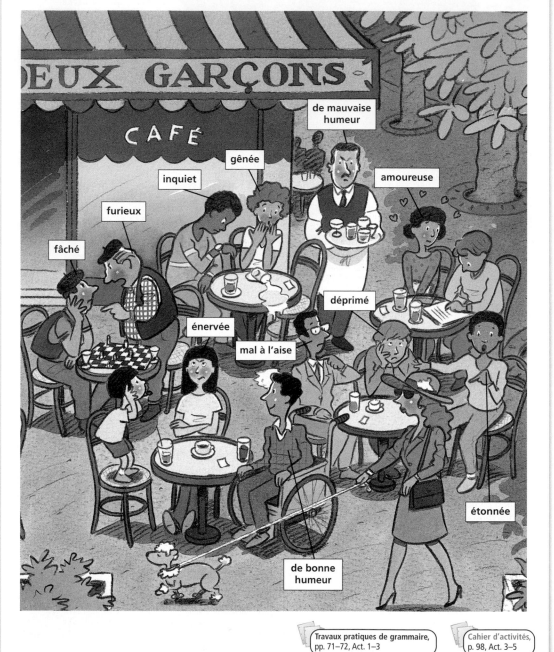

DEUX GARÇONS
CAFÉ
de mauvaise humeur
gênée
inquiet
amoureuse
furieux
fâché
déprimé
énervée
mal à l'aise
étonnée
de bonne humeur

Travaux pratiques de grammaire, pp. 71–72, Act. 1–3

Cahier d'activités, p. 98, Act. 3–5

Communication for All Students

Kinesthetic Learners
Ask for volunteers to act out an emotion for their classmates to guess. **(Il/Elle est de bonne humeur.)**

Visual Learners
Have students gather or draw pictures of people showing the emotions in the **Vocabulaire.** Have them write the words that describe the emotions of the people in their pictures on separate index cards. Then, have students pass their shuffled pictures and cards to a partner, who will match the pictures to the cards. Afterwards, display the pictures and labels around the classroom.

STANDARDS: 1.3

Note de grammaire

Remember that you use the **imparfait** to tell what people were like in the past.

Il **était** triste.

You can also use the expression **avoir l'air** + an adjective to tell how people *seem(ed)* to be.

Ils **ont l'air** furieux.
Elle **avait l'air fâchée.**

The adjective agrees with the person you're describing.

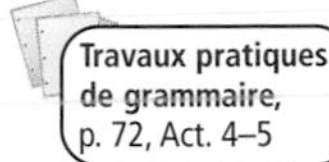

Travaux pratiques de grammaire, p. 72, Act. 4–5

Grammaire supplémentaire, pp. 272–273, Act. 1–3

7 Grammaire en contexte

See scripts on p. 251G.

CD 9 Tr. 3

Ecoutons Ecoute Raoul et Philippe qui sont au café Les Deux Garçons en train de parler de la fête d'hier soir. D'après leur conversation, comment étaient leurs amis?

1. Kim f
2. Serge b
3. Maria e
4. Maud d
5. Victor g
6. Guillaume c

a. énervé(e)
b. mal à l'aise
c. inquiet (inquiète)
d. gêné(e)
e. de bonne humeur
f. déprimé(e)
g. furieux (furieuse)
h. de mauvaise humeur

8 Qu'est-ce qui s'est passé?

Ecrivons Décris les réactions de tes amis dans ces situations. Complète chaque phrase avec un adjectif qui convient. Possible answers:

1. Pierre est tombé devant son prof d'histoire. Il était _____. gêné
2. Marion est allée à une boum où elle ne connaissait personne. Elle était _____. mal à l'aise
3. Jean a eu 20 à l'interro d'anglais. Il était _____. de bonne humeur
4. Le chat d'Alice est mort soudainement. Alice avait l'air _____. déprimée
5. Li est sortie avec un beau garçon. Elle avait l'air _____. amoureuse
6. Jean-Michel n'a pas pu trouver son portefeuille ce matin. Il était _____. de mauvaise humeur
7. On a fait une surprise-partie pour Eric. Il était vachement _____! étonné

9 Mon journal

Ecrivons Complète les phrases suivantes pour décrire ta personnalité. Possible answers:

Je suis ___1___ quand je rate le bus. Quand mes amis ne m'invitent pas à sortir avec eux, je suis ___2___. Quand j'ai une mauvaise note à une interro, je suis ___3___. Quand mon chien est malade, je suis ___4___. Quand je vais manger dans un restaurant très élégant, je suis un peu ___5___. Et quand je suis en vacances, je suis ___6___.

1. furieux(se) 2. fâché(e) 3. déprimé(e) 4. inquiet (inquiète) 5. mal à l'aise 6. de bonne humeur

10 Alors, raconte!

Ecrivons Avec qui as-tu parlé hier? Fais une liste et décris l'humeur de ces personnes.

Melissa était de bonne
humeur mais Manuel
avait l'air plutôt déprimé.
Sheryl était vachement
inquiète parce qu'elle
...it en ret...

A la française

To better describe people and things, you can use words like **assez** *(sort of)* and **plutôt** *(rather)* to modify adjectives. When you're talking to people your own age, you can use the informal expressions **vachement** *(really)* and **super** *(really, ultra-)* before adjectives for emphasis: Elle était **vachement énervée.** Il est **super sympa.**

Connections and Comparisons

Language Notes

- Another colloquial way to say *very* or *really* is **hyper. (Il/Elle était hyper fâché(e).)**
- Tell students that **une vache** is *a cow.* The term **vachement** developed from the use of **vache** as an adjective, meaning **méchant. (Il/Elle est vache.)** The word **méchant** is also used to mean *great.* **(Il a une méchante moto.) Vachement** came to be used as **méchamment** *(really)* as in **Ce gâteau est vachement bon,** similar to *You make a mean cake.*

Challenge

Have students describe a character in the **Vocabulaire,** without using the adjective that labels the person. **(Son petit frère l'énerve parce qu'il est pénible.)** A partner will try to guess who it is. **(C'est la fille qui est énervée.)**

Presenting
Note de grammaire

***Avoir l'air* + an adjective**
Use the pictures of various people showing emotion that students gathered (see Visual Learners on page 258). Show each picture, asking **Il/Elle a l'air comment?** Have students tell you how the person seems to be feeling.
(Il a l'air déprimé. Elle a l'air étonnée.)

Tactile Learners

7 Have students list the emotions on a sheet of paper and the names of the people on small pieces of paper. As they listen to the recording, have them place the names next to the appropriate emotion.

Challenge

7 Have students listen to the recording a second time and tell why the people felt or appeared to feel the way they did, according to Raoul or Philippe.

Group Work

8 Have groups of students create other sentences about imaginary people and call on another group to guess how the people might have felt.

STANDARDS: 1.2, 4.1

Première étape

CHAPITRE 9

Presenting Comment dit-on... ?

Bring to class magazine pictures of people showing various emotions. Write possible explanations for the people's emotions on large index cards **(Elle a trouvé deux cents euros.)** and place them face down on your desk. Show a picture and ask why the person feels the way he or she appears to. **(Je me demande pourquoi elle est de mauvaise humeur.)** Then, pick a card from the stack on your desk and read the explanation on the card **(Je crois qu'elle a trouvé deux cents euros).** Have students give the thumbs-up gesture if the explanation is logical or the thumbs-down gesture if it isn't. Based on students' responses, accept **(Evidemment.)** or reject **(Non, je ne crois pas.)** the explanation you gave.

Teaching Suggestion

To close this **étape,** tape to the board five pictures of people who are showing different emotions. Have students choose three pictures and write a short paragraph for each one, telling how the person feels and offering an explanation. Then, ask volunteers to read one of their paragraphs aloud and have the other students guess which picture it describes.

Assess

- Testing Program, pp. 223–226 Quiz 9-1A, Quiz 9-1B Audio CD 9, Tr. 13
- Student Make-Up Assignments, Chapter 9, Alternative Quiz
- Alternative Assessment Guide, p. 40

Comment dit-on...?

Wondering what happened; offering possible explanations; accepting or rejecting explanations

CD-ROM 3 DVD 2

To wonder what happened:

Je me demande pourquoi elle parle comme ça. *I wonder . . .*

To accept an explanation:

Tu as peut-être raison. *Maybe you're right.*
C'est possible. *That's possible.*
Ça se voit. *That's obvious.*
Evidemment. *Obviously.*

To offer possible explanations:

A mon avis, elle est amoureuse. *In my opinion, . . .*
Peut-être qu'elle a passé une bonne journée. *Maybe . . .*
Je crois qu'elle a gagné cent euros. *I think that . . .*
Je parie qu'elle a mangé trop vite. *I bet that . . .*

To reject an explanation:

A mon avis, tu te trompes. *In my opinion, you're mistaken.*
Ce n'est pas possible. *That's not possible.*
Je ne crois pas. *I don't think so.*

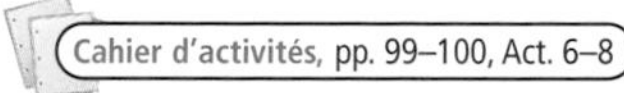
Cahier d'activités, pp. 99–100, Act. 6–8

11 Pourquoi est-ce que Pascale est de mauvaise humeur?

See scripts and answers on p. 251G.

Ecoutons Listen as Cédric asks his friends why Pascale doesn't talk to him. Does he accept or reject the explanations they offer?

CD 9 Tr. 4

12 Je me demande pourquoi!

Parlons Qu'est-ce qui est arrivé à Nora, à Thierry et à Didier? Imagine trois événements qui peuvent expliquer leur humeur. Parles-en avec un(e) camarade qui va te dire s'il/si elle est d'accord avec toi ou pas.

EXEMPLE **—Je me demande pourquoi Nora a l'air fatiguée aujourd'hui.**
—Peut-être qu'elle a mal à la tête.
—Non, je ne crois pas. Je parie qu'elle...

Nora

Thierry

Didier

13 Un petit mot

Ecrivons Tu devais retrouver ton/ta meilleur(e) ami(e) pour faire une randonnée hier, mais tu as eu des problèmes et tu n'as pas pu retrouvé ton ami(e). Ecris-lui un petit mot pour t'excuser. Explique ce qui s'est passé et dis à ton ami(e) comment tu t'es senti(e).

EXEMPLE **Excuse-moi pour hier. Tu sais, tout a été de travers. Mon réveil n'a pas sonné et je me suis réveillé(e) en retard. Alors, j'étais de mauvaise humeur...**

Communication for All Students

Challenge

Make statements in which you wonder why the people feel the way they do in the **Vocabulaire** on page 258. **(Je me demande pourquoi le serveur est de mauvaise humeur.)** Encourage students to respond, using the expressions in **Comment dit-on... ? (Je parie qu'il est...)**

STANDARDS: 1.1, 1.2, 1.3, 3.1, 5.1, 5.2

Comment est l'ami idéal?

We talked to some French-speaking teenagers about friendships. Here's what they had to say.

Marius, Côte d'Ivoire

«Pour moi, un ami idéal, c'est l'ami qui sait t'écouter, qui sait te comprendre et puis qui a beaucoup d'attentions pour toi. Et aussi, cet ami-là cherche toujours à t'aider quand tu as des problèmes... et qui ne trahit pas tes secrets et puis aussi c'est un ami qui te soutient toujours. Voilà.» Tr. 6

Yannick, Martinique

«L'amie parfaite, eh bien, c'est celle qui ne sera pas fayot, c'est-à-dire, enfin, fayotte, du moins c'est celle qui n'ira pas répéter à tout bout de champ «Mais oui, tiens, elle a tel et tel problème.» C'est l'idéal à la fin. Moi, je crois que, l'idéal comme amie, c'est, enfin, qu'elle me ressemble un peu.»

Quelle est la différence entre un copain et un ami?

«Eh ben, une copine, c'est par exemple... je ne sais pas, elle est dans la même classe. On discute avec elle des cours... je sais pas, moi... des bobards qu'on raconte à tout le monde. Et l'amie, on lui confie plus ce qui se passe dans l'intimité, ce qu'on ne veut pas dire à sa mère ou à quelqu'un d'autre. Si on a envie, je ne sais pas, de se confier vraiment, on irait plutôt vers l'amie que vers la copine.» Tr. 7

Jennifer, France

«Je pense qu'un copain, c'est quelqu'un qu'on voit un peu tous les jours, à qui on dit bonjour, mais sans vraiment se confier. Alors qu'une amie, on lui confie beaucoup de choses, on reste souvent avec elle, on est très proches.» Tr. 8

Qu'en penses-tu? See answers below.

1. What are the qualities of a good friend according to these people?
2. What characteristics do you look for in a friend?
3. According to these people, what is the difference between **un copain** and **un ami?**

CHAPITRE 9

Teaching Resources
p. 261

PRINT 
- Video Guide, pp. 61–63
- Cahier d'activités, p. 108

MEDIA
- One-Stop Planner
- Video Program, Videocassette 3, 48:39–53:09
- DVD Tutor, Disc 2
- Audio Compact Discs, CD 9, Trs. 5–8
- Interactive CD-ROM Tutor, Disc 3

Presenting Panorama Culturel

Have students view the video. Ask them if they can discern from the interviews whether **un(e) ami(e)** is the equivalent of *a friend* or *an acquaintance.*

Questions

1. **Qui pense que l'amie idéale doit lui ressembler un peu?** (Yannick)
2. **D'après Yannick, une camarade de classe est une amie ou plutôt une copine?** (une copine)
3. **Selon Jennifer, à qui est-ce qu'on se confie?** (à un ami ou une amie)

Connections and Comparisons

Language Note
Point out that **un fayot (une fayotte)** is slang for a student who is *a tattletale* or *a teacher's pet.* **Un bobard** is slang for *a fib* or *a tall tale.*

Teacher Note
For more practice with the **Panorama Culturel**, have students complete the **Compréhension** questions on Disc 2 of the *DVD Tutor.*

Answers

1 someone who listens to you, understands you, helps when you have problems, doesn't betray your confidence, and supports you

3 **Un ami** is a closer friend than **un copain. Un copain** might be a classmate or an acquaintance, but **un ami** is someone you confide in and trust.

STANDARDS: 1.2, 2.1, 3.2, 4.2

Teaching Resources
pp. 262–266

PRINT

- Lesson Planner, p. 43
- TPR Storytelling Book, pp. 66–67
- Listening Activities, pp. 68, 72
- Activities for Communication, pp. 51–52, 116, 118–119, 153–154
- Travaux pratiques de grammaire, pp. 73–76
- Grammar Tutor for Students of French, Chapter 9
- Cahier d'activités, pp. 101–103
- Testing Program, pp. 227–230
- Alternative Assessment Guide, p. 40
- Student Make-Up Assignments, Chapter 9

MEDIA 

- One-Stop Planner
- Audio Compact Discs, CD 9, Trs. 9–10, 14, 21–22
- Teaching Transparencies: 9-2, 9-B; **Grammaire supplémentaire** Answers; Travaux pratiques de grammaire Answers
- Interactive CD-ROM Tutor, Disc 3

Bell Work
Write some suppositions on the board or on a transparency. **(Je parie que le prof est étonné parce que tout le monde a fait ses devoirs.)** Have students either accept or reject them in writing.

Teaching Suggestion
Have students guess the relationships of the people to each other and where they are. Then, ask questions in the **passé composé** about the speakers.

Language Note
Un coup de foudre (literally *a bolt of lightning)* is an idiomatic expression meaning *love at first sight.* **(J'ai eu le coup de foudre pour...** *I fell head over heels in love with . . .)*

Deuxième étape

Objectives Breaking some news; showing interest

WA3 PROVENCE-9

J'avais rendez-vous avec une copine, mais j'ai eu un petit accident de vélo. Pendant que je réparais mon vélo, j'ai trouvé un billet de 20 euros! Super, non?

Marie

Romain

Thibaut

Amina

Didier

14 Tu as compris?

Lisons Qui a passé un bon week-end? Un mauvais week-end?

Bon week-end : Marie, Didier
Mauvais week-end : Romain, Thibaut, Amina

Cultures and Communities

Career Path
Professional reporters and journalists often have to travel to other countries to work on a story. While they may find people there who speak their language and can act as interpreters, they would gather more interesting and accurate information if they were able to communicate directly with local people. Ask students to think of other reasons why it would be beneficial for a journalist to have knowledge of the language and culture of a country he or she is visiting on assignment.

STANDARDS: 1.2, 5.1

Vocabulaire

avoir un accident	*to have an accident*
avoir (prendre) rendez-vous (avec quelqu'un)	*to have a date/make an appointment (with someone)*
se disputer (avec quelqu'un)	*to have an argument (with someone)*
casser (avec quelqu'un)	*to break up (with someone)*
être privé(e) de sortie	*to be "grounded"*
faire la tête	*to sulk*
tomber en panne	*to break down (in a vehicle)*
se perdre	*to get lost*
rencontrer	*to meet*
tomber amoureux(-euse) (de quelqu'un)	*to fall in love (with someone)*

CD-ROM 3
DVD 2

Cahier d'activités, pp. 101–102, Act. 10–12

Travaux pratiques de grammaire, p. 73, Act. 6–7

15 C'est arrivé le week-end dernier

See scripts and answers on p. 251G.

Ecoutons Regarde les images à la page 262. Ecoute Catherine qui décrit ses amis. De qui parle-t-elle?

CD 9 Tr. 9

16 Et toi?

Ecrivons Le week-end de ton ami ne s'est pas très bien passé! Complète sa carte postale avec des expressions du Vocabulaire. Utilise le passé composé dans tes réponses.

Possible answers: **1.** est tombés en panne **2.** s'est perdus **3.** ont fait la tête **4.** se sont disputés **5.** a cassé

Mon week-end à Lyon ne s'est pas très bien passé. Pour commencer, on ___1___ sur la route. Alors, on a dû faire réparer la voiture. Après ça, on n'a pas trouvé la gare Perrache et on ___2___. Tu sais, c'est une très grande ville, Lyon. On avait rendez-vous avec mes cousins à dix heures, mais bien sûr, on était en retard. Quand on est enfin arrivés, ils étaient très fâchés et ils ___3___ tout le week-end! Ensuite, Sophie et Martin ___4___ parce que Martin ne voulait pas venir au musée. Sophie était furieuse et elle ___5___ avec Martin! Quel week-end horrible!

Comment dit-on...?

Breaking some news; showing interest

To break some news:

Tu connais la nouvelle?
Did you hear the latest?
Tu ne devineras jamais ce qui s'est passé.
You'll never guess what happened.
Tu sais qui j'ai vu? *Do you know who . . . ?*
Tu sais ce que Robert a fait?
Do you know what . . . ?
Devine qui Marion a vu! *Guess who . . .*
Devine ce que j'ai fait! *Guess what . . .*

To show interest:

Raconte!
Dis vite! *Let's hear it!*
Aucune idée. *No idea.*

Si tu as oublié
ce qui and ce que
va à la page 108.

Cahier d'activités, p. 102, Act. 13

Connections and Comparisons

Language Note

Students might be interested in the following expressions related to **tomber en panne: tomber en panne d'essence** *(to run out of gas);* **une panne d'électricité** *(a power failure);* **dépanner** *(to repair);* **un dépanneur** *(a repairman);* **une dépanneuse** *(a tow truck).*

Deuxième étape

CHAPITRE 9

Presenting Vocabulaire

Model the expressions, using gestures. Write each expression and its English equivalent on an index card. Give one card to each pair of students or to groups of three. The partners or groups must devise a way to teach that expression to their classmates, without using English. They may mime the expressions. In large classes, you might write the same expression on two or three cards.

Comment dit-on... ?

Write the expressions for showing interest on the board and prompt three students to say them after each of three "news-breaking" statements you make. **(Tu connais la nouvelle?)** After the first student responds **(Raconte!),** tell a far-fetched story. Repeat the process with the other two students. Then, ask the class to guess the meanings of the expressions that you used and the responses that students gave.

Additional Practice

To re-enter the **passé composé** of verbs with **avoir** or **être** as their helping verbs and the **passé composé** of reflexive verbs, prepare several flashcards. On one side, write sentences in the present tense. **(Eric cherche son livre. Les filles sortent. Je me perds.)** Have students repeat the sentence(s) in the **passé composé.** After students respond, show the other side of the card on which you've written the sentence(s) in the **passé composé.**

Deuxième étape

CHAPITRE 9

Teaching Resources
pp. 262–266

PRINT

- Lesson Planner, p. 43
- TPR Storytelling Book, pp. 66–67
- Listening Activities, pp. 68, 72
- Activities for Communication, pp. 51–52, 116, 118–119, 153–154
- Travaux pratiques de grammaire, pp. 73–76
- Grammar Tutor for Students of French, Chapter 9
- Cahier d'activités, pp. 101–103
- Testing Program, pp. 227–230
- Alternative Assessment Guide, p. 40
- Student Make-Up Assignments, Chapter 9

MEDIA 

- One-Stop Planner
- Audio Compact Discs, CD 9, Trs. 9–10, 14, 21–22
- Teaching Transparencies: 9-2, 9-B; **Grammaire supplémentaire** Answers; Travaux pratiques de grammaire Answers
- Interactive CD-ROM Tutor, Disc 3

Additional Practice

18 Ask the following questions about the news article:

1. **Qu'est-ce que l'habitante d'Aix faisait quand elle a vu Elvis?** (Elle promenait son chien.)
2. **Qu'est-ce qu'Elvis a acheté?** (des pains au chocolat)
3. **Quand est-ce que les habitants de la région provençale ont vu un OVNI?** (vers dix-sept heures hier après-midi)
4. **Comment était l'OVNI que le témoin** *(eyewitness)* **a vu?** (comme un ballon de football)

Language Note

OVNI stands for **objet volant non-identifié.**

17 Tu ne devineras jamais... See scripts and answers on p. 251G.

CD 9 Tr. 10

Ecoutons Ecoute ces conversations et choisis l'image qui correspond à chaque conversation.

a.

b.

c.

d.

18 Tu connais la nouvelle?

Parlons Annonce les nouvelles de **Sur le vif!** à un(e) camarade. Il/Elle va réagir à ces histoires. Ensuite, changez de rôle.

SUR LE VIF

LE «KING» PARMI NOUS

Une habitante d'Aix-en-Provence a eu la surprise de sa vie ce matin. Elle promenait son chien au centre-ville quand elle a aperçu Elvis Presley en personne qui sortait d'une boulangerie. Elle a dit que le roi du rock avait un sac plein de pains au chocolat.

UNE VRAIE HISTOIRE MARSEILLAISE

Plusieurs habitants de la région provençale déclarent avoir vu un OVNI vers 17 heures hier après-midi. Un témoin a dit : « J'ai vu un énorme objet dans le ciel. Je savais que ce n'était pas un avion parce qu'il y avait des lumières vertes, jaunes et violettes qui clignotaient. C'était comme un ballon de football! C'était un spectacle incroyable! »

Note culturelle

In France, exaggerated stories, or "tall tales", are called **des histoires marseillaises.** Just as people from certain parts of the United States have a reputation—true or not—for exaggerating stories, people from Provence, particularly from the city of Marseilles, are known for their improbable tales.

Communication for All Students

Slower Pace

17 Have students look at the illustrations and predict what each conversation might be about.

Challenge

17 Before students listen to the recording, have partners write a short dialogue to accompany each illustration. Tell students that the illustrations represent the news they are going to break in the dialogue. Then, play the recording and have students complete the activity. Play the recording again and have students compare their dialogues with those in the recording.

STANDARDS: 1.1, 2.2, 3.2, 4.2, 5.1

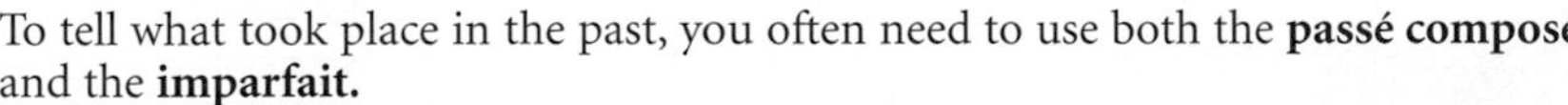

Grammaire

The *passé composé* vs. the *imparfait*

To tell what took place in the past, you often need to use both the **passé composé** and the **imparfait.**

You use the **passé composé** to tell *what happened.*

Elle **a eu** un accident. Nous **avons joué** au tennis.

- Words that indicate a specific moment in the past, like **soudain** *(suddenly),* **tout à coup** *(suddenly),* and **au moment où** *(just when),* usually signal the **passé composé.**

Tout à coup, on **est tombés** en panne.

- Words that tell in what order events happened, like **d'abord, puis,** and **ensuite,** often signal the **passé composé** as well.

D'abord, on **a rencontré** l'étudiant américain.

You use the **imparfait . . .**

—to describe *how people or things were* in the past.

Quand elle **avait** cinq ans, elle **était** pénible.

—to talk about repeated actions in the past, to tell *what used to happen.*

Quand j'**avais** huit ans, je **faisais** toujours des bêtises.

—to describe general conditions in the past, to *set the scene.*

Il **était** deux heures de l'après-midi; il **faisait** beau.

- Words that indicate a repeated action, like **toujours, d'habitude, tous les jours, souvent,** and **de temps en temps,** usually signal the **imparfait.**

On **allait** souvent au théâtre.

Grammaire supplémentaire, pp. 273–275, Act. 4–7

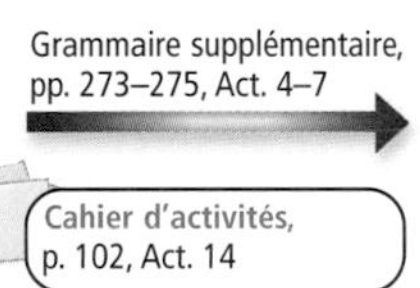

Cahier d'activités, p. 102, Act. 14

Travaux pratiques de grammaire, pp. 74–76, Act. 8–12

19 Grammaire en contexte

Lisons Read Nora's account of a rainy day and tell whether each underlined verb is in the **passé composé** or the **imparfait** and why. See answers below.

Il faisait gris et il pleuvait. J'étais de mauvaise humeur; ma mère travaillait et mon frère, qui était privé de sortie, faisait la tête. Soudain, j'ai pris une décision: pourquoi ne pas aller au cinéma? Je suis allée au Ciné 4 voir le nouveau film de Gérard Depardieu. Après, j'ai rencontré des copains et on est allés au café. Bref, j'ai passé une bonne journée!

Connections and Comparisons

Language Notes

- Point out that the expression **je jouais du piano** means *I played piano, I would play piano,* or *I used to play piano.* All imply that *playing piano* took place often and over an indefinite period of time.
- You might tell students that the imperfect of **être** means *was* and *were* and that the imperfect of other verbs sometimes means *was/were* + verb + *ing.* **(Ma mère travaillait.** *My mother was working.)*

Presenting Grammaire

The *imparfait* and the *passé composé* Read the **Grammaire** with students. Then, draw a timeline on the board, mark events, and label them. **(Je me suis levé(e) à 6h30. J'ai pris mon petit déjeuner à 7h30. Je suis parti(e) à 8h.)** Then, write sentences randomly around the timeline. **(Il faisait beau. Mon frère m'embêtait. J'étais content(e).)** Explain that these sentences can't be placed on the line at a specific time, because they express background circumstances, feelings, or occurrences over an extended period of time.

Teacher Note

Point out to students that when someone asks what they did over the weekend, they usually talk about completed activities, using the **passé composé.** However, when someone asks for further information about the event, they are asking for *background information* or a *description* of the event. *(What was the party like? Who was there? Who was driving when you had the accident? Was it raining?)* In French, these questions and their responses would be in the **imparfait.**

Answers

19 Il **faisait** gris et il **pleuvait:** *sets the scene*
J'**étais:** *describes how people were in the past*
ma mère **travaillait:** *sets the scene*
mon frère, qui **était:** *describes how people were in the past*
faisait la tête: *sets the scene*
j'ai pris une décision; Je **suis allée** au Ciné 4; j'**ai rencontré** des copains; on **est allés;** j'**ai passé:** *tells what happened*

Deuxième étape

Teaching Suggestion

20 Write the story with the blanks on a transparency and project it. Have a volunteer call on students to tell which form of the verb to write in each blank and why.

Speaking Assessment

21 You might use the following rubric when grading your students on this activity.

Speaking Rubric	Points			
	4	3	2	1
Content (Complete–Incomplete)				
Comprehension (Total–Little)				
Comprehensibility (Comprehensible–Incomprehensible)				
Accuracy (Accurate–Seldom accurate)				
Fluency (Fluent–Not fluent)				

18–20: A 14–15: C Under 12: F
16–17: B 12–13: D

Assess

- Testing Program, pp. 227–230
  Quiz 9-2A, Quiz 9-2B
  Audio CD 9, Tr. 14
- Student Make-Up Assignments, Chapter 9, Alternative Quiz
- Alternative Assessment Guide, p. 40

Answers

20
1. était
2. sont allés
3. ont eu
4. était
5. est entré
6. était
7. a demandé
8. semblait
9. riait
10. mettaient
11. donnaient
12. a regardé
13. a commandé
14. a bu
15. a payé
16. est parti
17. ne regrettait pas

Sur le vif

Ecrivons Complète cet article de **Sur le vif!** avec le passé composé ou l'imparfait des verbes entre parenthèses. See answers below.

Patrick Bruel continue sa tournée de concerts dans le sud de la France. Hier, le chanteur __1__ (être) à Montpellier où des centaines de jeunes __2__ (aller) l'applaudir. A leur grande joie, quelques-uns __3__ (avoir) la chance de le rencontrer en personne. Il __4__ (être) environ minuit au restaurant La Côte à l'Os quand tout à coup, Patrick lui-même __5__ (entrer). Il __6__ (être) accompagné de quelques-uns de ses musiciens. Il __7__ (demander) la carte au serveur qui n'en croyait pas ses yeux. Bruel __8__ (sembler) très content et il __9__ (rire) beaucoup. Il a dit au serveur que les concerts le __10__ (mettre) toujours de bonne humeur mais lui __11__ (donner) aussi très faim. Il __12__ (regarder) la carte que le serveur lui avait apportée, puis il __13__ (commander) des escargots et un steak au poivre. Après le repas, il __14__ (boire) un café. Ensuite, Bruel __15__ (payer) l'addition et il __16__ (partir) après avoir donné son autographe au serveur qui __17__ (ne pas regretter) d'avoir travaillé ce soir-là.

21 Tu plaisantes!

Parlons Raconte des histoires marseillaises à un(e) camarade, puis changez de rôle. Vous pouvez utiliser les suggestions suivantes.

EXEMPLE

—Tu sais qui j'ai rencontré?
—Non, raconte!
—J'ai rencontré le président des Etats-Unis!
—Mon œil! Tu étais où?
—J'étais à Washington, évidemment!
—Mais qu'est-ce que tu faisais?
—Je visitais la Maison Blanche.
—Alors, qu'est-ce que tu as fait?
—J'ai dîné avec lui.

rencontrer le président
à Washington
visiter la Maison Blanche
dîner avec lui

1. voir un extra-terrestre
   chez moi
   regarder la télé
   visiter sa planète
2. rencontrer le loup du Gévaudan *(the Bigfoot of France)*
   dans la forêt
   faire du camping
   prendre une photo
3. trouver 100 €
   dans le parc
   promener le chien
   faire du shopping
4. avoir rendez-vous avec ta star préférée
   sur le cours Mirabeau
   écouter de la musique
   demander son autographe

Mon œil!

Ecrivons Fais la liste de trois activités, d'un endroit et d'une émotion. Ensuite, échange ta liste avec celle d'un(e) camarade. Invente une histoire marseillaise avec les éléments de la liste de ton/ta camarade.

rencontrer un extra-terrestre
manger une boîte de chocolats
faire du ski nautique
à la boulangerie
déprimé(e)

Connections and Comparisons

Poetry Link

After presenting the **Grammaire** on page 265, divide the class into several groups. Give each group a copy of the poem *Le Petit Chameau* by Maurice Carême (*Listening Activities,* Level 3, page 66). Have students read the poem and underline the verbs that are in the **imparfait.** Then, have students use the information in the **Grammaire** to explain why each verb is in the **imparfait.** Finally, ask students to rewrite the second, the fifth, and the eleventh lines, replacing the **imparfait** with the **passé composé.** Remind students that they will need to alter the sentences in order to justify the use of the **passé composé.** You might refer students to the first part of the **Grammaire** for ideas on how to change the three sentences.

STANDARDS: 1.2, 1.3, 3.1, 5.2

Troisième étape

Objectives Beginning, continuing, and ending a story

go.hrw.com WA3 PROVENCE-9

Antoine

Pascale téléphone à Antoine . . .

— A propos, Antoine, qu'est-ce que tu as fait hier soir?

— Je m'ennuyais chez moi, alors, j'ai décidé d'aller au cinéma. A ce moment-là, le téléphone a sonné. C'était Arlette. Elle s'ennuyait aussi et voulait faire quelque chose avec moi.

— Donc, vous êtes allés au cinéma!

— Eh bien... c'est-à-dire que... je suis timide.

— Tu veux dire que tu ne l'as pas invitée?!

— Je n'ai pas eu le courage!

— Mais tu es dingue!

— Attends! Elle m'a proposé d'aller voir *Germinal* au Cinéma Cézanne.

— Heureusement!

— Oui, mais tu vois, ce cinéma est à l'autre bout d'Aix.

— Et alors?

— Ben, on a décidé de s'y retrouver une demi-heure plus tard. Alors, j'ai pris le bus, mais à cette heure-là, il y avait beaucoup de circulation et je suis arrivé très en retard. Arlette était déjà partie.

— Pauvre vieux! Maintenant, c'est à toi de l'inviter quelque part.

— Tu crois?

Pascale

23 Tu as compris?

Lisons Qu'est-ce qui est arrivé à Antoine hier soir? Pourquoi n'a-t-il pas invité Arlette? A ton avis, qu'est-ce qu'il va faire maintenant? Arlette called Antoine and asked him to go to a movie. Because of traffic, Antoine arrived very late, and Arlette has already left. He is shy; Answers will vary.

Comment dit-on...?

Beginning, continuing, and ending a story

CD-ROM 3 DVD 2

To begin a story:

A propos,... *By the way, . . .*

To continue a story:

Donc,... *Therefore, . . .*
Alors,... *So . . .*
A ce moment-là,... *At that point, . . .*
Bref,... *Anyway, . . .*
C'est-à-dire que... *That is, . . .*
... quoi. *. . . you know.*
... tu vois. *. . . you see.*

To end a story:

Heureusement,... *Fortunately, . . .*
Malheureusement,... *Unfortunately, . . .*
Enfin/Finalement,...

Cahier d'activités, p. 104, Act. 16–17

Teacher to Teacher

Pam Seccombe
Nathan Hale High School
West Allis, WI

Pam suggests the following activity to practice the *passé composé* and the *imparfait*.

"Show students a short video segment. You might use the **Mise en train** story or **suite** from this chapter or another chapter. While viewing, have half the class take notes about what the scene and people looked like **(imparfait)**, and have the other half take notes on the actions they observed **(passé composé)**. Students should first write 8–10 sentences on their observations. Then pair an "**imparfait** student" with a "**passé composé** student" and have them write a paragraph summary of the video segment."

Troisième étape

CHAPITRE 9

Teaching Resources
pp. 267–269

PRINT

- Lesson Planner, p. 44
- TPR Storytelling Book, pp. 68–69
- Listening Activities, pp. 69, 73
- Activities for Communication, pp. 53–54, 117, 119, 153–154
- Travaux pratiques de grammaire, p. 77
- Grammar Tutor for Students of French, Chapter 9
- Cahier d'activités, pp. 104–106
- Testing Program, pp. 231–234
- Alternative Assessment Guide, p. 40
- Student Make-Up Assignments, Chapter 9

MEDIA 

- One-Stop Planner
- Audio Compact Discs, CD 9, Trs. 11, 15, 23–24
- Teaching Transparencies: 9-3; **Grammaire supplémentaire** Answers; Travaux pratiques de grammaire Answers
- Interactive CD-ROM Tutor, Disc 3

Bell Work

Have students complete the following paragraph with the **imparfait** or the **passé composé**.

Tu sais qui j'ai vu? Je (J') ____ (rencontrer) Michael Jordan! J' ____ (être) au fast-food quand il ____ (entrer). Il m'a dit qu'il ____ (s'ennuyer) chez lui, et il ____ (aller) jouer au basket.

Presenting
Comment dit-on... ?

Tell students that you are going to tell a story, using certain expressions to begin, continue, and end it. Then, tell the story, raising your hand each time you use one of the expressions.

Troisième étape

CHAPITRE 9

Teaching Resources
pp. 267–269

PRINT 

- Lesson Planner, p. 44
- TPR Storytelling Book, pp. 68–69
- Listening Activities, pp. 69, 73
- Activities for Communication, pp. 53–54, 117, 119, 153–154
- Travaux pratiques de grammaire, p. 77
- Grammar Tutor for Students of French, Chapter 9
- Cahier d'activités, pp. 104–106
- Testing Program, pp. 231–234
- Alternative Assessment Guide, p. 40
- Student Make-Up Assignments, Chapter 9

MEDIA

- One-Stop Planner
- Audio Compact Discs, CD 9, Trs. 11, 15, 23–24
- Teaching Transparencies: 9-3; **Grammaire supplémentaire** Answers; Travaux pratiques de grammaire Answers
- Interactive CD-ROM Tutor, Disc 3

Teaching Suggestion

25 After students complete this activity, ask them the following comprehension questions.

1. **Qui a téléphoné à Odile?** (Pascale)
2. **Comment Odile est-elle allée au parc?** (en bus)
3. **Combien de temps est-ce qu'Odile a attendu au parc?** (vingt minutes)
4. **Odile était de bonne humeur après avoir attendu?** (non, fâchée)
5. **Qu'est-ce qu'elle a fait ensuite?** (Elle a essayé de téléphoner à Pascale et elle est rentrée chez elle.)
6. **Qui a téléphoné à Odile la deuxième fois?** (Pascale)

24 La journée de Caroline See scripts and answers on p. 251H.

Ecoutons Ecoute l'histoire de Caroline. Remets les images suivantes en ordre d'après son histoire.

CD 9 Tr. 11

a.

b.

c.

d.

25 Qu'est-ce qu'ils disent?

Ecrivons Complète la conversation entre Odile et Arlette.

heureusement	alors
à propos	aucune idée
dis vite	bref
devineras	malheureusement

— Salut, Odile.
— Salut, Arlette. Tu sais ce qui m'est arrivé hier?
— __1__. Raconte! Aucune idée
— Je faisais mes devoirs chez moi quand Pascale m'a téléphoné. Elle s'ennuyait chez elle et elle voulait aller faire du roller en ligne. Moi, j'étais d'accord. Simple, tu vois? Mais non! J'ai pris le bus pour aller au parc, mais Pascale n'était pas là.
— Vraiment? Mais elle est toujours à l'heure!
— Exactement! Donc, j'ai attendu vingt minutes...
— Vingt minutes!
— __2__, elle n'est jamais arrivée et j'étais fâchée. J'ai essayé de lui téléphoner, mais elle n'était pas là. Malheureusement/Bref
— Et alors?
— __3__, j'ai décidé de rentrer chez moi. Après ça, tu ne __4__ jamais ce qui s'est passé! 3. Alors, 4. devineras
— __5__! Dis vite
— Le téléphone a sonné. C'était Pascale!
— Qu'est-ce qu'elle t'a dit?
— Euh... tu vois, c'était de ma faute. Elle était au Jardin Rambot, et moi, je suis allée au Parc Joseph Jourdan! __6__, elle n'était pas trop fâchée contre moi. __7__, on s'est donné rendez-vous pour demain au Jardin Rambot. 6. Heureusement 7. Bref
— Tout est bien qui finit bien!

26 Le jeu du cadavre exquis

Lisons/Ecrivons In your group, choose a main character for a story. One person begins by writing the first sentence or two of the story, folds the paper to cover all but the last line, and passes it to the next person who writes another sentence, folds the paper again, and passes it on. Remember, anything can happen! When you've finished, read the story to the class.

Donc, elle a cassé avec Martin.

Communication for All Students

Challenge

25 First, have all students cover the word box on this page with a sheet of paper. Then have students work in pairs to complete the activity. Have one partner refer to the **Comment dit-on... ?** on pages 263 and 267. Have students decide together which words to use to complete the sentences. Afterwards, compile a list on the board or on a transparency of the words students chose. Have the class decide which are logical choices.

 STANDARDS: 1.2, 1.3, 3.1, 5.2

Note de grammaire

- Sometimes you have to use both the **imparfait** and the **passé composé** in the same sentence. For example, you might want to say that one action *was going on* (**imparfait**) when another action *happened* (**passé composé**).

CD-ROM 3 DVD 2

Je **faisais** mes devoirs quand le téléphone **a sonné.**

- To emphasize that you were *in the middle of* or *busy doing* something, you can use the imperfect of the expression **être en train de** with an infinitive.

J'étais en train de faire mes devoirs quand le téléphone **a sonné.**

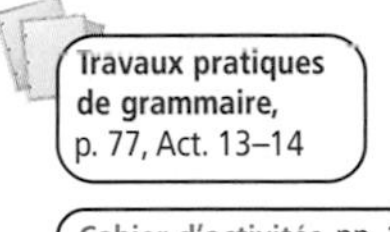

Travaux pratiques de grammaire, p. 77, Act. 13–14

Grammaire supplémentaire, p. 275, Act. 8–9

Cahier d'activités, pp. 105–106, Act. 18–20

27 Grammaire en contexte

Ecrivons Crée au moins dix phrases où tu utilises le passé composé et l'imparfait.

EXEMPLE —**Je faisais mes devoirs quand un extra-terrestre est entré dans ma chambre.**

faire mes devoirs danser le zouk manger de la pizza se disputer avec... visiter... faire la tête conduire la voiture faire la sieste faire des pompes être collé(e) être à... se promener ?	quand	rencontrer... avoir un accident décider de... voir... recevoir... tomber amoureux (amoureuse) de... perdre... casser (avec...) se casser... déguster... ?

28 Grammaire en contexte

Ecrivons Hier soir, un(e) invité(e) surprise est venu(e) chez toi. Raconte ce que tout le monde faisait à la maison quand cette personne est arrivée. Ensuite, décris cet(te) invité(e) et dis pourquoi il/elle est venu(e) chez toi.

Tu ne devineras jamais ce qui s'est passé hier soir! Mon père regardait la télé et moi, j'écoutais mon CD préféré de Céline Dion quand elle est entrée dans...

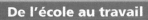

29 De l'école au travail

Ecrivons You work for a French publishing company specializing in books for children. Create a short fairy tale beginning with **"Il était une fois, dans un pays très lointain, ...".** You might refer to page R18 for additional fairy tale vocabulary.

Cendrillon *(Cinderella)*

La Belle et la Bête *(Beauty and the Beast)*

Blanche-Neige *(Snow White)*

la pantoufle de verre *(glass slipper)*
tuer *(to kill)*
le bal *(dance)*
la marraine *(godmother)*
la citrouille *(pumpkin)*
se cacher *(to hide)*
la sorcière *(witch)*
les souris *(mice)*
transformer en *(to turn into)*
se marier *(to get married)*
les sept nains *(the seven dwarfs)*
embrasser *(to kiss)*

Presenting Note de grammaire

The *imparfait* and the *passé composé* Write the following activities on the board: **faire les devoirs, écrire au tableau, regarder par la fenêtre, lire une bande dessinée, dormir, parler à un(e) camarade.** As you leave the classroom, tell six volunteers to do these activities. Then, after leaving for a few moments, make a grand entrance and ask each volunteer what he or she was doing when you came in. **(Qu'est-ce que tu faisais quand je suis entré(e) dans la classe?)** Finally, ask the other students what the volunteers were doing. **(Qu'est-ce que... faisait?)** Involve the other students by asking them what they were doing when you came in. You might repeat this, using **être en train de.**

Teaching Suggestion

29 Try to obtain one of the suggested fairy tales in French from the public library or from a foreign language bookstore. You might read it aloud to the class in one sitting or over several days. Students might follow along, reading photocopies you've distributed. Often, the French and English story lines will differ. Students might tell how the two versions differ, if they are familiar with the story in English.

Connections and Comparisons

Literature Link

26 Point out the title of the activity: **Le jeu du cadavre exquis.** André Breton (1896–1966), Louis Aragon (1897–1982), and Philippe Soupault (1897–1990) were co-founders of the Surrealist movement, which sought to eliminate the distinction between dream and reality, objectivity and subjectivity, and reason and madness. Together, they experimented with the revolutionary technique of *automatic writing* and were known to sit in cafés and practice this process, using **le jeu du cadavre exquis.**

Assess

- Testing Program, pp. 231–234
  Quiz 9-3A, Quiz 9-3B
  Audio CD 9, Tr. 15
- Student Make-Up Assignments, Chapter 9, Alternative Quiz
- Alternative Assessment Guide, p. 40

Lisons!

CHAPITRE 9

Teaching Resources
pp. 270–271

PRINT 

- Lesson Planner, p. 45
- Cahier d'activités, p. 107
- Reading Strategies and Skills Handbook, Chapter 9
- Joie de lire 2, Chapter 9
- Standardized Assessment Tutor, Chapter 9

MEDIA

- One-Stop Planner

Prereading
Activities A–B

Teacher Note
Eugène Ionesco, the author of *La Cantatrice chauve,* began to learn English in 1948, using a method that required him to memorize dialogues. The dialogues were supposed to reflect daily life, but in fact, had little to do with real life or authentic conversation. Ionesco noticed that people say many things every day that make little sense when taken out of context. It was this experience that inspired the writing of *La Cantatrice chauve.*

Challenge
B. Have students use a French dictionary to find synonyms for **absurde (futile, inconscient, dérangé, désarticulé, sot, sans sens)** and **banal (commun, quotidien, ordinaire, rebattu, usé).** Have students write sentences using these words.

Answers

A. The main characters are M. and Mme Martin. They're sitting across from each other, without speaking and smiling timidly, when the scene begins. Answers will vary.

Lisons!

La Cantatrice chauve par Eugene Ionesco

Stratégie pour lire
Before you read, make some theories about what the reading will be about or what's going to happen. Remember what you've learned about how the genre of a text can give you clues about what you're going to read. You'll understand and remember much more if you read with a purpose.

Misunderstandings can occur between friends. What do you think of the misunderstanding in this scene from the play ***La Cantatrice chauve?***

A. Before you read the play carefully, skim the scene to guess what the reading will be about. Who are the main characters? What are they doing when the scene begins? Do you think this will be a humorous scene or a sad one? Why? See answers below.

B. Have you ever had the experience of saying something over and over and suddenly realizing that what you were saying seemed completely meaningless? The playwright Eugène Ionesco had just such an experience in the late 1940s and wrote about it in ***La Cantatrice chauve.*** When you read this scene from the play, keep in mind that this is an example of the theater of the absurd. Then, reread the scene to see if you think Ionesco has made his point: the endless repetition of common, polite words and phrases makes them sound absurd.

SCENE IV

Mme et M. Martin, s'assoient l'un en face de l'autre, sans se parler. Ils se sourient, avec timidité.

M. MARTIN (le dialogue qui suit doit être dit d'une voix traînante, monotone, un peu chantante, nullement nuancée).
– Mes excuses, Madame, mais il me semble, si je ne me trompe, que je vous ai déjà rencontrée quelque part.

Mme MARTIN. – A moi aussi, Monsieur, il me semble que je vous ai déjà rencontré quelque part.

M. MARTIN. – Ne vous aurais-je pas déjà aperçue, Madame, à Manchester, par hasard?

Mme MARTIN. – C'est très possible. Moi, je suis originaire de la ville de Manchester! Mais je ne me souviens pas très bien, Monsieur, je ne pourrais pas dire si je vous y ai aperçu, ou non!

M. MARTIN. – Mon Dieu, comme c'est curieux! moi aussi je suis originaire de la ville de Manchester, Madame!

Mme MARTIN. – Comme c'est curieux!

. . .

M. MARTIN. – Depuis que je suis arrivé à Londres, j'habite rue Bromfield, chère Madame.

Mme MARTIN. – Comme c'est curieux, comme c'est bizarre! moi aussi, depuis mon arrivée à Londres j'habite rue Bromfield, cher Monsieur.

M. MARTIN. – Comme c'est curieux, mais alors, mais alors, nous nous sommes peut-être rencontrés rue Bromfield, chère Madame.

Mme MARTIN. – Comme c'est curieux; comme c'est bizarre! c'est bien possible, après tout! Mais je ne m'en souviens pas, cher Monsieur.

M. MARTIN. – Je demeure au n° 19, chère Madame.

Mme MARTIN. – Comme c'est curieux, moi aussi j'habite au n° 19, cher Monsieur.

M. MARTIN. – Mais alors, mais alors, mais alors, mais alors, mais alors, nous nous sommes peut-être vus dans cette maison, chère Madame?

Mme MARTIN. – C'est bien possible, mais je ne m'en souviens pas, cher Monsieur.

M. MARTIN. – Mon appartement est au cinquième étage, c'est le n° 8, chère Madame.

Mme MARTIN. – Comme c'est curieux, mon Dieu, comme c'est bizarre! et quelle coïncidence! moi aussi j'habite au cinquième étage, dans l'appartement n° 8, cher Monsieur!

Cultures and Communities

Culture Note
Ionesco was born in 1912 in Romania. From the age of six, he lived in France and witnessed the First World War. Ionesco was disturbed by the rise of Nazism in Romania and France and revolted against it in his writing. He became one of Europe's foremost playwrights and wrote *Rhinocéros,* one of the definitive plays of the theater of the absurd. When he died in Paris in 1994, his plays were still in production.

Multicultural Link
Have students research playwrights from other cultures to see if any have made significant contributions to the theater of the absurd.

STANDARDS: 1.2, 2.2, 3.1

M. MARTIN, *songeur.* –

Comme c'est curieux,
comme c'est curieux, comme c'est curieux et quelle coïncidence! vous savez, dans ma chambre à coucher j'ai un lit. Mon lit est couvert d'un édredon vert. Cette chambre, avec ce lit et son édredon vert, se trouve au fond du corridor, entre les water et la bibliothèque, chère Madame!

Mme MARTIN. – Quelle coïncidence, ah mon Dieu, quelle coïncidence! Ma chambre à coucher a, elle aussi, un lit avec un édredon vert et se trouve au fond du corridor, entre les water, cher Monsieur, et la bibliothèque!

M. MARTIN. – Comme c'est bizarre, curieux, étrange! alors, Madame, nous habitons dans la même chambre et nous dormons dans le même lit, chère Madame. C'est peut-être là que nous nous sommes rencontrés!

Mme MARTIN. – Comme c'est curieux et quelle coïncidence! C'est bien possible que nous nous y soyons rencontrés, et peut-être même la nuit dernière. Mais je ne m'en souviens pas, cher Monsieur!

M. MARTIN. – J'ai une petite fille, ma petite fille, elle habite avec moi, chère Madame. Elle a deux ans, elle est blonde, elle a un œil blanc et un œil rouge, elle est très jolie, elle s'appelle Alice, chère Madame.

Mme MARTIN. – Quelle bizarre coïncidence! moi aussi j'ai une petite fille, elle a deux ans, un œil blanc et un œil rouge, elle est très jolie et s'appelle aussi Alice, cher Monsieur!

M. MARTIN, *même voix traînante, monotone.* – Comme c'est curieux et quelle coïncidence! et bizarre! c'est peut-être la même, chère Madame!

Mme MARTIN. – Comme c'est curieux! c'est bien possible cher Monsieur.

Un assez long moment de silence...
La pendule sonne vingt-neuf fois.

M. MARTIN, *après avoir longuement réfléchi, se lève lentement et, sans se presser, se dirige vers Mme Martin qui, surprise par l'air solennel de M. Martin, s'est levée, elle aussi, tout doucement; M. Martin a la même voix rare, monotone, vaguement chantante.* – Alors, chère Madame, je crois qu'il n'y a pas de doute, nous nous sommes déjà vus et vous êtes ma propre épouse... Elisabeth, je t'ai retrouvée!

Mme MARTIN *s'approche de M. Martin sans se presser. Ils s'embrassent sans expression. La pendule sonne une fois, très fort. Le coup de la pendule doit être si fort qu'il doit faire sursauter les spectateurs. Les époux Martin ne l'entendent pas.*

Mme MARTIN. – Donald, c'est toi, darling!

For Activities C–I, see answers below.

C. What phrases do you find in the first few lines that indicate the Martins are strangers when the scene begins, in spite of the fact they are married?

D. In the first 20 lines, find two things that Mr. and Mrs. Martin have in common. Based on what you've just read, what do you think will happen in the scene?

E. Find examples of phrases that are repeated throughout this scene. What is the effect of the repetition of these phrases?

F. Why are the remarks **Comme c'est curieux** and **Quelle coïncidence** ridiculous as used here by the Martins? What is curious and bizarre about their conversation?

G. Reread the last lines of Mr. Martin and Mrs. Martin. What is the significant change in their attitude toward each other? How is this change signaled in their language? Give two examples.

H. Reread the stage directions. Why does Ionesco want the characters to present their lines in this way? Find the lines punctuated with an exclamation point. Practice reading them aloud with a monotone, singsong, expressionless voice. How easy is this to do?

I. What is the main point that Ionesco is trying to make? Can you find enough evidence to prove that the play is about the absurdity of daily life? Do you think that Ionesco has successfully created a scene that convinces you of this absurdity?

J. Using some of the small talk and polite phrases you noted in Activity B, write a brief, absurd dialogue with a partner. Then, perform your scene for the class.

Cahier d'activités, p. 107, Act. 22

Lisons!

CHAPITRE 9

Reading

Activities C–I

Group Work

C.–I. You might have students work in small groups to find and discuss the answers.

Postreading

Activity J

Teaching Suggestion

J. Since plays are meant to be read aloud and performed, give students ample opportunity to practice reading this scene aloud with appropriate intonation and facial expressions. You might have partners volunteer to present half or all of the scene to the class. You might consider staging it for other French classes.

Possible Answers

C. Mes excuses, Madame, mais il me semble... que je vous ai déjà rencontrée quelque part; A moi aussi, Monsieur; Ne vous aurais-je pas déjà aperçue, Madame, à Manchester... ?

D. Both are originally from Manchester. Both live on Bromfield Street; Answers will vary.

E. Comme c'est curieux! Comme c'est bizarre! Mais alors... ! Quelle coïncidence; The repetition of the phrases increases the absurdity of the situation and satirizes polite conversation.

F. The Martins are married, so there is nothing curious or coincidental about the things they have in common. They do not recognize each other immediately.

G. The Martins act like husband and wife; They use **tu** instead of **vous.** Mme Martin calls M. Martin "darling."

H. The lines are presented in a monotone voice to exaggerate the banality of polite conversation.

I. Daily life is full of absurdities. Our lives become mundane and empty when we speak to each other in platitudes and meaningless phrases.

Connections and Comparisons

Drama Link

C. Ask students to read the opening directions of this scene in lines one through four. Ask them what information they would get from reading the play as opposed to seeing it produced. (They would know what the playwright intended as opposed to a director's or actor's interpretation.) Ask students why it is important to read stage directions and other directions interspersed in the text in italics. If there are students in your class who have acted in some of the school plays or are in a drama or theater class, ask them to give advice on following stage directions.

Grammaire supplémentaire

CHAPITRE 9

For **Grammaire supplémentaire** Answer Transparencies, see the *Teaching Transparencies* binder.

Grammaire supplémentaire

Première étape

Objectives Wondering what happened; offering possible explanations; accepting or rejecting explanations

1 Vanessa te parle de ses amis. De qui est-ce qu'elle parle? Ecris le(s) nom(s) dans le blanc qui correspond à la description. (**p. 259**)

Sylvie et Julie — Martine — Bruno et Francine — Jérôme

1. ___________ avait l'air déprimée.
2. ___________ avaient l'air contents.
3. ___________ avaient l'air surprises.
4. ___________ avait l'air fâché.
5. ___________ avaient l'air de bonne humeur.

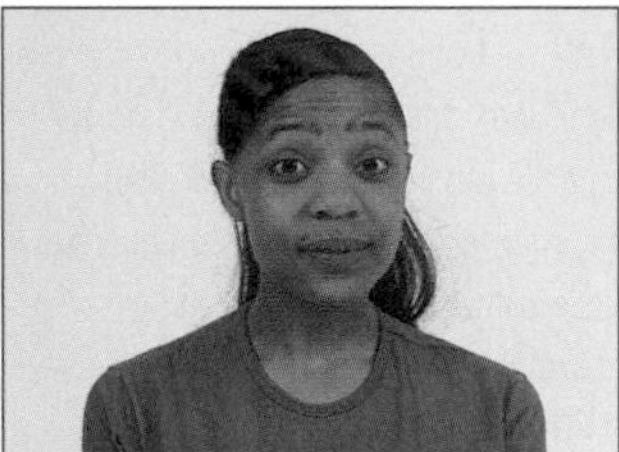

2 You and Frédéric both went to the same party, but you don't agree on what the people there were like. Disagree with each of Frédéric's statements, based on the model. Use the expression **ne pas avoir l'air** and an adjective in your answers. (**p. 259**)

EXEMPLE Nos amis étaient gênés. **Non, ils n'avaient pas l'air gênés.**

1. Sophie était énervée.
2. Claudine et Monique étaient furieuses.
3. Tu étais mal à l'aise.
4. Patricia et Nathan étaient déprimés.
5. J'étais de bonne humeur.
6. Jean était étonné.

Answers

1
1. Martine
2. Bruno et Francine
3. Sylvie et Julie
4. Jérôme
5. Sylvie et Julie OR Bruno et Francine

2
1. Non, elle n'avait pas l'air énervée.
2. Non, elles n'avaient pas l'air furieuses.
3. Non, je n'avais pas l'air mal à l'aise.
4. Non, ils n'avaient pas l'air déprimés.
5. Non, tu n'avais pas l'air d'être de bonne humeur.
6. Non, il n'avait pas l'air étonné.

Grammar Resources for Chapter 9

The **Grammaire supplémentaire** activities were designed as supplemental activities for the grammatical concepts presented in the chapter. You might use them as additional practice, for review, or for assessment.

For more grammar presentations, review, and practice, refer to the following:

- Travaux pratiques de grammaire
- Grammar Tutor for Students of French
- Grammar Summary on pp. R23–R42
- Cahier d'activités
- Grammar and Vocabulary quizzes (Testing Program)
- Test Generator
- Interactive CD-ROM Tutor
- DVD Tutor
- **Jeux interactifs** at go.hrw.com

3 You are a very observant person. Tell what the following people seemed like based on what happened to them. (**p. 259**)

gêné · triste · inquiet · amoureux · malheureux · heureux · content

Exemple Simone a raté une marche. Elle avait l'air gênée.

1. Marius et sa copine se sont disputés.
2. Christian et Cécile ont eu de bonnes notes.
3. Laurent a rencontré une jolie fille à la boum.
4. Odile a trouvé 20 € dans la rue.
5. Cassandre et Solange se sont perdues en ville.
6. Alexandre s'est cassé la jambe, alors il ne pouvait pas s'amuser avec ses amis.

Deuxième étape

Objective Breaking some news; showing interest

4 Complete the passage below by filling in the suggested verbs in the **passé composé** or the **imparfait.** Then, reread the passage and give the name of this fairy tale. When you've decided what the story is, check back over your verbs to make sure you've chosen the right tense and made the necessary agreements of the past participles. (**p. 265**)

Il ___1___ (faire) très beau hier matin. Je/J' ___2___ (décider) d'aller chez ma grand-mère. Je/J' ___3___ (vouloir) lui offrir un cadeau. En route, je/j' ___4___ (rencontrer) un type bizarre dans la forêt. Quand je/j' ___5___ (arriver) chez ma grand-mère, je/j' ___6___ (voir) qu'elle ___7___ (être) un peu plus poilue que d'habitude. Je/J' ___8___ (crier)—Mère-grand, ce que vous avez de grandes dents!—Elle ___9___ (avoir) l'air énervée. Quand soudain, elle ___10___ (déchirer) sa robe et je/j' ___11___ (voir) que c' ___12___ (être) un grand méchant loup! C' ___13___ (être) le type de la forêt! Alors, je/j' ___14___ (partir) en courant à toutes jambes.

Le nom de cette histoire, c'est ____________________.

Teacher to Teacher

Nancy Rodman
The Blake School
Minneapolis, MN

Nancy suggests this activity to practice grammar from the chapter.

"Students get the impression that feelings are always expressed by the **imparfait** in past tense narration. To practice the use of the **passé composé** to express a reaction that signals a change in a state of mind, have students brainstorm situations in which they "got scared" versus situations when they "were scared." Share examples on the board and ask students to explain the difference: **1. Quand le chien est entré dans notre maison, j'ai eu très peur. 2. Il pleuvait beaucoup et j'avais peur.** For homework, they write a short paragraph describing a scary situation in the past."

Answers

3
1. Ils avaient l'air malheureux.
2. Ils avaient l'air contents.
3. Il avait l'air amoureux.
4. Elle avait l'air heureuse.
5. Elles avaient l'air inquiètes.
6. Il avait l'air triste.

4
1. faisait
2. ai décidé
3. voulais
4. ai rencontré
5. suis arrivée
6. ai vu
7. était
8. ai crié
9. avait
10. a déchiré
11. ai vu
12. était
13. était
14. suis partie; *Little Red Riding Hood (Le Petit Chaperon rouge)*

For **Grammaire supplémentaire** Answer Transparencies, see the *Teaching Transparencies* binder.

Answers

5
1. ai vu
2. avais / étais
3. a téléphoné
4. étaient / allaient
5. a gagné
6. faisait

6
1. me suis disputée
2. a cassé
3. allais
4. suis tombée
5. a réparé
6. voulais
7. ai invité
8. s'est perdus
9. est arrivés
10. a décidé
11. mangeait
12. est arrivé

Grammaire supplémentaire

WA3 PROVENCE-9

5 Robert aime raconter des histoires. Complète ses phrases avec la forme correcte du verbe. (**p. 265**)

1. Hier, je (j') _____ Elvis au supermarché.
   ai vu   voyais   vois
2. Quand j' _____ cinq ans, j' _____ plus grand que mes parents.
   avait / était   ai eu / ai été   avais / étais
3. Tout à coup, le Président _____ chez moi.
   téléphone   a téléphoné   téléphonait
4. Quand mes parents _____ jeunes, ils _____ à l'école le samedi soir.
   ont été / allaient   étaient / allaient   étaient / sont allés
5. Ton frère _____ son match mercredi.
   a gagné   gagne   gagnait
6. De temps en temps, mon grand-père _____ la vaisselle pour ma grand-mère.
   a fait   fait   faisait

6 Complète le message électronique que ton amie Anne a envoyé avec les formes correctes de **l'imparfait** et du **passé composé** des verbes entre parenthèses. Mets les participes passés des verbes conjugués avec **être** au masculin, féminin ou pluriel quand c'est nécessaire. (**p. 265**)

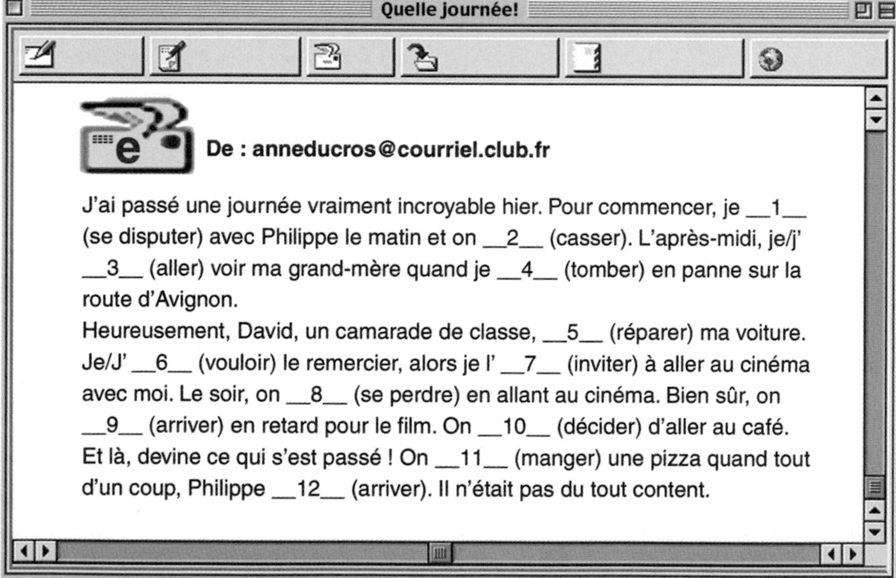

Quelle journée!

De : anneducros@courriel.club.fr

J'ai passé une journée vraiment incroyable hier. Pour commencer, je __1__ (se disputer) avec Philippe le matin et on __2__ (casser). L'après-midi, je/j' __3__ (aller) voir ma grand-mère quand je __4__ (tomber) en panne sur la route d'Avignon.

Heureusement, David, un camarade de classe, __5__ (réparer) ma voiture. Je/J' __6__ (vouloir) le remercier, alors je l' __7__ (inviter) à aller au cinéma avec moi. Le soir, on __8__ (se perdre) en allant au cinéma. Bien sûr, on __9__ (arriver) en retard pour le film. On __10__ (décider) d'aller au café. Et là, devine ce qui s'est passé ! On __11__ (manger) une pizza quand tout d'un coup, Philippe __12__ (arriver). Il n'était pas du tout content.

Review and Assess

Additional Practice

7 After students have completed Activity 7, you might have them expand this activity by writing about weekend activities from their own point of view. Have them write several sentences describing their weekend. Encourage them to provide details (they can make up their weekend activities if they wish) and use both the **passé composé** and **imparfait** in their responses. Have them exchange papers with a partner to see if they agree on the tenses used to describe the weekend.

7 Tu écris une histoire en français sur ce que tu as fait vendredi dernier. Indique si tu dois utiliser le **passé composé (PC)** ou **l'imparfait (I)** dans les phrases suivantes, puis récris les phrases avec le temps du verbe qui convient. (**p. 265**)

EXEMPLE Il fait froid.
I **Il faisait froid.**

1. Je vais au cinéma avec mes amis.
2. Le film est bien.
3. Gérard Depardieu est dans le film.
4. Après le film, mes amis et moi, nous allons au café.
5. Lucien prend un café et je prends une eau minérale.
6. Je rentre à dix heures et je me couche.
7. Je suis fatigué(e).

Troisième étape

Objectives Beginning, continuing, and ending a story

8 Il s'est passé quelque chose hier. Choisis une expression pour compléter chaque phrase. Utilise **l'imparfait** ou **le passé composé** dans tes réponses. (**p. 269**)

se disputer — aller — avoir un petit accident — avoir rendez-vous — tomber en panne — être en train de — rencontrer — faire du jogging

1. Magali _____ faire du vélo quand elle _____.
2. Olivia mangeait au café avec Hervé quand ils _____. Alors, ils ont cassé.
3. Hugues et Sylvain _____ chez leurs grands-parents en voiture quand ils _____.
4. Isabelle étudiait à la bibliothèque quand elle _____ Maxime.
5. Patrick _____ avec Eléonora, mais quand il est arrivé, elle était déjà partie.
6. Victor et moi, nous _____ dans la forêt quand nous nous sommes perdus.

9 Yesterday was not your day. Tell what you were doing and what happened to interrupt you. Use the **imparfait** and the **passé composé.** (**p. 269**)

EXEMPLE laver la voiture / le téléphone sonner
Je lavais la voiture quand le téléphone a sonné.

1. faire du jogging / avoir un accident
2. faire mes devoirs / Luc arriver
3. se laver / tomber
4. me promener / perdre ma clé
5. manger au restaurant / mes amis entrer

Review and Assess

You may wish to assign the **Grammaire supplémentaire** activities as additional practice or homework after presenting material throughout the chapter. Assign Activities 1–3 after **Note de grammaire** (p. 259), Activities 4–7 after **Grammaire** (p. 265), and Activities 8–9 after **Note de grammaire** (p. 269).

To prepare students for the **Etape** Quizzes and Chapter Test, we suggest doing the **Grammaire supplémentaire** activities in the following order. Have students complete Activities 1–3 before Quiz 9-1A or 9-1B; Activities 4–7 before Quiz 9-2A or 9-2B; and Activities 8–9 before Quiz 9-3A or 9-3B.

Answers

7
1. PC Je suis allé(e) au cinéma avec mes amis.
2. I Le film était bien.
3. I Gérard Depardieu était dans le film.
4. PC Nous sommes allé(e)s au café.
5. PC Lucien a pris un café et j'ai pris une eau minérale.
6. PC Je suis rentré(e) à dix heures et je me suis couché(e).
7. I J'étais fatigué(e).

8
1. était en train de; a eu un petit accident
2. se sont disputés
3. allaient; sont tombés en panne
4. a rencontré
5. avait rendez-vous
6. faisions du jogging

9
1. Je faisais du jogging quand j'ai eu un accident.
2. Je faisais mes devoirs quand Luc est arrivé.
3. Je me lavais quand je suis tombé(e).
4. Je me promenais quand j'ai perdu ma clé.
5. Je mangeais au restaurant quand mes amis sont entrés.

CHAPITRE 9

The **Mise en pratique** reviews and integrates all four skills and culture in preparation for the Chapter Test.

Teaching Resources
pp. 276–277

PRINT

- Lesson Planner, p. 45
- TPR Storytelling Book, pp. 70–71
- Listening Activities, p. 69
- Video Guide, pp. 61, 64
- Grammar Tutor for Students of French, Chapter 9
- Standardized Assessment Tutor, Chapter 9

MEDIA 

- One-Stop Planner
- Video Program
  Videocassette 3, 53:11–57:12
- DVD Tutor, Disc 2
- Audio Compact Discs, CD 9, Tr. 12
- Interactive CD-ROM Tutor, Disc 3

Challenge

1 Have students work in pairs to create a conversation in which Paul tells his best friend about his incredible adventure. Paul should break the news to his friend, explain what happened to him, and tell how he felt throughout the event. His friend should show interest and react to Paul's story. You might have volunteers perform their skit for the class.

Answers

1. He was going to meet some friends from school.
2. He had a bicycle accident in the park.
3. in a castle from the Middle Ages; He felt a little worried and uncomfortable.
4. the king's daughter, with whom Paul fell in love
5. They think he just had a dream.
6. When the police found him, he was wearing a scarf with the name "Mylena" printed on it.

Mise en pratique

internet
ADRESSE: go.hrw.com
MOT-CLE: WA3 PROVENCE-9

UN LYCEEN VOYAGE DANS LE TEMPS

Paul Daquin, le lycéen lyonnais qui avait disparu la semaine dernière, vient d'être retrouvé sain et sauf dans le parc de la Tête d'Or. Une interview avec des journalistes a révélé une histoire incroyable : Paul Daquin a peut-être voyagé dans le temps!

Tout a commencé jeudi dernier. Paul avait rendez-vous avec des amis du lycée. Mais il n'est jamais arrivé à son rendez-vous. D'après Paul, il a eu un petit accident de vélo dans le parc. Ensuite, il ne sait pas ce qui s'est passé. Il raconte que tout à coup, il s'est réveillé dans un château magnifique. Il s'est levé, puis il s'est promené dans le château. Il était mal à l'aise parce que les gens étaient habillés comme au Moyen Age et ils le regardaient d'une façon bizarre. Il est entré dans une très grande salle à manger où il y avait une fête. A ce moment-là, Paul a rencontré une très belle jeune fille, Mylena, la fille du roi. Paul et Mylena ont dansé toute la soirée et Paul est tombé amoureux de Mylena. Après ça, Paul a oublié ce qui s'est passé. Tout ce qu'il sait, c'est que les policiers l'ont retrouvé dans le parc de la Tête d'Or. Il dormait sous un arbre.

Cette histoire incroyable intéresse beaucoup de monde. Des experts du monde entier sont venus à Lyon pour essayer de comprendre ce qui est arrivé au jeune Paul Daquin. Beaucoup pensent que toute cette histoire incroyable n'est qu'un rêve. Mais si c'est un rêve, il reste un mystère : quand la police a retrouvé Paul, il avait un foulard en soie autour du cou. Plus étrange encore, le nom «Mylena» était écrit sur le foulard...

1 Read *Un lycéen voyage dans le temps* and answer the questions below. See answers below.

1. Where was Paul Daquin going last Thursday?
2. What happened to him on his way there?
3. Where was he when he woke up? How did he feel about the situation?
4. Who is Mylena?
5. What do experts think really happened to Paul?
6. According to the journalist who wrote the article, what proof is there that Paul's story is true?

2 Manon and Tristan are discussing what happened to their friend Eléonore yesterday. Listen to their conversation, and then answer the questions below. See scripts and answers on p. 251H.

CD 9 Tr. 12

1. What happened to Eléonore on her way to meet Laurent?
2. Was Laurent in a good mood at the café? Why or why not?
3. What happened when Eléonore finally arrived at the café?
4. Why does Manon think Laurent reacted the way he did? What explanation does she give?
5. Does Tristan agree with Manon in the end?

Apply and Assess

Teaching Suggestion

1 After students have completed the activity, have them read the article again. Then, ask them to close their textbooks and have them tell whether the following statements are true or false:

1. **On a retrouvé Paul dans le parc de la Tête d'Or.**
2. **Paul est parti de chez lui jeudi matin.**
3. **La voiture de Paul est tombée en panne.**
4. **Paul était mal à l'aise quand il s'est promené dans le château.**
5. **Il y avait une grande fête au château.**
6. **Paul a rencontré le roi.**
7. **Mylena a trouvé Paul dans la forêt.**
8. **A la fin, Paul et Mylena se sont disputés.**

STANDARDS: 1.2

Ecrivons!

A French literary magazine is showcasing the works of American students learning French language and culture. You've been asked to write your own **histoire marseillaise** for publication in the magazine.

Stratégie pour écrire
Setting is one of the first considerations when writing any type of story. Once you've decided what the subject of your histoire marseillaise will be, think about where and when it will take place.

Préparation

To help you get started, ask yourself the following questions: Will the setting be just a backdrop or will it play a more important role in the story? Can the setting be used to create a particular atmosphere? What details about the setting will you need to describe?

Based on your answers to the questions, select the time and place that would be best suited to your **histoire marseillaise.**

Rédaction

Once you've chosen the setting, begin to construct your story. When writing your **histoire marseillaise,** there are several points that you'll want to keep in mind. First, make sure that the events in your story follow a logical order. Also, be sure to remain consistent with verb tenses; try not to switch between the past and the present in your story. Next, try to help your reader "see" the story. In other words, use specific and vivid details when telling your story. Finally, try to use language you know. You may not know all the French words and phrases you'll need, but chances are there's a way to use what you do know to get your story across. You might also want to add illustrations to your story.

Evaluation

A good way to catch all the mistakes when you proofread is to create a checklist of things to look for. This can make the editing less overwhelming, and it allows you to focus on one aspect of your writing at a time. Some items to include on your checklist are punctuation, capitalization, spelling, and use of the **passé composé** and the **imparfait.**

4

Jeu de rôle

With your classmates, create an informal television news broadcast about the happenings in your school. Break the top news stories for your class. You might assign "correspondents" who report from the scene. Be sure to:

- break the news to the class.
- begin, continue, and end the stories.
- offer possible explanations for anything strange that happened.

Mise en pratique

CHAPITRE 9

Process Writing

3 To help students prepare to write their **histoires marseillaises,** you might have the class brainstorm to come up with a list of American tall tales, their characters, and the traits for which these characters are known. You might also ask for examples of this type of tale from students of other cultures represented in your class.

Portfolio

3 **Written** You might have students include their **histoire marseillaise** in their written portfolios. For portfolio information, see the *Alternative Assessment Guide,* pages iv–17.

Teaching Suggestion

4 This activity is expanded in the project on page 251C.

Teacher Note

For additional practice and review, you might use the **Histoire Finale** for Chapter 9 on pages 70–71 of the *TPR Storytelling Book.*

Apply and Assess

Cooperative Learning

Have groups of students write and stage a play in which they use as many of the words and expressions from the chapter as possible. Have each group choose a playwright to invent the story line, a writer to script the play in French, a director to create the stage directions, and the actors and actresses.

STANDARDS: 1.1, 1.3, 3.1, 5.1, 5.2

Que sais-je?

CHAPITRE 9

Teaching Resources
p. 278

PRINT
- Grammar Tutor for Students of French, Chapter 9

MEDIA
- Interactive CD-ROM Tutor, Disc 3
- Online self-test

go.hrw.com
WA3 PROVENCE-9

Teaching Suggestion

2 **3** You might have small groups work together to complete these activities. Have students create additional situations for Activity 2, and the other group members will try to offer possible explanations for them. For Activity 3, have students invent additional quotes for group members to respond to.

Que sais-je?

WA3 PROVENCE-9

Can you use what you've learned in this chapter?

Can you wonder what happened and offer possible explanations? p. 260

1 If you didn't know why your friend was late for your meeting after school, how would you say that you wonder what happened? Je me demande...

2 What possible explanations could you give for each of these situations?
1. Ton ami(e) était déprimé(e). A mon avis,...
2. Tes parents avaient l'air fâchés aujourd'hui. Peut-être que...
3. Ton prof était de bonne humeur. Je crois que...
4. Tes amis étaient étonnés. Je parie que...

Can you accept and reject explanations? p. 260

3 How would you respond if your friends made these remarks? Possible answers:
1. «A mon avis, il va faire beau aujourd'hui.» Tu as peut-être raison.
2. «Je crois que Paris est la plus grande ville de France.» Evidemment.
3. «Je parie que j'ai raté mon interro d'anglais.» Je ne crois pas.
4. «Peut-être que notre prof est en retard.» C'est possible.
5. «J'ai vu un extra-terrestre dans le jardin.» Ce n'est pas possible.

Can you break some news? p. 263

4 How would you break the following news to a friend? Possible answers:

1. Tu sais qui j'ai vu?

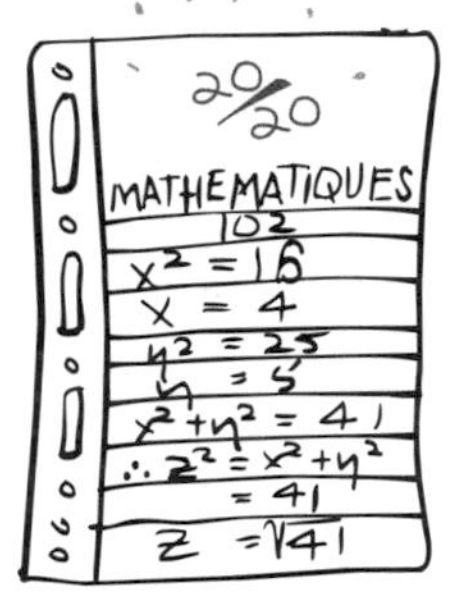

2. Tu ne devineras jamais ce qui s'est passé!

3. Devine ce que j'ai vu!

Can you show interest? p. 263

5 How would you respond if your friend said **Devine ce qui s'est passé hier!?** Aucune idée. Dis vite! Raconte!

Can you begin, continue, and end a story? p. 267

6 What would you say to begin a story you'd like to tell? A propos,...

7 What would you say to continue the story you began in number 6? Donc,... ; Alors,... ; A ce moment-là,...

8 What would you say if your story ended well? Badly? Heureusement,... ; Malheureusement,...

Review and Assess

Game

Je l'ai trouvée Write the answers to the questions in the **Que sais-je?** on separate index cards and scatter them face up on the floor. Form two teams. Call out a question at random. Have one student from each team race to try to find the card that contains the answer to that question. The first student to find the correct answer calls out **Je l'ai trouvée** and scores a point for his or her team.

Vocabulaire

Première étape

Wondering what happened; offering possible explanations

Je me demande...	*I wonder...*
A mon avis,...	*In my opinion,...*
Peut-être que...	*Maybe...*
Je crois que...	*I think that...*
Je parie que...	*I bet that...*

Accepting or rejecting explanations

Tu as peut-être raison.	*Maybe you're right.*
C'est possible.	*That's possible.*
Ça se voit.	*That's obvious.*
Evidemment.	*Obviously.*
A mon avis, tu te trompes.	*In my opinion, you're mistaken.*
Ce n'est pas possible.	*That's not possible.*
Je ne crois pas.	*I don't think so.*

Feelings

amoureux (amoureuse)	*in love*
de bonne humeur	*in a good mood*
de mauvaise humeur	*in a bad mood*
déprimé(e)	*depressed*
énervé(e)	*annoyed*
étonné(e)	*surprised*
fâché(e)	*angry*
furieux (furieuse)	*furious*
gêné(e)	*embarrassed*
inquiet (inquiète)	*worried*
mal à l'aise	*uncomfortable*

Other useful expressions

assez	*sort of*
plutôt	*rather*
vachement	*really*
super	*really, ultra-*
avoir l'air	*to seem*

Deuxième étape

Breaking some news; showing interest

Tu connais la nouvelle?	*Did you hear the latest?*
Tu ne devineras jamais ce qui s'est passé.	*You'll never guess what happened.*
Tu sais qui... ?	*Do you know who...?*
Tu sais ce que... ?	*Do you know what...?*
Devine qui...	*Guess who...*
Devine ce que...	*Guess what...*
Raconte!	*Tell me!*
Aucune idée.	*No idea.*
Dis vite!	*Let's hear it!*

Personal happenings

avoir un accident	*to have an accident*
avoir (prendre) rendez-vous (avec quelqu'un)	*to have a date/make an appointment (with someone)*
être privé(e) de sortie	*to be "grounded"*
faire la tête	*to sulk*
casser (avec quelqu'un)	*to break up (with someone)*
rencontrer	*to meet*
se disputer (avec quelqu'un)	*to have an argument (with someone)*
se perdre	*to get lost*
tomber amoureux (amoureuse) (de quelqu'un)	*to fall in love (with someone)*
tomber en panne	*to break down (vehicle)*

Troisième étape

Beginning, continuing, and ending a story

A propos,...	*By the way,...*
Donc,...	*Therefore,...*
Alors,...	*So,...*
A ce moment-là,...	*At that point,...*
Bref,...	*Anyway,...*
C'est-à-dire que...	*That is,...*
... quoi.	*...you know.*
... tu vois.	*...you see.*
Heureusement,...	*Fortunately,...*
Malheureusement,...	*Unfortunately,...*
Enfin/Finalement,...	*Finally,...*
être en train de	*to be in the process of (doing something)*

Review and Assess

Circumlocution

Have students work in pairs. Have each pair write the vocabulary for personal experiences on separate slips of paper, fold the slips, and mix them up. One partner will draw a slip of paper and describe the event as if it happened to one of his or her friends, without naming the event. The other student will try to guess the event from the description. When he or she guesses correctly, the players switch roles. (**—La mère de Paul était très fâchée. Il ne pouvait pas aller au cinéma ce week-end. —Il était privé de sortie? —Oui.**)

Vocabulaire

CHAPITRE 9

Game

Catégories Form rows of five or six students. Write the categories from the **Vocabulaire** on the board. The first person in each row has a sheet of paper, and everyone has a pen or pencil. First, name a category and secretly write five words or expressions from it on a transparency. Then, call out **Commencez!** The first student in the row writes one word or expression from the category and quickly passes the paper to the next student, who writes a different one, and so on. The last student in the row returns the paper to the first student. After one minute, call time and project your transparency. The student who has the paper tells you how many of the expressions on the transparency appear on the paper and are written correctly. The row that most closely matches your transparency wins that round.

Chapter 9 Assessment

- **Testing Program**
  Chapter Test, pp. 235–240

  Audio Compact Discs, CD 9, Trs. 16–18
  Speaking Test, p. 347
- **Alternative Assessment Guide**
  Performance Assessment, p. 40
  Portfolio Assessment, p. 26
  CD-ROM Assessment, p. 54
- **Interactive CD-ROM Tutor, Disc 3**
  CD-ROM 3 A toi de parler
  DVD 2 A toi d'écrire
- **Standardized Assessment Tutor**
  Chapter 9
- **One-Stop Planner, Disc 3**

  Test Generator
  Chapter 9

STANDARDS: 1.3

Chapitre 10 : Je peux te parler?

Chapter Overview

Mise en train pp. 282–284	***Qu'est-ce que je dois faire?***

	FUNCTIONS	GRAMMAR	VOCABULARY	RE-ENTRY
Première étape pp. 285–289	• Sharing a confidence, p. 286 • Asking for and giving advice, p. 286	• Placement of object pronouns, p. 288	• Apologetic actions, p. 287	• Giving, accepting, and rejecting advice **(Chapitre 7,** II) • The imperative **(Chapitre 5,** I)
Deuxième étape pp. 290–293	• Asking for and granting a favor; making excuses, p. 291	• Direct object pronouns with the **passé composé,** p. 293	• Party preparations, p. 291	• Pronunciation: the nasal sound **[ã]** **(Chapitre 5,** I) • Object pronouns **(Chapitre 9,** I)
Troisième étape pp. 294–297	• Apologizing and accepting an apology; reproaching someone, p. 294	• Object pronouns before an infinitive, p. 295		• Chores **(Chapitre 7,** I) • Object pronouns **(Chapitre 9,** I)

Lisons! pp. 298–299	**L'amitié**	**Reading Strategy:** Using supporting details	
Grammaire supplémentaire	**pp. 300–303** **Première étape,** pp. 300–301	**Deuxième étape,** pp. 302–303	**Troisième étape,** p. 303
Review pp. 304–307	**Mise en pratique,** pp. 304–305 **Ecrivons!** Tone Writing a poem	**Que sais-je?** p. 306	**Vocabulaire,** p. 307

CULTURE

- **Note culturelle, Le parc des Thermes,** p. 290
- **Note culturelle,** Provençale cuisine, p. 293
- **Panorama Culturel,** Talking about personal problems, p. 297

Chapitre 10 : Je peux te parler?

Chapter Resources

Lesson Planning

One-Stop Planner

Lesson Planner with Substitute Teacher

Lesson Plans, pp. 46–50, 72

Student Make-Up Assignments

- Make-Up Assignment Copying Masters, Chapter 10

Listening and Speaking

TPR Storytelling Book, pp. 72–79

Listening Activities

- Student Response Forms for Listening Activities, pp. 75–77
- Additional Listening Activities 10-1 to 10-6, pp. 79–81
- Additional Listening Activities (song), p. 82
- Scripts and Answers, pp. 147–151

Video Guide

- Teaching Suggestions, pp. 66–67
- Activity Masters, pp. 68–70
- Script and Answers, pp. 107–110, 122

Activities for Communication

- Communicative Activities, pp. 55–60
- Realia and Teaching Suggestions, pp. 120–124
- Situation Cards, pp. 155–156

Reading and Writing

Reading Strategies and Skills Handbook, Chapter 10

Joie de lire 2, Chapter 10

Cahier d'activités, pp. 109–120

Grammar

Travaux pratiques de grammaire, pp. 78–86

Grammar Tutor for Students of French, Chapter 10

Assessment

Testing Program

- Grammar and Vocabulary Quizzes, **Etape** Quizzes, and Chapter Test, pp. 249–266
- Score Sheet, Scripts and Answers, pp. 267–274

Alternative Assessment Guide

- Portfolio Assessment, p. 27
- Performance Assessment, p. 41
- CD-ROM Assessment, p. 55

Student Make-Up Assignments

- Alternative Quizzes, Chapter 10

Standardized Assessment Tutor

- Reading, pp. 39–41
- Writing, p. 42
- Math, pp. 51–52

MEDIA

Online Activities

- **Jeux interactifs**
- **Activités Internet**

Video Program

- Videocassette 4
- Videocassette 5 (captioned version)

Interactive CD-ROM Tutor, Disc 3

DVD Tutor, Disc 2

Audio Compact Discs

- Textbook Listening Activities, CD 10, Tracks 1–12
- Additional Listening Activities, CD 10, Tracks 19–25
- Assessment Items, CD 10, Tracks 13–18

Teaching Transparencies

- Situation 10-1 to 10-3
- Vocabulary 10-A to 10-B
- **Mise en train**
- **Grammaire supplémentaire** Answers
- **Travaux pratiques de grammaire** Answers

One-Stop Planner CD-ROM

Use the **One-Stop Planner CD-ROM with Test Generator** to aid in lesson planning and pacing.

For each chapter, the **One-Stop Planner** includes:

- Editable lesson plans with direct links to teaching resources
- Printable worksheets from resource books
- Direct launches to the HRW Internet activities
- Video and audio segments
- Test Generator
- Clip Art for vocabulary items

Projects

Une causerie télévisée

Working in groups of six, students will create and videotape a television talk show.

MATERIALS

✂ **Students may need**
- Video camera/Videocassette
- Banners or signs
- Costumes or props

SUGGESTED SEQUENCE

1. Each group decides on a name for the talk show and its topic.
2. Students assign roles within the group. There should be a host, a psychologist, and several panel members whose specific roles will be determined by the content of the show.
3. The group outlines the program. The panel members must be free to interact with one another and to respond to questions from the audience. Therefore, an outline of what will be discussed should be prepared, rather than an actual script.
4. Students rehearse the discussion in the order established in the outline.
5. To enhance their presentations, the groups may decide to create a set for the show, use some props or costumes, or simply display a banner bearing the name of the show.
6. For the presentation, you might allow students to carry index cards with an outline of the show and possible questions and answers, but they should not read from the cards. The host should allow each person to speak and should encourage interaction among the guests. The host should also elicit questions from the audience (the rest of the class). If possible, videotape the shows and then play them for the class. Have students provide constructive feedback.

GRADING THE PROJECT

Suggested Point Distribution: (total = 100 points)

Content (inclusion of functions)	20
Language use	20
Creativity/Presentation	20
Comprehensibility	20
Effort/Participation	20

Games

Carrés hollywoodiens

In this game, which is played like the game Hollywood Squares®, students will practice the functions and vocabulary from this chapter.

Preparation The day before playing the game, ask each student to prepare five true-false statements or multiple-choice questions based on what they've learned in the chapter. The questions might focus on vocabulary, grammar, or culture, and should be in French. For example, students might write:

1. **Vrai ou Faux? On sert des amuse-gueule après le dîner.**
2. **Quelle est la meilleure réponse à la question «Tu peux m'aider?»**
   a) **C'est de ma faute.**
   b) **Ça ne fait rien.**
   c) **Avec plaisir.**

Collect the questions. Then, prepare nine large cards. On one side of each card, write a large X, and on the other side, write a large O.

Procedure Ask for nine volunteers to serve as panelists. Seat them in chairs at the front of the class in three rows of three to form a tic tac toe grid. Give one of the nine cards to each panelist, and then form two teams. To play the game, a contestant from one team chooses a panelist. Read a question for the panelist to answer. The panelist may choose to respond correctly or incorrectly. The contestant then either agrees or disagrees with the panelist's response. If the contestant agrees with a correct answer, or disagrees with an incorrect response, the panelist holds up an X or O in the square for the contestant's team. However, if the contestant agrees with an incorrect response or disagrees with a correct response, the turn passes to the other team. Teams alternate trying to get an X or an O in a square. The first team to get three Xs or Os in a row diagonally, horizontally, or vertically wins.

 STANDARDS: 1.1, 1.3, 5.1

Storytelling

Mini-histoire

This story accompanies Teaching Transparency 10-1. The ***mini-histoire*** *can be told and retold in different formats, acted out, written down, and read aloud to give students additional opportunities to practice all four skills. The following story relates an eventful party organized by Antoine.*

Antoine est au téléphone avec un de ses meilleurs amis qui habite dans une autre ville. Il lui raconte ce qu'il a fait le week-end précédent : «Mes parents n'étaient pas là le week-end dernier. J'ai donc organisé une fête pour l'anniversaire de Philippe. J'ai invité toute la classe et aussi ma copine, Véronique. On a commencé à sortir ensemble il y a deux mois. Tout le monde s'amusait bien. Et puis, j'ai commencé à danser avec Emilie. Soudain, j'ai vu que Véronique nous regardait très méchamment. J'avais oublié qu'elle était très jalouse! Vers minuit, tout le monde est parti. J'ai commencé à ranger, je ne voulais pas que mes parents voient la maison en désordre. Mais j'étais très fatigué et je me suis endormi. Quand ils sont rentrés, la maison était encore sale. Maintenant, je n'ai plus le droit de sortir pendant un mois!»

Traditions

Lavande

During the summer months in Provence, the air is filled with the smell of **lavande fine** *(lavender)* and **lavandin** *(lavandin)*, a hybrid of fine lavender and aspic. Every July and August, the flowers are harvested and then distilled into essential oils used in fine perfumes. It takes approximately 130 kilos of lavender or 26 kilos of lavandin to produce one liter of oil. The oils are then sold to various perfume houses where a master perfumer, or **nez,** blends them with the essential oils from other flowers and other natural resources to create an essence. Have students find out more about the distillation process of lavender and other flowers used in perfumes and report to the class.

Recette

The name ***pissaladière*** *comes from the word* ***pissala*** *in provençal.* ***Piscis*** *meant fish in latin and* ***sal*** *meant salt. It is very similar to an Italian pizza. Anchovies are very common in cooking in the south of France.*

PISSALADIERE

Pâte

2 tasses de farine

une pincée de sel

1 cuillère à soupe de sucre

1/2 tasse de beurre froid en petits morceaux

3 cuillères à soupe d'eau (ou un petit verre)

2 cuillères d'huile d'olive

Garniture

3 cuillères d'huile olive

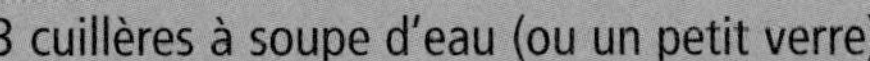

2 tasses d'oignons coupés

3 gousses d'ail

1 feuille de laurier

1 cuillère à soupe de thym

20 à 30 olives noires

15 filets d'anchois

Pâte

Mettre la farine, le sucre et le sel dans un bol. Couper le beurre en petits morceaux. Mélanger le beurre et la farine avec les doigts. Ajouter l'eau et l'huile petit à petit. Faire une boule avec la pâte. Laisser reposer pendant 30 minutes au frigidaire.

Garniture

Faire revenir à feu doux les oignons, l'ail, le thym et le laurier dans une poêle avec l'huile d'olive pendant environ 45 minutes. Pendant ce temps, étaler la pâte dans un moule. Faire chauffer au four pendant 10 minutes. Retirer du four. Etaler les oignons sur la pâte avec les olives et les anchois. Arroser avec un filet d'huile d'olive. Mettre au four à 400° F pendant 15 minutes.

Servir chaud ou froid.

Chapitre 10 : Je peux te parler?
Technology

DVD/Video

Videocassette 4, Videocassette 5 (captioned version)
DVD Tutor, Disc 2
See Video Guide, pages 65–70.

Mise en train • Qu'est-ce que je dois faire?

Pascale wants to give a party for her birthday and asks Arlette for advice on how to plan one. Pascale also wants to invite Cédric, but she hasn't spoken to him since their misunderstanding. Arlette gives her advice and promises to arrive early to help. Later Antoine gives Arlette advice on what to buy Pascale for her birthday. He also invites her to a concert taking place the same night as Pascale's party! Arlette doesn't know what to do.

Mise en train (suite)

Antoine urges Arlette to go with him to the concert, but Arlette doesn't want to disappoint Pascale. Later Cédric tells Arlette that he is planning to invite Pascale to the same concert. Arlette advises him to call and invite Pascale right away. At a café, both girls are reluctant to reveal that they would rather go to the concert. As they come to realize each other's true feelings, Antoine and Cédric arrive, and everyone is happy.

Qu'est-ce que tu fais quand tu as un problème? Tu parles à qui?

Students from Côte d'Ivoire, France, and Vietnam talk about what they do when they have a problem.

Vidéoclip

- *J'te l'dis quand même* performed by Patrick Bruel: music video

Interactive CD-ROM Tutor

Activity	Activity Type	Pupil's Edition Page
En contexte	*Interactive conversation*	
1. Comment dit-on... ?	Le bon choix	p. 286
2. Vocabulaire	Méli-mélo	p. 287
3. Grammaire	Méli-mélo	p. 288
4. Vocabulaire	Chasse au trésor	p. 291
5. Grammaire	Les mots qui manquent	p. 293
6. Comment dit-on... ?	Chacun à sa place Explorons!/Vérifions!	pp. 291, 294
Panorama Culturel	Qu'est-ce que tu fais quand tu as un problème? Tu parles à qui?	p. 297
A toi de parler	*Guided recording*	pp. 304–305
A toi d'écrire	*Guided writing*	pp. 304–305

Teacher Management System

Launch the program, type "admin" in the password area, and press RETURN. Log on to www.hrw.com/CDROMTUTOR for a detailed explanation of the Teacher Management System.

DVD Tutor

The *DVD Tutor* contains all material from the *Video Program* as described above. French captions are available for use at your discretion for all sections of the video. The *DVD Tutor* also provides a variety of video-based activities that assess students' understanding of the **Mise en train, Suite,** and **Panorama Culturel.**

This part of the *DVD Tutor* may be used on any DVD video player connected to a television, video monitor, or on a computer with a DVD-ROM drive.

In addition to the video material and the video-based comprehension activities, the *DVD Tutor* also contains the entire *Interactive CD-ROM Tutor* in DVD-ROM format. Each DVD disc contains the activities from all 12 chapters of the *Interactive CD-ROM Tutor.*

This part of the *DVD Tutor* may be used on a Macintosh® or Windows® computer with a DVD-ROM drive.

To preview all resources available for this chapter, use the **One-Stop Planner CD-ROM**, Disc 3.

Internet Connection

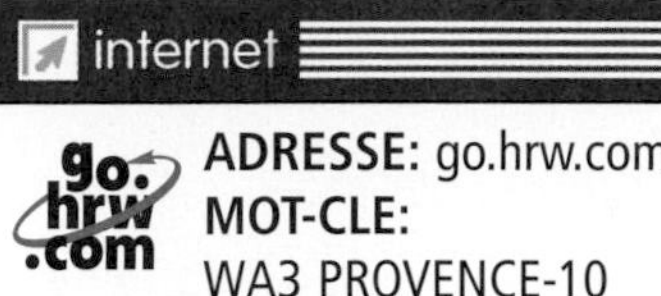

*Have students explore the **go.hrw.com** Web site for many online resources covering all chapters. All Chapter 10 resources are available under the keyword **WA3 PROVENCE-10.** Interactive games help students practice the material and provide them with immediate feedback. You'll also find a printable worksheet that provides Internet activities that lead to a comprehensive online research project.*

Jeux interactifs

You can use the interactive activities in this chapter

- to practice grammar, vocabulary, and chapter functions
- as homework
- as an assessment option
- as a self-test
- to prepare for the Chapter Test

Activités Internet

Students look for information on Provençal traditions and specialties online and record their findings, using the vocabulary from the chapter.

- In preparation for the **Activités Internet,** have students reread the **Notes culturelles** throughout the chapter. After completing the activity sheet, have students work with a partner and peer-edit Section D.

Location: http://

Nom ______ Classe ______ Date ______

10 *Je peux te parler?*

Level 2

Avant d'explorer

A. Tu dois organiser une fête d'anniversaire avec la Provence pour thème. Fais une liste des choses dont tu vas avoir besoin pour bien réussir ta fête.

En ligne!

B. Comment organiser une fête vraiment «provençale»? Explore Internet pour en savoir plus sur la Provence, ses traditions, ses spécialités culinaires et ses produits typiques.

Traditions	
Spécialités culinaires	

Projet

Have students choose one typical dish from Provence and research it on the Internet. Students should compile the information on a posterboard to present to the class. The posterboard should include a picture or drawing of the dish, the recipe, and some historical background. Have students document their sources by noting the URLs of all the sites that they consulted.

Chapitre 10 : Je peux te parler?

Textbook Listening Activities Scripts 

Première étape

7 p. 286

1. —Mohammed, je peux te parler?
   —Oui, qu'est-ce qu'il y a?
   —Tu vois, Li m'a prêté son livre d'histoire.
   —C'est gentil.
   —Le problème, c'est que je l'ai perdu!
2. —Tu as une minute?
   —Oui, je t'écoute.
   —Je suis embêtée. Hier soir, je devais retrouver Emile au café, mais j'ai été privée de sortie, et j'ai pas pu y aller. Il ne me parle plus, mais ce n'était pas de ma faute!
3. —J'ai un problème.
   —Je peux peut-être faire quelque chose?
   —Ben... c'est que j'ai eu dix en histoire-géo.
   —Tu avais étudié?

Answers to Activity 7
1. b
2. c
3. a

10 p. 288

1. —Salut, Hubert. Je peux te parler?
   —Oui, je t'écoute.
   —Je me suis disputée avec Luc. C'était un petit malentendu, mais il ne me parle plus.
   —C'est ridicule! Tu devrais lui téléphoner pour te réconcilier avec lui.
2. —Salut, Florence. Tu sais que je me suis disputée avec Luc?
   —Non! Qu'est-ce qui s'est passé?
   —Ben, tu vois, il était en retard à notre rendez-vous au ciné.
   —Mais c'est pas grave, ça! Tu devrais lui pardonner.
3. —Salut, Jacques. Tu as une minute? Je me suis disputée avec Luc, et j'ai besoin de conseils.
   —Qu'est-ce qu'il a fait?
   —Il était en retard pour notre rendez-vous au ciné.
   —Alors ça, c'est impardonnable! Il ne te respecte pas. A mon avis, tu devrais casser.
4. —Eh, Marie, tu as une minute? Je ne sais pas quoi faire.
   —Luc était en retard à notre rendez-vous hier soir et on s'est disputés.
   —Tu t'es fâchée contre lui?
   —Oui, mais c'était tellement bête.
   —Ecoute. Tu devrais t'excuser et lui dire que tu l'aimes. C'est vrai, non?

Answers to Activity 10
1. Call Luc and make up with him.
2. Forgive him.
3. Break up with him.
4. Apologize and tell him you love him.

Deuxième étape

16 p. 291

1. —Gisèle, tu peux me prêter ta jupe bleue pour la fête ce soir?
   —Bien sûr! Je peux te la prêter sans problème.
2. —Stéphane, ça t'ennuie de sortir la poubelle?
   —Désolé, je n'ai pas le temps. Je dois retrouver des amis dans dix minutes!
3. —Chantal, tu pourrais faire la vaisselle pour moi?
   —Je voudrais bien, sœurette, mais je dois faire mes devoirs.
4. —Papa, tu as une minute pour m'aider à ranger le salon?
   —Désolé, mais j'ai quelque chose d'important à faire. Demande à ta mère.
5. —Maman, ça t'embête de m'aider à ranger le salon?
   —Pas du tout.

Answers to Activity 16
1. helps
2. makes excuse
3. makes excuse
4. makes excuse
5. helps

The following scripts are for the listening activities found in the *Pupil's Edition.* For Student Response Forms, see *Listening Activities,* pages 75–77. To provide students with additional listening practice, see *Listening Activities,* pages 79–82.

To preview all resources available for this chapter, use the **One-Stop Planner CD-ROM**, Disc 3.

18 **p. 292**

PASCALE Vraiment, je ne sais pas par où commencer!
JEAN-CLAUDE Calme-toi, Pascale, c'est facile. D'abord, tu dois fixer la date.
PASCALE D'accord... samedi quatorze, ça va?
JEAN-CLAUDE Oui. Après, tu dois demander la permission à tes parents, bien sûr.
PASCALE Je suis sûre qu'ils seront d'accord. Mais je leur demanderai ce soir.
JEAN-CLAUDE Bon. Si tu veux, moi, je peux envoyer les invitations.
PASCALE Vraiment? C'est gentil!
JEAN-CLAUDE Pour le reste... euh... , il faut surtout penser à choisir de la bonne musique. Si tu veux que tout le monde danse, c'est vachement important!
PASCALE Mais je n'ai pas beaucoup de disques, moi.
JEAN-CLAUDE C'est pas grave. Je peux apporter mes CD, et je choisirai la musique. D'accord?
PASCALE D'accord.
JEAN-CLAUDE Ça va être une fête super, tu vas voir!

Answers to Activity 18
Pascale va fixer la date et demander la permission à ses parents.
Jean-Claude va envoyer les invitations et choisir la musique.

Troisième étape

25 **p. 295**

1. —Oh, Serge! Je voulais te dire... Je suis désolée pour hier soir. J'aurais dû te téléphoner.
   —Oh, t'en fais pas.
   —J'ai été privée de sortie, c'est pour ça que je ne suis pas venue à ta boum.
2. —Dis, Cécile...
   —Ouais?
   —Excuse-moi pour ce matin... Je n'aurais pas dû dire à tous tes copains que tu avais eu cinq en maths.
   —J'étais vraiment gênée, tu sais?
   —Tu ne m'en veux pas, dis?
   —Non... enfin, il n'y a pas de mal.
3. —Frédéric... à propos de ton Walkman®... C'est de ma faute. Je me suis disputé avec Roland, il m'a poussé, et j'ai cassé ton Walkman.
   —Quoi? T'exagères quand même! Tu aurais pu faire attention!
   —Oh, je suis vraiment désolé. Je t'en achèterai un autre si tu veux.

Answers to Activity 25
1. unable to go to party because she was grounded; apology accepted
2. told friends that Cécile got a five in math; apology accepted
3. dropped and broke Frédéric's Walkman; He is reproached.

Mise en pratique

1 **p. 304**

1. Bonjour, je m'appelle Désiré. Je suis déprimé parce que mes parents m'ont privé de sortie. Je suis rentré trop tard vendredi soir, et maintenant, ils ne veulent plus me laisser sortir le soir. Ce n'est pas de ma faute. J'avais oublié ma montre! Qu'est-ce que je peux faire?
2. Bonjour, mon nom est Murielle. Je suis embêtée parce que j'ai eu une très mauvaise note à ma dernière interro d'anglais. Je sais que mes parents vont être fâchés. Mais j'avais oublié mon livre au lycée, et je n'ai pas pu étudier pour l'interro. Qu'est-ce que je pourrais faire?
3. Salut. Moi, c'est Jérôme! J'ai rencontré une fille super sympa au parc l'autre jour. Je sais qu'elle habite à côté de chez moi, mais je ne lui ai pas demandé son numéro de téléphone, et maintenant, je voudrais bien la revoir. Qu'est-ce que je peux faire?
4. Je m'appelle Eric. Je suis invité à une boum ce week-end, mais je ne sais pas si je devrais y aller. Tu vois, mon amie Julie est invitée aussi, et... ben... on s'est disputés, et on ne se parle plus depuis trois jours. Elle est sans doute encore fâchée contre moi. Qu'est-ce que tu me conseilles de faire?

Answers to Activity 1
1. c 2. b 3. a 4. d

Chapitre 10 : Je peux te parler?

Suggested Lesson Plans 50-Minute Schedule

Day 1

CHAPTER OPENER 5 min.
- Present Chapter Objectives, p. 281.
- Photo Flash! and Culture Note, ATE, p. 280

MISE EN TRAIN 40 min.
- Presenting **Mise en train,** ATE, p. 283
- Teaching Suggestions: Post-viewing Suggestions 1–3, Video Guide, p. 66
- Thinking Critically, ATE, p. 283
- Do Activities 1–4, p. 284.
- Read and discuss **Note culturelle,** p. 284.

Wrap-Up 5 min.
- Do Thinking Critically for Activity 5, ATE, p. 284.

Homework Options
Cahier d'activités, Acts. 1–2, p. 109

Day 2

PREMIERE ETAPE
Quick Review 5 min.
- Bell Work, ATE, p. 285

Comment dit-on... ?, p. 286 15 min.
- Complete Activity 6, p. 285.
- Presenting **Comment dit-on... ?,** ATE, p. 286
- Play Audio CD for Activity 7, p. 286.
- Cahier d'activités, Activity 3, p. 110

Comment dit-on... ?, p. 286 25 min.
- Presenting **Comment dit-on... ?,** ATE, p. 287
- Cahier d'activités, Activity 4, p. 110
- Do Activity 8, p. 287.
- Have students do Activity 9, p. 287, in groups.

Wrap-Up 5 min.
- TPR, ATE, p. 287

Homework Options
Cahier d'activités, Act. 5, p. 111

Day 3

PREMIERE ETAPE
Quick Review 5 min.
- Check homework.

Vocabulaire, p. 287 20 min.
- Presenting **Vocabulaire,** ATE, p. 287
- Play Audio CD for Activity 10, p. 288.
- Travaux pratiques de grammaire, Activities 1–4, pp. 78–80
- Have students do Activity 11, p. 288, in groups.

Grammaire, p. 288 20 min.
- Presenting **Grammaire,** ATE, p. 288
- Visual Learners, ATE, p. 288
- Do Activity 12, p. 289.
- Cahier d'activités, Activity 8, p. 112
- Travaux pratiques de grammaire, Activities 5–7, pp. 80–81

Wrap-Up 5 min.
- Teaching Suggestions, ATE, p. 289

Homework Options
Study for Quiz 10-1.
Pupil's Edition, Act. 13, p. 289
Grammaire supplémentaire, Acts. 1–3, p. 300

Day 4

PREMIERE ETAPE
Quiz 10-1 20 min.
- Administer Quiz 10-1A or 10-1B.

DEUXIEME ETAPE
Note culturelle, p. 290 10 min.
- Complete Activity 15, p. 290.
- Read and discuss **Note culturelle,** p. 290.
- History Link, ATE, p. 290

Comment dit-on... ?, p. 291 15 min.
- Presenting **Comment dit-on... ?,** ATE, p. 291
- Play Audio CD for Activity 16, p. 291.
- Cahier d'activités, Activity 11, p. 114

Wrap-Up 5 min.
- Begin Activity 17, p. 291.

Homework Options
Finish Act. 17, p. 291.

Day 5

DEUXIEME ETAPE
Quick Review 5 min.
- Have volunteers share their notes from Activity 17, p. 291.

Vocabulaire, p. 291 20 min.
- Presenting Vocabulaire, ATE, p. 291
- Play Audio CD for Activity 18, p. 292.
- Cahier d'activités, Activity 12, p. 114
- Do Activity 19, p. 292.
- Have students do Activity 21, p. 292, in groups.

Note de grammaire, p. 293 15 min.
- Read and discuss **Note de grammaire,** p. 293.
- Cahier d'activités, Activities 14–15, p. 115
- **Grammaire supplémentaire,** Activities 7–10, pp. 302–303
- Do Activity 22, p. 293.

Note culturelle, p. 293 5 min.
- Read and discuss **Note culturelle,** p. 293.

Wrap-Up 5 min.
- Teaching Suggestion, ATE, p. 293

Homework Options
Study for Quiz 10-2.
Travaux pratiques de grammaire, Acts. 11–14, pp. 84–85

Day 6

DEUXIEME ETAPE
Quiz 10-2 20 min.
- Administer Quiz 10-2A or 10-2B.

TROISIEME ETAPE
Comment dit-on... ?, p. 294 25 min.
- Complete Activity 24, p. 294.
- Presenting **Comment dit-on... ?,** ATE, p. 294
- Play Audio CD for Activity 25, p. 295.
- Language-to-Language, ATE, p. 294
- Cahier d'activités, Activities 16–17, p. 116
- Do Activities 26–27, p. 295.

Wrap-Up 5 min.
- Read and discuss **A la française,** p. 295.

Homework Options
Cahier d'activités, Act. 18, p. 117

For alternative lesson plans by chapter section, to create your own customized plans, or to preview all resources available for this chapter, use the **One-Stop Planner CD-ROM**, Disc 3.

For additional homework suggestions, see activities accompanied by this symbol throughout the chapter.

Day 7

TROISIEME ETAPE

Quick Review 5 min.
- Check homework.

Note de grammaire, p. 295 15 min.
- Read and discuss **Note de grammaire,** p. 295.
- Travaux pratiques de grammaire, Activities 15–16, p. 86
- Cahier d'activités, Activity 19, p. 117
- Do Activity 28, p. 296.
- Have students do Activity 29, p. 296, in pairs.

PANORAMA CULTUREL 20 min.
- Presenting **Panorama Culturel,** ATE, p. 297
- Do Questions, ATE, p. 297.
- Discuss **Qu'en penses-tu?,** p. 297.
- See Teaching Suggestions: Post-viewing Suggestion, Video Guide, p. 67.

Wrap-Up 10 min.
- Teaching Suggestion, ATE, p. 296

Homework Options
Study for Quiz 10-3.
Pupil's Edition, Act. 30, p. 296
Grammaire supplémentaire, Acts. 11–12, p. 303

Day 8

TROISIEME ETAPE

Quiz 10-3 20 min.
- Administer Quiz 10-3A or 10-3B.

LISONS!, 25 min.
- Read and discuss **Stratégie pour lire,** p. 298.
- Complete Prereading Activities A–B, p. 298.
- Terms in **Lisons!,** ATE, p. 298
- Have students read **L'amitié,** pp. 298–299.
- Do Reading Activities C–F, pp. 298–299.

Wrap-Up 5 min.
- Have students check their answers for Activities C–F with a partner.

Homework Options
Cahier d'activités, Act. 22, p. 119

Day 9

LISONS!

Quick Review 5 min.
- Check homework.

Postreading Activity 20 min.
- Do Postreading Activity G, p. 299.
- Cooperative Learning: Activity H, ATE, p. 299

MISE EN PRATIQUE 15 min.
- Play Audio CD for Activity 1, p. 304.
- Challenge, ATE, p. 304
- Complete Activity 2, p. 304.
- Thinking Critically, ATE, p. 304
- Do Activity 3, p. 304.

Wrap-Up 10 min.
- Game: **Des trous,** ATE, p. 305

Homework Options
Cahier d'activités, Acts. 23–24, p. 120

Day 10

MISE EN PRATIQUE

Quick Review 5 min.
- Check homework.

Chapter Review 35 min.
- Discuss the strategy for **Ecrivons!,** p. 305, as a class, then have students work on their poems.
- Process Writing, ATE, p. 305
- Have students work in groups on **Jeu de rôle,** p. 305.

Wrap-Up 10 min.
- Have volunteers share scenes from **Jeu de rôle** with the class.

Homework Options
Have students finish poems for **Ecrivons!**, Pupil's Edition, p. 305.

Day 11

MISE EN PRATIQUE

Chapter Review 45 min.
- Have volunteers share their poems from **Ecrivons!**.
- Have students complete **A toi de parler**, CD-ROM Tutor, Disc 3.
- Have students do **A toi d'écrire,** CD-ROM Tutor, Disc 3.
- Show ***Qu'est-ce que je dois faire? (suite),*** Video Program, Videocassette 4.
- See Teaching Suggestions, Viewing Suggestions 1–2, Video Guide, p. 67.
- Complete Activities 7–8, Video Guide, p. 70.
- See Teaching Suggestions, Post-viewing Suggestions 1–2, Video Guide, p. 67.

Wrap-Up 5 min.
- Have students begin **Que sais-je?,** p. 306.

Homework Options
Pupil's Edition, **Que sais-je?,** p. 306

Day 12

MISE EN PRATIQUE

Quick Review 15 min.
- Go over **Que sais-je?,** p. 306.

Chapter Review 35 min.
- Review Chapter 10. Choose from **Grammaire supplémentaire,** Grammar Tutor for Students of French, Activities for Communication, Listening Activities, Interactive CD-ROM Tutor, or **Jeux interactifs.**

Homework Options
Study for Chapter 10 Test.

Assessment

Chapter Test 40–45 min.
- Administer Chapter 10 Test. Select from Testing Program, Alternative Assessment Guide, Test Generator, or Standardized Assessment Tutor.

Chapitre 10 : Je peux te parler?

Suggested Lesson Plans *90-Minute Block Schedule*

Block 1

CHAPTER OPENER **5 min.**
- Present Chapter Objectives, p. 281.
- Culture Note, ATE, p. 280

MISE EN TRAIN **45 min.**
- Preteaching Vocabulary, ATE, p. 282
- Presenting **Mise en train,** ATE, p. 283
- Do Activities 2–4, p. 284, using Teaching Suggestion, ATE, p. 284.
- Discuss **Note culturelle,** p. 284.

PREMIERE ETAPE

Comment dit-on... ?, p. 286 20 min.
- Presenting **Comment dit-on... ?,** ATE, p. 286
- Play Audio CD for Activity 7, p. 286. See Slower Pace for Activity 7, ATE, p. 287.

Comment dit-on?, p. 286 15 min.
- Presenting **Comment dit-on... ?,** ATE, p. 287

Wrap-Up 5 min.
- Write the headings "Sharing a Confidence" and "Responding" on the board. Pass out the cards used in Presenting **Comment dit-on... ?** to students and have them tape each card under the apppropriate heading.

Homework Options
Cahier d'activités, Acts. 1–4, pp. 109–110

Block 2

PREMIERE ETAPE

Quick Review 10 min.
- Teaching Transparency 10-1, using Suggestion #5 in Suggestions for Using Teaching Transparency 10-1

Comment dit-on… ?, p. 286 20 min.
- Do Activities 8–9, p. 287.

Vocabulaire, p. 287 35 min.
- Presenting **Vocabulaire,** ATE, p. 287
- TPR, ATE, p. 287
- Play Audio CD for Activity 10, p. 288.
- Do Activity 11, p. 288.

Grammaire, p. 288 15 min.
- Presenting **Grammaire,** ATE, p. 288
- Visual Learners, ATE, p. 288

Wrap-Up 10 min.
- Teaching Transparency 10-1, using Suggestion #6 in Suggestions for Using Teaching Transparency 10-1

Homework Options
Grammaire supplémentaire, Acts. 1–3, p. 300
Cahier d'activités, Acts. 5–7, p. 111
Travaux pratiques de grammaire, Acts. 1–5, pp. 78–80

Block 3

PREMIERE ETAPE

Quick Review 5 min.
- Teaching Transparency 10-A, using Suggestion #2 in Suggestions for Using Teaching Transparency 10-A

Grammaire, p. 288 20 min.
- Do Activities 12–13, p. 289.

PANORAMA CULTUREL 15 min.
- Presenting **Panorama Culturel,** ATE, p. 297
- Discuss the questions in **Qu'en penses-tu?,** p. 297.

DEUXIEME ETAPE

Comment dit-on... ?, p. 291 30 min.
- Presenting **Comment dit-on... ?,** ATE, p. 291
- Play Audio CD for Activity 16, p. 291.
- Activity 17, p. 291
- Discuss **Note culturelle,** p. 290.
- History Link, ATE, p. 290

Vocabulaire, p. 291 15 min.
- Presenting **Vocabulaire,** ATE, p. 291
- Do Activity 18, p. 292.

Wrap-Up 5 min.
- Teaching Suggestion, ATE, p. 291

Homework Options
Have students study for Quiz 10-1.
Grammaire supplémentaire, Act. 3, p. 300
Cahier d'activités, Acts. 8–11, pp. 112–114
Travaux pratiques de grammaire, Acts. 6–9, pp. 81–83

For alternative lesson plans by chapter section, to create your own customized plans, or to preview all resources available for this chapter, use the **One-Stop Planner CD-ROM,** Disc 3.

For additional homework suggestions, see activities accompanied by this symbol throughout the chapter.

Block 4

PREMIERE ETAPE

Quick Review 10 min.
- Communicative Activities 10-1A and 10-1B, Activities for Communication, pp. 55–56

Quiz 10-1 20 min.
- Administer Quiz 10-1A or 10-1B.

DEUXIEME ETAPE

Vocabulaire, p. 291 35 min.
- TPR, ATE, p. 291
- Do Activities 19–20, p. 292.

Note de grammaire, p. 293 20 min.
- Present **Note de grammaire,** p. 293.
- Do Activity 22, p. 293.
- **Note culturelle,** p. 293

Wrap-Up 5 min.
- Teaching Transparency 10-B, using Suggestion #3 on Suggestions for Using Teaching Transparency 10-B

Homework Options
Have students study for Quiz 10-2.
Grammaire supplémentaire, Acts. 7–9, p. 302
Cahier d'activités, Acts. 12–15, pp. 114–115
Travaux pratiques de grammaire, Acts. 10–14, pp. 83–85

Block 5

DEUXIEME ETAPE

Quick Review 10 min.
- Communicative Activities 10-2A and 10-2B, Activities for Communication, pp. 57–58

Quiz 10-2 20 min.
- Administer Quiz 10-2A or 10-2B.

TROISIEME ETAPE

Comment dit-on... ?, p. 294 20 min.
- Presenting **Comment dit-on... ?,** ATE, p. 294
- Play Audio CD for Activity 25, p. 295.
- Do Activity 26, p. 295.
- **A la française,** p. 295

Note de grammaire, p. 295 30 min.
- Present **Note de grammaire,** p. 295.
- Do Activities 27–28, pp. 295–296.

Wrap-Up 10 min.
- Communicative Activity 10-3, Activities for Communication, pp. 59–60

Homework Options
Have students study for Quiz 10-3.
Pupil's Edition, Activity 30, p. 296
Grammaire supplémentaire, Acts. 11–12, p. 303
Cahier d'activités, Acts. 16–21, pp. 116–118
Travaux pratiques de grammaire, Acts. 15–16, p. 86

Block 6

TROISIEME ETAPE

Quick Review 15 min.
- Do Activity 29, p. 296.

Quiz 10-3 20 min.
- Administer Quiz 10-3A or 10-3B.

LISONS! 30 min.
- Discuss **Stratégie pour lire,** p. 298.
- Prereading/Reading Activities A–B, p. 298
- Activities C–E, pp. 298–299

MISE EN PRATIQUE 25 min.
- Play Audio CD for Activity 1, p. 304.
- Activities 2–3, p. 304

Homework Options
Que sais-je?, p. 306
Pupil's Edition, Act. 4, p. 305
Have students prepare for **Carrés hollywoodiens,** ATE, p. 279C.
CD-ROM/Interactive Games
Study for Chapter 10 Test.

Block 7

MISE EN PRATIQUE

Quick Review 5 min.
- Check homework.

Chapter Review 35 min.
- Review Chapter 10. Choose from **Grammaire supplémentaire,** Grammar Tutor for Students of French, Activities for Communication, Listening Activities, Interactive CD-ROM Tutor, or **Jeux interactifs.**

Chapter Test 40–45 min.
- Administer Chapter 10 Test. Select from Testing Program, Alternative Assessment Guide, Test Generator, or Standardized Assessment Tutor.

Chapter Opener

CHAPITRE 10

For resource information, see the **One-Stop Planner,** Disc 3.

Pacing Tips

Chapter 10 presents many functional expressions that are relevant to students' daily lives. This is an ideal chapter for suggestions and activities from the *Activities for Communication.* For suggested Lesson Plans and timing suggestions, see pages 279I–279L.

Photo Flash!

Arlette and Pascale are talking at a café in Aix-en-Provence. The French often go to cafés for conversation with friends, as well as for something to eat or drink.

Meeting the Standards

Communication

- Sharing a confidence, p. 286
- Asking for and giving advice, p. 286
- Asking for and granting a favor; making excuses, p. 291
- Apologizing and accepting an apology; reproaching someone, p. 294

Culture

- Culture Note, pp. 280, 293
- Note culturelle, pp. 284, 290, 293
- Panorama Culturel, p. 297

Connections

- History Link, p. 290

Comparisons

- Thinking Critically: Analyzing, p. 283
- Thinking Critically: Synthesizing, p. 284
- Thinking Critically: Synthesizing, p. 304

Communities

- Career Path, p. 293
- De l'école au travail, p. 296

Cultures and Communities

Culture Note

Point out to students that the girls in the photo are at a café. You might tell students that in French cafés, beverages are not usually served with ice **(avec des glaçons)** unless it's requested. French people usually do not put ice in their drinks as is customary in the United States.

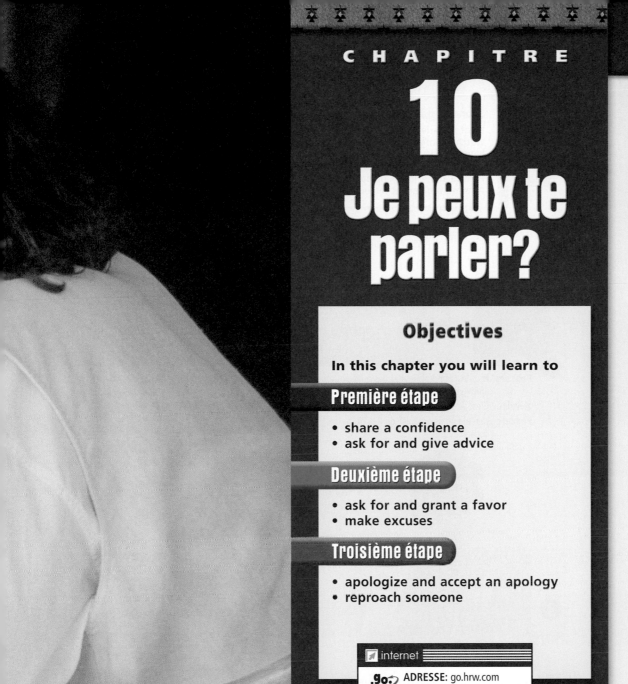

CHAPITRE

10 Je peux te parler?

Objectives

In this chapter you will learn to

Première étape

- share a confidence
- ask for and give advice

Deuxième étape

- ask for and grant a favor
- make excuses

Troisième étape

- apologize and accept an apology
- reproach someone

internet

ADRESSE: go.hrw.com
MOT-CLE:
WA3 PROVENCE-10

◀ **A ton avis, qu'est-ce que je dois faire?**

CHAPITRE 10

Focusing on Outcomes

Have students look at the photo and say as much as they can about it in French. Then read the caption in English and have students decide which outcome best describes the photo and why. NOTE: The self-check activities in **Que sais-je?** on page 306 help students assess their achievement of the objectives.

Chapter Sequence

Teacher to Teacher

Maxine suggests the following activity to integrate culture in her lessons.

Maxine Stewart
Genesis Preparatory School
New Port Richey, FL

"Students do reports each quarter on assigned cultural topics. The first quarter, they each prepare a written report on a museum or landmark in the Paris region. For other quarters, they report on other regions in France, such as Provence, various French-speaking countries, or various well-known French-speaking people, either modern or historical. Each student then gives an oral presentation to the class about the topic, sometimes using a poster or brochures to illustrate the presentation."

Mise en train

CHAPITRE 10

Teaching Resources
pp. 282–284

PRINT 

- Lesson Planner, p. 46
- Video Guide, pp. 66, 68
- Cahier d'activités, p. 109

MEDIA  

- One-Stop Planner
- Video Program
  Mise en train
  Videocassette 4, 00:50–05:53
  Videocassette 5 (captioned version), 1:25:02–1:30:05
  Suite
  Videocassette 4, 05:57–10:12
  Videocassette 5 (captioned version), 1:30:11–1:34:26
- DVD Tutor, Disc 2
- Audio Compact Discs, CD 10, Trs. 1–2
- **Mise en train** Transparencies

Teaching Suggestion
For additional listening practice, read aloud the sentences of the **Mise en train** one at a time, replacing one word or expression in each by blowing a whistle or ringing a bell. Students try to guess which words are missing. You should try to choose omissions that can be easily guessed from the context.

The **roman-photo** is an abridged version of the video episode.

MISE EN TRAIN ▪ *Qu'est-ce que je dois faire?*

CD 10 Trs. 1–2
DVD

Stratégie pour comprendre
What are Arlette and Pascale talking about? Watch for cognates and familiar words to help you get an idea of what is going on in this episode. What sort of problems do Pascale and Arlette talk about? What is Arlette's problem at the end?

Arlette

Pascale

Antoine

1
Pascale Ecoute, j'aimerais inviter des amis pour mon anniversaire. Qu'en penses-tu?
Arlette C'est une excellente idée! J'adore les fêtes.
Pascale Je n'ai jamais organisé de fête. Tu as des conseils?

2
Arlette D'abord, n'oublie pas d'envoyer des invitations. Ensuite, je te conseille d'acheter des assiettes en carton. C'est pratique. Tu n'as pas à faire la vaisselle. Et tu devrais demander à chacun d'apporter quelque chose.
Pascale C'est pas bête, ça…

3
Pascale Euh, je peux te parler?
Arlette Oui. Je t'écoute.
Pascale Est-ce que tu crois que je devrais inviter Cédric?
Arlette Bien sûr. Pourquoi pas?

4
Pascale Tu sais, on a eu une dispute. C'était tellement bête, un malentendu. Qu'est-ce que je dois faire?
Arlette C'est ridicule. Téléphone-lui et invite-le.
Pascale Tes conseils sont toujours bons!

Preteaching Vocabulary

Guessing words from context
First, have students skim the text and images in the **Mise en train.** Have them tell you how many conversations are going on in the story (two). What do they think is the topic of each conversation? Have them identify words and phrases related to party planning in Arlette and Pascale's conversation:

- ❷ **invitations**
- ❷ **assiettes en carton**
- ❸ **Est-ce que tu crois que je devrais inviter… ?**
- ❺ **Alors, qu'est-ce que tu vas mettre pour ta soirée?**

Have students use this context to guess what might be Arlette's problem in the second conversation.

5

Arlette Alors, qu'est-ce que tu vas mettre pour ta soirée?

Pascale Je n'ai pas encore réfléchi. Voyons, je ne sais pas quoi mettre.

6

Pascale Eh! Tu pourrais me prêter ta robe rose? Elle est superbe.

Arlette Je voudrais bien, mais je l'ai déchirée. Je suis désolée.

Pascale Ça ne fait rien.

7

Arlette Si tu veux, je peux te prêter ma jupe bleue plissée.

Pascale C'est mignon! Mais, qu'est-ce que je peux mettre avec?

Arlette Tu pourrais mettre un chemisier blanc.

Pascale Tu as toujours de bonnes idées!

8

Le lendemain, Arlette rencontre son copain Antoine en ville.

Arlette Je cherche un cadeau d'anniversaire pour Pascale. Je ne sais pas quoi lui offrir. Tu as une idée?

Antoine Offre-lui un CD. Elle adore la musique.

Arlette Non, je lui ai déjà offert un CD de Mylène Farmer l'année dernière.

9

Antoine Tu devrais lui offrir un poster de Cézanne. Elle l'aime beaucoup.

Arlette Ça, c'est une idée! Je te remercie. Qu'est-ce que je ferais sans toi?

Antoine Ecoute, j'ai deux places pour aller au concert des Vagabonds. Tu veux venir avec moi?

Pascale Je veux bien. C'est quand?

10

Antoine Samedi soir.

Arlette Samedi! Aïe!

Antoine Qu'est-ce qu'il y a?

Arlette Je voudrais bien, mais je suis invitée à la fête de Pascale. Je lui ai promis de l'aider à organiser sa fête. Je ne sais pas quoi faire!

Cahier d'activités, p. 109, Act. 1

Using the Captioned Video/DVD

If students have difficulty understanding French spoken at a normal speed, use Videocassette 5 to allow students to see the French captions for ***Qu'est-ce que je dois faire?*** and ***Qu'est-ce que je dois faire? (suite).*** Hearing the language and watching the story will reduce anxiety about the new language and facilitate comprehension. The reinforcement of seeing the written vocabulary words as they watch the gestures and actions will help prepare students to do the comprehension activities on page 284.

NOTE: The *DVD Tutor* contains captions for all sections of the *Video Program.*

Mise en train

CHAPITRE 10

Presenting Mise en train

Have students read the questions in Activity 1 on page 284 before they view the video or have them complete the Preteaching Vocabulary suggestion on page 282. Play the video, and then ask the questions in Activity 1. If students can't answer a question, play the corresponding part of the video again. Next, have students make a list of the party preparations Arlette advises Pascale to make.

Mise en train Transparencies

Thinking Critically

Analyzing Ask students what advice Arlette gave Pascale concerning Cédric (to call him and to invite him to the party). Ask them if they agree with the advice and why or why not. Ask students what they would do in this situation.

Mise en train (suite)

When the story continues, Antoine urges Arlette to go to the concert, but Arlette does not want to disappoint Pascale. Later, Arlette sees Cédric, who is planning to invite Pascale to the concert. Arlette advises him to call and invite Pascale right away. Arlette and Pascale are reluctant to tell each other that they would rather go to the concert than have the party. As they come to realize each other's true feelings, Antoine and Cédric show up, and all four are delighted.

Mise en train

CHAPITRE 10

Auditory Learners

2 Read aloud the three complete statements for each item and have students identify the statement that is true.

Visual/Tactile Learners

3 Have students write several quotes from the **Mise en train** on index cards. Then, have students shuffle the cards and pass them to a partner, who will organize them by speaker: Arlette, Pascale, or Antoine.

Thinking Critically

5 **Synthesizing** Poll the class to find out who would go to the concert and who would help Pascale with her party. Ask students to imagine the consequences of either decision for all of the characters involved.

These activities check for comprehension only. Students should not yet be expected to produce language modeled in **Mise en train.**

1 Tu as compris? See answers below.

1. Why is Pascale having a party?
2. What advice does Arlette offer her?
3. What favor does Pascale ask? Does Arlette agree to help?
4. What does Arlette ask Antoine for advice about? What does he suggest?
5. What decision does Arlette have to make at the end of ***Qu'est-ce que je dois faire?***

2 Complète les phrases

1. Pascale n'a jamais...
   a. organisé de fête.
   b. demandé de conseils.
   c. écouté de musique.
2. Pascale et Cédric...
   a. se sont réconciliés.
   b. se sont disputés.
   c. se sont rencontrés.
3. Pascale va mettre...
   a. une robe rose.
   b. une jupe bleue.
   c. un anorak vert.
4. Comme cadeau, Antoine suggère...
   a. du parfum.
   b. des fleurs.
   c. un poster.
5. Antoine invite Arlette à...
   a. une fête.
   b. un concert.
   c. faire les magasins.

3 Qui dit quoi?

Pascale

Arlette

Antoine

Arlette — Téléphone-lui et invite-le.

Arlette — Je ne sais pas quoi lui offrir. Tu as une idée?

Antoine — J'ai deux places pour aller au concert des Vagabonds.

Antoine — Tu devrais lui offrir un poster de Cézanne.

Arlette — Qu'est-ce que je ferais sans toi!

Pascale — Je devrais inviter Cédric?

4 Cherche les expressions

What do the people in ***Qu'est-ce que je dois faire?*** say to . . . See answers below.

1. ask for advice?
2. share a confidence?
3. give advice?
4. ask for a favor?
5. invite someone?
6. make excuses?

5 Et maintenant, à toi

Imagine que tu es Arlette. Qu'est-ce que tu décides de faire? Pourquoi?

Paul Cézanne, un des peintres post-impressionnistes les plus influents, est né à Aix-en-Provence en 1839. Il a rendu célèbre la **Montagne Sainte-Victoire** qui se trouve à quelques kilomètres d'Aix en la peignant une douzaine de fois. A Aix, vous pouvez marcher sur les pas de Cézanne en suivant le parcours de deux heures indiqué par des plaques de bronze sur le trottoir ; vous pouvez ainsi découvrir la maison où Cézanne est né, la cathédrale où il allait à la messe et son studio, qui est resté le même depuis sa mort en 1906.

Comprehension Check

Teaching Suggestion

4 Play the video, pausing each time a functional expression is used. Have students write down the number of the function as it is used. Students can also raise their hands to signal you to pause the video when they hear a function being used.

Answers

1
1. to celebrate her birthday
2. to send invitations, to buy paper plates, to ask each person to bring something
3. Pascale asks to borrow Arlette's pink dress; Yes, she helps by loaning Pascale her blue pleated skirt.
4. what to get Pascale for her birthday; a CD, a Cézanne poster
5. Arlette must decide whether to help organize Pascale's party or go to the concert with Antoine.

4
1. Tu as des conseils? Est-ce que tu crois que je devrais... ? Qu'est-ce que je dois faire? Tu as une idée?
2. ... je peux te parler?
3. N'oublie pas de... ; ... je te conseille de... ; Tu devrais... ; Téléphone-lui et invite-le; Tu pourrais... ; Offre-lui...
4. Tu pourrais... ?
5. Tu veux venir avec moi?
6. Je voudrais bien, mais...

STANDARDS: 1.2, 2.2

Objectives Sharing a confidence; asking for and giving advice

WA3 PROVENCE-10

QU'EN PENSES-TU?

Amitiés, amours, parents, études... Chaque semaine, posez votre question aux lecteurs.

VOICI LA QUESTION DE FERDINAND (Aix-en-Provence)

J'ai un petit problème. Dans ma classe, il y a une fille que j'aime bien. Elle s'appelle Myriam. Elle est toujours avec ses copines et je ne sais pas comment l'aborder. Je suis bien embêté. J'ai l'impression qu'elle m'aime bien, mais je n'ose pas lui parler. Je suis très timide. Qu'est-ce que vous me conseillez? Aidez-moi!

ET VOICI LES RÉPONSES DE...

MATHILDE (Pointe-à-Pitre, Guadeloupe)

A mon avis, tu devrais lui proposer d'aller au café après l'école. Parle-lui. Demande-lui si elle aime aller au cinéma. Ensuite, invite-la à voir un film. Si elle accepte, c'est parfait. Si elle refuse, tu devrais l'oublier.

FABIEN (Biarritz, Pyrénées-Atlantiques)

Si tu n'oses pas lui parler, écris-lui un petit mot. Sois sincère. Peut-être qu'elle est timide, elle aussi. C'est une bonne façon de faire connaissance avec elle.

IRÈNE (Dijon, Côte-d'Or)

Ce que tu devrais faire, c'est organiser une fête. Comme ça, tu as un prétexte pour l'inviter. Ensuite, ça va être plus facile de faire connaissance. Si tu ne sais pas quoi dire, tu peux l'inviter à danser!

LÉONARD (Toulouse, Haute-Garonne)

A mon avis, tu devrais faire l'indifférent. Ne lui montre pas que tu es amoureux et fais semblant de t'intéresser à une de ses copines. Tu vas voir, elle va tout de suite te remarquer!

6 Les conseils

Lisons

1. Quel est le problème de Ferdinand? Il y a une fille qu'il aime bien, mais il est très timide et il n'ose pas lui parler.
2. Quels conseils est-ce que chaque personne lui a donnés?
   a. Mathilde b. Fabien c. Irène d. Léonard

b — Sois sincère.
d — Tu devrais faire l'indifférent.
a — Invite-la au café.
b — Ecris-lui un petit mot.
a — Si elle refuse, tu devrais l'oublier.
c — Tu peux l'inviter à danser!
c — Ce que tu devrais faire, c'est organiser une fête.

3. A ton avis, quels sont les meilleurs conseils?

Communication for All Students

Visual/Auditory Learners

6 Write each of the expressions on large strips of posterboard or construction paper. Then, write the names of the four teenagers who offered advice on the board. Show each piece of advice and read it aloud. Have a student tape the expression to the board under the appropriate name.

Première étape

CHAPITRE 10

Teaching Resources
pp. 285–289

PRINT
- Lesson Planner, p. 47
- TPR Storytelling Book, pp. 72–73
- Listening Activities, pp. 75, 79
- Activities for Communication, pp. 55–56, 120, 123, 155–156
- Travaux pratiques de grammaire, pp. 78–81
- Grammar Tutor for Students of French, Chapter 10
- Cahier d'activités, pp. 110–113
- Testing Program, pp. 249–252
- Alternative Assessment Guide, p. 41
- Student Make-Up Assignments, Chapter 10

MEDIA
- One-Stop Planner
- Audio Compact Discs, CD 10, Trs. 3–4, 13, 19–20
- Teaching Transparencies: 10-1, 10-A; **Grammaire supplémentaire** Answers; Travaux pratiques de grammaire Answers
- Interactive CD-ROM Tutor, Disc 3

Bell Work

Have students write down two party preparations Arlette suggested to Pascale and two gift ideas that Antoine gave Arlette in the **Mise en train.**

Language Note

Students may want to know the following vocabulary from **Qu'en penses-tu? Aborder** means *to approach.* **Faire semblant** is an expression meaning *to pretend.*

Première étape

CHAPITRE 10

Teaching Resources
pp. 285–289

PRINT

- Lesson Planner, p. 47
- TPR Storytelling Book, pp. 72–73
- Listening Activities, pp. 75, 79
- Activities for Communication, pp. 55–56, 120, 123, 155–156
- Travaux pratiques de grammaire, pp. 78–81
- Grammar Tutor for Students of French, Chapter 10
- Cahier d'activités, pp. 110–113
- Testing Program, pp. 249–252
- Alternative Assessment Guide, p. 41
- Student Make-Up Assignments, Chapter 10

MEDIA 

- One-Stop Planner
- Audio Compact Discs, CD 10, Trs. 3–4, 13, 19–20
- Teaching Transparencies: 10-1, 10-A; **Grammaire supplémentaire** Answers; Travaux pratiques de grammaire Answers
- Interactive CD-ROM Tutor, Disc 3

Presenting
Comment dit-on... ?

To present the expressions for sharing a confidence, write the new expressions on large index cards and tape them to the board. Then, prepare two sets of additional cards. On one set, write several sentences telling about problems you're having, and on the other, sentences responding to a problem. Act out a conversation in which you share a confidence with a friend, using a card from each set you made. Tape the cards to the board to form a logical conversation as you use them. Have students repeat the new expressions. Repeat this process until all cards have been used.

Comment dit-on...?

Sharing a confidence

To share a confidence:

Je ne sais pas quoi faire.
I don't know what to do.
J'ai un problème.
Tu as une minute?
Je peux te parler?

To respond:

Qu'est-ce qu'il y a? *What's wrong?*
Qu'est-ce que je peux faire?
What can I do?
Je t'écoute.

Cahier d'activités, p. 110, Act. 3

7 Je peux te parler? See scripts and answers on p. 279G.

CD 10 Tr. 3

Ecoutons Mohammed's friends all come to him with their problems. Choose the picture that illustrates each friend's problem. Then, imagine the dialogue about the remaining picture. **1.** b **2.** c **3.** a

a.

b.

c.

d.

Comment dit-on...?

Asking for and giving advice

CD-ROM 3 DVD 2

To ask for advice:

A ton avis, qu'est-ce que je dois faire?
In your opinion, what should I do?
Qu'est-ce que tu ferais, toi?
What would you do?
Qu'est-ce que tu me conseilles?

To give advice:

Invite-le/-la/-les.
Invite him/her/them.
Parle-lui/-leur.
Talk to him/her/them.
Dis-lui/-leur que tu es fâché.
Tell him/her/them that . . .
Ecris-lui/-leur.
Write to him/her/them.
Explique-lui/-leur.
Explain to him/her/them.
Excuse-toi. *Apologize.*
Téléphone-lui/-leur.
Oublie-le/-la/-les.
Tu devrais lui écrire un petit mot.

Cahier d'activités, pp. 110–111, Act. 4–5

Connections and Comparisons

Teaching Suggestion

7 Have students look at illustration **a.** Ask them how they can tell it's a French paper. (It's written on graph paper, and it has a grade of 10.) Ask them what kind of textbook is pictured in illustration **b** (a history book) and what Parisian monument is depicted on its cover **(l'Arc de triomphe).**

STANDARDS: 1.2

8 Les deux font la paire

Lisons Choisis les meilleures réponses à chaque phrase ou question. Possible answers:

1. J'ai cassé avec ma petite amie! A ton avis, qu'est-ce que je dois faire? e
2. J'ai rencontré un garçon très sympa et je veux le revoir. b
3. J'ai de mauvaises notes en maths et je ne comprends pas le prof. Qu'est-ce que tu ferais, toi? i
4. J'ai été collé et mes parents m'ont privé de sortie. Mais ce n'était pas de ma faute! a
5. J'ai un problème et je ne sais pas quoi faire. g
6. Je suis tombé amoureux d'une fille qui habite à la Martinique. j
7. Tu as une minute? Je peux te parler? c

- **a.** Explique-leur.
- **b.** Dis-lui bonjour.
- **c.** Bien sûr. Je t'écoute.
- **d.** Invite-le au cinéma.
- **e.** Oublie-la!
- **f.** Invite-les chez toi.
- **g.** Qu'est-ce qu'il y a?
- **h.** Excuse-toi!
- **i.** Parle-lui.
- **j.** Ecris-lui une lettre.
- **k.** Téléphone-leur.
- **l.** Tu devrais leur dire que tu es fâché.

9 Jeu de conseils

Ecrivons/Parlons Think of a problem and write it down in French on a sheet of paper. Then, read it aloud to your group. The other group members have one minute to come up with as many solutions in French as possible. Who has the most answers? The craziest? The worst advice?

Vocabulaire

CD-ROM 3 DVD 2

lui expliquer ce qui s'est passé.

lui demander pardon.

lui offrir un cadeau.

lui dire que tu l'aimes.

te réconcilier avec elle.

téléphoner (à quelqu'un) *to call (someone)*
s'excuser *to apologize*
pardonner (à quelqu'un) *to forgive (someone)*
écouter ce qu'il/elle dit *to listen to what he/she says*

Travaux pratiques de grammaire, pp. 78–80, Act. 1–4

Première étape

CHAPITRE 10

Presenting
Comment dit-on... ?

To present the expressions for asking for and giving advice, draw three columns on the board and label them **oui, non,** and **peut-être.** Write the expressions for giving advice on separate large index cards. Describe several problems that would elicit some of the advice in **Comment dit-on... ?** and ask for advice, using the new expressions. Then, hold up the cards you prepared one at a time, read the advice, and tape the card under the appropriate column on the board, based on whether the advice is appropriate for the problem described. Once you've used all the cards, repeat this process, using new problems and new volunteers.

Vocabulaire

Use three stuffed animals or puppets to present the new vocabulary. Introduce **le garçon, sa petite amie,** and **son amie.** Demonstrate the conversation between **le garçon** and **son amie** and the advice she gives him. **(Tu devrais lui expliquer ce qui s'est passé.)** Act out the different scenes in which he follows her advice. **(Tu vois, j'étais privé de sortie, et c'est pour ça que je ne suis pas venu.)** Continue presenting the remaining expressions in this manner.

TPR Have partners act out the advice you give them. For example, if you say **Demande-lui pardon,** one partner might make an imploring gesture and facial expression. To show they understand **Réconcilie-toi avec ton ami(e),** students could shake hands. Students might say **Je t'aime** in response to **Dis-lui que tu l'aimes.**

Communication for All Students

Slower Pace

7 Before you play the recording, have students describe each of the pictures.

8 Have students copy the problems and write the appropriate advice next to each one. Then, have a student read the problems aloud and call on volunteers to offer the advice they chose.

Première étape

CHAPITRE 10

Teaching Resources
pp. 285–289

PRINT
- Lesson Planner, p. 47
- TPR Storytelling Book, pp. 72–73
- Listening Activities, pp. 75, 79
- Activities for Communication, pp. 55–56, 120, 123, 155–156
- Travaux pratiques de grammaire, pp. 78–81
- Grammar Tutor for Students of French, Chapter 10
- Cahier d'activités, pp. 110–113
- Testing Program, pp. 249–252
- Alternative Assessment Guide, p. 41
- Student Make-Up Assignments, Chapter 10

MEDIA 
- One-Stop Planner
- Audio Compact Discs, CD 10, Trs. 3–4, 13, 19–20
- Teaching Transparencies: 10-1, 10-A; **Grammaire supplémentaire** Answers; Travaux pratiques de grammaire Answers
- Interactive CD-ROM Tutor, Disc 3

Presenting Grammaire

Object pronouns and their placement Give a pen to one student, saying **Tiens, je te donne un stylo,** and some pencils to two students, saying **Tenez, je vous donne des crayons.** Then, tell one student to give you a pen. **(Donne-moi un stylo.)** Ask **Tu me donnes un stylo?** and prompt **Oui, je vous donne un stylo.** With a student by your side, tell another to give both of you a pencil, saying **Donne-nous un crayon.** Then ask the student **Tu nous donnes un crayon?** and so on.

10 Je ne sais pas quoi faire! See scripts and answers on p. 279G.

CD 10 Tr. 4

Ecoutons Lucie s'est disputée avec son copain Luc et elle demande des conseils à ses amis. Qu'est-ce que chaque personne lui conseille de faire? Qu'est-ce que toi, tu lui conseillerais de faire?

11 Un sondage

Lisons/Parlons Lis ce sondage et choisis les conseils que tu donnerais à chaque personne. Puis, fais le sondage auprès de cinq camarades. Est-ce que vous êtes tous d'accord? Finalement, pense à deux autres conseils pour chaque problème.

DONNE TES CONSEILS!

1 Mon copain Thomas ne me parle plus. Qu'est-ce que tu me conseilles?
a. Oublie-le.
b. Ecris-lui un petit mot.
c. Téléphone-lui et demande-lui de t'expliquer pourquoi.

2 Je voudrais faire une fête pour mon anniversaire, mais je ne sais pas par où commencer. Tu as une idée?
a. Tu devrais envoyer des invitations, puis faire les courses. Et n'oublie pas de faire le ménage et de choisir la musique!
b. Tu devrais plutôt sortir seul(e). Tu seras plus tranquille.
c. C'est facile. Tu devrais téléphoner à tous tes amis. Ils pourraient t'aider.

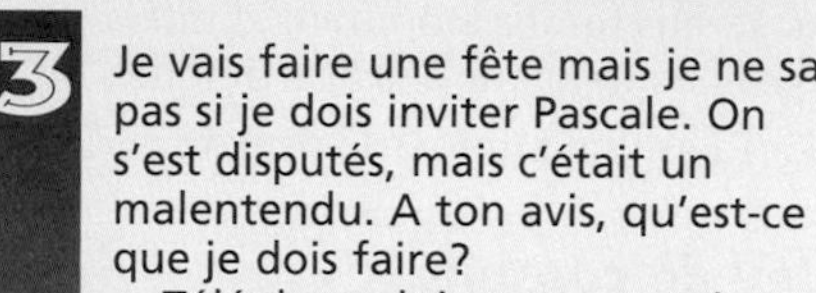

3 Je vais faire une fête mais je ne sais pas si je dois inviter Pascale. On s'est disputés, mais c'était un malentendu. A ton avis, qu'est-ce que je dois faire?
a. Téléphone-lui et excuse-toi.
b. Téléphone-lui et invite-la à ta fête.
c. Oublie-la et amuse-toi bien!

4 Mes parents sont fâchés contre moi parce que j'ai cassé la chaîne stéréo. Qu'est-ce que je peux faire?
a. Achète-leur une autre chaîne.
b. Parle-leur et explique-leur ce qui s'est passé.
c. Fais la tête dans ta chambre. Ce n'est pas de ta faute!

Grammaire

Object pronouns and their placement

CD-ROM 3 DVD 2

You've already learned that the direct object pronouns **le, la, l',** and **les** *(him, her, it,* or *them)* are used to replace people and things. You've also learned that the indirect object pronouns **lui** and **leur** *(to, for him/her/them)* are used to replace à + a person or people. Here are some new pronouns: **me** *(me, to/for me);* **te** *(you, to/for you);* **nous** *(us, to/for us);* **vous** *(you, to/for you).*

- You usually place these object pronouns before the conjugated verb.

  Tu **me** parles? Il **le** mettait tous les jours.
  Je **lui** ai parlé. Ne **nous** parle plus!

- In affirmative commands, put all pronouns after the verb, connected with a hyphen. In this position, **me** and **te** change to **moi** and **toi.**

  Invite-**le!** Parle-**moi!** Excuse-**toi!**

- If a pronoun is the object of an infinitive, put the pronoun before the infinitive.

  Tu devrais **lui** parler.

Grammaire supplémentaire, pp. 300–301, Act. 1–6

Cahier d'activités, p. 112, Act. 8

Travaux pratiques de grammaire, pp. 80–81, Act. 5–7

Communication for All Students

Slower Pace

10 Write the advice mentioned in the recording on the board or on a transparency in random order (see script on page 279G). Then, play the recording and have students number the advice in the order in which they hear it given.

Visual Learners

Show flashcards of questions containing object pronouns. **(Tu me parles?)** After students respond **(Oui, je vous parle),** show the answer you've written on the other side of the card.

STANDARDS: 1.1, 1.2, 3.1, 4.1, 5.2

12 Grammaire en contexte

Ecrivons Complète l'histoire de Van avec les pronoms qui conviennent.

Hier après-midi, j'ai vu ma copine Lien avec un autre garçon! Et moi qui voulais ___1___ inviter au cinéma! l'

Parle-lui!

J'étais vraiment fâché! J'ai téléphoné à Emmanuel qui ___2___ m' a conseillé de ___3___ lui parler.

Mais pourquoi?

Alors, je suis allé chez Lien. Je ___4___ ai dit lui que c'était fini entre nous. Elle n'a pas compris. J'ai commencé à ___5___ expliquer. lui

Enfin, devine qui est entré dans le salon! Le nouveau copain de Lien! Je ne pouvais pas ___6___ croire! le

Je te présente mon cousin Tuan.
Oh! Je pensais que...

Quel imbécile! C'était le cousin de Lien! Je ___7___ ai expliqué que je ___8___ avais vus au café ensemble. 7. leur 8. les

Alors, Lien a compris pourquoi j'étais fâché. Je ___9___ ai lui demandé pardon. Elle ___10___ a pardonné et elle a même dit qu'elle ___11___ aimait malgré tout! 10. m' 11. m'

13 Grammaire en contexte  See answers below.

Lisons/Ecrivons Ferdinand, (qui a parlé de son problème dans **Qu'en penses-tu?** à la page 285), a enfin invité Myriam à sortir avec lui. Malheureusement, tout a été de travers pendant leur sortie! Pour chaque problème, suggère deux choses que Ferdinand peut faire. Utilise les pronoms d'objet que tu as appris.

1. J'ai invité Myriam au restaurant, mais elle n'aime pas sortir au restaurant.
2. J'ai raté le bus et je suis arrivé à notre rendez-vous en retard. Myriam était déjà partie.
3. Le lendemain, j'ai téléphoné à Myriam pour m'excuser, mais son père m'a dit qu'elle était partie en vacances chez ses grands-parents en Belgique.
4. Finalement, je lui ai parlé, mais elle était très fâchée et elle ne veut plus me voir.

14 J'ai un problème...

Parlons Invente un problème que tu pourrais avoir à l'école, à la maison ou avec tes amis. Raconte ce qui se passe à un(e) camarade. Il/Elle va te consoler et te donner des conseils. Ensuite, changez de rôle.

Première étape

CHAPITRE 10

Teaching Suggestions

12 You might have students work in pairs to complete this activity. Write the sentences on a transparency and project them. Ask for volunteers to supply the correct pronouns, which another volunteer will write on the transparency.

14 To close this **étape,** use Activity 14. Have each student write his or her problem on a slip of paper. Collect them, read them to yourself, and put them in a box. Have students draw a slip of paper, read the problem aloud, and offer advice.

Assess

- Testing Program, pp. 249–252 Quiz 10-1A, Quiz 10-1B Audio CD 10, Tr. 13
- Student Make-Up Assignments, Chapter 10, Alternative Quiz
- Alternative Assessment Guide, p. 41

Connections and Comparisons

Additional Practice/Music Link

After presenting the **Grammaire,** play the song *A la claire fontaine* (Level 1, Audio CD 4, Track 31). Have students try to keep track of how many object pronouns they hear as they listen to the song. Then, distribute copies of the lyrics (*Listening Activities,* Level 1, page 34) and ask students to circle the object pronouns they see. Finally, have them count the pronouns they circled and compare the number they obtain with the number they counted when listening to the song.

Possible Answers

13
1. Invite-la au parc pour faire un pique-nique. Demande-lui si elle veut faire du sport.
2. Dis-lui que le bus était en retard. Demande-lui pardon.
3. Téléphone-lui ou parle à ses parents. Explique-leur la situation.
4. Achète-lui des fleurs! Ne pense pas à elle!

STANDARDS: 1.1, 1.2, 5.1

Teaching Resources
pp. 290–293

PRINT

- Lesson Planner, p. 48
- TPR Storytelling Book, pp. 74–75
- Listening Activities, pp. 76, 80
- Activities for Communication, pp. 57–58, 121, 123–124, 155–156
- Travaux pratiques de grammaire, pp. 82–85
- Grammar Tutor for Students of French, Chapter 10
- Cahier d'activités, pp. 114–115
- Testing Program, pp. 253–256
- Alternative Assessment Guide, p. 41
- Student Make-Up Assignments, Chapter 10

MEDIA 

- One-Stop Planner
- Audio Compact Discs, CD 10, Trs. 5–6, 14, 21–22
- Teaching Transparencies: 10-2, 10-B; **Grammaire supplémentaire** Answers; Travaux pratiques de grammaire Answers
- Interactive CD-ROM Tutor, Disc 3

Bell Work

Write the following problems on the board and have students write advice for each one.

1. **J'ai perdu mes devoirs pour mon cours d'anglais aujourd'hui.**
2. **J'ai deux rendez-vous le même soir.**
3. **Je suis trop timide pour inviter quelqu'un à sortir.**
4. **J'ai une interro en maths demain, mais j'ai oublié mon livre au lycée.**

Deuxième étape

Objectives Asking for and granting a favor; making excuses

go.hrw.com
WA3 PROVENCE-10

15 1. repairing his moped; Yes; She likes to work on motors, and she invites Patrick to the movies.
2. that Monique babysit for her; because she made a date with Patrick for the same time.
3. Possible answer: Hélène and Danielle are both planning to go out with Patrick the same afternoon.

Hélène,
Tu es libre demain après-midi? J'ai un grand service à te demander. Ma mobylette est en panne. J'ai passé le week-end à essayer de la réparer, mais tu sais la mécanique, c'est pas mon truc. Tu peux me donner un coup de main? Ça serait sympa de ta part.
Patrick

Cher Patrick,
Je n'ai rien à faire mercredi après-midi. A vrai dire, j'allais te demander si tu voulais aller au cinéma avec moi! Oui, je sais que toi et la mécanique, ça fait deux. Bien sûr que je peux t'aider à réparer ta mobylette. Ça ne m'ennuie pas du tout. Tu sais que j'adore mettre le nez dans les moteurs! Et ensuite, si on a le temps, on pourrait aller au cinéma. Qu'est-ce que tu en dis?
Hélène

Très, très chère Monique,
J'ai rendez-vous avec Patrick au parc des Thermes demain après-midi. On va faire le tour des ruines. Enfin! Notre premier rendez-vous! J'étais tellement contente que j'ai complètement oublié que j'avais promis à Mme Dumont de garder ses enfants. Tu pourrais le faire à ma place? Les enfants sont mignons et c'est bien payé. Ça ne t'embête pas, dis? Dis-moi que c'est possible! Je t'aiderai à faire tous tes devoirs de maths jusqu'à la fin de l'année. Promis.
Réponds-moi vite. Merci mille fois!
Danielle

15 Tu as compris? See answers above.
Lisons/Parlons

1. What does Patrick need help with? Does Hélène agree to help him? Why or why not?
2. What favor is Danielle asking? Why?
3. What problem do you anticipate?

Note culturelle

Le parc des Thermes, où les romains avaient à l'origine construits les bains, est un des sites touristiques d'Aix-en-Provence. Vous pouvez encore y admirer les ruines de villas romaines. Les sources thermales qui avaient attiré les romains vers cette ville au premier siècle av. J.-C. alimentent encore des douzaines de fontaines publiques.

Cultures and Communities

History Link

Around 1500 B.C. the Gauls migrated from the Rhine Valley to what is now France and northern Italy. The Romans began their conquest of Gaul in 125 B.C., which Julius Caesar accomplished in 52 B.C. Throughout France, the Romans left vestiges of their sophisticated use of water in elaborate aqueduct and sewer systems and baths, such as those in **le parc des Thermes.**

STANDARDS: 1.2, 2.2, 3.1

Comment dit-on...?

Asking for and granting a favor; making excuses

To ask for a favor:

Tu peux m'aider? *Can you help me?*
Tu pourrais inviter Michel?
Ça t'ennuie de téléphoner à Léonard?
Would you mind . . . ?
Ça t'embête de ranger le salon?
Would you mind . . . ?

To grant a favor:

Avec plaisir. *With pleasure.*
Bien sûr.
Pas de problème. *No problem.*
Bien sûr que non. *Of course not.*
Pas du tout.

To make excuses:

Désolé(e).
J'ai quelque chose à faire. *I have something (else) to do.*
Je n'ai pas le temps. *I don't have time.*
Je suis très occupé(e). *I'm very busy.*
C'est impossible. *It's impossible.*

Cahier d'activités, p. 114, Act. 11

16 La boum

See scripts and answers on p. 279G.

CD 10 Tr. 5

Ecoutons Caroline is asking her family to help her get ready for her party tonight. Do they say they'll help or do they make excuses?

17 Tu peux m'aider?

Ecrivons Comment est-ce que tu peux répondre au petit mot de Danielle à la page 290? Ecris-lui pour accepter ou refuser ce qu'elle te demande. Si tu refuses, donne une excuse.

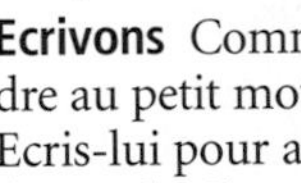

Vocabulaire

Les préparatifs

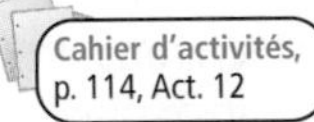

Travaux pratiques de grammaire, pp. 82–83, Act. 8–10

Cahier d'activités, p. 114, Act. 12

CD-ROM 3 DVD 2

Je voudrais faire une boum, mais je ne sais pas quoi faire.
C'est facile! Pour faire les préparatifs, tu dois...
POSTES

envoyer les invitations.

fixer la date.

demander la permission à tes parents.

choisir la musique.

préparer les amuse-gueule.

faire le ménage.

Communication for All Students

Slower Pace

17 Have students work in small groups to answer one of the letters.

TPR Have students show their comprehension of the vocabulary by acting out the party preparations with props as you tell them what to do. **(D'abord, fixe la date. Puis, demande la permission à tes parents.)**

Deuxième étape

CHAPITRE 10

Presenting Comment dit-on... ?

On the board or on a transparency, label three columns *To ask for a favor, To make excuses,* and *To grant a favor.* Then, have students look at the letters on page 290 and tell which sentences illustrate these functions. Have a volunteer write the sentences in the appropriate columns as his or her classmates suggest them.

Teaching Suggestion

Write on the board the four expressions used to ask a favor. Have students use these expressions to ask you to do something for them. Either grant each favor or make an excuse, using the appropriate expressions. Do this several times. Then, ask students for favors and have them try to recall the expressions they heard you use.

Presenting Vocabulaire

Tell students in French that you're planning a party. **(Je vais faire une boum.)** Then, describe and demonstrate all of the preparations you will make, using props (a calendar, CDs, a feather duster) and gestures.

Teaching Suggestion

Vocabulaire Ask students if they have made these preparations. Tell them to answer yes and add details. If you ask **Tu as fixé la date?**, a student might answer **Oui, c'est le vingt-sept.**

STANDARDS: 1.2, 1.3

Teaching Resources
pp. 290–293

PRINT

- Lesson Planner, p. 48
- TPR Storytelling Book, pp. 74–75
- Listening Activities, pp. 76, 80
- Activities for Communication, pp. 57–58, 121, 123–124, 155–156
- Travaux pratiques de grammaire, pp. 82–85
- Grammar Tutor for Students of French, Chapter 10
- Cahier d'activités, pp. 114–115
- Testing Program, pp. 253–256
- Alternative Assessment Guide, p. 41
- Student Make-Up Assignments, Chapter 10

MEDIA 

- One-Stop Planner
- Audio Compact Discs, CD 10, Trs. 5–6, 14, 21–22
- Teaching Transparencies: 10-2, 10-B; **Grammaire supplémentaire** Answers; Travaux pratiques de grammaire Answers
- Interactive CD-ROM Tutor, Disc 3

Teaching Suggestion

Tu te rappelles? Form small groups and assign each one a letter from page 290. Have them find and write down the words that contain nasal sounds.

Building on Previous Skills

19 Re-enter the functions of *reminding* **(N'oublie pas... ; Tu n'as pas oublié... ?)** and *reassuring* **(Ne t'en fais pas. J'ai pensé à tout. Je n'ai rien oublié.)** by having partners take turns reminding each other about the preparations pictured here.

Answers

19 Tu devrais préparer les amuse-gueule/faire le ménage/envoyer les invitations/choisir la musique.

18 La fête de Pascale

See scripts and answers on p. 279H.

CD 10 Tr. 6

Ecoutons Pascale et Jean-Claude font des préparatifs pour la fête de Pascale. Qu'est-ce que Pascale va faire? Et Jean-Claude?

Tu te rappelles?

Remember that the nasal sound [ã] that you hear in **parents, envoyer,** and **embête** is a pure nasal sound, with no trace of the *n* or *m* sound as in English. You usually pronounce [ã] whenever you see the letters **an, am, en,** and **em** in French.

19 Tu devrais...

Parlons/Ecrivons Patrick demande des conseils à Monique pour savoir comment organiser une boum. Qu'est-ce qu'elle lui conseille de faire? See answers below.

20 Quand tu fais une boum...

Parlons/Ecrivons Réponds aux questions suivantes, puis pose ces questions à un(e) ami(e). Est-ce que vous faites les mêmes préparatifs? Fais la liste des réponses que vous avez en commun.

1. Quand tu veux faire une boum, est-ce que tu demandes la permission à tes parents?
2. Est-ce que tu envoies des invitations, ou est-ce que tu téléphones à tes copains?
3. Qui est-ce que tu invites?
4. Est-ce que tu fais le ménage avant ta boum?
5. Qu'est-ce que tu prépares comme amuse-gueule?
6. Qu'est-ce que tu choisis comme musique?
7. Qu'est-ce qu'on fait à tes fêtes préférées? On discute? On écoute de la musique? On regarde des vidéos?
8. A ta boum idéale, qui sont les invités? Quel groupe joue? Qu'est-ce qu'on mange?

21 Jeu!

Parlons Tu prépares une soirée du Club de français chez toi et tu as besoin d'aide. Fais la liste de quatre choses du Vocabulaire à la page 291 que tu n'as pas envie de faire. Demande à des camarades de faire ces choses pour toi. Si un(e) camarade a la même chose sur sa liste, il/elle doit refuser de t'aider. Si cette chose n'est pas sur sa liste, il/elle doit accepter. Note le nom de chaque personne qui va t'aider sur ta liste. La première personne qui trouve quatre camarades pour l'aider gagne le jeu.

Connections and Comparisons

Language Note

21 You might tell students that **Bien sûr que non** and **Pas du tout** are responses used to grant a favor when the request begins with **Ça t'ennuie de... ?** or **Ça t'embête de... ?**

STANDARDS: 1.1, 1.2, 5.2

Note de grammaire

When you use the direct object pronouns **le, la, l', les, me, te, nous,** or **vous** in the **passé composé,** the past participle agrees with the direct object pronoun. Add **-e** if the pronoun is feminine, **-s** if the pronoun is masculine and plural, and **-es** if the pronoun is feminine and plural.

CD-ROM 3 DVD 2

La poubelle? Je **l'**ai sorti**e.**
Les chiens? Je **les** ai promené**s.**
Il **nous** a oublié**(e)s.**
Mais, Cécile, il **t'**a invité**e!**

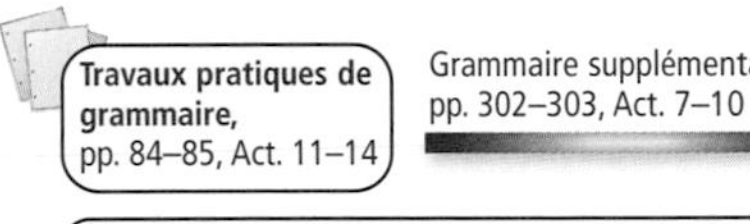

Travaux pratiques de grammaire, pp. 84–85, Act. 11–14

Grammaire supplémentaire, pp. 302–303, Act. 7–10

Cahier d'activités, p. 115, Act. 14–15

22 Grammaire en contexte

Ecrivons Ton ami Joël va faire une fête pour l'anniversaire de sa copine. La sœur de Joël lui demande si tout est prêt pour la fête. Crée la conversation entre Joël et sa sœur. Utilise les expressions proposées. See answers below.

EXEMPLE **—Est-ce que tu as fait les préparatifs?**
—Oui, je les ai tous faits!

demander	Sophie et Julie
fixer	les invitations
inviter	la musique
préparer	la permission à Maman
faire	le ménage
envoyer	la date
choisir	les amuse-gueule

Note culturelle

If you were to go to Provence, you would have the opportunity to try **provençale** cuisine. For an **amuse-gueule,** you might be served olives or **tapenade,** an aromatic paste of olives, garlic, and anchovies. At a dinner party, a typical **hors-d'œuvre** would be **pissaladière,** a type of pizza made with onions, anchovies, and olives. With fish, you would be likely to try **aïoli,** made of egg yolk, olive oil, and garlic. **Ratatouille** is a casserole of eggplant, tomatoes, zucchini, green peppers, and onions in a spicy tomato sauce. As you can tell, **provençale** cuisine uses a lot of garlic, olives, onions, tomatoes, and eggplant, all of which grow well in the soil of Provence.

23 Une soirée provençale

Parlons Des élèves d'Aix vont venir à ton école. La Club de français organise une fête pour les accueillir. En groupe, créez une scène où tout le monde fait les préparatifs pour la fête. Discutez des personnes que vous allez inviter et de la date de la fête. Parlez aussi de la musique que vous allez choisir et des amuse-gueule que vous allez préparer. (N'oubliez pas! Vos amis français aiment sûrement la cuisine provençale.) Ensuite, décidez qui va faire chaque chose. Certaines personnes du groupe vont accepter d'aider et d'autres vont refuser et donner des excuses. Jouez cette scène pour la classe.

Cultures and Communities

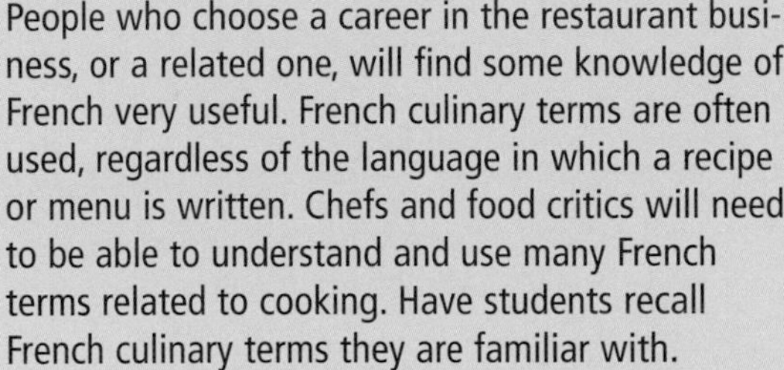

Career Path

People who choose a career in the restaurant business, or a related one, will find some knowledge of French very useful. French culinary terms are often used, regardless of the language in which a recipe or menu is written. Chefs and food critics will need to be able to understand and use many French terms related to cooking. Have students recall French culinary terms they are familiar with.

Culture Note

The black olives, tomatoes, and garlic pictured on this page are essential ingredients of Provençale cuisine. The rich land, coupled with a warm climate, produce an abundance of olive trees, spices, and vegetables. The tomato-based dishes flavored with olive oil, a variety of herbs and spices, and garlic are characteristic of Provence.

Teaching Suggestion

To close this **étape,** write a request for a favor on an index card for each student. Have students stand in two lines facing one another. Each student reads the request aloud and the person opposite must respond within ten seconds. At your signal, the students in one line move down one, and the student at the end of the line moves to the front, so that each student is facing a new partner. Repeat the process until the original partners are opposite each other again.

Assess

- Testing Program, pp. 253–256
  Quiz 10-2A, Quiz 10-2B
  Audio CD 10, Tr. 14
- Student Make-Up Assignments, Chapter 10, Alternative Quiz
- Alternative Assessment Guide, p. 41

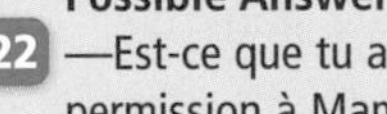

Possible Answers

22 —Est-ce que tu as demandé la permission à Maman? —Oui, je l'ai demandée!; —Est-ce que tu as fixé la date? —Oui, je l'ai déjà fixée!; —Est-ce que tu as invité Sophie et Julie? —Oui, je les ai invitées!; —Est-ce que tu as préparé les amuse-gueule? —Oui, je les ai préparés!; —Est-ce que tu as fait le ménage? —Oui, je l'ai fait!; —Est-ce que tu as envoyé les invitations? —Oui, je les ai envoyées!; —Est-ce que tu as choisi la musique?; —Oui, je l'ai choisie!

STANDARDS: 1.1, 2.2, 3.2, 5.1

Teaching Resources
pp. 294–296

PRINT

- Lesson Planner, p. 49
- TPR Storytelling Book, pp. 76–77
- Listening Activities, pp. 77, 81
- Activities for Communication, pp. 59–60, 122, 124, 155–156
- Travaux pratiques de grammaire, p. 86
- Grammar Tutor for Students of French, Chapter 10
- Cahier d'activités, pp. 116–118
- Testing Program, pp. 257–260
- Alternative Assessment Guide, p. 41
- Student Make-Up Assignments, Chapter 10

MEDIA 

- One-Stop Planner
- Audio Compact Discs, CD 10, Trs. 7, 15, 23–24
- Teaching Transparencies: 10-3; **Grammaire supplémentaire** Answers; Travaux pratiques de grammaire Answers
- Interactive CD-ROM Tutor, Disc 3

Bell Work

Have students answer these questions, using object pronouns and saying that they already did what was asked. (**Tu vas sortir la poubelle? Je l'ai déjà sortie.**)

1. Tu vas passer l'aspirateur?
2. Tu vas choisir la musique?
3. Tu vas faire tes devoirs?
4. Tu vas téléphoner à ta copine?
5. Tu vas parler à tes parents?

Presenting
Comment dit-on… ?

Write the functions and the expressions on strips of transparency. Use each expression with appropriate intonation and gestures as you place each strip under the function it serves.

Troisième étape

Objectives Apologizing and accepting an apology; reproaching someone

WA3 PROVENCE-10

CEDRIC Aurélie? Excuse-moi pour hier.
AURELIE Pourquoi?
CEDRIC Je suis vraiment désolé. Je voulais aller à ta boum, mais…
AURELIE Mais c'est pas grave.
CEDRIC Je sais que j'aurais dû te téléphoner. Tu ne m'en veux pas?
AURELIE Mais non. T'en fais pas. Isabelle m'a dit que tu ne venais pas.
CEDRIC Isabelle? Ouf, ça me rassure!
AURELIE Bon, alors, ça sera pour la prochaine fois.

24 La boum manquée
Lisons

1. Why did Cédric call Aurélie? to apologize for missing her party
2. Why is he worried? He is afraid that Aurélie is mad at him for missing her party.
3. Why isn't she mad? Isabelle had told her that Cédric wasn't coming.

Comment dit-on…?

Apologizing and accepting an apology; reproaching someone

To apologize:

C'est de ma faute. *It's my fault.*
Excuse-moi. *Forgive me.*
Désolé(e).
Tu ne m'en veux pas? *No hard feelings?*
J'aurais dû vous téléphoner. *I should have . . .*
J'aurais pu attendre dix minutes de plus. *I could have . . .*

To accept an apology:

Ça ne fait rien. *It doesn't matter.*
C'est pas grave.
Il n'y a pas de mal. *No harm done.*
T'en fais pas.
Je ne t'en veux pas. *No hard feelings.*

To reproach someone:

Tu aurais pu m'écouter.
You could have . . .
Tu aurais dû leur téléphoner.
You should have . . .

Cahier d'activités, pp. 116–117, Act. 16–18

Connections and Comparisons

Language-to-Language

The word **pardon** is common in several languages, especially those related to Latin. Both French and English use the expression **pardon** to mean *sorry* or *excuse me.* In Spanish, one can use **perdón** to say *excuse me,* and in Italian, the verb **perdonare** means *to excuse* or *to forgive.*

STANDARDS: 1.2, 4.1

Troisième étape

CHAPITRE 10

25 Excuse-moi.
See scripts and answers on p. 279H.

Ecoutons Listen to the following conversations you overhear in the hall. Why is each person apologizing? Does the other person accept the apology or reproach him or her?

CD 10 Tr. 7

A la française

You can say **Pardon** or **Excuse(z)-moi** to apologize politely in most situations. If you feel really sorry for something you did, however, say **Désolé(e)** or **Je regrette.**

Note de grammaire

Remember that when a conjugated verb is followed by an infinitive, all object pronouns come before the infinitive.

—J'ai invité les voisins.
—Tu n'aurais pas dû **les** inviter.

—Je n'ai pas parlé à Lucien.
—Tu aurais dû **lui** parler.

Travaux pratiques de grammaire, p. 86, Act. 15–16

Grammaire supplémentaire, p. 303, Act. 11–12

Cahier d'activités, p. 117, Act. 19

26 Grammaire en contexte
Possible answers:

Parlons/Ecrivons

1. Pardon./Ça ne fait rien.

2. Désolé!/Tu aurais dû téléphoner.

3. Je regrette!/T'en fais pas.

27 Grammaire en contexte

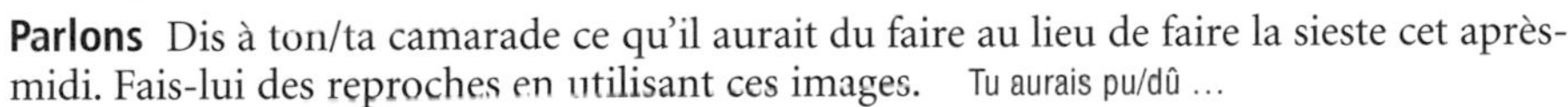

Parlons Dis à ton/ta camarade ce qu'il aurait du faire au lieu de faire la sieste cet après-midi. Fais-lui des reproches en utilisant ces images. Tu aurais pu/dû ...

EXEMPLE **—Tu aurais dû faire le ménage.**
—Mais je l'ai fait!

1. promener le chien.

2. faire tes devoirs.

3. faire du jogging.

4. me téléphoner.

5. faire la vaisselle.

Challenge

25 Play the recording again. Stop the recording after each of the three conversations. Have students give the opposite reaction to each apology than the one they heard.

Auditory Learners

25 Have students copy all the expressions from **Comment dit-on... ?** on page 294. As they listen to the recording, have them place a check mark next to an expression when they hear it. Ask them which of the expressions they heard twice **(Désolé.** and **J'aurais dû...)** and which were not used at all **(J'aurais pu... ; Ça ne fait rien. C'est pas grave. Je ne t'en veux pas. Tu aurais dû...).**

Slower Pace

26 Have students say as much as they can in French about the illustrations before they tell what the people are saying. Have students imagine who the people are, where they are, and what is happening.

27 Before students begin the activity, have them name activities that the photos suggest.

Teaching Suggestion

Prepare flashcards on which you've written the first sentences of various two-line dialogues (see **Note de grammaire** on this page). After students read the sentence and respond orally, show the response on the other side of the card to help visual learners. Afterwards, read the sentence and response to help auditory learners.

Communication for All Students

Challenge/Auditory Learners

Note de grammaire Call out the first sentence of a dialogue similar to the ones in the **Note de grammaire (J'ai oublié mes devoirs.)** and have students respond. **(Tu n'aurais pas dû les oublier.)**

STANDARDS: 1.2, 4.1

Troisième étape

CHAPITRE 10

Teaching Suggestion

28 For listening practice, read the letter aloud as students listen with their books closed. Ask them to identify as many things as they can that Denis did wrong. They might jot these down in French or in English as they listen.

Additional Practice

28 Have students use the letter in the activity as a model to write a letter explaining what an imaginary friend did wrong in a certain situation. Then, have a partner read and respond to the letter.

Portfolio

29 **Oral** This activity is appropriate for students' oral portfolios. For suggestions, see the *Alternative Assessment Guide,* page 27.

Mon journal

30 For an additional journal entry suggestion for Chapter 10, see *Cahier d'activités,* page 154.

Teaching Suggestion

To close this **étape,** have pairs of students choose one of the following situations to act out.

1. **Tu arrives au cinéma en retard et ton ami(e) est fâché(e).**
2. **Tu renverses ton coca sur la personne à côté de toi au café.**
3. **Dans le couloir, tu marches sur les pieds de quelqu'un.**

Assess

- Testing Program, pp. 257–260
  Quiz 10-3A, Quiz 10-3B
  Audio CD 10, Tr. 15
- Student Make-Up Assignments, Chapter 10, Alternative Quiz
- Alternative Assessment Guide, p. 41

---

28 Une catastrophe

Ecrivons Ton ami Denis n'est pas content parce que tout a été de travers hier soir. Lis son petit mot et écris ta réponse. Fais-lui des reproches. Dis-lui ce qu'il aurait dû et ce qu'il aurait pu faire.

EXEMPLE **Tu aurais pu faire tes devoirs. Et tu n'aurais pas dû sortir...**

Hier soir, j'avais des devoirs à faire, mais je suis quand même sorti avec des copains. Je suis parti sans avertir mes parents - j'ai oublié de leur dire à quelle heure j'allais rentrer. En route, j'ai vu Caroline, une amie de ma copine Elodie. Je lui ai parlé pendant quelques minutes. Donc, j'étais en retard pour le film et je n'ai pas pu trouver mes amis au ciné. J'ai décidé d'attendre la séance suivante. Le film était super, mais je suis rentré chez moi très tard. Mes parents étaient furieux et ils m'ont privé de sortie pendant deux semaines. Ensuite, le téléphone a sonné. C'était Elodie, ma copine, qui n'était pas contente parce qu'elle m'avait vu en tête-à-tête avec Caroline! Je lui ai dit que je ne savais pas de quoi elle parlait et de me rappeler plus tard. Tout le monde est fâché contre moi mais, en fait, je n'ai rien fait de mal!

29 Jeu de rôle

Parlons Avec un(e) camarade, choisissez une des scènes suivantes et jouez-la. Tu vas t'excuser et ton/ta camarade va te pardonner ou te faire un reproche. Puis, choisissez une autre scène et inversez les rôles.

1. Tu as perdu le livre de maths de ton ami(e).
2. Tu rentres chez toi à minuit et ton père (ta mère) n'est pas content(e)!
3. Tu as oublié de rendre le CD que ton ami(e) t'a prêté.
4. Tu n'es pas allé(e) à la boum de ton ami(e) parce que tu étais privé(e) de sortie.

30 Mon journal

Ecrivons In your journal, describe what happened the last time you had a misunderstanding or a disagreement with someone. Write about everything that happened and tell how you resolved it.

Tu te rappelles?

You already know how to make excuses, and sometimes you have to use them in the past tense.

J'avais quelque chose à faire.
Je n'ai pas eu le temps.
J'étais très occupé(e).
Je voulais le faire, mais j'ai dû...

31 De l'école au travail

Ecrivons You are working for a magazine publishing company this summer. You and some other interns have been assigned to work on the advice column for a youth-oriented magazine. Compose some letters from the readers and the responses of the columnist.

Communication for All Students

Slower Pace

30 Write a short example of the journal entry with some words omitted. Have students work in pairs, reading the journal to each other while filling in the blanks. Then have different groups read their completed entries aloud. Have students correct each other. Finally, collect the papers and have students write their own journal entries as instructed in Activity 30.

STANDARDS: 1.1, 1.2, 1.3, 3.1, 5.1, 5.2

Qu'est-ce que tu fais quand tu as un problème? Tu parles à qui?

What do you do when you have a problem? To whom do you talk? We asked some French-speaking teenagers what they do when they have a problem. Here's what they told us.

Antoine, France

«Quand j'ai des problèmes, en général je les garde pour moi. Mais, sinon, quand ça va pas du tout, j'en parle à une amie qui m'aide. C'est tout.» Tr. 9

Anselme, Côte d'Ivoire

«Au village, quand tu as un problème, quand tu as un malheur, c'est le malheur de tout le village et personne ne peut passer au village sans te dire bonjour.» Tr. 10

Céline, Viêt-nam

«J'en parle souvent à ma mère. Même si c'est pas très commun, enfin. Tout le monde en parle... Le plus souvent, les filles en parlent à leurs amies et ne se confient pas tellement à leurs parents. Mais moi, c'est le contraire.» Tr. 11

Qu'en penses-tu?

1. How do these students deal with their problems? Do you have a similar way of dealing with problems?
2. When you ask someone for help with a problem, what kind of help do you usually want? New ideas? Sympathy? Moral support? Advice? An honest opinion?
3. When your friends have problems, what do you do? How do you help them find a solution?

CHAPITRE 10

Teaching Resources
p. 297

PRINT 

- Video Guide, pp. 67–69
- Cahier d'activités, p. 120

MEDIA

- One-Stop Planner
- Video Program, Videocassette 4, 10:15–13:13
- DVD Tutor, Disc 2
- Audio Compact Discs, CD 10, Trs. 8–11
- Interactive CD-ROM Tutor, Disc 3

Presenting Panorama Culturel

Write the following on the board:

1. **Je parle à ma mère.**
2. **Je garde mes problèmes pour moi.**
3. **Tout le village m'aide.**
4. **Quelquefois, je parle à une amie qui m'aide.**

Have students view the video and match the paraphrased remarks to the interviewees (Céline, Antoine, Anselme, Antoine).

Questions

1. **Qui parle souvent à sa mère de ses problèmes?** (Céline)
2. **Qui garde ses problèmes pour lui?** (Antoine)
3. **Qui a tout un village pour l'aider avec ses problèmes?** (Anselme)
4. **D'après Céline, à qui est-ce que les filles se confient, en général?** (à leurs amies)

Connections and Comparisons

Teaching Suggestion

After students view the video, distribute typed copies of the interviews in which you've omitted some words. Then, play the recording and have students try to fill in the missing words. For a slower pace, write the missing words at the bottom of the page in random order.

Teacher Note

For more practice with the **Panorama Culturel**, have students complete the **Compréhension** questions on Disc 2 of the *DVD Tutor.*

Lisons!

CHAPITRE 10

Teaching Resources
pp. 298–299

PRINT 
- Lesson Planner, p. 50
- Cahier d'activités, p. 119
- Reading Strategies and Skills Handbook, Chapter 10
- Joie de lire 2, Chapter 10
- Standardized Assessment Tutor, Chapter 10

MEDIA
- One-Stop Planner

Prereading
Activities A–B

Motivating Activity
Have students imagine they're building a house. At first, it may seem like a difficult task, but when broken down into smaller, more manageable tasks, it's not so daunting. Have them tell how the same might be true of tackling an unfamiliar reading. (First, they build the foundation by looking at the title and main idea. Then, they construct the framework by identifying supporting details.)

Building on Previous Skills
Remind students to try to guess the meaning of an unfamiliar word from the context. Emphasize the importance of concentrating on what they do know rather than on what they don't know.

Teaching Suggestion
B. Once students have recognized **ami** in **amitié**, have them look for related words in the text, to help them determine the meaning of **amitié. (copine, aime, fidélité, confiance)**

Possible Answers

A. The article will be about friendship. There are quotes from various people telling what they feel friendship is.

B. **ami**; friendship

Lisons!

L'amitié

C'est quoi au juste, un meilleur ami? Un grand écrivain français, Michel de Montaigne, qui pourtant avait la plume facile, quand on lui demandait de dire pourquoi il était ami avec son ami La Boétie, répondait tout simplement "parce que c'était lui, parce que c'était moi... " comme s'il n'avait rien d'autre à dire. Il n'y a rien d'autre à dire, en effet. Parce que chez l'ami, le plus important, c'est son existence même, c'est le fait qu'il existe et qu'il soit qui il est. On n'aime pas un ami parce qu'il fait vos devoirs de maths ou qu'il vous paie le ciné, parce qu'il a une super Nintendo® ou un chalet à la montagne, parce qu'il a une sœur canon ou un frère si mignon...

On l'aime pour rien, pour lui, pour elle

Alors il y a autant de définitions de meilleur ami que de meilleurs amis sur cette terre. Mais ce qu'on peut dire c'est qu'avec l'amitié on va découvrir des choses très importantes. On découvre d'abord qu'on est libres. Libres de choisir ses amis. Cela ne va d'ailleurs pas sans mal. En effet, quand on est petit, en général on est "ami" avec celui ou celle qui est assis à côté de nous en classe ou celui ou celle qu'on voit souvent parce que ses parents sont amis avec les nôtres.

"Moi, ma meilleure copine est tout le contraire de moi : je suis petite, elle est grande, elle aime Céline Dion, pas moi... Ça ne nous empêche pas d'être des super copines."
Geneviève,

L'amitié

Stratégie pour lire
Once you get the gist or main idea of a text by using strategies you've already learned, look for the supporting details. Specific facts and phrases from the text will help you flesh out the main idea and give you a more complete picture of what you're reading about.

A. Skim the title and quotes to get the gist of the article. What type of information do you think you will find? See answers below.

B. What word do you recognize in the word **amitié**? What do you think **amitié** means? See answers below.

C. Read the article and decide whether the following statements are true or false, according to the information presented in the article.
1. Friends must share the same interests. false
2. We are free to choose our friends. true
3. Friends are important because of what they can do for you. false
4. Friendship should be easy. false

Connections and Comparisons

Terms in Lisons!
Students may want to know the following additional vocabulary: **empêcher** *(to prevent, stop);* **attiré** *(drawn);* **de mieux en mieux** *(better and better);* **écartelé** *(torn);* **bousculer** *(to shake up, to jostle someone).*

Paraphrasing
Have students paraphrase in one sentence the thoughts of the four teens whose reflections are highlighted in boxes. Write the names of the teens on the board and have students close their books. Collect their papers and read the sentences aloud. Have students identify to whom each sentence pertains.

L'amitié, ça nous engage, ça nous bouscule

Mais à l'adolescence, on choisit réellement ses amis. On remarque ce garçon ou cette fille qui vient d'arriver dans la classe ou au club de foot ou à la danse. On a envie de le connaître mieux, on est attiré. Choisir un(e) ami(e), c'est souvent un des premiers actes que l'on réalise sans demander leur avis aux parents...

> *"L'amitié, c'est essentiel pour être heureux dans une vie. Ce qu'il y a de bien dans l'amitié, c'est qu'on peut se confier à son ami(e) en toute sécurité. Une bonne amitié doit durer toute la vie."*
>
> **Julie**

On va ensuite découvrir de mieux en mieux qui on est. On ressent des sentiments tellement différents pour les personnes qui nous entourent. Certaines nous énervent sans qu'on puisse dire pourquoi, d'autres nous attirent au contraire. Réaliser petit à petit qu'on préfère les jeunes qui aiment le sport ou les voyages ou les jeux vidéos ou l'astronomie, cela nous fait comprendre ce que, nous aussi, on aime ou, au contraire, ce qu'on déteste. Cela ne veut pas dire non plus qu'on s'assemble uniquement avec ce qui nous ressemble. C'est vrai qu'un ami c'est quelqu'un avec qui on partage tout, alors si on n'a pas grand-chose à partager, ça va être difficile. Mais souvent, avec l'amitié, on découvre "l'autre" justement. L'autre qui a beaucoup de choses en commun avec nous, mais qui a quand même des goûts parfois très différents. Quelle idée de se passionner pour les trains, comment peut-on passer trois heures par semaine à répéter des mouvements de gym, ou des heures chaque jour devant un écran!? Chacun ses goûts.

> *"Je pense qu'on a besoin d'amis pour nous soutenir dans les moments difficiles et pour bien rigoler avec nous. On se confie à eux, on leur fait confiance et même chose pour eux envers nous."*
>
> **Séverine**

On découvre encore que nos sentiments sont complexes et changeants. Parfois très beaux et très forts, comme la fidélité, la confiance, l'estime, parfois violents, contradictoires, comme la jalousie, l'envie... Ce n'est pas toujours facile à vivre : si nos parents ne veulent pas voir notre meilleur ami, on se sent écartelé; quand on rencontre une nouvelle amitié, comment la faire accepter par les amis qu'on a déjà, et quand un ami s'éloigne comment ne pas lui en vouloir... L'amitié, ça nous fait prendre des risques, ça nous engage, ça nous bouscule, ça nous fait grandir en somme.

> *"Avec ma meilleure amie, on parle de tout. Quand une de nous deux a un coup de blues ou quelque chose qui ne va pas, l'autre est toujours là pour l'écouter, l'aider. Ça pour moi, c'est vraiment de l'amitié."*
>
> **Catherine**

Montaigne avait raison. Un véritable ami on ne peut pas dire pour "quoi" on l'aime, maintenant, on sait très bien pourquoi...

D. Match each of the following statements with the person who is most likely to make each one.

Geneviève Catherine Séverine Julie

1. Friends are there for you during hard times. Séverine
2. You can safely confide in a good friend. Julie
3. Friends are always there to listen. Catherine
4. Friendship should last forever. Julie
5. You can be different from your friend and still be good friends. Geneviève

E. What does **On l'aime pour rien, pour lui, pour elle** mean? What does the article say to support this statement? See answers below.

F. According to the article, what can make friendship difficult at times? See answers below.

G. Lis l'article encore une fois et puis écris trois idées sur l'amitié qu'on trouve dans l'article. Essaie de trouver des mots et des phrases dans le texte pour soutenir tes idées. See answers below.

H. Maintenant, écris ton propre essai sur l'amitié. Demande à quelques camarades de classe ce qu'ils pensent de l'amitié et écris leurs réponses. Après, en utilisant leurs réponses, écris un paragraphe sur l'amitié. Si tu veux, tu peux trouver des images ou des photos pour illustrer ton essai.

Cahier d'activités, p. 119, Act. 22

Communication for All Students

Cooperative Learning

H. Have students work in groups to write their own article on **l'amitié.** Each group should interview the members of another group about their views on friendship. Assign an interviewer to conduct the interviews, a recorder to record the interviewees' responses, a writer to compile the results into an article, and a reviewer to proofread and edit the article. You might have each group present its article to the class.

Lisons!

CHAPITRE 10

Reading

Activities C–F

Teaching Suggestions

C. Have students identify the phrases and/or sentences that either support or disprove each statement.

E. Have students determine what **"parce que c'était moi, parce que c'était lui"** means. Then, have them tell how this idea relates to the article and identify details in the article that support this perspective of **l'amitié.** Have them also identify any details that are in contrast to this point of view.

F. You might do this activity as a class and have a volunteer make a list of student responses on the board. Then, ask students to add to this list based on their own experiences.

Postreading

Activities G–H

Teaching Suggestion

G. Have students work in pairs to find three additional ideas about **l'amitié.** Then, have each pair present its findings and compare them to those of the other pairs.

Possible Answers

E. You love a friend for nothing but for him or for her. Answers will vary.

F. feelings of jealousy, having parents who don't like your best friend, making new friends

G. You care for a friend because of who he or she is, not what he or she can do for you; We are free to choose our friends; Friendship can make you grow. Answers will vary.

Grammaire supplémentaire

CHAPITRE 10

For **Grammaire supplémentaire** Answer Transparencies, see the *Teaching Transparencies* binder.

Grammaire supplémentaire

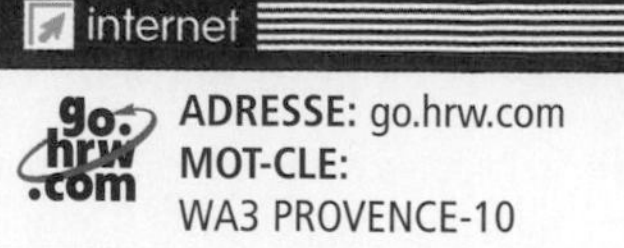

Première étape

Objectives Sharing a confidence; asking for and giving advice

1 Camille a eu un malentendu avec son petit ami, Frédéric. Ses copines lui donne des conseils. Récris les phrases suivantes et remplace les références à Frédéric avec des pronoms objets appropriés. (**p. 288**)

EXEMPLE Ecris à Frédéric **Ecris-lui.**

1. Dis à Frédéric que tu es désolée.
2. Il faut que tu oublies Frédéric.
3. Non, je ne suis pas d'accord. Parle à Frédéric.
4. A mon avis, tu devrais téléphoner à Frédéric.
5. Tu peux offrir un cadeau à Frédéric.
6. Invite Frédéric à la boum de Michèle.

2 Ta petite sœur te pose des questions et elle te demande de faire des choses pour elle. Réponds à ses questions par **oui** ou **non** et une phrase complète. Utilise un pronom objet pour remplacer les expressions en caractères gras. (**p. 288**)

EXEMPLE Tu lis cette histoire **à Luc et à moi?** (oui)
Oui, je vous lis cette histoire.

1. Tu vas parler **à Sylvie** ce soir? (oui)
2. Tu donnes une invitation **à nos voisins?** (non)
3. Tu peux **m'**aider avec mes devoirs? (oui)
4. Tu invites **Luc et moi** à ta boum? (non)
5. Tu vas **m'**acheter un cadeau pour mon anniversaire? (oui)

3 Choisis la photo qui correspond avec le conseil suggéré. (**p. 288**)

a.

b.

c.

d.

1. Achète-le.
2. Offre-lui…
3. Explique-leur.
4. Mets-le.

Answers

1
1. Dis-lui que tu es désolée.
2. Oublie-le.
3. Parle-lui.
4. Téléphone-lui.
5. Offre-lui un cadeau.
6. Invite-le.

2
1. Oui, je vais lui parler ce soir.
2. Non, je ne leur donne pas d'invitation.
3. Oui, je peux t'aider avec tes devoirs.
4. Non, je ne vous invite pas à ma boum.
5. Oui, je vais t'acheter un cadeau.

3
1. c
2. d
3. b
4. a

Grammar Resources for Chapter 10

The **Grammaire supplémentaire** activities were designed as supplemental activities for the grammatical concepts presented in the chapter. You might use them as additional practice, for review, or for assessment.

For more grammar presentations, review, and practice, refer to the following:

- Travaux pratiques de grammaire
- Grammar Tutor for Students of French
- Grammar Summary on pp. R23–R42
- Cahier d'activités
- Grammar and Vocabulary quizzes (Testing Program)
- Test Generator
- Interactive CD-ROM Tutor
- DVD Tutor
- **Jeux interactifs** at go.hrw.com

STANDARDS: 1.2

4 Tu vas faire une fête ce soir. Il y a des tas de choses à faire. Demande à ta sœur Claire et à ton frère François de t'aider. Utilise des pronoms dans tes réponses. (**p. 288**)

EXEMPLE téléphoner **à Luc** (Claire et François)
Téléphonez-lui.

1. expliquer à Jean comment aller chez nous (François)
2. inviter tous mes amis (Claire et François)
3. demander à nos parents de partir (Claire et François)
4. téléphoner à Jeanne et à Colette (Claire et François)
5. ne pas oublier les gâteaux (Claire)
6. ne pas parler aux invités (François)

5 Choisis le meilleur conseil pour chaque problème. (**p. 288**)

1. J'ai raté mon examen et mes parents sont fâchés.
2. Je suis privé de sortir et je ne peux pas aller à la boum de ma petite amie.
3. Je suis arrivée en retard au dîner.
4. Ma copine est fâchée et je ne sais pas pourquoi.
5. J'aime une fille dans ma classe, mais je suis trop timide de lui parler.
6. Victor m'a demandé de sortir avec lui le soir de la boum d'Agnès.
7. J'ai cassé avec mon petit ami. Il n'était pas sympa.
8. Mon petit ami a oublié mon anniversaire, mais il s'est excusé et m'a offert un cadeau.

a. Téléphone-lui et demande-lui pardon.
b. Ecris-lui.
c. Oublie-le.
d. Explique-leur.
e. Invite-le.
f. Excuse-toi.
g. Parle-lui.
h. Pardonne-lui.

6 Your friends are asking for your advice. Write a sentence telling them what you think they should do. Be sure to use pronouns in your response. (**p. 288**)

EXEMPLE Je me suis disputée avec mon petit ami. **Excuse-toi.** *or* **Tu devrais t'excuser.**

1. C'est l'anniversaire de mon père.
2. J'ai eu une mauvaise note en biologie et mes parents vont être fâchés.
3. J'ai oublié mes devoirs à la maison et le prof va me donner une mauvaise note.
4. J'ai cassé le CD que j'ai emprunté à Jean-Luc.
5. J'ai rencontré une fille super et je veux lui parler.

Grammaire supplémentaire

CHAPITRE 10

Answers

4
1. Explique-lui comment aller chez nous.
2. Invitez-les.
3. Demandez-leur de partir.
4. Téléphonez-leur.
5. Ne les oublie pas.
6. Ne leur parle pas.

5
1. d
2. a
3. f
4. g
5. b
6. e
7. c
8. h

6
1. Tu devrais lui offrir une cravate. OR Offre-lui une cravate.
2. Explique-leur ce qui s'est passé. OR Tu devrais leur expliquer ce qui s'est passé.
3. Dis-lui que tu as oublié tes devoirs à la maison. OR Tu devrais lui dire que tu as oublié tes devoirs à la maison.
4. Excuse-toi. OR Tu devrais t'excuser. Achète-lui un autre CD. OR Tu devrais lui acheter un autre CD.
5. Téléphone-lui. OR Tu devrais lui téléphoner. Invite-la à la boum. OR Tu devrais l'inviter à la boum samedi.

Review and Assess

Additional Practice

Prepare a set of index cards equal to the number of students in the class. On half of the cards, write questions **(Tu me pardonnes?)**, and on the other half, write the responses to the questions. **(Oui, je te pardonne.)** Distribute one card to each student. Without showing their cards, students circulate around the room, trying to find the appropriate question or answer to match their card. They should say whatever is on their card to every person they encounter. When they find a match, they read both the question and the answer to you. Continue until everyone has found a match. In large classes, you might make two identical sets of cards and have half of the students interact on one side of the room, and the other half on the other side of the room.

STANDARDS: 1.2

Grammaire supplémentaire

CHAPITRE 10

For **Grammaire supplémentaire** Answer Transparencies, see the *Teaching Transparencies* binder.

Grammaire supplémentaire

CD-ROM 3 DVD 2 go.hrw.com WA3 PROVENCE-10

Deuxième étape

Objectives Asking for and granting a favor; making excuses

7 You are at a party where there is a lot of noise, and you hear only parts of various conversations. Match what was said to the subject of the conversation. (**p. 293**)

1. — Je les ai écrites à la maison.
2. — Je l'ai faite avant de venir.
3. — Paul les a invités à la boum.
4. — Tu les as apportés dans ton sac.
5. — Je l'ai tondu hier.
6. — Ils les ont promenés dans le parc.

les invitations	les cadeaux	les chiens
Claire et Michel	le gazon	la cuisine

8 Rien ne change. Dis ce que tu as fait hier selon ce que tu fais aujourd'hui. Utilise des pronoms compléments d'objet dans tes réponses. (**p. 293**)

EXEMPLE Je prends le bus.
Je l'ai pris hier.

1. Je fais mes devoirs.
2. Je range ma chambre.
3. Je sors la poubelle.
4. Je ne regarde pas la télé.
5. Je lis le journal.
6. Je vois mes amis.
7. Je passe l'aspirateur.
8. Je ne perds pas mes clés.

9 Tu as invité des amis à une boum chez toi. Tu vérifies que tu as fait tous les préparatifs. Si la phrase est marquée, dis que tu l'as déjà faite. Si elle n'est pas marquée, dis que tu ne l'as pas encore faite. Utilise des pronoms. (**p. 293**)

EXEMPLE __√__ Acheter les boissons — **Je les ai achetées.**
_____ Faire le menage — **Je ne l'ai pas fait.**

1. __√__ Envoyer les invitations.
2. _____ Nettoyer la cuisine.
3. __√__ Acheter un cadeau.
4. _____ Préparer les amuse-gueule.
5. __√__ Ranger le salon.
6. __√__ Préparer le gâteau.
7. _____ Choisir la musique.

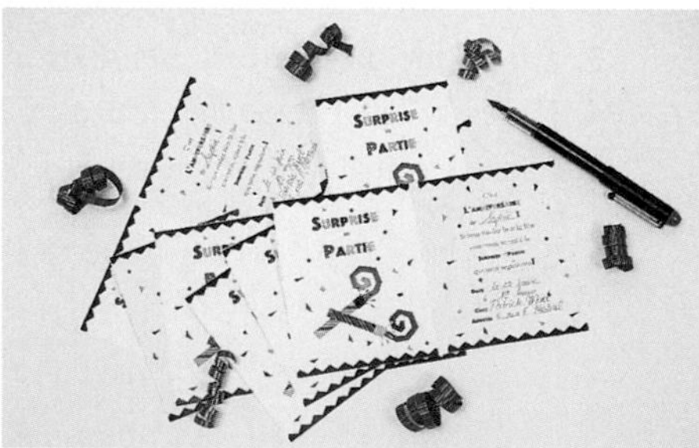

Answers

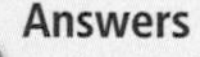

7
1. les invitations
2. la cuisine
3. Claire et Michel
4. les cadeaux
5. le gazon
6. les chiens

8
1. Je les ai faits hier.
2. Je l'ai rangée hier.
3. Je l'ai sortie hier.
4. Je ne l'ai pas regardée hier.
5. Je l'ai lu hier.
6. Je les ai vus hier.
7. Je l'ai passé hier.
8. Je ne les ai pas perdues hier.

9
1. Je les ai envoyées.
2. Je ne l'ai pas nettoyée.
3. Je l'ai acheté.
4. Je ne les ai pas préparés.
5. Je l'ai rangé.
6. Je l'ai préparé.
7. Je ne l'ai pas choisie.

Communication for All Students

Slower Pace

7 Before students complete this activity, write the following sentences on the board or on a transparency and have students choose the noun to which each object pronoun refers. Have students explain why they selected the answers.

1. **Je les ai invités à la boum. (les garçons, les filles)**
2. **Je l'ai invitée à la boum. (Marie, Cédric)**
3. **Je l'ai vu au cinéma. (ton ami, ton amie)**
4. **Je les ai mangées très vite. (les poires, les sandwiches)**

STANDARDS: 1.2

10 Elisabeth demande à sa sœur de l'aider avec les préparations pour sa boum. Sa sœur lui pose quelques questions. Réponds à ses questions par **oui** ou **non** et une phrase complète. (**p. 293**)

EXEMPLE Est-ce que tu as invités tes amis? (oui)
<u>Oui, je les ai invités.</u>

1. Est-ce que tu as envoyé les invitations? (oui)
2. Est-ce que tu as reçu les réponses? (non)
3. Est-ce que tu as écrit ton numéro de téléphone sur les invitations? (oui)
4. Est-ce tu as oublié la musique? (non)
5. Est-ce que tu as fait la vaisselle? (oui)

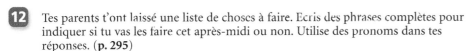

Troisième étape

Objectives Apologizing and accepting an apology; reproaching someone

11 Annick always forgets to do things. Reproach her for the following things. Remember to use pronouns in your responses. (**p. 295**)

EXEMPLE Je n'ai pas fait la vaisselle.
<u>Tu aurais dû la faire.</u>

1. Je n'ai pas fait mes devoirs.
2. Je n'ai pas parlé au professeur.
3. Je n'ai pas demandé la permission à mes parents.
4. Je n'ai pas invité Martin.
5. J'ai oublié mes livres à la maison.
6. Je n'ai pas envoyé les invitations pour la boum.
7. Je n'ai pas rangé ma chambre.
8. Je t'ai téléphoné après minuit hier soir.

12 Tes parents t'ont laissé une liste de choses à faire. Ecris des phrases complètes pour indiquer si tu vas les faire cet après-midi ou non. Utilise des pronoms dans tes réponses. (**p. 295**)

EXEMPLE faire le ménage?
<u>Oui, je vais le faire cet après-midi.</u>

1. envoyer les invitations pour la boum? (non)
2. lire le livre à tes frères? (oui)
3. recevoir ton bulletin trimestriel? (oui)
4. écrire la lettre à tes grands-parents? (non)
5. acheter le cadeau pour ton frère? (non)
6. sortir la poubelle? (oui)
7. rendre les CD à ton ami? (non)

Review and Assess

You may wish to assign the **Grammaire supplémentaire** activities as additional practice or homework after presenting material throughout the chapter. Assign Activities 1–6 after **Grammaire** (p. 288), Activities 7–10 after **Note de grammaire** (p. 293), and Activities 11–12 after **Note de grammaire** (p. 295).

To prepare students for the **Etape** Quizzes and Chapter Test, we suggest doing the **Grammaire supplémentaire** activities in the following order. Have students complete Activities 1–6 before Quiz 10-1A or 10-1B; Activities 7–10 before Quiz 10-2A or 10-2B; and Activities 11–12 before Quiz 10-3A or 10-3B.

Grammaire supplémentaire

CHAPITRE 10

Answers

10
1. Oui, je les ai envoyées.
2. Non, je ne les ai pas reçues.
3. Oui, je l'ai écrit sur les invitations.
4. Non, je ne l'ai pas oubliée.
5. Oui, je l'ai faite.

11
1. Tu aurais dû les faire.
2. Tu aurais dû lui parler.
3. Tu aurais dû leur demander la permission.
4. Tu aurais dû l'inviter.
5. Tu n'aurais pas dû les oublier à la maison.
6. Tu aurais dû les envoyer.
7. Tu aurais dû la ranger.
8. Tu n'aurais pas dû me téléphoner après minuit.

12 *Possible answers:*
1. Non, je ne vais pas les envoyer.
2. Oui, je vais leur lire le livre.
3. Oui, je vais le recevoir.
4. Non, je ne vais pas l'écrire.
5. Non, je ne vais pas lui acheter le cadeau.
6. Oui, je vais la sortir.
7. Non, je ne vais pas lui rendre les CD.

Mise en pratique

CHAPITRE 10

The **Mise en pratique** reviews and integrates all four skills and culture in preparation for the Chapter Test.

Teaching Resources
pp. 304–305

PRINT

- Lesson Planner, p. 50
- TPR Storytelling Book, pp. 78–79
- Listening Activities, p. 77
- Video Guide, pp. 67, 70
- Grammar Tutor for Students of French, Chapter 10
- Standardized Assessment Tutor, Chapter 10

MEDIA 

- One-Stop Planner
- Video Program Videocassette 4, 13:15–16:33
- DVD Tutor, Disc 2
- Audio Compact Discs, CD 10, Tr. 12
- Interactive CD-ROM Tutor, Disc 3

Thinking Critically

2 **Synthesizing** Distribute the following list of proverbs and ask students which ones apply to each writer and why. **Aide-toi, le ciel t'aidera.** *(Heaven helps those who help themselves.)*; **Il faut battre le fer quand il est chaud.** *(Strike while the iron is hot.)*; **Qui ne dit mot consent.** *(Silence gives consent.)*; **Qui cherche trouve.** *(He who seeks, finds.)*

Answers

2
1. He is trying to talk to his friend, who is always busy; He wants to talk to his friend about a problem.
2. **La chipie** is the author's little sister; She is called this because she is always getting into her brother's things; The author feels it is not fair that his sister can get away with mischief because she is little.
3. The poem is about a lost love; She can't forget about him even though he has a new girlfriend; Her friends say she should hate him.

Mise en pratique

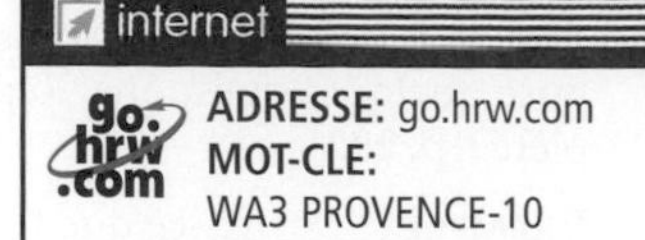

1 Listen as several teenagers call in to a radio talk show for advice. Match the host's responses to the problems. What other advice would you give? See scripts and answers on p. 279H.

CD 10 Tr. 12

a. Tu devrais aller la chercher au parc.

b. D'abord, tu aurais dû étudier! Maintenant, tu devrais leur dire combien tu as eu à ton interro.

c. Explique-leur ce qui s'est passé.

d. C'est ridicule! Va à la fête et parle-lui.

PARLONS-EN!

OCCUPÉ

Je téléphone
Occupé
«Plus tard, peut-être»
Encore occupé
J'ai un problème
Je peux te parler?
«J'ai trente-six choses...
Désolé...
Occupé.»
Je dois te parler!
Mon copain
est occupé.
Que faire?
Tu peux t'occuper de
moi?

-- Pierre, Arles

LA CHIPIE

Ma petite sœur est une chipie
Qui fait toujours des bêtises.
Est-ce qu'on la punit?
Mais non! Elle est «trop petite,
trop jeune», bien sûr!

Hier, dans ma chambre
Mon lieu sacré
Elle a écouté ma musique à moi
Pourquoi? Pour m'énerver.

Mes CD partout, par terre,
une catastrophe,
J'entre, incrédule, elle me sourit
Je suis furieux, sans recours,
Parce qu'elle sait qu'elle est
«trop petite».

Que faire? Vraiment, que faire?
Je suis tellement énervé
Ce n'est pas juste, cette petite,
trop petite.
Amis, avez-vous une idée?

-- Jean-Paul, Avignon

IMPOSSIBLE

Je devrais l'oublier
Le rayer de ma mémoire,
Mais je pense toujours à lui
Toute la journée, tous les
jours, tous les soirs.

Sa nouvelle petite amie
Est blonde, sympa, super.
De l'avis de tout le monde,
Ces deux-là, "Ils font la
paire!"

Tout le monde me dit
Que je dois le détester
Mais je souffre, souffre tant
Que je ne peux pas l'oublier.

D'un regard je suis tombée
amoureuse
Je l'aimais, je l'aime toujours.
Je ne sais vraiment plus quoi
faire
Pour oublier ce chagrin
d'amour.

-- Félicité, Aix-en-Provence

See answers below.

2
1. What is the problem for the writer of **Occupé?** What does he want?
2. Who is **la Chipie?** Why is she named this? How does the author of the poem feel?
3. Look through the poem **Impossible** to find words that you recognize. What is the poem about? Read the first line and the last two lines. What is Félicité's problem? What advice have her friends given her?

3 If you were to go to a restaurant in Provence, what local specialties could you order?
tapenade, pissaladière, ratatouille

Apply and Assess

Challenge

1 Play the recording a second time, pausing after each caller to ask the following questions: **1. Pourquoi est-ce que Désiré est déprimé? Pourquoi est-ce que ses parents sont fâchés? Pourquoi est-ce qu'il est rentré en retard? 2. Pourquoi est-ce que Murielle est embêtée? Pourquoi est-ce qu'elle a eu une mauvaise note? 3. Qui est-ce que Jérôme a rencontré? Où? 4. Où est-ce qu'Eric est invité? Pourquoi est-ce qu'il ne veut pas y aller?**

Language Note

You might call attention to the word **chipie,** which is slang for *vixen* or *little devil.*

Ecrivons!

A foreign-exchange program in France is holding its annual poetry contest for American and French students. All American students' entries must be in French. This year's theme is **C'est toute une affaire!** *(It's such a big deal!)*. Write a poem to enter in the contest that describes a problem or misunderstanding that is common among teenagers.

Stratégie pour écrire
Tone reveals a speaker's or writer's attitude toward his or her subject. Think of some ways you might be able to convey a particular attitude or emotion in your poem.

Préparation

First, list several problems or misunderstandings you might write about. Once you've decided on a topic for your poem, think about your own attitude towards the topic. Does it make you angry or sad? Do you find anything humorous about it? What other emotions does it stir in you?

Next, decide which of the emotions you listed you want to convey in your poem. This decision will determine the tone of your poem (humorous, sad, and so on). Jot down any French words and expressions you know that will help you convey that tone to the reader.

Rédaction

There are several techniques that can help you communicate your attitude. First, the images you use can affect the tone of your poem; for example **ma chambre** conveys a different feeling than **la boîte où je dors.** Choice of imagery goes hand in hand with diction, or word choice (**mon professeur** vs. **mon prof**). Repetition of certain words, alliteration (repetition of an initial consonant sound), and assonance (repetition of similar vowel sounds) can also greatly affect tone. Finally, rhythm and rhyme (or lack of rhyme) can make a big difference in the tone.

Evaluation

Read aloud the first draft of your poem to a classmate. Have your partner tell you his or her impression of the tone of your poem. If your partner's impression is different from the tone you were aiming for, ask what you might change to achieve the expected tone.

5

Jeu de rôle

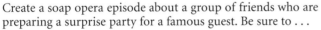

Create a soap opera episode about a group of friends who are preparing a surprise party for a famous guest. Be sure to . . .

- decide whom to invite.
- ask for and give advice about the preparations.
- include some type of misunderstanding, like a lost invitation or an old grudge.

Mise en pratique

CHAPITRE 10

Process Writing

4 Make several columns on the board and give each of them a label that describes a different mood (humorous, sad, and so on). Then, have the class brainstorm several French words and phrases that they know might convey the tone in each category (sad: **pas content**). Have a volunteer write their suggestions in the appropriate column. Students may then refer to this list as a starting point for developing the tone of their poems.

Writing Assessment

4 You might use the following rubric when grading your students on this activity.

Writing Rubric	Points			
	4	3	2	1
Content (Complete–Incomplete)				
Comprehensibility (Comprehensible–Incomprehensible)				
Accuracy (Accurate–Seldom accurate)				
Organization (Well organized–Poorly organized)				
Effort (Excellent–Minimal)				

18–20: A 16–17: B 14–15: C 12–13: D Under 12: F

Teacher Note

For additional practice and review, you might use the **Histoire Finale** for Chapter 10 on pages 78–79 of the *TPR Storytelling Book.*

Apply and Assess

Game

Des trous To prepare for the game, form five teams and give a transparency to each one. Assign each team five vocabulary expressions and have them write a sentence with each one. Then, have them copy the sentences onto a transparency, leaving blanks where the vocabulary items should appear. Collect the transparencies. To play the game, project the transparencies one at a time for thirty seconds each. Teams will write down the words they would use to fill in the blanks. They should sit out the round involving the transparency they created, so that each team will have four sets of answers. After you have shown the last transparency, have teams read their answers aloud and either verify or correct them. The team that filled in the most blanks correctly wins.

STANDARDS: 1.1, 1.3, 3.1, 5.1, 5.2

Que sais-je?

CHAPITRE 10

Teaching Resources
p. 306

PRINT 
- Grammar Tutor for Students of French, Chapter 10

MEDIA
- Interactive CD-ROM Tutor, Disc 3
- Online self-test

go.hrw.com
WA3 PROVENCE-10

Game
Lève-toi! Prepare a stack of yellow and red cards and form two teams. Read aloud questions from **Que sais-je?** at random. Tell students to stand if they know the answer. The first person to stand is recognized and tries to answer. If the student gives an appropriate answer, his or her team scores a point. If not, repeat the question for the other team, and anyone may answer. The first time a student answers correctly, give him or her a yellow card. The second time a student answers correctly, he or she gets a red card and may no longer answer questions for the team. Students with red cards will help keep score, determine who stood first, and judge the accuracy of the answers. When all the questions have been answered, the team with the most points wins.

Possible Answers

6
1. Bien sûr que non.
2. Bien sûr. Pas de problème.
3. Non, pas du tout.

8
1. Ça ne fait rien. C'est pas grave.
2. Il n'y a pas de mal. T'en fais pas.
3. Je ne t'en veux pas.

Que sais-je?

WA3 PROVENCE-10

Can you use what you've learned in this chapter?

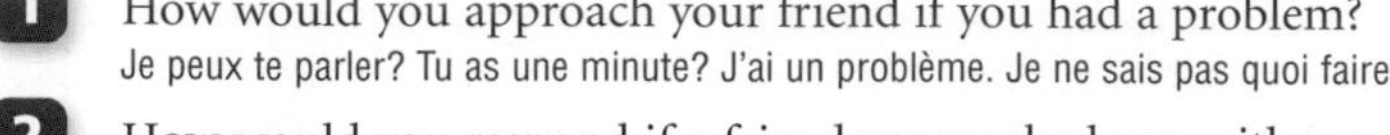

Can you share a confidence? p. 286

1 How would you approach your friend if you had a problem?
Je peux te parler? Tu as une minute? J'ai un problème. Je ne sais pas quoi faire.

2 How would you respond if a friend approached you with a problem?
Qu'est-ce qu'il y a? Qu'est-ce que je peux faire? Je t'écoute.

Can you ask for and give advice? p. 286

3 How would you ask a friend for advice about doing better in one of your classes? A ton avis, qu'est-ce que je dois faire? Qu'est-ce que tu ferais, toi? Qu'est-ce que tu me conseilles?

4 How would you advise your friend to. . .
1. apologize? Excuse-toi.
2. forgive her boyfriend? Pardonne-lui.
3. telephone his parents? Téléphone-leur.

Can you ask for a favor? p. 291

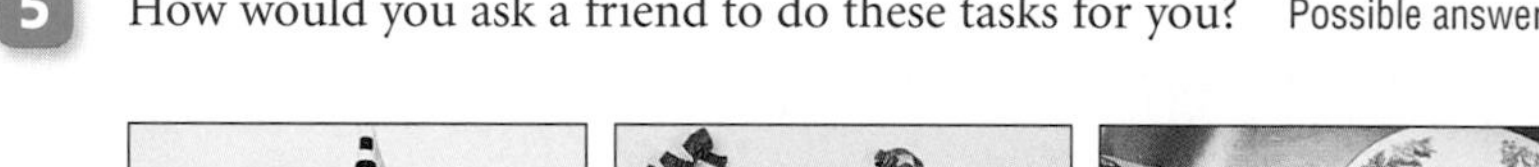

5 How would you ask a friend to do these tasks for you? Possible answers:

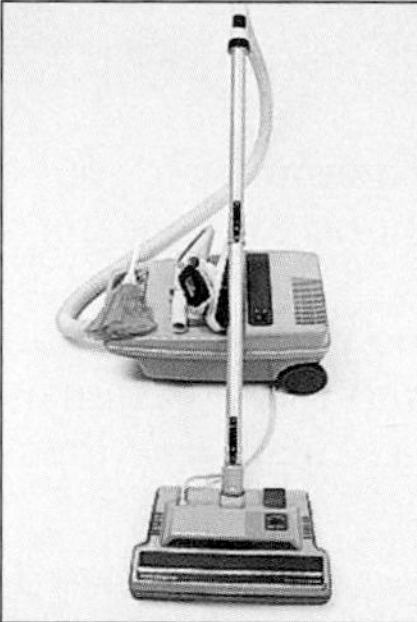
1. Tu pourrais faire le ménage?

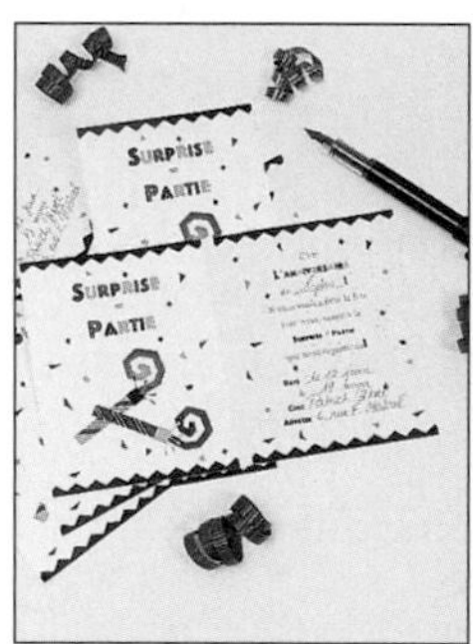
2. Ça t'ennuie d'envoyer les invitations?

3. Ça t'embête de faire la vaisselle?

Can you grant a favor and make excuses? p. 291

6 How would you respond if your friend asked you for the following favors? See answers below.
1. «Ça t'embête de téléphoner à Catherine?»
2. «Tu pourrais sortir la poubelle, s'il te plaît?»
3. «Ça t'ennuie de me prêter 20 €?»

Can you apologize and accept an apology? p. 294

7 How would you apologize to a friend with whom you had a misunderstanding? Possible answers: C'est de ma faute. Excuse-moi. Désolé(e). Tu ne m'en veux pas? J'aurais dû... ; J'aurais pu...

8 How would you respond if your friend said . . . See answers below.
1. «J'ai perdu ton livre. C'est de ma faute.»
2. «Je suis désolée de ne pas être venue à ta fête hier soir.»
3. «Tu ne m'en veux pas?»

Can you reproach someone? p. 294

9 How would you reproach a friend who was late meeting you at the movies?
Tu aurais pu... ; Tu aurais dû...

Review and Assess

Game
Je l'ai trouvée! Write the questions from **Que sais-je?** on one set of cards and the answers on another set. Tape the question cards on the board at random and put the answer cards in a bag. Then, form two teams. Have the first player from each team select one card from the bag, find the matching question on the board, and call out **Je l'ai trouvée!** The first player to find the correct question reads the question and the answer and wins a point for his or her team. Repeat the process with the remaining players.

Vocabulaire

Première étape

Sharing a confidence

Je ne sais pas quoi faire.	*I don't know what to do.*
J'ai un problème.	*I have a problem.*
Tu as une minute?	*Do you have a minute?*
Je peux te parler?	*Can I talk to you?*
Qu'est-ce qu'il y a?	*What's wrong?*
Qu'est-ce que je peux faire?	*What can I do?*
Je t'écoute.	*I'm listening.*

Asking for and giving advice

A ton avis, qu'est-ce que je dois faire?	*In your opinion, what should I do?*
Qu'est-ce que tu ferais, toi?	*What would you do?*
Qu'est-ce que tu me conseilles?	*What do you think I should do?*
Invite-le/-la/-les.	*Invite him/her/them.*
Parle-lui/-leur.	*Talk to him/her/them.*
Dis-lui/-leur que...	*Tell him/her/them that…*
Ecris-lui/-leur.	*Write to him/her/them.*
Explique-lui/-leur.	*Explain to him/her/them.*
Excuse-toi.	*Apologize.*
Téléphone-lui/-leur.	*Phone him/her/them.*
Oublie-le/-la/-les.	*Forget him/her/them.*
Tu devrais...	*You should…*

Apologetic actions

un petit malentendu	*a little misunderstanding*
expliquer ce qui s'est passé (à quelqu'un)	*to explain what happened (to someone)*
demander pardon (à quelqu'un)	*to ask (someone's) forgiveness*
se réconcilier (avec quelqu'un)	*to make up (with someone)*
dire (à quelqu'un) que...	*to tell (someone) that…*
téléphoner (à quelqu'un)	*to call (someone)*
s'excuser	*to apologize*
pardonner (à quelqu'un)	*to forgive (someone)*
offrir (à quelqu'un)	*to give (to someone)*
écouter ce qu'il/elle dit	*to listen to what he/she says*

Deuxième étape

Asking for and granting a favor; making excuses

Tu peux m'aider?	*Can you help me?*
Tu pourrais... ?	*Could you…?*
Ça t'ennuie de... ?	*Would you mind…?*
Ça t'embête de... ?	*Would you mind…?*
Avec plaisir.	*With pleasure.*
Bien sûr.	*Of course.*
Pas du tout.	*Not at all.*
Bien sûr que non.	*Of course not.*
Pas de problème.	*No problem.*
Désolé(e).	*Sorry.*
J'ai quelque chose à faire.	*I have something (else) to do.*
Je n'ai pas le temps.	*I don't have time.*
Je suis très occupé(e).	*I'm very busy.*
C'est impossible.	*It's impossible.*

Party preparations

faire une boum	*to give a party*
faire les préparatifs	*to get ready*
demander la permission à tes parents	*to ask your parents' permission*
fixer la date	*to choose the date*
envoyer les invitations	*to send the invitations*
choisir la musique	*to choose the music*
préparer les amuse-gueule	*to make party snacks*
faire le ménage	*to do housework*

Troisième étape

Apologizing and accepting an apology; reproaching someone

C'est de ma faute.	*It's my fault.*
Excuse-moi.	*Forgive me.*
Tu ne m'en veux pas?	*No hard feelings?*
J'aurais dû...	*I should have…*
J'aurais pu...	*I could have…*
Ça ne fait rien.	*It doesn't matter.*
C'est pas grave.	*It's not serious.*
Il n'y a pas de mal.	*No harm done.*
T'en fais pas.	*Don't worry about it.*
Je ne t'en veux pas.	*No hard feelings.*
Tu aurais pu...	*You could have…*
Tu aurais dû...	*You should have…*

Review and Assess

Game

Concours de vocabulaire Write the six categories from the **Vocabulaire** on separate slips of paper and place them in a box. Form two teams. Have a player from one team draw a category from the box. Set a timer for 30 seconds or designate a timekeeper. Within 30 seconds, the team calls out as many words or expressions as possible that fit the category. Players must pronounce the words or expressions clearly in order to receive credit. Award one point for each correctly delivered expression. At the end of 30 seconds, the turn passes to another team.

Vocabulaire

CHAPITRE 10

Circumlocution

Tell students to imagine that they're planning a party to celebrate the end of the school year. They're asking their partner, the French exchange student, to help them make plans for the party, but they don't remember the words for party preparations. Have them describe to the exchange student what needs to be done, without using the actual terms. Once the exchange student has guessed three of the preparations, have students change roles.

Chapter 10 Assessment

- **Testing Program**
  Chapter Test, pp. 261–266

  Audio Compact Discs, CD 10, Trs. 16–18
  Speaking Test, p. 347
- **Alternative Assessment Guide**
  Performance Assessment, p. 41
  Portfolio Assessment, p. 27
  CD-ROM Assessment, p. 55
- **Interactive CD-ROM Tutor, Disc 3**
  CD-ROM 3 A toi de parler
  DVD 2 A toi d'écrire
- **Standardized Assessment Tutor**
  Chapter 10
- **One-Stop Planner, Disc 3**

  Test Generator
  Chapter 10

STANDARDS: 1.1

Chapitre 11 : Chacun ses goûts
Chapter Overview

Mise en train pp. 310–312	***Bientôt la Fête de la musique!***

	FUNCTIONS	GRAMMAR	VOCABULARY	RE-ENTRY
Première étape pp. 313–318	• Identifying people and things, p. 313	• The verb **connaître,** p. 314 • **C'est** versus **il/elle est,** p. 315	• Nationalities, p. 314 • Types of music, p. 316	• Emphasizing likes and dislikes **(Chapitre 4,** II) • Making and responding to suggestions **(Chapitre 8,** II)
Deuxième étape pp. 319–323	• Asking for and giving information, p. 320		• Types of movies, p. 321	• Asking for and giving information **(Chapitre 6,** II)
Troisième étape pp. 324–327	• Giving opinions, p. 324 • Summarizing, p. 326	• The relative pronouns **qui** and **que,** p. 327	• Types of books, p. 325	• Asking for opinions **(Chapitre 6,** II) • Describing and characterizing yourself and others **(Chapitre 1,** II)

Lisons! pp. 328–329	**Cinq films qui ont fait date**	**Reading Strategy:** Combining reading strategies	
Grammaire supplémentaire	**pp. 330–333** **Première étape,** pp. 330–331	**Deuxième étape,** p. 331	**Troisième étape,** pp. 332–333
Review pp. 334–337	**Mise en pratique,** pp. 334–335 Ecrivons! Characterization Writing a movie proposal	**Que sais-je?** p. 336	**Vocabulaire,** p. 337

CULTURE

- **Panorama Culturel,** Musical tastes, p. 318
- **Note culturelle,** Movie theaters in France, p. 322
- **Rencontre culturelle, Minitel,** p. 323

Chapitre 11 : Chacun ses goûts
Chapter Resources

PRINT

Lesson Planning

One-Stop Planner

Lesson Planner with Substitute Teacher

Lesson Plans, pp. 51–55, 73

Student Make-Up Assignments
- Make-Up Assignment Copying Masters, Chapter 11

Listening and Speaking

TPR Storytelling Book, pp. 80–87

Listening Activities
- Student Response Forms for Listening Activities, pp. 83–85
- Additional Listening Activities 11-1 to 11-6, pp. 87–89
- Additional Listening Activities (song), p. 90
- Scripts and Answers, pp. 152–156

Video Guide
- Teaching Suggestions, pp. 72–73
- Activity Masters, pp. 74–76
- Scripts and Answers, pp. 110–112, 122–123

Activities for Communication
- Communicative Activities, pp. 61–66
- Realia and Teaching Suggestions, pp. 125–129
- Situation Cards, pp. 157–158

Reading and Writing

Reading Strategies and Skills Handbook, Chapter 11

Joie de lire 2, Chapter 11

Cahier d'activités, pp. 121–132

Grammar

Travaux pratiques de grammaire, pp. 87–97

Grammar Tutor for Students of French, Chapter 11

Assessment

Testing Program
- Grammar and Vocabulary Quizzes, **Etape** Quizzes, and Chapter Test, pp. 275–292
- Score Sheet, Scripts and Answers, pp. 293–300

Alternative Assessment Guide
- Portfolio Assessment, p. 28
- Performance Assessment, p. 42
- CD-ROM Assessment, p. 56

Student Make-Up Assignments
- Alternative Quizzes, Chapter 11

Standardized Assessment Tutor
- Reading, pp. 43–45
- Writing, p. 46
- Math, pp. 51–52

MEDIA

Online Activities
- **Jeux interactifs**
- **Activités Internet**

Video Program
- Videocassette 4
- Videocassette 5 (captioned version)

Interactive CD-ROM Tutor, Disc 3

DVD Tutor, Disc 2

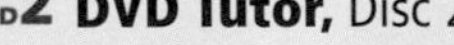

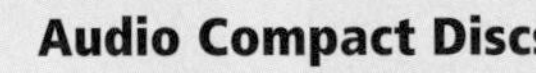

Audio Compact Discs
- Textbook Listening Activities, CD 11, Tracks 1–13
- Additional Listening Activities, CD 11, Tracks 20–26
- Assessment Items, CD 11, Tracks 14–19

Teaching Transparencies
- Situation 11-1 to 11-3
- Vocabulary 11-A to 11-D
- **Mise en train**
- **Grammaire supplémentaire** Answers
- **Travaux pratiques de grammaire** Answers

One-Stop Planner CD-ROM

Use the **One-Stop Planner CD-ROM with Test Generator** to aid in lesson planning and pacing.

For each chapter, the **One-Stop Planner** includes:
- Editable lesson plans with direct links to teaching resources
- Printable worksheets from resource books
- Direct launches to the HRW Internet activities
- Video and audio segments
- Test Generator
- Clip Art for vocabulary items

Chapitre 11 : Chacun ses goûts

Projects

Couverture de livre

Students will design and make a book jacket for their favorite book. The jacket will be designed as follows:

- *Front cover: Illustration, title, and author*
- *Inside front flap: Summary of the book*
- *Inside back flap: Critical reviews and list of other works by the same author*
- *Back cover: Picture and description of the author, price*
- *Spine: Title and author*

MATERIALS

Students may need

- Construction or unlined paper
- Colored markers or pencils
- Scissors
- Tape or glue
- Typewriter or word processor
- Magazines or catalogues

SUGGESTED SEQUENCE

1. Have students choose a book they have read and enjoyed. If it's in English, they will need to translate the title into French. They should acquire a copy of the book to refresh their memory about the characters and the story. Have students research the author's background, residence, family, hobbies, and other works.
2. Students write the text for the book jacket, including a summary of the story for the inside front flap of the book jacket, a description of the author for the back cover, and three favorable reviews and French titles of other works by the author (if available) for the inside back flap. The back flap should include a price in euros. The summary should entice others to read the book without revealing the ending of the story. Students might exchange papers for peer editing. After making corrections and recopying, students should hand in these drafts for final corrections before they type them. Allow students to write the text neatly if they don't have access to a typewriter or a word processor.
3. While you correct the rough drafts, have students prepare the illustrations for their book jackets. They might use magazine or catalogue pictures to create a collage or cut out letters to spell the title and the author's name.
4. After students have corrected their rough draft, they should type or write it, cut it apart, and paste the sections in the proper places on the book jacket. You might display the finished jackets in the library.

GRADING THE PROJECT

Suggested Point Distribution: (total = 100 points)

Content	20
Language use	20
Variety of vocabulary	20
Creativity/Effort	20
Overall appearance	20

Games

Faire la paire

In this game, students will practice using relative pronouns.

Preparation The day before playing the game, have each student write three or four incomplete sentences about celebrities, musicians, books, or movies. The sentence starters should end with a relative pronoun. (**Mel Gibson est un acteur qui** ________ .) Have students write the incomplete sentences on strips of paper. Collect and read them, choose some to use for the game, and put them in a box.

Procedure Have four contestants sit facing the class. The other students will be panelists. To play the game, a contestant draws an incomplete sentence from the box and reads it aloud. The contestant and all the panelists write the sentence starter and complete it as they wish. Then, the contestant reads aloud the complete sentence he or she wrote. Any panelist whose completed sentence matches the contestant's raises his or her hand. The contestant receives a point for every panelist's sentence that matches his or hers. Continue in this manner with the other three contestants. After several rounds, the contestant with the most points wins.

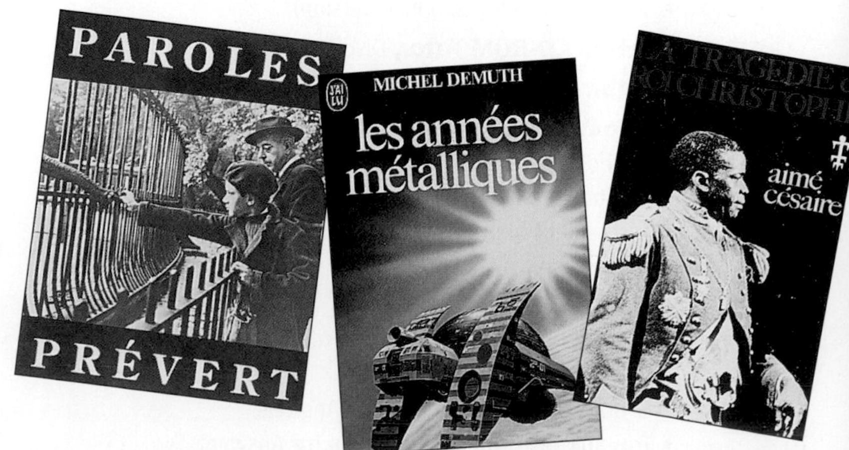

STANDARDS: 1.3, 3.1, 5.1

Storytelling

Mini-histoire

*This story accompanies Teaching Transparency 11-2. The **mini-histoire** can be told and retold in different formats, acted out, written down, and read aloud to give students additional opportunities to practice all four skills. The following story relates Marina's experience at the cinema festival.*

Marina est allée à la Fête du cinéma avec ses amis hier. Au cinéma, ils ont eu beaucoup de mal à se décider pour un film. Heureusement, la Fête du cinéma dure deux jours, et ils ont pu voir tous les films qu'ils voulaient voir. Après une longue discussion, ils ont décidé de commencer par voir *Le Trésor.* C'était génial. Après, ils sont allés voir le western *Un Homme, un revolver et un cheval.* C'était un très mauvais film. A la sortie du film, personne n'était d'accord sur le prochain film à voir. Alors, ils se sont séparés en deux groupes. Un groupe est allé voir *Un Petit malentendu* et le second groupe est allé voir *Un Suspect dans la ville.* Le lendemain, seuls deux des amis de Marina ont voulu retourner au cinéma avec elle. Ils n'ont pas aimé du tout les deux films qu'ils ont vus : *Le Ver gigantesque* et *Le Voyage des petits hommes verts.*

Traditions

La Pétanque

«Tu tires ou tu pointes?» is a question you might hear quite often in Provence. It is asked when people play the game of **pétanque,** or **boules.** Players form teams of two (**doublettes**) or three (**triplettes**). The object of the game is to get as many boules as close as possible to the **cochonnet** (literally *piglet).* The boules are usually made of heavy metal and measure a little over 3 inches in diameter. Each team has a set of boules marked with a distinctive pattern. The cochonnet is a small wooden ball. The player can **pointer,** which means to aim at the cochonnet, or, if an adversary already has a boule close to the cochonnet, the player must **tirer** to try to hit the opponent's ball out of the way. Sets of boules also are made for children. They are usually lighter and more colorful.

Recette

*Almond trees are the first to bloom at the end of winter in Provence. The almond is at the center of numerous candies in France: **pâte d'amande** (marzipan), **nougat, nougatine, dragées** (sugared almonds), **pralines,** and chocolate almonds.*

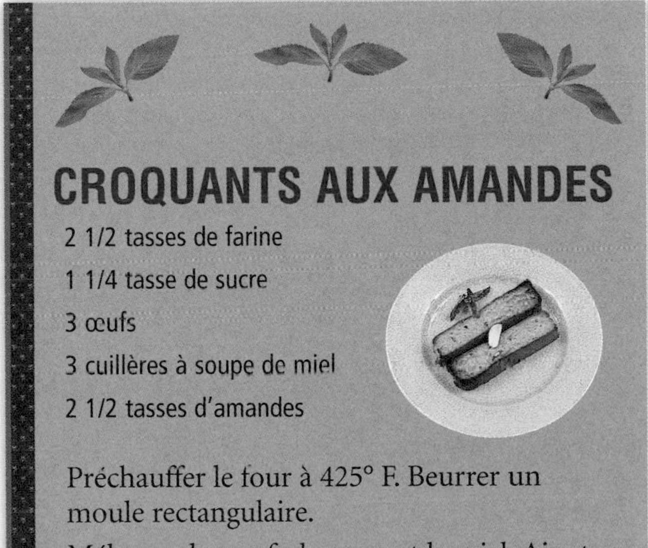

CROQUANTS AUX AMANDES

2 1/2 tasses de farine
1 1/4 tasse de sucre
3 œufs
3 cuillères à soupe de miel
2 1/2 tasses d'amandes

Préchauffer le four à 425° F. Beurrer un moule rectangulaire.

Mélanger les œufs, le sucre et le miel. Ajouter la farine petit à petit.

Ajouter les amandes. Mettre dans le moule. Faire cuire au four pendant environ 20 minutes.

Retirer du four. Laisser refroidir cinq minutes. Démouler. Découper le gâteau en tranches de 1 pouce (1 inch). Placer chaque tranche sur une plaque à gâteau et remettre au four pendant environ 15 minutes.

Les croquants aux amandes se conservent très bien pendant plusieurs jours.

Servir avec le café ou le thé.

STANDARDS: 1.2, 1.3, 2.2, 3.2, 5.1

Chapitre 11 : Chacun ses goûts

Technology

DVD/Video

Videocassette 4, Videocassette 5 (captioned version)
DVD Tutor, Disc 2
See Video Guide, pages 71–76.

Mise en train • Bientôt la Fête de la musique!
Cédric, Pascale, and Odile are deciding what to do during the annual **Fête de la musique** in Aix-en-Provence. A man overhears their discussion and offers his copy of *Aix en musique,* a weekly guide to musical events in the city. Cédric and Pascale want to see one of the rock groups listed, but Odile, who prefers classical music, isn't at all interested.

Mise en train (suite)
Cédric, Pascale, and Odile continue deciding which musical group to see during the **Fête de la musique.** A man appears, distributing flyers and announcing that several different groups will be appearing at a café that evening. The young people make plans to go. We see them later that evening at the café, and they are all happy with their choice.

Qu'est-ce que tu aimes comme musique?
Students from Côte d'Ivoire and Quebec talk about the kind of music they like to listen to.

Vidéoclips
- **Virgin Megastore®:** advertisement for a music store
- **Reynolds®:** advertisement for writing instruments

Interactive CD-ROM Tutor

Activity	Activity Type	Pupil's Edition Page
En contexte	*Interactive conversation*	
1. Grammaire	Les mots qui manquent	pp. 314–315
2. Vocabulaire	Jeu des paires	p. 316
3. Comment dit-on... ?	Le bon choix	p. 320
4. Vocabulaire	Chasse au trésor Explorons!/Vérifions!	p. 325
5. Comment dit-on... ?	Chacun à sa place	pp. 324, 326
6. Grammaire	Les mots qui manquent	p. 327
Panorama Culturel	Qu'est-ce que tu aimes comme musique?	p. 318
A toi de parler	*Guided recording*	pp. 334–335
A toi d'écrire	*Guided writing*	pp. 334–335

Teacher Management System

Launch the program, type "admin" in the password area, and press RETURN. Log on to www.hrw.com/CDROMTUTOR for a detailed explanation of the Teacher Management System.

DVD Tutor

The *DVD Tutor* contains all material from the *Video Program* as described above. French captions are available for use at your discretion for all sections of the video. The *DVD Tutor* also provides a variety of video-based activities that assess students' understanding of the **Mise en train, Suite,** and **Panorama Culturel.**

This part of the *DVD Tutor* may be used on any DVD video player connected to a television, video monitor, or on a computer with a DVD-ROM drive.

In addition to the video material and the video-based comprehension activities, the *DVD Tutor* also contains the entire *Interactive CD-ROM Tutor* in DVD-ROM format. Each DVD disc contains the activities from all 12 chapters of the *Interactive CD-ROM Tutor.*

This part of the *DVD Tutor* may be used on a Macintosh® or Windows® computer with a DVD-ROM drive.

To preview all resources available for this chapter, use the **One-Stop Planner CD-ROM**, Disc 3.

Internet Connection

Have students explore the ***go.hrw.com*** *Web site for many online resources covering all chapters. All Chapter 11 resources are available under the keyword* ***WA3 PROVENCE-11.*** *Interactive games help students practice the material and provide them with immediate feedback. You'll also find a printable worksheet that provides Internet activities that lead to a comprehensive online research project.*

Jeux interactifs

You can use the interactive activities in this chapter

- to practice grammar, vocabulary, and chapter functions
- as homework
- as an assessment option
- as a self-test
- to prepare for the Chapter Test

Activités Internet

Students look online for books and music CDs as gifts for friends, using the vocabulary from the chapter.

- In preparation for the **Activités Internet,** have students review the dramatic episode on Videocassette 4, or complete the activities in the **Panorama Culturel** on page 318.
- After completing the activity sheet, have students work with a partner and peer-edit Section D.

Location: http://

Nom ________ Classe ________ Date ________

11 *Chacun ses goûts*

Level 2

Avant d'explorer

A. Tu es en Provence et tu vas bientôt retourner aux Etats-Unis. Tu veux acheter des cadeaux pour tes camarades de classe. Tu as décidé de leur acheter des livres et des CD. Pense à quatre ami(e)s et écris ce qu'ils/elles aiment lire et écouter comme musique.

Ami(e) 1: ________
Ami(e) 2: ________
Ami(e) 3: ________
Ami(e) 4: ________

En ligne!

B. Explore Internet pour trouver cinq livres que tu peux offrir à tes camarades. Dans le tableau suivant, écris les titres des livres et mentionne le genre de chaque livre et son prix.

Titre	Genre	Prix (francs ou euros)
1.		
2.		
3.		
4.		
5.		

Maintenant, choisis un de ces livres et réponds aux questions suivantes:

Projet

In groups of three, students will create a newspaper. The newspaper will contain three reviews, one targeting each of the following: movie, book, music group. Have the students choose one topic, research it, write a review, and include a picture. Students will then compile their reviews into their newspaper. Have students document their sources by noting the URLs of all the sites that they consulted.

STANDARDS: 1.3, 5.1, 5.2

Chapitre 11 : Chacun ses goûts
Textbook Listening Activities Scripts 

Première étape

7 **p. 314** **Answers to Activity 7**
Vanessa Paradis, Patrick Bruel

ROMAIN Dis, Djé Djé, tu connais Vanessa Paradis?

DJE DJE Mais bien sûr! Tout le monde connaît. Je suis allé à son dernier concert. Elle est super!

ROMAIN Vraiment? Tu en as de la chance! Mais mon groupe préféré, c'est Zouk Machine. Tu connais?

DJE DJE Non, je ne connais pas. Ils sont d'où?

ROMAIN C'est un groupe antillais qui chante le zouk. J'adore danser le zouk, c'est sensass! Mais toi, tu préfères la pop, non? Tu connais Céline Dion?

DJE DJE Non, pas du tout.

ROMAIN Ah, je parie que tu connais Patrick Bruel!

DJE DJE Mais bien sûr que je connais! J'ai tous ses albums, et j'ai aussi vu son dernier film, *Profil bas!*

ROMAIN Super! Tu sais, je crois qu'il passe en concert mercredi soir.

12 **p. 316**

1. — Qu'est-ce qui te plaît comme musique, Arnaud?
— Moi, j'aime bien le jazz.
— Tu aimes la musique classique aussi?
— Bof, pas tellement. Mais le blues, c'est génial!

2. — Et toi, Magali? Qu'est-ce que tu aimes comme musique?
— Moi? Ben, ce que j'aime bien, c'est le rock. J'adore Jean-Jacques Goldman.
— Tu écoutes autre chose?
— Ça dépend. Parfois, j'écoute du reggae.

3. — Qu'est-ce que tu aimes comme musique, Thierry?
— Je suis plutôt du genre country ou rock. En général, j'aime bien la musique américaine.
— Tu n'aimes pas le rap?
— Bof, pas vraiment.

4. — Et toi, Elodie?
— Moi, j'aime tout. J'écoute de la musique classique le matin, et de la pop quand je fais mes devoirs.

5. — Et toi, Christian, tu aimes quel genre de musique?
— Ben, ce que j'adore, c'est le rap. Je suis fou de MC Solaar, et j'ai plein de CD de rap!
— C'est tout?
— Non, j'écoute aussi du rock.

Answers to Activity 12
1. *Arnaud:* jazz, blues
2. *Magali:* rock, reggae
3. *Thierry:* country, rock, American music
4. *Elodie:* classical music, pop
5. *Christian:* rap, rock

Deuxième étape

 **19** **p. 320** **Answers to Activity 19**
1. b 2. c 3. b 4. a

— J'ai envie d'aller au ciné ce soir. Qu'est-ce qu'on joue comme films?

— Attends... euh, on joue *Astérix chez les Bretons.*

— Bof, je n'aime pas tellement les dessins animés. Quoi d'autre?

— Bon... on joue *Le Fugitif* et *Germinal.*

— *Germinal?* D'après le roman de Zola? C'est avec qui?

— C'est avec Gérard Depardieu et...

— Gérard Depardieu! C'est mon acteur préféré! Ça passe où?

— Partout! Ça passe au Gaumont Les Halles, au Quatorze Juillet, au Gaumont Alésia...

— Ben, Gaumont Les Halles, c'est le plus proche.

— Ça commence à dix-huit heures vingt et à vingt heures cinquante.

— Oh, zut! Il est déjà six heures! Dépêchons-nous!

22 **p. 322** **Answers to Activity 22**
film d'horreur, film classique, film comique

NADEGE Salut, Emile. Dis, j'ai envie de voir un film. Pas toi?

EMILE Si, c'est une bonne idée. Alors... *Zombie et le train fantôme,* ça te dit? C'est un bon film d'horreur.

NADEGE Pas question! C'est trop bizarre. Je préfère les films classiques.

EMILE Les films classiques... Tiens, j'ai une idée! Tu as envie de voir *Jules et Jim?* Ça passe à l'UGC Biarritz.

NADEGE Non, ça ne me dit pas trop. Je l'ai déjà vu plusieurs fois.

EMILE Ben... *Monty Python sacré graal,* alors. C'est un film comique anglais. C'est vachement bien.

NADEGE Ben, comme tu veux. Vraiment, je n'ai pas de préférence.

EMILE Oh là là! Que tu es pénible! Bon, alors c'est moi qui décide! On va voir *Monty Python.* Allez, viens!

The following scripts are for the listening activities found in the *Pupil's Edition.* For Student Response Forms, see *Listening Activities,* pages 83–85. To provide students with additional listening practice, see *Listening Activities,* pages 87–90.

To preview all resources available for this chapter, use the **One-Stop Planner CD-ROM**, Disc 3.

Troisième étape

29 **p. 325**

Answers to Activity 29
Luc aime *Calvin and Hobbes.* Perrine aime *Daïren, La Cantatrice chauve.*

LUC Dis donc, tu connais *Calvin et Hobbes?* Tu trouves pas ça génial, toi?

PERRINE Bof, ça ne casse pas des briques. Et puis, les histoires de tigre en peluche, c'est pas mon truc. Moi, je préfère la science-fiction. Tu connais *Daïren* par exemple?

LUC Non, qu'est-ce que ça raconte?

PERRINE Ça se passe au dix-septième millénaire, sur la planète Uyuni. Il y a plein de batailles intergalactiques. On ne s'ennuie pas une seconde. Tu vas voir, c'est plein de rebondissements.

LUC Ah! C'est un peu comme *La Guerre des étoiles,* non?

PERRINE Si tu veux. On appelle ça un «space opéra.»

LUC Dis donc, est-ce que tu as lu *La Cantatrice chauve* pour le cours de français?

PERRINE Bien sûr. J'adore le théâtre. Et puis, c'est très drôle.

LUC Tu trouves? Moi, j'ai rien compris. Il n'y a pas d'histoire, et il n'y a même pas de cantatrice! A mon avis, c'est nul.

PERRINE Mais non! C'est parce que c'est absurde!

LUC C'est bien ce que je dis : c'est nul. Moi, de toute façon, je préfère les romans.

PERRINE Eh bien moi, je pense que la science-fiction, c'est l'avenir de la littérature!

31 **p. 325**

Answers to Activity 31
1. c 2. e 3. d 4. b 5. a

1. — Bonjour, monsieur. Je cherche des romans de Simenon, s'il vous plaît.
— Oui, les policiers sont tous au même endroit, sur ce rayon, et ils sont classés par auteur.
— Merci.

2. — Je viens de voir le film *La Reine Margot,* et je voudrais lire le livre maintenant. Où est-ce que je pourrais le trouver?
— Dans les romans classiques. A Dumas.
— Merci beaucoup, monsieur.

3. — Notre professeur de français prend sa retraite, et nous voudrions lui offrir les œuvres de Rimbaud. Elles se trouvent où, s'il vous plaît?
— Toute la poésie est sur le mur de gauche.

4. — Bonjour, monsieur. Est-ce que vous pourriez m'aider, s'il vous plaît?
— Oui?
— Je cherche *La Florentine* de Juliette Benzoni pour une amie.
— C'est un roman policier?
— Non, c'est une histoire d'amour, je crois.
— Les romans d'amour sont au fond du magasin.
— Merci.

5. — Bonjour, monsieur. Je cherche la collection complète des œuvres de Tintin. C'est pour offrir.
— Les bandes dessinées sont à l'entrée du magasin, juste derrière vous.
— Merci, monsieur.

Mise en pratique

2 **p. 334**

Answers to Mise en pratique Activity 2
1. Martinique
2. A boy is raised by his grandmother, who encourages him to pursue a better life than that of a sugar cane worker.
3. *Martin:* good story; *Janine:* long, depressing, boring.

MARTIN Bonsoir, mesdames et messieurs. Bienvenue à la Revue de Films avec Martin Blondeau et Janine Neuville.

JANINE Ce soir, nous parlerons du premier film du festival, *La Rue Cases-Nègres,* qui se passe dans les années trente à la Martinique.

MARTIN Ce film parle d'un jeune garçon, José Hassam, qui est élevé par sa grand-mère qui travaille dans les champs de canne à sucre.

JANINE La grand-mère rêve d'une meilleure vie pour José et l'encourage dans ses études pour qu'il ne soit pas condamné à travailler dans les champs de canne à sucre.

MARTIN José va souvent voir Monsieur Méduse, une sorte de père spirituel, qui lui parle de ses ancêtres en Afrique. Mais celui-ci finit par mourir dans les champs de canne à sucre. Enfin, José reçoit une bourse pour faire ses études à Fort-de-France et quitte la rue Cases-Nègres pour aller vivre à la grande ville.

JANINE Une bonne fin pour un mauvais film.

MARTIN Moi, j'ai bien aimé ce petit film.

JANINE Moi, je l'ai trouvé trop long.

MARTIN En tout cas, c'est une belle histoire.

JANINE Mais non, c'est déprimant! Et on s'ennuie.

MARTIN Pas du tout! Je recommande ce film à tous ceux qui aiment les films classiques.

JANINE Et moi, si c'est le seul film qui passe!

Chapitre 11 : Chacun ses goûts

Suggested Lesson Plans 50-Minute Schedule

Day 1

CHAPTER OPENER 5 min.

- Present Chapter Objectives, p. 309.
- Culture Note, ATE, p. 308
- Photo Flash! and Radio-Television-Film Link, ATE, p. 309

MISE EN TRAIN 40 min.

- Presenting **Mise en train,** ATE, p. 311
- Teaching Suggestions: Post-viewing Suggestions 1–2, Video Guide, p. 72
- Thinking Critically, ATE, p. 310
- Culture Note, ATE, p. 312
- Do Activities 1–4, p. 312.

Wrap-Up 5 min.

- Activity 5, p. 312

Homework Options

Cahier d'activités, Act. 1, p. 121

Day 2

PREMIERE ETAPE

Quick Review 5 min.

- Bell Work, ATE, p. 313

Comment dit-on... ?, p. 313 10 min.

- Complete Activity 6, p. 313.
- Presenting **Comment dit-on... ?,** ATE, p. 313
- Play Audio CD for Activity 7, p. 314.
- Cahier d'activités, Activity 2, p. 122

Note de grammaire, p. 314 15 min.

- Presenting **Note de grammaire,** ATE, p. 314
- Travaux pratiques de grammaire, Activities 1–2, pp. 87–88
- Cahier d'activités, Activity 3, p. 122
- Have students do Activity 8, p. 314, in pairs.

Vocabulaire, p. 314 15 min.

- Presenting **Vocabulaire,** ATE, p. 315
- Travaux pratiques de grammaire, Activities 3–4, p. 88
- Do Activities 9–10, p. 315.

Wrap-Up, 5 min.

- Geography Link, ATE, p. 314

Homework Options

Grammaire supplémentaire, Act. 1, p. 330
Cahier d'activités, Act. 4, p. 123

Day 3

PREMIERE ETAPE

Quick Review 5 min.

- Check homework.

Note de grammaire, p. 315 20 min.

- Presenting **Note de grammaire,** ATE, p. 315
- Do Activity 11, p. 315.
- Travaux pratiques de grammaire, Activities 5–7, p. 89
- **Grammaire supplémentaire,** Activities 2–3, pp. 330–331
- Additional Practice, ATE, p. 315

Vocabulaire, p. 316 20 min.

- Presenting **Vocabulaire,** ATE, p. 316
- Play Audio CD for Activity 12, p. 316.
- Do Activity 13, p. 316.
- Cahier d'activités, Activities 7–8, p. 124
- Do Activity 14 and Activity 15, p. 317, in small groups.

Wrap-Up 5 min.

- Language-to-Language, ATE, p. 317

Homework Options

Study for Quiz 11-1.
Activity 16, p. 317
Travaux pratiques de grammaire, Acts. 8–11, pp. 90–91

Day 4

PREMIERE ETAPE

Quiz 11-1 20 min.

- Administer Quiz 11-1A or 11-1B.

PANORAMA CULTUREL 20 min.

- Presenting **Panorama Culturel,** ATE, p. 318
- Have students complete Activity 4, Video Guide, p. 75, as they watch.
- Complete Activity 5, Video Guide, p. 75.
- Questions, ATE, p. 318
- Discuss **Qu'en penses-tu?,** p. 318.
- See Teaching Suggestions: Post-viewing Suggestion 1, Video Guide, p. 73.

Wrap-Up 10 min.

- Viewing Activity 3, Video Guide, p. 74

Homework Options

Multicultural Link, ATE, p. 318

Day 5

DEUXIEME ETAPE

Quick Review 5 min.

- Check homework.

Comment dit-on... ?, p. 320 20 min.

- Do Activity 18, p. 319.
- Presenting **Comment dit-on... ?,** ATE, p. 320
- Play Audio CD for Activity 19, p. 320.
- Cahier d'activités, Activities 10–11, pp. 125–126
- Do Activities 20–21, p. 320, in pairs.

Vocabulaire, p. 321 20 min.

- Presenting **Vocabulaire,** ATE, p. 321
- Culture Note, ATE, p. 321
- Play Audio CD for Activity 22, p. 322.
- Cahier d'activités, Activities 12–13, pp. 126–127
- Do Activity 24, p. 322, in groups and Activity 26, p. 322, in pairs.

Wrap-Up 5 min.

- Read and discuss **Note culturelle,** p. 322.

Homework Options

Study for Quiz 11-2.
Pupil's Edition, Acts. 25 and 27, p. 322
Travaux pratiques de grammaire, Acts. 12–15, pp. 92–93

Day 6

DEUXIEME ETAPE

Quiz 11-2 20 min.

- Administer Quiz 11-2A or 11-2B.

RENCONTRE CULTURELLE 10 min.

- Presenting **Rencontre culturelle,** ATE, p. 323
- Discuss **Qu'en penses-tu?,** p. 323.
- Read and discuss **Savais-tu que... ?,** p. 323.
- Thinking Critically, ATE, p. 323

TROISIEME ETAPE

Comment dit-on... ?, p. 324 15 min.

- Complete Activity 28, p. 324.
- Presenting **Comment dit-on... ?,** ATE, p. 324

Wrap-Up 5 min.

- Use Transparency 11-3 to practice expressions from **Comment dit-on... ?,** p. 324.

Homework Options

Cahier d'activités, Act. 15, p. 128

For alternative lesson plans by chapter section, to create your own customized plans, or to preview all resources available for this chapter, use the **One-Stop Planner CD-ROM,** Disc 3.

For additional homework suggestions, see activities accompanied by this symbol throughout the chapter.

Day 7

TROISIEME ETAPE

Quick Review 5 min.
- Check homework.

Vocabulaire, p. 325 25 min.
- Presenting **Vocabulaire,** ATE, p. 325
- Play Audio CD for Activity 29, p. 325.
- Travaux pratiques de grammaire, Activities 16–18, pp. 94–95
- Do Activity 30, p. 325.
- Play Audio CD for Activity 31, p. 325.
- Have students do Activity 32, p. 325, in pairs.

Comment dit-on... ?, p. 326 15 min.
- Presenting **Comment dit-on... ?,** ATE, p. 326
- Cahier d'activités, Activity 20, p. 129
- Do Activity 33, p. 326.
- Culture Notes, ATE, p. 326

Wrap-Up 5 min.
- Read and discuss **De bons conseils,** p. 326.

Homework Options
Cahier d'activités, Act. 16, p. 128

Day 8

TROISIEME ETAPE

Quick Review 5 min.
- Check homework.

Grammaire, p. 327 25 min.
- Presenting **Grammaire,** ATE, p. 327
- Travaux pratiques de grammaire, Activities 19–21, pp. 96–97
- Do Activity 34, p. 327.
- Cahier d'activités, Activities 21–22, p. 130
- Music Link, ATE, p. 327
- Have students do Activity 36, p. 327, in groups.

Wrap-Up 20 min.
- Do Activity 37, p. 327.
- Write several well-known film and book titles on the board and have students tell the genre, describe the characters, and summarize the plot.

Homework Options
Study for Quiz 11-3.
Pupil's Edition, Act. 35, p. 327
Grammaire supplémentaire, Acts. 5–6, p. 332

Day 9

TROISIEME ETAPE

Quiz 11-3 20 min.
- Administer Quiz 11-3A or 11-3B.

LISONS! 25 min.
- Read and discuss **Stratégie pour lire,** p. 328.
- Do Prereading Activity A, p. 328.
- Have students read **Cinq films qui ont fait date,** pp. 328–329.
- Complete Reading Activities B–E, pp. 328–329.
- Culture Notes and Radio-Television-Film Link, ATE, pp. 328–329

Wrap-Up 5 min.
- Read and discuss Career Path, ATE, p. 329.

Homework Options
Cahier d'activités, Act. 24, p. 131

Day 10

LISONS!

Quick Review 5 min.
- Check homework.

Postreading Activity 10 min.
- Do Postreading Activity F, p. 329.
- Thinking Critically, ATE, p. 329

MISE EN PRATIQUE 30 min.
- Do Activity 1, p. 334.
- Play Audio CD for Activity 2, p. 334.
- Discuss the strategy for **Ecrivons!,** p. 335, then have students work on their proposals.
- Have students do **Jeu de rôle,** p. 335, in pairs.

Wrap-Up 5 min.
- Have volunteers share interviews from **Jeu de rôle** with the class.

Homework Options
Have students finish final drafts for **Ecrivons!,** Pupil's Edition, p. 335.

Day 11

MISE EN PRATIQUE

Review 45 min.
- Have volunteers share their proposals from **Ecrivons!**
- Have students complete **A toi de parler,** CD-ROM Tutor, Disc 3.
- Have students do **A toi d'écrire,** CD-ROM Tutor, Disc 3.
- Show ***Bientôt la fête de musique! (suite),*** Video Program, Videocassette 4.
- See Teaching Suggestions, Viewing Suggestions 1–2, Video Guide, p. 72.
- Complete Activity 7, Video Guide, p. 76.
- See Teaching Suggestions, Post-viewing Suggestions 1–2, Video Guide, p. 72.

Wrap-Up 5 min.
- Have students begin **Que sais-je?,** p. 336.

Homework Options
Que sais-je?, p. 336

Day 12

MISE EN PRATIQUE

Quick Review 15 min.
- Go over **Que sais-je?,** p. 336.

Chapter Review 35 min.
- Review Chapter 11. Choose from **Grammaire supplémentaire,** Grammar Tutor for Students of French, Activities for Communication, Listening Activities, Interactive CD-ROM Tutor, or **Jeux interactifs.**

Homework Options
Study for Chapter 11 Test.

Assessment

Chapter Test 40–45 min.
- Administer Chapter 11 Test. Select from Testing Program, Alternative Assessment Guide, Test Generator, or Standardized Assessment Tutor.

Chapitre 11 : Chacun ses goûts

Suggested Lesson Plans *90-Minute Block Schedule*

Block 1

CHAPTER OPENER **10 min.**
- Photo Flash! and Teaching Suggestion, ATE, p. 309
- Present Chapter Objectives, p. 309.
- Culture Note, ATE, p. 308

MISE EN TRAIN **45 min.**
- Preteaching Vocabulary, ATE, p. 310
- Presenting **Mise en train,** ATE, p. 311
- Do Activities 1–4, p. 312.
- Discuss **Note culturelle,** p. 312.

PREMIERE ETAPE

Comment dit-on... ?, p. 313 **15 min.**
- Presenting **Comment dit-on... ?,** ATE, p. 313
- Play Audio CD for Activity 7, p. 314.

Note de grammaire, p. 314 **15 min.**
- Presenting **Note de grammaire,** ATE, p. 314
- Do Activity 8, p. 314.

Wrap-Up **5 min.**
- Do Activity 5, p. 312.

Homework Options
Grammaire supplémentaire, Act. 1, p. 330
Cahier d'activités, Acts. 1–3, pp. 121–122
Travaux pratiques de grammaire, Acts. 1–2, pp. 87–88

Block 2

PREMIERE ETAPE

Quick Review **5 min.**
- On a transparency, write several fill-in-the-blank sentences. Have students complete each sentence with the appropriate form of **connaître.**

Vocabulaire, p. 314 **20 min.**
- Presenting **Vocabulaire,** ATE, p. 315
- Do Activities 9–10, p. 315.

Note de grammaire, p. 315 **20 min.**
- Presenting **Note de grammaire,** ATE, p. 315
- Do Activity 11, p. 315.

Vocabulaire, p. 316 **40 min.**
- Presenting **Vocabulaire,** ATE, p. 316
- Play Audio CD for Activity 12, p. 316.
- Activity 13, p. 316
- Review **Tu te rappelles?,** p. 317.
- Do Activities 14–15, p. 317.

Wrap-Up **5 min.**
- Teaching Transparency 11-1, using Suggestion #2 in Suggestions for Using Teaching Transparency 11-1

Homework Options
Have students study for Quiz 11-1.
Pupil's Edition, Activity 16, p. 317
Grammaire supplémentaire, Act. 2, p. 330
Cahier d'activités, Acts. 4–9, pp. 123–124
Travaux pratiques de grammaire, Acts. 3–11, pp. 88–91

Block 3

PREMIERE ETAPE

Quick Review **10 min.**
- Communicative Activities 11-1A and 11-1B, Activities for Communication, pp. 61–62

Quiz 11-1 **20 min.**
- Administer Quiz 11-1A or 11-1B.

PANORAMA CULTUREL **15 min.**
- Presenting **Panorama Culturel,** ATE, p. 318
- Discuss **Qu'en penses-tu?,** p. 318.

DEUXIEME ETAPE

Comment dit-on... ?, p. 320 **25 min.**
- Presenting **Comment dit-on... ?,** ATE, p. 320
- Play Audio CD for Activity 19, p. 320.
- Activity 20, p. 320

Vocabulaire, p. 321 **10 min.**
- Presenting **Vocabulaire,** ATE, p. 321
- Play Audio CD for Activity 22, p. 322.

Wrap-Up **10 min.**
- Challenge, ATE, p. 320

Homework Options
Cahier d'activités, Acts. 10–12, pp. 125–126
Travaux pratiques de grammaire, Acts. 12–13, pp. 92–93

For alternative lesson plans by chapter section, to create your own customized plans, or to preview all resources available for this chapter, use the **One-Stop Planner CD-ROM,** Disc 3.

For additional homework suggestions, see activities accompanied by this symbol throughout the chapter.

Block 4

DEUXIEME ETAPE

Quick Review 5 min.

- Teaching Suggestion, ATE, p. 321

Vocabulaire, p. 321 25 min.

- Do Activity 23, p. 322.
- Read and discuss **Note culturelle,** p. 322.
- Do Activity 25, p. 322.

TROISIEME ETAPE

Comment dit-on... ?, p. 324 25 min.

- Presenting **Comment dit-on... ?,** ATE, p. 324
- Play Audio CD for Activity 29, p. 325.
- Do Activity 30, p. 325.

Vocabulaire, p. 325 25 min.

- Presenting **Vocabulaire,** ATE, p. 325
- Play Audio CD for Activity 31, p. 325.
- Do Activity 32, p. 325.

Wrap-Up 10 min.

- Teaching Transparency 11-2, using Suggestion #1 in Suggestions for Using Teaching Transparency 11-2

Homework Options

Have students study for Quiz 11-2.
Pupil's Edition, Activity 27, p. 322
Grammaire supplémentaire, Act. 4, p. 331
Cahier d'activités, Acts. 13–16, pp. 127–128
Travaux pratiques de grammaire, Acts. 14–18, pp. 93–95

Block 5

DEUXIEME ETAPE

Quick Review 10 min.

- Communicative Activity 11-2, Activities for Communication, pp. 63–64

Quiz 11-2 20 min.

- Administer Quiz 11-2A or 11-2B.

TROISIEME ETAPE

Comment dit-on... ?, p. 326 25 min.

- Presenting **Comment dit-on... ?,** ATE, p. 326
- **De bons conseils,** p. 326
- Do Activity 33, p. 326.

Grammaire, p. 327 30 min.

- Presenting **Grammaire,** ATE, p. 327
- Do Activities 34–35, p. 327.

Wrap-Up 5 min.

- Teaching Transparency 11-3, using Suggestion #2 in Suggestions for Using Teaching Transparency 11-3

Homework Options

Have students study for Quiz 11-3.
Grammaire supplémentaire, Acts. 5–7, pp. 332–333
Cahier d'activités, Acts. 17–23, pp. 128–130
Travaux pratiques de grammaire, Acts. 19–21, pp. 96–97

Block 6

TROISIEME ETAPE

Quick Review 10 min.

- Communicative Activity 11-3, Activities for Communication, pp. 65–66

Quiz 11-3 20 min.

- Administer Quiz 11-3A or 11-3B.

RENCONTRE CULTURELLE 15 min.

- Presenting **Rencontre culturelle,** ATE, p. 323
- Read and discuss **Qu'en penses-tu?** and **Savais-tu que...?,** p. 323.

MISE EN PRATIQUE 20 min.

- Do Activity 1, p. 334.
- Play Audio CD for Activity 2, p. 334.
- Do Activity 4, p. 335.

LISONS! 25 min.

- **Stratégie pour lire,** p. 328
- Do Prereading Activity A, p. 328.
- Do Reading Activities B–E, pp. 328–329, using Teaching Suggestion, ATE, p. 328.

Homework Options

Que sais-je?, p. 336
CD-ROM/Interactive Games
Study for Chapter 11 Test.

Block 7

MISE EN PRATIQUE

Chapter Review 35 min.

- Review Chapter 11. Choose from **Grammaire supplémentaire,** Grammar Tutor for Students of French, Activities for Communication, Listening Activities, Interactive CD-ROM Tutor, or **Jeux interactifs.**

Chapter Test 40–45 min.

- Administer Chapter 11 Test. Select from Testing Program, Alternative Assessment Guide, Test Generator, or Standardized Assessment Tutor.

Chapter Opener

CHAPITRE 11

For resource information, see the **One-Stop Planner,** Disc 3.

Pacing Tips

In this chapter, students will learn many new vocabulary words. However, many of the vocabulary items are cognates and thus will be easier for students to master. Most of the functional expressions and vocabulary items will be presented again in Level 3, should you need to spend less time on this chapter. For suggested Lesson Plans and timing suggestions, see pages 307I–307L.

Meeting the Standards

Communication

- Identifying people and things, p. 313
- Asking for and giving information, p. 320
- Giving opinions, p. 324
- Summarizing, p. 326

Culture

- Culture Note, pp. 308, 310, 312, 321, 323, 325, 326, 328, 329
- Note culturelle, pp. 312, 322
- Panorama Culturel, p. 318
- Rencontre culturelle, p. 323

Connections

- Radio-Television-Film Link, pp. 309, 328
- Geography Link, p. 314
- Multicultural Link, pp. 318, 323
- Computer Science Link, p. 323
- Music Link, p. 327

Comparisons

- Thinking Critically: Drawing Inferences, p. 310
- Thinking Critically: Synthesizing, p. 323

Communities

- Career Path, p. 329
- De l'école au travail, p. 327

Cultures and Communities

Culture Note

In this chapter, students will learn about types of music. Most French schools do not offer courses for learning to play a musical instrument. Students who wish to learn to play an instrument must take private lessons or classes at a club or community center. If a student has studied music before entering the **lycée,** he or she can choose a course of study that includes fine arts and musical instruction.

STANDARDS: 2.1

CHAPITRE 11
Chacun ses goûts

Objectives

In this chapter you will learn to

Première étape
- identify people and things

Deuxième étape
- ask for and give information

Troisième étape
- give opinions
- summarize

internet
ADRESSE: go.hrw.com
MOT-CLE:
WA3 PROVENCE-11

◀ Qu'est-ce qu'on joue comme films?

Connections and Comparisons

Radio-Television-Film Link

During the Occupation and postwar era, French cinema focused on script and literary themes. During the postwar period of renewal, however, there emerged a new movement in film production called **la nouvelle vague,** or New Wave. The influential writings of Alexandre Astruc and André Bazin molded an entire generation of filmmakers. Astruc created the concept of the **caméra-stylo,** in which film became an audiovisual language, and the filmmaker, its writer. Bazin advocated rejecting mainstream cinematography in favor of hand-held cameras and elliptical, or *invisible,* editing. The New Wave was over by 1965, but certain directors of this movement continued to dominate French cinema well into the 1970s. French New Wave is one of the few national movements that heavily influenced cinematic development world-wide.

Chapter Opener

CHAPITRE 11

Focusing on Outcomes

Have students read the chapter outcomes and match the photo to the one that best describes it. NOTE: The self-check activities in **Que sais-je?** on page 336 help students assess their achievement of the objectives.

Photo Flash!

A French movie theater typically displays large posters on its marquee. American films are very popular in France. Although the movie titles are sometimes in French, these movies could be showing either in **v.o. (version originale)** or in **v.f. (version française).** See **Note culturelle** on page 322.

Teaching Suggestion

Poll the class about their tastes in books, movies, and music. Then, ask students if they can guess the meaning of the title of the chapter, **Chacun ses goûts** *(To each his own).* If they can't guess the meaning, tell them that **goûts** is related to **déguster** (from Chapter 4) and means *tastes.* Then, ask them to try again.

Chapter Sequence

Mise en train

CHAPITRE 11

Teaching Resources
pp. 310–312

PRINT 

- Lesson Planner, p. 51
- Video Guide, pp. 72, 74
- Cahier d'activités, p. 121

MEDIA

- One-Stop Planner
- Video Program
  Mise en train
  Videocassette 4, 16:49–19:26
  Videocassette 5 (captioned version), 1:34:33–1:37:10
  Suite
  Videocassette 4, 19:28–23:34
  Videocassette 5 (captioned version), 1:37:12–1:41:18
- DVD Tutor, Disc 2
- Audio Compact Discs, CD 11, Trs. 1–2
- **Mise en train** Transparencies

Language Note
Call attention to the cobblestones where Cédric, Pascale, and Odile are standing in Photo 4. *Cobblestones* are called **des pavés,** *cobblestone streets* are **des rues pavées,** and *round cobblestones,* such as the ones pictured in the photos here, are called **des pavés ronds.**

Thinking Critically
Drawing Inferences Ask students to infer from the conversation what *Aix en musique* is. Ask them what kind of information they would find in such a publication.

Culture Note
When traveling in France, you can find out what's going on in the town you're visiting by looking for entertainment guides at a **kiosque.** A **kiosque** is a newsstand that sells newspapers, magazines, and often postcards and candy, in addition to entertainment guides.

The **roman-photo** is an abridged version of the video episode.

MISE EN TRAIN • *Bientôt la Fête de la musique!*

CD 11 Trs. 1–2

Stratégie pour comprendre
Look below at the pantomimes that Cédric, Odile, and Pascale do to imitate their favorite kinds of music. What kind does each prefer, and how do you say the name of that musical genre in French? Why is Pascale displeased at the end of the story?

Pascale

Cédric

Odile

Le passant

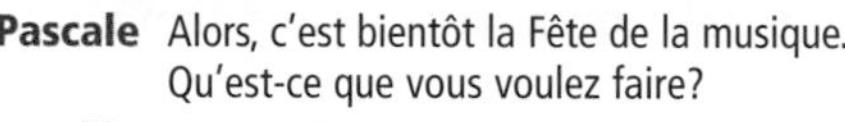

1
Pascale Alors, c'est bientôt la Fête de la musique. Qu'est-ce que vous voulez faire?
Odile Moi, je n'ai rien de prévu.
Cédric J'ai des courses à faire, mais à part ça, je suis libre. Qu'est-ce que tu veux faire?

2
Odile On pourrait faire quelque chose ensemble. Ça vous dit?
Cédric Oui, qu'est-ce que tu proposes?
Pascale J'ai entendu dire qu'on va faire la fête sur le cours Mirabeau. Il y aura des tas de groupes musicaux. Qu'est-ce que vous en pensez?
Odile Ça, c'est nul.

3
Cédric J'aimerais bien aller voir un concert de jazz.

4
Pascale Mouais... Moi, j'ai envie d'aller voir un groupe de rock.

Preteaching Vocabulary

Identifying Keywords
First, have students skim the text and images in the **Mise en train.** Have them list words they can find that relate to music. Ask them which words are cognates. Then have students match the types of music to the characters that like or dislike each one.

❸ **concert de jazz**	**a. Cédric**
❹ **groupe de rock**	**b. Odile**
❺ **la musique classique**	**c. Pascale**

STANDARDS: 1.2

5 **Odile** Ce qui me plaît, moi, c'est la musique classique. On va jouer la symphonie numéro cinq de Beethoven.

6 **Le passant** Excusez-moi... Vous avez regardé *Aix en musique?*
Pascale Non. C'est une bonne idée, ça.

7 **Le passant** Tenez. Je n'en ai plus besoin.
Odile Mais, non. Il n'y a pas de raison.
Le passant Si, si. Allez-y.
Cédric C'est très gentil. Merci, monsieur.

8 **Cédric** Eh! Il y a des tas de concerts.
Pascale Tiens, il y a l'Affaire Louis Trio. C'est génial comme groupe! J'adore!
Cédric Ça serait super! J'espère qu'il y a encore des places.

9 **Cédric** Odile, ça te dit? Tu les connais?
Odile Non, je ne les connais pas, mais je n'aime pas tellement la musique rock. A vrai dire, ça ne me dit rien.
Pascale Oh là là, ce que tu es pénible! Tu n'es jamais contente!

Cahier d'activités, p. 121, Act. 1

Using the Captioned Video/DVD

If students have difficulty understanding French spoken at a normal speed, use Videocassette 5 to allow students to see the French captions for ***Bientôt la Fête de la musique!*** and ***Bientôt la Fête de la musique! (suite).*** Hearing the language and watching the story will reduce anxiety about the new language and facilitate comprehension. The reinforcement of seeing the written vocabulary words as they watch the gestures and actions will help prepare students to do the comprehension activities on page 312.

NOTE: The *DVD Tutor* contains captions for all sections of the *Video Program.*

Mise en train

CHAPITRE 11

Presenting Mise en train

Have students view the video with their books closed. Afterwards, have them tell in French what they were able to understand about the story. Next, form four groups and have them read the **Mise en train.** You might present the Preteaching Vocabulary suggestion on page 310. Assign each group one of the following functions: 1) expressing your preference in music; 2) giving a favorable opinion; 3) giving an unfavorable opinion; and 4) telling who is playing when and where. Have group members list the expressions they read that accomplish their assigned function. Have groups exchange their lists to verify their work.

Mise en train Transparencies

Mise en train (suite)

When the story continues, Pascal, Cédric, and Odile are still trying to decide which group to see, but they can't agree. They each make suggestions and give their opinions about the kind of music they like. A man appears, distributing programs for the festival, and Pascale, Cédric, and Odile ask him about the groups. They finally decide on a group to see. Next, we see them at the festival, listening to the group. Everyone seems satisfied!

Mise en train

CHAPITRE 11

Building on Previous Skills

4 Have partners suggest attending a certain concert and respond to the suggestion, using expressions they learned in Chapter 1: **Qu'est-ce qu'on fait? Si tu veux, on peut... ; On pourrait... ; Tu as envie de... ?; Ça te dit de... ?; D'accord. C'est une bonne idée. Je veux bien. Je ne peux pas. Ça ne me dit rien. Non, je préfère... ; Pas question!**

Culture Note

The Cannes International Film Festival takes place every year for two weeks in May. It was held for the first time in 1939, but was interrupted by World War II and was not resumed until 1946. The **Palme d'or,** awarded at the festival, is one of the most important awards in the film industry. Another important award in the French film industry is the **César,** the equivalent of the American Oscar.

Teacher Note

For more practice with the **Mise en train,** have students complete the **Compréhension** questions on Disc 2 of the *DVD Tutor.*

These activities check for comprehension only. Students should not yet be expected to produce language modeled in **Mise en train.**

1 Tu as compris?

1. What event are the teenagers discussing? a music festival
2. What are they trying to decide? which type of musical group to see
3. What do they do to help them decide? They consult *Aix en musique.*
4. What is the problem at the end of ***Bientôt la Fête de la musique?*** Odile doesn't like rock music, and she doesn't want to see l'Affaire Louis Trio.

2 Qu'est-ce qu'ils aiment comme musique?

Pascale
rock music

Odile
classical music

Cédric
jazz

3 Vrai ou faux?

1. Odile est libre pour la Fête de la musique. vrai
2. Pascale veut faire la fête sur le cours Mirabeau. vrai
3. Cédric voudrait aller voir un groupe de blues. faux
4. Les jeunes achètent *Aix en musique.* faux
5. Ils décident d'aller voir l'Affaire Louis Trio. faux
6. Pascale n'est jamais contente. faux

4 Cherche les expressions

What do the people in ***Bientôt la Fête de la musique!*** say to . . .

1. make a suggestion?
2. emphasize what they like?
3. give unfavorable opinions?
4. give favorable opinions?
5. refuse a gift?
6. accept a gift?
7. express annoyance with someone?

See answers below.

Note culturelle

La Fête de la musique est un festival de musique de renommée mondiale qui a lieu chaque année en France le premier jour de l'été. Musiciens, connus ou non, descendent dans les rues des villages et des villes pour y faire partager leur musique. Le printemps et l'été sont l'occasion de nombreux festivals en tout genre partout en France. Le festival le plus connu est sans doute Le Festival International du Film à Cannes qui rassemblent réalisateurs, acteurs et producteurs du monde entier venus montrer leurs derniers films et essayer de remporter la Palme d'or du meilleur films et autres prix.

5 Et maintenant, à toi

Imagine que tu aides ces amis à choisir ce qu'ils veulent faire. Est-ce que tu es d'accord avec Odile, Cédric ou Pascale? Est-ce que tu as une autre suggestion?

Answers

4
1. On pourrait faire...
2. Ce qui me plaît, moi, c'est la musique classique. J'adore!
3. Ça, c'est nul;... je n'aime pas tellement la musique rock; ... ça ne me dit rien.
4. C'est génial... ! Ça serait super! J'adore!
5. Mais, non. Il n'y a pas de raison.
6. C'est très gentil. Merci.
7. Oh là là, ce que tu es pénible!

Comprehension Check

Teaching Suggestion

2 Label three columns on the board **Cédric, Pascale,** and **Odile.** On separate strips of posterboard or construction paper, write the following sentences:

1. **J'ai des courses à faire.**
2. **J'aimerais voir un concert de jazz.**
3. **J'ai envie d'aller voir un groupe de rock.**
4. **On pourrait voir l'Affaire Louis Trio.**
5. **Ce qui me plaît, c'est la musique classique.**
6. **Je n'aime pas tellement la musique rock.**

Read aloud each sentence and ask students which character in the **Mise en train** said it. Have a student tape the sentence to the board as his or her classmates suggest the correct column.

STANDARDS: 1.2, 2.1

Première étape

Objective Identifying people and things

WA3 PROVENCE-11

AIX - en - PROVENCE
Fête de la Musique
21 juin
Café Concert du Cours
Cours Mirabeau

17h - 18h30 TRIO CLASSIQUE
Cantates de Bach

19h - 20h30 Groupe MARACAS
Jazz Brésilien

21h - 22h30 DIABOLO
Rock Blues

Toute la nuit
De nombreux autres groupes
Rap
Heavy Metal
Reggae
Zouk
Rock
Jazz
Funk
Soul
Blues

6 Tu as compris?

Lisons Quels genres de groupes est-ce qu'il y a? A quel concert est-ce que tu voudrais aller? classical, jazz, rock, blues, rap, heavy metal, reggae, zouk, funk, soul

Comment dit-on...?

Identifying people and things

To identify people and things:

Tu connais le groupe Maracas? *Are you familiar with . . . ?*
Bien sûr! C'est un groupe brésilien. *Of course! They are (He/She/It is) . . .*
Non, **je ne connais pas.** *I'm not familiar with them/him/her/it.*

Cahier d'activités, p. 122, Act. 2

Teacher to Teacher

Sharron Saam
Barrett Middle School
Urban Academy
Columbus, OH

Sharron suggests the following to help plan your lessons.

"Using very simple and readily accessible Websites available at both **www.schoolnotes.com** and **www.quia.com,** I post homework updates and copies of project guidelines. The project guideline pages and the homework pages also contain links to information students find useful in completing their assignments and to sources of enrichment activities."

Première étape

CHAPITRE 11

Teaching Resources
pp. 313–317

PRINT

- Lesson Planner, p. 52
- TPR Storytelling Book, pp. 80–81
- Listening Activities, pp. 83, 87
- Activities for Communication, pp. 61–62, 125, 128, 157–158
- Travaux pratiques de grammaire, pp. 87–91
- Grammar Tutor for Students of French, Chapter 11
- Cahier d'activités, pp. 122–124
- Testing Program, pp. 275–278
- Alternative Assessment Guide, p. 42
- Student Make-Up Assignments, Chapter 11

MEDIA

- One-Stop Planner
- Audio Compact Discs, CD 11, Trs. 3–4, 14, 20–21
- Teaching Transparencies: 11-1, 11-A, 11-B; **Grammaire supplémentaire** Answers; Travaux pratiques de grammaire Answers
- Interactive CD-ROM Tutor, Disc 3

Bell Work

Select a short segment from the **Mise en train** and write the sentences from the segment on a transparency in scrambled order. Have students rewrite the conversation in the correct order and check their answers with a partner.

Presenting
Comment dit-on... ?

Have students suggest groups and musicians for different categories of music. Then, explain the meaning of the verb **connaître** and ask students if they know the groups. **(Tu connais... ?)**

CHAPITRE 11

Teaching Resources
pp. 313–317

PRINT

- Lesson Planner, p. 52
- TPR Storytelling Book, pp. 80–81
- Listening Activities, pp. 83, 87
- Activities for Communication, pp. 61–62, 125, 128, 157–158
- Travaux pratiques de grammaire, pp. 87–91
- Grammar Tutor for Students of French, Chapter 11
- Cahier d'activités, pp. 122–124
- Testing Program, pp. 275–278
- Alternative Assessment Guide, p. 42
- Student Make-Up Assignments, Chapter 11

MEDIA 

- One-Stop Planner
- Audio Compact Discs, CD 11, Trs. 3–4, 14, 20–21
- Teaching Transparencies: 11-1, 11-A, 11-B; **Grammaire supplémentaire** Answers; Travaux pratiques de grammaire Answers
- Interactive CD-ROM Tutor, Disc 3

Presenting
Note de grammaire

The verb *connaître* Write the forms of the verb **connaître** and several subjects on the board or on a transparency in random order. Have students match the subjects with the verb forms. Then, ask students to make complete sentences, using the subjects and verbs and adding appropriate complements. You might have students ask one another if they are familiar with a place, a person, or a group, historical or contemporary.

Note de grammaire

Connaître is an irregular verb that means *to know, to be familiar with.*

je conn**ais**
tu conn**ais**
il/elle/on conn**aît**
nous conn**aissons**
vous conn**aissez**
ils/elles conn**aissent**

The past participle of **connaître** is **connu.**

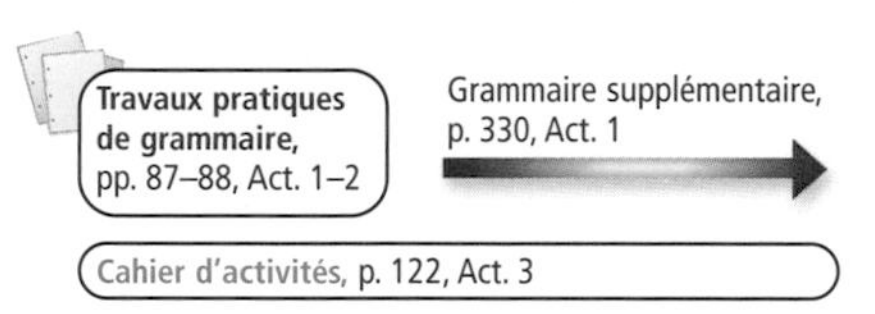

Travaux pratiques de grammaire, pp. 87–88, Act. 1–2

Grammaire supplémentaire, p. 330, Act. 1

Cahier d'activités, p. 122, Act. 3

 **Grammaire en contexte** See scripts and answers on p. 307G.

CD 11 Tr. 3

Ecoutons Romain and his friend Djé Djé, who is visiting from Côte d'Ivoire, are trying to decide which concert to go to during the **Fête de la musique.** Which singers and groups is Djé Djé familiar with?

Patrick Bruel
Céline Dion
Zouk Machine
Vanessa Paradis

8 Grammaire en contexte

Parlons Ecris le nom de trois de tes professeurs et demande à un(e) camarade s'il/si elle les connaît. S'il/Si elle ne les connaît pas, explique-lui qui c'est.

EXEMPLE **—Tu connais M. Miller?**
—Non, c'est qui?
—C'est mon prof de maths.

Vocabulaire

une chanteuse canadienne (un chanteur canadien)

un groupe antillais

une chanson américaine

un musicien africain (une musicienne africaine)

Travaux pratiques de grammaire, p. 88, Act. 3–4

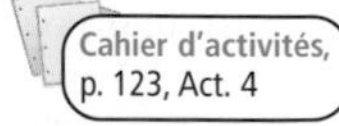

Cahier d'activités, p. 123, Act. 4

Connections and Comparisons

Geography Link

Have students name songs and artists from several different countries, or you might prepare a list in advance (Sade, Sting, Kassav', The Gipsy Kings, Céline Dion, *La Vie en rose, An sèl zouk*). Mark all the countries on a world map with pins. Then, give students the French words for the nationalities represented. For additional countries, see page R18.

Building on Previous Skills

8 If students don't know the teacher their partners mention, have them ask **Il/Elle est comment?** and have their partners describe the teacher. **(Il/Elle a les cheveux noirs. Il/Elle est de taille moyenne.)**

STANDARDS: 1.1, 1.2, 3.1

9 C'est à qui?

Parlons/Ecrivons Some of the performers for a benefit concert left their things backstage. What type of performer do the items suggest?

Answers may vary.

C'est la guitare <u>d'un musicien américain.</u>

1. C'est la musique... d'une chanteuse française.

2. 

C'est le tam-tam... d'un musicien africain.

3. Ce sont les instruments... d'un groupe canadien.

4. 

C'est la musique... d'un chanteur antillais.

10 Tu les connais? See answers below.

Parlons Tu connais les chansons, les groupes ou les chanteurs suivants? Identifie-les!

1. Zouk Machine
2. MC Solaar
3. *An sèl zouk*
4. Jean-Jacques Goldman
5. George Strait
6. *Alouette*

Note de grammaire

Remember that in French you can use **il est** or **c'est** to mean *he is,* and **elle est** or **c'est** to mean *she is,* depending on the situation.

- You can identify someone by profession or nationality with **il est/elle est** followed by a noun or adjective. In this case, you do not use an article before the noun.

  Roch Voisine **est** chanteur.
  Virginie Ledoyen? **Elle est** française.

- You can also use **c'est** followed by an article and a noun.

  Virginie Ledoyen? **C'est une** Française.

- Whenever you use <u>both</u> a noun and adjective, use **c'est.**

  Roch Voisine? **C'est un** chanteur canadien.

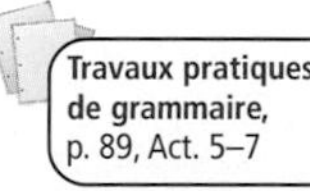

Travaux pratiques de grammaire, p. 89, Act. 5–7

Grammaire supplémentaire, pp. 330–331, Act. 2–3

Cahier d'activités, p. 123, Act. 6

11 Grammaire en contexte

Lisons Complète la conversation entre Marc et Ali avec **c'est, il est** ou **elle est.**

MARC Dis, qu'est-ce que tu voudrais écouter comme musique? J'ai plein de CD!

ALI Euh... attends. Tu connais Jeanne Mas?

MARC Non, pas très bien. Qui c'est?

ALI __1__ une chanteuse. Elle chante *En rouge et noir.* C'est

MARC __2__ française? Elle est

ALI Non, je crois qu' __3__ italienne. En tout cas, c'est pas important. elle est

MARC Tu connais Patricia Kaas?

ALI Mais bien sûr que je connais! Mais moi, je préfère Patrick Bruel. __4__ un chanteur formidable et __5__ acteur aussi! C'est; il est

MARC Oui, __6__ super! J'ai son dernier CD. Tu veux l'écouter? il est

Première étape

CHAPITRE 11

Presenting Vocabulaire

Gather pictures of singers and musicians from magazines, or have students bring these pictures to class. Show the pictures and identify the people in them. **(C'est Whitney Houston. C'est une chanteuse américaine.)** Write the titles of some songs on the board, such as *Alouette* and *This Land is Your Land* and identify them. **(C'est une chanson canadienne/américaine.)**

Note de grammaire

C'est* vs. *il/elle est Have the class name ten to fifteen celebrities and write their suggestions on the board. Then, have students choose five celebrities and write three sentences for each one, the first beginning with **Il/Elle est** to identify the celebrity's profession **(George Clooney? Il est acteur.)**; the second with **C'est un(e)** to identify his or her nationality **(C'est un Anglais.)**; and the third with **C'est un(e)**, combining the first two sentences. **(C'est un acteur anglais.)**

Communication for All Students

Teaching Suggestion

10 Have students ask their classmates if they know other musicians or songs. **(Tu connais Los Lobos, Simon?)**

Additional Practice

Gather pictures of celebrities from magazines and tape them to students' backs without their seeing them. Have students ask one another questions with **Il/Elle est** and **C'est un(e)** until they can identify the person taped to their back. **(C'est une femme? C'est une actrice? Elle est américaine?)** Students may only ask questions that can be answered with **Oui** or **Non.**

Answers

10
1. C'est un groupe antillais.
2. C'est un chanteur français.
3. C'est une chanson antillaise.
4. C'est un chanteur français.
5. C'est un chanteur américain.
6. C'est une chanson canadienne.

STANDARDS: 4.1, 5.2

Première étape

CHAPITRE 11

Teaching Resources
pp. 313–317

PRINT 

- Lesson Planner, p. 52
- TPR Storytelling Book, pp. 80–81
- Listening Activities, pp. 83, 87
- Activities for Communication, pp. 61–62, 125, 128, 157–158
- Travaux pratiques de grammaire, pp. 87–91
- Grammar Tutor for Students of French, Chapter 11
- Cahier d'activités, pp. 122–124
- Testing Program, pp. 275–278
- Alternative Assessment Guide, p. 42
- Student Make-Up Assignments, Chapter 11

MEDIA

- One-Stop Planner
- Audio Compact Discs, CD 11, Trs. 3–4, 14, 20–21
- Teaching Transparencies: 11-1, 11-A, 11-B; **Grammaire supplémentaire** Answers; Travaux pratiques de grammaire Answers
- Interactive CD-ROM Tutor, Disc 3

Presenting Vocabulaire

Have students bring in several recordings of the types of music listed in the **Vocabulaire.** Play a brief segment of classical music and ask students **C'est du rock, ça?** After they answer, tell them what type of music it is **(Non, ce n'est pas du rock! C'est de la musique classique).** Have students repeat the type of music as you play each selection. Then, play short segments of each of the different types of music and have students identify them, using the vocabulary. **(C'est du rap.)**

Vocabulaire

CD-ROM 3 DVD 2

Qu'est-ce qui te plaît comme musique?

la musique classique

le jazz

le rock

le rap

le blues

le country/le folk

la pop

le reggae

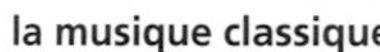

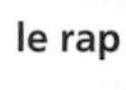

Travaux pratiques de grammaire, pp. 90–91, Act. 8–11

Cahier d'activités, p. 124, Act. 7–8

12 A chacun sa musique
See scripts and answers on p. 307G.

Ecoutons Listen as Pascale asks her friends what music they like. What type(s) of music does each one like best?
CD 11 Tr. 4

13 Qu'est-ce qui vous plaît comme musique?

Parlons/Ecrivons Comment est-ce que chaque personne répondrait à la question **Qu'est-ce qui vous plaît comme musique?** Possible answers:

J'aime le country.

1.

J'aime la musique classique.

2.

Nous aimons le rock/la musique pop.

3.

Communication for All Students

TPR Gather several record-club advertisements in magazines that picture miniature album covers for a variety of types of music, or bring in some album covers. Then, have each student cut out several album covers. Prepare a list of commands, such as the ones that follow. Then, call out the commands and have students respond with the appropriate actions.

- **Si tu as un disque de country, passe-le à l'élève devant toi.**
- **Si tu as un disque de jazz, prends un des disques de l'élève à ta gauche.**
- **Si tu as un disque de rock, donne un de tes disques à l'élève derrière toi.**

 STANDARDS: 1.2, 3.1

Tu te rappelles?

You already know several expressions to emphasize your likes and dislikes.

Ce que j'aime bien, c'est... **Ce que je n'aime pas, c'est...**
Ce qui me plaît, c'est... **Ce qui ne me plaît pas, c'est...**
Ce que je préfère, c'est...

14 Sondage

Parlons Demande à tes camarades ce qu'ils aiment comme musique. Quel genre de musique est le plus populaire? Le moins populaire?

15 Jeu

Parlons Draw a grid of nine squares, three across and three down. Write the name of one of your favorite groups, singers, musicians, or songs in each square. Find someone in your class who's familiar with one of the artists or songs in your grid. Have that person sign the appropriate box and write the type of music associated with the artist or song in French. The first person to get five different signatures that form an **x** or a **+** wins.

EXEMPLE **—Tu connais LeAnn Rimes?**
—Non. *ou* **Oui, c'est une chanteuse de country.**
—Tu connais ***Beethoven's 9th?***
—Non. *ou* **Oui, c'est de la musique classique.**

16 Post-express 

Ecrivons Ecris une réponse à une des lettres de **Post-Express.** Dis quels genres de musique tu aimes et n'aimes pas. Dis aussi quels chanteurs, groupes ou musiciens tu écoutes. Explique qui est chaque personne que tu mentionnes. N'oublie pas que les jeunes Français ne connaissent peut-être pas les mêmes genres de musique que toi.

POST-EXPRESS

Tu cherches des amis, des disques, des posters? Cette rubrique est pour toi!

Recherche tout sur...

LE COUNTRY.
Je voudrais correspondre avec des F. de 13 à 15 ans. J'aime le country et je recherche des posters et des photos de musiciens et de chanteurs. J'aime aussi le rock et un peu le blues. Contre tout sur Roch Voisine, Vanessa Paradis et Paula Abdul.
Jérôme LEGER, 13 allée Paul Eluard, 44400 REZE.

LA MUSIQUE CLASSIQUE ET LE BLUES.
Je suis fan de Patrick Bruel et de Harry Connick Jr. Mais je recherche tout sur tout. Faites éclater ma boîte aux lettres! Réponse assurée à 100%!
Florence PANIER, 200 rue de la Cité, 62370 SAINT FOLQUIN.

LE ROCK, LE POP.
Je m'appelle Damien. J'adore écrire, j'adore le sport, Elsa, le rock et surtout les animaux, la nature... Je suis fan de Mariah Carey et de toute la musique des U.S. Réponse assurée. A vos plumes!
Damien JARRE, 78 allée Bayard, 93190 LIVRY-GARGAN.

    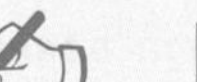 

17 Bientôt la Fête de la musique!

Parlons Avec un(e) camarade, invente ta propre **Fête de la musique.** Chaque personne suggère plusieurs musiciens qui pourraient jouer. Vous pouvez aussi suggérer des chansons ou des albums.

Si tu as oublié
making and responding to suggestions
va à la page 237.

Connections and Comparisons

Thinking Critically

16 Comparing and Contrasting Ask students what the teenagers who have written to **Post-Express** are looking for. What kind of magazine might this page have come from? Do American teen magazines feature this sort of column? If not, what kinds of columns do they feature?

Language-to-Language

Many languages borrow terms from other languages. Ask students why they think the music vocabulary presented here uses English terms. (Most of these types of music originated in the United Kingdom or the United States, so English terms are used.) Ask students if they can think of words English has borrowed from French (terms related to ballet and cuisine).

Building on Previous Skills

13 Have students ask their classmates what kinds of music they like. **(Qu'est-ce qui te plaît comme musique?)** Have students respond, using the expression they learned for emphasizing in Chapter 4. **(Ce qui me plaît, c'est le country.)** Have students refer to **Tu te rappelles?** on page 317.

Additional Practice

16 Ask questions about **Post-Express,** such as **Quel genre de musique est-ce que Jérôme aime? Qu'est-ce qu'il recherche? Quelle est l'adresse de Florence? Qu'est-ce que Damien aime faire?**

Assess

- Testing Program, pp. 275–278
  Quiz 11-1A, Quiz 11-1B
  Audio CD 11, Tr. 14
- Student Make-Up Assignments, Chapter 11, Alternative Quiz
- Alternative Assessment Guide, p. 42

STANDARDS: 1.1, 1.3, 4.2, 5.1

CHAPITRE 11

Teaching Resources
p. 318

PRINT 

- Video Guide, pp. 73–75
- Cahier d'activités, p. 132

MEDIA  

- One-Stop Planner
- Video Program
  Videocassette 4, 23:38–26:41
- DVD Tutor, Disc 2
- Audio Compact Discs, CD 11, Trs. 5–8
- Interactive CD-ROM Tutor, Disc 3

Presenting Panorama Culturel

Show the video and have students tell what they understood. Then, have students discuss the questions in **Qu'en penses-tu?** Finally, ask the **Questions** below to check for comprehension.

Questions

1. **Quels sont les groupes préférés de Marco?** (U2, Duran [Duran], Bon Jovi)
2. **Quelle sorte de musique est-ce que Flaure aime?** (toutes sortes de musique, surtout celles qui font danser)
3. **Catherine préfère la musique qui vient de quels pays?** (des Etats-Unis, du Québec, de la France)

Qu'est-ce que tu aimes comme musique?

We asked some francophone people what kind of music they like to listen to. Here's what they had to say.

Marco, Québec

«J'aime beaucoup le rock'n'roll. J'aime beaucoup les groupes comme U2, Duran [Duran], Bon Jovi. Maintenant, depuis quelques années, la musique française est rendue beaucoup meilleure. On a maintenant de la bonne musique en français. Il y a de bons groupes qui sont sortis, comme Vilain Pingouin, mais la musique américaine est très populaire ici.» Tr. 6

Flaure, Côte d'Ivoire

«La musique que j'aime, euh... J'aime à peu près toutes les musiques et puis, j'aime les musiques qui font danser, quoi.» Tr. 7

Catherine, Québec

«J'ai bien des misères à classifier les sortes de musique, mais je crois que j'aime le rock, le rock folk, le québécois. J'aime beaucoup de sortes de musique.»

Qui est ton chanteur préféré?

«Mon chanteur préféré, j'en ai beaucoup. J'aime beaucoup Renaud mais j'aime aussi un groupe : Jethro Tull. J'aime Edie Brickell, Brenda Kane et des chanteurs des Etats-Unis, du Québec et de la France surtout.» Tr. 8

Qu'en penses-tu?

1. What kind of music do these people like? See answers below.
2. Which person shares your tastes in music?
3. What French musical artists have you heard?
4. Where can you go in your area to hear or buy music from foreign countries?

Cultures and Communities

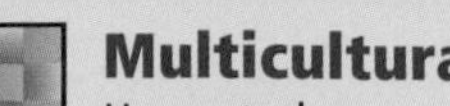

Multicultural Link

Have students try to obtain a variety of recorded international music from the library, exchange students, acquaintances, or relatives.

Teacher Note

For more practice with the **Panorama Culturel,** have students complete the **Compréhension** questions on Disc 2 of the *DVD Tutor.*

Answers

1 Marco likes rock; Flaure likes all music, especially dance music; Catherine likes rock, folk-rock, and French-Canadian music.

STANDARDS: 1.2, 2.2, 3.2, 4.2

 Objectives Asking for and giving information

WA3 PROVENCE-11

FA CHICKEN RUN. 2000. 1h25. Dessin animé américain en couleurs de Peter Lord et Nick Park. Ce film de conception très originale (les personnages sont en pâte à modeler) raconte l'histoire du destin tragique des poules qui ne pondent pas leur œuf quotidien à la ferme de madame Tweedy... En effet, ces malheureuses risquent de se retrouver au menu du dîner, comme plat principal. Leur situation semble désespérée... C'est alors qu'un coq venu d'ailleurs leur redonne espoir. ✦ **Studio Galande 21 v.f.** ✦ **Denfert 82 v.f.** ✦ **Le Grand Pavois 94 v.f.** ✦ **Saint Lambert 96 v.f.**

CO LES RANDONNEURS. 1996. 1h35. Comédie française en couleurs de Philippe Harel avec Benoît Poelvoorde, Karin Viard, Geraldine Pailhas, Vincent Elbaz, Philippe Harel.
Les kilomètres à pied, ça n'use pas que les souliers : les nerfs aussi parfois. C'est ce que découvrent trois garçons et deux filles, sur un chemin de grande randonnée corse, quand se mêlent les problèmes de cœur et les rivalités. La meilleure façon de marcher : celle, rigolote, du réalisateur de «Un été sans histoires». ✦ **Studio Galande 21** ✦ **Denfert 82** ✦ **Le Grand Pavois 94**

DR JEAN DE FLORETTE. 1986. 2h02. Drame français de Claude Berri avec Gérard Depardieu, Yves Montand et Daniel Auteuil.
Dans un petit village du sud de la France, un paysan et son neveu convoitent la propriété de leurs voisins. Ils veulent en effet utiliser la source qui s'y trouve pour arroser leurs champs. Ils décident alors de bloquer la source pour obliger leurs voisins à quitter les lieux et, pendant tout l'été torride, ils observent les efforts désespérés de leurs voisins pour s'approvisionner en eau. ✦ **Saint Lambert 96 v.f.**

AV LES TROIS MOUSQUETAIRES. 1993. 1h45. Film d'aventures américain en couleurs de Stephen Herek avec Chris O'Donnell, Charlie Sheen, Kiefer Sutherland, Oliver Platt, Tim Curry, Rebecca de Mornay.
Arrivant de sa Gascogne natale, le jeune et fringant d'Artagnan rêve d'entrer dans la célèbre compagnie des mousquetaires du roi. Hélas! Le fourbe Richelieu vient de la dissoudre... D'Artagnan, en compagnie d'Athos, Porthos et Aramis, saura néanmoins prouver son courage au cours d'une mission très périlleuse... Nouvelle version librement adaptée du roman d'Alexandre Dumas. ✦ **Le Grand Pavois 94 v.f.**

DC UNE BREVE HISTOIRE DU TEMPS. A Brief History of Time. 1992. 1h20. Documentaire américain en couleurs de Errol Morris.
L'univers a-t-il eu un commencement? Le temps s'achèvera-t-il un jour ? Adapté du best-seller de Stephen Hawking, le réalisateur de «Dossier Adams» met en images des théories scientifiques au cours d'un voyage en compagnie d'un savant d'exception, que certains comparent à Einstein. ✦ **Denfert 82 v.o.**

CO EMMA. L'entremetteuse. 1996. 1h55. Comédie américaine en couleurs de Douglas MacGrath avec Gwyneth Paltrow, Toni Collette, Alan Cumming, Jeremy Northam, Ewan MacGregor, Greta Scacchi.
Dans l'Angleterre du XIXème siècle, une délicieuse jeune fille décide de s'occuper en jouant les marieuses. D'erreurs en catastrophes, de gaffes en maladresses, elle apprend à se connaître et à aimer les autres... D'après le roman de Jane Austen, une comédie qui mêle humour et romantisme. ✦ **Le Grand Pavois 94 v.o.**

18 Si on allait au ciné?

Lisons Look at the movie listings and answer these questions. See answers below.

1. What information is given in the first paragraph of every entry? How can you tell the type of film?
2. What information is given in the second paragraph of every entry?
3. What information is given at the end of every entry after the diamond symbol?
4. Which film(s) would you like to see or have you already seen?

Communication for All Students

Challenge

Ask questions about the movie guide, such as the following: *Les Randonneurs* **a été fait en quelle année? (en 1996) Ça dure combien de temps? (1h35) Ça passe dans combien de cinémas? (dans trois cinémas)** You might ask similar questions about the remaining movies in the guide.

Teaching Resources
pp. 319–322

PRINT

- Lesson Planner, p. 53
- TPR Storytelling Book, pp. 82–83
- Listening Activities, pp. 84, 88
- Activities for Communication, pp. 63–64, 126, 128–129, 157–158
- Travaux pratiques de grammaire, pp. 92–93
- Grammar Tutor for Students of French, Chapter 11
- Cahier d'activités, pp. 125–127
- Testing Program, pp. 279–282
- Alternative Assessment Guide, p. 42
- Student Make-Up Assignments, Chapter 11

MEDIA 

- One-Stop Planner
- Audio Compact Discs, CD 11, Trs. 9–10, 15, 22–23
- Teaching Transparencies: 11-2, 11-C; **Grammaire supplémentaire** Answers; Travaux pratiques de grammaire Answers
- Interactive CD-ROM Tutor, Disc 3

Bell Work

Write the following paragraph on the board or on a transparency and have students complete the sentences with **Il est** or **C'est.**

Tu connais le film *Air Force One?* ____ un film d'aventures avec Harrison Ford. Tu ne connais pas Harrison Ford? ____ super. ____ un acteur américain. ____ très intelligent. Tu veux aller le voir? ____ un très bon film, je t'assure.

Answers

18
1. type of film, title, year made, length, country of origin, color or black and white, director, principal actors; by the abbreviations in the black boxes before the titles
2. plot summary, description
3. where the film is playing

Deuxième étape

CHAPITRE 11

Teaching Resources
pp. 319–322

PRINT 

- Lesson Planner, p. 53
- TPR Storytelling Book, pp. 82–83
- Listening Activities, pp. 84, 88
- Activities for Communication, pp. 63–64, 126, 128–129, 157–158
- Travaux pratiques de grammaire, pp. 92–93
- Grammar Tutor for Students of French, Chapter 11
- Cahier d'activités, pp. 125–127
- Testing Program, pp. 279–282
- Alternative Assessment Guide, p. 42
- Student Make-Up Assignments, Chapter 11

MEDIA 

- One-Stop Planner
- Audio Compact Discs, CD 11, Trs. 9–10, 15, 22–23
- Teaching Transparencies: 11-2, 11-C; **Grammaire supplémentaire** Answers; Travaux pratiques de grammaire Answers
- Interactive CD-ROM Tutor, Disc 3

Presenting
Comment dit-on... ?

Have students look at the movie listings on page 319. Then, ask questions about the films, using the expressions in **Comment dit-on... ?** Finally, distribute copies of movie listings from the newspaper and have partners ask each other about them, using the expressions in **Comment dit-on... ?**

Comment dit-on...?

Asking for and giving information

CD-ROM 3 DVD 2

To ask about films:

Qu'est-ce qu'on joue comme films?
What films are playing?
C'est avec qui?
Ça passe où?
Where is it playing?
Ça commence à quelle heure?

To respond:

On joue *Profil bas.*
. . . is showing.
C'est avec Patrick Bruel.
Ça passe au Gaumont.
It's playing at the . . .
A 18h30.

 Cahier d'activités, pp. 125–126, Act. 10–11

19 **J'ai envie d'aller au ciné...** See scripts on p. 307G.

Ecoutons Ecoute la conversation entre Béatrice et Fabien qui essaient de décider quel film aller voir. Puis, complète les phrases suivantes.

CD 11 Tr. 9

1. On joue...
   a. *Astérix chez les Bretons, Germinal, Jules et Jim.*
   b. *Astérix chez les Bretons, Le Fugitif, Germinal.*
   c. *Astérix chez les Bretons, Profil bas, Germinal.*
2. *Germinal,* c'est avec...
   a. Patrick Bruel.
   b. Isabelle Adjani.
   c. Gérard Depardieu.
3. Ça passe au...
   a. Gaumont Gobelins, Gaumont Les Halles, 14 Juillet.
   b. Gaumont Les Halles, 14 Juillet, Gaumont Alésia.
   c. Gaumont Alésia, Gaumont Gobelins, UGC Georges V.
4. Ça commence à...
   a. 18h20 et à 20h50.
   b. 18h15 et à 19h50.
   c. 17h20 et à 20h30.

20 **Méli-mélo!** See answers below.

Lisons Trouve la bonne réponse pour chaque question, puis mets le dialogue dans le bon ordre. Ensuite, lis le dialogue avec un(e) camarade.

Ça passe où? C'est avec qui? Qu'est-ce qu'on joue comme films? Ça commence à quelle heure?	*Camille Claudel.* Euh... à 17h05 ou à 20h10. A l'UGC Triomphe et au Gaumont Opéra. Gérard Depardieu et Isabelle Adjani.

21 **Qu'est-ce qu'on joue comme films?**

Lisons/Parlons Choisis un des films de la page 319. Un(e) camarade va te demander quels films on joue, dans quels cinémas et qui sont les acteurs principaux. Ensuite, changez de rôle.

Communication for All Students

Tactile/Visual Learners

20 Have students write the sentences and questions on separate strips of paper, arrange them in logical order, and copy the dialogue on a sheet of paper before reading it aloud with a partner.

Challenge

21 Have students choose a film from page 319 and give some information about it to a partner who will try to guess the title of the film.
— **Ça dure 1h45. C'est avec Chris O'Donnell et Charlie Sheen.**
— **C'est** *Les Trois Mousquetaires.*

STANDARDS: 1.1, 1.2, 5.1

Vocabulaire

Au cinéma

les westerns — *Le Train sifflera trois fois*
les films comiques — *Trois Hommes et un couffin*
les films d'horreur — *Frankenstein*

les films de science-fiction — *Le Monde perdu*
les films d'amour — *La Mariée est en fuite*
les films policiers — *Demain ne meurt jamais*

les films classiques — *La Belle et la Bête*
les films d'aventures — *Titanic*
les films d'action — *Mission Impossible*

Travaux pratiques de grammaire, pp. 92–93, Act. 12–15

Cahier d'activités, pp.126–127, Act. 12–13

Cultures and Communities

Culture Note

In Paris, there are over 100 movie theaters that offer approximately 300 films to see every week. There are two main entertainment guides that feature movie listings: *Pariscope* and *L'Officiel des spectacles.* Movies are listed alphabetically by genre and by movie theater. There is also information about movie theaters outside of Paris in the suburbs **(en banlieue)**. The guides also tell you which metro station is closest to the movie theater. In addition, these guides contain information about museum exhibitions, club happenings, cabaret shows, plays, sports activities, concerts, and much more.

Presenting Vocabulaire

Write the different film genres on the board. Photocopy and distribute the movie listings from a newspaper and ask which genre each film represents. **(C'est quel genre de film, ça?)** Write the titles of the movies under the appropriate categories as students suggest them. If a genre is not represented, ask students to name some films of that genre.

Teaching Suggestion

Have partners ask each other about the films in the **Vocabulaire.** For each film, they should ask **Tu connais... ?** and **C'est avec qui?** Students might also identify the actors shown in the scenes here and give their nationalities.

Challenge

Ask students why they like a certain genre of film **(Pourquoi est-ce que tu aimes les films classiques?)** and have them answer in French.

Game

Les genres Form small groups and give each one a transparency. Then, call out a type of film **(les films comiques).** Groups have thirty seconds to list films of that genre. Call time and have each group count the number of films they listed. The group with the most films listed projects its transparency to the class.

Possible Answers

20 — Qu'est-ce qu'on joue comme films?
— *Camille Claudel.*
— C'est avec qui?
— Gérard Depardieu et Isabelle Adjani.
— Ça passe où?
— Ça passe à l'UGC Triomphe et au Gaumont Opéra.
— Ça commence à quelle heure?
— Euh... à 17h05 ou à 20h10.

Deuxième étape

CHAPITRE 11

Slower Pace

22 Before you play the recording, give students the names and genres of the films in the activity (see script on page 307G). Have students write them on a sheet of paper.

Building on Previous Skills

24 Encourage students to use the vocabulary they learned in the **Première étape** to identify the movies and actors in their discussions. **(Tu connais... ? Il est/Elle est... ; C'est un/C'est une...)**

Portfolio

24 **Oral** This activity is appropriate for students' oral portfolios. For portfolio suggestions, see the *Alternative Assessment Guide,* page 28.

Teaching Suggestion

To close this **étape,** have students present the review they wrote for Activity 27 as if they were a TV film critic.

Assess

- Testing Program, pp. 279–282 Quiz 11-2A, Quiz 11-2B Audio CD 11, Tr. 15
- Student Make-Up Assignments Chapter 11, Alternative Quiz
- Alternative Assessment Guide, p. 42

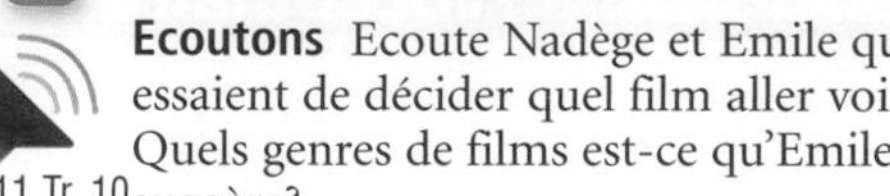

22 A l'affiche cette semaine

See scripts and answers on p. 307G.

CD 11 Tr. 10

Ecoutons Ecoute Nadège et Emile qui essaient de décider quel film aller voir. Quels genres de films est-ce qu'Emile suggère?

23 Le Hit-Parade

Ecrivons Fais une liste de tes dix films préférés. Ensuite, classe-les par genre. D'après ta liste, quel genre de films préfères-tu?

24 Ça te dit?

Parlons Tu organises une soirée vidéo où tu vas passer ton film préféré. Invite plusieurs camarades de classe à venir regarder ce film avec toi. S'ils ne veulent pas venir ou s'ils ne connaissent pas ce film, explique quel genre de film tu vas passer et qui sont les acteurs. Donne-leur aussi ton opinion sur ce film.

25 Au Gaumont Alésia

See answers below.

Lisons

a. Look at the first paragraph in the movie listings at the right. Find four types of information given.

b. Now look at the movie listings.

1. How much is the full price for *L'Enfant lion?* How much is the reduced price for students?
2. Is *Aladdin* in French or in English?
3. At the 2:00 P.M. showing of *Grosse Fatigue,* what time does the feature film actually begin?
4. Which of the movies listed here are dubbed in French?

26 Qu'est-ce qui passe au Gaumont?

Parlons Un(e) camarade et toi, vous avez envie de voir un film mercredi soir au Gaumont Alésia. Choisissez quel film vous voulez voir et à quelle heure.

27 C'est toi, le critique

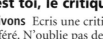

Ecrivons Ecris une critique de ton film préféré. N'oublie pas de préciser de quel genre de film il s'agit et qui sont le réalisateur et les acteurs principaux, puis donne ton opinion sur le film.

Note culturelle

Before you go to the movies in France, check the local newspaper or movie guide. You'll notice that you can see many foreign films. Look for **v.o. (version originale)** to see a film in the original language with French subtitles, and **v.f. (version française)** to see a film dubbed in French. Look for ticket prices. Most theaters offer a discount **(tarif réduit)** for students and a lower ticket price for everyone on Mondays and/or Wednesdays. Check the time of the showing **(séance),** and be aware that there are 10–20 minutes of commercials before the movie actually starts.

84 GAUMONT ALESIA. 73, avenue du Général Leclerc. 01.43.27.84.50; Résa : 01.40.30.30.31 **(#114)** M° Alésia. Perm de 14h à 24h. Pl : de 6, 50 à 7, 00 €. Mer, tarif unique : 5, 50 et 5, 25 €; Etud, CV : 5, 50 et 5, 25 € (Du Lun au Ven 18h) ; -12 ans : 4, 75 €. Carte Gaumont : 5 places : 27, 00 € (valables 2 mois, tlj à toutes les séances). Carte bleue acceptée. Rens : 3615 Gaumont. 1 salle équipée pour les malentendants et deux salles pour les handicapés.

L'Incroyable Voyage v.f. Dolby stéréo.
Séances : 13h35, 15h45, 17h55, 20h05, 22h15. Film 10 mn après.

J'ai pas sommeil Dolby stéréo
Séances : 13h35, 15h45, 17h55, 20h05, 22h15. Film 10 mn après.

L'Enfant lion Dolby stéréo. (Pl : 7, 50 et 5, 75€).
Séances : 14h, 17h20, 21h. Film 25 mn après.

Aladdin v.f.
Séances : Mer, Sam, Dim 13h25, 15h35. Film 15 mn après.

Une Pure Formalité
Séances : Mer, Sam, Dim 17h50, 20h, 22h10 ; Jeu, Ven, Lun, Mar 13h30, 15h40, 17h50, 20h, 22h10. Film 15 mn après.

Le Jardin secret v.f.
Séances : 14h, 16h40, 19h20, 21h55. Film 20 mn après.

Les Aristochats v.f. Dolby stéréo
Séances : Mer, Sam, Dim 19h15, 21h50. Jeu, Ven, Lun, Mar 13h55, 16h30, 19h15, 21h50. Film 15 mn après.

Salle Gaumontrama (Pl : 7, 00 et 5, 50€):

Grosse Fatigue Dolby stéréo.
Séances : 14h, 16h, 18h, 20h, 22h. Film 20 mn après.

Possible Answers

25 a. address, phone number, métro stop, price, name of the theater

b. 1. 7,50 €, 5,75 €
2. French
3. 2:20
4. *L'Incroyable Voyage, Aladdin, Le Jardin secret, Les Aristochats*

Connections and Comparisons

Language Notes

- The **M°** in the movie listing stands for **métro** and indicates the subway stop nearest the movie theater.
- **CV (Carte Vermeille)** is a senior-citizen discount card.
- **Tlj** means **tous les jours.**
- **Une carte bleue** is a debit card.
- **Les malentendants** are *the hard-of-hearing.*

STANDARDS: 1.1, 1.2, 1.3, 2.1, 3.2, 5.2

1. The screens provide information on movies, concerts, etc. The Minitel is an online information service like the World Wide Web.
2. The expressions correspond to these words in English: *a chat room, a window (on a computer desktop), a server, virtual, a personal page, to surf the Web, a (computer) bug, a (Web) surfer*

Qu'en penses-tu?

1. Look at these photos of **Minitel**® screens. What do you think the Minitel is?
2. Have you ever visited a French-language Web site? What do you think the following expressions might mean? **un chat, une fenêtre, un serveur, virtuel, une page perso, surfer le Web, un bogue, un cybernaute**

Savais-tu que... ?

Since 1984, the French have used the online information service called the **Minitel** to shop their favorite catalogues, buy movie tickets, look up phone numbers, or read magazine articles. Sounds like the World Wide Web, doesn't it? The Minitel was the first widely distributed online information service found in people's homes—before the Web could be found there. How do you think the Minitel will evolve in the coming years in response to the technology of the Internet?

The Web is becoming as popular in France as it is in the United States. In recent years, there has been a debate in France over Web terminology: should French speakers use English words, or make up their own? For every Internet term in English, you'll find many words (and creative spellings!) in French. For instance, a French speaker might use any one of the following expressions to mean *e-mail:* **le courrier électronique, le courriel, la messagerie électronique, l'e-mail,** or **l'imèle.**

Teacher Note

Minitel service is currently available to French classrooms in the United States for the price of a local information service. If Internet is available somewhere in the school, then the Minitel software is available free from Minitel Services Company, but there is a charge for online time.

Presenting Rencontre culturelle

Have students look at the computer screens to try to guess what types of services **Minitel** offers. Then, have them look more closely and list specific services and types of information available. Ask students to find other Internet-related expressions in French.

Thinking Critically

Synthesizing Ask students if such technology was available to their parents when they were in high school. Ask them to name technological advances that have occurred since they were young children. Have them anticipate what new technologies, particularly information systems, might be available for their own children.

Computer Science Link

Ask students if they know of any computer-related innovations that have been made recently and if they anticipate any in the future.

Cultures and Communities

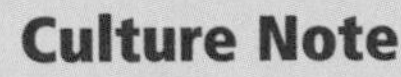

Culture Note

One difference between **Minitel** and many American information systems is that the French customers don't need a modem or a computer to subscribe to the service. Small monitors that connect to the phone line are available for a modest fee, making Minitel easily accessible.

Multicultural Link

If some of your students have access to Internet through various computer networks, have them do some research to find out what kinds of online information systems are available in other countries. (I.EARN® is one international network.)

STANDARDS: 2.1, 2.2, 3.2, 4.2

Teaching Resources
pp. 324–327

PRINT 

- Lesson Planner, p. 54
- TPR Storytelling Book, pp. 84–85
- Listening Activities, pp. 85, 89
- Activities for Communication, pp. 65–66, 127, 129, 157–158
- Travaux pratiques de grammaire, pp. 94–97
- Grammar Tutor for Students of French, Chapter 11
- Cahier d'activités, pp. 128–130
- Testing Program, pp. 283–286
- Alternative Assessment Guide, p. 42
- Student Make-Up Assignments, Chapter 11

MEDIA

- One-Stop Planner
- Audio Compact Discs, CD 11, Trs. 11–12, 16, 24–25
- Teaching Transparencies: 11-3, 11-D; **Grammaire supplémentaire** Answers; Travaux pratiques de grammaire Answers
- Interactive CD-ROM Tutor, Disc 3

Bell Work

Have students unscramble the following: **C'est avec qui?/** *Le Fugitif* **/Ça passe où?/A 2h25 et à 5h10./Qu'est-ce qu'on joue comme films?/Aux Halles./Harrison Ford./Ça commence à quelle heure?**

Presenting
Comment dit-on... ?

Gather several books. Label two columns on the board: *Favorable* and *Unfavorable.* Give your opinion of a book, using the expressions in **Comment dit-on... ?** Write the book title in the appropriate column as you talk about it.

Troisième étape

Objectives Giving opinions; summarizing

go.hrw.com
WA3 PROVENCE-11

S. F.

DAIREN
Alain Paris (J'ai Lu).
S'appuyant sur des structures sociales très hiérarchisées, l'humanité du XVIIe millénaire pratique une politique galactique conquérante. Mais cette expansion musclée est freinée par la résistance des Zyis sur la planète Uyuni et par une légende, celle de la Terre mythique, qui prône l'entente entre toutes les races de l'univers. Daïren est un solide «Space Opera» relevé d'un zeste de mysticisme, qui a parfaitement assimilé les leçons de son glorieux modèle, *la Guerre des étoiles.*

Denis Guiot

B.D.

CALVIN ET HOBBES
Bill Waterson (Hachette)
Calvin, c'est le garçon dynamique, intrépide, insupportable. Hobbes, c'est son faire-valoir... un tigre en peluche! Waterson, un des plus célèbres dessinateurs de presse américain, utilise seulement deux à quatre images par gag. Un trait simple et nerveux, un humour sympathique. Voilà une B.D. bien agréable et une traduction excellente, puisqu'elle est due au scénariste Frank Reichert.

Yves Frémion

28 Tu as compris?

Lisons 2. absurdes, dérisoire, comique

1. How many categories of books are presented? What are they? three; science fiction, comic strip, humorous plays
2. Look at the review of *La Leçon* and *La Cantatrice chauve.* List the words that you recognize.
3. Scan the commentary on *Daïren.* What is this book about? a battle in outer space
4. How does Yves Frémion describe the heroes of *Calvin et Hobbes?* Calvin is dynamic, intolerable. Hobbes is Calvin's sidekick: a stuffed tiger.

DECOUVRIR DES LIVRES POUR RIRE

LA LEÇON, LA CANTATRICE CHAUVE,
de Eugène Ionesco

Ionesco a composé la tragédie du langage. En rire majeur. Chez lui tout s'effondre : ses héros énoncent doctement des lieux communs éculés, entassent des axiomes absurdes dans leur conversation. Jusqu'au délire. De cette cacophonie burlesque naît l'image d'un monde en miettes, dérisoire et comique. (Folio.)

S.F.

Comment dit-on...?

Giving opinions

Favorable:

C'est drôle/amusant. *It's funny.*
C'est une belle histoire. *It's a great story.*
C'est plein de rebondissements. *It's full of plot twists.*
Il y a du suspense. *It's suspenseful.*
On ne s'ennuie pas. *You're never bored.*
C'est une histoire passionnante. *It's an exciting story.*
Je te le/la recommande. *I recommend it.*

Unfavorable:

C'est trop violent/long. *It's too violent/long.*
C'est déprimant. *It's depressing.*
C'est bête. *It's stupid.*
C'est un navet. *It's a dud.*
C'est du n'importe quoi. *It's worthless.*
Il n'y a pas d'histoire. *It has no plot.*
C'est gentillet, sans plus. *It's cute, but that's all.*
Ça casse pas des briques. *It's not earth-shattering.*

Cahier d'activités, p. 128, Act. 15

Connections and Comparisons

Language-to-Language

The expression **C'est un navet** refers only to movies, while **C'est du n'importe quoi** can be used for movies, books, or other printed material. You might tell students that the literal meaning of the word **navet** is *turnip.* Ask students if they use food expressions in English to give opinions of people or things. *(You bought a lemon (bad car). He's a couch potato.)*

STANDARDS: 1.2, 2.2, 4.1

Vocabulaire

Ton livre préféré, c'est quel genre? 

un roman policier (un polar)?

une autobiographie?

un roman d'amour?

un roman de science-fiction?

une bande dessinée (une B.D.)?

un livre de poésie?

un (roman) classique?

une pièce de théâtre?

Travaux pratiques de grammaire, pp. 94–95, Act. 16–18

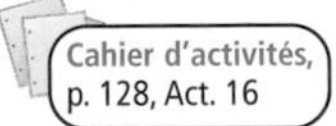
Cahier d'activités, p. 128, Act. 16

29 Pas d'accord! See scripts and answers on p. 307H.

CD 11 Tr. 11

Ecoutons Ecoute Luc et Perrine parler de *La Cantatrice chauve, Daïren* et *Calvin et Hobbes.* Qu'est-ce que Luc aime? Et Perrine?

30 A mon avis

Ecrivons Fais une liste des trois derniers livres (ou pièces de théâtre) que tu as lus. Fais une description de ces livres. Utilise les phrases du Comment dit-on... ? à la page 324.

31 Pardon, monsieur... See scripts on p. 307H.

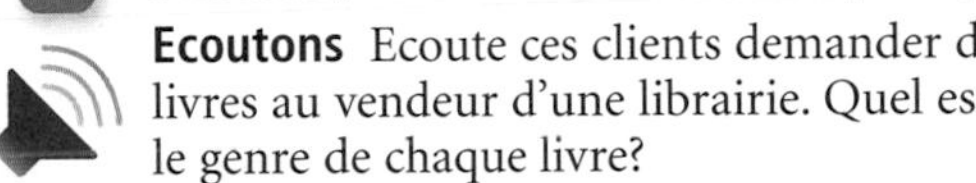

Ecoutons Ecoute ces clients demander des livres au vendeur d'une librairie. Quel est le genre de chaque livre?

CD 11 Tr. 12

1. un roman de Simenon c
2. *La Reine Margot* e
3. les œuvres de Rimbaud d
4. *La Florentine* b
5. les œuvres complètes de Tintin a

a. une B.D.
b. un roman d'amour
c. un polar
d. un livre de poésie
e. un classique

32 Une interview

Parlons Tu dois faire la critique d'un livre pour ton cours de français. Demande à un(e) camarade quel livre il/elle a lu récemment, de quel genre de livre il s'agit et son opinion sur ce livre.

EXEMPLE
—Qu'est-ce que tu as lu récemment?
—On a lu *Huckleberry Finn* pour le cours d'anglais.
—C'est quel genre de livre?
—C'est un classique.
—Tu as aimé?
—Oui, c'est une belle histoire et en plus, c'est très amusant.

Presenting Vocabulaire

Gather several books that are representative of the genres given in the **Vocabulaire.** Write the names of the different genres side-by-side across the board. Show each book, ask the students what kind of book it is **(C'est quel genre de livre?),** and place the book on the chalk ledge beneath the appropriate genre written on the board. Ask students if they have read the books, and if so, have them give their opinions of the books, using the expressions in **Comment dit-on... ?** on page 324.

Culture Note

In francophone countries, as in the United States, comic books are not just for children. There are many **bandes dessinées** written for teenagers and adults. These comics often contain sophisticated humor and a complex story. It is not unusual for people to collect entire series of comic books; in fact, for some, it's a major hobby.

Teaching Suggestion

32 You might have volunteers present their conversations to the class as a skit in the form of a TV program that reviews books.

Communication for All Students

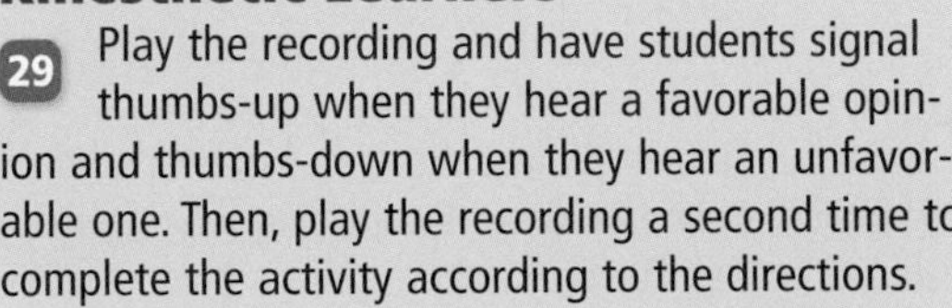

Kinesthetic Learners

29 Play the recording and have students signal thumbs-up when they hear a favorable opinion and thumbs-down when they hear an unfavorable one. Then, play the recording a second time to complete the activity according to the directions.

Slower Pace

31 On a sheet of paper, have students list the names of the novels in one column and the genres in a second column. As they listen to the recording, they should draw lines matching the books to the appropriate genres.

Teaching Resources
pp. 324–327

PRINT 

- Lesson Planner, p. 54
- TPR Storytelling Book, pp. 84–85
- Listening Activities, pp. 85, 89
- Activities for Communication, pp. 65–66, 127, 129, 157–158
- Travaux pratiques de grammaire, pp. 94–97
- Grammar Tutor for Students of French, Chapter 11
- Cahier d'activités, pp. 128–130
- Testing Program, pp. 283–286
- Alternative Assessment Guide, p. 42
- Student Make-Up Assignments, Chapter 11

MEDIA

- One-Stop Planner
- Audio Compact Discs, CD 11, Trs. 11–12, 16, 24–25
- Teaching Transparencies: 11-3, 11-D; **Grammaire supplémentaire** Answers; Travaux pratiques de grammaire Answers
- Interactive CD-ROM Tutor, Disc 3

Presenting
Comment dit-on... ?

Draw two columns on the board. In one column, write movie titles. In a second column, write a one-sentence description of each plot. Then, ask about and summarize each film plot, pointing to the information as you discuss it. Finally, describe each film again in random order and have students try to guess the film title from your description.

Comment dit-on...?

Summarizing

To ask what something is about:

De quoi ça parle? *What's it about?*
Qu'est-ce que ça raconte? *What's the story?*

To tell what something's about:

Ça parle d'une femme qui devient actrice. *It's about . . .*
C'est l'histoire d'un chien qui cherche son père. *It's the story of . . .*

Cahier d'activités, p. 129, Act. 20

TROIS HOMMES ET UN COUFFIN 3
(FRANCE - 1985)
(couleurs) 1 h 40
Comédie de Coline Serreau
avec Roland Giraud, Michel Boujenah, André Dussollier

Jacques, Michel et Pierre sont des célibataires endurcis qui chérissent leur indépendance... jusqu'au jour où ils trouvent un bébé de six mois sur leur paillasson! Peu à peu, les trois hommes apprennent leur nouveau rôle de pères, pour le meilleur et pour le pire. Bientôt ils ne peuvent plus se passer de la petite Marie. Que feront-ils quand sa mère reviendra?

AU REVOIR LES ENFANTS 4
(FRANCE - 1987)
(couleurs) 1 h 42
Comédie dramatique de Louis Malle
avec Gaspard Manesse, Raphael Fejto

Pendant la Deuxième Guerre Mondiale, deux adolescents français se rencontrent et deviennent amis. Julien, le personnage principal, découvre l'absurdité du monde adulte à travers la triste histoire de son ami Jean qui est persécuté par les Allemands. Julien, enfant de bonne famille, et Jean, enfant prodige, vivent ensemble quelques aventures qu'on n'est pas près d'oublier.

NOTRE-DAME DE PARIS 2
(FRANCE-ITALIE - 1956) **CINÉ CINÉMAS**
(couleurs) 1 h 40
Drame parisien de J. Delannoy d'après V. Hugo
avec G. Lollobrigida, A. Quinn, A. Cuny, R. Hirsch

C'est la fête des fous sur le parvis de Notre-Dame. Tout le monde y remarque Esmeralda, la danseuse gitane. Le capitaine Phœbus en tombe amoureux ainsi que Quasimodo, le bossu monstrueux qui habite la cathédrale. Mais le perfide Frollo a décidé d'enlever Esmeralda et est prêt à toutes les bassesses pour la conquérir.

L'ETERNEL RETOUR 1
(FRANCE - 1943) **RTL**
(noir et blanc) 1 h 45
Drame de Jean Delannoy
avec J. Marais, M. Sologne, J. Murat, A. Rignault.

C'est le mythe de Tristan et Yseult revisité par Jean Delannoy, et par Jean Cocteau qui a signé le scénario. Les héros de la légende sont devenus Patrice et Nathalie, deux jeunes gens contemporains qui tombent amoureux l'un de l'autre sous l'effet d'un élixir magique qu'ils n'auraient jamais dû boire. Car Nathalie est mariée à l'oncle de Patrice.

33 De quoi ça parle? See numbers placed in the ads above.

Lisons Lis les critiques des quatre films ci-dessus. Puis, lis les phrases suivantes et choisis le film qui correspond à chaque phrase.

1. C'est l'histoire de deux jeunes qui tombent amoureux.
2. Ce film parle de trois hommes qui tombent amoureux d'une danseuse gitane.
3. Ce film parle de trois hommes qui doivent s'occuper d'un bébé.
4. C'est l'histoire d'une amitié entre deux garçons.

When you summarize the plot of a book or movie, you use the present tense instead of the past tense, just as you do in English.
C'est l'histoire d'un jeune homme français qui veut être mousquetaire. Il va à Paris pour devenir mousquetaire du roi et en route, il prend part à trois duels.

Cultures and Communities

Culture Notes

- Jean Delannoy directed both *Notre-Dame de Paris* and *L'Eternel Retour. Notre-Dame de Paris* is based on the historical novel by Victor Hugo. The novel depicted medieval life under the reign of Louis XI and condemned a society that wrought misery on the hunchback and the gypsy.
- Jean Cocteau wrote the screenplay for *L'Eternel Retour,* in which the characters Patrice and Nathalie are set against the forces of evil, personified by the dwarf, Achilles. In making this film, Cocteau surrounded himself with some of the greatest talent in the French film industry: Roger Hubert, photography; Georges Wakhévitch, decor; and Georges Auric, musical score.

STANDARDS: 1.2, 2.2, 3.2, 4.1

Grammaire

The relative pronouns *qui* and *que*

You can use clauses that begin with **qui** or **que** *(that, which, who,* or *whom)* to describe something or someone you've already mentioned.

- **Qui** is the subject of a clause and is followed by a singular or plural verb, depending on the subject of the main clause that **qui** represents.

  C'est l'histoire d'un garçon **qui tombe** amoureux d'une fille.
  Ça parle de deux garçons **qui tombent** amoureux de la même fille.

- **Que (qu')** is the direct object of a clause. It's always followed by a subject and a verb.

  Il aime une fille **que sa mère déteste.**
  Le film **qu'elle a vu était intéressant?**

- When the **passé composé** follows **que,** the past participle always agrees with the noun **que** represents.

  La pièce que j'ai vu**e** était amusante.

Grammaire supplémentaire, pp. 332–333, Act. 5–7

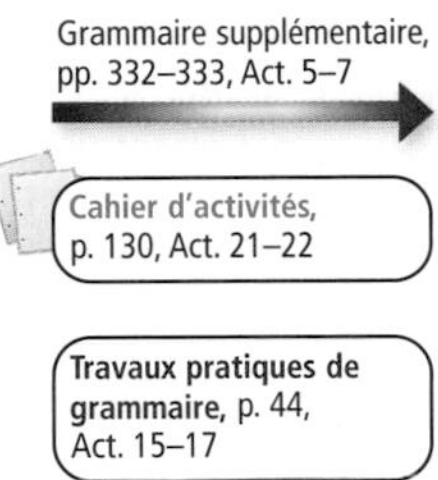

Cahier d'activités, p. 130, Act. 21–22

Travaux pratiques de grammaire, p. 44, Act. 15–17

34 Grammaire en contexte

1. que 2. qui 3. qui 4. que 5. qui 6. qui 7. que 8. qui

Lisons Lis cette critique d'un nouveau livre et complète les phrases avec **qui** ou **que.**

L'Agent secret est un livre plein de rebondissements __1__ j'ai beaucoup aimé. C'est un roman policier __2__ parle d'un détective __3__ aide une jeune fille à retrouver son père. Le détective découvre __4__ le père de la fille est un agent secret __5__ travaille sur un projet très dangereux. La fille reçoit une lettre __6__ dit que son père est en France, mais le détective pense __7__ c'est un piège. Alors, c'est lui __8__ va en France... Une histoire passionnante à lire absolument!

35 Grammaire en contexte

See answers below.

Parlons/Ecrivons Lisa a lu une bonne bande dessinée ce week-end et elle en a écrit une description pour son cours de français. Aide Lisa à écrire une description moins répétitive. Pour combiner les phrases utilise **qui** et **que.** Parfois, tu vas peut-être devoir ajouter des mots comme **mais** ou **et.** D'autres fois, tu ne vas pas utiliser tous les mots des phrases de Lisa.

1. Ce week-end j'ai lu une B.D. J'ai adoré cette B.D.
2. C'est une des aventures de Tintin. Tintin est un personnage très connu en France.
3. C'est un reporter. Il voyage dans tous les pays du monde.
4. Il a deux très bons amis. Ils s'appellent Capitaine Haddock et Professeur Tournesol.

36 Devine!

Ecrivons/Parlons Ecris un résumé du dernier livre que tu as lu. Ensuite, donne des détails sur ce livre à tes camarades. Ils vont deviner le titre du livre. Ensuite, la personne qui a deviné le titre de ton livre va résumer un autre livre.

37 De l'école au travail

Ecrivons You're a critic working for a journal distributed for French speakers interested in American culture. Write a review in French of a book you've read recently.

Presenting Grammaire

The relative pronouns *qui* and *que* Write two sentences on the board or on a transparency. Rewrite the sentences, joining them with **qui.** Do the same with two other sentences, joining them with **que.** Ask students what you did. Then, ask them why they think you used **qui** in one instance and **que** in the other. Point out that **qui** is the subject in the clause it introduces and that **que** is the direct object in the clause it begins. Finally, write other sentences, deleting the **qui** or **que,** and have students supply the relative pronouns. Point out that **qui** and **que** are used for both people and things.

Mon journal

37 For an additional journal entry suggestion for Chapter 11, see *Cahier d'activités,* page 155.

Assess

- Testing Program, pp. 283–286 Quiz 11-3A, Quiz 11-3B Audio CD 11, Tr. 16
- Student Make-Up Assignments, Chapter 11, Alternative Quiz
- Alternative Assessment Guide, p. 42

Connections and Comparisons

Music Link

After presenting the **Grammaire,** play the song *Il était une bergère* (Level 1, Audio CD 10, Track 32) and have students raise their hands when they hear a relative pronoun. Then, project the first and third stanzas on a transparency and have volunteers circle the relative pronouns.

Answers

35
1. Ce week-end, j'ai lu une B.D. que j'ai adorée.
2. C'est une des aventures de Tintin, qui est un personnage très connu en France.
3. C'est un reporter qui voyage dans tous les pays du monde.
4. Il a deux très bons amis qui s'appellent Capitaine Haddock et Professeur Tournesol.

STANDARDS: 1.3, 4.1, 5.2

CHAPITRE 11

Teaching Resources
pp. 328–329

PRINT 
- Lesson Planner, p. 55
- Cahier d'activités, p. 131
- Reading Strategies and Skills Handbook, Chapter 11
- Joie de lire 2, Chapter 11
- Standardized Assessment Tutor, Chapter 11

MEDIA
- One-Stop Planner

Prereading
Activity A

Teaching Suggestion
A. Have students research how the cinema was born in 1895. Have them also find out what the other six arts are if the cinema is considered to be the "seventh art."

Reading
Activities B–E

Teaching Suggestion
You might have students work in groups of three to find and discuss the answers to Activities B–E.

Culture Note
France imports many more American films than the United States does French films. The French rarely produce high budget, high action films, as Hollywood often does, so this may account for some of the appeal American films have for the French.

Cooperative Learning
B. You might have students work in groups of three to complete the activity. Each student might be responsible for the information that follows one of the stars in each review.

Lisons!

Cinq films qui ont fait date

Stratégie pour lire
Let's review some of the basic reading strategies you used in earlier chapters. In this reading, you will need to get oriented to the text, figure out its organization, and answer some questions to check your understanding of it.

A. Read the first and last sentences in the introduction. What will the reading be about?
1. special effects in films
2. some important films from the first 100 years of filmmaking
3. the history of filmmaking since 1895

B. Examine the organization of the descriptions of the five films.
1. What does the information following the first star tell you about the film?
   a. country of origin
   b. director
   c. date of film
   d. principal actors
   e. all of the above
2. What do you find after the second star?
   a. a critique of the film
   b. a summary of the plot
   c. an interview with the star
3. After the third star?
   a. importance of the film in the history of filmmaking

Le cinéma est né en 1895 : "le 7e art" s'apprête à fêter un siècle d'existence. En cent ans, que de progrès, que d'évolutions techniques, que de films ! Voici quelques-uns des films, qui, chacun à leur manière, ont marqué un tournant dans l'histoire du cinéma.

5 FILMS QUI ONT FAIT DATE

2001, L'ODYSSEE DE L'ESPACE

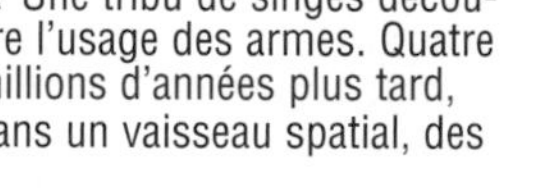

★ Grande-Bretagne-Etats-Unis, 1968. De Stanley Kubrick. Avec Keir Dullea, Gary Lockwood.
★ Une tribu de singes découvre l'usage des armes. Quatre millions d'années plus tard, dans un vaisseau spatial, des hommes sont confrontés à l'ordinateur HAL.
★ Kubrick a réalisé une fable sur l'Homme face au progrès et à l'Univers. Ce film est aussi l'une des premières œuvres importantes en matière de science-fiction.

IL ETAIT UNE FOIS DANS L'OUEST

★ Italie, 1968. De Sergio Leone. Avec Henry Fonda, Charles Bronson.
★ Le film se passe dans l'Ouest américain, à la fin du siècle dernier. « *Il était une fois dans l'Ouest* est, sous le prétexte d'une histoire presque nulle, avec des personnages de convention, une tentative pour reconstruire l'Amérique de cette époque», explique le réalisateur italien Sergio Leone.
★ Jusqu'alors, les westerns étaient la chasse gardée des Américains. Sergio Leone renouvela complètement le genre, avec ce que l'on a appelé, le "western-spaghetti", une parodie du western classique. Avec des bons et des méchants. Mais sans réelle authenticité historique. Ce film, particulièrement célèbre pour la musique d'Ennio Morricone, fait partie d'une longue série, dont le premier, *Pour une poignée de dollars*, fut réalisé en 1964.

Connections and Comparisons

Radio-Television-Film Link
Most French films are not exported to the United States, but Hollywood will often remake a French film. Some examples of American remakes of French films are: *Cousins,* starring Ted Danson and Isabella Rossellini, from the French film *Cousin, Cousine; Three Men and a Baby,* with Ted Danson, Tom Selleck, and Steve Guttenberg, from *Trois Hommes et un couffin (cradle); Paradise,* with Don Johnson and Melanie Griffith, from *Le Grand Chemin; Pure Luck,* starring Martin Short and Danny Glover, from *La Chèvre; Sommersby,* with Richard Gere and Jodie Foster, from *Le Retour de Martin Guerre;* and *Nell,* starring Jodie Foster and Liam Neeson, from *L'Enfant sauvage.*

STANDARDS: 1.2, 2.2, 3.1

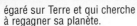

E.T., L'EXTRA-TERRESTRE

★ Etats-Unis, 1982. De Steven Spielberg. Avec Dee Wallace, Henry Thomas, Peter Coyote.

★ Eliott, un jeune Américain de 10 ans, se prend d'amitié pour E.T., un extra-terrestre égaré sur Terre et qui cherche à regagner sa planète.

★ La fable est belle ; le message de Steven Spielberg est simple mais essentiel : apprenez à respecter autrui, en dépit des différences...

STAR WARS: UN NOUVEL ESPOIR

★ Etats-Unis, 1977. De George Lucas. Avec Harrison Ford, Carrie Fisher, Mark Hamill.

★ La princesse Leia est tenue en otage par les forces Impériales malfaisantes qui veulent réprimer une révolte contre l'Empire Galactique. Luke Skywalker et le Capitaine Han Solo s'allient avec Obi-wan Kenobi et les androïdes R2D2 et C3PO pour sauver la belle princesse et rétablir la justice dans la Galaxie.

★ "Le feuilleton de l'espace" de Lucas décrit l'opposition classique entre le bien et le mal, le jour et les ténèbres. C'est aussi un pionnier dans l'art des effets spéciaux. Avec ce mélange de symbolisme mythologique et historique, le film transporte les spectateurs dans un monde fantastique tout en rappelant le temps passé.

CYRANO DE BERGERAC

★ France, 1989. De Jean-Paul Rappeneau. Avec Gérard Depardieu, Anne Brochet.

★ Cyrano aime sa cousine Roxane, qui lui préfère Christian, un jeune soldat. Le premier écrira pour le second les lettres d'amour qui séduiront la belle...

★ Qui aurait cru qu'on puisse tirer un film de la pièce en vers d'Edmond Rostand ? Pourtant, c'est un film plein de vie et de panache. Cyrano a fait découvrir les œuvres classiques à beaucoup !

---

b. the evolution of film techniques
c. a biography of the director

C. Read the information after the first star.
1. How many of these films were made in the United States? In France? 2; 1
2. How many were joint productions? 1
3. What other two countries were involved in these films? 3. Great Britain, Italy

D. Read the information after the second star. Where and when does the story take place in *Il était une fois dans l'Ouest?* See answers below.

E. Complète les phrases suivantes avec les descriptions correctes.
1. *Star Wars* est... d
2. *Il était une fois dans l'Ouest* est... a
3. *2001, l'Odyssée de l'espace* est... b
4. *Cyrano de Bergerac* est... c
   a. une parodie du western classique.
   b. une fable sur l'homme face au progrès.
   c. tiré d'une pièce en vers.
   d. célèbre pour ses effets spéciaux.

F. Trouve dans un journal une annonce pour un film que tu aimes et que tu trouves important. Ensuite, écris un article sur ce film. Donne les mêmes informations que celles qui se trouvent dans les présentations des cinq films de gauche. Deux ou trois élèves vont lire ton article et le corriger avant de le donner au professeur. Ta classe peut aussi faire un journal avec tous les articles que les élèves ont faits.

Cahier d'activités, p. 131, Act. 24

Lisons!

CHAPITRE 11

Postreading
Activity F

Thinking Critically
F. Analyzing Have students include in their article a justification of their opinion of the film they have chosen.

F. Slower Pace Have students limit the information that follows the second and third stars to one sentence.

F. Challenge Have pairs of students use the information in this activity to create and present a dialogue between film critics.

Terms in Lisons!
Students might want to know the following vocabulary from the movie guides: *2001, L'Odyssée de l'espace:* **un singe** *(a monkey);* **un vaisseau spatial** *(a space ship);* **une œuvre** *(a work); Il était une fois dans l'Ouest:* **un siècle** *(a century);* **une tentative** *(an attempt);* **la chasse gardée** *(literally private hunting grounds—here, exclusive domain) E. T., L'extraterrestre:* **égaré** *(lost);* **regagner** *(to get back to);* **autrui** *(others);* **en dépit de** *(in spite of); Star Wars :* **otage** *(hostage);* **malfaisantes** *(evil);* **réprimer** *(to suppress);* **s'allient** *(join);* **rétablir** *(re-establish);* **ténèbres** *(darkness);* **pionnier** *(pioneer);* **mélange** *(mix);* **en rappelant** *(in remembering); Cyrano de Bergerac:* **séduire** *(to seduce);* **Qui aurait cru... ?** *(Who would have believed . . . ?);* **une pièce en vers** *(a play in verse);* **du panache** *(gallantry).*

Answers
D. *Il était une fois dans l'Ouest:* in the western United States; at the end of the 19th century

Cultures and Communities

Career Path
Ask students if they've ever considered a career in the movie industry. As they probably know, most movies are dubbed in the languages spoken in the countries where they will be shown. Therefore, knowledge of a foreign language would be an important skill to have for people interested in pursuing a career as a film translator.

Culture Note
Students may have seen the comedy *Roxanne,* starring Steve Martin and Darryl Hannah. *Roxanne* is based on the French play *Cyrano de Bergerac* by Edmond Rostand (1897). *Roxanne* was released before the 1990 French film, *Cyrano de Bergerac,* with Gérard Depardieu and Anne Brochet.

STANDARDS: 1.2, 2.2, 3.1, 5.1

Grammaire supplémentaire

CHAPITRE 11

For **Grammaire supplémentaire** Answer Transparencies, see the *Teaching Transparencies* binder.

Grammaire supplémentaire

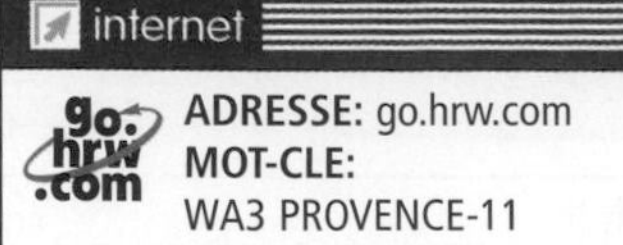

ADRESSE: go.hrw.com
MOT-CLE:
WA3 PROVENCE-11

Première étape

Objective Identifying people and things

1 Simon et ses amis Serge et Bruno parlent des élèves et des professeurs de leur école. Complète leur conversation avec les formes correctes du verbe **connaître.** (**p. 314**)

SIMON Salut, Bruno et Serge. C'est qui, cette fille qui parle à Luc? Vous la __1__?

BRUNO Bien sûr, je la __2__. Elle s'appelle Suzanne. Elle est dans mon cours de maths.

SIMON C'est qui, ton prof? M. Martin?

BRUNO Non, c'est M. Dubois. Tu le __3__, Serge?

SERGE Non, je ne le __4__ pas, mais mon frère aîné le __5__. C'était son prof de maths l'année dernière. Il est cool comme prof.

SIMON Sophie et Marius le __6__ aussi. Ils m'ont dit que c'était leur cours préféré. Tu as de la chance d'être dans ce cours.

BRUNO Oui, c'est vrai. En fait, je dois faire mes devoirs. A plus tard.

2 Tu regardes un magazine de musique populaire avec un ami. Identifie les photos que tu regardes et complète chaque phrase avec **c'est, il est** ou **elle est.** (**p. 315**)

EXEMPLE <u>C'est</u> un chanteur africain.

1. _____ américaine.
2. _____ un musicien.
3. _____ africain.
4. _____ une bonne chanteuse.
5. _____ un Français.
6. _____ canadienne.

Answers

1
1. connaissez
2. connais
3. connais
4. connais
5. connaît
6. connaissent

2
1. Elle est
2. C'est
3. Il est
4. C'est
5. C'est
6. Elle est

Grammar Resources for Chapter 11

The **Grammaire supplémentaire** activities were designed as supplemental activities for the grammatical concepts presented in the chapter. You might use them as additional practice, for review, or for assessment.
For more grammar presentations, review, and practice, refer to the following:

- Travaux pratiques de grammaire
- Grammar Tutor for Students of French
- Grammar Summary on pp. R23–R42
- Cahier d'activités
- Grammar and Vocabulary quizzes (Testing Program)
- Test Generator
- Interactive CD-ROM Tutor
- DVD Tutor
- **Jeux interactifs** at **<u>go.hrw.com</u>**

STANDARDS: 1.2

3 Complète les questions suivantes avec **C'** ou **Il/Elle.** Ensuite, devine de laquelle des célébrités proposées on parle. (**p. 315**)

1. _____ est une chanteuse.
   _____ est canadienne.
   _____ est très connue en France.
   _____ est _____ .
2. _____ est un acteur très populaire.
   _____ est français.
   _____ est connu aux Etats-Unis.
   _____ est _____ .

Céline Dion	Vanessa Paradis	Gérard Depardieu
Patricia Kaas	Isabelle Adjani	
Patrick Bruel	Roch Voisine	

Deuxième étape

Objectives Asking for and giving information

4 Choisis quatre films et écris des phrases avec **c'est, il est** ou **elle est** pour parler de l'histoire dans le film et des acteurs. Choisis quatre films dans la liste ou parle d'autres films que tu as vus. (**pp. 315, 321**)

Trois Hommes et un couffin	*Titanic*	*La Belle et la Bête*
Frankenstein	*Hercule*	*Demain ne meurt jamais*

EXEMPLE *Demain ne meurt jamais,* **c'est un film d'action...**

1. ...
2. ...
3. ...
4. ...

Teacher to Teacher

Jeanne suggests the following activity to practice grammar from the chapter.

Jeanne S. Jendrzejewski
LSU Lab School
Baton Rouge, LA

"Students email me twice a week, using the grammar that we are focusing on in class. They usually email a few comments about their day, etc. I do not correct the emails, but I do respond in the correct form to reinforce the structure. Emails can target vocabulary and functions from the current chapter as well as review material from previous chapters."

Answers

3 1. C'
Elle
Elle
C' —— Céline Dion
2. C'
Il
Il
C' —— Gérard Depardieu

4 *Possible answers:*
1. *Hercule,* c'est un film classique. Hercule, il est amusant.
2. *Titanic,* c'est un film d'aventures. Leonardo DiCaprio, il est super.
3. *La Belle et la Bête,* c'est un film d'amour. La Belle, elle est jolie.
4. *Frankenstein,* c'est un film d'horreur. Frankenstein, il n'est pas beau.

Grammaire supplémentaire

CHAPITRE 11

For **Grammaire supplémentaire** Answer Transparencies, see the *Teaching Transparencies* binder.

Answers

5
1. que
2. qui
3. que
4. qui
5. que
6. que
7. qui
8. qui
9. que
10. qui

6
1. J'aime le cadeau que tu m'as donné.
2. J'ai rencontré un garçon qui est sympa.
3. Tu connais le monsieur qui est arrivé.
4. Voilà les livres que tu as perdus.
5. Ce sont les devoirs que tu dois finir ce soir.
6. C'est l'histoire d'une jeune fille qui tombe amoureuse d'un beau garçon.
7. Tu n'as pas envie de revoir le film que tu as vu hier?
8. Dans ce livre, il s'agit d'un homme fou qui s'habille en clown pour aller chez le dentiste.
9. C'est la femme mystérieuse qu'il a rencontrée hier dans la rue.
10. C'est l'histoire d'un homme qui s'échappe d'une prison à l'aide d'une cuillère.

Grammaire supplémentaire

Troisième étape

Objectives Giving opinions; summarizing

5 Complète les phrases suivantes avec **qui** ou **que.** (**p. 327**)

1. C'est la fille _____ j'ai rencontrée à la boum.
2. C'est un livre _____ est très intéressant.
3. J'ai vu le film _____ Gérard Depardieu a tourné.
4. J'ai acheté les fleurs _____ étaient jolies.
5. Luc a parlé à la fille _____ tu aimes.
6. Tu as fait les devoirs _____ le professeur nous a donnés?
7. C'est l'histoire d'un jeune homme _____ rencontre la fille de ses rêves.
8. C'est un groupe américain _____ joue du rock.
9. C'est le roman policier _____ Marc a lu.
10. Je connais un Français _____ habite aux Etats-Unis.

6 Récris les phrases suivantes en utilisant **qui** ou **que.** (**p. 327**)

EXEMPLE Ce week-end j'ai lu un livre. Le livre était très intéressant.
Ce week-end j'ai lu un livre qui était très intéressant.

1. J'aime le cadeau. Tu m'as donné le cadeau.
2. J'ai rencontré un garçon. Le garçon est sympa.
3. Tu connais le monsieur. Le monsieur est arrivé.
4. Voilà les livres. Tu as perdu les livres.
5. Ce sont les devoirs. Tu dois finir les devoirs ce soir.
6. C'est l'histoire d'une jeune fille. La jeune fille tombe amoureuse d'un beau garçon.
7. Tu n'as pas envie de revoir le film? Tu as vu le film hier.
8. Dans ce livre, il s'agit d'un homme fou. L'homme s'habille en clown pour aller chez le dentiste.
9. C'est la femme mystérieuse. Il a rencontré la femme hier dans la rue.
10. C'est l'histoire d'un homme. L'homme s'échappe d'une prison à l'aide d'une cuillère.

Communication for All Students

Additional Practice

To provide students additional practice with the grammar and vocabulary in this **étape,** write several well-known film and book titles on the board or on a transparency. For each title, have students identify the genre, describe the characters, and summarize the plot. You might also have students retell the story from the **Troisième étape** of the *TPR Storytelling Book.*

Grammaire supplémentaire

CHAPITRE 11

7 Complète les phrases suivantes avec le pronom relatif approprié (**qui, que** ou **qu'**). Ensuite, regarde les posters et donne le titre du film décrit. Attention! Il y a une phrase qui ne correspond à aucun poster. A toi de la trouver! (**p. 327**)

1. Ça raconte l'histoire d'un homme (qui/que) est attaqué par un ver gigantesque.
2. C'est l'histoire de petits hommes verts (que/qui) arrivent sur la terre pour nous kidnapper.
3. Ça parle d'un homme (qu'/qui) on ne voit plus parce qu'il devient invisible.
4. C'est l'histoire d'une femme (qui/que) devient détective pour trouver des documents volés.
5. Ce film, (qui/que) je vous recommande, parle d'un cow-boy (que/qui) arrive dans une ville fantôme pour attraper un bandit.

Review and Assess

You may wish to assign the **Grammaire supplémentaire** activities as additional practice or homework after presenting material throughout the chapter. Assign Activity 1 after **Note de grammaire** (p. 314), Activities 2–3 after **Note de grammaire** (p. 315), and Activities 5–7 after **Grammaire** (p. 327).

To prepare students for the **Etape** Quizzes and Chapter Test, we suggest doing the **Grammaire supplémentaire** activities in the following order. Have students complete Activities 1–3 before Quiz 11-1A or 11-1B; Activity 4 before Quiz 11-2A or 11-2B; and Activities 5–7 before Quiz 11-3A or 11-3B.

Answers

7
1. qui, *Le Ver gigantesque*
2. qui, *Le Voyage des petits hommes verts*
3. qu', no film
4. qui, *Un Suspect dans la ville*
5. que, qui, *Un homme, un revolver et un cheval*

Mise en pratique

CHAPITRE 11

The **Mise en pratique** reviews and integrates all four skills and culture in preparation for the Chapter Test.

Teaching Resources
pp. 334–335

PRINT 

- Lesson Planner, p. 55
- TPR Storytelling Book, pp. 86–87
- Listening Activities, p. 85
- Video Guide, pp. 73, 76
- Grammar Tutor for Students of French, Chapter 11
- Standardized Assessment Tutor, Chapter 11

MEDIA

- One-Stop Planner
- Video Program Videocassette 4, 26:43–28:36
- DVD Tutor, Disc 2
- Audio Compact Discs, CD 11, Tr. 13
- Interactive CD-ROM Tutor, Disc 3

Language Note

Students might want to know the following vocabulary words from the *Guide de l'été.* Tell students that these words might change meaning in another context: **une œuvre** *(work);* **saluer** *(to pay tribute to);* **des dérives** *(variations);* **un périple** *(trip).*

Mise en pratique

internet

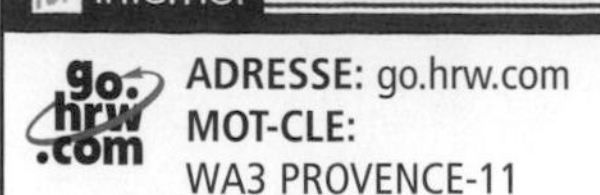

ADRESSE: go.hrw.com
MOT-CLE:
WA3 PROVENCE-11

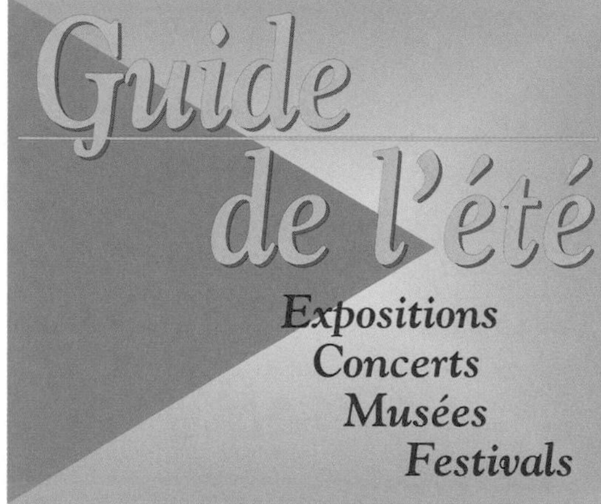

PROVENCE-COTE-D'AZUR

EXPOSITIONS

● Nice

2 juillet - 30 octobre
Marc Chagall, 1945-1985 : les années méditerranéennes.
L'exposition est une manière de saluer l'importance de la couleur dans l'œuvre du maître.
Musée national du message biblique - Marc Chagall. 36, avenue du Docteur-Ménard, 06000 Nice.
✆ **04.93.81.75.75.**

● Saint-Paul-de-Vence

2 juillet - 15 octobre
Braque : rétrospective.
Pour fêter son trentième anniversaire, la Fondation ne pouvait mieux choisir : Braque, au travers de plus de cent vingt œuvres.
Fondation Maeght, 06570 Saint-Paul-de-Vence.
✆ **04.93.32.81.63.**

● Vence

2 juillet - 30 octobre
Marc Chagall, 1945-1985: les années méditerranéennes.
Château de Villeneuve. Fondation Emile Hugues. 3, place du Frêne, 06140 Vence.
✆ **04.93.58.15.78.**

JAZZ

● Juan-les-Pins

19 - 27 juillet
Festival international de jazz d'Antibes-Juan-les-Pins.
Pour sa trente-quatrième édition, le célèbre festival permettra de retrouver Pat Metheny, Dee Dee Bridgewater, Gilberto Gil, Steve Grossman...
Pinède Gould, 06160 Juan-les-Pins.
✆ **04.92.90.53.00.**

THEATRE

● Avignon

8 juillet - 1er août
Festival d'Avignon.
In ou *off*, c'est le roi des festivals, la fête totale du théâtre avec ses beautés et ses dérives. En officiel, on pourra voir, entre autres, l'*Andromaque* d'Euripide monté par Jacques Lasalle et le très remarquable *Henry VI* de Shakespeare, que Start Seide reprend ici après son périple parisien.

35

See answers below.

1

1. Look at this page from the *Guide de l'été* on Provence-Côte d'Azur. What information is given for each event? Name four things.
2. Where would you go to see a Shakespeare play?
3. Which artists are exhibited in Provence in July?
4. Which musicians will be playing at Juan-les-Pins? What type of music do they play?
5. If you were in the Provence-Côte d'Azur area on July 4, what could you go see?
6. If you had five days to spend in the Provence-Côte d'Azur area this summer, when would you go and what would you see?

2

Listen as Martin and Janine, two radio film reviewers, give their opinions of *La Rue Cases-Nègres,* which is playing at the **Festival français de musique de films.** Then, answer the questions. See scripts and answers on p. 307H.

CD 11
Tr. 13

1. Where does the film take place?
2. What happens in the movie?
3. Did Martin like the film? Did Janine? Why or why not?

Answers

1

1. the subject of the exposition/type of festival, the dates, where the event is being held, and the phone number
2. the Festival d'Avignon
3. Marc Chagall and Braque
4. Pat Metheny, Dee Dee Bridgewater, Gilberto Gil, and Steve Grossman; jazz
5. any of the art exhibits
6. Answers will vary.

Apply and Assess

Challenge

2 After students have listened to the recording and answered the questions, write these additional questions on the board or on a transparency. Play the recording again and have students write their answers in French.

1. **En quelle année se passe ce film?** (dans les années trente)
2. **Qui a élevé José?** (sa grand-mère)
3. **Où est-ce que la grand-mère de José travaille?** (dans les champs de canne à sucre)
4. **Qui est Monsieur Méduse?** (une sorte de père spirituel)
5. **Où est-ce que José fait ses études?** (à Fort-de-France)

3

Ecrivons!

You've been hired by a French movie studio to submit proposals for books that you feel would make good screenplays. You've just finished a book that you feel could be a blockbuster movie. Write a proposal in which you briefly describe the plot and the main characters and tell why this book would make a great movie.

Stratégie pour écrire
Characterization is the way an author or playwright reveals the personality of the characters in a story or play. Think about what types of personalities the characters in the book have and how you might describe them.

Préparation

Before you write your proposal, jot down all the basic information you'll need to include about your book: the genre, the basic plot, and the time and place of the action. You might organize your information in an outline format.

Now think about the main characters. What does the author tell you directly about each of them? What are their physical characteristics? What do they do and say that reveals their personalities? A good way to organize your notes is to create a character map of each character using cluster diagrams.

Rédaction

After you've completed your character maps, you'll be ready to write the first draft. You should describe the plot of the story in as few words as possible; try to avoid unnecessary details.

As you write your character descriptions, recall from Chapter 1 the French words and phrases you've learned to describe and characterize others. The key to good characterization is to accurately describe a character's mental and emotional states, as well as how he or she looks. A character's mental state will often dictate how he or she appears on the outside. You might review the vocabulary for describing emotions in Chapter 9. Suggest actors and actresses who would be good for the roles and tell convincingly why you think this book would be a great movie.

Evaluation

Once your first draft is complete, read each part separately. Are your reasons for recommending the book convincing? Is your plot summary accurate and informative? Do you adequately describe the appearance and personality of each of the main characters? Make any changes that you feel are necessary. Be sure to proofread your work before you write the final draft.

4

Jeu de rôle

You have received an interview with the movie director about the screenplay you wrote. Act out this conversation, and then change roles. In your conversation, you should . . .

- discuss the book you wrote about in your screen play. Talk about the plot, the characters, and why you like it. Decide where the movie will take place and who will be the actors.
- make plans for a sequel to the movie you're making.

Mise en pratique

CHAPITRE 11

Speaking Assessment

4 You might use the following rubric when grading your students on this activity.

Speaking Rubric	Points			
	4	3	2	1
Content (Complete–Incomplete)				
Comprehension (Total–Little)				
Comprehensibility (Comprehensible–Incomprehensible)				
Accuracy (Accurate–Seldom accurate)				
Fluency (Fluent–Not fluent)				

18–20: A 16–17: B 14–15: C 12–13: D Under 12: F

Teacher Note

For additional practice and review, you might use the **Histoire Finale** for Chapter 11 on pages 86–87 of the *TPR Storytelling Book.*

Apply and Assess

Process Writing

3 Instead of using cluster diagrams for their character descriptions, students could create a chart for each character in which they cite specific details from the text that define that particular character. For example, have students write the name of a character at the top of a sheet of paper and then divide the sheet into four columns. They should label the first column *Physical Traits* and the third column *Emotional/Mental Traits.* The second and fourth columns should be labeled *How Do I Know?;* in these two columns students can give specific examples of how the author reveals the character's physical and emotional/mental attributes.

Que sais-je?

CHAPITRE 11

Teaching Resources
p. 336

PRINT 
- Grammar Tutor for Students of French, Chapter 11

MEDIA
- Interactive CD-ROM Tutor, Disc 3
- Online self-test

go.hrw.com
WA3 PROVENCE-11

Que sais-je?

WA3 PROVENCE-11

Can you use what you've learned in this chapter?

Can you identify people and things? p. 313

1 How would you ask a friend if she's familiar with your favorite singer? If she isn't, how would you identify the person? Tu connais... ? C'est un/une... Il/Elle est...

2 How would you respond if someone asked you if you were familiar with . . . Bien sûr, c'est... ; Non, je ne connais pas.
1. *La vie en rose?*
2. Téléphone?
3. Jeanne Mas?
4. Kassav'?

Can you ask for and give information? p. 320

3 How would you ask a friend . . .
1. what movies are playing?
2. where a movie is playing?
3. who stars in a movie?
4. what time something starts? See answers below.

4 According to this movie listing, how would you tell a friend what is playing tonight, where, and at what time? See answers below.

LE PLUMEREAU 10, place Plumereau. Pl : 6, 10 €. Mer et Lun : 4, 60 €.; -26 ans, 3, 90 €. Séances sur réserv. Salle accessible aux handicapés.

Aladdin v.f. 15h30 ; 17h30 ; 20h10

Beaucoup de bruit pour rien v.o. Séances : 19h25 ; 21h40. Film 15 min après.

Les Quatre Cents Coups Dolby stéréo Séances : 14h15 ; 18h15 ; 21h25. Film 10 min après.

Les Trois Mousquetaires v.f. Dolby stéréo. Séances : 14h ; 15h45 ; 18h30; 20h45. Film 15 min après.

Au revoir les enfants Séances : 14h ; 16h ; 18h ; 20h. Film 10 min après.

Can you give opinions? p. 324

5 What's your opinion of . . .
1. the play *Romeo and Juliet?*
2. romance novels?
3. westerns?
4. *To Kill a Mockingbird?*
5. classical music?
6. *La Cantatrice chauve?*

6 What would you say about the last book you read that you liked? The last movie you saw that you didn't like?

Can you summarize? p. 326

7 How would you summarize the plot of . . .
1. your favorite film?
2. your favorite book?

Review and Assess

Additional Practice
For additional listening, reading, and speaking practice, ask the following questions about the movie guide: **Quelle est l'adresse du cinéma? (10, place Plumereau); Combien coûte une place? (10 euros); Quels jours est-ce qu'il y a un tarif réduit? (le mercredi et le lundi); Combien coûte une place pour les moins de 26 ans? (3, 90 euros);** ***Aladdin*** **est en version française ou en version originale? (en version française); A quelle heure commence la première séance pour** ***Aladdin?*** **(à quinze heures trente); Il y a combien de séances pour** *Les Trois Mousquetaires?* **(quatre)**

Answers

3
1. Qu'est-ce qu'on joue comme films?
2. Ça passe où?
3. C'est avec qui?
4. Ça commence à quelle heure?

4 *Possible answer: Aladdin* passe au Plumereau à quinze heures trente, à dix-sept heures trente et à vingt heures dix.

Vocabulaire

Première étape

Identifying people and things

Tu connais... ?	*Are you familiar with...?*
Bien sûr. C'est...	*Of course. They are (He/She/It is)...*
Je ne connais pas.	*I'm not familiar with them/him/her/it.*

Music

une chanteuse (un chanteur)	*singer*
un musicien (une musicienne)	*musician*
un groupe	*(music) group*
une chanson	*song*
la musique classique	*classical music*
le jazz	*jazz*
le rock	*rock*
le rap	*rap*
le blues	*blues*
le country/le folk	*country/folk*
la pop	*popular, mainstream music*
le reggae	*reggae*

Adjectives

canadien(ne)	*Canadian*
africain(e)	*African*
antillais(e)	*from the Antilles*
américain(e)	*American*

Deuxième étape

Asking for and giving information

Qu'est-ce qu'on joue comme films?	*What films are playing?*
On joue...	*...is showing.*
Ça passe où?	*Where is it playing?*
Ça passe à/au...	*It's playing at...*
C'est avec qui?	*Who's in it?*
C'est avec...	*...is (are) in it.*
Ça commence à quelle heure?	*What time does it start?*
A...	*At...*

Types of films

un genre	*a type (of film, literature, or music)*
un western	*western*
un film comique	*comedy*
un film d'horreur	*horror movie*
un film de science-fiction	*science-fiction movie*
un film d'amour	*romantic movie*
un film policier	*detective or mystery movie*
un film classique	*classic movie*
un film d'aventures	*adventure movie*
un film d'action	*action movie*

Troisième étape

Giving opinions

C'est drôle/amusant.	*It's funny.*
C'est une belle histoire.	*It's a great story.*
C'est plein de rebondissements.	*It's full of plot twists.*
Il y a du suspense.	*It's suspenseful.*
On ne s'ennuie pas.	*You're never bored.*
C'est une histoire passionnante.	*It's an exciting story.*
Je te le/la recommande.	*I recommend it.*
Il n'y a pas d'histoire.	*It has no plot.*
Ça casse pas des briques.	*It's not earth-shattering.*
C'est...	*It's...*
trop violent.	*too violent.*
trop long.	*too long.*
bête.	*stupid.*
un navet.	*a dud.*
du n'importe quoi.	*worthless.*
gentillet, sans plus.	*cute, but that's all.*
déprimant.	*depressing.*

Summarizing

De quoi ça parle?	*What's it about?*
Qu'est-ce que ça raconte?	*What's the story?*
Ça parle de...	*It's about...*
C'est l'histoire de...	*It's the story of...*

Types of books

un roman policier (un polar)	*detective or mystery novel*
une (auto) biographie	*(auto)biography*
une bande dessinée (une B.D.)	*comic book*
un livre de poésie	*book of poetry*
un roman d'amour	*romance novel*
un roman de science-fiction	*science-fiction novel*
un (roman) classique	*classic*
une pièce de théâtre	*play*

Vocabulaire

CHAPITRE 11

Circumlocution

Have students work in pairs. One student will play the role of a shopper in a video store, while the other is the clerk. The shopper is looking for a particular type of movie, but can't remember the specific term for it. He or she should describe the type of film to the clerk, who will try to determine what the shopper is looking for and then point out where that type of film is located. Then, have students switch roles. This may also be done in a bookstore or a music store.

Review and Assess

Tactile/Visual Learners

Have students work in groups of six, with two members working on the vocabulary of each **étape.** Students should write each word or expression from their **étape** on separate index cards. For each card, they should prepare another card bearing a word, a name, or an expression that is associated with it. For example, in the **Première étape,** they might write **le rap** on one card and **MC Solaar** on another. In the **Deuxième étape,** students might also match questions **(Ça passe où?)** to answers **(Au Gaumont).** In the **Troisième étape,** students might name a type of film or book **(les films d'Alfred Hitchcock)** to fit the description. **(Il y a du suspense.)** Then, students shuffle the cards, exchange them with another group, and match the new cards they receive.

Chapter 11 Assessment

- **Testing Program**
  Chapter Test, pp. 287–292

  Audio Compact Discs, CD 11, Trs. 17–19
  Speaking Test, p. 348
- **Alternative Assessment Guide**
  Performance Assessment, p. 42
  Portfolio Assessment, p. 28
  CD-ROM Assessment, p. 56
- **Interactive CD-ROM Tutor, Disc 3**

  A toi de parler
  A toi d'écrire
- **Standardized Assessment Tutor**
  Chapter 11
- **One-Stop Planner, Disc 3**
  Test Generator
  Chapter 11

Location Opener

CHAPTER 12

Teaching Resources
pp. 338–341

PRINT 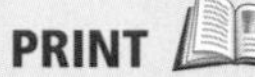

- Lesson Planner, p. 56
- Video Guide, pp. 77–78

MEDIA  

- One-Stop Planner
- Video Program
  Videocassette 4, 29:07–31:48
- DVD Tutor, Disc 2
- Interactive CD-ROM Tutor, Disc 3
- Map Transparencies 3, 4

 go.hrw.com
WA3 QUEBEC

Using the Almanac and Map

Terms in the Almanac

- **Québec,** the capital of Quebec province, is referred to as the "cradle of French civilization in North America." It is the only fortified city north of Mexico.
- **Chicoutimi,** located on the Saguenay River, is an industrial city whose Amerindian name means "up to where the water runs deep."
- **Le parc olympique de Montréal,** built for the 1976 Summer Olympics, is the site of a 169-meter inclining tower and the Olympic Stadium, home to the Montreal Expos baseball team.
- **Le Festival des Films du monde** is a well-known film festival held every August in Montreal.
- **Manon Rhéaume** was the first woman to play in the National Hockey League.

CHAPITRE 12

Allez, viens au Québec!

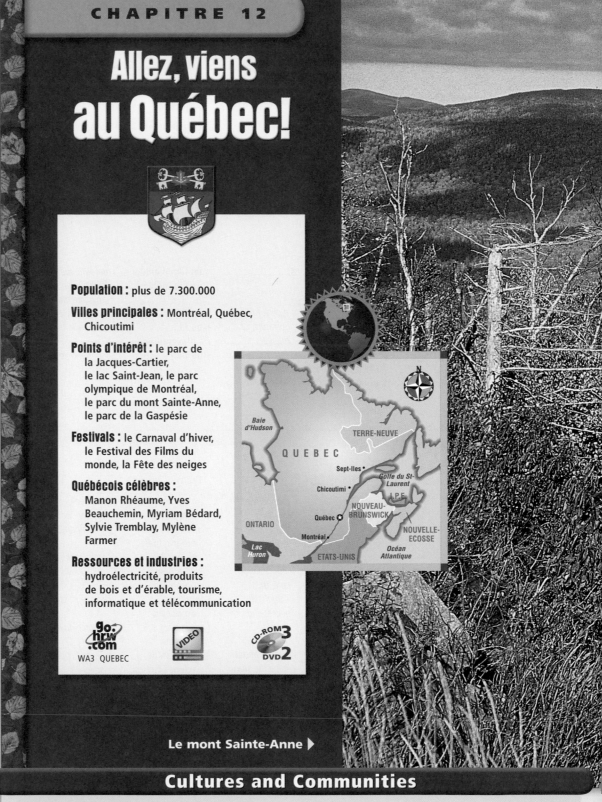

Population : plus de 7.300.000

Villes principales : Montréal, Québec, Chicoutimi

Points d'intérêt : le parc de la Jacques-Cartier, le lac Saint-Jean, le parc olympique de Montréal, le parc du mont Sainte-Anne, le parc de la Gaspésie

Festivals : le Carnaval d'hiver, le Festival des Films du monde, la Fête des neiges

Québécois célèbres : Manon Rhéaume, Yves Beauchemin, Myriam Bédard, Sylvie Tremblay, Mylène Farmer

Ressources et industries : hydroélectricité, produits de bois et d'érable, tourisme, informatique et télécommunication

go.hrw.com WA3 QUEBEC — VIDEO — CD-ROM 3 DVD 2

Le mont Sainte-Anne

Cultures and Communities

Background Information

The province of **Québec,** originally **la Nouvelle-France,** is the largest province in Canada. Explored first by Jacques Cartier in 1534, Quebec was later settled by fur traders, missionaries, and soldiers. The **Québécois** people and culture have been influenced by a variety of factors, including contact with the Amerindian population, the harsh winter climate, proximity to the St. Lawrence River and the sea, and their isolation as a French-speaking province.

STANDARDS: 2.2

Location Opener

CHAPTER 12

Science Link

The Olympic **Vélodrome** has been converted into a **Biodôme,** which recreates four distinct North American ecosystems: a tropical rain forest, a polar habitat, the St. Lawrence River, and the Laurentian Forest.

Language Notes

- The name *Tremblay* in Quebec is a very common family name, similar to *Smith* in the United States.
- Much of the French engineering terminology related to hydroelectric power has been developed by the **Québécois** and is now used in France.

Teacher Note

For more practice with the Location Opener, have students complete the **Compréhension** questions on Disc 2 of the *DVD Tutor.*

Connections and Comparisons

Geography Link

- **Le parc du mont Sainte-Anne,** located 40 kilometers east of Quebec, was created in 1969 as a recreational area for the city. At the top of **le mont Sainte-Anne,** which is 320 meters high, there is a statue of Saint Anne, the mother of the Virgin Mary. The mountain offers excellent skiing and is even lit for nighttime skiing. From the summit, one can see the entire coastline along the **baie de Percé** (part of the Gulf of St. Lawrence), which includes the **Rocher Percé,** a large rock made of limestone. It is one of Canada's most famous natural phenomena.
- **Le lac Saint-Jean** serves as a basin into which all the area rivers flow, except the Saguenay, which is the only river that drains water from the lake.

Using the Photo Essay

1 Vieux-Québec, the old section of Quebec City, is known for its narrow streets and quaint cafés. The horse-drawn carriages **(calèches),** generally found in the Place d'Armes, provide a relaxing, informative tour of the city.

2 Le parc de la Jacques-Cartier is a paradise for sports enthusiasts. They can go down the river in rafts or kayaks, hike in the summer, and ski in the winter. The park is located in the highest part of the Laurentides and is one of over 16 major parks in Quebec. It was begun by conservationists in order to protect the area from hydroelectric development. Naturalists regularly lead canoe trips, teaching visitors how the Montaignais Amerindians (part of the larger Algonquin community) traveled the **rivière Jacques-Cartier.**

3 La péninsule de Gaspé is where the explorer Jacques Cartier first landed. Because the peninsula's interior was so rugged, most of the inhabitants lived in small fishing villages scattered around the coast, and they were quite isolated from one another. Several English-speaking communities were established on the peninsula's south shore along the **baie des Chaleurs.**

4 Montréal, Canada's second largest metropolitan area, is a multicultural island city. Despite the fact that Montreal is the largest French-speaking city outside of Paris, the majority of Montrealers speak both French and English, unlike the inhabitants of Quebec City, who are predominantly French-speakers. Montreal's flag reflects the city's cosmopolitan nature. The English rose, the Irish shamrock, the Scottish thistle, and the French **fleur de lys** each occupy a quarter of the flag. They are symbols of the four countries that influenced Montreal's development during the nineteenth century.

Le Québec

La province du Québec a un statut très indépendant. Trois fois plus grande que la France, elle compte pourtant moins de huit millions d'habitants. La langue officielle est le français, mais pour le commerce, la plupart des Québécois doivent aussi parler anglais. Montréal est la ville qui a le plus grand nombre d'habitants bilingues du monde. Pourquoi est-ce qu'on parle français au Québec? Parce que ce sont les Français qui l'ont fondé. Jacques Cartier a exploré le fleuve Saint-Laurent en 1534 et Samuel de Champlain a fondé La Nouvelle-France en 1608.

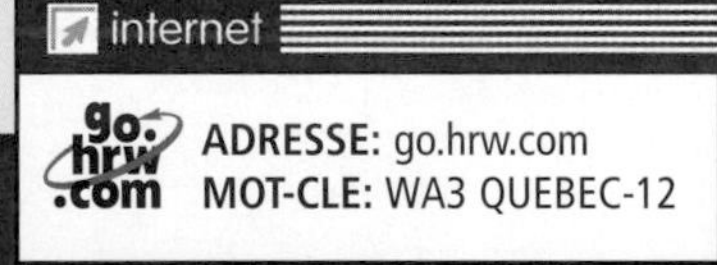

1 Le Vieux-Québec
On peut le visiter en calèche.

2 Le parc de la Jacques-Cartier
Au nord de la ville de Québec, ce parc offre une grande variété d'activités en pleine réserve naturelle.

3 La péninsule de Gaspé
C'est l'une des plus anciennes régions touristiques du Québec, avec ses forêts et sa belle côte sauvage.

Connections and Comparisons

Geography Links

3 La péninsule de Gaspé, bounded by the St. Lawrence River and the **baie des Chaleurs,** is approximately 550 kilometers long and sparsely populated. The peninsula has two popular parks: the mountainous **parc de la Gaspésie,** and the **parc national de Forillon,** with its well-traveled hiking paths and abundant wildlife.

6 Beluga whales come to feed where the Saguenay's warmer river water empties into the colder waters of the St. Lawrence.

4 Montréal
Au bord du Saint-Laurent, Montréal est la plus grande ville du Québec.

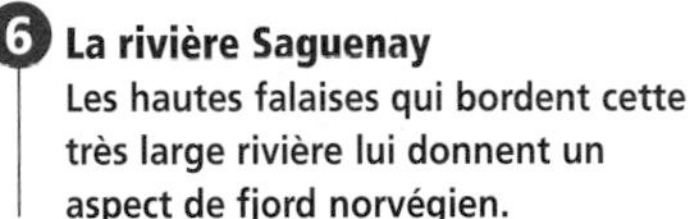

5 Les Laurentides
On y trouve la plus grande concentration de stations de ski d'Amérique du nord.

6 La rivière Saguenay
Les hautes falaises qui bordent cette très large rivière lui donnent un aspect de fjord norvégien.

7 Les Inuits
Les Inuits sont un des peuples indigènes du Québec.

Au chapitre 12,

tu vas faire la connaissance de Michèle, Francine, René, Paul et Denis, cinq jeunes Québécois qui vont t'emmener faire une randonnée au parc de la Jacques-Cartier. C'est un vrai paradis pour les amoureux de la nature. Tu vas avoir l'occasion de voir des paysages d'une beauté sauvage et plein d'animaux tels que des mouffettes, des orignaux et même des ours!

5 Les Laurentides, among the world's oldest mountains, extend along the north side of the St. Lawrence from the Ottawa River to the Saguenay River. They are sprinkled with clear blue lakes, hills for skiing, and vast forests. This large region is known as one of North America's largest ski areas.

6 La rivière Saguenay, which empties out of **le lac Saint-Jean,** is 104 kilometers long and navigable by ocean-going vessels to Chicoutimi. It has an average depth of 240 meters. **Le fjord Saguenay,** the world's southernmost fjord, and one of the longest, was made by glaciers.

7 Les Inuits, native Arctic inhabitants, were thought to be Asian hunters who migrated across the Bering Strait thousands of years ago. They are known as whale hunters, who developed the igloo for winter housing and live in tents made of hides in warmer weather.

Thinking Critically

Observing Ask students to look at the photos for examples of both ancient traditions and modern innovations.

Cultures and Communities

Geography Link

4 Montréal, located downstream from where the **rivière des Outaouais** empties into the St. Lawrence, is truly surrounded by water. The St. Lawrence passes on the south side, and the **rivière des Prairies** separates it from Laval, a Montreal suburb. Laval is itself an island bounded by the **rivière des Mille Iles** on the north.

History Link

4 Montréal was known as **Hochelaga** by the Amerindians. **Ville-Marie de Montréal** was founded on an island in the St. Lawrence in 1642 and was settled by fur traders. Its later phenomenal growth was due to the development of the lumber and paper industries after fur trading declined.

STANDARDS: 2.2, 3.1

Chapitre 12 : A la belle étoile

Review Chapter

Chapter Overview

Mise en train pp. 344–346	***Promenons-nous dans les bois***		

	FUNCTIONS	GRAMMAR	VOCABULARY	RE-ENTRY
Première étape pp. 347–351	• Asking for and giving information; giving directions, p. 348		• Animals, p. 349 • Outdoor activities, p. 350	• Pointing out where things are **(Chapitre 2,** II) • Locations **(Chapitre 12,** I) • Activities **(Chapitres 4, 6,** II)
Deuxième étape pp. 352–357	• Complaining; expressing discouragement and offering encouragement, p. 354 • Asking for and giving advice, p. 356	• The verb **emporter,** p. 354	• Camping equipment, p. 353	• Clothing vocabulary **(Chapitre I,** II) • Expressing discouragement and offering encouragement **(Chapitre 7,** II) • Giving advice **(Chapitre 7,** II)
Troisième étape pp. 358–361	• Relating a series of events; describing people and places, p. 358	• The **passé composé** versus the **imparfait,** p. 359		• Relating a series of events **(Chapitre 4,** II) • The **imparfait (Chapitre 8,** II)

Lisons! pp. 362–363	French-Canadian poetry by Anne Hébert	**Reading Strategy:** Using imagery and metaphor	
Grammaire supplémentaire	**pp. 364–367** **Première étape,** pp. 364–365	**Deuxième étape,** pp. 365–366	**Troisième étape,** p. 366–367
Review pp. 368–371	**Mise en pratique,** pp. 368–369 **Ecrivons!** Story mapping Writing an account of adventures as a pioneer explorer in Canada	**Que sais-je?** p. 370	**Vocabulaire,** p. 371

CULTURE

- **Note culturelle, Le parc de la Jacques-Cartier,** p. 348
- Realia: **Les parcs québécois,** p. 350
- Realia: **Bienvenue dans le parc de la Jacques-Cartier,** p. 355
- **Note culturelle,** Ecology in Canada, p. 356
- **Panorama Culturel,** Endangered animals, p. 357
- **Rencontre culturelle,** French-Canadian expressions, p. 361

Chapter Resources

PRINT

Lesson Planning

One-Stop Planner

Lesson Planner with Substitute Teacher

Lesson Plans, pp. 56–60, p. 74

Student Make-Up Assignments

- Make-Up Assignment Copying Masters, Chapter 12

Listening and Speaking

TPR Storytelling Book, pp. 88–95

Listening Activities

- Student Response Forms for Listening Activities, pp. 91–93
- Additional Listening Activities 12-1 to 12-6, pp. 95–97
- Additional Listening Activities (song), p. 98
- Scripts and Answers, pp. 157–161

Video Guide

- Teaching Suggestions, pp. 80–81
- Activity Masters, pp. 82–84
- Scripts and Answers, pp. 113–116, 123

Activities for Communication

- Communicative Activities, pp. 67–72
- Realia and Teaching Suggestions, pp. 130–134
- Situation Cards, pp. 159–160

Reading and Writing

Reading Strategies and Skills Handbook, Chapter 12

Joie de lire 2, Chapter 12

Cahier d'activités, pp. 133–144

Grammar

Travaux pratiques de grammaire, pp. 98–107

Grammar Tutor for Students of French, Chapter 12

Assessment

Testing Program

- Grammar and Vocabulary Quizzes, **Etape** Quizzes, and Chapter Test, pp. 301–318
- Score Sheet, Scripts and Answers, pp. 319–326
- Final Exam, pp. 327–334
- Score Sheet, Scripts and Answers, pp. 335–340

Alternative Assessment Guide

- Portfolio Assessment, p. 29
- Performance Assessment, p. 43
- CD-ROM Assessment, p. 57

Student Make-Up Assignments

- Alternative Quizzes, Chapter 12

Standardized Assessment Tutor

- Reading, pp. 47–49
- Writing, p. 50
- Math, pp. 51–52

MEDIA

Online Activities

- Jeux interactifs
- Activités Internet

Video Program

- Videocassette 4
- Videocassette 5 (captioned version)

Interactive CD-ROM Tutor, Disc 3

DVD Tutor, Disc 2

Audio Compact Discs

- Textbook Listening Activities, CD 12, Tracks 1–12
- Additional Listening Activities, CD 12, Tracks 24–30
- Assessment Items, CD 12, Tracks 13–23

Teaching Transparencies

- Situation 12-1 to 12-3
- Vocabulary 12-A to 12-D
- **Mise en train**
- **Grammaire supplémentaire** Answers
- **Travaux pratiques de grammaire** Answers

One-Stop Planner CD-ROM

Use the **One-Stop Planner CD-ROM with Test Generator** to aid in lesson planning and pacing.

For each chapter, the **One-Stop Planner** includes:

- Editable lesson plans with direct links to teaching resources
- Printable worksheets from resource books
- Direct launches to the HRW Internet activities
- Video and audio segments
- Test Generator
- Clip Art for vocabulary items

Projects

Album de photos en vidéo

Students will make a "photo album" of an imaginary camping trip in a public park. They will record the album on videocassette. The "photos," which students will create, will be mounted on construction paper with a caption below each one. Each group will make ten "photos" to describe their camping trip. The first "photo" in the album should show a map of the country and the park's location.

MATERIALS

Students may need

- Construction paper
- Markers
- Magazines or catalogues
- Scissors
- Videocamera and Videocassette
- Overhead projector

SUGGESTED SEQUENCE

1. Each group will choose a national or regional park in any francophone country, department, or province as the site of their imaginary camping trip. You might reserve one or two class periods in the library and have the librarian select books on francophone countries, departments, or provinces for your use.
2. Students should select or draw their "photos" and write a one- or two-sentence caption for each one.
3. When the photos and captions are finished, students begin recording their "photo album" on videocassette.
4. To record the photos, tape one photo to the board or to the wall and focus the video camera only on the photo. Turn on the camera, have a student read the caption for that photo, and pause the camera. Follow the same procedure for each photo. The result is a series of pictures, similar to a slide show, with narration on videocassette.
5. While groups are videotaping their album, all other students will work quietly on their own.
6. Show the video to the class and to other French classes.

GRADING THE PROJECT

Suggested Point Distribution: (total = 100 points)

Content	20
Language use	20
Overall presentation	20
Comprehensibility	20
Effort/Participation	20

Games

Péril

In this game, students will practice the vocabulary and expressions from this chapter and all previous chapters.

Preparation (This game is similar to the game Jeopardy®.)

1. Draw a "Jeopardy" game board on a transparency: five columns with five squares in each. Write five categories across the top, such as *Animals, Camping, Complaining, Clothes,* and *Sports.*
2. In each column, write numerical values in the squares from 100 in the first squares to 500 in the fifth squares.
3. For each square in each category, prepare a clue and the correct response. Write the clues on a sheet of paper. Write the corresponding category and point value next to each clue. For example, for one of the squares in the *Clothes* category, you might write the clue **On la met autour du cou quand il fait froid** to elicit the answer **C'est une écharpe.**
4. The object of the game is to win the number of points in a square by giving the answer suggested by the clue.
5. Form three teams. Team members will take turns playing during a round. They may volunteer to participate, or you might draw names at random. If possible, obtain three buzzers or bells for the three players (one from each team) to sound when they know the answer. Have a judge determine who was the first to sound the buzzer or bell.
6. Prepare several transparencies for different rounds.

Procedure

1. To begin, a player from one team chooses a category and a specific point value. (**Je voudrais** *Complaining* **pour 300, s'il vous plaît.**)
2. Read aloud the clue you prepared for that square. (**On dit ça quand on a été debout pendant toute la journée.**)
3. The player who sounds his or her buzzer or bell first may answer. (**J'ai mal aux pieds.**)
4. If the first contestant answers incorrectly, the others may sound their buzzer or bell to try to answer. If no contestant answers correctly, the last contestant to try to answer chooses the next category and point value.
5. The contestant who answers correctly earns the designated number of points and chooses another category and point value. The team with the most points at the end of the game wins.

Storytelling

Mini-histoire

*This story accompanies Teaching Transparency 12-1. The **mini-histoire** can be told and retold in different formats, acted out, written down, and read aloud to give students additional opportunities to practice all four skills. The following story is about some park animals who want to have a party.*

Les animaux du Parc du Québec ont décidé d'organiser une petite fête sportive. Malheureusement, ils n'ont pas de tente, pas de skis, rien! Ils partent donc à la recherche du site idéal. Ils le trouvent rapidement. Il y a des raquettes, un canoë, des skis, un vélo, des sièges et même de la nourriture. L'ours demande : «Pardon, nous voudrions organi... » «AAHHH!» L'ours dit : «Et, voilà. Je leur ai encore fait peur. Mais, voilà, monsieur est trop timide... » A ce moment, le renard dit : «Eh, regardez comme je sais bien faire du vélo!» L'orignal demande alors aux deux jeunes filles qui sont dans l'arbre : «Pardon mesdemoiselles, je peux vous emprunter vos raquettes?» Elles répondent : «Heuuuu, oui.» «Regardez, on peut faire des hot-dogs!» dit le raton laveur. Une des jeunes filles demande à l'autre : «Dis, tu crois qu'on peut descendre ?» L'autre répond : «Oui, ils n'ont pas l'air trop méchants, et puis j'aimerais bien manger quelque chose.» Alors la mouffette leur dit : «Mais oui, venez. On ne vous fera pas de mal. On veut juste faire la fête!»

Traditions

Le français au Québec

Why is French still spoken in Quebec? The province of Quebec was founded by French immigrants and when France ceded the colony to Great Britain in 1760, it retained its religion and language. In 1791, the Canadian Constitution Act established two provinces: Upper Canada (primarily English-speaking Ontario), and Lower Canada (primarily French-speaking Quebec) with Quebec City as its capital. After the World War II, facing increasing economic supremacy from the English speaking world, the Quebecers decided to affirm their French-speaking status. In 1974, the French language became the official language of the province. Now more than 80% of the people living in Quebec speak French. Despite all efforts to keep their French-speaking identity, Quebec voters rejected twice the proposition of having an independent Quebec. The second referendum on Quebec's independence was defeated by only a narrow margin in October 1995.

Recette

Quebec inherited the anglo-saxon tradition of painting eggs for Easter. The egg has been traditionally associated with Easter for many years. In the 4th century, the Church forbade Christians from eating eggs during the 40 days of Lent. During these forty days, however, the hens kept laying eggs. People had so many eggs that they started giving them away as presents. Since the eggs became presents, people decided to paint them.

TARTE AUX ŒUFS

Pâte à tarte	Garniture
2 tasses de farine	3 œufs + un blanc d'œuf
1/2 tasse de sucre	2 tasses de lait
1/2 tasse de beurre	1 tasse de sucre
1 œuf	1 gousse de vanille (ou 1 sachet de sucre vanillé)

Pâte à tarte

Faire fondre le beurre. Placer la farine dans un saladier. Faire un puits. Y mettre le sucre et l'œuf. Commencer à mélanger doucement. Ajouter le beurre petit à petit. Faire une boule du mélange. Si la boule est trop beurrée, ajouter une ou deux cuillères à soupe de farine.

Garniture

Faire chauffer le lait. Dans un bol mélanger le sucre, les œufs et le sucre vanillé. Ajouter le lait chaud petit à petit.

Etaler la pâte dans le moule et badigeonner avec le blanc d'œuf. Mettre au four chaud pendant 2 minutes. Retirer du four. Verser la garniture sur la pâte. Remettre au four à 425° F jusqu'à ce que la tarte soit ferme.

Technology

DVD/Video

Videocassette 4, Videocassette 5 (captioned version)
DVD Tutor, Disc 2
See Video Guide, pages 79–84.

Mise en train • Promenons-nous dans les bois
Francine, René, Michèle, and Denis are at the **parc de la Jacques-Cartier** with Francine's parents. The young people go for a hike in the woods, during which Michèle and Denis disagree on environmental issues. When the teenagers are ready to return to camp, they decide to take a shortcut and are soon lost. They discuss the advantages and disadvantages of staying where they are or continuing on.

Mise en train (suite)
The young people decide to build a fire to stay warm. Denis leaves to go fishing and later returns with a small fish. A park ranger finds the group seated around the fire and warns them that building fires and fishing without a permit are against the park rules. When they tell the ranger they're lost, she leads them back to the campground, where Francine's parents are waiting anxiously.

Quels sont les animaux en voie de disparition dans ta région?
Students from Martinique, Côte d'Ivoire, and Quebec talk about endangered animals in their area.

Vidéoclip
- *Les dinosaures* performed by Michel Rivard: music video

Interactive CD-ROM Tutor

Activity	Activity Type	Pupil's Edition Page
En contexte	*Interactive conversation*	
1. Comment dit-on... ?	Le bon choix	p. 348
2. Vocabulaire	Chasse au trésor Explorons!/Vérifions	p. 349
3. Vocabulaire	Jeu des paires	p. 353
4. Comment dit-on... ?	Chacun à sa place	p. 354
5. Comment dit-on... ?	Méli-mélo	p. 358
6. Grammaire	Les mots qui manquent	p. 359
Panorama Culturel	Quels sont les animaux en voie de disparition dans ta région?	p. 357
A toi de parler	*Guided recording*	pp. 368–371
A toi d'écrire	*Guided writing*	pp. 368–371

Teacher Management System
Launch the program, type "admin" in the password area, and press RETURN. Log on to www.hrw.com/CDROMTUTOR for a detailed explanation of the Teacher Management System.

DVD Tutor

The *DVD Tutor* contains all material from the *Video Program* as described above. French captions are available for use at your discretion for all sections of the video. The *DVD Tutor* also provides a variety of video-based activities that assess students' understanding of the **Mise en train, Suite,** and **Panorama Culturel.**

This part of the *DVD Tutor* may be used on any DVD video player connected to a television, video monitor, or on a computer with a DVD-ROM drive.

In addition to the video material and the video-based comprehension activities, the *DVD Tutor* also contains the entire *Interactive CD-ROM Tutor* in DVD-ROM format. Each DVD disc contains the activities from all 12 chapters of the *Interactive CD-ROM Tutor.*

This part of the *DVD Tutor* may be used on a Macintosh® or Windows® computer with a DVD-ROM drive.

To preview all resources available for this chapter, use the **One-Stop Planner CD-ROM,** Disc 3.

Internet Connection

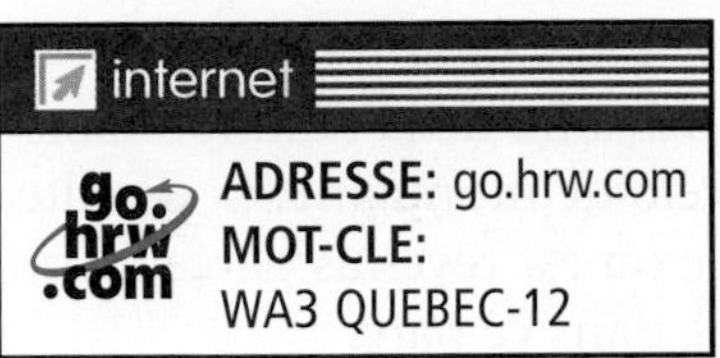

*Have students explore the **go.hrw.com** Web site for many online resources covering all chapters. All Chapter 12 resources are available under the keyword **WA3 QUEBEC-12.** Interactive games help students practice the material and provide them with immediate feedback. You'll also find a printable worksheet that provides Internet activities that lead to a comprehensive online research project.*

Jeux interactifs

You can use the interactive activities in this chapter

- to practice grammar, vocabulary, and chapter functions
- as homework
- as an assessment option
- as a self-test
- to prepare for the Chapter Test

Activités Internet

Students look for information about natural parks in Quebec online and record some information about each park, using the vocabulary from the chapter.

- In preparation for the **Activités Internet,** have students complete the activities in the **Panorama Culturel** on page 357 and read the **Notes culturelles** throughout the chapter. After completing the activity sheet, have students share their responses with the class.

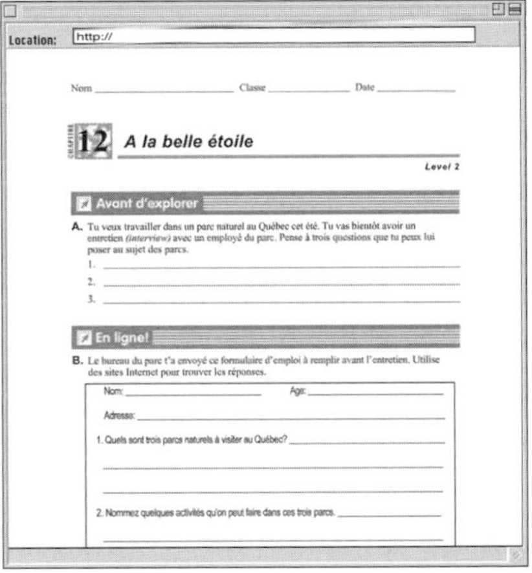

Location: http://

Nom ______ Classe ______ Date ______

12 A la belle étoile

Level 2

Avant d'explorer

A. Tu veux travailler dans un parc naturel au Québec cet été. Tu vas bientôt avoir un entretien (*interview*) avec un employé du parc. Pense à trois questions que tu peux lui poser au sujet des parcs.

1. ______
2. ______
3. ______

En ligne!

B. Le bureau du parc t'a envoyé ce formulaire d'emploi à remplir avant l'entretien. Utilise des sites Internet pour trouver les réponses.

Nom: ______ Age: ______

Adresse: ______

1. Quels sont trois parcs naturels à visiter au Québec? ______

2. Nommez quelques activités qu'on peut faire dans ces trois parcs. ______

Projet

Have students look up information on parks, animals, and outdoor activities in Quebec. Students will use this information to create a brochure directed to teenagers who like the outdoors. Have students document their sources by noting the URLs of all the sites that they consulted.

Textbook Listening Activities Scripts 

Première étape

7 p. 348

1. Ça se trouve au bord du lac Saint-Jean, en face de la ville d'Alma.
2. Oui, c'est dans le nord du Québec, à l'est de Matane. C'est très beau, là-bas.
3. C'est pas loin d'ici. Vous allez à Thetford Mines, et c'est à l'est, au bord d'un très beau lac.
4. Oui, c'est un parc très célèbre. Ça se trouve au nord de Québec ville.
5. C'est assez loin. C'est une île dans l'Océan Atlantique. C'est dans le nord-est du Québec, près de Gaspé.

Answers to Activity 7

1. parc de la Pointe-Taillon
2. parc de la Gaspésie
3. parc de Frontenac
4. parc de la Jacques-Cartier
5. parc de l'Ile-Bonaventure-et-du-Rocher-Percé

10 p. 349

SON AMI Alors, Francine, ce week-end au parc de la Jacques-Cartier, c'était comment?

FRANCINE Super! On s'est vraiment bien amusés!

SON AMI Ah, oui? Et qu'est-ce que vous avez fait?

FRANCINE D'abord, on a fait une randonnée pédestre. On a vu un renard et plein d'orignaux. Je les ai même pris en photo.

SON AMI Très bien. Comme ça, on pourra aussi les voir.

FRANCINE Après ça, on avait faim, alors on a fait un pique-nique. Jérôme voulait donner à manger aux écureuils et aux canards, mais c'était interdit. Ensuite, on est allés nager dans la rivière. C'était génial! Et puis, on a fait du camping.

SON AMI Est-ce que vous avez vu d'autres animaux?

FRANCINE Ah! J'oubliais! Au retour, nous avons vu un ours énorme!

Answers to Activity 10

a fox, moose, squirrels, ducks, a bear

14 p. 351

1. Samedi, on s'est bien amusés! On a fait du canotage; c'était super! Mais on ne peut pas faire de la natation dans ce parc. Donc, on a fait du vélo de montagne. Et ensuite, on a fait de la voile. Après ça, on est revenus parce qu'on ne peut pas faire du camping dans ce parc.
2. Quel week-end! Tout a été de travers. On a fait du camping, bien sûr, mais il n'y avait pas grand-chose à faire comme sports. Tout le monde voulait faire du vélo de montagne, mais c'était impossible : interdit. Et le canotage, c'était impossible aussi! Enfin, on a fait une randonnée pédestre, et après, nous sommes allés à la pêche. Nous, les filles, on voulait se baigner, mais on ne peut pas là-bas! On n'a vraiment pas eu de chance!
3. On a passé un week-end très chouette. On est allés à la pêche, on a fait du vélo de montagne et on a vu une chute d'eau magnifique. En hiver, là-bas, on peut faire du ski alpin, mais en juillet, on a juste pu faire un pique-nique en plein air. Et puis après, on s'est reposés. Que la nature est belle!

Answers to Activity 14

1. canoeing, mountain biking, sailing
2. camping, hiking, fishing
3. fishing, mountain biking, picnic

The following scripts are for the listening activities found in the *Pupil's Edition*. For Student Response Forms, see *Listening Activities,* pages 91–93. To provide students with additional listening practice, see *Listening Activities,* pages 95–98.

To preview all resources available for this chapter, use the **One-Stop Planner CD-ROM**, Disc 3.

Deuxième étape

24 **p. 355**

1. — Mais qu'est-ce que tu fais, Elodie?
— J'emporte des carottes pour les donner aux écureuils. Ils sont si mignons!
— Mais tu ne dois pas nourrir les animaux! C'est interdit!
— Vraiment? Ben, alors, je les mangerai.

2. — Romain! Arrête!
— Mais qu'est-ce que tu as, toi, à crier comme ça?
— Ne mutile pas les arbres! Tu devrais plutôt en prendre une photo pour en préserver le souvenir. Tiens, voilà mon appareil-photo.

3. — Tu ne vas pas jeter ces papiers, j'espère.
— Mais... il n'y a pas de poubelle, Bénédicte. Qu'est-ce que je dois en faire?
— Pourquoi tu ne les remportes pas avec toi? Tu peux les jeter plus tard. Il faut respecter la nature!

Answers to Activity 24
1. b 2. c 3. a

Troisième étape

29 **p. 359**

GUILLAUME Qu'est-ce que tu as fait le week-end dernier?
SEVERINE Je suis allée camper au parc du Saguenay avec des amies. Nous sommes allées en voiture jusqu'au parc, puis nous avons marché.
GUILLAUME Ah oui? Vous avez dû beaucoup vous amuser, surtout avec ce beau temps.
SEVERINE Oui, il faisait très beau, et nous avons pu faire du canotage, des randonnées...
GUILLAUME Quelle chance! Ça doit être magnifique là-bas, surtout les fjords!
SEVERINE Oui, tu verras, j'ai pris beaucoup de photos. Le seul problème, c'était Monique.
GUILLAUME Monique? Mais elle est super sympa, non?
SEVERINE En général, oui, mais ce week-end, elle était de très mauvaise humeur. Elle se plaignait constamment. D'abord, elle avait mal aux pieds, ensuite, elle crevait de faim, après ça, son sac à dos était trop lourd. Et puis, elle ne voulait rien faire.
GUILLAUME Alors, qu'est-ce que tu as fait?
SÉVERINE Je lui ai parlé, et elle m'a expliqué ce qui s'était passé. C'était un malentendu avec son copain. Enfin, on s'est bien amusées.

Answers to Activity 29
1. Il faisait très beau.
2. Elles ont fait du canotage et des randonnées. Séverine a pris des photos.
3. Elle était de mauvaise humeur; Elle s'est disputée avec son copain.

Mise en pratique

2 **p. 368**

ETIENNE Dis, Béatrix, on va bientôt finir? Je n'en peux plus, moi!
BEATRIX Courage! On y est presque!
ETIENNE Je suis fatigué, moi. Et je meurs de faim en plus. Tu sais, cette randonnée pédestre de cinq kilomètres, c'était peut-être pas une si bonne idée!
BEATRIX Oh là là! Mais arrête un peu!
ETIENNE Aïe!
BEATRIX Quoi? Qu'est-ce qu'il y a maintenant?
ETIENNE Je ne sais pas. J'ai mal au bras. Tu as emporté la trousse de premiers soins?
BEATRIX Bien sûr. Fais-moi voir... Mais, tu n'as rien du tout! Qu'est-ce que tu racontes! Allez, dépêche-toi un peu!
ETIENNE Eh ben, en tout cas, moi, cet après-midi, je vais rester au camping et je vais faire la sieste.
BEATRIX Ah toi, vraiment! Tu as la chance de passer le week-end dans un des plus beaux parcs du Québec et tu veux faire la sieste!
ETIENNE Et alors? Je suis fatigué et j'en ai marre de marcher.
BEATRIX Comme tu veux. Moi, je vais faire du canotage et ensuite, je vais faire du vélo de montagne.
ETIENNE Eh ben, bon courage!

Answers to Mise en pratique Activity 2
1. They're hiking.
2. He's tired and hungry.
3. His arm hurts.
4. She is going canoeing and mountain-biking.
5. He is going to stay at the campsite and take a nap.

Suggested Lesson Plans 50-Minute Schedule

Day 1

CHAPTER OPENER 5 min.
- Present Chapter Objectives, p. 343.
- Photo Flash!, Culture Notes, and Math Link, ATE, pp. 342–343

MISE EN TRAIN 40 min.
- Presenting **Mise en train,** ATE, p. 345
- Teaching Suggestions: Post-viewing Suggestions 1–2, Video Guide, p. 80
- Career Path, ATE, p. 344
- Do Activities 1–4, p. 346.

Wrap-Up 5 min.
- Do Activity 5, p. 346.

Homework Options
Cahier d'activités, Act. 1, p. 133

Day 2

PREMIERE ETAPE
Quick Review 5 min.
- Bell Work, ATE, p. 347

Comment dit-on... ?, p. 348 25 min.
- Complete Activity 6, p. 347.
- Presenting **Comment dit-on... ?,** ATE, p. 348
- Play Audio CD for Activity 7, p. 348.
- Cahier d'activités, Activities 2–4, pp. 134–135
- Have students do Activities 8–9, pp. 348–349, in pairs.
- Read and discuss **Note culturelle,** p. 348.

Vocabulaire, p. 349 15 min.
- Presenting **Vocabulaire,** ATE, p. 349
- Play Audio CD for Activity 10, p. 349.
- Do Activity 11, p. 350.
- Travaux pratiques de grammaire, Activities 1–3, p. 98
- Have students do Activity 12, p. 350, in pairs.

Wrap-Up 5 min.
- Language-to-Language, ATE, p. 350, and TPR, ATE, p. 349

Homework Options
Cahier d'activités, Act. 5, p. 135

Day 3

PREMIERE ETAPE
Quick Review 5 min.
- Check homework.

Vocabulaire, p. 350 25 min.
- Presenting **Vocabulaire,** ATE, p. 350
- Do Activity 13, p. 351.
- Play Audio CD for Activity 14, p. 351.
- Travaux pratiques de grammaire, Activities 4–6, p. 99
- Do Activity 15, p. 351.

Wrap-Up 20 min.
- Do Activity 16, p. 351.
- Have students do Activity 17, p. 351, in small groups.

Homework Options
Study for Quiz 12-1.
Cahier d'activités, Act. 6, p. 136

Day 4

PREMIERE ETAPE
Quiz 12-1 20 min.
- Administer Quiz 12-1A or 12-1B.

DEUXIEME ETAPE
Vocabulaire and **Note de grammaire, pp. 353–354** 20 min.
- Presenting **Vocabulaire,** ATE, p. 353
- TPR, ATE, p. 353
- Do Activity 19, p. 353
- Travaux pratiques de grammaire, Activity 8, p. 101
- Presenting **Note de grammaire,** ATE, p. 354
- Travaux pratiques de grammaire, Activities 10–11, p. 102
- Do Activity 20, p. 354.

Wrap-Up 10 min.
- Building on Previous Skills, ATE, p. 353

Homework Options
Cahier d'activités, Acts. 8–9, p. 137
Grammaire supplémentaire, Act. 4, p. 365

Day 5

DEUXIEME ETAPE
Quick Review 5 min.
- Check homework.

Comment dit-on... ?, p. 354 15 min.
- Presenting **Comment dit-on... ?,** ATE, p. 354
- Cahier d'activités, Activity 11, p. 138
- Do Activity 21, p. 354.
- Have students do Activity 22, p. 354, in groups.

Vocabulaire, p. 355 10 min.
- Presenting **Vocabulaire,** ATE, p. 355
- Do Activity 23, p. 355.
- Play Audio CD for Activity 24, p. 355.
- Travaux pratiques de grammaire, Activities 12–14, p. 103

Comment dit-on... ?, p. 356 15 min.
- Presenting **Comment dit-on... ?,** ATE, p. 356
- Cahier d'activités, Activity 13, p. 139
- Do Activity 25, p. 356.

Wrap-Up 5 min.
- Read and discuss **Note culturelle,** p. 356.

Homework Options
Study for Quiz 12-2.
Cahier d'activités, Act. 12, p. 139

Day 6

DEUXIEME ETAPE
Quiz 12-2 20 min.
- Administer Quiz 12-2A or 12-2B.

PANORAMA CULTUREL 20 min.
- Presenting **Panorama Culturel,** ATE, p. 357
- Discuss **Qu'en penses-tu?,** p. 357.
- Questions, ATE, p. 357
- See Teaching Suggestions: Post-viewing Suggestions 1–2, Video Guide, p. 81.

Wrap-Up 10 min.
- **Panorama Culturel** Activity, Interactive CD-ROM Tutor, Disc 3

Homework Options
Cahier d'activités, Acts. 21–22, p. 144

One-Stop Planner CD-ROM

For alternative lesson plans by chapter section, to create your own customized plans, or to preview all resources available for this chapter, use the **One-Stop Planner CD-ROM,** Disc 3.

For additional homework suggestions, see activities accompanied by this symbol throughout the chapter.

Day 7

TROISIEME ETAPE

Quick Review 5 min.
- Check homework.

Comment dit-on... ?, p. 358 15 min.
- Presenting **Comment dit-on... ?,** ATE, p. 358
- Play Audio CD for Activity 29, p. 359.
- Cahier d'activités, Activities 15–16, p. 140

Grammaire, p. 359 25 min.
- Presenting **Grammaire,** ATE, p. 359
- Travaux pratiques de grammaire, Activities 15–17, pp. 104–105
- Do Activity 30, p. 359.
- Travaux pratiques de grammaire, Activities 18–20, pp. 106–107

Wrap-Up 5 min.
- Do Activity 31, p. 360.

Homework Options
Study for Quiz 12-3
Pupil's Edition, Act. 32, p. 360
Cahier d'activités, Acts. 17–19, pp. 140–142

Day 8

TROISIEME ETAPE

Quiz 12-3 20 min.
- Administer Quiz 12-3A or 12-3B.

RENCONTRE CULTURELLE 10 min.
- Motivating Activity, ATE, p. 361
- Presenting **Rencontre culturelle,** ATE, p. 361
- Discuss **Qu'en penses-tu?,** p. 361.
- Read and discuss **Savais-tu que... ?,** p. 361.
- Thinking Critically: Analyzing, ATE, p. 361
- Thinking Critically: Comparing and Contrasting, ATE, p. 361

LISONS! 15 min.
- Making Connections, ATE, p. 362
- Read and discuss **Stratégie pour lire,** p. 362.
- Do Activity A, p. 362.

Wrap-Up 5 min.
- Culture Note, ATE, p. 362

Homework Options
Cahier d'activités, Act. 20, p. 143

Day 9

LISONS!

Quick Review 10 min.
- Check homework.

Reading and Postreading Activities 35 min.
- Have students read **Tombée du jour** and **Nos mains au jardin,** pp. 362–363.
- Complete Reading Activities B–H, pp. 362–363.
- Have students do Activity I, p. 363, using Group Work, ATE, p. 363.
- Complete Activity J, p. 363.
- Literature Link, ATE, p. 363

Wrap-Up 5 min.
- Have volunteers share their answers to Activity J, p. 363.

Homework Options
Have students write their own poems about nature.

Day 10

LISONS!

Quick Review 5 min.
- Have students share their poems about nature.

MISE EN PRATIQUE 40 min.
- Do Activity 1, p. 368.
- Play Audio CD for Activity 2, p. 368.
- Do Activity 3, p. 368.
- Discuss the strategy for **Ecrivons!,** p. 369, then have students work on their compositions.
- Have students do **Jeu de rôle,** p. 369, in pairs.

Wrap-Up 5 min.
- Have volunteers share conversations from **Jeu de rôle** with the class.

Homework Options
Have students finish final drafts for **Ecrivons!,** Pupil's Edition, p. 369.

Day 11

MISE EN PRATIQUE 45 min.
- Have volunteers share their compositions from **Ecrivons!**
- Have students complete **A toi de parler,** CD-ROM Tutor, Disc 3.
- Have students do **A toi d'écrire,** CD-ROM Tutor, Disc 3.
- Show ***Promenons-nous dans les bois (suite),*** Video Program, Videocassette 4/DVD, Disc 2.
- See Teaching Suggestions, Viewing Suggestions 1–2, Video Guide, p. 80.
- Complete Activities 8–9, Video Guide, p. 84.
- See Teaching Suggestions, Post-viewing Suggestions 1–2, Video Guide, p. 80.

Wrap-Up 5 min.
- Have students begin **Que sais-je?,** p. 370.

Homework Options
Que sais-je?, p. 370

Day 12

MISE EN PRATIQUE

Quick Review 15 min.
- Go over **Que sais-je?,** p. 370.

Chapter Review 35 min.
- Review Chapter 12. Choose from **Grammaire supplémentaire,** Grammar Tutor for Students of French, Activities for Communication, Listening Activities, Interactive CD-ROM Tutor, or **Jeux interactifs.**
- Circumlocution, ATE, p. 371

Homework Options
Study for Chapter 12 Test.

Assessment

Chapter Test 40–45 min.
- Administer Chapter 12 Test. Select from Testing Program, Alternative Assessment Guide, Test Generator, or Standardized Assessment Tutor.

Suggested Lesson Plans 90-Minute Block Schedule

Block 1

CHAPTER OPENER 10 min.
- Photo Flash!, ATE, p. 343
- Present Chapter Objectives, p. 343.
- Math Link, ATE, p. 343

MISE EN TRAIN 45 min.
- Preteaching Vocabulary, ATE, p. 344
- Presenting **Mise en train,** ATE, p. 345
- Do Activities 1–4, p. 346.

PREMIERE ETAPE

Comment dit-on... ?, p. 348 30 min.
- Presenting **Comment dit-on... ?,** ATE, p. 348
- Play Audio CD for Activity 7, p. 348.
- Activity 8, p. 348

Wrap-Up 5 min.
- **Note culturelle,** p. 348

Homework Options

Cahier d'activités, Acts. 1–4, pp. 133–135

Block 2

PREMIERE ETAPE

Quick Review 5 min.
- Ask questions about the map on page 347. Have students answer the questions, using expressions from **Comment dit-on... ?,** p. 348.

Comment dit-on... ?, p. 348 10 min.
- Do Activity 9, p. 349.

Vocabulaire, p. 349 20 min.
- Presenting **Vocabulaire,** ATE, p. 349
- TPR, ATE, p. 349
- Play Audio CD for Activity 10, p. 349.
- Do Activity 11, p. 350.

Vocabulaire, p. 350 20 min.
- Presenting **Vocabulaire,** ATE, p. 350
- Do Activity 13, p. 351.
- Play Audio CD for Activity 14, p. 351.
- Do Activity 15, p. 351.

PANORAMA CULTUREL 15 min.
- Presenting **Panorama Culturel,** ATE, p. 357
- Have students discuss the questions in **Qu'en penses-tu?,** p. 357.

DEUXIEME ETAPE

Vocabulaire, p. 353 15 min.
- Presenting **Vocabulaire,** ATE, p. 353
- Do Activity 19, p. 353.
- Presenting **Note de grammaire,** ATE, p. 354

Wrap-Up 5 min.
- TPR, ATE, p. 353

Homework Options

Have students study for Quiz 12-1.
Pupil's Edition, Act. 20, p. 354
Grammaire supplémentaire, Acts. 1–4, pp. 364–365
Cahier d'activités, Acts. 5–10, pp. 135–138
Travaux pratiques de grammaire, Acts. 1–11, pp. 98–102

Block 3

PREMIERE ETAPE

Quick Review 10 min.
- Communicative Activities 12-1A and 12-1B, Activities for Communication, pp. 67–68

Quiz 12-1 20 min.
- Administer Quiz 12-1A or 12-1B.

DEUXIEME ETAPE

Comment dit-on... ?, p. 354 25 min.
- Presenting **Comment dit-on... ?,** ATE, p. 354
- Do Activities 21–22, p. 354.

Vocabulaire, p. 355 25 min.
- Presenting **Vocabulaire,** ATE, p. 355
- Activity 23, p. 355
- Play Audio CD for Activity 24, p. 355.

Wrap-Up 10 min.
- Game: **Je m'en souviens!,** ATE, p. 365

Homework Options

Cahier d'activités, Acts. 11–12, pp. 138–139
Travaux pratiques de grammaire, Act. 12, p. 103

One-Stop Planner CD-ROM

For alternative lesson plans by chapter section, to create your own customized plans, or to preview all resources available for this chapter, use the **One-Stop Planner CD-ROM,** Disc 3.

For additional homework suggestions, see activities accompanied by this symbol throughout the chapter.

Block 4

DEUXIEME ETAPE

Quick Review 10 min.

- Teaching Transparency 12-2, using Suggestion #2 in Suggestions for Using Teaching Transparency 12-2

Comment dit-on... ?, p. 356 25 min.

- **Note culturelle,** p. 356
- Presenting **Comment dit-on... ?,** ATE, p. 356
- Do Activity 25, p. 356.

RENCONTRE CULTURELLE 25 min.

- Ask students if they know any British words or expressions that are different from American English words.
- Presenting **Rencontre culturelle,** ATE, p. 361
- Read and discuss **Qu'en penses-tu?** and **Savais-tu que... ?,** p. 361.
- Thinking Critically: Analyzing, ATE, p. 361

TROISIEME ETAPE

Comment dit-on... ?, p. 358 20 min.

- Presenting **Comment dit-on... ?,** ATE, p. 358
- Play Audio CD for Activity 29, p. 359.

Wrap-Up 10 min.

- Teaching Transparency 12-D, using Suggestion #3 from Suggestions for Using Teaching Transparency 12-D

Homework Options

Have students study for Quiz 12-2.
Cahier d'activités, Acts. 13–16, pp. 139–140
Travaux pratiques de grammaire, Acts. 13–14, p. 103

Block 5

DEUXIEME ETAPE

Quick Review 10 min.

- Communicative Activity 12-2, Activities for Communication, pp. 69–70

Quiz 12-2 20 min.

- Administer Quiz 12-2A or 12-2B.

TROISIEME ETAPE

Comment dit-on... ?, p. 358 10 min.

- Teaching Transparency 12-3, using suggestion #1 on Suggestions for Using Teaching Transparency 12-3

Grammaire, p. 359 40 min.

- Presenting **Grammaire,** ATE, p. 359
- Do Activity 30, p. 359.
- Do Activity 31, p. 360.

Wrap-Up 10 min.

- Activities for Communication, pp. 71–72, Communicative Activity 12-3

Homework Options

Have students study for Quiz 12-3.
Grammaire supplémentaire, Acts. 5–6, p. 366
Cahier d'activités, Acts. 17–19, pp. 140–142
Travaux pratiques de grammaire, Acts. 15–20, pp. 104–107

Block 6

TROISIEME ETAPE

Quick Review 15 min.

- Additional Practice, ATE, p. 366

Quiz 12-3 20 min.

- Administer Quiz 12-3A or 12-3B.

MISE EN PRATIQUE 25 min.

- Do Activities 1–3, p. 368.
- Play Audio CD for Activity 2, p. 368.
- Do Activity 3, p. 368.

LISONS! 30 min.

- **Stratégie pour lire,** p. 362
- Do Activities A–G, pp. 362–363.

Homework Options

Que sais-je?, p. 370
Pupil's Edition, Activity 4, p. 369
CD-ROM/Interactive Games
Study for Chapter 12 Test.

Block 7

MISE EN PRATIQUE

Quick Review 15 min.

- Game: **Cercle de mots,** ATE, p. 369

Chapter Review

- Review Chapter 12. Choose from **Grammaire supplémentaire,** Grammar Tutor for Students of French, Activities for Communication, Listening Activities, Interactive CD-ROM Tutor, or **Jeux interactifs.**

Chapter Test 40–45 min.

- Administer Chapter 12 Test. Select from Testing Program, Alternative Assessment Guide, Test Generator, or Standardized Assessment Tutor.

Chapter Opener

CHAPITRE 12

One-Stop Planner CD-ROM

For resource information, see the **One-Stop Planner,** Disc 3.

Pacing Tips

Chapter 12 is a review chapter set within a new cultural context. While students will recognize most of the functions and grammatical structures, there is some new vocabulary as well as new cultural information for them to master for the chapter quizzes and test. After Chapter 12, you might administer the Final Exam. For suggested Lesson Plans and timing suggestions, see pages 341I–341L.

Meeting the Standards

Communication

- Asking for and giving information; giving directions, p. 348
- Complaining; expressing discouragement and offering encouragement, p. 354
- Asking for and giving advice, p. 356
- Relating a series of events; describing people and places, p. 358

Culture

- Culture Note, pp. 342, 348
- Note culturelle, pp. 348, 356
- Panorama Culturel, p. 357
- Rencontre culturelle, p. 361

Connections

- Multicultural Link, p. 356
- Math Link, pp. 343, 352
- Science Link, p. 356
- Music Link, p. 359
- Literature Link, p. 363

Comparisons

- Thinking Critically: Analyzing, p. 361
- Thinking Critically: Comparing and Contrasting, p. 361

Communities

- Career Path, p. 344

Cultures and Communities

Culture Notes

- The **parc de la Jacques-Cartier** is open from the end of May to mid-October. There are eleven semi-equipped or primitive camping sites in the park. Rock climbing, hiking, and mountain biking are available throughout the park season. Canoeing, kayaking, and mini-rafting are permitted on the river, and equipment can be rented. The Information Center offers guided nature activities, slide shows, lectures, and exhibits.
- **La rivière Jacques-Cartier** is the major river running through the park. Fishing is allowed from May until September with a permit. The Information Center offers guided observations of salmon and trout during spawning season in mid-October. There are over 100 kilometers (62 miles) of hiking and biking trails in the park.

Le Draveur Nord

CHAPITRE 12

A la belle étoile

Objectives

In this chapter you will review and practice how to

Première étape

- ask for and give information
- give directions

Deuxième étape

- complain
- express discouragement and offer encouragement
- ask for and give advice

Troisième étape

- relate a series of events
- describe people and places

internet

go.hrw.com
ADRESSE: go.hrw.com
MOT-CLE:
WA3 QUEBEC-12

◀ **Au Québec, il y a des forêts magnifiques!**

Chapter Opener

CHAPITRE 12

Focusing on Outcomes

Help students recall some of the expressions they learned in previous chapters that accomplish the chapter outcomes. NOTE: The self-check activities in **Que sais-je?** on page 370 help students assess their achievement of the objectives.

Photo Flash!

Paul, Denis, René, Michèle, and Francine stop during their hike to admire the beauty of the **parc de la Jacques-Cartier.** The park, located 40 kilometers north of Quebec City, is one of sixteen provincial parks in Quebec. It was created in 1981 in order to preserve the natural beauty of the area, which comprises 670 square kilometers. The maple tree is the Canadian national tree. The manufacturing of maple syrup is a major Canadian industry.

Chapter Sequence

Connections and Comparisons

Math Link

Have students convert the distance and area in the **Photo Flash!** from kilometers to miles. One kilometer equals 0.62 miles. To convert the distance from kilometers to miles, multiply the number of kilometers by 0.62. (The park is 24.8 miles north of Quebec.) You might also have students convert the distance between two cities in their area from miles to kilometers. One mile equals 1.609 kilometers. To convert miles to kilometers, multiply the number of miles by 1.609 (or divide the number of miles by 0.62).

Language Note

The article **la** is used in **parc de la Jacques-Cartier** because it refers to **la rivière Jacques-Cartier.**

Mise en train

CHAPITRE 12

Teaching Resources
pp. 344–346

PRINT 
- Lesson Planner, p. 56
- Video Guide, pp. 80, 82
- Cahier d'activités, p. 133

MEDIA  
- One-Stop Planner, Disc 3
- Video Program
  Mise en train
  Videocassette 4, 31:52–39:50
  Videocassette 5 (captioned version), 1:41:25–1:49:23
  Suite
  Videocassette 4, 39:54–47:08
  Videocassette 5 (captioned version), 1:49:27–1:56:41
- DVD Tutor, Disc 2
- Audio Compact Discs, CD 12, Trs. 1–2
- **Mise en train** Transparencies

Career Path

A heightened awareness of the importance of preserving the environment has led to the development of many new jobs in the field of ecology. Professionals in this field, as well as in biology and climatology, work to lessen the causes and effects of tropical deforestation. Ecotourism has become a popular way for tourists to visit these beautiful regions without causing harm to their delicate environments. Have students name some countries with tropical forests. Ask students what languages would be important to know for environmentalists in these regions.

This is an abridged version of the video episode.

MISE EN TRAIN • *Promenons-nous dans les bois*

CD 12 Trs. 1–2

Stratégie pour comprendre
Have you ever kept a journal on vacation before? What did you record in it? What do you think happened to René and his friends?

Michèle
Francine

René

Mme Desrochers

Paul

Denis

Le matin, au camping du parc de la Jacques-Cartier. René, Francine, Michèle, Denis et Paul s'apprêtent à partir pour une randonnée. Les parents de Francine, M. et Mme Desrochers, vont rester au camping. René, lui, commence son journal.

1

26 septembre.
8H15 - Tout le monde est prêt. On a l'eau, le pique-nique et des allumettes. Moi, j'ai mon appareil-photo. Mme Desrochers nous a donné une lampe de poche. A mon avis, ce n'est pas la peine. On va rentrer avant la nuit.

Mme Desrochers Vous avez tout?
Francine On devrait peut-être prendre une lampe de poche?
René Oh, c'est pas la peine. On va rentrer avant la nuit.
Francine La nuit tombe tôt. Moi, je préférerais en avoir une.
Michèle Bien. On y va?
Paul On y va!
René J'arrive!

2 **Mme Desrochers** Tiens, Francine. On ne sait jamais.

Preteaching Vocabulary

Guessing words from context

In the **Mise en train** story, students will see vocabulary related to nature. Have students first identify what types of vocabulary they would need to describe an outdoor adventure in a park. (Animals, nature descriptions, directions, camping equipment, etc.) Then have students identify vocabulary words from the text on pages 344–345 for the categories they suggested. Have them give examples from the context that helped them reach their conclusions.

STANDARDS: 1.2, 5.1

12H30 – Nous avons marché toute la matinée. Une balade superbe. C'est magnifique ici. C'est tellement calme et tellement beau. Il y a autant de bruit qu'à Québec, mais c'est le bruit de la nature : le chant des oiseaux, les coin-coin des canards... Et si on écoutait bien, on entendrait peut-être le grognement d'un ours!... A propos d'animaux, Michèle et Denis se disputent... comme d'habitude.

3
Francine Eh, vous avez vu! Superbe, non? Qu'en pensez-vous?
Michèle C'est magnifique.
Denis Il doit y avoir des tas d'animaux. C'est idéal pour la chasse.

3H10 – Si on veut arriver avant la nuit, il faut partir maintenant. Paul est fatigué. Il n'est pas habitué à ces longues marches... Francine veut prendre un raccourci. C'est une bonne idée, mais on risque de se perdre! Allons, faisons confiance à Francine!

4
Michèle Tu n'as pas honte? Tu devrais plutôt préserver les animaux.
Denis Il y a plus d'un million d'orignaux par ici. Un orignal de plus ou de moins, hein? Qu'est-ce que ça fait?
Michèle Si tout le monde pensait comme toi, il n'y aurait plus d'orignaux ici!
Denis Et si tout le monde pensait comme toi, il n'y aurait que des orignaux!

5
Francine On devrait peut-être prendre un raccourci?
René Tu as raison, il est déjà tard. Mais il ne faudrait pas se perdre.
Francine T'inquiète pas. Si on marche vers le sud, on ne peut pas se perdre.

5H20 – Ça y est! Nous sommes perdus! Nous ne savons plus où nous sommes. C'est malin!... Paul a faim. Francine est embêtée. Et Denis est ravi! Lui, il adore l'aventure! Il faudrait trouver une solution. On ne peut pas dormir ici. Et si on continuait à marcher? Paul ne veut pas. Il a mal aux pieds. Je pourrais les laisser ici et chercher le chemin. Mais si je me perdais? Ce n'est peut-être pas une très bonne idée... Alors? Que faire?

6
René Alors, qu'est-ce que tu proposes, Francine?
Francine Je ne sais pas trop. Si on continue, on risque de se perdre encore plus. Si on reste ici, on risque d'avoir très froid et mes parents vont s'inquiéter. Je ne sais pas trop quoi faire.

Cahier d'activités, p. 133, Act. 1

Using the Captioned Video/DVD

If students have difficulty understanding French spoken at a normal speed, use Videocassette 5 to allow students to see the French captions for ***Promenons-nous dans les bois*** and ***Promenons-nous dans les bois (suite).*** Hearing the language and watching the story will reduce anxiety about the new language and facilitate comprehension. The reinforcement of seeing the written vocabulary words as they watch the gestures and actions will help prepare students to do the comprehension activities on page 346.

NOTE: The *DVD Tutor* contains captions for all sections of the *Video Program.*

Mise en train

CHAPITRE 12

Presenting Mise en train

Have students view the video with their books closed and then summarize the story in English. You might also present the Preteaching Vocabulary suggestion on page 344. Then, play the audio recording and have students read along as they listen. Finally, ask the questions in Activity 1 on page 346.

Mise en train Transparencies

Kinesthetic Learners

Have groups of six act out the dialogue in the **Mise en train.**

Mise en train (suite)

When the story continues, Francine and her friends decide to build a fire to stay warm. Denis leaves to go fishing and returns later with a small fish. A park ranger finds everyone seated around the fire and informs them that building fires and fishing without a permit are against park regulations! They're unaware that they are only a short distance from the campground, and the ranger leads them back, where they find Francine's parents anxiously waiting.

Mise en train

CHAPITRE 12

Auditory/Visual Learners

2 Have students work in pairs. One student reads a sentence from the journal entries. The other student finds the appropriate journal entry and tells at what time René wrote that sentence.

Tactile Learners

3 Have students write the characters' names on a sheet of paper and the sentences on small strips of paper. Have them place the sentences next to the name of the person who might have said them. Then, have them write additional clues to the characters' identities on strips of paper. Partners will place the strips next to the names of the appropriate people.

Answers

1
1. at Jacques-Cartier Park
2. preparing to go on a hike
3. whether people should hunt
4. The campers get lost.

4
1. Superbe, non? Qu'en pensez-vous?
2. C'est magnifique ici. C'est tellement calme. Tellement beau.
3. On devrait peut-être prendre une lampe de poche? On devrait peut-être prendre un raccourci? Si on marche... ?
4. Tu as raison. C'est une bonne idée.
5. Ce n'est peut-être pas une bonne idée. Ce n'est pas la peine.
6. Qu'est-ce que tu proposes?

These activities check for comprehension only. Students should not yet be expected to produce language modeled in **Mise en train.**

1 Tu as compris? See answers below.

1. Where are the young people?
2. What are they doing?
3. What do Michèle and Denis disagree about?
4. What happens at the end of ***Promenons-nous dans les bois?***

2 Il est quelle heure?

A quelle heure est-ce que René a écrit les phrases suivantes dans son journal?

1. Ça y est! Nous sommes perdus! à cinq heures vingt
2. Mme Desrochers nous a donné une lampe de poche. à huit heures quinze
3. A propos d'animaux, Michèle et Denis se disputent... comme d'habitude. à midi et demi
4. Il faudrait trouver une solution. à cinq heures vingt
5. Allons, faisons confiance à Francine! à trois heures dix
6. C'est tellement calme et tellement beau. à midi et demi

3 Qui suis-je?

Michèle

Denis

René

Francine

Paul

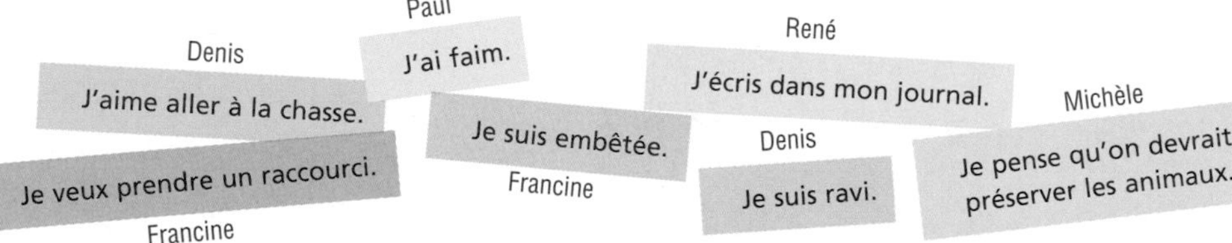

4 Cherche les expressions See answers below.

What do the people in ***Promenons-nous dans les bois*** say or write to . . .

1. ask for an opinion?
2. describe a place?
3. make a suggestion?
4. agree?
5. disagree?
6. ask for a suggestion?

5 Et maintenant, à toi

A ton avis, qu'est-ce qui va se passer maintenant? Imagine que tu fais du camping ou une randonnée et que tu te perds. Quelle est ta réaction?

Comprehension Check

Teaching Suggestion

4 Once students have found the answers to this activity, have them call out one of the expressions at random and ask another student to name the function it accomplishes.

Captioned Video/DVD

5 Have small groups write their own ending to the story. Then, play the captioned version of ***Promenons-nous dans les bois (suite)*** on Videocassette 5 or DVD Disc 2, so groups can compare their endings to what really happened.

STANDARDS: 1.2, 2.2

Objectives Asking for and giving information; giving directions

WA3 QUEBEC-12

6 **Destination nature** Possible answers:

Lisons

1. What geographical features do you see on the map? What cities? 1. the St. Lawrence river, lakes, mountains . . . ; Québec, Montréal, Alma, Matane . . .
2. What animals would you expect to find in Quebec? whales, lobsters, geese, bears, deer . . .
3. What types of parks can you find in Quebec? recreational parks and nature preserves

Communication for All Students

Challenge

- After students complete Activity 6, ask questions about the map: **Combien de parcs voyez-vous? (seize) Il y a combien de villes sur cette carte? (huit) Comment s'appelle le lac qu'on voit sur la carte? (le lac Saint-Jean) Qu'est-ce qu'il y a au sud de la ville de Nouvelle? (le parc de Miguasha)**
- For extra listening practice, make true-false statements about the locations of cities, lakes, and parks. **(Gaspé est à l'ouest de Matane. (faux) Le parc de Frontenac est au sud de Thetford Mines. (vrai))**

Première étape

CHAPITRE 12

Teaching Resources
pp. 347–351

PRINT

- Lesson Planner, p. 57
- TPR Storytelling Book, pp. 88–89
- Listening Activities, pp. 91–92, 95
- Activities for Communication, pp. 67–68, 130, 133, 159–160
- Travaux pratiques de grammaire, pp. 98–99
- Grammar Tutor for Students of French, Chapter 12
- Cahier d'activités, pp. 134–136
- Testing Program, pp. 301–304
- Alternative Assessment Guide, p. 43
- Student Make-Up Assignments, Chapter 12

MEDIA 

- One-Stop Planner
- Audio Compact Discs, CD 12, Trs. 3–5, 13, 24–25
- Teaching Transparencies: 12-1, 12-A, 12-B; **Grammaire supplémentaire** Answers; Travaux pratiques de grammaire Answers
- Interactive CD-ROM Tutor, Disc 3

Bell Work

Write the following descriptions on the board or on a transparency and have students identify the corresponding characters from the **Mise en train.**

1. Il adore l'aventure.
2. Ses parents vont s'inquiéter.
3. Elle n'est pas d'accord avec Denis.
4. Il n'est pas habitué aux longues marches.
5. Elle propose un raccourci.
6. Il écrit dans son journal.

(*Answers:* 1. Denis 2. Francine 3. Michèle 4. Paul 5. Francine 6. René)

STANDARDS: 1.2

Première étape

CHAPITRE 12

Teaching Resources
pp. 347–351

PRINT 

- Lesson Planner, p. 57
- TPR Storytelling Book, pp. 88–89
- Listening Activities, pp. 91–92, 95
- Activities for Communication, pp. 67–68, 130, 133, 159–160
- Travaux pratiques de grammaire, pp. 98–99
- Grammar Tutor for Students of French, Chapter 12
- Cahier d'activités, pp. 134–136
- Testing Program, pp. 301–304
- Alternative Assessment Guide, p. 43
- Student Make-Up Assignments, Chapter 12

MEDIA

- One-Stop Planner
- Audio Compact Discs, CD 12, Trs. 3–5, 13, 24–25
- Teaching Transparencies: 12-1, 12-A, 12-B; **Grammaire supplémentaire** Answers; Travaux pratiques de grammaire Answers
- Interactive CD-ROM Tutor, Disc 3

Presenting Comment dit-on... ?

Point out a national park on a map of the United States. Describe the park and the surrounding area, using the expressions in **Comment dit-on... ?** Re-enter the vocabulary for nature and activities that students know **(les moustiques, une chute d'eau, une île, une rivière, la forêt, faire du vélo, aller à la pêche, faire du ski, faire de la natation, se promener).** Finally, point out another park and make true-false statements about it, using the new expressions.

Comment dit-on...?

Asking for and giving information; giving directions

To ask for information:

Où se trouve le parc de la Jacques-Cartier?
Qu'est-ce qu'il y a à voir au parc?
Qu'est-ce qu'il y a à faire?

To give information:

Le parc **se trouve** près du lac Saint-Jean.
Il y a des forêts magnifiques et beaucoup d'animaux.
On peut faire des pique-niques, des safaris d'observation,...

To give directions:

C'est au nord/au sud/à l'est/à l'ouest de la ville de Québec.
It's to the north/south/east/west of . . .
C'est dans le nord/le sud/l'est/l'ouest du Québec.
It's in the northern/southern/eastern/western part of . . .

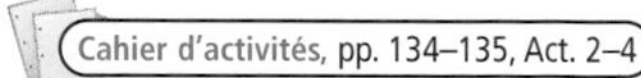
Cahier d'activités, pp. 134–135, Act. 2–4

7 **Les parcs nationaux** See scripts and answers on p. 341G.

CD 12 Tr. 3

Ecoutons Stéphane est à Montréal. Il essaie de choisir quel parc il veut visiter. Ecoute les informations que l'office de tourisme lui donne et décide de quel parc on parle. Aide-toi du plan à la page 347.

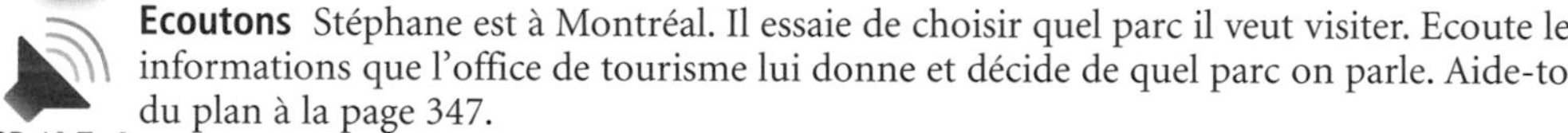

Note culturelle

Il y a beaucoup d'endroits sauvages à visiter au Québec. Un parc fameux, le parc de la Jacques-Cartier, tient son nom de l'explorateur Jacques Cartier qui a découvert et apporté au roi de France en 1534 ce qui est maintenant le Canada. Dans le parc vous pouvez suivre la route des draveurs, hommes qui transportaient, sur les rivières, les trappeurs et les bûcherons venus faire fortune après que Cartier ait dressé la carte de la région. Pendant l'été, vous pouvez aussi faire de la pêche avec un permis.

8 **C'est tellement beau!**

Parlons Demande à ton/ta camarade où sont les parcs suivants et ce qu'on peut y faire et y voir. Il/Elle va te répondre en s'aidant du plan à la page 347. Puis, changez de rôles.

le parc du Mont-Tremblant

le parc du Saguenay

le parc de la Jacques-Cartier

Cultures and Communities

Culture Note

Le parc du Mont-Tremblant, created in 1895, is used throughout the year. The most popular winter activities include skiing, snowmobiling **(de la motoneige),** and snowshoeing. In the summer, camping and canoeing are popular. Moose hunting in season is permitted. There are twenty-two cottages available for rent, as well as primitive campgrounds at **lac Monroe, lac Chat,** and **lac Lajoie.**

Language Note

Remind students to use definite articles when naming countries and provinces, but not cities. Therefore, **du Québec** and **au Québec** refer to the province of Quebec, but **de Québec** and **à Québec** refer to Quebec City.

On pourrait aller...

Parlons Ton ami(e) et toi, vous essayez de décider où vous voulez aller en vacances. Suggère un endroit et réponds aux questions de ton/ta camarade qui te demande ce qu'il y a à voir et à faire là-bas. Puis, changez de rôle.

au Québec | à Paris | à Abidjan | à la Martinique | en Touraine | en Provence

You've learned a lot of words and phrases. To review them, remember vocabulary in thematic groups. Think of a topic or situation that you've studied, such as making suggestions about what to see and do in Martinique. Then, list the vocabulary and phrases that you would need in that situation. Keep the lists you make and use them to study for your next test—and your final exam!

Vocabulaire

Qu'est-ce qu'on peut voir dans les parcs du Québec?

un orignal

un ours

un loup

un écureuil

un renard

un raton laveur

une mouffette

un canard

Travaux pratiques de grammaire, p. 98, Act. 1–3

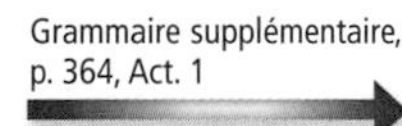

Cahier d'activités, p. 135, Act. 5

Grammaire supplémentaire, p. 364, Act. 1

10 Les animaux du parc

See scripts and answers on p. 341G.

Ecoutons Francine est revenue d'une excursion dans le parc de la Jacques-Cartier. Quels animaux est-ce qu'elle a vus?

CD 12 Tr. 4

Communication for All Students

Slower Pace

9 To prepare students for this activity, have them recall what there is to see and do in each of the places listed in the word box. Write these on the board for students to refer to as they decide where to go on vacation.

Tactile/Visual Learners

10 Have students trace the photos in the **Vocabulaire** or draw quick sketches of each of the animals. Then, play the recording and have students put a check mark next to the pictures of the animals they hear mentioned.

Première étape

CHAPITRE 12

Building on Previous Skills

9 Before they begin this activity, have students recall the expressions they learned in Chapter 8 for making and responding to suggestions. **(Si on allait... ? Si on visitait... ? D'accord. Bonne idée! Bof! Ça m'est égal. Non, je préfère... ; Non, je ne veux pas.)**

Presenting Vocabulaire

Gather or draw pictures of these animals. You might also use *Teaching Transparency 12-A.* Show a picture, name the animal, and tell students a little about it. **(Il est très féroce.)** Then, make animal noises or mime the actions of each animal and have students identify it.

TPR Name an animal and have students show their comprehension by making the appropriate animal call, by miming an action typical of that animal, or by going to the board and drawing it.

Language Notes

- The following are common French idiomatic expressions involving animals: **vivre comme un ours** *(to live like a hermit);* **vendre la peau de l'ours avant de l'avoir tué** *(to count your chickens before they're hatched);* **avoir une faim de loup** *(to be hungry as a wolf);* **avancer à pas de loup** *(to move stealthily);* **Il faut hurler avec des loups** *(When in Rome, do as the Romans do);* **être futé(e) comme un renard** *(to be sly as a fox);* **un canard** *(a false rumor);* **faire un froid de canard** *(to be freezing cold);* **ne pas casser quatre pattes à un canard** *(not to be worth writing home about).*
- **Mon petit canard** is a term of endearment that is often used with children.

Teaching Resources
pp. 347–351

PRINT 

- Lesson Planner, p. 57
- TPR Storytelling Book, pp. 88–89
- Listening Activities, pp. 91–92, 95
- Activities for Communication, pp. 67–68, 130, 133, 159–160
- Travaux pratiques de grammaire, pp. 98–99
- Grammar Tutor for Students of French, Chapter 12
- Cahier d'activités, pp. 134–136
- Testing Program, pp. 301–304
- Alternative Assessment Guide, p. 43
- Student Make-Up Assignments, Chapter 12

MEDIA

- One-Stop Planner
- Audio Compact Discs, CD 12, Trs. 3–5, 13, 24–25
- Teaching Transparencies: 12-1, 12-A, 12-B; **Grammaire supplémentaire** Answers; Travaux pratiques de grammaire Answers
- Interactive CD-ROM Tutor, Disc 3

Presenting Vocabulaire

Draw and number pictures of each activity on a transparency. Project the transparency, say the captions at random, and ask students to try to match each caption to the number of its corresponding picture. Then, ask questions, such as **Tu as déjà fait une randonnée en skis? Où est-ce qu'on peut faire du canotage?**

11 Qui suis-je?

Lisons **1.** une mouffette **2.** un renard **3.** un raton laveur **4.** un ours **5.** un canard

1. Je suis noir et blanc et j'ai une grande queue. Certains disent que je sens mauvais.
2. J'ai le museau et les oreilles pointus et une grande queue rousse. J'adore les poules!
3. Je suis gris et noir. J'ai une queue à rayures et j'ai l'air de porter un masque.
4. Je suis noir ou brun et les gens ont peur de moi parce que je suis grand et fort.
5. J'habite les lacs et les rivières. Les enfants adorent me donner à manger.

12 Et toi?

Parlons Réponds aux questions suivantes, puis interviewe un(e) camarade.

1. Quels animaux du Vocabulaire à la page 349 est-ce que tu as déjà vus?
2. Où est-ce que tu les as vus?
3. Est-ce que tu leur as donné à manger?
4. Quels animaux est-ce que tu n'as jamais vus?
5. Si tu pouvais être un de ces animaux, lequel choisirais-tu? Pourquoi?

Vocabulaire

Qu'est-ce qu'on peut faire au Québec? On peut...

faire du camping.

faire du canotage.

faire du vélo de montagne.

faire une randonnée en skis.

Cette liste ne représente pas tous les parcs du Québec.

LES PARCS QUÉBÉCOIS

Activités et services offerts dans les parcs québécois	Activités															Services							
	Baignade	Canotage, canot-camping	Escalade	Golf	Interprétation	Observation	Pêche	Randonnée à bicyclette	Randonnée à raquettes	Randonnée à skis (courte)	Randonnée à skis (longue)	Randonnée équestre	Randonnée pédestre	Ski alpin	Voile, planche à voile	Aire de pique-nique	Camping	Chalet	Location d'équipement (été)	Location d'équipement (hiver)	Rampe de mise à l'eau	Refuge	Restauration
Bas-Saint-Laurent – Gaspésie																							
1. Bic					✓	✓		✓	❄				✓		✓	✓	✓	✓	✓		✓		✓
2. Gaspésie		✓			✓	✓	✓	✓	❄	❄	❄		✓	✓		✓	✓	✓	✓	❄			✓
3. Île-Bonaventure-et-du-Rocher-Percé					✓	✓							✓			✓					✓		✓
4. Miguasha					✓								✓			✓							✓
Saguenay – Lac-Saint-Jean																							
5. Pointe-Taillon	✓	✓			✓	✓		✓					✓			✓	✓		✓				
6. Saguenay					✓	✓	✓		❄		❄	✓	✓			✓	✓		✓			✓	✓
Parc marin du Saguenay – Saint-Laurent					✓	✓															✓		
Québec																							
7. Grands-Jardins		✓	✓		✓	✓	✓		❄	❄	❄		✓			✓	✓	✓	✓		✓	✓	
8. Jacques-Cartier		✓	✓		✓	✓	✓	✓			❄	✓	✓			✓	✓	✓	✓			✓	

faire une randonnée en raquettes.

faire une randonnée pédestre.

Travaux pratiques de grammaire, p. 99, Act. 4–6

Cahier d'activités, p. 135, Act. 6

Grammaire supplémentaire, p. 365, Act. 2–3

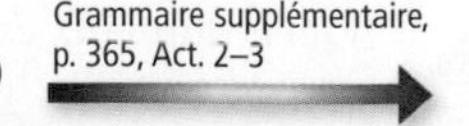

Connections and Comparisons

Language-to-Language

Representations of animal noises differ from language to language. Cats say *Meow!* in English, but they say **Miaou! Miaou!** in French. Dogs say *Bow Wow!* or *Ruff! Ruff!* in English, **Ouah! Ouah!** in French, and **Bau! Bau!** in Italian. And while roosters say *Cockadoodledoo!* in English, they say **Cocorico!** in French, and **Kikeriki!** in German. Ducks in French say **Coin-coin!** as opposed to *Quack! Quack!* Ask speakers of Spanish or other languages in your class how animal sounds are expressed in their native languages.

STANDARDS: 1.1, 4.1, 5.2

13 Vrai ou faux?

Lisons Regarde le tableau à la page 350 et décide si les phrases suivantes sont vraies ou fausses.

1. On peut se baigner au parc du Saguenay. faux
2. On peut faire du camping et de la pêche au parc du Miguasha. faux **3.** vrai
3. Au parc du Pointe-Taillon, on peut faire une randonnée pédestre et du canotage.
4. On peut faire une randonnée en raquettes au parc du Saguenay, mais on ne peut pas faire de canotage. vrai
5. Au parc de la Gaspésie, on ne peut pas faire de ski alpin, mais on peut faire une randonnée en skis. faux
6. Dans tous les parcs, il est possible de faire un pique-nique et une randonnée pédestre. vrai

14 Mon week-end au parc See scripts and answers on p. 341G.

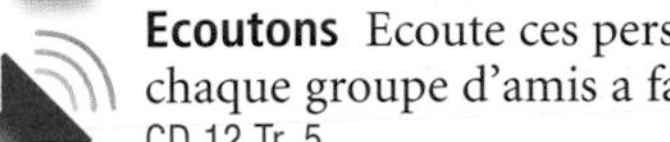

Ecoutons Ecoute ces personnes qui parlent de leurs week-ends. Fais une liste de ce que chaque groupe d'amis a fait.

CD 12 Tr. 5

15 Un week-end sportif

Parlons/Ecrivons Des groupes de copains font du camping. Compare leurs activités. Qu'est-ce qu'ils font de semblable? Et de différent? See answers below.

Jules et Romain

Marie et Jeanne

16 Moi, j'aime bien...

Ecrivons Fais une liste des activités que tu aimerais pratiquer si tu allais au Québec. Quels sont les parcs qui offrent ces activités?

17 Si on allait... ?

Parlons En utilisant les listes que vous avez faites pour l'activité 16, choisissez un parc québécois où votre classe de français peut aller pour le voyage de fin d'année. Créez une publicité pour le parc pour persuader le reste de la classe d'y aller.

Communication for All Students

Challenge

14 Have students listen a second time to determine what the groups were *not* able to do. Challenge the students to write in French the activities mentioned.
(Answers: **1. de la natation, du camping; 2. du vélo de montagne, du canotage, se baigner; 3. du ski alpin)**

Première étape

CHAPITRE 12

Additional Practice

As a homework assignment, have students imagine they went on a camping trip, and draw pictures of the activities they did and the animals they saw, or they may choose to cut them out of magazines or catalogues. In class, have students pass their drawings or pictures to a partner, who will tell or write what the classmate did and saw. **(Il/Elle a fait du vélo de montagne, et il/elle a vu un renard.)**

Teaching Suggestion

To close this **étape**, have students trace the map on page 347, including all the parks and towns. Then, have them choose four parks, four activities, and four animals and tell a partner where they went, what they did, and what they saw in each park. **(Je suis allé(e) au parc du Bic. Il se trouve au sud de Matane. Là, j'ai fait une randonnée pédestre, et j'y ai vu un orignal!)** The partner will sketch what the student did or saw next to the park mentioned on his or her map.

Assess

- Testing Program, pp. 301–304
  Quiz 12-1A, Quiz 12-1B
  Audio CD 12, Tr. 13
- Student Make-Up Assignments, Chapter 12, Alternative Quiz
- Alternative Assessment Guide, p. 43

Answers

15 *Tous:* la pêche, une randonnée pédestre, un pique-nique; *Les garçons:* du canotage, des photos; *Les filles:* du vélo de montagne, de la natation

Teaching Resources
pp. 352–356

PRINT

- Lesson Planner, p. 58
- TPR Storytelling Book, pp. 90–91
- Listening Activities, pp. 92, 96
- Activities for Communication, pp. 69–70, 131, 133, 159–160
- Travaux pratiques de grammaire, pp. 100–103
- Grammar Tutor for Students of French, Chapter 12
- Cahier d'activités, pp. 137–139
- Testing Program, pp. 305–308
- Alternative Assessment Guide, p. 43
- Student Make-Up Assignments, Chapter 12

MEDIA 

- One-Stop Planner
- Audio Compact Discs, CD 12, Trs. 6, 14, 26–27
- Teaching Transparencies: 12-2, 12-C, 12-D; **Grammaire supplémentaire** Answers; Travaux pratiques de grammaire Answers
- Interactive CD-ROM Tutor, Disc 3

Bell Work
Have students describe a national park in the United States. Have them give the location and tell about the activities they can do there and the animals they might see.

Language Note
Students might want to know the following vocabulary from the advertisement: **une poignée** *(handle);* **un moulinet** *(reel);* **une cartouche** *(cartridge);* **le sol** *(floor);* **plié** *(folded);* **le toit** *(roof);* **matelassé** *(quilted);* **une fermeture éclair** *(zipper);* **une poche** *(pocket);* **des bretelles ajustables** *(adjustable straps);* **l'épaisseur** *(thickness).*

Deuxième étape

Objectives Complaining; expressing discouragement and offering encouragement; asking for and giving advice

WA3 QUEBEC-12

AU BON CAMPEUR
① TUE-INSECTES
Appréciez une soirée à l'extérieur sans moustiques grâce à ce tue-insectes portable.
Hauteur : 25 cm
4 watts, 220 volts
8, 80 €
② SAC DE COUCHAGE
Dimensions : 2 m x 80 cm
Extérieur nylon, intérieur coton. Fermeture éclair.
Peut être aussi utilisé comme couverture.
Six coloris.
Lavable à la machine.
36, 51 €
③ CANNE A PECHE
Poignée et bobine en plastique et moulinet en métal. Vendue avec un flotteur et un mini-lancer téléscopique.
7, 00 €
④ LAMPE DE CAMPING
Indispensable pour les soirées autour du feu de camp.
80 watts, nécessite une cartouche 200 grs.
14, 17 €
⑤ SAC A DOS
Parfait pour emporter tout son matériel de randonnée. Nylon renforcé, fermeture éclair, cinq poches à fermetures velcro. Bretelles ajustables et matelassées pour votre confort.
Existe en six couleurs.
22, 71 €
⑥ TENTE A AVANCEE
Trois places. Intérieur et toit en nylon.
Sol en mousse de polyéthylène.
Deux fenêtres.
Dimensions pliée : 35 cm x 12 cm
Poids : 2 kg.
60, 83 €
⑦ TAPIS DE SOL
Parfait pour le camping, la gym ou la plage.
100% polyéthylène. Dimensions : 2 m x 60 cm.
Deux épaisseurs au choix: 1 cm ou 2,5 cm
Coloris : bleu, rouge, noir et vert.
5, 63 €

18 Tu as compris?

Lisons Regarde la publicité et réponds aux questions suivantes.

1. Cette publicité est pour quelle sorte d'équipement? équipement de camping
2. Combien de poches a le sac à dos? Combien coûte-t-il? cinq; 22, 71 €
3. Comment dit-on *sleeping bag* en français? Quelles sont les dimensions de celui sur la publicité? Combien coûte-t-il? sac de couchage; 2 m x 80 cm; 36, 51 €
4. Comment est-ce qu'on peut utiliser le tapis de sol? pour le camping, la gym et la plage
5. Est-ce que la tente a des fenêtres? Elle peut loger combien de personnes? oui; trois

Connections and Comparisons

Math Link
Have students convert the prices in the advertisement to American dollars. You can find the current rate of exchange in the business section of the newspaper or on the Internet. For additional practice, have students convert the American prices into Canadian dollars.

Vocabulaire

Tu as pensé à tout?
Tu n'as rien oublié?
Ne vous en faites pas. J'emporte...

CD-ROM 3 DVD 2

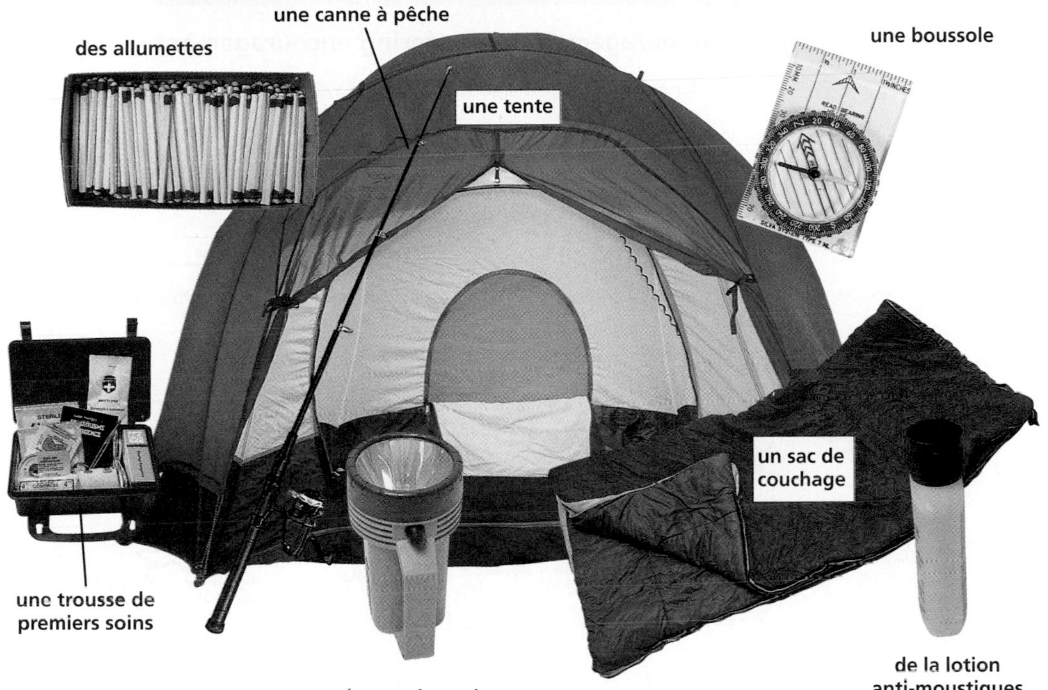

Travaux pratiques de grammaire, pp. 100–101, Act. 7–8

Cahier d'activités, p. 137, Act. 8–9

19 J'en ai besoin!

Parlons/Ecrivons Si tu vas faire du camping, qu'est-ce qu'il faut que tu emportes pour...

1. dormir? un sac de couchage
2. attraper des poissons? une canne à pêche
3. ne pas te perdre? une boussole
4. ne pas te faire piquer par les insectes? de la lotion anti-moustiques
5. soigner quelqu'un qui s'est fait mal? 5. une trousse de premiers soins
6. bien voir la nuit? une lampe de poche
7. faire la cuisine? des allumettes

Communication for All Students

Building on Previous Skills

Have each student gather or draw pictures of the vocabulary items. One partner arranges them on his or her desk without letting the other partner see the arrangement. Then, to re-enter prepositions, have students describe the arrangement of the items to a partner. **(La tente est à gauche de la boussole. Les allumettes sont sur la tente.)** The partner will position his or her pictures according to the description. Then, have partners switch roles.

Deuxième étape

CHAPITRE 12

Presenting Vocabulaire

Gather the items shown here or find pictures of them and place them on a table. Tell students you're going camping **(Je vais faire du camping)** and tell what you're going to bring **(J'emporte...)**. Show each item as you name it. Then, to check comprehension, hold up the items or pictures and make true-false statements about them. For example, as you hold up the flashlight, you might say **Je vais emporter des allumettes.**

TPR Put the vocabulary items on a table. Then, give commands involving the items and have students show their comprehension by performing the actions. **(Donne-moi la boussole. Allume la lampe de poche. Ouvre la trousse de premiers soins.)**

Additional Practice

19 Reverse the procedure and have partners take inventory of their camping gear, taking turns naming the objects and their purpose. **(Voyons... une lampe de poche pour voir la nuit.)**

Language Notes

- You might caution students not to confuse **une boussole,** a directional compass, with **un compas,** a device for drawing circles.
- Call students' attention to the use of the word **trousse** in **une trousse de premiers soins.** Ask them if they know of another **trousse** *(a pencil case)* and what it might contain.
- In Canada, **la lotion anti-moustiques** is spelled with an **-s,** while in France, it is spelled without an **-s.**

Deuxième étape

CHAPITRE 12

Teaching Resources
pp. 352–356

PRINT 

- Lesson Planner, p. 58
- TPR Storytelling Book, pp. 90–91
- Listening Activities, pp. 92, 96
- Activities for Communication, pp. 69–70, 131, 133, 159–160
- Travaux pratiques de grammaire, pp. 100–103
- Grammar Tutor for Students of French, Chapter 12
- Cahier d'activités, pp. 137–139
- Testing Program, pp. 305–308
- Alternative Assessment Guide, p. 43
- Student Make-Up Assignments, Chapter 12

MEDIA 

- One-Stop Planner
- Audio Compact Discs, CD 12, Trs. 6, 14, 26–27
- Teaching Transparencies: 12-2, 12-C, 12-D; **Grammaire supplémentaire** Answers; Travaux pratiques de grammaire Answers
- Interactive CD-ROM Tutor, Disc 3

Presenting
Note de grammaire

The verb *emporter* Demonstrate the meaning of **emporter** by telling what you're going to take with you to various places as you pack each item. **(Je vais faire du camping. J'emporte...)**

Comment dit-on... ?

Have students recall the expressions they learned to express discouragement and those to offer encouragement. Write them on the board. Then, act out the complaints, using appropriate facial expressions.

Note de grammaire

The verb **emporter** means *to take something with you.* It's a regular **-er** verb. You can use it to advise someone what to bring: **Emporte** une boussole!

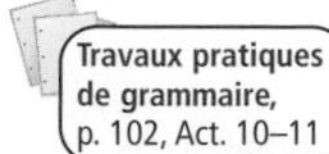
Travaux pratiques de grammaire, p. 102, Act. 10–11

Grammaire supplémentaire, p. 365, Act. 4

20 Grammaire en contexte

Ecrivons Ton ami(e) va aller faire du camping avec toi. Ecris-lui une lettre dans laquelle tu lui donnes des conseils sur ce qu'il/elle doit emporter et mettre.

Si tu as oublié
clothing vocabulary
va à la page R14.

Travaux pratiques de grammaire, p. 101, Act. 9

Comment dit-on...?

Complaining; expressing discouragement and offering encouragement

CD-ROM 3 DVD 2

To complain:	To express discouragement:	To offer encouragement:
Je crève de faim!	**Je n'en peux plus!**	**Courage!**
Je meurs de soif!	**J'abandonne!**	**Tu y es presque!**
Je suis fatigué(e).	**Je craque!**	**On y est presque!**
J'ai peur des loups! *I'm scared of . . . !*		**Allez!**

Cahier d'activités, p. 138, Act. 11

21 Qu'est-ce qu'ils disent?

Parlons/Ecrivons

1. Je suis fatiguée./Allez! On y est presque!

2. J'ai peur des ours!

3. Je meurs de soif! Je n'en peux plus.

22 Jeu de rôle

Parlons Ecris et joue une scène dans laquelle des amis partent camper et se perdent. Parmi tes amis, une personne est toujours en train de se plaindre, une autre personne est découragée et elle a peur dans les bois et la dernière personne essaie d'encourager les deux autres.

Teacher to Teacher

Todd Losié
Renaissance High School
Detroit, Michigan

Todd suggests the following activity to practice material from this *étape.*

"To practice **emporter** and camping equipment vocabulary, I use an activity called "Inside/Outside Circles." I divide the class in half and give one half a card with a place and a season. Those students form the inside circle facing out. The remaining students form the outside circle facing in. A student on the inside circle will say **Je vais à Montréal en hiver, qu'est-ce que j'emporte?** The outside circle must provide three suggestions. The outside circle then moves to the right. At some point, I have the circles switch."

STANDARDS: 1.1, 1.3, 4.1, 5.1

Vocabulaire

respecter la nature	*to respect nature*
jeter (remporter) les déchets	*to throw away (to take back with you) your trash*
nourrir les animaux	*to feed the animals*
mutiler les arbres	*to deface the trees*
suivre les sentiers balisés	*to follow the marked trails*

Travaux pratiques de grammaire, p. 103, Act. 12–14

Cahier d'activités, p. 139, Act. 12

PARC DE LA JACQUES-CARTIER

BIENVENUE DANS LE PARC DE LA JACQUES-CARTIER

«LA PROTECTION DU PARC, C'EST L'AFFAIRE DE TOUS»

Lorsque tu viens dans le parc, prends soin de:

• laisser chez toi les animaux domestiques

• garer ta voiture dans les aires de stationnement

• admirer les animaux sauvages sans les déranger ni tenter de les nourrir;
• jeter tes déchets dans les contenants prévus à cette fin;
• contempler les arbres, arbustes et autres plantes sans les prélever, ni les mutiler;
• ramener chez toi toute substance nocive tels savon, huile, combustible ou pesticide;

• éviter de peinturer, d'altérer ou de prélever les roches et autres formations naturelles

Québec

23 Au parc de la Jacques-Cartier

Lisons

1. Look at the words in bold type at the top and bottom of the poster. What is this poster about? Who is it for?
2. If you were going to a state park, what things do you think would be forbidden? What would be encouraged?
3. According to the illustrations and text below each one, what are three things you shouldn't do at the **parc de la Jacques-Cartier?**
4. Read the poster carefully to find two other things you shouldn't do, and two you should do. See answers below.

24 Le règlement du parc See scripts and answers on p. 341H.

Ecoutons Ecoute Bénédicte et ses copains qui font une randonnée dans le parc. Choisis le dessin qui correspond à chaque conversation.

CD 12 Tr. 6

a. b. c.

Presenting Vocabulaire

Make drawings on the board to represent these activities, such as a tree with initials carved into it and a forest with marked trails. Then, tell students what one should or shouldn't do in the forest. **(Il faut respecter la nature. Il ne faut pas mutiler les arbres.)** Repeat the vocabulary and have students give a thumbs-up or a thumbs-down gesture to indicate whether one should or shouldn't do what you suggest.

Teaching Suggestion

23 After students do Activity 23, ask the following questions about the brochure: **Qu'est-ce qu'il faut laisser chez toi? (les animaux domestiques) Qu'est-ce qu'il faut faire de tes déchets? (les jeter dans les contenants prévus à cette fin) Qu'est-ce qu'il faut éviter de faire? (de peinturer, d'altérer ou de prélever les roches et autres formations naturelles)**

Communication for All Students

Challenge

24 Before you play the recording, have students tell as much as they can about the pictures in French. They should tell what the people are doing and then tell whether they should or shouldn't do it.

Answers

23
1. park rules; visitors
2. Answers will vary.
3. *Possible answers:* bring pets to the park, park your car outside of the parking lot, deface or remove rocks or other forms of nature
4. *Shouldn't do:* bother or feed the animals, deface the trees or plants
   Should do: put litter in garbage cans, take with you any toxic substances, contemplate the trees and plants

Deuxième étape

CHAPITRE 12

Presenting
Comment dit-on... ?

Help students recall expressions from Chapter 7 for giving advice **(Tu devrais... , Tu ferais bien de... , Evite de... , Tu ne devrais pas...)**. Ask students what advice they would give a friend who eats a lot of junk food. Write the expressions on the board or on a transparency, and have students use them and the **Vocabulaire** on page 355 to give advice about appropriate behavior in parks. Then, have them use these expressions to give advice about school, table manners, and friendship.

Mon journal

27 For an additional journal entry suggestion for Chapter 12, see *Cahier d'activités,* page 156.

Assess

- Testing Program, pp. 305–308 Quiz 12-2A, Quiz 12-2B Audio CD 12, Tr. 14
- Student Make-Up Assignments, Chapter 12, Alternative Quiz
- Alternative Assessment Guide, p. 43

Possible Answers

25 *(from left to right):* Tu ne devrais pas mutiler les arbres. Tu devrais utiliser de la lotion anti-moustiques. Evite de nourrir les animaux. Tu devrais respecter la nature. Tu devrais remporter les déchets. Tu ferais bien de suivre les sentiers balisés.

Comment dit-on...?

Asking for and giving advice

To ask for advice:

Qu'est-ce que je dois faire?

To give advice:

Tu devrais respecter la nature.
Tu ferais bien de suivre les sentiers balisés.
Evite de nourrir les animaux.
Tu ne devrais pas mutiler les arbres.

Cahier d'activités, p. 139, Act. 13

25 Qu'est-ce qu'ils font, ces enfants?!

Parlons/Ecrivons Tu fais du camping avec un groupe d'enfants... mais ils font des bêtises. Qu'est-ce que tu leur conseilles? See answers below.

26 Tu dois respecter les règles!

Ecrivons Fais un poster comme celui du parc de la Jacques-Cartier à la page 355. Ecris la liste des règles que l'on doit respecter dans un parc près de chez toi, dans ton école, dans ta classe ou dans ta chambre à la maison. Utilise des illustrations ou des extraits de magazines.

27 Mon journal

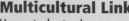

Ecrivons Est-ce que l'idée de faire du camping te plaît? Ecris ce que tu aimes et ce que tu n'aimes pas au sujet du camping.

Note culturelle

L'écologie est devenue une des priorités au Canada. Il y a plus de 500 groupes dédiés à la recherche et à la protection de l'environnement au Canada. Ces groupes ne travaillent pas seuls; le gouvernement aussi cherche à protéger les ressources naturelles du pays en créant des réserves naturelles et écologiques et des parcs nationaux. Un programme télévisé appelé La Semaine Verte fournie des mises à jour régulières concernant les problèmes d'environnement.

Connections and Comparisons

Multicultural Link

Have students choose a country and research its ecological problems and programs that are in place to solve them.

Science Link

Have students ask their science teachers or do research to find out what advances are being made in the field of environmental preservation.

STANDARDS: 1.3, 2.1, 3.1, 3.2, 5.2

Quels sont les animaux en voie de disparition dans ta région?

We asked some francophone people about endangered animals in their areas. Here's what they had to say.

Max, Martinique

«Il y en a beaucoup qui ont déjà complètement disparu, mais l'animal qui est en voie de disparition en ce moment, c'est l'iguane. Il en reste une dizaine d'unités. Ils sont au fort Saint-Louis. Je crois que c'est plutôt ceux-là qui sont vraiment en voie de disparition.»

Qu'est-ce qu'on fait pour les protéger?

«J'ai l'impression qu'on ne s'en occupe pas beaucoup. Ils sont là. Ils sont livrés à eux-mêmes et je pense qu'ils vont disparaître dans très peu de temps.» Tr. 8

Marius, Côte d'Ivoire

«Il y a des animaux en voie de disparition comme l'éléphant. L'éléphant en Côte d'Ivoire, il y en avait plein avant, mais maintenant ils commencent à disparaître et puis aussi il y a... il y a plein d'animaux hein... Je ne sais pas, l'hippopotame, le crocodile et puis le singe et puis les jolis oiseaux, les petits oiseaux comme les grands. Bon, maintenant on n'en a pas trop. Pour les voir, il faut aller soit à l'intérieur du pays ou aller au zoo.»
Tr. 9

Mathieu, Québec

«Qui sont en voie de disparition? Dans le fleuve Saint-Laurent, ici, en bas du Québec, il y a les baleines. Il y a les bélugas qui sont en voie de disparition. A l'extérieur, il y en a plusieurs. Il y en a beaucoup qui ont déjà disparu aussi. Et puis, il y a beaucoup d'oiseaux aussi qui disparaissent, à cause des produits qu'on envoie dans l'environnement.»

Qu'est-ce qu'on fait pour les protéger?

«Le gouvernement, ils pensent, enfin ils veulent faire dépolluer le fleuve Saint-Laurent ici, mais ils [ne] font pas grand-chose.»
Tr. 10

Qu'en penses-tu?

1. Are there any endangered animals in your community? What endangered species have you read about or heard about in the news lately?
2. What is being done to protect endangered species?

CHAPITRE 12

Teaching Resources
p. 357

PRINT
- Video Guide, pp. 81–83
- Cahier d'activités, p. 144

MEDIA 
- One-Stop Planner
- Video Program
  Videocassette 4, 47:11–51:27
- DVD Tutor, Disc 2
- Audio Compact Discs, CD 12, Trs. 7–10
- Interactive CD-ROM Tutor, Disc 3

Presenting
Panorama Culturel

Write on the board or on a transparency the following names of animals: **les orignaux, l'éléphant, le crocodile, l'iguane, les lions, les oiseaux, les orangs-outangs, les bélugas, le singe, les baleines, les ours, l'hippopotame, les perroquets, les poissons.**
Show the video and have students check off the animals they hear mentioned and tell where (country, department, or province) they are found.

Questions

1. **A la Martinique, où est-ce qu'on trouve des iguanes?** (au fort Saint-Louis)
2. **D'après Marius, où faut-il aller pour voir certains animaux en Côte d'Ivoire?** (soit à l'intérieur du pays, soit au zoo)
3. **D'après Mathieu, pourquoi est-ce que les oiseaux disparaissent?** (à cause des produits qu'on envoie dans l'environnement)

Communication for All Students

Challenge

Before students read the **Panorama Culturel** interviews, have them make a list of reasons animals are becoming extinct. Help students with vocabulary they do not know or provide dictionaries. List these reasons on the board. Then, read the interviews and have students see if any of the interviewees' responses matched their own.

STANDARDS: 1.2, 2.1, 3.2, 4.2

CHAPITRE 12

Teaching Resources
pp. 358–361

PRINT

- Lesson Planner, p. 59
- TPR Storytelling Book, pp. 92–93
- Listening Activities, pp. 93, 97
- Activities for Communication, pp. 71–72, 132, 134, 159–160
- Travaux pratiques de grammaire, pp. 104–107
- Grammar Tutor for Students of French, Chapter 12
- Cahier d'activités, pp. 140–142
- Testing Program, pp. 309–312
- Alternative Assessment Guide, p. 43
- Student Make-Up Assignments, Chapter 12

MEDIA 

- One-Stop Planner
- Audio Compact Discs, CD 12, Trs. 11, 15, 28–29
- Teaching Transparencies: 12-3; **Grammaire supplémentaire** Answers; Travaux pratiques de grammaire Answers
- Interactive CD-ROM Tutor, Disc 3

Bell Work

Have students write three complaints a camper might make and an expression of encouragement in response to each one.

Presenting
Comment dit-on... ?

Ask students to recall the expressions in Chapters 1 and 4 to relate a series of events and the expressions in Chapter 8 to tell what things were like. Then, tell a story, using the expressions. Have students raise their right hands when they hear an expression that relates a series of events, and raise their left hands when they hear an expression that describes people or places.

Troisième étape

Objectives Relating a series of events; describing people and places

WA3 QUEBEC-12

Lundi 12 septembre 20h 15

Cher journal,

Me voici donc revenue de mon week-end de camping! Il faisait un temps horrible quand nous sommes partis mais heureusement ça n'a pas duré. A midi, il faisait beau et chaud, un temps magnifique, surtout pour les randonnées. Alors, on s'est mis en route! D'abord, on a fait une randonnée super et Marc a pris des tas de photos. Il y avait une chute d'eau géniale; il a pris une photo de moi devant. Nous avons même vu un ours! Après ça, on est allés se baigner dans la rivière. Ensuite, Julie est allée à la pêche, Marc est rentré au terrain de camping et moi, je suis restée nager. Malheureusement, les moustiques sont restés aussi! Ils m'ont piquée partout! Julie m'a prêté sa lotion anti-moustiques, mais c'était trop tard! Enfin, on a fait un pique-nique super. On a mangé les poissons que Julie avait attrapés. Quelle journée! Malgré les piqûres, c'était super génial. Vive le camping!

Sophie

28 Tu as compris?

Lisons

1. Où est-ce que Sophie et ses amis sont allés? faire du camping
2. Quel temps faisait-il? Il faisait un temps horrible quand ils sont partis, mais à midi, il faisait beau et chaud.
3. Qu'est-ce qu'ils ont fait là-bas? Ils ont fait une randonnée. Ils ont pris des photos. Ils ont vu un ours. Ils sont allés se baigner. Julie est allée à la pêche. Sophie a nagé. Ils ont fait un pique-nique.
4. Le week-end s'est bien passé? Oui. C'était super-génial.

Comment dit-on...?

Relating a series of events; describing people and places

CD-ROM 3 DVD 2

To relate a series of events:

D'abord, j'ai acheté des bottes et une casquette.
Ensuite, je suis parti(e) au parc avec Francine et Denis.
Après ça, on a fait une randonnée pédestre.
Finalement, je me suis couché(e) très tôt.

To describe people and places:

Il y avait beaucoup d'arbres et une chute d'eau.
Paul **était** pénible parce qu'il **avait** faim.
Francine **avait l'air** embêtée.
Moi, j'**étais** ravi(e)!

Cahier d'activités, p. 140, Act. 15–16

Communication for All Students

Auditory/Visual Learners

Find or draw pictures of the activities Sophie does during her camping experience. (For printable drawings of camping activities, see the Clip Art section on the *One-Stop Planner CD-ROM.)* Put the drawings in random order on a sheet of paper and give a copy to each student. Then, read Sophie's postcard to the class with their books closed. Have students number the drawings in the order that Sophie does them.

29 Le week-end de Séverine

See scripts and answers on p. 341H.

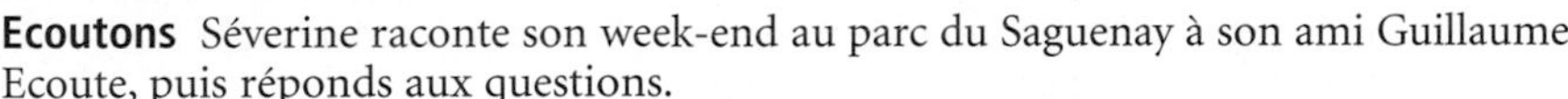

Ecoutons Séverine raconte son week-end au parc du Saguenay à son ami Guillaume. Ecoute, puis réponds aux questions.

CD 12 Tr. 11

1. Quel temps faisait-il?
2. Qu'est-ce qu'elles ont fait là-bas?
3. Est-ce que Monique était de bonne ou de mauvaise humeur? Pourquoi?

Grammaire

The *passé composé* and the *imparfait*

CD-ROM 3 DVD 2

Remember that you use the **passé composé** to tell what happened in the past.

- When you use **être** as the helping verb, the past participle agrees with the subject.
- Words that often signal the **passé composé** are **un jour, une fois, soudain,** and the words you've learned to use to relate a series of events.

You use the **imparfait** to describe what people or things were like; to describe repeated or habitual actions in the past, what used to happen; and to describe general conditions in the past, to tell what was going on.

- Words that often signal the **imparfait** are **toujours, d'habitude, souvent,** and **de temps en temps.**

Grammaire supplémentaire, pp. 366–367, Act. 5–9

Cahier d'activités, pp. 140–142, Act. 17–19

Travaux pratiques de grammaire, pp. 104–107, Act. 15–20

30 Grammaire en contexte

Lisons Francine raconte une histoire de fantômes à ses amis réunis autour d'un feu de camp. Complète son histoire en mettant les verbes au passé composé ou à l'imparfait. Est-ce que c'était un vrai fantôme? Qu'est-ce que c'était? See answers below.

À PROPOS, VOUS CONNAISSEZ LA VIEILLE MAISON DUCHARME?

C' __1__ (être) un soir d'automne. Je (J') __2__ (rentrer) chez moi. Je (J') __3__ (être) un peu en retard parce que je (j') __4__ (chercher) mon chat, Minou. Je (J') __5__ (passer) devant la maison Ducharme quand soudain, je (j') __6__ (entendre) un bruit. On aurait dit un fantôme! Je (J') __7__ (décider) de faire une enquête. D'abord, je (j') __8__ (monter) par l'escalier jusqu'à la terrasse — « CRICK, CRICK, CRICK, », puis je (j') __9__ (ouvrir) la porte « JOUIIIING » et je (j') __10__ (entrer) dans la maison. A l'intérieur, il y __11__ (avoir) de la poussière et des toiles d'araignée partout. Je (J') __12__ (faire) un pas vers le salon quand, tout à coup, quelque chose __13__ (tomber) derrière moi! Je (J') __14__ (être) verte de peur! Le fantôme avait essayé de me tuer!

HEUREUSEMENT, JE ME SUIS ÉCHAPPÉE, SAINE ET SAUVE!

Presenting Grammaire

The *passé composé* and the *imparfait* Ask students to recall what they know about the **passé composé** and the **imparfait.** Then, write the following paragraph on the board, underlining the **passé composé** and the **imparfait** verb forms in two different colors. Have students explain the tense of each verb.

Quand j'étais petit(e), d'habitude on allait à la plage. Mais une fois, on est allés camper. D'abord, on a fait une randonnée pédestre. Il faisait froid! J'avais très faim. Après ça, on a cuisiné sur un feu de bois (heureusement). On était en train de dîner quand soudain, une mouffette est entrée dans notre tente! Mon père avait très peur! Finalement, la mouffette est partie, et tout le monde était content. C'était un week-end super!

Answers

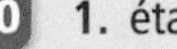

30

1. était
2. rentrais
3. étais
4. cherchais
5. passais
6. ai entendu
7. ai décidé
8. suis montée
9. ai ouvert
10. suis entrée
11. avait
12. ai fait
13. est tombé
14. étais

Connections and Comparisons

Music Link

To review the **Grammaire,** have students draw two columns on a sheet of paper and label them **passé composé** and **imparfait.** Play the song *Le Bon Roi Dagobert* (Level 2, Audio CD 9, Track 25). Ask students to mark the appropriate column each time they hear a verb in the **passé composé** or the **imparfait.** Finally, distribute copies of the lyrics *(Listening Activities,* Level 2, page 74) so students can check their work.

STANDARDS: 1.2, 4.1, 5.2

Troisième étape

CHAPITRE 12

Teaching Suggestion

32 You might refer students to the Additional Vocabulary on page R19 for outdoor activities.

Writing Assessment

32 You might use the following rubric when grading your students on this activity.

Writing Rubric	Points			
	4	3	2	1
Content (Complete–Incomplete)				
Comprehensibility (Comprehensible–Incomprehensible)				
Accuracy (Accurate–Seldom accurate)				
Organization (Well organized–Poorly organized)				
Effort (Excellent–Minimal)				

18–20: A 14–15: C Under
16–17: B 12–13: D 12: F

Assess

- Testing Program, pp. 309–312 Quiz 12-3A, Quiz 12-3B Audio CD 12, Tr. 15
- Student Make-Up Assignments, Chapter 12, Alternative Quiz
- Alternative Assessment Guide, p. 43

31 La journée de Pierre

Parlons/Ecrivons Aujourd'hui, Pierre a fait une randonnée dans le parc. Mets en ordre ses activités et raconte sa journée. See answers below.

a.

b.

c.

d.

e.

f.

32 Quelle aventure! 

Ecrivons Imagine que tu as passé le week-end avec un groupe d'amis dans un des parcs québécois. Décris le temps qu'il a fait là-bas, ce que tu as vu et ce que tout le monde a fait. Décris tes impressions de cette expérience dans la nature.

33  **De l'école au travail** 

Parlons Tu travailles pour le bureau d'information du parc de la Jacques-Cartier. Tu dois interviewer ton ami(e) au sujet du week-end décrit dans l'activité 32. Demande-lui où il/elle est allé(e), avec qui, quel temps il a fait, comment était le parc, ce qu'il/elle a fait et si c'était bien.

Communication for All Students

Slower Pace

To help students complete Activity 32, have them answer the following questions in complete sentences. **1. Dans quel parc est-ce que tu es allé(e)? 2. Tu y es allé(e) avec qui? 3. Quel temps est-ce qu'il a fait? 4. Comment était le parc? 5. Qu'est-ce que tu as fait?** Then have students put their answers in paragraph form. Encourage them to use words like **d'abord, ensuite,** etc. to sequence their events.

Possible Answers

31 e, a, f, d, c, b; Pierre est allé au parc. Il faisait beau et il était très content. D'abord, il a fait une randonnée. Ensuite, il a fait un pique-nique. Un écureuil a mangé son sandwich et il a vu une mouffette qui lui a fait une surprise! Pierre sentait mauvais, et il n'était pas très content. Alors, il s'est baigné dans la rivière. Finalement, il est rentré chez lui.

STANDARDS: 1.1, 1.3, 3.1, 5.1

Rencontre culturelle

If you visit Quebec, you might be surprised at some of the French-Canadian words and expressions you'll hear. See if you can match the French expressions on the left with their French-Canadian equivalents on the right.

1. maïs	**a.** bonjour
2. dîner	**b.** breuvage
3. stop	**c.** patate
4. au revoir	**d.** bienvenue
5. boisson	**e.** fin de semaine
6. pomme de terre	**f.** arrêt
7. week-end	**g.** souper
8. ça va	**h.** blé d'Inde
9. de rien	**i.** c'est correct
10. hot-dog	**j.** chien chaud

Qu'en penses-tu?

stop, week-end, hot-dog; arrêt, fin de semaine, chien chaud

1. Which French expressions use English words? What do French Canadians use instead?
2. Which French-Canadian expressions show the influence of North American culture?

bonjour *(used for "goodbye," lit., "goodday")*, **bienvenue** *(used for "you're welcome," lit., "welcome")*, and **patate** *(potato)*

Savais-tu que... ?

If you visit Quebec, some of the words and expressions you will hear may be different from those you would hear in many parts of France. Some words and expressions heard in Quebec were used only in certain regions of France and may no longer be used in France. Other more modern expressions originated separately in France and Quebec. For example, in France, English words such as **hot-dog, week-end,** and **stop** are commonly used. In Quebec you are more likely to hear **patate, fin de semaine,** and **arrêt.** Some expressions you will hear in Quebec reflect the influence of English, such as **bienvenue,** which literally means "welcome," and is often used instead of **de rien** to mean "you're welcome."

(answers: 1 h, 2 g, 3 f, 4 a, 5 b, 6 c, 7 e, 8 i, 9 d, 10 j)

Cultures and Communities

Language Note

Some French people might be surprised to hear **Bonjour, bienvenue!** when they leave a place of business in Quebec. In France, a merchant would say **Bonjour, bienvenue** to mean *Hello, welcome!* and **Merci, au revoir** to mean *Thank you, goodbye!* French-Canadians say **Bonjour** to mean *Have a nice day* and **bienvenue** to mean *You're welcome* at the end of a business transaction after the customer has said **merci.**

CHAPITRE 12

Motivating Activity

Ask students if they know any British words or expressions that are different from American English words (lift/*elevator;* lorry/*truck;* bonnet/*hood of a car;* wee/*little;* bloke, chap/*man;* lass/*girl;* lad/*boy;* loo/*bathroom*). Ask students in what other ways the United States and Great Britain differ.

Presenting Rencontre culturelle

Write the two columns of words on the board. Call for volunteers to draw a line between each French expression and its French-Canadian equivalent. If students can't match them all, discuss the remaining words and have the class decide together how to match them.

Thinking Critically

Analyzing Ask students why they think the same language evolves differently in different parts of the world. (Language changes continually, so when people who speak the same language are separated geographically, their language evolves differently.) Ask students to imagine why the same languages in different parts of the world are changing less now than they did in the past. (Global communication links people together now despite geographical separation.)

Comparing and Contrasting
Ask students to consider how accents differ in various regions of the United States. Then, ask them if they know of any region-specific vocabulary that has developed in the United States and even in different communities of the same city. (For example, in New England one says *pocketbook* and *soda* or *tonic,* whereas in the Midwest one says *purse* and *pop.*)

STANDARDS: 3.2, 4.1, 4.2

CHAPITRE 12

Teaching Resources
pp. 362–363

PRINT 
- Lesson Planner, p. 60
- Cahier d'activités, p. 143
- Reading Strategies and Skills Handbook, Chapter 12
- Joie de lire 2, Chapter 12
- Standardized Assessment Tutor, Chapter 12

MEDIA
- One-Stop Planner

Prereading
Activity A

Making Connections
Give students two different descriptions of something in nature, one that is direct and one that uses a metaphor. For example, you might describe a starry night by telling them, "It was a starry, starry night." and then "The night was a black velvet blanket, scattered with sequins winking and glittering on its surface." Ask students which description creates a more vivid image in their minds. Which one would be more effective in a poem?

Reading
Activities B–H

Challenge
C. Have the students cover the list of terms with a sheet of paper. Then, write the French terms on the board or on a transparency and have students try to determine their meanings from context. Have volunteers come to the board or the overhead and write their definitions beside each term. Then, have students uncover the list in their books and compare it with their definitions.

Possible Answers

A. Both poems relate to nature; the day and the garden; Answers will vary.

Lisons!

Poèmes de Anne Hérbert

Stratégie pour lire
What makes a group of words a poem? The *imagery* in the poem, or the pictures the words create in your mind, is part of what makes a poem come to life. One way a writer creates these images is to use *metaphors,* phrases that suggest a likeness or relationship between two things by stating that one thing is another. Before you look closely at the poem, read it aloud and note the images and metaphors the poet uses.

Nature is a theme for many poets, including Canadian writer Anne Hébert, author of several prize-winning novels, screenplays, and poems.

A. What do both poem titles relate to? Can you think of any poems or songs you're familiar with whose titles suggest the same themes? See answers below.

B. Lis les premières strophes de chaque poème. Tu penses à quelles images en lisant ces strophes? Answers will vary.

C. Lis les mots suivants et trouve chacun dans *Tombée du jour* ou *Nos Mains au jardin.*

Tombée du jour	
soleil évanoui	*vanishing sun*
ramasse	*pick up*
grisonne	*greys, is greying*
pourrir	*to rot away, to spoil*
sol	*ground*
survienne	*appears, arrives*
aubes	*dawns, daybreaks*
sauvage	*wild*
paroles	*words*

Tombee du jour

Le jour tombe
De l'arbre rond
Comme une orange ronde
Soleil évanoui

Nul ne le ramasse
Dans l'air qui grisonne
Le laisse là pourrir
Sur le sol noir

Survienne la nuit confuse
Rumination des aubes
incertaines
Magma sauvage des
paroles jamais dites

Germe la plus étonnante
des fleurs vives
Et peut-être même le
sang de la terre
Tout entière
En sa naissance reconduite

Cultures and Communities

Culture Note
Canada has a rich literary history reaching back to the late 1600s. Anne Hébert is a **Québécois** writer, playwright, and poet who utilizes nature in many of her poems, including *Tombée du jour* and *Nos mains au jardin.* At first glance, her poetry may appear to be very straightforward. However, Hébert's use of sympathetic nature, or the use of a force of nature to reflect the internal emotions of the speaker, challenges readers to unravel complex themes of alienation and uncertainty.

STANDARDS: 1.2, 2.2, 3.1, 3.2, 4.2

NOS MAINS AU JARDIN

Nous avons eu cette idée
De planter nos mains au jardin

Branches des dix doigts
Petits arbres d'ossements
Chère plate-bande.

Tout le jour
Nous avons attendu l'oiseau roux
Et les feuilles fraîches
A nos ongles polis.

Nul oiseau
Nul printemps
Ne se sont pris au piège de nos mains coupées.

Pour une seule fleur
Une seule minuscule étoile de couleur
Un seul vol d'aile calme
Pour une seule note pure
Répétée trois fois.

Il faudra la saison prochaine
Et nos mains fondues comme l'eau.

étonnante	***surprising***
sang de la terre	***blood of the earth***
naissance	***birth***
Nos Mains au jardin	
ossements	***bones***
plate-bande	***flower/garden bed***
ongles	***fingernails***
ne se sont pris au piège	***didn't fall in the trap of . . .***

Tombée du jour

D. How does the poet describe the end of the day? What images does she use? See answers below.

E. What tone does the poem have after the sun has set? The poet uses powerful images to describe the night. Find examples from the poem of some of these images. See answers below.

Nos Mains au jardin

F. What type of images does the author use in the first two stanzas of the poem? Whom do you think **nous** represents? See answers below.

G. What does the author want or long for? Does she get what she wants? Why or why not? See answers below.

H. Comment est-ce que la nature est représentée dans le poème *Nos Mains au jardin?* Explique ta réponse en utilisant le vocabulaire trouvé dans le poème. See answers below.

I. Think of how weather or nature affects you. What type of weather makes you happy? Sad? Make a list of these feelings and think about what you would associate with each one. Then, write a poem about these feelings. Try to use metaphors to create mental images for your reader.

J. Quel poème est-ce que tu préfères? Pourquoi?

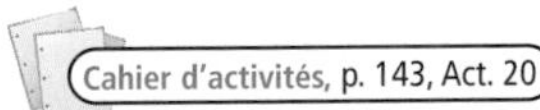
Cahier d'activités, p. 143, Act. 20

Lisons!

CHAPITRE 12

Teaching Suggestion

G. Have students cite specific lines in the poem that justify their answers.

Language Arts Link

H. Have students identify in each of the two poems examples of nature being personified, as well as instances in which it is only compared to something else metaphorically.

Postreading

Activities I–J

Group Work

I. Form an even number of groups. Each group should brainstorm a list of feelings and associations about weather or nature as described in the activity. Then, each group should write the first stanza of their poem. When the first stanza is complete, have them exchange with another group who will write the second stanza based solely on their impression of the first stanza. The groups then return the poems and write their own third stanza. They exchange a final time to write the fourth stanza. Have each group share their finished poem.

Possible Answers

D. The end of the day is a vanishing sun, falling from the tree.

E. The tone is somber and serious. Images of night: graying air, black ground, confused night

F. The physical image of planting one's hand in the garden. Answers will vary.

G. The author longs for her hand to grow and become a part of nature. She doesn't get her wish; Answers will vary.

H. fresh (les feuilles fraîches), calm (un seul vol d'aile calme), pure (une seule note pure)

Connections and Comparisons

Literature Link

The theme of nature played an important part in the romantic movement in French literature. In 1820, the French poet Alphonse de Lamartine published a volume of poetry entitled *Méditations poétiques* that is considered a pillar among French romantic works. It includes the poems **"Le Lac,"** **"Le Vallon,"** and **"L'Automne,"** in which nature serves as a metaphor for life, death, and the destiny of humankind. You might distribute copies of these poems and ask students to compare how nature is treated by both poets.

STANDARDS: 1.2, 2.2, 3.1, 3.2, 4.2

Grammaire supplémentaire

CHAPITRE 12

For **Grammaire supplémentaire** Answer Transparencies, see the *Teaching Transparencies* binder.

Grammaire supplémentaire

Première étape

Objectives Asking for and giving information; giving directions

1 Ta classe a fait une excursion à la montagne et quelques étudiants parlent de ce qu'ils ont vu. Dis ce que chacun a vu en employant ces fragments de phrases et ces photos. (**pp. 136, 140, 167, 305, 349**)

Exemple  traverser/le chemin
<u>Un raton laveur a traversé le chemin.</u>

1.  /entrer/dans le lac/pour boire
2. Julien et Lucien/voir/ 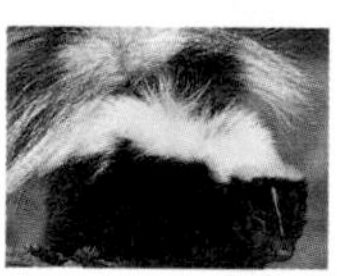 /à côté d'un arbre
3.  /faire coin-coin/quand/ il/ passer/près de Stéphanie
4.  /se cacher/derrière un arbre
5. Dominique/voir/  /sur la colline/à gauche/du chemin
6. Nous/entendre/  /et ça nous a fait peur

Answers

1
1. Un orignal est entré dans le lac pour boire.
2. Julien et Lucien ont vu une mouffette à côté d'un arbre.
3. Un canard a fait coin-coin quand il est passé près de Stéphanie.
4. Un écureuil s'est caché derrière un arbre.
5. Dominique a vu un renard sur la colline, à gauche du chemin.
6. Nous avons entendu un loup et ça nous a fait peur.

Grammar Resources for Chapter 12

The **Grammaire supplémentaire** activities were designed as supplemental activities for the grammatical concepts presented in the chapter. You might use them as additional practice, for review, or for assessment.
For more grammar presentations, review, and practice, refer to the following:
- Travaux pratiques de grammaire
- Grammar Tutor for Students of French
- Grammar Summary on pp. R23–R42
- Cahier d'activités
- Grammar and Vocabulary quizzes (Testing Program)
- Test Generator
- Interactive CD-ROM Tutor
- DVD Tutor
- **Jeux interactifs** at <u>go.hrw.com</u>

STANDARDS: 1.2

2 Ta classe de sciences fait une étude sur les différents animaux que les élèves ont déjà vus. Dis ce que chaque personne faisait quand elle a vu chaque animal. Utilise les verbes au **passé composé** ou à **l'imparfait** quand c'est nécessaire. (**pp. 269, 350**)

1. Francine et Monique / faire du canotage / un canard
2. Marie et Julien / faire du vélo de montagne / une mouffette
3. Je / faire une randonnée pédestre / un raton laveur
4. Nous / se baigner / un orignal
5. Sasha / faire un pique-nique / un écureuil
6. Tu / faire du ski alpin / un loup

3 Toi et tes amis, vous allez au parc du Saguenay. Suggère une activité que vous pouvez faire selon ce que chaque personne emporte. Utilise l'expression **si on + imparfait.** (**pp. 237, 350**)

Exemple François: hiking boots **Si on faisait une randonnée pédestre?**

1. Luc: a canoe
2. Christian: a tent
3. Martin: ski poles
4. Annick: a mountain bike
5. Yves: snowshoes
6. Laurent: fishing pole
7. Michelle: sandwiches and trail mix
8. Antoine: a camera
9. Isabelle: cross-country skis

Deuxième étape

Objectives Complaining; expressing discouragement and offering encouragement; asking for and giving advice

4 Ta famille fait des préparatifs pour un week-end de camping. Décide ce que chaque personne doit emporter pour faire les choses suivantes. (**p. 354**)

Exemple ta mère / faire la cuisine
Elle emporte des allumettes.

des allumettes — une tente — une lampe de poche — un sac de couchage — une boussole — une trousse de premiers soins — de la lotion anti-moustiques — une canne à pêche — un canoë — des vélos de montagne — des raquettes

1. tes frères / dormir
2. ton père / ne pas se perdre
3. toi / attraper des poissons
4. on / bien voir la nuit
5. nous / soigner quelqu'un qui s'est fait mal
6. vous / ne pas se faire piquer par les moustiques
7. ton père et toi / faire du canotage
8. ta sœur / faire une randonnée pédestre dans la neige
9. ta mère et toi / faire du vélo de montagne
10. on / se protéger de la pluie

Review and Assess

Game

Je m'en souviens! One student begins by saying **Je vais faire du camping. J'emporte une boussole.** The next student must repeat what was said and add another item. **(Je vais faire du camping. J'emporte une boussole et une tente.)** Continue in this manner until someone makes a mistake. The student who makes a mistake is out, but is then responsible for keeping track of what the players say. Start a new vocabulary round when someone makes a mistake, but the students who are out stay out. The winner is the last one remaining. You might also form small groups to play this game.

Grammaire supplémentaire

CHAPITRE 12

Answers

2
1. Francine et Monique faisaient du canotage quand elles ont vu un canard.
2. Marie et Julien faisaient du vélo de montagne quand ils ont vu une mouffette.
3. Je faisais une randonnée pédestre quand j'ai vu un raton laveur.
4. Nous nous baignions quand nous avons vu un orignal.
5. Sasha faisait un pique-nique quand il a vu un écureuil.
6. Tu faisais du ski alpin quand tu as vu un loup.

3
1. Si on faisait du canotage?
2. Si on faisait du camping?
3. Si on faisait du ski?
4. Si on faisait du vélo de montagne?
5. Si on faisait une randonnée en raquettes?
6. Si on allait à la pêche?
7. Si on faisait un pique-nique?
8. Si on faisait de la photo?
9. Si on faisait une randonnée à skis?

4
1. Ils emportent des sacs de couchage.
2. Il emporte une boussole.
3. J'emporte une canne à pêche.
4. On emporte une lampe de poche.
5. Nous emportons une trousse de premiers soins.
6. Vous emportez de la lotion anti-moustiques.
7. Vous emportez un canoë.
8. Elle emporte des raquettes.
9. Vous emportez des vélos de montagne.
10. On emporte une tente.

Grammaire supplémentaire

CHAPITRE 12

For **Grammaire supplémentaire** Answer Transparencies, see the *Teaching Transparencies* binder.

Answers

5
1. emportait
2. a emporté
3. emportait
4. ai emporté
5. n'a pas emporté
6. emportions
7. n'avons pas emporté
8. emportais
9. n'ai pas emporté
10. a emporté

6
1. étais
2. jouais
3. était
4. aimions
5. habitait
6. aimaient
7. avait
8. faisait
9. passions
10. amusais
11. étais

Grammaire supplémentaire

WA3 QUEBEC-12

Troisième étape

Objectives Relating a series of events; describing people and places

5 Tu aides ton cousin à écrire une histoire de camping pour son cours de français. Complète le paragraphe avec l'imparfait ou le passé composé du verbe **emporter.** (**pp. 136, 230, 354, 359**)

Quand j'étais petit, mon père et moi, on faisait du camping tout le temps et on __1__ beaucoup de choses avec nous. La semaine dernière, Johan et moi, on a fait du camping et on __2__ beaucoup de choses aussi, mais pas assez. Mon père __3__ toujours une tente. Alors, je (j') __4__ une tente aussi. Johan devait emporter plusieurs choses, mais il (ne... pas) __5__ la plus importante : une boussole. D'habitude, mon père et moi, nous __6__ toujours une lampe de poche, mais Johan et moi, nous (ne... pas) __7__ de lampe. Au moins, on n'a pas oublié les sacs de couchage. Quand j'étais petit, je (j') __8__ toujours ma canne à pêche, mais cette fois, je (ne... pas) __9__ de canne. Heureusement, Johan __10__ sa canne.

6 Christine décrit ce qu'elle faisait quand elle avait cinq ans. Complète sa description avec l'imparfait des verbes entre parenthèses. (**p. 359**)

Quand je(j') __1__ (être) petite, je(j') __2__ (jouer) souvent avec mon frère. Il __3__ (être) parfois pénible, mais nous __4__ (aimer) jouer ensemble. On __5__ (habiter) une petite maison près d'un parc et en général mes parents __6__ (aimer) aller au parc avec nous. Il y __7__ (avoir) toujours beaucoup d'enfants au parc. Quand il __8__ (faire) beau, nous y __9__ (passer) l'après-midi. Je me(m') __10__ (amuser) beaucoup quand je (j') __11__ (être) petite.

Review and Assess

Additional Practice

Distribute copies of the following paragraph and have students supply the correct verb forms.

Le week-end passé, je (j') _____ (faire) du vélo de montagne avec des copains. Ça (C') _____ (être) génial! Il _____ (faire) un temps superbe, et tout le monde _____ (être) de bonne humeur. Ça (C') _____ (être) dur, le vélo, mais on _____ (s'arrêter) souvent pour se reposer. Comme d'habitude, Jacques _____ (aller) moins vite que les autres et en plus, il _____ (se perdre)! Heureusement, il nous _____ (retrouver). Tout est bien qui finit bien! (*Answers:* **ai fait, était, faisait, était, était, s'est arrêtés, allait, s'est perdu, a retrouvés)**

STANDARDS: 1.2

Grammaire supplémentaire

CHAPITRE 12

7 Tes camarades de classe racontent ce qui est arrivé quand ils faisaient du camping. Complète les phrases suivantes avec l'imparfait ou le passé composé du verbe. (**p. 359**)

1. On faisait une randonnée pédestre quand soudain, un ours énorme _____ le sentier.
   a. traversait **b.** a traversé
2. Quand nous étions petits, mes frères et moi, nous _____ toujours à la montagne.
   a. sommes allés **b.** allions
3. Un jour, on _____ un gros loup gris dans la forêt.
   a. voyait **b.** a vu
4. De temps en temps, les mouffettes _____ dormir dans notre tente.
   a. venaient **b.** sont venues
5. Vendredi, ils _____ du parc de la Gaspésie vers dix heures du matin.
   a. sont partis **b.** partaient
6. Paul _____ les déchets dans la poubelle quand il a vu un orignal.
   a. a jeté **b.** jetait

8 Ahmed fait du camping avec des amis et il écrit une lettre à ses parents pour décrire ce qui s'est passé. Complète sa lettre en mettant les verbes au passé composé ou à l'imparfait. (**p. 359**)

> Chers Maman et Papa,
>
> Je m'amuse beaucoup avec mes amis. Chaque jour, il y a beaucoup de choses à faire. D'abord, en arrivant, je (j') ___1___ (préparer) la tente avec Robert. Ensuite, tout le monde ___2___ (ranger) ses affaires. Je ___3___ (ne pas emporter) de lampe de poche, alors je (j') ___4___ (devoir) emprunter celle de Robert. Le premier jour, il ___5___ (pleuvoir), mais samedi et hier, il ___6___ (faire) du soleil. Lorette et moi, nous ___7___ (apporter) nos cannes à pêche et hier, on ___8___ (aller) au lac pour attraper des poissons. Mais, on ___9___ (ne rien attraper)! Claude et Benoît ___10___ (se perdre) parce qu'ils ___11___ (ne pas suivre) les sentiers balisés. Ils ___12___ (être) fatigués et ils ___13___ (avoir) très faim quand ils ___14___ (revenir) au terrain de camping. On va rentrer vendredi, mais j'ai envie de rester ici encore une semaine!
>
> Je vous embrasse,
> Ahmed

9 Jean-Pierre a fait du camping le week-end dernier. Fais des phrases complètes pour décrire son week-end. Utilise le passé composé et l'imparfait. (**p. 359**)

1. ce / être le week-end dernier
2. il / faire beau
3. Anaïs et Christophe / venir avec moi
4. d'abord / je / acheter les provisions
5. ensuite / on / partir pour le terrain de camping
6. au parc / nous / décider / de faire une randonnée pédestre
7. Christophe / être pénible / parce que / il / être fatigué
8. je / voir beaucoup de renards et de canards
9. au lac / Christophe et Anaïs / attraper des poissons pour le dîner
10. je / ne pas emporter la tente / alors / on / dormir à la belle étoile

Answers

7
1. b
2. b
3. b
4. a
5. a
6. b

8
1. ai préparé
2. a rangé
3. n'ai pas emporté
4. ai dû
5. a plu
6. a fait
7. avons apporté
8. est allés
9. n'a rien attrapé
10. se sont perdus
11. n'ont pas suivi
12. étaient
13. avaient
14. sont revenus

9
1. C'était le week-end dernier.
2. Il faisait beau.
3. Annaïs et Christophe sont venus avec moi.
4. D'abord, j'ai acheté les provisions.
5. Ensuite, on est partis pour le terrain de camping.
6. Au parc, nous avons décidé de faire une randonnée pédestre.
7. Christophe était pénible parce qu'il était fatigué.
8. J'ai vu beaucoup de renards et de canards.
9. Au lac, Christophe et Anaïs ont attrapé des poissons pour le dîner.
10. Je n'ai pas emporté de tente alors on a dormi à la belle étoile.

Review and Assess

You may wish to assign the **Grammaire supplémentaire** activities as additional practice or homework after presenting material throughout the chapter. Assign Activity 4 after **Note de grammaire** (p. 354) and Activities 5–9 after **Grammaire** (p. 359).

To prepare students for the **Etape** Quizzes and Chapter Test, we suggest doing the **Grammaire supplémentaire** activities in the following order. Have students complete Activities 1–3 before Quiz 12-1A or 12-1B; Activity 4 before Quiz 12-2A or 12-2B; and Activities 5–9 before Quiz 12-3A or 12-3B.

Mise en pratique

CHAPITRE 12

The **Mise en pratique** reviews and integrates all four skills and culture in preparation for the Chapter Test.

Teaching Resources
pp. 368–369

PRINT 

- Lesson Planner, p. 60
- TPR Storytelling Book, pp. 94–95
- Listening Activities, p. 93
- Video Guide, pp. 81, 84
- Grammar Tutor for Students of French, Chapter 12
- Standardized Assessment Tutor, Chapter 12

MEDIA

- One-Stop Planner
- Video Program Videocassette 4, 51:30–55:56
- DVD Tutor, Disc 2
- Audio Compact Discs, CD 12, Tr. 12
- Interactive CD-ROM Tutor, Disc 3

Teaching Suggestion

1 Have students explain why it would be important to bring insect repellent and light-colored clothes when visiting the park. Have them also tell why they shouldn't eat bananas or use perfumed products. Students might want to know that the parasite Giardia is a protozoan that can cause prolonged pain in the intestines.

Answers

1
1. mid-June to the end of August
2. bring insect repellant, wear light-colored clothing, don't eat bananas, don't use perfumed products
3. water from rivers, lakes, streams
4. boil it for five minutes

Mise en pratique

1 Your friends decided to "rough it" on a camping trip, so you're off to the **parc de la Jacques-Cartier.** Before you go, read the **Conseils pratiques** of the lynx, the mascot of the park. See answers below.

1. When are you most likely to be bothered by insects at the park?
2. What should you do to protect yourself against bites?
3. **Non potable** means *not drinkable.* What water at the park is not drinkable?
4. What can you do to make the water drinkable?

Conseils pratiques

Comme la période des insectes piqueurs s'étend de la mi-juin à la fin août, nous vous conseillons, pour un séjour agréable :

- d'apporter de l'huile à mouches;
- de porter des vêtements de couleur pâle;
- de ne pas consommer de bananes;
- d'éviter les produits parfumés.

Avertissement :
L'eau de surface (lacs, rivières et ruisseaux) est non potable et doit être bouillie pendant cinq minutes avant consommation. Veuillez noter que le parasite Giardia est résistant aux comprimés de chlore et d'iode utilisés pour purifier l'eau.

2 Béatrix and her brother Etienne are spending the weekend at the **parc de la Gaspésie.** Listen to their conversation and answer the questions below. See scripts and answers on p. 341H.

CD 12 Tr. 12

1. What are Etienne and Béatrix doing?
2. What are two things Etienne complains about?
3. Why does Etienne ask Béatrix if she brought the first-aid kit?
4. What are Béatrix's plans for the afternoon?
5. What are Etienne's plans for the afternoon?

3 What comparisons can you make among the people and places you've learned about this year? Make a chart with **France, Martinique, Côte d'Ivoire, Quebec,** and the **United States** in a column on the left. Across the top of the chart, write these headings for six columns: **Location and Size, Language(s), History, Teenage Life, Leisure Activities,** and **Food.** Fill in the chart, using your book as a reference. Compare your chart with a partner's. What similarities and differences do you find among these cultures?

Apply and Assess

Challenge

2 After students have completed the activity, create several statements describing Béatrix or Etienne **(Cette personne veut faire la sieste. Cette personne a emporté une trousse de premiers soins...),** read them aloud, and have students identify the person each statement describes.

STANDARDS: 1.2, 2.1

4 **Ecrivons!**

Imagine that you're one of the first pioneers who explored the unsettled wilderness of Canada. Write an account of your adventures, making sure to include descriptions of the landscape, of any animals you encountered, and of any problems you faced.

Stratégie pour écrire
Story mapping can help you decide in which direction you want your story to go. A story map provides you with different situations and possible solutions or problems that might arise from each one.

Préparation

A story map in writing works much like a flow chart does in computer programming: it begins at a certain point and flows in different directions based on the action taken. First, decide how you want your story to begin. On a sheet of paper, jot down a short phrase that describes your beginning and draw a circle around it. Next, think about several things that might happen as a result of the beginning of the story. Jot these down, draw circles around them, and draw lines connecting them to your first circle. Now write down several things that might result from this second set of actions and connect them also with lines. Continue mapping out your story until you reach a conclusion for each action.

Je marchais dans la forêt.
J'ai rencontré une mouffette.
Je l'ai évitée.
J'ai vu un ours.

Rédaction

When your story map is complete, you'll be ready to write about your adventures in the Canadian wilderness. Look at your map and choose the direction that you want your story to take. As you write the first draft of your story, add appropriate details to make it more appealing to your reader. Also, don't forget to use the expressions you've learned for relating a series of events to help your story flow more smoothly and logically.

Evaluation

One key to good writing is listening carefully to how the words sound. Read your story aloud to yourself and listen to what you've written. This can often alert you to awkward sentences and to areas where your ideas don't flow smoothly. A variation of this might be to have a classmate read your work aloud to you.

5 **Jeu de rôle**

It's your job to convince a reluctant friend to come with you to the **parc de la Jacques-Cartier.** He or she has never been camping and is a bit fearful. You should tell your friend what you know about the park's history, what there is to see and do at the park, what to bring, and what to do and what not to do at the park.

Mise en pratique

CHAPITRE 12

Process Writing/Challenge

4 Instead of writing a single plot and ending to their stories, have students create a choose-your-own-adventure story. To do this, students write different outcomes for each action in the story and give their reader the option of deciding the direction the story takes. For example, if the main character discovers an abandoned house, the reader might have the following options: **Si Jean entre dans la maison pour l'explorer, allez à la page 2; s'il évite la maison et continue sur la route, allez à la page 3.** The reader chooses the outcome, reads what happens, and is given a choice of where the story goes from there.

Teacher Note

For additional practice and review, you might use the **Histoire Finale** for Chapter 12 on pages 94–95 of the *TPR Storytelling Book.*

Portfolio

5 **Oral** This activity is suitable for students' oral portfolios. For portfolio information, see the *Alternative Assessment Guide,* page iv–17.

Apply and Assess

Game

Cercle de mots Have students make two identical sets of flashcards with French words or expressions on one side and the English equivalents on the other. Form two teams and have them each sit in a circle. Then, distribute one card to each student. One student in each team begins by showing the English equivalent on his or her card to the teammate on his or her left. That student responds by giving the French expression. Then, he or she shows the English equivalent on his or her card to the student on his or her left. The first team to complete the circle wins.

Que sais-je?

CHAPITRE 12

Teaching Resources
p. 370

PRINT 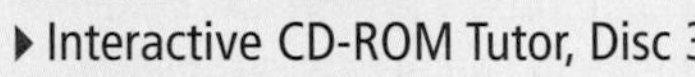

- Grammar Tutor for Students of French, Chapter 12

MEDIA

- Interactive CD-ROM Tutor, Disc 3
- Online self-test

go.hrw.com
WA3 QUEBEC-12

Possible Answers

2 Où se trouve... ?
1. Il se trouve au nord de Québec.
2. Elle se trouve dans l'ouest de l'Afrique.
3. ... au sud des Etats-Unis.

3 1. Je n'en peux plus! J'abandonne! Je craque!
2. Je crève de faim!
3. J'ai peur des... !

6 1. Tu devrais emporter un short, des lunettes de soleil, un maillot de bain, une tente, un sac de couchage, une boussole, une canne à pêche et de la lotion anti-moustiques.
2. Tu ferais bien d'emporter un anorak, un pull, des bottes, des raquettes, des skis, une tente, un sac de couchage et une boussole.

7 1. Tu devrais mettre de la lotion anti-moustiques.
2. Evite de nourrir les animaux.
3. Tu devrais remporter tes déchets.

8 D'abord, nous avons fait de la muscu-lation. Ensuite, nous avons fait une randonnée. Finalement, nous avons fait du canotage.

Que sais-je?

WA3 QUEBEC-12

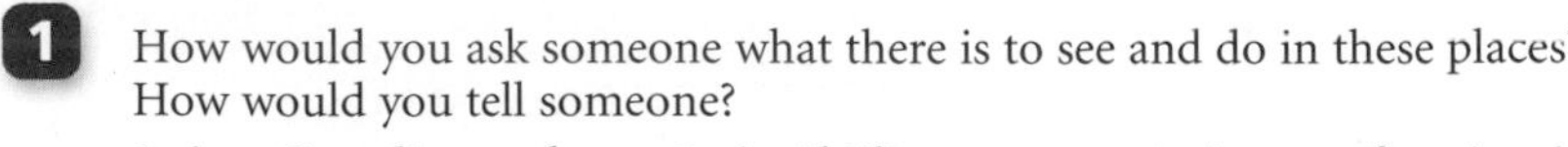

Can you use what you've learned in this chapter?

Can you ask for and give information? p. 348

1 How would you ask someone what there is to see and do in these places? How would you tell someone?
1. in a Canadian park **2.** in Abidjan **3.** in your favorite city
Qu'est-ce qu'il y a à voir/faire... ? ; Il y a... ; On peut...

Can you give directions? p. 348

2 How would you ask where these places are? How would you tell where they are? See answers below.
1. le parc de la Jacques-Cartier **2.** la Côte d'Ivoire **3.** la Martinique

Can you complain and express discouragement? p. 354

3 What would you say if . . . See answers below.
1. you were on a hike and just couldn't go on?
2. you hadn't eaten since 5:00 this morning?
3. you were afraid of a certain animal?

Can you offer encouragement? p. 354

4 How would you encourage your tired friend to finish the hike?
Possible answers: Courage! Tu y es presque! On y est presque! Allez!

Can you ask for and give advice? p. 356

5 How would you ask someone for advice? Qu'est-ce que je dois faire?

6 What would you advise a friend to pack for a camping trip . . .
1. in the summer? **2.** in the winter? See answers below.

7 What advice would you give a friend who . . . See answers below.
1. is being bitten by mosquitos?
2. is offering some potato chips to a squirrel?
3. just threw the potato chip bag on the ground?

Can you relate a series of events and describe people and places? p. 358

8 How would you say that you did these things in this order?

9 How would you describe . . .
1. the weather yesterday? Hier, il faisait...
2. how you felt this morning? Ce matin, j'étais...

Review and Assess

Game

Allez-y! Form four teams and give a transparency and a transparency pen to each one. Then, make four sets of nine index cards, each set bearing the numbers 1–9 (36 cards total), and put the cards in a bag. Have one member from each team select three cards and place them face-down on his or her desk. Once all the teams have selected cards, call out **Allez-y!** and have them turn their cards over. Teams should then write on their transparency the answers to the questions from **Que sais-je?** that correspond to the numbers they drew. After two minutes, have students put down their pens. Have one member from each team bring their cards and transparency to the front. Show the cards and the transparency and have the class verify that the questions were answered correctly.

Vocabulaire

Première étape

Asking for and giving information; giving directions

Où se trouve... ?	*Where is... located?*
Qu'est-ce qu'il y a à voir/faire... ?	*What is there to see/do...?*
... se trouve...	*...is located...*
Il y a...	*There is/are...*
On peut...	*You can...*
C'est au nord/au sud/à l'est/à l'ouest de...	*It's to the north/south/east/west of...*
C'est dans le nord/le sud/l'est/l'ouest de...	*It's in the northern/southern/eastern/western part of...*

Animals

un orignal	*moose*
un ours	*bear*
un loup	*wolf*
un écureuil	*squirrel*
un renard	*fox*
un raton laveur	*raccoon*
une mouffette	*skunk*
un canard	*duck*

Outdoor activities

faire du camping	*to go camping*
faire du canotage	*to go canoeing*
faire du vélo de montagne	*to go mountain-bike riding*
faire une randonnée pédestre	*to go for a hike*
... en raquettes	*...snow-shoeing*
... en skis	*...cross-country skiing*

Deuxième étape

Complaining; expressing discouragement and offering encouragement

Je crève de faim!	*I'm dying of hunger!*
Je meurs de soif!	*I'm dying of thirst!*
Je suis fatigué(e).	*I'm tired.*
J'ai peur (de la, du, des)...	*I'm scared (of)...*
Je n'en peux plus!	*I just can't do any more!*
J'abandonne!	*I'm giving up!*
Je craque!	*I'm losing it!*
Courage!	*Hang in there!*
Tu y es (On y est) presque!	*You're (we're) almost there!*
Allez!	*Come on!*

Asking for and giving advice

Qu'est-ce que je dois faire?	*What should I do?*
Tu devrais...	*You should...*
Tu ferais bien de...	*You would do well to...*
Evite de...	*Avoid...*
Tu ne devrais pas...	*You shouldn't...*
respecter la nature	*to respect nature*
jeter (remporter) les déchets	*to throw away (to take with you) your trash*
nourrir les animaux	*to feed the animals*
mutiler les arbres	*to deface the trees*
suivre les sentiers balisés	*to follow the marked trails*

Camping equipment

emporter	*to bring (with you)*
une lampe de poche	*flashlight*
une tente	*tent*
un sac de couchage	*sleeping bag*
une boussole	*compass*
une trousse de premiers soins	*first-aid kit*
une canne à pêche	*fishing pole*
des allumettes	*matches*
de la lotion anti-moustiques	*insect repellent*

Troisième étape

Relating a series of events; describing people and places

D'abord,...	*First,...*
Ensuite,...	*Then,...*
Après ça,...	*After that,...*
Finalement,...	*Finally,...*
Il y avait...	*There was/were...*
Il était...	*He was...*
Elle avait l'air...	*She seemed...*
J'étais...	*I was...*

Review and Assess

Game

Catégories Type five games on a sheet of paper, each having five categories. For example, **Jeu #1** might have: 1. an animal; 2. an outdoor activity; 3. camping supplies; 4. complaining; 5. offering encouragement. Form groups of five and distribute a game sheet to each group. The groups try to give an answer for each category that no one else gives. For example, if the category is *an animal* and three teams name **un loup,** the fourth team names **un renard,** and the fifth team names **un ours,** only the fourth and fifth teams score a point. To start, each group uncovers **Jeu #1.** Players have three minutes to write something for each category. Call time and have each group name what they wrote for the first category. Tally the points and repeat for the other categories. Next, have students uncover and begin **Jeu #2,** and so on.

Vocabulaire

CHAPITRE 12

Circumlocution

Have students work in pairs. One student will play the role of a shopper in a sporting goods store, while the other is a salesperson. The shopper is looking for items to take on a camping trip. However, he or she can't remember the exact French words for the items and must describe them to the salesperson. When an item is identified, the salesperson shows the customer where it is located. (**—Ce que je cherche, c'est des trucs qu'on utilise pour faire du feu. —Vous cherchez des allumettes? —Oui, c'est ça. —Voici les allumettes. —Merci.)** Then, have students switch roles.

Chapter 12 Assessment

- **Testing Program**
  Chapter Test, pp. 313–318

  Audio Compact Discs, CD 12, Trs. 16–23
  Speaking Test, p. 348
  Final Exam, pp. 327–334

  Audio Compact Discs, CD 12, Trs. 19–23
- **Alternative Assessment Guide**
  Performance Assessment, p. 43
  Portfolio Assessment, p. 29
  CD-ROM Assessment, p. 57
- **Interactive CD-ROM Tutor, Disc 3**

  A toi de parler
  A toi d'écrire
- **Standardized Assessment Tutor**
  Chapter 12
- **One-Stop Planner, Disc 3**
  Test Generator, Chapter 12

STANDARDS: 1.1

Reference Section

Summary of Functions

Function is another word for the way in which you use language for a specific purpose. When you find yourself in specific situations, such as in a restaurant, in a grocery store, or at school, you'll want to communicate with those around you. In order to communicate in French, you have to "function" in the language.

Each chapter in this book focuses on language functions. You can easily find them in boxes labeled **Comment dit-on... ?** The other features in the chapter—grammar, vocabulary, culture notes—support the functions you're learning.

Here is a list of the functions presented in Levels 1 and 2 of the ***Allez, viens!*** program and their French expressions. You'll need them in order to communicate in a wide range of situations. Following each function are the numbers of the level, the chapter, and the page where the function was first introduced.

Socializing

Greeting people **I Ch. 1, p. 22**
Bonjour.
Salut.

Saying goodbye **I Ch. 1, p. 22**
Salut.
Au revoir.
A tout à l'heure.
A bientôt.
A demain.
Tchao.

Asking how people are **I Ch. 1, p. 23**
(Comment) ça va?
Et toi?

Telling how you are **I Ch. 1, p. 23**
Ça va.
Super!
Très bien.
Comme ci comme ça.
Bof.
Pas mal.
Pas terrible.

Expressing thanks **I Ch. 3, p. 90**
Merci.
A votre service.

Extending invitations **I Ch. 6, p. 179**
Allons... !
Tu veux... ?
Tu viens?
On peut...

Accepting invitations **I Ch. 6, p. 179**
Je veux bien.
Pourquoi pas?
D'accord.
Bonne idée.

Refusing invitations **I Ch. 6, p. 179**
Désolé(e), je suis occupé(e).
Ça ne me dit rien.
J'ai des trucs à faire.
Désolé(e), je ne peux pas.

Identifying people **I Ch. 7, p. 203**
C'est...
Ce sont...
Voici...
Voilà...

II Ch. 11, p. 313
Tu connais...
Bien sûr. C'est...
Je ne connais pas.

Introducing people **I Ch. 7, p. 207**
C'est...
Je te/vous présente...
Très heureux (heureuse). (FORMAL)

Seeing someone off **I Ch. 11, p. 336**
Bon voyage!
Bonnes vacances!
Amuse-toi bien!
Bonne chance!

Welcoming someone **II Ch. 2, p. 37**
Bienvenue chez moi (chez nous).
Faites (Fais) comme chez vous (toi).
Vous avez (Tu as) fait bon voyage?

Responding to someone's welcome **II Ch. 2, p. 37**
Merci.

C'est gentil de votre (ta) part.
Oui, excellent.
C'était fatigant!

Extending good wishes **II Ch. 3, p. 79**
Bonne fête!
Joyeux (Bon) anniversaire!
Bonne fête de Hanoukkah!
Joyeux Noël!
Bonne année!
Meilleurs vœux!
Félicitations!
Bon voyage!
Bonne route!
Bonne santé!

Congratulating someone **II Ch. 5, p. 143**
Félicitations!
Bravo!
Chapeau!

Exchanging Information

Asking someone's name and giving yours
I Ch. 1, p. 24
Tu t'appelles comment?
Je m'appelle...

Asking and giving someone else's name
I Ch. 1, p. 24
Il/Elle s'appelle comment?
Il/Elle s'appelle...

Asking someone's age and giving yours
I Ch. 1, p. 25
Tu as quel âge?
J'ai... ans.

Asking for information (about classes)
I Ch. 2, pp. 55, 58
Tu as quels cours... ?
Vous avez... ?
Tu as quoi... ?
Tu as... à quelle heure?

(about places) **II Ch. 4, p. 102**
Où se trouve... ?
Qu'est-ce qu'il y a... ?
C'est comment?

II Ch. 12, p. 348
Où se trouve... ?
Qu'est-ce qu'il y a à voir... ?
Qu'est-ce qu'il y a à faire?

(about travel) **II Ch. 6, p. 172**
A quelle heure est-ce que le train (le car) pour... part?
De quel quai... ?
A quelle heure est-ce que vous ouvrez (fermez)?
Combien coûte... ?
un aller-retour
un aller simple
C'est combien, l'entrée?

(about movies) **II Ch. 11, p. 320**
Qu'est-ce qu'on joue comme films?
Ça passe où?
C'est avec qui?
Ça commence à quelle heure?

Giving information (about classes) **I Ch. 2, p. 55**
Nous avons...
J'ai...

Telling when you have class **I Ch. 2, p. 58**
à... heures
à... heures quinze
à... heures trente
à... heures quarante-cinq

Describing a place **II Ch. 4, p. 102**
dans le nord
dans le sud
dans l'est
dans l'ouest
plus grand(e) que
moins grand(e) que
charmant(e)
coloré(e)
vivant(e)

II Ch. 12, p. 358
Il y avait...
Il était...

Giving information (about travel)
II Ch. 6, p. 172
Du quai...
Je voudrais...
Un..., s'il vous plaît.
... tickets, s'il vous plaît.

II Ch. 12, p. 348
...se trouve...
Il y a...
On peut...

(about movies) **II Ch. 11, p. 320**
On joue...
Ça passe à...
C'est avec...
A...

Making requests **I Ch. 3, p. 80**
Tu as... ?
Vous avez... ?

Responding to requests **I Ch. 3, p. 80**
Voilà.
Je regrette.
Je n'ai pas de...

Asking others what they need **I Ch. 3, p. 82**
Qu'est-ce qu'il te faut pour... ?
Qu'est-ce qu'il vous faut pour... ?

Expressing need **I Ch. 8, p. 238**
Qu'est-ce qu'il te faut?
Il me faut...
De quoi est-ce que tu as besoin?
J'ai besoin de...

Expressing need (shopping) **I Ch. 10, p. 301**
Oui, il me faut...
Oui, vous avez... ?
Je cherche quelque chose pour...
J'aimerais... pour aller avec...

Getting someone's attention **I Ch. 3, p. 90**
Pardon.
Excusez-moi.

I Ch. 5, p. 151
... s'il vous plaît.
Excusez-moi.
Monsieur!
Madame!
Mademoiselle!

Exchanging information (about leisure activities)
I Ch. 4, p. 116
Qu'est-ce que tu fais comme sport?
Qu'est-ce que tu fais pour t'amuser?
Je fais...
Je ne fais pas de...
Je joue...

II Ch. 1, p. 12
Qu'est-ce que tu aimes faire?
Qu'est-ce que tu fais comme sport?
Qu'est-ce que tu aimes comme musique?
Quel(le) est ton/ta... préféré(e)?
Qui est ton/ta... préféré(e)?

Ordering food and beverages **I Ch. 5, p. 151**
Vous avez choisi?
Vous prenez?
Je voudrais...
Je vais prendre..., s'il vous plaît.
Un sandwich, s'il vous plaît.
Donnez-moi..., s'il vous plaît.
Apportez-moi..., s'il vous plaît.
Vous avez... ?
Qu'est-ce que vous avez comme... ?

Paying the check **I Ch. 5, p. 155**
L'addition, s'il vous plaît.
Oui, tout de suite.
Un moment, s'il vous plaît.
Ça fait combien, s'il vous plaît?
Ça fait... euros.
C'est combien,... ?
C'est... euros.

Making plans **I Ch. 6, p. 173**
Qu'est-ce que tu vas faire... ?
Tu vas faire quoi... ?
Je vais...
Pas grand-chose.
Rien de spécial.

Arranging to meet someone **I Ch. 6, p. 183**
Quand (ça)?
tout de suite
Où (ça)?
devant
au métro...
chez...
dans...
Avec qui?
A quelle heure?
A cinq heures...
et demie
et quart
moins le quart
moins cinq
midi (et demi)
minuit (et demi)
vers...
On se retrouve...
Rendez-vous...
Entendu.

Describing and characterizing people
I Ch. 7, p. 209
Il/Elle est comment?
Ils/Elles sont comment?
Il est...
Elle est...
Ils sont...

II Ch. 1, p. 10
avoir... ans
J'ai...
Il/Elle a...
Ils/Elles ont...
Je suis...

Il/Elle est...
Ils/Elles sont...

Describing people **II Ch. 12, p. 358**
Il avait...
Elle avait l'air...
J'étais...

Making a telephone call **I Ch. 9, p. 276**
Bonjour.
Je suis bien chez... ?
C'est...
(Est-ce que)... est là, s'il vous plaît?
(Est-ce que) je peux parler à... ?
Je peux laisser un message?
Vous pouvez lui dire que j'ai téléphoné?
Ça ne répond pas.
C'est occupé.

Answering a telephone call **I Ch. 9, p. 276**
Allô?
Bonjour.
Qui est à l'appareil?
Vous pouvez rappeler plus tard?
Une seconde, s'il vous plaît.
D'accord.
Bien sûr.
Ne quittez pas.

Inquiring (shopping) **I Ch. 10, p. 301**
(Est-ce que) je peux vous aider?
Vous désirez?
Je peux l'(les) essayer?
Je peux essayer... ?
C'est combien,... ?
Ça fait combien?
Vous avez ça en... ?

Pointing out places and things **I Ch. 12, p. 361**
Là, tu vois, c'est...
Regarde, voilà...
Ça, c'est...
Là, c'est...
Voici...

Asking for advice (directions)
I Ch. 12, p. 366
Comment est-ce qu'on y va?

Making suggestions **I Ch. 12, p. 366**
On peut y aller...
On peut prendre...

Asking for directions **I Ch. 12, p. 371**
Pardon,... s'il vous plaît?
Pardon,... Où est..., s'il vous plaît?
Pardon,... Je cherche..., s'il vous plaît.

II Ch. 2, p. 49
Où est..., s'il vous plaît?

Giving directions **I Ch. 12, p. 317**
Vous continuez jusqu'au prochain feu rouge.
Vous tournez...
Vous allez tout droit jusqu'à...
Vous prenez la rue..., puis traversez la rue...
Vous passez devant...
C'est tout de suite à...

II Ch. 2, p. 49
Traversez...
Prenez...
Puis, tournez à gauche dans/sur...
Allez (continuez) tout droit.
sur la droite (gauche)

II Ch. 12, p. 348
C'est au nord/au sud/à l'est/à l'ouest de...
C'est dans le nord/le sud/l'est/l'ouest de...

Inquiring about past events **I Ch. 9, p. 270**
Qu'est-ce que tu as fait... ?
Tu es allé(e) où?
Et après?
Qu'est-ce qui s'est passé?

Inquiring about future plans **I Ch. 11, p. 329**
Qu'est-ce que tu vas faire... ?
Où est-ce que tu vas aller... ?

Sharing future plans **I Ch. 11, p. 329**
J'ai l'intention de...
Je vais...

Relating a series of events **II Ch. 1, p. 20**
Qu'est-ce que tu vas faire... ?
D'abord, je vais...
Ensuite,...
Puis,...
Enfin,...

II Ch. 4, p. 111
Après ça...
Finalement...
Vers...

II Ch. 12, p. 358
D'abord,...
Ensuite,...
Puis,...
Après ça,...
Enfin,/Finalement,...

Pointing out where things are **II Ch. 2, p. 43**
Là, c'est...
A côté de...
Il y a...

Ça, c'est...
en face de
à gauche de
à droite de
près de

Making purchases **II Ch. 3, p. 66**
Combien coûte(nt)... ?
Combien en voulez-vous?
Je vais (en) prendre...
Ça fait combien?

Asking what things were like **II Ch. 8, p. 226**
C'était comment?
C'était tellement différent?

Describing what things were like **II Ch. 8, p. 226**
C'était...
Il y avait...
La vie était plus..., moins...

Reminiscing **II Ch. 8, p. 229**
Quand j'étais petit(e),...
Quand il/elle était petit(e),...
Quand j'avais... ans,...

Breaking some news **II Ch. 9, p. 263**
Tu connais la nouvelle?
Tu ne devineras jamais ce qui s'est passé.
Tu sais qui... ?
Tu sais ce que... ?
Devine qui...
Devine ce que...

Showing interest **II Ch. 9, p. 263**
Raconte!
Aucune idée.
Dis vite!

Beginning a story **II Ch. 9, p. 267**
A propos,...

Continuing a story **II Ch. 9, p. 267**
Donc,...
Alors,...
Bref,...
C'est-à-dire que...
... quoi.
A ce moment-là,...
... tu vois.

Ending a story **II Ch. 9, p. 267**
Heureusement,...
Malheureusement,...
Finalement,...

Summarizing **II Ch. 11, p. 326**
De quoi ça parle?
Qu'est-ce que ça raconte?
Ça parle de...
C'est l'histoire de...

Expressing Feelings and Emotions

Expressing likes and preferences about things
I Ch. 1, p. 26
J'aime (bien)...
J'aime mieux...
J'adore...
Je préfère...

I Ch. 5, p. 154
C'est...

Expressing dislikes about things **I Ch. 1, p. 26**
Je n'aime pas...

I Ch. 5, p. 154
C'est...

Telling what you'd like and what you'd like to do
I Ch. 3, p. 85
Je voudrais...
Je voudrais acheter...

Telling how much you like or dislike something
I Ch. 4, p. 114
Beaucoup.
Pas beaucoup.
Pas tellement.
Pas du tout.
surtout

Inquiring about likes and dislikes
I Ch. 5, p. 154
Comment tu trouves ça?

Sharing confidences **I Ch. 9, p. 279**
J'ai un petit problème.
Je peux te parler?
Tu as une minute?

II Ch. 10, p. 286
Je ne sais pas quoi faire.
J'ai un problème.
Tu as une minute?
Je peux te parler?
Qu'est-ce qu'il y a?
Je t'écoute.
Qu'est-ce que je peux faire?

Consoling others **I Ch. 9, p. 279**
Ne t'en fais pas!
Je t'écoute.
Ça va aller mieux!
Qu'est-ce que je peux faire?

II Ch. 5, p. 141
Ça va aller mieux.
T'en fais pas.
C'est pas grave.
Courage!

Hesitating **I Ch. 10, p. 310**
Euh... J'hésite.
Je ne sais pas.
Il/Elle me plaît, mais il/elle est...

Making a decision **I Ch. 10, p. 310**
Vous avez décidé de prendre... ?
Vous avez choisi?
Vous le/la/les prenez?
Je le/la/les prends.
Non, c'est trop cher.

Expressing indecision **I Ch. 11, p. 329**
J'hésite.
Je ne sais pas.
Je n'en sais rien.
Je n'ai rien de prévu.

Expressing wishes **I Ch. 11, p. 329**
J'ai envie de...
Je voudrais bien...

Asking how someone is feeling
II Ch. 2, p. 38
Pas trop fatigué(e)?
Vous n'avez pas (Tu n'as pas) faim?
Vous n'avez pas (Tu n'as pas) soif?

Telling how you are feeling
II Ch. 2, p. 38
Non, ça va.
Si, un peu.
Si, je suis crevé(e).
Si, j'ai très faim (soif)!
Si, je meurs de faim (soif)!

Inquiring **II Ch. 5, p. 139**
Comment ça s'est passé?
Comment s'est passée ta journée (hier)?
Comment s'est passé ton week-end?
Comment se sont passées tes vacances?

Expressing satisfaction **II Ch. 5, p. 139**
Ça s'est très bien passé!
C'était incroyable!
Quelle journée!
Quel week-end!

Expressing frustration **II Ch. 5, p. 139**
Quelle journée!
Quel week-end!
J'ai passé une journée épouvantable!
C'est pas mon jour!
Tout a été de travers!

Sympathizing with someone **II Ch. 5, p. 141**
Oh là là!
C'est pas de chance, ça!
Pauvre vieux (vieille)!

Making excuses **II Ch. 5, p. 143**
Je suis nul (nulle) en maths.
Je suis assez bon (bonne) en histoire.
Je suis le/la meilleur(e) en informatique.
Ce n'est pas mon fort.
J'ai du mal à comprendre.

Expressing disbelief and doubt **II Ch. 6, p. 168**
Tu plaisantes!
Pas possible!
Ça m'étonnerait!
C'est pas vrai!
N'importe quoi!
Mon œil!

Expressing concern for someone **II Ch. 5, p. 135**
Ça n'a pas l'air d'aller.
Qu'est-ce qui se passe?
Qu'est-ce qui t'arrive?
Raconte!

II Ch. 7, p. 189
Quelque chose ne va pas?
Qu'est-ce que tu as?
Tu n'as pas l'air en forme.

Complaining **II Ch. 7, p. 189**
Je ne me sens pas bien.
Je suis tout(e) raplapla.
J'ai mal dormi.
J'ai mal partout!

II Ch. 12, p. 354
Je crève de faim!
Je meurs de soif!
Je suis fatigué(e).
J'ai peur (de la, du, des)...

Expressing discouragement **II Ch. 7, p. 198**
Je n'en peux plus!
J'abandonne.
Je craque!

II Ch. 12, p. 354
Je n'en peux plus!
J'abandonne!
Je craque!

Offering encouragement **II Ch. 7, p. 198**
Allez!
Encore un effort!

Tu y es presque!
Courage!

II Ch. 12, p. 354
Courage!
Tu y es (On y est) presque!
Allez!

Telling what or whom you miss **II Ch. 8, p. 225**
Je regrette...
... me manque.
... me manquent.
Ce qui me manque, c'est (de)...!

Persuading

Asking for suggestions **II Ch. 1, p. 18**
Qu'est-ce qu'on fait?

II Ch. 4, p. 106
Qu'est-ce qu'on peut faire?

Making suggestions **I Ch. 12, p. 366**
On peut y aller...
On peut prendre...

I Ch. 5, p. 145
On va... ?
On fait... ?
On joue... ?

II Ch. 1, p. 18
Si tu veux, on peut...
On pourrait...
Tu as envie de... ?
Ça te dit de... ?

II Ch. 4, p. 106
On peut...
Ça te dit d'aller... ?
Si on allait... ?

II Ch. 8, p. 237
Si on achetait... ?
Si on visitait... ?
Si on jouait... ?
Si on allait... ?

Accepting suggestions **I Ch. 4, p. 122**
D'accord.
Bonne idée.
Allons-y!
Oui, c'est...

Turning down suggestions **I Ch. 4, p. 122**
Non, c'est...
Ça ne me dit rien.
Désolé(e), mais je ne peux pas.

Responding to suggestions **II Ch. 1, p. 18**
D'accord.
C'est une bonne (excellente) idée.
Je veux bien.
Je ne peux pas.
Ça ne me dit rien.
Non, je préfère...
Pas question!

II Ch. 8, p. 237
D'accord.
C'est une bonne idée.
Bof.
Non, je préfère...
Non, je ne veux pas.

Making excuses **I Ch. 5, p. 149**
Désolé(e), j'ai des devoirs à faire.
J'ai des courses à faire.
J'ai des trucs à faire.
J'ai des tas de choses à faire.

II Ch. 5, p. 143
..., c'est pas mon fort.
J'ai du mal à comprendre.
Je suis pas doué(e) pour...

II Ch. 10, p. 291
Désolé(e).
J'ai quelque chose à faire.
Je n'ai pas le temps.
Je suis très occupé(e).
C'est impossible.

Giving reasons **II Ch. 5, p. 143**
Je suis assez bon (bonne) en...
C'est en... que je suis le/la meilleur(e).
..., c'est mon fort.

Making a recommendation
I Ch. 5, p. 148
Prends/Prenez...

Asking for permission **I Ch. 7, p. 213**
(Est-ce que) je peux... ?
Tu es d'accord?

Giving permission **I Ch. 7, p. 213**
Oui, si tu veux.
Pourquoi pas?
Oui, bien sûr.
D'accord, si tu... d'abord...

Refusing permission **I Ch. 7, p. 213**
Pas question!
Je ne suis pas d'accord.
Non, tu as... à...
Pas ce soir.

Making requests **I Ch. 8, p. 240**
Tu peux aller faire les courses?
Tu me rapportes... ?

I Ch. 12, p. 364
Est-ce que tu peux... ?
Tu pourrais passer à... ?

Accepting requests **I Ch. 8, p. 240**
Bon, d'accord.
Je veux bien.
J'y vais tout de suite.

I Ch. 12, p. 364
D'accord.
Je veux bien.
Si tu veux.

Declining requests **I Ch. 8, p. 240**
Je ne peux pas maintenant.
Je regrette, mais je n'ai pas le temps.

I Ch. 12, p. 364
Désolé(e), mais je n'ai pas le temps.
J'ai des tas de choses (trucs) à faire.

Telling someone what to do
I Ch. 8, p. 240
Rapporte-moi...
Prends...
Achète(-moi)...
N'oublie pas.

Asking for food **II Ch. 3, p. 72**
Je pourrais avoir... ?
Vous pourriez (Tu pourrais) me passer... ?

Offering food **I Ch. 8, p. 247**
Tu veux... ?
Vous voulez... ?
Vous prenez... ?
Tu prends... ?
Encore de... ?

II Ch. 3, p. 72
Voilà.
Vous voulez (Tu veux)... ?
Encore... ?
Tenez (Tiens).

Accepting food **I Ch. 8, p. 247**
Oui, s'il vous (te) plaît.
Oui, avec plaisir.

II Ch. 3, p. 72
Oui, je veux bien.

Refusing food **I Ch. 8, p. 247**
Non, merci.
Non, merci. Je n'ai plus faim.
Je n'en veux plus.

II Ch. 3, p. 72
Merci, ça va.
Je n'ai plus faim (soif).

Asking for advice **I Ch. 12, p. 366**
Comment est-ce qu'on y va?

I Ch. 9, p. 279
A ton avis, qu'est-ce que je fais?
Qu'est-ce que tu me conseilles?

I Ch. 10, p. 300
Je ne sais pas quoi mettre pour...
Qu'est-ce que je mets?

II Ch. 3, p. 76
Tu as une idée de cadeau pour... ?
Qu'est-ce que je pourrais offrir à... ?
Bonne idée!

II Ch. 10, p. 286
A ton avis, qu'est-ce que je dois faire?
Qu'est-ce que tu ferais, toi?
Qu'est-ce que tu me conseilles?

II Ch. 12, p. 356
Qu'est-ce que je dois faire?

Giving advice **I Ch. 9, p. 279**
Oublie-le/-la/-les!
Téléphone-lui/-leur!
Tu devrais...
Pourquoi tu ne... pas?

I Ch. 10, p. 300
Pourquoi est-ce que tu ne mets pas... ?
Mets...

II Ch. 1, p. 15
Pense à prendre...
Prends...
N'oublie pas...

II Ch. 3, p. 76
Offre-lui (leur)...
Tu pourrais lui (leur) offrir...
... peut-être?

II Ch. 7, p. 197
Tu devrais...
Tu ferais bien de...
Tu n'as qu'à...
Pourquoi tu ne... pas... ?

II Ch. 10, p. 286
Oublie-le/-la/-les.
Invite-le/-la/-les.

Parle-lui/-leur.
Dis-lui/-leur que...
Ecris-lui/-leur.
Explique-lui/-leur.
Excuse-toi.
Téléphone-lui/-leur.
Tu devrais...

II Ch. 7, p. 202
Evite de...
Ne saute pas...
Tu ne devrais pas...

II Ch. 12, p. 356
Tu devrais...
Tu ferais bien de...
Evite de...
Tu ne devrais pas...

Accepting advice **II Ch. 3, p. 76**
Bonne idée!
C'est original.
Tu as raison...
D'accord.

II Ch. 7, p. 197
Tu as raison.
Bonne idée.
D'accord.

Rejecting advice **II Ch. 3, p. 76**
C'est trop cher.
C'est banal.
Ce n'est pas son style.
Il/Elle en a déjà un(e).

II Ch. 7, p. 197
Non, je n'ai pas très envie.
Je ne peux pas.
Ce n'est pas mon truc.
Non, je préfère...

Reminding **I Ch. 11, p. 333**
N'oublie pas...
Tu n'as pas oublié... ?
Tu ne peux pas partir sans...
Tu prends... ?

Reassuring **I Ch. 11, p. 333**
Ne t'en fais pas.
J'ai pensé à tout.
Je n'ai rien oublié.

II Ch. 8, p. 225
Tu vas t'y faire.
Fais-toi une raison.
Tu vas te plaire ici.
Tu vas voir que...

Asking a favor **I Ch. 12, p. 364**
Est-ce que tu peux... ?
(Est-ce que) tu pourrais me rendre un petit service?
Tu pourrais passer à... ?

Agreeing to a request **I Ch. 12, p. 364**
D'accord.
Je veux bien.
Si tu veux.

Refusing a request **I Ch. 12, p. 364**
Désolé(e), mais je n'ai pas le temps.
J'ai des tas de choses (trucs) à faire.
Non, je ne peux pas.

Reprimanding someone **II Ch. 5, p. 143**
C'est inadmissible.
Il faut mieux travailler en classe.
Il ne faut pas faire le clown en classe!
Ne recommence pas.

Justifying your recommendations
II Ch. 7, p. 202
C'est bon pour toi.
C'est mieux que...
Ça te fera du bien.

Advising against something **II Ch. 7, p. 202**
Evite de...
Ne saute pas...
Tu ne devrais pas...

Asking for a favor **II Ch. 10, p. 291**
Tu peux m'aider?
Tu pourrais... ?
Ça t'ennuie de... ?
Ça t'embête de... ?

Granting a favor **II Ch. 10, p. 291**
Avec plaisir.
Bien sûr.
Pas du tout.
Bien sûr que non.
Pas de problème.

Apologizing **II Ch. 10, p. 294**
C'est de ma faute.
Excuse-moi.
Désolé(e).
J'aurais dû...
J'aurais pu...
Tu ne m'en veux pas?

Accepting an apology **II Ch. 10, p. 294**
Ça ne fait rien.
Je ne t'en veux pas.
Il n'y a pas de mal.

Reproaching someone **II Ch. 10, p. 294**
Tu aurais dû...
Tu aurais pu...!

Expressing Attitudes and Opinions

Agreeing **I Ch. 2, p. 54**
Oui, beaucoup.
Moi aussi.
Moi non plus.

Disagreeing **I Ch. 2, p. 54**
Moi, non.
Non, pas trop.
Moi, si.
Pas moi.

Asking for opinions **I Ch. 2, p. 61**
Comment tu trouves... ?
Comment tu trouves ça?

I Ch. 9, p. 269
Tu as passé un bon week-end?

I Ch. 10, p. 306
Comment tu trouves... ?
Il/Elle me va?
Il/Elle te (vous) plaît?
Tu aimes mieux... ou... ?

I Ch. 11, p. 337
Tu as passé un bon... ?
Ça s'est bien passé?
Tu t'es bien amusé(e)?

II Ch. 6, p. 164
C'était comment?
Ça t'a plu?
Tu t'es amusé(e)?

Expressing opinions **I Ch. 2, p. 61**
C'est...

I Ch. 9, p. 269
Oui, très chouette.
Oui, excellent.
Oui, très bon.
Oui, ça a été.
Oh, pas mauvais.
C'était épouvantable.
Très mal.

I Ch. 11, p. 337
Oui, très chouette.
C'était formidable!
Non, pas vraiment.
Oui, ça a été.
Oh, pas mauvais.
C'était épouvantable.
Je suis embêté(e).
C'était un véritable cauchemar!

Paying a compliment **I Ch. 10, p. 306**
C'est tout à fait ton/votre style.
Il/Elle te (vous) va très bien.
Il/Elle va très bien avec...
Je le/la/les trouve...
sensass (sensationnel)
C'est parfait.

II Ch. 3, p. 72
C'est vraiment bon!
C'était délicieux!

II Ch. 2, p. 44
Il (Elle) est vraiment bien, ton (ta)...
Il (Elle) est cool, ton (ta)...
beau (belle)
génial(e)
chouette

Responding to compliments **II Ch. 2, p. 44; II Ch. 3, p. 72**
Ce n'est pas grand-chose.
C'est gentil!
Tu trouves?
C'est vrai? (Vraiment?)

Criticizing **I Ch. 10, p. 306**
Il/Elle ne te (vous) va pas du tout.
Il/Elle ne va pas du tout avec...
Il/Elle est (Ils/Elles sont) trop...
Je le/la/les trouve moche(s).

Emphasizing likes **II Ch. 4, p. 107**
Ce que j'aime bien, c'est...
Ce que je préfère, c'est...
Ce qui me plaît, c'est (de)...

Emphasizing dislikes **II Ch. 4, p. 107**
Ce que je n'aime pas, c'est...
Ce qui m'ennuie, c'est (de)...
Ce qui ne me plaît pas, c'est (de)...

Expressing enthusiasm **II Ch. 6, p. 164**
C'était...
magnifique.
incroyable.
superbe.
sensass.
Ça m'a beaucoup plu.
Je me suis beaucoup amusé(e).

Expressing indifference **II Ch. 6, p. 164**
C'était...
assez bien.

comme ci comme ça.
pas mal.
Plus ou moins.

Expressing dissatisfaction **II Ch. 6, p. 164**
C'était...
ennuyeux.
mortel.
nul.
sinistre.
Sûrement pas!
Je me suis ennuyé(e).

Wondering what happened and offering possible explanations **II Ch. 9, p. 260**
Je me demande...
A mon avis,...
Peut-être que...
Je crois que...
Je parie que...

Accepting explanations **II Ch. 9, p. 260**
Tu as peut-être raison.
C'est possible.
Ça se voit.
Evidemment.

Rejecting explanations **II Ch. 9, p. 260**
A mon avis, tu te trompes.
Ce n'est pas possible.
Je ne crois pas.

Giving opinions **II Ch. 11, p. 324**
C'est drôle (amusant).
C'est une belle histoire.
C'est plein de rebondissements.
Il y a du suspense.
On ne s'ennuie pas.
C'est une histoire passionnante.
Je te le recommande.
Il n'y a pas d'histoire.
Ça casse pas des briques.
C'est...
trop violent.
trop long.
bête.
un navet.
du n'importe quoi.
gentillet, sans plus.
déprimant.

Si tu as oublié...

Family and Pets

le beau-père	*stepfather/father-in-law*
la belle-fille	*stepdaughter/ daughter-in-law*
la belle-mère	*stepmother/mother-in-law*
le beau-frère	*brother-in-law/stepbrother*
la belle-sœur	*stepsister/sister-in-law*
le cousin (la cousine)	*cousin*
le demi-frère	*half-brother*
la demi-sœur	*half-sister*
l'enfant unique	*only child*
le frère	*brother*
la grand-mère	*grandmother*
le grand-père	*grandfather*
la mère	*mother*
l'oncle (m.)	*uncle*
le père	*father*
la sœur	*sister*
la tante	*aunt*
le canari	*canary*
le chat	*cat*
le chien	*dog*
le poisson	*fish*

Clothing and Colors

un blouson	*a jacket*
des boucles (f.) **d'oreilles**(f.)	*earrings*
un bracelet	*a bracelet*
un cardigan	*a sweater*
une casquette	*a cap*
une ceinture	*a belt*
un chapeau	*a hat*
des chaussettes (f.)	*socks*
des chaussures (f.)	*shoes*
une chemise	*a shirt (men's)*
un chemisier	*a shirt (women's)*

un collant	*hose*
une cravate	*a tie*
une jupe	*a skirt*
des lunettes (f.) **de soleil**	*sunglasses*
un maillot de bain	*a bathing suit*
un manteau	*a coat*
un pantalon	*a pair of pants*
une robe	*a dress*
des sandales (f.)	*sandals*
un short	*a pair of shorts*
un sweat-shirt	*a sweatshirt*
une veste	*a suit jacket, a blazer*
blanc(he)(s)	*white*
bleu(e)(s)	*blue*
gris(e)(s)	*grey*
jaune(s)	*yellow*
marron	*brown*
noir(e)(s)	*black*
orange	*orange*
rose(s)	*pink*
rouge(s)	*red*
vert(e)(s)	*green*
violet(te)(s)	*purple*

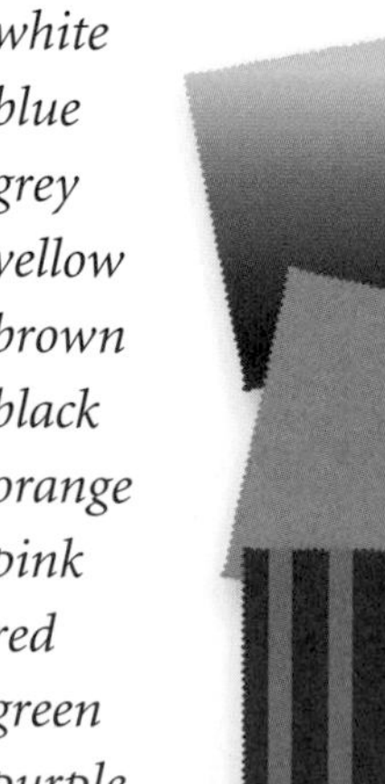

Weather and Seasons

Il fait beau.	*It's nice weather.*
Il fait chaud.	*It's hot.*
Il fait frais.	*It's cool.*
Il fait froid.	*It's cold.*
Il neige.	*It's snowing.*
Il pleut.	*It's raining.*

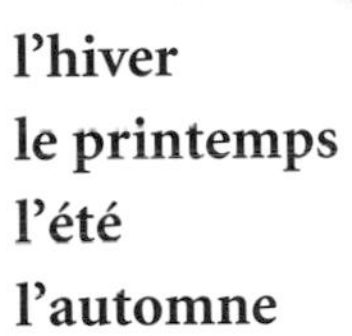

l'hiver	*winter*
le printemps	*spring*
l'été	*summer*
l'automne	*fall*

How to Tell Time

A quelle heure?	*At what time?*
à... heure(s)	*at . . . o'clock*
à... heure(s) quinze	*at . . . fifteen*
à... heure(s) trente	*at . . . thirty*
à... heure(s) quarante-cinq	*at . . . forty-five*
à... heure(s) et demie	*at half past . . .*
à... heure(s) et quart	*at quarter past . . .*
à... heure(s) moins le quart	*at quarter to . . .*
à... heure(s) moins cinq	*at five to . . .*
à midi	*at noon*
à minuit	*at midnight*
à midi (minuit) et demi	*at half past noon (midnight)*

Sports

faire de l'aérobic	*to do aerobics*
faire de l'athlétisme	*to do track and field*

faire du jogging	*to jog*
faire de la natation	*to swim*
faire du patin à glace	*to ice-skate*
faire des/de la photo(s)	*to take pictures/to do photography*
faire du roller en ligne	*to in-line skate*
faire du ski	*to ski*
faire du ski nautique	*to water ski*
faire du théâtre	*to do drama*
faire du vélo	*to bike*

faire de la vidéo	*to make videos*
jouer au base-ball	*to play baseball*
jouer au basket(-ball)	*to play basketball*
jouer au foot(ball)	*to play soccer*
jouer au football américain	*to play football*
jouer au golf	*to play golf*
jouer au hockey	*to play hockey*
jouer à des jeux vidéo	*to play video games*
jouer au tennis	*to play tennis*
jouer au volley(-ball)	*to play volleyball*

Additional Vocabulary

This list presents additional vocabulary you may want to use when you're doing the activities in the textbook and in the workbooks. If you can't find the words you need here, try the French-English and English-French vocabulary lists beginning on page R47.

Adjectives

absurd	*absurde*
agile	*agile*
awesome (impressive)	*impressionnant(e), imposant(e)*
boring	*ennuyeux (ennuyeuse)*
chilly (weather)	*froid; frais*
colorful (person) (thing)	*vif (vive); pittoresque; coloré(e)*
despicable	*abject(e); ignoble; méprisable*
eccentric	*excentrique; original(e); bizarre*
horrifying	*horrifiant(e)*
incredible	*incroyable*
phenomenal	*phénoménal(e)*
scandalous	*scandaleux (scandaleuse)*
tasteful (remark, object)	*de bon goût*
tasteless (flavor)	*sans goût/insipide*
tasteless (remark)	*de mauvais goût*
terrifying	*terrifiant(e), épouvantable*
threatening	*menaçant(e)*
tremendous (size)	*énorme; (excellent) formidable; fantastique*
unbearable	*insupportable*
unforgettable	*inoubliable*
unique	*unique*

Rooms of the House and Furnishings

garage	*le garage*
office	*le bureau*
basement	*la cave/le sous-sol*
attic	*le grenier*
patio	*la terrasse*
closet	*le placard*
couch	*le divan; le canapé*
easy chair	*le fauteuil*
mirror	*le miroir*
nightstand	*la table de nuit*
painting	*le tableau*
refrigerator	*le réfrigérateur (le frigo)*
oven	*le four*
microwave	*le micro-ondes*
dishwasher	*le lave-vaisselle*
washing machine	*le lave-linge, la machine à laver*
dryer	*le sèche-linge*
wall-to-wall carpeting	*la moquette*

Shops and Gifts

mall	*le centre commercial*
jewelry shop	*la bijouterie*
perfume shop	*la parfumerie*
clothing store	*la boutique de vêtements*
bookstore	*la librairie*
music store	*le disquaire*
jewelry	*des bijoux* (m.)
ring	*une bague*
watch	*une montre*
necklace	*un collier*
earrings	*des boucles* (f.) *d'oreilles*
bracelet	*un bracelet*
perfume	*un parfum*
outfit (matching; women)	*un ensemble*

Daily Activities

to wake up	*se réveiller*
to get ready	*se préparer*
to comb your hair	*se peigner*
to fix your hair	*se coiffer*
to shave	*se raser*
to put on makeup	*se maquiller*

to put perfume on	*se parfumer*
to look at yourself in the mirror	*se regarder dans le miroir*
to hurry	*se dépêcher*
to shower	*se doucher, prendre une douche*

School Day Activities

to get a good grade	*avoir une bonne note*
to see friends	*retrouver ses amis*
to have a substitute	*avoir un(e) remplaçant(e)*
to be quizzed	*être interrogé(e) par le prof*
to win a game	*gagner un match*
to have an argument with a friend	*se disputer avec un copain (une copine)*
to miss a class	*manquer un cours*
to be called to the principal's office	*être convoqué(e) chez le proviseur*
to receive a warning	*recevoir un avertissement*

Weekend Activities

to visit friends	*rendre visite à des amis*
to go to a concert	*aller au concert*
to rent some movies	*louer des vidéos*
to go to a party	*aller à une soirée/ boum/fête*
to go to a botanical garden	*aller au jardin botanique*
to go to an art exhibit	*aller voir une exposition*
to go to a festival	*aller voir un festival*

Illnesses

to cough	*tousser*
bronchitis	*une bronchite*
tonsillitis	*une angine*
indigestion	*une indigestion*
sore neck	*un torticolis*
to be sick to your stomach	*avoir une crise de foie*

Injuries

to have a bruise	*avoir un bleu*
to have a cut/wound	*avoir une coupure/plaie*
to strain a muscle	*se froisser un muscle*
to bump into	*se cogner contre*
to injure (something)	*se blesser (à la) (au)*

Childhood Events, Toys, and Games

to get in trouble	*faire des bêtises*
to have a slumber party	*passer la nuit chez un copain (une copine)*
to jump Chinese jump rope	*jouer à l'élastique*
to jump rope	*sauter à la corde*

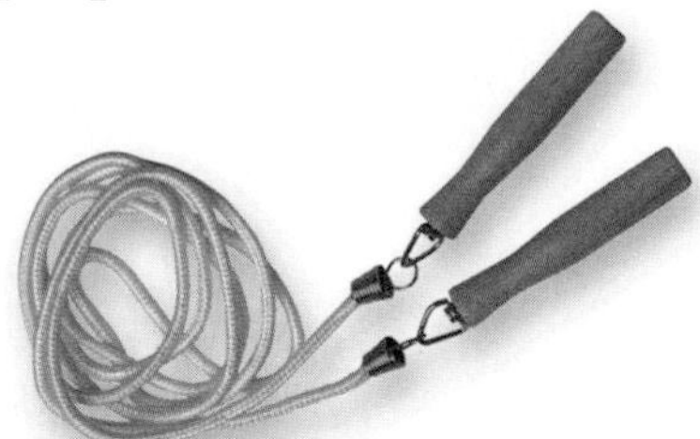

to lose a tooth	*perdre une dent de lait*
to play blind man's bluff	*jouer à colin-maillard*
to play hopscotch	*jouer à la marelle*
to put one's tooth under one's pillow	*mettre sa dent sous l'oreiller*
to run away	*faire une fugue*
to start school for the first time	*entrer à l'école*
to swing	*faire de la balançoire*
to wait for the Tooth Fairy	*attendre que la souris passe*

Fairy Tales

Once upon a time . . .	*Il était une fois...*
bears	*des ours* (m.)
big bad wolf	*le grand méchant loup*
castle	*un château*
enchanted	*enchanté(e)*
fairy	*la fée*
golden hair	*les cheveux d'or*
king	*le roi*
knight	*le chevalier*
magic mirror	*le miroir magique*
magician	*le magicien*
poisoned apple	*la pomme empoisonnée*
prince	*le prince*
Prince Charming	*le Prince Charmant*
princess	*la princesse*
seven dwarfs	*les sept nains*
slipper	*le soulier*
sword	*l'épée* (f.)
queen	*la reine*
wicked stepmother	*la marâtre*
And they lived happily ever after.	*Ils vécurent heureux et eurent beaucoup d'enfants.*

Friendship

to be sorry	*être désolé(e)*
to confide in someone	*se confier à quelqu'un*
to feel guilty	*se sentir coupable*

to get along with someone	*s'entendre bien avec quelqu'un*
to help someone do something	*aider quelqu'un à faire quelque chose*
to make friends	*se faire des amis*
to meet after school	*se retrouver après l'école*
to misunderstand	*mal comprendre*
to take the first step	*faire le premier pas*
to talk with friends	*discuter avec des amis*

More Music, Movies, Books

latest (music) **hits**	*les derniers tubes*
movie soundtrack	*la bande originale d'un film*
music videos	*les clips* (m.)
new wave	*la new wave, la nouvelle vague*
opera	*l'opéra* (m.)
fantasy film	*un film fantastique*
historic film	*un film historique*
psychological drama	*un drame psychologique*
war movie	*un film de guerre*
biography	*une biographie*
comedy	*une comédie*
drama	*un drame*
fable	*une fable*
fairy tale	*un conte de fées*
novel	*un roman*
tragedy	*une tragédie*

Outdoor Activities

to climb mountains	*faire de l'alpinisme*
to go rock-climbing	*faire de l'escalade*
to go rafting	*faire la descente d'une rivière*
to do archery	*faire du tir à l'arc*
to go spelunking	*faire de la spéléologie*
to go on a photo safari	*faire un safari-photo*
to collect rocks	*ramasser des pierres*
to collect butterflies	*aller à la chasse aux papillons*
to pick wildflowers	*cueillir des fleurs sauvages*
to collect wood	*ramasser du bois*
to build a fire	*faire un feu*
to sing around the campfire	*chanter autour du feu de camp*

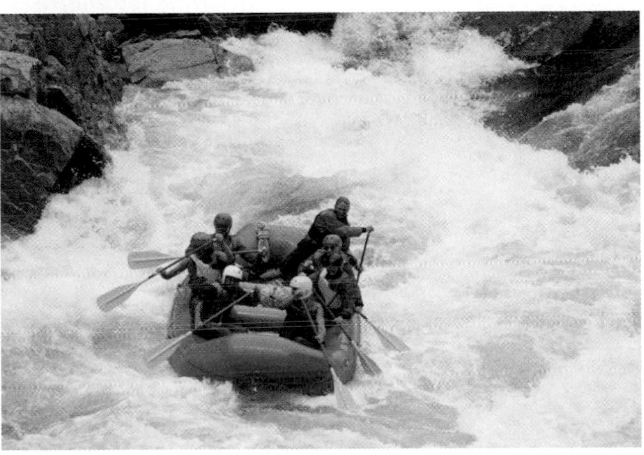

Computers

CD-ROM	*le CD-ROM, le disque optique compact*
CD-ROM drive	*le lecteur de CD-ROM, l'unité* (f.) *de CD-ROM*
to click	*cliquer*
computer	*l'ordinateur* (m.)

delete key	*la touche d'effacement*
disk drive	*le lecteur de disquette, l'unité* (f.) *de disquettes*
diskette, floppy disk	*la disquette, la disquette souple*
to drag	*glisser, déplacer*
e-mail	*le courrier électronique, la messagerie électronique*
file (folder)	*le fichier*
hard drive	*le disque dur*
homepage	*la page d'accueil*
Internet	*Internet* (m.)
keyboard	*le clavier*
keyword	*le mot-clé*
log on	*l'ouverture* (f.) *de session*
modem	*le modem*
monitor	*le moniteur, le logimètre*
mouse	*la souris*
password	*le mot de passe*
to print	*imprimer*
printer	*l'imprimante* (f.)
to quit	*quitter*
to record	*enregistrer*
return key	*la touche de retour*
to save	*sauvegarder, enregistrer*
screen	*l'écran* (m.)
to search	*chercher, rechercher*
search engine	*le moteur de recherche, l'outil* (m.) *de recherche*
to send	*envoyer*
software	*le logiciel*
Web site	*le site du Web, le site W3*
World Wide Web	*le World Wide Web, le Web, le W3*

Geographical Terms

The Continents

Africa	*l'Afrique* (f.)
Antarctica	*l'Antarctique* (f.)
Asia	*l'Asie* (f.)
Australia	*l'Australie* (f.)
Europe	*l'Europe* (f.)

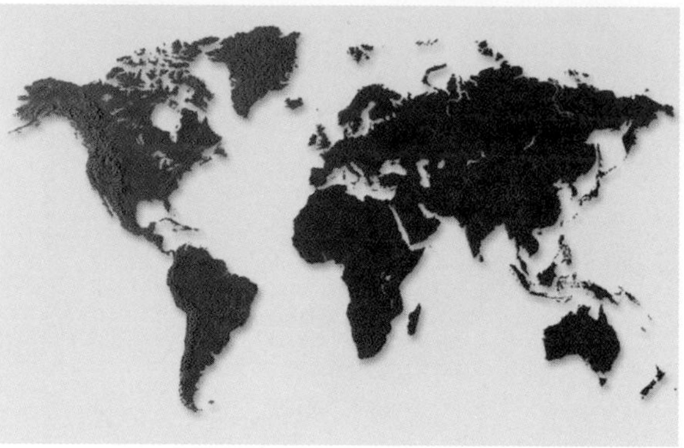

North America	*l'Amérique* (f.) *du Nord*
South America	*l'Amérique* (f.) *du Sud*

Countries

Algeria	*l'Algérie* (f.)
Argentina	*l'Argentine* (f.)
Australia	*l'Australie* (f.)
Austria	*l'Autriche* (f.)
Belgium	*la Belgique*
Brazil	*le Brésil*
Canada	*le Canada*
China	*la Chine*
Egypt	*l'Egypte* (f.)
England	*l'Angleterre* (f.)
France	*la France*
Germany	*l'Allemagne* (f.)
Greece	*la Grèce*
Holland	*la Hollande*
India	*l'Inde* (f.)
Ireland	*l'Irlande* (f.)
Israel	*Israël* (m.) (no article)
Italy	*l'Italie* (f.)
Jamaica	*la Jamaïque*
Japan	*le Japon*
Jordan	*la Jordanie*
Lebanon	*le Liban*
Libya	*la Libye*
Luxembourg	*le Luxembourg*
Mexico	*le Mexique*
Monaco	*Monaco* (f.) (no article)
Morocco	*le Maroc*
Netherlands	*les Pays-Bas* (m.)
North Korea	*la Corée du Nord*

Peru	*le Pérou*
Philippines	*les Philippines* (f.)
Poland	*la Pologne*
Portugal	*le Portugal*
Republic of Côte d'Ivoire	*la République de Côte d'Ivoire*
Russia	*la Russie*
Senegal	*le Sénégal*
South Korea	*la Corée du Sud*
Spain	*l'Espagne* (f.)
Switzerland	*la Suisse*
Syria	*la Syrie*
Tunisia	*la Tunisie*
Turkey	*la Turquie*
United States	*les Etats-Unis* (m.pl.)
Vietnam	*le Viêt-nam*

States

Alabama	*l'Alabama* (m.)
Alaska	*l'Alaska* (m.)
Arizona	*l'Arizona* (m.)
Arkansas	*l'Arkansas* (m.)
California	*la Californie*
Colorado	*le Colorado*
Connecticut	*le Connecticut*
Delaware	*le Delaware*
Florida	*la Floride*
Georgia	*la Géorgie*
Hawaii	*Hawaii* (m.) (no article)
Idaho	*l'Idaho* (m.)
Illinois	*l'Illinois* (m.)
Indiana	*l'Indiana* (m.)
Iowa	*l'Iowa* (m.)
Kansas	*le Kansas*
Kentucky	*le Kentucky*
Louisiana	*la Louisiane*
Maine	*le Maine*
Maryland	*le Maryland*
Massachusetts	*le Massachusetts*
Michigan	*le Michigan*
Minnesota	*le Minnesota*
Mississippi	*le Mississippi*
Missouri	*le Missouri*
Montana	*le Montana*
Nebraska	*le Nebraska*
Nevada	*le Nevada*
New Hampshire	*le New Hampshire*
New Jersey	*le New Jersey*
New Mexico	*le Nouveau Mexique*
New York	*l'état de New York*
North Carolina	*la Caroline du Nord*
North Dakota	*le Dakota du Nord*
Ohio	*l'Ohio* (m.)
Oklahoma	*l'Oklahoma* (m.)
Oregon	*l'Oregon* (m.)
Pennsylvania	*la Pennsylvanie*
Rhode Island	*le Rhode Island*
South Carolina	*la Caroline du Sud*
South Dakota	*le Dakota du Sud*
Tennessee	*le Tennessee*
Texas	*le Texas*
Utah	*l'Utah* (m.)
Vermont	*le Vermont*
Virginia	*la Virginie*
Washington	*l'état de Washington*
West Virginia	*la Virginie de l'Ouest*
Wisconsin	*le Wisconsin*
Wyoming	*le Wyoming*

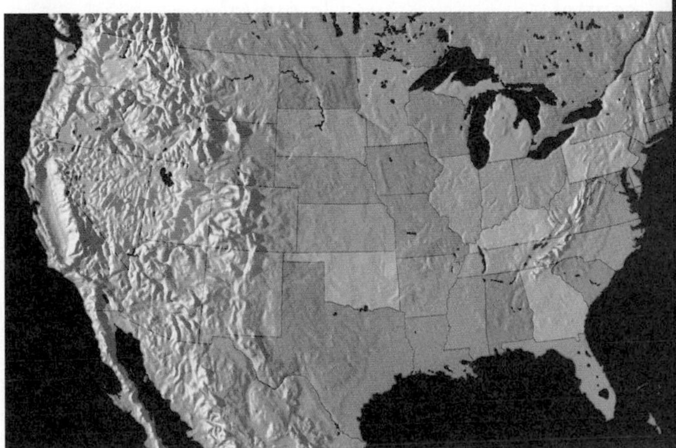

Cities

Algiers	*Alger*
Brussels	*Bruxelles*
Cairo	*Le Caire*
Geneva	*Genève*
Lisbon	*Lisbonne*
London	*Londres*
Montreal	*Montréal*
Moscow	*Moscou*
New Orleans	*La Nouvelle-Orléans*

Quebec City	*Québec*
Tangier	*Tanger*
Venice	*Venise*
Vienna	*Vienne*

Other Geographical Terms

Alps	*les Alpes* (f.)
Atlantic Ocean	*l'Atlantique* (m.), *l'océan* (m.) *Atlantique*
border	*la frontière*
capital	*la capitale*
continent	*un continent*

country	*un pays*
English Channel	*la Manche*
hill	*une colline*
lake	*un lac*
latitude	*la latitude*
longitude	*la longitude*
Mediterranean Sea	*la mer Méditerranée*
mountain	*une montagne*
North Africa	*l'Afrique* (f.) *du Nord*
North Pole	*le pôle Nord*
ocean	*l'océan* (m.)
Pacific Ocean	*le Pacifique, l'océan* (m.) *Pacifique*
plain	*une plaine*
Pyrenees	*les Pyrénées* (f.)
river	*une rivière, un fleuve*
sea	*la mer*
South Pole	*le pôle Sud*
state	*un état*
valley	*une vallée*

ADJECTIVES

REGULAR ADJECTIVES

In French, adjectives agree in gender and number with the nouns that they modify. A regular adjective has four forms: masculine singular, feminine singular, masculine plural, and feminine plural. To make a regular adjective agree with a feminine noun, add an **-e** to the masculine singular form of the adjective. To make an adjective agree with a plural noun, add an **-s** to the masculine singular form. To make an adjective agree with a feminine plural noun, add **-es** to the masculine singular form. Adjectives ending in **-é,** like **étonné,** also follow these rules.

	SINGULAR	PLURAL
MASCULINE	un homme **gourmand**	des hommes **gourmands**
FEMININE	une femme **gourmande**	des femmes **gourmandes**

ADJECTIVES THAT END IN AN UNACCENTED -E

When an adjective ends in an unaccented **-e,** the masculine singular and feminine singular forms are the same. To form the plural of these adjectives, add an **-s** to the singular forms.

	SINGULAR	PLURAL
MASCULINE	un frère **pénible**	des garçons **pénibles**
FEMININE	une sœur **pénible**	des filles **pénibles**

ADJECTIVES THAT END IN -S

When the masculine singular form of an adjective ends in an **-s,** the masculine plural form does not change. The feminine forms follow the regular adjective rules.

	SINGULAR	PLURAL
MASCULINE	un tapis **gris**	des tapis **gris**
FEMININE	une robe **grise**	des robes **grises**

ADJECTIVES THAT END IN -EUX

Adjectives that end in **-eux** do not change in the masculine plural. The feminine singular form of these adjectives is made by replacing the **-x** with **-se.** To form the feminine plural, replace the **-x** with **-ses.**

	SINGULAR	PLURAL
MASCULINE	un homme **furieux**	des hommes **furieux**
FEMININE	une femme **furieuse**	des filles **furieuses**

ADJECTIVES THAT END IN -IF

To make the feminine singular form of adjectives that end in **-if,** replace **-if** with **-ive.** To make the plural forms of these adjectives, add an **-s** to the singular forms.

	SINGULAR	PLURAL
MASCULINE	un garçon **sportif**	des garçons **sportifs**
FEMININE	une fille **sportive**	des filles **sportives**

ADJECTIVES THAT END IN -IEN

To make the feminine singular and feminine plural forms of adjectives that end in **-ien** in their masculine singular form, add **-ne** and **-nes.** Add an **-s** to form the masculine plural.

	SINGULAR	PLURAL
MASCULINE	un garçon **canadien**	des garçons **canadiens**
FEMININE	une fille **canadienne**	des filles **canadiennes**

ADJECTIVES THAT DOUBLE THE LAST CONSONANT

To make the adjectives **bon, gentil, gros, mignon, mortel, nul,** and **violet** agree with a feminine noun, double the last consonant and add an **-e.** To make the plural forms, add an **-s** to the singular forms. Notice that with **gros,** the masculine singular and masculine plural forms are the same.

	SINGULAR				
MASCULINE	**bon**	**gentil**	**gros**	**mignon**	**violet**
FEMININE	**bonne**	**gentille**	**grosse**	**mignonne**	**violette**

	PLURAL				
MASCULINE	**bons**	**gentils**	**gros**	**mignons**	**violets**
FEMININE	**bonnes**	**gentilles**	**grosses**	**mignonnes**	**violettes**

INVARIABLE ADJECTIVES

Some adjectives are invariable. They never change form. **Marron, orange,** and **super** are examples of invariable adjectives.

Véronique est une fille **super.** Elle a les yeux **marron.**

Note that **sympa** doesn't change form in the feminine, but you add an **-s** to the plural.

Véronique est une fille très **sympa.** Ses sœurs sont **sympas** aussi.

IRREGULAR ADJECTIVES

The adjectives **beau, nouveau,** and **vieux,** have irregular feminine forms: **belle, nouvelle,** and **vieille.** They also have irregular masculine forms when they modify singular nouns that begin with a vowel sound: **bel, nouvel,** and **vieil.** To form the masculine plural of **beau** and **nouveau,** add an **-x. Vieux** does not change in the masculine plural. To make **belle, nouvelle,** and **vieille** plural, simply add an **-s. Des** changes to **de** when you have an adjective that precedes a plural noun.

	beau	**nouveau**	**vieux**
MASCULINE SINGULAR	un **beau** jardin	un **nouveau** lit	un **vieux** musée
BEFORE VOWEL SOUND	un **bel** homme	un **nouvel** anorak	un **vieil** imperméable
FEMININE SINGULAR	une **belle** maison	une **nouvelle** lampe	une **vieille** gare
MASCULINE PLURAL	de **beaux** jardins	de **nouveaux** lits	de **vieux** musées
FEMININE PLURAL	de **belles** maisons	de **nouvelles** lampes	de **vieilles** gares

POSITION OF ADJECTIVES

In French, adjectives are usually placed after the noun that they modify.

C'est un film **déprimant!**

However, there are certain adjectives that you usually place before the noun. These are adjectives that refer to the beauty, age, goodness, or size of the nouns they modify. Some of these adjectives are **beau (belle), bon, grand, jeune, joli, nouveau, petit,** and **vieux (vieille).**

DEMONSTRATIVE ADJECTIVES

This, that, these, and *those* are demonstrative adjectives. In French there are two masculine singular forms: **ce** and **cet.** You use **cet** before a masculine singular noun that begins with a vowel sound. Some examples are **cet homme** and **cet imperméable**. Demonstrative adjectives always precede the nouns that they modify.

	Singular Before a Consonant	**Singular Before a Vowel Sound**	**Plural**
MASCULINE	**ce** cadre	**cet** imperméable	**ces** vases
FEMININE	**cette** main	**cette** écharpe	**ces** chansons

POSSESSIVE ADJECTIVES

Possessive adjectives come before the noun that they modify, and agree in number and gender with that noun. Before singular nouns that begin with a vowel sound, use the masculine singular form, **mon ami(e), ton ami(e), son ami(e).**

	Masculine Singular	Feminine Singular	Masc./Fem. Singular Before a Vowel Sound	Masc./Fem. Plural
my	**mon** jardin	**ma** maison	**mon** armoire	**mes** étagères
your	**ton** salon	**ta** cuisine	**ton** anorak	**tes** bottes
his, her, its	**son** tapis	**sa** lampe	**son** imperméable	**ses** mains

The possessive adjectives for *our, your,* and *their* have only two forms, singular and plural.

	SINGULAR	PLURAL
our	**notre** jardin	**nos** armoires
your	**votre** maison	**vos** chambres
their	**leur** salon	**leurs** posters

ADJECTIVES AS NOUNS

To use a color or an adjective as a noun, add a definite article before the adjective. The article and the adjective that you use agree in number and gender with the noun that they are replacing.

—Tu aimes le tapis bleu ou **le gris?**
Do you like the blue rug or the grey one?

—J'aime **le bleu.**
I like the blue one.

—Vous préférez **les bottes noires** ou **les grises?**
Do you prefer the black boots or the grey ones?

—Je préfère **les noires.**
I like the black ones.

ADVERBS

ADVERBS OF FREQUENCY

To tell how often you do or used to do something, you use adverbs of frequency. Some adverbs of frequency are **de temps en temps** *(from time to time)*, **d'habitude** *(usually)*, ... **fois par semaine** *(. . . time(s) a week)*, **souvent** *(often)*, **quelquefois** *(sometimes)*, **rarement** *(rarely)*, and **ne... jamais** *(never)*.

Most adverbs follow the conjugated verb.

Nathalie téléphone **souvent** à ses amis.
Quand j'étais petit, je mangeais **rarement** des légumes.

Adverbs made up of more than one word can be placed at the beginning or the end of a sentence. **Ne (N')... jamais** is placed around the conjugated verb. With the **passé composé,** the adverb is placed before the past participle.

D'habitude, je ne mange pas de viande.

Je fais des abdominaux **trois fois par semaine.**

Je **n'**ai **jamais** fait de plongée.

J'ai **beaucoup** mangé.

ARTICLES

INDEFINITE ARTICLES

To refer to whole items, you use the indefinite articles **un, une,** and **des.** Remember that the indefinite articles agree in number and gender with the nouns they modify.

	SINGULAR	PLURAL
MASCULINE	**un** rôti	**des** œufs
FEMININE	**une** tarte	**des** crevettes

PARTITIVE ARTICLES

To refer to only some of or a portion of an item, you use the partitive articles **du, de la,** and **de l'. Du** and **de la** modify masculine and feminine singular nouns, respectively. **De l'** is used to modify a masculine or feminine noun that begins with a vowel sound.

Donne-moi **du** poisson, s'il te plaît. — *Give me some fish, please.*
Je voudrais **de la** mousse au chocolat. — *I'd like some chocolate mousse.*
Tu veux **de l'**omelette, Marc? — *Do you want some omelette, Marc?*

NEGATION WITH ARTICLES

When the main verb of the sentence is negated, the indefinite and the partitive articles usually change to **de.** Definite articles remain the same after a negative verb.

Karim prend **de** l'eau minérale. —> Karim ne prend pas **d'**eau minérale.
Je vais acheter **des** fleurs. —> Je ne vais pas acheter **de** fleurs.
J'ai **le** nouveau CD de MC Solaar. —> Je n'ai pas **le** nouveau CD de MC Solaar.

INTERROGATIVES

INTONATION

Just as in English, your voice generally falls at the end of a statement or a question in French. However, when asking a yes-or-no question, your voice rises at the end of the question; this is called *intonation.*

Tu vas acheter cette vieille maison?

Another way to form a yes-or-no question is to add **est-ce que** to the beginning of the sentence.

Est-ce que tu vas acheter cette vieille maison?

FORMAL AND INFORMAL QUESTIONS

To say *which* or *what,* use the correct form of the interrogative adjective **quel** before a noun.

	SINGULAR	PLURAL
MASCULINE	**Quel** livre?	**Quels** films?
FEMININE	**Quelle** robe?	**Quelles** bottes?

To ask for specific kinds of information, use the following question words:

A quelle heure?	*At what time?*	**Où?**	*Where?*
Avec qui?	*With whom?*	**Quand?**	*When?*

To ask a question in a formal situation, use the question words above followed by **est-ce que.** You should also use **est-ce que** when you ask formal yes-or-no questions.

A quelle heure est-ce que le train part?

Avec qui est-ce qu'on va à la bibliothèque?

Est-ce que vous avez des anoraks?

In informal situations, you may place the question words at the beginning or the end of the question. For yes-or-no questions, simply raise your voice at the end without using **est-ce que.**

Le train part **à quelle heure?**

Avec qui on va à la bibliothèque?

Tu vas acheter cette vieille maison?

NOUNS

PLURAL FORMS OF NOUNS

In French, you make most nouns plural by adding an **-s** to the end of the word, unless they already end in **-s** or **-x.** Nouns that end in **-eau** are made plural by adding an **-x,** and nouns that end in **-al** are generally made plural by replacing the **-al** with **-aux.**

	Regular nouns	-s or -x	-eau	-al
SINGULAR	cadre	tapis	bureau	animal
PLURAL	cadres	tapis	bureaux	animaux

PREPOSITIONS

THE PREPOSITIONS A AND DE

The preposition **à** means *to, at,* or *in,* and **de** means *from* or *of.* When **à** and **de** precede the definite articles **le** and **les,** they form the contractions **au, aux, du,** and **des.** If they precede any other definite article, there is no contraction.

Nous allons **à la** plage et **au** zoo. Tu es loin **du** marché, mais près **des** musées.

	Masculine Article	Feminine Article	Vowel Sound	Plural
à	à + le = **au**	**à la**	**à l'**	à + les = **aux**
de	de + le = **du**	**de la**	**de l'**	de + les = **des**

De is also used to indicate possession or ownership.

Là, c'est la boulangerie **de** ma tante. *That's my aunt's bakery over there.*

C'est le bureau **du** prof. *It's the teacher's desk.*

PREPOSITIONS AND PLACES

To say that you are at or going to a place, you need to use a preposition. With cities, use the preposition **à: à Paris.** One notable exception is **en Arles.** When speaking about masculine countries, use **au: au Viêt-nam.** With names of plural countries, use **aux: aux Etats-Unis.** Most countries ending in **-e** are feminine; in these cases, use **en: en Italie. Le Mexique** is an exception. If a country begins with a vowel, like **Inde,** use **en: en Inde.**

Cities	Masculine Countries	Feminine or Masculine Countries that begin with a vowel	Plural Countries
à Nantes **à** Paris **en** Arles	**au** Canada **au** Maroc **au** Mexique	**en** Italie **en** Espagne **en** Israël	**aux** Etats-Unis **aux** Philippines **aux** Pays-Bas

PRONOUNS

SUBJECT PRONOUNS: TU AND VOUS

The pronoun **tu** is used when you are addressing someone your own age or younger; **tu** is also often used when speaking to family members. **Vous,** on the other hand, is used when addressing someone older than you, someone you don't know very well, or groups of people.

DIRECT OBJECT PRONOUNS: LE, LA, AND LES

	SINGULAR	PLURAL
MASCULINE	**le / l'**	**les**
FEMININE	**la / l'**	**les**

A direct object is a noun or pronoun that receives the action of the verb. A direct object pronoun replaces a direct object that has already been mentioned. The direct object pronoun agrees in gender and number with the noun it refers to. You place the direct object pronoun in front of the conjugated verb.

— Il mange **la tarte?**

— Oui, il **la** mange.

If the pronoun is the direct object of an infinitive, it precedes the infinitive.

— Tu vas attendre **le bus?**

— Oui, je vais **l'**attendre.

In an affirmative command, the direct object pronoun follows the verb and is connected to it with a hyphen. In a negative command, the pronoun precedes the verb.

— Je voudrais acheter **le pull** bleu.

— Achète-**le!**

— Et **la cravate** verte?

— Ne **l'**achète pas! Elle est horrible!

DIRECT OBJECT PRONOUNS AND THE PASSE COMPOSE

When using the direct object pronouns **le, la, l', les, me, te, nous,** and **vous** with the **passé composé,** you must often change the spelling of the past participle to agree in number and gender with the preceding direct object pronoun.

— Tu as rangé **ta chambre?**

— Oui, je **l'**ai rangée ce matin.

— Pierre a acheté **les boissons?**

— Non, il ne **les** a pas achetées**es.**

THE PRONOUN Y

To replace a phrase meaning *to, on, at,* or *in* any place that has already been mentioned, use the pronoun **y.** It can replace phrases beginning with prepositions of location such as **à, sur, chez, dans,** and **en + a place or thing.** Place **y** before the conjugated verb or before an infinitive.

— Elle va **à la confiserie?**

— Oui, elle **y** va.

If there is an infinitive in the sentence, **y** precedes the infinitive.

— Tu vas aller **à l'épicerie** ce matin?

— Oui, je vais **y** aller.

THE PRONOUN EN

The object pronoun **en** can be used to replace phrases that begin with **du, de la, de l'**, or **des.** These phrases might refer to activities:

— Tu fais **de la plongée?**

— Non, je n'**en** fais pas.

or to quantities:

— Tu veux **des œufs** pour le dîner?

— Oui, j'**en** veux bien.

— Est-ce qu'il te faut **du café?**

— Non, j'**en** ai acheté hier.

Like other object pronouns, **en** precedes the conjugated verb. If the sentence contains an infinitive, **en** is placed between the conjugated verb and the infinitive.

— Nous avons **des crevettes?**

— Non, mais je vais **en** acheter aujourd'hui.

THE REFLEXIVE PRONOUNS

Reflexive pronouns accompany a reflexive verb, a verb whose action is done by the subject to itself. These pronouns reflect the subject, and they change depending upon the subject of the sentence. The reflexive pronoun **se** is part of the infinitive of a reflexive verb. The verb **se laver** *(to wash oneself)* is conjugated below.

Subject	Reflexive Pronoun	se laver
je	**me**	Je **me** lave.
tu	**te**	Tu **te** laves.
il/elle/on	**se**	Il/Elle/On **se** lave.
nous	**nous**	Nous **nous** lavons.
vous	**vous**	Vous **vous** lavez.
ils/elles	**se**	Ils/Elles **se** lavent.

INDIRECT OBJECT PRONOUNS: LUI, LEUR

The pronouns **lui** *(to/for him, to/for her)* and **leur** *(to/for them)* replace nouns that are indirect objects of a verb. They are used to replace a phrase that begins with **à** or **pour** followed by a person or persons, never by things.

The pronoun is placed before the conjugated verb . . .

Tu offres un cadeau **à ta mère?** —> Tu **lui** offres un cadeau?

or before an infinitive, when it is the object of that infinitive.

Je vais offrir des bonbons **à mes amis.** —> Je vais **leur** offrir des bonbons.

In affirmative commands, the pronouns follow the verb and are connected to it with a hyphen.

Offre un cadre **à ta sœur!** —> **Offre-lui** un cadre!

POSITION OF OBJECT PRONOUNS

Object pronouns like **le, la, l', les, lui, leur, me, te, nous,** and **vous** usually precede the conjugated verb in a sentence.

Tu **me** donnes un cadeau?
Paul **leur** parle tout le temps.
Mon livre? Je **l'**ai oublié à l'école.
Qui **vous** a donné ce bracelet?

In affirmative commands, the object pronoun follows the verb and is connected to it by a hyphen. In this case, **me** and **te** change to **moi** and **toi.** In negative commands, the object pronoun precedes the conjugated verb.

Téléphone-**moi** ce soir!
Ne **me** donne pas de tarte!
Donne-**le** à ta sœur!
Ne **les** invite pas!

When the object pronoun is the object of the infinitive, the object pronoun directly precedes the infinitive.

Je voudrais **l'**inviter à la boum.
Tu aurais dû **lui** téléphoner.

IL/ELLE EST VERSUS C'EST

Both **il/elle est** and **c'est** can mean *he/she is.* **Il/Elle est** can be used to identify someone by the person's profession or nationality. In this case, no article precedes the noun.

Harrison Ford? **Il est** acteur.
Céline Dion? **Elle est** québécoise.

If **c'est** is used for the same purpose, the noun must be preceded by an appropriate article.

Harrison Ford? **C'est un** acteur.
Céline Dion? **C'est une** Québécoise.

When you use both an adjective and a noun, you must use **c'est.**

Céline Dion? **C'est une** chanteuse québécoise.

RELATIVE PRONOUNS: CE QUI AND CE QUE

Ce qui and **ce que** are relative pronouns that mean *what.* However, **ce qui** is the subject of the verb in the clause it introduces:

Ce qui est embêtant, c'est de devoir se coucher très tôt.

Ce que, on the other hand, is the object of the verb in the clause it introduces and it is usually followed by a subject:

Ce que je n'aime pas, c'est aller à la pêche quand il pleut.

RELATIVE PRONOUNS: QUI AND QUE

The relative pronouns **qui** and **que** introduce clauses that give more information about a subject that you've already mentioned. **Qui** is the subject of the verb in the clause it introduces. The verb agrees with the person or object in the main clause that it refers to.

Isabelle Adjani est une actrice **qui est** très connue en France.

J'ai deux amis **qui s'appellent** Hervé et Guillaume.

Que is the direct object of the verb in the clause; therefore, it is followed by a subject. When the verb in the clause introduced by **que** is in the **passé composé,** the past participle agrees with the noun that **que** represents.

Voici le CD **que** je voudrais acheter.
La tente que j'ai **achetée** hier est très chouette!

VERBS

REGULAR -ER VERBS

To form the present tense of most **-er** verbs, drop the **-er** and add the following endings to the stem.

	aimer *(to like, love)*	
Subject	**Stem**	**Ending**
j'	aim	**-e**
tu		**-es**
il/elle/on		**-e**
nous		**-ons**
vous		**-ez**
ils/elles		**-ent**

For the **nous** form of the verbs **manger, nager,** and **voyager,** only the **-r** is dropped from the infinitive, the **-e** is retained: **nous mangeons, nous nageons, nous voyageons.** For the **nous** form of **commencer,** the second **c** is changed to a **ç** in the stem: **nous commençons.**

Some **-er** verbs that are presented for the first time in Level 2 are: **déguster** *(to taste, enjoy),* **se baigner** *(to go swimming),* **s'habiller** *(to get dressed),* **se lever** *(to get up),* **se laver** *(to wash),* **tomber** *(to fall),* and **emporter** *(to take something with you).*

REGULAR -IR VERBS

To form the present tense of most **-ir** verbs, drop the **-ir** and add the following endings to the stem.

	choisir *(to choose)*	
Subject	**Stem**	**Ending**
je	chois	**-is**
tu		**-is**
il/elle/on		**-it**
nous		**-issons**
vous		**-issez**
ils/elles		**-issent**

Other **-ir** verbs that follow this pattern are **grandir, maigrir, grossir,** and **se nourrir.** To form the past participle of these verbs, you simply drop the **-ir** from the infinitive and add **-i** to the stem (**choisir —> choisi).**

REGULAR -RE VERBS

The present tense of most **-re** verbs is formed by dropping the **-re** and adding the following endings to the stem.

	attendre *(to wait)*	
Subject	**Stem**	**Ending**
j'	attend	**-s**
tu	attend	**-s**
il/elle/on	attend	-(no ending)
nous	attend	**-ons**
vous	attend	**-ez**
ils/elles	attend	**-ent**

VERBS LIKE DORMIR

These verbs follow a different pattern from the one you learned for regular **-ir** verbs. These verbs have two stems: one for the singular subjects, and one for the plural ones.

	dormir *(to sleep)*	**partir** *(to leave)*	**sortir** *(to go out, to take out)*
je	dor**s**	par**s**	sor**s**
tu	dor**s**	par**s**	sor**s**
il/elle/on	dor**t**	par**t**	sor**t**
nous	dorm**ons**	part**ons**	sort**ons**
vous	dorm**ez**	part**ez**	sort**ez**
ils/elles	dorm**ent**	part**ent**	sort**ent**
Past Participle	dormi	parti	sorti

IRREGULAR VERBS

The verbs **avoir, être, aller,** and **faire** are irregular because they do not follow the conjugation patterns that **-er, -ir,** and **-re** verbs do.

	avoir *(to have)*	**être** *(to be)*
je/j' tu il/elle/on	**ai** **as** **a**	**suis** **es** **est**
nous vous ils/elles	**avons** **avez** **ont**	**sommes** **êtes** **sont**
Past Participle	**eu**	**été**

	aller *(to go)*	**faire** *(to do, make)*
je tu il/elle/on	**vais** **vas** **va**	**fais** **fais** **fait**
nous vous ils/elles	**allons** **allez** **vont**	**faisons** **faites** **font**
Past Participle	**allé**	**fait**

Devoir, pouvoir, and **vouloir** are also irregular. They are usually followed by an infinitive.

Je peux chanter. *I can sing.*

	devoir *(to have to, must)*	**pouvoir** *(be able to, can)*	**vouloir** *(to want)*
je tu il/elle/on	**dois** **dois** **doit**	**peux** **peux** **peut**	**veux** **veux** **veut**
nous vous ils/elles	**devons** **devez** **doivent**	**pouvons** **pouvez** **peuvent**	**voulons** **voulez** **veulent**
Past Participle	**dû**	**pu**	**voulu**

These verbs also have irregular forms.

	dire *(to say)*	**écrire** *(to write)*	**lire** *(to read)*
je/j' tu il/elle/on nous vous ils/elles	**dis** **dis** **dit** **disons** **dites** **disent**	**écris** **écris** **écrit** **écrivons** **écrivez** **écrivent**	**lis** **lis** **lit** **lisons** **lisez** **lisent**
Past Participle	**dit**	**écrit**	**lu**

	mettre *(to put, to put on, to wear)*	**prendre** *(to take, to have food or drink)*	**voir** *(to see)*
je tu il/elle/on nous vous ils/elles	**mets** **mets** **met** **mettons** **mettez** **mettent**	**prends** **prends** **prend** **prenons** **prenez** **prennent**	**vois** **vois** **voit** **voyons** **voyez** **voient**
Past Participle	**mis**	**pris**	**vu**

THE VERB CONNAITRE

Some French verbs do not follow any of the regular verb patterns you've learned. They are referred to as *irregular verbs.* **Connaître** *(to know, to be familiar with)* is an irregular verb. Here are the forms of **connaître** in the present tense:

connaître *(to know, to be acquainted with)*	
je tu il/elle/on nous vous ils/elles	**connais** **connais** **connaît** **connaissons** **connaissez** **connaissent**

The past participle of **connaître** is **connu. Connaître** uses **avoir** as its helping verb in the **passé composé.** The **passé composé** of **connaître** has a special meaning.

J'ai connu Sophie au lycée. *I met Sophie (for the first time) at school.*

THE VERB OUVRIR

While the verb **ouvrir** ends in **-ir,** it is conjugated like a regular **-er** verb.

ouvrir *(to open)*	
j'	**ouvre**
tu	**ouvres**
il/elle/on	**ouvre**
nous	**ouvrons**
vous	**ouvrez**
ils/elles	**ouvrent**

The past participle of **ouvrir** is **ouvert. Ouvrir** uses **avoir** as its helping verb in the **passé composé.**

J'ai ouvert la porte pour mon père.

VERBS WITH STEM AND SPELLING CHANGES

Verbs listed in this section are not irregular, but they do have some stem and spelling changes. When you write the forms of **acheter** and **promener,** add an **accent grave** over the second-to-last **e** in all forms except **nous** and **vous.** Notice that the second **é** in **préférer** changes from **é** to **è** in all forms except the **nous** and **vous** forms.

	acheter *(to buy)*	**préférer** *(to prefer)*	**promener** *(to walk) (an animal))*
je/j'	**achète**	**préfère**	**promène**
tu	**achètes**	**préfères**	**promènes**
il/elle/on	**achète**	**préfère**	**promène**
nous	**achetons**	**préférons**	**promenons**
vous	**achetez**	**préférez**	**promenez**
ils/elles	**achètent**	**préfèrent**	**promènent**
Past Participle	**acheté**	**préféré**	**promené**

The following verbs have different stems for the **nous** and **vous** forms.

	appeler *(to call)*	**essayer** *(to try)*
j'	**appelle**	**essaie**
tu	**appelles**	**essaies**
il/elle/on	**appelle**	**essaie**
nous	**appelons**	**essayons**
vous	**appelez**	**essayez**
ils/elles	**appellent**	**essaient**
Past Participle	**appelé**	**essayé**

REFLEXIVE VERBS

French verbs that require a reflexive pronoun are called *reflexive verbs.* The subject of the sentence receives the action of a reflexive verb. The reflexive pronoun must change with the subject, as shown in the table below.

To make a reflexive verb negative, place **ne... pas** around the reflexive pronoun and the verb **(Je ne me lève pas tôt le week-end.)**

se laver *(to wash)*		
je	**me**	**lave**
tu	**te**	**laves**
il/elle/on	**se**	**lave**
nous	**nous**	**lavons**
vous	**vous**	**lavez**
ils/elles	**se**	**lavent**

To make the **passé composé** of a reflexive verb, you need to use **être** as the helping verb. The past participle must agree in number and gender with the subject when there's no direct object following the verb. (**Elle s'est lavée.** but **Elle s'est lavé les mains.**)

To make a reflexive verb negative in the **passé composé,** place **ne... pas** around the reflexive pronoun and the helping verb. **(Je ne me suis pas levée tôt samedi.)**

se laver			
je	**me**	**suis**	**lavé (e)**
tu	**t'**	**es**	**lavé (e)**
il/elle/on	**s'**	**est**	**lavé (e) (s)**
nous	**nous**	**sommes**	**lavé (e)s**
vous	**vous**	**êtes**	**lavé (e) (s)**
ils/elles	**se**	**sont**	**lavé (e)s**

THE PASSE COMPOSE WITH AVOIR

The **passé composé** of most verbs consists of two parts: the present tense form of the helping verb **avoir** and the past participle of the main verb. To form the past participle, use the formulas below. To make a sentence negative in the **passé composé,** place the **ne... pas** around the helping verb **avoir.**

Infinitive	**aimer** *(to love, to like)*		**choisir** *(to choose)*		**vendre** *(to sell)*	
	Stem	**Ending**	**Stem**	**Ending**	**Stem**	**Ending**
Past Participle	aim	-é	chois	-i	vend	-u
	aimé		choisi		vendu	
Passé Composé	**j'ai aimé**		**j'ai choisi**		**j'ai vendu**	

J'**ai mangé** au fast-food. Nous n'**avons** pas encore **choisi** la musique.
Elle **a choisi** un anorak rouge. Elle n'**a** pas **répondu** à sa lettre.

Some verbs have irregular past participles.

être —> **été**
avoir —> **eu**
prendre —> **pris**
faire —> **fait**
lire —> **lu**
mettre —> **mis**
faire —> **fait**
recevoir —> **reçu**
boire —> **bu**
voir —> **vu**

THE PASSE COMPOSE WITH ETRE

While most French verbs use **avoir** as the helping verb in the **passé composé,** two groups of verbs use **être** as their helping verb. The first group includes verbs of motion, like **aller, descendre, monter, tomber, venir,** and so on. You form the **passé composé** of these verbs with two parts: the present tense form of the helping verb **être** and the past participle of the main verb. When using **être,** the past participle has to agree in gender and number with the subject. To make a sentence negative, put **ne... pas** around the helping verb. (**Je ne suis pas allé à l'école hier.**)

aller *(to go)*		
je	suis	allé(e)
tu	es	allé(e)
il/elle/on	est	allé(e)(s)
nous	sommes	allé(e)s
vous	êtes	allé(e)(s)
ils/elles	sont	allé(e)s

The second group, reflexive verbs, also uses **être** as the helping verb. For more information on the **passé composé** with reflexive verbs, see the heading "Reflexive Verbs" on page R38.

THE IMPARFAIT

To talk about what used to happen in the past or to describe what things were like, you use the **imparfait** (imperfect tense.) The stem you use to form the imperfect is the **nous** form of the verb in the present tense without **-ons** (**écrire** —> **nous écrivons** —> **écriv-**). For verbs like **manger,** drop the final **-e** from the stem for the **nous** and **vous** forms (**nous mangions, vous mangiez**). The endings are listed below. To make the imperfect form negative, place **ne... pas** around the verb.

écrire *(to write)*		
	Stem	**Endings**
j'	écriv	**-ais**
tu		**-ais**
il/elle/on		**-ait**
nous		**-ions**
vous		**-iez**
ils/elles		**-aient**

Je n'**écrivais** pas de lettres.
Tu **mangeais** bien?
Elles **achetaient** des bonbons.
Nous n'**allions** pas à l'école le samedi.

You will often need to use the verbs **avoir** and **être** in the **imparfait** to talk about the past. The table below gives you the **imparfait** forms of both verbs. Notice that **être** uses the irregular stem **ét-.**

avoir *(to have)*	
j'	**avais**
tu	**avais**
il/elle/on	**avait**
nous	**avions**
vous	**aviez**
ils/elles	**avaient**

être*(to be)*	
j'	**étais**
tu	**étais**
il/elle/on	**était**
nous	**étions**
vous	**étiez**
ils/elles	**étaient**

- The phrase **C'était...** *(It was . . .)* can be used in a variety of situations to describe how something was or used to be, including: expressing enthusiasm (**C'était magnifique!**), expressing indifference (**C'était assez bien.**), and expressing dissatisfaction (**C'était mortel.**).
- To tell how people seemed, use the expression **avoir l'air** in the **imparfait** followed by an adjective.

  Ils **avaient l'air** contents.
- You can also use the expression **si on** followed by a verb in the **imparfait** to make a suggestion.

  Si on jouait au volley?

THE IMPARFAIT VS. THE PASSE COMPOSE

In French, there are two tenses you can use to talk about the past: the **imparfait** and the **passé composé.** The table below lists the uses of each tense.

Imparfait	Passé Composé
• to describe how things and people were in the past **Il était petit.** • to describe general conditions or to set the scene **Il faisait froid.** • to talk about what used to happen or to tell about repeated or habitual actions **J'allais à l'école le samedi.** • after words that indicate a repeated action in the past, like **toujours, d'habitude, souvent, tous les jours,** and **de temps en temps** **Je jouais souvent au foot.** • to tell what was going on when something else happened **Je regardais la télé quand Pierre est arrivé.** • to emphasize that you were in the middle of doing something when something else happpened, you can use the expression **être en train de** in the **imparfait** followed by an infinitive **J'étais en train de manger quand Jacques est arrivé.** • to make a suggestion, you can use the expression **si on** followed by a verb in the **imparfait** **Si on allait à la plage?** • to tell how someone seemed to be, you can use the expression **avoir l'air** in the **imparfait** followed by an adjective **Elle avait l'air triste.**	• to tell what happened **Il est tombé.** • after words that indicate a specific moment in the past, like **un jour, soudain, tout d'un coup, au moment où,** and **une fois** **Un jour, elle est partie.** • after words that indicate in which order a series of events occurred, like **d'abord, après, ensuite, enfin,** and **finalement** **Ensuite, on a payé.** • to talk about an event that occurred while another action was going on **Il a téléphoné quand tu dormais.**

THE IMPERATIVE (COMMANDS)

To make a request or a command of most verbs, use the **tu, nous,** or **vous** form of the present tense of the verb without the subject. Remember to drop the final **-s** in the **tu** form of an **-er** verb.

Prends un jus de fruit!

Range ta chambre!

Allons en colonie de vacances!

Continuez tout droit.

To make a command negative, simply place **ne... pas** around the verb.

Ne sors **pas** sans faire tes devoirs!

THE NEAR FUTURE (LE FUTUR PROCHE)

To say that something is going to happen, use the near future (**le futur proche**). It is made up of two parts: the present tense of the verb **aller** and the infinitive of the main verb.

Je **vais faire** de la plongée demain.

I'm going to go scuba diving tomorrow.

To make a sentence in the **futur proche** negative, place **ne... pas** around the conjugated verb (**aller**).

Monique **ne** va **pas** lire la biographie de Napoléon.

Monique isn't going to read Napoleon's biography.

Pronunciation Index

Sound	Letter Combination	IPA Symbol	Example
The sounds [y] and [u]	the letter **u**	/y/	une
	the letter combination **ou**	/u/	nous
The nasal sound [ã]	the letter combination **an**	/ã/	anglais
	the letter combination **am**		jambon
	the letter combination **en**		comment
	the letter combination **em**		temps
The vowel sounds [ø] and [œ]	the letter combination **eu**	/ø/	deux
	the letter combination **eu**	/œ/	heure
The nasal sounds [ɔ̃], [ɛ̃], and [œ̃]	the letter combination **on**	/ɔ̃/	pardon
	the letter combination **om**		nombre
	the letter combination **in**	/ɛ̃/	cousin
	the letter combination **im**		impossible
	the letter combination **ain**		copain
	the letter combination **aim**		faim
	the letter combination **(i)en**		bien
	the letter combination **un**	/œ̃/	lundi
	the letter combination **um**		humble
The sounds [o] and [ɔ]	the letter combination **au**	/o/	jaune
	the letter combination **eau**		beau
	the letter **ô**		rôle
	the letter **o**	/ɔ/	carotte
The vowel sounds [e] and [ɛ]	the letter combination **ez**	/e/	apportez
	the letter combination **er**		trouver
	the letter combination **ait**	/ɛ/	fait
	the letter combination **ais**		français
	the letter combination **ei**		neige
	the letter **ê**		bête
The glides [j], [w], and [ɥ]	the letter **i**	/j/	mieux
	the letter combination **ill**		maillot
	the letter combination **oi**	/w/	moi
	the letter combination **oui**		Louis
	the letter combination **ui**	/ɥ/	huit
h, th, ch, and gn	the letter **h**	/ʼ/	les halls
	the letter combination **th**	/t/	théâtre
	the letter combination **ch**	/ʃ/	chocolat
	the letter combination **gn**	/ɲ/	oignon
The **r** sound	the letter **r**	/ʀ/	rouge vert

Numbers

Les Nombres Cardinaux

0	zéro	**20**	vingt	**80**	quatre-vingts
1	un(e)	**21**	vingt et un(e)	**81**	quatre-vingt-un(e)
2	deux	**22**	vingt-deux	**82**	quatre-vingt-deux
3	trois	**23**	vingt-trois	**90**	quatre-vingt-dix
4	quatre	**24**	vingt-quatre	**91**	quatre-vingt-onze
5	cinq	**25**	vingt-cinq	**92**	quatre-vingt-douze
6	six	**26**	vingt-six	**100**	cent
7	sept	**27**	vingt-sept	**101**	cent un
8	huit	**28**	vingt-huit	**200**	deux cents
9	neuf	**29**	vingt-neuf	**201**	deux cent un
10	dix	**30**	trente	**300**	trois cents
11	onze	**31**	trente et un(e)	**800**	huit cents
12	douze	**32**	trente-deux	**1.000**	mille
13	treize	**40**	quarante	**2.000**	deux mille
14	quatorze	**50**	cinquante	**3.000**	trois mille
15	quinze	**60**	soixante	**10.000**	dix mille
16	seize	**70**	soixante-dix	**19.000**	dix-neuf mille
17	dix-sept	**71**	soixante et onze	**40.000**	quarante mille
18	dix-huit	**72**	soixante-douze	**500.000**	cinq cent mille
19	dix-neuf	**73**	soixante-treize	**1.000.000**	un million

- The word **et** is used only in 21, 31, 41, 51, 61, and 71.
- **Vingt (trente, quarante,** and so on) **et une** is used when the number refers to a feminine noun: **trente et une cassettes.**
- The **s** is dropped from **quatre-vingts** and is not added to multiples of **cent** when these numbers are followed by another number: **quatre-vingt-cinq; deux cents,** *but* **deux cent six.** The number **mille** never takes an **s** to agree with a noun: **deux mille insectes.**
- **Un million** is followed by **de** + a noun: **un million d'euros.**
- In writing numbers, a period is used in French where a comma is used in English.

Les Nombres Ordinaux

1er, 1ère	premier, première	**9e**	neuvième	**17e**	dix-septième
2^{e}	deuxième	**10e**	dixième	**18e**	dix-huitième
3^{e}	troisième	**11e**	onzième	**19e**	dix-neuvième
4^{e}	quatrième	**12e**	douzième	**20e**	vingtième
5^{e}	cinquième	**13e**	treizième	**21e**	vingt et unième
6^{e}	sixième	**14e**	quatorzième	**22e**	vingt-deuxième
7^{e}	septième	**15e**	quinzième	**30e**	trentième
8^{e}	huitième	**16e**	seizième	**40e**	quarantième

French-English Vocabulary

English-French Vocabulary

French-English Vocabulary

This list includes both active and passive vocabulary in this textbook. Active words and phrases are those listed in the **Vocabulaire** section at the end of each chapter. You are expected to know and be able to use active vocabulary. All entries in heavy black type in this list are active. All other words are passive. Passive vocabulary is for recognition only.

The number after each entry refers to the chapter where the word or phrase is introduced. Nouns are always given with an article. If it is not clear whether the noun is masculine or feminine, *m.* (masculine) or *f.* (feminine) follows the noun. Some nouns that are generally seen only in the plural, as well as ones that have an irregular plural form, are also given with gender indications and the abbreviation *pl.* (plural) following them. An asterisk (*) before a word beginning with *h* indicates an aspirate *h*. Phrases are alphabetized by the key word(s) in the phrase.

The following abbreviations are also used in this vocabulary: *pp.* (past participle), *inv.* (invariable), *adj.* (adjective), *obj.* (object), and *subj.* (subject).

à *to, in (a city or place),* I, 11; **A...** *At...,* II, 11; **A bientôt.** *See you soon.* I, 1; **à la** *to, at,* I, 6; **à côté de...** *next to,* II, 2; **A demain.** *See you tomorrow.* I, 1; **à droite de** *to the right of,* II, 2; **à gauche de** *to the left of,* II, 2; à l'autre bout *at the other end,* II, 9; **à la mode** *in style,* I, 10; à la place de *in the place of,* II, 6; à peu près *nearly,* II, 11; **A propos,...** *By the way,...,* II, 9; **A quelle heure?** *At what time?* I, 6; **A tout à l'heure!** *See you later (the same day)!* I, 1; **A votre service.** *At your service. (You're welcome.),* I, 3; **Tu n'as qu'à...** *All you have to do is...,* II, 7

a: Il/Elle a... *He/She has...,* II, 1

abandonne: J'abandonne. *I give up.* II, 7

les abdominaux (m. pl.): **faire des abdominaux** *to do sit-ups,* II, 7

aborder *to approach,* II, 10

l' acajou (m.) *mahogany*

accepter *to accept,* II, 10

l' accès (m.) *access,* II, 2

l' accident (m.): **avoir un accident** *to have an accident,* II, 9

l' accord (m.) *agreement,* II, 1

D' accord. *OK.* I, 9; II, 7; **D'accord, si tu... d'abord.** *OK, if you..., first.* I, 7; **Bon, d'accord.** *Well, OK.* I, 8; **Je ne suis pas d'accord.** *I don't agree.* I, 7; **Tu es d'accord?** *Is that OK with you?* I, 7

accordons: Accordons nos violons. *Let's come to an understanding.* II, 4

accueillant *welcoming,* II, 1

accueillir *to welcome,* II, 2

achetait: Si on achetait...? *How about buying...?* II, 8

acheter *to buy,* I, 9; **Achète (-moi)...** *Buy (me)...,* I, 8

l' acier (m.) *steel,* II, 12

l' acteur (m.) *actor,* II, 11

l' activité (f.) *activity,* II, 1

l' addition (f.) *check, bill,* I, 5; **L'addition, s'il vous plaît.** *The check, please.* I, 5

l' adjectif (m.) *adjective,* II, 1

adorer *to adore,* I, 1; **J'adore...** *I adore...,* I, 1; *I love...,* II, 1

l' adresse (f.) *skill,* II, 7

l' aérobic (f.) *aerobics,* I, 4; **faire de l'aérobic** *to do aerobics,* I, 4; II, 7

les affaires (f. pl.) *things, belongings,* II, 11

africain(e) *African* (adj.), II, 11

l' âge (m.) *age;* **Tu as quel âge?** *How old are you?* I, 1

âgé(e) *older,* I, 7

l' agence de voyages (f.) *travel agency,* II, 8

l' agneau (m.) *lamb,* II, 3

ai: J'ai... *I have...* I, 2; II, 1; **J'ai... ans.** *I am...years old.* I, 1; **J'ai besoin de...** *I need...,* I, 8; **J'ai de la fièvre.** *I have a fever.* II, 7; **J'ai faim.** *I'm hungry.* I, 5; **J'ai l'intention de...** *I intend to...,* I, 11; **J'ai mal au genou.** *My knee hurts.* II, 7; **J'ai soif.** *I'm thirsty.* I, 5; **Je n'ai pas de...** *I don't have...,* I, 3

aider *to help,* II, 8; **(Est-ce que) je peux vous aider?** *May I help you?* I, 10; **Tu peux m'aider?** *Can you help me?* II, 10; l'aide: à l'aide d'une cuillère *using a spoon,* II, 11

aïe! *ouch!,* II, 7

l' ail (m.) *garlic,* II, 3

l' aile (f.) *wing,* II, 12

ailleurs *elsewhere,* II, 4

aimer *to like,* I, 1; **Ce que j'aime bien, c'est...** *What I like is...,* II, 4; **Ce que je n'aime pas, c'est...** *What I don't like is...,* II, 4; **J'aime bien...** *I like...,* II, 1; **J'aime mieux...** *I prefer...,* I, 1; II, 1; **Je n'aime pas...** *I don't like...,* I, 1; II, 1; **Moi, j'aime (bien)...** *I (really) like...,* I, 1; **Qu'est-ce que tu aimes comme musique?** *What music do you like?* II, 1; **Qu'est-ce que tu aimes faire?** *What do you like to do?* II, 1; **Tu aimes mieux... ou...?** *Do you prefer...or...?* I, 10; **Tu aimes...?** *Do you like...?* I, 1

aimerais: J'aimerais... pour aller avec... *I'd like... to go with...,* I, 10

ainsi que *as well as,* II, 1

l' air (m.): **avoir l'air...** *to seem...,* II, 9; **Ça n'a pas l'air d'aller.** *Something's wrong?* II, 5; **Elle avait l'air...** *She seemed...,* II, 12; **Tu n'as pas l'air en forme.** *You don't look well.* II, 7

ajouter *to add,* II, 3

l' album (m.) *album,* II, 11

l' algèbre (f.) *algebra,* I, 2

l' aliment (m.) *food,* II, 7
l' alimentation (f.): le magasin d'alimentation *food store,* II, 3
allait: Si on allait...? *How about going...?* II, 4
allé(e) (pp. of aller) *went,* I, 9; **Je suis allé(e)...** *I went...,* I, 9; **Tu es allé(e) où?** *Where did you go?* I, 9
l' allemand (m.) *German (language),* I, 2
aller *to go,* I, 6; **l'aller-retour** (m.) *round-trip ticket,* II, 6; **l'aller simple** (m.) *one-way ticket,* II, 6; **aller à la pêche** *to go fishing,* II, 4; **Ça n'a pas l'air d'aller.** *Something's wrong?* II, 5; **Ça te dit d'aller...?** *What do you think about going...?* II, 4; **Ça va aller mieux!** *It's going to get better!* I, 9; II, 5; **On peut y aller...** *We can go there...,* I, 12
l' allergie (f.) *allergy,* II, 7; **J'ai des allergies.** *I have allergies.* II, 7
Allez! *Come on!* II, 7; **Allez tout droit.** *Go straight ahead.* II, 2; **Allez au tableau!** *Go to the blackboard!* I, 0
Allô? *Hello?* I, 9
Allons... *Let's go...,* I, 6; **Allons-y!** *Let's go!* I, 4
l' allumette (f.) *match,* II, 12
l' allure (f.) *style, elegance,* II, 4
Alors,... *So,...* II, 9
amener: amener à ébullition *bring to a boil,* II, 3
américain(e) *American* (adj.), II, 11
l' ami(e) *friend,* I, 1
l' amitié (f.) *friendship,* II, 10
amoureux (-euse) *in love,* II, 9; **tomber amoureux (-euse) (de quelqu'un)** *to fall in love (with someone),* II, 9
amusant(e) *funny,* I, 7; II, 1; *fun,* II, 11
l' amuse-gueule (m.) *appetizer, snack,* II, 10; **préparer les amuse-gueule** *to make party snacks,* II, 10
amusé(e) (pp. of s'amuser): **Je me suis beaucoup amusé(e).** *I had a lot of fun.* II, 6; **Tu t'es amusé(e)?** *Did you have fun?* II, 6; **Tu t'es bien amusé(e)?** *Did you have fun?* I, 11
amuser *to amuse, entertain,* II, 1
s' amuser *to have fun,* II, 4; **Amuse-toi bien!** *Have fun!* I, 11; **Qu'est-ce que tu fais pour t'amuser?** *What do you do to have fun?* I, 4
l' an (m.) *year,* I, 1; **avoir... ans** *to be...years old,* II, 1; **J'ai... ans.** *I am...years old.* I, 1; **Quand j'avais... ans,...** *When I was...years old,...,* II, 8

l' ananas (m.) *pineapple,* I, 8; II, 4
l' anglais (m.) *English (language),* I, 1
l' animal (m.) *animal,* II, 12; **donner à manger aux animaux** *to feed the animals,* II, 6; **nourrir les animaux** *to feed the animals,* II, 12
animé(e) *exciting,* II, 8
l' anneau (m.) *ring,* II, 12
l' année (f.) *year,* II, 1; **Bonne année!** *Happy New Year!* II, 3
l' anniversaire (m.) *anniversary; birthday,* I, 7; **Joyeux (Bon) anniversaire!** *Happy birthday!* II, 3
l' annonce (f.) *advertisement,* II, 2
l' anorak (m.) *ski jacket,* II, 1
antillais(e) *from the Antilles,* II, 11
les Antilles *the West Indies,* II, 4
août *August,* I, 4; **en août** *in August,* I, 4
apercevoir *to notice,* II, 8
aplatir *to flatten,* II, 3
l' appareil (m.) *phone,* I, 9; **Qui est à l'appareil?** *Who's calling?* I, 9
l' appareil-photo (m.) *camera,* I, 11; II, 1
appartient *belongs to,* II, 8
appartenir *to belong to,* II, 8
s' appeler *to call oneself, to be called,* I, 1; **Il/Elle s'appelle comment?** *What's his/her name?* I, 1; **Il/Elle s'appelle...** *His/Her name is...,* I, 1; **Je m'appelle...** *My name is...,* I, 1; **Tu t'appelles comment?** *What's your name?* I, 1
apporter *to bring,* I, 9; **Apportez-moi..., s'il vous plaît.** *Please bring me...,* I, 5
apprécier *to appreciate,* II, 1
apprendre *to learn,* I, 0
s' apprêter *to get ready,* II, 12
approprié(e) *appropriate,* II, 1
s' approvisionner *to provide oneself, to supply oneself,* II, 11
l' après-midi (m.) *afternoon,* I, 2; *in the afternoon,* I, 2; **l'après-midi libre** (m.) *afternoon off,* I, 2
après *after,* I, 9; **Après ça,...** *After that,...* II, 4; **Après, je suis sorti(e).** *Afterwards, I went out.* I, 9; **Et après?** *And afterwards?* I, 9
d' après *according to,* II, 2
l' arbre (m.) *tree,* II, 12; **mutiler les arbres** *to deface the trees,* II, 12
l' argent (m.) *money,* I, 11
l' armoire (f.) *armoire/wardrobe,* II, 2
arracher *to grab, snatch,* II, 8
l' arrêt (m.) *stop,* II, 12
arrêter *to stop,* II, 7

arriver *to arrive,* II, 5; **Qu'est-ce qui t'arrive?** *What's wrong?* II, 5
l' article (m.) *article,* II, 1
l' artisanat (m.) *craft industry,* II, 8
l' artiste (m./f.) *artist,* II, 11
les arts martiaux (m. pl.), *martial arts,* II, 7
les arts plastiques (m. pl.) *art class,* I, 2
as: De quoi est-ce que tu as besoin? *What do you need?* I, 8; **Qu'est-ce que tu as?** *What's wrong?* II, 7; **Qu'est-ce que tu as fait?** *What did you do?* I, 9; **Tu as...?** *Do you have...?* I, 3; **Tu as... à quelle heure?** *At what time do you have...?* I, 2; **Tu as quel âge?** *How old are you?* I, 1
l' ascenseur (m.) *elevator,* II, 2
Asseyez-vous! *Sit down!* I, 0
assez *sort of,* II, 9; **assez bien** *OK,* II, 6
l' assiette (f.) *plate,* I, 5; les assiettes en carton *paper plates,* II, 10
assister: assister à un spectacle son et lumière *to attend a sound and light show,* II, 6
l' astuce (f.) cleverness, II, 7
l' athlète (m./f.) *athlete,* II, 7
l' athlétisme (m.) *track and field,* I, 4; **faire de l'athlétisme** *to do track and field,* I, 4
attendre *to wait for,* I, 9
l' attention (f.) *attention,* II, 11
l' attitude (f.) *attitude,* II, 9
l' attrait (m.) *attraction,* II, 11
attraper *to catch,* II, 11
au *to, at,* I, 6; *to, in (before a masculine noun),* I, 11; **Au revoir!** *Goodbye!* I, 1; **au métro...** *at the...metro stop,* I, 6
l' auberge de jeunesse (f.) *youth hostel,* II, 2
aucun(e) *no, none, any,* II, 9; **Aucune idée.** *No idea.* II, 9
aujourd'hui *today,* I, 2
aurais: J'aurais dû... *I should have...,* II, 10; **J'aurais pu...** *I could have...,* II, 10; **Tu aurais dû...** *You should have...,* II, 10; **Tu aurais pu...** *You could have...,* II, 10
aussi *also,* I, 1; **Moi aussi.** *Me too.* I, 2
autant de *as much, as many,* II, 10
l' autobiographie (f.) *autobiography,* II, 11
l' automne (m.) *autumn, fall,* I, 4; **en automne** *in the fall,* I, 4
l' autre (m./f.) *another,* II, 2
autrefois *in the past,* II, 4
autrui *others, other people,* II, 11

aux *to, in (before a plural noun),* I, 11
l' auxiliaire (m.) *auxilary* (verb), II, 5
avais: Quand j'avais... ans,... *When I was...years old,...,* II, 8
avait: Elle avait l'air... *She seemed...,* II, 12; **Il y avait...** *There was/were...,* II, 8
l' avantage (m.) *advantage,* II, 8
avec *with,* I, 6; **avec moi** *with me,* I, 6; **Avec qui?** *With whom?* I, 6; **C'est avec qui?** *Who's in it?* II, 11; **C'est avec...** *...is (are) in it.* II, 11
l' avenir (m.) *future,* II, 1
l' aventure (f.) *adventure,* II, 11
avez: Oui, vous avez... ? *Yes, do you have...?* I, 10; **Qu'est-ce que vous avez comme... ?** *What kind of...do you have?* I, 5; **Vous avez... ?** *Do you have...?* I, 2
l' avion (m.) *plane,* I, 12; **en avion** *by plane,* I, 12
l' avis (m.) *opinion,* I, 9; **A mon avis,...** *In my opinion,...,* II, 9; **A mon avis, tu te trompes.** *In my opinion, you're mistaken.* II, 9; **A ton avis, qu'est-ce que je dois faire?** *In your opinion, what should I do?* II, 10; **A ton avis, qu'est-ce que je fais?** *In your opinion, what do I do?* I, 9
l' avocat (m.) *avocado,* I, 8
avoir *to have,* I, 2 ; **avoir rendez-vous (avec quelqu'un)** *to have an appointment/a date (with someone),* II, 9; **avoir des responsabilités** *to have responsibilities,* II, 8; **avoir des soucis** *to have worries,* II, 8; **avoir faim** *to be hungry,* I, 5; **avoir l'air...** *to seem ...,* II, 9; **avoir soif** *to be thirsty,* I, 5; **avoir un accident** *to have an accident,* II, 9; **avoir... ans** *to be...years old,* II, 1
avons: Nous avons... *We have...,* I, 2; **Nous avons parlé.** *We talked.* I, 9
avril *April,* I, 4; **en avril** *in April,* I, 4
ayant: ayant pu donner *having been able to give,* I, 2

B

la baguette *long, thin loaf of bread,* I, 12; II, 3; la baguette magique *magic wand,* II, 6
se baigner *to go swimming,* II, 4
le bal *dance, prom,* II, 1
le balcon *balcony,* II, 2
la baleine *whale,* II, 12
le ballon *ball,* II, 5
banal(e) *ordinary,* II, 3; **C'est banal.** *That's ordinary.* II, 3
la banane *banana,* I, 8
le bananier *banana tree,* II, 4
la bande *group of friends,* II, 10
la bande dessinée (la B.D.) *comic book,* II, 11
le bandit *bandit,* II, 11
la banlieue *suburbs*
la banque *bank,* I, 12
le baptême *christening,* II, 6
barbant(e) *boring,* I, 2
le base-ball *baseball,* I, 4; **jouer au base-ball** *to play baseball,* I, 4
le basket(-ball) *basketball,* I, 4; **jouer au basket(-ball)** *to play basketball,* I, 4
les baskets (f. pl.) *a pair of sneakers,* I, 3; II, 1
le bateau *boat,* I, 12; **en bateau** *by boat,* I, 12; **faire du bateau** *to go sailing,* I, 11
le bâtiment *building,* II, 8
Bd (abbrev. of boulevard) (m.) *boulevard,* I, 6
B.D. (la bande dessinée) *comic book,* II, 11
beau (bel) *handsome,* II, 1; **Il fait beau.** *It's nice weather.* I, 4
Beaucoup. *A lot.* I, 4; **Oui, beaucoup.** *Yes, very much.* I, 2; **Pas beaucoup.** *Not very much.* I, 4
beaux: les beaux-arts (m. pl.) *fine arts,* II, 2
belle *beautiful,* II, 1; **C'est une belle histoire.** *It's a great story.* II, 11
le besoin: De quoi est-ce que tu as besoin? *What do you need?* I, 8; **J'ai besoin de...** *I need...,* I, 8
la bête *beast, animal,* II, 6; **bête** (adj.) *stupid,* II, 1
la bêtise *silly thing, blunder,* II, 8; **faire des bêtises** *to do silly things,* II, 8
le beurre *butter,* I, 8; II, 3
la bibliothèque *library,* I, 6; II, 2
la bicyclette *bicycle,* II, 4
bien *well,* I, 1; **bien se nourrir** *to eat well,* II, 7; **Ça te fera du bien.** *It'll do you good.* II, 7; **Il/Elle est vraiment bien, ton/ta...** *Your...is really great.* II, 2 ; **J'aime bien...** *I like...,* II, 1; **J'en veux bien.** *I'd like some.* I, 8; **Je ne me sens pas bien.** *I don't feel well.* II, 7; **Je veux bien.** *Gladly.* I, 8; *I'd like to.* II, 1; *I'd really like to.* I, 6; **Moi, j'aime (bien)...** *I (really) like...,* I, 1; **Très bien.** *Very well.* I, 1
Bien sûr. *Of course,* I, 3; II, 10; *Certainly,* I, 9; **Bien sûr que non.** *Of course not.* II, 10; **Bien sûr. C'est...** *Of course. They are (He/She/It is)...,* II, 11
bientôt *soon,* I, 1; **A bientôt.** *See you soon.* I, 1
Bienvenue chez moi (chez nous). *Welcome to my home (our home),* II, 2
le bifteck *steak,* II, 3
bilingue *bilingual,* II, 1
le billet *ticket,* I, 11; **un billet d'avion** *plane ticket,* I, 11; II, 1; le billet de retard *tardy slip,* II, 5; **un billet de train** *train ticket,* I, 11
la biographie *biography,* II, 11
la biologie *biology,* I, 2
la bise *kiss,* II, 1
bizarre *strange,* II, 10
blanc(he) *white,* I, 3
bleu(e) *blue,* I, 3; II, 1
le bleuet *blueberry,* II, 3
blond(e) *blond,* I, 7; II, 1
le blouson *jacket,* I, 10
le blues *blues (music),* II, 11
le bobard *lie, fib,* II, 9
le bœuf *beef,* I, 8; II, 3
Bof! *(expression of indifference),* I, 1; II, 8
le bogue *computer bug,* II, 11
boire *to drink,* I, 5; II, 3; **Qu'est-ce qu'il y a à boire?** *What is there to drink?* I, 5
le bois *wood,* II, 2; en bois *made of wood,* II, 2
la boisson *drink,* I, 5; **Qu'est-ce que vous avez comme boissons?** *What do you have to drink?* I, 5
la boîte *box,* II, 3; **une boîte de** *a can of,* I, 8; **une boîte de chocolats** *box of chocolates,* II, 3
le bol *bowl,* II, 3
bon *good,* I, 5; **Bon, d'accord.** *Well, OK.* I, 8; **Bon courage!** *Good luck!* I, 2; **Bon rétablissement!** *Get well soon!* II, 3; **Bon voyage!** *Have a good trip!* I, 11; **C'est bon pour toi.** *It's good for you.* II, 7; **C'est vraiment bon!** *It's really good!* II, 3; **Oui, très bon.** *Yes, very good.* I, 9; **pas bon** *not good,* I, 5; **Vous avez (Tu as) fait bon voyage?** *Did you have a good trip?* II, 2
bonne *good,* I, 4; **Bonne chance!** *Good luck!* I, 11; **Bonne fête!** *Happy holiday! (Happy saint's day!)* II, 3; **Bonne idée.** *Good idea.* I, 4; II, 3; **Bonnes vacances!** *Have a good vacation!* I, 11; **C'est une bonne idée.** *That's a good*

idea. II, 1; **de bonne humeur** *in a good mood,* II, 9
le bonbon *candy,* II, 3
le bonheur *happiness,* II, 1
Bonjour. *Hello.* I, 1
le bord: au bord de la mer *to/at the coast,* I, 11
le bossu *hunchback,* II, 11
la botte *boot,* I, 10; II, 1
la boucherie *butcher shop,* II, 3
la boucle d'oreille *earring,* I, 10
la bougie *candle,* II, 3
le bouillon *broth,* II, 3
la boulangerie *bakery,* I, 12; II, 3
le boulgour *bulgur wheat,* II, 3
la boum *party,* I, 6; **aller à une boum** *to go to a party,* I, 6; **faire une boum** *to give a party,* II, 10
le bouquet *bouquet,* II, 3
la bourse *purse,* II, 4
bousculer *to be swept off one's feet,* II, 10
la boussole *compass,* II, 12
le bout *end,* II, 9; à l'autre bout *at the other end,* II, 9
la bouteille *bottle,* I, 8; **une bouteille de** *a bottle of,* I, 8
la boutique de cadeaux *gift shop,* II, 3
le bracelet *bracelet,* I, 3
la branche *branch,* II, 12
le bras *arm,* II, 7; **J'ai mal au bras.** *My arm hurts.* II, 7
Bravo! *Terrific!* II, 5
Bref,... *Anyway,...,* II, 9
le bretzel *pretzel,* II, 7
le breuvage *drink,* II, 8
la brique: **Ça casse pas des briques.** *It's not earth-shattering.* II, 11
la brochure *brochure,* II, 4
se brosser: **se brosser les dents** *to brush one's teeth,* II, 4
la brousse *the bush,* II, 8
le bruit *noise,* II, 2
brûler *to burn,* II, 6
brun(e) *brunette,* I, 7; *dark brown (hair),* II, 1
bruyant(e) *noisy,* II, 8
la bulle *speech bubble,* II, 2
le bureau *desk,* II, 2; office, II, 8
le bulletin trimestriel *report card,* II, 5
le bus *bus,* I, 12; **en bus** *by bus,* I, 12; **rater le bus** *to miss the bus,* II, 5
le but *goal,* II, 7

C

ça: Ça fait combien? *How much does that make?* II, 3; **Ça fait combien, s'il vous plaît?** *How much is it, please?* I, 5; **Ça fait... euros.** *It's...euros.* I, 5; **Ça ne me dit rien.** *I don't feel like it.* I, 4; *That doesn't interest me.* II, 1; **Ça se voit.** *That's obvious.* II, 9; **Ça te dit d'aller... ?** *What do you think about going...?* II, 4; **Ça te dit de... ?** *Does... sound good to you?* II, 1; **Ça va.** *Fine.* I, 1; **Ça va?** *How are things going?* I, 1; **Ça, c'est...** *This is...,* I, 12; II, 2; **Comment ça s'est passé?** *How did it go?* II, 5; **Et après ça,...** *And after that,...,* I, 9; **Merci, ça va.** *No thank you, I've had enough.* II, 3; **Non, ça va.** *No, I'm fine.* II, 2; **Oui, ça a été.** *Yes, it was fine.* I, 9
la cacahuète *peanut,* II, 7
le cacao *cocoa,* II, 8
cacher *to hide,* II, 5
le cachot *dungeon,* II, 6
le caddie® *shopping cart,* II, 3
le cadeau *gift,* I, 11; **Tu as une idée de cadeau pour... ?** *Do you have a gift idea for ...?* II, 3; **la boutique de cadeaux** *gift shop,* II, 3
le cadre *photo frame,* II, 3; *setting, surroundings,* II, 6, 12; un cadre rustique *a country (rustic) atmosphere,* II, 1
le café *coffee,* I, 5; *café,* I, 5; **le café au lait** *coffee with milk,* II, 3
le cahier *notebook,* I, 3
la caisse *ticket window,* II, 6
la calculatrice *calculator,* I, 3
la calèche *four-wheeled carriage*
le calisson *calisson (a type of sweet made with ground almonds)*
calme *calm,* II, 8
le camarade (la camarade) *(class)mate, friend,* II, 1
cambodgien(ne) *Cambodian* (adj.), II, 1
le caméscope *camcorder,* II, 4
le camp: ficher le camp *to leave quickly, "scram,"* II, 5
la campagne *countryside,* I, 11; **à la campagne** *to/at the countryside,* I, 11
le camping *camping,* I, 11; **faire du camping** *to go camping,* I, 11; II, 12; **terrain de camping** (m.) *campground,* II, 2
canadien(ne) *Canadian* (adj.), II, 11
le canard *duck,* II, 12
le canari *canary,* I, 7
la canne à pêche *fishing pole,* II, 12
la cannelle *cinnamon,* II, 3
le canotage *canoeing,* II, 12; **faire du canotage** *to go canoeing,* II, 12
la cantine *cafeteria,* I, 9; **à la cantine** *at the school cafeteria,* I, 9
la capitale *capital,* II, 4
le car *bus (intercity),* II, 6
les caractères gras (m.) *boldface,* II, 10
le cardigan *sweater,* I, 10
la carence *deficiency,* II, 7
la carotte *carrot,* I, 8
carré(e) *square,* II, 1
le carré d'agneau *rack of lamb,* II, 3
la carte *map,* I, 0; **La carte, s'il vous plaît.** *The menu, please.* I, 5
la carte postale *postcard,* II, 6
les cartes (f. pl.) *cards,* I, 4; **jouer aux cartes** *to play cards,* I, 4
la cascade *waterfall,* II, 4
la case *box,* II, 10; *hut,* II, 11
la casquette *cap,* I, 10
casser (avec quelqu'un) *to break up (with someone),* II, 9; **Ça casse pas des briques.** *It's not earth-shattering.* II, 11; **se casser...** *to break one's...,* II, 7
la cassette *cassette tape,* I, 3
la catégorie *category,* II, 3
la cathédrale *cathedral,* II, 2
le cauchemar *nightmare,* I, 11; **C'était un véritable cauchemar!** *It was a real nightmare!* I, 11
ce *this; that,* I, 3; **Ce sont...** *These/those are...,* I, 7
ce que *what* (obj.), II, 4; **Ce que j'aime bien, c'est...** *What I like is...,* II, 4; **Ce que je n'aime pas, c'est...** *What I don't like is...,* II, 4; **Ce que je préfère, c'est...** *What I prefer is...,* II, 4; **Tu sais ce que... ?** *Do you know what...?* II, 9
ce qui *what* (subj.), II, 4; **Ce qui m'ennuie, c'est (de)...** *What bothers me is...,* II, 4; **Ce qui me plaît, c'est (de)...** *What I like is...,* II, 4; **Ce qui ne me plaît pas, c'est (de)...** *What I don't care for is...,* II, 4
la ceinture *belt,* I, 10
célèbre *famous; well-known,* II, 1
le centre commercial *mall,* I, 6
les céréales (f. pl.) *cereal,* II, 3
certain(e) *certain,* II, 10
le cerveau *brain,* II, 7
ces *these; those,* I, 3
C'est... *It's...,* I, 2; II, 11; *This is...,* I, 7; **C'est-à-dire que...** *That is,...,* II, 9; **C'est combien?** *How much is it?* I, 3; **C'est comment?** *What's it like?* II, 4; **Ça, c'est...** *This is...,* II, 2; **Non, c'est...** *No, it's...,* I, 4; **Non, c'est impossible.** *No, that's impossible.* I, 7; **Oui, c'est...** *Yes, it's...,* I, 4
cet *this; that,* I, 3

C'était... *It was...*, II, 6
cette *this; that,* I, 3
chacun(e) *each person,* II, 11
la chaîne stéréo *stereo,* II, 2
la chaise *chair,* I, 0
la chaleur *warmth,* II, 4
la chambre *bedroom,* I, 7; II, 2; **ranger ta chambre** *to pick up your room,* I, 7
le champignon *mushroom,* I, 8
le champ de canne à sucre (m.) *sugar cane field,* II, 4
la chance *luck,* I, 11; **Bonne chance!** *Good luck!* I, 11; **C'est pas de chance, ça!** *Tough luck!* II, 5
changer *to change,* II, 2
la chanson *song,* II, 11
le chant *song,* II, 12
chanter *to sing,* I, 9
le chanteur *(male) singer,* II, 11
la chanteuse *(female) singer,* II, 11
le chapeau *hat,* I, 10; **Chapeau!** *Well done!* II, 5
le chapitre *chapter,* II, 5
chaque *each,* II, 1
la charcuterie *delicatessen,* II, 3
charmant(e) *charming,* II, 4
la chasse gardée *private ground,* II, 11
le chat *cat,* I, 7; *chat room,* II, 11
châtain *brown (hair),* II, 1
le château *château/castle,* II, 6
la châtelaine *lady of the nobility,* II, 6
chaud(e) *hot,* I, 4; **Il fait chaud.** *It's hot.* I, 4
chauffer *to heat,* II, 3
la chaussette *sock,* I, 10
la chaussure *shoe,* I, 10
la chemise *shirt (men's),* I, 10
le chemisier *shirt (women's),* I, 10
le chèque de voyage *traveler's check,* II, 1
cher (chère) *expensive,* I, 10; **C'est trop cher.** *It's too expensive.* I, 10; II, 3
chercher *to look for,* I, 9; **Je cherche quelque chose pour...** *I'm looking for something for...,* I, 10
les cheveux (m. pl.) *hair,* II, 1
la cheville *ankle,* II, 7; **se fouler la cheville** *to sprain one's ankle,* II, 7
le chèvre *goat cheese,* II, 3
chez... *to/at...'s house,* I, 6; **Bienvenue chez moi (chez nous).** *Welcome to my home (our home),* II, 2; **chez le disquaire** *at the record store,* I, 12; **Faites/Fais comme chez vous/toi.** *Make yourself at home.* II, 2; **Je suis bien chez...?** *Is this...'s house?* I, 9
chic *chic,* I, 10
le chien *dog,* I, 7; **promener le chien** *to walk the dog,* I, 7
le chien chaud *hot dog,* II, 12
le chiffre *number,* II, 1
la chimie *chemistry,* I, 2
la chipie *rascal (for a girl only),* II, 10
les chips (f.) *chips,* II, 7
le chocolat *chocolate,* I, 1; *hot chocolate,* I, 5
choisi (e) (pp. of choisir) *decided, chosen,* I, 5; **Vous avez choisi?** *Have you decided/chosen?* I, 5
choisir *to choose, to pick,* I, 10; **choisir la musique** *to choose the music,* II, 10
la chorale *choir,* I, 2
la chose *thing,* I, 12; **J'ai quelque chose à faire.** *I have something else to do.* II, 10; **J'ai des tas de choses (trucs) à faire.** *I have lots of things to do.* I, 12; **Quelque chose ne va pas?** *Is something wrong?* II, 7
le chou *cabbage,* II, 3
le chou-fleur *cauliflower,* II, 3
chouette *very cool,* II, 2; **Oui, très chouette.** *Yes, very cool.* I, 9
la chute d'eau *waterfall,* II, 4
le ciel *sky,* II, 5
le cimetière *cemetery,* II, 2
le cinéma *the movies,* I, 1; *movie theater,* I, 6
le circuit *tour,* II, 6; **faire un circuit des châteaux** *to tour some châteaux,* II, 6
le citron *lemon,* I, 8
le citron pressé *lemonade,* I, 5
la classe *class,* II, 1
le classeur *loose-leaf binder,* I, 3
le clavecin *harpsicord,* II, 2
le client *client,* II, 3
clignoter *to blink,* II, 9
climatisé(e) *air-conditioned,* II, 2
le clin d'œil *the blink of an eye,* II, 8
le clocher *church tower,* II, 2
le clown *clown,* II, 11 **Tu ne dois pas faire le clown en classe!** *You shouldn't goof off in class!* II, 5
le coca *cola,* I, 5
cocher *to check off,* II, 10
le cocotier *coconut tree,* II, 4
le cœur *heart,* II, 5; **J'ai mal au cœur.** *I'm sick to my stomach.* II, 7
le coin *corner;* I, 12; **au coin de** *on the corner of,* I, 12
coin-coin *quack-quack,* II, 12
le collant *hose,* I, 10
collé(e): être collé(e) *to have detention,* II, 5
le collège *middle-school,* II, 8
la colline *hill,* II, 12
le colombo de cabri *a type of spicy goat stew,* II, 3
la colonie: en colonie de vacances *to/at a summer camp,* I, 11
la colonne *column,* II, 2
coloré(e) *colorful,* II, 4
le combat *fight,* II, 7
combien *how much, how many,* I, 5; **C'est combien,...?** *How much is...?* I, 5; **C'est combien?** *How much is it?* I, 3; **C'est combien, l'entrée?** *How much is the entrance fee?* II, 6; **Ça fait combien?** *How much is it?* I, 10; *How much does that make?* II, 3; **Ça fait combien, s'il vous plaît?** *How much is it, please?* I, 5; **Combien coûte(nt)...?** *How much is (are)...?* II, 3; **Combien en voulez-vous?** *How many (much) do you want?* II, 3
combiner *to combine,* II, 11
la comédie *comedy,* II, 11
comme *like, as,* II, 11; **Comme ci comme ça.** *So-so.* I, 1; II, 6; **Qu'est-ce que tu fais comme sport?** *What sports do you play?* I, 4; **Qu'est-ce que vous avez comme...?** *What kind of...do you have?* I, 5; **Qu'est-ce que vous avez comme boissons?** *What do you have to drink?* I, 5
commencer *to begin, to start,* I, 9; **Ça commence à quelle heure?** *At what time does it start?* II, 11
comment *what,* I, 0; *how,* I, 1; **(Comment) ça va?** *How's it going?* I, 1; **C'est comment?** *What's it like?* II, 4; **C'était comment?** *How was it?* II, 6; *What was it like?* II, 8; **Comment tu trouves...?** *What do you think of...?* I, 2; **Comment tu trouves ça?** *What do you think of that/it?* I, 2 ; *How do you like it?* I, 5; **Il/Elle est comment?** *What is he/she like?* I, 7; **Ils/Elles sont comment?** *What are they like?* I, 7; **Tu t'appelles comment?** *What is your name?* I, 0
le commentaire *comment,* II, 2
commenté(e): un circuit commenté *guided walk,* II, 2
la commode *chest of drawers,* II, 2
comparer *to compare,* II, 8
compléter *to complete,* II, 1
le compliment *compliment,* II, 2
comprendre *to understand,* II, 5; **J'ai du mal à comprendre.** *I have a hard time understanding.* II, 5
compris (pp. of comprendre): Tu as compris? *Did you understand?* II, 1

concassé(e) *crushed,* II, 3
la conception *concept, idea,* II, 11
le concentré *purée,* II, 3
le concert *concert,* I, 1
le concombre *cucumber,* II, 3
le concours *competition,* II, 4
la condition *condition, shape,* II, 7; **se mettre en condition** *to get into shape,* II, 7
conduire *to drive,* II, 8; **conduire une voiture** *to drive a car,* II, 8
se confier à *to confide in,* II, 10
la confiserie *candy shop,* II, 3
la confiture *jam,* I, 8
connais: Je ne connais pas. *I'm not familiar with them (him/her/it).* II, 11; **Tu connais la nouvelle?** *Did you hear the latest?* II, 9; **Tu connais...?** *Are you familiar with…?* II, 11
la connaissance *acquaintance,* II, 5; faire la connaissance de *to make someone's acquaintance,* II, 5
connaître *to know; to be acquainted with,* II, 1, 11
conseiller *to advise, to counsel;* **Qu'est-ce que tu me conseilles?** *What do you advise me to do?* I, 9; *What do you think I should do?* II, 10
les conseils (m.pl.) *advice,* II, 1
consoler *to console,* II, 5
consommer *to eat, to consume,* II, 7; **consommer trop de sucre** *to eat too much sugar,* II, 7
le conte de fée *fairy tale,* II, 9
content(e) *happy,* I, 7
continuer *to continue,* I, 12; **Vous continuez jusqu'au prochain feu rouge.** *You keep going until the next light.* I, 12
contre *against,* II, 2
convaincre *to convince,* II, 8
convenir *to agree with,* II, 5
convient *agrees with,* II, 5
la conversation *conversation,* II, 2
convoitent (convoiter) *to covet, to envy, to desire,* II, 11
cool *cool,* I, 2; **Il/Elle est cool, ton/ta...** *Your…is cool.* II, 2
le copain (la copine) *friend,* II, 10
le coq *rooster,* II, 11
le coquillage *shellfish,* II, 7
le correspondant (la correspondante) *pen pal,* II, 1
correspondre *to correspond,* II, 2
corriger *to correct,* II, 8
le costume *costume,* II, 1
la côte *coast,* II, 8
le côté: à côté de *next to,* I, 12; II, 2
le coton *cotton,* I, 10; **en coton** *(made of) cotton,* I, 10
le cou *neck,* II, 7; **J'ai mal au cou.** *My neck hurts.* II, 7
la couche *layer,* II, 3
se coucher *to go to bed,* II, 4
coule: J'ai le nez qui coule. *I've got a runny nose.* II, 7
la couleur *color,* I, 3; **De quelle couleur est...?** *What color is…?* I, 3
le couloir *hallway,* II, 2
le country *country (music),* II, 11
le coup *strike, blow, hit,* II, 7, 9; un coup de main *a helping hand,* II, 10
coupé(e) *cut,* II, 3
coupe: Ça coupe l'appétit. *It spoils your appetite.* II, 3
se couper *to cut one's (part of the body),* II, 7; **se couper le doigt** *to cut one's finger,* II, 7
la cour *court (of a king or queen),* II, 6
Courage! *Hang in there!* II, 5
le coureur *runner,* II, 4
le courriel *e-mail,* II, 11
le courrier électronique *e-mail,* II, 11
le cours *course,* I, 2; **cours de développement personnel et social (DPS)** *health,* I, 2; **Tu as quels cours...?** *What classes do you have…?* I, 2
les courses (f. pl.) *shopping; errands,* I, 8; **faire les courses** *to do the shopping,* I, 7; **J'ai des courses à faire.** *I have errands to do.* I, 5; **Tu peux aller faire les courses?** *Can you do the shopping?* I, 8
court(e) *short (objects),* I, 10; *(hair),* II, 1
le cousin *male cousin,* I, 7
la cousine *female cousin,* I, 7
coûte: Combien coûte(nt)...? *How much is (are)…?* II, 3
craque: Je craque! *I'm losing it!* II, 7
la cravate *tie,* I, 10
le crayon *pencil,* I, 3
créer *to create,* II, 3
la crème *cream,* II, 3; crème fraîche *a type of thick, heavy cream,* II, 3; **de la crème contre les insectes** *insect repellent,* II, 12
la crémerie *dairy,* II, 3
la crêpe *a very thin pancake,* I, 5
creuser *to dig,* II, 8
crève: Je crève de faim! *I'm dying of hunger!* II, 12
crevé(e): Si, je suis crevé(e). *Yes, I'm exhausted.* II, 2
la crevette *shrimp,* II, 3
crier *to yell, scream,* II, 5
croire *to believe,* II, 6, 9
crois: Je crois que... *I think that…,* II, 9; **Je ne crois pas.** *I don't think so.* II, 9
la croissance *growth, development,* II, 7
le croissant *croissant,* II, 3
la croix *cross,* II, 7
le croque-monsieur *toasted ham and cheese sandwich,* I, 5
cru(e) *uncooked,* I, 5
le cube *block,* II, 8
la cuillerée *spoonful,* II, 3; cuillerée à soupe *tablespoonful,* II, 3; cuillerée à thé *teaspoonful,* II, 3
le cuir *leather,* I, 10; **en cuir** *(made of) leather,* I, 10
cuire *to cook, to bake,* II, 3
la cuisine *kitchen,* II, 2
la culture *culture,* II, 6
la culture physique *physical training,* II, 7
cybernaute *(Web) surfer,* II, 11

D

D'abord,... *First,…,* II, 1; **D'abord, j'ai fait...** *First, I did…,* I, 9
D'accord. *OK.* I, 4; II, 1; **Bon, d'accord.** *Well, OK.* I, 8; **D'accord, si tu... d'abord.** *OK, if you…, first.* I, 7; **Je ne suis pas d'accord.** *I don't agree.* I, 7; **Tu es d'accord?** *Is that OK with you?* I, 7
d' après *according to,* II, 2
d'habitude *usually,* I, 4
dangereux (-euse) *dangerous,* II, 8
dans *in,* I, 6
la danse *dance,* I, 2
danser *to dance,* I, 1; **danser le zouk** *to dance the zouk,* II, 4
la date *date,* II, 10
la daube de lapin *rabbit stew,* II, 3
la daurade *sea bream (a type of fish),* II, 4
davantage *more,* II, 5
de *from,* I, 0; *of,* I, 0; **de l'** *some,* I, 8; **de la** *some,* I, 8; **de taille moyenne** *of medium height,* II, 1; **Je n'ai pas de...** *I don't have…,* I, 3; **Je ne fais pas de...** *I don't play/do…,* I, 4
débarrasser la table *to clear the table,* I, 7
debout *standing up,* II, 5
se débrouiller *to manage,* II, 8
le début *beginning,* II, 1
décembre *December,* I, 4; **en décembre** *in December,* I, 4
les déchets (m. pl.) *trash,* II, 12; **jeter (remporter) les déchets** *to throw away (to take with you) your trash,* II, 12

déchirer *to rip,* II, 5
décidé (pp. of décider): **Vous avez décidé de prendre... ?** *Have you decided to take...?* I, 10
la décoration *decoration,* II, 2
découper *to cut out,* II, 3
se décourager *to become discouraged,* II, 1
la découverte *discovery,* II, 6
découvrir *to discover,* II, 2
décrire *to describe,* II, 1
la défaite *defeat,* II, 7
le dégât *damage,* II, 7
dégoûtant(e) *gross,* I, 5
déguster *to taste, enjoy,* II, 4
déjà *already,* I, 9; **Il/Elle en a déjà un(e).** *He/She already has one (of them).* II, 3
le déjeuner *lunch,* I, 2; **déjeuner** *to have lunch,* I, 9
le délice *delight,* II, 3
délicieux (-euse) *delicious,* I, 5; **C'était délicieux!** *That was delicious!* II, 3
le deltaplane: faire du deltaplane *to hang glide,* II, 4
demain *tomorrow,* I, 2; **A demain.** *See you tomorrow.* I, 1
demande: Je me demande... *I wonder...,* II, 9
demander *to ask,* II, 2; **demander la permission à tes parents** *to ask your parents' permission,* II, 10; **demander pardon à (quelqu'un)** *to ask (someone's) forgiveness,* II, 10
déménager *to move,* II, 8
la demeure *residence,* II, 6
demi(e): et demi *half past (after midi and minuit),* I, 6; **et demie** *half past,* I, 6; une demi-heure *half an hour,* II, 4
démodé(e) *out of style,* I, 10
la dent *tooth,* II, 7; **J'ai mal aux dents.** *My teeth hurt.* II, 7; **se brosser les dents** *to brush one's teeth,* II, 4
le dépaysement *change of scenery*
déposer *to deposit,* I, 12
déprimant(e) *depressing*, II, 11
déprimé(e) *depressed,* II, 9
depuis *since,* II, 5
le dernier (la dernière) *last,* II, 9
se dérouler *to take place,* II, 4
derrière *behind,* I, 12
des *some,* I, 3
se désaltérer *to quench one's thirst,* II, 5
descendre *to go down,* II, 6
la description *description,* II, 1
désert(e) *deserted,* II, 12
désespéré(e) *desperate,* II, 11
désirer: Vous désirez? *What would you like?* I, 10
Désolé(e). *Sorry.* I, 5; II, 10; **Désolé(e), je suis occupé(e).** *Sorry, I'm busy.* I, 6; **Désolé(e), mais je ne peux pas.** *Sorry, but I can't.* I, 4
le dessert *dessert,* II, 3
le dessin *drawing,* II, 2
dessiner *to draw,* II, 2
le destin *fate,* II, 11
la destination *destination,* II, 4
le détail *detail,* II, 6
se détendre *to relax*
devant *in front of,* I, 6
devenir *to become,* II, 6
devine: Devine ce que... *Guess what...,* II, 9; **Devine qui...** *Guess who...,* II, 9
devineras: Tu ne devineras jamais ce qui s'est passé. *You'll never guess what happened.* II, 9
devoir *to have to, must,* II, 7
les devoirs (m. pl.) *homework,* I, 2; **faire ses devoirs** *to do homework,* I, 7
devrais: Tu devrais... *You should...,* I, 9; II, 7; **Tu ne devrais pas...** *You shouldn't...,* II, 7
le dictionnaire *dictionary,* I, 3
différent(e) *different,* II, 8
difficile *hard,* I, 2
dimanche *Sunday,* I, 2; **le dimanche** *on Sundays,* I, 2
le dîner *dinner,* I, 8; **dîner** *to have dinner,* I, 9
dingue *crazy,* II, 9
dire *to say, to tell,* I, 9; **Ça ne me dit rien.** *That doesn't interest me.* I, 4; II, 1; **Ça te dit d'aller... ?** *What do you think about going...?* II, 4; **Ça te dit de... ?** *Does...sound good to you?* II, 1; **dire à (quelqu'un) que...** *to tell (someone) that...,* II, 10; **Dis vite!** *Let's hear it!* II, 9; **Dis-lui/-leur que...** *Tell him/her/ them that...,* II, 10; **écouter ce qu'il/elle dit** *to listen to what he/she says,* II, 10; il dit *he says,* II, 5; **Vous pouvez lui dire que j'ai téléphoné?** *Can you tell her/ him that I called?* I, 9
la direction (f.) *directions,* II, 2
disparaître *to disappear,* II, 8
disponible *available,* II, 2
la dispute *argument,* II, 10
se disputer (avec quelqu'un) *to have an argument (with someone),* II, 9
le disquaire *record store,* I, 12; **chez le disquaire** *at the record store,* I, 12
le disque compact/le CD *compact disc/CD,* I, 3
dissoudre *to disband, to dissolve,* II, 11
la diversité *diversity,* II, 2
le documentaire *documentary,* II, 11
le doigt *finger,* II, 7; **se couper le doigt** *to cut one's finger,* II, 7
dois: A ton avis, qu'est-ce que je dois faire? *In your opinion, what should I do?* II, 10; **Non, tu dois...** *No, you've got to...,* I, 7; **Qu'est-ce que je dois... ?** *What should I...?* II, 1
doit: On doit... *Everyone should...,* II, 7
le don *gift,* II, 6
Donc,... *Therefore,...,* II, 9
le donjon *castle keep,* II, 6
donner *to give,* I, 5; **donner à manger aux animaux** *to feed the animals,* II, 6; **Donnez-moi..., s'il vous plaît.** *Please give me...,* I, 5
dorer *to brown,* II, 3
dormi (pp. of dormir) *slept,* II, 7; **J'ai mal dormi.** *I didn't sleep well.* II, 7
dormir *to sleep,* I, 1
le dos *back,* II, 7; **J'ai mal au dos.** *My back hurts.* II, 7
la douane *customs,* II, 1
la douceur *sweetness,* II, 4
doué(e) *talented,* II, 5
le doute *doubt,* II, 6
doux (douce) *mild,* II, 1
la douzaine *dozen,* I, 8; **une douzaine de** *a dozen,* I, 8
le drame *drama,* II, 11
le droit *the right to do something,* II, 8
la droite *right (direction),* I, 12; **à droite** *to the right,* I, 12; **à droite de** *to the right of,* II, 2; **sur la droite** *on the right,* II, 2
drôle *funny,* II, 11; **C'est drôle.** *It's funny.* II, 11
du *some,* I, 8
dû (pp. of devoir): **J'aurais dû...** *I should have...,* II, 10; **Tu aurais dû...** *You should have...,* II, 10
dur(e) *hard,* II, 3; *tough, difficult,* II, 4

l' eau (f.) *water,* I, 5; **l'eau minérale** *mineral water,* I, 5; **la chute d'eau** *waterfall,* II, 4; **le sirop de fraise (à l'eau)** *water with strawberry syrup,* I, 5
l' ébène (f.) *ebony,* II, 8
l' ébullition (f.) *boiling, a boil,* II, 3; amener à ébullition *bring*

to a boil, II, 3
écartelé(e) *to be torn (between two things),* II, 10
l' échange (m.) *exchange;* échanges franco-américains *Franco-American exchange programs,* II, 1
s' échapper: s'échapper d'une prison *to escape from prison,* II, 11
échanger *to exchange,* II, 2
l' écharpe (f.) *scarf,* I, 10; II, 1
éclater *to burst,* II, 4
l' école (f.) *school,* I, 1
écouter *to listen,* I, 1; **écouter ce qu'il/elle dit** *to listen to what he/she says,* II, 10; **écouter de la musique** *to listen to music,* I, 1; **Ecoutez!** *Listen!* I, 0; **Je t'écoute.** *I'm listening.* I, 9; II, 10
l' écran (m.) *screen,* II, 1
écrasé(e) *crushed,* II, 3
écris: Ecris-lui/-leur. *Write to him/her/them.* II, 10
l' écrivain (m.) *writer, author,* II, 4
s' écrouler *to collapse, fall down,* II, 5
l' écureuil (m.) *squirrel,* II, 12
l' édredon (m.) *comforter,* II, 9
l' éducation physique et sportive (EPS) (f.) *physical education,* I, 2
en effet *indeed,* II, 11
l' effort (m.) *effort, try,* II, 7; **Encore un effort!** *One more try!* II, 7
égaré(e) *lost,* II, 11
l' église (f.) *church,* II, 2
l' élève (m./f.) *student,* I, 2
s' éloigner *to distance oneself,* II, 10
l' e-mail (m.) *e-mail,* II, 11
l' émail (les émaux) (m.) *enamel work,* II, 2
embêtant(e) *annoying,* I, 7; II, 1
embête: Ça t'embête de...? *Would you mind...?* II, 10
embêté(e) *worried,* II, 10
emmener *to take (someone) along,* II, 8
l' émotion (f.) *emotion,* II, 9
empêcher *to stop (from doing something),* II, 10
employer *to use,* II, 3
l' employé (l'employée) *employee,* II, 6
emporter *to bring (with you),* II, 12
emprunter *to borrow,* I, 12
en *some, of it, of them, any, none,* I, 8; *to, in (before a feminine country),* I, 11; **Combien en voulez-vous?** *How many (much) do you want?* II, 3; **en coton** *(made of) cotton,* I, 10; **en cuir** *(made of) leather,* I, 10; en dépit de *in spite of,* II, 11; en effet *indeed,* II, 10; **en face de** *across from,* II, 2; **en jean** *(made of) denim,* I, 10; en voie de *in the process of,* II, 12; **Il/Elle en a déjà un(e).** *He/She already has one (of them).* II, 3; **Je n'en peux plus!** *I just can't do any more!* II, 7; **Je n'en veux plus.** *I don't want anymore.* I, 8; **Je ne t'en veux pas.** *No hard feelings.* II, 10; **J'en veux bien.** *I'd like some.* I, 8; **Je vais (en) prendre...** *I'll take...,* II, 3; **Oui, j'en veux bien.** *Yes, I'd like some.* I, 8; **T'en fais pas.** *Don't worry.* II, 5; **Tu n'as pas l'air en forme.** *You don't seem too well.* II, 7; **Tu ne m'en veux pas?** *No hard feelings?* II, 10; **Vous avez ça en...?** *Do you have that in...? (size, fabric, color),* I, 10
encore *again;* **Encore de...?** *More...?* I, 8; **Encore un effort!** *One more try!* II, 7; **Encore...?** *Some more...?* II, 3
l' endroit (m.) *place,* I, 12
énervé(e) *annoyed,* II, 9
l' enfance (f.) *childhood,* II, 8
l' enfant (m./f.) *child,* I, 7
Enfin,... *Finally,...,* II, 1; **Enfin, je suis allé(e)...** *Finally, I went...,* I, 9
ennuie: Ça t'ennuie de...? *Would you mind...?* II, 10; **Ce qui m'ennuie, c'est (de)...** *What bores me is...,* II, 4; **On ne s'ennuie pas.** *You're never bored. (One does not get bored.)* II, 11
ennuyé(e) *bored,* II, 6; **Je me suis ennuyé(e).** *I was bored.* II, 6
ennuyer *to bother,* II, 8
ennuyeux (-euse) *boring,* II, 6; **C'était ennuyeux.** *It was boring.* I, 5
l' ensemble (m.) *group,* II, 8
ensemble (adv.) *together,* II, 8
enseveli(e) *buried,* II, 8
Ensuite,... *Next,...,* II, 1; *Then,...,* II, 12
entendre *to hear,* II, 5; **entendre le réveil** *to hear the alarm clock,* II, 5
Entendu. *OK.; Agreed.* I, 6
l' entente (f.) *harmony,* II, 11
enterrer *to bury,* II, 8
s' entraider *to help each other,* II, 10
l' entraînement (m.) *training,* II, 7
entraîner *to carry along,* II, 12
s' entraîner à... *to train for (a sport),* II, 7
l' entraîneur (m.) *trainer, coach,* II, 7
entre *between,* I, 12
l' entrée (f.) *first course,* II, 3; *entrance fee,* II, 6; **C'est combien, l'entrée?** *How much is the entrance fee?* II, 6
entrer *to enter,* II, 6
l' enveloppe (f.) *envelope,* I, 12
l' envie (f.) *desire, need;* **J'ai envie de...** *I feel like...,* I, 11; **Non, je n'ai pas très envie.** *No, I don't feel like it.* II, 7; **Tu as envie de...?** *Do you feel like...?* II, 1
les environs (m. pl.) *surroundings,* II, 12
envoyer *to send,* I, 12; **envoyer des lettres** *to send letters,* I, 12; **envoyer les invitations** *to send the invitations,* II, 10
l' épicerie (f.) *(small) grocery store,* I, 12
l'épisode (m.) *episode,* II, 1
épouser *to marry,* II, 8
épouvantable *horrible, terrible,* I, 11; **passer une journée épouvantable** *to have a horrible day,* II, 5; **C'était épouvantable.** *It was horrible.* I, 11; II, 9
l' épreuve (f.): à toute épreuve *solid, unfailing,* II, 10
l' équilibre (m.) *balance,* II, 7
l' équipe (f.) *team,* II, 7
l' équitation (f.) *horseback riding,* I, 1; **faire de l'équitation** *to go horseback riding,* I, 1
l' érable (m.) *maple*
es: Tu es allé(e) où? *Where did you go?* I, 9; **Tu es d'accord?** *Is that OK with you?* I, 7
l' escalier (m.) *stairs,* II, 2
les escargots (m.) *snails,* I, 1; II, 3
l' espagnol (m.) *Spanish (language),* I, 2
l' espoir (m.) *hope,* II, 11
essayer *to try; to try on,* I, 10; **Je peux essayer...?** *Can I try on...?* I, 10; **Je peux l'(les) essayer?** *Can I try it (them) on?* I, 10
est: Il/Elle est... *He/She is...,* I, 7; **Il/Elle est comment?** *What is he/she like?* I, 7; **Qu'est-ce qui s'est passé?** *What happened?* I, 9; **Quelle heure est-il?** *What time is it?* I, 6; **Qui est à l'appareil?** *Who's calling?* I, 9
Est-ce que *(Introduces a yes-or-no question),* I, 4; **(Est-ce que) je peux...?** *May I...?* I, 7
l' est (m.) *east,* II, 4; **dans l'est** *in the east,* II, 4; **C'est à l'est de...** *It's to the east of...,* II, 12
et *and,* I, 1; **Et après ça,...** *And after that,...,* I, 9; **Et toi?** *And you?* I, 1
l' étage (m.) *floor (of a building),* II, 2; **le premier étage** *second floor,* II, 2
l' étagère (f.) *shelf,* II, 2
étais: J'étais... *I was...,* II, 12

était: C'était comment? *What was it like?* II, 8; **C'était épouvantable.** *It was horrible.* I, 9; **C'était tellement différent?** *Was it really so different?* II, 8
l' état (m.) *state,* II, 4
les Etats-Unis (m. pl.) *the United States,* II, 1
l' été (m.) *summer,* I, 4; **en été** *in the summer,* I, 4
été (pp. of être): **Oui, ça a été.** *Yes, it was fine.* I, 9
étendu(e) *vast,* II, 8
éternue: J'éternue beaucoup. *I'm sneezing a lot.* II, 7
l' ethnie (f.) *ethnic group,* II, 8
l' étoile (f.) *star,* II, 4
étonné(e) *surprised,* II, 9
étonnerait: Ça m'étonnerait! *I doubt it!* II, 6
étrange *strange,* II, 12
l' étranger (m.): à l'étranger *abroad,* II, 1
être *to be,* I, 7; **Ça s'est très bien passé!** *It went really well!* II, 5; **Comment ça s'est passé?** *How did it go?* II, 5; **être collé(e)** *to have detention,* II, 5; **être en train de** *to be in the process of (doing something),* II, 9; **Il/Elle est...** *He/She is...,* I, 7; II, 1
l' étude (f.) *study hall,* I, 2
étudier *to study,* I, 1
l' euro (m.), European Community monetary unit, I, 3; II, 3
Evidemment. *Obviously.* II, 9
éviter *to avoid,* II, 3; **Evite/Evitez de fumer.** *Avoid smoking.* II, 7
l' examen (m.) *exam, test,* I, 1; **passer un examen** *to take a test,* I, 9
excellent(e) *excellent,* I, 5; **Oui, excellent.** *Yes, excellent.* I, 9; II, 2
l' excitant (m.) *stimulant,* II, 7
l' excursion (f.) *excursion,* II, 12
l' excuse (f.) *excuse,* II, 5
s' excuser *to apologize,* II, 10; **Excuse-moi.** *Forgive me.* II, 10; **Excuse-toi.** *Apologize.* II, 10
excusez: Excusez-moi. *Excuse me.* I, 3
l' exercice (m.) *exercise,* II, 7; **faire de l'exercice** *to exercise,* II, 7
expliquer *to explain,* II, 2; **Explique-lui/-leur.** *Explain to him/her/them.* II, 10; **expliquer ce qui s'est passé (à quelqu'un)** *to explain what happened (to someone),* II, 10
l' exportateur (m.) *exporter,* II, 8
l' exposé (m.) *oral presentation,* II, 5
l' expression (f.) *expression,* II, 1

F

face: en face de *across from,* I, 12; II, 2
fâché(e) *angry,* II, 9
facile *easy,* I, 2
faciliter *to make easier, facilitate,* II, 7
la façon *way,* II, 1
le faible *weakness,* II, 7
la faïence *glazed pottery,* II, 2
la faim *hunger,* II, 2; **avoir faim** *to be hungry,* I, 5; **Je n'ai plus faim.** *I'm not hungry anymore.* II, 3; **Non, merci. Je n'ai plus faim.** *No thanks. I'm not hungry anymore.* I, 8; **Si, j'ai très faim!** *Yes, I'm very hungry!* II, 2; **Vous n'avez pas (Tu n'as pas) faim?** *Aren't you hungry?* II, 2
faire *to do, to make, to play,* I, 4; **Désolé(e) j'ai des devoirs à faire.** *Sorry, I have homework to do.* I, 5; faire la connaissance de *to make someone's acquaintance,* II, 10; faire la cuisine *to cook,* II, 8; **faire la tête** *to sulk,* II, 9; **faire les préparatifs** *to get ready,* II, 10; faire semblant de *to pretend to (do something),* II, 10; **Fais-toi une raison.** *Make the best of it.* II, 8; **Faites/Fais comme chez vous (toi).** *Make yourself at home.* II, 2; **J'ai des courses à faire.** *I have errands to do.* I, 5; **J'ai des tas de choses à faire.** *I have lots of things to do.* I, 5; **J'ai des trucs à faire.** *I have some things to do.* I, 5; **Je ne sais pas quoi faire.** *I don't know what to do.* II, 10; **Qu'est-ce qu'on peut faire?** *What can we do?* II, 4; **Qu'est-ce que je dois faire?** *What should I do?* II, 12; **Qu'est-ce que tu aimes faire?** *What do you like to do?* II, 1; **Qu'est-ce que tu vas faire...?** *What are you going to do...?* I, 6; **se faire mal à...** *to hurt one's...,* II, 7; **Tu peux aller faire les courses?** *Can you do the shopping?* I, 8; **Tu vas faire quoi...?** *What are you going to do...?* I, 6; **Tu vas t'y faire.** *You'll get used to it.* II, 8
fais: A ton avis, qu'est-ce que je fais? *In your opinion, what do I do?* I, 9; **Fais-toi une raison.** *Make the best of it.* II, 8; **Ne t'en fais pas!** *Don't worry!* I, 9; I, 11; **Faites (Fais) comme chez vous (toi).** *Make yourself at home.* II, 2; **Je fais...** *I play/do...,* I, 4; **Je ne fais pas de...** *I don't play/do...,* I, 4; **Ne t'en fais pas!** *Don't worry!* I, 9; **Qu'est-ce que tu fais comme sport?** *What sports do you play?* II, 1; **Qu'est-ce que tu fais pour t'amuser?** *What do you do to have fun?* I, 4; **Qu'est-ce que tu fais...?** *What do you do...?* I, 4; **Qu'est-ce que tu fais quand...?** *What do you do when...?* I, 4; **T'en fais pas.** *Don't worry.* II, 5
fait: Ça fait combien? *How much does that make?* II, 3; **Ça ne fait rien.** *It doesn't matter.* II, 10; **D'abord, j'ai fait...** *First, I did...,* I, 9; **Il fait beau.** *It's nice weather.* I, 4; **Il fait frais.** *It's cool.* I, 4; **Il fait froid.** *It's cold.* I, 4; **Il fait chaud.** *It's hot.* I, 4; **Qu'est-ce qu'on fait?** *What should we do?* II, 1
fait (pp. of faire) *done, made,* I, 9; **J'ai fait...** *I did/made...,* I, 9; **Qu'est-ce que tu as fait...?** *What did you do...?* I, 9
faites: Faites/Fais comme chez vous/toi. *Make yourself at home.* II, 2
la falaise *cliff,* II, 5
la famille *family,* I, 7
un fantôme *ghost,* II, 11
la farine *flour,* I, 8
fatigant(e) *tiring,* II, 2; **C'était fatigant!** *It was tiring!* II, 2
fatigué(e) *tired,* II, 2; **Je suis fatigué(e)** *I'm tired.* II, 12; **Pas trop fatigué(e)?** *(You're) not too tired?* II, 2
faudra: Il faudra... *It will be necessary...,* II, 12
faut: Il faut mieux travailler en classe. *You have to work harder in class.* II, 5; **Il me faut...** *I need...,* I, 3; **Il ne faut pas faire le clown en classe!** *You can't be goofing off in class!* II, 5; **Oui, il me faut...** *Yes, I need...,* I, 10; **Qu'est-ce qu'il te faut?** *What do you need?* I, 8; **Qu'est-ce qu'il te faut pour...?** *What do you need for...? (informal),* I, 3; **Qu'est-ce qu'il vous faut pour...?** *What do you need for...? (formal),* I, 3
la faute *fault,* II, 10; **C'est de ma faute.** *It's my fault.* II, 10
faux (fausse) *false,* II, 2
le féculent *carbohydrate,* II, 7
la fée *fairy,* II, 6
Félicitations! *Congratulations!* II, 3
la femme *wife,* I, 7
la fenêtre *window,* I, 0
fera: Ça te fera du bien. *It'll do you good.* II, 7

ferais: Qu'est-ce que tu ferais, toi? *What would you do?* II, 10; **Tu ferais bien de...** *You would do well to...,* II, 7
la ferme *farm,* II, 11
fermer: *to close,* II, 6; **A quelle heure est-ce que vous fermez?** *At what time do you close?* II, 6; **Fermez la porte.** *Close the door.* I, 0
la fête *party,* I, 1; *holiday,* II, 3; **Bonne fête!** *Happy holiday! (Happy saint's day!),* II, 3; **Bonne fête de Hanoukkah!** *Happy Hanukkah!* II, 3; la fête des Mères *Mother's Day,* II, 3; la fête des Pères *Father's Day,* II, 3
le feu *flame (heat),* II, 3
la feuille: une feuille de papier *a sheet of paper,* I, 0; *leaf,* II, 12
février *February,* I, 4; **en février** *in February,* I, 4
ficher: ficher le camp *to leave quickly, "scram,"* II, 5
fier (fière) *proud,* II, 1
la fièvre: J'ai de la fièvre. *I have a fever.* II, 7
la figure *face,* II, 5
filer *to spin,* II, 6
la fille *daughter,* I, 7
le film *movie,* I, 6; **film classique** *classic movie,* II, 11; **film comique** *comedy,* II, 11; **film d'action** *action movie,* II, 11; **film d'amour** *romantic movie,* II, 11; **film d'aventures** *adventure movie,* II, 11; **film d'horreur** *horror movie,* II, 11; **film de science-fiction** *science-fiction movie,* II, 11; **film policier** *detective or mystery movie,* II, 11; **voir un film** *to see a movie,* I, 6
le fils *son,* I, 7
la fin *end,* II, 4
Finalement,... *Finally,...* I, 9; II, 4
fixer: fixer la date *to choose the date,* II, 10
le flamant *flamingo*
le fleuriste *florist's shop,* II, 3
la fleur *flower,* II, 3
le fleuve river
la fois *time,* I, 4; **une fois par semaine** *once a week,* I, 4
le folk *folk music,* II, 11
fonder *to found,* II, 12
fondu(e) *melted,* II, 3
le foot(ball) *soccer,* I, 1; **le football américain** *football,* I, 4; **jouer au foot** *to play soccer,* I, 4; **jouer au football américain** *to play football,* I, 4
la forêt *forest,* I, 11: **en forêt** *to the forest,* I, 11; **la forêt tropicale** *tropical rainforest,* II, 4
la forme *form,* II, 1; **Tu n'as pas l'air en forme.** *You don't look well.* II, 7
formidable *great,* I, 11; **C'était formidable!** *It was great!* I, 11
fort(e) *strong,* I, 7; II, 1; **C'est pas mon fort.** *It's not my strong point.* II, 5; **C'est mon fort.** *It's my strong point.* II, 5
la fosse *grave,* II, 8
le fou *fool, jester,* II, 3; *crazy,* II, 11; Plus on est de fous, plus on rit. *The more the merrier.* II, 3
le foulard *scarf,* II, 3
se fouler *to sprain one's (part of the body),* II, 7; **se fouler la cheville** *to sprain one's ankle,* II, 7
le four *oven,* II, 3; au four *baked,* II, 3
fourbe *treacherous,* II, 11
fraîche (f. of **frais**) *cool, fresh,* II, 12
frais *cool (weather),* I, 4; **Il fait frais.** *It's cool.* I, 4
la fraise *strawberry,* I, 8
le franc *(the former French monetary unit),* I, 3
le français *French (language),* I, 1
français(e) *French* (adj), II, 1
francophone, *French-speaking,* II, 3
frapper *to knock,* II, 2
freiné(e) *held up, slowed down,* II, 11
le frère *brother,* I, 7
fringant(e) *dashing,* II, 11
les frites (f. pl.) *French fries,* I, 1
froid(e) *cold,* I, 4; **Il fait froid.** *It's cold.* I, 4
le fromage *cheese,* I, 5; II, 3
les fruits de mer (m. pl.) *seafood,* II, 3
fumer: Evite/Evitez de fumer. *Avoid smoking.* II, 7
furieux (-euse) *furious,* II, 9
le fuseau *spindle,* II, 6

G

gagner *to win, to earn,* I, 9
les gants (m.) *a pair of gloves,* II, 1
le garçon *boy,* I, 9
garder: garder ta petite sœur *to look after your little sister,* I, 7
la gare *train station,* II, 2
la gare routière *bus station,* II, 6
garni(e) *garnished,* II, 3
le gâteau *cake,* I, 8
la gauche *left (direction),* I, 12; **à gauche** *to the left,* I, 12; **à gauche de** *to the left of,* II, 2; **sur la gauche** *on the left,* II, 2
gazeuse *carbonated,* II, 7
gêné(e) *embarrassed,* II, 9
en général *in general,* II, 8
génial(e) *great,* I, 2; II, 2
le genou: J'ai mal au genou. *My knee hurts.* II, 7
le genre *type (of film, literature, or music),* II, 11
les gens (m.pl.) *people,* II, 1
gentil(le) *nice,* I, 7; II, 1; **C'est gentil de votre (ta) part.** *That's so nice of you.* II, 2; **Merci, c'est gentil!** *Thanks, that's nice of you!* II, 2
gentillet: gentillet, sans plus *cute (but that's all),* II, 11
la géographie *geography,* I, 2
la géométrie *geometry,* I, 2
le gibier *game (animals)*
le gingembre *ginger,* II, 3
gitan(e) (adj.) *gypsy,* II, 11
la glace *ice cream,* I, 1
la glace: faire du patin à glace *to ice-skate,* I, 4
glacé(e) *iced,* II, 3
le golf *golf,* I, 4; **jouer au golf** *to play golf,* I, 4
les gombos (m.pl.) *okra,* I, 8
la gomme *eraser,* I, 3
la gorge *throat,* II, 7; **J'ai mal à la gorge.** *I have a sore throat.* II, 7
gourmand(e) *someone who loves to eat,* II, 1
la gousse d'ail *clove of garlic,* II, 3
le goût: Chacun ses goûts. *To each his own.* II, 11
le goûter *afternoon snack,* I, 8
la goutte *drop,* II, 8
la goyave *guava,* I, 8
la graisse *fat,* II, 7
la grammaire *grammar,* II, 1
grand(e) *tall,* I, 7; II, 1; *big,* I, 10; II, 1; **moins grand(e) que** *smaller than...,* II, 4; **plus grand(e) que** *bigger than...,* II, 4
grand-chose: Ce n'est pas grand-chose. *It's nothing special.* II, 3; **Pas grand-chose.** *Not much.* I, 6
la grand-mère *grandmother,* I, 7
le grand-père *grandfather,* I, 7
les grands-parents (m. pl.) *grandparents,* II, 6
grandir *to grow,* I, 10
gras(se): des matières grasses *fat,* II, 7
le gratin *cheese-toppped dish,* II, 3
gratuit(e) *free,* II, 1
grave *serious,* II, 5; **C'est pas grave.** *It's not serious.* II, 5
grec (grecque) *Greek* (adj.), II, 1
grignoter: grignoter entre les repas *to snack between meals,*

II, 7
grillé(e) *grilled,* II, 3
la **grippe** *flu,* II, 7; **J'ai la grippe.** *I've got the flu.* II, 7
gris(e) *grey,* I, 3
le grognement *growl,* II, 12
gros(se) *fat,* I, 7
grossir *to gain weight,* I, 10
la grotte *cave,* II, 8
le groupe *(musical) group,* II, 11
guidé(e) *guided,* II, 6; **une visite guidée** *a guided tour,* II, 6
la gymnastique *gymnastics,* II, 7; **faire de la gymnastique** *to do gymnastics,* II, 7

H

s' habiller *to get dressed,* II, 4
habiter *to live,* II, 1
l' habitude (f.) *habit,* II, 7; les habitudes alimentaires (f. pl.) *eating habits,* II, 7
d' habitude *usually,* I, 4
s' habituer à *to get used to,* II, 1
haché(e) *ground (meat),* I, 4
***le hamburger** *hamburger,* I, 1
Hanoukkah *Hanukkah,* II, 3; **Bonne fête de Hanoukkah!** *Happy Hanukkah!* II, 3
***les haricots verts** (m.pl.) *green beans,* I, 8
l' hébergement (m.) *lodging,* II, 6, 12
hésite: Euh... J'hésite. *Oh, I'm not sure.* I, 10
l' heure (f.) *hour; time,* I, 1; **à l'heure de** *at the time of,* I, 1; **A quelle heure?** *At what time?* I, 6; **A tout à l'heure!** *See you later (the same day)!* I, 1; **Quelle heure est-il?** *What time is it?* I, 6; **Tu as... à quelle heure?** *At what time do you have…?* I, 2
heures *…o'clock,* I, 2; **à... heures** *at…o'clock,* I, 2; **à... heures quarante-cinq** *at…forty-five,* I, 2; **à... heures quinze** *at…fifteen,* I, 2; **à... heures trente** *at… thirty,* I, 2
heureusement *fortunately,* II, 9
heureux (-euse): Très heureux (heureuse). *Pleased to meet you.* I, 7
hier *yesterday,* I, 9
l' histoire (f.) *history,* I, 2; *story,* II, 11; les histoires marseillaises (f. pl.) *tall tales,* II, 9; **C'est l'histoire de...** *It's the story of…,* II, 11; **C'est une belle histoire.** *It's a great story.* II, 11; **C'est une histoire passionnante.** *It's an exciting story.* II, 11; **Il n'y a pas d'histoire.** *It has no plot.* II, 11
l' hiver (m.) *winter,* I, 4; **en hiver** *in the winter,* I, 4
***le hockey** *hockey,* I, 4; **jouer au hockey** *to play hockey,* I, 4
horrible *terrible,* I, 10
hors: hors du feu *away from the flame,* II, 3
***le hot-dog** *hot dog,* I, 5
l' hôtel particulier (m.) *mansion,* II, 9
*la huée *boo, hoot,* II, 5
l' huile (f.) *oil,* II, 3
les huîtres (f.) *oysters,* II, 3
l' humeur (f.) *mood,* II, 9; **de mauvaise humeur** *in a bad mood,* II, 9; **de bonne humeur** *in a good mood,* II, 9
humoristique *humorous,* II, 2

I

ici *here,* II, 1
idéal(e) *ideal,* II, 2
l' idée (f.) *idea,* II, 3; **Bonne idée!** *Good idea!* I, 4; II, 3; **C'est une bonne (excellente) idée.** *That's a good (excellent) idea.* II, 1; **Tu as une idée de cadeau pour...?** *Have you got a gift idea for…?* II, 3
l' ile (f.) *island,* II, 4
l' illustration (f.) *illustration,* II, 7
il y a *there is/there are,* I, 5; **Il n'y a pas de mal.** *No harm done.* II, 10; **Qu'est-ce qu'il y a à boire?** *What is there to drink?* I, 5
Il y avait... *there was/were…,* II, 12
l' image (f.) *image,* II, 2
imaginaire *imaginary,* II, 1
imaginer *to imagine,* II, 1
l' imèle (m.) *e-mail,* II, 11
l' immeuble (m.) *building,* II, 2
l' impératrice (f.) *empress,* II, 6
l' imperméable (m.) *raincoat,* II, 1
important(e) *important,* II, 6
importe: du n'importe quoi *worthless,* II, 11; **N'importe quoi!** *That's ridiculous!* II, 6
impossible *impossible,* II, 10; **C'est impossible.** *It's impossible.* II, 10
inadmissible: C'est inadmissible. *That's not acceptable.* II, 5
inattendu(e) *unexpected,* II, 9
s' incorporer *to incorporate/integrate oneself,* II, 1
incrédule *unbelieving,* II, 10
incroyable *incredible,* II, 6; **C'était incroyable!** *It was amazing/unbelievably bad!* II, 5
indien(ne) *Indian (adj.),* II, 1
indigène *native*
individuel(le) *individual,* II, 7
indonésien(ne) *Indonesian (adj.),* II, 1
l' infirmerie (f.) *infirmary,* II, 5
l' information (f.) *information,* II, 5
l' informatique (f.) *computer science,* I, 2
les ingrédients (m. pl.) *ingredients,* II, 3
inquiet (inquiète) *worried,* II, 9
insolite *unusual,* II, 2
intelligent(e) *smart,* I, 7; II, 1
l' intention (f.)**: J'ai l'intention de...** *I intend to…,* I, 11
intéressant(e) *interesting,* I, 2
intéresser *to interest,* II, 1
l' intérieur (m.) *interior,* II, 2
l' interro (f.) *quiz,* I, 9
l' interview (f.) *interview,* II, 1
interviewer *to interview,* II, 1
l' invitation (f.) *invitation,* II, 10; **envoyer les invitations** *to send the invitations,* II, 10
invite: Invite-le/-la/-les. *Invite him/her/them.* II, 10
l' invité(e) *guest,* II, 1
Ivoirien(ne) *native of the Ivory Coast,* II, 8

J

jamais: ne... jamais *never,* I, 4
la jambe *leg,* II, 7; **J'ai mal à la jambe.** *My leg hurts.* II, 7
le jambon *ham,* I, 5; II, 3
janvier *January,* I, 4; **en janvier** *in January,* I, 4
le jardin *yard,* II, 2
jaune *yellow,* I, 3
le jazz *jazz,* II, 11
je *I,* I, 1
le jean *(a pair of) jeans,* I, 3; II, 1; **en jean** *denim,* I, 10
jeter *to throw;* **jeter les déchets** *to throw away your trash,* II, 12
le jeu *game,* II, 1; les jeux de société *board games,* II, 4; **jouer à des jeux vidéo** *to play video games,* I, 4
jeudi *Thursday,* I, 2; **le jeudi** *on Thursdays,* I, 2
jeune *young,* I, 7; II, 1
la jeunesse: l'auberge (f.) **de jeunesse** *youth hostel,* II, 2
la Joconde *the Mona Lisa,* II, 1

le **jogging** *jogging,* I, 4; **faire du jogging** *to jog,* I, 4
la joie *joy,* II, 1
jouait: Si on jouait... ? *How about playing...?* II, 8
jouer *to play,* I, 4; **Je joue...** *I play...,* I, 4; **Je ne joue pas...** *I don't play...,* I, 4; **jouer à...** *to play...(a game),* I, 4; **On joue...** *...[film] is showing.* II, 11; **Qu'est-ce qu'on joue comme films?** *What films are playing?* II, 11
le jouet *toy,* II, 8
le jour *day,* I, 2; II, 5; **C'est pas mon jour!** *It's just not my day!* II, 5. tous les jours *everyday,* II, 1
le journal *journal,* II, 1
journaliste (m./f.) *journalist,* II, 8
la journée *day,* II, 5; **passer une journée épouvantable** *to have a horrible day,* II, 5; **Comment s'est passée ta journée (hier)?** *How was your day (yesterday)?* II, 5; **Quelle journée!** *What a good/bad day!* II, 5
joyeux (-euse) *happy, merry,* II, 3; **Joyeux (Bon) anniversaire!** *Happy birthday!* II, 3; **Joyeux Noël!** *Merry Christmas!* II, 3
juillet *July,* I, 4; **en juillet** *in July,* I, 4
juin *June,* I, 4; **en juin** *in June,* I, 4
le jumeau (la jumelle) *twin,* II, 4
la jupe *skirt,* I, 10
le jus *juice,* I, 5; **le jus d'orange** *orange juice,* I, 5; **le jus de pomme** *apple juice,* I, 5
jusqu'à *up to; until,* I, 12; **Vous allez tout droit jusqu'à...** *You go straight ahead until you get to...,* 12
juste *just, only,* II, 5

K

le kilo *kilogram,* I, 8; **un kilo de** *a kilogram of,* I, 8

L

la *her, it,* I, 9
là *there,* I, 9; **-là** *there (noun suffix),* I, 3; **(Est-ce que)... est là, s'il vous plaît?** *Is..., there, please?* I, 9; **Là, c'est...** *Here (There) is...,* II, 2; là-bas *(over) there,* II, 1
le lac *lake,* II, 1
laisser *to permit,* II, 6, 8 *to leave,* I, 9; II, 12; **Je peux laisser un message?** *Can I leave a message?* I, 9
le lait *milk,* I, 8; II, 3; lait gélifié *sweetened, yogurt-like pudding,* II, 3
la laitue *lettuce,* II, 3
la lampe *lamp,* II, 2; **la lampe de poche** *flashlight,* II, 12
le lapin chasseur *rabbit in tomato-mushroom sauce,* II, 3
large *baggy,* I, 10
les larmes (f.) *tears,* II, 7
le latin *Latin (language),* I, 2
la lavande *lavender*
laver *to wash,* I, 7; **laver la voiture** *to wash the car,* I, 7; **se laver** *to wash oneself,* II, 4
le *him, it,* I, 9
les légumes (m.) *vegetables,* I, 8; II, 7
lent(e) *slow,* II, 12
les *them,* I, 9
la lettre *letter,* II, 1
leur (indirect object) *to them,* I, 9
leur(s) *their,* I, 7
se lever *to get up,* II, 4; **Levez-vous!** *Stand up!* I, 0
Levez la main! *Raise your hand!* I, 0
libanais(e) *Lebanese* (adj.), II, 1
la librairie *bookstore,* I, 12
libre *free,* II, 8
lié(e) *bound, tied,* II, 10
le lieu *place,* II, 1
le lièvre *hare,* II, 8
la limonade *lemon soda,* I, 5
lire *to read,* I, 1
la liste *list,* II, 3
le lit *bed,* II, 2
le litre *liter,* I, 8; **un litre de** *a liter of,* I, 8
livré(e) *delivered,* II, 12
la livre *pound,* I, 8; **une livre de** *a pound of,* I, 8
le livre *book,* I, 3; **le livre de poésie** *book of poetry,* II, 11
local(e) *local,* II, 4
le logement *lodging,* II, 2
logique *logical,* II, 2
loin *far,* I, 12; **loin de** *far from,* I, 12
long(ue) *long,* II, 1; **trop long(ue)** *too long,* II, 11
longtemps *(for) a long time,* II, 6
lorsque *when,* II, 4
la lotion: la lotion anti-moustiques *insect repellent,* II, 12
louer *to rent,* II, 6
le loup *wolf,* II, 12
lu (pp. of **lire**) *read,* I, 9
lui *to him, to her,* I, 9
la lumière *light,* II, 6
lundi *Monday,* I, 2; **le lundi** *on Mondays,* I, 2
luné(e): toujours mal luné(e) *always in a bad mood,* II, 8
les lunettes de soleil (f. pl.) *sunglasses,* I, 10
le lycée *high school,* II, 2
le lycéen (la lycéenne), *high school student* II, 5

ma *my,* I, 7
madame (Mme) *ma'am; Mrs,* I, 1; **Madame!** *Waitress!* I, 5
mademoiselle (Mlle) *miss; Miss,* I, 1; **Mademoiselle!** *Waitress!* I, 5
le magasin *store,* I, 1; **faire les magasins** *to go shopping,* I, 1; un grand magasin *department store,* II, 3
le magazine *magazine,* I, 3
le magnétoscope *videocassette recorder, VCR,* I, 0
magnifique *beautiful,* II, 6
mai *May,* I, 4; **en mai** *in May,* I, 4
maigrir *to lose weight,* I, 10
le maillot de bain *bathing suit,* I, 10
la main *hand,* I, 0; **J'ai mal à la main.** *My hand hurts.* II, 7; se serrer la main *to shake hands,* II, 8; un coup de main *a helping hand,* II, 10
maintenant *now,* I, 2; **Je ne peux pas maintenant.** *I can't right now.* I, 8
mais *but,* I, 1
le maïs *corn,* I, 8
la Maison des jeunes et de la culture *recreation center,* I, 6
maîtriser, *to master* II, 4
mal *bad,* I, 1; **Il n'y a pas de mal.** *No harm done.* II, 10; **J'ai mal à...** *My...hurts.* II, 7; **J'ai mal à la gorge.** *I have a sore throat.* II, 7; **J'ai mal à la jambe.** *My leg hurts.* II, 7; **J'ai mal à la main.** *My hand hurts.* II, 7; **J'ai mal à la tête.** *My head hurts.* II, 7; **J'ai mal au bras.** *My arm hurts.* II, 7; **J'ai mal au cœur.** *I'm sick to my stomach.* II, 7; **J'ai mal au cou.** *My neck hurts.* II, 7; **J'ai mal au dos.** *My back hurts.* II, 7; **J'ai mal au ventre.** *My stomach hurts.* II, 7; **J'ai mal aux dents.** *My*

teeth hurt. II, 7; **J'ai mal à l'oreille.** *My ear hurts.* II, 7; **J'ai mal au pied.** *My foot hurts.* II, 7; **J'ai mal dormi.** *I didn't sleep well.* II, 7; **J'ai mal partout!** *I hurt all over!* II, 7; **mal à l'aise** *uncomfortable,* II, 9; **pas mal** *not bad,* I, 1; *all right,* II, 6; **se faire mal à...** *to hurt one's...,* II, 7; toujours mal luné(e) *always in a bad mood,* II, 8; **Très mal.** *Very badly.* I, 9
le mal du pays: avoir le mal du pays, *to be homesick* II, 8
malade *sick,* II, 7; **Je suis malade.** *I'm sick.* II, 7
le malentendu *misunderstanding,* II, 10; **un petit malentendu** *a little misunderstanding,* II, 10
malgré *in spite of,* II, 5
le malheur *misfortune,* II, 10
Malheureusement,... *Unfortunately,...,* II, 9
le malheureux (la malheureuse) *unfortunate, unlucky person,* II, 11
la mandarine *mandarin orange,* II, 3
manger *to eat,* I, 6; II, 7; **donner à manger aux animaux** *to feed the animals,* II, 6; **manger quelque chose** *to eat something,* I, 6
la mangue *mango,* I, 8
la manière *way,* II, 1
le manoir *manor,* II, 5
manque: ... me manque. *I miss... (singular),* II, 8; **Ce qui me manque, c'est (de)...** *What I miss is...,* II, 8
manquent: ... me manquent. *I miss... (plural),* II, 8
le manteau *coat,* I, 10
le maquis *popular Ivorian outdoor restaurant,* II, 8
le marchand *shopkeeper,* II, 3
la marche *step,* II, 5; **rater une marche** *to miss a step,* II, 5
le marché *market,* I, 8
mardi *Tuesday,* I, 2; **le mardi** *on Tuesdays,* I, 2
le mari *husband,* I, 7
marocain(e) *Moroccan* (adj.), II, 1
la maroquinerie *leather-goods shop,* II, 3
la marraine *godmother,* II, 6
marron (inv.) *brown,* I, 3; II, 1
le marron *chestnut,* II, 3
mars *March,* I, 4; **en mars** *in March,* I, 4
le Martiniquais (la Martiniquaise), *native of Martinique* II, 4
la Martinique, *Martinique* II, 4
le masque *mask,* II, 8
le match *game,* I, 6; **regarder un match** *to watch a game (on TV),* I, 6; **voir un match** *to see a game (in person),* I, 6
les maths (f. pl.) *math,* I, 1
les matières grasses (f. pl.) *fat,* II, 7
le matin *morning, in the morning,* I, 2
mauvais(e) *bad,* I, 9; **C'est pas mauvais!** *It's pretty good!* I, 5; **Oh, pas mauvais.** *Oh, not bad.* I, 9; **Très mauvais.** *Very bad.* I, 9; **avoir une mauvaise note** *to get a bad grade,* II, 5; **de mauvaise humeur** *in a bad mood,* II, 9
me *me, to me,* II, 1
la mécanique *mechanics,* II, 10
méchant(e) *mean,* I, 7; II, 1
les médicaments (m.) *medicine,* I, 12
meilleur(e) *better,* II, 7; **C'est meilleur que(de)...** *It's better than...,* II, 7; **Meilleurs vœux!** *Best wishes!* II, 3; **C'est en... que je suis le/la meilleur(e).** *I'm best in...,* II, 5
mélanger *to mix,* II, 3
le membre *member,* II, 5
même *same,* II, 2; le/la même *the same,* II, 9; quand même *anyway,* II, 1
le ménage *housework,* I, 1; **faire le ménage** *to do housework,* I, 1; II, 10
mentionné(e) *mentioned,* II, 2
le menu *menu,* II, 3
la méprise *mistake, error,* II, 1
la mer *sea,* II, 4; **au bord de la mer** *to/at the coast,* I, 11
Merci. *Thank you.* I, 3; II, 2; **Merci, ça va.** *No thank you, I've had enough.* II, 3; **Merci, c'est gentil!** *Thanks, that's nice of you!* II, 3; **Non, merci.** *No, thank you.* I, 8
mercredi *Wednesday,* I, 2; **le mercredi** *on Wednesdays,* I, 2
la mère *mother,* I, 7
la merveille *wonder,* II, 8
merveilleux (-euse) *marvelous, wonderful,* II, 1
mes *my,* I, 7
le message *message,* II, 6
la messagerie électronique *emailer,* II, 11
le métro *subway,* I, 12; **au métro...** *at the... metro stop,* I, 6; **en métro** *by subway,* I, 12
le metteur en scène *director,* II, 11
mettre *to put, to put on, to wear,* I, 10; **Je ne sais pas quoi mettre pour...** *I don't know what to wear for...,* I, 10; **Mets...** *Wear...,* I, 10; **Qu'est-ce que je mets?** *What shall I wear?* I, 10; **se mettre en condition** se mettre en forme *to get into shape,* II, 7
meublé(e) *furnished,* II, 2
les meubles (m.) *furniture,* II, 2
meurs: Je meurs de soif! *I'm dying of thirst!* II, 12; **Si, je meurs de faim/soif!** *Yes, I'm dying of hunger/thirst!* II, 2
mexicain(e) *Mexican* (adj.), II, 1
midi *noon,* I, 6; **Il est midi.** *It's noon.* I, 6; **Il est midi et demi.** *It's half past noon.* I, 6
mieux *better,* I, 9; **Ça va aller mieux!** *It's going to get better!* I, 9; *It'll get better.* II, 5; **J'aime mieux...** *I prefer...,* I, 1; II, 1; **Tu aimes mieux... ou... ?** *Do you prefer... or...?* I, 10
mignon(ne) *cute,* I, 7; II, 1
mijoter *to simmer,* II, 3
milieu: au milieu de *in the middle of*
le millefeuille *layered pastry,* II, 3
les milliers (m. pl.) *thousands,* II, 4
mince *slender,* I, 7
le minimum *minimum,* II, 4
minuscule *minuscule, tiny,* II, 12
minuit *midnight,* I, 6; **Il est minuit.** *It's midnight.* I, 6; **Il est minuit et demi.** *It's half past midnight.* I, 6
la minute *minute,* I, 9; **Tu as une minute?** *Do you have a minute?* I, 9; II, 10
le mobilier *furniture,* II, 2
moche *tacky,* I, 10; **Je le/la/les trouve moche(s).** *I think it's (they're) really tacky.* I, 10
la mode *style, fashion,* I, 10; **à la mode** *in style,* I, 10
moi *me,* I, 2; **Moi aussi.** *Me too.* I, 2; **Moi, non.** *I don't.* I, 2; **Moi non plus.** *Neither do I.* I, 2; **Moi, si.** *I do.* I, 2; **Pas moi.** *Not me.* I, 2
moins *minus; less,* II, 8; *lower,* I, 0; **La vie était moins...** *Life was less...,* II, 8; **moins cinq** *five to,* I, 6; **moins grand(e) que** *smaller than...,* II, 4; **moins le quart** *quarter to,* I, 6; au moins *at least,* II, 3; **Plus ou moins.** *More or less.* II, 6
le mois *month,* I, 4
la moitié *half,* II, 3; la moitié de *half of,* II, 3
le moment *moment,* I, 5; *point,* II, 9; **A ce moment-là,...** *At that point,...,* II, 9; **Un moment, s'il vous plaît.** *One moment, please.* I, 5
mon *my,* I, 7
le monde *world;* beaucoup de monde, *a lot of people,* II, 9
monsieur (M.) *sir; Mr.* I, 1; **Monsieur!** *Waiter!* I, 5
la montagne *mountain,* I, 11; **à la montagne** *to/at the mountains,* I, 11; **faire du vélo de montagne** *to go mountain-bike riding,* II, 12; **les**

montagnes russes *roller coaster,* II, 6
monter *to go up,* II, 6; **monter dans une tour** *to go up in a tower,* II, 6
la montre *watch,* I, 3
Montréal *Montreal,* II, 1
montrer *to show,* I, 9
le morceau *piece,* I, 8; **un morceau de** *a piece of,* I, 8
mortel(le) *deadly dull,* II, 6
la mosquée *mosque,* II, 8
le mot *word;* un petit mot *a short note,* II, 2
motivé (e) *motivated,* II, 4
Mouais. *Yeah.* II, 6
la mouffette *skunk,* II, 12
le moulin *mill, windmill,* II, 12
mourir *to die,* II, 6
le moustique *mosquito,* II, 4
le mouton *mutton,* II, 3
le moyen *means, way to do something,* II, 8
le Moyen Age *Middle Ages,* II, 6
moyen(ne) *average, medium,* II, 1; **de taille moyenne** *of medium height,* II, 1
le mur *wall,* II, 5
la musculation *weightlifting;* **faire de la musculation** *to lift weights,* II, 7
le musée *museum,* I, 6; II, 2
le musicien (la musicienne) *musician,* II, 11
la musique *music,* I, 2; **la musique classique** *classical music,* II, 11; **écouter de la musique** *to listen to music,* I, 1; **Qu'est-ce que tu aimes comme musique?** *What music do you like?* II, 1
mutiler *to deface, to mutilate,* II, 12; **mutiler les arbres** *to deface the trees,* II, 12
mystérieux (mystérieuse) *mysterious,* II, 11

N

nager *to swim,* I, 1
naître *to be born,* II, 6
la narine *nostril,* II, 8
la natation *swimming,* I, 4; **faire de la natation** *to swim,* I, 4
la nature *nature,* II, 12
nautique *nautical;* **faire du ski nautique** *to water-ski,* I, 4
le navet *turnip;* **C'est un navet.** *It's a dud.* II, 11
ne: ne... jamais *never,* I, 4; **ne... ni grand(e) ni petit(e)** *neither tall nor short,* I, 7; **ne... pas encore** *not yet,* I, 9; **ne... pas** *not,* I, 1; **Pourquoi tu ne... pas... ?** *Why don't you...?* II, 7; **Tu n'as qu'à...** *All you have to do is...,* II, 7
néanmoins *nevertheless,* II, 11
nécessaire *necessary,* II, 5
négative (négatif) *negative,* II, 5
la neige *snow,* II, 8
neige: Il neige. *It's snowing.* I, 4
nettoyer *to clean,* II, 10
le nez *nose,* II, 7; **J'ai le nez qui coule.** *I've got a runny nose.* II, 7
nocif (-ive) *harmful,* II, 12
le Noël *Christmas,* II, 3; **Joyeux Noël!** *Merry Christmas!* II, 3
noir(e) *black,* I, 3; II, 1
la noix de coco *coconut,* I, 8
le nom *(last) name,* II, 1
nommer *to name,* II, 8
non *no,* I, 1; **Moi, non.** *I don't.* I, 2; **Moi non plus.** *Neither do I.* I, 2; **Non, c'est...** *No, it's...,* I, 4; **Non, merci.** *No, thank you.* I, 8; **Non, pas trop.** *No, not too much.* I, 2
le nord *north,* II, 4; **dans le nord** *in the north,* II, 4; **C'est au nord de...** *It's to the north of...,* II, 12
norvégien(ne) *Norwegian,* II, 12
nos *our,* I, 7
la nostalgie *nostalgia,* II, 8
la note *grade,* II, 5; **avoir une mauvaise note** *to get a bad grade,* II, 5; *note (music),* II, 12
noter *to write down,* II, 10
notre *our,* I, 7
nourrir *to feed,* II, 12; **nourrir les animaux** *to feed the animals,* II, 12; **bien se nourrir** *to eat well,* II, 7
nouveau (nouvel/nouvelle) *new,* II, 2
la nouvelle: Tu connais la nouvelle? *Did you hear the latest?* II, 9
novembre *November,* I, 4; **en novembre** *in November,* I, 4
nul(le) *useless,* I, 2; *lame,* II, 6; *worthless,* II, 8; *no (non-existent),* II, 12
nullement *not at all,* II, 9
le numéro *number,* II, 4

O

l' objet (m.) *object,* II, 1
obliger *to force, to oblige,* II, 11
observer *to observe, to watch,* II, 11
l' occasion (f.) *chance,* II, 1
occupé(e): C'est occupé. *It's busy.* I, 9; **Désolé(e), je suis occupé(e).** *Sorry, I'm busy.* I, 6; **Je suis très occupé(e).** *I'm very busy.* II, 10
s' occuper de *to take care of someone or something,* II, 10
octobre *October,* I, 4; **en octobre** *in October,* I, 4
l' œil (m.) (pl. les yeux) *eye,* II, 1; **Mon œil!** *Yeah, right!* II, 6
l' œillet (m.) *carnation,* II, 3
l' œuf (m.) *egg,* I, 8; II, 3
l' œuvre (f.) *work, piece of art,* II, 11
l' office de tourisme (m.) *tourist information office,* II, 2
offre: Offre-lui (-leur)... *Give him/her (them)...,* II, 3
offrir (à quelqu'un) *to give (to someone),* II, 10; **Qu'est-ce que je pourrais offrir à... ?** *What could I give to...?* II, 3; **Tu pourrais lui (leur) offrir...** *You could give him/her (them)...,* II, 3
oh: Oh là là! *Oh no!* II, 5; **Oh, pas mauvais.** *Oh, not bad.* I, 9
l' oignon (m.) *onion,* I, 8
l' oiseau (m.) *bird,* II, 5
ombragé(e) *shaded,* II, 3
l' ombre (f.) *shade,* II, 1
l' omelette (f.) *omelette,* I, 5
on: On... ? *How about...?* I, 4; **On fait du ski?** *How about skiing?* I, 5; **On joue au base-ball?** *How about playing baseball?* I, 5; **On peut...** *We can...,* I, 6; **On pourrait...** *We could...,* II, 1; **On va au café?** *Shall we go to the café?* I, 5
l' oncle (m.) *uncle,* I, 7
l' ongle (m.) *fingernail,* II, 12
l' opinion (f.) *opinion,* II, 8
optimiste *optimistic,* II, 10
orange (inv.) *orange (color),* I, 3
l' orange (f.) *orange,* I, 8
l' ordinateur (m.) *computer,* I, 3
l' ordre (m.) *order,* II, 3
l' oreille (f.) *ear,* II, 7; **J'ai mal à l'oreille.** *My ear hurts.* II, 7
l' oreiller (m.) *pillow,* II, 2
organiser *to organize,* II, 8
original(e) *original, unique,* II, 3; **C'est original.** *That's unique.* II, 3
l' orignal (m.) *moose,* II, 12
l' os (m.) *bone,* II, 7
oser *to dare (to do something),* II, 10
les ossements (m. pl.) *bones,* II, 12
ou *or,* I, 1; ou bien *or (else),* II, 7
où *where,* I, 6; **Où (ça)?** *Where?* I, 6; **Où est-ce que tu vas aller... ?** *Where are you going to go...?* I, 11; **Où est... s'il vous plaît?** *Where is..., please?* II, 2; **Où se trouve... ?**

Where is...? II, 4; **Tu es allé(e) où?** *Where did you go?* I, 9
oublier *to forget,* I, 9; **Je n'ai rien oublié.** *I didn't forget anything.* I, 11; **N'oublie pas...** *Don't forget...,* I, 8; II, 1; **Oublie-le/-la/-les!** *Forget him/her/them!* I, 9; II, 10; **Tu n'as pas oublié... ?** *You didn't forget...?* I, 11
l' ouest (m.) *west,* II, 4; **dans l'ouest** *in the west,* II, 4; **C'est à l'ouest de...** *It's to the west of...,* II, 12
ouf *whew,* II, 7
oui *yes,* I, 1; **Oui, c'est...** *Yes, it's...,* I, 4; **Oui, s'il te/vous plaît.** *Yes, please.* I, 8
l' ours (m.) *bear,* II, 12
ouvert(e) *open,* II, 1
ouvrez: A quelle heure est-ce que vous ouvrez? *When do you open?* II, 6; **Ouvrez vos livres à la page...** *Open your books to page...,* I, 0
ouvrir *to open,* II, 6

P

la page *page,* I, 0
la page perso *personal web page,* II, 11
le pagne *a piece of Ivorian cloth,* II, 8
le paillasson *doormat,* II, 11
le pain *bread,* I, 8; II, 3; **le pain au chocolat** *croissant with a chocolate filling,* II, 3
la paire *pair,* II, 2
le palmier *palm tree,* II, 4
le panier *basket,* II, 8
la panne *breakdown (car);* **tomber en panne** *to break down,* II, 9
la panoplie *range,* II, 11
le pantalon *pair of pants,* I, 10
la papaye *papaya,* I, 8
la papeterie *stationery store,* I, 12
le papier *paper,* I, 0
le paquet *package, box,* I, 8; **un paquet de** *a package/box of,* I, 8
le paragraphe *paragraph,* II, 1
le parapluie *umbrella,* I, 11
le parc *park,* I, 6; II, 2; **visiter un parc d'attractions** *to visit an amusement park,* II, 6
parce que *because,* I, 5; **Je ne peux pas parce que...** *I can't because...,* I, 5
Pardon. *Pardon me,* I, 3; **demander pardon à (quelqu'un)** *to ask (someone's) forgiveness,* II, 10; **Pardon, madame. ... s'il vous plaît?** *Excuse me, ma'am... please?* I, 12; **Pardon, mademoiselle. Où est... s'il vous plaît?** *Excuse me, miss. Where is...please?* I, 12; **Pardon, monsieur. Je cherche..., s'il vous plaît.** *Excuse me, sir. I'm looking for..., please.* I, 12
pardonner à (quelqu'un) *to forgive (someone),* II, 10
le parent *parent, relative,* I, 7
la parenthèse *parenthesis,* II, 1
parfait(e) *perfect,* I, 10; **C'est parfait.** *It's perfect.* I, 10
parfois *sometimes, occasionally,* II, 2
parie: Je parie que... *I bet that...,* II, 9
parisien(ne) *Parisian,* II, 1
parlé (pp. of parler) *talked, spoke,* I, 9; **Nous avons parlé.** *We talked.* I, 9
parler *to talk, to speak,* I, 1; **(Est-ce que) je peux parler à... ?** *Could I speak to...?* I, 9; **Ça parle de...** *It's about...,* II, 11; **De quoi ça parle?** *What's it about?* II, 11; **Je peux te parler?** *Can I talk to you?* I, 9; II, 10; **Parle-lui/-leur.** *Talk to him/her/them.* II, 10; **parler au téléphone** *to talk on the phone,* I, 1
parmi *among,* II, 12
parquer *to pen up,* II, 11
la part *part,* II, 2; **C'est gentil de votre (ta) part.** *That's nice of you.* II, 2
partager *to share,* II, 7
le partenaire (la partenaire) *partner,* II, 1
le participe passé *past participle,* II, 7
partir *to leave,* I, 11; II, 6; **A quelle heure est-ce que le train (le car) pour... part?** *What time does the train (the bus) for...leave?* II, 6; à partir de *from;* **Tu ne peux pas partir sans...** *You can't leave without...,* II, 11
partout: J'ai mal partout! *I hurt all over!* II, 7
pas: Il/Elle ne va pas du tout avec... *It doesn't go at all with...,* I, 10; **Pas bon.** *Not good.* I, 5; **Pas ce soir.** *Not tonight.* I, 7; **Pas du tout.** *Not at all.* II, 10; **Pas grand-chose.** *Not much.* I, 6; **Pas mal.** *Not bad.* I, 1; **pas mauvais** *pretty good,* I, 5; *not bad,* I, 9; **Pas moi.** *Not me.* I, 2; **Pas question!** *No way!* II, 1; *Out of the question!* I, 7; **pas super** *not so hot,* I, 2; **Pas terrible.** *Not so great.* I, 1
passé (pp. of passer): **Ça s'est bien passé?** *Did it go well?* I, 11; **Ça s'est très bien passé!** *It went really well!* II, 5; **Comment ça s'est passé?** *How did it go?* II, 5; **expliquer ce qui s'est passé (à quelqu'un)** *to explain what happened (to someone),* II, 10; **J'ai passé une journée épouvantable!** *I had a terrible day!* II, 5; **Qu'est-ce qui s'est passé?** *What happened?* I, 9; **Tu as passé un bon week-end?** *Did you have a good weekend?* I, 9; **Tu as passé un bon... ?** *Did you have a good...?* I, 11
passer *to take,* I, 9; *to go by, to pass,* I, 12; **Ça passe à...** *It's playing at...,* II, 11; **Ça passe où?** *Where is that playing?* II, 11; **passer l'aspirateur** *to vacuum,* I, 7; **passer un examen** *to take a test,* I, 9; **Tu pourrais passer à... ?** *Could you go by...?* I, 12; **Vous passez devant...** *You'll pass...,* I, 12
se passer: Qu'est-ce qui se passe? *What's going on?* II, 5
le passeport *passport,* I, 11; II, 1
le passe-temps *hobby,* II, 4
passionnant(e) *fascinating,* I, 2; **C'est une histoire passionnante.** *It's an exciting story.* II, 11
la patate *potato,* II, 12
la pâte à modeler *modeling clay,* II, 11
le pâté *pâté,* II, 3
les pâtes (f. pl.) *pasta,* II, 7
le patin *skating;* **faire du patin à glace** *to ice skate,* I, 4
la pâtisserie *pastry,* I, 12; *pastry shop,* I, 12; II, 3
pauvre *poor;* **Pauvre vieux/vieille!** *You poor thing!* II, 5
le pays *country,* II, 6
le paysan *farmer,* II, 11
la peau *skin,* II, 7
la pêche *fishing;* **aller à la pêche** *to go fishing,* II, 4; **la canne à pêche** *fishing pole,* II, 12
la pêche *peach,* I, 8
les pêcheurs (m.) *fishermen;* **le village de pêcheurs** *fishing village,* II, 4
pédestre: faire une randonnée pédestre *to go for a hike,* II, 12
le peintre *painter,* II, 2
la peinture *painting,* II, 2
pendant *during, for,* II, 4; pendant ce temps *meanwhile,* II, 1
la pendule *clock,* II, 9
pénible *a pain in the neck,* I, 7

penser: J'ai pensé à tout. *I've thought of everything.* I, 11; **Pense à prendre...** *Remember to take...*, II, 1
la pension *board and lodging,* II, 12
perché(e) *set high up in the mountains,* II, 9
perdre *to lose,* II, 5; **se perdre** *to get lost,* II, 9
le père *father,* I, 7
perfide *deceitful,* II, 11
la permission *permission,* II, 10; **demander la permission à tes parents** *to ask your parents' permission,* II, 10
le personnage principal *main character,* II, 9
la personne *person,* II, 1
personnel(le) *personal* II, 8
pessimiste *pessimistic,* II, 10
le petit déjeuner *breakfast,* I, 8
petit(e) *short (height),* I, 7; II, 1; *small,* I, 10; II, 1; petit à petit *little by little,* II, 3; **Quand il/elle était petit(e),...** *When he/she was little,...*, II, 8; **Quand j'étais petit(e),...** *When I was little, ...*, II, 8
les petits pois (m.) *peas,* I, 8
un peu *a little,* II, 2; **Si, un peu.** *Yes, a little.* II, 2
la peur: J'ai peur (de la, du, des)... *I'm scared (of)...*, II, 12
peut: On peut... *We can...*, I, 6
peut-être *maybe,* II, 3; **Tu as peut-être raison.** *Maybe you're right.* II, 9
peux: Désolé(e), mais je ne peux pas. *Sorry, but I can't.* I, 4; **Tu peux... ?** *Can you...?* I, 8
la pharmacie *drugstore,* I, 12
le philtre *potion,* II, 8
la photo *picture, photo,* I, 4; **faire de la photo** *to do photography,* I, 4; **faire des photos** *to take pictures,* I, 4
photographique *photographic,* II, 4
la phrase *sentence,* II, 1
la physique *physics,* I, 2
la pièce *room (of a house),* II, 2; *play (theatrical),* I, 6; **voir une pièce** *to see a play,* I, 6; une pièce (d'or ou d'argent) *coin,* II, 4
le pied *foot,* I, 12; **à pied** *on foot,* I, 12; **J'ai mal au pied.** *My foot hurts.* II, 7
le piège *trap,* II, 5
piétonnier(-ière) *pedestrian* (adj.), II, 2
le pique-nique *picnic,* I, 6; **faire un pique-nique** *to have a picnic,* I, 6; II, 6
pique-niquer *to have a picnic,* II, 6
pire: de pire en pire *worse and worse,* II, 5
la piscine *swimming pool,* I, 6; II, 2
la piste *track,* II, 7
le pitre: faire le pitre *to clown around,* II, 5
la pizza *pizza,* I, 1
le placard *closet,* II, 2
la plage *beach,* I, 1; II, 4
se plaindre *to complain,* II, 12
plaire: Il/Elle me plaît, mais c'est cher. *I like it, but it's expensive.* I, 10; **Il/Elle te/vous plaît?** *Do you like it?* I, 10; **Ce qui me plaît, c'est (de)...** *What I like is...*, II, 4; **Ce qui ne me plaît pas, c'est (de)...** *What I don't care for is...*, II, 4; **s'il vous/te plaît** *please,* I, 3; **Un..., s'il vous plaît.** *A(n)..., please.* II, 6
se plaire: Tu vas te plaire ici. *You're going to like it here.* II, 8
plaisanter *to joke;* **Tu plaisantes!** *You're joking!* II, 6
le plaisir *pleasure,* I, 8; **Avec plaisir.** *With pleasure.* II, 10; **Oui, avec plaisir.** *Yes, with pleasure.* I, 8
le plan *map,* II, 2
le plan d'entraînement individuel *personal training program,* II, 7
la planche: faire de la planche à voile *to go windsurfing,* I, 11; II, 4
planter *to plant,* II, 12
le plat *dish,* II, 3
le plat principal *main course,* II, 3
la plate-bande *flower bed,* II, 12
plein(e) *full,* II, 8; **C'est plein de rebondissements.** *It's full of plot twists.* II, 11; plein tarif *full admission price,* II, 2
pleurer *to cry,* II, 6
pleut: Il pleut. *It's raining.* I, 4
plat(e) *flat;* eau plate *non-carbonated water,* II, 7
la plongée: faire de la plongée *to go scuba diving,* I, 11; **faire de la plongée avec un tuba** *to snorkel,* II, 4; **faire de la plongée sous-marine** *to scuba dive,* II, 4
plu (pp. of plaire): **Ça m'a beaucoup plu.** *I really liked it.* II, 6; **Ça t'a plu?** *Did you like it?* II, 6
la pluie *rain,* II, 9
plus *more,* II, 1; **Je n'ai plus faim/soif.** *I'm not hungry/ thirsty anymore.* II, 3; **Je n'en peux plus!** *I just can't do any more!* II, 7; **Je n'en veux plus.** *I don't want anymore.* I, 8; **La vie était plus...** *Life was more...*, II, 8; **Moi non plus.** *Neither do I.* I, 2; **Non, merci. Je n'ai plus faim.** *No thanks. I'm not hungry anymore.* I, 8; **plus grand(e) que** *bigger than...*, II, 4; Plus on est de fous, plus on rit. *The more the merrier.* II, 3; **Plus ou moins.** *More or less.* II, 6
plusieurs *several,* II, 1
plutôt *rather,* II, 9
la poêle *frying pan,* II, 3
la poésie *poetry,* II, 11
le poids *weight,* II, 7
poilu(e) *hairy, furry,* II, 9
le point de départ *starting point,* II, 2
le point de vue *point of view,* II, 9
la poire *pear,* I, 8
les pois chiches *chickpeas,* II, 3
le poisson *fish,* I, 7; II, 3
la poissonnerie *fish shop,* II, 3
poli(e) *polite,* II, 3; *polished,* II, 12
poliment *politely,* II, 3
polisson *naughty,* II, 8
la pomme *apple,* I, 8
la pomme de terre *potato,* I, 8
les pompes (f.) *push-ups,* II, 7; **faire des pompes** *to do push-ups,* II, 7
pondent un œuf (pondre) *to lay (an egg),* II, 11
le pont *bridge*
la pop *popular, mainstream music,* II, 11
populaire *popular,* II, 5
le porc *pork,* I, 8
la porte *door,* I, 0
le portefeuille *wallet,* I, 3; II, 3
porter *to wear,* I, 10
le portrait *portrait, description,* II, 1
poser (un problème, une question) *to present or ask,* II, 1
positif (positive) *positive,* II, 5
possible *possible,* II, 9; **C'est possible.** *That's possible.* II, 9; **Ce n'est pas possible.** *That's not possible.* II, 9; **Pas possible!** *No way!* II, 6
la poste *post office,* I, 12; II, 2
le poster *poster,* I, 3; II, 2
la poterie *pottery,* II, 8
la poubelle *trash can,* I, 7; **sortir la poubelle** *to take out the trash,* I, 7
le pouding *pudding,* II, 3
la poule *live chicken (hen),* I, 8
le poulet *chicken meat,* I, 8; II, 3
pour *for,* I, 3; **Qu'est-ce qu'il te faut pour... ?** *What do you need for...? (informal),* I, 3; **Qu'est-ce que tu fais pour t'amuser?** *What do you do to have fun?* I, 4
pourquoi *why,* I, 6; **Pourquoi est-ce que tu ne mets pas... ?** *Why don't you wear...?* I, 10;

Pourquoi pas? *Why not?* I, 6; **Pourquoi tu ne... pas?** *Why don't you...?* I, 9; II, 7
pourrais: Je pourrais avoir... ? *May I have some...?* II, 3; (Est-ce que) tu pourrais me rendre un petit service? *Could you do me a favor?* I, 12; **Qu'est-ce que je pourrais offrir à... ?** *What could I give to...?* II, 3; **Tu pourrais... ?** *Could you...?* II, 10; **Tu pourrais lui (leur) offrir...** *You could give him/her (them)...,* II, 3; **Tu pourrais passer à... ?** *Could you go by...?* I, 12
pourrait: On pourrait... *We could...,* II, 1
pourriez: Vous pourriez (Tu pourrais) me passer... ? *Would you pass me...?* II, 3
pouvoir *to be able to, can,* I, 8; **Est-ce que tu peux... ?** *Can you...?* I, 12; **(Est-ce que) je peux... ?** *May I...?* I, 7; **Je n'en peux plus!** *I just can't do any more!* II, 7; **Je ne peux pas.** *I can't.* II, 1; **Je ne peux pas maintenant.** *I can't right now.* I, 8; **Je peux te parler?** *Can I talk to you?* II, 10; **Non, je ne peux pas.** *No, I can't.* I, 12; **On peut...** *We can...,* II, 4; *You can...,* II, 12; **Qu'est-ce qu'on peut faire?** *What can we do?* II, 4; **Si tu veux, on peut...** *If you like, we can...,* II, 1; **Qu'est-ce que je peux faire?** *What can I do?* I, 9; **Tu peux m'aider?** *Can you help me?* II, 10
le pouvoir *power,* II, 8
pratiquer *to practice,* II, 1
préférer *to prefer,* I, 1; **Ce que je préfère, c'est...** *What I prefer is...,* II, 4; **Je préfère...** *I prefer...,* I, 1; II, 1; **Non, je préfère...** *No, I'd rather...,* II, 1
préféré(e) *favorite,* II, 1; **Quel(le) est ton/ta... préféré(e)?** *What is your favorite...?* II, 1; **Qui est ton/ta... préféré(e)?** *Who is your favorite...?* II, 1
le premier étage *second floor,* II, 2
prendre *to take or to have (food or drink),* I, 5; **avoir (prendre) rendez-vous (avec quelqu'un)** *to have (make) a date/an appointment (with someone),* II, 9; **Je le/la/les prends.** *I'll take it/them.* I, 10; **Je vais (en) prendre...** *I'll take...,* II, 3; **Je vais prendre..., s'il vous plaît.** *I'll have..., please.* I, 5; *I'm going to have..., please.* I, 5; **On peut prendre...** *We can take...,* II, 12; **Pense à prendre...** *Remember to take...,* II, 1; **Prends/Prenez...** *Get...,* I, 8; *Have...,* I, 5; *Take...,* II, 1; **Prenez une feuille de papier.** *Take out a sheet of paper.* I, 0; **Tu prends... ?** *Are you taking...?* I, 11; *Will you have...?* I, 8; **Vous avez décidé de prendre... ?** *Have you decided to take...?* I, 10; **Vous le/la/les prenez?** *Are you going to take it/them?* I, 10; **Vous prenez?** *What are you having?* I, 5; *Will you have...?* I, 8; **Prenez la rue..., puis traversez la rue...** *Take... Street, then cross... Street.* I, 12
le prénom *first name,* II, 1
les préparatifs (m. pl.): **faire les préparatifs** *to get ready,* II, 10
préparer *to make, to prepare,* II, 10; **préparer les amuse-gueule** *to make party snacks,* II, 10
près *close,* I, 12; **près de** *close to,* I, 12; *near,* II, 2
présenter: Je te/vous présente... *I'd like you to meet...,* I, 7
presque *almost,* II, 7; **Tu y es (On y est) presque!** *You're (we're) almost there!* II, 7
pressé(e) *in a hurry,* II, 7
prêt(e) *ready,* II, 10
le prétendant *suitor,* II, 8
prévu(e): Je n'ai rien de prévu. *I don't have any plans.* I, 11
principal(e) *main,* II, 7
le printemps *spring,* I, 4; **au printemps** *in the spring,* I, 4
pris (pp. of **prendre**) *took,* I, 9
privé(e): être privé(e) de sortie *to be "grounded,"* II, 9
le prix *price,* II, 3
le problème *problem,* I, 9; **J'ai un petit problème.** *I've got a problem.* I, 9; **J'ai un problème.** *I have a problem.* II, 10; **Pas de problème.** *No problem.* II, 10
prochain(e) *next,* I, 12; **Vous continuez jusqu'au prochain feu rouge.** *You keep going until the next light.* I, 12
proche *nearby,* II, 1; *close,* II, 5
le produit *product,* II, 3
les produits laitiers (m. pl.) *dairy products,* I, 8
le prof(esseur) *teacher,* I, 2
profiter *to take advantage of,* II, 1
le pronom *pronoun,* II, 3; le pronom objet *object pronoun,* II, 10
le projet *projects, plans,* II, 1
la promenade *walk,* I, 6; **faire une promenade** *to go for a walk,* I, 6
se promener *to go for a walk,* II, 4; **promener le chien** *to walk the dog,* I, 7
promouvoir *to promote,* II, 2
prôner *to advocate,* II, 11
propos: A propos,... *By the way,...,* II, 9
proposé(e) *suggested,* II, 1
propre *(one's) own,* II, 1; **propre** *clean,* II, 8
la propriété *property,* II, 11
provençal(e) *from Provence,* II, 10
le proviseur *school principal,* II, 5
pu (pp. of pouvoir): **J'aurais pu...** *I could have...,* II, 10; **Tu aurais pu...** *You could have...,* II, 10
la publicité *advertisement,* II, 3
puis *then,* II, 1; **Puis, tournez à gauche dans/sur...** *Then, turn left on...,* II, 2; **Prenez la rue..., puis traversez la rue...** *Take... Street, then cross... Street.* I, 12
le pull(-over) *pullover sweater,* I, 3; II, 1
pur(e) *pure,* II, 12

Q

qu'est-ce que *what* (obj.), I, 4; **Qu'est-ce que tu as?** *What's wrong?* II, 7; **Qu'est-ce qu'il te/vous faut pour... ?** *What do you need for...?* I, 3; **Qu'est-ce qu'il y a... ?** *What is there...?* II, 4; **Qu'est-ce qu'il y a?** *What's wrong?* II, 10; **Qu'est-ce qu'on fait?** *What should we do?* II, 1; **Qu'est-ce qu'on peut faire?** *What can we do?* II, 4; **Qu'est-ce que je peux faire?** *What can I do?* I, 9; II, 10; **Qu'est-ce que tu aimes faire?** *What do you like to do?* II, 1; **Qu'est-ce que tu as fait... ?** *What did you do...?* I, 9; **Qu'est-ce que tu fais... ?** *What do you do...?* I, 4; **Qu'est-ce que tu fais comme sport?** *What sports do you play?* I, 4; **Qu'est-ce que tu fais pour t'amuser?** *What do you do to have fun?* I, 4; **Qu'est-ce que tu fais quand... ?** *What do you do when...?* I, 4; **Qu'est-ce que tu vas faire... ?** *What are you going to do...?* I, 6; **Qu'est-ce que vous avez comme... ?** *What kind of...do you have?* I, 5; **Qu'est-ce que vous avez comme boissons?** *What do you have to drink?* I, 5
qu'est-ce qui *what* (subj.), I, 9; **Qu'est-ce qui s'est passé?**

What happened? I, 9; **Qu'est-ce qui se passe?** *What's going on?* II, 5; **Qu'est-ce qui t'arrive?** *What's wrong?* II, 5
le **quai** *platform,* II, 6; **De quel quai... ?** *From which platform...?* II, 6; **Du quai...** *From platform...,* II, 6
quand *when,* I, 6; **Quand (ça)?** *When?* I, 6; quand même *anyway,* II, 1
quant: quant à *with respect to,* II, 1
la quantité *quantity,* II, 3
le **quart** *quarter,* I, 6; **et quart** *quarter past,* I, 6; **moins le quart** *quarter to,* I, 6
le quartier *neighborhood,* II, 8
quel(le) *which,* I, 1; *what,* I, 2; **De quelle couleur est... ?** *What color is...?* I,3; **Quel(le) est ton/ta... préféré?** *What is your favorite...?* II, 1; **Quel temps fait-il?** *What's the weather like?* I, 4; **Quel week-end formidable!** *What a great weekend!* II, 5; **Quel week-end!** *What a good/bad weekend!* II, 5; **Quelle journée!** *What a good/bad day!* II, 5; **Quelle journée formidable!** *What a great day!* II, 5; **Tu as... à quelle heure?** *At what time do you have...?* I, 2; **Tu as quel âge?** *How old are you?* I, 1; **Tu as quels cours... ?** *What classes do you have...?* I, 2
quelques *some, a few,* II, 3
quelqu'un *someone,* II, 3
quelque chose *something,* I, 10; **J'ai quelque chose à faire.** *I have something (else) to do.* II, 10; **Je cherche quelque chose pour...** *I'm looking for something for...,* I, 10; **Quelque chose ne va pas?** *Is something wrong?* II, 7
quelque part *somewhere,* II, 9
quelquefois *sometimes,* I, 4
la **question: Pas question!** *No way!* II, 1; *Out of the question!* I, 7
le questionnaire *questionnaire,* II, 8
qui *who,* II, 1; *whom,* I, 6; **Avec qui?** *With whom?* I, 6; **Qui est ton/ta... préféré(e)?** *Who is your favorite ...?* II, 1
la **quiche** *quiche: a type of custard pie, usually with savory filling, such as ham, bacon, cheese, or spinach,* I, 5
quitter *to leave,* II, 6; quitter les lieux *to leave the place,* II, 2, 11
quittez: Ne quittez pas. *Hold on.* I, 9
quoi *what,* I, 2; **... quoi.** *...you know.* II, 9; **De quoi est-ce que tu as besoin?** *What do you need?* I, 5; **Je ne sais pas quoi faire.** *I don't know what to do.* II, 10; **Je ne sais pas quoi mettre pour...** *I don't know what to wear for...,* I, 10; **N'importe quoi!** *That's ridiculous!* II, 6; **Tu as quoi... ?** *What do you have...?* I, 2; **Tu vas faire quoi?** *What are you going to do?* I, 6
quotidien(ne) *daily,* II, 4

R

le raccourci *short cut,* II, 12
raconte: Raconte! *Tell me!* II, 5; **Qu'est-ce que ça raconte?** *What's the story?* II, 11
raconter *to tell (a story),* II, 1
la radio *radio,* I, 3
le raisin *grapes,* I, 8
la raison *reason,* II, 5; **Fais-toi une raison.** *Make the best of it.* II, 8; **Tu as raison...** *You're right...,* II, 3
rajouter *to add,* II, 7
le ramasseur de balles *ballboy,* II, 8
ramener *to bring back,* II, 8
la randonnée *hike,* I, 11; **faire de la randonnée** *to go hiking,* I, 11; **faire une randonnée en raquettes** *to go snow-shoeing,* II, 12; **faire une randonnée en skis** *to go cross- country skiing,* II, 12; **faire une randonnée pédestre** *to go for a hike,* II, 12
le rang *row,* II, 3
ranger *to arrange, to straighten;* **ranger ta chambre** *to pick up your room,* I, 7
le rap *rap music,* II, 11
râpé(e) *grated,* II, 3
raplapla *wiped out,* II, 7; **Je suis tout raplapla.** *I'm wiped out.* II, 7
rappeler *to call back,* I, 9; **Vous pouvez rappeler plus tard?** *Can you call back later?* I, 9
se rappeler *to remember,* II, 6
rapporter *to bring back,* I, 8; **Rapporte-moi...** *Bring me back...,* I, 8; **Tu me rapportes... ?** *Will you bring me...?* I, 8
la raquette: faire une randonnée en raquettes *to go snow-shoeing,* II, 12
rarement *rarely,* I, 4
rassurer *to reassure,* II, 8
rater *to fail,* I, 9; *to miss,* I, 9; **rater le bus** *to miss the bus,* I, 9; II, 5; **rater un examen** *to fail a test,* I, 9; **rater une interro** *to fail a quiz,* I, 9; **rater une marche** *to miss a step,* II, 5
le raton laveur *raccoon,* II, 12
rayer *to blot out, to erase,* II, 10
réagir *to react,* II, 9
le réalisateur *director,* II, 11
le rebondissement: C'est plein de rebondissements. *It's full of plot twists.* II, 11
recevoir *to receive,* II, 5; **recevoir le bulletin trimestriel** *to receive one's report card,* II, 5
la recherche *search,* II, 11
recommande: Je te le recommande. *I recommend it.* II, 11
recommence: Ne recommence pas. *Don't do it again.* II, 5
se **réconcilier: se réconcilier avec (quelqu'un)** *to make up (with someone),* II, 10
réconforter *to comfort,* II, 8
reconnaître *to recognize,* II, 3
la récréation *break,* I, 2
récrire *to rewrite,* II, 3
récupérer *to recover,* II, 1
la rédaction *essay,* II, 5
redonner *to give back,* II, 11
réduit(e) *reduced,* II, 2
réel (réelle) *real,* II, 6
refuser *to refuse,* II, 10
se régaler *to treat oneself,* II, 3
le regard *look, glance,* II, 10
regarder *to watch, to look at,* I, 1; **Non, merci, je regarde.** *No, thanks, I'm just looking.* I, 10; **Regarde, c'est...** *Look, here's (there's)(it's)...,* I, 12; **Regarde, voilà...** *Look, here's (there's) (it's)...,* I, 12; **regarder la télé(vision)** *to watch TV,* I, 1; **regarder un match** *to watch a game (on TV),* I, 6; **Regardez la carte!** *Look at the map!* I, 0
le régent (la régente) *regent; someone who rules in place of the king or queen,* II, 6
le reggae *reggae music,* II, 11
le régime *diet,* II, 7; **suivre un régime trop strict** *to follow a diet that's too strict,* II, 7
la région *region,* II, 3
la règle *ruler,* I, 3; les règles *rules,* II, 7
regrette: Je regrette. *Sorry.* I, 3; **Je regrette...** *I miss...,* II, 8; **Je regrette, mais je n'ai pas le temps.** *I'm sorry, but I don't have time.* I, 8
le rein *kidney,* II, 7
la reine *queen,* II, 6
relaxant(e) *relaxing,* II, 8
la relaxation *relaxation,* II, 7

la religieuse *cream puff pastry,* II, 3
relire *to reread,* II, 8
remarquer *to notice,* II, 10
remplacer *to replace,* II, 3
remplir *to fill,* II, 5
remporter: remporter les déchets *to take your trash with you,* II, 12
le renard *fox,* II, 12
rencontrer *to meet,* I, 9; II, 9
le rendez-vous *appointment, date,* II, 9; **avoir (prendre) rendez-vous (avec quelqu'un)** *to have (make) a date/appointment (with someone),* II, 9; **Rendez-vous...** *We'll meet…,* I, 6
rendre *to return something,* I, 12; **rendre les interros** *to return tests,* II, 5
rendre visite à *to visit (someone),* II, 8
rentrer *to go back (home),* II, 6
renverser *to knock over, spill,* II, 5
répartir *to spread evenly,* II, 3
le repas *meal,* II, 7; **sauter un repas** *to skip a meal,* II, 7
répéter *to rehearse, to practice,* I, 9; **Répétez!** *Repeat!* I, 0
la répétition *repetition,* II, 3
répétitif/répétitive *repetitive,* II, 11
répondre *to answer,* I, 9; **Ça ne répond pas.** *There's no answer.* I, 9
la réponse *response, answer,* II, 1
le reportage *report,* II, 4
reprendre *to have a second helping,* II, 3
représenter *to represent,* II, 4
réprimander *to reprimand,* II, 5
reprochant *reproaching,* II, 10
le reproche *reproach,* II, 10
la résolution *resolution,* II, 1
respecter *to respect,* II, 12; **respecter la nature** *to respect nature,* II, 12
la responsabilité *responsibility,* II, 8; **avoir des responsabilités** *to have responsibilities,* II, 8
ressembler à *to resemble,* II, 1
la ressource *resource,* II, 8
ressusciter *to bring back to life,* II, 8
le restaurant *restaurant,* I, 6
rester *to stay,* II, 6
le resto *restaurant,* II, 1
le résumé *summary,* II, 11
le rétablissement: Bon rétablissement! *Get well soon!* II, 3
en retard *late,* II, 5
retirer: retirer de l'argent *to withdraw money,* I, 12
retourner *to return,* II, 6
rétro (inv.) *retro,* I, 10
se retrouver *to meet,* I, 6; **Bon, on se retrouve...** *We'll meet…,* I, 6
le rêve *dream,* II, 1
le réveil *alarm clock,* II, 5; **entendre le réveil** *to hear the alarm clock,* II, 5
revenir *to come back,* II, 6; faire revenir dans le beurre *to sauté in butter,* II, 3
revoir *to watch again, to see again,* II, 11
le rez-de-chaussée *first (ground) floor,* II, 2
le rhume *cold,* II, 7; **J'ai un rhume.** *I've got a cold.* II, 7
rien *anything,* I, 11; *nothing,* I, 6; **Ça ne fait rien.** *It doesn't matter.* II, 10; **Ça ne me dit rien.** *I don't feel like it.* I, 4; *That doesn't interest me.* II, 1; **Je n'ai rien oublié.** *I didn't forget anything.* I, 11; **Rien de spécial.** *Nothing special.* I, 6
rigoler *to laugh,* II, 10
le risque *risk,* II, 5
risquent de se retrouver (risquer) *risk ending up,* II, 11
riverain(e) *riverside* (adj.), II, 8
la rivière *river,* II, 12
le riz *rice,* I, 8
la robe *dress,* I, 10
le rock *rock music,* II, 11
le roi *king,* II, 6
le roller: faire du roller en ligne *to in-line skate,* I, 4
le roman *novel,* I, 3; **le roman classique** *classic (novel),* II, 11; **le roman d'amour** *romance novel,* II, 11; **le roman de science-fiction** *science-fiction novel,* II, 11; **le roman policier (le polar)** *detective or mystery novel,* II, 11
la rondelle *slice,* II, 3
rose *pink,* I, 3
le rossignol *nightingale,* II, 6
le rôti de bœuf *roast beef,* II, 3
la roue: la grande roue *ferris wheel,* II, 6
rouge *red,* I, 3
la route: Bonne route! *Have a good (car) trip!* II, 3
la routine *routine,* II, 4
roux (rousse) *red-headed,* I, 7; II, 1
la rue *street,* II, 11
russe *Russian* (adj.), II, 1; **les montagnes russes** *roller coaster,* II, 6

S

s'il vous/te plaît *please,* I, 3; **Oui, s'il te/vous plaît.** *Yes, please.* I, 8
sa *his, her,* I, 7
le sable *sand,* II, 4
le sac (à dos) *bag; backpack,* I, 3; **le sac à main** *purse,* II, 3; **le sac de couchage** *sleeping bag,* II, 12
le sachet *small bag,* II, 3
sais: Je n'en sais rien. *I have no idea.* I, 11; **Je ne sais pas quoi faire.** *I don't know what to do.* II, 10; **Je ne sais pas.** *I don't know.* I, 10; **Tu sais ce que... ?** *Do you know what…?* II, 9; **Tu sais qui... ?** *Do you know who…?* II, 9
la saison *season,* II, 4
la salade *salad, lettuce,* I, 8; II, 3
sale *dirty,* II, 8
saler *to salt,* II, 3
la salle à manger *dining room,* II, 2; **la salle de bains** *bathroom,* II, 2; la salle de jeux *game room,* II, 2; la salle de lavage *laundry room,* II, 2
le salon *living room,* II, 2
saluer *to greet,* II, 8
Salut! *Hi!* or *Goodbye!* I, 1
samedi *Saturday,* I, 2; **le samedi** *on Saturdays,* I, 2
la sandale *sandal,* I, 10
le sandwich *sandwich,* I, 5; **un sandwich au fromage** *cheese sandwich,* I, 5; **un sandwich au jambon** *ham sandwich,* I, 5; **un sandwich au saucisson** *salami sandwich,* I, 5
le sang *blood,* II, 7
la santé *health,* II, 7; **C'est bon pour la santé.** *It's healthy.* II, 7
la sauce *sauce,* II, 7
le saucisson *salami,* I, 5; II, 3
sauf *except,* II, 2
saupoudrer *to sprinkle (with),* II, 3
saute: Ne saute pas... *Don't skip…,* II, 7
sauter *to jump; to skip,* II, 7; **sauter un repas** *to skip a meal,* II, 7
sauver *to save,* II, 5
le savoir *knowledge,* II, 8
savoir *to know,* II, 8
le scénario *scenario,* II, 11
la scène *scene,* II, 2
les sciences naturelles (f. pl.) *natural science,* I, 2
la séance *film show,* II, 11
sec (sèche) *dry, dried,* II, 7

la seconde *second,* I, 9; **Une seconde, s'il vous plaît.** *One second, please.* I, 9
la section *section,* II, 2
le séjour *visit, stay,* II, 1
séjourner *to stay*
le sel *salt,* II, 7
selon *according to,* II, 10
la semaine *week,* I, 4; **une fois par semaine** *once a week,* I, 4
semblable *similar,* II, 2
semblant: faire semblant de *to pretend to (do something),* II, 10
sembler *to seem,* II, 11
sens: Je ne me sens pas bien. *I don't feel well.* II, 7
sensass (sensationnel) *fantastic,* I, 10; *sensational,* II, 6
la sensation *sensation,* II, 9
le sentier *path, trail,* II, 12; **suivre les sentiers balisés** *to follow the marked trails,* II, 12
se sentir *to feel,* II, 6
septembre *September,* I, 4; **en septembre** *in September,* I, 4
serré(e) *tight,* I, 10
serrer: serrer la main *to shake hands,* II, 8
le serveur *server (computer),* II, 11
le service *service,* I, 3; **A votre service.** *At your service; You're welcome,* I, 3
servir *to serve,* II, 3
ses *his, her,* I, 7
seul(e) *only (one),* II, 4
seulement *only,* II, 4
le short *(a pair of) shorts,* I, 3
si *yes (to contradict a negative question),* I, 2; *if,* II, 1; **Moi, si.** *I do.* I, 2; **Si on achetait...?** *How about buying...?* II, 8; **Si on allait...?** *How about going...?* II, 4; **Si on jouait...?** *How about playing...?* II, 8; **Si on visitait...?** *How about visiting...?* II, 8; **Si tu veux, on peut...** *If you like, we can...,* II, 1
le siècle *century,* II, 6
la sieste *nap,* II, 8; **faire la sieste** *to take a nap,* II, 8
la signature *signature,* II, 11
simple *simple,* II, 8
le singe *monkey,* II, 11
sinistre *awful,* II, 6
le sirop de fraise (à l'eau) *water with strawberry syrup,* I, 5
la situation *situation,* II, 5
situé(e) à *situated in,* II, 5
le ski *skiing,* I, 1; **faire du ski** *to ski,* I, 4; **faire du ski nautique** *to water-ski,* I, 4
les skis (m.): **faire une randonnée en skis** *to go cross-country skiing,* II, 12
la sœur *sister,* I, 7
la soif: avoir soif *to be thirsty,* I, 5; **Je n'ai plus soif.** *I'm not thirsty anymore.* II, 3; **Si, j'ai très soif!** *Yes, I'm very thirsty.* II, 2; **Vous n'avez pas (Tu n'as pas) soif?** *Aren't you thirsty?* II, 2
le soir *evening; in the evening,* I, 4; **Pas ce soir.** *Not tonight.* I, 7
la soirée *evening,* II, 10
la solution *solution,* II, 10
son *his, her,* I, 7
le sondage *poll,* II, 1
sont: Ce sont... *These/those are...,* I, 7; **Ils/Elles sont...** *They're...,* I, 7; II, 1; **Ils/Elles sont comment?** *What are they like?* I, 7
la sorcière *witch,* II, 8
sorti(e) (pp. of **sortir**) *went out,* I, 9; **Après, je suis sorti(e).** *Afterwards, I went out.* I, 9
la sortie *dismissal,* I, 2; **être privé(e) de sortie** *to be "grounded,"* II, 9
sortir *to go out,* II, 6; **sortir avec les copains** *to go out with friends,* I, 1; **sortir la poubelle** *to take out the trash,* I, 7
le souci *worry,* II, 8; **avoir des soucis** *to have worries,* II, 8
soudain *suddenly,* II, 5
souhaits: A tes souhaits! *Bless you!* II, 7
souligner *to underline,* II, 9
la soupe au pistou *vegetable soup with basil*
le souper *dinner,* II, 12
la source *source of water, spring,* II, 11
sous *under,* II, 4
sous-marin(e): faire de la plongée sous-marine *to scuba dive,* II, 4
soutenir *to support,* II, 10
se souvenir *to remember,* II, 9
souvent *often,* I, 4
spécial(e) *special,* I, 6; **Rien de spécial.** *Nothing special.* I, 6
la spécialité *specialty,* II, 8
le spectacle *show,* II, 6; **assister à un spectacle son et lumière** *to attend a sound and light show,* II, 6
le sport *gym class,* I, 2; *sports,* I, 1; **faire du sport** *to play sports,* I, 1; **Qu'est-ce que tu fais comme sport?** *What sports do you play?* I, 4
les sports d'hiver *winter sports,* II, 7
sportif (sportive) *athletic,* II, 1
le stade *stadium,* I, 6
le statut *status*
le steak-frites *steak and French fries,* I, 5
stressant(e) *stressful,* II, 8
strict(e) *strict,* II, 7
le style *style,* II, 3; **C'est tout à fait ton style.** *It looks great on you!* I, 10; **Ce n'est pas son style.** *That's not his/her style.* II, 3
le stylo *pen,* I, 3
le sucre *sugar,* I, 8
sucré(e) *sweet,* II, 7
le sud *south,* II, 4; **dans le sud** *in the south,* II, 4; **C'est au sud de...** *It's to the south of...,* II, 12
la sueur *sweat,* II, 7
suggérer *to suggest,* II, 4
la suggestion *suggestion,* II, 3
suis: Désolé(e), je suis occupé(e). *Sorry, I'm busy.* I, 6; **Après, je suis sorti(e).** *Afterwards, I went out.* I, 9; **Je suis bien chez...?** *Is this ...'s house?* I, 9
suite: C'est tout de suite à... *It's right there on the...,* I, 12; **J'y vais tout de suite.** *I'll go right away.* I, 8; **tout de suite** *right away,* I, 6
suivant(e) *following,* II, 1
suivre *to follow,* II, 7; **suivre les sentiers balisés** *to follow the marked trails,* II, 12; **suivre un régime trop strict** *to follow a diet that's too strict.* II, 7
le sujet *subject;* au sujet de *about,* II, 2
super *super* (adj.), I, 2; *really, ultra-* (adv.), II, 9; **Super!** *Great!* I, 1; **pas super** *not so hot,* I, 2
superbe *great,* II, 6
le supermarché *supermarket,* I, 8
sur *on,* II, 2; **sur la droite/gauche** *on the right/left,* II, 2; sur le vif *live, on the spot,* II, 9
sûr: Bien sûr. *Of course.* II, 10; **Bien sûr. C'est...** *Of course. They are (He/She is)...,* II, 11
sûrement *certainly,* II, 1; **Sûrement pas!** *Definitely not!* II, 6
surfer le web *to surf the net,* II, 11
surprenant(e) *surprising,* II, 2
la surprise *surprise,* II, 3
sursauter *to jump,* II, 9
surtout *especially,* I, 1
le surveillant *university student who supervises younger students at school,* II, 5
le suspense: Il y a du suspense. *It's suspenseful.* II, 11
le sweat(-shirt) *sweatshirt,* I, 3; II, 1
le symbole *symbol,* II, 7
sympa (abbrev. of **sympathique**) *nice,* I, 7; II, 1
sympathique *nice,* I, 7

ta *your,* I, 7
le tabac *tobacco,* II, 1
le tableau *blackboard,* I, 0
la taille *size,* I, 10; **de taille moyenne** *of medium height,* II, 1
le taille-crayon *pencil sharpener,* I, 3
le tam-tam (inv.) *an African drum,* II, 8
tamisé(e) *subdued,* II, 3
tant *so much,* II, 8
la tante *aunt,* I, 7
le tapis *rug,* II, 2
la tapisserie *tapestry,* II, 2
taquiner *to tease,* II, 8
tard *late,* II, 4
le tarif *admission price,* II, 2
la tarte *pie,* I, 8; **la tarte aux pommes** *apple tart,* II, 3
la tartine *bread, butter, and jam,* II, 3
le tas: J'ai des tas de choses à faire. *I have lots of things to do.* I, 5
la tasse *cup,* II, 3
le taxi *taxi,* I, 12; **en taxi** *by taxi,* I, 12
Tchao! *Bye!* I, 1
la techno *techno,* II, 3
le tee-shirt *T-shirt,* II, 1
la télé(vision) *television, TV,* I, 1; **regarder la télé(vision)** *to watch TV,* I, 1
le téléphone *telephone,* I, 1; **parler au téléphone** *to talk on the phone,* I, 1; **Téléphone-lui/-leur.** *Phone him/her/them.* II, 10
téléphoné (pp. of téléphoner) *called, phoned,* I, 9; **Vous pouvez lui dire que j'ai téléphoné?** *Can you tell him/her that I called?* I, 9
téléphoner à (quelqu'un) *to call (someone),* II, 10; **Téléphone-lui/-leur!** *Call him/her/them!* I, 9
tellement: C'était tellement différent? *Was it really so different?* II, 8; **Pas tellement.** *Not too much.* I, 4
le témoignage *display,* II, 2
le témoin *witness,* II, 9
la tempête *storm,* II, 12
temps *time,* I, 4; *weather,* I, 4; **de temps en temps** *from time to time,* I, 4; **Je regrette, mais je n'ai pas le temps.** *I'm sorry, but I don't have time.* I, 8; **Je suis désolé(e), mais je n'ai pas le temps.** *Sorry, but I don't have time.* I, 12; **Je n'ai pas le temps.** *I don't have time.* II, 10; **Quel temps fait-il?** *What's the weather like?* I, 4
Tenez. *Here you are* (formal, plural). II, 3
le tennis *tennis,* I, 4; **jouer au tennis** *to play tennis,* I, 4
la tentative *attempt,* II, 11
la tente *tent,* II, 12
tenter *to tempt,* II, 4
la tenue *outfit,* II, 1
le terrain de camping *campground,* II, 2
la terrasse *terrace,* II, 2
la terre *Earth,* II, 10
terrible: Pas terrible. *Not so great.* I, 1
tes *your,* I, 7
la tête *head,* II, 7; **J'ai mal à la tête.** *My head hurts.* II, 7; **faire la tête** *to sulk,* II, 9
thaïlandais(e) *Thai* (adj.), II, 1
le thé *tea,* II, 3
le théâtre *theater,* I, 6; II, 2; **faire du théâtre** *to do drama,* I, 4
le thème *theme,* II, 4
le ticket *ticket,* II, 6; **Trois tickets, s'il vous plaît.** *Three (entrance) tickets, please.* II, 6
Tiens. *Here you are (familiar).* II, 3
le timbre *stamp,* I, 12
timide *shy,* I, 7
le tissu *fabric, cloth,* II, 8
le titre *title,* II, 7
toi *you,* I, 1; **Et toi?** *And you?* I, 1
la toile d'araignée *spider web,* II, 12
les toilettes (f.) **(les W.-C.** (m. pl.)**)** *toilet, restroom,* II, 2
la tomate *tomato,* I, 8
tomber *to fall,* II, 5; **tomber amoureux (-euse) (de quelqu'un)** *to fall in love (with someone),* II, 9; **tomber en panne** *to break down (car),* II, 9
ton *your,* I, 7
tondre *to mow, to cut,* I, 7; **tondre le gazon** *to mow the lawn,* I, 7
le tonus *vigor,* II, 7
torride *very hot,* II, 11
tôt *early,* II, 4
toujours: toujours mal luné(e) *always in a bad mood,* II, 8
la tour *tower,* II, 6
le tour: faire un tour sur la grande roue *to take a ride on the ferris wheel,* II, 6; **faire un tour sur les montagnes russes** *to take a ride on the roller coaster,* II, 6
le touriste (la touriste) *tourist,* II, 6
touristique *with tourist appeal,* II, 2
tourner *to turn,* I, 12; **Puis, tournez à gauche dans/sur...** *Then, turn left on…,* II, 2; **Vous tournez...** *You turn…,* I, 12
le tournoi de joute *jousting tournament,* II, 6
tout(e) *all,* I, 2; **A tout à l'heure!** *See you later (the same day)!* I, 1; à toute épreuve *solid, unfailing,* II, 10; **Allez (continuez) tout droit.** *Go (keep going) straight ahead.* II, 2; **C'est tout à fait ton style.** *It looks great on you!* I, 10; **C'est tout de suite à...** *It's right there on the…,* I, 12; **Il/Elle ne va pas du tout avec...** *It doesn't go at all with…,* I, 10; **J'ai pensé à tout.** *I've thought of everything.* I, 11; **J'y vais tout de suite.** *I'll go right away.* I, 8; **Oui, tout de suite.** *Yes, right away.* I, 5; **Pas du tout.** *Not at all.* I, 4; II, 10; tout à coup *suddenly,* II, 9; **Tout a été de travers!** *Everything went wrong!* II, 5; **tout de suite** *right away,* I, 5; **Vous allez tout droit jusqu'à...** *You go straight ahead until you get to…,* I, 12
tout le monde *everybody,* II, 9
tragique *tragic,* II, 11
le train *train,* I, 12; **en train** *by train,* I, 12; **être en train de** *to be in the process of (doing something),* II, 9
traînant(e) *trailing,* II, 9
la tranche *slice,* I, 8; **une tranche de** *a slice of,* I, 8
tranquille *peaceful,* II, 8
le travail *work,* II, 8
travailler *to work,* I, 9; **Tu dois mieux travailler en classe.** *You have to work harder in class.* II, 5
les travaux pratiques (m. pl.) *lab,* I, 2
travers: Tout a été de travers! *Everything went wrong!* II, 5
Traversez... *Cross…,* II, 2
le traversin *bolster pillow,* II, 2
très *very,* I, 1; **Ça s'est très bien passé!** *It went really well!* II, 5; **Très bien.** *Very well.* I, 1; **Très heureux (-euse).** *Pleased to meet you.* I, 7
trompes: A mon avis, tu te trompes. *In my opinion, you're mistaken.* II, 9
trop *too (much),* I, 10; **C'est trop cher.** *It's too expensive.* I, 10; II, 3; **Non, pas trop.** *No, not too much.* I, 2
tropical(e) *tropical,* II, 4
la trousse *pencil case,* I, 3; **la trousse de premiers soins**

first-aid kit, II, 12
trouver *to find,* I, 9; **Comment tu trouves...?** *How do you like...?* I, 10; *What do you think of...?* I, 2; **Je le/la/les trouve...** *I think it's/they're...,* I, 10; **Où se trouve...?** *Where is...?* II, 4; **Tu trouves?** *Do you think so?* II, 2
le truc *thing,* I, 5; **Ce n'est pas mon truc.** *It's not my thing.* II, 7; **J'ai des tas de choses (trucs) à faire.** *I have lots of things to do.* I, 12; **J'ai des trucs à faire.** *I have some things to do.* I, 5
tu *you,* I, 0
le tuba: faire de la plongée avec un tuba *to snorkel,* II, 4
tutoyer *to use **tu** when speaking to someone,* II, 2
le type *type,* II, 9

un, *a, an,* I, 3
une, *a, an,* I, 3
utile *useful,* II, 9
utiliser *to use,* II, 1

va: Ça me va? *Does it suit me?* I, 10; **(Comment) ça va?** *How's it going?* I, 1; **Ça ne te/vous va pas du tout.** *That doesn't look good on you.* I, 10; **Ça te/vous va très bien.** *That suits you really well.* I, 10; **Ça va.** *Fine.* I, 1; **Ça va aller mieux.** *It'll get better.* II, 5; **Ça va très bien avec...** *It goes very well with...,* I, 10; **Comment est-ce qu'on y va?** *How can we get there?* I, 12; **Il/Elle me va?** *Does it suit me?* I, 10; **Il/Elle ne va pas du tout avec..** It doesn't go at all with..., I, 10; **Il/Elle te/vous va très bien.** *It suits you really well.* I, 10; **Il/Elle va très bien avec...** *It goes very well with...,* I, 10; **Quelque chose ne va pas?** *Is something wrong?* II, 7
vachement *really (informal),* II, 9
les vacances (f. pl.) *vacation,* I, 1; **Bonnes vacances!** *Have a good vacation!* I, 11; **Comment se sont passées tes vacances?** *How was your vacation?* II, 5; **en colonie de vacances** *to/at a summer camp,* I, 11; **en vacances** *on vacation,* I, 4
vais: D'abord, je vais... *First, I'm going to...,* II, 1; **Je vais...** *I'm going...,* I, 6; *I'm going to...,* I, 11; **Je vais (en) prendre...** *I'll take...,* II, 3; **J'y vais tout de suite.** *I'll go right away.* I, 8
le vaisseau spatial *spacecraft,* II, 11
la vaisselle *dishes,* I, 7; **faire la vaisselle** *to do the dishes,* I, 7
la valise *suitcase,* I, 11
varier *to vary,* II, 4
vas: Qu'est-ce que tu vas faire...? *What are you going to do...?* II, 1
le vase *vase,* II, 3
végétarien(ne) *vegetarian,* II, 3
le vélo *bike,* I, 1; **à vélo** *by bike,* I, 12; **faire du vélo** *to bike,* I, 4; **faire du vélo de montagne** *to go mountain-bike riding,* II, 12
vendre *to sell,* I, 10
vendredi *Friday,* I, 2; **le vendredi** *on Fridays,* I, 2
venir *to come,* II, 6
le vent *wind,* II, 12
venu (past participle of venir) *to come,* II, 7
le ventre *stomach,* II, 7; **J'ai mal au ventre** *My stomach hurts.* II, 7
le ver *worm,* II, 11
le verbe *verb,* II, 1
véritable *real,* I, 11; **C'était un véritable cauchemar!** *It was a real nightmare!* I, 11
le verre *glass,* II, 2
vers *around,* I, 6; **Vers...** *About (a certain time)...,* II, 4
verser *to pour,* II, 3
la version *version,* II, 9
vert(e) *green,* I, 3; II, 1
la veste *suit jacket, blazer,* I, 10
le vêtement *clothing item,* I, 10
veux: Je veux bien. *I'd really like to.* I, 6; **Tu veux... avec moi?** *Do you want...with me?* I, 6
la viande *meat,* I, 8
la vidéo *video,* I, 4; **faire de la vidéo** *to make videos,* I, 4; **jouer à des jeux vidéo** *to play video games,* I, 4
la vidéocassette *videotape,* I, 3
la vie *life,* II, 8; **La vie était plus... moins...** *Life was more..., less...,* II, 8
viens: Tu viens? *Will you come?* I, 6
vietnamien(ne) *Vietnamese* (adj.), II, 1
vieux (vieil, vieille) *old,* II, 2; **Pauvre vieux/vieille!** *You poor thing!* II, 5
vif: sur le vif *live, on the spot,* II, 9
la vigne *vineyard*
le village de pêcheurs *fishing village,* II, 4
la ville *city,* II, 2
violent(e) *violent,* II, 11; **trop violent** *too violent,* II, 11
violet(te) *purple,* I, 3
le violon: Accordons nos violons. *Let's come to an understanding.* II, 4
virtuel *virtual,* II, 11
visitait: Si on visitait...? *How about visiting...?* II, 8
la visite: une visite guidée *a guided tour,* II, 6
visiter *to visit (a place),* I, 9; II, 6
vite: Dis vite! *Let's hear it!* II, 9
le vitrail *stained glass,* II, 2
la vitrine: faire les vitrines *to window-shop,* I, 6
vivant(e) *lively,* II, 4
vivre *to live,* II, 4
le vocabulaire *vocabulary,* II, 2
les vœux (m. pl.) *wishes,* II, 3; **Meilleurs vœux!** *Best wishes!* II, 3; une carte de vœux *greeting card,* II, 3
Voici... *This is...,* I, 7
Voilà. *Here it is.* II, 3; *Here,* I, 3; **Voilà...** *There's...,* I, 7
la voile *sailing,* I, 11; **faire de la planche à voile** *to windsurf,* I, 11; **faire de la voile** *to go sailing,* I, 11
voir *to see,* I, 6; **Qu'est-ce qu'il y a à voir...?** *What is there to see...?* II, 12; **Tu vas voir que...** *You'll see that...,* II, 8; **voir un film** *to see a movie,* I, 6; **aller voir un match** *to go see a game,* I, 6; **voir une pièce** *to see a play,* I, 6
vois: ... tu vois. *...you see.* II, 9
le voisin neighbor, II, 11
voit: Ça se voit. *That's obvious.* II, 9
la voiture *car,* I, 7; **en voiture** *by car,* I, 12; **laver la voiture** *to wash the car,* I, 7
le vol *flight,* II, 12
la volaille *poultry,* II, 3
le volcan *volcano,* II, 4
volé(e), stolen, II, 11
le volet *shutter,* II, 12
le voleur *thief,* II, 8
le volley(-ball) *volleyball,* I, 4; **jouer au volley(-ball)** *to play volleyball,* I, 4
vos *your,* I, 7
votre *your,* I, 7
voudrais: Je voudrais... *I'd like...,* I, 3; II, 6; **Je voudrais acheter...** *I'd like to buy...,* I, 3;

Je voudrais bien... *I'd really like to...*, I, 11
vouloir *to want,* I, 6; **J'en veux bien.** *I'd like some.* I, 8; Je n'en veux plus. *I don't want anymore.* I, 8; **Je ne t'en veux pas.** *No hard feelings.* II, 10; **Je veux bien.** *Gladly.* I, 12; *I'd like to.* II, 1; *I'd really like to.* I, 6; **Non, je ne veux pas.** *No, I don't want to.* II, 8; **Oui, je veux bien.** *Yes, I would.* II, 3; **Oui, si tu veux.** *Yes, if you want to.* I, 7; **Si tu veux, on peut...** *If you like, we can...*, II, 1; **Tu ne m'en veux pas?** *No hard feelings?* II, 10; **Tu veux... ?** *Do you want...?* I, 6; II, 3; **Vous voulez... ?** *Do you want...?* I, 8; II, 3
vous *you,* I, 0
le voyage *trip, voyage,* I, 11; **Bon voyage!** *Have a good trip! (by plane, ship),* I, 11; II, 3; **Vous avez (Tu as) fait bon voyage?** *Did you have a good trip?* II, 2
voyager *to travel,* I, 1
vrai(e) *true,* I, 2; **C'est pas vrai!** *You're kidding!* II, 6; **C'est vrai?** *Really?* II, 2
vraiment *really,* I, 11; **C'est vraiment bon!** *It's really good!* II, 3; **Il/Elle est vraiment bien, ton/ta...** *Your...is really great.* II, 2 ; **Non, pas vraiment.** *No, not really.* I, 11
vu (pp. of **voir**) *seen,* I, 9
vue *with a view of,* II, 2

les W.-C. (m. pl.) *restroom,* II, 2
le week-end *weekend; on weekends,* I, 4; **ce week-end** *this weekend,* I, 6; **Comment s'est passé ton week-end?** *How was your weekend?* II, 5
le western *western (movie),* II, 11

y *there,* I, 12; **Allons-y!** *Let's go!* I, 4; **Comment est-ce qu'on y va?** *How can we get there?* I, 12; **Il y avait...** *There was/were...*, II, 8; **Je n'y comprends rien.** *I don't understand anything about it.* II, 5; **J'y vais tout de suite.** *I'll go right away.* I, 8; **On peut y aller...** *We can go there...*, I, 12; **Tu vas t'y faire.** *You'll get used to it.* II, 8
le yaourt *yogurt,* I, 8
les yeux (m. pl.) *eyes,* II, 1

zéro *a waste of time,* I, 2
le zoo *zoo,* I, 6; II, 6
le zouk: danser le zouk *to dance the zouk,* II, 4
Zut! *Darn!* I, 3

English-French Vocabulary

In this vocabulary, the English definitions of all active French words in the book have been listed, followed by their French equivalent. The number after each entry refers to the chapter in which the entry is introduced. The roman numeral accompanying each chapter number indicates the level in which the entry is presented. It is important to use a French word in its correct context. The use of a word can be checked easily by referring to the chapter where it appears.

French words and phrases are presented in the same way as in the French-English vocabulary.

a *un, une,* I, 3
able: to be able to *pouvoir,* I, 8
about *vers,* II, 4; **about (a certain time)...** *vers...,* II, 4; **It's about...** *Ça parle de...,* II, 11; **What's it about?** *De quoi ça parle?* II, 11
acceptable: That's not acceptable. *C'est inadmissible.* II, 5
accident *l'accident* (m.), II, 9; **to have an accident** *avoir un accident,* II, 9
across from *en face de,* I, 12; II, 2
action *l'action* (f.), II, 11; **action movie** *un film d'action,* II, 11
adore *adorer,* I, 1; **I adore...,** *J'adore...,* I, 1
adventure *l'aventure* (f.), II, 11; **adventure movie** *un film d'aventures,* II, 11
advise *conseiller,* I, 9; **What do you advise me to do?** *Qu'est-ce que tu me conseilles?* I, 9
aerobics *l'aérobic* (f.), I, 4; **to do aerobics** *faire de l'aérobic,* I, 4; II, 7
African (adj.) *africain(e),* II, 11
after *après,* I, 9; **And after that,...** *Et après ça,...* I, 9; II, 4
afternoon *l'après-midi* (m.), I, 2; **afternoon off** *l'après-midi libre,* I, 2; **in the afternoon** *l'après-midi,* I, 2
afterwards *après,* I, 9; **Afterwards, I went out.** *Après, je suis sorti(e).* I, 9; **And afterwards?** *Et après?* I, 9
again: Don't do it again! *Ne recommence pas!* II, 5
agree *être d'accord,* I, 7; **I don't agree.** *Je ne suis pas d'accord.* I, 7
Agreed. *Entendu.* I, 6
ahead: Go (Keep going) straight ahead. *Allez (Continuez) tout droit.* II, 2
alarm clock *le réveil,* II, 5; **to hear the alarm clock** *entendre le réveil,* II, 5
algebra *l'algèbre* (f.), I, 2
all: All you have to do is... *Tu n'as qu'à...,* II, 7; **Not at all.** *Pas du tout.* I, 4; II, 10; **I hurt all over!** *J'ai mal partout!* II, 7; **all right** *pas mal,* II, 6
allergy *l'allergie* (f.), II, 7; **I have allergies.** *J'ai des allergies.* II, 7
almost *presque,* II, 7; **You're (We're) almost there!** *Tu y es (On y est) presque!* II, 7
already *déjà,* I, 9
also *aussi,* I, 1
am: I am... *Je suis...,* II, 1; **I am... years old.** *J'ai... ans.* I, 1
amazing *incroyable,* II, 5; **It was amazing!** *C'était incroyable!* II, 5
American (adj.) *américain(e),* II, 11
amusement park *le parc d'attractions,* II, 6
an *un, une,* I, 3
and *et,* I, 1
angry *fâché(e),* II, 9
ankle *la cheville,* II, 7; **to sprain one's ankle** *se fouler la cheville,* II, 7
annoyed *énervé(e),* II, 9
annoying *embêtant(e),* I, 7; II, 1
answer *répondre,* I, 9; **There's no answer.** *Ça ne répond pas.* I, 9
any (of it) *en,* I, 8
any more: I don't want any more. *Je n'en veux plus.* I, 8; **I just can't do any more!** *Je n'en peux plus!* II, 7
anymore *ne... plus,* II, 3; **I'm not hungry/thirsty anymore.** *Je n'ai plus faim/soif.* II, 3
anything *ne... rien,* I, 11; **I didn't forget anything.** *Je n'ai rien oublié.* I, 11
Anyway,... *Bref, ...,* II, 9
apologize *s'excuser,* II, 10; **Apologize.** *Excuse-toi.* II, 10
apple *la pomme,* I, 8; **apple juice** *le jus de pomme,* I, 5; **apple tart** *la tarte aux pommes,* II, 3
April *avril,* I, 4
are: These/Those are... *Ce sont...,* I, 7; **They're...** *Ils/Elles sont...,* I, 7
argument: to have an argument (with someone) *se disputer (avec quelqu'un),* II, 9
arm *le bras,* II, 7
armoire *l'armoire* (f.), II, 2
around *vers,* II, 4
arrive *arriver,* II, 5
art class *les arts plastiques* (m. pl.), I, 2
ask *demander,* II, 10; **to ask (someone's) forgiveness** *demander pardon à (quelqu'un),* II, 10; **to ask your parents' permission** *demander la permission à tes parents,* II, 10
at *à,* I, 6; II, 2; **at... fifteen** *à... heure(s) quinze,* I, 2; **at... forty-five** *à... heure(s) quarante-cinq,* I, 2; **at... thirty** *à... heure(s) trente,* I, 2; **at... 's house** *chez...,* I, 6; **At that point,...** *A ce moment-là,...,* II, 9; **at the record store** *chez le disquaire,* I, 12; **At what time?** *A quelle heure?* I, 6

athletic *sportif (sportive),* II, 1
attend *assister à,* II, 6; **to attend a sound and light show** *assister à un spectacle son et lumière,* II, 6
August *août,* I, 4
aunt *la tante,* I, 7
autobiography *l'autobiographie* (f.), II, 11
avocado *l'avocat* (m.), I, 8
Avoid… *Evitez de…,* II, 7; *Evite de…,* II, 12; **Avoid smoking.** *Evitez de fumer.* II, 7
away: Yes, right away. *Oui, tout de suite.* I, 5
awful *sinistre,* II, 6

B

back *le dos,* II, 7
back: come back *revenir,* II, 6; **go back (home)** *rentrer,* II, 6
backpack *le sac à dos,* I, 3
bad *mauvais(e),* I, 9; **It was unbelievably bad!** *C'était incroyable!* II, 5; **not bad** *pas mal,* I, 2; **Oh, not bad.** *Oh, pas mauvais.* I, 9; **Very bad.** *Très mauvais.* I, 9; **What a bad day!** *Quelle journée!* II, 5; **What a bad weekend!** *Quel week-end!* II, 5
bag le sac, I, 3; **sleeping bag** *sac de couchage,* 12
baggy *large,* I, 10
bakery *la boulangerie,* I, 12; II, 3
balcony *le balcon,* II, 2
banana *la banane,* I, 8; **banana tree** *le bananier,* II, 4
bank *la banque,* I, 12
baseball *le base-ball,* I, 4; **to play baseball** *jouer au base-ball,* I, 4
basketball *le basket(-ball),* I, 4; **to play basketball** *jouer au basket (-ball),* I, 4
basket *le panier,* II, 8
bathing suit *le maillot de bain,* I, 10
bathroom *la salle de bains,* II, 2
be *être,* I, 7
be able to, can *pouvoir,* I, 8; **Can you…?** *Est-ce que tu peux…?* I, 12; **I can't.** *Je ne peux pas.* II, 7
to be in the process of (doing something) *être en train de (+ infinitive),* II, 9
beach *la plage,* I, 1
beans *les haricots* (m.), I, 8; **green beans** *les haricots verts,* I, 8
bear *l'ours* (m.), II, 12
beautiful *beau (belle) (bel),* II, 2; *magnifique,* II, 6
because *parce que,* I, 5
become *devenir,* II, 6
bed *le lit,* II, 2; **to go to bed** *se coucher,* II, 4
bedroom *la chambre,* II, 2
beef *le bœuf,* I, 8
begin *commencer,* I, 9
behind *derrière,* I, 12
belt *la ceinture,* I, 10
best: Best wishes! *Meilleurs vœux!* II, 3; **Make the best of it.** *Fais-toi une raison.* II, 8
bet *parier,* II, 9; **I bet that…** *Je parie que…,* II, 9
better *mieux,* II, 5; *meilleur(e),* II, 7; **It'll get better.** *Ça va aller mieux.* II, 5; **It's better than…** *C'est meilleur que…,* II, 7; **It's going to get better!** *Ça va aller mieux!* I, 9; **You have work harder in class.** *Il faut mieux travailler en classe.* II, 5
between *entre,* I, 12
big *grand(e),* I, 10; II, 1
bigger *plus grand(e),* II, 4; **bigger than…** *plus grand(e) que…,* II, 4
bike *le vélo; faire du vélo,* I, 4; **by bike** *à vélo,* I, 12
biking *le vélo,* I, 1
binder: loose-leaf binder *le classeur,* I, 3
biography *la biographie,* II, 11
biology *la biologie,* I, 2
birthday *l'anniversaire* (m.), II, 3; **Happy birthday!** *Joyeux (Bon) anniversaire!* II, 3
black *noir(e),* I, 3; **black hair** *les cheveux noirs,* II, 1
blackboard *le tableau,* I, 0; **Go to the blackboard!** *Allez au tableau!* I, 0
blazer *la veste,* I, 10
bless: Bless you! *A tes souhaits!* II, 7
blond *blond(e),* I, 7; **blond hair** *les cheveux blonds,* II, 1
blue *bleu(e),* I, 3
blues (music) *le blues,* II, 11
boat *le bateau,* I, 12; **by boat** *en bateau,* I, 12
book *le livre,* I, 0
bookstore *la librairie,* I, 12
boots *les bottes* (f.), I, 10
bored *ennuyé(e),* II, 6; **I was bored.** *Je me suis ennuyé(e).* II, 6; **You're never bored.** *On ne s'ennuie pas.* II, 11
boring *barbant(e),* I, 2; *ennuyeux (-euse),* II, 6; **It was boring.** *C'était ennuyeux.* I, 5; *C'était barbant!* I, 12
born: to be born *naître,* II, 6
borrow *emprunter,* I, 12
bother *ennuyer,* II, 8; **What bothers me is…** *Ce qui m'ennuie, c'est (de)…,* II, 4
bottle *la bouteille,* I, 8; **a bottle of** *une bouteille de,* I, 8
box: a box/package of *un paquet de,* I, 8
boy *le garçon,* I, 0
bracelet *le bracelet,* I, 3
bread *le pain,* I, 8; II, 3; **long, thin loaf of bread** *la baguette,* I, 12
break *la récréation,* I, 2; **to break down (car)** *tomber en panne,* II, 9; **to break up (with someone)** *casser (avec quelqu'un),* II, 9; **to break one's (leg)** *se casser (la jambe),* II, 7
breakfast *le petit déjeuner,* I, 8
bring *apporter,* I, 9; **Bring me back…** *Rapporte-moi…,* I, 8; **Please bring me…** *Apportez-moi…, s'il vous plaît.* I, 5; **to bring (with you)** *emporter,* II, 12; **Will you bring me…?** *Tu me rapportes…?* I, 8
brother *le frère,* I, 7
brown *marron* (inv.), I, 3; **brown hair** *les cheveux châtain,* II, 1; **dark brown hair** *les cheveux bruns,* II, 1
brunette *brun(e),* I, 7
brush: to brush one's teeth *se brosser les dents,* II, 4
bus *le bus,* I, 12; *le car* (intercity), II, 6; **by bus** *en bus,* I, 12; **to miss the bus** *rater le bus,* II, 5
busy *occupé(e),* I, 6; **I'm very busy.** *Je suis très occupé(e).* II, 10; **It's busy.** *C'est occupé.* I, 9; **Sorry, I'm busy.** *Désolé(e), je suis occupé(e).* I, 6
but *mais,* I, 1
butcher shop *la boucherie,* II, 3
butter *le beurre,* I, 8; II, 3
buy *acheter,* I, 9; **Buy (me)…** *Achète(-moi)…,* I, 8; **How about buying…?** *Si on achetait…?* II, 8
by: By the way,… *A propos,…,* II, 9
Bye! *Tchao!* I, 1

C

cafeteria *la cantine,* I, 9; **at the school cafeteria** *à la cantine,* I, 9
cake *le gâteau,* I, 8
calculator *la calculatrice,* I, 3

call (someone) *téléphoner à (quelqu'un),* II, 10; **Call him/her/them!** *Téléphone-lui/-leur!* I, 9; **Can you call back later?** *Vous pouvez rappeler plus tard?* I, 9; **Then I called...** *Ensuite, j'ai téléphoné à...,* I, 9; **Who's calling?** *Qui est à l'appareil?* I, 9
calm *calme,* II, 8
camera *l'appareil-photo* (m.), I, 11; II, 1
camp: to/at a summer camp *en colonie de vacances,* I, 11
campground *le terrain de camping,* II, 2
camping *le camping,* I, 11; **to go camping** *faire du camping,* I, 11
can (to be able to) *pouvoir,* I, 8; **Can you do the shopping?** *Tu peux aller faire les courses?* I, 8; **Can I try on...?** *Je peux essayer...?* I, 10; **Can you...?** *Est-ce que tu peux...?* I, 12; *Tu peux...,* I, 8; **Can I talk to you?** *Je peux te parler?* II, 10; **If you like, we can...** *Si tu veux, on peut...,* II, 1; **We can...** *On peut...,* II, 4; **What can I do?** *Qu'est-ce que je peux faire?* II, 10; **What can we do?** *Qu'est-ce qu'on peut faire?* II, 4
can *la boîte,* I, 8; **a can of** *une boîte de,* I, 8
Canadian (adj.) *canadien(ne),* II, 11
canary *le canari,* I, 7
candy *le bonbon,* II, 3
candy shop *la confiserie,* II, 3
canoe: to go canoeing *faire du canotage* (Canada), II, 12
can't: I can't. *Je ne peux pas.* II, 1; **I can't right now.** *Je ne peux pas maintenant.* I, 8; **No, I can't.** *Non, je ne peux pas.* I, 12
cap *la casquette,* I, 10
capital *la capitale,* II, 4
car *la voiture,* I, 7; **by car** *en voiture,* I, 12; **to wash the car** *laver la voiture,* I, 7
cards *les cartes* (f.), I, 4; **to play cards** *jouer aux cartes,* I, 4
care: What I don't care for is... *Ce qui ne me plaît pas, c'est (de)...,* II, 4
carrot *la carotte,* I, 8
cassette tape *la cassette,* I, 3
cat *le chat,* I, 7
cathedral *la cathédrale,* II, 2
CD (compact disc) *le disque compact/le CD,* I, 3
cereal *les céréales* (f. pl.), II, 3
Certainly. *Bien sûr.* I, 9
chair *la chaise,* I, 0
charming *charmant(e),* II, 4
check *l'addition* (f.), I, 5; **The check, please.** *L'addition, s'il vous plaît.* I, 5; **traveler's check** *le chèque de voyage,* II, 1
cheese *le fromage,* I, 5, II, 3; **toasted ham and cheese sandwich** *le croque-monsieur,* I, 5
chemistry *la chimie,* I, 2
chest: chest of drawers *la commode,* II, 2
chic *chic,* I, 10
chicken *le poulet,* II, 3; **chicken meat** *le poulet,* I, 8; **live chickens** *les poules* (f.), I, 8
child *l'enfant* (m./f.), I, 7
chocolate *le chocolat,* I, 1; **box of chocolates** *la boîte de chocolats,* II, 3
choir *la chorale,* I, 2
choose *choisir,* I, 10; **to choose the date** *fixer la date,* II, 10; **to choose the music** *choisir la musique,* II, 10
Christmas *Noël,* II, 3; **Merry Christmas!** *Joyeux Noël!* II, 3
church *l'église* (f.), II, 2
class *le cours,* I, 2; **What classes do you have...?** *Tu as quels cours...?* I, 2
classic (novel) *un (roman) classique,* II, 11; **classic movie** *un film classique,* II, 11
classical *classique,* II, 11; **classical music** *la musique classique,* II, 11
clean *propre,* II, 8; **to clean house** *faire le ménage,* I, 7
clear the table *débarrasser la table,* I, 7
clock: to hear the alarm clock *entendre le réveil,* II, 5
close *fermer,* I, 0; **Close the door!** *Fermez la porte!* I, 0; **At what time do you close?** *A quelle heure est-ce que vous fermez?* II, 6
close to *près de,* I, 12
cloth *le tissu,* II, 8
clothing *les vêtements* (m.), I, 10
coast *le bord de la mer,* I, 11; **to/at the coast** *au bord de la mer,* I, 11
coat *le manteau,* I, 10
coconut *la noix de coco,* I, 8; **coconut tree** *le cocotier,* II, 4
coffee *le café,* I, 5
cola *le coca,* I, 5
cold *le rhume,* II, 7; **I've got a cold.** *J'ai un rhume.* II, 7; **It's cold.** *Il fait froid.*
color *la couleur,* I, 3; **What color is...?** *De quelle couleur est...?* I, 3
colorful *coloré(e),* II, 4
come *venir,* II, 6; **Come on!** *Allez!* II, 7; **Will you come?** *Tu viens?* I, 6
come back *revenir,* II, 6
comedy (film) *le film comique,* II, 11
comic book *la bande dessinée (la B. D.),* II, 11
compact disc/CD *le disque compact/le CD,* I, 3
compass *la boussole,* II, 12
computer *l'ordinateur* (m.), I, 3
computer science *l'informatique* (f.), I, 2
concert *le concert,* I, 1
Congratulations! *Félicitations!* II, 3
continue *continuer,* I, 12
cool *cool,* I, 2; **very cool** *chouette,* II, 2; **Your... is cool.** *Il/Elle est cool, ton/ta...,* II, 2; **It's cool (outside).** *Il fait frais.* I, 4
corn *le maïs,* I, 8
corner *le coin,* I, 12; **on the corner of** *au coin de,* I, 12
cotton *le coton,* I, 10; **in cotton** *en coton,* I, 10
could: Could you...? *Tu pourrais...?* II, 10; **Could you do me a favor?** *(Est-ce que) tu pourrais me rendre un petit service?* I, 12; **Could you go by...?** *Tu pourrais passer à...?* I, 12; **I could have...** *J'aurais pu...,* II, 10; **We could...** *On pourrait...,* II, 1; **You could give him/her (them)...** *Tu pourrais lui (leur) offrir...,* II, 3; **You could have...** *Tu aurais pu...,* II, 10
country (music) *le country,* II, 11
countryside *la campagne,* I, 11; **to/at the countryside** *à la campagne,* I, 11
course *le cours,* I, 2; **first course of a meal** *l'entrée* (f.), II, 3; **main course of a meal** *le plat principal,* II, 3; **Of course.** *Bien sûr.* I, 3; **Of course not.** *Bien sûr que non.* II, 10
cousin *le cousin (la cousine),* I, 7
cream puff pastry *la religieuse,* II, 3
croissant *le croissant,* II, 3; **croissant with a chocolate filling** *le pain au chocolat,* II, 3
cross *traverser,* II, 2; **Cross...** *Traversez...,* II, 2
cross-country: to go cross-country skiing *faire une randonnée en skis,* II, 12
cut: to cut one's finger *se couper le doigt,* II, 7
cute *mignon(ne),* I, 7; II, 1; *gentillet(te),* II, 11; **cute (but that's all)** *gentillet, sans plus,* II, 11

D

dairy *la crémerie,* II, 3; **dairy products** *les produits laitiers* (m. pl.), I, 8
dance *danser* (v.), I, 1; *la danse* (n.), I, 2; **to dance the zouk** *danser le zouk,* II, 4
dangerous *dangereux (-euse),* II, 8
Darn! *Zut!* I, 3
date *le rendez-vous,* II, 9; **to have (make) a date/an appointment (with someone)** *avoir (prendre) rendez-vous (avec quelqu'un),* II, 9
daughter *la fille,* I, 7
day *le jour,* I, 2; **I had a terrible day!** *J'ai passé une journée épouvantable!* II, 5; **It's just not my day!** *C'est pas mon jour!* II, 5; **What a bad day!** *Quelle journée!* II, 5
deadly dull *mortel(le),* II, 6
December *décembre,* I, 4; **in December** *en décembre,* I, 4
decided *décidé(e),* I, 10; **Have you decided to take...?** *Vous avez décidé de prendre...?* I, 10; **Have you decided?** *Vous avez choisi?* I, 5
deface *mutiler,* II, 12; **to deface the trees** *mutiler les arbres,* II, 12
Definitely not! *Sûrement pas!* II, 6
delicatessen *la charcuterie,* II, 3
delicious *délicieux (-euse),* I, 5; **That was delicious!** *C'était délicieux!* II, 3
denim *le jean,* I, 10; **in denim** *en jean,* I, 10
deposit *déposer,* I, 12; **to deposit money** *déposer de l'argent,* I, 12
depressed *déprimé(e),* II, 9
depressing *déprimant(e),* II, 11
desk *le bureau,* II, 2
dessert *le dessert,* II, 3
detective or mystery movie *le film policier,* II, 11; **detective or mystery novel** *le roman policier (le polar),* II, 11
detention: to have detention *être collé(e),* II, 5
dictionary *le dictionnaire,* I, 3
die *mourir,* II, 6
diet *le régime,* II, 7; **follow a diet that's too strict.** *suivre un régime trop strict,* II, 7
different *différent(e),* II, 8; **Was it really so different?** *C'était tellement différent?* II, 8
dining room *la salle à manger,* II, 2
dinner *le dîner,* I, 8; **to have dinner** *dîner,* I, 9
dirty *sale,* II, 8
dishes *la vaisselle,* I, 7; **to do the dishes** *faire la vaisselle,* I, 7
dismissal (when school gets out) *la sortie,* I, 2
do *faire,* I, 4; **All you have to do is...** *Tu n'as qu'à...,* II, 7; **Do you play/do...?** *Est-ce que tu fais...?* I, 4; **Don't do it again.** *Ne recommence pas.* II, 5; **I do.** *Moi, si.* I, 2; **I don't know what to do.** *Je ne sais pas quoi faire.* II, 10; **I don't play/do...** *Je ne fais pas de...,* I, 4; **I have errands to do.** *J'ai des courses à faire.* I, 5; **I just can't do any more!** *Je n'en peux plus!* II, 7; **I play/do...** *Je fais...,* I, 4; **In your opinion, what do I do?** *A ton avis, qu'est-ce que je fais?* I, 9; **It'll do you good.** *Ça te fera du bien.* II, 7; **Sorry. I have homework to do.** *Désolé(e). J'ai des devoirs à faire.* I, 5; **to do homework** *faire les devoirs,* I, 7; **to do the dishes** *faire la vaisselle,* I, 7; **What are you going to do...?** *Qu'est-ce que tu vas faire...?* I, 6, II, 1; **What are you going to do...?** *Tu vas faire quoi...?* I, 6; **What can I do?** *Qu'est-ce que je peux faire?* I, 9; **What can we do?** *Qu'est-ce qu'on peut faire?* II, 4; **What did you do...?** *Qu'est-ce que tu as fait...?* I, 9; **What do you advise me to do?** *Qu'est-ce que tu me conseilles?* I, 9; **What do you do...?** *Qu'est-ce que tu fais...?* I, 4; **What do you do when...?** *Qu'est-ce que tu fais quand...?* I, 4; **What do you like to do?** *Qu'est-ce que tu aimes faire?* II, 1; **What should we do?** *Qu'est-ce qu'on fait?* II, 1
dog *le chien,* I, 7; **to walk the dog** *promener le chien,* I, 7
done, made *fait* (pp. of faire), I, 9
door *la porte,* I, 0
down: go down *descendre,* II, 6; **You go down this street to the next light.** *Vous continuez jusqu'au prochain feu rouge.* I, 12
dozen *la douzaine,* I, 8; **a dozen** *une douzaine de,* I, 8
drama: to do drama *faire du théâtre,* I, 4
dress *la robe,* I, 10
dressed: to get dressed *s'habiller,* II, 4
drink *boire,* I, 5; **What do you have to drink?** *Qu'est-ce que vous avez comme boissons?* I, 5; **What is there to drink?** *Qu'est-ce qu'il y a à boire?* I, 5
drive *conduire,* II, 8; **to drive a car** *conduire une voiture,* II, 8
drugstore *la pharmacie,* I, 12
drum (from Africa) *le tam-tam,* II, 8
duck *le canard,* II, 12
dud: It's a dud. *C'est un navet.* II, 11
dull: deadly dull *mortel(le),* II, 6
dying: I'm dying of hunger! *Je crève de faim!* II, 12; **I'm dying of thirst!** *Je meurs de soif!* II, 12

ear *l'oreille* (f.), II, 7; **My ear hurts.** *J'ai mal à l'oreille.* II, 7
early *tôt,* II, 4
earn *gagner,* I, 9
earrings *les boucles d'oreilles* (f.), I, 10
earth-shattering: It's not earth-shattering. *Ça casse pas des briques.* II, 11
east *l'est,* II, 4; **in the east** *dans l'est,* II, 4; **It's to the east of...** *C'est à l'est de...,* II, 12
easy *facile,* I, 2
eat *manger,* I, 6; II, 7; **to eat too much sugar** *consommer trop de sucre,* II, 7; **someone who loves to eat** *gourmand(e),* II, 1; **to eat well** *bien se nourrir,* II, 7
egg *l'œuf* (m.), I, 8; II, 3
embarrassed *gêné(e),* II, 9
English (language) *l'anglais* (m.), I, 1
enjoy *déguster,* II, 4
enter *entrer,* II, 6
entrance *l'entrée* (f.), II, 6; **How much is the entrance fee?** *C'est combien, l'entrée?* II, 6
envelope *l'enveloppe* (f.), I, 12
eraser *la gomme,* I, 3
errands *les courses* (f. pl.), I, 7; **I have errands to do.** *J'ai des courses à faire.* I, 5
especially *surtout,* I, 1
euro *l'euro* (m.), I, 5; II, 3
evening *le soir,* I, 2; **in the evening** *le soir,* I, 2
everyone: Everyone should... *On doit...,* II, 7
everything *tout,* I, 11; **Everything went wrong!** *Tout a été de travers!* II, 5; **I've thought of everything.** *J'ai pensé à tout.* I, 11
exam *l'examen* (m.), I, 1

excellent *excellent(e),* I, 5; II, 2; **Yes, excellent.** *Oui, excellent.* I, 9
exciting *passionnant(e),* II, 11; **It's an exciting story.** *C'est une histoire passionnante.* II, 11
excuse: Excuse me. *Excusez-moi.* I, 3; **Excuse me,..., please?** *Pardon,..., s'il vous plaît?* I, 12; **Excuse me, ma'am,..., please?** *Pardon, madame,... s'il vous plaît?* I, 12; **Excuse me, miss. Where is..., please?** *Pardon, mademoiselle. Où est..., s'il vous plaît?* I, 12; **Excuse me, sir. I'm looking for...** *Pardon, monsieur. Je cherche...,* I, 12
exercise *faire de l'exercice,* II, 7
exhausted *crevé(e),* II, 2; **Yes, I'm exhausted.** *Si, je suis crevé(e).* II, 2
expensive *cher (chère),* II, 3; **It's too expensive.** *C'est trop cher.* II, 3
explain *expliquer,* II, 10; **Explain to him/her/them.** *Explique-lui/-leur.* II, 10; **to explain what happened (to someone)** *expliquer ce qui s'est passé (à quelqu'un),* II, 10
eye *l'œil* (m.), II, 1; **eyes** *les yeux* (m. pl.), II, 1

F

fabric *le tissu,* II, 8
fail *rater,* I, 9; **to fail a test** *rater un examen,* I, 9; **to fail a quiz** *rater une interro,* I, 9
fall *l'automne* (m.), I, 4; **in the fall** *en automne,* I, 4
fall *tomber,* II, 5, **to fall in love (with someone)** *tomber amoureux(-euse) (de quelqu'un),* II, 9
familiar: Are you familiar with...? *Tu connais...?* II, 11; **I'm not familiar with them (him/her).** *Je ne connais pas.* II, 11
family *la famille,* I, 7
fantastic *sensass (sensationnel),* I, 10; II, 6
far from *loin de,* I, 12
fascinating *passionnant(e),* I, 2
fat *gros(se)* (adj.), I, 7; *les matières grasses* (f. pl.), II, 7
father *le père,* I, 7
fault *la faute,* II, 10; **It's my fault.** *C'est de ma faute.* II, 10
favor *le petit service,* I, 12; **Could you do me a favor?** *(Est-ce que) tu pourrais me rendre un petit service?* I, 12
favorite *préféré(e),* II, 1; **What is your favorite...?** *Quel(le) est ton/ta... préféré(e)?* II, 1; **Who is your favorite...?** *Qui est ton/ta... préféré(e)?* II, 1
February *février,* I, 4; **in February** *en février,* I, 4
fee: How much is the entrance fee? *C'est combien, l'entrée?* II, 6
feed *donner à manger,* II, 6; *nourrir,* II, 12; **to feed the animals** *donner à manger aux animaux,* II, 6; *nourrir les animaux,* II, 12
feel *se sentir,* II, 7; **Do you feel like...?** *Tu as envie de...?* II, 1; **I don't feel well.** *Je ne me sens pas bien.* II, 7; **I feel like...** *J'ai envie de...,* I, 11; **No, I don't feel like it.** *Non, je n'ai pas très envie.* II, 7
feelings: No hard feelings. *Je ne t'en veux pas.* II, 10; **No hard feelings?** *Tu ne m'en veux pas?* II, 10
ferris wheel *la grande roue,* II, 6
fever: I have a fever. *J'ai de la fièvre.* II, 7
film *le film,* II, 11; **What films are playing?** *Qu'est-ce qu'on joue comme films?* II, 11
Finally,... *Enfin,...,* I, 9; II, 1; *Finalement...,* I, 9; II, 4
find *trouver,* I, 9
Fine. *Ça va.* I, 1; **Yes, it was fine.** *Oui, ça a été.* I, 9
first *d'abord,* I, 7, II, 1; **OK, if you... first.** *D'accord, si tu... d'abord.* I, 7
first-aid kit *la trousse de premiers soins,* II, 12
fish *le poisson,* I, 7; II, 3
fish shop *la poissonnerie,* II, 3
fishing *la pêche,* II, 4; **to go fishing** *aller à la pêche,* II, 4; **fishing pole** *la canne à pêche,* II, 12; **fishing village** *le village de pêcheurs,* II, 4
flashlight *la lampe de poche,* II, 12
floor (of a building) *l'étage* (m.), II, 2; **first (ground) floor** *le rez-de-chaussée,* II, 2; **second floor** *le premier étage,* II, 2
florist's shop *le fleuriste,* II, 3
flour *la farine,* I, 8
flower *la fleur,* II, 3
flu *la grippe,* II, 7; **I've got the flu.** *J'ai la grippe.* II, 7
folk (music) *le folk,* II, 11
follow *suivre,* II, 7; **to follow a diet that's too strict** *suivre un régime trop strict,* II, 7; **to follow the marked trails** *suivre les sentiers balisés,* II, 12
foot *le pied,* II, 7; **on foot** *à pied,* I, 12; **My foot hurts.** *J'ai mal au pied.* II, 7
football *le football américain,* II, 4; **to play football** *jouer au football américain,* I, 4
for *pour,* I, 3; **It's good for you.** *C'est bon pour toi.* II, 7; **What do you need for...?** (informal) *Qu'est-ce qu'il te faut pour...?* I, 3
forest *la forêt,* I, 11; **to the forest** *en forêt,* I, 11
forget *oublier,* I, 9; **Don't forget.** *N'oublie pas.* I, 8; II, 1; **Forget him/her/them!** *Oublie-le/-la/-les!* I, 9; II, 10; **I didn't forget anything.** *Je n'ai rien oublié.* I, 11; **You didn't forget your...?** *Tu n'as pas oublié ton/ta/tes...?* I, 11
forgive *excuser,* II, 10; *pardonner,* II, 10; **Forgive me.** *Excuse-moi.* II, 10; **to forgive (someone)** *pardonner à (quelqu'un),* II, 10
forgiveness *le pardon,* II, 10; **to ask (someone's) forgiveness** *demander pardon à (quelqu'un),* II, 10
Fortunately,... *Heureusement,...,* II, 9
fox *le renard,* II, 12
frame: photo frame *le cadre,* II, 3
franc (the former French monetary unit) *le franc,* I, 3
French (language) *le français,* I, 1; **French fries** *les frites* (f. pl.), I, 1
Friday *vendredi,* I, 2; **on Fridays** *le vendredi,* I, 2
friend *l'ami(e),* I, 1; **to go out with friends** *sortir avec les copains,* I, 1
from *de,* I, 0; **From platform...** *Du quai...,* II, 6
front: in front of *devant,* I, 6
fun *amusant(e),* II, 8 **to have fun** *s'amuser,* II, 4; **Did you have fun?** *Tu t'es amusé(e)?* I, 11; II, 6; **Have fun!** *Amuse-toi bien!* I, 11; **I had a lot of fun.** *Je me suis beaucoup amusé(e).* II, 6; **What do you do to have fun?** *Qu'est-ce que tu fais pour t'amuser?* I, 4
funny *amusant(e),* I, 7, II, 1; **It's funny.** *C'est drôle (amusant).* II, 11
furious *furieux (-euse),* II, 9

G

gain *gagner;* **to gain weight** *grossir,* I, 10
game *le match,* I, 6; **to watch a game (on TV)** *regarder un match,* I, 6; **to go see a game** *aller voir un match,* I, 6
geography *la géographie,* I, 2
geometry *la géométrie,* I, 2
German (language) *l'allemand* (m.), I, 2
get: Get... *Prends...,* I, 8; **to get up** *se lever,* II, 4; **You'll get used to it.** *Tu vas t'y faire.* II, 8; **Get well soon!** *Bon rétablissement!* II, 3; **How can we get there?** *Comment est-ce qu'on y va?* I, 12; **It'll get better.** *Ça va aller mieux.* II, 5; **to get a bad grade** *avoir une mauvaise note,* II, 5; **to get lost** *se perdre,* II, 9; **to get ready** *faire les préparatifs,* II, 10
gift *le cadeau,* I, 11; **gift shop** *la boutique de cadeaux,* II, 3; **Have you got a gift idea for...?** *Tu as une idée de cadeau pour...?* II, 3
girl *la fille,* I, 0
give *donner,* I, 5; *offrir (à quelqu'un),* II, 10; **Give him/her (them)...** *Offre-lui (-leur)...,* II, 3; **Please give me...** *Donnez-moi..., s'il vous plaît.* I, 5; **What could I give to...?** *Qu'est-ce que je pourrais offrir à...?* II, 3; **You could give him/her (them)...** *Tu pourrais lui (leur) offrir...,* II, 3; **I'm giving up.** *J'abandonne.* II, 7
Gladly. *Je veux bien.* I, 8
glove *le gant,* II, 1
go *aller,* I, 6; **Could you go by...?** *Tu pourrais passer à...?* I, 12; **Did it go well?** *Ça s'est bien passé?* I, 11; **First, I'm going to...** *D'abord, je vais...,* II, 1; **Go straight ahead.** *Allez tout droit.* II, 2; **Go to the blackboard!** *Allez au tableau!* I, 0; **How about going...?** *Si on allait...?* II, 4; **How did it go?** *Comment ça s'est passé?* II, 5; **How's it going?** *(Comment) ça va?* I, 1; **I'd like... to go with...** *J'aimerais... pour aller avec...,* I, 10; **I'm going...** *Je vais...,* I, 6; **I'm going to...** *Je vais...,* I, 11; **I'm going to have..., please.** *Je vais prendre..., s'il vous plaît.* I, 5; **It doesn't go at all with...** *Il/Elle ne va pas du tout avec...,* I, 10; **It goes very well with...** *Ça va très bien avec...,* I, 10; **Let's go...** *Allons...,* I, 6; **to go back (home)** *rentrer,* II, 6; **to go down** *descendre,* II, 6; **to go for a walk** *faire une promenade,* I, 6; *se promener,* II, 4; **to go out** *sortir,* II, 6; **to go out with friends** *sortir avec les copains,* I, 1; **to go up** *monter,* II, 6; **We can go there...** *On peut y aller...,* I, 12; **What are you going to do...?** *Qu'est-ce que tu vas faire...?* I, 6; II, 1; *Tu vas faire quoi...?* I, 6; **What do you think about going...?** *Ça te dit d'aller...?* II, 4; **Where are you going to go...?** *Où est-ce que tu vas aller...?* I, 11; **Where did you go?** *Tu es allé(e) où?* I, 9; **You're going to like it here.** *Tu vas te plaire ici.* II, 8; **You keep going until the next light.** *Vous continuez jusqu'au prochain feu rouge.* I, 12
golf *le golf,* I, 4; **to play golf** *jouer au golf,* I, 4
good *bon(ne),* I, 5; **Did you have a good...?** *Tu as passé un bon...?* I, 11; **Did you have a good trip?** *Vous avez (Tu as) fait bon voyage?* II, 2; **Good idea!** *Bonne idée!* II, 3, 7; **Have a good trip! (by car)** *Bonne route!* II, 3; **(by plane ship)** *Bon voyage!* I, 11; **It doesn't look good on you at all.** *Il/Elle ne te/vous va pas du tout.* I, 10; **It'll do you good.** *Ça te fera du bien.* II, 7; **It's good for you.** *C'est bon pour toi.* II, 7; **It's really good!** *C'est vraiment bon!* II, 3; **not very good** *pas bon,* I, 5; **pretty good** *pas mauvais,* I, 5; **That's a good idea.** *C'est une bonne idée.* II, 1; **Yes, very good.** *Oui, très bon.* I, 9
Goodbye! *Au revoir!, Salut!* I, 1
goof off *faire le clown,* II, 5; **You can't be goofing off in class!** *Tu ne dois pas faire le clown en classe!* II, 5
got: No, you've got to... *Non, tu dois...,* I, 7
grade *la note,* II, 5; **to get a bad grade** *avoir une mauvaise note,* II, 5
grandfather *le grand-père,* I, 7
grandmother *la grand-mère,* I, 7
grapes *le raisin,* I, 8
great *génial(e),* I, 2; II, 2; *superbe,* II, 6; **Great!** *Super!* I, 1; **It looks great on you!** *C'est tout à fait ton style!* I, 10; **It was great!** *C'était formidable!* I, 11; **Not so great.** *Pas terrible.* I, 1; **What a great day!** *Quelle journée formidable!* II, 5; **What a great weekend!** *Quel week-end formidable!* II, 5; **Your... is really great.** *Il/Elle est vraiment bien, ton/ta...,* II, 2
green *vert(e),* I, 3; **green beans** *les haricots verts* (m.), I, 8
grey *gris(e),* I, 3
grocery store *l'épicerie* (f.), I, 12
gross *dégoûtant(e),* I, 5
grounded: to be "grounded" *être privé(e) de sortie,* II, 9
group *le groupe,* II, 11
grow up *grandir,* I, 10
guava *la goyave,* I, 8
guess *deviner,* II, 9; **Guess what...** *Devine ce que...,* II, 9; **Guess who...** *Devine qui...,* II, 9; **You'll never guess what happened.** *Tu ne devineras jamais ce qui s'est passé.* II, 9
guided *guidé(e),* II, 6; **to take a guided tour** *faire une visite guidée,* II, 6
gym *le sport,* I, 2
gymnastics *la gymnastique,* II, 7; **to do gymnastics** *faire de la gymnastique,* II, 7

H

hair *les cheveux* (m. pl.), II, 1; **black hair** *les cheveux noirs,* II, 1; **blond hair** *les cheveux blonds,* II, 1; **brown hair** *les cheveux châtain,* II, 1; **dark brown hair** *les cheveux bruns,* II, 1; **long hair** *les cheveux longs,* II, 1; **red hair** *les cheveux roux,* II, 1; **short hair** *les cheveux courts,* II, 1
half *demi(e),* I, 6; **half past** *et demie,* I, 6; **(after midi and minuit)** *et demi,* I, 6
ham *le jambon,* I, 5; **toasted ham and cheese sandwich** *le croque-monsieur,* I, 5
hamburger *le hamburger* , I, 1
hand *la main,* I, 0
handsome (beautiful) *beau (belle) (bel),* II, 1
hang glide *faire du deltaplane,* II, 4
hang: Hang in there! *Courage!* II, 5
Hanukkah *le Hanoukkah,* II, 3; **Happy Hanukkah!** *Bonne fête de Hanoukkah!* II, 3
happen *se passer,* I, 9; **What**

happened? *Qu'est-ce qui s'est passé?* I, 9; **to explain what happened (to someone)** *expliquer ce qui s'est passé (à quelqu'un),* II, 10; **You'll never guess what happened.** *Tu ne devineras jamais ce qui s'est passé.* II, 9
happy *content(e),* I, 7; *joyeux (-euse),* II, 3; **Happy birthday!** *Joyeux (Bon) anniversaire!* II, 3; **Happy Hanukkah!** *Bonne fête de Hanoukkah!* II, 3; **Happy holiday! (Happy saint's day!)** *Bonne fête!* II, 3; **Happy New Year!** *Bonne année!* II, 3
hard *difficile,* I, 2; **No hard feelings.** *Je ne t'en veux pas.* II, 10; **No hard feelings?** *Tu ne m'en veux pas?* II, 10
harm *le mal,* II, 10; **No harm done.** *Il n'y a pas de mal.* II, 10
has: He/She has... *Il/Elle a...,* II, 1
hat *le chapeau,* I, 10
have *avoir,* I, 2; **All you have to do is...** *Tu n'as qu'à...,* II, 7; **At what time do you have...?** *Tu as... à quelle heure?* I, 2; **Do you have...?** *Tu as...?* I, 3; *Vous avez...?* I, 2; **Do you have that in...? (size, fabric, color)** *Vous avez ça en...?* I, 10; **Have...** *Prends/Prenez...,* I, 5; **Have a good trip! (by car)** *Bonne route!;* **(by plane, ship)** *Bon voyage!* II, 3; **I don't have...** *Je n'ai pas de...,* I, 3; **I have...** *J'ai...,* I, 2; **I have some things to do.** *J'ai des trucs à faire.* I, 5; **I'll have/I'm going to have..., please.** *Je vais prendre..., s'il vous plaît.* I, 5; **May I have some...?** *Je pourrais avoir...?* II, 3; **to have an accident** *avoir un accident,* II, 9; **to have an argument (with someone)** *se disputer (avec quelqu'un),* II, 9; **to have fun** *s'amuser,* II, 4; **to take or to have (food, drink)** *prendre,* I, 5; **We have...** *Nous avons...,* I, 2; **What are you having?** *Vous prenez?* I, 5; **What classes do you have...?** *Tu as quels cours...?* I, 2; **What do you have...?** *Tu as quoi...?* I, 2; **What kind of... do you have?** *Qu'est-ce que vous avez comme...?* I, 5; **Will you have...** *Tu prends...?* I, 8; *Vous prenez...?* I, 8; **You have to work harder in class.** *Il faut mieux travailler en classe.* II, 5
have to *devoir,* II, 7
head *la tête,* II, 7
health *le cours de développement personnel et social (DPS),* I, 2
healthy: It's healthy. *C'est bon pour la santé.* II, 7
hear *entendre,* II, 5; **Did you hear the latest?** *Tu connais la nouvelle?* II, 9; **Let's hear it!** *Dis vite!* II, 9; **to hear the alarm clock** *entendre le réveil,* II, 5
height *la taille,* II, 1; **of medium height** *de taille moyenne,* II, 1
Hello. *Bonjour.* I, 1; **Hello? (on the phone)** *Allô?* I, 9
help *aider,* II, 8; **Can you help me?** *Tu peux m'aider?* II, 10; **May I help you?** *(Est-ce que) je peux vous aider?* I, 10
her *la,* I, 9; **her...** *son/sa/ses...,* I, 7; **to her** *lui,* I, 9
Here. *Voilà.* I, 3; *ici,* II, 8; **Here (There) is...** *Là, c'est...,* II, 2; **Here it is.** *Voilà.* II, 3; **Here you are.** *Tenez (Tiens).* II, 3
Hi! *Salut!* I, 1
high school *le lycée,* II, 2
hike *la randonnée,* I, 11; **to go for a hike** *faire une randonnée pédestre,* II, 12; **to go hiking** *faire de la randonnée,* I, 11
him *le,* I, 9; **to him** *lui,* I, 9
his *son/sa/ses,* I, 7
history *l'histoire* (f.), I, 2
hockey *le hockey,* I, 4; **to play hockey** *jouer au hockey,* I, 4
Hold on. (on the phone) *Ne quittez pas.* I, 9
holiday *la fête,* II, 3; **Happy holiday! (Happy saint's day!)** *Bonne fête!* II, 3
home: Make yourself at home. *Faites (Fais) comme chez vous (toi).* II, 2; **Welcome to my home (our home).** *Bienvenue chez moi (chez nous).* II, 2
homework *les devoirs* (m. pl.), I, 2; **I've got homework to do.** *J'ai des devoirs à faire.* I, 5; **to do homework** *faire les devoirs,* I, 7
horrible *épouvantable,* I, 9; **It was horrible.** *C'était épouvantable.* I, 9; **to have a horrible day** *passer une journée épouvantable,* II, 5
horror movie *le film d'horreur,* II, 11
horseback riding *l'équitation* (f.), I, 1; **to go horseback riding** *faire de l'équitation,* I, 1
hose *le collant,* I, 10
hostel: youth hostel *l'auberge de jeunesse* (f.), II, 2
hot *chaud(e),* I, 4; **hot chocolate** *le chocolat,* I, 5; **hot dog** *le hot-dog,* I, 5; **It's hot (outside).** *Il fait chaud.* I, 4; **not so hot** *pas super,* I, 2
house *la maison,* II, 2; **at my house** *chez moi,* I, 6; **Is this... 's house?** *Je suis bien chez...?* I, 9; **to clean house** *faire le ménage,* I, 7; **to/at... 's** *chez...,* I, 11
housework *le ménage,* I, 1; **to do housework** *faire le ménage,* I, 1
how *comment,* I, 1; **How did it go?** *Comment ça s'est passé?* II, 5; **How do you like it?** *Comment tu trouves ça?* I, 5; **How old are you?** *Tu as quel âge?* I, 1; **How was it?** *C'était comment?* II, 6; **How was your day (yesterday)?** *Comment s'est passée ta journée (hier)?* II, 5; **How was your vacation?** *Comment se sont passées tes vacances?* II, 5; **How was your weekend?** *Comment s'est passé ton week-end?* II, 5; **How's it going?** *(Comment) ça va?* I, 1
how about: How about...? *On...?* I, 4; **How about buying...?** *Si on achetait...?* II, 8; **How about going...?** *Si on allait...?* II, 4; **How about playing...?** *Si on jouait...?* II, 8; **How about playing baseball?** *On joue au base-ball?* I, 5; **How about skiing?** *On fait du ski?* I, 5; **How about visiting...?** *Si on visitait...?* II, 8
how much *combien,* I, 3; **How much is...?** *C'est combien,...?* I, 3; *Combien coûte...?* II, 3; **How much are...?** *Combien coûtent...?* II, 3; **How much does that make?** *Ça fait combien?* I, 5; **How many (much) do you want?** *Combien en voulez-vous?* II, 3
hundred *cent,* I, 3; **two hundred** *deux cents,* I, 3
hunger *la faim,* II, 2; **I'm dying of hunger!** *Je crève de faim!* II, 12; *Je meurs de faim!* II, 2
hungry: to be hungry *avoir faim,* I, 5; **Aren't you hungry?** *Vous n'avez pas (Tu n'as pas) faim?* II, 2; **He was hungry.** *Il avait faim.* II, 12; **I'm very hungry.** *J'ai très faim!* II, 2; **No thanks. I'm not hungry anymore.** *Non, merci. Je n'ai plus faim.* I, 8
hurt *avoir mal,* II, 7; **I hurt all over!** *J'ai mal partout!* II, 7; **My... hurts.** *J'ai mal à...,* II, 7; **to hurt one's...** *se faire mal à...,* II, 7
husband *le mari,* I, 7

I

I *je,* I, 1; **I do.** *Moi, si.* I, 2; **I don't.** *Moi, non.* I, 2
ice cream *la glace,* I, 1
ice-skate *faire du patin à glace,* I, 4
idea *l'idée* (f.), I, 4; **Good idea.** *Bonne idée.* I, 4; **I have no idea.** *Je n'en sais rien.* I, 11; **No idea.** *Aucune idée.* II, 9; **That's a good (excellent) idea.** *C'est une bonne (excellente) idée.* II, 1
if *si,* I, 7; **OK, if you… first.** *D'accord, si tu… d'abord.* I, 7
impossible *impossible,* I, 7; II, 10; **It's impossible.** *C'est impossible.* II, 10; **No, that's impossible.** *Non, c'est impossible.* I, 7
in *dans,* I, 6; **(a city or place)** *à,* I, 11; **(before a feminine country)** *en,* I, 11; **(before a masculine country)** *au,* I, 11; **(before a plural noun)** *aux,* I, 11; **in front of** *devant,* I, 6; **in the afternoon** *l'après-midi,* I, 2; **in the evening** *le soir,* I, 2; **in the morning** *le matin,* I, 2; **... is (are) in it.** *C'est avec…,* II, 11; **Who's in it?** *C'est avec qui?* II, 11
in-line skate *le roller en ligne,* I, 4; **to in-line skate** *faire du roller en ligne,* I, 4
incredible *incroyable,* II, 6
indifference: (expression of indifference) *Bof!* I, 1
insect repellent *la lotion anti-moustiques,* II, 12
intend *avoir l'intention de,* I, 11; **I intend to…** *J'ai l'intention de…,* I, 11
interesting *intéressant(e),* I, 2
invitation *l'invitation* (f.), II, 10;
invite *inviter,* II, 10; **Invite him/her/them.** *Invite-le/-la/-les.* II, 10
is: He is… *Il est…,* I, 7; **She is…** *Elle est…,* I, 7; **There's…** *Voilà…,* I, 7; **This is…** *C'est…; Voici…,* I, 7
island *l'île* (f.), II, 4
it *le, la,* I, 9
it's: It's… *C'est…,* I, 2; **It's… euros.** *Ça fait… euros.* I, 5

J

jacket *le blouson,* I, 10; **ski jacket** *l'anorak* (m.), II, 1; **suit jacket** *la veste,* I, 10
jam *la confiture,* I, 8
January *janvier,* I, 4; **in January** *en janvier,* I, 4
jazz *le jazz,* II, 11
jeans *le jean,* I, 3
jog *faire du jogging,* I, 4
joking: You're joking! *Tu plaisantes!* II, 6
July *juillet,* I, 4; **in July** *en juillet,* I, 4
June *juin,* I, 4; **in June** *en juin,* I, 4

K

kidding: You're kidding! *C'est pas vrai!* II, 6
kilogram *le kilo,* I, 8; **a kilogram of** *un kilo de,* I, 8
kind: What kind of… do you have? *Qu'est-ce que vous avez comme…?* I, 5
kitchen *la cuisine,* II, 2
knee *le genou,* II, 7; **My knee hurts.** *J'ai mal au genou.* II, 7
know *savoir,* I, 10; **..., you know.** *…, quoi.* II, 9; **Do you know what…?** *Tu sais ce que…?* II, 9; **Do you know who…?** *Tu sais qui…?* II, 9; **I don't know what to do.** *Je ne sais pas quoi faire.* II, 10; **I don't know.** *Je ne sais pas.* I, 10

L

lab *les travaux pratiques* (m. pl.), I, 2
lame *nul(le),* II, 6
lamp *la lampe,* II, 2
late *tard,* II, 4
later *plus tard,* I, 9; **Can you call back later?** *Vous pouvez rappeler plus tard?* I, 9; **See you later (the same day)!** *A tout à l'heure!* I, 1
latest: Did you hear the latest? *Tu connais la nouvelle?* II, 9
Latin (language) *le latin,* I, 2
lawn *le gazon,* I, 7; **to mow the lawn** *tondre le gazon,* I, 7
learn *apprendre,* I, 0
leather *le cuir,* I, 10; **in leather** *en cuir,* I, 10
leather-goods shop *la maroquinerie,* II, 3
leave *partir,* I, 11; **Can I leave a message?** *Je peux laisser un message?* I, 9; **You can't leave without…** *Tu ne peux pas partir sans…,* I, 11
left *la gauche,* I, 12; **to the left** *à gauche,* I, 12; **on the left** *sur la gauche,* II, 2; **to the left of** *à gauche de,* II, 2
leg *la jambe,* II, 7
lemon *le citron,* I, 8; **lemon soda** *la limonade,* I, 5
lemonade *le citron pressé,* I, 5
less *moins,* II, 6; **Life was more…, less…** *La vie était plus… moins…,* II, 8; **More or less.** *Plus ou moins.* II, 6
let's: Let's go! *Allons-y!* I, 4; **Let's go…** *Allons…,* I, 6; **Let's hear it!** *Dis vite!* II, 9
letter *la lettre,* I, 12; **to send letters** *envoyer des lettres,* I, 12
lettuce *la salade,* I, 8
library *la bibliothèque,* I, 6
life *la vie,* II, 8
lift weights *faire de la musculation,* II, 7
like *aimer,* I, 1; **Did you like it?** *Ça t'a plu?* II, 6; **Do you like…?** *Tu aimes…?* I, 1; **Do you like it?** *Il/Elle te/vous plaît?* I, 10; **How do you like…?** *Comment tu trouves…?* I, 10; **How do you like it?** *Comment tu trouves ça?* I, 5; **I (really) like…** *Moi, j'aime (bien)…,* I, 1; **I don't like…** *Je n'aime pas…,* I, 1; **I like…** *J'aime bien…,* II, 1; **I like it, but it's expensive.** *Il/Elle me plaît, mais c'est cher.* I, 10; **I really liked it.** *Ça m'a beaucoup plu.* II, 6; **I'd like…** *Je voudrais…,* I, 3; **I'd like… to go with…** *J'aimerais… pour aller avec…,* I, 10; **I'd like to.** *Je veux bien.* II, 1; **I'd really like…** *Je voudrais bien…,* I, 11; **I'd really like to.** *Je veux bien.* I, 6; **I'd like to buy…** *Je voudrais acheter…,* I, 3; **If you like,…** *Si tu veux,…,* II, 1; **What are they like?** *Ils/Elles sont comment?* I, 7; **What do you like to do?** *Qu'est-ce que tu aimes faire?* II, 1; **What I don't like is…** *Ce que je n'aime pas, c'est…,* II, 4; **What I like is…** *Ce que j'aime bien, c'est…,* II, 4; *Ce qui me plaît, c'est (de)…,* II, 4; **What is he/she like?** *Il /Elle est comment?* I, 7; **What music do you like?** *Qu'est-ce que tu aimes comme musique?* II, 1; **What was it like?** *C'était comment?* II, 8; **What would you like?** *Vous désirez?* I, 10;

You're going to like it here. *Tu vas te plaire ici.* II, 8
listen *écouter,* I, 1; **I'm listening.** *Je t'écoute.* I, 9; **Listen!** *Ecoutez!* I, 0; **to listen to music** *écouter de la musique,* I, 1; **to listen to what he/she says** *écouter ce qu'il/elle dit,* II, 10
liter *le litre,* I, 8; **a liter of** *un litre de,* I, 8
little *petit(e),* I, 10; **When he/she was little,...** *Quand il/elle était petit(e),...,* II, 8; **When I was little,...** *Quand j'étais petit(e),...* , II, 8; **Yes, a little.** *Si, un peu.* II, 2
lively *vivant(e),* II, 4
living room *le salon,* II, 2
located: ...is located... *...se trouve...,* II, 12; **Where is... located?** *Où se trouve...?* II, 12
long *long(ue),* II, 11; **long hair** *les cheveux longs,* II, 1
look *regarder,* I, 0; **I'm looking for something for...** *Je cherche quelque chose pour...,* I, 10; **It doesn't look good on you at all.** *Il/Elle ne te/vous va pas du tout.* I, 10; **It looks great on you!** *C'est tout à fait ton style.* I, 10; **Look at the map!** *Regardez la carte!* I, 0; **Look, here's (there's) (it's)...** *Regarde, c'est...,* I, 12; **No, thanks, I'm just looking.** *Non, merci, je regarde.* I, 10; **That doesn't look good on you.** *Ça ne te (vous) va pas du tout.* I, 10; **to look after someone** *garder (quelqu'un),* I, 7; **to look for** *chercher,* I, 9
loose-leaf binder *le classeur,* I, 3
lose *perdre,* II, 5; **I'm losing it!** *Je craque!* II, 7; **to lose weight** *maigrir,* I, 10
lost: to get lost *se perdre,* II, 9
lot: A lot. *Beaucoup.* I, 4; **I had a lot of fun.** *Je me suis beaucoup amusé(e).* II, 6
lots: I have lots of things to do. *J'ai des tas de choses (trucs) à faire.* I, 12
love *adorer, aimer,* I, 1; **I love...** *J'adore...,* II, 1; **in love** *amoureux (-euse),* II, 9; **to fall in love (with someone)** *tomber amoureux (-euse) (de quelqu'un),* II, 9
lower *moins,* I, 0
luck *la chance,* I, 11; **Good luck!** *Bonne chance!* I, 11; *Bon courage!* I, 2; **Tough luck!** *C'est pas de chance, ça!* II, 5
lunch *le déjeuner,* I, 2; **to have lunch** *déjeuner,* I, 9

ma'am *madame (Mme),* I, 1
made *fait* (pp. of faire), I, 9
magazine *le magazine,* I, 3
make *faire,* I, 4; **make up (with someone)** *se réconcilier (avec quelqu'un),* II, 10; **How much does that make?** *Ça fait combien?* II, 3; **Make the best of it.** *Fais-toi une raison.* II, 8; **to make a date/an appointment (with someone)** *prendre rendez-vous (avec quelqu'un),* II, 9
mall *le centre commercial,* I, 6
mango *la mangue,* I, 8
many: How many (much) do you want? *Combien en voulez-vous?* II, 3
map *la carte,* I, 0
March *mars,* I, 4; **in March** *en mars,* I, 4
market *le marché,* I, 8
mask *le masque,* II, 8
matches *les allumettes* (f.), II, 12
math *les maths* (f. pl.), I, 1
matter: It doesn't matter. *Ça ne fait rien.* II, 10
May *mai,* I, 4; **in May** *en mai,* I, 4
may: May I...? *(Est-ce que) je peux...?* I, 7; **May I have some...?** *Je pourrais avoir...?* II, 3; **May I help you?** *(Est-ce que) je peux vous aider?* I, 10
maybe *peut-être,* II, 3; **Maybe...** *Peut-être que...,* II, 9; **Maybe you're right.** *Tu as peut-être raison.* II, 9
me *moi,* I, 2; **Me, too.** *Moi aussi.* I, 2; **Not me.** *Pas moi.* I, 2
meal *le repas,* II, 7
mean *méchant(e),* I, 7
meat *la viande,* I, 8
medicine *les médicaments* (m.), I, 12
meet *rencontrer,* I, 9; **I'd like you to meet...** *Je te (vous) présente...,* I, 7; **Pleased to meet you.** *Très heureux (-euse).* I, 7; **OK, we'll meet...** *Bon, on se retrouve...,* I, 6; **We'll meet...** *Rendez-vous...,* I, 6
menu *la carte,* I, 5; **The menu, please.** *La carte, s'il vous plaît.* I, 5
merry *joyeux (-euse),* II, 3; **Merry Christmas!** *Joyeux Noël!* II, 3
message *le message,* I, 9; **Can I leave a message?** *Je peux laisser un message?* I, 9
metro *le métro,* I, 6; **at the... metro stop** *au métro...,* I, 6

midnight *minuit,* I, 6; **It's midnight.** *Il est minuit.* I, 6; **It's half past midnight.** *Il est minuit et demi.* I, 6
milk *le lait,* I, 8; II, 3
mind: Would you mind...? *Ça t'embête de...?* II, 10; *Ça t'ennuie de...?* II, 10
mineral water *l'eau minérale* (f.), I, 5
minute *la minute,* I, 9; **Do you have a minute?** *Tu as une minute?* I, 9
miss (Miss) *mademoiselle (Mlle),* I, 1
miss *rater,* II, 5; *regretter,* II, 8; **I miss...** *Je regrette...,* II, 8; **I miss... (plural subject)** *...me manquent.* II, 8; **(singular subject)** *...me manque.* II, 8; **to miss the bus** *rater le bus,* II, 5; **What I miss is...** *Ce qui me manque, c'est (de)...,* II, 8
mistaken: In my opinion, you're mistaken. *A mon avis, tu te trompes.* II, 9
misunderstanding *le malentendu,* II, 10; **a little misunderstanding** *un petit malentendu,* II, 10
moment *le moment,* I, 5; **One moment, please.** *Un moment, s'il vous plaît.* I, 5
Monday *lundi,* I, 2; **on Mondays** *le lundi,* I, 2
money *l'argent* (m.), I, 11
month *le mois,* I, 4
mood *l'humeur* (f.), II, 9; **in a bad/good mood** *de mauvaise/bonne humeur,* II, 9; **always in a bad mood** *toujours mal luné(e),* II, 8
moose *l'orignal* (m.), II, 12
more *plus,* II, 6; **I don't want any more.** *Je n'en veux plus.* I, 8; **I just can't do any more!** *Je n'en peux plus!* II, 7; **Life was more..., less...** *La vie était plus... moins...,* II, 8; **More...?** *Encore de...?* I, 8; **More or less.** *Plus ou moins.* II, 6; **One more try!** *Encore un effort!* II, 7; **Some more...?** *Encore ...?* II, 3
morning *le matin,* I, 2; **in the morning** *le matin,* I, 2
mosque *la mosquée,* II, 8
mosquito *le moustique,* II, 4
mother *la mère,* I, 7
mountain *la montagne,* I, 11; **to go mountain-bike riding** *faire du vélo de montagne,* II, 12; **to/at the mountains** *à la montagne,* I, 11
movie *le film,* I, 6; **movie theater** *le cinéma,* I, 6; **the movies** *le cinéma,* I, 1; **to go**

see a movie *aller voir un film,* I, 6

mow: to mow the lawn *tondre le gazon,* I, 7

Mr. *monsieur (M.),* I, 1

Mrs. *madame (Mme),* I, 1

much: How much is (are)...? *Combien coûte(nt)...?* II, 3; **How much is...?** *C'est combien,...?* I, 3; **How much is it?** *C'est combien?* I, 3; **How much is it, please?** *Ça fait combien, s'il vous plaît?* I, 5; **How much is the entrance fee?** *C'est combien, l'entrée?* II, 6; **No, not too much.** *Non, pas trop.* I, 2; **Not much.** *Pas grand-chose.* I, 6; **Not too much.** *Pas tellement.* I, 4; **Not very much.** *Pas beaucoup.* I, 4; **Yes, very much.** *Oui, beaucoup.* I, 2

museum *le musée,* I, 6

mushroom *le champignon,* I, 8

music *la musique,* I, 2; **music group** *le groupe,* II, 11; **classical music** *la musique classique,* II, 11; **What music do you like?** *Qu'est-ce que tu aimes comme musique?* II, 1

musician *le musicien (la musicienne),* II, 11

my *mon/ma/mes,* I, 7; **It's just not my day!** *C'est pas mon jour!* II, 5

N

name: His/Her name is... *Il/Elle s'appelle...,* I, 1; **My name is...** *Je m'appelle...,* I, 1; **What's your name?** *Tu t'appelles comment?* I, 1

nap *la sieste,* II, 8; **to take a nap** *faire la sieste,* II, 8

nature *la nature,* II, 12

natural science *les sciences naturelles* (f. pl.), I, 2

near *près de,* II, 2

neck *le cou,* II, 7; **a pain in the neck** *pénible,* I, 7

need *avoir besoin de,* I, 8; **I need...** *Il me faut...,* I, 3; *J'ai besoin de...,* I, 8; **What do you need for...?** *Qu'est-ce qu'il te/vous faut pour...?* I, 3; **What do you need?** *De quoi est-ce que tu as besoin?* I, 8; *Qu'est-ce qu'il te faut?* I, 8; **Yes, I need...** *Oui, il me faut...,* I, 10

neither: Neither do I. *Moi non plus.* I, 2; **neither tall nor short** *ne... ni grand(e) ni petit(e),* I, 7

never *ne... jamais,* I, 4

new *nouveau (nouvelle) (nouvel),* II, 2; **Happy New Year!** *Bonne année!* II, 3

next *prochain(e),* I, 12; **Next,...** *Ensuite,...,* II, 1; **You go down this street to the next light.** *Vous continuez jusqu'au prochain feu rouge.* I, 12

next to *à côté de,* I, 12; II, 2

nice *gentil(le),* I, 7; II, 1; *sympa, sympathique,* I, 7; II, 1; **It's nice weather.** *Il fait beau.* I, 4; **That's nice of you.** *C'est gentil!* II, 2

nightmare *le cauchemar,* I, 11; **It was a real nightmare!** *C'était un véritable cauchemar!* I, 11

ninety *quatre-vingt-dix,* I, 3

no *non,* I, 1; **No way!** *Pas question!* II, 1

noisy *bruyant(e),* II, 8

none (of it) *en,* I, 8

noon *midi,* I, 6; **It's noon.** *Il est midi.* I, 6; **It's half past noon.** *Il est midi et demi.* I, 6

north *le nord,* II, 4; **in the north** *dans le nord,* II, 4; **It's to the north of...** *C'est au nord de...,* II, 12

nose *le nez,* II, 7; **I've got a runny nose.** *J'ai le nez qui coule.* II, 7

not *pas,* I, 4; **Definitely not!** *Sûrement pas!* II, 6; **No, not really.** *Non, pas vraiment.* I, 11; **No, not too much.** *Non, pas trop.* I, 2; **Not at all.** *Pas du tout.* I, 4; II, 10; **Not me.** *Pas moi.* I, 2; **not so great** *pas terrible,* I, 5; **not very good** *pas bon,* I, 5; **not yet** *ne... pas encore,* I, 9; **Oh, not bad.** *Oh, pas mauvais.* I, 9

notebook *le cahier,* I, 0

nothing *rien,* I, 6; **It's nothing special.** *Ce n'est pas grand-chose.* II, 3; **Nothing special.** *Rien de spécial.* I, 6

novel *le roman,* I, 3

November *novembre,* I, 4; **in November** *en novembre,* I, 4

now *maintenant,* I, 2; **I can't right now.** *Je ne peux pas maintenant.* I, 8

obviously *évidemment,* II, 9; **That's obvious.** *Ça se voit.* II, 9

o'clock *... heure(s),* I, 2; **at... o'clock** *à... heure(s),* I, 2

October *octobre,* I, 4; **in October** *en octobre,* I, 4

of *de,* I, 0; **Of course.** *Bien sûr.* I, 3; II, 10; **Of course not.** *Bien sûr que non.* II, 10; **of it** *en,* I, 8; **of them** *en,* I, 8

off (free) *libre,* I, 2; **afternoon off** *l'après-midi* (m.) *libre,* I, 2

often *souvent,* I, 4

oh: Oh no! *Oh là là!* II, 5

OK. *D'accord.* I, 4; II, 1; *Entendu.* I, 6; **Is that OK with you?** *Tu es d'accord?* I, 7; **It was OK.** *C'était assez bien.* II, 6; **No, I'm OK.** *Non, ça va.* II, 2; **Well, OK.** *Bon, d'accord.* I, 8; **Yes, it was OK.** *Oui, ça a été.* I, 9

okra *les gombos* (m.), I, 8

old *vieux (vieille) (vieil),* II, 2; **How old are you?** *Tu as quel âge?* I, 1; **to be... years old** *avoir... ans,* II, 1; **When I was... years old,...** *Quand j'avais... ans,...,* II, 8

older *âgé(e),* I, 7

omelette *l'omelette* (f.), I, 5

on *sur,* II, 2; **Can I try on...?** *Je peux essayer...?* I, 10; **on foot** *à pied,* I, 12; **on Fridays** *le vendredi,* I, 2; **on Mondays** *le lundi,* I, 2; **on Saturdays** *le samedi,* I, 2; **on Sundays** *le dimanche,* I, 2; **on the right (left)** *sur la droite (gauche),* II, 2; **on Thursdays** *le jeudi,* I, 2; **on Tuesdays** *le mardi,* I, 2; **on Wednesdays** *le mercredi,* I, 2

once: once a week *une fois par semaine,* I, 4

one *un(e),* I, 0; **He/She already has one (of them).** *Il/Elle en a déjà un(e).* II, 3

one-way: a one-way ticket *un aller simple,* II, 6

onion *l'oignon* (m.), I, 5

open *ouvrir,* I, 0; II, 6 **Open your books to page...** *Ouvrez vos livres à la page...,* I, 0; **At what time do you open?** *A quelle heure est-ce que vous ouvrez?* II, 6

opinion *l'avis* (m.), I, 9; **In my opinion, you're mistaken.** *A mon avis, tu te trompes.* II, 9; **In your opinion, what do I do?** *A ton avis, qu'est-ce que je fais?* I, 9; **In your opinion, what should I do?** *A ton avis, qu'est-ce que je dois faire?* II, 10

or *ou,* I, 1

orange *orange* (adj.), I, 3; **orange** *l'orange* (f.), I, 8; **orange juice** *le jus d'orange,* I, 5

ordinary *banal(e),* II, 3; **That's**

ordinary. *C'est banal.* II, 3
our *notre/nos,* I, 7
out: go out *sortir,* II, 6; **Out of the question!** *Pas question!* I, 7; **out of style** *démodé(e),* I, 10
oyster *l'huître* (f.), II, 3

P

package *le paquet,* I, 8; **a package/box of** *un paquet de,* I, 8
page *la page,* I, 0
pain: a pain in the neck *pénible* (adj.), II, 1
pair: (a pair of) jeans *le jean,* I, 3; **(a pair of) shorts** *le short,* I, 3; **(a pair of) boots** *les bottes* (f.), II, 1; **(a pair of) gloves** *les gants* (m.), II, 1; **(a pair of) pants** *le pantalon,* I, 10; **(a pair of) sneakers** *les baskets* (f. pl.), II, 1
palm tree *le palmier,* II, 4
pancake: a very thin pancake *la crêpe,* I, 5
papaya *la papaye,* I, 8
paper *le papier,* I, 0; **sheets of paper** *les feuilles de papier* (f.), I, 3
pardon *le pardon,* II, 10; **Pardon me.** *Pardon,* I, 3
parent *le parent,* I, 7
park *le parc,* I, 6; II, 2
party *la boum,* I, 6; **to give a party** *faire une boum,* II, 10; **to go to a party** *aller à une boum,* I, 6
pass *passer,* I, 12; **Would you pass...?** *Vous pourriez (tu pourrais) me passer...?* II, 3; **You'll pass...** *Vous passez devant...?* I, 12
passport *le passeport,* I, 11; II, 1
pasta *les pâtes* (f. pl.), II, 7
pastry *la pâtisserie,* I, 12; **pastry shop** *la pâtisserie;* I, 12; II, 3
pâté *le pâté,* II, 3
peaceful *tranquille,* II, 8
peach *la pêche,* I, 8
pear *la poire,* I, 8
peas *les petits pois* (m.), I, 8
pen *le stylo,* I, 0
pencil *le crayon,* I, 3; **pencil case** *la trousse,* I, 3; **pencil sharpener** *le taille-crayon,* I, 3
perfect *parfait(e),* I, 10; **It's perfect.** *C'est parfait.* I, 10
permission *la permission,* II, 10; **to ask your parents' permission** *demander la permission à tes parents,* II, 10
phone *le téléphone,* I, 1; **Phone him/her/them.** *Téléphone-lui/-leur.* II, 10; **to talk on the phone** *parler au téléphone,* I, 1
photo *la photo,* I, 4; **photo frame** *le cadre,* II, 3
photography: to do photography *faire de la photo,* I, 4
physical education *l'éducation physique et sportive (EPS)* (f.), I, 2
physics *la physique,* I, 2
pick *choisir,* I, 10; **to pick up your room** *ranger ta chambre,* I, 7
picnic *le pique-nique,* I, 6; **to have a picnic** *faire un pique-nique,* I, 6; II, 6
picture *la photo,* I, 4; **to take pictures** *faire des photos,* I, 4; *faire de la photo,* I, 4
pie *la tarte,* I, 8; II, 3
piece *le morceau,* I, 8; **a piece of** *un morceau de,* I, 8
pineapple *l'ananas* (m.), I, 8; II, 4
pink *rose,* I, 3
pizza *la pizza,* I, 1
place *l'endroit* (m.), I, 12
plane *l'avion* (m.), I, 12; **by plane** *en avion,* I, 12; **plane ticket** *le billet d'avion,* I, 11
plans: I don't have any plans. *Je n'ai rien de prévu.* I, 11
plate *l'assiette* (f.), I, 5
platform *le quai,* II, 6; **From which platform...?** *De quel quai...?* II, 6; **From platform...** *Du quai...,* II, 6
play (theatrical) *la pièce,* I, 6; **to see a play** *voir une pièce,* I, 6
play *faire,* I, 4; *jouer,* I, 4; **How about playing...?** *Si on jouait...?* II, 8; **I don't play/do...** *Je ne fais pas de...,* I, 4; **I play...** *Je joue...,* I, 4; **to play (a game)** *jouer à...,* I, 4; **to play sports** *faire du sport,* I, 1; **What sports do you play?** *Qu'est-ce que tu fais comme sport?* I, 4; II, 1
playing: It's playing at... *Ça passe à...,* II, 11; **What films are playing?** *Qu'est-ce qu'on joue comme films?* II, 11; **Where is that playing?** *Ça passe où?* II, 11
please *s'il te/vous plaît,* I, 3; **Yes, please.** *Oui, s'il te/vous plaît.* I, 8
pleased *heureux (-euse),* I, 7; **Pleased to meet you.** *Très heureux (-euse).* I, 7
pleasure *le plaisir,* I, 8; **With pleasure.** *Avec plaisir.* I, 8; II, 10
plot *l'histoire* (f.), II, 11; **It has no plot.** *Il n'y a pas d'histoire.* II, 11; **It's full of plot twists.** *C'est plein de rebondissements.* II, 11
poetry *la poésie,* II, 11; **book of poetry** *le livre de poésie,* II, 11
point (in time) *le moment,* II, 9; **At that point,...** *A ce moment-là,...,* II, 9
pool *la piscine,* II, 2
poor *pauvre,* II, 5; **You poor thing!** *Pauvre vieux (vieille)!* II, 5
popular (pop), mainstream music *la pop,* II, 11
pork *le porc,* I, 8
possible *possible,* II, 9; **That's not possible.** *Ce n'est pas possible.* II, 9; **That's possible.** *C'est possible.* II, 9
post office *la poste,* I, 12; II, 2
poster *le poster,* I, 0; II, 2
potato *la pomme de terre,* I, 8
pottery *les poteries* (f. pl.), II, 8; **to make pottery** *faire de la poterie*
poultry *la volaille,* II, 3
pound *la livre,* I, 8; **a pound of** *une livre de,* I, 8
practice *répéter,* I, 9
prefer *préférer,* I, 1; **Do you prefer... or...?** *Tu aimes mieux... ou...?* I, 10; **I prefer...** *Je préfère...,* I, 1; II, 1; *J'aime mieux...,* I, 1; II, 1; **No, I prefer...** *Non, je préfère...,* II, 7; **What I prefer is...** *Ce que je préfère, c'est...,* II, 4
problem *le problème,* I, 9; **I have a (little) problem.** *J'ai un (petit) problème.* I, 9; I, 10; **No problem.** *Pas de problème.* II, 10
process: to be in the process of (doing something) *être en train de,* II, 9
pullover (sweater) *le pull-over,* I, 3
purple *violet(te),* I, 3
purse *le sac à main,* II, 3
push-ups *les pompes* (f.); **to do push-ups** *faire des pompes,* II, 7
put *mettre,* I, 10; **put on (clothing)** *mettre,* I, 10

quarter *le quart,* I, 6; **quarter past** *et quart,* I, 6; **quarter to** *moins le quart,* I, 6

question *la question,* I, 7; **Out of the question!** *Pas question!* I, 7
quiche *la quiche,* I, 5
quiz *l'interro* (f.), I, 9

raccoon *le raton laveur,* II, 12
radio *la radio,* I, 3
raincoat *l'imperméable* (m.), II, 1
rainforest: tropical rainforest *la forêt tropicale,* II, 4
raining: It's raining. *Il pleut.* I, 4
raise *lever,* I, 0; **Raise your hand!** *Levez la main!* I, 0
rap *le rap,* II, 11
rarely *rarement,* I, 4
rather *plutôt,* II, 9; **No, I'd rather…** *Non, je préfère…,* II, 1
read *lire,* I, 1
read *lu* (pp. of lire), I, 9
ready: to get ready *faire les préparatifs,* II, 10
really *vraiment,* I, 11; **I (really) like…** *Moi, j'aime (bien)…,* I, 1; **I really liked it.** *Ça m'a beaucoup plu.* II, 6; **I'd really like…** *Je voudrais bien…,* I, 11; **I'd really like to.** *Je veux bien.* I, 6; **No, not really.** *Non, pas vraiment.* I, 11; **Really?** *C'est vrai? (Vraiment?),* II, 2; **Was it really so different?** *C'était tellement différent?* II, 8; **Your… is really great.** *Il (Elle) est vraiment bien, ton (ta)…* II, 2; **really** *vachement,* II, 9; **really, ultra-** *super,* II, 9
receive *recevoir,* II, 5; **to receive one's report card** *recevoir le bulletin trimestriel,* II, 5
recommend *recommander,* II, 11; **I recommend it.** *Je te le (la) recommande.* II, 11
record store *le disquaire,* I, 12; **at the record store** *chez le disquaire,* I, 12
recreation center *la Maison des jeunes et de la culture (MJC),* I, 6
red *rouge,* I, 3; **red hair** *les cheveux roux,* II, 1; **red-headed** *roux (rousse),* I, 7
reggae music *le reggae,* II, 11
rehearse *répéter,* I, 9
relative *le parent,* I, 7
relaxing *relaxant(e),* II, 8
remember: Remember to take… *Pense à prendre…,* II, 1
repeat *répéter,* I, 0; **Repeat!** *Répétez!* I, 0
report card *le bulletin trimestriel,* II, 5; **to receive one's report card** *recevoir le bulletin trimestriel,* II, 5
respect *respecter,* II, 12; **to respect nature** *respecter la nature,* II, 12
responsibility *la responsabilité,* II, 8; **to have responsibilities** *avoir des responsabilités,* II, 8
restaurant *le restaurant,* I, 6
restroom *les toilettes* (f.) *(les W.-C.)* (m.), II, 2
retro (style) *rétro* (inv.), I, 10
return *retourner,* II, 6; **to return something** *rendre,* I, 12; **to return tests** *rendre les interros,* II, 5
rice *le riz,* I, 8
ride *le tour,* II, 6; **to go horseback riding** *faire de l'équitation,* I, 1; **to take a ride on the ferris wheel** *faire un tour sur la grande roue,* II, 6; **to take a ride on the roller coaster** *faire un tour sur les montagnes russes,* II, 6
ridiculous: That's ridiculous! *N'importe quoi!* II, 6
riding: to go horseback riding *faire de l'équitation,* I, 1
right (direction) *la droite,* I, 12; **on the right** *sur la droite,* II, 2; **to the right** *à droite,* I, 12; **to the right of** *à droite de,* II, 2
right: right away *tout de suite,* I, 6; **I'll go right away.** *J'y vais tout de suite.* I, 8; **I can't right now.** *Je ne peux pas maintenant.* I, 8; **It's right there on the…** *C'est tout de suite à…,* I, 12; **Yeah, right!** *Mon œil!* II, 6; **Yes, right away.** *Oui, tout de suite.* I, 5; **You're right…** *Tu as raison…,* II, 3
rip *déchirer,* II, 5
rock (music) *le rock,* II, 11
roller coaster *les montagnes russes* (f. pl.), II, 6
romance novel *le roman d'amour,* II, 11
romantic movie *le film d'amour,* II, 11
room (of a house) *la pièce,* II, 2
room (bedroom) *la chambre,* I, 7; **to pick up your room** *ranger ta chambre,* I, 7
round-trip ticket *l'aller-retour* (m.), II, 6
rug *le tapis,* II, 2
ruler *la règle,* I, 3
runny: I've got a runny nose. *J'ai le nez qui coule.* II, 7

S

sailing *la voile,* I, 11; **to go sailing** *faire de la voile,* I, 11; *faire du bateau,* I, 11
salad *la salade,* I, 8; II, 3
salami *le saucisson,* I, 5
salt *le sel,* II, 7
sand *le sable,* II, 4
sandals *les sandales* (f.), I, 10
sandwich *le sandwich,* I, 5; **cheese sandwich** *le sandwich au fromage,* I, 5; **ham sandwich** *le sandwich au jambon,* I, 5; **salami sandwich** *le sandwich au saucisson,* I, 5; **toasted ham and cheese sandwich** *le croque-monsieur,* I, 5
Saturday *samedi,* I, 2; **on Saturdays** *le samedi,* I, 2
scared: I'm scared (of)… *J'ai peur (de la, du, des)…,* II, 12
scarf (for outdoor wear) *l'écharpe* (f.), I, 10; **(dressy)** *le foulard,* II, 3
school *l'école* (f.), I, 1; **high school** *le lycée,* II, 2
science fiction *la science-fiction,* II, 11; **science-fiction novel** *le roman de science-fiction,* II, 11; **science-fiction movie** *le film de science-fiction,* II, 11
scuba dive *faire de la plongée,* I, 11; *faire de la plongée sous-marine,* II, 4
sea *la mer,* II, 4
seafood *les fruits de mer* (m. pl.), II, 3
second *la seconde,* I, 9; **One second, please.** *Une seconde, s'il vous plaît.* I, 9
see *voir,* I, 6, **…you see.** *…tu vois.* II, 9; **See you later (the same day)!** *À tout à l'heure!* I, 1; **See you soon.** *À bientôt.* I, 1; **See you tomorrow.** *À demain.* I, 1; **to go see a game** *aller voir un match,* I, 6; **to go see a movie** *aller voir un film,* I, 6; **to see a play** *voir une pièce,* I, 6; **What is there to see…?** *Qu'est-ce qu'il y a à voir…?* II, 12; **You'll see that…** *Tu vas voir que…,* II, 8
seem *avoir l'air,* II, 9; **You don't look/seem too well.** *Tu n'as pas l'air en forme.* II, 7; **She seemed…** *Elle avait l'air…,* II, 12
seen *vu* (pp. of voir), I, 9
sell *vendre,* I, 9
send *envoyer,* I, 12; **to send letters** *envoyer des lettres,* I, 12; **to send the invitations** *envoyer les invitations,* II, 10

sensational *sensass* (inv.), II, 6
September *septembre,* I, 4; **in September** *en septembre,* I, 4
serious *grave,* II, 5; **It's not serious.** *C'est pas grave.* II, 5
service *le service,* I, 3; **At your service. (You're welcome.)** *A votre service.* I, 3
seventeen *dix-sept,* I, 1
seventy *soixante-dix,* I, 3
shall: Shall we go to the café? *On va au café?* I, 5
shape *la condition,* II, 7; **to get into shape** *se mettre en condition,* II, 7
sheet of paper *la feuille de papier,* I, 0
shelves *les étagères* (f.), II, 2
shirt (men's) *la chemise,* I, 10; **shirt (women's)** *le chemisier,* I, 10
shoes *les chaussures* (f.), I, 10
shop: to window-shop *faire les vitrines,* I, 6
shopping: Can you do the shopping? *Tu peux aller faire les courses?* I, 8; **to go shopping** *faire les courses,* I, 8; *faire les magasins,* I, 1
short (height) *petit(e),* I, 7; **(length)** *court(e),* I, 10; **short hair** *les cheveux courts,* II, 1
shorts: (a pair of) shorts *le short,* I, 3; II, 1
should: Everyone should... *On doit...,* II, 7; **I should have...** *J'aurais dû...,* II, 10; **In your opinion, what should I do?** *A ton avis, qu'est-ce que je dois faire?* II, 10; **What do you think I should do?** *Qu'est-ce que tu me conseilles?* II, 10; **What should I...?** *Qu'est-ce que je dois...?* II, 1; **What should we do?** *Qu'est-ce qu'on fait?* II, 1; **You should...** *Tu devrais...,* I, 9; II, 7; **You should have...** *Tu aurais dû...,* II, 10; **You should talk to him/her/them.** *Tu devrais lui/leur parler.* I, 9
shouldn't: You shouldn't... *Tu ne devrais pas...,* II, 7
show *montrer* (v.), I, 9; **sound and light show** *un spectacle son et lumière,* II, 6
showing:... is showing/playing. *On joue...,* II, 11
shrimp *la crevette,* II, 3
shy *timide,* I, 7
sick *malade,* II, 7; **I'm sick to my stomach.** *J'ai mal au cœur.* II, 7; **I'm sick.** *Je suis malade.* II, 7
silly: to do silly things *faire des bêtises,* II, 8
simple *simple,* II, 8
sing *chanter,* I, 9
singer *le chanteur (la chanteuse),* II, 11
sir *monsieur (M.),* I, 1
sister *la sœur,* I, 7
sit-ups *les abdominaux* (m.), II, 7; **to do sit-ups** *faire des abdominaux,* II, 7
Sit down! *Asseyez-vous!* I, 0
sixty *soixante,* I, 3
size *la taille,* I, 10
skate: to ice-skate *faire du patin à glace,* I, 4; **to in-line skate** *faire du roller en ligne,* I, 4
ski *faire du ski,* I, 4; **to water-ski** *faire du ski nautique,* I, 4; **ski jacket** *l'anorak* (m.), II, 1
skiing *le ski,* I, 1; **How about skiing?** *On fait du ski?* I, 5
skip *sauter,* II, 7; **Don't skip...** *Ne saute pas...,* II, 7; **skip a meal** *sauter un repas,* II, 7
skirt *la jupe,* I, 10
skunk *la mouffette,* II, 12
sleep *dormir,* I, 1; **I didn't sleep well.** *J'ai mal dormi.* II, 7
sleeping bag *le sac de couchage,* II, 12
slender *mince,* I, 7
slice *la tranche,* I, 8; **a slice of** *une tranche de,* I, 8
small, short *petit(e),* I, 10; II, 1
smaller *moins grand(e),* II, 4; **smaller than...** *moins grand(e) que...,* II, 4
smart *intelligent(e),* I, 7; II, 1
smoking: Avoid smoking. *Evitez de fumer.* II, 7
snack: afternoon snack *le goûter,* I, 8; **snacking between meals** *grignoter entre les repas,* II, 7; **party snacks** *les amuse-gueule* (m.), II, 10
snails *les escargots* (m.), I, 1; II, 3
sneakers *les baskets* (f. pl.), I, 3; II, 1
sneeze *éternuer,* II, 7; **I'm sneezing a lot.** *J'éternue beaucoup.* II, 7
snorkel *faire de la plongée avec un tuba,* II, 4
snowing: It's snowing. *Il neige.* I, 4; **to go snow-shoeing** *faire une randonnée en raquettes,* II, 12
So... *Alors...,* II, 9; **so-so** *comme ci comme ça,* I, 1; II, 6; **not so great** *pas terrible,* I, 5
soccer *le football,* I, 1; **to play soccer** *jouer au foot(ball),* I, 4
socks *les chaussettes* (f.), I, 10
some *du, de la, de l', des,* I, 8; **Yes, I'd like some.** *Oui j'en veux bien.* I, 8; **Some more...?** *Encore...?* II, 3; **some (of it)** *en,* I, 8; II, 3
something *quelque chose,* II, 10; **I have something to do.** *J'ai quelque chose à faire.* II, 10; **I'm looking for something for...** *Je cherche quelque chose pour...,* I, 10
sometimes *quelquefois,* I, 4
son *le fils,* I, 7
song *la chanson,* II, 11
soon *bientôt,* I, 1; **See you soon.** *A bientôt.* I, 1
Sorry. *Je regrette.* I, 3; *Désolé(e).* I, 5; II, 10; **I'm sorry, but I don't have time.** *Je regrette, mais je n'ai pas le temps.* I, 8; **Sorry, but I can't.** *Désolé(e), mais je ne peux pas.* I, 4; **Sorry, I'm busy.** *Désolé(e), je suis occupé(e).* I, 6
sort of *assez,* II, 9
sound *le son,* II, 6; **Does... sound good to you?** *Ça te dit de...?* II, 1; **sound and light show** *le spectacle son et lumière,* II, 6
south *le sud,* II, 4; **in the south** *dans le sud,* II, 4; **It's to the south of...** *C'est au sud de...,* II, 12
Spanish (language) *l'espagnol* (m.), I, 2
speak *parler,* I, 9; **Could I speak to...?** *(Est-ce que) je peux parler à...?* I, 9
special *spécial(e),* I, 6; **It's nothing special.** *Ce n'est pas grand-chose.* II, 3; **Nothing special.** *Rien de spécial.* I, 6
sports *le sport,* I, 1; **to play sports** *faire du sport,* I, 1; **What sports do you play?** *Qu'est-ce que tu fais comme sport?* I, 4; II, 1
sprain *se fouler,* II, 7; **to sprain one's ankle** *se fouler la cheville,* II, 7
spring *le printemps,* I, 4; **in the spring** *au printemps,* I, 4
squirrel *l'écureuil* (m.), II, 12
stadium *le stade,* I, 6
stamp *le timbre,* I, 12
Stand up! *Levez-vous!* I, 0
start *commencer,* I, 9; **At what time does it start?** *Ça commence à quelle heure?* II, 11
station (train) *la gare,* II, 2
stationery store *la papeterie,* I, 12
stay *rester,* II, 6
steak *le bifteck,* II, 3; **steak and French fries** *le steak-frites,* I, 5
step *la marche,* II, 5; **to miss a step** *rater une marche,* II, 5
stereo *la chaîne stéréo,* II, 2
stomach *le ventre,* II, 7; **I'm sick to my stomach.** *J'ai mal au cœur.* II, 7
stop: at the metro stop... *au métro...,* I, 6

store *le magasin,* I, 1
story *l'histoire* (f.), II, 11; **It's a great story.** *C'est une belle histoire.* II, 11; **It's the story of...** *C'est l'histoire de...*, II, 11; **What's the story?** *Qu'est-ce que ça raconte?* II, 11
straight ahead *tout droit,* I, 12; **You go straight ahead until you get to...** *Vous allez tout droit jusqu'à...*, I, 12; **Go (Keep going) straight ahead.** *Allez (Continuez) tout droit.* II, 2
strawberry *la fraise,* I, 8; **water with strawberry syrup** *le sirop de fraise (à l'eau),* I, 5
street *la rue,* I, 12; **You take... Street, then... Street.** *Prenez la rue..., puis traversez la rue...*, I, 12
stressful *stressant(e),* II, 8
strict *strict(e),* II, 7; **to follow a diet that's too strict** *suivre un régime trop strict,* II, 7
strong *fort(e),* I, 7; II, 1; **It's not my strong point.** *Ce n'est pas mon fort.* II, 5
student *l'élève* (m./f.), I, 2
study *étudier,* I, 1
study hall *l'étude* (f.), I, 2
stupid *bête,* II, 1
style *la mode,* I, 10; *le style,* II, 3; **in style** *à la mode,* I, 10; **That's not his/her style.** *Ce n'est pas son style.* II, 3
subway *le métro,* I, 12; **by subway** *en métro,* I, 12
sugar *le sucre,* I, 8; **sugar cane fields** *les champs* (m.) *de canne à sucre,* II, 4
suit jacket, blazer *la veste,* I, 10
suit: Does it suit me? *Ça me va?* I, 10; **It suits you really well.** *Il/Elle te/vous va très bien.* I, 10
suitcase *la valise,* I, 11
sulk *faire la tête,* II, 9
summer *l'été* (m.), I, 4; **in the summer** *en été,* I, 4
summer camp *la colonie de vacances,* I, 11; **to/at a summer camp** *en colonie de vacances,* I, 11
Sunday *dimanche,* I, 4; **on Sundays** *le dimanche,* I, 2
sunglasses *les lunettes de soleil* (f. pl.), I, 10
super *super,* I, 2
supermarket *le supermarché,* I, 8
sure: Oh, I'm not sure. *Euh... J'hésite.* I, 10
surprised *étonné(e),* II, 9
suspenseful: It's suspenseful. *Il y a du suspense.* II, 11
sweater *le cardigan,* I, 10; *le pull,* I, 10
sweatshirt *le sweat(-shirt),* II, 1
swim *nager,* I, 1; *faire de la natation,* I, 4; **to go swimming** *se baigner,* II, 4
swimming pool *la piscine,* I, 6
syrup: water with strawberry syrup *le sirop de fraise à l'eau,* I, 5

T

table *la table,* I, 7; **to clear the table** *débarrasser la table,* I, 7
tacky *moche,* I, 10; **I think it's (they're) really tacky.** *Je le/la/les trouve moche(s).* I, 10
take or have (food or drink) *prendre,* I, 5; **Are you going to take it/them?** *Vous le/la/les prenez?* I, 10; **Are you taking...?** *Tu prends...?* I, 11; **Have you decided to take...?** *Vous avez décidé de prendre...?* I, 10; **I'll take... (of them).** *Je vais en prendre...*, II, 3; **I'll take it/them.** *Je le/la/les prends.* I, 10; **Remember to take...** *Pense à prendre...*, II, 1; **Take...** *Prends... ; Prenez...*, II, 2; **to take a test** *passer un examen,* I, 9; **to take pictures** *faire des photos,* I, 4; **We can take...** *On peut prendre...*, I, 12; **You take... Street, then... cross Street.** *Prenez la rue..., puis traversez la rue...*, I, 12
take out: Take out a sheet of paper. *Prenez une feuille de papier.* I, 0; **to take out the trash** *sortir la poubelle,* I, 7
taken *pris* (pp. of prendre), I, 9
talk *parler,* I, 1; **Can I talk to you?** *Je peux te parler?* I, 9; II, 10; **Talk to him/her/them.** *Parle-lui/-leur.* II, 10; **to talk on the phone** *parler au téléphone,* I, 1; **We talked.** *Nous avons parlé.* I, 9
tall *grand(e),* I, 7; II, 1
tart *la tarte,* II, 3; **apple tart** *la tarte aux pommes,* II, 3
taste *déguster,* II, 4
taxi *le taxi,* I, 12; **by taxi** *en taxi,* I, 12
teacher *le professeur,* I, 0
tease *taquiner,* II, 8
teeth *les dents* (f.), II, 7
telephone *le téléphone,* I, 0
television *la télévision,* I, 0
tell *dire,* I, 9; *raconter,* II, 5; **Can you tell her/ him that I called?** *Vous pouvez lui dire que j'ai téléphoné?* I, 9; **Tell him/her/them that...** *Dis-lui/-leur que...*, II, 10; **Tell me!** *Raconte!* II, 5; **to tell (someone) that...** *dire à (quelqu'un) que...*, II, 10
tennis *le tennis,* I, 4; **to play tennis** *jouer au tennis,* I, 4
tent *la tente,* II, 12
terrible *horrible,* I, 10; **I had a terrible day!** *J'ai passé une journée horrible!* II, 5
Terrific! *Bravo!* II, 5
test *l'examen* (m.), I, 1; **to take a test** *passer un examen,* I, 9
than *que,* II, 4; **bigger than...** *plus grand(e) que...*, II, 4; **It's better than...** *C'est meilleur que...*, II, 7; **smaller than...** *moins grand(e) que...*, II, 4
Thank you. *Merci.* I, 3, II, 2; **No, thank you.** *Non, merci.* I, 8; **Yes, thank you.** *Oui, s'il vous (te) plaît.* I, 8; **No thank you, I've had enough.** *Merci, ça va.* II, 3; **No thanks. I'm not hungry anymore.** *Non, merci. Je n'ai plus faim.* I, 8
that *ce, cet, cette,* I, 3; **That is,...** *C'est-à-dire que...*, II, 9; **This/That is...** *Ça, c'est...*, I, 12
theater *le théâtre,* I, 6; II, 2
their *leur/leurs,* I, 7
them *les,* I, 9, **to them** *leur,* I, 9
then *ensuite,* I, 9; *puis,* II, 1; **Then I called...** *Ensuite, j'ai téléphoné à...*, I, 9; II, 1; **Then,...** *Puis,...* , II, 1
there *-là (noun suffix),* I, 3; *y,* I, 12; **Here (There) is...** *Là, c'est...*, II, 2; **Is... there, please?** *(Est-ce que)... est là, s'il vous plaît?* I, 9; **There is/are...** *Il y a...*, I, 5; II, 2; **There's...** *Voilà...*, I, 7; **You're almost there!** *Tu y es presque!* II, 7; **What is there to drink?** *Qu'est-ce qu'il y a à boire?* I, 5
Therefore,... *Donc,...*, II, 9
these *ces,* I, 3; **These/Those are...** *Ce sont...*, I, 7
thing *la chose,* I, 5; *le truc,* I, 5; **It's not my thing.** *Ce n'est pas mon truc.* II, 7; **I have lots of things to do.** *J'ai des tas de choses à faire.* I, 5; **I have some things to do.** *J'ai des trucs à faire.* I, 5
think *penser,* I, 11; **Do you think so?** *Tu trouves?* II, 2; **I don't think so.** *Je ne crois pas.* II, 9; **I think it's/they're...** *Je le/la/les trouve...*, I, 10; **I think that...** *Je crois que...*, II, 9; **I've thought of everything.** *J'ai pensé à tout.* I, 11; **What do you think about going...?** *Ça te dit d'aller...?* II, 4; **What do**

you think I should do? *Qu'est-ce que tu me conseilles?* II, 10; **What do you think of...?** *Comment tu trouves...?* I, 2; **What do you think of that/it?** *Comment tu trouves ça?* I, 2
thirst *la soif,* II, 2; **I'm dying of thirst!** *Je meurs de soif!* II, 2
thirsty: to be thirsty *avoir soif,* I, 5; **Aren't you thirsty?** *Vous n'avez pas (Tu n'as pas) soif?* II, 2; **I'm not hungry/thirsty anymore.** *Je n'ai plus faim/soif.* II, 3
this *ce, cet, cette,* I, 3; **This is...** *C'est...,* I, 7; **This is...** *Voici...,* I, 7; **This/That is...** *Ça, c'est...,* I, 12
those *ces,* I, 3; **These (those) are...** *Ce sont...,* I, 7
thought *pensé* (pp. of penser), I, 11; **I've thought of everything.** *J'ai pensé à tout.* I, 11
throat *la gorge,* II, 7
throw *jeter,* II, 12; **to throw away (to take with you) your trash** *jeter (remporter) les déchets,* II, 12
Thursday *jeudi,* I, 2; **on Thursdays** *le jeudi,* I, 2
ticket *le billet,* I, 11; *le ticket,* II, 6; **plane ticket** *le billet d'avion,* I, 11; II, 1; **Three (entrance) tickets, please.** *Trois tickets, s'il vous plaît.* II, 6; **train ticket** *le billet de train,* I, 11
tie *la cravate,* I, 10
tight *serré(e),* I, 10
time *l'heure* (f.), I, 6; *le temps,* I, 4; II, 10; **a waste of time** *zéro,* I, 2; **at the time of** *à l'heure de,* I, 1; **At what time?** *A quelle heure?* I, 6; **At what time do you have...?** *Tu as... à quelle heure?* I, 2; **from time to time** *de temps en temps,* I, 4; **I don't have time.** *Je n'ai pas le temps.* II, 10; **I'm sorry, but I don't have time.** *Je regrette, mais je n'ai pas le temps.* I, 8; *Je suis désolé(e), mais je n'ai pas le temps.* I, 12; **At what time does it start?** *Ça commence à quelle heure?* II, 11; **At what time does the train (the bus) for... leave?** *A quelle heure est-ce que le train (le car) pour... part?* II, 6; **What time is it?** *Quelle heure est-il?* I, 6
tired *fatigué(e),* II, 2; **(You're) not too tired?** *Pas trop fatigué(e)?* II, 2; **I'm tired.** *Je suis fatigué(e).* II, 12
tiring *fatigant(e),* II, 2; **It was tiring!** *C'était fatigant!* II, 2
to *à la, à l', au, aux,* I, 6; **(a city or place)** *à,* I, 11; **(before a feminine country)** *en,* I, 11; **(before a masculine country/noun)** *au,* I, 11; **(before a plural country/noun)** *aux,* I, 11; **to him/her** *lui,* I, 9; **to them** *leur,* I, 9; **five to** *moins cinq,* I, 6
today *aujourd'hui,* I, 2
toilet *les toilettes* (f.) *(les W.-C.)* (m.), II, 2
tomato *la tomate,* I, 8
tomorrow *demain,* I, 2; **See you tomorrow.** *A demain.* I, 1
tonight *ce soir,* I, 7; **Not tonight.** *Pas ce soir.* I, 7
too *aussi,* I, 2; **Me too.** *Moi aussi.* I, 2
too *trop,* I, 10; **It's/They're too...** *Il/Elle est (Ils/Elles sont) trop...,* I, 10; **No it's too expensive.** *Non c'est trop cher.* I, 10; II, 3; **No, not too much.** *Non, pas trop.* I, 2; **Not too much.** *Pas tellement.* I, 4; **too violent** *trop violent,* II, 11
tough: Tough luck! *C'est pas de chance, ça!* II, 5
tour *le circuit,* II, 6; *la visite,* II, 6; **to take a guided tour** *faire une visite guidée,* II, 6; **to tour some châteaux** *faire un circuit des châteaux,* II, 6
tourist information office *l'office de tourisme* (m.), II, 2
tower *la tour,* II, 6; **to go up in a tower** *monter dans une tour,* II, 6
track and field *l'athlétisme* (m.), I, 4; **to do track and field** *faire de l'athlétisme,* I, 4
trail *le sentier,* II, 12; **to follow the marked trails** *suivre les sentiers balisés,* II, 12
train *le train,* I, 12; **by train** *en train,* I, 12; **train station** *la gare,* II, 2; **train ticket** *le billet de train,* I, 11
train for (a sport) *s'entraîner à...,* II, 7
trash *les déchets* (m. pl.), II, 12; **to take out the trash** *sortir la poubelle,* I, 7
trash can *la poubelle,* I, 7
travel *voyager,* I, 1
trip *la route,* II, 3; *le voyage,* II, 2; **Did you have a good trip?** *Vous avez (Tu as) fait bon voyage?* II, 2; **Have a good (car) trip!** *Bonne route!* II, 3; **Have a good trip! (by plane, ship)** *Bon voyage!* II, 3
tropical rainforest *la forêt tropicale,* II, 4
true *vrai(e),* I, 2
try *essayer* (v.), I, 10; *l'effort* (m.), II, 7; **Can I try on...?** *Je peux essayer...?* I, 10; **Can I try it (them) on ?** *Je peux l'(les) essayer?* I, 10; **One more try!** *Encore un effort!* II, 7
T-shirt *le tee-shirt,* I, 3; II, 1
Tuesday *mardi,* I, 2; **on Tuesdays** *le mardi,* I, 2
turn *tourner,* I, 12; **Then, turn left on...** *Puis, tournez à gauche dans/sur...,* II, 2; **You turn...** *Vous tournez...,* I, 12
TV *la télé(vision),* I, 1; **to watch TV** *regarder la télé(vision),* I, 1
twelve *douze,* I, 1
twist *le rebondissement,* II, 11; **It's full of plot twists.** *C'est plein de rebondissements.* II, 11

umbrella *le parapluie,* I, 11
unbelievable *incroyable,* II, 5
uncle *l'oncle* (m.), I, 7
uncomfortable *mal à l'aise,* II, 9
uncooked *cru(e),* I, 5
understand *comprendre,* II, 5
Unfortunately,... *Malheureusement, ...,* II, 9
unique *original(e),* II, 3; **That's unique.** *C'est original.* II, 3
until *jusqu'à,* I, 12; **You go straight ahead until you get to...** *Vous allez tout droit jusqu'à...,* I, 12
up: go up *monter,* II, 6
used: You'll get used to it. *Tu vas t'y faire.* II, 8
useless *nul(le),* I, 2
usually *d'habitude,* I, 4

vacation *les vacances* (f. pl.), I, 1; **Have a good vacation!** *Bonnes vacances!* I, 11; **on vacation** *en vacances,* I, 4
vacuum *passer l'aspirateur,* I, 7
vase *le vase,* II, 3
VCR (videocassette recorder) *le magnétoscope,* I, 0
vegetables *les légumes* (m.), I, 8; II, 7
very *très,* I, 1; **very cool** *chouette,* II, 2; **Yes, very much.** *Oui, beaucoup.* I, 2; **very well** *très bien,* I, 1
video *la vidéo,* I, 4; **to make**

videos *faire de la vidéo,* I, 4; **to play video games** *jouer à des jeux vidéo,* I, 4
videotape *la vidéocassette,* I, 3
village *le village,* II, 4; **fishing village** *le village de pêcheurs,* II, 4
violent *violent(e),* II, 11
visit (a place) *visiter,* I, 9; II, 6; **How about visiting...?** *Si on visitait...?* II, 8
volcano *le volcan,* II, 4
volleyball *le volley(-ball),* I, 4; **to play volleyball** *jouer au volley (-ball),* I, 4

wait for *attendre,* I, 9
Waiter! *Monsieur!* I, 5
Waitress! *Madame!* I, 5, *Mademoiselle!* I, 5
walk *se promener,* II, 4; **to go for a walk** *faire une promenade,* I, 6; **to walk the dog** *promener le chien,* I, 7
wallet *le portefeuille,* I, 3; II, 3
want *vouloir,* I, 6; **Do you want...?** *Tu veux...?* I, 6; II, 3; *Vous voulez...?* I, 8; II, 3; **I don't want any more.** *Je n'en veux plus.* I, 8; **No, I don't want to.** *Non, je ne veux pas.* II, 8; **Yes, if you want to.** *Oui, si tu veux.* I, 7
wardrobe (armoire) *l'armoire* (f.), II, 2
wash *laver,* I, 7; **to wash oneself** *se laver,* II, 4; **to wash the car** *laver la voiture,* I, 7
waste: a waste of time *zéro,* I, 2
watch *la montre,* I, 3; **to watch a game (on TV)** *regarder un match,* I, 6; **to watch TV** *regarder la télé(vision),* I, 1
water *l'eau* (f.), I, 5; **mineral water** *l'eau minérale,* I, 5; **water with strawberry syrup** *le sirop de fraise (à l'eau),* I, 5
water-skiing *le ski nautique,* I, 4; **to go water-skiing** *faire du ski nautique,* I, 4
waterfall *une chute d'eau,* II, 4
way: No way! *Pas question!* II, 1; *Pas possible!* II, 6
wear *mettre, porter,* I, 10; **I don't know what to wear for...** *Je ne sais pas quoi mettre pour...,* I, 10; **Wear...** *Mets...,* I, 10; **What shall I wear?** *Qu'est-ce que je mets?* I, 10; **Why don't you wear...?** *Pourquoi est-ce que tu ne mets pas...?* I, 10
weather *le temps,* I, 4; **What's the weather like?** *Quel temps fait-il?* I, 4
Wednesday *mercredi,* I, 2; **on Wednesdays** *le mercredi,* I, 2
week *la semaine,* I, 4; **once a week** *une fois par semaine,* I, 4
weekend *le week-end,* I, 4; **Did you have a good weekend?** *Tu as passé un bon week-end?* I, 9; **on weekends** *le week-end,* I, 4; **this weekend** *ce week-end,* I, 6; **What a (bad) weekend!** *Quel week-end!* II, 5
weight : to lift weights *faire de la musculation,* II, 7
welcome: You're welcome. (At your service.) *A votre service.* I, 3; **Welcome to my home (our home)** *Bienvenue chez moi (chez nous).* II, 2
well *bien,* I, 1; **Did it go well?** *Ça s'est bien passé?* I, 11; **Get well soon!** *Bon rétablissement!* II, 3; **I don't feel well.** *Je ne me sens pas bien.* II, 7; **It went really well!** *Ça s'est très bien passé!* II, 5; **Very well.** *Très bien.* I, 1; **Well done!** *Chapeau!* II, 5; **You don't look well.** *Tu n'as pas l'air en forme.* II, 7; **You would do well to...** *Tu ferais bien de...,* II, 7
went *allé(e)* (pp. of aller), I, 9; **Afterwards, I went out.** *Après, je suis sorti(e).* I, 9; **I went...** *Je suis allé(e)...,* I, 9
west *l'ouest* (m.), II, 4; **in the west** *dans l'ouest,* II, 4; **It's to the west of...** *C'est à l'ouest de...,* II, 12
western (film) *le western,* II, 11
what *comment,* I, 0; *ce qui* (subj.), II, 4; *ce que* (obj.), II, 4; **What bores me is...** *Ce qui m'ennuie, c'est (de)...,* II, 4; **What do you think of...?** *Comment tu trouves...?* I, 2; **What do you think of that/it?** *Comment tu trouves ça?* I, 2; **What I don't like is...** *Ce que je n'aime pas, c'est...,* II, 4; **What I like is...** *Ce qui me plaît, c'est (de)...,* II, 4; **What is your name?** *Tu t'appelles comment?* I, 0; **What's his/her name?** *Il/Elle s'appelle comment?* I, 1; **What's it like?** *C'est comment?* II, 4
what *qu'est-ce que,* I, 1; **What are you going to do...?** *Qu'est-ce que tu vas faire...?* I, 6; **What can we do?** *Qu'est-ce qu'on peut faire?* II, 4; **What do you do to have fun?** *Qu'est-ce que tu fais pour t'amuser?* I, 4; **What do you have to drink?** *Qu'est-ce que vous avez comme boissons?* I, 5; **What do you need for...?** *Qu'est-ce qu'il te/vous faut pour...?* I, 3; **What happened?** *Qu'est-ce qui s'est passé?* I, 9; **What is there...?** *Qu'est-ce qu'il y a...?* II, 4; **What is there to drink?** *Qu'est-ce qu'il y a à boire?* I, 5; **What kind of... do you have?** *Qu'est-ce que vous avez comme...?* I, 5;
what *quoi,* I, 2; **I don't know what to do.** *Je ne sais pas quoi faire.* II, 10; **I don't know what to wear for...** *Je ne sais pas quoi mettre pour...,* I, 10; **What are you going to do...?** *Tu vas faire quoi...?* I, 6; **What do you have...?** *Tu as quoi...?* I, 2; **What do you need?** *De quoi est-ce que tu as besoin?* I, 5
when *quand,* I, 6; **When?** *Quand (ça)?* I, 6
where *où,* I, 6; **Where?** *Où (ça)?* I, 6; **Where are you going to go...?** *Où est-ce que tu vas aller...?* I, 11; **Where did you go?** *Tu es allé(e) où?* I, 9; **Where is..., please?** *Où est..., s'il vous plaît?* II, 2
which *quel(le),* II, 6; **From which platform...?** *De quel quai...?* II, 6
white *blanc(he),* I, 3
who *qui,* I, 9; **Who's calling?** *Qui est à l'appareil?* I, 9
whom *qui,* I, 6; **With whom?** *Avec qui?* I, 6
why *pourquoi,* I, 6; **Why don't you...?** *Pourquoi tu ne... pas?* I, 9; II, 7; **Why not?** *Pourquoi pas?* I, 6
wife *la femme,* I, 7
win *gagner,* I, 9
window *la fenêtre,* I, 0; **to window-shop** *faire les vitrines,* I, 6
windsurfing *la planche à voile,* I, 11; **to windsurf** *faire de la planche à voile,* I, 11; II, 4
winter *l'hiver* (m.), I, 4; **in the winter** *en hiver,* I, 4
wiped out *raplapla,* II, 7; **I'm wiped out.** *Je suis tout(e) raplapla.* II, 7
wishes *les vœux* (m. pl.), II, 3; **Best wishes!** *Meilleurs vœux!* II, 3
with *avec,* I, 6; **with me** *avec moi,* I, 6; **With whom?** *Avec qui?* I, 6
withdraw *retirer,* I, 12; **to withdraw money** *retirer de l'argent,* I, 12

without *sans,* I, 11; **You can't leave without...** *Tu ne peux pas partir sans...,* I, 11
wolf *le loup,* II, 12
wonder *se demander,* II, 9; **I wonder...** *Je me demande...,* II, 9
work *travailler,* I, 9
worried *inquiet (inquiète),* II, 9
worries *les soucis* (m.), II, 8; **to have worries** *avoir des soucis,* II, 8
worry: Don't worry! *Ne t'en fais pas!* I, 9; *T'en fais pas.* II, 5
worthless *nul(le),* II, 8; **It's worthless.** *C'est du n'importe quoi.* II, 11
would: What would you do? *Qu'est-ce que tu ferais, toi?* II, 10; **Would you mind...?** *Ça t'embête de...?* II, 10; *Ça t'ennuie de...?* II, 10; **Would you pass me...?** *Vous pourriez (Tu pourrais) me passer...,* II, 3; **Yes, I would.** *Oui, je veux bien.* II, 3; **You would do well to...** *Tu ferais bien de...,* II, 7
would like: I'd like to buy... *Je voudrais acheter...,* I, 3
write *écrire,* II, 10; **Write to him/her/them.** *Ecris-lui/-leur.* II, 10
wrong: Everything went wrong! *Tout a été de travers!* II, 5; **Is something wrong?** *Quelque chose ne va pas?* II, 7; **You look like something's wrong.** *Ça n'a pas l'air d'aller.* II, 5; **What's wrong?** *Qu'est-ce qui t'arrive?* II, 5; *Qu'est-ce que tu as?* II, 7; *Qu'est-ce qu'il y a?* II, 10

yard *le jardin,* II, 2
Yeah. *Mouais.* II, 6; **Yeah, right!** *Mon œil!* II, 6
year *l'an* (m.), I, 1; *l'année* (f.), I, 4; **Happy New Year!** *Bonne année!* II, 3; **I am... years old.** *J'ai ... ans.* I, 1; **When I was... years old,...** *Quand j'avais... ans,...,* II, 8
yellow *jaune,* I, 3
yes *oui,* I, 1; **Yes, please.** *Oui, s'il te/vous plaît.* I, 8
yesterday *hier,* I, 9
yet: not yet *ne... pas encore,* I, 9
yogurt *les yaourts* (m.), I, 8
you *tu, vous,* I, 0; **And you?** *Et toi?* I, 1
young *jeune,* I, 7
your *ton/ta/tes/votre/vos,* I, 7

zoo *le zoo,* I, 6; II, 6

Grammar Index

This grammar index includes topics introduced in **Allez, viens!** Levels 1 and 2. The roman numeral I preceding the page numbers indicates Level 1; the Roman numeral II indicates Level 2. Page numbers in boldface type refer to **Grammaire** and **Note de grammaire** presentations. Other page numbers refer to grammar structures presented in the **Comment dit-on... ?, Tu te rappelles?, Vocabulaire,** and **A la française** sections. Page numbers beginning with R refer to the Grammar Summary in this reference section (pages R23–R42) or in the Level 1 Grammar Summary.

Credits

ACKNOWLEDGMENTS

For permission to reprint copyrighted material, grateful acknowledgment is made to the following sources:

Au Plaisir d'offrir: Advertisement, "Au Plaisir d'offrir," from *Chartres: Ville d'Art.*

Bayard Presse International: From "A Table: pourquoi manger?" and "Gare au régime!" from *Okapi,* no. 550, November 12, 1994. Copyright © 1994 by Bayard Presse International. From "L'Amitié" by Sylvaine de Paulin from *Le dossier Okapi,* no. 602, March 8, 1997. Copyright © 1997 by Bayard Presse International. Text from "2001, L'Odyssée de l'espace," text from "Il était une fois dans l'ouest," text from "E.T., l'extra-terrestre," and text from "Cyrano de Bergerac" from "10 films qui ont fait date" from *Okapi: Cinéma mon plaisir,* May 1993. Copyright © 1993 by Bayard Presse International. From "*La leçon, La cantatrice chauve* by Eugène Ionesco" by Rémy Lillet from *Phosphore,* no. 94, November 1988. Copyright © 1988 by Bayard Presse International. From "B.D.: 'Calvin et Hobbes' by Bill Waterson" by Yves Frémion and from "*Daïren* by Alain Paris" by Denis Guiot from *Phosphore,* no. 97, February 1989. Copyright © 1989 by Bayard Presse International.

Comité Français d'Education pour la Santé: From the poster "Code des enfants pour les enfants," edited and distributed by CFES at 2, rue Auguste Comte, 92170 Vanves.

Crêperie du Cygne: Advertisement, "Crêperie du Cygne," from *Chartres: Ville d'Art.*

Antoine Dubroux: Photo by Antoine Dubroux from "L' Amitié" from *Le dossier Okapi,* no. 602, March 8, 1997.

EDICEF: "78. Les questions difficiles (suite)" and jacket cover from *La Belle Histoire de Leuk-le-Lièvre* by Léopold Sédar Senghor and Abdoulaye Sadji. Copyright © 1953 by Librairie Hachette.

Editions du Boréal: "Tombée du jour" from *Poèmes pour la main gauche* by Anne Hébert. Copyright © 1997 by Editions du Boréal.

Editions du Seuil: "Nos Mains au jardin" from *Poèmes* by Anne Hébert. Copyright © 1948 by Editions du Seuil.

Editions Gallimard: From *La cantatrice chauve* by Eugène Ionesco. Copyright © 1954 by Editions Gallimard. "Le Cancre" and "Page d'écriture" from *Paroles* by Jacques Prévert. Copyright © 1980 by Editions Gallimard.

Editions J.M. Fuzeau and Lycée Alfred Kastler: Cover of "Carnet de correspondance" from Lycée Alfred Kastler.

EF Foundation: From "Votre année en High School aux USA" from *Une année scolaire à l'étranger,* 1993–94.

France Télévision Distribution: Logo for television channel "France 2."

S.C. Galec: Nine photographs of fruits and vegetables and E. Leclerc logo from *Grande fraîcheur à petits prix,* October 13–23, 1993.

La Napolitaine Restaurant–Pizzeria: Advertisement, "La Napolitaine Restaurant–Pizzeria," from *Chartres: Ville d'Art.*

La Passacaille: Advertisement, "La Passacaille," from *Chartres: Ville d'Art.*

Le Chêne Fleuri: Advertisement, "Le Chêne Fleuri," from *Chartres: Ville d'Art.*

Le Figaro Magazine: From "Provence, Côte d'Azur" from *Le Figaro Magazine: Guide de l'été,* 1994. Copyright © 1994 by Figaro Magazine.

Le Figaro TV Magazine: From "Urgences" and from "X-Files: aux frontières du réel" from *Le Figaro TV Magazine,* no. 16.534. Copyright © by Figaro Magazine.

M6: Logo for French television channel M6.

Marilyn Agency: Advertisement for Gymnase Club.

Office de Tourisme de Chartres: Map of Chartres from *Chartres: Ville d'Art.* Copyright © by the Office de Tourisme de Chartres. Advertisements for "Le Centre International du Vitrail," "La Maison Picassiette," "Le Musée des Beaux-Arts," and "Les Tours de la Cathédrale" from *Passeport Culturel pour Chartres.* Copyright © by the Office de Tourisme de Chartres.

Office de Tourisme de Fontainebleau: "Renseignements Pratiques" from *Fontainebleau.*

Parc Bromont: Advertisement, "Parc Bromont," from *Camping/Caravaning.*

Pariscope: une semaine de Paris: "Géronimo," "Les Trois mousquetaires," et "Une brève histoire du temps" from *Pariscope: une semaine de Paris,* no. 1357, May 25–31, 1994. Copyright © 1994 by Pariscope. "Les Randonneurs" from *Pariscope: une semaine de Paris,* no. 1529, September 10, 1997. Copyright © 1997 by Pariscope.

Promotrain: Advertisement, "Promotrain," from *Chartres: Ville d'Art.*

Protéines SA: "Vive l'eau" from *Les Secrets de la Forme—Guides Pratiques,* no. 14.

Restaurant La Sellerie: Advertisement, "La Sellerie," from *Chartres: Ville d'Art.*

Services Touristiques de Touraine: From "Circuits d'une journée," from "Circuits d'une demi-journée," and from "Spectacles son et lumière" from *Châteaux de la Loire: Circuits en autocars au départ de Tours du 10 avril au 30 septembre 1993.*

SNCF: Direction Grandes Lignes: Excerpts from SNCF train schedule, 1997.

Société Gestion Activités Commerciales Parc de la Jacques-Cartier: From "Les Parcs Québécois" from *Les Parcs du Québec* and "Bienvenue dans le Parc de la Jacques-Cartier" and "Conseils Pratiques" from *Parc de la Jacques-Cartier.*

Sony Music Publishing France: Lyrics from "Un Sèl Zouk" by César Durcin from *Tékit Izi* by Kassav'. Copyright © 1992 by Sony Music Publishing. Cover of CD *Tékit Izi* by Kassav'. Designed and illustrated by F.A.W. Copyright © and ℗ 1992 by Sony Music Entertainment (France).

Sony/ATV Tunes LLC: Lyrics from "Un Sèl Zouk" by César Durcin from *Tékit Izi* by Kassav'. Copyright © 1992 by Sony Music Publishing.

STS Student Travel Schools AB: Text and photographs from *Une année scolaire aux USA 1993/1994.* Copyright © 1993 by STS Student Travel Schools AB.

Télé Câble Hebdo: "L'Eternel retour" and "Notre-Dame de Paris" from "Films de mars: le choix de Cinémaniac" from *Télé Câble,* no. 2. Copyright © by Télé Câble.

ILLUSTRATION AND CARTOGRAPHY CREDITS

Abbreviated as follows: (t) top, (b) bottom, (l) left, (r) right, (c) center.

All art, unless otherwise noted, by Holt, Rinehart and Winston.

Front Matter: Page xxii, MapQuest.com; xxiii, MapQuest.com; xxiv, MapQuest.com; xxv, MapQuest.com.

LOCATION: PARIS REGION

Page 1, MapQuest.com. **Chapter 1:** Page 9, Jocelyne Bouchard; 13, Maria Lyle; 16, Yves Larvor; 20 (t), Bruce Roberts; 20 (c), Vincent Rio; 24, Guy Maestracci; 25, Jocelyne Bouchard; 28, Jocelyne Bouchard; 30, Jocelyne Bouchard. **Chapter 2:** Page 37, Bruce Roberts; 39, Jocelyne Bouchard; 41, Neil Wilson; 42, Jocelyne Bouchard; 54, Jocelyne Bouchard; 55, Anne Stanely. **Chapter 3:** Page 67, Jean-Jacques Larrière; 73, Fançoise Amadieu; 77 (l), Jocelyne Bouchard; 77 (cr), Jean-Jacques Larrière; 78, Jean-Jacques Larrière.

LOCATION: MARTINIQUE

Page 90, MapQuest.com. **Chapter 4:** Page 100, Anne Stanley; 106, Anne de Masson; 110, Anne de Masson; 111, Lynne Russell; 118, Lynnn Russell; 120, Anne Stanley; 122, Anne de Masson.

LOCATION: TOURAINE

Page 124, MapQuest.com. **Chapter 5:** Page 134, Gilles-Marie Baur; 135, Françoise Amadieu; 136, Gilles-Marie Baur; 148, Gilles-Marie Baur; 151, Jocelyne Bouchard; 154, Gilles-Marie Baur. **Chapter 6:** Page 165, Guy Maestracci; 166, Gilles-Marie Baur; 174–175, Pat Lucas Morris; **Chapter 7:** Page 189 (tr, cl), Bruce Roberts; 189 (br), Gilles-Marie Baur; 190 (tr), Gilles-Marie Baur; 190 (b), Jocelyne Bouchard; 191, Gilles-Marie Baur; 192, Jocelyne Bouchard; 193, Bruce Roberts; 198, Jocelyne Bouchard; 200, Fançoise Amadieu; 206, Jocelyne Bouchard.

LOCATION: COTE D'IVOIRE

Page 214, MapQuest.com. Chapter 8: 222, Gilbert Gnangbel; 228, Gilbert Gnangbel; 232, Gilles-Marie Baur; 236, Gilbert Gnangbel; 241; Gilles-Marie Baur; 242, Gilbert Gnangbel; 244, Gilbert Gnangbel; 246, Gilbert Gnangbel.

LOCATION: PROVENCE

Page 248, MapQuest.com. **Chapter 9:** Page 258, Gilles-Marie Baur; 260, Jocelyne Bouchard; 262, Jean-Jacques Larrière; 264 (t), Jocelyne Bouchard; 264 (br), Bruce Roberts; 268, Jocelyne Bouchard; 276, Guy Maestracci; 278, Bruce Roberts. **Chapter 10:** Page 286, Jocelyne Bouchard; 287, Gilles-Marie Baur; 289, Anne de Masson; 292, Jocelyne Bouchard; 295, Vincent Rio; 303, Jean-Pierre Foissy. **Chapter 11:** Page 315, Yves Larvor; 316, Bruce Roberts; 331, Bruce Roberts; 333, Jocelyne Bouchard.

LOCATION: QUEBEC

Page 338, GeoSystems. **Chapter 12:** Page 347, Anne Stanley; 351, Yves Larvor; 354, Gilles-Marie Baur; 355, Bruce Roberts; 356, Gilles-Marie Baur; 360, Jocelyne Bouchard; 362-363, Hilber Nelson; 366, Jocelyne Bouchard; 370, Jocelyne Bouchard.

PHOTO CREDITS

Abbreviations used: (t) top, (c) center, (b) bottom, (l) left, (r) right
Rencontre culturelle students: HRW Photo/ John Langford
Panorama fabric: Copyright (c) 1992 by Dover Publications, Inc.
Remaining fabric: HRW Photo
All globes: Mountain High Maps(r) Copyright (c)1997 Digital Wisdom, Inc.
All euros: (c)European Communities
Jeu de rôle masks: (c)PhotoSpin, Inc.

TABLE OF CONTENTS: vii (t), HRW photo/Marty Granger/Edge Productions; (b), Eric Beggs; viii, © Ulrike Welsch; ix, HRW Photo/Marty Granger/Edge Productions; x (both), HRW Photo/Marty Granger/Edge Productions;xi (t), HRW Photo/Marty Granger/Edge Productions; (b), © Lawrence Manning/CORBIS; xii, © Audrey Gottlieb; xiii, © Tony Freeman/PhotoEdit; xiv (both), HRW Photo/Louis Boireau; xv (t), HRW Photo/ Marty Granger/Edge Productions; (b), Robert Fried; xvi (t), Bokelberg/The Image Bank; (b), HRW Photo/ Marty Granger/Edge Productions; xvii, Owen Franken/ Stock Boston; xviii (t), HRW Photo/Eric Beggs; (b), HRW Photo/Marty Granger/Edge Productions; xix, Corbis Images; xx, HRW Photo/Marty Granger/Edge Productions; xxi (both), HRW Photo/Marty Granger/ Edge Productions.

LOCATION: PARIS REGION: xxvi–1, Phillipe Chardon/ Option Photo; 2 (t), Bill Wassman/The Stock Market; (c), George Seurat, French, 1859–1891, A Sunday on La Grande Jatte-1884, oil on canvas, 1884–86, 207.6 x 308 cm, Helen Birch Bartlett Memorial Collection, 1926.224; (bl), Brigitte Perigois/Option Photo; (br), Marc Deville/Gamma Liaison; 3 (tl), HRW Photo/Marty Granger/Edge Productions; (tr), J. Reznicki/The Stock Market; (bl), S. Kanno/FPG International; (br), Steve Elmore/Stone. **Chapter 1:** 4–5, Eric Beggs; 6 (all), HRW Photo/Marty Granger/Edge Productions; 7 (all), HRW Photo/Marty Granger/Edge Productions; 8 (all), HRW Photo/Marty Granger/Edge Productions; 9 (l), Walter Chandoha; (c), HRW Photo by May Polycarpe; (cl, cr, r), HRW Photo/Marty Granger/Edge Productions; 10 (l), Banaroch/Sipa Press; (cl), Philippe Denis/Sipa Press; (cr), Sebastien Raymond/Sipa Press; (r), Toussaint/Sipa Press; 12, HRW Photo/May Polycarpe; 13 (both), Mark Antman/The Image Works; 14 (both), HRW Photo by Sam Dudgeon; 16 (l), Serge Côté/L'Imagier; (r), HBJ Photo/Pierre Capretz; 17 (l), HRW photo/Louis Boireau/ Edge Productions; (c, r), HRW Photo/Marty Granger/ Edge Productions; 18 (both), HRW Photo/Marty Granger/ Edge Productions; 19 (l), Ulrike Welsch/PhotoEdit; (r), Emmanuel Rongieras d'Usseau; 21 (both), Everett Collection; 22 (b), HRW Photo/Peter Van Steen; 23 (br), © VCG/FPG International; 26 (tl), HRW Photo/Victoria Smith; (tc, tr), Digital imagery® © 2003 PhotoDisc, Inc.; (bl), HRW Photo/Sam Dudgeon; (br), HRW Photo/ Russell Dian; 30 (l), HRW Photo/Russell Dian; (c), HRW Photo/Henry Friedman; (r), Tony Freeman/PhotoEdit. **Chapter 2:** 32–33, © Ulrike Welsch; 34–36 (all), HRW Photo/Marty Granger/Edge Productions; 38 (tl), HRW Photo/Marty Granger/Edge Productions; (tr), R. Lucas/ The Image Works; (bl), HRW Photo/Sam Dudgeon; (br), Chapman/IPA/The Image Works; 39 (l), HRW Photo/ Marty Granger/Edge Productions; (c), Michelle Bridwell/ Frontera Fotos; (r), HRW Photo/Sam Dudgeon; 40 (l, cl, cr), HRW Photo/Marty Granger/Edge Productions; (r), HRW Photo/Sam Dugeon; 42 (tl), HRW Photo; (tc), HRW Photo/Sam Dugeon; (tr, bl), HRW Photo/ Marty Granger/Edge Productions; (br), John Miller/ Leo de Wys, Inc.; 45 (all), HRW Photo/Marty Granger/ Edge Productions; 47 (tl), HRW Photo/John Langford; (tc, tr, br), HRW Photo/Marty Granger/Edge Productions; (bl), HBJ Photo/Oscar Buitrago; (bc), IPA/The Image Works; 48 (both) HRW Photo/Marty Granger/Edge Productions; 50, HRW Photo/Marty Granger/Edge Productions; 53 (l), Michelle Bridwell/Frontera Fotos; (cl, cr), HRW Photo/Marty Granger/Edge Productions; (r), Chapman/IPA/The Image Works; 58 (l), HRW Photo/Sam Dudgeon; (c), UPI Photo/UPI/Bettmann; (r), Michelle Bridwell/Fronteras Fotos. **Chapter 3:** 60–64 (all), HRW Photo/Marty Granger/Edge Productions; 69 (all), HRW Photo/Marty Granger/Edge Productions; 70, HRW Photo; 71 (t), HRW Photo/Sam Dudgeon; (b), HRW Photo/ Cooke Photographic; 74, © European Communities; 76, HRW Photo/Marty Granger/Edge Productions; 78 (c), HRW Photo/Marty Granger/Edge Productions; 78 (remaining), HRW Photo/Sam Dudgeon; 80 (t), Paul Lanue; (b), Amy Reichman/Envision; 81 (both), HRW Photo/Sam Dudgeon; 82, HRW Photo/Marty Granger/Edge Productions; 84, HRW Photo/Victoria Smith; 88 (all), HRW Photo/Sam Dudgeon.

LOCATION: MARTINIQUE: 90–93, HRW Photo/Marty Granger/Edge Productions. **Chapter 4:** 94–97, HRW Photo/Marty Granger/Edge Productions; 98 (cr), Pamela Pate; (remaining), HRW Photo/Marty Granger/Edge Productions; 99 (t,c), HRW Photo/Marty Granger/Edge Productions; (b), Bettmann/CORBIS; 101 (cl), Robert Rattner; (remaining), HRW Photo/Marty Granger/Edge Productions; 103 (l), HRW Photo/Edge Productions; 103 (c, r), HRW Photo/Marty Granger/Edge Productions; 104 (tl, tr), HRW Photo/Marty Granger/Edge Productions; (b), Allan A. Philiba; 105 (Row 1 l), Robert Fried; (Row 1 c), Allan A. Philiba; (Row 1 r), Robert Fried; (Row 2 l), HRW Photo/Marty Granger/Edge Productions; (Row 2 c), Kit Kittle/Viesti Associates; (Row 2 r), HRW Photo/ Marty Granger/Edge Productions; (Row 3 l), Robert Fried; (Row 3 c, r), HRW Photo/Marty Granger/Edge Productions; (Row 4), Robert Fried; 107, HRW Photo/

Marty Granger/Edge Productions; 109 (all), Joe Viesti/ Viesti Associates; 114 (both), HRW Photo/Sam Dudgeon; 115, HRW Photo/Sam Dudgeon; 116 (all), HRW Photo/ Marty Granger/Edge Productions; 119, HRW Photo/ Marty Granger/Edge Productions; 120, Allan A. Philiba

LOCATION: TOURAINE: 124–125, HRW Photo/Marty Granger/Edge Productions; 126 (t), HRW Photo/Marty Granger/Edge Productions; (cl), Giraudon/Art Resource, NY; (cr), Culver Pictures, Inc.; (b), Steve Vidler/Super Stock; 127 (tl), HRW Photo/Marty Granger/Edge Productions; (tr), Dennis Hallinan/FPG International; (tc, cl), SuperStock; (cr), Four By Five/Superstock; (b), E. Scorcelletti/Liaison Agency. **Chapter 5:** 128–129, © Lawrence Manning/CORBIS; 130–131 (all), HRW Photo/ Marty Granger/Edge Productions; 138, HRW Photo/Sam Dudgeon; 141 (l), HRW Photo/Marty Granger/Edge Productions; (c, r), HRW Photo/Sam Dudgeon; 144 (all), HRW Photo; 145 (all), HRW Photo/Marty Granger/Edge Productions; 149, Corbis Images. **Chapter 6:** 156–157, © Audrey Gottlieb; 158–160 (all), HRW Photo/Marty Granger/Edge Productions; 161 (tl), Paul Barton/The Stock Market; (tr, bl), © AFP/CORBIS; (br), T. Mogi/ Superstock; 162 (tl), Robert Fried/Stock Boston; (tc), Jose Carrillo/PhotoEdit; (tr), W. Bertsch/Bruce Coleman; (cl), Owen Franken/Stock Boston; (ccl), Michael Melford/The Image Bank; (ccr), HRW Photo/Marty Granger/Edge Productions; (cr), The Image Bank; (bl), Robert Fried; (bc), H. Kanus/Superstock; (br), Adam Woolfitt/Woodfin Camp & Associates; 163 (l), Charlie Waite/ Stone; (cl), SuperStock; (cr), Don Smetzer/Click/ Stone; (r), Bruce Fier/Liaison International; 170 (all), HRW Photo/Marty Granger/Edge Productions; 176 (l), HRW Photo/Marty Granger/Edge Productions; (r), © AFP/CORBIS; 178 (all), HRW Photo/Marty Granger/Edge Productions; 180, Culver Pictures, Inc.; 182 (l, c), HRW Photo/Marty Granger/Edge Productions; (r), Tony Freeman/PhotoEdit. **Chapter 7:** 184–185, © Tony Freeman/PhotoEdit; 186–188 (all), HRW Photo/Marty Granger/Edge Productions; 191, HRW Photo/Marty Granger/Edge Productions; 195 (tl, tr), HRW Photo/Marty Granger/Edge Productions; (tc), Richard Hutchings/PhotoEdit; (bl), Tony Freeman/ PhotoEdit; (bc), Robert Fried; (br), HRW Photo/ Michelle Bridwell; 196 (l), Al Tielemans/Duomo Photography; (c), Vandystadt/AllSport; (r), Chris Trotman/Duomo Photography; 199 (all), HRW Photo/ Marty Granger/Edge Productions; 203 (l), HRW Photo/ Sam Dudgeon; (c), Robert Fried; (r), Michelle Bridwell/ Frontera Fotos; 209 (tl), HRW Photo/Richard Haynes; (tc), HRW Photo/Michelle Bridwell; (tr), HRW Photo/ Park Street; (bl), HRW Photo/Russell Dian; (br), HRW Photo/Patrick Courtault; 212 (l, r), HRW Photo/Marty Granger/Edge Productions; (c), Richard Hutchings/ PhotoEdit.

LOCATION: COTE D'IVOIRE: 214–217 (all), HRW Photo/ Louis Boireau. **Chapter 8:** 218–219, HRW Photo/Louis Boireau; 220 (tc, tr), HRW Photo; 220 (remaining), HRW Photo/Louis Boireau; 221 (cl), HRW Photo; (remaining), HRW Photo/Louis Boireau; 223–224 (all), HRW Photo/Louis Boireau; 225 (tr), Marc & Evelyne Bernheim/Woodfin Camp & Associates; (c), Kevin Syms/ David R. Frazier Photolibrary; (l, br), HRW Photo/Louis Boireau; 226, HRW Photo/Louis Boireau; 231 (tl, tr, bl), Marc & Evelyne Bernheim/Woodfin Camp & Associates; (bc), HRW Photo; (br), William Stevens/Gamma Liaison; 233 (all), HRW Photo/Marty Granger/Edge Productions; 234–235 (all), HRW Photo/Louis Boireau; 237 (l), Richard Wood/The Picture Cube; 237 (remaining), HRW Photo/Louis Boireau; 240, Jacky Gucia/The Image Bank; 246 (l), Mary Kate Denny/PhotoEdit; (c), HRW Photo/ Sam Dudgeon; (r), Cleo Freelance Photo/PhotoEdit.

LOCATION: PROVENCE: 248–249, P Jacques/FOC Photo; 250 (t), Nik Wheeler; (b), R. Palomba/FOC Photo; 251 (tl), Robert Fried; (tr), Nik Wheeler; (c), Allan A. Philiba; (bl), Scala/Art Resource, New York; (bl frame), © 2003 Image Farm Inc.; (br), HRW Photo/Marty Granger/Edge Productions. **Chapter 9:** 252–253, Robert Fried; 254–257 (all), HRW Photo/Marty Granger/Edge Productions; 261 (l), HRW Photo/Louis Boireau; (c, r), HRW Photo/Marty Granger/Edge Productions; 266, Sebastien Raymond/ Sipa Press; 267 (both), HRW Photo/Marty Granger/Edge Productions; 270–271 (background), Daniel J. Schaefer; 270–271 (masks) Digital imagery® © 2003 PhotoDisc, Inc.; 272 (l), HRW Photo/John Langford; (c), HRW Photo/Sam Dudgeon; (r), HRW Photo/Victoria Smith. **Chapter 10:** 280–281, Bokelberg/The Image Bank; 282–284 (all), HRW Photo/Marty Granger/Edge Productions; 285 (t, bl, br), HRW Photo/Mark Antman; (cl), HRW Photo/Russell Dian; (cr), Mat Jacob/ The Image Works; 291 (tl), HRW Photo/Marty Granger/ Edge Productions; (tr), HRW Photo/Russell Dian; (bl), HBJ Photo/Mark Antman; (remaining), HRW Photo/ Sam Dudgeon; 293 (all), HRW Photo/Sam Dudgeon; 294 (l), HRW Photo/Marty Granger/Edge Productions; (b), HRW Photo/Daniel Aubry; 295 (tl), HRW Photo/ François Vikar; (tc), HRW Photo/Patrick Courtault; (tr), HRW Photo/Sam Dudgeon; (bl), HRW Photo/Daniel Aubry; (br), Michelle Bridwell/Frontera Fotos; 297 (l), HRW Photo/Marty Granger/Edge Productions; (c), HRW Photo/Louis Boireau; (r), HRW Photo; 300 (l, r), HRW Photo/Marty Granger/Edge Productions; (cl), HRW Photo/Russell Dian; (cr), Robert Fried/Stock Boston; 302, HRW photo/Sam Dudgeon; 306 (l, c), HRW Photo/Sam Dugeon; (r), Michelle Bridwell/ Frontera Fotos. **Chapter 11:** 308–309, Owen Franken/ Stock Boston; 310–311 (all), HRW Photo/Marty Granger/Edge Productions; 312 (b), HRW Photo/Patrice Maurin; (remaining), HRW Photo/Marty Granger/Edge Productions; 314 (tl), Benainous-Scorcellett/Liaison International; (tr), Allen/Liaison International; (bl), HRW Photo/Sam Dudgeon; (br), Michel Renaudeau/

Liaison International; 316 (l), HRW Photo/Sam Dudgeon; (c), Bob Riha/Liaison International; (r), © TRIP/ASK Images; 318 (l, r), HRW Photo/Marty Granger/Edge Productions; (c), HRW Photo/Louis Boireau; 321 (tl, tr), Motion Picture and TV Photo Archive; (tc, bl), Ciné-Plus Photothèque; (cl), ILM/Universal/Shooting Star; (c), Paramount/Voyeur Coll./Shooting Star International; (cr), © 1997 Danjaq, LLC and United Artists Pictures, Inc. All Right Reserved/Keith Hamshere/Photofest; (bc), © 1997 Paramount Pictures/Twentieth Century Fox/ Photofest; (br), Photofest; 323 (both), HRW Photo/ Cherie Mitschke; 324 (t), *Daïren* by Alain Paris. HRW Photo/Sam Dudgeon; (b), *La Cantatrice Chave,* suivi *de La Leçon,* Courtesy folio books, HRW Photo/Sam Dudgeon; 325 (Row 1 l), *Mort sur le Nil* by Agatha Christie, translated by Louis Postif. Copyright © 1948 by Agatha Christie, Librairie des Champs-Elysées. Reprinted by permission of Librairie des Champs-Elysées. HRW Photo/Sam Dudgeon; (Row 2 l), *Un amour de Swann* by Marcel Proust. Copyright © 1954 by Editions Gallimard. Reprinted by permission of Editions Gaillimard. HRW Photo/Sam Dudgeon; (Row 2 r), *Les années métalliques* by Michel Demuth. Copyright © 1977 by Editions Robert Laffont, S.A. Reprinted by permission of Editions J'ai Lu. HRW Photo/Sam Dudgeon; (Row4 l), *Les Misérables* by Victor Hugo. Copyright © 1985 by Le Livre Poche. Reprinted by permission of Le Livre Poche. HRW Photo/Sam Dudgeon; (Row 1 r), *L'enfant noir* by Camara Laye. Copyright © 1953 by Librairie Plon. Reprinted by permission of Pocket Books. HRW Photo/Sam Dudgeon; (Row 3 l), *Les aventures de Tintin: Le Secret de la Licorne* by Hergé. Copyright © 1947, 1974 by Casterman. Reprinted by permission of Casterman and Moulinsart SA. HRW Photo/Sam Dudgeon; (Row 3 r), Cover of *Paroles: Selected Poems* by Jacques Prévert, translated by Lawrence Ferlinghetti. Translation copyright © 1958 by Lawrence Ferlinghetti. Cover photo by Izis Bidermanas. Reprinted by permission of City Lights Books. HRW Photo/Sam Dudgeon; (Row 4 r), Cover of *La tragédie du Roi Christophe* by Aimé Césaire. Copyright © 1963 by Présence Africaine. Reprinted by permission of Présence Africaine. HRW Photo/Sam Dudgeon; 326 (all), Ciné-Plus Photothèque; 327, cartoon of TINTIN © Hergé/ MOULINSART 1998; 328–329 (background) HRW Photo; (t), Motion Picture & TV Archive; (b), Ciné Plus; 329 (t), Fotos International/Archive Photos; (c), Twentieth Century Fox/Shooting Star; (b) Ciné Plus; 330, Pono Presse/Liaison International

LOCATION: QUEBEC: 338–339, HRW Photo/Marty Granger/Edge Productions; 340 (b), Winston Fraser; (remaining), HRW Photo/Marty Granger/Edge Productions; 341 (t, cl), Winston Fraser; (cr), Maryo Goudreault/L'Imagier; (b), P. H. Cornut/ Stone. **Chapter 12:** 342–346, (all) HRW Photo/Marty Granger/Edge Productions; 348 (l), Winston Fraser; (r), HRW Photo/ Marty Granger/Edge Productions; (c), L'imagier; 349 (tl, br), Serge Côté/L'imagier; (tlc), Stephen J. Krasemann/ AllStock/Stone; (trc), L.L. Rue/SuperStock; (tr), HRW Photo/Marty Granger/Edge Productions; (bl), Darrell Gulin/AllStock/Stone; (bcl), Daniel J. Cox/AllStock/ Stone; (bcr), Renee Lynn/AllStock; 350 (tl, tcr, b), HRW Photo/Marty Granger/Edge Productions; (tcl), L'imagier; (tr), Winston Fraser; (c), N. Paquin/L'imagier; 352 (all), HRW Photo/Victoria Smith; 353 (t), HRW Photo/Marty Granger/Edge Productions; (c), HRW Photo/Eric Beggs; (remaining), HRW Photo/Sam Dudgeon; 357 (l, r), HRW Photo/Marty Granger/Edge Productions; (c), HRW Photo/Louis Boireau; 358, Winston Fraser; 361 (both), HRW Photo/Marty Granger/Edge Productions; 364 (row 1), Daniel J. Cox/AllStock/ Stone; (row 2), Serge Côté/ L'imagier; (row 3), Renee Lynn/AllStock; (row 4), Serge Côté/L'imagier; (row 5), HRW Photo/Marty Granger/ Edge Productions; (row 6), Darrell Gulin/AllStock/Stone; (row 7), L.L. Rue/SuperStock.

SI TU AS OUBLIÉ: R14 (t, bl. bc. br), HRW Photo/Sam Dudgeon; (cl, c, cr), Digital imagery ® © 2003 PhotoDisc, Inc.; R15 (tc, ctl, c), Corbis Images; (cbl), EyeWire, Inc.; (remaining), Digital imagery ® © 2003 PhotoDisc, Inc.

ADDITIONAL VOCABULARY: R16 (t), HRW Photo/ Patrick Courtault; (c, br), HRW Photo/Sam Dudgeon; (bl), © Stockbyte; R17 (tl, b), HRW Photo/Sam Dudgeon; (tc), Digital imagery ® © 2003 PhotoDisc, Inc.; (cl), Greg Meadors/Stock Boston; (c), Robert Fried/Stock Boston; (tr), EyeWire, Inc.; (cr), Corbis Images; R18 (bl), ©1997 Radlund & Associates for Artville; (br), ©PhotoSpin, Inc.; (remaining), Digital imagery ® © 2003 PhotoDisc, Inc.; R19 (t), EyeWire, Inc.; (remaining), Digital imagery ® © 2003 PhotoDisc, Inc.; R20 (tr), © Digital Vision; (remaining), Digital imagery ® © 2003 PhotoDisc, Inc.; R21 (b), Mountain High Maps ® © 1997 Digital Wisdom, Inc.; (remaining), Digital imagery ® © 2003 PhotoDisc, Inc.; R22 (t), EyeWire, Inc. Image Club Graphics © 1997 Adobe Systems, Inc.; (c), Corbis Images; (b), Digital imagery® copyright (current©here) PhotoDisc, Inc.